HARPER'S

NEW MONTHLY MAGAZINE.

VOLUME LXIX.

JUNE TO NOVEMBER, 1884.

NEW YORK:

HARPER & BROTHERS, PUBLISHERS,

327 to 335 PEARL STREET,

FRANKLIN SQUARE.

1884.

CONTENTS OF VOLUME LXIX.

JUNE TO NOVEMBER, 1884.

EDITOR'S EASY CHAIR.

Clubs in Court, 147. Kindergartens for the Blind, 148. The Copyright Question in Congress, 149. Dangers from Fire in Flats, 150. Mr. Gladstone, 151. The Wagner Concerts in New York, 307. Close of the Theatrical Season, 308. Vulgar Manners at public Amusements, 309. "Tom Appleton," 310. National Conventions, 470. A Retrospect of Rochester, 471. Phariseeism, 472. Foolish Extravagance, 473. The College Commencement, 474. Charles Fenno Hoffman, 629. An old Scrap- Book, 630. George Augustus Sala and M. Blowitz, 631. The University of the State of New York, 632. Cui Bono ? 793. Letters of the Princess Alice, 794. The House of Lords, 795. Matthew Arnold as Writer and Lecturer, 796. A Movement against certain Malefactors, 959. Recollections of the old Traveller, 961. The coming Opera Season, 962. Some Masculine Peculiarities not to be imitated by Women, 963. Taking our Pleasures sadly, 964.

EDITOR'S HISTORICAL RECORD.

UNITED STATES.—Congress: Post-office Appropriation, 158, 319 ; Deficiency Appropriation, 158, 482, 642 ; Mississippi Floods Appropriation, 158, 482 ; Naval Appropriation, 158 ; Indian Appropriation, 158, 319 ; Pension Appropriation, 319 ; New Orleans Exhibition, 319, 482 ; Army Appropriation, 482, 642 ; Consular and Diplomatic Appropriation, 482 ; Agricultural Appropriation, 482 ; River and Harbor Appropriation, 482 ; Legislative Appropriation, 482, 642 ; Sundry Civil Appropriation, 642 ; Mexican Pension Appropriation, 642 ; Fortifications, 642 ; Lands to Indians in Severalty, 158 ; Greely Search Expedition, 158 ; Trade Dollars, 158 ; Blair Education Bill, 158 ; Labor Statistics Bureau, 319, 482 ; Bankruptcy, 319 ; Pensions, 319 ; Bureau of Navigation, 319 ; Shipping, 319, 642 ; Pleuro-Pneumonia, 319 ; Anti-Chinese, 319, 642 ; General Grant, 319 ; Alaska, 319 ; Morrison Tariff Bill, 158, 319 ; Alaska, 319 ; Newspaper Postage, 482 ; Opium, 482 ; Duty on Works of Art, 482 ; Utah, 642 ; Pacific Railroad, 642 ; Soldiers' Home, 642 ; Atlantic and Pacific Railroad Grants, 642 ; Mr. Mayo unseated, 158 ; Minister Sargent, 158 ; Bonded Whiskey, 158 ; President Arthur's Message on Reconstruction of the Navy, 158 ; Fitz-John Porter Bill vetoed, 642 ; Passed over Veto by House, 642 ; Veto Sustained by Senate, 642. Nominations by the President: John A. Kasson, Minister to Germany, Alphonso Taft, Minister to Russia, John M. Francis, Minister to Austria, Lewis Richmond, Minister Resident to Portugal, Ward McAllister, Jun., United States Judge of Alaska, and John Jarrett, Commissioner of Labor, 642. Adjournment of Congress, 642. United States Debt, 158, 642, 970. Prohibition and Woman's suffrage voted down by New Jersey Assembly, 158. National Greenback Convention, 482. National Prohibition Convention, 805. State Conventions: 158, 319, 482, 642, 805, 970. State Elections : 319, 805, 970. Cincinnati Riot, 158. Rescue of the Greely Explorers, 805. Corner-Stone of Bartholdi Statue laid, 805. Earthquake in the United States, 805.

EUROPE, ASIA, AFRICA, NORTH AND SOUTH AMERICA.— Great Britain : British Army Estimates Bill, 158 ; Failure to censure Gladstone, 319 ; Gladstone's Franchise Bill, 642, 805 ; Egyptian Conference, 642 ; Irish Constabulary Bill, 805 ; Expedition for Relief of General Gordon, 805 ; Henry M. Stanley's Return to England, 805 ; British Budget, 970. Pan-Presbyterian Council, Belfast, 642. Holland : Queen Emma appointed Regent, 805. France : Bartholdi Statue presented to the United States, 642 ; Epidemic of Cholera, 642, 805 ; Revised Constitutional Bill passed by French Chamber of Deputies, 805 ; Tonquin Credit voted, 970. Spain : Election of Deputies, 319. Italy : Resignation of Ministry, 158. China : Capture of Hong-Hoa by the French, 158 ; Treaty of Peace between France and Anam, 319 ; French attacked by Chinese, 642 ; New King of Anam crowned, 970 ; Foo-Chow bombarded, 970. Egypt : Burning of Tamanieh, 158 ; Massacre of Refugees from Khartoom, 319 ; Capture of Berber and Massacre of the Garrison, 482. General Diaz declared President of Mexico, 642. Attempt to assassinate the President of Guatemala, 158. Resignation of President Iglesias, of Peru, 642.

DISASTERS : Explosion Thompson's Point, Pennsylvania, 158 ; Oakville, Indiana, destroyed by Wind Storm, 158 ; Steamer Rebecca Everingham burned, 158 ; Steamer Daniel Steinmann wrecked, 158 ; Steamer State of Florida and Bark Ponema sunk in collision, 319 ; Circus Panic, Bucharest, 319 ; Fall of Train into the River, Spain, 319 ; Paquebot sunk, 319 ; Poor-House in Michigan burned, 319 ; Explosion of Powder-Magazine near Havana, 319 ; Destructive Forest Fires, New York, New Jersey, and Pennsylvania, 319 ; Accident on Baltimore and Ohio Railroad, near Connellsville, 482 ; Earthquake, Island of Kishur, 482 ; French Brig Senorine wrecked, 482 ; drowning by Cloud-Burst, 482 ; Schooner Six Brothers lost, 482 ; drowning at Thompson's Falls, Montana, 482 ; Danish Brig Elena lost, 482 ; Accident on Mexican Railroad, 482 ; Accident on Burlington and Missouri Railroad, 642 ; Killed by Lightning, 642 ; Accident, Manchester and Sheffield Railway, 642 ; Steamers Gijon and Laxham sunk, 805 ; Steamer Amsterdam wrecked, 805 ; suffocated in under-ground Canal, 970 ; United States Ship Tallapoosa sunk, 970 ; Colliery Accident, Shamokin, Pennsylvania, 970 ; Steam-Ship City of Merida burned, 970 ; Steamer Belmont sunk, 970 ; Cleveland Fire, 970 ; Mexican Central Railroad Accident, 970 ; Distillery Explosion, 970 ; Chippewa River Floods, 970 ; Inundation in China, 970.

OBITUARY : 158, 319, 482, 642, 805, 970.—Abbot, Dr. Ezra, 158 ; Anna, ex-Empress, 319 ; Anthony, Hon. Henry B., 970 ; Appleton, T. G., 319 ; Beebe, ex-Judge W. R., 482 ; Benjamin, Judah P., 319 ; Bishop, Anna, 158 ; Bohn, Henry George, 970 ; Bosworth, J. S., 482 ; Brown, Rev. John, 970 ; Chatfield, Levi B., 805 ; Cisco, John J., 158 ; Claghorn, J. L., 970 ; Clymer, Heister, 482 ; Costa, Sir Michael, 319 ; Dickson, Thomas, 805 ; Droysen, Professor J. G., 642 ; Emmons, Rear-Admiral George F., 805 ; Folger, Hon. Charles J., 970 ; Frere, Sir Henry E. B., 482 ; Fuller, George, 158 ; Gross, Dr. S. D., 319 ; Harriman, ex-Governor Walker, 805 ; Harwood, Rear-Admiral A. A., 970 ; Hill, Hon. John, 805 ; Hoe, Robert, 970 ; Horne, R. H., 158 ; Hudson, Mary Clemmer, 970 ; Hunt, Dr. S. B., 319 ; Johnson, Alvin J., 319 ; Kavanagh, Bishop H. H., 158 ; Laube, Henri, 805 ; Leopold, Prince, 158 ; Leypoldt, Frederick, 158 ; Lord Ampthill, 970 ; Lovell, General Mansfield, 482 ; McCormick, Cyrus H., 319 ; Midhat Pasha, 319 ; Mignet, François A. M., 158 ; O'Conor, Charles, 319 ; Opdycke, General E., 319 ; Parker, Dr. Willard, 319 ; Phelps, Royal, 805 ; Pierce, Bishop George F., 970 ; Pinkerton, Allan, 642 ; Pool, Hon. John, 970 ; Pratt, ex-Attorney-General Daniel, 805 ; Prince of Orange, 642 ; Reade, Charles, 158 ; Richter, Gustav, 158 ; Schell, Augustus, 158 ; Sheldon, Smith, 970 ; Simpson, Bishop Matthew, 642 ; Slater, J. F., 319 ; Smith, Bishop Benjamin Bosworth, 482 ; Sowerby, George B., 805 ; Sultan Pasha, 970 ; Swayne, Noah H., 482 ; Swisshelm, Jane Grey, 805 ; Taglioni, Maria, 319 ; Todleben, General F. E., 642 ; Trübner, Nicholas, 158 ; Ward, ex-Governor M. L., 319 ; Ward, Samuel, 482 ; Webb, James Watson, 482 ; Weitzel, Major-General Godfrey, 158 ; Wellesley, Arthur R., 805 ; White, R. C., 970 ; Wikoff, Chevalier, 319 ; Woodward, Colonel J. J., 970.

EDITOR'S LITERARY RECORD.

POETRY.

BY THE RIVER.—From a Drawing by E. A. Abbey.

[See "Judith Shakespeare," Page 133.]

HARPER'S
NEW MONTHLY MAGAZINE.

No. CCCCIX.—JUNE, 1884.—Vol. LXIX.

BIARRITZ.

IT was only February when we left Bordeaux for the Pyrenees, but everywhere were signs of early bloom: the fields were green, the hedge-rows beginning to deepen, and here and there were orchards touched with pink and white. The fragrant almond-tree was in full blossom. We whirled by many garden walls within which were some yellow and red flowers growing gayly; and once I remember seeing a group of children climbing a slope with long branches of feathery purple bloom in their little hands. All these tokens of spring-time came upon us like a sudden waking up after a wintry sleep, for we had left London shrouded in fog and mist, with not a sign that summer ever meant to come again. It was with new delight we observed that on nearing Bayonne, a large town four miles from Biarritz, the verdure deepened: indeed, there was a look as of June brilliancy about the country we finally rested in. Our destination was Biarritz, but, to reach it, one goes first to a little sunny railway station called La Négresse, for what reason we always forgot to inquire. There was the name, however, in big painted letters above a picture of a dark lady with ear-rings and a heavy smile—mysterious, but no doubt the most impressive feature of the little place. There were a great many idlers about, watching, with the same interest shown by such people all the world over, for new arrivals; but we noticed at once a certain picturesqueness of dress and attitude among the people—something which redeemed the most worthless from looking commonplace. Carriages, landaus, hotel omnibuses, stood in waiting. Ahead of us stretched a long white road bordered by a pretty and very fertile country, beyond which rose occasional glimpses of the hills, shining in rather a fierce light, that made it hard just then to gather distinct impressions of form and color. The long roadway was softened here and there by the green of some feathery-looking trees, which cast only faint shadows on the hot white ground, yet swayed now and then daintily in the breeze. This road led to Biarritz, and we were very soon seated in a big landau driving comfortably in that direction. Our driver wore the gay dress of his class in the Pyrenees. It had a very good effect, although on a short, stout man it looked a little fantastic. There were a great many silver buttons on his short little coat; the horses wore bells, and somehow during our stay in Biarritz we never felt quite sure whether the driver or the horse produced the little cheerful tinkling sound which accompanied all our excursions.

We drove through a beautiful though quiet country. The features of the landscape were clearly marked: a rich sweep of green lay between soft undulations, diversified by trees, vagrant hedge-rows, villas, and gardens, with their stone walls hung with vines; a bend in the road would bring us sometimes in sudden view of a little inn, with a court-yard full of cheerful clatter. "Madame" was frequently to be seen leaning out of a window on the ground-floor, handing some tired customer a drink of beer or *eau sucrée*, while her strong-limbed maidens moved about, dusky shadows within.

The customers seemed chiefly men who were driving teams or wagons in and out between Biarritz and neighboring villages. Any one of these men might have stepped on to the "boards" in the character of a brigand, yet I know not where a more peaceable, good-humored people are to be found. Their *al fresco* life, bringing bronzed cheeks, strong limbs, and a certain swaggering gait, seems also to have made them cheerful and gay-tempered, and, from what we overheard them saying, they appeared to enjoy the beautiful weather with an appreciation curious in such a land of bloom. Everywhere the sunshine seemed almost unbroken. It lay in

FLOWER-GATHERING.

OUR POSTILION.

wide, flowing streams of light, emphasizing every bit of color, deepening every bit of green, and, in spite of the cool, soft winds, giving us an impression of midsummer. Overhead, the trails of cloud were fretted, making their way with delicate, languid movements across the radiant bosom of the sky. I think it was in that first drive from La Négresse to Biarritz that we received the impression of perpetual smiling youth and gladness in the old, old country, which we never lost; everywhere Nature seemed to lift this joyous look to heaven; her face seemed to flush and pale, to laugh and dimple, with the divine tenderness and light of happy youth; nothing then or later suggested the possibility of decay. It was all bloom and perfection, untouched, unfettered; and even after days and nights of storm, the land always awoke again with the same laugh of spring-time in every bud and blossom. Our drive seemed scarcely begun, though we had gone over three miles, when the straggling signs of a town grew closer. We came in sight of some beautiful villas with fine gardens and stone walls covered with vines and flowers, of groups of simpler houses, and one or two more pretentious inns. The passers-by were more frequent and various. The women of the middle class were especially noticeable. They were handsome, dark, and vivacious, dressing well, and wearing a sort of bandana handkerchief bound about their abundant coils of hair. The men strongly suggested the chorus of the French opera. Like the team-drivers we had seen, they were bronzed and ruddy, but they combined a certain townish manner with an air of genial audacity, nodding to us politely as we passed, yet smiling, as much as to say, "We too may enjoy Biarritz and the gayety there."

A turn in the road brought us suddenly to the town itself. Biarritz at the first glance seemed to mean one wide, sunshiny street, with hotels to the right and left, cafés and casinos, a few *lingerie* shops, and a moving population of fashionable ladies and gentlemen walking about the hotel gardens or up and down the street, with all the conventional indications of people at a "resort." All in a moment we seemed to have left the primitive country, with its background of silent, "everlasting hills," behind us, and to have come into a veritable watering-place, in which,

WATER-CARRIER.

however, the Basque element so far predominated that the sense of mere fashion was not oppressive. We wondered, for a moment longer, where could be the sea; for nowhere in this gay little town could we see any signs of nearing the water. We were, indeed, almost at our hotel before we saw that Biarritz slopes upward on a blooming cliff, below which rolls in wide, boundless expanse the Bay of Biscay—a stretch of sailless, tempestuous water, beating upon high rocks, dashing furiously against the cliffs, roaring and surging past the sweep of yellow sands as though uttering a perpetual protest against the verdant serenity above.

I think there is no more striking contrast than that offered to the mind and eye in such a drive as led us to Biarritz, and the sudden movement and activity of a fashionable hotel. The one-o'clock breakfast was about to be served, and as we strolled up and down the luxurious corridors leading to the salon and dining-room, we saw figures and heard voices and sentences that brought us back with cruel directness to the world of fashion and youthful frivolity. A great many young ladies had come in from playing tennis or croquet, or walking about the sands. They wore pretty, summery-looking gowns, straw hats, and a great deal of Breton lace on their neck-ties and parasols. They were full of the social animation of the place. From the fragments of conversation which drifted toward us we gathered that Madame De B—— had issued invitations for a fancy-dress ball.

"And I need five-and-twenty bangles for my costume," said a very pretty girl, with the seal of death clearly on her eyes and thin, flushed cheek. "Bob says I sha'n't have them. Didn't you, Bob?"

This to a heavy young swell of Britain who was reading *Galignani* in a window.

"Can't I have five-and-twenty bangles, Bob?" persisted his young wife, while the third of their party—a languid English girl with a big coronet in diamonds on her locket—listened and laughed good-humoredly.

"You have forty now," said Bob, not moving his eyes from his paper. "Hasn't she, Bell?" Bell only laughed again softly.

"I want five-and-twenty more," persisted the wife; "I want all my arms just run over with them—Vaudeau says I must." She stretched out her thin young arms with a gay little gesture. "Can't I have five-and-twenty more bangles, Bob?" she resumed. "I can get them in Bayonne."

"Oh, they're to be had anywhere," rejoined Bob, with light scorn. "All the shops know women's ways."

"Are five-and-twenty bangles sinful?" she asked, flippantly. She was so exquisitely lovely, but so evidently dying, and dying fast of that dreadful foe of England, consumption, that there was something positively grotesque in her persistence for the five-and-twenty bangles with which, added to her own forty, her arms were to "run over" on the night of the ball.

"*You* have everything for your dress, haven't you?" she said to Bell.

"I dare say," rejoined that calm young lady. "Come, Alicia," she added; "breakfast is ready;" and away they went, the invalid shaking out her airy draperies, and talking rapidly to Bob, with gestures that showed her mind still ran upon the five-and-twenty bangles.

Nearly every one goes to the *table d'hôte* in these foreign hotels. Somebody said the peerage seemed to have flung its contents into that one dining-room; but certain it is, at least three members of the Queen's household, one or two well-known royal equerries, some dowager duchesses, three members of the fast-vanishing cabinet, and a dozen young noblemen circled about the table. Conversation was rather general, but not particularly interesting, as the people, who were in Biarritz for health's sake, generally seemed depressed at table. The gentlemen of her Majesty's government were anxious, and the noble young men had some burdens of the card-table rather heavy upon their minds. Everybody, however, seemed anxious to ask every one else what excursions they had been taking, and eager to know if any new place had been discovered. The Englishman abroad is certainly indefatigable in the way of sight-seeing, and the most languid person was to be roused, we found, by being told of any unvisited point of interest. The first question, "Dear me, how does one go?" was generally followed by, "Oh, really, I must manage it"; and it was noticeable that he usually *did* manage it, rewarded, perhaps, only by a sense of duty done.

When we were in our rooms again we went out upon the balcony fronting them, fairly overawed by the spectacle before

FLOWER GIRL AND MAN.

THE BEACH AND THE CASINO.

us. Far away, bounding the western shore, rose the Lower Pyrenees, their dim heights crowning the picture, and contrasting strangely with the wild waters at their feet. To two of our party this was an unknown country, and to them it seemed as if some dream had taken possession of the land. The splendor and yet the calm of it all made this first day go by like an hour. The sunset came, flooding the whole scene with a marvellous light. Trails of amber and amethyst and opal went sweeping across the sky like colors of some hidden king, trembling with a divine radiance on the waters and the distant hills, and even when the last gleam of color faded, leaving a curious quality of light in the grayness filling earth and sky. When night fell, and the moon rose, the whole scene changed. The sea shone under the cold light with a glamour which seemed to influence all the distant country of fading hills. The sky was full of passionate throbbing from a million stars. We could only look and wonder what new glories this world might contain.

"As for sketching or *painting* this sort of thing," says the voice of the artist, in a minor key, "why, it can't be done. Who could even tell of what we have seen to-day? And this moonlight!—one reads, you know, of what moonlight can do, but was there ever anything so wonderful as the way in which it glorifies the water? Ah! there—there is the White Maiden of Biarritz!"

We all looked, but could only see, at the foot of one of the boldest rocks, a tall, thin spray of water which rose and fell on the impassive stone with a little wailing sound. Now one member of our party was particularly fond of the legendary, though he objected strongly to calling it a taste for the supernatural. He certainly found out the lore of a place almost by instinct.

"Yes," he continued, "that is the White Maiden of Biarritz."

"And what was her story?"

"It was a *very* sad one," said the erudite person, thoughtfully. "Her lover— he was a Basque knight — discovered a rival whom the girl favored, and one moonlight night—so runs the legend—he enticed her to that rock, and there flung her over. This was about—about 1307. Ever since, at every full moon, she rises, moaning and making ineffectual attempts to be free."

"To be *free*?" says a young person who always enjoys the weird—"to be *free*? But isn't she dead—drowned—and in heaven?"

The story-teller smiles calmly. "That's the most singular part of it," he says. "It's most horribly fantastic; perhaps I ought not to have told it at all. No; she can never *really drown*—so they believe; and he is supposed to sit chained to that rock, compelled through all ages to hear her cries. The Basques are a highly organized people."

After this we sit silent, and as we leave

the balcony, about midnight, the most composed of us remarks:

"Whatever you may say, I dread tomorrow. I am so sure we shall wake up to find the place all a dream; a glimpse of something unearthly; a maddening suggestion of what *might be*."

But the next day the most brilliant sunshine welcomed us, and we went out early into the town, full of vigor and belief in its existence. What is there about the influence of such a place as Biarritz which compels one to feel himself a holiday-maker? One wonders always whether humdrum commonplace lives are ever led in it, whether the most colorless existence does not derive some warmth from the ebb and flow of pleasure-seeking humanity always at its threshold. We walked by the splendid hotels, in the gardens of which some ladies in fine morning toilets were moving about, evidently waking

INVALIDS.

WOMAN WITH BASKET.

"courts" at the Casino; but I am afraid we were a vagabond party, too fond of roaming about the beach and the cliffs to enter with any ardor into such country-house occupations as filled hours of every day for many visitors. Past the hotels, that first morning, we walked, down into the gay street where the business activity of the town concentrated. It was such a pretty place, half idle, half busy; the shop people stood in their open doorways, nodding and smiling good-humoredly, not exactly asking one's custom, but certainly evincing every readiness to be attentive. Parisian taste was everywhere about the shops; the signs and indications had not a touch of provincialism; only in the market-place did we feel that we had put a metropolis far behind us. It is a big, cheerful *halle*, that of Biarritz. There is an iron railing all around it, with a deep stone ledge inside heaped up with flowers, behind which the sellers stand, dangling roses at you encouragingly.

"Buy, buy, madame, m'sieur," a voice called after us, and there was a picturesque, dark old woman within the railing, with her head tied up in a bandana, and her brown hands full of the loveliest red and yellow roses. "Buy, madame. See, *quite* twenty for ten sous." And for this trifle we became possessed of a great bunch of Maréchal Niels and "Jacques," such as would seem priceless this season over the water. At this hour half of Biarritz is at the market, buying and selling fruit, flowers, eggs and butter and fowls, and a clamor of voices fills the air, French and Spanish and Basque mingling now and then with English sounds. Away past the market we strolled, up into one of the hilly streets of the town. Here the houses were very good, though extremely unpicturesque. They were mostly built of yellowish or gray stone, with painted blinds. Sometimes a bit of garden ran in front,

up the fashion of the day. The main windows of the hotels front the sea, and toward the town are spacious court-yards or gardens, with every variety of wicker chairs and tables, sometimes terraces and balconies laden with flowers. Sometimes on moonlight nights one finds the gardens peopled, and always early in the day. There is a Casino somewhere—a club; there are dark rumors of rouge et noir and piquet, and all the time we remained in Biarritz we heard of "tennis" going on somewhere at a maddening rate; young ladies appeared at the mid-day *table d'hôte* in tennis costumes, flushed with triumph, exchanging significant expressions, and ready to rush off at two o'clock to the

OUT ON THE BAY.

but generally the house door opened, with one or two steps, on to the street. Some were largely advertised "à louer," others were devoted to lodgings or private residences, but all partook of the general brightness of the town. Winding our way up the pleasant street, we passed several times impromptu shops: women had opened their wares on clothes-horses or lines directly across the sidewalks, greatly to the inconvenience of passers-by, but I must say no one seemed to resent it. Bright bandanas, shawls, linens, even heavier articles of dress, were thus displayed, in the midst of which the owner sat knitting contentedly, looking up now and then with an appeal for a purchaser: "Is it not that messieurs et dames wishes something?" and on being answered in the negative, the shop-keeper would only lower her eyes, knit on, catching the attention of the next passer-by with equal civility.

Beyond this first hilly street the town wound in and out, up and down, with graceful irregularity. We followed a certain lazy course of streets which brought us finally up on the cliffs and sea-walk. The ground was very irregular here, rising into green knolls, jutting out into a base of stone, or stretching from point to point in a grassy ledge, but all overlooking the water, which, lighted up now by dancing gleams of sunlight, seemed to

have forgotten the unearthly glow and vibrations of the night before. We saw the bold coast to very good advantage in this clear light. The rocky lines were sharply defined; the wild character of the shore became apparent, with the "stone monsters" at whose feet the waters tumbled furiously; the fierce crags stood out with the sun shining on them as though they wished the fishermen who tempted them in stormy times to see how deadly a peril they would risk.

I suppose that nearly every one knows the character of the Pyrenean and Basque sea-ports. Fishing is the common avocation of a large class; the men and boys go out, bringing in heavy boat-loads, for which the women wait eagerly upon the shore, buying of the fishermen, and selling readily in the town.

Our first morning on the cliffs we were, as later, greatly interested in watching the groups of fisher-women waiting for the return of the boats on the sands below. Some were moving about; some half lying or sitting on the rocks and sands; most of them knitting, their brown fingers moving deftly, while their eyes now and then were eagerly strained seaward, watching for the first speck of the boats' heads to appear. They were very handsome women in a strong, muscular way. Their bare feet and ankles, bronzed and roughened as they were, would have served a sculptor

HOUSE OF LOUIS XIV.

admirably, and the litheness of limb, strong waists and shoulders, and free play of the arms showed how little trace of physical weakness they or their ancestry knew. The women, young and old, were dressed in short, dark skirts and loose, short-sleeved blouses. On their heads they wore the usual gay bandanas. Now and then a brown old face looked out from the handkerchief knotted under the chin, but chiefly the bit of colored linen was wound about the back of the head, and frequently fastened by long brass or silver pins. A great deal of shrill, good-humored talking went on. The groups engaged in conversation gesticulated in a way that looked denunciatory at times, but was in fact only roughly emphatic. Presently every group scattered; the knitters thrust their work into their belts, as they ran hither and thither on the beach taking their accustomed places. The boats were dimly to be seen coming in — tiny specks at first—tossing and tumbling on the line of the horizon. The interest among the women grew loud and eager, and as the boats drew nearer, and finally were fairly in, it was astonishing with what rapidity every basket was filled and placed upon the linen cushion each woman carried for her head. The whole company trooped up the cliff, dispersing in different directions, each following her accustomed track.

Now this was early in the day. We lingered a little while, watching the fishermen in their boats within a sort of haven of water walled in by firm stones, which was their safeguard often in stormy weather. They were active, sturdy-limbed men, an excellent type of Basque peasantry—if peasant the man can be called whose days are passed upon the water. They sang out now and then; they had a way of chaffing one another; they talked and laughed; and of all the people of the lower classes whom we saw, seemed most indifferent to spectators, above all to strangers. Their work and themselves seemed very exclusive. One day I ventured to talk to a fine-looking lad, whose oarsmanship I had admired. He answered in a perfectly unabashed, frank tone.

"Was he Basque?"

"Well, he came from St.-Jean-de-Luz. It was a town not far away."

"And do you work here always?" I asked.

"Yes, madame; but one day I hope to go very much further—when the grandfather dies."

"How far ?"

day with a real gold watch of her own."

"And what did she think of St.-Jean ?" The lad was really puzzled.

STREET IN ST.-JEAN-DE-LUZ.

The boy's dark face looked comically expressive.

"Who can say, madame, if Jacques and I may not reach Bordeaux ? We knew a boy who went from St.-Jean there. He married Lepoline, the daughter of Pierre Gaudin. She came back to St.-Jean one

"Oh, she thought it all very well, no doubt, for her mother and father, but she gladly went back to Bordeaux. Perhaps madame may have been there ?"

The lad's simple discourse, and he himself, interested me greatly; and it impressed upon me a strong desire to see St.-Jean-

VIEW ON THE BASQUE COAST.

de-Luz. One could, I thought, fancy the simplicity of a people to whom Bordeaux seemed an *ultima thule*, and Lepoline's gold watch an evidence of its luxuriousness. I told him a little about the large, noisy city. I am afraid I did not make it seem very alluring to him, for my memories were of its heat and noise, the wrangling of its wharves, the air of provincial vulgarity noticeable in many of its streets; but I softened some points in my description. I could not look at the dark, eager young face before me, the slim, active figure in blue and white linen, the brown hands burning for movement, and be cruel enough to dash all his hopes. On the whole, he seemed pleased. Perhaps he liked to hear of noise and bustle and a big city's animation. At all events, he thanked me with the air of one who feels a new impetus given to an old desire. I asked him some questions about St.-Jean, to which he cordially responded, and for the first time I saw evidences of the Basque power of language—the improvisatore's talent which so many of them possess. The boy grew quite eloquent as he told me of his native town, and he threw over it a glamour of pathos which, indeed, we felt later when we walked in its sad old streets. He told me that there was constant danger of its being washed away by the sea; that no walls could be built to resist the merciless barbarity of those waves. Twice it had nearly all been destroyed. It has suffered in old times by sword and famine as well. Yet it holds its own to-

day, proudly, confidently Basque; cherishing its great memories, honoring its old customs, although the people well know that at any hour or day all traces of its present being may be washed away.

We were very anxious to visit the old town, and found that the drive formed one of the favorite excursions from Biarritz. Meanwhile we studied up a little history—not guide-book exactly, but a quaint story of the town loaned us by a friend—a long, narrow little book, with faded yellow leaves between shining brown covers. St.-Jean-de-Luz, we therein learned, was a well-built and flourishing town when Columbus, who visited it, was thinking of his western voyage. The sailors of St.-Jean knew Iceland well, and it is said that one of their number, Sancho de Huelva, gave Columbus the first suggestion for his explorations. De Huelva knew many remote places, and had in his own mind determined that a land untrodden by European feet must lie somewhere to the west. Just what he knew or guessed at is not recorded, but that he talked navigation and adventure with the discoverer of our country seems tolerably certain, and that the people of St.-Jean were accustomed to hear of new lands toward the west seems very evident from their traditions and earlier literature. All sorts of interesting and picturesque incidents color the story of St.-Jean. Thither came Francis I. in his proud captivity; there was celebrated the splendid marriage of Louis XIV. and the Infanta; battles were fought again and again in the streets, stout resistance made to the most formidable foes. That the people were brave is shown not only in the history of their wars, but in the way in which they bore the loss of their noted whale-fisheries. For generations whaling had been the chief support of St.-Jean, but gradually these monsters of the deep disappeared from the Bay of Biscay. Nothing daunted, the sailors of St.-Jean pursued them to the Spitzbergen seas. Later their cod-fisheries in Newfoundland became most profitable. It was in 1675 that the first disaster occurred: the waves rose, to the partial destruction of the town. On the 22d of January, 1749, a great flood of waters poured upon the town, and its old people now relate with bated breath the

INTERIOR OF CHURCH IN ST.-JEAN-DE-LUZ.

stories of that terrible time told them by their grandsires. Such as could escape speedily abandoned their houses, but the havoc in life and property was terrible; and then it was known that the doom of the town was sealed. Over and again attempts have been made to guard against the invasion of this relentless foe, but nearly all are in vain. Something, it is true, has been done with the high sea-wall, yet year by year the waters steadily advance.

A town with such traditions, with such a future, must necessarily possess a certain mournful charm, a dignity of splendid and saddening melancholy. I think we enjoyed dwelling upon the depressing features of its history to a neighbor of ours at the *table d'hôte*, who was the most briskly animated and analytical person I have ever met. In journeying about we found he was typical of a class—a small class, perhaps, yet large enough to be generalized about. He pounced, as it were, upon the slightest suggestion of sentiment in anything, whether in architecture or the customs or relics of a place or people. He was one of those persons who seem to believe the grand old monuments of the past are left solely that such as he may come and laugh their intricacies or suggestions to scorn. But he was the most indefatigable sight-seer I ever beheld. He went about the sunny, carelessly happy little town of Biarritz, I believe, aggrieved that the stones he turned up with his perpetually moving cane did not present cabalistic characters which he might find it worth his while to decipher and scoff at; and it became my dear delight to indulge in all the sentiment possible over any "sight" or any excursion in his hearing, as well as to resolutely decline the use of any guide-book, however useful. The traditionary interest of St.-Jean-de-Luz, as dwelt upon by certain members of our party, drove this personage to the borders of despair. I have said his conversation was analytical; possibly the term does not describe his power of wearing a subject so threadbare that you utterly forgot the opinion you had originally expressed. He tortured you to explain yourself; he called upon you to render him an account for the meaning of every chance syllable your lips had formed, and when you had civilly tried to state your reasons for the faith within you, and explain in bald terms just why you felt thus and so, his manner

plainly indicated, "By Jove! what a lot of rubbish *some* people take in!" That we were going to St.-Jean-de-Luz without reading his yellow-covered guide-book, with its pencil marks, nearly crazed him, and he talked dates and events to us during three meals with the air of one who feels that the persistently ignorant are his special mission in life. We never told him the secret of our little shining brown book; we never told him about our young friend the sailor-boy whose destiny was Bordeaux. We thoroughly enjoyed appearing to have the vaguest of reasons for our sentimental behavior in regard to St.-Jean-de-Luz, and we exasperated him almost beyond endurance by saying we had no fixed date for our journey to the old town: we were waiting for the clouds to look just a certain way, for the sunshine to come at just the right angle, for our pulsations to "feel" St.-Jean-de-Luz; the impulse to go was to be purely æsthetic. As for our neighbor, he loudly declared, as he grasped his cane and umbrella, he "did" so many sights a day, rain or shine, warm or cold, and *I know* that he uttered to himself an expressive "Dammy."

Any idea of gloom connected with the old town was dispelled by the radiant day on which we started to see it. I use "radiant" in its tersest significance; for what other term can express the weather during that journey through a land of light and color, warmth and richness? We left the town by a road bordered by the low stone walls behind which villas are to be seen protected by graceful shrubberies. There are two roads to St.-Jean-de-Luz, and we chose the one which took us into a country rimmed by the mountains—a land half verdure and blossom, half wilderness of crags and sea-beach. Sometimes for half a mile or more the road was quite shut in by hedges, tall trees, and garden walls, but even these could not tone down the color that seemed to flow in streams of light on all around us; for the hedges near Biarritz run riot with vines and wild flowers; over the garden walls hang languid trails of roses—Jacques and Maréchal Niels, and a pale white rose, blushing faintly at its heart like some newly wooed maiden. As we drove along, a pretty picture suddenly presented itself before us. Above an old garden wall the shrubbery clustered thickly, but as we slowly passed, the green was parted by a pair of quick dark hands, and a girl's face and figure came in view.

THE ARCHED BRIDGE.

She was a veritable Spaniard, charmingly pretty, her dark hair loosely bound in a dull blue bandana, her red and black dress a mixture of the peasant and serving-maid. She bent forward, reaching with her slim brown fingers for a spray of the yellow blossoms tangled along the wall, and as she did so she bent her head back slightly, answering a call from the garden behind her. For an unconscious "study" it was the most perfect picture I have ever seen; and where else, we wondered, could it have been given us? Now and then on our drive we passed a bank of feathery willows; again some grander trees arched overhead, shutting out all the rich perfumes of the fields and flowers behind us. Breaking away from these sheltered places, we came at intervals into sudden view of the water sweeping wildly against the craggy shore, dashing against the rocks, uttering the same defiant message to the land, and receding with that long-drawn moan which makes the music of the Bay of Biscay so unutterably plaintive. To the left of such wild scenes we could always turn our eyes to a peaceful upland, where peasants, men and women, were toiling, their brown figures sharply defined against the sky—models, we often thought, for a Bréton or Lepage, impressive from the contrast they afforded to fiercer elements in the landscape, but of themselves charming studies, their very activity possessing an element of crude grace in keeping with their form and color, harmonizing with the wide stretches of upland field waiting to be tilled or sown, as the case may be, shining duskily brown and green in the morning light. Now and then, as we drove by a group of these hill-side toilers, a weather-beaten kindly face would turn to look at us; sometimes a little child would start forward, fling a handful of wild flowers into the carriage, and look up with pretty, smiling eyes and lips for the sous one could not help tossing him; occasionally a man or woman trudging along would offer a good-humored salutation, but in general the natives take but little heed of the foreign visitors who come and go in their lovely land.

Curving in and out of the hilly road to St.-Jean, we had recurrent glimpses of the mountains, finally beholding in the distance the snowy heights, so much sung and painted, but never, it seems to me, to be adequately described. A something imperial, triumphant, and proudly self-conscious dominates those hills; they seem to lift an eternal message from earth to sky. As we drove along we looked almost with reverence at the glistening heights, fading into an ethereal vapor that seemed heaven itself, and we felt it was a scene not to be transcribed by pen or pencil—only to be witnessed, to be felt. Below, the bosom of the hills varies with a hundred restless lights, now brown, now purple, now flushed with a trembling rosy tint; but look at and admire these as one may, the eye seeks that unwritten glory above; it vanishes into air, seeming to penetrate the mystery of the very sun itself.

Perhaps it was as well that we sometimes lost sight of this shining vision of "God's hills"; we could not have otherwise found ardor for the minor objects along the road, which had in them perpetually varying elements of human and picturesque interest. There were many undulations in the road, and as we drove along we passed on the rise or fall of verdure many dwellings, those of the very poor being rudely built of stone, sometimes perched on a hill-top in the midst of straggling, wind-blown farm lands. Better dwellings marked the entrance to some tiny village, and these, though rarely pretty, had usually some characteristic which made them picturesque, and inclined one of the party to produce a sketch-book and pencil: a bit of tumble-down balcony; a court, grass-grown and ill kept; a gable end; a doorway with heavy oaken beams—something, at all events, worth remembering; and when animated by two or three active, handsome young people, the doorways and yards looked very well. Sometimes we passed a bourgeois garden which was trimly kept—a contrast to its neighbors, for flowers do not seem to be cultivated in the windows and at the doorways of the poor in the Pyrenees as they are in England. A rose-tree may run wildly if it will, covering half the side of a house, or green vines may tangle themselves wantonly over door and window and porch, but there is none of the jea-

lously loving care bestowed upon a blossom's growth such as makes the humblest cottage in Great Britain pleasing. This may be because flowers in the Basque country are taken as matters of course as much as the richly rolling sea, the green slopes, or the fair blue sky.

En route to St.-Jean we passed the quaint little village of Bidart. I don't know what the guide-books have to say of it. We had known of it in the vaguest fashion before starting, and somehow I always associate it with the change that suddenly filled the earth and sky: the day suddenly turned gray, the sunshine fitful though luminous. Some boys, active over the national game, *jeu de paume*, stopped short, evidently reading from familiarity the tokens of the sky. For ourselves, we felt at once, in the midst of all the springing green and blossom, that one of the sudden Pyrenean storms was imminent. We drove on quickly, anxious to take shelter, and our coachman seemed to share our very worst apprehensions of a drenching. It was then that we curved about and entered Bidart. Everything had a lurid intensity; objects stood out as though upon some curiously contrived canvas; the houses, quaint and oddly shaped, were lighted up or cast into shadow in unexpected places; where the ground sloped roughly to the sea there were ridges of black tones, while, just above, fierce gleams of light would color the walls of some old house, or lie in fantastic zigzag across the roadway; people moved hither and thither, their importance in size and color won-

BASQUE OX-TEAM.

derfully strengthened by the lurid quality in the heavens; strange things grew prominent; road-side daisies and buttercups started into sudden dilation as we passed them by. Perhaps the utmost significance of this strange yellow light and fantastic shade centred about one building. It was a beer merchant's establishment. There was a curious rambling gallery, in which three or four men and women were grouped like people in Froissart. Below, two or three strong peasants were rolling casks into a vast, dim room, and in strong contrast to these figures was a young woman above. She had on a dark green gown, and a big silver cross on her breast. She ran to the end of the balcony, and shading her eyes from a too vivid gleam of light, she called out to some old people in a field below to make haste and take shelter. The old people— a group of thin, irregular, brown figures —seemed listless, or unaware of what the heavens meant. The girl above flung her arms about with the wild gestures we learned to understand as only a sort of underscoring to Basque feelings and sentiments. She was very pretty, in a rough, dark way, and I don't know what could have been more effective than her figure in the stormy light against the brown old house, the wind flapping her skirts and moving the waves of hair on her forehead. Her cross was shining in a spot of light.

Upon a hilly slope at Bidart is a little gray stone church, the bell of which was tolling as we drove into the town. Some pious old people were going in up a flight of well-worn stone steps just above a curious mediæval gateway. The patient figures toiling up the steps seemed to take no heed of the fact that the storm had already broken and the rain was pelting down furiously against the doorway, mingling with the sound of the organ within. We hastily took shelter in one of those inns which abound along the road, but which are devoted to the accommodation of very simple travellers.

But from Bidart to St.-Jean the drive was full of serene loveliness; the day was not too far advanced for us to enter the solemn old city with clear, still lines of sunlight in the open spaces. We left the range of hills and the quiet uplands rather suddenly behind us, and our first impression of St.-Jean-de-Luz was of silent, melancholy buildings, full of a pathetic dignity and jealously guarded splendors.

A wide irregular square gave on to the wharves and sea. Prominently to the right, and among the sombre houses, was the old church—that which witnessed the bravery and pomp of the royal marriage in 1660. Further on, as I have said, was the sea. There was an old wall, and fishermen were lounging about. Some nets were dragged in, boats turned up, and other idle signs of the craft which still characterizes the town. It was the hour for the afternoon service, and we entered the ponderous old church, our tourist sense merging into something comparatively personal. The pathos of the people seemed to find its concentration in this vast old house of God, and we had a curious feeling that we might be intruding upon some prayer, though mutely uttered, for the city's salvation.

The church is a splendid building, vast, dark, and peculiar in architecture. Tiers of oaken galleries, black with age, rise on either side, giving a peculiar effect when filled with people. The men and women, according to the established custom of the country, were divided. The whole suggestion of place and people was mediæval, for so much of the past clings to these Basques, both in dress and bearing, that one almost expected to hear the strains of old-time music when the organ pealed forth. It seemed as if we might have come in to witness the pompous march of King Louis's wedding up the aisle toward that altar, with its wax lights flickering yellow spots among the blackening oak. Could we not by lingering see it all, catch the shouts of a rejoicing crowd without, see a king made happy, and a queen given to the nation? But it was only March, 1880, after all, and two centuries had clouded St.-Jean, had doubtless changed the character, if not some of the instincts, of the people since that day of fair magnificence. If in their time-honored old church they seemed to bring back the meanings of the past, to-day grew present when they drifted out into the old square after the service ended. We stood among them for a little while, watching certain picturesque groups which formed unconsciously here and there. The old people clattered away in their sabots down the sharply paved streets; the younger ones stood about, laughing and talking gayly.

The residence of Louis XIV. was across the square, and presented deeper suggestions of antiquity; at least the windows were better, the stone-work more rugged; but the lower part to-day is devoted to merchandise; and the people of St.-Jean are so listless about their historic sights that we found no one who could even tell us whether it would be possible to obtain admittance to the old houses.

We drove back to Biarritz by the second road of which I have spoken, and found its elements rather wilder than the road by which we had gone; the stretch of hills was more unbroken; there were fields of grain and pasture-lands in great level sweeps of yellow and green, and one or two bits of roadway arched by the most splendid old trees. Thence we curved into the little village of La Négresse, and on over the now familiar white road to Biarritz. Here all was animation, for on Sunday evening the population of Biarritz is wont to assemble in its principal street, the young women dressing with dainty Parisian touches in gowns and parasols, but wearing no hats; the men in rather stiff corduroys, with red and green vests, and something picturesque or characteristic in their caps and knee-breeches. A great deal of laughing and talking was going on, sometimes briefly suspended while the gay chatterers stopped to watch some open carriage roll by with its burden of fashionable ladies and gentlemen. Visitors to Biarritz used to be heard complaining that Sunday was intolerably dull; but to me it seemed only an idea, for after service there were drives and walks to take, the sands were always free from a crowd, and if there was no special amusement for the evening, there came the quiet of a long, still watch of the starlight above that wonderful throbbing water. I remember one or two Sundays when we strolled out upon the sands to watch the marvellous moonlight effects upon the crags. What could have been grander than that sweeping shore, weirdly fascinating under the cold guardianship of the moon? We sat on one of the benches on a high cliff, and allowed our limbs to grow stiff and our necks to ache while we watched the unutterable splendors of the night before us.

Away stretched the water, rolling toward what might be the Infinite, for all it indicated of a distant shore; there were the hills, the crags, the sands, yellow-green in this delusive light. We moved away from our cold bench to look down into some rocky caverns where the waters moaned and gurgled, where it seemed as if a misstep would be so easy, where death would be so swift, yet so hideous and fantastic. Out on to one of the stone walls we ventured, growing reckless under the moon's sway, and there we beheld, shining in the pure white light, the statue of the Virgin, raised by reverent hands as a signal to sailors. Something curiously unearthly filled all this shore at moonlight; we always tried to smile at our own fantasies concerning it, yet we never could quite defy them; we knew that each occasion would revive the same bewildering, fascinating sensations.

I think I must not leave these fragmentary notes of that part of the Basque country without a few words about the curious legends of the people which we heard on very good authority. How far they are believed in is difficult to say, but they are certainly related by old dames over winter fires, told by mothers to refractory children, and so far influence the minds of the people as to tinge them with that air of half credulity, half timidity about the unknown which any traditionally superstitious nation is sure to possess. For the most part the legends are merely fantastic or absurdly foolish, but some are amusing, while certain legendary characters constantly appear in different stories, as, for example, Bassa-Jaun, the wild man, and Bassa-Audre, the wild woman. Bassa-Jaun is sometimes represented as a vampire, then as a faun or satyr, and again as a kind of brownie. His wife, Bassa-Audre, figures in various disguises, and one can trace in her likenesses to the legendary characters of the fairy lore of Northern nations. The Laminak constantly appear, and seem to be considered as fairies, both good and evil. The stories are told in the most primitive language, whether they appear in print or are related by the people themselves, and are curiously lacking in all descriptive power, analysis, or even the graphic force so often found in simple beginnings of a literature. For instance, one of the tales about Bassa-Jaun opens thus;

"Once upon a time there lived in one house the landlady and the farmer's wife. The farmer's wife had three sons. One day they said to their mother to give each of them a ball and a penny roll; that they wished to go from country to country. The mother was sorry to part with her three much-loved sons, but all three started off." This highly popular story goes on to relate, in the baldest, most meaning-less language, the wanderings of the three sons, their final appearance at Bassa-Jaun's castle, where they are transform-ed by the wild man, and their subsequent release by the efforts of their young sis-ter. The stories are utterly devoid of in-terest except as specimens of primitive literature, and expressing the simplicity of the people. One very popular fireside tale is so characteristic and so absurd that I will give it entire.

" There were a man and wife who were very poor. The man used to sit sadly at a cross-road. There came to him a gentle-man who asked, ' Why are you so sad ?'

" ' Because I have not wherewith to live,' he said to him.

" ' I will give you as much money as you like, if, at such a time, you tell me the age of the devil.'

" Our man goes off happy. He leads a merry life with his wife, for they wanted for nothing. They lived at a great rate. But time went on, and the time was ap-proaching. The man recollected that he had not busied himself at all about the devil's age. He became pensive. His wife asked him what was the matter with him—why is he not happy ? they wanted for nothing—why is he so sad ? He tells her how it is that he got rich, and what compact he had made with the gentle-man. His wife said to him:

" ' If you have nothing but that, it is nothing at all. Get into a barrel of honey, and when you come out of it get into another barrel of feathers, and, dress-ed like that, go to the cross-roads and wait for the devil there. You will put your-self on all fours, and walk backward and forward, and go between his legs, and walk all around him.'

" The man does as his wife had told him. The devil comes, and draws back when he sees him, and our man goes up quite close to the devil. The devil, being frightened, said to him:

" ' I am so many years old, and I have never seen any animal like that, and such a *frightful* one !'

" Our man had heard enough. He went off home at full speed, and told his wife that they would want for nothing ; that he had done as she had told him, just as if she had been a witch, and that he was no longer afraid of the devil. They lived rich and happily ; and if they lived well, they died well too."

The faculty of rhyming is very common among the people. Old men will go on sometimes for two hours at a time re-lating the events of the day in sing-song doggerel, while the improvisator, dying out elsewhere, is still a well-known char-acter at Basque fêtes, prizes being given for the best impromptu verses on a given theme. Some of the songs of the people are extremely plaintive and pretty ; when literally translated, their simplicity is very sweet, but rather monotonous.

It is hard, even when one has a strong interest in the subject, to get very near these Basques. Their reserve is good-hu-mored, but it is often impenetrable ; yet they are a most fascinating people, and one longs to solve the mystery of their origin.* It is curious to observe how many of their very oldest traits they yet preserve —even physical characteristics, which we read of as belonging to perhaps the Abys-sinians, whence some of them came, re-ap-pear now and then with surprising clear-ness. What they believe in the way of their legends they cling to with absolute faith, or at least with that refusal to disbelieve which operates forcibly on any untutored mind. I found among the Basques pre-cisely such influences as I had observed in the peasants of Devon and Somerset, the same belief in witchcraft and demon power—indeed, in the fantastic sway of fairies ; for the Basque "brownie" is the Devonshire were-woman, and the doings of the one are as much respected and feared as those of the other. In the neigh-borhood of St.-Jean-de-Luz a woman will tell you her child has been bewitched and is ill, and a Devon woman will say with equal gravity and faith that her child has had the evil-eye upon her. Witchcraft seems to be the prevailing Basque super-stition, though happily the day has gone by when St.-Jean-de-Luz glowed with the fires kindled for the unhappy victims sus-pected of employing witchcraft.

There had been cool winds, mornings and evenings, when a wood fire was not unacceptable, before we talked of leaving the lower Pyrenees, but these were follow-

* It is considered probable that the Basques were of Iberian origin, and " preceded the Celts by twenty centuries. They were called Euskarians when the Phœnicians came in the year 1100 B.C." The ori-gin of their language is little known, but it bears close analogy to Oriental tongues, especially to San-skrit. Their numbers in France and Spain are about 840,000. There are about 100,000 Basques in South America.

ed by days of summery stillness. In them we drove all over the country near Biarritz, taking in those final impressions which, as I have said, were like our first. The morning that we left it seemed to me as if I had never seen anything lovelier than the Judas-trees that were richly pink in all the gardens. We left at sunrise to take a train for the upper Pyrenees, and drove to Bayonne over a country gay with the voices of birds, and exquisitely lovely in the first flush of a perfect day. The fields, the hedges, the gardens, the road-side daisies, all had awakened with trembling pulsations of the deepening spring—the air was deliciously soft and cool, the glory in the east was a distant flood of color, flaming the mountain-tops, glorifying their shining heights with an unreal, awful majesty; but nearer to us the reflections were more delicately cast. Biarritz receded from view —the plaint of its ineffable shore grew more and more distant as we journeyed along in the morning; yet we found, on looking about us, and later, on recalling that day, and all others spent among these lower Pyrenean hills, that we had preserved all our first impressions. Light and color and fragrance were an abiding association with the country of the Basques.

A HUMBLE ROMANCE.

SHE was stooping over the great kitchen sink, washing the breakfast dishes. Under fostering circumstances her slenderness of build might have resulted in delicacy or daintiness; now the harmony between strength and task had been repeatedly broken, and the result was ugliness. Her finger joints and wrist bones were knotty and out of proportion, her elbows, which her rolled-up sleeves displayed, were pointed and knobby, her shoulders bent, her feet spread beyond their natural bounds—from head to foot she was a little discordant note. She had a pale, peaked face, her scanty fair hair was strained tightly back, and twisted into a tiny knot, and her expression was at once passive and eager.

There came a ringing knock at the kitchen door, and a face of another description, large, strong-featured, and assured, peered out of the pantry, which was over against the sink.

"Who is it, Sally?"

"I don' know, Mis' King."

"Well, go to the door, can't you, an' not stan' thar gapin'. I can't; my hands are in the butter."

Sally shook the dish-water off her red, sodden fingers, and shuffled to the door.

A tall man with a scraggy sandy mustache stood there. He had some scales in his hand.

"Good mornin', marm," he said. "Hev you got any rags?"

"I'll see," said the girl. Then she went over to the pantry, and whispered to her mistress that it was the tin peddler.

"Botheration!" cried Mrs. King, impatiently; "why couldn't he hev come an-

other day? Here I am right in the midst of butter, an' I've got lots of rags, an' I've got to hev some new milk pans right away."

All of this reached the ears of the tin peddler, but he merely stood waiting, the corners of his large mouth curving up good-naturedly, and scrutinized with pleasant blue eyes the belongings of the kitchen, and especially the slight, slouching figure at the sink, to which Sally had returned.

"I s'pose," said Mrs. King, approaching the peddler at length, with decision thinly veiled by doubt, "that I shall hev to trade with you, though I don' know how to stop this mornin', for I'm right in the midst of butter-making. I wish you'd 'a happened along some other day."

"Wa'al," replied the peddler, laughing, "an' so I would, marm, ef I'd only known. But I don't see jest how I could hev, unless you'd 'a pasted it up on the fences, or had it put in the newspaper, or mebbe in the almanac."

He lounged smilingly against the door-casing, jingling his scales, and waiting for the woman to make up her mind.

She smiled unwillingly, with knitted brows.

"Well," said she, "of course you ain't to blame. I guess I'll go an' pick up my rags, up in the garret. There's quite a lot of 'em, an' it 'll take some time. I don't know as you'll want to wait."

"Lor', I don't keer," answered the peddler. "I'd jest as soon rest a leetle as not. It's a powerful hot mornin' for this time o' year, an' I've got all the day afore me."

He came in and seated himself on a chair near the door with a loose-jointed sprawl.

After Mrs. King had gone out he sat a few minutes eying the girl at the sink intently. She kept steadily on with her work, though there was a little embarrassment and uncertainty in her face.

"Would it be too much trouble ef I should ask you to give me a tumbler of water, miss?"

She filled one of her hot, newly washed glasses with water from a pail standing on a shelf at one end of the sink, and brought it over to him. "It's cold," she said. "I drawed it myself jest a few minutes ago, or I'd get some right out of the well for you."

"This is all right, an' thanky kindly, miss; it's proper good water."

He drained the glass, and carried it back to her at the sink, where she had returned. She did not seem to dare absent herself from her dish-washing task an instant.

He set the empty glass down beside the pail; then he caught hold of the girl by her slender shoulders and faced her round toward him. She turned pale, and gave a smothered scream.

"Thar! thar! don't you go to being afeard of me," said the peddler. "I wouldn't hurt you for the whole world. I jest want to take a squar look at you. You're the worst-off-lookin' little cretur I ever set my eyes on."

She looked up at him pitifully, still only half re-assured. There were inflamed circles around her dilated blue eyes.

"You've been cryin', 'ain't you?"

The girl nodded meekly. "Please let me go," she said.

"Yes, I'll let you go; but I'm a-goin' to ask you a few questions first, an' I want you to answer 'em, for I'll be hanged ef I ever see— Ain't she good to you?"—indicating Mrs. King with a wave of his hand toward the door through which she had departed.

"Yes, she's good enough, I guess."

"Don't ever scold you, hey?"

"I don' know; I guess so, sometimes."

"Did this mornin', didn't she?"

"A little. I was kinder behind with the work."

"Keeps you workin' pretty stiddy, don't she?"

"Yes: thar's consider'ble to do this time o' year."

"Cookin' for hired men, I s'pose, and butter an' milk?"

"Yes."

"How long hev you been livin' here?"

"She took me when I was little."

"Do you do anything besides work?—go round like other gals?—hev any good times?"

"Sometimes." She said it doubtfully, as if casting about in her mind for reminiscences to prove the truth of it.

"Git good wages?"

"A dollar a week sence I was eighteen. I worked for my board an' close afore."

"Got any folks?"

"I guess I've got some brothers an' sisters somewhar. I don' know jest whar. Two of 'em went West, an' one is married somewhar in York State. We was scattered when father died. Thar was ten of us, an' we was awful poor. Mis' King took me. I was the youngest; 'bout four, they said I was. I 'ain't never known any folks but Mis' King."

The peddler walked up and down the kitchen floor twice; Sally kept on with her dishes; then he came back to her.

"Look a-here," he said; "leave your dish-washin' alone a minute. I want you to give me a good look in the face, an' tell me what you think of me."

She looked up shyly in his florid, freckled face, with its high cheek-bones and scraggy sandy mustache; then she plunged her hands into the dish-tub again.

"I don' know," she said, bashfully.

"Well mebbe you do know, only you can't put it into words. Now jest take a look out the window at my tin cart thar. That's all my own, a private consarn. I ain't runnin' for no company. I owns the cart an' horse, an' disposes of the rags, an' sells the tin, all on my own hook. An' I'm a-doin' pretty well at it; I'm a-layin' up a leetle money. I ain't got no family. Now this was what I was a-comin' at: s'pose you should jest leave the dishes, an' the scoldin' woman, an' the butter, an' everything, an' go a-ridin' off with me on my tin cart. I wouldn't know you, an' *she* wouldn't know you, an' you wouldn't know yourself, in a week. You wouldn't hev a bit of work to do, but jest set up thar like a queen, a-ridin' and seein' the country. For that's the way we'd live, you know. I wouldn't hev you keepin' house an' slavin'. We'd stop along the road for vittles, and bring up at taverns nights. What d'ye say to it?"

She stopped her dish-washing now, and stood staring at him, her lips slightly parted and her cheeks flushed.

"I know I ain't much in the way of

looks," the peddler went on, "an' I'm older than you—I'm near forty—an' I've been married afore. I don't s'pose you kin take a likin' to me right off, but you might arter a while. An' I'd take keer of you, you poor leetle thing. An' I don't b'lieve you know anything about how nice it is to be taken keer of, an' hev the hard, rough things kep' off by somebody that likes yer."

Still she said nothing, but stood staring at him.

"You 'ain't got no beau, hev you?" asked the peddler, as a sudden thought struck him.

"No." She shook her head, and her cheeks flushed redder.

"Well, what do you say to goin' with me? You'll hev to hurry up an' make up your mind, or the old lady'll be back."

The girl was almost foolishly ignorant of the world, but her instincts were as brave and innocent as an angel's. Tainted with the shiftless weariness and phlegm of her parents, in one direction she was vigorous enough.

Whether it was by the grace of God, or an inheritance from some far-off Puritan ancestor, the fire in whose veins had not burned low, she could see, if she saw nothing else, the distinction between right and wrong with awful plainness. Nobody had ever called her anything but a *good* girl. It was said with a disparagement, maybe, but it was always "a good girl."

She looked up at the man before her, her cheeks burning painfully hot, her eyes at once drooping and searching. "I—don't know jest—how you mean," she stammered. "I wouldn't go with the king, ef—it wasn't to—go honest—"

The peddler's face flushed as red as hers. "Now, look a-here, little un," he said. "You jest listen, an' it's God's own truth; ef I hadn't 'a meant all right I wouldn't 'a come to you, but to some other gal, hansumer, an' pearter, an'—but, oh Lord! I ain't that kind, anyway. What I want is to merry you honest, an' take keer of you, an' git that look off your face. I know it's awful sudden, an' it's askin' a good deal of a gal to trust so much in a fellow she never set eyes on afore. Ef you can't do it, I'll never blame you; but ef you kin, well, I don't b'lieve you'll ever be sorry. Most folks would think I was a fool, too, an' mebbe I am, but I wanted to take keer on you the minute I set eyes on you; an'

afore I know it the wantin' to take keer on you will be growin' into lovin' you. Now you hurry and make up your mind, or she will be back."

Sally had little imagination, and a loving nature. In her heart, as in all girls' hearts, the shy, secret longing for a lover had strengthened with her growth, but she had never dreamed definitely of one. Now she surveyed the homely, scrawny, good-natured visage before her, and it filled the longing nature had placed in her helpless heart well enough. His appearance dispelled no previous illusion, for previous illusion there had been none. No one had ever spoken to her in this way. Rough and precipitate though it was, it was skillful wooing; for it made its sincerity felt, and a girl more sophisticated than this one could not have listened to it wholly untouched.

The erratic nature of the whole proceeding did not dismay her. She had no conscience for conventionalities; she was too simple; hers only provided for pure right and wrong. Strange to say, the possible injury she would do her mistress by leaving her in this way did not occur to her till afterward. Now she looked at her lover, and began to believe in him, and as soon as she began to believe in him —poor, unattractive, ignorant little thing that she was!—she began to love just like other girls. All over her crimson face flashed the signs of yielding. The peddler saw and understood them.

"You will—won't you, little un?" he cried. Then, as her eyes drooped more before his, and her mouth quivered between a sob and a smile, he took a step forward and stretched out his arms toward her. Then he stepped back, and his arms fell.

"No," he cried, "I won't; I'd like to give you a hug, but I won't; I won't so much as touch that little lean hand of yours till you're my wife. You shall see I mean honest. But come along now, little un, or she will be back. I declar' ef I don't more'n half believe she's fell in a fit, or she'd ha' been back afore now. Come now, dear, be spry!"

"Now?" said Sally in turn.

"Now! why, of course now: what's the use of waitin'? Mebbe you want to make some weddin' cake, but I reckon we'd better buy some over in Derby, for it might put the old lady out;" and the peddler chuckled. "Why, I'm jest a-goin' to stow you away in that 'ere tin cart of mine—there's plenty of room, for I've been on the road a-sellin' nigh a week. An' then I'm a-goin' to drive out of this yard, arter I've traded with your missis, as innocent as the very innocentest lamb you ever see, an' I'm a-goin' to drive along a piece till it's safe; an' then you're a-goin' to git out an' set up on the seat alongside of me, an' we're goin' to keep on till we git to Derby, an' then we'll git merried, jest as soon as we kin find a minister as wants to airn a ten-dollar bill."

"But," gasped Sally, "she'll ask whar I am."

"I'll fix that. You lay there in the cart an' hear what I say. Lor, I'd jest as soon tell her to her face, myself, what we was goin' to do, an' set you right up on the seat aside of me, afore her eyes; but she'd talk hard, most likely, an' you look scared enough now, an' you'd cry, an' your eyes would git redder; an' she might sass you so you'd be ready to back out, too. Women kin say hard things to other women, an' they ain't likely to understan' any woman but themselves trustin' a man overmuch. I reckon this is the best way." He went toward the door, and motioned her to come.

"But I wants my bonnet."

"Never mind the bunnit; I'll buy you one in Derby."

"But I don't want to ride into Derby bare-headed," said Sally, almost crying.

"Well, I don' know as you do, little un, that's a fact; but hurry an' git the bunnit, or she *will* be here. I thought I heard her a minute ago."

"Thar's a leetle money I've saved, too."

"Well, git that; we don't want to make the old lady vallyble presents, an' you kin buy yourself sugar-plums with it. But be spry."

She gave him one more scared glance, and hastened out of the room, her limp calico accommodating itself to every ungraceful hitch of her thin limbs and sharp hips.

"I'll git her a gown with puckers in the back," mused the peddler, gazing after her. Then he hastened out to his tin cart, and arranged a vacant space in the body of it. He had a great-coat which he spread over the floor.

"Thar, little un, let me put you right in," he whispered, when Sally emerged, her bonnet on her head, a figured green delaine shawl over her shoulders, and her little hoard dangling from her hand in an old stocking.

She turned round and faced him once more, her eyes like a child's peering into a dark room. "You mean *honest*?"

"Before God, I do, little un. Now git in quick, for she *is* comin'!"

He had to lift her in, for her poor little limbs were too weak to support her. They were not a moment too soon, for Mrs. King stood in the kitchen door a second later.

"Here! you ain't goin', air you?" she called out.

"No, marm; I jest stepped out to look arter my hoss; he was a trifle uneasy with the flies, an' thar was a yaller wasp buzzin' round." And the peddler stepped up to the door with an open and artless visage.

"Well, I didn't know but you'd git tired waitin'. You spoke so about not bein' in a hurry that I stopped to pick my white rags out from the colored ones. I knew they'd bring more ef I did. I'd been meanin' to hev 'em all sorted out afore a peddler come along. I thought I'd hev Sally pick 'em over last week, but she was sick— Why, whar is Sally?"

"Who?"

"Sally—the girl that was washin' dishes when you come—she went to the door."

"Oh, the gal! I b'lieve I saw her go out the door a minute afore I went out to see to my hoss."

"Well, I'll call her, for she'll never git the dishes done, I guess, an' then we'll see about the rags."

Mrs. King strode toward the door, but the peddler stopped her.

"Now, marm, ef you please," said he, "I'd a leetle rayther you'd attend to business first, and call Sally arterward, ef it's jest the same to you, for I am gittin' in a leetle of a hurry, and don't feel as ef I could afford to wait much longer."

"Well," said Mrs. King, reluctantly, "I don't suppose I orter ask you to, but I do hev such discouragin' times with help. I declare it don't seem to me as ef Sally ever would git them dishes done."

"Wa'al, it don't seem to me, from what I've seen, that she ever will, either," said the peddler, as he gathered up Mrs. King's rag-bags and started for the cart.

"Anybody wouldn't need to watch her for more'n two minutes to see how slow she was," assented Mrs. King, following. "She's a girl I took when she was a baby to bring up, an' I've wished more'n fifty times I hadn't. She's a good girl enough, but she's awful slow—no snap to her. How much is them milk pans?"

Mrs. King was reputedly a sharp woman at a bargain. To trade with her was ordinarily a long job for any peddler, but to-day it was shortened through skillful management. The tinman came down with astonishing alacrity from his first price at the merest suggestion from his customer, and in a much shorter time than usual she bustled into the house, her arms full of pans, and the radiant and triumphant conviction of a good bargain in her face.

The peddler whirled rapidly into his seat, and snatched up the lines; but even then he heard Mrs. King calling the girl as he rattled around the corner.

A quarter of a mile from Mrs. King's there was a house; a little beyond, the road ran through a considerable stretch of woods. This was a very thinly settled neighborhood. The peddler drove rapidly until he reached the woods; then he stopped, got down, and peered into the cart.

Sally's white face and round eyes peered piteously back at him.

"How're you gittin' along, little un?"

"Oh, let me git out an' go back!"

"Lor', no, little un, you don't want to go back now! Bless your heart, she's all primed for an awful sassin'. I tell you what 'tis, you sha'n't ride cooped up in thar any longer; you shall git out, an' set up here with me. We'll keep our ears pricked up, an' ef we hear anybody comin', I'll stow you in the box under the seat afore you kin say Jack Robinson, an' thar ain't any houses for three mile."

He helped the poor shivering little thing out, and lifted her up to the high seat. When he had seated himself beside her, and gathered up the lines, he looked down at her curiously. Her bonnet the severe taste of Mrs. King had regulated. It was a brown straw, trimmed with brown ribbon. He eyed it disapprovingly. "I'll git you a white bunnit, sich as brides wear, in Derby," said he.

She blushed a little at that, and glanced up at him, a little grateful light over her face.

"You poor little thing!" said the peddler, and put out his hand toward her, then drew it back again.

Derby was a town with the prestige of a city. It was the centre of trade for a large circle of little country towns; its main street was crowded on a fair day, when the roads were good, with any quantity of nondescript and antediluvian-looking vehicles, and the owners thereof presented a wide variety of quaintness in person and attire.

So this eloping pair, the tall, bony, shambling man, and the thin, cowed-looking girl, her scant skirts slipping too far below her waist line in the back, and following the movements of her awkward heels, excited no particular attention.

After the tin cart had been put up in the hotel stable, and the two had been legally pronounced man and wife, or specifically Mr. and Mrs. Jake Russell, they proceeded on foot down the principal street, in which all the shops were congregated, in search of some amendments to the bride's attire.

If it was comparatively unnoticed, Sally was fully alive to the unsuitableness of her costume. She turned around, and followed with wistful eyes the prettily dressed girls they met. There was a great regret in her heart over her best gown, a brown delaine, with a flounce on the bottom, and a shiny back. She had so confidently believed in its grandeur so long, that now, seen by her mental vision, it hardly paled before these splendors of pleating and draping. It compared advantageously, in her mind, with a brown velvet suit whose wearer looked with amusement in her eyes at Sally's forlorn figure. If she only had on her brown delaine, she felt that she could walk more confidently through this strangeness. But, nervously snatching her bonnet and her money, she had, in fact, heard Mrs. King's tread on the attic stairs, and had not dared to stop longer to secure it.

She knew they were out on a search for a new dress for her now, but she felt a sorrowful conviction that nothing could be found which could fully make up for the loss of her own beloved best gown. And then Sally was not very quick with her needle; she thought with dismay of the making up; the possibility of being aided by a dressmaker, or a ready-made costume, never entered her simple mind.

Jake shambled loosely down the street, and she followed meekly after him, a pace or two behind.

At length the peddler stopped before a large establishment, in whose windows some ready-made ladies' garments were displayed. "Here we air," said he, triumphantly.

Sally stepped weakly after him up the broad steps.

One particular dress in the window had excited the peddler's warm admiration. It was a trifle florid in design, with dashes of red here and there.

Sally eyed it a little doubtfully, when the clerk, at Jake's request, had taken it down to show them. Untutored as her taste was, she turned as naturally to quiet plumage as a wood-pigeon. The red slashes rather alarmed her. However, she said nothing against her husband's decision to purchase the dress. She turned pale at the price; it was nearly the whole of her precious store. But she took up her stocking-purse determinedly when Jake began examining his pocket-book.

"I pays for this," said she to the clerk, lifting up her little face to him with scared resolve.

"Why, no, you don't, little un," cried Jake, catching hold of her arm. "I'm a-goin' to pay for it, o' course. It's a pity ef I can't buy my own wife a dress."

Sally flushed all over her lean throat, but she resolutely held out the money.

"No," she said again, shaking her head obstinately, "*I* pays for it."

The peddler let her have her way then, though he bit his scraggy mustache with amaze and vexation as he watched her pay her bill, and stare with a sort of frightened wistfulness after her beloved money as it disappeared in the clerk's grasp.

When they emerged from the store, the new dress under his arm, he burst out, "What on airth made you do that, little un?"

"Other folks does that way. When they gits merried they buys their own close, ef they kin."

"But it took pretty near all you'd got, didn't it?"

"That ain't no matter."

The peddler stared at her, half in consternation, half in admiration.

"Well," said he, "I guess you've got a little will o' your own, arter all, little un, an' I'm glad on't. A woman'd orter hev a little will to back her sweetness; it's all too soft an' slushy otherways. But I'll git even with you about the dress."

Which he proceeded to do by ushering his startled bride into the next dry-goods establishment, and purchasing a dress pattern of robin's-egg blue silk, and a delicate white bonnet. Sally, however, insisted on buying a plain sun-hat with the remainder of her own money. She was keenly alive to the absurdity and peril of that airy white structure on the top of a tin cart.

The pair remained in Derby about a week; then they started forth on their travels, the blue silk, which a Derby dressmaker had made up after the prevailing mode, and the white bonnet, stowed away in a little new trunk in the body of the cart.

The peddler, having only himself to consult as to his motions, struck a new route now. Sally wished to keep away from her late mistress's vicinity. She had always a nervous dread of meeting her in some unlikely fashion.

She wrote a curious little ill-spelled note to her at the first town where they stopped after leaving Derby. Whether or no Mrs. King was consoled or mollified by it she never knew.

Their way still lay through a thinly settled country. The tin peddler found readier customers in those farmers' wives who were far from stores. It was late spring. Often they rode for a mile or two through the lovely fresh woods without coming to a single house.

The girl had never heard of Arcadia, but she was riding through it under gold-green boughs, to the sweet broken jangling of tin-ware, all unexpressed to herself.

When they stopped to trade at the farmhouses, how proudly she sat, a new erectness in her slender back, and held her husband's horse tightly while he talked with the woman of the house, with now and then a careful glance toward her to see if she was safe. They always contrived to bring up at some town where there was a place of worship on a Sabbath-day. Then the blue silk and the white bonnet were taken reverently from their hiding-place, and Sally, full of happy consciousness, went to church with her husband in all her bridal bravery.

These two simple pilgrims, with all the beauty and grace there was in either of them turned only toward each other, and seen rightly only in each other's untutored, uncritical eyes, had journeyed together blissfully for about three months, when one afternoon Jake came out of a little country tavern, where they had proposed stopping for the night, with a pale face. Sally had been waiting on the cart outside until he should see if they could be accommodated. He jumped up beside her and took the lines.

"We'll go on to Ware," he said, in a dry voice; "it's only three mile further. They're full here."

Jake drove rapidly along, an awful look on his homely face, giving it the beauty of tragedy.

Sally kept looking up at him with pathetic wonder, but he never looked at her or spoke till they reached the last stretch of woods before Ware village. Then, just before they left the leafy cover, he slackened his speed a little, and threw his arm around her.

"See here, little un," he said, brokenly. "You've — got — consider'ble backbone, 'ain't you? Ef anything awful should happen, it wouldn't — kill you — you'd bear up?"

"Ef you told me to."

He caught at her words eagerly. "I would tell you to, little un—I do tell you to," he cried. "Ef anything awful ever should—happen—you'll remember that I told you to bear up."

"Yes, I'll bear up." Then she clung to him trembling. "Oh, what is it, Jake?"

"Never mind now, little un," he answered; " p'rhaps nothin' awful's goin' to happen; I didn't say thar was. Chirk up an' give us a kiss, an' look at that 'ere sky thar, all pink an' yaller."

He tried to be cheerful, and comfort her with joking endearments then, but the awful lines in his face staid rigid and unchanged under the smiles.

Sally, however, had not much discernment, and little of the sensitiveness of temperament which takes impressions of coming evil. She soon recovered her spirits, and was unusually merry for her the whole evening, making, out of the excess of her innocence and happiness, several little jokes, which made Jake laugh loyally, and set his stricken face harder the next minute.

In the course of the evening he took out his pocket-book and displayed his money, and counted it jokingly. Then he spoke, in a careless, casual manner, of a certain sum he had deposited in a country bank, and how, if he was taken sick and needed it, Sally could draw it out as well as he. Then he spoke of the value of his stock in trade and horse and cart. When they went to bed that night he had told

his wife, without her suspecting he was telling her, all about his affairs.

She fell asleep as easily as a child. Jake lay rigid and motionless till he had listened to her regular breathing an hour. Then he rose softly, lit a candle, which he shaded from her face, and sat down at a little table with a pencil and paper. He wrote painfully, with cramped muscles, his head bent on one side, following every movement of his pen, yet with a confident steadiness which seemed to show that all the subject-matter had been learned by heart beforehand. Then he folded the paper carefully around a little book which he took from his pocket, and approached the bed, keeping his face turned away from his sleeping wife. He laid the little package on his vacant pillow, still keeping his face aside.

Then he got into his clothes quickly, his head turned persistently from the bed, and opened the door softly, and went out, never once looking back.

When Sally awoke the next morning she found her husband gone, and the little package on the pillow. She opened it, more curious than frightened. There was a note folded around a bank-book. Sally spelled out the note laboriously, with whitening lips and dilating eyes. It was a singular composition, its deep feeling pricking through its illiterate stiffness.

"DEAR WIFE,—I've got to go and leve you. It's the only way. Ef I kin ever come back, I will. I told you bout my bizness last night. You'd better drive the cart to Derby to that Mister Arms I told you bout, an' he'll help you sell it an' the hoss. Tell him your husband had to go away, an' left them orders. I've left you my bank-book, so you can git the money out of the bank the way I told you, an' my watch an' pocket-book is under the pillow. I left you all the money, cept what little I couldn't git long without. You'd better git boarded somewhar in Derby. You'll hev enough money to keep you awhile, an' I'll send you some more when thet's gone, ef I hev to work my fingers to the bone. Don't ye go to worryin' an' workin' hard. An' bear up. Don't forgit thet you promised me to bear up. When you gits to feelin' awful bad, an' you will, jest say it over to yourself—'He told me to bear up, an' I said as I would bear up.' Scuse poor writin' an' a bad pen.
                    Yours till death,
                         "JAKE RUSSELL."

When Sally had read the letter quite through, she sat still a few minutes on the edge of the bed, her lean, round-shouldered figure showing painfully through her clinging night dress, her eyes staring straight before her.

Then she rose, dressed herself, put the bank-book, with the letter folded around it, and her husband's pocket-book, in her bosom, and went down-stairs quietly. Just before she went out her room door she paused with her hand on the latch, and muttered to herself, "He told me to bear up, an' I said as I would bear up."

She sought the landlord to pay her bill, and found that it was already paid, and that her recreant husband had smoothed over matters in one direction for her by telling the landlord that he was called away on urgent business, and that his wife was to take the tin cart next morning, and meet him at a certain point.

So she drove away on her tin cart in solitary state without exciting any of the wondering comments which would have been agony to her.

When she gathered up the lines and went rattling down the country road, if ever there was a zealous disciple of a new religion, she was one. Her prophet was her raw-boned peddler husband, and her creed and whole confession of faith his parting words to her.

She did not take the road to Derby; she had made up her mind about that as she sat on the edge of the bed after reading the letter. She drove straight along the originally prescribed route, stopping at the farm-houses, taking rags and selling tin, just as she had seen her husband do. There were much astonishment and many curious questions among her customers. A woman running a tin cart was an unprecedented spectacle, but she explained matters, with meek dignity, to all who questioned her. Her husband had gone away, and she was to attend to his customers until he should return. She could not always quite allay the suspicion that there must needs be something wrong, but she managed the trading satisfactorily, and gave good bargains, and so went on her way unmolested. But not a farm-yard did she enter or leave without the words sounding in her beating little heart, like a strong, encouraging chant, "He told me to bear up, an' I said as I would bear up."

When her stock ran low, she drove to Derby to replenish it. Here she had opposition from the dealers, but her almost abnormal persistence overcame it.

She showed Jake's letter to Mr. Arms, the tin dealer with whom she traded, and he urged her to take up with the advice in it, promising her a good bargain; but she was resolute.

Soon she found that she was doing as well as her husband had done, if not better. Her customers, after they had grown used to the novelty of a tinwoman, instead of a tinman, liked her. In addition to the regular stock, she carried various little notions needed frequently by housewives, such as pins, needles, thread, etc.

She oftener staid at a farm-house overnight than a tavern, and frequently stopped over at one a few days in severe weather.

After her trip to Derby she carried always a little pistol, probably more to guard Jake's watch and property than herself.

Whatever money she did not absolutely require for current expenses went to swell Jake's little hoard in the Derby bank. During the three years she kept up her lonely travelling little remittances came directed to her from time to time, in the care of Mr. Arms. When one came, Sally cried pitifully, and put it into the bank with the rest.

She never gave up expecting her husband. She never woke up one morning without the hope in her heart that he would come that day. Every golden dawn showed a fair possibility to her, and so did every red sunset. She scanned every distant, approaching figure in the sweet country roads with the half conviction in her heart that it was he, and when nearness dispelled the illusion, her heart bounded bravely back from its momentary sinking, and she looked ahead for another traveller.

Still he did not come for three years from the spring he went away. Except through the money remittances, which gave no clew but the New York postmark on the envelope, she had not heard from him.

One June afternoon a poor lonely maiden, now without her beloved swain, driving through her old Arcadian solitudes, whose enchanted meaning was lost to her, heard a voice from behind calling to her, above the jangling of tin, "Sally! Sally! Sally!"

She turned, and there he was, running after her. She turned her head quickly, and, stopping the horse, sat perfectly still, her breath almost gone with suspense. She did not dare look again for fear she had not seen aright.

The hurrying steps came nearer and nearer; she looked when they came abreast the cart. It was he. It always seemed to her that she would have died if it had not been that time.

"Jake! Jake!"

"Oh, Sally!"

He was up on the seat before she could breathe again, and his arms around her.

"Jake, I did—bear up—I did."

"I know you did, little un. Mr. Arms told me all about it. Oh, you dear little un, you poor little un, a-drivin' round on this cart all alone!"

Jake laid his cheek against Sally's and sobbed.

"Don't cry, Jake. I've airned money, I hev, an' it's in the bank for you."

"Oh, you blessed little un! Sally, they said hard things 'bout me to you in Derby, didn't they?"

She started violently at that. There was one thing which had been said to her in Derby, and the memory of it had been a repressed terror ever since.

"Yes: they said as how you'd run off with—another woman."

"What did you say?"

"I didn't believe it."

"I did, Sally."

"Well, you've come back."

"Afore I married you I'd been married afore. By all that's good an' great, little un, I thought my wife was dead. Her folks said she was. When I come home from peddlin', one time, she was gone, an' they said she was off on a visit. I found out in a few weeks she'd run off with another fellow. I went off peddlin' agin without carin' much what become of me. 'Bout a year arterward I saw her death in a paper, an' I wrote to her folks, an' they said 'twas true. They were a bad lot, the whole of 'em. I got took in. But she had a mighty pretty face, an' a tongue like honey, an' I s'pose I was green. Three year ago, when I went into that 'ere tavern in Grover, thar she was in the kitchin a-cookin'. The fellow she run off with had left her, an' she'd been tryin' to hunt me up. She was awful poor, an' had come across this place an' took it. She was allers a good cook, an' she suited the customers fust rate. I

guess they liked to see her pretty face 'round too, confound her!

"Well, little un, she knew me right off, an' hung on to me, an' cried, an' begged me to forgive her; and when she spied you a-settin' thar on the cart, she tore. I hed to hold her to keep her from goin' out an' tellin' you the whole story. I thought you'd die ef she did. I didn't know then how you could bear up, little un. *Ef* you 'ain't got backbone!"

"Jake, I did bear up."

"I know you did, you blessed little cretur. Well, she said ef I didn't leave you, an' go with her, she'd expose me. As soon as she found she'd got the weapons in her own hands, an' could hev me up for bigamy, she didn't cry so much, an' wa'n't quite so humble.

"Well, little un, then I run off an' left you. I couldn't stay with you ef you wa'n't my wife, an' 'twas all the way to stop her tongue. I met her that night, an' we went to New York. I got lodgin's for her; then I went to work in a box factory, an' supported her. I never went nigh her from one week's end to the other; I couldn't do it without hevin' murder in my heart; but I kep' her in money. Every scrap I could save I sent to you, but I used to lay awake nights worryin' for fear you'd want things. Well, it's all over. She died a month ago, an' I saw her buried."

"I knowed she was dead when you begun to tell about her, because you'd come."

"Yes, she's dead this time, an' I'm glad. Don't you look scared, little un. I hope the Lord 'll forgive me, but *I'm glad*. She was a bad un, you know, Sally."

"Was she sorry?"

"I don' know, little un."

Sally's head was resting peacefully on Jake's shoulder; golden flecks of light sifted down on them through the rustling maple and locust boughs; the horse, with bent head, was cropping the tender young grass at the side of the road.

"Now we'll start up the horse, an' go to Derby an' git married over agin, Sally."

She raised her head suddenly, and looked up at him with eager eyes.

"Jake."

"Well, little un?"

"Oh, Jake, my blue silk dress an' the white bonnet is in the trunk in the cart jest the same, an' I can git 'em out, an' put 'em on under the trees thar, an' wear 'em to be married in!"

THE DAGGER.

A STORY OF THE TIME OF SEXTUS POMPEY.

IT was in the old, old days when Sextus Pompey ruled the Mediterranean from Antioch to the Pillars of Hercules that a war galley of fine proportions was speeding northward along the lower Italian coast not far from Sicily.

There was a pleasant breeze from the west, and as her sharp brazen beak clove through the foaming water her rowers, with their oars all drawn inboard, lay stretched upon their benches enjoying the breeze that drew in through the open oar-ports, for the huge square mainsail, her only sail upon her only mast, with the fresh wind abeam, superseded all their labor, and, with every reef let out, bore them right gallantly upon their course.

Her deck, flush fore and aft, was protected by strong bulwarks, along which on either side was a line of catapults, each having beside it a large tub of rounded stones of the proper size mingled with leaden balls, all covered, like the catapult, with a tarpaulin. Her belaying-pins and all her metal fittings were of the finest bronze, and so well cared for that they shone like burnished gold. Forward of the mast, on a revolving platform, was a strong ballista that could thus be turned in any direction. On each side of this were two large boxes full of heavy arrows, and two tubs full of stout linen bags containing stones and leaden balls that could be discharged from the machine with deadly effect at short range upon an enemy's deck. The fine bronze figure of a lark, with its wings extended, to typify the swiftness of the ship, which indeed was evident from her model, was fastened upon the topmost part of the prow, just above the foaming waves, and explained the name *Alauda* in bronze letters on her stern.

Two young men tended the tiller, while a wrinkled and bronzed old pilot sat near to keep them straight. The rest of the crew were at work forward, repairing and refitting the running and standing rigging, and doing those thousand little things that must be done on board a ship, and which prevent the men from suffering all the ills of idleness. Their uniform was of dark blue edged with white, which, besides its neat appearance, was advantageous in a night attack from the strong contrast of the colors.

An awning was stretched above the quarter-deck, and under it four officers, two on either side, were pacing to and fro. Of the two on the right, the commander seemed about twenty-eight years of age, and was evidently of superior mould.

His fine head, well set on his broad shoulders, his broad and deep chest, his fine, upright figure, his firm, easy, and alert step, his short, curling, coal-black hair and beard, his dark, penetrating, and expressive eyes, and the quiet energy that marked his every movement, showed him born to lead and to command. His clothing consisted of an under-tunic of the fine linen of Egypt, of unsullied whiteness, which appeared at the neck and wrists, where it was adorned with a finely embroidered border of rich purple. Over this was the ordinary Roman tunic of the whitest and finest woollen stuff, adorned with the broad stripe of purple that told of senatorial rank. A pair of light sandals completed his attire.

The belt that girt his tunic sustained a sword of the best Spanish steel, just such as are still made at Toledo, straight, double-edged, strong, light, and elastic. Its silver hilt was finely wrought, yet so that its ornaments should not interfere with, but rather aid, the grasp. A separate, slender belt of the finest leather, richly embroidered, supported at his right side a dagger, the flashing gems upon whose hilt told of its value. This gift of an Eastern potentate to Sextus Pompey had been presented by him to his favorite young commander, Titus Aurelius Cotta, who, in spite of his good old Roman name, had rather the features of a Greek, for his father, while pursuing his studies at Athens, as was then the custom of the better educated Roman nobles, had fallen in love with a beautiful Greek girl, and had finally succeeded in overcoming the opposition of his family to their union. His Greek blood had perhaps inclined him toward the sea, and a boyish voyage with a sailor uncle had made that inclination so strong that he was at length allowed to enter the Roman navy at sixteen, just one year before the battle of Pharsalia.

When war actually broke out, his father's death having left him free, he joined the side of Pompey, and by showing a very unusual combination of courage and of judgment had risen thus early to his present position.

His mother and sister lived in quiet security in Rome, and during that brief time of peace when Sextus met Augustus and Antony at Misenum he had gone to Rome to gladden their hearts by his visit. The gay young sailor was as happy as a big boy let loose on shore, and they were delighted with his intense enjoyment of everything. Meeting a beautiful friend of his sister, he fell most deeply in love, and was so impetuous that he wished to carry her heart by storm. She was not prepared for such terrible rapidity, and so resisted, until finally he tore himself away in a rage of disappointment, and sought his solace on the sea.

The fair Julia Sabina was half sorry as soon as he had gone, but the short-lived truce was quickly over, and she heard of him no more.

His second in command, who paced beside him, was of another mould of mind and body. Sturdy, muscular, square-built, and very powerful, he was a fair specimen of

"the black-eyed Roman with
The eagle's beak between those eyes which ne'er
Beheld a conqueror or looked along
The land he made not Rome's."

His firm-shut but rather thick-lipped mouth, his keen and penetrating glance, that saw and noted everything, and the promptness of his every movement, showed him to be a man of action rather than of thought. His name was Marcus Claudius Pulcher. He was indeed descended from that bluff old sailor Appius Claudius Pulcher, who when he wished to give battle to the enemy, having been informed by the augurs that he must not fight because the sacred chickens had refused to eat, swore by the gods that if they would not eat they should drink, and ordered both coops and chickens to be thrown into the sea.

Turning to his commander, he said:

"Hast thou yet read thy sealed instructions, and hast thou any orders now to give?"

"I have. My orders are to wait for night, and then to get as near the promontory of Misenum as may consist with safety; to send a well-manned boat on shore to seize whoever may be in the official residence at the extremity of the promontory, and bring him back to Sicily as a hostage for one of our officers recently taken by the enemy. I am also ordered to remain with the ship, and to send ashore my second in command. Thou wilt find there either the admiral of the fleet that is in port near by, or the Procurator of Campania, or some other high official. Seize him, bind him quickly, and bring him on board. No great force is needed. Our large boat's crew will be sufficient. Thou canst take the eight rowers, and leave the steersman and the bow-boy to tend boat; for swiftness and not strength is the soul of such an enterprise. Thou wilt take with thee two lanterns, and when thou comest away light them, and let the bow-boy hold them one above the other. As soon as thy lights are seen we will show the same. At present we are bowling along too rapidly. Let the sail be double reefed, so that we get near the house at the right time."

The house he spoke of had been built with care so as to be a most luxurious mansion. A space about eight hundred by two hundred feet on the bare rock had been inclosed by a strong stone wall some eight feet high. This had all been filled in with rich earth and planted with trees, at the same time the house was built near the end toward the sea, with trees enough to shield it from the westering sun, but not to interfere with the seaward view.

The house was built in the usual style, with a short hall leading into the atrium, a square apartment whose roof sloped inward toward a large square opening in the centre, thus allowing the rain-water to fall into a square cistern, and securing in this way both air and moisture to cool the house. Beyond the atrium was the tablinum, or small parlor, separated from the atrium by heavy curtains, and by sliding doors on the other side toward the peristyle, whose roof sloped outward from a large central opening, around which were set columns for support and ornament. Beyond the peristyle was the garden wall.

The day had been warm, and all the doors were open to admit the cooling western breeze. The servants were mostly outside under the trees, and the fair Julia, whose father had been appointed Procurator of Campania, was sitting on a chair in the tablinum. The heavy curtain was lifted and the sliding doors drawn back to admit the pleasant breeze; and as the tender twilight came on, Julia dismissed her attendant, and sat there in that musing mood that comes at times to all of us.

First memory took her gently by the hand, and led her to her girlish days among the Sabine hills, with all the dear delights of vineyard and of orchard, of the rich milk, the cream, the butter, and the cheese-cakes; the grass so green in spring, and then the new-mown hay, and then the gathered sheaves of autumn; and how her mother, now two years dead, had enjoyed all these.

Then she thought of Rome, and of its pleasures and its shows; and then she naturally fell to passing in review, as young women will, the young men she had seen. Each had his good and bad points, which, with the quick appreciation of her sex, she had observed and noted. Among these she thought of Titus Cotta and his family, and half regretted that he had been so hasty, for he seemed, during the short time she knew him, so superior to the young men around her.

Very beautiful was she as she sat there in her chair, with her clasped hands in her lap, her fine soft white dress falling in graceful folds around the beautiful outlines of her exquisitely proportioned form, her beautiful feet just appearing with their light sandals, while her Grecian sleeve, loose from the elbow, and fastened above with loops and buttons, showed through the openings her rounded arm. Her beautiful neck was finely set upon her well-proportioned bust. Her abundant dark brown hair was gathered in long braids that were then wound around each other at the back of the head. Through these braids was passed a long golden pin shaped like a slender lance, which also passed through the middle of a veil, the upper part of which could be drawn over the forehead, or allowed to fall back so as to form a graceful drapery for the shoulders. Her fair and beautifully clear complexion, with her large dark hazel eyes, as well as her brown hair and eyebrows, showed that the blood of the mountaineers had mingled with that of the darker inhabitants of the lowlands. As the daylight gradually disappeared, so absorbed was she in these thronging memories, sitting there with her eyes fixed upon the floor, that she did not hear the stealthy steps, she did not see the gliding forms, until a hand was placed upon her mouth, while others pressed her down upon her chair. She heard a voice say:

"Cut a strip from the curtain to put into her mouth, and tie behind her head, but not so tight as to choke her. Tie her hands and feet, and bind her fast upon her chair. Pass a strong strip around the back of the chair, and let Darius, who is the strongest, bend down and fasten this strip around his chest, so as to carry the chair and its contents on his back. Thus we shall lose the use of only one man's sword if we must fight."

The servants outside, who had seen these men enter the house, gazed at them at first in stupid wonder. Then, crowding to the entrance, they were soon driven back by the sharp words and sharper swords that met them. Some fled in terror to the nearest villa—toward Baiæ—to call for aid. Some few of the boldest lurked behind the trees to see what might be done. Their mistress had not called for lights, so they saw nothing till the men appeared bearing her thus strangely in their midst. They were surprised to hear no outcry, but stole along, concealing themselves as best they could, until they saw the boat push off, with their mistress still silent in the stern. Returning to the house, they procured lights and, taking the best horse from the stable, they mounted one of their number, who was to ride as fast as possible to Port Julian to inform the commander of the fleet what had taken place, and to give the alarm at the different villas as he passed. The rest, taking down from the walls the swords and shields that had been hung there as ornaments, returned thus armed to the shore, and sat down behind some rocks to watch, with the vague hope that something might be seen of their young mistress, whose kindness they had all experienced.

The boat meantime was pulled directly outward from the shore. The bow lights were set as directed, and when they were at a safe distance Julia felt the strip that gagged her cut and removed. Waiting for a moment until she had somewhat recovered from its effects, she exclaimed:

"Oh, tell me who you are, and why you have thus taken me from my father's house! Oh, do not harm me! My father is rich, and will give abundant ransom. I am his only child. His name is Caius Sempronius Sabinus. He is the Procurator of Campania. He went to Capua to hold his monthly court. He will be home to-morrow. You can easily communicate with him, and if I write to him, he will not harm your messenger."

No answer was vouchsafed, but a boat-cloak was thrown over her, as if to show some touch of kindness. It was terrible for a young woman to be thus torn from a luxurious and protected home, and to find herself in the power of pirates. What horrible fate might await her she could not tell, but she nerved herself to seek some mode of sudden death, if that should prove her only refuge. Her mother had read with her the old chronicles of Rome, her nurse had sung to her its old, old legends, and she was familiar with the lives of all the worthy women of Rome from Clœlia to Cornelia. Her spirits rose, in spite of her terrible position, as she thought of these, and nerved herself to emulate them.

They soon reached the galley; a rope was lowered, and the chair and its contents were transferred to the commander's cabin, while Marcus made his report to him.

"Thou hast done wrong, Marcus, a great wrong. We can do nothing with a woman. The enemy would laugh at us were we to propose such an exchange. We are not pirates to carry off young women. We must restore her, or at least land her, as soon as possible. I must see her."

Opening the door of his well-lighted cabin, he saw, to his great astonishment, Julia Sabina. While his astonishment prevented speech, she exclaimed:

"What! Titus Cotta! Thou commander of these pirates! Thou seizing helpless women! Oh, shame! Oh, shame! Think upon thy mother and thy sister! Oh, restore me to my father and my home, or if thou canst not, give me at least that dagger at thy girdle, that it may give me a sharp but sure remedy against all ills."

"Fair Julia, thy words are bitter and not true. I am no pirate. Thou shalt be returned immediately to thy father, even if I lose by so doing my liberty or my life. I did not know that he was Procurator here. My orders were to seize him as a hostage. My officer, not finding him, took thee. The instant that he told me I reproved him for his folly and his crime. Thou shalt have this dagger to use if I can not protect thee, but first let me cut therewith thy bonds."

So saying, he severed the strips that bound her hands and feet. While he was busy unbuckling the small belt, Julia attempted to rise to enjoy her new-found freedom; but her benumbed ankles gave way, and as Titus caught her and replaced her gently in the chair, her emotion overcame her, and she burst into tears. Kneeling before her, he exclaimed:

"Do not weep, fair Julia. Thy tears seem to fall on me like melted lead. Thou shalt be returned immediately, no matter what the risk. But, fool that I am, I have not yet changed the vessel's course."

Touching a bell, he said to the man who appeared:

"Tell the chief officer to change the vessel's course so as to bring her back as quickly as possible to the place from which we came. Let out every reef, and double man each oar. Get ready the four-oared barge with muffled oars and a picked crew. Away, and let these things be done instantly."

Then kneeling before her, without daring to touch even the hem of her garment, he besought her again and again not to weep. Calmed at length by his entreaties, her sobs subsided, and he left her to expedite the execution of his orders.

Meantime the slaves and freedmen that constituted the household sat upon the rocks discussing the event, and some, of course, began to swagger and to boast of what they would have done if they had only known that these men were pirates. Yet it was strange that they had stolen nothing. They therefore felt convinced that they would soon be back to secure all the rich plunder of the house.

The two freedmen, Stasimus and Demipho, were naturally the leaders of the party, which consisted of three Greek slaves, three common ones, and the two cooks, Anthrax and Congrio. They were all armed with shields and swords of antique pattern taken from the ornamented walls, except the cooks, of whom Anthrax was armed with a long and formidable spit, as his more natural weapon, while his aid, Congrio, with a shorter one, had followed his example.

Suddenly Charinus, the young Greek, who had been a sailor-boy, exclaimed:

"There is a boat coming!"

"Nonsense!" said Stasimus; "I hear nothing."

"No; because their oars are muffled; but bend your head down low and see the outline of that boat against the sky."

"It is so. Now listen. We will stay here to see where they touch the shore. If they go toward the house, and we are

"OPENING THE DOOR OF HIS WELL-LIGHTED CABIN, HE SAW, TO HIS GREAT ASTONISHMENT, JULIA SABINA."

strong enough, we may get behind them as they pass the big rock after the first turn. Strobilus, run thou to the house and put out all the lights, to give them as much delay and trouble as possible."

Seeing the boat come to at the same place as before, they ran for the big rock, some even extending their course to the garden behind the house, where the women-servants were hiding in terror. About half remained with Stasimus in ambuscade.

As the boat neared the shore, Titus said to his steersman:

"After we land, see that all stay by the boat, and keep her off shore within easy call. If I come not back within half an hour, save yourselves, and return to the ship, for you can not then help me."

Oh, how gladly Julia stepped upon the rock whence she had embarked! What joy and wild delight thrilled through all her frame to think that she had indeed escaped the horrible fate that seemed to await her! And as she climbed the well-known rocky pathway that led to her house beneath the faint light of the stars, other feelings began to take the place of that terror and anxiety that had hitherto pervaded her bosom. Titus still loved her. She saw it in his eyes, she heard it in his voice, she felt it in her whole being; and must they now separate forever? What could she do?

He had been so kind and so manly in the full and instantaneous reparation that he sought to make for the error of his subordinate, he had such a beautiful and powerful face and head, he was such a model of manliness in every respect, and he did love her so that it seemed a thousand pities that they must part. What could she do?

She began to pour forth her warmest thanks. The relief and the joy that thrilled in her bosom began to thrill in her voice as her expressions became warmer and warmer.

It was very pleasant to him, and he bent his head to hear, when, just as they passed the big rock at the first turn of the road, she heard the dull sound of a blow, and a voice saying, "Death to the pirate!" as Titus fell like a log before her. A piercing shriek tore through the air. She recognized the voice, and exclaimed:

"What! is it thou, Stasimus? He was no pirate. He was protecting me. How couldst thou do it?—how couldst thou do it? If he be dead, I must die too."

Kneeling down, Stasimus felt of his heart.

"He is not dead, lady. His heart beats. We have a large old-fashioned shield here that was taken from the wall. Two of us can carry him on that, and other two can hold his head and feet. His thick leather boarding cap has saved him."

"Take him up tenderly, then, and I will hold his head. Let some one bring lights and light the house. O Æsculapius, save him! save him!"

They put the broad old shield under him, and gently lifted him up all together. Julia, by a strong exertion of her will, res-

olutely put down all the natural nervousness she felt, and determined to do her utmost for him. Supporting tenderly the head that had now become so dear to her, with her hands that trembled somewhat in spite of all her resolution, she soon reached the house, and had him laid upon the bed in the best and largest of the guest-chambers. Then removing the stiff leather boarding cap that had done such good service, and washing off the clotted blood from the curling hair, she found to her great joy that the skull was not broken; but the blow must have been a powerful one, for he lay in complete torpor. Calling one of the most active of the men-servants, she dispatched him on the swiftest horse to her cousin Marcus Aurelius Sabinus at Baiæ, who owned a very able Greek physician, and who hired him out at a high price to those who needed him. He had been purchased by the father of his present owner, who had remarked him as a very bright and intelligent young slave. Noticing his turn for medicine, he had him carefully educated in that art, in which he became an enthusiast; but he was never allowed to purchase his freedom, though he offered a high price for himself, his former as well as his present owner both preferring to hire him out at high prices, and thus repay themselves for their expenditure. The messenger fortunately found him at home, and he returned with him.

His clear, penetrating eyes, with the calm consciousness of ability that marked his whole bearing, impressed Julia most favorably, though this was qualified by the subdued demeanor of a slave, and the necessary sadness of a highly educated man who is still retained in a servile condition. Having carefully examined into the condition of the patient, he said:

"Brain-fever seems to be commencing. He may suddenly pass from this stupor into strong delirium. Have ready four of the strongest men you can command, for possibly we may need all their strength."

His prediction was soon verified. After some convulsive movements Titus sat up in bed and gazed around. Seeing Julia near the door, he exclaimed:

"What! cruel one, art thou still there to persecute me? My head is all on fire. It burns; it burns. My blood boils in my veins. Give me the dagger that I gave thee, that I may prick my heart and let the hot blood out."

He started up as if to approach her, but the four strong men seized him, and passing strong bands over him, they bound him securely to the bed, while Julia fled in terror to her own room, and buried her face in the cushions of her couch.

"Must he die," she thought—"die now, and thus be lost when just regained? Oh no! the gods could not be so cruel. O Æsculapius," she exclaimed, "save him! save him! and I will enrich thy altar. Be merciful, and send relief!"

She could not help hearing the delirious shouts that rang through the house. She could not stay away in spite of the sharp pain it gave to hear him. Now he called on his mother and his sister; now she heard her own name, and complaints of her cruelty; then he was evidently, in imagination, in all the heady tumult of a fight, leading on his brave boarders to sweep the enemy from their deck.

She sent for the physician, and entreated him to do his best. He understood of course her feelings, and re-assured her to the best of his ability. Toward noon of the next day she heard the sound of horses' hoofs upon the rocks, and looking out of a window, saw her father approaching with his attendants. Running down to meet him, she was soon in his arms, and told him hurriedly of what had happened while their dinner was preparing.

"Well," he said, "we shall run no more such risks, for Agrippa has his fleet now ready. I heard as I came by the naval station that they are to sail to-morrow to attack that foolish sluggard Sextus Pompey, on the Sicilian coast, and that will be the last of him; but you must have some doors shut, for this shouting is too troublesome, and if this continues the small house at the garden's end must be fitted up for him, so that we can get some sleep at night. Now hurry dinner, my child, for I am hungry. I mounted just after daybreak, having eaten little, so that I am quite sharp-set with my long morning ride. I have to send a messenger to Rome with my report about my province, and he can bear thy message to the mother or sister of Titus. Write it to-day, for my messenger must leave to-morrow morning."

Directions were immediately given to prepare the garden house. The letter was written and dispatched. For a week the young man raved, with scarcely any sleep, carefully watched by the skillful Greek. Then the change came. The inflammation subsided, and the patient lay exhausted on his couch. Slowly, slowly his strength returned, the terrible wear and tear was gradually made up again, the wasted tissues were restored, and the mute sufferer's tongue was unloosed.

Oh, what joy was Julia's when at last she was told that he was really recovering! She had received an answer from his sister, stating that his mother, in consequence of exposure, had caught a cold, which changed into a fever, so that neither could come to him. She felt, therefore, that she must take their place. When the physician said that he was strong enough to see her, she sent to ask if she might come.

At first he received her with constraint and embarrassment; but her ardent eyes, her warm expressions of thankfulness and delight at his recovery, her abundant and cordial gratitude for what he had done, all spread like a balmy and invigorating cordial through his frame. When she told him of the letter from Rome, and said that she must be both mother and sister to him until they could come, he smiled and thanked her, as she took her leave, at the instance of the physician, who refused a longer interview.

At her second visit he was much stronger, and asked if he was a prisoner.

"Yes," said she; "you are my prisoner."

"But tell me of Sextus Pompey," he exclaimed.

"He has been utterly defeated off the northern coast of Sicily by Agrippa, and has fled toward the east."

Covering his face with his hands, he bowed down his head and was silent. Sitting down beside him, she said, tenderly: "Do not be cast down. If thou hast lost one friend, thou hast many others left, and none warmer than we are. Think how much, how very much, I owe thee."

He raised his head, and looking at her, with her glistening eyes moist with tears for his sorrow, and beaming evidently with the warmest affection for him, he said, softly, "Julia, dost thou love me?"

She bent down her head, and a slight tremor passed over her, but she answered, firmly, "I do, Titus."

And as he drew her to his bosom the happiest pair that morning's sun lit with his beams was on the rocky promontory of Misenum.

They neither of them wished then to try the sharp point of the dagger.

THE NEW YORK CUSTOM-HOUSE.

THREE things are perfectly clear to citizens of New York : first, the United States of America constitute the greatest country on earth; second, New York is the greatest city in the country; third, the Custom-house is the greatest institution in the city.

The Custom-house is a plain Doric building, of Quincy granite, with a portico of twelve front, four middle, and two rear granite columns, each thirty-eight feet high and four and a half feet in diameter. It has a frontage of 200 feet on Wall Street, a depth of about 160 feet on William and Hanover streets, and is 77 feet high. The rotunda has a height of 80 feet, and the dome is supported on eight pilasters of fine variegated Italian marble. Constructed for a Merchants' Exchange, at a cost of $1,800,000, it was purchased and occupied by the national government in 1862, and ought to be sold at the earliest opportunity. It is dark, damp, inconvenient, badly ventilated, and altogether inadequate for present uses. President Arthur, when Collector of the Port of New York, wisely advocated the erection of a suitable edifice on the block bounded by Whitehall and State streets, Bowling Green, and Whitehall Square. That would be a more eligible site. It is near to the Barge Office, which covers the water-front sold by the city to the government for $5000.

Plain as the Custom-house is, it is the commercial heart of the American people. What passes there is felt by every man, woman, and child in the land. There most of the duties are collected on the foreign woollens, silks, linens, cottons, and on the hats, bonnets, and furs they wear; on the carpets and mattings they tread; on the sugars, molasses, confectionery, spices, fruits, and breadstuffs they eat; on the spirits, wines, and malt liquors they drink; on the watches and jewelry they carry; on the earthenware, china, and glass that cover their tables; on the paintings that adorn their walls, the books that fill up their libraries, and the iron, steel, and other metallic instruments indispensable to their uses. All these articles cost the consumer more because of the work that is done at the Custom-house.

The total value of merchandise, free and dutiable, imported into the United States during the year ending June 30, 1883, was $723,180,914. The total value of dutiable merchandise entered for consumption, on arrival and after withdrawal from warehouse, in the United States during the same period, was $493,916,384. The entire value of dutiable merchandise imported into the United States, entered for consumption, and warehoused for payment of duties, in the fiscal year ending June 30, 1883, was $515,676,196. The total amount of duties collected thereon

was $214,706,496, or 43.49 per cent. of the whole value as officially stated.

This enormous revenue from duties on imported goods is the principal means wherewith the United States government maintains the army, the navy, and the civil service, pays the interest on the national debt, reduces the principal, and effects needed improvements.

In the fiscal year ending June 30, 1883, there were collected at the port of New York in duties on foreign merchandise no less than $146,483,964, or 68.5 per cent. of the aggregate amount collected in all the ports of the country. This fact shows the great national importance of the New York Custom-house. Another fact of similar bearing is that the foreign commerce of the United States, which has increased nearly one hundred per cent. since 1866, must in the future, as in the past, be mainly carried on through New York.

With the exception of Mexico and Canada, our commercial intercourse with other nations is conducted by means of steam and sailing vessels. By far the greater portion of these is owned by foreigners. The tonnage of foreign vessels entered at American ports increased from 3,117,034 tons in 1866 to 10,526,176 tons in 1883; whereas the American tonnage entered from foreign ports only increased from 1,891,453 tons in 1866 to 2,834,681 tons in 1883.

Great Britain, which, independently of her colonial and other possessions, is our largest commercial correspondent, and which imported from us goods valued at $425,424,174 in the year ending June 30,

EXHIBIT SHOWING THE IMPORTS FROM GREAT BRITAIN AND HER DEPENDENCIES INTO THE PORTS OF THE UNITED STATES DURING THE YEAR ENDING JUNE 30, 1883.

Country.	Number of Vessels.	Tonnage.	Steam Vessels.	Sailing Vessels.	Value of Imports.
England	2,783	6,309,498	1,189	1,594	$161,960,672
Scotland	377	915,416	172	205	18,702,898
Ireland	39	30,328	....	39	7,959,049
Gibraltar	97	160,184	48	49	4,573
Nova Scotia, New Brunswick, and Prince Edward Island	3,562	489,910	125	3,437	6,091,406
Newfoundland and Labrador	40	12,258	7	33	446,718
British West Indies	631	397,372	160	471	8,736,112
British Guiana	137	64,281	14	123	5,946,429
British Honduras	13	6,868	3	10	531,839
British East Indies	85	97,738	3	82	19,467,800
British Hong-Kong	77	159,007	36	41	1,918,894
British Possessions in Africa	27	26,551	7	20	1,840,020
British Possessions in Australasia	135	169,171	....	135	4,021,395
All other British Possessions	....	......	....	....	1,017,281
	8,003	8,838,582	1,764	6,239	$238,645,086

THE BARGE OFFICE.

1883, exporting to us within the same period goods amounting to $188,622,619, is, naturally enough, the principal owner of this shipping. She takes 51.6 per cent. of the total value of American exports, and sends to us 26 per cent. of all our imports.

In 1883 the total value of merchandise imported and exported at the port of New York was $857,430,637, or 55.43 per cent. of the whole value of our foreign commerce.

The tonnage of British vessels entering at United States ports in the last fiscal year amounted to 6,775,526 tons, a falling off in two years of 1,682,271 tons, but still constituting nearly two-thirds of the entire foreign tonnage entering at our ports.

EXHIBIT SHOWING NUMBER AND TONNAGE OF AMERICAN AND FOREIGN VESSELS WHICH ENTERED THE PORT OF NEW YORK FROM GREAT BRITAIN AND HER DEPENDENCIES IN THE YEAR ENDING JUNE 30, 1883; ALSO VALUE OF IMPORTS.

	American Vessels.		Foreign Vessels.		Aggregate.		Imports at New York.
	No.	Tons.	No.	Tons.	No.	Tons.	
England.......................	64	86,679	756	1,838,438	820	1,925,117	$92,252,820
Scotland......................	..	....	128	326,290	128	326,290	16,082,713
Ireland.......................	5	5,558	28	17,557	33	23,115	7,487,061
Gibraltar.....................	..	....	44	75,776	44	75,776	4,573
Nova Scotia, New Brunswick, and Prince Edward Island	298	52,689	517	104,840	815	157,529	798,090
Quebec, Ontario, Manitoba, and Northwest Territory	..	....	1	118	1	118	1,873
Newfoundland and Labrador	..	....	10	3,437	10	3,437	339,652
British West Indies	142	45,882	254	185,798	396	231,680	6,140,133
British Guiana	38	11,159	35	16,329	73	27,488	2,489,261
British Honduras	1	105	9	3,174	10	3,279	146,890
British East Indies	30	32,933	81	88,644	111	121,577	17,113,230
Hong-Kong	17	16,235	7	7,407	24	23,642	1,755,216
British Possessions in Africa and adjacent Islands	4	1,746	22	10,640	26	12,386	1,329,695
British Possessions in Australasia ..	3	1,372	8	2,791	11	4,163	1,803,334
All other British Possessions	..	....	1	287	1	287	1,005,964
	602	254,358	1,901	2,681,526	2,503	2,935,884	$148,750,505

Mr. George Hillier, superintendent of the Custom-house building, who entered the revenue service in 1841, keeps record of all the steam-ships entering New York from Europe. The average number of weekly arrivals is *forty*. This is a marvellous exhibit, in view of the fact that in 1845, only thirty-nine years ago, there cer, a Surveyor, and an Appraiser of the port of New York. Each is nominated for office by the President of the United States, confirmed therein by vote of the national Senate, and may retain his position for four years, unless removed for satisfactory reasons by joint Executive and Senatorial authority.

WILLIAM H. ROBERTSON, COLLECTOR OF THE PORT OF NEW YORK.

was only one steamer, the *Syria*, plying between New York and Liverpool.

The local administration of the national statutes regulating this vast and rapidly growing commerce, together with the collection of the differential duties imposed on imported merchandise, is intrusted to a Collector, assisted by a Naval Offi- Collector William H. Robertson, a vigorous and robust gentleman of sixty years, was commissioned by President Garfield, June 29, 1881, and brought to his new office the experience acquired in a long and honorable legal, judicial, and legislative career. Whether as Congressman, State Senator, or judge, his reputation was of the highest character, and justified the expectations that have since been so abundantly realized. The discussions in the national Senate pertinent to his nomination, and the results to which they gave birth, will ever constitute one of the most memorable chapters in American political history.

The Collector's duty is to see that all vessels and the merchandise therein contained, coming within the jurisdiction of his district, are duly entered at the Custom-house; that legally responsible parties be held to their liabilities; that the other branches of the customs service be enabled to do their duty as by law required; that the duties be properly assessed and collected, and that the legal disposition be made of goods entered in bond, or otherwise, or which are unclaimed; that smuggling and other frauds be prevented; that claims for drawback or refund be paid upon due proof only; that just fines, penalties, and forfeitures be imposed and enforced; and to report fully, as by law required, on all that pertains to the customs revenue, to the Treasury Department at Washington.

It is the duty of the Naval Officer to verify the clerical work done in the Collector's office. The latter is performed under laws and regulations so complicated as to render independent revision, in order to insure perfect accuracy, indispensably necessary. The Naval Officer is sworn to correct errors, inadvertencies, and neglect; and to enforce strict compliance with the national statutes. His action is co-ordinate with that of the Collector "in all matters affecting the collection of customs revenue, so far as they involve the amount of money collectable and collected; the proper record, adjustment, correction, and certification of accounts, including those of drawbacks and refunds; the enforcement of all laws and regulations for the safety of the revenue, and excluding any and all concern in the administration of the machinery of collection." General Charles K. Graham, formerly Surveyor of the Port, is now at the head of this department. The average cost per annum of the Naval Officer's department in New York for the past twelve or thirteen years does not exceed one-tenth of one per cent. of the duties collected at that port, and it certainly yields vastly more than that sum to the government in return.

The Surveyor is charged with the duty—subject in all cases to the Collector—of superintending and directing all inspectors, weighers, measurers, and gaugers within the port; of weekly reporting all neglect of duty to the Collector; of visiting, by proxy, all arriving vessels, and reporting in writing every morning to his superior all that have arrived from foreign ports on the preceding day; specifying the names and denominations of the vessels, the masters' names, whence arrived, whether laden or in ballast, to what nation belonging, and, if American vessels, whether the masters have or have not complied with the law requiring a definite number of manifests of the cargo on board. He may act in certain cases with the Collector and Naval Officer in allowing ships' manifests to be corrected. He must also put one or more inspectors on board each vessel immediately after its arrival in port; ascertain and rate, acording to law, the proof, quantities, and kinds of distilled spirits imported; examine into the correspondency between the goods imported in any vessel and the deliveries thereof, according to the inspectors' returns and the permits for landing the same, and report any error or discrepancy to the Collector and the Naval Officer; superintend the lading for exportation of all goods entered for the benefit of any drawback, bounty, or allowance, and report on the correspondency between the kind, quantity, and quality of the goods so laded with the entries and permits granted therefor; test the weights, measures, and other instruments used in ascertaining the duties on imports, with public standards; report disagreements, and execute directions for correcting them agreeably to the standard. The duties of this office devolve upon Mr. James L. Benedict, formerly Auditor of the department.

It is the duty of the Appraiser to ascertain and report to the Collector, under that official's orders, the quantity, description, and value of all imported merchandise, and to give his opinion as to what rate of duty such goods are liable to pay.

The duties of the Collector and his assistants not only include the collection of the tariff on goods entered for consumption, and the proper entry and clearance of vessels, but also the surveillance, appraisement, and forwarding of goods imported by citizens in other sections of the country, through the port of New York,.

INSPECTION OF CABIN PASSENGERS' BAGGAGE ON THE DOCK.

and on which the imposts are collected at the places of destination. In the due discharge of these onerous, delicate, and often difficult duties, ability, faithfulness, and integrity in all the officials are essentially necessary. Added to these quali- ties, expert knowledge, careful training, judicial experience, and culture are also requisite in many instances. All these qualifications are sought — and should uniformly be sought — by subjecting applicants for office, and for promotion in

INSPECTION OF IMMIGRANTS' BAGGAGE.

office, to judicious competitive examinations, under regulations prescribed by the Civil Service Commission.

In February, 1884, there were 1538 public servants employed in the New York Custom-house, at salaries amounting to $1,988,237 per annum. Of these, 232, with salaries amounting to $311,513, in the Collector's special department, had been appointed under the Civil Service regulations. There were also 34, with salaries amounting to $50,800, in the Naval Office, and 126, with salaries amounting to $176,083, in the Appraiser's department, who had been appointed under the same regulations. Of the 1538 employés in the Custom-house, 470 were in the Collector's office, 95 in the Naval Office, 321 in the Appraiser's, 11 in the General Appraiser's, and 35 in the Surveyor's; while there were 322 inspectors, 9 inspectresses, 117 night inspectors, 94 weighers and gaugers, and 64 store-keepers.

Among the officials not subjected to competitive examinations are the Collector, Deputy Collectors, Naval Officer, Deputy Naval Officers, Surveyor, appraisers, engineers, ushers, laborers, etc.

The members of the large force belonging to the Collector's office are distributed into eight divisions, including the Auditor's, Cashier's, Warehouse, Navigation, Entry, Invoice and Order, Law, and Public Store departments. Besides these, there is a Customs Bureau at Castle Garden, with a superintendent in charge; and a Correspondence Bureau at the Custom-house, in charge of the Chief Clerk of Customs. Mr. Joseph Treloar, the latter official, enjoyed twenty-one years of training under the tutelage of Assistant-Collector Clinch; has been in office more than thirty years; is an encyclopædia of customs law and literature; holds all his knowledge at instantaneous command, and has the courage of his convictions. Each of the last six departments is in charge of a deputy collector, has a chief clerk, and a suitable number of subordinates. The Bureau of Statistics is included in the Auditor's department. There are also two deputy collectors for the current business of the office, an assistant collector at Jersey City, and a special deputy collector, Mr. Joseph Barrett, who is also the Collector's private secretary.

How the functionaries in these several departments come into active service is apparent as the progress of passengers and goods through the Custom-house is traced.

Armed with a pass from the Surveyor, the inquirer proceeds to the Barge Office, at the Battery. This is a granite and iron building of irregular shape, with rooms for the Surveyor's staff, day, night, and female inspectors, examiners, officials from the Collector's, Naval Officer's, and Appraiser's offices, and for the safe-keep-ing of public documents and records. A capacious shed, with 10,000 square feet of area, projects seaward from the building. Close by is the dock where he takes the revenue-cutter, in command of a uniformed officer of the revenue marine service, who is also a customs official, and subject to the Collector's orders. The sail down the bay on a bright, breezy May morning is a pleasurable experience not soon to be forgotten. The boarding in-

SEARCHING A FEMALE SMUGGLER.

spectors, as well as the revenue marine officer, willingly impart information.

The incoming steamer—the *Servia*, of the Cunard Line, will answer as an example for all—reported by telegraph from Fire Island, is soon met as she slowly enters port under the guidance of a skillful pilot. The breathing ocean monster, bearing still on her nostrils the salt of much tempestuous spray, is covered with eager Americans returning home, curious foreign tourists, and anxious immigrants gazing for the first time on the shores of the promised land that henceforth is to be their home.

The revenue marine officer assigned to boarding duty, and the inspectors of passengers' baggage, ascend the rope-ladder, as soon as the sanitary examination of the vessel has been completed by the Health Officer of the port. The revenue marine officer demands from the master the manifests of his cargo; and, if the vessel be American, he also demands the crew list, and has the crew mustered and compared with the list. He also identifies, by means of the consul's certificate, any destitute American seamen who may have been brought home in the vessel. Then he certifies the manifests, crew list, and consul's certificates, seals or secures the hatches and openings until the necessary permits for unlading are obtained, and hands over the charge of the vessel to the inspectors who have been temporarily assigned to her, or to superintend the delivery of cargo. At the Barge Office he subsequently makes report of his procedure, and delivers all duplicate manifests and other papers received from the master of the vessel to the boarding officer for transmission to the Collector at the Custom-house.

The examination of personal baggage belonging to returning Americans and to foreign visitors is a matter of great interest to the parties concerned. As soon as the staff officer in charge receives the passenger list from the purser, he and his fellow-officials take their seats at the end of one of the long tables in the saloon. Blanks containing declarations of the different trunks, valises, rugs, etc., and of the dutiable goods contained in them, are on hand, and are filled out consecutively as the passengers, in long lines, present themselves to the inspectors. When the blank is filled out, agreeably to the representations of each individual, or of the head of a family who acts for the whole, he solemnly swears that his statements are true, and signs the document. This is handed to another member of the staff, who numbers and retains it, and gives to the signer a ticket bearing a corresponding number. The signer's name is at the same time checked off on the passenger list by a third officer.

Under the inquiries propounded by the inspectors, the idiosyncrasies of the parties questioned not unfrequently become markedly apparent. Some are jolly, others sulky, and others nervous. Some promptly and others hesitantly respond to the query: "Have you any new or dutiable goods?" Honest men at once blurt out: "Yes; twelve pairs of kid gloves for a friend;" "A piece of silk for my wife;" "A cloak for my daughter;" "A service of china—here are the bills." The answers are at once entered under the appropriate heading, together with the value of the articles specified, if known by the owner. A peculiar mark is also put on the back of the paper to indicate to the examining inspector that something "declared" is in the baggage of that individual. Experienced travellers pass the ordeal quietly; others are occasionally restive under the pointed inquisition. While thus engaged, the inspectors answer a thousand and one questions, endlessly varied, about required forms, when the baggage will be examined, the rates of duty, and when the worrying querists will be able to leave the dock. Patience has, or ought to have, her perfect work in these pachydermatous gentlemen.

While this lively scene is in progress the steamer is proceeding up the bay, enters the North River, and slowly moves into her dock. There matters wear a still more exciting aspect. Crowds of expectant friends are in waiting. Eager salutations are exchanged. The voyagers are as willing to quit the luxurious steamer as was Dr. Johnson the ship that he defined as "a prison, with a chance of being drowned." The movable gangway is run from the dock to the deck. The cabin passengers pour down it in ceaseless streams, while the steerage passengers wait wistfully for later debarkation at Castle Garden. The staff officers, declarations in hand, follow. Baggage is landed and deposited in separate piles, according to the initials of the owners' names, the proper label having been affixed on the steamer.

LANDING IMMIGRANTS AT CASTLE GARDEN.

The places are designated by huge letters on the wall of the shed. If there are many Smiths aboard, for instance, there will be a crowded congregation of trunks and owners about S. The examining inspectors are already drawn up in line across the dock, and nothing passes them without due scrutiny. Wearied travellers, who can leave their matters in the hands of friends, are relieved of further waiting, and after quick search of wraps and valises are allowed to depart in peace. As each individual's baggage is brought together, he notifies the staff officer, and hands over his ticket. The officer selects the corresponding declaration, writes the name of an inspector—whom he calls from the line—upon it, and directs immediate examination. This is usually sufficiently thorough. Inspectors, through long practice, become involuntary disciples of Lavater, and such expert critics of human nature that they almost intuitively detect attempted fraud. Dutiable articles, not declared as such, are brought out, valued by the attendant appraiser, entered, with value attached on the declaration, and the owner is obliged to pay the requisite duty to a clerk in attendance for the purpose of receiving it. The inspector also signs his name to the declaration.

The efficiency and courtesy of the Dep-

THE SEIZURE-ROOM.

uty Surveyor, and also of the inspectors on the dock, together with the delicate discharge of their not particularly pleasing duties, are worthy of high praise. Exceptions are few and far between. The questions asked about dresses, laces, cloaks, etc., are not invariably met with precisely truthful rejoinders. To cheat Uncle Sam in revenue matters is regarded as a decidedly venial sin by most of his children, native or adopted. This notion is doubtless an unconscious remnant of the freebooting ethics of forgotten ancestors. It is slowly yielding to higher and better ideas. Even the wealthiest are not exempt from the smuggling mania. One gentleman, whose name is synonymous with almost fabulous wealth, returning from Europe in company with his wife, was compelled to pay about $1800 in duties on her enormous stock of wearing apparel, which he contended was not dutiable, whether it had or had not been worn. He appealed to the Secretary of the Treasury, who decided against him. He then brought suit within ninety days in the United States court. His wife swore that a portion of the whole had been worn in good faith. The duties paid on that portion

were refunded, while those on the remainder were retained.

Smuggling is carried on in many ways, and will be carried on while human nature continues to be what it is. Foreign retail traders are adept instructors in the art of evading the payment of duties, as any one who has been in the lace establishment of Des Marets and other merchants at Brussels can testify. The ingenuity of inspectors is taxed to the uttermost to defeat their schemes. Female inspectors are employed to search persons of their own sex who are sent to them by the Deputy Surveyor for that purpose. Of these inspectresses there are nine. In 1866 there were only four. The inspectresses perform their duties, both at Castle Garden and on the docks, in rooms set apart for such searches. Recitals of their experiences are at once amusing and humiliating to believers in the natural goodness of men. German Jews are more addicted to smuggling than people of other nationalities, but none are altogether free from the vice. Modistes and dressmakers are naturally the most frequent and flagrant offenders. Extra gold watches; laces, silks, linens, wound around the body or limbs; human hair in toupees, wigs, and switches sewn into skirts; new dresses stitched to old ones; silks and laces made up into several voluminous skirts—are among ordinary discoveries. One unlucky wight, suspected of complicity in feminine designs, was found to have two sets of point lace in the crown of his hat.

By the 346 saloon passengers arriving at New York in the *Servia*, 230 entries of dutiable goods were made, and on them $946 85 in imposts were collected. The Collector's representative on the dock retains the declarations, makes the entries in his own name, and pays the duties received to the cashier, who receipts for them and checks his account. The revenue from this single source is quite considerable in the course of twelve months.

When all the work of the examining officers on the dock has been performed they return to the Barge Office, and the inspectors assigned to superintend the discharge of the cargo take charge of the vessel.

But what of the immigrants in the steer-age? Their turn comes next. In the *Servia* their accommodations have been sumptuous compared with those provided in steamers of Continental lines, and especially in those sailing from Holland. All the oxygen of the Atlantic is needed to save them from the diseases that foul air, unaccustomed food, close contact, and unavoidable uncleanliness induce. But even this must be denied in stormy voyages, and many of them arrive in physical condition that imperatively calls for medical assistance. "Man's inhumanity to man" is often painfully visible on steamship and sailing vessel alike. Matters improve, it is true, but all too slowly. The dens in which many are cribbed, cabined, and confined are often unfit for the use of human beings. The smell of the ship is in the clothing of the unhappy occupants for long weeks after their escape. One vessel brought 1155 steerage passengers from Amsterdam in May, 1882. Spar deck and lower deck were crowded. An average of sixteen people occupied each room. The marvel is that the five deaths on the voyage had not been fifty.

These immigrants are a motley crowd. New York contains representatives of for-

SMUGGLING CIGARS ON THE JERSEY COAST.

ty-four different nationalities. Those Armenians in red fez and Oriental costume will swell the number to forty-five. Small steamers, under the control of a landing agent who contracts with the steam-ship companies, take off the Babel crowd in detachments from all steamers, and convey them to Castle Garden. There, at the inspectors' office, record is kept of the steamers arriving, the dates of

THE ROTUNDA OF THE CUSTOM-HOUSE.

steerage passengers, were thus recorded; 3791 packages were sent to the public store for appraisement, and somewhat less than $10,000 in duties collected upon them. In 1883 the number of immigrants recorded was 405,352. Smuggling among the steerage passengers is mainly confined to persons who have been visiting their friends in Europe. Minute examination occasionally detects pieces of silk and velvet, rings, watches, gold chains, and liquors. Discretion is wisely intrusted to the officials, and is sparingly exercised

arrival, the name of each vessel, the port from which she sailed, the number and names of the passengers, the births and deaths during the voyage, the number of packages sent to the public store at Castle Garden, and the names of the inspectors and inspectresses who examined each vessel. In 1881, 941 steamers, bringing 441,110

toward genuine immigrants. Here is one young Teuton whose trunk reveals, now that its false bottom has been knocked out, a formidable array of little phials containing *Magentropfen*, or stomach drops, and oils wherewith to lubricate rheumatic limbs. The value of the whole is about twelve shillings — certainly not an inordinate supply for a dyspeptic Dutchman, and hardly enough to last a hypochondriac Yankee for a single month. The value of the 710 seizures of goods of all classes smuggled by incoming passengers in the year ending June 30, 1883, was $125,519.

For each package sent in for appraisement a check is given to the owner, and also a receipt by the United States Public Store-keeper. This check is returned when the package is taken away. Immigrants being poorer now than formerly, only $9360 were collected in duties in 1883. Free baggage is sent into another department, and is duly checked. After the immigrants have been duly registered, their uncurrent funds exchanged for American currency, and their railroad tickets purchased, the baggage is forwarded, after presentation of tickets at the office, to their destinations in the West, or in other parts of the country. The Castle Garden Express delivers such as is addressed to New York, Newark, and other near cities.

Castle Garden is one of the most beneficent institutions in the world, and owes its present uses largely to Dr. Friedrich Kapp, now a member of the Imperial German Reichsrath, but formerly a resident of New York. It is under the control of nine Commissioners of Emigration, appointed for the term of six years by the Governor and confirmed by the Senate of the State of New York. Thither let us follow a portion of the 6730 immigrants who arrived by seven different steamers on the 15th of May, 1882. The name of each, the date of his arrival, place of departure, number of his family (if any), whither bound, his business, and other particulars, are all registered. This record, together with that of the cabin passengers, is compared with the manifest of each captain, which manifest ought to exhibit the names of all the persons he had on board. It thus becomes a check on the greed of some who have brought more passengers than the law permits, or than were named in the manifests.

Not only do the Commissioners of Emi-

gration protect their often helpless charges against the extortions, robberies, and unspeakable villainies of the human harpies who formerly infested the docks, and preyed upon the luckless incomers—not only do they supply interpreters, maintain an employment bureau, assist in the exchange of funds, purchase of tickets, forwarding of immigrants and baggage—but they also license the boarding-house runners, and subject them to rigid supervision. They further provide for the sick and disabled, the lunatics, and the pregnant women whose husbands, if sick, are sent to the hospital on Ward's Island, furnish medicine to the ailing and trusses to the ruptured, and preserve recorded particulars of all thus coming under their special care by which they may be found and identified in the future.

Near the Information Bureau from 2000 to 2500 people waiting inquiringly for their friends have sometimes been congregated at one time.

The grandly beneficent work of the Emigration Commissioners deserves better medical facilities than the miserably inadequate hospital accommodations at their immediate command in Castle Garden. New York does the work and bears the expense connected with foreign immigration, but the whole country shares in its benefits. The railroads especially profit by it. The cash value of tickets purchased by inward-bound immigrants in 1881 was more than five million dollars. Moneys to the value of eleven millions were exchanged in Castle Garden, and the estimated amount of the drafts, bonds, and other representatives of specie value brought in during the same year was no less than one hundred million dollars. Castle Garden ought to be a national institution.

While all this busy, anxious work is going on at the dock and immigrant landing depot, the captain of the vessel repairs to the Custom-house and enters his vessel by delivering its register, together with his clearance and other papers, and particularly the original manifest of his cargo, to the Collector. He also affirms under oath that he sailed from the port of departure on a certain day, and that his manifest is truthful to the best of his knowledge and belief. He further signs this sworn affirmation, and attaches it to his manifest. Until this is done the bulk of his cargo can not be broken. The manifest is in writing, and contains the name of the vessel, where she is owned, master's name, tonnage, where built, whither bound, where cargo was shipped, the marks and numbers of the several packages, the contents of the packages, consignees' names and residences, and ports of destination, number of passengers, and the nature and amount of the vessel and cabin stores. The manifest is usually in the national language of the vessel, and is made up from the bills of lading, or copies of them, given to shippers of goods, and signed by the captain or his representative. It is an essential document, and copies of it are made to meet the several requisitions of the customs revenue. This statement of the captain or master is noted at once in the register of entries of vessels, and a copy of it is furnished next day to the appraisers.

Within forty-eight hours after arrival the master must also report in writing all necessary information about his vessel to the Surveyor, and particularly the quantities and kinds of spirits, wines, and teas he has on board, the number of packages in which they are contained, together with the marks and numbers, and also his sea stores of spirits, wines, and teas. If the vessel belong to the United States, the master must give to the Collector a true account of the number of persons employed on board since it was last in a United States port, and must pay forty cents per month, for every person so employed, into the Marine Hospital Fund before it can be admitted to entry. Fees and charges are about as numerous in New York as at Niagara. These paid, and legal demands all satisfied, the Collector issues a general order for the delivery of the cargo. This is effected under the supervision of the inspectors in care of the vessel. All cargoes must be unladed between sunrise and sunset. Special permits, however, may be granted by the Collector and Naval Officer to unlade between sunset and sunrise. In this and in many other cases indemnity bonds are required by the Collector.

The scene on the dock during the unlading and delivery of the cargo is one of great interest and suggestiveness. The two discharging inspectors in charge superintend the transfer of the goods from the vessel to the dock; see to it that all goods requiring to be weighed, gauged, measured, or proved are manipulated only by the proper officers; send sample goods and goods ordered for appraisement to the Public Store, and other merchandise to warehouse or elsewhere as directed; allow no goods to leave the dock without due permits; deliver packages to authorized persons; and enter all permits, with specified particulars, to take away goods, and all goods taken away or sent to the Public Store, warehouse, or elsewhere, by marks, numbers, and descriptions, and what goods were apparently damaged on the voyage, in a discharging book. They also take charge of all the specie and valuables on board the vessel; compare the list of stores on board with those furnished by the master at the Collector's office; report dutiable goods and necessary stores to the Collector or Surveyor; seize all articles imported in violation of law, and close and lock the hatches of the vessel at night. They also, within three days after the delivery of the discharging book to the Surveyor, make another return of the discharge of the vessel, supported by permits, orders, and other vouchers, showing what goods were called for and not found, what did not agree with permit or order, what were damaged, what were not included in manifest, what sea stores were on board, and also the names of all officials who performed any duty in connection with the cargo. Discrepancies between ships' manifests and inspectors' returns are subsequently corrected by specific process in case no intention to defraud the government is apparent on the surface. Both manifests and inspectors' returns go through the Bureau of Liquidation and Closing of Vessels' Accounts, and ultimately find their way into that orderly cemetery of dead enterprises known as the Record Room.

When the discharging inspectors close their labors for the day, they are relieved as custodians of revenue interests by the night inspectors, who number 117 men, and are officered by Captain P. C. Bensel and three assistants. This force is composed of vigorous and active men, and includes medical and other students, who in this way acquire the funds necessary to complete their professional education. It is divided into two watches, which alternate in the discharge of duty from sunset to midnight, and from midnight to sunrise. Should any be detailed for all-night duty on vessels lying in the stream, they are excused from service on the following night. The sphere of these duties includes the waters and portions of the shores of New Jersey, Long Island, and New York city.

The night inspectors are appointed to prevent smuggling, are uniformed and armed, and are authorized to stop and search reasonably suspected persons who may go on board or come from the vessel. Their office is by no means a sinecure. It involves watching, exposure, and fatigue. The Cuban steamers have been wont to bring men who inclosed cigars in rubber bags and threw them into the waters of the lower bay. Confederates in boats then picked them up, placed them in express wagons waiting on the shore, and then drove rapidly away. There is something contagious in the glee of wide-awake officials as they relate how they had watched unseen the whole operation until the wagon was ready to start, when they seized the reins, and landed the spoils at the Seizure Room. One French steamer, notorious for smuggling by dribblets, when searched by this force, was found to contain thirteen hundred bottles of spirits, which it was intended to send ashore bottle by bottle. Tins about an inch deep, and fitted to the body under the armpits, have been taken from the bodies of men who were thus stealthily bringing in valuable bay oil. One dealer in human hair, who died in possession of about $200,000, was detected in illicit importations under the shirts of his agents. Another vivacious fellow, belonging to a French steamer, rejoiced in a profitable trade in kid gloves secreted by the dozen in his immense boots. Sailing vessels are watched by special agents, whose duties are irksome enough to render special supervision by superiors a matter of positive necessity. Dealers in contraband goods, scamps who live by their wits, and unscrupulous traders of many kinds tax the resources of human ingenuity and craft to the uttermost. Logs of foreign wood, cunningly excavated and packed with cigars or spirits; cases of boots and shoes, in the heels of which watches and jewelry are hidden; miraculous trunks, false as Machiavelli, being thinly hollow on side and end, top and bottom, concealing laces, hair, trinkets, etc., etc., are among the common devices of ingenious freebooters. Keen, honest, true men—such as may be seen on any tour of night inspection, like mastiffs at their posts, and especially if visitors be expected—are needed to baffle

the plots of the rascals. Political affiliations constitute no guarantee of efficiency. The best attainable is through rigid adherence to the rules of the civil service reform.

All seizures of whatever value are sent to the Seizure Room at the Custom-house. This is under the authority of General G. W. Palmer, formerly Appraiser of the port, and now the learned and effective head of the Law Department. It embraces a singular collection. Here a jeweller's pack; there dresses, silks, shawls, laces, bundles of cigarettes, row-boats captured with contraband goods on board, cutlery, wines, liquors, cigars, and obscene literature. Contaminating articles are destroyed, unclaimed goods may be obtained by the owner in the course of twelve months if they are detained in the General Order Store, or within three years if warehoused, on payment of duty and order of the Secretary of the Treasury. Perishable articles are sold at auction as soon as possible. Other condemned and unclaimed goods are sold by auction at Collector's sale, after being kept in custody as just stated. Complete records of all transactions are carefully preserved.

A disappointed raiser of church debts said that he needed no evidence of total depravity additional to that of the unpaid subscription on his list. If he did, the Seizure Room would furnish it. Humanity, after all, is redeemable. Charles Reade maintains that it is "never too late to mend." The records of the Custom-house illustrate the theory of the novelist. In May, 1882, a check for $87 came to hand from a troubled individual who had imported silks, laces, and linens in 1873, and which he then believed to be free, but had since discovered to be dutiable to that amount; $50 to correct an undervaluation arrived the week before. Collector Schell once received $1500 from a burdened conscience, the owner of which requested him to acknowledge the receipt in a daily paper, which he did. Smaller sums appear in the list of the Conscience Fund, such as $36, $10, $7 27. Most commendable of all is an item of $10 transmitted to the Collector by an inspector, into whose pocket it had been thrust by a passenger. Tender conscience or something else would not allow it to stay there, and the bribe was "covered into the Treasury." With these facts before him, Collector Robertson may still hope to find out the author of the infamously celebrated "forged telegram," and more particularly since he himself received in the month of October, 1882, a check for $10,000 from a most excellent merchant whose clerk, unknown to him, had defrauded the government of about that sum by undervaluations. The fact of undervaluation had not been suspected at the Custom-house, and the length of time that had elapsed since it took place had placed the loss beyond the limits of legal recovery. New York has many such high-minded and sternly principled merchant princes.

Returning from the Seizure Room to the Rotunda, it is obvious that the concentrated activity on the dock receiving the cargo has many counterparts in that of the consignees and their agents. These are naturally anxious to obtain possession of their merchandise as quickly as possible. They therefore hasten to the Custom-house and make entry of their respective consignments. This is usually, but not always, done through the instrumentality of a class of men known as Custom-house brokers.

Custom-house brokers are principally pushing young men bent on the attainment of fortune. The fees charged for their assistance are matters of bargain between themselves and customers. If fraudulent and untrustworthy, they are sure to be extruded from the building. Some are men of high moral character and excellent business abilities. True policy would dictate their enrollment, and invest the Collector with power to exclude from practice all who are shown to be incapable or unjust. Self-interest would then hold the broker to the strictest honesty and probity.

At the Custom-house, the consignee or owner states under oath that he has certain merchandise on board the steamer, and verifies his statement by the production of an invoice, bill of lading, and consular certificate to the invoice given in the country whence the goods were exported. Invoices are made and certified in triplicate, the consul filing one in his office, sending a second to the Collector of the port whither the goods are shipped, and giving a third to the consignor. The last forwards his to the consignee. He also forwards the bill of lading, or copy of it, given by the steam-ship company for goods shipped. The consignee or owner attaches the bill of lading to the entry of the goods he wishes to take away from the dock. All entries are made in duplicate. Every entry must be of all goods coming by the same vessel to the same consignee, even if they come from ten, twenty, thirty, or more consignors. This requirement often makes it necessary for consumption entries to be made upon *pro forma* invoices, which practice has been used by dishonest men to further schemes for undervaluation and fraud.

The marks and numbers inserted in the entry must correspond with those in the bill of lading, and the description of contents of each package must tally with that found in the invoice. The invoice itself is also compared with that sent to the Collector by the consul. If the consignee wishes to have part of the dutiable goods claimed by him sent to a bonded warehouse, he makes a separate and specific entry of them. These papers are next examined as to their correctness by an entry clerk, and are then stamped with consecutive numbers. The entry clerk also indorses on the back of the invoice the value of the goods thus entered. In determining approximately this value, the consul's and commissioner's fees are deducted from the amount specified in the invoice, and the shipping charges, and proper commissions prescribed by law, are added to it. The rate of duty and the date of examination of entry are also inscribed on the invoice. The entry clerk then issues a consumption permit for the duty-free and duty-paid goods, and a bonded warehouse permit for those on which the consignee does not wish to pay the duty at once, each permit agreeing with the contents of the entry, the bill of lading, and the invoice. All these papers, except the original entry, which remains in the Collector's office, are then taken to the Naval Office, where the clerical work is verified. On their return a deputy collector compares the contents of the documents with each other, and ascertains whether the invoice is properly made, and the consular certificate duly attached. If the latter be not attached, the claimant is required to give bonds to produce a proper consular invoice. If all the papers be correct, the deputy collector then designates certain packages of dutiable goods—about 10 per cent. of the whole—and orders them to be sent to the Public Store for appraisement. Where this is inexpedient, as in the case of iron, marble, gypsum, soda-ash, soda crystals, live animals, grains, bones, building stones, etc., he orders an appraisement on the wharf; or in the case of glass-ware, etc., at the merchant's store. The number of the packages to be examined are described by indorsement on the invoice; which indorsement constitutes an order to the Appraiser to decide their dutiable character and value. A similar indorsement is written on the entry, and also on the permit. The last is an order to the discharging inspector to send the packages indicated to the Public Store for appraisement. The numbers written on invoice, entry, and permit must agree, inasmuch as they are designed to be safeguards against collusion and fraud, and guides to officers who act independently of each other.

The consignee, or his broker, papers in hand, next repairs to the cashier's office, and pays the estimated duty on the whole invoice of goods wanted for immediate consumption, together with the legal fees. The cashier affixes his check, in token of payment, to invoice and permit both. Then the merchant, compliant with law, gives what is termed a "return bond" that he will hold the packages intact for ten days after the Appraiser has passed upon the cases sent to his department, and that he will return to the custody of the Collector within that time any or all of the goods so received by him upon due notice so to do. All these preliminaries having been duly observed, the consignee leaves all his papers, except the permit, at the Custom-house. To the permit he procures the signature of the deputy collector, and the counter-signature of the Naval Officer, and at length presents it to the inspector in charge of the vessel, and receives his goods.

Record is kept of all invoices, of the kinds and numbers of the packages sent to the Public Store, and of the ship in which they came. The invoices, together with copies of record and entries, are sent to the Appraiser by the revenue cab running between the Custom-house and the Appraiser's office, so that by them he may identify the parcels sent to him for examination and appraisal. These are so numerous as to keep himself and the assistant appraisers in a state of decided activity during the spring and fall importations. In 1873 the number of packages appraised was 181,068; in 1881 it was

249,593; and in 1883 it was 267,202. The largest number of packages received in a single day was on the 16th of September, 1881, when it reached the total of 1542.

The United States Public Store occupies an entire block, owned by the heirs of a deceased New York merchant, and fronts on the Hudson River, between Hubert and Laight streets. The number of public servants employed therein is 349, of whom about 100 have held office for upward of ten years. Assistant Appraiser John A. Baush, who died in 1883, held office for forty-one years, and other officials have kept their places over twenty years. One hundred and seventy-seven other officers, watchmen, and laborers belonging to the Eighth Division of the Collector's office, and under the immediate orders of Deputy Collector Colonel William A. Jones, co-operate with them. The rules of the civil service are here applied with strict regularity. No temporary appointments have been made since the appointment of Colonel A. P. Ketchum to the office of Appraiser, except to positions of which the annual salary is under $900, and therefore below the grade to which civil service regulations apply. Papers different from those employed at the Collector's office are used in the examination of candidates. Goods and merchandise are assigned, on arrival for examination and appraisal, to one or more of the ten divisions in the office, each of which is under the supervision of an assistant appraiser, whose salary is $3000. Samples of textile and other fabrics sent to this country by foreign manufacturers for the inspection of merchants who order supplies, yet to be made, from them, are promptly examined and appraised in the sample office: 31,993 packages of samples were received in 1881, and 63,479 in 1883.

The tariff is an abstruse science. Heyl's work entitled *United States Import Duties*, or Morgan's *United States Tariff*, must be mastered to understand its application. Even then its principles are not readily comprehended. Some goods are subjected to specific, others to *ad valorem*, and still others to specific and *ad valorem* duties combined. The typical Philadelphia lawyer is needed to unravel all its mysteries. There are doubtless reasons of some sort why silk and wool dress goods should be charged a specific duty of eight cents per square yard, and forty per cent. *ad valorem;* why, if such goods weigh over four ounces to the square yard, they should pay fifty cents per pound, and thirty-five per cent. *ad valorem;* why one textile fabric with thirty-four warp and twenty-six woof threads to the quarter of a square inch, or 240 warp and woof threads to the square inch, should pay a specific duty of seven and a half cents per square yard, and fifteen per cent. of its value additionally; why, if there be less than 201 threads to a square inch, it should pay six and a half cents per square yard, and fifteen per cent. *ad valorem;* and why, if not exceeding 200 threads to the square inch (the difference of a single thread may and sometimes does determine the rate of duty), and costing over twenty-five cents per square yard, it should pay an *ad valorem* duty of thirty-five per cent.; but to the uninitiated these reasons appear to be inscrutable. As the laws of a nation are the crystallizations of its historical experiences, so the customs regulations of a people are the residual crystallization of its commercial relations with foreigners, its efforts at industrial development and self-preservation, and its bitter acquaintance with greed, guile, and guilt.

Passing through other departments of the Public Store we paused to criticise the costly, exquisitely beautiful, and marvellously constructed dresses imported from Worth and from Camus, in Paris; the paintings by Meissonier, son of the famous artist, whose "Charge des Cuirassiers" adorns the stately mansion of Mrs. A. T. Stewart, and other distinguished painters; the statuary, bronzes, watches, and jewelry; the carpets, rugs, and curtains; the cigars and tobacco, wines, spirits, and liqueurs; and specimens of all other articles proper and improper to high and wealthy civilization.

All packages are seemingly handled with skill and care. The contents of not a few are manifestly injured by injudicious nailing on the part of the consignor's employés; and from some, portions of the contents have been extracted *in transitu* by thievish hands.

When the invoices of imported goods arrive at the Public Store they are sent to the Invoice Bureau, and are there distributed to the appropriate divisions. The head of each division in turn distributes his allotment among the respective examiners, and charges each with the invoices assigned to him. Deft, cautious,

and expert examination of each and every parcel follows. The standard of value for each article in the foreign market where it was purchased is ascertained by correspondence with consular agents, by extensive comparison of invoices, and more especially from the invoices of the more prominent American merchants, whose reputation for integrity and square dealing is unimpeached and unassailable.

The most persistent attempts to defraud the government of its just dues take the forms of undermeasurement and undervaluation. Merchandise is frequently undervalued by foreign consignors. The consignees, aware of the fact, and instructed by previous failures, usually correct the fault by entering the goods at figures nearer to their true value. One case of merchandise exhibited an increased statement of value to the average extent of ten per cent. When the Appraiser raises the dutiable value of goods as much as ten per cent., the estimate carries with it an additional penalty to the importer of twenty per cent. The Chinese importers doing business in New York have not yet, in every instance, learned how business is done at the Custom-house. Their undervaluations are occasionally outrageous. Seven packages of silk fabrics had just been appraised at from 50 to 300 per cent. above the invoice price.

As soon as the examiners finish their inspection of the goods appraised, the quantity and quality thereof are noted on the invoice, and that document is sent to the Appraiser for his approval. Correct invoices are returned to the Entry and Invoice Department of the Collector's office on a black list, and corrected ones on a red list. No parcels are permitted to leave the Public Store without being corded and sealed and checked by the examiner. This is a precaution against possible theft. In the Entry Department the returned invoices are placed in the hands of the liquidating clerks, by whom the work of the Appraiser as to classification of goods and the true amount of duties to be paid is carefully revised. If either or both should be incorrect, the invoice is sent back to the Appraiser for reclassification and amendment. After this is done, and the exact amount of duty is ascertained, the amendment is revised by the amendment clerk in the Naval Office, and on his indorsement is again returned to the Bureau of Liquidation. If the importer have already paid the right sum on entering his goods, he is notified of the fact, applies for a delivery permit, and receives his goods. If a balance yet be due to the government, he is informed of the fact, and immediate payment is demanded. If he have paid more than the proper amount, he is notified of the fact, receives a refunding check from the Auditor, and payment thereof from the Assistant Treasurer of the United States.

The national government does business wisely, and always secures itself beforehand against possible loss. If the importer when apprised of the classification as to rate of duty made by the Collector be dissatisfied with it, he must make a written protest within ten days, appeal to the Secretary of the Treasury within thirty days, and if the Secretary's decision sustain the action of the Collector, must, within ninety days from said decision, bring suit in court in order to save any remedy to which he may be legally entitled. Or, if dissatisfied with the valuation noted and certified on the invoice, he may ask for a re-appraisement, or merchant appraisal. If he should do so, then the Collector selects one discreet and experienced merchant, a citizen of the United States, familiar with the character and value of the goods in question, and notifies him of his appointment. The General Appraiser is also notified of the appeal, and of the name of the merchant appraiser. A day is fixed for the appraisal, and the merchant selected is sworn to do his duty. Other merchants may be subpœnaed to act as mercantile experts at the examination. The importer or his agent presents his views of the case, and the decision of the General Appraiser and merchant appraiser is final. Ordinarily the judgment of the Appraiser of the port is sustained. Should they disagree, the Collector decides the matter. Only in the event of informality in the procedure can the importer institute further proceedings in the United States District or Circuit Court. The importer usually accepts the decision, pays the duty, and receives his goods. So accurately is the work of the General Appraiser's office done that not more than two per cent. of all its transactions is found to be incorrect by the Liquidating Bureau.

Damage appraisements are demanded where goods have been injured on the voyage of importation. When the damages claimed exceed $100 the percentage of damage to the goods is subtracted from the amount of duty assessed. Green fruit must be damaged in excess of twenty-five per cent. of the invoice value in order to admit of any reduction of duty, and then the reduction is only on the damage above twenty-five per cent. of injury.

A bulletin of correct entries, increased appraisements, and refunds to importers who paid more than the real duty at the time of entering their merchandise is hung up in the Rotunda for the inspection of interested parties. All invoices are stamped after final examination in the Liquidating Bureau, and are thence sent to the custody of a clerk, who records the date of reception, arranges them in packages according to the initial and terminal letters of importers' names, classifies them as miscellaneous, free, or duty-paid, and warehoused, and ties the several packages together with differently colored tapes. Invoices thus preserved are in constant demand for reference, re-appraisement, etc., and are always brought forward, on proper requisitions, by the heads or chief clerks of divisions. Responsible parties are also permitted to consult them on matters of business. After being retained for six months they are deposited in the Record Room.

The entry papers accompanying the invoices to the cashier's office are there separated from them, and sent to an official, who imposts them, or, in other words, classifies the articles therein described in separate columns according to the rate of duty that each is liable to pay. Articles paying duty by the yard are also classified in appropriate columns. The duties on the wholes are then calculated. The totals added together must correspond with the totals of the cashier's and Naval Officer's offices. This is another efficient safeguard against inadvertencies and inaccuracies. From the imposter the entries pass to other hands, which tabulate the contents for statistical purposes; from thence they pass to a third official, who therefrom prepares the statistics for publication in the newspapers. From him the Bureau of Liquidation receives them for examination and correction, reunites them with the corresponding invoices, sends them to the Naval Office, and receives them again after due revision by the amendment clerks. Again they pass into the hands of the imposting and statistical clerks, who correct their own work, in case any error should have been detected. The entry papers are then filed away.

Tedious and complicated as are the investigations connected with the appraisal of composite textile fabrics, and of wares whose dutiable value is based upon weighers' and gaugers' returns, still greater difficulties attach to the valuation of other articles, such as sugars, chemicals, etc., etc. Appeals from the decisions of the Collector and litigation in United States Courts often delay final settlement for some time. In these cases the aid of the United States Chemical Laboratory, situated in the Public Store, is invoked. This institution is conducted by Dr. Edward Sherer.

Not satisfied with all the precautions hitherto described in order to obtain a proximate approach to absolutely certain knowledge of the commerce of New York, the accounts of each vessel are put into the hands of a class of officials known as liquidators of vessels, about thirteen months after her arrival in port. The liquidators bring together all the papers connected with a single voyage of that vessel, compare and check off the officer's return and the ship's manifest, ascertain what disposition has been made of goods for which no entries or papers were filed, and, if such goods are still in general order stores, cause them to be put upon the sale list, and sold for the benefit of the government. They examine the accounts of the liquidators of entries, and inquire whether any refunds ought to be made or increase of duty assessed. All the entries of each vessel are tabulated upon a duty list, showing the original, additional, and liquidated duties, the increase and excess of duty, and the penalties exacted. All these are footed up, and referred to the Naval Officer for comparison. If found correct, the Naval Officer checks the duty list, which is then filed in the Record Room for statistical or other purposes.

To the same repository the documents associated with entries for warehousing, transportation, and exportation in bond, warehouse and immediate exportation, immediate transportation, and withdrawal for transportation and export to Canada or Mexico, ultimately find their way. Merchants entering imported goods, on which the duties are not paid, for warehousing, give bonds to the amount of twice the value of the goods with the duty added. Receipts for such goods, given

by bonded warehouse proprietors, are negotiable, and available as collateral securities for the eventual liquidation of indebtedness. When importers wish to withdraw their merchandise, in part or in whole, from warehouse, withdrawal entries are made for that purpose, the estimated duties paid, and delivery permits obtained. A regular debtor and creditor account with them is kept by the warehouse department. It also keeps account of all goods received and delivered for transportation or export, including descriptions of marks, numbers, and contents of all packages.

Of bonded warehouses (most of which include from three to six buildings each) in New York, Brooklyn, Jersey City, and Hoboken, the number is fifty-nine. The United States government grants the privilege of private bonded warehouses to importers; but only one firm, that of Lanman and Kemp, the great drug importers, avail themselves of it. All the rest are for public use. Each is double locked every evening, the proprietors using one set of locks, and the United States storekeepers another. Any one may hire or erect a building for a bonded warehouse, and enter upon the business of conducting it, after having given a bond of $25,000 for each independent edifice, 25 by 100 feet in area, and an additional bond of from $10,000 to $15,000 for each building connected with the original structure by internal doors. Should the proprietor discontinue business, his books are compared with those of the warehouse department, and in case of correspondency his pecuniary liability ceases, but no bond is ever cancelled. All are preserved in anticipation of possible need. No suit, however, has as yet been brought against a proprietor on his bond. The store-keepers are United States officials, under the control and orders of the Collector, and number sixty-five persons.

On the 1st of February, 1884, there were 241 lighters and 1501 carts employed in the transfer of merchandise to and from the bonded warehouses. The owner of each lighter gives a bond for it by name. The 397 owners of the carts also give bonds that their vehicles shall be faithfully used for revenue purposes only while in government employ.

In the four bonded manufacturing warehouses—one in Brooklyn, and three in New York—merchandise such as Florida water, sarsaparilla, life syrup, and tricopherous is manufactured for export only. All dutiable goods imported for these purposes are sent into general storage warehouses, class 3, where the duties are ascertained, and are thence forwarded to manufacturing bonded warehouses, without payment of duties, but under the prescribed bonds. There they are manufactured, and are thence exported. None can be sold in the United States. The manufacturers file formulas specifying the nature of their manufactures with the Secretary of the Treasury. Government chemists detailed to test the quality and percentage of the alcohol used have free access to these establishments at all times, and on their favorable reports permits for exportation are issued to the proprietors. Each manufacturing bonded warehouse is under the charge of a United States store-keeper.

On many dutiable articles of commerce drawbacks of duties paid are allowed to exporters. Imported merchandise, exported within three years direct from the custody of the United States store-keepers, is entitled to drawback, less one per cent. to defray necessary expenses. Drawback of duties paid, less one per cent., is allowed on imported goods that have been withdrawn from warehouse to enter into the construction or repair of American vessels, or less ten per cent. if manufactured into articles for export to foreign countries. Rebate of internal revenue taxes is allowed on certain taxable articles of domestic production that are entered for export. The object of drawbacks is the encouragement of domestic manufactures, and the promotion of the influx of precious metals. The amount of drawback upon imported goods, afterward manufactured and exported from New York, in the fiscal year ending June 30, 1883, was $1,663,297; of drawback and remission of tax upon domestic and foreign goods, $4,816,659.

Bonds are required by the government in order to secure its rights and dues from individuals, corporations, and business firms who seek its protective aid and indorsement in the transaction of their business, to insure honesty and fair dealing, and to prevent frauds. Such bonds are never cancelled unless satisfactory proof be adduced that the legal conditions have been fulfilled. If the proof of fulfilled stipulations be not sufficient, then the importer often applies to the Secretary of the Treasury, who has discretionary power, to cancel the bonds. Should the Secretary decline to cancel them, the cases are then prepared in the law department of the Collector's office, and forwarded by him to the United States District Attorney for prosecution. The number of such suits instituted in the year ending June 30, 1883, was 280. The entire number of bonds of all kinds duly executed in connection with the public revenue at the port of New York in the same year was 140,963.

The Law Department of the Collector's office also reviews with critical legal eye the entire course of the revenue business and its results; interferes to correct irregularities; perfects it in a legal sense; prepares all the papers and evidence necessary to the defense of the Collector in the suits instituted against him by dissatisfied or fraudulent importers, or other persons whose business relations with him have not been agreeable to themselves; and prepares the documents and evidence needful to the prosecution of criminal offenders and the redress of irregularities. The number of suits instituted against Collector W. H. Robertson in the fiscal year ending June 30, 1883, was 586; and of suits brought by him against others for other causes than on bonds was 161.

Ship-building in the United States is one of the relatively decadent industries. Politico-economical reasons are readily adduced to account for it. But what vessels the country does possess in the locality of New York are cared for with minute fullness at the Custom-house. There United States vessels are documented, or registered, enrolled, and licensed. In the registry of each vessel the managing owner or president of the proprietary company deposes under oath to the names of the owners, to the share of each in the vessel, to the place of his residence, and to the fact that he is a citizen of the United States. The master of the vessel also makes oath that he is himself a citizen. No foreigner can own a recorded interest in a foreign-going American vessel, although he may own an interest in a steamer running on inland waters, rivers, or bays. The managing owner and master then unite in giving a bond, with sureties satisfactory to the Collector, that the certificate of register shall be used exclusively within the limits of the law.

The registers of all American vessels,

while in port, are deposited with the Collector at the registry desk. The owner's and master's oath and bond for registry are all included in a bound volume afterward preserved in the depository of records. Each foreign-bound vessel also deposits articles of agreement, signed by master and crew, and a copy thereof, which is certified by the Collector. A list of the persons composing the crew is also deposited with the Collector, and a certified copy thereof is given by him to the master. A crew bond is further executed by the master and sureties, binding them to produce the persons named as composing the crew to the first boarding officer at the first port of the United States at which the vessel shall arrive, unless the said persons shall have been discharged by consent of an American consul. If sailors are discharged, or desert in foreign countries, the fact is certified by the nearest American consul. Crew lists and articles of vessels are bound together in volumes. Returned crew lists are placed on file. If a vessel should discharge her crew at a port other than that from which she sailed, notification of the fact that the crew is accounted for is sent to the original port of departure, and the crew bond is thereupon cancelled. When a change of master of any vessel occurs, the new master makes oath that he is a citizen of the United States, and the certificate of this oath is attached to the certificate of the vessel's register. Particulars of all such changes are recorded. Abstracts of surrendered registers issued at other ports are also kept in book form, and monthly reports of them are sent to Washington.

Certificates of record are issued to vessels built in the United States and owned by foreigners, to enable such vessels, should they become the property of American citizens, to be documented and receive an American register. Bills of sale and mortgages of vessels are also received and recorded in books that describe the species and name of each vessel, names of grantors and mortgagors, parts owned, parts conveyed, species of conveyance (bill of sale, etc.), when made, amounts received for sale or mortgage, when received for record, dates of record, dates of cancellation, and names of parties who take the documents away from the office.

Certificates of register, if lost, must be replaced by new ones; and new certificates must also be issued in correspondency with changes in the characteristics or occupation of vessels. Record is kept of all these registers, and of all issues and surrenders of documents, and copies of such records are sent quarterly to the Secretary of the Treasury.

Rebates of duties paid on imported goods are allowed by law to the extent in which these goods enter into the construction of American vessels. The rebate in one instance, in 1882, amounted to $3622. In the case of some Boston vessels it was still larger. In the registration of a new vessel, the production of the master carpenter's certificate, of the certificate of measurement, and of the inspector's certificate, as well as the oath of ownership, etc., are required in order to documentation. Application is then made to the Secretary of the Treasury at Washington for an official number, and for letters to be used in signaling at sea. Thus 130,052 is the official number, and *J. R. K. W.* the official letters, of the little schooner *Nettie Dobbins;* 10,456 the number, and *H. J. G. W.* the letters, of the barque *Gemsbok*, of New York. When any number and set of letters are exhibited by flags at sea, the officers of passing vessels who observe them can turn to the list of United States merchant vessels and learn what the name of the signaling vessel is.

The total registered tonnage of the port of New York, according to the latest report, is as follows:

VESSELS REGISTERED FOR FOREIGN TRADE.

Sailing vessels	540,	with a tonnage of 346,485
Steam "	50,	" 82,490
Total	590,	with a tonnage of 428,975

VESSELS OF FIVE TONS AND UPWARD ENGAGED IN THE COASTING TRADE AND UNDER ENROLLMENT AND LICENSE.

Sailing vessels	1452,	with a tonnage of 132,260
Barges, etc.	375,	" 68,246
Steamers	741,	" 203,054
Total	2568,	with a tonnage of 403,560

RECAPITULATION.

Registered vessels	590;	tonnage, 428,975
Enrolled and licensed	2568;	" 403,560
Total	3158;	" 832,535

Eighty-six of the above-mentioned steamers are constructed wholly of iron.

American vessels engaged in domestic trade are enrolled and licensed. The process of enrollment and license is very similar to that of registration for foreign commerce. Records of steam vessels owned in New York and engaged in domestic trade are preserved in the Custom-house, whose officers enforce the execution of the navigation laws, including those relating to the inspection of vessels, the licensing of pilots, engineers, and masters, and the entrance and clearance of coastwise vessels. Particulars of all the wrecks and casualties of American vessels documented at New York are also preserved, and often prove to be of great service.

All receipts of duties, penalties, fees, etc., are revised and tabulated in the office of Colonel Charles Treichel, the Auditor. There all checks for refund of money paid in excess of the true amount of duty are drawn and furnished to the importers. Uncle Sam scarcely ever fails to assure himself against loss. In 1880 the sum of $2,256,487 73 was disbursed in refunds, $1,594,833 37 in 1881, and $3,313,159 73 in the first eleven months of 1882. The whole of the refunds made since 1870 is upward of $18,000,000. The average annual number of entries on which refunds are made is 28,512. Receipts for refunds are taken in duplicate; one copy is sent to Washington, and the other is preserved in the Collector's office for reference. All checks paid for refunds are reported to the Naval Officer, who compares the reports with his own books of record. Full particulars of all matters connected with each refund are also reported to Washington. All record books are kept in the Auditor's office for seven or eight years, and are then sent to the Record Room. Only lately a dispute as to which of two merchants a certain check had been paid was settled by appeal to the records. It was paid to the importer.

Prior to the advent of Mr. S. G. Ogden, who served in the Auditor's department for more than forty years, the Collectors were often placed in the position of defaulters by faulty book-keeping. But so thoroughly has the system of keeping accounts been revised and perfected that for many years they have balanced exactly at the end of every week. The system of checks and balances in use at the New York Custom-house, if not absolutely perfect, is at least a close approximate approach to perfection. Accounts of all receipts and disbursements by the Collector are rendered monthly to the Commissioner of Customs and to the First Auditor of the Treasury.

The multitudinous records and papers appertaining to the customs service in New York have been preserved from the commencement, and are now so classified and arranged that any of them can be readily found when sought, unless it be some very old papers packed away in the dark rooms. The record rooms occupy the entire upper story of the Custom-house, and a portion of the story immediately below it. The custody and care of all these papers and documents require a genius for classification and arrangement. Hundreds if not thousands of tons of account books, bond books, cargo and passenger manifests, entries, inspectors' returns, official certificates, withdrawals, invoices, consular certificates, permits, shipping articles, crew lists, pay rolls, check-book stubs, registers, etc., etc., are here stowed away in such order as to be almost immediately available when wanted.

Directly but independently related to the customs revenue in New York is a class of about twenty United States officials, three of whom are known as special agents. All are under the charge of an intelligent, active, and energetic head—Captain C. H. Brackett. The special agents keep vigilant watch over sailors, importers, and officials alike, and are, in fact, practical and practiced detectives. Suspicion of wrong may be awakened by personal observation, or by confidential information from different sources. Once on the track of offenders they are sure to run them down, unless the criminals be endowed with almost supernatural shrewdness and cunning.

Nothing that human ingenuity can devise appears to be left out of the machinery of this, the greatest revenue establishment in the United States. It is the most scientifically organized and economically administered of American national institutions. Under Collector W. H. Robertson's presidency the cost of collecting the public revenue at this point is 1.78½ per cent. of the whole sum—less than in the administration of any of his predecessors.

NOTE.—In the preparation of this article the writer has been indebted to the courtesy of several officials, and particularly of K. N. Prince, Esq., Chief of the Bureau of Statistics, for indispensable assistance. Whatever discrepancies may appear between the figures in this article and those in the Annual Report on the Foreign Commerce of the United States are due to the fact that the latter are largely made up from the duties estimated at the time of entry, whereas the former have been made up since the entries were finally liquidated and the due amount of duties paid.

ABRAHAM LINCOLN AT CINCINNATI.

IN the summer of 1857 Mr. Lincoln made his first visit to Cincinnati. He was original counsel for the defendant in a patent reaper suit pending in the United States Circuit Court for Northern Illinois. The argument of the case was adjourned to Cincinnati, the home of Judge McLean, at his suggestion and for his accommodation.

Mr. Lincoln came to the city a few days before the argument took place, and remained during his stay at the house of a friend. The case was one of large importance pecuniarily, and in the law questions involved. Reverdy Johnson represented the plaintiff. Mr. Lincoln had prepared himself with the greatest care; his ambition was up to speak in the case, and to measure swords with the renowned lawyer from Baltimore. It was understood between his client and himself before his coming that Mr. Harding, of Philadelphia, was to be associated with him in the case, and was to make the "mechanical argument." Mr. Lincoln was a little surprised and annoyed, after reaching here, to learn that his client had also associated with him Mr. Edwin M. Stanton, of Pittsburgh, and a lawyer of our own bar, the reason assigned being that the importance of the case required a man of the experience and power of Mr. Stanton to meet Mr. Johnson. The Cincinnati lawyer was appointed "for his local influence." These reasons did not remove the slight conveyed in the employment, without consultation with him, of this additional counsel. He keenly felt it, but acquiesced. The trial of the case came on; the counsel for defense met each morning for consultation. On one of these occasions one of the counsel moved that only two of them should speak in the case. This motion was acquiesced in. It had always been understood that Mr. Harding was to speak to explain the mechanism of the reapers. So this motion excluded either Mr. Lincoln or Mr. Stanton from speaking— which? By the custom of the bar, as between counsel of equal standing, and in the absence of any action of the client, the original counsel speaks. By this rule Mr. Lincoln had precedence. Mr. Stanton suggested to Mr. Lincoln to make the speech. Mr. Lincoln answered, "No; do you speak." Mr. Stanton promptly replied, "I will," and, taking up his hat,

said he would go and make preparation. Mr. Lincoln acquiesced in this, but was deeply grieved and mortified; he took but little more interest in the case, though remaining until the conclusion of the trial. He seemed to be greatly depressed, and gave evidence of that tendency to melancholy which so marked his character. His parting on leaving the city can not be forgotten. Cordially shaking the hand of his hostess, he said: "You have made my stay here most agreeable, and I am a thousand times obliged to you; but in reply to your request for me to come again I must say to you I never expect to be in Cincinnati again. I have nothing against the city, but things have so happened here as to make it undesirable for me ever to return here."

Thus untowardly met the first time Mr. Lincoln and Mr. Stanton. Little did either then suspect that they were to meet again on a larger theatre, to become the chief actors in a great historical epoch.

While in the city he visited its lions, among other places of interest the grounds and conservatories of the late Nicholas Longworth, then living. The meeting of these remarkable men is worthy of a passing note. Nor can it be given without allusion to their dress and bearing. Mr. Lincoln entered the open yard, with towering form and ungainly gait, dressed in plain clothing cut too small. His hands and feet seemed to be growing out of their environment, conspicuously seen from their uncommon size. Mr. Longworth happened at the time to be near the entrance, engaged in weeding the shrubbery by the walk. His alert eye quickly observed the coming of a person of unusual appearance. He rose and confronted him.

"Will a stranger be permitted to walk through your grounds and conservatories?" inquired Mr. Lincoln.

"Y-e-s," haltingly, half unconsciously, was the reply, so fixed was the gaze of Mr. Longworth.

As they stood thus face to face the contrast was striking, so short in stature was the one that he seemed scarcely to reach the elbow of the other. If the dress of Mr. Lincoln seemed too small for him, the other seemed lost in the baggy bulkiness of his costume; the overflowing sleeves concealed the hands, and the extremities of the pantaloons were piled in heavy folds upon the open ears of the untied shoes. His survey of Mr. Lincoln was searching : beginning with the feet, he slowly raised his head, closely observing, until his upturned face met the eye of Mr. Lincoln. Thus for a moment gazed at each other in mutual and mute astonishment the millionaire pioneer and the now forever famous President. Mr. Lincoln passed on, nor did Mr. Longworth ever become aware that he had seen Mr. Lincoln.

The grounds and conservatories were viewed and admired. And so afterward the suburbs of the city—Walnut Hills, Mount Auburn, Clifton, and Spring Grove Cemetery. He lingered long in the grounds of Mr. Hoffner in study of the statuary. He sought to find out whom the statues represented, and was much worried when he found himself unable to name correctly a single one.

A day was given to the county and city courts. An entire morning was spent in Room No. 1 of the Superior Court, then presided over by Bellamy Storer, eccentric and versatile, in the maturity of his extraordinary powers. His manner of conducting the business of that room, miscellaneous, demurrers, motions, submitted docket, etc., was unique. The older members of the bar remember it well. To describe it literally would do gross injustice to that really great judge. To mingle in the same hour the gravity of the judge and the jest of the clown was a feat that only he could perform without loss of dignity, personal or judicial.

On this morning the judge was in his happiest vein, in exuberant spirits, keeping the bar "in a roar," assisted much in this by the lively humor of poor Bob McCook.

Mr. Lincoln greatly enjoyed this morning, and was loath to depart when the curtain dropped. He said to the gentleman accompanying him: "I wish we had that judge in Illinois. I think he would share with me the fatherhood of the legal jokes of the Illinois bar. As it is now, they put them all on me, while I am not the author of one-half of them. By-the-way, however, I got off one last week that I think really good. I was retained in the defense of a man charged before a justice of the peace with assault and battery. It was in the country, and when I got to the place of trial I found the whole neighborhood excited, and the feeling was strong against my client. I saw the only way

was to get up a laugh, and get the people in a good humor. It turned out that the prosecuting witness was talkative; he described the fight at great length, how they fought over a field, now by the barn, again down to the creek, and over it, and so on. I asked him, on cross-examination, how large that field was; he said it was ten acres, he knew it was, for he and some one else had stepped it off with a pole. 'Well, then,' I inquired, 'was not that the smallest *crap* of a fight you have ever seen raised off of ten acres?' The hit took. The laughter was uproarious, and in half an hour the prosecuting witness was retreating amid the jeers of the crowd."

Mr. Lincoln remained in the city about a week. Freed from any care in the law case that brought him here, it was to him a week of relaxation. He was then not thinking of becoming President, and gave himself up to unrestrained social intercourse.

His conversation at this time related principally to the politics and politicians of Illinois—a theme of which he never seemed to weary. A strange chapter in the story of our country that is. What a crowd of great men arose with the first generation of white people on the broad Illinois prairie! There were Hardin, Logan the judge, Bissel, Trumbull, Douglas, Lincoln, and many other scarcely lesser names. Of these he discoursed as only he could. The Kansas-Nebraska agitation was at its height, and Douglas the prominent figure. Of him he spoke much.

Indeed, the story of Lincoln interlaces with that of Douglas. They are inseparable. It is the relation of antagonism. Parties might come and go—Whig, Know-Nothing, Union, Republican—they were never on the same side until, amid the throes of revolution, they met in the defense of the Union. Douglas was a perennial stimulus to Lincoln. Webster was wont to say, if he had attained any excellence in his profession, he owed it to his early conflicts with Jeremiah Mason. In his public speeches Lincoln seemed ever addressing Douglas; even to the last, as seen in his great speech at New York, when he made the words of Douglas his text.

When Lincoln was driving an ox-team at four dollars a month, and splitting rails, he first met Douglas, then teaching school in central Illinois.

Mr. Lincoln loved to tell the story of Douglas. It is indelibly written in my memory. Not in the very words can I repeat it, and yet even that in the salient points.

He said Douglas, when he first met him, was the smallest man he had ever seen—in stature under five feet, in weight under ninety pounds. He was teaching a country school, and lodging with a violent Democratic politician, a local celebrity. From him Douglas got his political bias. Douglas was his protégé. He encouraged Douglas in the study of the law, procured the books for him, had him admitted to the bar before a year, pushed him into the office of prosecuting attorney, and into the Legislature.

When Van Buren became President, the patron wanted the office of Register at the Land-office, and sent Douglas to Washington to procure the place for him. In due time Douglas returned with the commission in his pocket, but not for his patron. It was to himself. The old man was enraged at the ingratitude, and swore vengeance. He listened to no explanations. It was not long before he had an opportunity to gratify his feelings.

Douglas became the Democratic candidate for Congress, the whole State constituting one Congressional district. His opponent was Mr. Stewart—still living, a relative of Mrs. Lincoln. After an animated contest Douglas was defeated by one vote in a poll of 36,000. The old patron rejoiced in the belief that that one vote was his.

Mr. Douglas's sensitive nature was overwhelmed by this defeat. He gave way to uncontrollable grief, sought consolation in excessive drink, and his career seemed at an end. But time brought its accustomed relief, and he re-appeared in the arena, again the thunderer of the scene. The years to follow were to him years of unbroken prosperity. He became successively Judge of the Supreme Court, Representative in Congress, and Senator. The name and fame of the "Little Giant" overspread the land. These, however, were cheerless years to Mr. Lincoln, yet with unshaken fortitude he bore the banner of Whiggery. It was his custom to follow Mr. Douglas about the State, replying to him.

But a change came; the Kansas-Nebraska Bill awakened the moral sense of the State, and by common consent Mr. Lincoln became its representative. Mr. Douglas, in Washington, was alarmed at the uprising, and hurried home to educate the people up to conquering their prejudice against slavery. He made a canvass of the State, Mr. Lincoln following him and replying to him. "After having spoken at a number of places," said Mr. Lincoln, "I was surprised one evening, before the speaking began, at Mr. Douglas entering my room at the hotel. He threw himself on the bed, and seemed in distress. 'Abe, the tide is against me,' said he. 'It is all up with me. I can do nothing. Don't reply to me this evening. I can not speak, but I must, and it is my last. Let me alone tonight.' I saw he was in great distress; he could not bear adversity; and I acquiesced in his request and went home."

They did not meet again in debate, if I mistake not, until the great contest of 1858.

Mr. Lincoln had a high admiration for the abilities of Mr. Douglas, and afterward was glad to have his aid in behalf of the Union, and commissioned him a major-general; but he thought him in debate and in politics adroit, unscrupulous, and of an amazing audacity. "It is impossible," said he, "to get the advantage of him; even if he is worsted, he so bears himself that the people are bewildered and uncertain as to who has the better of it."

"When I," said Thucydides, "in wrestling have thrown Pericles and given him a fall, by persisting that he had no fall he gets the better of me, and makes the bystanders, in spite of their own eyes, believe him." Thus doth man from age to age repeat himself; and yet not quite always. We hear of Gladstone felling trees, but it is not reported that he and Froude have wrestling matches.

Some weeks after this conversation with Mr. Lincoln I met Mr. Douglas, and drew from him his opinion of Mr. Lincoln. His very words, terse and emphatic as they were, I give: "Of all the —— —— Whig rascals about Springfield, Abe Lincoln is the ablest and most honest."

The Kansas-Nebraska Bill had indeed turned the tide against Douglas; the Republicans were successful, having a majority of one on joint ballot in the Legislature, thus securing the Senator.

With a common voice the Republicans of the State proclaimed Lincoln Senator. In caucus he received forty-nine votes out of the fifty-one Republican majority. If I recall the figures aright, Mr. Trumbull the other two. But these refused in any contingency to vote for Mr. Lincoln. "After balloting for some time, I learned from a trustworthy source," said Mr. Lincoln, "that on a certain future ballot these two men would cast their votes for the Democratic candidate, and elect him. I called a meeting of my friends, explained the situation to them, and requested them on the next ballot, after these two men had voted for Mr. Trumbull, to change their votes and elect him. At this there was a murmur of disapprobation and declarations never to do it. I resumed and said: 'Gentlemen, I am not here to play a part; you can not elect me; you can elect Mr. Trumbull, who is a good Republican. You put me in a false position if you use my name to the injury of the Republican party, and whoever does it is not my friend.' They then reluctantly acquiesced, and Mr. Trumbull was elected."

This is the most significant act in the merely personal history of Mr. Lincoln. It exhibited the self-control and equilibrium of his character, as well as his party fidelity. There is now before me a letter of his in which he announces his motto in political affairs, "Bear and forbear." This self-poise, self-abnegation, and forbearance enabled him to bring the ship of state safely through the stormy seas before him. He never labored for effect; there was nothing theatrical in him; he was not concerned about his personal relations to affairs; smiled when he was told that Seward was using him and getting all the glory. He sought nothing fantastical; but felt it to be his supreme duty to bring peace with honor to his distracted country.

A picturesque administration may please the unskillful, but it makes the judicious grieve. The machinery of government, like that of the human body, is usually working best when it is attracting no attention.

The bread thus thrown upon the waters by Mr. Lincoln in securing the election of Trumbull returned, and not after many days. But when he had these conversations it was unknown to him. To the suggestion he would certainly be selected as the next Senator, he quietly replied, "I don't know." But when the time came the Republican Convention unanimously nominated him for Senator—an act without precedent in our Senatorial history.

The debate followed. At that time, under the influence of a strong partisan enthusiasm, I felt that Lincoln had greatly the advantage. But upon reading the debate now, its moral bearings aside, as a mere intellectual feat, the advantage of either is not apparent. The argument of slavery is put with all the telling force of Douglas's vigorous mind and intense nature. He was a veritable "little giant."

Mr. Lincoln, as we have seen, remained in Cincinnati about a week, moving freely around. Yet not twenty men in the city knew him personally, or knew that he was here; not a hundred would have known who he was had his name been given them.

He came with the fond hope of making fame in a forensic contest with Reverdy Johnson. He was pushed aside, humiliated, and mortified. He attached to the innocent city the displeasure that filled his bosom, shook its dust from his feet, and departed never to return. How dark and impenetrable to him then was the thin veil soon to rise, revealing to him a resplendent future! He did return to the city, two years thereafter, with a fame wide as the continent, with the laurels of the Douglas contest on his brow, and the Presidency in his grasp. He returned, greeted with the thunder of cannon, the strains of martial music, and the joyous plaudits of thousands of citizens thronging the streets. He addressed a vast concourse on Fifth Street Market; was entertained in princely style at the Burnet House; and there received with courtesy the foremost citizens, come to greet this rising star.

The manner of the man was changed. The free conversation of unrestraint had given place to the vague phrase of the wary politician, the repose of ease to the agitation of unaccustomed elevation.

Two men have I known on the eve of a Presidential nomination, each expecting it—Chase and Lincoln. With each, but in different degrees, there was an all-absorbing egotism. To hear, every waking moment, one's hopes and prospects canvassed, develops in one the feeling that he is the most important thing in the universe. Accompanying this is a lofty exaltation of spirits; the blood mounts to the brain, and the mind reels in delirium. Pity the Presidential aspirant.

With high hope and happy heart Mr. Lincoln left Cincinnati after a three days' sojourn. But a perverse fortune attended him and Cincinnati in their intercourse. Nine months after Mr. Lincoln left us, after he had been nominated for the Presidency, when he was tranquilly waiting in his cottage home at Springfield the verdict of the people, his last visit to Cincinnati and the good things he had had at the Burnet House were rudely brought to his memory by a bill presented to him from its proprietors. Before leaving the hotel he had applied to the clerk for his bill; was told that it was paid, or words to that effect. This the committee had directed, but afterward neglected its payment. The proprietors shrewdly surmised that a letter to the nominee for the Presidency would bring the money.

The only significance in this incident is in the letter it brought from Mr. Lincoln, revealing his indignation at the seeming imputation against his honor, and his greater indignation at one item of the bill. "*As to wines, liquors, and cigars, we had none—absolutely none.* These last may have been in 'Room 15' by order of committee, but I do not recollect them at all."

Mr. Lincoln again visited Cincinnati on his way to Washington. His coming was not heralded by the roar of cannon, but it was greeted by an outpouring of the people such as no man here ever before or since has received; they thronged in countless thousands about the station, along the line of his march, covering the house-tops. They welcomed him with one continuous and unbroken storm of applause. Coming events were then casting their dark shadows before them. All men instinctively desired to look upon and cheer him who was to be their leader in the coming conflict.

There was an informal reception at the Burnet House, the people, in line, filing through and shaking his hand until a late hour in the evening. His manner was quiet, calm, resolute, and observant. All exaltation of feeling was gone. His reception amused and instructed him. As they passed before him, this one eagerly and enthusiastically grasped his hand, speaking out, "Be firm; don't back down." He was a good Republican. But this one takes his hand quietly, releases it slowly, while whispering, "The country expects a conservative administration." This is a Bell and Everett man. Another touches his hand with the tips of his fingers, and, with a curious gaze, passes on in silence. That is a Douglas man.

The reception over, Mr. Lincoln passes to his room to find his little son fretfully waiting his coming to be put to bed. The father lovingly takes him in his arms and retires to an adjoining room, undresses him, and puts him to bed. As he gazes upon the placid features of his sleeping child for a moment his mind turns from all around him and all before him, back to his quiet life and home, to the grave of the little one not with him. Its last sickness is before him; also the dream that warned him that his child could not live—the dream that ever came to him before coming calamity—that was once again to startle him, presaging his tragic end.

One may lift himself out of his early environment, but its impress is enduring.

About this weird and wonderful man—one of those unique characters that do not repeat themselves in history—is fast gathering a cloud of myth and legend, obscuring the real man. That we may retain some glimpses of this is the apology for these reminiscences.

LITTLE ELSIE.

Ah, don't come a-wooing with your long, long face,
    And your longer purse behind:
I'm a bright young girl, and I know my place,
    And I think I know my mind.
I like to laugh, and to dance and sing,
    And to tease my parents dear.
My brothers call me a "tiresome thing";
    But they wouldn't miss me here.

O 'tis I am my mother's heart's delight,
    And my father's right hand brave.
Would I leave my home so free and bright
    To be a rich man's slave?

Would I buy myself a gown of silk
    In a grand dull house to pine,
When I've boys to play with and cows to milk,
    And the whole fair world is mine?

Ah, don't come talking of the cares of life:
    My head is gold, not gray;
And it's my desire to be no man's wife—
    At least, not just to-day.
But I've a heart, and it's warm and true,
    And I'll keep it safe, at ease;
And if one I love should come to woo,
    I'll give it—when I please!

SHEFFIELD.

ONE beauty of Sheffield is that you can see very little of it at a time. The greatest altitude and the clearest day combined do not considerably affect this circumstance. No matter which point of view is selected, the foreground is dim, yellow, and confined; the distance is spectral, muffled, and deplorably gloomy. Down below us, from every height, is a nest of dark, unornamental houses; a complication of narrow, winding streets; the lofty spire or dome of a church; the urgent traffic of pedestrians and vehicles. Beyond, in every direction, is a screen of torpid smoke which obscures the sky, and tones the warm radiance behind it to a mellow and sometimes golden twilight. Out of the clinging folds countless slender chimneys immensely high streak the monotonous color that surrounds them, and from each issues a woolly black stream that, lacking the natural buoyancy and regard of the conveniences of approach. As the population has multiplied, and as the sons of the old cutler of a hundred years ago have grown into a firm employ-

SHEFFIELD FROM THE HIGH LEVEL AT VICTORIA STATION.

diffusiveness of smoke, seems to clot in the sultry air. The uninformed traveller who glances through the town by railway without alighting is kept in ignorance of its topography by the persistence of these fumes: he can not tell, from all that is visible, whether it is built upon a plain, a slope, or a ridge; whether it is compact or scattered, wide or narrow in area. Only the elongated chimneys with their smoky pennons are lifted into prominence; all below them is vague.

It is a blessing even yet that not much of Sheffield can be seen at a time, for all that makes a city attractive is only now being provided. The streets were tortuous and incongruous, having been built without any prevision. The builders seem never to have thought that the plans which suited them might obstruct in the future, or, thinking, they did not care; and when any new edifices were put up, it was with American indifference to the harmony of environment, and un-American dis-

ing hundreds of workmen, larger dwellings and more commodious factories have been necessary; but the modern structures have not been erected with a cohesive design or appropriate sequence; the new music hall is here, and the new hotel there, with shabby blocks of antiquated houses between. The manifest inconvenience of such a state of things at length forced itself upon the attention of the authorities, who, armed with power and provided with the necessary funds, have entirely revised large portions of the early plan of the centre of the town. Blind alleys and curvilinear lanes, with all their misleading sinuosities, have been razed to open the continuous and spacious streets which the ever-increasing traffic requires. The authorities have aimed to secure a main avenue, broad and well lighted, in its business centre, with well-planned streets running at right angles with it. In them stately piles of buildings, of some architectural pretensions, are being erected, and the centre of the town in the future will present a very different appearance from what it has done in the past. Sheffield possesses no town-hall, court-house, museum, or other public building really worth looking at, and until recently it had only one public park; now it has three. A brief digression will enable us to see what there is commendable in the town besides its commerce.

The atmosphere of Sheffield is not favorable to the development of genius, but a few notable men have grown under the smoky skies whose fame has reached all English readers. Chantrey, the sculptor, was born within two or three miles of the town; Montgomery, the poet, spent most of his life in it; and Elliott, whose facile versification contributed as much to the repeal of the corn laws as the most logical eloquence of prose, carried on a business within its precincts.

When he was a mere boy, and an unsuccessful one, having failed in London, the rock that breaks so many hearts, Montgomery saw an advertisement in a Sheffield newspaper which led to his engagement upon its staff. The paper was the *Register*, which was in disfavor with the government on account of its sympathy with the disaffection created in England by the French Revolution; and the embryo poet had not been long enough in an editorial chair to perceive what Dead Sea fruit its rewards are, when (the proprietor having fled) he was arrested on the charge of having written a seditious ballad, and sentenced to three months' imprisonment. Soon after his release his sense of humanity was touched and his indignation aroused by the violence of a military officer in quelling a disturbance, for a description of which he was again arrested, and imprisoned six months. But he survived these penalties, and prospered. Under the name of the *Iris*, the *Register* became a great pecuniary success, and Montgomery died in April, 1854, at the age of eighty-three years, wealthy and honored, after a residence in Sheffield of sixty-two years. A bronze statue upon a granite pedestal has been erected to his memory in the General Cemetery. His paper was published and most of his poems were written in an old house in the Hartshead, which was recently occupied as a tavern, but now is used as offices. It is related that Howitt once called his attention to the number of authors whose homes had become public drinking places, among others Burns's, Scott's, Shelley's, and Coleridge's at Nether Stowey. Montgomery laughed, but he lived to see his own sanctum become the resort of disreputable old topers.

Ebenezer Elliott, the "Corn-law Rhymer," entered the steel business in Sheffield with a capital of one hundred pounds, and after many struggles acquired a respectable fortune. His corn-law rhymes had an extraordinary success,

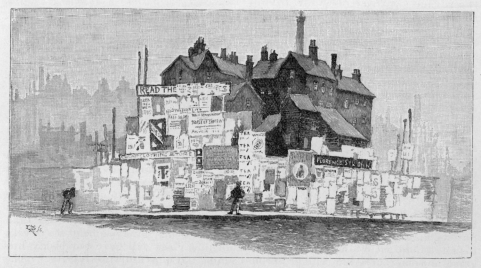

A CORNER.

and if his other works were not satisfactory in form they showed in some degree real inspiration.

THE MANOR CASTLE.

Chantrey was a milk-boy in Sheffield, and when released from this occupation he was transferred to the scarcely more congenial shop of a grocer, and then apprenticed to a carver and gilder, with whom he remained only a short time. Afterward he started out on his own account as a portrait painter, and modestly set forth his claims to patronage through an advertisement in Montgomery's paper, which stated that "he hoped to meet with the liberal sentiments of an impartial public." His advancement was rapid, and from a humble portrait painter he soon developed into a great sculptor. He was knighted by William the Fourth, and was buried in a suburb of Sheffield. Thomas Creswick, the landscape painter, was also a native of the town, as were Archbishop Secker, Sir Sterndale Bennett, and several other celebrities.

Another thing which uplifts the town above the sordid commonplaces of its commerce is its history, which has a varied interest. Its site was known to the Romans, of whom many traces have been found; and when they had departed the land was occupied by a succession of Saxon lords, from whom it passed to the famous Shrewsburys. The fourth earl was custodian of Cardinal Wolsey during his disgrace, and entertained him with great consideration at the Manor Castle, in which

Mary, Queen of Scots, was imprisoned twelve years out of the nineteen which she spent in England. She was in custody of the sixth earl, and was guarded by forty men. There is extant the following document, issued by the earl for the government of her household, which comprised thirty personal attendants.

"*To the Master of the Scotts Queenes Household, Mr. Beton.*

"*First.*—That all your people which appertayneth to the Queene shall depart from the Queene's chamber or chambers to their own lodging at IX of the clock at night, winter and summer, whatsoever he or she; either to their lodging within the house or without in the towne, and there to remain till the next day at VI of the clock. *Item.* That none of the Queenes people shall at no tyme wear his sword neither within the house nor when her grace rydeth or goeth abroad; unless the master of the household himself do weare a sword and no more without special licence. *Item.* That there shall none of the Queenes people carry any bow or shaftes at no tyme, neither to the fields nor to the butts, unless it be four or fyve and no more in the Queenes companye. *Item.* That none of the Queenes people shall ryde or go at no tyme out of the house or towne without my special licence; and if he or they so doeth, they or he shall come no more in at the gates, neither in the towne, whatsoever he or she or they be. *Item.* That you or some of the Queenes chamber, when her grace will walke abroad, shall advertyse the officiar of my warde, who shall declare the messuage to me one houer before she goeth forth. *Item.* That none of the Queenes people, whatsoever he or they be, not once offer at no tyme to come forth of their chamber or lodging when anie alarum is given by night or daie, whether they be in the Queenes chamber or in their chambers within the house or without in the towne, and yf he or they keep not their chambers or lodging whatsoever that be he or they shall stande at their perill for deathe.

"*At Shefeild the 26th daie of April,* 1571, *per me,*
"SHREWSBURIE."

The earl's orthography was not always so "symmetrical," as Matthew Arnold would say, however, as may be seen in a letter which he wrote describing the unhappy lady's condition: "She is within a few dayes become more malincholy than of long before, and complenes of her wronges and imprisonments. I am sure her malyncholy and grefe is grattar than she in words uttars; and yett, rather than contynew this imprisonment she stycks not to say she will gyve hur boddy, hur sonne, and hur cuntry for lyberty." The Queen remained at the castle until September, 1584, and three years later her career was ended by the executioner's axe. Wolsey died within three days of his departure from the town.

which received the Queen while alterations were being made in the main building, remains, in a state of extreme dilapidation, having been occupied as a road-

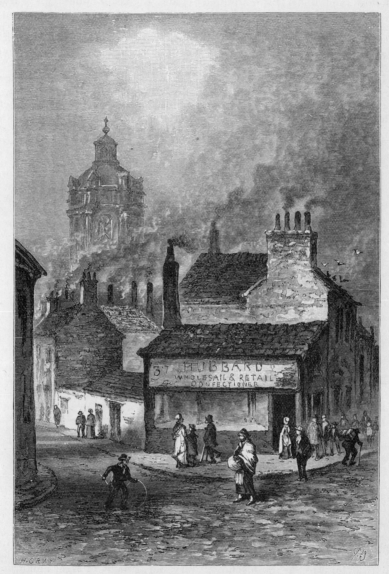

A BIT OF OLD SHEFFIELD.

With the extinction of the male Shrewsburys in the civil war, the estate became the property of the Howards, and the Duke of Norfolk now owns much of the ground upon which Sheffield is built. The castle is levelled, but the manor attached to it, side ale-house until its walls became too insecure for the shelter even of the most reckless. The parish church was founded in the reign of Henry I. It is rectangular in shape, with a crocketed tower and a spire near the centre. The nave and chancel have north and south aisles, and the nave is divided into five bays with stone pillars and arches. In the southeast corner is the Shrewsbury Chapel, an elaborately fitted alcove with a stained-glass window, and under its sculptured vault is the tomb of Wolsey's noble custodian, whose figure is reproduced in recumbent marble, with similar statues of his two wives by his side.

The Hall, the property of the Cutlers' Company of Hallamshire, is most interesting for its associations. The reputation of Sheffield steel-ware had even reached

pany "for the good order and government of the makers of knives, sickles, shears, scissors, and other cutlery wares"—an organization which still exists in a prosperous condition. The body-corporate includes a master-cutler, two wardens, six searchers, and twenty-four assistant searchers, the latter being empowered to seize all defective wares produced by inferior workmen. For a long time the government of the Cutlers' Company pursued a very exclusive policy, excluding all except freemen from their handicraft; but in 1814 an act of Parliament limited its functions to the granting of trade-marks.

BLOOMSPRING LANE BOARD SCHOOL.

old Chaucer's ears, who, describing a character in the *Canterbury Tales*, says, "A Sheffield thwytel bare he in his hose," the "thwytel" or "whittle" having been a fourteenth-century bowie-knife; and in the Middle Ages the staple business of the town was the manufacture of arrow-heads, some of which were used on Bosworth Field. Nearly two hundred years ago the population included seven thousand cutlers, and in 1624 the operatives formed themselves into a protective com-

By a still more recent act the functions of the company have been extended to every department of steel and iron in the district, and it now occupies a position of equality with the Registrar-General of Trade-marks in London. The revenue of the company is derived from the granting of marks, the lettings of their rooms, and dividends on invested stocks. The first Thursday in September is a memorable day in connection with the company. The master-cutler-elect is then ceremoniously installed in office, and in the evening he gives his time-honored "feast"—one of the most celebrated events in northern England. His guests number 350; and happy is the master-cutler who can secure the presence at his festive

well-equipped charities. The Shrewsbury Hospital began its beneficence over two hundred years ago, and has since accommodated twenty poor gentlewomen and twenty poor gentlemen, providing them with lodgings, coal, clothing, and a small

WESLEYAN COLLEGE.

board of one or more of the cabinet ministers of the day, with a sprinkling of dukes, earls, and noble lords. The hall is in the Italian style, and includes a dining-room one hundred feet long and fifty feet wide, and an assembly-room eighty feet long by thirty feet wide.

At one time Sheffield was deplorably behind in educational matters; but since the Education Act was passed in 1872 Herculean efforts have been made to supply felt deficiencies. The School Board have erected twenty-three schools in different parts of the town, which are alike an ornament and a credit to it. The attendance at the elementary schools within the borough has increased since 1872 from 12,000 to 36,317. There is no more handsome pile of buildings in the town than the central schools, the offices of the board, and the college erected through the munificence of the late Mr. Mark Firth. Much attention is also being given to technical education. Then there is the new Albert Hall, which, in proportions at least, is somewhat noteworthy. In Arundel Street a school of art is established under the auspices of the South Kensington Museum, the directors of which place it at the head of all similar schools in the United Kingdom; and in Darkhouse Road is the classic front of the Wesleyan College.

Another count in Sheffield's favor is that it has many firmly established and

amount of cash each week. Besides the inmates, it has sixty out-door pensioners, twenty of whom (males) receive seven shillings a week each, and forty of whom (females) receive five shillings a week each. The Deakin Institute is both novel in its aims and admirable in its administration. It was founded by a merchant, who bequeathed three thousand pounds toward its establishment, on condition that a like sum should be subscribed within two years of his death. Its object is to assist unmarried women of good character, who are members of the Episcopal Church, Evangelical, or Dissenters, over forty years of age, and thirty-nine such women are now annuitants, twenty-five of the number receiving twenty-five pounds each annually, and fourteen twenty pounds each annually. The most unusual and commendable feature of the charity is its privacy and unostentation. On election the annuitants immediately receive one-half of the yearly sum, and the details of the payment are so arranged that no one is the wiser for it except the recipient.

At Ranmoor, one of the loveliest suburbs of Sheffield, is a group of almshouses which were built and adequately endowed by the late Mr. Mark Firth at a cost of £30,000. There are thirty-six houses for the accommodation of forty-eight persons, with chapel and house for the chaplain and governor. Besides the free occupancy of the house, each married couple receives ten shillings and each single inmate seven shillings per week. The Sheffield General Infirmary, which has been established for nearly a century, relieves from 12,000 to 14,000 in and out patients every year. It contains 186 beds for patients, of which forty are set apart exclusively for children's cases in separate wards. The Public Hospital and Dispensary accommodates about forty thousand patients, in-door and out, annually; and the town also has a special hospital for women, built at a cost of more than £30,000 by Mr. Thomas Jessop; a free hospital for children, an Institute and manufactory for the blind, a home for nurses, an asylum for decayed licensed victuallers (the euphemistic calling in Great Britain of dealers in alcoholic liquors), a school of medicine, and various "funds" bequeathed under more or less narrow, eccentric, or oddly generous conditions. Among the hills outside the town, in an old dwelling, is the nucleus of Mr. Ruskin's art museum of the St. George's Society; and among the things we have to admit is that the desire for wealth has not been so eager nor the hold of it so tenacious that the unfortunate or necessitous have been overlooked in Sheffield.

But now that we have enumerated such of its possessions, historical, biographical, and architectural, as weigh in a tourist's estimate of a town's desirability, let us emphasize what is fairly evident — that Sheffield is not to be discovered in museums, churches, or municipal palaces; that its vitality, its influence on the world, all that makes it great, and the causes of its reputation, are by no means æsthetical, religious, or philanthropic. Its significance is in its immense trade and the absolute excellence of its metallic manufactures, the knowledge of which is circulated everywhere by a medium less mutable than literature. We question if there is a savage so benighted who, however ignorant he may be of its import, can not see Sheffield deeply branded on his knife, and it is quite possible at this very moment, while the ink is drying on this manuscript, that with a Sheffield blade of one kind or another some fugitive Bannocks are hiding in the fastnesses of Montana, with a view to anatomic experiments upon the "whites";

that many a Jack Tar, perched in the foretop, surveying the gray uncertainty of antipodal seas, is shaving his "plug" for a fresh "quid"; that princes are sitting down to dinner; that some convicts are scraping the cement out of the walls of their cells; and that the readers of *Harper's Magazine* are cutting the leaves of the last number. Scarcely any limitation can be set to the variety of purposes served by Sheffield manufactures. Travellers in Russia and Austria are whirled over Sheffield rails; the twenty-four inch armor plates of England's newest ironclads were rolled in Sheffield; the scissors that myriads of pale seamstresses are plying bear the Sheffield brand; the velocipedes upon which numerous young athletes are flying between the bloom of English lanes have come from under the big Sheffield chimneys; the scythes that are levelling fields of ripe grain in Iowa and Minnesota were ground on Sheffield stones; the rotary saws that are hissing in lumbering settlements among the California sierras were cut by Sheffield hands; the mortars and cannons that bristle along many a fortress, with the pyramids of shot and shell for their consumption beside them, represent an extensive part of Sheffield's industry; the superb repoussé work of silver épergnes that adorn banquet tables was hammered out by Sheffield artisans; and every variety of electro-plate and silver-ware, beautiful in design and enormous in price, is wrought under Sheffield roofs. We have not nearly exhausted a catalogue which includes many other products, such as railway tires, axles, springs, buffers, and engines, all sorts of tools, sewing-machines, fire-irons, and stoves; but we have mentioned enough to indicate where Sheffield *is* to be found, if its interest is invisible in the places to which a tourist usually looks for a city's attractions.

The labor has few rests, and whenever we are carried into the dark limits of the town from the green hills of Yorkshire by the Manchester, Sheffield, and Lincolnshire line, the grewsome spectres of chimneys are still wearing their funereal banners. At night the smoke pulsates with the fervid glow of the furnaces at the base, around which hoarse, complexionless, sweating men are toiling, not for the price of a ransom, but for a brief respite. We see Sheffield in hundreds of blackened little cottages, built in alleys, courts, and

A BIT OF SHEFFIELD ON THE HILL.

is less of a problem with it than the adjustment of work and wages. The steam-hammer shapes the destinies of the populace as well as the metal upon which its blows fall and ring.

In whichever direction we walk we can not escape the throbbing of labor. Now it is audible in the hissing whirl of a steam-saw that tears its way through a plate of steel as though it were the softest wood; now in the strident friction of a grinding-wheel; now in the measured beat of a hundred hammers; then in the ravenous breathing of a blast-furnace; and once more in the terrible splashings of molten metals. Nor can we wander far away from the presence of labor, which is visible from the pleasure-parks, the cemeteries, and the homes of the citizens. A prodigious exhibit of industries is that which Sheffield presents; one that, if it were taken in the details of all its branches, would fill a volume of description—an absorbingly interesting volume, too, for while every appliance that human ingenuity has devised

thoroughfares; again, in the groups of citizens who with their wives fill the streets and markets in the evenings; again, in the modern factories built to accommodate from one to five thousand hands; now in the scorching glow of a red-hot armor plate, then in the dust of a "hull" of grinding "troughs." It has little time for refinement or amusement, and immortality

A VERY CLEAR DAY.

may be seen in operation, the purely mechanical or economic aspect which engages the engineer is superseded in the estimation of a layman by the picturesque side of the works, the high colors, the unintermittent activity, and the metamorphoses of some of the workmen, who seem like imps in a region which only needs perpetuity to realize the inferno. Only of a Sunday does the hum of toil cease, the smoke begin to clear away, and Sheffield for a few hours of respite become quiet and visible.

Containing a population of 286,289, mostly artisans, Sheffield has particular interest to the student of social science. Notwithstanding its great and varied industries, and the abundant opportunities for employment that are afforded, there are in the more crowded parts of the town much destitution and immorality. Employers complain that their people will not work full time, but waste their days at cricket and foot-ball matches, at handicaps and coursing matches; and betting on almost every conceivable event has spread amongst them like an epidemic. Others are ardent fishermen. There are hundreds of fishing clubs in the town, which

rent miles of water away in Nottinghamshire, Lincolnshire, and elsewhere. Co-operation, improved dwellings, cafés, clubs, and so forth, are doing much to improve the social life of the people.

The more respectable Sheffield artisan is not tentative by nature, and the course of a river is not more submissive to the thralldom of habit than he is. Living in a two-storied cottage well seasoned with the homogeneous blackness, he is usually enabled by ordinary sobriety and industry to maintain himself and his family in a respectable and comfortable position. The cottage has two stories, a kitchen and sitting-room on the first floor, and two or three bedrooms above, such a dwelling being obtainable for about five shillings, or one dollar and twenty-five cents, a week. His wife is apt to be a stout Lancashire or Yorkshire woman, thrifty, industrious, and cleanly, whose good qualities are conspicuous in the whitened door-step, the speckless windows, and the orderly arrangement of the furniture. The neatness of these cottages is very noticeable, and an exception to the rule in most manufacturing towns.

Once a year even the poorest try to take

a holiday by the sea-side at Bridlington, Morecambe Bay, or Scarborough, and evening amusements are provided by several theatres and music halls, though it is to be confessed that the entertainment most patronized during our visit to the town was not of an edifying character. The programme consisted of a farce called *An Old Woman in a Fix* (the very title of which seemed to strike the audience as being humorous to a side-splitting degree), and a novel exhibition in which the spectators took part. A new silk hat ("one of Tyler's best") was offered to the "gastronomic prodigy" who could eat one of "Fiddlestick's celebrated all-hot pies" the quickest; and the contest provoked an uproar of mirth that must have warmed the managerial heart. But the more sedate citizens resort to the neighboring tap-room for the discussion of affairs of state. Sometimes there are flashes of rough wit, and the stolid Yorkshire mechanic becomes as eager a politician as the most eloquent members of the Bull-dog Coterie, Sixth Ward, New York. "Wheer's tha off to?" inquires his opponent, as a disgusted Liberal angrily makes for the door. "I'm goin' to see if th' 'sylum's open," retorts Mr. Gladstone's disciple, delicately insinuating the appropriateness of that institution for the gentleman opposite. "Well,

want to answer it, and it 'ud ta-ake thee a' neet."

A survey of all the trades that are plied in Sheffield is impossible here, and we must confine our observations to the three largest, which are in steel manufactures, electro-plating, and cutlery. The last is first in history, extent, and importance, the value of its exports to the United States being about one million dollars annually. The oldest firm began its business one hundred and fifty years ago, with workshops in the rear of the dwellings of its two partners. It made only the plainest goods, but the steel in them was of the best quality, and it has now become an establishment employing over seventeen hundred mechanics, who produce weekly five thousand dozen table knives and forks, eighteen hundred pairs of carvers, sixteen hundred dozen pocket-knives, fourteen hundred dozen razors, and fifteen hundred dozen scissors. The quantity of finished cutlery exported by this one firm to the United States annually weighs more than twelve tons, and the intimacy engendered between Sheffield and the West by the traffic causes an American to be treated in that city with a little less wonderment than his advent excites in some other English provinces.

A SUNDAY EVENING.

they'll ta-ake thee in, anyway, I'll bet," loudly asserts the Conservative; and the audience, whether they believe it or not, are vastly tickled by the sally. "What argement canst th' make on it?" demands another Conservative of a Liberal, referring to a question that he has put. "A good enough one," is the reply, "but thou'd

The "pioneer establishment," as they would call it on the Pacific coast, was willingly opened for our inspection, and an intelligent artisan was appointed to act as our guide, who first took us into the ivory room, in which twenty-five tons of elephant tusks are made fit for handles every year. It is not a pleasant place by

WORKS AT SHEFFIELD.

any means; the air is filled with white dust, which is thrown out like a spray from the saws, and the pale brown tusks piled upon the shelves have no reminiscence of the spicy Indies in their odor. The best quality is African, the second East Indian, and each tusk contains eight different qualities in itself, the yellowish part near the centre being most valuable. Every bit is utilized, and as the sawyer is paid according to the thrift he displays with his materials, he is sometimes so ingenious that not a scrap of waste remains. Besides the ivory, four hundred-weight of stag-horn is used every week for pocket-knives, and of this only the rough brown outside is available. The inside is put in solution for the gelatinous substances which it contains; the extraction is sold for the stiffening of cloth, and the residue is an excellent fertilizer. In the next department, which is in a court-yard, six men, each in a separate alcove, like mediæval alchemists, are bending over little forges, and here the blades are shaped out of purposeless-looking bars, under the tinkling rain of the hammers; the form is given, without the polish or edge of the finished article, and at this stage of the manufacture the steel is a variable blue or purple, with rings and blots of rusty brown upon it. Every blade is branded with the individual mark of its maker, who is thus held accountable for its quality to his employers, and the same sign shows at the end of the day exactly how much work he has done, the labor in all the branches of cutlery being paid for by the piece. The blade made, it is welded, in the case of a dinner knife, to a piece of iron, which forms the "tang," or the part that is inserted in the handle, and the shoulder, or the projecting part between the handle and the blade. It is then heated to incandescence, and plunged perpendicularly into cold water, by which a sudden hardening is effected, and the gradual application of further heat afterward "tempers" it. The next process is grinding. We are led across the court-yard into a dismal workshop, which is so poorly lighted that for a few moments we can only discern the whirring bands on many wheels, an occasional white flash, or a shower of sparks, and when our sight becomes accustomed to the gloom, a fantastic scene is visible. From the back of the room to the front there are several separate rows of grinding-stones, and these massive disks are revolving with a busy murmur, the power being communicated from the shafting near the ceiling by leather bands. The lower part of the stones touches a long vessel containing water, and by a technical peculiarity each stone is called a "trough." Immediately behind every stone there is a solid block of wood with a saddle in it, which forms the seat of the grinder, who, scarcely ever straightening himself, bends to his task, and accompanies the humming of the stone with a song or a whistle. The stone spins steadily and tirelessly; myriads of minute sparks fly out from it mixed with particles of sand that make the apartment misty, and the grinder gently draws the blade to and fro across it until the steel loses the dark color the forge gave it, and becomes lustrously white under the friction. Now and then he lifts the blade from the stone, and quickly runs his eye along its lambent surface, or touches the edge with his finger—an experiment repeated several times before he transfers it into other hands. After it has been applied to the rough sandstone, it is ground upon a wheel of hard blue-stone, next upon an emery wheel, and finally upon a wheel of what our amiable guide very deliberately called "rhinoc'us" hide, the different kinds of friction leaving it sharp and brilliant.

The grinders work under an unusual system: the troughs and the tools belong to them, having been a heritage through an unknown number of generations, and they pay the employers seven shillings a week for the power supplied to each trough. Not every grinder is a proprietor, however. Some have no direct relations with the master-cutlers, being hired by their fellows, who adjust and settle their wages, and these agents are paid so much a dozen for the blades ground. The custom is old and incongruous; it has no apparent advantages to either party; but a Sheffield grinder inflexibly adheres to established usage, and resists every innovation. He suffers severely from a painful disease caused by the entrance of steel and stone dust into the lungs, and when fans were applied to create draughts that would suck the dust away, he objected to them because they would lengthen the average life of the trade, and lead to a surplus of labor! The grounds upon which a grinder stands have not often a more rational

FORGING THE BLADES OF CLASP-KNIVES.

FINISHING POCKET-KNIVES.

foundation. A very notable characteristic of his class, and one that has sprung in recent years from the dissemination of cheap literature and the facilities for travel and observation, is an independence of attitude and utterance which, however repugnant it may be to those followers of Mr. Ruskin whose watch-word is "Obey," contrasts refreshingly with the obsequiousness of former days.

Passing from the dark interior of the grinding-room, where each wheel has a sound of its own, one spluttering, another whirring, and another singing, we are led up and down stairways, along close corridors, and through interminable workrooms, where men, women, and children are silently putting the various parts of the knives together; and the division of labor is so complete that one knife is handled, or "taken up," to use the local expression, about seventy times, by different artisans, from the moment the blade is forged until the instrument is finished and

smoothly wrapped up for market. At one long bench we find a party of men cutting files on the blades of pocket-knives with such dexterity that the threads, each less than the hundredth part of an inch in thickness, and exactly equidistant, are as true as if they were graven with the aid of a rule and a magnifying-glass, while the only implements used in the work are a chisel and a mallet, the mechanic being guided by his eye and an almost marvellous sensitiveness and accuracy of touch. The chisel is put upon the blade near the tip, and struck with the mallet, leaving the initial thread, which is followed by others until the flat steel becomes a perfect file. The men employed in this are fairly considered skilled workmen, but their earnings are small, and do not reach two pounds, or ten dollars, a week, under the most favorable circumstances. At another bench a row of men are putting together the parts of ivory, pearl, and buckhorn clasps, riveting them and jointing them with a like quickness and sureness of touch that would not be suspected from the clumsiness of their fingers; and in a separate room more wheels are revolving, each operated by a man or a boy, who is putting the finishing polish on the blades. The custom previously mentioned of making some mark on a knife by which each of the various processes may be traced to the artisan who has done the work, and a check put upon carelessness or incapacity, is continued through all the branches, and ever resource the work-people find outside the abstraction of their toil must be in the imagination. Here and there the benches have been decorated by scraps from illustrated newspapers, or the very chromatic portrait of some houri that has adorned a baking-powder box. An ascetic-looking old gentleman has a familiar hymn pasted on the wall before him, and the youth next to him, whose face indicates much pent-up levity, has a ballad under his eye, the easy rhyme having an

GRINDING THE BLADES OF POCKET-KNIVES.

when a knife passes into the packing-room or storehouse it bears a succinct history of itself from its shaping at the forge to its chastening on the polishing-wheel.

The hours are long—from seven in the morning until noon, when there is an intermission for a frugal dinner, and from one o'clock until six. We grow pitiful in contemplating their tedium. All the windows show an unvarying prospect of roofs and smoking chimneys, without a bit of blue sky or any silver lining to the clouds —a contraction of the horizon, a despondence of color, unspeakably monotonous. Conversation is not allowed, and what- inexhaustible fascination for him. The intelligence of some, their comfortableness of dress and well-taken-care-of appearance, are very noticeable, and yet more so is the interest evinced in politics by the men, who, between their bites at dinner, pore over the "leaders" of the morning papers with great eagerness.

From the cutlers—and, by-the-way, let us say that, technically, the cutler is the man who puts the knife together, to the exclusion from the name of grinders and others—from the cutlers, whose buildings loom up on an entire block, we traverse several little alleys and broad thoroughfares, with smoke-discolored houses and shops bordering them, until we stand before a massive gateway, with a tremendous knocker not less than five pounds in weight affixed to it, and in response to a laborious rat-tat and a word of explanation, we are admitted into a laboratory where Vulcan and Titan are partners, and the Cyclops, disembodied, re-appear in machines of modern devising; where feats of strength are performed every minute that make play of those recorded in the classic fables; where Sheffield is again seen in five thousand mechanics, clothed in fustian, begrimed, and translated, to all appearances, from decent humanity to a hybrid condition between that of gnomes and that of demons. Within these noisy precincts the materials of the toil are steel and iron, and the productions are armor plates, tools, and railway metals.

The space covered by the workshops is more than fourteen acres, subdivided by long avenues, and all over this vast area, which is piteously black and execrably dusty, the labor assumes heroic proportions, which elevate it and fill an observer with the almost obsolete sense of amazement—even an observer of nineteenth-century ubiquitousness, who has been everywhere, seen everything, and cares nothing about ordinary mechanical pro-cesses. No wild vision of the supernatural, no Crystal Palace exhibition of pyrotechnics, no brilliant achievement of scenic art, could approach in weirdness, picturesqueness, and startling quality of effect the simple business of making Bessemer steel, which is a staple and every-day industry.

Our final exploration is through the work-rooms of an electro-plate factory—another scene, another act, and a new set of characters in Sheffield life. We watch the inferior metals in pale green and yellow baths assuming the whiteness of silver; we see shapeless pieces of metal transformed into beautiful dishes embossed with fruits, flowers, and other artistic designs, under the instantaneous pressure of an insensate machine; we are charmed by the exquisite skill of the repoussé workman, under whose hammer Nature is imitated in her loveliest forms.

Though Sheffield is itself so sombre, it is environed by some of the fairest scenery in England. Chatsworth and Beauchief Abbey are in its vicinity. Proceeding in any direction, the traveller is sure to find within a few miles of the town a picturesque charm in an embowered rivulet, a quaint old church, an ancient manor-house covered with ivy, a cool expanse of woodland, or a sweep of velvety pasturage.

A SHEFFIELD FOUNDRY.

WHIT-SUNDAY.

VII.

DURING the week which followed Easter the season moved forward as if there were to be no more regress. An efficient ally in the form of a southwest wind came to the aid of the sun, and every day nature responded with increasing fervor. Amy no more complained that an American April was like early March in England; and as the surface of the land grew warm and dry it was hard for her to remain in-doors, there was so much life, bustle, and movement without. Buds were swelling on every side. Those of the lilac were nearly an inch long, and emitted a perfume of the rarest delicacy, that was far superior to that of the blossoms to come. The nests of the earlier birds were in all stages of construction, and could be seen readily in the leafless trees. Snakes were crawling from their holes, and lay sunning themselves in the roads, to her and Johnnie's dismay. Alf

captured turtles that, deep in the mud, had learned the advent of spring as readily as the creatures of the air. The fish were ascending the swollen streams. "Each rill," as Thoreau wrote, "is peopled with new life rushing up it." Abram and Alf were planning a momentous expedition to a tumbling dam on the Moodna, the favorite resort of the sluggish suckers. New chicks were daily breaking their shells, and their soft, downy, ball-like little bodies were more to Amy's taste than the peepers of the marsh.

One Saturday morning Alf rushed in, announcing with breathless haste that "Kitten had a calf." Kitten was a fawn-colored Alderney, the favorite of the barnyard, and so gentle that even Johnnie did not fear to rub her rough nose, scratch her between her horns, or to bring her wisps of grass when she was tied near the house, and her calf was unlike all other calves. There was no rest until Amy had seen it, and she admitted that she had never looked upon a more innocent and droll little visage. At the children's pleading the infant cow was given to them, but they were warned to leave it for the present to

Abram and Kitten's care, for the latter was inclined to act like a veritable old cat when any one made too free with her bovine baby.

This bright Saturday, occurring about the middle of the month, completely enthroned spring in the children's hearts. The air was sweet with the fragrance from the springing grass, swelling buds, and so still and humid that sounds from other farms and gardens and songs from distant fields and groves blended softly yet distinctly with those of the immediate vicinage. The sunshine was warm, but veiled by fleecy clouds; and as the day advanced every member of the family was out-of-doors, even to Mrs. Clifford, for whom had been constructed, under her husband's direction, a low garden-chair which was so light that even Alf or Amy could draw it easily along the walks. From it she stepped down on her first visit of the year to her beloved flower beds, which Alf and Burt were putting in order for her, the latter blending with his filial attentions the hope of seeing more of Amy. Nor was he unrewarded, for his manner toward his mother, whom he alternately petted and chaffed, while at the same time doing her bidding with manly tenderness, won the young girl's hearty good-will. At last Mrs. Clifford, after she had gloated over the blooming crocuses, daffodils, and the budding hyacinths and tulips, expressed a wish to join her husband.

A wide path bordered on either side by old-fashioned perennials and shrubbery led down through the garden. There Amy gave herself up to the enjoyment of the pleasing sights and sounds on every side. Mr. Clifford was the picture of placid content as he sat on a box in the sun, cutting potatoes into the proper size for planting. Johnnie was perched on another box near, chattering incessantly as she handed him the tubers, and asking no other response than the old gentleman's amused smile. Leonard with a pair of stout horses was turning up the rich black mould, sinking his plough to the beam, and going twice in a furrow. It would require a very severe drought to affect land pulverized thus deeply, for under Leonard's thorough work the root pasturage was extended downward eighteen inches. On one side of the garden plot Webb was planting seeds. Leaving Mrs. Clifford chatting and laughing with her

husband and Johnnie, Amy sauntered along the broad path until she came in the neighborhood of Webb, and lingered there, enjoying an April day that lacked few elements of perfection.

The garden is one of the favorite haunts of the song-sparrow. In the flower border near, she would hear such a vigorous scratching among the leaves that she might well believe that a motherly hen was at work, but presently one of these little sober-coated creatures that Thoreau well calls a "ground-bird" would fly to the top of a plum-tree and trill out a song as sweet as the perfume that came from the blossoming willows not far away. The busy ploughs made it a high festival for the robins, for with a confidence not misplaced they followed near in the furrows that Leonard was making in the garden, and that Abram was turning on an adjacent hill-side, and not only the comparatively harmless earth-worms suffered, but also the pestiferous larvæ of the May-beetle, the archenemy of the strawberry plant. Even on that day of such varied and etherealized fragrance the fresh, wholesome odor of the upturned earth was grateful. Suddenly Webb straightened himself from the sowing of the scale-like parsnip seed in which he was then engaged, and said, "Listen." Remote yet distinct, like a dream of a bird-song, came a simple melody from a distant field. Then he took off his hat and said: "Welcome. That's our meadow-lark, Amy: not equal to your skylark, I admit. Indeed, it is not a lark at all, for Dr. Marvin says it belongs to the oriole family. Brief and simple as is its song, I think you will agree with me that spring brings few more lovely sounds. That is the first one that I have heard this year."

She scarcely more than caught the ethereal song before Burt and Alf came down the path, trundling immense wheelbarrow-loads of the prunings of the shrubbery around the house. These were added to a great pile of brush and refuse that had accumulated on the other side of the walk, and to Alf was given the wild excitement of igniting the inflammable mass, and soon there was a fierce crackling as the flames devoured their way into the loose dry centre of the rejected débris of the previous year. Then to Alf and Johnnie's unmeasured delight they were permitted to improvise a miniature prairie fire. A part of the garden had been left

"THERE WAS NO REST UNTIL AMY HAD SEEN IT."

to grow very weedy in the preceding summer, and they were shown how, by lighting the dry, dead material on the windward side, the flames, driven by a gentle western breeze, would sweep across the entire plot. With merry cries they followed the advancing line of fire, aiding it forward by catching up on iron rakes burning wisps and transferring them to spots in the weedy plot that did not kindle readily. Little Ned, clinging to the hand of Maggie, who had joined the family in the garden, looked on with awe-stricken eyes. From the bonfire and the consuming weeds great volumes of smoke poured up and floated away, the air was full of pungent odors, and the robins called vociferously back and forth through the garden, their alarmed and excited cries vying with the children's shouts. In half an hour only a faint haze of smoke to the eastward indicated the brief conflagration; the family had gone to the house for their one-o'clock dinner, and the birds were content with the normal aspect of the old garden in April.

The last Saturday of the month was looked forward to with hopeful expectations, as a genial earnest of May, and a chance for out-door pleasures; but with it came a dismal rain-storm, which left the ground as cold, wet, and sodden as it had been a month before.

The next day was one of sunshine. The birds took heart, and their songs of exultation resounded far and near. A warm south breeze sprang up and fanned Amy's cheek, as she, with the children and Burt, went out for their usual Sunday afternoon walk. They found the flowers looking up hopefully, but with melted snow hanging like tears on their pale little faces. The sun at last sank into the unclouded west, illumining the sky with a warm golden promise for the future. Amy gazed at its departing glory, but Burt looked at her—looked so earnestly, so wistfully, that she was full of compunction even while she welcomed the return of the children, which delayed the words that were trembling at his lips. He was ready, she was not; and he walked homeward at her side silent and depressed, feeling that the receptive, responsive spring was later in her heart than in nature.

According to the almanac, May was on time to a second, but Nature seemed unaware of the fact. Great bodies of snow covered the Adirondack region, and not a little still remained all the way southward through the Catskills and the Highlands, about the head-waters of the Delaware, and its cold breath benumbed the land. Johnnie's chosen intimates had given her their suffrages as May-queen; but prudent Maggie had decided that the crowning ceremonies should not take place until May truly appeared with its warmth and floral wealth. Therefore, on the first Saturday of the month, Leonard planned a half-holiday, which should not only compensate the disappointed children, but also give his busy wife a little outing. He had learned that the tide was right for crossing the shallows of the Moodna Creek, and they would all go fishing. Johnnie's friends and Dr. and Mrs. Marvin were invited, and great were the preparations. Reed and all kinds of poles were taken down from their hooks, or cut in a neighboring thicket, the stock of rusty hooks depleted at the country store, and stray corks were fastened on the brown linen lines for floats. Burt disdained to take his scientific tackle, and indeed there was little use for it in Moodna Creek, but he joined readily in the frolic. He would be willing to fish for even minnows indefinitely if at the same time there was a chance to angle for Amy. Some preferred to walk to the river, and with the aid of the family rockaway the entire party were at the boat-house before the sun had passed much beyond the zenith. Burt, from his intimate knowledge of the channel, acted as pilot, and was jubilant over the fact that Amy consented to take an oar with him and receive a lesson in rowing. Mrs. Marvin held the tiller-ropes, and the doctor was to use a pair of oars when requested to do so. Webb and Leonard took charge of the larger boat, of which Johnnie, as hostess, was captain, and a jolly group of little boys and girls made the echoes ring, while Ned, with his thumb in his mouth, clung close to his mother, and regarded the nautical expedition rather dubiously. They swept across the flats to the deeper water near Plum Point, and so up the Moodna, whose shores were becoming green with the rank growth of the bordering marsh, and passing under an old covered bridge they soon were skirting an island from which rose a noble grove of trees, whose swollen buds were only waiting for a warmer caress of the sun to unfold. Returning, they beached their boats below

THE UPLAND MEADOW.

the bridge, under whose shadow the fish were fond of lying. The little people were disembarked, and placed at safe distances; for, if near, they would surely hook each other, if never a fin. Silence was enjoined, and there was a breathless hush for the space of two minutes; then began whispers more resonant than those of the stage, followed by acclamations as Johnnie pulled up a wriggling eel, of which she was in mortal terror. They all had good sport, however, for the smaller fry of the finny tribes that haunted the vicinity of the old bridge suffered from the well-known tendency of extreme youth to take everything into its mouth. The day was good for fishing, for thin clouds obscured the light and darkened the water. Indeed, at that season an immature sunfish will take a hook if there is but a remnant of a worm upon it. Amy was the heroine of the party, for Burt had furnished her with a long light pole, and taught her to throw her line well away from the others. As a result she soon took, amidst excited plaudits, several fine yellow perch. At last Leonard shouted:

"You shall not have all the honors, Amy. I have a hook in my pocket that will catch bigger fish than you have seen to-day. Come, the tide is going out, and we must go out of the creek with it, unless we wish to spend the night on a sand-bar. I shall now try my luck at shad-fishing over by Pollopol's Island."

The prospect of crossing the river and following the drift-nets down into the Highlands was a glad surprise to all, and they were soon out into Newburgh Bay, whose broad, lake-like surface was unruffled by a breath. The sun, declining toward the west, scattered rose hues among the clouds. Sloops and schooners had lost steerage-way, and their sails flapped idly against their masts. The grind of oars between the thole-pins came distinct-ly across the water from far distant boats, while songs and calls of birds, faint and etherealized, reached them from the shores. Rowing toward a man rapidly paying out a net from the stern of his boat, they were soon hailed by Mr. Marks, who with genial good-nature invited them to see the sport. He had begun throwing his net over in the middle of the river, his oarsman rowing eastward with a slight inclination toward the south, for the reason that the tide is swifter on the western side. The aim is to keep the net as straight as possible and at right angles with the tide. The two boats were soon following Mr. Marks on either side, the smooth water and absence of wind enabling them to keep near and converse without effort. Away in their wake bobbed the cork floats in an irregular line, and from these floats, about twenty feet below the surface, was suspended the net, which extended down thirty or forty feet further, being kept in a vertical position by iron rings strung along its lower edge at regular intervals; thus the lowest side of the net was from fifty to sixty feet from the surface. In shallow water narrower nets are rigged to float vertically much nearer the surface. Mr. Marks explained that his net was about half a mile long, adding:

"It's fun fishing on a day like this, but it's rather tough in a gale of wind, with your eyes half blinded by rain, and the waves breaking into your boat. Yes, we catch just as many then; perhaps more, for there are fewer men out; and I suppose the weather is always about the same, except as to temperature, down where the shad are. The fish don't mind wet weather; neither must we if we make a business of catching them."

"Do you always throw out your net from the west shore toward the east?" Webb asked.

"No; we usually pay out against the

wind. With the wind, the boat is apt to go too fast. The great point is to keep the net straight, and not all tangled and wobbled up. Passing boats bother us, too. Sometimes a float will catch on a paddle-wheel, and like enough half of the net will be torn away. A pilot with any human feeling will usually steer one side and give a fellow a chance, and we can often bribe the skipper of sailing craft by holding up shad and throwing it aboard as he tacks around us. As a rule, however, boats of all kinds pass over a net without doing any harm. Occasionally a net breaks from the floats and drags on the bottom. This is covered with cinders thrown out by steamers, and they play the mischief."

"Do the fish swim against the tide ?"

"Usually; but they come in on both sides."

" Mr. Marks, how can you catch fish in a net that is straight up and down ?" Amy asked.

"You'll soon see; but I'll explain. The meshes of the net will stretch five inches. A shad swims into one of these, and then, like many others that go into things, finds he can't back out, for his gills catch on the sides of the mesh, and there he hangs. Occasionally a shad will just tangle himself up, and so be caught, and sometimes we take a large striped bass in this way."

In answer to a question of Burt's he continued: "I just let my net float with the tide, as you see, giving it a pull from one end or the other now and then to keep it as straight and as near at right angles with the river as possible. When the tide stops running out, and turns a little, we begin at one end of the net and pull it up, taking out the fish, at the same time laying it carefully in folds on the gunnel, so as to prevent all tangles. If the net comes up clear and free, I may throw it in again, and float back with the tide. So far from being able to depend on this, we often have to go ashore where there is a smooth beach, before our drift is over, and untangle our net. There, now, I'm through paying out. Haven't you noticed the floats bobbing here and there ?"

" We've been too busy listening and watching you," said Leonard.

" Well, now, watch the floats. If you see one bob under and wobble, a shad has struck the net near it, and I can go and take him out. In smooth water it's like fishing with one of your little cork bob-

bers there on your lines. I'll give the shad to the first one that sees a float bob under."

Alf nearly sprang out of the boat as he pointed and shouted, "There! there!"

Laughing good-naturedly, Mr. Marks lifted the net beneath the float, and sure enough there was a great roe-shad hanging by his gills, and Alf gloated over his supper already secured.

The fish were running well, and there were excited calls and frantic pointings, in which at first even the older members of the party joined, and every few moments a writhing shad flashed in the slanting rays as it was tossed into the boat. Up and down the long irregular line of floats the boats passed and repassed until excitement verged toward satiety, and the sun, near the horizon, with a cloud canopy of crimson and gold, warned the merry fishers by proxy that their boats should be turned homeward. Leonard pulled out what he termed his silver hook, and supplied not only the Clifford family, but all of Johnnie's guests, with fish so fresh that they had as yet scarcely realized that they were out of water.

"Now, Amy," said Burt, "keep stroke with me," adding, in a whisper, "no fear but that we can pull well together."

Her response was: "One always associates a song with rowing. Come, strike up, and let us keep the boats abreast, that all may join."

He, well content, started a familiar boating song, to which the splash of their oars made musical accompaniment. A passing steamer saluted them, and a moment later the boats bowed gracefully over the swells. The glassy river flashed back the crimson of the clouds, the eastern slopes of the mountains donned their royal purple, the intervening shadows of valleys making the folds of their robes. As they approached the shore the resonant song of the robins blended with the human voice. Burt, however, heard only Amy's girlish soprano, and saw but the pearl of her teeth through her parted lips, the rose in her cheeks, and the snow of her neck.

Final words were spoken, and all were soon at home. Maggie took the household helm with a fresh and vigorous grasp. What a supper she improvised! The maids never dawdled when she directed, and by the time the hungry fishermen were ready, the shad that two hours before had been swimming deep in the Hudson lay browned to a turn on the ample platter. "It is this quick transition that gives to game fish their most exquisite flavor," Burt remarked.

"Are shad put down among the game fish?" his father asked.

"Yes; they were included not very long ago, and most justly, too, as I can testify to-night. I never tasted anything more delicious, except trout. If a shad were not so bony, it would be almost perfection when eaten under the right conditions. Not many on the Hudson are aware of the fact, perhaps, but angling for them is fine sport in some rivers. They will take a fly in the Connecticut and Housatonic; but angle-worms and other bait are employed in the Delaware and Southern rivers. The best time to catch them is early in the morning, and from six to eight in the evening. At dusk one may cast for them in still water as for trout. The Hudson is too big, I suppose, and the water too deep, although I see no reason why the young fry should not be caught in our river as well as in the Delaware. I have read of their biting voraciously in September at a short distance above Philadelphia."

"Do you mean to say that our rivers are full of shad in August and September?" Leonard asked.

"Yes; that is, of young shad on the way to the sea. The females that are running up now will spawn in the upper and shallow waters of the river, and return to the ocean by the end of June, and in the autumn the small fry will also go to the sea, the females to remain there two years. The males will come back next spring, and these young males are called 'chicken shad' on the Connecticut. Multitudes of these half-grown fish are taken in seines and sold as herrings or 'alewives.' The true herring does not run up into fresh-water. Young shad are said to have teeth, and they live largely on insects, while the full-grown fish have no teeth, and feed chiefly on animalcules that form the greater part of the slimy growths that cover nearly everything that is long under water."

"Well, I never had so much shad before in my life," said his father, laughing and pushing back his chair; "and, Burt, I have enjoyed those you have served up in the water almost as much as those dished under Maggie's superintendence."

"I should suppose that the present mode of fishing with drift-nets was cheaper and more profitable than the old method of suspending the nets between poles," Leonard remarked.

"It is indeed," Burt continued, vivaciously, for he observed that Amy was

SHAD-FISHING ON THE HUDSON.

listening with interest. "Poles, too, form a serious obstruction. Once, years ago, I was standing near the guards of a steamboat, when I heard the most awful grating, rasping sound, and a moment later a shad-pole gyrated past me with force enough to brain an elephant had it struck him. It was good fun, though, in old times, to see the shad-fishers raise the nets, for they often came up heavy with fish.

Strange to say, a loon was once pulled up with the shad. Driven by fear, it must have dived so vigorously as to entangle itself, for there it hung with its head and one leg fast. I suppose that the last moment of consciousness that the poor bird had was one of strong surprise."

May came in reality the follow-

THE BEE HARVEST.

ing morning. Perhaps she thought that the leisure of Sunday would secure her a more appreciative welcome. The wind no longer blew from the chill and still snowy north, but from lands that had long since responded to the sun's genial power. Therefore the breeze that came and went fitfully was like a warm, fragrant breath, and truly it seemed to breathe life and beauty into all things. During the morning hours the cluster buds of the cherry burst their varnished-looking sheaths, revealing one-third of the little green stems on which the blossoms would soon appear. The currant bushes were hanging out their lengthening racemes, and the hum of many bees proved that honey may be gathered even from gooseberry bushes, thus suggesting a genial philosophy. The sugar-maples were beginning to unfold their leaves, and to dangle their emerald-gold flowers from long drooping pedicels. There are few objects of more exquisite and delicate beauty than this inflorescence lighted up by the low afternoon sun. The meadows and oat fields were passing into a vivid green, and the hardy rye had pushed on so resolutely in all weather that it was beginning to grow billowy under the wind. All through the week the hues of life and beauty became more and more apparent upon the face of nature, and by the following Saturday May had provided everything in perfection for Johnnie's coronation ceremonies.

For weeks past there had been distinguished arrivals from the South almost daily. Some of these songsters, like the fox-sparrow, sojourned a few weeks, favoring all who listened with their sweet and simple melodies; but the chief musician of the American forests, the hermit-thrush, passed silently, and would not deign to utter a note of his unrivalled minstrelsy until he had reached his remote haunts at the North. Dr. Marvin evidently had a little grudge against this shy, distant bird, and often complained: "Why can't he give us a song or two as he lingers here in his journey? I often see him flitting about in the mountains, and have watched him by the hour with the curiosity that one would look at a great soprano or tenor, hoping that he might indulge me with a brief song as a sample of what he could do; but he was always royally indifferent and reserved. I am going to the Adirondacks on purpose to hear him some

6*

day. There's the winter wren, too—saucy, inquisitive little imp!—he was here all winter, and has left us without vouchsafing a note. But then great singers are a law unto themselves the world over."

The week which preceded the May party was a memorable one to Amy, for during its sunny days she saw an American spring in its perfection. Each morning brought rich surprises to her, Johnnie, and Alf, and to Webb an increasing wonder that he had never before truly seen the world in which he lived. The pent-up forces of nature, long restrained, seemed finding new expression every hour. Tulips opened their gaudy chalices to catch the morning dew. Massive spikes of hyacinths distilled a rich perfume that was none too sweet in the open air. Whenever Amy stepped from the door it seemed that some new flower had opened and some new development of greenery and beauty had been revealed. But the crowning glory in the near landscape were the fruit trees. The cherry boughs grew whiter every day, and were closely followed by the plum and pear and the pink-hued peach blossoms. Even Squire Bartley's unattractive place was transformed for a time into fairy-land; but he, poor man, saw not the blossoms, and the birds and boys stole his fruit. Amy wondered at the wealth of flowers that made many of the trees as white as they had been on the snowiest day of winter, and Johnnie revelled in them, often climbing up into some low-branched tree that she might bury herself in their beauty, and inhale their fragrance in long breaths of delight. The bees that filled the air about her with their busy hum never molested her, believing, no doubt, that she had as good a right to enjoy the sweets in her way as themselves. After all, it was Mrs. Clifford, perhaps, who obtained the profoundest enjoyment from the season. Seated by her window or on a sunny corner of the piazza, she would watch the unfolding buds as if she were listening to some sweet old story that had grown dearer with every repetition. Indeed, this was true, for with the blossoms of every year were interwoven the memories of a long life, and their associations had scarcely ever been more to her heart than the new ones now forming. She often saw with her children and grandchildren the form of a tall girl passing to and fro, and to her loving eyes Amy seemed to be the fairest and most perfect flower of this gala period. She, and indeed they all, had observed Burt's strongly manifested preference, but with innate refinement and good sense there had been a tacit agreement to appear blind. The orphan girl should not be annoyed by even the most delicate raillery; but the old lady and her husband could not but feel the deepest satisfaction that Burt—the one child that gave them solicitude—was making so wise a choice. They liked Amy all the better because she was so little disposed to sentiment, and proved that she was not to be won easily.

But they all failed to understand her, and gave her credit for a maturity that she did not possess. In her happy, healthful country life the girlish form that had seemed so fragile when she first came to them was taking on the rounded lines of womanhood. Why should she not be wooed like other girls at her age? Burt was farther astray than any one, and was even inclined to complain mentally that her nature was cold and unresponsive. And yet her very reserve and elusiveness increased his passion, which daily acquired a stronger mastery. Webb alone half guessed the truth in regard to her. As time passed, and he saw the increasing evidences of Burt's feeling, he was careful that his manner should be strictly fraternal toward Amy, for his impetuous brother was not always disposed to be reasonable in his most normal condition, and now was afflicted with a malady that had often brought to shame the wisdom of the wisest. He saw how easily Burt's jealousy could be aroused, and therefore denied himself many an hour of the young girl's society, although it caused him a strange little heart-ache to do so. But he was very observant, for Amy was becoming a deeply interesting study. He saw and appreciated her delicate fence with Burt, in which tact, kindness, and a little girlish brusqueness were almost equally blended. Was it the natural coyness of a high-spirited girl who could be won only by long and patient effort, or was it an instinctive self-defense from a suit that she could not repulse decisively without giving pain to those she loved? Why was she so averse? Their home life, even at that busy season, gave him opportunities to see her often, and glimmerings of the truth began to dawn upon him. He saw that she enjoyed the society of Alf and Johnnie almost

as much as that of the older members of the family, that her delight at every new manifestation of spring was as unforced as that of the children, while at the same time it was an intelligent and questioning interest. The beauty of the world without impressed her deeply, as it did Johnnie, but to the latter it was a matter of course, while with Amy it was becoming an inviting mystery. The little girl would bring some new flower from the woods or garden, the first of the season, in contented triumph, but to Amy the flower had a stronger interest. It represented something unknown, a phase of life which it was the impulse of her developing mind to explore. Her botany was not altogether satisfactory, for analysis and classification do not reveal to us a flower or plant any more than the mention of a name and family connection makes known individual character. She felt this, and her love for natural objects was too real to be satisfied with a few scientific facts about them. If a plant, tree, or bird interested her, she would look at it with a loving, lingering glance until she felt that she was learning to know it somewhat as she would recognize a friend. The rapid changes which each day brought were like new chapters in a story or new verses in a poem. She watched the transition of buds into blossoms with their changes of form and color with admiring wonder. She shared in Alf's excitement over the arrival of every new bird from the South, and having a good ear for music, found absorbing pleasure in learning and estimating the quality and characteristics of their various songs. With her sense of humor their little oddities amused her. A pair of cat-birds that had begun their nest near the house received from her more ridicule than admiration. "They seem to be regular society birds and gossips," she said, "and I can never step out-of-doors but I feel that they are watching me, and trying to attract my attention. They have a pretty song, but they seem to have learned it by heart, and as soon as they are through they make that horrid noise, as if in their own natural tone they were saying something disagreeable about you."

But on the morning of Johnnie's coronation she was wakened by songs as entrancing as they were unfamiliar. Running to her window, she saw darting through the trees birds of such a brilliant flame-color that they seemed direct from the tropics, and their notes were almost as varied as their colors. She speedily ceased to heed them, however, for from the edge of the nearest grove came a melody so ethereal and sustained that it thrilled her with the delight that one experiences when some great singer lifts up her voice with a power and sweetness that we feel to be divine. At the same moment she saw Alf running toward the house. Seeing her at the window, he shouted: "Amy, the orioles and wood-thrushes—the finest birds of the year—have come. Hurry up, and go with me to the grove yonder."

Soon after, Webb, returning from a distant field to breakfast, met her near the grove. She was almost as breathless and excited as the boy, and passed him with a bright hurried smile, while she pressed on after her guide with noiseless steps lest the shy songster should be frightened. He looked after her and listened, feeling that eye and ear could ask for no fuller enchantment. At last she came back to him with the fresh loveliness of the morning in her face, and exclaimed: "I have seen an ideal bird, and he wears his plumage like a quiet-toned elegant costume that simply suggests a perfect form. He was superbly indifferent, and scarcely looked at us until we came too near, and then, with a reserved dignity, flew away. He is the true poet of the woods, and would sing just as sweetly were there never a listener."

"I knew he would not disappoint you. Yes, he is a poet, and your true aristocrat, who commands admiration without seeking it," Webb replied.

"I am sure he justifies all your praises, past and present. Oh, isn't the morning lovely—so fresh, dewy, and fragrant, and the world looks so young and glad!"

"You also look young and glad this morning, Amy."

"How can one help it? This May beauty makes me feel as young as Alf," she replied, placing her hand on the boy's shoulder.

Her face was flushed with exercise, her step buoyant; her eyes were roaming over the landscape tinted with fruit blossoms and the expanding foliage. Webb saw in what deep accord her spirit was with the season, and he thought: "She *is* young—in the very May of her life. She is scarcely more ready for the words that Burt

would speak than little Johnnie. I wish he would wait till the girl becomes a woman;" and then for some reason he sighed deeply. Amy gave him an arch look, and said:

"That came from the depths, Webb. What secret sorrow can you have on a day like this?"

He laughed, but made no reply.

"Ah, listen!" she cried. "What bird is that? Oh, isn't it beautiful!—almost equal to the thrush's song. He seems to sing as if his notes were written for him in couplets." She spoke at intervals, looking toward the grove they had just left; and when the bird paused, Webb replied:

"That is the wood-thrush's own cousin, and a distinguished member of the thrush family, the brown-thrasher. Well, Johnnie," he added, to the little girl who had come to meet them, "you are honored to-day. Three of our most noted minstrels have arrived just in time to furnish music for the May-queen."

But Johnnie was not surprised, only pleased, as Webb and others congratulated her. She would be queen that day with scarcely more self-consciousness than one of the flowers that decked her. It was the occasion, the carnival of spring, that occupied her thoughts, and, since the fairest blossoms of the season were to be gathered, why should not the finest birds be present also?

For the children, May-day was a revel that left nothing to be desired. They had decided that it should be a congress of flowers from the earliest that had bloomed to those now opening in their sunniest haunts. Alf, with one or two other adventurous boys, had climbed the northern face of old Storm King, and brought away the last hepaticas and fragrant clusters of arbutus and diceutras, for "pattykers, arbuties, and dutcher's butchers," as Ned called them, were favorites that could not be spared. On a sunny slope dogwood well advanced was found. There were banks white with the rue-anemone, and they were marked, that some of the little tuber-like roots might be taken up in the fall for forcing in the house. Myriads of violets gave a purple tinge to parts of a low meadow near, and chubby hands were stained with the last of the star-like blood-root blossoms, many of which dropped their white petals on their way to Johnnie's throne. Some brought handfuls of columbine from rocky nooks, and others the

purple trillium, that is near of kin to Burroughs's white "wake-robin." There were
so many jacks-in-the-pulpit that one might
fear a controversy, but the innumerable
dandelions and dog-tooth-violets which
carpeted the ground around the throne
diffused so mellow a light that all the
flowers felt that they looked well and
were amiable. But it would require pages
even to mention all the flowers that were
brought from gardens, orchards, meadows
and groves, and rugged mountain slopes.
Each delegation of blossoms and young
tinted foliage was received by Amy as
mistress of ceremonies, and arranged in
harmonious positions; while Johnnie, quite
forgetful of her royalty, was as ready to
help at anything as the humblest maid-of-
honor. All the flowers were treated tenderly except the poor purple violets, and
these were slaughtered by hundreds, for
the projecting spur under the curved stem
at the base of the flower enabled the boys
to hook them together and "fight roosters," as they termed it. Now and then
some tough-stemmed violet would "hook
off" a dozen blue heads before losing its
own, and it became the temporary hero.
At last the little queen asserted her power
by saying, with a sudden flash in her dark
eyes, that she "wouldn't have any more
fighting roosters; she didn't think it was
nice."

By one o'clock the queen had been
crowned, the lunch had met the capacity
of even the boys, and the children, circling round the throne, were singing:
"Oats, pease, beans, and barley grows,"
and kindred rhymes, their voices rising
and falling with the breeze, the birds war-
bling an accompaniment. Webb and Leonard, at work in a field not far away, often
paused to listen, the former never failing
to catch Amy's clear notes as she sat on a
rock, the gentle power behind the throne
that had maintained peace and good-will
among all the little fractious subjects.

The day had grown almost sultry, and
early in the afternoon there was a distant
jar of thunder. Burt started up from a
bed of dry leaves, from which he had been
watching Amy, and saw that there was
an ominous cloud in the west. She acceded at once to the prudence of returning, for she was growing weary and depressed. Burt, though he tried to seem
quietly and unobtrusively devoted, had
never permitted her to become unconscious of his presence and feeling. There-

fore her experience had been a divided
one. She could not abandon herself to
her hearty sympathy with the children
and their pleasure, for he, by manner at
least, ever insisted that she was a young
lady, and the object of his especial devotion. Her nature was so fine that it
was wounded and annoyed by an unwelcome admiration. She did not wish to
think about it, but was not permitted to
forget it. She had been genial, merry,
yet guarded toward him all day, and now
had begun to long for the rest and refuge
of her own room. He felt that he had
not made progress, and was also depressed, and he showed this so plainly on their
way home that she was still more perplexed and troubled. "If he would only be
sensible, and treat me as Webb does!" she
exclaimed, as she threw herself on a lounge
in her room, exhausted rather than exhilarated by the experience of the day.

During the hour she slept an ideal shower crossed the sky. In the lower strata
of air there was scarcely any wind, and
the rain came down vertically, copiously,
and without beating violence. The sun-
warmed earth took in every drop like a
great sponge. Beyond the first muttered
warning to the little May party in the
grove there was no thunder. The patter
of the rain was a gentle lullaby to Amy,
and at last she was wakened by a ray of
sunlight playing upon her face, yet she
still heard the soft fall of rain. With the
elasticity of youth she sprang up, feeling
that the other cloud that had shadowed
her thoughts might soon pass also. As
she went singing down the stairway Webb
called from the front door.

"Amy, look here. I was hoping you
would come. See that rainbow." The
cloud still hung heavily over the eastern
mountains, while against it was a magnificent arch, and so distinctly defined
that its feet appeared to rest on each bank
of the river. They watched it in silence
until it faded away, and the whole scene,
crowned with flowers and opening foliage
that was tinted like varied-hued flowers,
was gemmed with crystals by the now
unclouded sun, for the soft rain had clung
to everything, from the loftiest tree-top
to the tiniest spire of grass. Flame-like
orioles were flashing through the perfumed air. Robins with their heads lifted heavenward were singing as rapturously as if they were saints rather than
rollicking gormandizers. Every bird that

had a voice was lifting it up in thanks-giving, but clear, sweet, and distinct above them all came the notes of the wood-thrush with his Beethoven-like melody.

"Have you no words for a scene like this, Webb?" she asked at last.

"It is beyond all words, Amy. It is one of nature's miracles. My wonder is even greater than my admiration, for the greater part of this infinite variety of beauty is created out of so few materials and so simple yet mysterious a method that I can scarcely believe it, although I see it and know it. Men have always agreed to worship the genius which could achieve the most with the least. And yet the basis of nearly all we see is a mi-croscopic cell endowed with essential pow-ers. That large apple-tree yonder, whose buds are becoming so pink, started from one of these minute cells, and all the growth, beauty, and fruitfulness since at-tained were the result of the power of this one cell to add to itself myriads of like cells, which form the whole structure. It is cell adding cells that is transforming the world around us." He spoke earnestly, and almost as if he were thinking aloud, and he looked like one in the presence of a mystery that awed him. The hue of Amy's eyes darkened and deepened, and her face flushed in her quickened interest. Her own mind had been turning to kin-dred thoughts and questionings. She had too much mind, and she had passed be-yond the period when she could be satis-fied with the mere surface of things, and Webb's direct approach to the very foun-dation principles of what she saw sent a thrill through all her nerves as a heroic deed would have done.

"Can you not show me one of these cells with your microscope?" she asked, eagerly.

"Yes, easily, and some of its contents through the cell's transparent walls, as, for instance, the minute grains of *chloro-phyll*, that is, the green of leaves. All the hues of foliage and flowers are caused by what the cells contain, and these, to a certain extent, can be seen and analyzed. But there is one thing within the cell which I can not show you, and which has never been seen, and yet it accounts for everything, and is the architect of all —life. When we reach the cell we are at the threshold of this mysterious pre-sence. We know that it is within. We can see its work, for its workshop is under

our eye, and in this minute shop it is building all the vegetation of the world, but the artisan itself ever remains invis-ible."

"Ah, Webb, do not say artisan, but rather artist. Does not the beauty all around us prove it? Surely there is but one explanation, the one papa taught me: it is the power of God. He is in the lit-tle as well as in the great. Do you not believe so, Webb?"

"Well, Amy," he replied, smilingly, "the faith taught you by your father is, to my mind, more rational than any of the explanations that I have read, and I have studied several. But then my know-ledge is small indeed, compared with that of multitudes of others. I am sure, how-ever, that the life of God is in some way the source of all the life we see. But perplexing questions arise on every side. Much of life is so repulsive and noxious— but there! what a fog-bank I am leading you into this crystal May evening! Most young girls would vote me an insufferable bore should I talk to them in this style."

"So much the worse for the young girls, then. I should think they would feel that no compliment could exceed that of being talked to as if they had brains. But I do not wish to put on learned airs. You know how ignorant I am of even the be-ginnings of all this knowledge. All that I can say is that I am not content to be ignorant. The curiosity of Mother Eve is growing stronger every day; and is it strange that it should turn toward the ob-jects that are so beautiful and yet so mys-terious that meet my eyes on every side?"

"No," said he, musingly; "the strange thing is that people have so little curiosity in regard to their surroundings. Why, multitudes of intelligent persons are al-most as indifferent as the cattle that browse around among the trees and flow-ers. But I am a sorry one to preach. I once used to investigate things, but did not see them. I have thought about it very much this spring. It is said that great painters and sculptors study anato-my as well as outward form. Perhaps here is a good hint for those who are trying to appreciate nature. I am not so shallow as to imagine that I can ever un-derstand nature any more than I can you with your direct honest gaze. To the thoughtful, mystery is ever close at hand, but it seems no little thing to trace back what one sees as far as one can, and you have made me feel that it is a great thing to see the Divine artist's finished work."

They were now joined by others, and the perfect beauty of the evening as it slowly faded into night attracted much attention from all the family. The new moon hung in the after-glow of the western sky, and, as the dusk deepened, the weird notes of the whip-poor-will were heard for the first time from the mountain-sides.

At the supper table Leonard beamed on every one. "A rain like this, after a week of sunshine has warmed the earth," he exclaimed, "is worth millions to the country. We can plant our corn next week."

"Yes," added his father; "the old Indian sign, the unfolding of the oak leaves, indicates that it is now safe to plant. Next week will be a busy one. After long years of observation I am satisfied that the true secret of success in farming is the doing of everything at just the right time. Crops put in too early or too late often partially fail, but if the right conditions are complied with from the beginning, they start with a vigor which is not lost until maturity."

Burt indulged in a gayety that was phenomenal even for him, but after supper he disappeared. Amy retired to her room early, but she sat a long time at her window and looked out into the warm, fragrant night. She had forgotten poor Burt, who was thinking of her, as in his unrest he rode mile after mile, holding his spirited horse down to a walk. She had almost forgotten Webb, but she thought deeply of his words, of the life that was working all around her so silently and yet so powerfully. Unseen, it had created the beauty she had enjoyed that day. From the very contrast of ideas it made her think of death, of her father, who once had been so strong and full of life. The mystery of one seemed as great as that of the other, and a loneliness such as she had not felt before for months depressed her. "I wish I could talk to Webb again," she thought. "He says he does not understand me. Little wonder: I do not understand myself. It would seem that when one began to think, nothing that appeared simple before is understood. But his words are strong and assured; he leads one to the boundaries of the known, and then says, quietly, we can go no farther, but he makes you feel that

what is beyond is all right. Oh, I wish Burt was like him!"

But little chance had Amy to talk with Webb for the next few days. He had seen the cloud on Burt's brow, and had observed that he was suspicious, unhappy, and irritable, that reason and good sense were not in the ascendant; and he understood his brother sufficiently well to believe that his attack must run its natural course, as like fevers had before. From what he had seen he also thought that Amy could deal with Burt better than any one else, for although highstrung, he was also manly and generous when once he got his bearings. In his present mood he would bitterly resent interference from any one, but would be bound to obey Amy and to respect her wishes. Therefore he took especial pains to be most kindly, but also to appear busy and preoccupied.

It must not be thought that Burt was offensive or even openly obtrusive in his attentions. He was far too well bred for that. There was nothing for which even his mother could reprove him, or of which Amy herself could complain. It was the suit itself from which she shrank, or rather would put off indefinitely. But Burt was not disposed to put anything that he craved into the distance. Spring-tide impulses were in his veins, and his heart was so overcharged that it must find expression. His opportunity came unexpectedly. A long exquisite day had merged into a moonlight evening. The apple blossoms were in all of their white and pink glory, and filled the summer-like air with a fragrance as delicate as that of the arbutus. The petals of the cherry were flurrying down like snow in every passing breeze, glimmering momentarily in the pale radiance. The night was growing so beautiful that Amy was tempted to stroll over the grounds, and soon she yielded to a fancy to see the effect of moonlight through an apple-tree that towered like a mound of snow at some little distance from the house. She would not have been a human girl had the witchery of the May evening been without its influence. If Burt could have understood her, this was his opportunity. If he had come with step and tone that accorded with the quiet evening, and simply said, "Amy, you know, you have seen, that I love you; what hope can you give me?" she in her present mood would have answered him as gently and frankly as a child. She might have laughingly pointed him to the tree, and said: "See, it is in blossom now. It will be a long time before you pick the apples. You must wait. If you will be sensible, and treat me as you would Johnnie, were she older, I will ride and walk with you, and be as nice to you as I can."

But this Burt could not do and still remain Burt. He was like an overcharged cloud, and when he spoke at last his words seemed to the sensitive girl to have the vividness and abruptness of the lightning. It was her custom to make a special toilet for the evening, and when she came down to supper with a rose in her hair, and dressed in some light clinging fabric, she proved so attractive to the young fellow that he felt that the limit of his restraint was reached. He would appeal to her so earnestly, so passionately, as to kindle her cold nature. In his lack of appreciation of Amy he had come to deem this his true course, and she unconsciously enabled him to carry out the rash plan. He had seen her stroll away, and had followed her until she should be so far from the house that she must listen. As she emerged from under the apple-tree, through which as a white cloud she had been looking at the moon, he appeared so suddenly as to startle her, and without any gentle re-assurance he seized her hand, and poured out his feelings in a way that at first wounded and frightened her.

"Burt," she cried, "why do you speak to me so? Can't you see that I do not feel as you do? I've given you no reason to say such words to me."

"Have you no heart, Amy? Are you as cold and elusive as this moonlight? I have waited patiently, and now I must and will speak. Every man has a right to speak and a right to an answer."

"Well, then," she replied, her spirit rising, "if you will insist on my being a woman instead of a young girl just coming from the shadow of a great sorrow, I also have my rights. I've tried to show you gently and with all the tact I possessed that I did not want to think about such things. I'm just at the beginning of my girlhood and I want to be a young girl as long as I can, and not an engaged young woman. No matter who spoke the words you have said, they would only pain me. Why couldn't you see this from my manner, and save both yourself and me

from this scene? I'll gladly be your loving sister, but you must not speak to me in this way again."

"You refuse me, then?" he said, throwing back his head haughtily.

"Refuse you? No. I simply tell you that I won't listen to such words from any one. Why can't you be sensible, and understand me? I no more wish to talk about such things than do Alf and Johnnie."

"I do understand you," he exclaimed, passionately, "and better perhaps than you understand yourself. You are not a child. You are a woman, but you seem to lack a woman's heart, as far as I am concerned;" and with a gesture that was very tragic and despairing he strode away.

She was deeply troubled, and incensed also, and she returned to the house with drooping head and fast-falling tears.

"Why, Amy, what is the matter?" Looking up, she saw Webb coming down the piazza steps. Yielding to her impulse she sprang forward and took his arm, as she said:

"Webb, you have always acted toward me like a brother. Tell me true. Am I cold? Am I heartless? Is it unnatural in me that I do not wish to hear such words as Burt would speak to-night? All I ask is that he will let me stay a happy young girl till I am ready for something else. This is no way for a flower to bloom"— she snatched the rose from her hair and pushed open the red petals—"and yet Burt expects me to respond at once to feelings that I do not even understand. If it's best in the future— But surely I've a right to my freedom for a long time yet. Tell me, do you think I'm unnatural?"

"No, Amy," he answered, gently. "It is because you are so perfectly natural, so true to your girlhood, that you feel as you do. In that little parable of the rose you explain yourself fully. You have no cause for self-reproach, nor has Burt for complaint. Will you do what I ask?"

"Yes, Webb. You say you do not understand me, and yet always prove that you do. If Burt would only treat me as you do, I should be perfectly happy."

"Well, Burt's good-hearted, but sometimes he mislays his judgment," said Webb, laughing. "Come, cheer up. There is no occasion for any high tragedy on his part nor for grieving on yours. You go and tell mother all about it, and just how you feel. She is the right one to manage this affair, and her influence over Burt is almost unbounded. Do this, and, take my word for it, all will soon be serene."

And so it proved. Amy felt that night what it was to have a mother's boundless love and sympathy, and she went to her rest comforted, soothed, and more assured as to the future than she had been for a long time. "How quiet and sensible Webb was about it all!" was her last smiling thought before she slept. His thought, as he strolled away in the moonlight after she left him, was: "It is just as I half believed. She has the mind of a woman, but the heart of a child. How apt was her use of that rose! It told all."

Burt did not stroll; he strode mile after mile, and the uncomfortable feeling that he had been very unwise, to say the least, and perhaps very unjust, was growing upon him. When at last he returned, his mother called to him through her open door. Sooner or later Mrs. Clifford always obtained the confidence of her children, and they ever found that it was sacred. All that can be said, therefore, was that he came from her presence penitent, ashamed, and hopeful. His mood may best be explained, perhaps, by a note written before he retired. "My dear sister Amy," it ran, "I wish to ask your pardon. I have been unjust and ungenerous. I was so blinded and engrossed by my own feelings that I did not understand you. I have proved myself unworthy of even a sister's love, but I will try to make amends. Do not judge me harshly because I was so headlong. There is no use of disguising the truth. What I have said so unwisely and prematurely, I can not unsay, and I shall always be true to my words. But I will wait patiently as long as you please, and if you find in future years that you can not feel as I do, I will not complain or blame you, however sad the truth may be to me. In the mean time let there be no constraint between us. Let me become once more your trusted brother Burt." This note he pushed under her door, and then slept too soundly for the blighted youth he deemed himself a few hours before.

He felt a little embarrassed at the prospect of meeting her the next morning, but she broke the ice at once by coming to him on the piazza and extending her hand in smiling frankness, as she said: "You are neither unjust nor ungenerous, Burt, or you would not have written me such a

note. I take you at your word. As you said the first evening I came, we shall have jolly times together."

The young fellow was immensely relieved and grateful, and showed it. Soon afterward he went about the affairs of the day happier than he had been for a long time. Indeed, it soon became evident that his explosion on the previous evening had cleared the air generally. Amy felt that the one threatening cloud had sunk below the horizon. As the days passed, and Burt proved that he could keep his promise, her thoughts grew as serene as those of Johnnie. Her household duties were not very many, and yet she did certain things regularly. The old people found that she rarely forgot them and she had the grace to see when she could help and cheer. Attentions that must be constantly asked for have little charm. A day rarely passed that she did not give one or more of its best hours to her music and drawing, for while she never expected to excel in these arts, she had already learned that they would enable her to give much pleasure to others. Her pencil also was of great assistance in her study of out-door life, for the fixed attention which it required to draw a plant, tree, or bit of scenery revealed its characteristics. She had been even more interested in the unfolding of the leaf buds than in the flowering of the trees, and the gradual advance of the foliage, like a tinted cloud up the mountain slopes, was something she never tired of watching. When speaking of this one day to Webb, he replied:

"I have often wondered that more is not said and written about our spring foliage before it passes into its general hue of green. To me it has a more delicate beauty and charm than anything seen in October. Different trees have their distinct coloring now as then, but it is evanescent, and the shades usually are less clearly marked. This very fact, however, teaches the eye to have a nicety of distinction that is pleasing."

The busy days passed quickly on. The blossoms faded from the trees, and the immature fruit was soon apparent, the strawberry rows, that had been like lines of snow, were now full of little promising cones. The grass grew so lusty and strong that the dandelions were almost hidden. At last the swelling buds on the rose-bushes proclaimed the advent of June.

GRACE SHERWOOD.
THE ONE VIRGINIA WITCH.

THE singular incident here related is almost unknown except to students. A few lines in the histories of the State are all that the annalists bestow upon it; and yet it seems that the historians ought not to have regarded it as beneath the dignity of history. What we wish to ascertain is the character of a people—to have the exact measure of their feelings and opinions; and this incident throws a curious and unexpected light on the Virginians of the old age. They were men neither better nor worse than their contemporaries: mingled childish credulity with generous instincts and the soundest good sense, and to get at their true portraits we must see the sense and folly as they actually mingled.

The scene of the event was as strange as the event itself; the weirdest of transactions had a frame-work in unison with it.

Princess Anne County, Virginia, extends from opposite Hampton Roads to the borders of North Carolina; and this long coast-line is broken on the Chesapeake and the Atlantic by numerous coves and inlets, one of which had a singular origin. A sluggish stream formerly crawled in a northerly direction toward the Chesapeake, emptied its waters into a small lagoon separated from the bay by a narrow sand bar, and escaped by an inlet at the western extremity of the lagoon. A gentleman residing in the vicinity was fond of boating on the Chesapeake, but to reach the open bay was obliged to make the long detour. In front was the low sand bar of very inconsiderable width, and, long meditating on the subject, he determined at last to dig a canal through the obstruction wide enough for the passage of his boat. This scheme was accomplished, but the result was disastrous. The Chesapeake, at the first high tide, rushed through the opening, and carried all before it. The little channel became an inlet half a mile wide, which would float a ship; and the waters of the bay were not even content with this feat of engineering science; they rolled steadily inland, following the course of the sluggish stream, encroached more and more, undermined what they did not overflow, and one of the results was the destruction of an ancient church on the west shore. The edifice, beaten by the waters, slowly crumbled, at last fell, and was completely submerged. The old tombstones, with their coats of arms and curious inscriptions, went with the rest; and bathers near the spot still occasionally touch them with their feet, and are able to read the names by the sense of touch.

Lynhaven Bay was thus formed—a wide expanse of water shut in by low shores. The surrounding country is wild and lonely. The chance traveller making his way over the roads of oyster-shells through the weird thickets sees the gleam of the white-winged water-fowl hovering above the ripples, and hears the murmur of the bay and the ocean. The waves lap on level shores clothed with junipers and ragged pines, and here and there the deep green leaves of the cypress stand out in vivid contrast with the oozy margin. A few shrubs only grow in the sandy soil, and relieve its barrenness, though it yields, with sufficient attention, all the vegetables for which the region is famous. Among these shrubs the most prominent is the rosemary, which grows to a large size, as on the banks of the Mediterranean; and its origin, well authenticated by ancient tradition, brings us to our subject. For a century after the settlement of Virginia no rosemary was ever seen there, but at last it was domesticated without the aid of government. Somewhere about the year 1700, or perhaps earlier, a certain young woman named Grace Sherwood resided in Princess Anne. She was a shy, secretive maid, and her neighbors told envious stories of her. Only one of these vague reports, however, was established on sufficient evidence, to wit, that she had crossed the Atlantic to the Mediterranean in an egg-shell, had been pleased with the odor of the rosemary growing on its shores, and on her return from this voyage in an open boat had brought some plants which she set out around her cottage "for remembrance."

The result of this harmless fancy was that Princess Anne was soon covered with rosemary; but the neighbors of young Grace Sherwood were ungrateful. For want of something better to occupy their minds, they began to gossip about her. Rosemary was sweet, but there was that voyage in the egg-shell boat! It was true it harmed nobody, but such proceedings were uncanny. Only witches who rode on broomsticks to midnight meetings could sail in egg - shells, and as witches cast spells and exerted malignant influences on honest people, it was plain that Grace Sherwood was a witch, and ought to be tried and punished.

Grave citizens, solid men of the county of Princess Anne, were ready to give their testimony. That egg-shell voyage was a fact established: might not the witch as easily bridle and saddle honest people, and ride them to her nocturnal revelries? Would not strange and malignant diseases, the result of spells, break out in the community? Nay, had not these dread inflictions already resulted from the toleration of Grace Sherwood? As worshipful Shallows and Slenders of the County Court of Princess Anne, it behooved them to institute proceedings for the extirpation of the witch, if she were a witch.

That was the question now solemnly examined into by their honors in the case of Grace Sherwood, the place being Princess Anne Court House, and the time July, 1706. The entry in the court record is the only remaining evidence of the event, and a copy of this entry from the yellow old sheet is here presented, with all the literary and other graces of the original carefully preserved: •

Princefs Annfs }
At a court held yᵉ 10th July 1706

Prefent { Colᵒ Mofeley,   Capt. Mofeley } Justices
{ Captⁿ Woodhouse, Jno Cornick }
{ Capt Chapman, Capt Wᵐ Smyth }

—— J.   Richafson—come late

Grace Sherwood to be Ducked

Whereas Grace Sherwood being Suspected of Witchcraft—have a long time waited for a fit opportunity for a further Examination—and by her Consent, & Approbation of yᵉ court, it is ordered yᵗ yᵉ Sherr take all such Convenient assistance of boats and men as shall be by him thought fit to meet & at John Harper's plantation in order to take yᵉ sᵈ Grace Sherwood forthwith & put her into water above mans Debth & try her how she swims. Therein always having Care of her life to preserve he [r] from Drowning & as soon as she comes Out yᵗ he request as many Ancient and Knowing women as possible to come to Serch her Carefully for teats spotts and marks about her body not usual on Others & yᵗ as they find yᵉ same to make report on oath To yᵉ truth there of to the Court, and further it is ordered yᵗ Four women be requested to Shift and Serch her before she goo into yᵉ water yᵗ she carry nothing about her to cause any further Suspicion.

Order XX

Grace Sherwood Ducked &c

Whereas on Complaint of Luke Hill in behalf of her Majesty yᵗ now is agᵗ Grace Sherwood for a person Suspected of Witch craft & having had Sundry Evidences sworn agᵗ her proving many Circumstances to which She could not make any Excuse Little or Nothing to Say in her own behalf only Seamed to Rely on wᵗ yᵉ Court should doo, and there upon Consented to be tryed in yᵉ Water & Like wise to be Serched again Bodily. Experiment being tried She swiming wᵉⁿ therein & bound Contrary to Custom & yᵉ judgᵗ of all yᵉ Spectators, & afterward being Serched, & five Ancient weomen who have all Declared on Oath yᵗ she is not like yᵉᵐ nor noo Other women yᵗ they know of . . . . all wᶜʰ Circumstances yᵉ Court weighing in there Consideration Doo there fore ordr yᵗ yᵉ Sherr take yᵉ sᵈ Grace Into his custody and to commᵗ her body to yᵉ Common Goal of this County, there to secure her by irons or other Wise, there to Remain till Such time as shall be otherwise Directed in order for her comming to yᵉ Common Goal of yᵉ County, to be brought to a future tryall there

EDWᴰ MOSELEY &
JNO. RICHASSON.

This literary performance, the work of that official Dogberry the clerk of the court, whose reading and writing probably came by nature, may be regarded by certain persons as obscure, even as bungling and stupid. But this criticism may involve injustice. A clear and direct writer is not necessarily a profound one, and the wise Lord Bacon tells us that all great literary beauty hath something of strangeness in it, requiring study. Applying this maxim to the production before us, and carefully collating the various portions, we perceive that the luminous record clearly sets forth the following facts:

That at Princess Anne Court House, Virginia, July 10, 1706, their worships the justices of that county, in serious mood and with spectacles on noses, did calmly take into consideration the case of a certain Grace Sherwood, charged with witchcraft. The historian does not pause to describe the imposing surroundings of the trial—the grave worships with contracted brows seated in a row on the elevated dais; the packed crowd of worthy people, in broad skirts and knee-breeches, behind the bar; himself, Dogberry, C. C., with possible nasal intonation, reading the indictment; and poor Grace Sherwood, the witch, standing up in the box of the accused, but bending down her head and weeping. The foliage of summer brushes the windows, and the birds are singing; but the stern representatives of the law are oblivious of this indifference of nature, and solemnly set about their duty as the servants of "her Majesty that now is"—that gracious Princess Anne from whom their county takes its name.

The prosecutor in the business is a certain Master Luke Hill, who doubtless scowls fiercely at poor Grace, awaiting the call to testify. It is not the first time that the witch has been arraigned. Collating carefully the detailed statements of Dogberry, C. C., we ascertain that the said Grace Sherwood, having previously been "suspected of witchcraft," had been arrested and examined, no doubt by a single justice of the peace; and that the result of this trial *extra curiam* in the justice's manor-house had been the committal of the accused to jail to undergo "further examination," for which the prisoner, we are informed, "awaited a fit opportunity."

The opportunity is now at hand, and the charges are duly investigated. To the damning array of testimony, by Master Luke Hill and others, the weeping witch has nothing to say; or, in the more concise style of Dogberry, "sundry evidences were sworn against her, proving many circumstances, to which she could not make any excuse." Alas! there were the terrible facts; her depravity was "proved," and what she faltered out piteously was not to the point. "She had little or nothing to say in her own behalf, and only seemed to rely on what the court should do"—a frail reliance it must have seemed after all the mass of proof clearly establishing the egg-shell business, and the spells she had inflicted on honest people. But what was she to do? She could only appeal to the mercy of the court. And then the witch no doubt covered her face and sank down weeping, sorely distrusting the result of their worships' consultation.

The court seems to have been in a quandary. There was the law, and there was the evidence. The latter "proved" that Grace Sherwood was a witch, and the former directed that witches should be burned. But then to burn women was a thing unknown in Virginia. Various persons might have their opinion of themselves, the worshipfuls, if Grace Sherwood were burned, and a certain flash of intelligence visits the minds of the Shallows and Slen-

ders. There was a means of infallibly determining the guilt or innocence of the accused. As she persisted in declaring her innocence, would she consent to be bound and thrown into the water as a conclusive test? If she swam, under these circumstances, the fact would be established that she was a witch; if she sank, and were drowned, her innocence would be as clearly demonstrated! That was fair, their worships intimated. Was the accused ready to undergo the ordeal? The reply is concisely indicated: judgment was entered "by her consent," and the court duly directed the character of the test. The sheriff is to take the necessary boats and men, to conduct the said Grace Sherwood to John Harper's plantation on the shore of Lynhaven Bay, and then and there these further directions of their worships are to be complied with. The said Grace Sherwood is to be committed to four ancient women, who are to remove her clothing, in order to ascertain "before she go into the water that she carry nothing about her to cause any further suspicion"—doubtless amulets or charms of virtue sufficient to cause a person to float while bound. Then, if nothing of this improper description is found concealed about her body, the said Grace is to be bound—her hands only it would seem—by the sheriff; he and his men are to conduct her in a boat to deep water, and there she is to be thrown in, "above a man's depth, to try her how she swims." If she is guilty, as this honorable court believes, she will swim in spite of her bonds; if she is innocent, she will sink; but the sheriff is to have "a care of her life to preserve her from drowning." A final ceremony, in accordance with her own request, is to be observed. When she comes out of the water, as many ancient and knowing women as possible are to search her person once more for evidences of witchcraft, and if such are found, the said ancients are to report the fact under oath to this court.

So the trial of the witch ends, and the supreme test is speedily applied. A crowd of "spectators" assemble at John Harper's plantation on Lynhaven Bay, and it is possible that their worships adjourned court and mingled with the rest. The scene was still and lonely—oozy banks skirted with pines, and lugubrious cypresses shining in the sun, white-winged sea-fowl flitting and screaming, the far lines of the Chesapeake coast, and the dim haze toward the shore of the Atlantic. On the banks are the crowd of people who have come to witness the punishment of the first Virginia witch, and the sheriff and his posse are ready to carry out the order of court. The waves are lapping in the grass and flags, and the odor of the pines mingles with the scent of rosemary—that rosemary brought in the egg-shell ship from the distant shores of the Mediterranean. And so the test begins.

The "ancient women," no doubt resembling their respectable prototypes in *Macbeth*, proceed to make their examination. Poor Grace Sherwood, no doubt weeping at the terrible ordeal before her, is divested of her clothing—in a place of privacy, it is to be hoped—and her person is closely inspected for some lurking amulet or other protection. None, it seems, was found, and, her clothing no doubt having been restored to her, the witch was ready to undergo the decreed test. Her hands were bound, and she was placed in the boat; the sheriff followed with his posse; the fleet rowed to deep water, and having reached a spot where it was over a man's head, the final ceremony took place. It is to be regretted that Dogberry, C. C., did not find it convenient to enter into details, but doubtless he depended upon the intelligence of his readers to imagine the scene. The sheriff, he informs us, was to take "boats" for his purpose, and a number filled with men probably formed a circle around the sheriff's with the view of rescuing the accused if she sank to the bottom. One and all of these honest Virginians, if we may hazard a conjecture, thought it a bad business. It was hard to drown a woman, and doubtless they were about to drown Grace Sherwood; for was it not "the judgment of all the spectators" that it was "contrary to custom" and the laws of nature that one bound as she was could swim or float in water? But there was the order of their worships, which must be obeyed; and suddenly Grace Sherwood is grasped in strong hands, in spite of her struggles, and thrown into "water above a man's depth."

The witch plunges and disappears, when doubtless the cry rises, "She was innocent!" But as suddenly she re-appears, and begins to swim in spite of her bonds! The witch is a witch, after all, as their wise worships declared; and never more should anybody presume to doubt those in authority! A shout from the crowd on shore proclaims the respect due to magistrates; the witch is dragged into the boats, which are rowed back to shore, and there the "five ancients" remove her wet garments and re-examine her. This time there is no more doubt. Conclusive and damning evidence is discovered of the witch's true character. Two moles are found on her person, and the hags hold up their hands in horror. When they come in due time to make oath as to what they have discovered, they will sum up all in the crushing statement that Grace Sherwood is a witch, for upon examination they had found that she "was not *like them*."

So Grace is taken back to jail, and their worships are in a greater quandary than ever. She is proved a witch—are they to burn her? Doubtless that were the true course, in accordance with the laws of the realm. But then it is a serious matter to burn people, and the court will consider it further. It may be that certain people outside of Princess Anne are laughing at the whole proceeding. To end: judgment will be reserved; Grace Sherwood shall be confined "in irons or otherwise" in the county jail, and shall be brought to "future trial"....

The facts here recorded are all that is known of this singular incident. A tradition has survived that the young witch died in prison before that future trial, but the statement only rests upon tradition. But for the entry in the journal of the court, and the name "Witch Duck" still attached to the scene on Lynhaven Bay where Grace Sherwood was "put into water," the whole story of this first and only Virginia witch would remain a mere legend.

LOVE'S RESURRECTION DAY.

ROUND among the quiet graves,
　　When the sun was low,
Love went grieving—Love who saves—
　　Did the sleepers know?

At his touch the flowers awoke,
　　At his tender call
Birds into sweet singing broke,
　　And it did befall

From the blooming, bursting sod
　　All Love's dead arose,
And went flying up to God
　　By a way Love knows.

THE NORTH SHORE.

AMONG European types there is none more interesting than the monks, who in popular conception, I believe, are supposed to have been vastly instrumental, in the Middle Ages, in preserving the foundations of modern art and learning. They are believed to have been even then, however, rather jovial fellows, fond of good living and a racy story, and are thus represented by the artists of the present.

I do not remember having seen a picture of the American monk, unless it be in the illustrations of Châteaubriand's Atala, and he is certainly not a familiar figure. But it has been my good fortune to have seen something of the climate and soil to which he appears to have become native, for, like nearly every one else in America, he has gone west, not west from Boston or New York, but from the St. Lawrence, and he went at a very early day.

The Northern region of which it is proposed to speak is, however, interesting for many other reasons than because the crucifix and gown stand out in sombre silhouettes against its historical horizon, for the monastic life formed only a part, though a very important part, of a vast and brilliant panorama of discovery and adventure, and the North Shore is interesting as a region toward which the eyes of the world were once turned throughout an extended period, and whose atmosphere is redolent of a somewhat venerable past; but which, in spite of it all, has these many years lain well-nigh forgotten behind pathless forests, and has had the unique fate to remain a perpetual frontier.

It happened that our tickets were on an American line of boats, and it happened also that while we had hoped to find on board some gentle Franciscan, or at least some weather-beaten *voyageur*, full of stories of the early trading days, to lend the beginning of our journey a characteristic flavor, the monotonous list of passengers was only relieved by the conspicuous figure of a venerable widower, who was distinguished by having married four wives of different nationalities, and was now out on wedding journey number five, bound, as a commercial traveller informed us, for "the great sea-side resort of the west, at Ashland," with a veritable travelling Babel of sons and daughters.

This somewhat ambitious expression is characteristic of the country, but not nearly so inaccurate as may appear, for not only is this wide way-side nook itself a surprise both in its surroundings and its unsurpassed accommodations, but Lake Superior, which was once mainly distinguished from the sea by its freshness, has now been found to contain all the essential salts, at least in the waters of Thunder Bay, a locality of which more will be said as our narrative continues, and as early as 1851 Professor Agassiz announced the fact that the beach pea is found along the North Shore, together with other plants and insects peculiar to the ocean.

The place of Lake Superior among all bodies of fresh-water is unique, with its vast expanse, its headlands that repeat Gibraltar, its islands that lie in the distance like mountains of opaque amethyst in beds of turquoise blue or silver, and its waters cold as the waters of the pole, and so clear that you look at a depth of fifty feet upon beds of rock white with silver veins, paved with phosphorescent spar, or glittering with copper, "where Isle Royale stretches her jewelled fingers beneath the waves."

Then, too, it has lain there these many million years, hemmed in by a rim of rocky heights which were twisted and marred by the fires which shaped the globe, and as a model about which the continent was formed, presents an epitome of antiquity before which the age of the eternal hills is but an instant in the march of time.

There was a pleasant surprise in entering Duluth. We had expected to find deserted warehouses and streets grown green since the fiasco of a premature beginning, but the prosperity inevitable upon its natural situation seems to have taken a new lease of life, and there is a strong impression in approaching from the water that the city has grown in a single night, almost every other one of the houses scattered well up the slope of the irregular and barren hills being still unpainted, and apparently occupied before completion.

The early French writers were fond of comparing Superior to a bended bow, and Keweenaw Point, stretching far into the lake, was not inaptly called an arrow; but the people of Duluth humorously speak of it, or at least of its western end, as a colossal hand, with the index finger pointing significantly toward their city as the outlet and feeder of the northern west, and the enthusiastic hope that it will become an important centre at no distant day bears every evidence of being realized, inasmuch as it lies at the head of navigation at the eastern extremity of the Northern Pacific, is surrounded by the largest pine forest east of the Rocky Mountains, and possesses in Vermilion Range a deposit of iron of great extent and undisputed value.

While at Duluth a delightful jaunt was made to the Dells of the St. Louis, where the river pours through broken, irregular gorges, which seem hewn from the solid rock, sweeping around enormous rugged bowlders, and tumbling with impetuous haste over frequent falls.

We were told that the river had lost much of its charm through the construction of dams for timber, but while one regrets these innovations from the point of view of the picturesque, the practical value of the stream becomes a matter of engaging interest, when we learn that with a fall of four hundred feet in four miles there is enough power to turn the twenty-five million spindles of England and Scotland combined.

Sieur Du Luth was by no means the first to explore the territory of Minnesota, but he was at one time actively engaged in trade at the western end of Lake Superior, and is said to have caused his Majesty the King of France's arms to be planted in a chief village of the Sioux in 1678. He may or he may not have been identified with the locality now called Duluth, though it is more than likely that he was, but however important the spot may have been at an early day, there is little in the modern city to remind one of the past.

It is true that in the palmy days of the fur trade there was a post at Fond du Lac, within sight of the hills behind the city, but even there every vestige of the past is gone; there is not even a rafter of the old banquet hall remaining, and we found no one with a personal recollection of the scenes along the great portage to the Mississippi, when the rivers were vocal with the songs of the *voyageurs*, and the wilderness, which they never touched with change, was populous with their half-savage and half-civilized existence, and one's consciousness of the antiquity of the place is strangely at variance with the impression of one's actual surroundings. The

prospects of to-day in this region are, however, curiously interwoven with the ideas of early discovery, and the mind reverts with a feeling of relief to that earlier phase of life which was remarkable alike for its picturesque scenes and its striking historical contrast with contemporaneous events. In 1600, after the failure of Raleigh's Virginia colony, there was not an Englishman in America. Washington was not born until 1732, and yet ninety years before, the Jesuit Jognes had landed at the Sault Ste. Marie. In 1659 two French traders had already penetrated to northern Minnesota, and in 1672, ten years before Penn landed on the Delaware, there was a mission at the Apostles Islands, and Marquette and his fellow-missionaries had not only learned the location of the Mississippi, but prepared an excellent map of the lake, which was published in Paris while the New England colonists were still struggling with King Philip.

It would seem that affairs went forward in those early days at a very modern rate of speed, for the missionaries were scarcely established on the lake before there were settlements of traders, with their quaint block-houses and stockades, and its waters were picturesque with bright and stirring scenes of life long before the first drum-tap of the Revolution. The priests were the heroic figures of the epoch, and seem to reproduce the age of saintship, as with exalted piety and fervor they penetrated among hostile tribes, taking possession of the country in the name of God by carving the word Jesus on the trees, and when tortured with diabolical ingenuity, weeping for those who could not find martyrdom a joy. It may be that they accomplished little among the Indians in proportion to their efforts, but the character of the performance remains the same, and the interest quickens as we fancy them treading the dense Northern forests, floating down silent shadowy rivers in their birch canoes, or sleeping in the snow beneath the stars, and often enough, with faces illumined with benignant piety, yielding up their lives.

Standing at Duluth, at the extremity of the great avenue of progress, the mists which hide the past seem to roll away, and the bright panorama of adventure is reproduced in fancy, with its brilliant coloring, and the buoyant freedom of an unrestrained existence; the priests always in the lead, the discoverers, the traders, all in the quaint and often gay costume of the time, in ever-ending and ever-renewed procession; and then the theatre of action, the magnificent approach to the country of the lakes, down foaming rivers, and over unknown inland seas, the St. Lawrence, the Ottawa, the islands of Huron, the Sault, and the new Pillars of Hercules at Gros Cap and Point Iroquois, which guard the entrance to the Kitchigami, with its mighty basalt hills, and its silver mists in which men floated forever in enchantment.

Eight miles from Montreal was the feudal castle of La Salle, with its palisades and bastions—not exactly like the castles of early European history in appearance, but, after all, with its tenantry and the whole movement of its life the same, and called La Chine, from his proposed route to China from the upper Mississippi—a project based on ideas of the nearness of China and Japan which now seem ludicrous enough, but were then so seriously entertained that on one occasion at least Chinese traders were expected to be found in what is now Wisconsin, and a certain explorer even prepared himself for a western expedition with garments of celestial hue.

Not the least interesting feature of the period, though remote from Lake Superior, was the strange spectacle of the grace and stateliness of a court in log cabins buried in the dark Canadian forests, and the quaint progress of the provincial governors with their fleets of brightly colored boats, when the chivalrous European knight, surrounded with barbaric splendor, appeared as a patriarch and protector in a region which, though far from populous, was already picturesque with the life of merry boatmen, and resounded with the joyous airs of France whenever the traders swept in their swift canoes along the rivers, or built their camp fires for the night's bivouac. On a certain occasion, something over two hundred years ago, the Intendant of Canada, with a view to an extension of the French dominions, sent envoys throughout the west to propose a congress of the nations at the Sault Ste. Marie, than which there can have been few more picturesque assemblies, as the tribes came in hosts in their birchen navies, with merry shouts and shining paddles, in all the glitter of savage decoration, and finally gathered on the shore in silent semicircles (sitting) about a group of black-gowned priests, stately braves in snowy turbans and eagle feathers, and French officials in plumed hats and scarlet cloaks, while above all were reared the cross, and a column "marked with the lilies of the Bourbons." Here was feudalism, the flavor of mediæval saintship, the gallantry of Paris and Versailles, and the buoyant, joyous life of the *bourgeois* class, all in the heart of the new continent, before Bunker Hill was dreamed of. The French incursion is, however, quite as interesting as a repetition and epitome of history, for the Latin race bore the cross and fleur-de-lis far beyond the heavy-footed Saxon, built forts, conciliated the savages, and laid the foundations of an empire, and then came the Norsemen, as of old when the south of Europe led the world. Again in the New World the Latin races were to lead, and again all that is left is the poetry and romance of the past, like the perfume of a rich and brilliant flower which lingers long after the substance has passed away; but the short route to China has been discovered, the sturdy Norsemen have laid the rails, and the fair dreams of those early days will be more than realized in the new belt of civilization and commerce along the boundary of Canada and the United States.

There are several ways of skirting along the coast eastward from Duluth. A journey through the interior would only be possible for experienced woodsmen; indeed, very much of the country has really never been thoroughly explored. We might have taken the government road along the shore, in comparison with which the roughest "corduroy" would appear a brilliant modern innovation. We learned, however, that it was merely a broad trail for dog teams, which carry the mail in winter to Thunder Bay and other places, and were willing to leave undisturbed a monopoly which could not excite the envy of the most communistically inclined.

It would require a week to reach Prince Arthur's Landing in a Mackinaw boat, and while we might have made the "run" in eighteen hours by steamer, it was preferred to combine pleasure with moderate expedition, and we accordingly took the mail tug which plies between Duluth, Grand Portage, and intermediate points, with a view to an occasional glimpse of the scenery, which increases in grandeur all the way to Thunder Cape.

In the dry atmosphere of this region the vision reaches very far. On the upward journey the northern coast had been visible nearly across the lake, stretching its faint outlines far along the horizon; and now, eighteen miles away, we could see every wrinkle and fold in the mighty wall rising hundreds of feet into the sunlight in shining escarpments and palisades, cleft by shadowy recesses, broken by bold headlands, and now and then opening into some exquisite rock-bound harbor radiant with imprisoned light.

In such a journey there is little incident, and one is content with impressions that can not be conveyed. One merely exists, exhilarated by the bracing air, and satisfied to bask in the sun, and follow the long irregular line of heights as they emerge in pale blue masses from their robe of misty light.

It is not safe to approach too near the coast. There were, however, occasional close glimpses, notably at Agate Bay, where picturesque groups of Indians were gathering the beautiful stones implied in the name, which in the rough are indistinguishable to the untrained eye from ordinary pebbles, but are gathered in quarts and bushels by these dusky-fingered *connoisseurs*.

It was not long, as we pushed merrily onward in our brusque and somewhat intrusive little craft, before we reached a bit of scenery well worthy of special notice in the palisades, which begin beyond a rock-bound bay, and once formed a wall which rose directly and continuously from the water. Their composition, however, is such that this could not long remain the case, the basaltic columns, of which the surface is composed, being loosened by storms and frost, and sliding down perpendicularly as the softer rock beneath is worn away, or crushed by the icy batteries which every winter's storm hurls against its base, with the result that the effect of grandeur is heightened on close inspection among the huge columns which lean against the wall, or lie shattered at its base in massive blocks, and the mind is awed by a vivid realization of the forces by which they were formed, and which have left the underlying portions twisted and curved in a manner which defies description.

It will be remembered that before 1842 the Great Lakes formed part of the boundary line of the United States. At Pigeon River we crossed the present line, which includes Isle Royale, and extends along a remarkable chain of lakes and streams reaching to the Lake of the Woods, which once formed an important highway, followed by the traders, who after a journey of several thousand miles, arrived at the Grand Portage in their canoes with more regularity than a modern steamer in its trip around the lakes.

The territory thus acquired is still virtually *terra incognita*. There are no settlements inland, and the few scattered towns along the lake are the result of mining, which has been encouraged by the geological surveys, but which, whether the deposits of silver and other metals be rich or otherwise, will not soon be carried forward without the utmost difficulty, and the mines can now only be reached from the coast by "packing."

At the Grand Marais, one of these towns, where there was considerable delay, it was our good fortune to catch a glimpse of local life, and see the trains of gaunt Indian figures, with "packs" on their backs, supported by straps around the forehead, ascending a rocky portage in single file, something like the carriers of South America, or the *arrieros* of Spain. A more novel make-shift for a team, however, used in winter, consists of a dog, a billy-goat, and a mule, a combination of character in the latter two animals which comically typifies the persistence necessary in local operations, and is oddly characteristic of a region where literally the earth's crust is so bare that, were the forests removed, a few heavy rains would wash away what little soil there is, and leave a continuous line of rocky hills all the way eastward from Duluth, not unlike the Riviera of southern France, except in elevation, and if recollection serves us rightly, even more jagged and splintered in their savage grandeur.

One of the most interesting places in the early history of Lake Superior was Grand Portage, on Grosselier or Pigeon River. In 1679 Du Luth built a fort there, the ruins of which were still visible a few years since, but the real importance of the place did not begin until after the establishment of the Northwest Company, though at the signing of the Declaration of Independence it is said to have already been a commercial emporium of the backwoods, bright with a motley and *bizarre* existence.

CLIFFS ON THE NORTH SHORE, ABOVE DULUTH.

LAMB ISLAND LIGHT, NEAR THUNDER CAPE.

Until the boundary treaty the Grand Portage was the general head-quarters and rendezvous of trade in this part of the world, and became a sort of home to the *voyageurs*, or was at least the one place in the wilderness in which their interests centred, and which was associated with social pleasures, and it is in places like Grand Portage and Fort William that one gets the best idea of these heroes of the paddle. They were gay, droll, braggart fellows, full of poetry and music, whose every passing mood found expression in verse, which was often enough doggerel in form, but more or less genuine in feeling. They were true believers, too, in the old German saying, "Ein anderes Städtchen, ein anderes Mädchen,"* and often enough had a sweetheart at every post from Montreal to the Pacific. It was therefore natural that some *ma Doudette* or *ma belle Rose* should often be made the theme of compositions, the body of which was made up of the impressions of the journey, the steersman touching every passing incident in his composition, and the others joining in a joyous chorus, keeping time with their paddles and their swaying bodies, and nothing could be more inspiriting than a brigade of canoes under full song sweeping down some rapid river. Theirs was, however, a life of hardships, and Lower Canada always remained the home to which they would some time return, but toward which they nevertheless always turned the longing eyes of exiles, and the result was a peculiar and pathetic sadness running in an under-tone through many of their songs,

* Another village, another maiden.

giving their *complaintes* in particular a peculiar interest, and they might often have been seen at evening slowly moving across the polished surface of some silent forest lake with slowly dipping paddles, chanting a *complainte*, which perhaps related the sufferings and misfortunes of some real or imaginary *voyageur*.

At certain seasons they came to the Grand Portage, and later to Fort William, in numbers swelling the population to several thousands, and it was invariably a season of festivity and rejoicing, when old friends met after scenes of danger, and old vows were renewed over brimming bumpers. During the day there were wrestling matches and Indian dances in the open air, and night after night the great banquet hall with its low ceiling was lighted for the dance, with blazing pine knots revealing its unstudied decoration—a few pairs of snow-shoes leaning in the corners, cutlasses crossed with muskets at intervals along the walls, and an occasional pair of branching antlers, which may have been the gift of some Highland laddie, for Sandy was by no means a stranger to the fur trade.

The ruling social element, however, was always French, and there are few more picturesque affairs than those border balls, with an orchestra composed of a bagpipe, a fiddle, and a flute, to the music of which the dark-eyed half-breed girls moved through the stately dances with the wild grace and freedom of the woods, with gay partners, who were doubtless very handsome in their soft brown deer-skin leggings, their blue capotes, and scarlet sashes, from which hung glittering knives and embroidered Indian pouches.

The steamer from Grand Portage brought us into Thunder Bay at night, and there were only passing glimpses in the evening of clusters of curiously indented islands, with long tapering points, and the irregular coast of the mainland, with an occasional Indian lodge, a few indistinct figures before a camp fire, and two or three canoes drawn up on the shore, or a solitary "light" on some wind-swept rock, run up on a pole, in lieu of a light-house, before a rickety hut, which looked the picture of exile and desolation.

We will frankly acknowledge a prejudice against Canadian towns. We had thought them rickety and shiftless, but Prince Arthur's Landing, on Thunder Bay, is a creation of New Canada. It is true it is not much of a place as yet, and there was the least suggestion in the tinkling bells of one-horse carts that jogged slowly along the village streets of the delicious drowsy life in those quaint old French towns along the St. Lawrence River, and the lawyer and banker walked about the streets in slippers.

One saw more of the life of the place in the long twilight of pleasant summer evenings, when all the town was out, and a little bevy of ladies and gentlemen went canoeing in craft that were quite luxurious enough for Quebec or Montreal, and a fleet of white-winged yachts rode buoyantly in the bay, dipping with the rising swells as a swallow dips and soars against a freshening breeze.

The Landing is, in fact, all sorts of a place. There were smart, tidy shops that remind one of an English village, where one can buy articles of luxury not to be found in our larger country towns, and not always in our cities. A ruined stockade, which the fancy connected with Indian massacres and a frontier life, was built to anticipate the Fenian invasion. The government yard contained the gig of Sir Garnet Wolseley, who once passed through here with troops; and as we strolled along the street that skirts the bay before the Queen's Hotel, groups of dusky figures basking in the sun along the beach, the brilliant atmosphere, the magnificent scenery, with Pie Island lying in the distance, very like Capri across the Bay of Naples, created a vivid impression of many a sunny nook along the Italian coast. There is not, in fact, much about the Landing to remind one of the frontier, except the sameness of the houses and a picturesque log bank, which, with its quaint gables, really looks as if it were built to please some idle fancy.

On learning, however, of the sums that are being laid out in docks and piers, and

THE DEVIL'S TOOTHPICK, PIE ISLAND.

A MINER—SILVER ISLAND.

that, with only 1300 people, the village has laid twelve miles of track against heavy odds to meet the Canadian Pacific, extending, as it were, a royal invitation to that line to make this its eastern terminus for the present in preference to the neighboring village of Fort William, we were whisked from idle fancies to the practical realities of the present, and felt the bracing atmosphere of enterprise and competition.

A friendly greeting at the landing had been assured through letters from Duluth, and as we happened into the post-office the evening of the day of our arrival, we were surrounded by the judge, a lawyer, two editors, and a sheriff—a combination which would naturally have a portentous aspect; but though we were arrested rather summarily in our course, it was only to be presented to the postmaster, and a civil engineer, said to be very familiar with the country, and it was not long before we were thoroughly at home among friends, many of whom devoted themselves to our service with engaging hospitality.

Accordingly the following morning we became their guests in an excursion to "the Nipigon," one hundred miles away. On this occasion we enjoyed the use of a private launch, a sort of propeller, tug, and yacht combined, provided by the president (reeve) of the village, and an intelligent and enterprising merchant, and nothing could have been more agreeable than our surroundings on setting forth; the exhilarating freshness of the Northern morning; the landscape gradually stealing from a silent world of mist, which broke up with shifting irregular patches of blue between its vapory masses; and then as we approached the pier, what a spectacle lay before the eye!—the bending lines of hills stretching in gentle curves far out to sea, with increasing elevation to Thunder Cape, and Pie Island in the foreground (the latter once a projection of the shore), inclosed with mural cliffs from eight to fourteen hundred feet in height a vast rock-rimmed basin, radiant with light and color. There it lay with undulating stretches of soft rich purple, followed by purplish-grays and greens a little farther out, and finally a pale blue bed about the distant islands, which lay dark and massive across our path, their huge crowns silhouetting in clear-cut outlines against the eastern sky, while a soft mirage lifted the distant heights of Isle Royale across the outer gaps in white and shining

PIE ISLAND.

light. But it was not until we gradually rounded Thunder Cape that we felt the full effect. Then how the mighty masses ruled us! What silent isolation! And how supreme they were as they seemed to look down upon us across these many million years since the earth was young, and their scarred and wrinkled fronts echoed the tumult of creation!

Parallel with Thunder Bay, and only separated from it by the cape, lies Black Bay, stretching inland nearly forty miles, some river like the Danube or Rhine; again the effect was of a submerged mountain chain, while still again the appearance was wholly like the sea as we swept by breezy headlands with projecting reefs of dark brown rock fringed with curling foam, or stopped to sketch some broken pile of blocks richly mottled with patches of yellow, brown, and green, and crispy with its brilliant lichen coat.

The following evening found us at Red Rock, at the head of Nipigon Bay, where

FORT WILLIAM.

while "the Nipigon," rock-bound like the rest, and equally extensive, lies close beyond.

At the foot of Thunder Cape we touched at Silver Islet, which at one time created a furor in the speculative world, and is unique, I believe, among silver mines, the shaft being sunk fifteen hundred feet through a rock which was originally only forty by seventy feet in extent, and until it was cribbed was submerged by every heavy sea.

Mr. Cabot, who wrote the narrative of the Agassiz expedition in 1851, estimated that there were nearly thirty-six thousand islands in the lake, most of which lie across the mouth of these three bays, and along Point Magnet, which bends westward from the western extremity of "the Nipigon," and as we passed between them and the mainland, there was at times the impression that one was floating down a river pours down from a chain of lakes linked by a series of boiling rapids. A visit was made to the house of the agent of the Hudson Bay Company a commodious modern building, curiously and rather elaborately finished throughout with hard pine in place of plaster. The register contained the names of a good many American fishermen, and a goodly list of speckled trout caught by different parties, single fish often tipping the scales at from five to seven pounds. In the course of our stay there was an interesting jaunt to an Indian settlement on Lake Helen, one of the expansions of the Nipigon River, two miles above. The wigwams lay scattered all along the shore, surrounded by scores of yelping Indian dogs blinking in the sun; and inasmuch as the Nipigon Indians were at one time exceedingly warlike and ferocious, the present peaceful settlement speaks well for the success of the Catholic

INDIAN BOY AT NIPIGON.

tation to the Manitoulin Islands, in Lake Huron, to ask the establishment of a mission on the North Shore, and two priests—Fathers Du Ranquet and Conin—were accordingly sent to the post at Pigeon River, but subsequently removed to the vicinity of Fort William, where there is now a considerable establishment, the school buildings, church, and monastery lying in green fields along the river-bank against a mountain background. Our first visit was made on a warm day in June. A few canoes were lying on the shore before a group of scattered cottages, and the place seemed silent, as all old places do. We passed a large field yellow with buttercups, and as we let down the bars on apparently deserted grounds, and ascended a narrow projecting wharf, a bright-eyed little Indian boy offered to ferry us across. There was an ascent of a steep and rickety pair of stairs on the opposite bank, and we found ourselves in the quaint porch of the little monastery, where a tall, spare priest with a pleasant face gave us welcome.

missions. There was a church, and a few substantial houses and barns belonging to half-breeds, but the full-blooded Indians invariably lived in wigwams, which were scattered in picturesque groups, usually with a few nets and brightly colored garments drying in the sun before them, and Indian women repairing canoes along the beach.

The Canadians have an English fondness for long jaunts, at least in this part of Canada, and we had scarcely returned from the Nipigon when our friends proposed an expedition inland to the Kakabikka Falls.

During the days spent in preparation for the inland journey (for our Canadian cousins have an English system in their business) the time was passed at the mission and Fort William.

Years ago the Chippeways sent a depu-

There were many pleasant hours spent at the mission, full of interesting information. In the conversion of the Indian it seems, curiously enough, that the main bulwark to be carried is his fondness for drumming—a ceremony senseless and monotonous enough to us, but full of mysterious importance to those who, in the simplicity of race childhood, are awed by natural phenomena, and especially in winter are lonely and full of a superstitious fear of tempests, and practice this pagan rite by way of solace and protection.

Sometimes in a storm a long smoky wigwam will be filled with Indians surrounding drummers, who continue their monotonous ceremony throughout the day and night, until the feeling becomes so intense that one may pass back and forth among them without attracting notice. However, when once thoroughly Christianized,

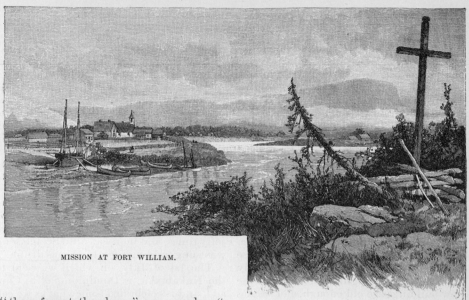

MISSION AT FORT WILLIAM.

"they forget the drum" even under (to them) the most trying circumstances, and I well remember an occasion when, coming down a wild rapid in a storm, the clouds were black, the wind blew in gusts, and the dark spruce woods rocked above us as we shot through the white foam, and my guide, who was a Christian, chanted a Latin hymn with a countenance full of wondering awe, and a curious mingling of savage feeling and Christian solace. In cases of great mortality, however, even these Christian Indians often return to the fetich of the drum.

The whole neighborhood of Fort William has a peculiar charm, and is indelibly impressed upon the mind. A mountain with bold cliffs, the straggling buildings of the mission, a few crosses, an ancient grave-yard, in which is buried many an old-time *voyageur;* up the river a sleepy village, with lazily droning mills and de-

serted docks; and below, where the river enters the lake through a delta, a broad bed of blue through the trees, and on the left, toward a low-lying light-house, the old fort, which grows upon one imperceptibly as it lies there in the sunshine, with its quaint peaked roofs, its mossy walls full of the mellow tones of age, and the last schooner of the "trade" lying before it on the river-bank, with crumbling cordage and gaping seams.

The chief glory of the fort has, however, passed away in the retirement of Mr. McIntyre, the last of the local factors, who looked like an old Scotch laird, with his ruddy face, shaggy eyebrows, and a tasselled cap that covered locks as white as the Northern snows among which he

NIPIGON STRAIT.

has spent his life. There was always something interesting in a visit to the fort with him. Sometimes it was old Lombard, who said he had had twelve wives and six running dogs in his day, "and if I were to live my life over, I would be a *voyageur* again"; sometimes it was the records, and sometimes an old rubbish chamber, from which we were permitted to carry away the bayonet of an "Old Brown Bess," bearing the Tower mark, and Louis Quatorze shoe-buckles, which were the more plentiful as they were sent over to sell to the Indians, who, strangely enough, it was thought, did not appreciate these then modern innovations.

Again it was the fort itself, for while, with the exception of a ruined block-house and a stone house for furs, there is really little left of the original fortification, the new buildings are old enough, and besides they have inherited their traits as a son inherits from his father. Best of all, however, was to hear the old factor renew the "auld lang syne," when the trade was in its glory, and the old gentleman's eyes sparkled as he recalled the meetings of the partners, when an Italian cook was sent from the club-house at Montreal with brandies oily with age and fine old port; on such occasions the table groaned with fish and game. Simon McGilvary, chief factor, presided, and a beaver was on the platter, and three hundred sat down to dine, in the order of their rank, with wines graded from champagne at the factors' places, to rum and water among the guides at the lower end. "Aye, mon, those were jolly times, and mony an auld Scotch song was sung, and mony a toast was drunk."

The 1st of July, on which we went to the Kakabikka, is Dominion-day in Canada, and is celebrated somewhat as we celebrate the Fourth, though it is only important as the anniversary of the recent provincial confederation. The celebration on this occasion was a mild one, but it was interesting to watch the Donalds and Johnnies as they came in on the little steamers from the mines, and the throngs of Indians and squaws seated in wondering groups along the shore and pier. Two large vessels were sailing below the cape, and with bright flags and buoys, and the snowy fleet of swiftly sailing yachts, the bay presented an unwonted scene of life; but the most interesting spectacle of all was the canoe race as the two Indian crews shot forward with lusty strokes and merry shouts, which continued till the goal was passed.

At evening we were to be ready for the start. As we assembled at the station a few awkward workmen— tyros on the still unused road — were moving about with lanterns, for what purpose no one could exactly tell, and a group of Indians waiting for their prizes curiously eyed our hand-car, which was loaded with two

HALLWAY IN PRIEST'S HOUSE.

KAKABIKKA FALLS.

well-secured canoes, and provisions and luggage for the journey.

The Canadian Pacific skirts along the bay as you leave the village, and the effect is unsurpassed as the moon rises large and red above the dark rocks across the gleaming water, and as we bowled along, the wash of the breakers soothed our ears, and the glancing waves seemed to smile and beckon in mystery through the slen-der second growth, which seemed etched against the light, until we entered the silence of the dark Muskeg. It was not long before we passed Fort William, and then followed a long ascent of nearly five hundred feet in twenty miles, until in the dim morning light a floating cloud of smoky mist appeared above the forest, and the journey was at an end. There were no changing scenes, only the deep shad-

owy woods, the white moonlight, the silence only broken by the continual rattle
of the car, and the shadows of our figures
slowly bending back and forth, and an
occasional relief by turns, when the one
most anxious to keep awake invariably
fell asleep as he rattled along on a hard
pine board across the keels of the over-
reaching boats.   At the as yet unused station of Kaministiquoia there was a short
nap, a brisk "bathe," as our Scotch friends
called it, in the river, a hearty breakfast,
and the canoes were launched for the
downward passage.

There was a dash of rapids at the outset.   A few swift, steady strokes brought
us to the clearest water, and the spout-
ing foam showered us with its refreshing
drops; then there was a lull, a stretch of
dimpling, eddying surface, and again a
roar and rush of water that looked the
whiter by contrast with the overhanging
green.

At one point there was a fall of twenty
feet, beyond which the river seemed to
lose itself among the trees.   The forest
lay all about us, and the impression was
that the broad smooth surface had ceased
to move, but on winding through a long
circuitous channel we dropped down a
glassy chute into an extensive basin, crossed by a curving line of islands with a luxurious growth of spruce interspersed with
modest satiny birches, and between the islands the river poured in picturesque cascades.

It was evening when we reached the
Indian trail above the Kakabikka, which
began with characteristic caution at a distance above the falls.   As we pushed
through the tangled brush and interlacing boughs the leaves were wet with
spray, and as we neared the brink there
was a dizzy rush of water, which seemed
to sink out of sight, and the mist overwhelmed us with its hurrying clouds.
There was a rough descent along the trail
of some two hundred feet, which brought
us to an ideal terrace surrounded by a
hedge of thickly blooming roses, but it
was nevertheless decided to camp on an
island which lay temptingly beneath the
falls.   There was a stiff struggle up the
rapids, a clinging here and there to roots
along the wall, with an occasional rest in
some deep eddy, the surface of which was
covered with thick foam, cut now and

then by the fins of slowly moving stur-
geon, then another struggle with the water, and in the course of an hour or so
the distance of a few hundred feet was
made.

It was dark above and darker still between the black walls of the gorge, which
rose two hundred feet above us, and little
could be seen except vague clouds of mist
that moved in spectral procession down
the valley.

In the quickly made camp a ruddy bonfire was surrounded by a floor of cedar
boughs, bacon was frying in pans on improvised stone ovens, and a surrounding
wall of wet gray blankets hung smoking
in the heat, relieved by red bandana
handkerchiefs, blue stockings, and soiled
white sombreros, while a little group of
tourists lay stretched at length before the
fire, for the last pipe and story, and finally lay down, with their heads under the
canoes, in wet clothing, between wet
blankets, beneath the ever-falling spray.

If Lake Superior were remarkable for
nothing else, it would still be remarkable
for the unnumbered cascades which stud
its coasts, and which are often of great
height and beauty.   Among them all
perhaps the grandest is the Kakabikka,
as, with a width of one hundred yards, it
flings itself over a precipice twenty feet
higher than Niagara.

The descent is perpendicular, but there
is a slight shelving of the slate, and the
water sinks in consequence in flaky foam
from the very top.

On the occasion of our visit the morning sun filled the fall with light, and the
projecting piers which form the caldron
were rich and dark against the snowy
mass, and the thundering torrent seemed
to disappear in an impalpable and seemingly incandescent spray.   Below the falls
there were ten miles of boiling rapids,
then long smooth slopes of water, where
at a few yards' distance we could overlook
the heads of those before us as they swept
down the rapid current; then an interminable maze of bends and curves, with
exquisite terraced banks, and luxurious
growths of elms; then the mission, the
fort, and light-house, a long stretch across
the bay in the dusk of evening; then occasional voices, a bell, and echoing hammers at the Landing, and as the moon
rose above the cape our journey ended.

TRANSCRIPTS FROM NATURE.

VIII.—THE GIANT BEECH.

MILLION little beech leaves sway
  In the warm wind above me here;
  A speckled mavis sings quite near,
The cuckoo calls from far away,
But only beech leaves can I see,
Trembling and tossing carelessly—

A world of green lost in the fair
Surrounding space of azure air.

IX.—OLD FISHER-BOAT.

Bright as a burnished shield, the sea
  In calm, in moveless peace doth sleep;
  Only the tide's faint ripples creep
Along the brown sands hushfully,
Till now they lap the old worn boat
That nevermore on them will float.

A year ago a wild storm made
The sands a grave where it was laid.

X.—A HERRING SHOAL, WEST HIGHLANDS.

Between dark hills on either side
  The salt sea-loch runs for a mile;
  And now, sun-charmèd to a smile,
Gleams bright its flowing, frothing tide.
But, lo! each wave to silver turns,
In dazzling fire the whole loch burns.

Millions of herring dart and splash,
Each one a living lightning-flash.

THE four years' administration of John Quincy Adams is commonly spoken of as a very uninteresting period, but it was in one respect more important than the twenty years that went before it or the ten years that followed. For the first time the inhabitants of the United States began to find out how very large a country they lived in. From occupying a mere strip of land on the Atlantic they had spread already through New York and Ohio; but it was by detached emigrations, of which the nation was hardly conscious, by great single waves of population sweeping here and there. After 1825 this development became a self-conscious and deliberate thing, recognized and legislated for, though never systematically organized by the nation. When, between 1820 and 1830, Michigan Territory increased 260 per cent., Illinois 180 per cent., Arkansas Territory 142 per cent., and Indiana 133 per cent., it indicated not a mere impulse but a steady progress, not a wave but a tide. Now that we are accustomed to the vast statistics of to-day, it may not seem exciting to know that the population of the whole nation rose from nearly ten millions (9,633,822) in 1820 to nearly thirteen (12,866,020) in 1830; but this gain of one-third was at the time the most astounding demonstration of national progress. It enables us to understand the immense importance attached in John Quincy Adams's time to a phrase now commonplace and almost meaningless—"internal improvements." It is true that under John Quincy Adams more commercial treaties were organized than under all his predecessors; but this, after all, was a minor benefit. The foreign commerce of the United States is now itself, comparatively speaking, subordinate; it is our vast internal development that makes us a nation. It is as the great epoch of internal improvements that the four years from 1825 to 1829 will forever be momentous in the history of the United States.

In 1825 the nation was in the position of a young man who has become aware that he owns a vast estate, but finds it to be mostly unproductive, and hardly even marketable. Such a person sometimes hits upon an energetic agent, who convinces him that the essential thing is to build a few roads, bridge a few streams, and lay out some building lots. It was

just in this capacity of courageous adviser that John Quincy Adams was quite ready to offer himself. On the day of his inauguration the greater part of Ohio was yet covered with forests, and Illinois was a wilderness. The vast size of the country was still a source rather of anxiety than of pride. Monroe had expressed the fear that no republican government could safely control a nation reaching as far as the Mississippi; and Livingston, after negotiating for the purchase of Louisiana, had comforted himself with the thought that a large part of it might probably be resold. At that time this enormous annexation was thought to endanger the very existence of the original thirteen States.

This was perhaps nowhere more frankly stated than by an able Fourth-of-July orator at Salem, Massachusetts, in 1813, Benjamin R. Nichols. He declares that to admit to the Union new States formed out of new territory is "to set up a principle which, if submitted to, will make us more dependent than we were as colonies of Great Britain. If a majority of Congress have a right of making new States where they please, we shall probably soon hear of States formed for us in East and West Florida; and, should it come within the scope of the policy of our rulers, of others as far as the Pacific Ocean. If all this be right, the consequence is that the people of New England, in case of any disturbances in these newly created States, may, under pretense of suppressing insurrections, be forced to march, in obedience to the Constitution, to the remotest corners of the globe." In other words, that which now makes the crowning pride of an American citizen, that the States of the Union are spread from the Atlantic to the Pacific, was then held up by a patriotic Federalist as the very extreme of danger. The antidote to this deadly peril, the means of establishing some communication with these "remotest corners of the globe," must be found first of all in internal improvements. At least, under these circumstances of alarm, a highway or two might be held a reasonable proposition, and the new President, in his inaugural address, approached the subject with something of the lingering stateliness of those days:

"The magnificence and splendor of their public works are among the imperishable glories of the ancient republics. The roads

JOHN QUINCY ADAMS.

From the painting by G. P. A. Healy, in the Corcoran Gallery, Washington.

and aqueducts of Rome have been the admiration of all after-ages, and have survived thousands of years, after all her conquests have been swallowed up in despotism, or become the spoil of barbarians. Some diversity of opinion has prevailed with regard to the powers of Congress for legislation upon subjects of this nature. The most respectful deference is due to doubts originating in pure patriotism, and sustained by venerated authority. But nearly twenty years have passed since the construction of the first national road was commenced. The authority for its construction was then unquestioned. To how many thousands of our countrymen has it proved a benefit? To what single individual has it ever proved an injury?"

We must remember that when John Quincy Adams became President the nation had been governed for a quarter of a century under a succession of Democratic administrations, acting more and more on Federalist principles. The tradition of States-rights had steadily receded, and the reality of a strong and expanding nation had taken its place. The very statesmen who had at first put into the most definite shape these States-rights opinions had, by their action, done most to overthrow them, Jefferson above all. By the purchase of Louisiana he had, perhaps unconsciously, done more to build up national feeling than any President before him. Having, by a happy impulse, and in spite of all his own theories, enormously enlarged the joint territory, he had recognized the need of opening and enlightening the new possession; he had set the example of proposing national appropriations for roads, canals, and even education; and had given his sanction (March 24, 1806) to building a national road from Maryland to Ohio, first obtaining the consent of the States through which it was to pass. To continue this policy would, he admitted, require constitutional amendments, but in his closing message he favored just these changes. It was but a step from favoring constitutional amendments for this purpose to doing without them; Jefferson, Madison, Monroe had done the one, John Quincy Adams did the other.

Of course it took the nation by surprise. Nothing astonishes people more than to be taken at their word, and have their own theories energetically put in practice. Others had talked in a general way about internal improvements; under President Monroe there had even been created (April 30, 1824) a national board to plan them; but John Quincy Adams really meant to have them; and his very first message looked formidable to those who supposed that because he had broken with the Federalists he was therefore about to behave like an old-fashioned Democrat. In truth he was more new-fashioned than anybody. This is the way he committed himself in this first message:

"While foreign nations, less blessed with that freedom which is power than ourselves, are advancing with gigantic strides in the career of public improvement, were we to slumber in indolence, or fold up our arms and proclaim to the world that we are palsied by the will of our constituents, would it not be to cast away the bounties of Providence, and doom ourselves to perpetual inferiority? In the course of the year now drawing to its close, we have beheld, under the auspices and at the expense of one State of this Union, a new university unfolding its portals to the sons of science, and holding up the torch of human improvement to eyes that seek the light. We have seen, under the persevering and enlightened enterprise of another State, the waters of our western lakes mingle with those of the ocean. If undertakings like these have been accomplished in the compass of a few years by the authority of single members of our confederation, can we, the representative authorities of the whole Union, fall behind our fellow-servants in the exercise of the trust committed to us for the benefit of our common sovereign, by the accomplishment of works important to the whole, and to which neither the authority nor the resources of any one State can be adequate?"

Nor was this all. It is curious to see that the President's faithful ally, Mr. Rush, Secretary of the Treasury, went far beyond his chief in the tone of his recommendations, and drifted into what would now be promptly labelled as Communism. When we read as an extreme proposition in these days, in the middle of some mildly socialistic manifesto, the suggestion that there should be a national bureau "whereby new fields can be opened, old ones developed, and every labor can be properly directed and located," we fancy it a novelty. But see how utterly Mr. Rush surpassed these moderate proposals in one of his reports as Secretary of the Treasury. He said that it was the duty of government

"to augment the number and variety of occupations for its inhabitants; to hold out to every degree of labor and to every manifestation of skill its appropriate object and inducement;

to organize the whole labor of a country; to entice into the widest ranges its mechanical and intellectual capacities, instead of suffering them to slumber; to call forth, wherever hidden, latent ingenuity, giving to effort activity, and to emulation ardor; to create employment for the greatest amount of numbers by adapting it to the diversified faculties, propensities, and situations of men, so that every particle of ability, every shade of genius, may come into requisition."

Let us now turn to the actual advances made under the guidance of Mr. Adams. Nothing in the history of the globe is so extraordinary in its topographical and moral results as the vast western march of the American people within a hundred years. Let us look, for instance, at the excellent French map of what constituted the northern part of the United States in 1798. The western boundary of visible settlement is the Genesee River of New York. The names on the Hudson are like the names of to-day; all beyond is strange. No railroad, no canal; only a turnpike running to the Genesee, and with no farther track to mark the way through the forest to "Buffaloe," on the far-off lake. Along this turnpike are settlements, "Schenectady," "Canajohary," "Schuyler or Utica," "Fort Stenwick or Rome," "Oneida Cassle," "Onondaga Cassle," "Geneva," and "Canandargue," where the road turns north to Lake Ontario. Forests cover all Western New York, all Northwestern Pennsylvania. Far off in Ohio is a detached region indicated as "the Connecticut Reserve, conceded to the families who had been ruined during the war of Independence"—whence our modern phrase "Western Reserve." The summary of the whole map is that the United States still consisted of the region east of the Alleghanies, with a few outlying settlements, and nothing more.

Now pass over twenty years. In the map prefixed to William Darby's *Tour from New York to Detroit*, in 1818—this Darby being the author of an emigrant's guide, and a member of the New York Historical Society—we find no State west of the Mississippi except Missouri, and scarcely any towns in Indiana or Illinois. Michigan Territory is designated, but across the whole western half of it is the inscription, "This part very imperfectly known." All beyond Lake Michigan and all west of the Mississippi is a nameless waste, except for a few names of rivers and of Indian villages. This marks the progress — and a very considerable progress—of twenty years. Writing from Buffalo (now spelled correctly), Darby says: "The beautiful and highly cultivated lands of the strait of Erie are now a specimen of what in forty years will be the landscape from Erie to Chicaga [*sic*]. It is a very gratifying anticipation to behold in fancy the epoch to come when this augmenting mass of the population will enjoy, in the interior of this vast continent, a choice collection of immense marts where the produce of the banks of innumerable rivers and lakes can be exchanged."

Already, it seems, travellers and mapmakers had got from misspelling "Buffaloe" to misspelling "Chicaga." It was a great deal. The *Edinburgh Review* for that same year (June, 1818), in reviewing Birkbeck's once celebrated *Travels in America*, said:

"Where is this prodigious increase of numbers, this vast extension of dominion, to end? What bounds has nature set to the progress of this mighty nation? Let our jealousy burn as it may, let our intolerance of America be as unreasonably violent as we please, still it is plain that she is a power in spite of us, rapidly rising to supremacy; or, at least, that each year so mightily augments her strength as to overtake, by a most sensible distance, even the most formidable of her competitors."

This was written, it must be remembered, when the whole population of the United States was but little more than nine millions, or about the present population of New York and Pennsylvania taken together.

What were the first channels for this great transfer of population? The great turnpike-road up the Mohawk Valley, in New York; and farther south, the "National Road," which ended at Wheeling, Virginia. Old men, now or recently living—as, for instance, Mr. Sewall Newhouse, the trapper and trap-maker of Oneida—can recall the long lines of broad-wheeled wagons, drawn by ten horses, forty of these teams sometimes coming in close succession; the stages, six of which were sometimes in sight at once; the casualties, the break-downs, the sloughs of despond, the passengers at work with fence rails to pry out the vehicle from a mud hole. These sights, now disappearing on the shores of the Pacific, were then familiar in the heart of what is now the

JOHN C. CALHOUN.
From the painting by De Block, owned by John C. Calhoun, Esq.

East. This was the tide flowing westward; while eastward, on the other hand, there soon began a counter current of flocks and herds sent from the new settlements to supply the older States. As early as 1824 Timothy Flint records meeting a drove of more than a thousand cattle and swine, rough and shaggy as wolves, guided toward the Philadelphia market by a herdsman looking as untamed as themselves, and coming from Ohio—"a name which still sounded in our ears," Flint says, "like the land of savages."

The group so well known in our literature, the emigrant family, the way-side fire, the high-peaked wagon, the exhausted oxen, this picture recedes steadily in space as we come nearer to our own time. In 1788 it set off with the first settlers from Massachusetts to seek Ohio; in 1798 it was just leaving the Hudson to ascend the Mohawk River; in 1815 the hero of *Lawrie Todd* saw it at Rochester, New York; in 1819 Darby met it near Detroit, Michigan; in 1824 Flint saw it in Missouri; in 1831 Alexander depicted it in Tennessee; in 1843 Margaret Fuller Ossoli sketched it beyond Chicago, Illinois; in 1856 I myself saw it in Nebraska and Kansas; in 1864 Clarence King described it in his admirable sketch, *Way-side Pikes*, in California; in 1882 Mrs. Leighton in her charming letters pictures it at Puget Sound; beyond which, as it has reached the Pacific, it can not advance. From this continent the emigrant group, in its original form, has almost vanished; the process of spreading emigration by steam is less picturesque, but more rapid.

The newly published volumes of the United States Census for 1880 give, with an accuracy of detail such as the world never before saw, the panorama of this vast westward march. It is a matter of national pride to see how its ever-changing phases have been caught and photographed in these masterly volumes, in a way such as the countries of the older world have never equalled, though it would seem so much easier to depict their more fixed conditions. The Austrian newspapers complain that no one in that nation knows at this moment, for instance, the centre of Austrian population; while the successive centres for the United States are here exhibited on a chart with a precision as great, and an impressiveness to the imagination as vast, as when astronomers represent for us the successive posi-

tions of a planet. Like the shadow thrown by the hand of some great clock, this inevitable point advances year by year across the continent, sometimes four miles a year, sometimes eight miles, but always advancing. And with this striking summary, the census report gives us a series of successive representations on colored charts, at ten-year intervals, of the gradual expansion and filling in of population over the whole territory of the United States. No romance is so fascinating as the thoughts suggested by these silent sheets, each line and tint representing the unspoken sacrifices and fatigues of thousands of nameless men and women. Let us consider for a moment these successive indications.

In the map for 1790 the whole population is on the eastern slope of the Appalachian range, except a slight spur of emigration reaching westward from Pennsylvania and Virginia, and a detached settlement in Kentucky. The average depth of the strip of civilization, measuring back from the Atlantic westward, is but three hundred and fifty-five miles. In 1800 there is some densening of population within the old lines, and a western movement along the Mohawk in New York State, while the Kentucky oasis of population has spread down into Tennessee. In 1810 all New York, Pennsylvania, and Kentucky are well sprinkled with population, which begins to invade southern Ohio also, while the territory of Orleans has a share; and Michigan, Indiana, Illinois, Missouri, the Mississippi territory—including Mississippi and Alabama—are still almost or quite untouched. In 1820 Ohio, or two-thirds of it, shows signs of civilized occupation; and the settlements around Detroit, which so impressed Darby, have joined those in Ohio; Tennessee is well occupied, as is southern Indiana; while Illinois, Wisconsin, Alabama, have rills of population adjoining the Indian tribes, not yet removed, still retarding Southern settlements. In 1830—Adams's administration being now closed—Indiana is nearly covered with population, Illinois more than half; there is hardly any unsettled land in Ohio, while Michigan is beginning to be occupied. Population has spread up the Missouri to the north of Kansas River; and, farther south, Louisiana, Alabama, and Arkansas begin to show for something. But even in 1830 the centre of population is in Moorefield, western Virginia, not yet moving westward at the rate of more than five miles a year.

This year of 1830 lying beyond the term of John Quincy Adams's administration, I shall here follow the statistics of the great migration no farther. Turn now to his annual message and see how, instead of the doubts or cautious hints of his predecessors, these state papers fairly bristle with suggestions of special improvements which an overflowing Treasury enabled him to secure. In his third

fourteen millions were expended under him for permanent objects, besides five million dollars for pensions; a million and a half for the Indian tribes; thirty millions for the reduction of the public debt; and a surplus of five millions for his successor. Here was patriotic housekeeping indeed, for the vast household of the nation, and yet this administration has very commonly been passed over as belonging to those times of peace that have proverbially but few historians.

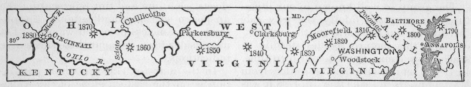

MAP SHOWING THE MOVEMENT OF THE CENTRE OF POPULATION WESTWARD ON THE THIRTY-NINTH PARALLEL.

annual message, for instance, he enumerates reports ready for Congress, and in some cases acted upon, in respect to the continuance of the national road from Cumberland eastward, and to Columbus and St. Louis westward; as to a national road from Washington to Buffalo, and a post-road from Baltimore to Philadelphia; as to a canal from Lake Pontchartrain to the Mississippi; another to be cut across Florida; another to connect Mobile and Pensacola; another to unite the Coosa and Hiwassee rivers in Alabama. There are reports also on Cape Fear; on the Swash in Pamlico Sound; on La Plaisance Bay in Michigan; on the Kennebec and Saugatuck rivers; on the harbors of Edgartown, Hyannis, and Newburyport. What has been already done, he says, in these and similar directions, has cost three or four million dollars annually; but has been done without creating a dollar of taxes or debt; nor has it diminished the payment of previous debts, which have indeed been reduced to the extent of $16,000,000 in three years. But this was only a partial estimate. During the whole administration of John Quincy Adams, according to the *American Annual Register*, more than a million dollars were devoted to the light-house system; half a million to public buildings; two millions to arsenals and armories; three millions to coast fortifications; three millions to the navy; and four millions to internal improvements and scientific surveys. Including smaller items, nearly

Let us return to the actual progress of the great western march. The Ohio River being once reached, the main channel of emigration lay in the water-courses. Steamboats as yet were but beginning their invasion, amid the general dismay and cursing of the population of boatmen that had rapidly established itself along the shore of every river. The early water life of the Ohio and its kindred streams was the very romance of emigration; no monotonous agriculture, no toilsome wood-chopping, could keep back the adventurous boys who found delight in the endless novelty, the alternate energy and repose of a floating existence on those delightful waters. The variety of river craft corresponded to the varied temperaments of the boatmen. There was the great barge with lofty deck requiring twenty-five men to work it up-stream; there was the long keel-boat, carrying from fifteen to thirty tons; there was the Kentucky "broad-horn," compared by the emigrants of that day to a New England pig-sty set afloat, and sometimes built one hundred feet long, and carrying seventy tons; there was the "family-boat," of like structure, and bearing a whole household, with cattle, hogs, horses, and sheep. Other boats were floating tin shops, blacksmiths' shops, whiskey shops, dry-goods shops. A few were propelled by horse-power. Of smaller vessels there were "covered sleds," "ferry flats," and "Alleghany skiffs"; "pirogues" made from two tree trunks, or "dug-outs" consisting of one.   These boats would set out from Pittsburgh for voyages of all lengths, sometimes extending over three thousand miles; and reaching points on the Missouri, Arkansas, and Red rivers.   Boats came to St. Louis from Montreal with but few "portages" or "carries" on the way; and sometimes arrived from Mackinaw, when the streams were high and morasses full, without being carried by hand at all.

The crews were carefully chosen; a "Kentuck," or Kentuckian, was considered the best man at a pole, and a "Kanuck," or French Canadian, at the oar or the "cordelle," the rope used to haul a boat up-stream.   Their talk was of the dangers of the river; of "planters and sawyers," meaning tree trunks imbedded more or less firmly in the river; of "riffles," meaning ripples; and of "shoots," or rapids (French, *chutes*).   It was as necessary to have violins on board as to have whiskey, and all the traditions in song or picture of "the jolly boatmen" date back to that by-gone day.   Between the two sides of the river there was already a jealousy.   Ohio was called "the Yankee State"; and Flint tells us that it was a standing joke among the Ohio boatmen, when asked their cargo, to reply, "Pit-coal indigo, wooden nutmegs, straw baskets, and Yankee notions."   The same authority describes this sort of questioning as being inexhaustible among the river people, and asserts that from one descending boat came this series of answers, all of which proved to be truthful: "Where are you from?" "Redstone." "What's your lading?" "Millstones." "What's your captain's name?" "Whetstone." "Where are you bound?" "To Limestone."

All this panorama of moving life was brought nearly to a close during the younger Adams's administration by the steamboats, though it was transferred for a time to the newly built canals.   Steamboats were therefore looked upon, as Flint tells us, with "detestation" by the inhabitants, though they soon learned to depend upon them, and to make social visits in them to friends a hundred miles away.   In 1812 Fulton's first Western boat, the *Orleans*, went down the Ohio, and in 1816 the *Washington* proved itself able to stem the current in returning. But for a time canals spread more rapidly than steamboats.   Gouverneur Morris had first suggested the Erie Canal in 1777, and

Washington had indeed proposed a system of such waterways in 1774.   But the first actual canal in the United States was that dug around Turner's Falls, in Massachusetts, soon after 1792.   In 1803 DeWitt Clinton again proposed the Erie Canal. It was begun in 1817, and opened July 4, 1825, being cut mainly through a wilderness.   The effect produced on public opinion was absolutely startling.   When men found that the time taken from Albany to Buffalo was reduced one-half, and that the freight on a ton of merchandise was brought down from $100 to $10, and ultimately to $3, similar enterprises sprang into being everywhere.   The most conspicuous of these was the Chesapeake and Ohio Canal, from Georgetown to Pittsburgh, which was surveyed and planned by the national board of internal improvements, created just before Mr. Adams's accession.   On July 4, 1828, the first blow was struck for the excavation by President Adams.   He had a habit of declining invitations to agricultural fairs and all public exhibitions, but was persuaded to make a speech and put the first spade in the ground for this great enterprise.   The soil was for some reason so hard that it would scarcely yield, so the President took off his coat, and tried again and again, at last raising the sod, amid general applause.   It was almost the only time during his arduous life when he paused to do a picturesque or symbolic act before the people.

Thus, by various means, the great wave swept westward.   Massachusetts, Connecticut, and New Jersey filled up Ohio; North Carolina and Virginia populated Kentucky and Tennessee; Canada sent its emigrants into Illinois and Indiana, and all down the Mississippi.   The new settlers, being once launched in the free career of the West, developed by degrees a new type of character.   Everywhere there was a love of the frontier life, of distance, isolation, of "range," as the Kentuckians of that day told it.   There was a charming side to it all.   There was no more fascinating existence anywhere than that of the pioneer hunters in the yet unfelled forests, and the lasting popularity of Cooper's novels proves the permanent spell exercised by this life over the imagination.   No time will ever diminish the picturesqueness of Daniel Boone's career in Kentucky, for instance, amid the exquisite beauty of the forests near Lexington; woods carpeted with turf like an English park, free from underbrush, with stately trees of every variety, and fresh, clear streams everywhere; or beside the salt springs of the Licking Valley, where Simon Kenton saw from twenty to thirty thousand buffaloes congregated at a time. What were the tame adventures of Robin Hood to the occasion when these two pioneer hunters, Boone and Kenton, approached the Licking Valley, each alone, from opposite points, each pausing to reconnoitre before leaving the shelter of the woods, and each recognizing the presence of another human being in the valley? Then began a long series of manœuvres on the part of each to discover who the other was, without self-betrayal; and such was their skill that it took forty-eight hours before each could make up his mind that the other was a white man and a friend, not an Indian and a foe.

But there was to all this picture a reverse side that was less charming. For those who were not content to spend their lives as woodsmen in Kentucky, and preferred to seek Ohio as agriculturists, how much of sacrifice there was! what weary years of cold, poverty, discomfort! This letter, quoted in Perkins's *Fifty Years of Ohio*, as written in 1818 from Marietta, gives a glimpse through the doorway of a thousand cabins:

"Marietta I find a poor, muddy hole; the mud here is more disagreeable than snow in Massachusetts. My advice to all my friends is not to come to this country. There is not one in a hundred but what is discontented; but they can not get back, having spent all their property in getting here. It is the most broken country that I ever saw. Poor, lean pork at twelve cents; salt, four cents; poor, dry fish, twenty cents. The corn is miserable, and we can not get it ground; we have to pound it. Those that have lanterns grate it. Rum, twenty-five cents a gill; sugar, thirty-seven cents a pound; and no molasses! This country has been the ruin of a great many poor people; it has undone a great many poor souls forever."

Meantime, at Washington, there had been a great increase in wealth and social refinement since the earlier days. Mr. Josiah Quincy, in his *Recollections of Washington Society in* 1826, presents for us a polished and delightful community, compared to that which had preceded it. Himself a handsome young Bostonian, with the prestige of a name already noted, he found nothing but sunshine and roses in his path through the metropolis. Names now historic glitter through his pages; he

went to balls under the escort of Mr. and Mrs. Daniel Webster; his first entertainment was at Mrs. William Wirt's, where he met Miss Henry, Patrick Henry's daughter, who played the piano and sang to the harp. The belles of the day smiled upon him; Miss Catherine van Rensselaer, of Albany, and Miss Cora Livingston, the same who in her old age, as Mrs. Barton, sold the great Shakespearean library to the city of Boston. The most conspicuous married belle of that day was known as Mrs. Florida White, so called because her husband represented that region, then new and strange. More eccentric than this *sobriquet* were the genuine names in the household of Mrs. Peter, granddaughter of Mrs. Washington, and the fiercest of Federalists, who had named her daughters America, Columbia, and Britannia—the last by way of defiance, it was said, to Jefferson. With these various charmers Mr. Quincy attended many a ball in Washington, these entertainments then keeping modest hours— from eight to eleven. He saw a sight not then considered so modest—the introduction, in 1826, of the first waltz, danced with enthusiasm by Baron Stackelburg, who whirled through it without removing his huge dragoon spurs, and was applauded at the end for the skill with which he avoided collisions that might have been rather murderous.

The young Bostonian also went to dinner parties; sometimes at the White House, either formal state dinners of forty gentlemen and ladies, or private occasions, less elaborate, where he alone among witnesses found the President "amusing." He gives also an agreeable picture of the home and household manners of Daniel Webster, not yet fallen into those questionable private habits which the French M. Bacourt, sixteen years afterward, too faithfully chronicled. Mr. Quincy also found the Vice-President, John C. Calhoun, a man most agreeable in his own house, while Miss Calhoun had an admirable gift for political discussion. The presence of these eminent men lent a charm even to the muddy streets and scattered houses of the Washington of that day. The two branches of government then met in small, ill-arranged halls, the House of Representatives having huge pillars to intercept sight and sound, with no gallery, but only a platform for visitors, but little higher than the floor. In this body the great Federal party had left scarcely a remnant of itself, Mr. Elisha Potter, of Rhode Island, describing vividly to Mr. Quincy a caucus held when the faithful few had been reduced to eleven, and could only cheer themselves with the thought that the Christian apostles, after the desertion of Judas, could number no more. The Houses of Congress were still rather an arena of debating than for set speeches, as now; and they had their leaders, mostly now fallen into that oblivion which waits so surely on merely political fame. Daniel Webster, to be sure, was the great ornament of the Senate; but McDuffie, of South Carolina, and Storrs, of New York, members of the House, had then a national reputation for eloquence, though they now are but the shadows of names. To these must be added Archer, of Virginia, too generally designated as "Insatiate Archer," from his fatal long-windedness.

For the first time for many years the White House was kept in decent order again; all about it had for years—if we may trust Samuel Breck's testimony—worn the slipshod, careless look of a Virginia plantation. Fence posts fell and lay broken on the ground for months, although they could have been repaired in half an hour, and the grass of the lawns, cut at long intervals, was piled in large stacks before the drawing-room windows. Fifty thousand dollars spent on the interior in Monroe's time had produced only a slovenly splendor, while the fourteen thousand appropriated to Adams produced neatness at least. Manners shared some of the improvement, in respect to order and decorum at least, though something of the profuse Virginia cordiality may have been wanting. It was an intermediate period, when, far more than now, the European forms were being tried, and sometimes found wanting. In Philadelphia, where the social ambition was highest, Mr. William Bingham had entertainments that were held to be the most showy in America. As in England, he had a row of liveried servants, who repeated in loud tone, from one to another, the name of every guest. A slight circumstance put an end to the practice. On the evening of a ball an eminent physician, Dr. Kuhn, drove to the door with his step-daughter, and was asked his name by the lackey. "The doctor and Miss Peggy," was the reply. "The doctor and Miss Peggy,"

was echoed by the man at the door, and hence by successive stages to the drawing-room. "The doctor and Miss Peggy" (Miss Markoe, afterward Mrs. Benjamin Franklin Bache) became the joke of the town; and the practice was soon after changed, carrying with it the humbler attempts at imitation in Washington. Samuel Breck, who tells the story, rejoices that among the other failures in aping foreign manners were "the repeated attempts of our young dandies to introduce the mustache on the upper lip." "And so," he adds, "with the broadcloth gaiters and other foreign costumes. They were neither useful nor ornamental, and would not take with us. So much the better."

The President himself, in the midst of all this, lived a life so simple that the word Spartan hardly describes it. He was now sixty years old. Rising at four or five, even in winter, he often built his own fire, and then worked upon his correspondence and his journal, while the main part of the day was given to public affairs, these being reluctantly interrupted to receive a stream of visitors. In the evening he worked again, sometimes going to bed at eight or nine even in summer. His recreations were few—bathing in the Potomac before sunrise, and taking a walk at the same hour, or a ride later in the day, or sometimes the theatre, such as it was. For social life he had little aptitude, though he went through the forms of it. This is well illustrated by one singular memorandum in his diary: "I went out this evening in search of conversation, an art of which I never had an adequate idea....I never knew how to make, control, or change it. I am by nature a silent animal, and my dear mother's constant lesson in childhood that little children should be seen and not heard confirmed me in what I now think a bad habit."

It is to be observed that the influence of political wire-pulling first began to be seriously felt at this period. We commonly attribute its origin to Jackson, but it really began, as was explained in a previous paper, with Crawford. When, in Monroe's time, this ambitious Secretary of the Treasury pressed the passage of a bill limiting the term of civil officers, he did it because he was a candidate for the Presidency; and all the Treasury officials at once became ardent Crawfordites. As the end of Monroe's administration drew near, there were, it must be remembered, five candidates in the field for the succession —Crawford, Clay, Calhoun, Adams, and Jackson. Calhoun withdrew, was nominated for Vice-President, and was triumphantly elected; but for President there was no choice. Jackson had 99 electoral votes, Adams 84, Crawford 41, Clay 37. The choice was thrown into the House of Representatives, and took place February 9, 1825. Two distinguished men were tellers, Daniel Webster and John Randolph. They reported that Mr. Adams had 13 votes, General Jackson 7, Mr. Crawford 4; and that Mr. Adams was therefore elected. The explanation was that Mr. Clay's forces had been transferred to Mr. Adams, and when, after his inauguration, Mr. Clay was made Secretary of State, the cry of "unholy coalition" was overwhelming. It was, John Randolph said, "a combination hitherto unheard of, of the Puritan and the Blackleg—of Blifil and Black George"—these being two characters in Fielding's *Tom Jones*. This led to a duel between Clay and Randolph, in which neither party fell. But the charge remained. Jackson and Calhoun believed it during their whole lives, though the publication of John Adams's *Diaries* has made it clear that there was no real foundation for it.

The method thus introduced by Crawford was one brought to bear systematically against John Quincy Adams during all the latter part of his administration. Having the reluctance of a high-minded statesman to win support by using patronage for it, he unluckily had not that better quality which enables a warm-hearted man to secure loyal aid without raising a finger. We know by the unerring evidence of his own diary that he saw clearly how his own rectitude was injuring him, yet never thought of swerving from his course. One by one the men dependent on him went over, beneath his eyes, to the camp of his rival; and yet so long as each man was a good officer he was left untouched. Mr. Adams says in his diary (under date of May 13, 1825), when describing his own entrance on office: "Of the custom-house officers throughout the Union two-thirds were probably opposed to my election. They were all now in my power, and I had been urged very earnestly from various quarters to sweep away my opponents, and provide with their places for my friends." This was what he absolutely refused to do. In these days of civil service reform we go back with pleasure to his example; but the general verdict of the period was that this course may have been very heroic, but it was not war.

It must always be remembered, moreover, in our effort to understand the excitement of politics fifty years ago, that the Presidential candidates were then nominated by Congressional caucus. The effect was to concentrate in one spot the excitement and the intrigues that must now be distributed through the nation. The result was almost wholly evil. "It places the President," John Quincy Adams wrote just before his election, "in a state of subserviency to the members of the Legislature, which . . . . leads to a thousand corrupt cabals between the members of Congress and heads of departments. . . . The only possible chance for a head of a department to attain the Presidency is by ingratiating himself with the members of Congress." The result was that these Congressmen practically selected the President. For political purposes, Washington was the focus of all that political agitation now distributed over various cities; it was New York, Cincinnati, Chicago, all in one. It was in a centre of politics like this, not in the present more metropolitan Washington, that John Quincy Adams stood impassive—the object of malice, of jealousy, of envy, of respect, and perhaps sometimes even of love.

He was that most unfortunate personage, an accidental President—one chosen not by a majority or even a plurality of popular or electoral votes, but only by the mechanism reluctantly employed in case these votes yield no choice. The popular feeling of the nation, by a plurality at least, had demanded the military favorite, Jackson; and through the four years of Adams's respectable but rather colorless administration it still persisted in this demand. The grave, undemonstrative President, not rewarding his friends, if indeed he had friends, had little chance against the popular favorite; his faults hindered him; his very virtues hindered him; and though he was not, like his father, defeated squarely on a clear political issue, he was defeated still. With him we leave behind the trained statesmen Presidents of the early period, and pass to the untrained, untamed, vigorous personality of Andrew Jackson.

CHAPTER XVI.

BY THE RIVER.

THE next morning she was unusually demure, and yet merry withal. In her own chamber, as she chose out a petticoat of pale blue taffeta, and laid on the bed her girdle of buff-colored leather, and proceeded to array herself in these and other braveries, it was to the usual accompaniment of thoughtless and quite inconsequent ballad-singing. At one moment it was "Green-sleeves was all my joy," and again "Fair, fair, and twice so fair," or perhaps—

> "An ambling nag, and a-down, a-down,
> We have borne her away to Dargison."

But when she came to take forth from the cupboard of boxes the portion of the play she had locked up there the night before, and when she carefully placed that in a satchel of dark blue velvet that she had attached to the girdle, she was silent; and when she went down-stairs and encountered her mother, there was a kind of anxious innocence on her face. The good parson (she explained) had remained so late on the previous afternoon, and there were so many things about the house she had to attend to, that she had been unable to get out into the fields, as her father had bade her, to bring him home some wild flowers. Besides, as every one knew, large dogs got weak in the hind-legs if they were kept chained up too continuously; and it was absolutely necessary she should take Don Roderigo out for a run with her through the meadows, if her father would permit.

"There be plenty of flowers in the garden, surely," her mother said, who was busy with some leather hangings, and wanted help.

"But he would liefer have some of the little wildlings, good mother," said Judith. "That I know right well; for he is pleased to see them lying on the table before him; and sometimes, too, he puts the names of them in his writing."

"How know you that?" was the immediate and sharp question.

"As I have heard, good mother," Judith said, with calm equanimity.

And then she went to the small mirror to see that her gray velvet cap and starched ruff were all right.

"What can your father want with wild flowers if he is to remain the whole day at Warwick?" her mother said.

"Is my father going to Warwick?" she asked, quickly.

"If he be not already set forth."

She glanced at the window; there was neither horse nor serving-man waiting there. And then she hastily went out and through the back yard into the garden; and there, sure enough, was her father, ready booted for the road, and giving a few parting directions to his bailiff.

"Well, wench," he said, when he had finished with the man, "what would you?"

She had taken from her purse all the money she could find there.

"Good father," said she, "will you do this errand for me at Warwick?"

"More vanities?" said he. "I wonder you have no commissioner to dispatch to Spain and Flanders. What is't, then? —a muff of satin—a gimmal ring—"

"No, no, not so, father; I would have you buy for me a clasp-knife—as good a one as the money will get; and the cutler must engrave on the blade, or on the handle, I care not which, a message—an inscription, as it were; 'tis but three words —For Judith's Sweetheart. Could you remember that, good father? Is't too much of a trouble?"

"How now?" said he. "For whom do you wish me to bring you such a token?"

"Nay, sir," said she, demurely, "would you have me name names? The gift of a sweetheart to a sweetheart is a secret thing."

"You are a mad wench," said he (though doubtless he guessed for whom the knife was intended), and he called to Matthew gardener to go round and see if Master Shawe were not yet ready. "But now I bethink me, child, I have a message for thee. Good Master Walter spoke to me yesternight about what much concerns him—and you."

Instantly all her gay self-confidence vanished; she became confused, anxious, timid; and she regarded him as if she feared what his look or manner might convey.

"Yes, sir," she said, in rather a low voice.

"Well, you know what the good man wishes," her father said, "and he speaks fairly, and reasoneth well. Your mother, too, would be right well pleased."

"And you, sir?" she said, rather faintly.

"I?" said he. "Nay, 'tis scarce a matter that I can say ought in. 'Tis for yourself to decide, wench; but were you inclined to favor the young parson, I should be well pleased enough—indeed 'tis so—a good man and honest, as I take him to be, of fair attainment, and I know of none that bear him ill-will, or have ought to say against him. Nay, if your heart be set that way, wench, I see no harm; you are getting on in years to be still in the unmarried state; and, as he himself says, there would be security in seeing you settled in a home of your own, and your future no longer open and undecided. Nay, nay, I see no harm. He reasons well."

"But, father, know you why he would have me become his wife?" Judith said, with a wild feeling overcoming her that she was drowning and must needs throw out her hands for help. "'Tis for no matter of affection that I can make out—or that he might not as well choose any other in the town; but 'tis that I should help him in his work, and—and labor in the vineyard, as he saith. In truth I am all unfit for such a task—there be many another far better fitted than I; my mother must know that right well. There is little that I would not do to please her; but surely we might all of us have just as much of the good man's company without this further bond. But what say you, father? What is your wish?" she added, humbly. "Perchance I could bring my mind to it if all were anxious that it should be so."

"Why, I have told thee, wench, thou must choose for thyself. 'Twould please your mother right well, as I say; and as for the duties of a parson's wife—nay, nay, they are none so difficult. Have no fears on that score, good lass; I dare be sworn you are as honest and well-minded as most, though perchance you make less profession of it." (The gratitude that sprang to her eyes, and shone there, in spite of her downcast face!) "Nor must you think the good parson has but that end in view; 'tis not in keeping with his calling that he should talk the language

of romances. Consider it, wench—consider. And there is more for you to think of. Even if Master Blaise be no vehement lover, as some of the young rattlepates might be, that is but a temporary thing; 'tis the long years of life that weigh for the most; and all through these you would be in an honorable station, well thought of, and respected. Nay, there be many, I can tell thee, lass, that might look askance now at the player's daughter, who would be right glad to welcome the parson's wife."

"What say you, father?" said she—and she was so startled that the blood forsook her lips for a moment. "That—that there be those—who scorn the player's daughter—and would favor the parson's wife?" And then she instantly added: "I pray you, sir, did not you say that I was to decide for myself?"

"Truly, child, truly," said he, somewhat wondering at her manner, for her face had grown quite pale.

"Then I have decided, father."

"And how? What answer will you have for Master Walter?"

She spoke slowly now, and with a distinctness that was almost harsh.

"This, so please you, sir—that the player's daughter shall not, and shall never, become the parson's wife, God helping her!"

"Why, how now? what a coil is this!" he exclaimed. "Good lass, 'twas not the parson that said ought of the kind. Lay not that to his charge, in fair honesty."

"I have decided," she said, proudly and coldly. "Father, the horses are brought round—I can hear them. You will not forget the knife, and the message on the blade?"

He looked at her, and laughed, but in a kindly way; and he took her by the shoulder.

"Nay, now, wench, thou shalt not throw over the good man for a matter that was none of his bringing forward. And why should you wish to have less than the respect of all your neighbors, all and sundry, whatever be their views? In good sooth I meant to speak for the parson, and not to harm him; and when I have more time I must undo the ill that I have done him. So soften your heart, you proud one, and be thankful for the honor he would do you; and think over it; and be civil and grateful."

"Nay, I will be civil enough to the

good minister," said she, with a return to her ordinary placid humor, "if he speak no more of making me his wife."

"He will win you yet, for as stubborn as you are," her father said, with a smile. "He hath a rare gift of reason; do not say nay too soon, wench, lest you have to recall your words. Fare you well, lass, fare you well!"

"And forget not the knife, good father. 'With Judith's Love,' or 'For Judith's Sweetheart,' or what you will." And then she added, daringly: "'Tis for the young prince Mamillius, if you must know, good sir."

He was just going away; but this caused him to stop for a second; and he glanced at her with a curious kind of suspicion. But her eyes had become quite inscrutable. Whatever of dark mischief was within them was not to be made out but by further questioning, and for that he had now no time. So she was left alone, mistress of the field, and rather inclined to laugh at her own temerity; until it occurred to her that now she could go leisurely forth for her stroll along the banks of the Avon, taking the great dog with her.

Indeed, her anger was always short-lived. Or perhaps it was the feeling that this danger was got rid of—that the decision was taken, and the parson finally and altogether left behind her—that now raised her spirits. At all events, as she went along the thoroughfare, and cheerfully greeted those that met her, the neighbors said 'twas little wonder that Master William Shakespeare's second daughter put off the choosing of a mate for herself, for that she seemed to grow younger and more winsome every day. And she knew all the children by name, and had a word for them—scolding or merry, as the case might be—when that she passed them by; and what with the clear sunlight of the morning, and the fresher atmosphere as she got out of the town, it seemed to herself as if all the air were filled with music.

"Then sigh not so, but let them go,
And be you blithe and bonny,"

she said or sung to herself; and she had not a trace of ill-will in her mind against the parson (although she did not fail to recollect that she was a player's daughter); and she was admonishing the Don to take good care of her, for that phantom conspirators and such like evil creatures might be about. And so she got down to the river-side; but she did not cross; she kept along by the path that followed the windings of the stream, between the wide meadows and the luxurious vegetation that overhung the current.

This English-looking landscape was at its fairest on this fair morning, for some heavy rain in the night had washed the atmosphere clear; everything seemed sharp and luminous; and the rows of trees along the summits of the distant and low-lying hills were almost black against the white and blue sky. Nearer her all the foliage of the wide-branching elms was stirring and rustling before a soft westerly breeze; the flooded river was of a tawny brown; while its banks were a wilderness of wild flowers between the stems of the stunted willows — straggling rose-bushes of white and red, tall masses of goose-grass all powdered over with cream-white blossom, a patch of fragrant meadow-sweet here and there, or an occasional blood-red poppy burning among the dark dull greens. And as for companions? Well, she caught a glimpse of a brood of ducks sidling along by the reeds, and tried to follow them, but the bushes shut them out from her sight. A mare and her foal, standing under the cool shadow of the trees, gazed blankly at her as she passed. Further off there were some shorn sheep in the meadows; but she could see no shepherd. The harsh note of the corn-crake sounded somewhere in the long grass; and the bees were busy; and now and again a blue-backed swallow would swoop by her and over the stream; while all around there was a smell of clover sweetening the westerly wind. At this moment, she convinced herself, she bore no ill-will at all against the good parson: only that she had it in her mind that she would be well content to remain a player's daughter. Her condition, she imagined, was one that she did not desire to have bettered. Why, the air that touched her cheek was like velvet; and there could be nothing in the world fairer than the pink and white roses bestarring the bushes there; and the very pulse of her blood seemed to beat to an unheard and rhythmical and subtle tune. What was it her father had said? "I dare be sworn you are as honest and well-minded as most, though perchance you make less profession of it." She laughed to herself, with a kind of pride. And she was so well content that she wished she had little

Willie Hart here, that she might put her hand on his shoulder and pet him, and convey to him some little of that satisfaction that reigned within her own bosom. No matter; he should have the clasp-knife —"*With Judith's Love*"; and right proud he would be of that, she made sure. And so she went idly on her way, sometimes with,

"*Fair, fair, and twice so fair,*
And fair as any may be,"

coming uncalled-for into her head; and always with an eye to the various wild flowers, to see what kind of a nosegay she would be able to gather on her homeward walk.

But by-and-by her glances began to go further afield. Master Leofric Hope, in his brief references to his own habits and condition at the farm, had incidentally remarked that of all his walks abroad he preferred the following of the path by the river-side; for there he was most secure from observation. Nay, he said that sometimes, after continued solitude, a longing possessed him to see a town—to see a populated place filled with a fair number of his fellow-creatures—and that he would come within sight of Stratford itself and have a look at the church, and the church spire, and the thin blue smoke rising over the houses. That, he said, was safer for him than coming over such an exposed thoroughfare as Bardon Hill; and then again, when he was of a mind to read— for this time he had brought one or two books with him—he could find many a sheltered nook by the side of the stream, where even a passer-by would not suspect his presence. Nor could Judith, on this fresh, warm, breezy morning, conceal from herself the true object of her coming forth. If she had tried to deceive herself, the contents of the blue velvet satchel would have borne crushing testimony against her. In truth she was now looking with some eagerness to find whether, on such a pleasant morning, it was possible that he could have remained within-doors, and with the very distinct belief that sooner or later she would encounter him.

Nor was she mistaken, though the manner of the meeting was unexpected. The mastiff happened to have gone on a yard or two in front of her, and she was paying but little attention to the beast, when all of a sudden it stopped, became rigid, and uttered a low growl. She sprang forward and seized it by the collar. At the same instant she caught sight of some one down by the water's edge, where, but for this occurrence, he would doubtless have escaped observation. It was Leofric Hope, without a doubt; for now he was clambering up through the bushes, and she saw that he had a small book in his hand.

"My good fortune pursues me, fair Mistress Judith," said he (but with a watchful eye on the dog), "that I should so soon again have an opportunity of meeting with you. But perchance your protector is jealous? He likes not strangers?"

"A lamb, sir—a very lamb!" Judith said, and she patted the dog and coaxed him, and got him into a more friendly— or at least neutral and watchful—frame of mind.

"I marvel not you have come forth on such a morning," said he, regarding the fresh color in her face. "'Tis a rare morning; and 'tis a rare chance for one that is a prisoner, as it were, that his dungeon is not four walls, but the wide spaces of Warwickshire. Will you go further? May I attend you?"

"Nay, sir," said she, "I but came forth to look at the country, and see what blossoms I could carry back to my father; I will go as far as the stile there, and rest a few minutes, and return."

"'Tis like your kindness, sweet lady, to vouchsafe me a moment's conversation; a book is but a dull companion," said he, as they walked along to the stile that formed part of a boundary hedge. And when they reached it she seated herself on the wooden bar with much content, and the mastiff lay down, stretching out his paws, while the young gentleman stood idly—but not carelessly—by. He seemed more than ever anxious to interest his fair neighbor, and so to beguile her into remaining.

"A dull companion," he repeated, "it is. One would rather hear the sound of one's voice occasionally. When I came along here this morning I should have been right glad even to have had a she shepherd say 'Good-morrow' to me—"

"A what, good sir?" she asked.

He laughed.

"Nay, 'tis a book the wits in London have much merriment over just now—a guide-book for the use of foreigners coming to this country—and there be plenty of them at present, in the train of the ambassadors. Marry, the good man's English is none of the best. '*For to ask the Way*' is a chapter of the book; and the one traveller saith to the other, '*Ask of that she shepherd*'—in truth the phrase hath been caught up by the town. But the traveller is of a pleasant and courteous turn; when that he would go to bed, he saith to the chamber-maid: 'Draw the curtains, and pin them with a pin. My she friend, kiss me once, and I shall sleep the better. I thank you, fair maiden.' Well, their English may be none of the best, but they have a royal way with them, some of those foreigners that come to our court. When the Constable of Castile was at the great banquet at Whitehall— doubtless you heard of it, sweet Mistress Judith?—he rose and drank the health of the Queen from a cup of agate of extraordinary value, all set with diamonds and rubies, and when the King had drank from the same cup the Constable called a servant, and desired that the cup should be placed on his Majesty's buffet, to remain there. Was't not a royal gift? And so likewise he drank the health of the King from a beautiful dragon-shaped cup of crystal all garnished with gold; but he drank from the cover only, for the Queen, standing up, drank the pledge from the cup itself; and then he would have that in turn transferred to her buffet, as he had given the other one to the King."

"My father," said she, with much complacent good-nature—for she had got into the way of talking to this young gentleman with a marvellous absence of restraint or country shyness, "hath a tankard of great age and value, and on the silver top of it is a tribute engraved from many of his friends—truly I would that you could come and see it, good sir—and— and—my father, too, he would make you welcome, I doubt not. And what book is it," she continued, with a smile, "that you have for companion, seeing that there be no she shepherd for you to converse withal?"

"'Tis but a dull affair," said he, scarce looking at it, for Judith's eyes were more attractive reading. "And yet if the book itself be dull, there is that within its boards that is less so. Perchance you have not heard of one Master Browne, a young Devonshire gentleman, that hath but late come to London, and that only for a space, as I reckon?"

"No, sir," she said, hesitatingly.

"The young man hath made some stir with his poems," he continued, "though there be none of them in the booksellers' hands as yet. And as it hath been my good fortune to see one or two of them— marry, I am no judge, but I would call them excellent, and of much modesty and grace—I took occasion to pencil down a few of the lines inside the cover of this little book. May I read them to you, Mistress Judith?"

"If it please you, good sir."

He opened the book, and she saw that there were some lines pencilled on the gray binding; but they must have been familiar to him, for he scarce took his eyes from Judith's face as he repeated them.

"They are a description," said he, "of one that must have been fair indeed:

"'*Her cheeks, the wonder of what eye beheld,*
Begot betwixt a lily and a rose,
In gentle rising plains divinely swelled,
Where all the graces and the loves repose.
Nature in this piece all her works excelled,
Yet showed herself imperfect in the close,
For she forgot (when she so fair did raise her)
To give the world a wit might duly praise her.

"'*When that she spoke, as at a voice from heaven,*
On her sweet words all ears and hearts attended;
When that she sung, they thought the planets seven
By her sweet voice might well their tunes have mended;
When she did sigh, all were of joy bereaven;
And when she smiled, heaven had them all befriended:
If that her voice, sighs, smiles, so many thrilled,
Oh, had she kissed, how many had she killed!'"

"'Tis a description of a lady of the court?" Judith asked, timidly.

"No, by heavens," he said, with warmth; "the bonniest of our English roses are they that grow in the country air!"—and his glance of admiration was so open and undisguised, and the application of his words so obvious, that her eyes fell, and in spite of herself the color mounted to her cheeks. In her embarrassment she sought safety in the blue velvet satchel. She had contemplated some other way of introducing this latest writing of her father's; but now that had all fled from her brain. She knew that the town gentlemen were given to flattery; but then she was not accustomed to it. And she could not but swiftly surmise that he had written down these lines with the especial object of addressing them to her when he should have the chance.

"Good sir," said she, endeavoring to hide this brief embarrassment by assuming a merry air, "a fair exchange, they say, is no robbery. Methinks you will find something here that will outweigh good Master Browne's verses—in bulk, if not in merit."

He gazed in astonishment at the parcel of sheets she handed to him, and he but glanced at the first page when he exclaimed,

"Why, I have heard naught of this before."

"Nay, sir," said she, with a calm smile, "the infant is but young — but a few weeks, as I take it; it hath had but little chance of making a noise in the world as yet. Will you say what you think of it?"

But now he was busy reading. Then by-and-by she recollected something of the manner in which she had meant to introduce the play.

"You see, sir, my father hath many affairs on his hands; 'tis not all his time he can give to such things. And yet I have heard that they be well spoken of in London—if not by the wits, perchance, or by the court ladies, at least by the common people and the 'prentices. We in these parts have but little skill of learning; but—but methinks 'tis a pretty story—is it not, good sir?—and perchance as interesting as a speech from a goddess among the clouds?"

"In truth it is a rare invention," said he, but absently, for his whole and rapt attention was fixed on the sheets.

She, seeing him so absorbed, did not interfere further. She sat still and content —perhaps with a certain sedate triumph in her eyes. She listened to the rustling of the elms overhead, and watched the white clouds slowly crossing the blue, and the tawny-hued river lazily and noiselessly stealing by below the bushes. The corn-crake was silent now—there was not even that interruption; and when the bell in the church tower began to toll, it was so soft and faint and distant that she thought it most likely he would not even hear it. And at what point was he now? At the story of how the sweet Miranda came to grow up in exile? Or listening to Ariel's song? Or watching the prince approach this new wonder of the magic island? Her eyes were full of triumph. "Ben Jonson!" she had said.

But suddenly he closed the sheets together.

"It were unmannerly so to keep you waiting," said he.

"Nay, heed not that, good sir," she said, instantly. "I pray you go on with the reading. How like you it? 'Tis a pretty story, methinks; but my father hath been so busy of late—what with acres, and tithes, and sheep, and malt, and the like —that perchance he hath not given all his mind to it."

"It is not for one such as I, fair Mistress Judith," said he, with much modesty, "to play the critic when it is your father's writing that comes forward. Beshrew me, there be plenty of that trade in London, and chiefly the feeble folk that he hath driven from our stage. No, sweet lady; rather consider me one of those that crowd to see each new piece of his, and are right thankful for aught he pleaseth to give us."

"Is that so?" said she; and she regarded him with much favor, which he was not slow to perceive.

"Why," said he, boldly, "what needs your father to heed if some worshipful Master Scoloker be of opinion that the play of the Prince Hamlet belongeth to the vulgar sort, and that the prince was but moon-sick; or that some one like Master Greene—God rest his soul, wherever it be!—should call him an upstart crow, and a Johannes factotum, and the like? 'Tis what the people of England think that is of import; and right sure am I what they would say—that there is no greater writer than your father now living in the land."

"Ah, think you so?" she said, quickly, and her face grew radiant, as it were, and her eyes were filled with gratitude.

"This Master Greene," he continued, "was ever gibing at the players, as I have heard, and bidding them be more humble, for that their labor was but mechanical, and them attracting notice through wearing borrowed plumes. Nay, he would have it that your father was no more than that—poor man, he lived but a sorry life, and 'twere ill done to cherish anger against him; but I remember to have seen the apology that he that published the book made thereafter to your father—in good truth it was fitting and right that it should be printed and given to the world; and though I forget the terms of it, 'twas in fair praise of Master William Shakespeare's gentle demeanor, and his uprightness of conduct, and the grace of his wit."

"Could you get that for me, good sir?" said she, eagerly. "Is't possible that I could get it?"

And then she stopped in some embarrassment, for she remembered that it was not becoming she should ask this stranger for a gift. "Nay, sir, 'twould be of little use to me, that have no skill of reading."

"But I pray you, sweet Mistress Judith, to permit me to bring you the book; 'twill be something, at least, for you to keep and show to your friends—"

"If I might show it to Prudence Shawe, I could return it to you, good sir," said she. And then she added, "Not that she—no, nor any one in Stratford town—would need any such testimony to my father's qualities, that are known to all."

"At least they seem to have won him the love and loyalty of his daughter," said he, gallantly; "and they know most about a man who live nearest him. Nay, but I will beg you to accept the book from me when I can with safety get to London again; 'twill be a charge I am not likely to forget. And in return, fair Mistress Judith, I would take of you another favor, and a greater."

"In what manner, gentle sir?"

"I have but glanced over this writing, for fear of detaining you, and but half know the value of it," said he. "I pray you let me have it with me to my lodging for an hour or two, that I may do it justice. When one hath such a chance come to him, 'tis not to be lightly treated; and I would give time and quiet to the making out the beauties of your father's latest work."

She was at first somewhat startled by this proposal, and almost involuntarily was for putting forth her hand to receive the sheets again into safe-keeping; but then she asked herself what harm there could be in acceding to his request. She was eagerly anxious that he should understand how her father—even amidst those multifarious occupations that were entailed on him by his prominent position in the town—could, when he chose, sit down and write a tale far exceeding in beauty and interest any of the mummeries that the court people seemed to talk about. Why should not he have a few hours' time to study this fragment withal? Her father was gone to Warwick for the day. Nay, more, she had taken so small a portion of what had been cast aside that she knew the absence of it would not be noticed, however long it might be kept. And then this young gentleman, who was so civil and courteous, and who spoke so

well of her father, was alone, and to be pitied for that he had so few means of beguiling the tedium of his hiding.

"In the afternoon," said he, seeing that she hesitated, "I could with safety leave it at your grandmother's cottage, and then, perchance, you might send some one for it. Nay, believe me, sweet Mistress Judith, I know the value of that I ask; but I would fain do justice to such a treasure."

"You would not fail me, sir, in leaving it at the cottage?" said she.

"You do me wrong, Mistress Judith, to doubt—in good sooth you do. If you can find a trusty messenger—"

"Nay, but I will come for it myself, good sir, and explain to my grandmother the nature of the thing, lest she suspect me of meddling with darker plots. Let it be so, then, good sir, for now I must get me back to the town. I pray you forget not to leave the package; and so—farewell!"

"But my thanks to you, dear lady—"

"Nay, sir," said she, with a bright look of her eyes, "bethink you you have not yet fairly made out the matter. Tarry till you have seen whether these sheets be worth the trouble—whether they remind you in aught of the work of your friend Master Jonson—and then your thanks will be welcome. Give ye good-day, gentle sir."

There was no thought in her mind that she had done anything imprudent in trusting him with this portion of the play for the matter of an hour or two; it was but a small equivalent, she recollected, for his promise to bring her from London the retractation or apology of one of those who had railed at her father, or abetted in that, and found himself constrained by his conscience to make amends. And now it occurred to her that it would look ill if, having come out to gather some wild flowers for the little table in the summer-house, she returned with empty hands; so, as she proceeded to walk leisurely along the winding path leading back to the town, she kept picking here and there such blossoms as came within her reach. If the nosegay promised to be somewhat large and straggling, at least it would be sweet-scented, and she felt pretty sure that her father would be well content with it. At first she was silent, however; her wonted singing was abandoned; perchance she was trying to recall something of the lines that Master Leofric Hope had repeated to her with so marked an emphasis.

"And what said he of our English roses?" she asked herself, with some faint color coming into her face at the mere thought of it.

But then she forcibly dismissed these recollections, feeling that that was due to her own modesty, and busied herself with her blossoms and sprays; and presently, as she set out in good earnest for the town, she strove to convince herself that there was nothing more serious in her brain than the tune of "Green-sleeves":

> "Green-sleeves, now farewell, adieu;
>   God I pray to prosper thee;
> For I am still thy lover true—
>   Come once again and love me!"

CHAPTER XVII.

WILD WORDS.

HER light-heartedness did not last long. In the wide clear landscape a human figure suddenly appeared, and the briefest turn of her head showed her that Tom Quiney was rapidly coming toward her across the fields. For a second her heart stood still. Had he been riding home from Ludington? Or from Bidford? Was it possible that he had come over Bardon Hill, and from that height espied the two down by the river? She could not even tell whether that was possible, or what he had done with his horse, or why he had not interfered sooner, if he was bent on interfering. But she had an alarmed impression that this rapid approach of his boded trouble, and she had not long to wait before that fear was confirmed.

"Judith, who is that man?" he demanded, with a fury that was but half held in.

She turned and faced him.

"I knew not," she said, coldly and slowly, "that we were on a speaking platform."

"'Tis no time to bandy words," said he; and his face was pale, for he was evidently striving to control the passion with which his whole figure seemed to quiver from head to heel. "Who is that man? I ask. Who is he, that you come here to seek him, and alone?"

"I know not by what right you put such questions to me," she said; but she was somewhat frightened.

"By what right? And you have no regard, then, for your good name?"

There was a flash in her eyes. She had been afraid: she was no longer afraid.

"My good name?" she repeated. "I thank God 'tis in none of your keeping!"

In his madness he caught her by the wrist.

"You shall tell me—"

"Unhand me, sir!" she exclaimed; and she threw off his grasp, while her cheeks burned with humiliation.

"Nay, I quarrel not with women," said he. "I crave your pardon. But, by God, I will get to know that man's name and purpose here if I rive it from his body!"

So he strode off in the direction that Leofric Hope had taken; and for a moment she stood quite terror-stricken and helpless, scarcely daring to think of what might happen. A murder on this fair morning? This young fellow, that was quite beside himself in his passion of jealous anger, was famed throughout the length and breadth of Warwickshire for his wrestling prowess. And the other— would he brook high words? These things flashed across her mind in one bewildering instant; and in her alarm she forgot all about her pride. She called to him,

"I pray you—stay!"

He turned and regarded her.

"Stay," said she, with her face afire. "I—I will tell you what I know of him— if you will have it so."

He approached her with seeming reluctance, and with anger and suspicion in his lowering look. He was silent, too.

"Indeed, there is no harm," said she (and still with her face showing her mortification that she was thus forced to defend herself). "'Tis a young gentleman that is in some trouble—his lodging near Bidford is also a hiding, as it were—and— and I know but little of him beyond his name, and that he is familiar with many of my father's friends in London."

"And how comes it that you seek him out here alone?" said he. "That is a becoming and maidenly thing!"

"I promised you I would tell you what I know of the young gentleman," said she, with scornful lips. "I did not promise to stand still and suffer your insolence."

"Insolence!" he exclaimed, as if her audacity bewildered him.

"How know you that I sought him out!" she said, indignantly. "May not one walk forth of a summer morning without being followed by suspicious eyes

—I warrant me, eyes that are only too glad to suspect! To think evil is an easy thing, it seems, with many: I wonder, sir, you are not ashamed."

"You brave it out well," said he, sullenly; but it was evident that her courage had impressed him, if it still left him angered and suspicious.

And then he asked:

"How comes it that none of your friends or your family know ought of this stranger?"

"I marvel you should speak of my family," she retorted. "I had thought you were inclined to remain in ignorance of them of late. But had you asked of Prudence Shawe she might have told you something of this young gentleman; or had you thought fit to call in at my grandmother's cottage, you might perchance have found him seated there, and a welcome guest at her board. Marry, 'tis easier far to keep aloof and to think evil, as one may see."

And then she added:

"Well, sir, are you satisfied? May I go home without farther threats?"

"I threatened you not, Judith," said he, rather more humbly. "I would have my threats kept for those that would harm you."

"I know of none such," she said, distinctly. "And as for this young gentleman—that is in misfortune—such as might happen to any one—and not only in hiding, but having intrusted his secret to one or two of us that pity him and see no harm in him—I say it were a cruel and unmanly thing to spy out his concealment, or to spread the rumor of his being in the neighborhood."

"Nay, you need not fear that of me, Judith," said he. "Man to man is my way, when there is occasion. But can you marvel if I would have you for your own sake avoid any further meetings with this stranger? If he be in hiding, let him remain there, in God's name; I for one will set no beagles to hunt him out. But as for you, I would have you meddle with no such dangerous traps."

"Good sir," said she, "I have my conduct in my own keeping, and can answer to those that have the guardianship of me."

He did not reply to this rebuke. He said:

"May I walk back to the town with you, Judith?"

"You forget," she said, coldly, "that if we were seen together the gossips might say I had come out hither to seek you, and alone."

But he paid no heed to this taunt.

"I care not," said he, with an affectation of indifference, "what the gossips in Stratford have to talk over. Stratford and I are soon to part."

"What say you?" said she, quickly—and they were walking on together now, the Don leisurely following at their heels.

"Nay, 'tis nothing," said he, carelessly; "there are wider lands beyond the seas, where a man can fight for his own and hold it."

"And you?" she said. "You have it in your mind to leave the country?"

"Marry, that have I!" said he, gayly. "My good friend Daniel Hutt hath gotten together a rare regiment, and I doubt not I shall be one of the captains of them ere many years be over."

Her eyes were downcast, and he could not see what impression this piece of news had made upon her—if, indeed, he cared to look. They walked for some time in silence.

"It is no light matter," said she at length, and in rather a low voice, "to leave one's native land."

"As for that," said he, "the land will soon be not worth the living in. Why, in former times, men spoke of the merry world of England. A merry world?—I trow the canting rogues of preachers have left but little merriment in it; and now they would seek to have all in their power, and to flood the land with their whining and psalm-singing, till we shall have no England left us, but only a vast conventicle. Think you that your father hath any sympathy with these? I tell you no; I take it he is an Englishman, and not a conventicle-man. 'Tis no longer the England of our forefathers when men may neither hawk nor hunt, and women are doomed to perdition for worshipping the false idol starch, and the very children be called in from their games of a Sunday afternoon. God-a-mercy, I have had enough of Brother Patience-in-suffering, and his dominion of grace!"

This seemed to Judith a strange reason for his going away, for he had never professed any strong bias one way or the other in these religious dissensions; his chief concern, like that of most of the young men in Stratford, lying rather in the direction of butt-shooting, or wrestling, or having a romp with some of the wenches to the tune of "Packington's Pound."

"Nay, as I hear," said he, "there be some of them in such discontent with the King and the Parliament that they even talk of transplanting themselves beyond seas, like those that went to Holland: 'twere a goodly riddance if the whole gang of the sour-faced hypocrites went, and left to us our own England. And a fair beginning for the new country across the Atlantic—half of them these Puritanical rogues, with their fastings and preachments; and the other half the constable's brats and broken men that such as Hutt are drafting out: a right good beginning, if they but keep from seizing each other by the throat in the end! No matter: we should have our England purged of the double scum!"

"But," said Judith, timidly, "methought you said you were going out with these same desperate men?"

"I can take my life in my hand as well as another," said he, gloomily. And then he added: "They be none so desperate, after all. Broken men there may be amongst them, and many against whom fortune would seem to have a spite: perchance their affairs may mend in the new country."

"But your affairs are prosperous," Judith said—though she never once regarded him. "Why should you link yourself with such men as these?"

"One must forth to see the world," said he; and he went on to speak in a gay and reckless fashion of the life that lay before him, and of its possible adventures and hazards and prizes. "And what," said he, "if one were to have good fortune in that far country, and become rich in land, and have good store of corn and fields of tobacco; what if one were to come back in twenty years' time to this same town of Stratford, and set up for the trade of gentleman?"

"Twenty years?" said she, rather breathlessly. "'Tis a long time; you will find changes."

"None that would matter much, methinks," said he, indifferently.

"There be those that will be sorry for your going away," she ventured to say—and she forced herself to think only of Prudence Shawe.

"Not one that will care a cracked three-farthings!" was the answer.

"You do ill to say so—indeed you do!" said she, with just a touch of warmth in her tone. "You have many friends; you serve them ill to say they would not heed your going."

"Friends?" said he. "Yes, they will miss me at the shovel-board, or when there is one short at the catches."

"There be others than those," said she, with some little hesitation.

"Who, then?" said he.

"You should know yourself," she answered. "Think you that Prudence, for one, will be careless as to your leaving the country?"

"Prudence?" said he, and he darted a quick glance at her. "Nay, I confess me wrong, then; for there is one that hath a gentle heart, and is full of kindness."

"Right well I know that—for who should know better than I?" said Judith. "As true a heart as any in Christendom, and a prize for him that wins it, I warrant you. If it be not won already," she added, quickly. "As to that, I know not."

They were now nearing the town—they could hear the dull sound of the mill, and before them was the church spire among the trees, and beyond that the gray and red huddled mass of houses, barns, and orchards.

"And when think you of going?" she said, after a while.

"I know not, and I care not," said he, absently. "When I spoke of my acquaintances being indifferent as to what might befall me, I did them wrong, for in truth there be none of them as indifferent as I am myself."

"'Tis not a hopeful mood," said she, "to begin the making of one's fortunes in a new country withal. I pray you, what ails this town of Stratford, that you are not content?"

"It boots not to say, since I am leaving it," he answered. "Perchance in times to come, when I am able to return to it, I shall be better content. And you?"

"And I?" she repeated, with some surprise.

"Nay, you will be content enough," said he, somewhat bitterly. "Mother Church will have a care of you. You will be in the fold by then. The faithful shepherd will have a charge over you, to keep you from communication with the children of anger and the devil, that rage without like lions seeking to destroy."

"I know not what you mean," said she, with a hot face.

"Right well you know," said he, coolly; but there was an angry resentment running through his affected disdain as he went on: "There be those that protest, and go forth from the Church. And there be those that protest, and remain within, eating the fat things, and well content with the milk and the honey, and their stores of corn and oil. Marry, you will be well provided for—the riches of the next world laid up in waiting for you, and a goodly share of the things of this world to beguile the time withal. Nay, I marvel not; 'tis the wisdom of the serpent along with the innocence of the dove. What matters the surplice, the cross in baptism, and the other relics of popery, if conformity will keep the larder full ? Better that than starvation in Holland, or seeking a home beyond the Atlantic, where, belike, the children of the devil might prove overrude companions. I marvel not, I; 'tis a foolish bird that forsakes a warm nest."

And now she well knew against whom his bitter speech was levelled; and some recollection of the slight he had put upon her in the church-yard came into her mind, with the memory that it had never been atoned for. And she was astounded that he had the audacity to walk with her now and here, talking as if he were the injured one. The sudden qualm that had filled her heart when he spoke of leaving the country was put aside; the kindly reference to Prudence was forgotten; she only knew that this sarcasm of his was very much out of place, and that this was far from being the tone in which he had any right to address her.

"I know not," said she, stiffly, "what quarrel you may have with this or that section of the Church; but it concerns me not. I pray you attack those who are better able to defend themselves than I am, or care to be. Methinks your studies in that line have come somewhat late."

"'Tis no greater marvel," said he, "than that you should have joined yourself to the assembly of the saints: it was not always so with you."

"I ?" she said; but her cheeks were burning; for well she knew that he referred to his having seen her with the parson on that Sunday morning, and she was far too proud to defend herself. "Heaven help me now, but I thought I was mistress of my own actions !"

"In truth you are, Mistress Judith," said he, humbly (and this was the first time that he had ever addressed her so, and it startled her, for it seemed to suggest a final separation between them—something as wide and irrevocable as that twenty years of absence beyond the seas). And then he said, "I crave your pardon if I have said ought to offend you; and would take my leave."

"God be wi' you," said she, civilly; and then he left, striking across the meadows toward the Bidford road, and, as she guessed, probably going to seek his horse from whomsoever he had left it with.

And as she went on, and into the town, she was wondering what Prudence had said to him that should so suddenly drive him to think of quitting the country. All had seemed going well. As for Master Leofric Hope, his secret was safe; this late companion of hers seemed to have forgotten him altogether in his anger against the good parson. And then she grew to think of the far land across the ocean, that she had heard vaguely of from time to time; and to think how twenty years could be spent there; and what Stratford would be like when that long space was over.

"Twenty years," she said to herself, with a kind of sigh. "There are many things will be settled, ere that time be passed, for good or ill."

CHAPTER XVIII.

A CONJECTURE.

WHEN she got back to New Place she found the house in considerable commotion. It appeared that the famous divine Master Elihu Izod had just come into the town, being on his way toward Leicestershire, and that he had been brought by the gentleman whose guest he was to pay a visit to Judith's mother. Judith had remarked ere now that the preachers and other godly persons who thus honored the New Place generally made their appearance a trifling time before the hour of dinner; and now, as she reached the house, she was not surprised to find that Prudence had been called in to entertain the two visitors—who were at present in the garden—while within-doors her mother and the maids were hastily making such preparations as were possible. To this latter work she quickly lent a helping hand; and in due course of time the board was spread with a copious and substantial repast, not forgetting an ample supply of wine and ale for those that were that way inclined. Then the two gentlemen were called in, Prudence was easily persuaded to stay, and, after a lengthened grace, the good preacher fell to, seasoning his food with much pious conversation.

At such times Judith had abundant opportunities for reverie, and for a general review of the situation of her own affairs. In fact, on this occasion she seemed in a manner to be debarred from participation in these informal services at the very outset. Master Izod, who was a tall, thin, dark, melancholy-visaged man—unlike his companion, Godfrey Buller, of the Leas, near to Hinckley, who, on the contrary, was a stout, yeoman-like person, whose small gray absent eyes remained motionless and vacant in the great breadth of his rubicund face—had taken for his text, as it were, a list he had found somewhere or other of those characters that were entitled to command the admiration and respect of all good people. These were: a young saint; an old martyr; a religious soldier; a conscionable statesman; a great man courteous; a learned man humble; a silent woman; a merry companion without vanity; a friend not changed with honor; a sick man cheerful; a soul departing with comfort and assurance. And as Judith did not make bold to claim to be any one of these—nor, indeed, to have any such merits or excellences as would extort the approval of the membership of the saints—she gradually fell away from listening; and her mind was busy with other things; and her imagination, which was vivid enough, intent upon other scenes. One thing that had struck her the moment she had returned was that Prudence seemed in an unusually cheerful mood. Of course the arrival of two visitors was an event in that quiet life of theirs; and no doubt Prudence was glad to be appointed to entertain the strangers—one of them, moreover, being of such great fame. But so pleased was she, and so cheerful in her manner, that Judith was straightway convinced there had been

no quarrel between her and Tom Quiney. Nay, when was there time for that? He could scarcely have seen her that morning; while the night before there had certainly been no mention of his projected migration to America, else Prudence would have said as much. What, then, had so suddenly driven him to the conclusion that England was no longer a land fit to live in? And why had he paid Prudence such marked attention—why had he presented her with the spaniel-gentle and offered her the emblazoned missal—one evening, only to resolve the next morning that he must needs leave the country? Nay, why had he so unexpectedly broken the scornful silence with which he had recently treated herself? He had given her to understand that, as far as he was concerned, she did not exist. He seemed determined to ignore her presence. And yet she could not but remember that, if this contemptuous silence on his part was broken by the amazement of his seeing her in the company of a stranger, his suspicions in that direction were very speedily disarmed. A few words, and they fled. It was his far more deadly jealousy of the parson that remained; and was like to remain, for she certainly would not stoop to explain that the meeting in the churchyard was quite accidental. But why should he trouble his head about either her or the parson? Had he not betaken himself elsewhere—and that with her right good will? Nay, on his own confession he had discovered how kind and gentle Prudence was: there was a fit mate for him—one to temper the wildness and hot-headedness of his youth. Judith had never seen the sea, and therefore had never seen moonlight on the sea; but the nearest to that she could go, in thinking of what Prudence's nature was like, in its restful and sweet and serious beauty, was the moonlight she had seen on the river Avon in the calm of a summer's night, the water unbroken by a ripple, and not a whisper among the reeds. Could he not perceive that too, and understand?

As for herself, she knew that she could at any moment cut the knot of any complications that might arise by allowing Master Walter to talk her over into marrying him. Her father had assured her that the clear-headed and energetic young parson was quite equal to that. Well, it was about time she should abandon the frivolities and coquetries of her youth;

and her yielding would please many good people, especially her mother and sister, and obtain for herself a secure and established position, with an end to all these quarrels and jealousies and uncertainties. Moreover, there would be safety there. For, if the truth must be told, she was becoming vaguely and uncomfortably conscious that her relations with this young gentleman who had come secretly into the neighborhood were no longer what they had been at first. Their friendship had ripened rapidly; for he was an audacious personage, with plenty of self-assurance; and with all his professions of modesty and deference, he seemed to know very well that he could make his society agreeable. Then those lines he had repeated: why, her face grew warm now as she thought of them. She could not remember them exactly, but she remembered their purport; and she remembered, too, the emphasis with which he had declared that the bonniest of our English roses were those that grew in the country air. Now a young man cut off from his fellows as he was might well be grateful for some little solace of companionship, or for this or the other little bit of courtesy; but he need not (she considered) show his gratitude just in that way. Doubtless his flattery might mean little; the town gentlemen, she understood, talked in that strain; and perhaps it was only by an accident that the verses were there in the book; but still she had the uneasy feeling that there was something in his manner and speech that, if encouraged, or suffered to continue without check, might lead to embarrassment. That is to say, if she continued to see him; and there was no need for that. She could cut short this acquaintance the moment she chose. But on the one hand she did not wish to appear uncivil; and on the other she was anxious that he should see the whole of this play that her father had written—thrown off, as it were, amid the various cares and duties that occupied his time. If Master Leofric Hope talked of Ben Jonson when he came into the country, she would have him furnished with something to say of her father when he returned to town.

These were idle and wandering thoughts; and in one respect they were not quite honest. In reality she was using them to cloak and hide, or to drive from her mind altogether, a suspicion that had suddenly occurred to her that morning, and that had set her brain afire in a wild way. It was not only the tune of "Green-sleeves" that was in her head as she set off to walk home, though she was trying to force herself to believe that. The fact is this: when Master Leofric Hope made the pretty speech about the country roses, he accompanied it, as has been said, by a glance of only too outspoken admiration; and there was something in this look—apart from the mere flattery of it—that puzzled her. She was confused, doubtless; but in her confusion it occurred to her that she had met that regard somewhere before. She had no time to pursue this fancy further; for in order to cover her embarrassment she had betaken herself to the sheets in her satchel; and thereafter she was so anxious that he should think well of the play that all her attention was fixed on that. But after leaving him, and having had a minute or two to think over what had happened, she recalled that look, and wondered why there should be something strange in it. And then a startling fancy flashed across her mind—the wizard! Was not that the same look—of the same black eyes —that she had encountered up at the corner of the field above the Weir Brake?— a glance of wondering admiration, as it were? And if these two were one and the same man? Of course that train, being lit, ran rapidly enough: there were all kinds of parallels—in the elaborate courtesy, in the suave voice, in the bold and eloquent eyes. And she had no magical theory to account for the transformation—it did not even occur to her that the wizard could have changed himself into a young man —there was no dismay or panic in that direction: she instantly took it for granted that it was the young man who had been personating the wizard. And why?—to what end, if this bewildering possibility were to be regarded for an instant? The sole object of the wizard's coming was to point out to her her future husband. And if this young man were himself the wizard? A trick to entrap her?

Ariel himself could not have flashed from place to place more swiftly than this wild conjecture; but the next moment she had collected herself. Her common-sense triumphed. She bethought her of the young man she had just left— of his respectful manners—of the letter he had brought for her father—of the circumstances of his hiding. It was not possible that he had come into the neighborhood for the deliberate purpose of making a jest of her. Did he look like one that would play such a trick; that would name himself as her future husband; that would cozen her into meeting him? She felt ashamed of herself for harboring such a thought for a single instant. Her wits had gone wool-gathering! Or was it that Prudence's fears had so far got hold of her brain that she could not regard the young man but as something other than an ordinary mortal? In fair justice, she would dismiss this absurd surmise from her mind forthwith; and so she proceeded with her gathering of the flowers; and when she did set forth for home, she had very nearly convinced herself that there was nothing in her head but the tune of "Green-sleeves." Nay, she was almost inclined to be angry with Prudence for teaching her to be so suspicious.

Nevertheless, during this protracted dinner, while good Master Izod was enlarging upon the catalogue of persons worthy of honor and emulation, Judith was attacked once more by the whisperings of the demon. For a while she fought against these, and would not admit to herself that any further doubt remained in her mind; but when at last she found herself, despite herself, going back and back to that possibility, she took heart of grace and boldly faced it. What if it were true? Supposing him to have adopted the disguise, and passed himself off as a wizard, and directed her to the spot where she should meet her future husband—what then? What ought she to do? How ought she to regard such conduct? As an idle frolic of youth? Or the device of one tired of the loneliness of living at the farm, and determined at all hazards to secure companionship? Or a darker snare still—with what ultimate aims she could not divine? Or again (for she was quite frank), if this were merely some one who had seen her from afar, at church, or fair, or market, and considered she was a good-looking maid, and wished to have further acquaintance, and could think of no other method than this audacious prank? She had heard of lovers' stratagems in plenty; she knew of one or two of such that had been resorted to in this same quiet town of Stratford. And supposing that this last was the case, ought she to be indignant? Should she resent his boldness in hazarding such a stroke to

win her? And then, when it suddenly occurred to her that, in discussing this possibility, she was calmly assuming that Master Leofric Hope was in love with her —he never having said a word in that direction, and being in a manner almost a stranger to her—she told herself that no audacity on his part could be greater than this on hers; and that the best thing she could do would be to get rid once and forever of such unmaidenly conjectures. No; she would go back to her original position. The facts of the case were simple enough. He would have brought no letter to her father had he been bent on any such fantastic enterprise. Was it likely he would suffer the thralldom of that farm-house, and live away from his friends and companions, for the mere chance of a few minutes' occasional talk with a Stratford wench? As for the similarity between his look and that of the wizard, the explanation lay no doubt in her own fancy, which had been excited by Prudence's superstitious fears. And if in his courtesy he had applied to herself the lines written by the young Devonshire poet—well, that was but a piece of civility and kindness, for which she ought to be more than usually grateful, seeing that she had not experienced too much of that species of treatment of late from one or two of her would-be suitors.

She was awakened from these dreams by the conversation suddenly ceasing; and in its place she heard the more solemn tones of the thanksgiving offered up by Master Izod:

"The God of glory and peace, who hath created, redeemed, and presently fed us, be blessed forever and ever! So be it. The God of all power, who hath called from death that great pastor of the sheep, our Lord Jesus, comfort and defend the flock which He hath redeemed by the blood of the eternal testament; increase the number of true preachers; repress the rage of obstinate tyrants; mitigate and lighten the hearts of the ignorant; relieve the pains of such as be afflicted, but specially of those that suffer for the testimony of Thy truth; and finally, confound Satan by the power of our Lord Jesus Christ. Amen."

And then, as the travellers were continuing their journey forthwith, they proposed to leave; and Master Buller expressed his sorrow that Judith's father had not been at home to have made the friendship of a man so famous as Master Izod; and the good parson, in his turn, as they departed, solemnly blessed the house and all that dwelt therein, whether present or absent. As soon as they were gone, Judith besought her mother for the key of the summer-house, for she wished to lay on her father's table the wild flowers she had brought; and having obtained it, she carried Prudence with her into the garden, and there they found themselves alone, for goodman Matthew had gone home for his dinner.

"Dear mouse," said she, quickly, "what is it hath happened to Tom Quiney?"

"I know not, Judith," the other said, in some surprise.

"It is in his mind to leave the country."

"I knew not that."

"I dare be sworn you did not, sweetheart," said she, "else surely you would have told me. But why? What drives him to such a thing? His business prospers well, as I hear them say; and yet must he forsake it for the company of those desperate men that are going away to fight the Indians beyond seas. Nothing will content him. England is no longer England; Stratford is no longer Stratford. Mercy on us, what is the meaning of it all?"

"In truth I know not, Judith."

Then Judith regarded her.

"Good cousin, I fear me you gave him but a cold welcome yesternight."

"I welcomed him as I would welcome any of my brother's friends," said Prudence, calmly and without embarrassment.

"But you do not understand," Judith said, with a touch of impatience. "Bless thy heart! young men are such strange creatures; and must have all to suit their humors; and are off and away in their peevish fits if you do not entertain them, and cringe, and say your worship to every sirrah of them! Oh, they be mighty men of valor in their own esteem; and they must have us poor handmaidens do them honor; and if all be not done to serve, 'tis boot and spur and off to the wars with them, and many a fine tale thereafter about the noble ladies that were kind to them abroad. Marry! they can crow loud enough; 'tis the poor hens that durst never utter a word; and all must give way before his worship! What, then? What did you do? Was not the claret to

his liking? Did not your brother offer him a pipe of Trinidado?"

"Indeed, Judith, it can not be through ought that happened last night, if he be speaking of leaving the country," Prudence said. "I thought he was well content, and right friendly in his manner."

"But you do not take my meaning," Judith said. "Dear heart, bear me no ill-will; but I would have you a little more free with your favors. You are too serious, sweet mouse. Could you not pluck up a little of the spirit that the pretty Rosalind showed—do you remember?—when she was teasing Orlando in the forest? In truth these men are fond of a varying mood; when they play with a kitten they like to know it has claws. And again, if you be too civil with them, they presume, and would become the master all at once; and then must everything be done to suit their lordships' fantasies, or else 'tis up and away with them, as this one goes."

"I pray you, Judith," her friend said, and now in great embarrassment, "forbear to speak of such things: in truth, my heart is not set that way. Right well I know that if he be leaving the country, 'tis through no discontent with me, nor that he would heed in any way how I received him. Nay, 'tis far otherwise; it is no secret whom he would choose for wife. If you are sorry to hear of his going away from his home, you know that a word from you would detain him."

"Good mouse, the folly of such thoughts!" Judith exclaimed. "Why, when he will not even give me a 'Goodday to you, wench'!"

"You best know what reasons he had for his silence, Judith; I know not."

"Reasons?" said she, with some quick color coming to her face. "We will let that alone, good gossip. I meddle not with any man's reasons, if he choose to be uncivil to me; God help us, the world is wide enough for all!"

"Did you not anger him, Judith, that he is going away from his home and his friends?"

"Anger him? Perchance his own suspicions have angered him," was the answer; and then she said, in a gentler tone: "But in truth, sweetheart, I hope he will change his mind. Twenty years—for so he speaks—is a long space to be away from one's native land; there would be many changes ere he came back. Twenty years, he said."

Judith rather timidly looked at her companion, but indeed there was neither surprise nor dismay depicted on the pale and gentle face. Her eyes were absent, it is true, but they did not seem to crave for sympathy.

"'Tis strange," said she. "He said nought of such a scheme last night, though he and Julius spoke of this very matter of the men who were preparing to cross the seas. I know not what can have moved him to such a purpose."

"Does he imagine, think you," said Judith, "that we shall all be here awaiting him at the end of twenty years, and as we are now? Or is he so sure of his own life? —they say there is great peril in the new lands they have taken possession of beyond sea, and that there will be many a bloody fight ere they can reap the fruit of their labors in peace. Nay, I will confess to thee, sweet mouse, I like not his going. Old friends are old friends, even if they have wayward humors; and fain would I have him remain with us here in Stratford—ay, and settled here, moreover, with a sweet Puritan wife by his side, that at present must keep everything hidden. Well, no matter," she continued, lightly. "I seek no secrets—except those that be in the oaken box within here."

She unlocked the door of the summerhouse, and entered, and put the flowers on the table. "Tell me, Prue," said she, "may we venture to take some more of the play, or must I wait till I have put back the other sheets?"

"You have not put them back?"

"In truth, no," said Judith, carelessly. "I lent them to the young gentleman, Leofric Hope."

"Judith!" her friend exclaimed, with frightened eyes.

"What, then?"

"To one you know nothing of? You have parted with these sheets—that are so valuable?"

"Nay, nay, good mouse," said she; "you know the sheets are cast away as useless. And I but lent them to him for an hour or two to lighten the tedium of his solitude. Nor was that all, good Prue, if I must tell thee the truth: I would fain have him know that my father can do something worth speaking of as well as his friend Ben Jonson, and perchance even better: what think you?"

"You have seen him again, then?— this morning?"

"Even so," Judith answered, calmly.

"Judith, why will you run into such danger?" her friend said, in obvious distress. "In truth I know not what 'twill come to. And now there is this farther bond in this secret commerce—think you that all this can remain unknown? Your meeting with him must come to some one's knowledge—indeed it must, sweetheart."

"Nay, but this time you have hit the mark," said Judith, complacently. "If you would assure yourself, good Prue, that the young gentleman is no grisly ghost or phantom, methinks you could not do better than ask Tom Quiney, who saw him this very morning—and saw us speaking together, as I guess."

"He saw you!" Prudence exclaimed. "And what said he?"

"He talked large and wild for a space," said Judith, coolly, "but soon I persuaded him there was no great harm in the stranger gentleman. In sooth his mind was so full of his own affairs—and so bitter against all preachers, ministers, and pastors—and he would have it that England was no longer fit to live in—marry, he told me so many things in so few minutes that I have half forgotten them!"

And then it suddenly occurred to her that this fantasy that had entered her mind in the morning, and that had haunted her during Master Elihu Izod's discourse, would be an excellent thing with which to frighten Prudence. 'Twas but a chimera, she assured herself; but there was enough substance in it for that. And so, when she had carefully arranged the flowers on the table, and cast another longing look at the oaken chest, she locked the door of the summer-house, and put her arm within the arm of her friend, and led her away for a walk in the garden.

"Prudence," said she, seriously, "I would have you give me counsel. Some one hath asked me what a young maiden should do in certain circumstances that I will put before you; but how can I tell, how can I judge of anything, when my head is in a whirligig of confusion with parsons' arguments, and people leaving the country, and I know not what else? But you, good mouse—your mind is ever calm and equable—you can speak sweet words in Israel—you are as Daniel that was so excellent a judge even in his youth—"

"Judith!" the other protested; but indeed Judith's eyes were perfectly grave and apparently sincere.

" Well, then, sweetheart, listen: let us say that a young man has seen a young maiden that is not known to him but by name—perchance at church it may have been, or as she was walking home to her own door. And there may be reasons why he should not go boldly to her father's house, though he would fain do so; his fancy being taken with her in a small measure, and he of a gentle disposition, and ready to esteem her higher than she deserved. And again it might be that he wished for private speech with her—to judge of her manners and her inclinations —before coming publicly forward to pay court to her: but alack, I can not tell the story as my father would; 'tis the veriest skeleton of a story, and I fear me you will scarce understand. But let us say that the young man is bold and ingenious, and bethinks him of a stratagem whereby to make acquaintance with the damsel. He writes to her as a wizard that has important news to tell her; and begs her to go forth and meet him; and that on a certain morning he will be awaiting her at such and such a place. Now this maiden that I am telling you of has no great faith in wizards, but being curious to see the juggling, she goes forth to meet him as he asks—"

" Judith, I pray you speak plain; what is't you mean?" Prudence exclaimed; for she had begun to suspect.

" You must listen, good mouse, before you can give judgment," said Judith, calmly; and she proceeded: " Now you must understand that it was the young gentleman himself whom she met, though she knew it not; for he had dressed himself up as an ancient wizard, and he had a solemn manner, and Latin speech, and what not. Then says the wizard to her, ' I can show you the man that is to be your lover and sweetheart and husband; that will win you and wear you in the time coming; and if you would see him, go to such and such a cross-road, and he will appear.' Do you perceive, now, sweet mouse, that it was a safe prophecy, seeing that he had appointed himself to be the very one who should meet her?"

Prudence had gradually slipped her arm away from that of her friend, and now stood still, regarding her breathlessly, while Judith, with eyes quite placid and inscrutable, continued her story:

" 'Twas a noteworthy stratagem, and successful withal; for the maiden goes to the cross-road, and there she meets the young gentleman—now in his proper costume. But she has no great faith in magic; she regards him not as a ghost summoned by the wizard; she would rather see in this meeting an ordinary accident; and the young man being most courteous and modest and civil-spoken, they become friends. Do you follow the story? You see, good mouse, there is much in his condition to demand sympathy and kindness—he being in hiding, and cut off from his friends; and she, not being too industrious, and fond rather of walking in the meadows and the like, meets him now here, now there, but with no other thought than friendliness. I pray you, bear that in mind, sweetheart; for though I esteem her not highly, yet would I do her justice: there was no thought in her mind but friendliness, and a wish to be civil to one that seemed grateful for any such communion. And then one morning something happens—beshrew me if I can tell thee how it happened, and that is the truth—but something happens— an idea jumps into her head—she suspects that this young gentleman is no other than the same who was the wizard, and that she has been entrapped by him, and that he, having played the wizard, would now fain play the lover—"

" Judith, is't possible!—is't possible!"

" Hold, cousin, hold; your time is not yet. I grant you 'tis a bold conjecture, and some would say not quite seemly and becoming to a maiden, seeing that he had never spoken any word to her of the kind; but there it was in her head—the suspicion that this young gentleman had tricked her, for his own amusement, or perchance to secure her company. Now, sweet judge in Israel, for your judgment! And on two points, please you. First, supposing this conjecture to be false, how is she to atone to the young gentleman? And how is she to punish herself? And how is she to be anything but uneasy should she chance to see him again? Nay, more, how is she to get this evil suspicion banished from her mind, seeing that she dare not go to him and confess, and beg him for the assurance that he had never heard of the wizard? Then the second point: supposing the conjecture to be true, ought she to be very indignant? How should she demean herself? Should she go to him and reproach him with his treachery? She would never forgive it, dear

mouse, would she, even as a lover's stratagem?"

"Judith, I can not understand you; I
can not understand how you can even regard such a possibility, and remain content and smiling—"

"Then I ought to be indignant?—good
cousin, I but asked for your advice," Judith said. "I must be angry; I must
fret and fume, and use hot language, and
play the tragedy part? In good sooth,
when I think on't, 'twas a piece of boldness to put himself forward as my future
husband—it was indeed—though 'twas
cunningly contrived. Marry, but I understand now why my goodman wizard would
take no money from me; 'twas myself
that he would have in payment of his
skill; and 'gracious lady' and 'sweet
lady,' these were the lures to lead me on;
and his shepherd's dial placed on the
ground! Then off go beard and cloak,
and a couple of days thereafter he is a
gay young gallant; and 'sweet lady' it is
again—or 'fair lady,' was't?—'know you
one Master Shakespeare in the town?'
And such modesty, and such downcast
eyes, and an appeal for one in misfortune:
Heaven save us, was it not well done?
Modesty! By my life, a rare modest gentleman! He comes down to Stratford,
armed with his London speech and his
London manners, and he looks around.
Which one, then? which of all the maidens will his lordship choose for wife?
'Oh!' saith he, 'there is Judith Shakespeare; she will do as well as another;
perchance better, for New Place is the fairest house in the town, and doubtless she
will have a goodly marriage portion. So
now how to secure her? how to charm
her away from any clownish sweetheart
she may chance to have? Easily done, i'
faith!—a country wench is sure to believe in magic; 'tis but raising my own
ghost out of the ground, and a summons
to her, and I have her sure and safe, to win
and to wear, for better or worse!'" She
looked at Prudence. "Heaven's blessings
on us all, good Prue, was there ever poor
maiden played such a scurril trick?"

"Then your eyes are opened, Judith?"
said Prudence, eagerly; "you will have
nought more to do with such a desperate
villain?"

Again Judith regarded her, and laughed.
"I but told a story to frighten thee, good
heart," said she. "A desperate villain?
Yes, truly; but 'tis I am a desperate vil-

lain to let such rascal suspicions possess
me for an instant. Nay, good mouse,
think of it!—is't possible that one would
dare so much for so poor a prize? That
the young gentleman hath some self-assurance, I know; and he can quickly
make friends; but do you think, if any
such dark design had been his, he would
have entered my grandmother's cottage,
and ate and drank there, and promised to
renew his visit? Sweet judge in Israel,
your decision on the other point, I pray
you! What penance must I do for letting such cruel thoughts stray into my
brain? How shall I purge them away?
To whom must I confess? Nay, methinks
I must go to the young gentleman himself, and say: 'Good sir, I have a friend
and gossip that is named Prudence Shawe,
who hath a strange belief in phantom-
men and conspirators. I pray you pardon me that through her my brain is somewhat distraught; and that I had half a
mind to accuse you of a plot for stealing
me away—me, who have generally this
stout mastiff with me. I speech you, sir,
steal me not—nay, forgive me that I ever
dreamed of your having any such purpose.
'Tis our rude country manners, good sir,
that teach a maid to believe a man may
not speak to her without intent to marry
her. I pray you pardon me—my heart is
kneeling to you, could you but see—and
give me such assurance that you meditated no such thing as will bring me back
my scattered senses.' Were not that well
done? Shall that be my penance, good
mouse?"

"Dear Judith, tell me true," her friend
said, almost piteously, "do you suspect
him of having played the wizard to cheat
you and entrap you?"

"Good cousin," said she, in her frank-
est manner, "I confess: I did suspect—for
an instant. I know not what put it into
my head. But sure I am I have done
him wrong—marry, 'twere no such deadly
sin even had he been guilty of such a
trick; but I believe it not—nay, he is too
civil and gentle for a jest of the kind.
When I see him again I must make him
amends for my evil thinking: do not I
owe him as much, good gossip?"

This was all she could say at present,
for Matthew gardener here made his appearance, and that was the signal for their
withdrawing into the house. But that
afternoon, as Judith bethought her that
Master Leofric Hope would be coming to

her grandmother's cottage with the manuscript he had promised to return, she became more and more anxious to see him again. Somehow she thought she could more effectually drive away this disquieting surmise if she could but look at him, and regard his manner, and hear him speak. As it turned out, however, it was not until somewhat late on in the evening that she found time to seek out little Willie Hart, and propose to him that he should walk with her as far as Shottery.

Editor's Easy Chair.

ONE of the effects of the universal publicity of the day is that clubs are calling upon the courts to settle the quarrels of club members, although a club is in its idea the most exclusive of realms. A club, indeed, may be defined as a society of like-minded gentlemen. Its fundamental law, like all laws of social intercourse, is more unwritten than written. It contemplates the social assembly of gentlemen of a common interest and taste, and the voluntary withdrawal of any one who openly violates the canons of good-breeding. If a member so far forgets himself as to assault another member, either with opprobrious epithets or actual blows, when he comes to himself he should at once offer his resignation; and for two reasons. The first is that he has plainly insulted the club by ungentlemanly conduct; and the second is that he should be unwilling to remain a member of the society if he holds the opinion of another member which he has expressed, yet a person whom the club thinks to be good enough for its membership.

To the public nothing can be more unimportant than the quarrel of two members of a club, and nothing was therefore more amusing a few months since than to see such a squabble treated at length as a piece of interesting news. Beyond the club and the small circle of personal acquaintance, the fact that Mr. A. had called Mr. B. a puppy, and that Mr. B. had called Mr. A. a liar, and that they had scowled, grappled, and tumbled down the stairs together, is stuff less valuable than the police reports. It is hardly possible to conceive of persons of less interest to the public than gentlemen—usually very young gentlemen—who quarrel in clubs. But having quarrelled, the club instinct should lead them to take themselves off. To insist upon staying to be formally requested to resign, or to be expelled and then refuse to go, is so droll a procedure that it seems to threaten the existence of clubs. "To take the law of" a club, and to insist upon remaining in a society which distinctly and formally declares that your room is better than your company, is an act which might bring the old habitués of White's and Brookes's to revisit the glimpses of the moon to see what kind of men had followed them.

It has been decided, however, in England, that a member must be re-instated who has been expelled without an opportunity of being heard. But as the courts can not compel social intercourse between persons who do not desire it, the return of the expelled member to the club under such circumstances is both a common misfortune and a comedy. But it is easy to carry the theory of a club farther than the actual facts will authorize. A club, as we said, is a society of like-minded gentlemen. But, in fact, there are a great many clubs which can not be so described. A club which would be finely housed and luxuriously appointed incurs necessarily very large expenses, and a large membership is necessary in order to supply adequate revenue. It is this necessity which changes the character of clubs by changing the condition of membership.

Many an old club-man, as he sits musing amid the later splendors of its estate, recalls the earlier days of its happy moderation with the ardor of Béranger in remembering his attic. He does not personally know all the members now as then. The peculiar character and tone of the club is not the same. That distinctive *cachet*, as in the days when he had recently left Paris he was wont to say, as if—*pardon!*—his native tongue were slipping a little from his grasp—that *cachet* is certainly changed. The excellent man yonder, you say, is in the cheese line? Yes; ah! well, the *cari luoghi* and the *belli giorni* are faded a little, are fast vanishing!

Or is the veteran mistaking a lament over his lost youth for the threnody of a changed club? Is it the club-man and not the club that is translated? However that may be, he is not mistaken in thinking that never in that ancient day of his youth would a fellow-member have asked a court of justice to keep him in a smoking-room or a chatting-room or a reading-room where he was not wanted; or invoke it to interpret the rules of the club respecting its own members. He may well feel that if a club is a luxurious lounging-house and nothing else, and that a member is not to be disturbed except upon strictly legal compulsion, like the occupant of a seat at the opera, *à la bonne heure*, as they used to say in Paris in his time, then the social bond which was the old charm of a club is gone. A club regulated by the courts is not the club that the veteran knew. Men who blackguard each other in the club-house, and appeal to the courts to prevent them from being expelled, are not the club-men of his youth. The club palace may be finer, but the club pleasure is less. Three blackballs used to make a gentleman wince, and gentlemen only were held to be clubbable men. But the order of a court to decide who is clubbable—does Dr. Johnson hear that?

New times, muses the veteran, as he hums the melody of an old opera—new times, new men, new clubs.

THE newspapers are so full of stories of crime and suffering that many a reader shakes his head in wonder whether the world is not getting more wretched as it grows older. Yet, if this impression becomes strong and disturbing, the remedy is history. Turn to the tale of other times, and be consoled. The war for the union, for instance, in this country was a civil war exciting the most bitter passions, and waged with relentless determination upon both sides. Yet those who recall it and those who read of it know that the march of the armies was followed close by sympathy and intelligence, and every form of relief for suffering. Whatever could be done to mitigate the inevitable misery was done. Contrast with the story of the Sanitary Commission and the Christian Commission and the vast system of local committees of assistance and succor which left no individual soldier uncared-for, the awful tale of the Thirty Years' War, the unspeakable suffering, desolation, and crime which seemed almost to extinguish civilization in Germany, and in the contrast humanity in these days will seem almost to have taken war itself under its protection. Or go with John Howard to the jails of a century ago in England, or explore the London prisons of the middle of the last century as they are described in the novels of the time, or in Lecky's review of the eighteenth century, or later in the life of Elizabeth Fry, or in the old memoirs, and compare the universal public apathy with the wise humanity and careful knowledge of to-day. There is a certain proportion in the general social condition at any particular time and in any place. If it is very bad in one way, it is seldom very good in any other, and when the prison was worst, so was the palace. In Lecky and Fielding and Smollett the tale of the Fleet is well completed by Hervey's memoirs of St. James's. The recent revelations of the Ludlow Street Jail in New York, indeed, and much that is disclosed of the management of county jails and poor-houses, are doubtless repulsive, and show how much yet remains to do. But the significant fact is that such revelations are made at all, for in the old day the situation was accepted as a matter of course; and not only that they are made, but that they instantly arouse an indignant protest, and a movement of relief to correct an abuse which is felt to be disgraceful to the age, not to be characteristic of it.

Indeed, the distinction of the nineteenth century, which is now drawing to a close, is a spirit of practical humanity—the study and

care and skill with which intelligent sympathy has sought to relieve and to prevent suffering and poverty and crime—a spirit infinitely patient, not to be balked or dismayed or diverted, which reverses Cain's question and gladly owns that it is its brother's keeper. This is a truth which must strongly impress the observer of the work of any efficient board of charity, or of any good special institution for relief, in any of the States of this country.

The very organized impostures and parodies of such institutions which are merely swindles for personal advantage, and which we have more than once mentioned as existing abundantly in New York, are a striking tribute to the universal prevalence of this humane spirit. Its best result, however, is not sentimental effusion, but scientific organization. It has led to a science of the relief of suffering, and of pauper and penal treatment. It deals with the social difficulties, with every form of physical and mental and moral deprivation, with poverty and crime in all their aspects, as a surgeon deals with the human body that requires his care, with coolness, precision, and knowledge, recognizing that nothing more effectually obstructs the good work of relief than hysterics, or any kind of unrestrained emotion.

This view is very vividly suggested by a late paper of the director of the Perkins Institution for the Blind, at South Boston. This is the famous institution which was so long under the control of Dr. Howe, and which is now managed, with Dr. Howe's devotion, intelligence, and interest, by his son-in-law, Mr. Anagnos. In the fifty-second report of the institution, which is just issued, Mr. Anagnos makes a very earnest and eloquent plea for a Kindergarten for the blind. And in no department has the modern spirit shown itself more attractively than in the care of the blind. Its methods may be truly said to have restored or given to the blind the pleasure of life, and the miracle has been accomplished mainly by an intelligent provision of employment, and teaching the sightless that they are not left by Providence to a soul-consuming despair.

Sorrowful as the misfortune of blindness is, it is doubly so to the children of the very poor. They are abandoned as helpless and hopeless, and they grow up neglected but surrounded with every pernicious influence, half fed, half clothed, hearing the sounds of a pleasure in which they can take no part, condemned to an ignorance and inactivity and desolation in which their poor little hearts break and their brains reel and sink into imbecility. To take the blind children and train them for four or five of their tender years in useful work and knowledge is to suffer them to come unto Him who bade His disciples feed His lambs.

The key of the value of Froebel's Kindergarten system is that the natural play and activity of childhood is turned to useful account.

Mr. Anagnos says that the average intelligence and mental activity of children taught in the Kindergarten are much greater than those of pupils who enter primary schools without such training. Froebel's system has the advantage for the blind that it especially trains the senses, and peculiarly the sense of touch. During the last three years the results of this system among the blind children have been "truly marvellous," and an admirable description of most touching and inspiring facts is given by Miss Poulssen, a graduate of the school and a skillful teacher.

The plan of Mr. Anagnos is a primary school for sightless children, with a board of trustees of public-spirited citizens, the school to be situated in the neighborhood of Boston, with nothing eleemosynary in its title, charter, or regulations. It should be free from political or sectarian influence, open to all sightless children, and to a small number of seeing ones as companions and playmates. By the age of twelve they would be amply trained in Froebel's system, and in the way to help themselves. It is a proposition so timely and humane, and one well-endowed and wisely managed institution of the kind would so stimulate the establishment of others, that the enterprise appeals most strongly to the philanthropic and generous everywhere. Nowhere could it begin so prosperously as in a community familiar with the great success of the Perkins Institution, and where it would have the great advantage of that institution as its immediate neighbor.

THE old debate upon international copyright was renewed this winter by the bill introduced in Congress by Mr. Dorsheimer, but which the middle of April saw still slumbering in that limbo where so many good propositions repose. The mystery of Congressional procedure is past finding out. A member of Congress once complained ruefully to the Easy Chair that it took all the salary of his term to pay the expenses of his election, and all its time to learn the way of doing business. "I was a poorer and a wiser man," he said, "when I was defeated for a renomination. But I thought with grim delight of the fate that awaited my successor." Mr. Dorsheimer is not responsible for the long slumber of his bill, and indeed, when these words are read, it may have been discussed and its fate decided.

It was natural that Mr. Dorsheimer, who is a man of educated tastes and sympathies, and who believes that the laborer is worthy of his hire, should have wished to associate his name with an enterprise already associated with the names of Everett and Clay, and with a cause which has had the most distinguished Americans for its friends. Free trade and sailors' rights was a patriotic war-cry seventy years ago, and justice and authors' rights is a good patriotic cry for a statesman to-day. But the battle-field is the floor of Congress itself. There is no doubt that public opinion at large

would instantly declare, were it polled, that even "littery fellers" had rights which ought to be respected, and that Scott and Dickens and Thackeray, and any Shakespeare or Milton, or Bacon or Newton, who might appear, ought not to be robbed without pity for no other offense than writing books which everybody wished to read.

Yet during the effort which was made by Mr. Dorsheimer to bring his bill before the House, the opposition took substantially the ground that this great and glorious country could not spare time upon its triumphant way to chaffer with authors. It evidently thinks that if people choose to write books, they must do so at their peril. With such immense opportunities in mining and manufacturing of every kind, if a man prefers to write a *Macbeth* or a *Paradise Lost*, a *Novum Organon* or a Gibbon's History, he must take the consequences. A man of mind so perverse, with Congress warning him to beware, who might manage a railroad, and who deliberately elects to write the *Heart of Mid-Lothian*, or *The Newcomes*, or *David Copperfield*, can not reasonably ask for clemency, and ought to expect that his foolish work will be confiscated for the public benefit.

Knowledge, Mr. Speaker, must not be taxed. The great and glorious American people are levers of the universe; and to what purpose do they maintain the public schools if, having taught the country to read, they make reading dear by paying authors? Sir, fame is the shining goal of the "littery" man. He does not work for vulgar, sordid gain. His reward is the consciousness that the immortal productions of his genius are—are, I say—appropriated by his grateful fellow-men without money and without price.

That was the lofty argument which opposed Mr. Dorsheimer's bill. We shall yet hear its later strain, that the foreign author is honored when his work is reprinted—not at his expense, sir; no sir, not at all, but at American risk, by American enterprise; and he has the happy consciousness that far over the ocean, sir, which the poet describes in poetry for which no proud American ever paid him a Continental penny, as "deeply, darkly, beautifully blue"—I say, sir, the consciousness of knowing that far over that ocean he is read and admired by a great people who mix no dross with their delight, and no pelf with their praise.

This was the noble strain of opposition. Deprived of its sheeny vans of rhetoric, the assertion was this: if a man three thousand miles from America writes in our language a book which is so great a work of genius, or so inspiring and useful and helpful or entertaining, that it is sure to be read by everybody in this country, then the moment a copy reaches our shores we will multiply it, and furnish it to the whole country without so much as thank ye. The man is paid for it three thousand miles off, where he writes it, isn't he? Well, that ought to content him, if he is such a mercenary writer that he wants money. Do you say that he is entitled to compensation upon equal terms from everybody who profits by his labor, and that if one man pays him for twenty years a consideration for that profit, everybody who enjoys under the same conditions ought to pay the same consideration? All I have to say to that is that you are talking metaphysics, and that England doesn't make laws for America. This great country, sir, is going to have cheap reading. No taxes on knowledge!—no taxes on knowledge!

This strenuous orator forgets that although America wants cheap goods, and although stolen goods are cheap, yet that America does not wish to steal in order to secure cheapness. Nor can he be allowed to escape by saying that the laws of England and of America acknowledge no other author's right in publication than the concession of a monopoly for a specified term, not for his own benefit, but for the advantage of the public. That is true; but the public advantage is the advantage of everybody who is benefited, not of the inhabitants of the Strand, or of Middlesex, or of England, but of the realm, of the language, and wherever the work is reproduced. If the theory of copyright be correct—not that it is a natural right of the author, but a bounty to induce him to write and benefit his reader—then every country which is benefited is equally interested to encourage him; and the more he is encouraged the better he will write and the more benefit he will confer.

But whatever may be the just interpretation of the law, and the theory of bounty is evidently the constitutional theory in this country, there is still the feeling that it is inexpressibly mean to use the fruit of another man's skill and labor and effort without making him the least acknowledgment. And if the inexpressibly mean could possibly be meaner, it would become so when this appropriation of another man's diligence and toil is accompanied with swaggering rhetoric about taxing knowledge and the necessity of cheap reading. Is cheap reading a greater necessity than cheap bread? and does the tumid orator propose to rob the baker?

Mr. Dorsheimer's bill has been approved, with some suggestions of amendment, by the great body of authors and publishers in the country. It will remove what has been long felt to be a reproach. It will bind in still closer comity the two great English-speaking nations; and should it become law, it will be an unfading laurel upon the brow of its author.

———

THE narrow streets of the "superb Genoa" are very striking and picturesque to the young American who sees them for the first time, especially if, like the Easy Chair, he sees them before he has become accustomed to the aspect of foreign cities. There are streets of palaces in that city which the traveller never forgets. So in Venice there are the narrow ways, so narrow and so still that they seem almost to steal along between the high houses, and to be fitting avenues of the mystery and crime and romance which are associated with the city in the sea.

But in both those cities the streets are sunless, and there is almost a gloomy shade, which is welcome only in the burning summer weather. Such shaded streets health does not love, and an invalid whose windows open only upon the unsunned rays must long for a glimpse of the bright open sky with the yearning of Austin Dobson's ballad of the thrush in the cage upon the city street:

"Sing on: what though thou beat
 On that dull bar, thy foe!
Somewhere the green boughs meet
 Beyond the roofs a-row;
Somewhere the blue skies show;
 Somewhere no black walls crush
Poor hearts with helpless woe—
 Sing on—sing on, O thrush!"

It is not, however, of streets, but of houses that we mean to speak, and of the huge towering houses which in New York are beginning to overhang the streets with gloom, and which, as they multiply, will injure both the cheerfulness and the healthfulness of the city. They are already among the most striking objects to strangers. The palaces in the Italian cities are massive and often picturesque, but they are seldom very lofty. It is very hard for the Fire Department to deal with a fire in the upper part of a building which is sixty-five or seventy feet in height, but there are more than a hundred in the city which exceed eighty feet, and already, in 1883, there were nine between one hundred and one hundred and fifty feet, and two between one hundred and fifty and one hundred and sixty feet. These are facts which reveal a wholly new situation; for the population of the apartment-houses is computed to be not less than twenty-five thousand, and the St. George, whose burning, although happily without loss of life, produced such consternation and apprehension, was as fire-proof, according to Inspector Esterbrook, as hundreds of them.

How fire-proof the St. George was appears from the fact that a lady returning from market saw that the house was on fire, and knew that her young children were upon the sixth floor. She hurried in at the street door, and happily found her husband and children, who had just descended, having left their rooms immediately upon discovering the fire. But the husband, instantly endeavoring to return to his rooms, was stopped by the smoke on the second floor, and everything was lost. Yet the fire occurred in the morning. Had it taken place at night, the tragedy would have been indescribable. This fire evidently apprised the community of a new peril. The papers at once sounded the alarm, and demanded further legislation to protect human life.

It is undoubtedly the interest of a man who hires a flat to ascertain whether it is fire-proof, but the safety of the community and of human life can not safely be intrusted altogether to the chance of his ascertaining. It is the interest of passengers upon a ferry-boat to know whether it is safe. But the community does not permit them to risk their lives upon the chance of knowing, and requires that official inspectors, who are responsible for the discharge of their duty, shall certify the safety of the boat, and without such a certificate no such boat may transport passengers. The reason is quite as strong with the apartment-house. The risk of life from fire in it is very great, and stringent building laws are essential to its safety.

We are not aware that the question has ever been judicially decided, what is a fire-proof house. But Inspector Esterbrook is reported to have given a very good definition of such a house. It is one, he said, in which a man who lives upon the top story when told that there was a fire in the lower story would go to bed as quietly as if the fire were in the next town. The community ought certainly to require any man who proposes to build a house one hundred and twenty feet high to accommodate many families—for some of the houses have nearly two hundred inhabitants—to build in a way which is a reasonable guarantee of the safety of human life. There are buildings in the city which are practically fire-proof, and it is not asking too much to demand that the huge caravansaries be made so, even although the cost of building be increased.

The architects and the builders whose views have been elicited by the destruction of the St. George are of opinion that the Legislature will move only in response to an emphatic public opinion. But their own feeling should assure them of the existence of such an opinion. The court, as the old judge thought, might be presumed to know some law. A legislator may be presumed to have some common-sense. And as the story of the burning of the St. George is now familiar, legislative action will doubtless be taken, unless, as the Inspector says, a holocaust of victims be necessary to produce the law.

Mr. GLADSTONE, at the age of seventy-three, Prime Minister of England, and the chief of English statesmen, no less eminent for weight of personal character and accomplished scholarship than for his extraordinary mastery of public affairs and his Parliamentary eloquence, is a fine illustration of the English genius in its most characteristic form. There is a certain sturdiness in Mr. Gladstone's nature showing itself in every way, except his reputed sensitiveness to personal criticism, which is in singular contrast with the Oriental character

of Lord Beaconsfield, so long his chief opponent. It was the want of this quality quite as much as an alien genius which made the late minister so apparently un-English. No one, indeed, cultivated English ways more assiduously, or celebrated with more gusto the distinctive English life, than Lord Beaconsfield, and he identified himself with the bucolic party—the squire, the country gentleman—and he seemed in every manner resolved —if resolution would accomplish it—to be an Englishman.

But the contrast between him and Mr. Gladstone was as apparent in every aspect as it is in the remarkable caricatures of *Punch*, in which, if Gladstone has sometimes the air of a prig, Disraeli has always the air of Cagliostro. When Disraeli was at the head of the ministry, the feeling was unavoidable that it was an accomplished foreign talent that was governing England. But with Gladstone, it is England governing herself. Much more than in any chief minister the English conscience is felt in Gladstone. In Lord Sidmouth and Mr. Percival, the two most ordinary and commonplace of Prime Ministers, there was the conventional English respectability and morality. But in Gladstone it is the power of rectitude which is remarkable. He believes in honest dealing, and in subordinating public policy to the moral law. He may not like to be personally criticised, but he is not ashamed to be called sentimental in his regard for the moral honor as well as for the "interest" of England.

Nothing could be more distasteful to Mr. Gladstone than the Egyptian complication. Nothing could have been more delightful to Lord Beaconsfield. The vagueness of the object to be attained by warlike operations, the difficulty of a possible protectorate of the country, the desire to respect the rights of a people so remote from English sympathy and habits, naturally oppress Mr. Gladstone, thus necessarily engaged in transactions in which his country should never have been involved. But they would have been exciting chapters of romance to Lord Beaconsfield, and he would have endeavored to turn the situation to the most dazzling account.

Coping at once with the elusive situation in Egypt, with the franchise in England, and with the discontent of Ireland, and goaded by a Tory party not greatly led, but officered by a brilliant cynic, a worthy squire, and a nondescript madcap, only a chief of the sturdiest moral and mental quality could hold at seventy-three a position which nobody else could fill. It is, as we said, his character no less than his genius which will give him a great place in English history. With the conquering Chatham and the accomplished Canning, with William Pitt and Sir Robert Peel, Gladstone must always be mentioned as an English statesman and minister who showed in his public and private life, in his masterly grasp of affairs, in his ascendency over a great, intelligent, and progressive party, in his high moral tone and his immense accomplishment, the power which any intelligent country would wish to see conducting its affairs.

This is the year in which the other great English-speaking nation calls one of its citizens to the Chief Executive Magistracy. Happy that country if it summon to that office a statesman so commanding, conscientious, and courageous, and a man so spotless as the Eng-lish Prime Minister! Looking at Gladstone, and then across the sea at our Presidential contest, the Englishman may be pardoned if he is not quite ready to abandon a political system which brings so great a man as Gladstone into the direction of the government, and even the American may wonder whether his system of selecting the Chief Magistrate is surer than the English method to bring the real chief of a party to the executive chair.

Editor's Literary Record.

THE literary merits of Queen Victoria's new book, *More Leaves from the Journal of a Life in the Highlands*,[1] are of the most modest kind. Its style is unadorned to plainness, and not a little monotonous; its matter, though sensible, is devoid of originality or depth of thought, and the reader will look in vain through its pages for any gleam of imagination or any exhibition of poetical sensibility. And yet the book is not wanting in attractiveness even from the literary stand-point. If its style is plain and repetitious, it is clear, concise, intelligible, and never ungraceful, and it is marked throughout by a tone of quiet, unassuming, and simple dignity. So, also, if its matter betrays no faculty for deep or lofty thinking, and is overladen on the one hand with tristful and somewhat trite ejaculatory references to Prince Albert, and on the other with unnecessarily multiplied recognitions and acknowledgments of John Brown's petty but useful services and functions, it is compact with sterling good sense, with clear intuitions of character, with sound judgments of men and things, and with unvarying gentleness, kindliness, and steadfastness; and its even tenor is often alleviated by brief and unlabored passages finely descriptive of the picturesque natural objects and social incidents peculiar to Scottish scenery and society. One very pleasing feature of the volume is its absolute freedom from bitterness and cynicism and ill-nature. Indeed, its sweetness and equability of temper and its delicate consideration for the feelings of others is one of its special charms. Nor is it lacking in occasional touches of dry and genial humor, though this is exercised with delicate reserve. After all is said, however, the chief attractiveness of the book does not depend upon its slender literary qualities, but upon the fullness with which it admits the outside world—"the million"—behind the scenes of royalty, and vouchsafes us a sight of the diurnal doings, occupations, diversions, haps and mishaps, of one who was born in the royal purple, and who is still wearing it, not only royally, but with wo-manly gentleness and dignity. Some of its revelations of the domestic and inner life of the Queen and her household, and of her daily round, are very tender and touching; and even those which are the most commonplace are of a kind to gratify the curiosity and excite the interest of that large body of people, even in republican America, who, consciously or unconsciously, recognize and reverence "the divinity that doth hedge a king."

IT is no disparagement to say of Mr. Eugene Schuyler's *Historical Biography of Peter the Great*[2] that it is less brilliant and ornate as a portraiture of character, less dramatic in its narrative, less skillful in its groupings and descriptions, and less richly endowed with philosophic historical insight than similar works that have proceeded from the pens of Lord Macaulay and our own gifted countrymen Mr. Prescott and Mr. Motley. That his literary workmanship is inferior to and will scarcely provoke comparison with that of these great writers is due not so much to his defects as a writer as to their incontestable superiority to all others in this department of literature. But if it must be admitted that he is surpassed by these and some others that might be named in the faculty of making a character seem to live and move before us, or of picturing incidents and events as if they were being really enacted before our eyes, or of extracting from history the vital principles that underlie and give significance to it, he is at least exceeded by none in the diligence of his research, in the intelligence with which it was prosecuted, in the fullness and minuteness of his recital of facts and descriptions of incidents and occurrences, or in the amplitude and variety of the materials he has gathered to illustrate the character and doings of the remarkable personage whose career he depicts, and by means of which he is enabled to give a comprehensive view of the state of the Russian Empire, its government and people, during the rapid development that signalized the transitional period in its history which was coincident with

---

[1] *More Leaves from the Journal of a Life in the Highlands.* From 1862 to 1882. With Portraits and Illustrations. 16mo, pp. 170. New York: Harper and Brothers.
The Same. "Franklin Square Library." 4to, pp. 42. New York: Harper and Brothers.

[2] *Peter the Great, Emperor of Russia.* A Study of Historical Biography. By EUGENE SCHUYLER, Ph.D., LL.D. Copiously Illustrated. In Two Volumes, 8vo, pp. 451 and 460. New York: Charles Scribner's Sons.

the reign of this phenomenal personage, and indeed was the natural and inevitable outcome of it. In these important respects Mr. Schuyler's work is worthy of very high praise. With his book before him the intelligent reader will have no difficulty in arriving at a just estimate of the faults and virtues, the vices, weaknesses, and greatnesses, the genius and talents, the temper and disposition, of the last and greatest of the Czars, and of his wonderful capacity for good and evil, for organization, and for the development of the national energies and power; and he will be enabled very satisfactorily to gauge the nature and genius of the Russian people, to fathom the depths and shoals of Russian society and Russian institutions, and to comprehend the portentous combination of barbarism and civilization which distinguishes the social and political institutions of Russia at this day, and stamps its millions a peculiar and exclusive people.

AMONG English and American scholars there is no higher authority on the history and progress of sculpture in Italy during the Renaissance than our fellow-countryman Mr. Charles C. Perkins. His researches have been so extensive, his knowledge is so large and accurate, and his criticisms and opinions have been so sound and discriminating, that all who have studied or written upon the subject of the renaissance of Italian art since the publication, some years ago, of his sterling works, *Tuscan Sculptors* and *Italian Sculptors*, recognize his pre-eminence in this department of historical investigation, and refer to his writings as standard authorities. In especial, one of the most distinguished of these later writers, Mr. John Addington Symonds, in the preface to one of the volumes in his masterly series on *The Renaissance in Italy*, being the one devoted to the consideration of *The Fine Arts in Italy*, has cordially acknowledged his indebtedness to the "two important works of Mr. Perkins" above named. And indeed it needs a glance only at Mr. Symonds's treatment of the historical portions of his subject to discern how largely he has profited by Mr. Perkins's researches, while the many analogies that are perceptible between the tasteful and tempered judgments and criticisms of the earlier and the later writer show that Mr. Perkins's opinions and conclusions on art, and on artists and their productions, have not been without influence upon the mind of the candid and cultured English scholar, wherever they have traversed common ground. Mr. Perkins has now prepared, largely from materials already made use of in his former works, and largely from new matter that has been added to the common stock of information since their publication, an exceedingly valuable supplementary volume, whose title, *A Historical Hand-Book of Italian Sculpture*,[3]

very accurately defines its scope and office, if a larger signification is accorded to the term "hand-book" than is usually associated with it, since it is not a mere elementary manual or synoptical summary, in which names, dates, facts, and events are recapitulated in bald outline, but, on the contrary, is a full and rounded epitome, replenished with historical and biographical details illustrating the modern beginnings and progress of sculpture, and enriched with brief and well-considered opinions, criticisms, and judgments upon the condition and character of the art in its several stages, as exhibited by the productions of the artists who flourished in each of them. Mr. Perkins's volume is an intelligent and instructive guide to all the best examples of the art that are extant in collections or edifices, or of which there is any record in engravings or in authentic works on art.

IN the preparation of his new volume, *Travels in Mexico, and Life among the Mexicans*,[4] Mr. Frederick A. Ober has brought into play the same practiced eye as a naturalist, the same zestful powers of observation as a traveller, and the same faculty for picturesque description that served him so well and were such important factors in the preparation of his former attractive book, *Camps in the Caribbees*. His present volume comprises the record of his travels in Yucatan, Southern and Central Mexico, and those bordering States of our own country which have a close relation to Mexico from their having originally formed a portion of its territory, from the similarity of their climate, productions, natural features, and historic remains, and also from their proximity, and their importance as natural avenues for the opening of closer relations between the two countries, through the agency of railroad, mining, and other commercial or industrial enterprises. A thousand miles of these travels— being that portion of them which extended through Yucatan and Central and Southern Mexico—were made on horseback by Mr. Ober, which gave him an opportunity for a close and comparatively leisurely observation of the country through which he passed, and for a careful study of its people, its flora and fauna, its volcanoes and other natural features, and its historic remains. His descriptions of these old-new fields are exhaustive of their material resources, and are interspersed with, and rendered highly attractive by, his indulgence in his taste for natural history, and for explorations and researches among the antiquities in which they abound. In his descriptions of these antiquities Mr. Ober reproduces much with which we have been made familiar by Humboldt, Catherwood, Stephens, Squier,

[3] *A Historical Hand-Book of Italian Sculpture.* By CHARLES C. PERKINS. Illustrated. 8vo, pp. 432. New York: Charles Scribner's Sons.

[4] *Travels in Mexico, and Life among the Mexicans.* By FREDERICK A. OBER. I. Yucatan. II. Central and Southern Mexico. III. The Border States. With 180 Illustrations. Large 8vo, pp. 672. Boston: Estes and Lauriat. New York: Western W. Wilson.

Brantz Meyer, and other travellers, supplemented by much more which is the fruit of his own observations and explorations. These antiquarian and archæological researches, though deeply interesting, were incidental, however, to his principal object in the volume, which is to draw attention to the present of this important region, its inexhaustible material capabilities and resources, and the inviting opportunities it offers to pioneers, settlers, miners, agriculturists, capitalists, and men of enterprise generally, in the work of the development and "opening up" of its territory to the trade, commerce, and industries of the United States and the other more energetic nations. Mr. Ober's accounts of the resources of Mexico and the region forming the border States; of the recently perfected railway system, which has penetrated Mexico and Central America over ten thousand miles, much of it traversing portions of the country that are seldom visited and are but little known; and of the people, the scenery, the mountains and plains, the lakes and volcanoes, the ruins and pyramids, the products of the soil, the minerals and mines, and the salubrious spots for those who are seeking health or pleasure—are invaluable for their stores of copious and exact information, and at the same time rich in spirited incidents of travel and adventure, and in picturesque descriptions of men and manners, of life among the aborigines, and of curious or stupendous natural objects. The volume is an important contribution to the already large catalogue of recent publications bearing upon a portion of the continent which promises to occupy the attention and engage the energies of the coming generation of Americans and Englishmen to the utmost. The work is profusely and admirably illustrated, mainly from photographs and sketches made by the author, and is equipped with excellent maps.

THE favor with which *The Franklin Square Song Collection* was received on its publication some three years ago has encouraged its compiler, Mr. J. P. McCaskey, to prepare another similar collection[5] on the same popular and eclectic plan. Like its predecessor, the new collection consists very largely of a tasteful selection from the fine old familiar tunes, glees, ballads, carols, songs, and hymns which are endeared to us by their associations, and whose rich or plaintive melodies have stood the test of time through many generations. Besides these it also contains a number of choice airs and songs and sacred melodies of a more recent date, by composers who have known how to touch the popular heart. The entire collection, both music and words, is made up of two hundred selections of that chaste and moving kind which is suitable for use in homes and schools, in the nursery and at the fireside, on

innocent festal occasions and for family and social worship. In connection with these old and new favorites the compiler has utilized the space before and after each of them so that no fragment of a page may be lost, by the introduction of well-chosen bits of suggestive and instructive reading matter, embodying some of the best thoughts of eminent writers and composers on musical subjects, together with brief and appropriate anecdotes of great musicians, and pithy historical or biographical incidents of their lives and careers. The two volumes form a musical repertory of great extent and the most sterling quality.

How much of the value of what we eat is destroyed or impaired by the manner in which it is prepared for the table, how often it is converted into slow but sure poison by the process of cooking, and how greatly, in either case, it contributes to physical ill health and to mental and moral impairment, few persons stop to consider; and yet the fact is patent to every intelligent physician, and might be equally so to every man of ordinary commonsense if he would give the subject the consideration it deserves. It is safe to say that a very considerable proportion—perhaps a moiety—of the nervous and stomach disorders with which our countrymen and country-women are plagued, of the feebleness, lassitude, indigestion, and lack of vitality that we experience, and of the fretfulness, discontent, ill-nature, and mental and moral obliquity of which we are the seemingly causeless victims, is chargeable directly upon the food we eat, not because the food itself is intrinsically unwholesome, but because it has been so prepared as inevitably to become so. We are therefore always disposed not only to extend a hearty welcome to a really good cookery book, but to rank its author among our philanthropists and public benefactors, the more especially if the book be one that is adapted for popular use, and teaches us, simply and intelligently, how to convert plain, cheap, and even contemned edibles into relishing, wholesome, nutritious, and elegant viands. After having subjected a book of this kind, entitled *The Virginia Cookery Book*,[6] which the Messrs. Harper have wisely included in their popular "Franklin Square Library," to the crucial test of trial by our own household divinities, we give it our grateful and unqualified commendation. The book has been compiled by Mrs. Mary Stuart Smith, or rather by two ladies of Virginia, who, under cover of her name, lay its excellent recipes before their "sisters in our American households," coupled with the assurance that "they have been constantly used in the families of Virginia for many years back, and have been tested by the experience of several generations." Our readers will find many

[5] *Franklin Square Song Collection.* Two Hundred Favorite Songs and Hymns for Schools and Homes, Nursery and Fireside. No. 2. Selected by J. P. McCaskey. 8vo, pp. 176. New York: Harper and Brothers.

[6] *Virginia Cookery Book.* Compiled by Mary Stuart Smith. "Franklin Square Library." 4to, pp. 70. New York: Harper and Brothers.

excellent dishes in this collection which have the rare merit of being savory and gustful, and yet adapted to the means of housekeepers with whom economy is a prime consideration.

AN exceedingly interesting contribution has been made to our knowledge of the history and character of the American Indians by a very full and exhaustive compilation of *Indian Myths*,[7] prepared by Ellen Russell Emerson. The volume consists of a large collection of myths, traditions, legends, stories, allegories, apologues, and symbols, illustrative of the religious conceptions and beliefs of the Indians; their poetical association of things seen and natural with those that are unseen and supernatural; their intellectual, social, and political condition; their methods of communicating their conceptions of the grand, the sublime, the beautiful, and the preternatural, by figurative symbols and pictorial representations; and the analogies that exist between these and the corresponding myths, traditions, words, symbols, and written or pictorial representations that have been discovered in the literature and remains of other primeval peoples, more especially those of Hindostan, Egypt, Persia, Assyria, and China. Many of these analogies are very striking, and fairly vindicate the positions advanced by the author in support of the evident capacity of the Indian race for intellectual and moral culture, and in proof of the unity of the human race, and the common origin of their religious conceptions and beliefs. The treatment of the subject is popular, yet with a sufficient infusion of the scientific to command the attention of scholars without perplexing the intelligent general reader; and it comprehends the ascertained myths, traditions, etc., that have been or continue to be prevalent among the North American Indians, arranged under specific heads, and compared under each head with those of other primitive peoples. The whole is illustrated by numerous interesting drawings from prehistoric and historic remains, and the results are summed up in a condensed epitome entitled "General Considerations," in which the origin and nature of the social, intellectual, and religious characteristics of the aborigines are analyzed, and their analogies and correspondencies with those of other peoples are reviewed and more closely traced. A very interesting feature of this portion of the work is that which describes the political institutions of the Indians; the relations, authority, and succession of their chiefs, sachems, and kings; the division of the various nations into clans; the restrictions and limitations that existed among the clans as to intermarriage and the punishment of offenses; the subordination of the clan to the

nation; and the functions and attributes severally of the clan, the tribe, and the confederacy—the latter being specially exemplified by an outline of the celebrated league or confederacy of the Iroquois. In this section quite full accounts are given of Indian councils and assemblies; considerable abstracts are presented of their debates, showing the native intelligence of the Indian, and his capacity for organization, statesmanship, and oratory; and much valuable information is accumulated illustrating the tribal dialects, the sensibility of the Indians to the influences of sounds and sights, and the operation of these influences upon their imaginations and beliefs, and also upon the formation, composition, pronunciation, and other characteristics of their language. The work is one of genuine and sustained interest.

IN several of the poems contained in a little volume entitled *The City of Success, and Other Poems*,[8] Mr. Henry Abbey exhibits a striking faculty for sustained and ingenious allegory. This is specially visible in the two more elaborate poems in the volume, "The City of Success" and "The City of Decay." In the first of these is symbolized, under a delicately veiled romance of love and ambition, the race for wealth, luxury, place, power, and fame, and the unsatisfying nature of each when the goal is won; and in the other is shadowed forth the indestructibility of truth—above all, of the truth that streams from the great Central Face "on dark Calvary lifted high"—amid the change and decay worked by Time and his companions, Life and Death, and his children, the moments, hours, days, months, seasons, years, and centuries. In both these poems Mr. Abbey demonstrates that he is endowed with a fertile and bold though irregular and untrained imagination; his language and versification are often rugged and unmelodious, and the general effect of his verse is cold, and awakens no response of passion or emotion. In two of his less ambitious efforts he reaches a higher plane, and touches the heart with a tenderer sympathy. We refer to the poems entitled "A Ballad of Consolation" and "Liberty," the former being a new and touching version of the old Spanish-Arabian story preserved in More's *Dialogues*, and afterward elaborated by Parnell in "The Hermit," illustrating the idea that under God's overruling providence the most heart-rending calamity, even the death of a beloved child, is often a blessing in disguise; and the latter, a pathetic romance based on the unrequited love of a beautiful Indian maiden for a young army officer, whose loyal heart had been already surrendered to a maiden of his own race. Besides the poems that we have singled out because of the germs of fine promise that are to be de-

[7] *Indian Myths; or, Legends, Traditions, and Symbols of the Aborigines of America compared with those of Other Countries, including Hindostan, Egypt, Persia, Assyria, and China.* By ELLEN RUSSELL EMERSON. Illustrated. 8vo, pp. 677. Boston: James R. Osgood and Co.

[8] *The City of Success, and Other Poems.* By HENRY ABBEY. 12mo, pp. 142. New York: D. Appleton and Co.

scried in them, there are many that Mr. Abbey should have had the resolution or the insight to suppress.

AMONG the recent additions to the already extensive literature that has grown out of the Revised Version of the New Testament is a useful and pre-eminently practical *Commentary*,[9] which has been prepared under the competent editorship of the Rev. Dr. Schaff, designed for the assistance and instruction of those who may adopt the Revised Version as their standard, and which is almost equally applicable to the needs of those who may adhere to the Authorized Version, its chief object being to explain the more difficult passages of the New Testament Scriptures, to interpret its historical, local, and Old Testament allusions, to unfold its lessons and teachings, to reconcile its apparent discrepancies, and to vindicate its title to be considered a divinely authorized revelation. Of this Commentary six volumes are now published, comprising the Gospels, the Acts of the Apostles, and the Epistle of St. Paul to the Romans. Each volume is accompanied by a complete apparatus for the use of Bible readers and Bible classes, consisting of an introduction supplying an outline of the contents of the book, an account of its design, composition, and authorship, an examination of its credibility, characteristics, evidential value, and chronology, and excursuses and textual notes.

THE fourth volume of Mr. Bancroft's last revision of his *History of the United States of America*,[10] now just published, covers the momentous period from May, 1774, when, the final estrangement of the colonies having been consummated by the unwise and arbitrary measures of the British King and Parliament, the use of armed force was resorted to by them to subjugate the people of Massachusetts Bay, until July 4, 1776, when all the colonies united in adopting the cause of Massachusetts as the common cause of the people of America, and forming themselves into a federal union, declared the colonies free, sovereign, and independent, and forever cut themselves loose from the ties that had bound them to the mother country. The

eventful story of this epochal period, when America took up arms in self-defense and arrived at independence, has never been told as eloquently and as philosophically as by Mr. Bancroft, or so fully and candidly. In this new edition some slight changes have been made in the text, where fuller information has been discovered, or where new light has suggested a modification of the coloring. But in the main, although revealing improving touches on nearly every page, the history is substantially unchanged in any prime essential, and remains an evidence of the thoroughness and conscientiousness of the author's researches while engaged in its original preparation.

THE Messrs. Harper have now completed the republication of the standard edition of *The Complete Works of Coleridge*,[11] to which we have adverted in this Record for previous months, by the issue, in a final volume, of the crowning flower of his writings, his poetical and dramatic works. To enter upon a detailed criticism of these would be an affectation and an impertinence, in view of their recognized position in our literature; but it may be said, without being guilty of either, that no modern poet has been more felicitous than he in the use of language, that few have produced more vivid, more impressive, or more enduring imaginative effects, that still fewer have equalled him in the grace, subtlety, and delicacy of his ideal creations, and that none have excelled him in the cleanliness, masculine beauty, and purity of his thoughts and teachings. No collection of poetry can be complete from which his poems are excluded, and no education in the art of poetry and in the canons of poetical taste and composition can be considered fully rounded and perfected from which the study of his inspiring verse has been omitted. The publishers have added materially to the value and convenience of the new edition by appending to the final volume a full and exhaustive topical index, arranged alphabetically, by means of which the great variety of subjects—literary, critical, theological, philosophical, and biographical—treated of in its seven volumes may be seen at a glance, and easily turned to.

THE Messrs. Carter have published a new edition, in popular form, of the *Life and Works*[12] of the late eminent Scottish preacher and theo-

[9] *The International Revision Commentary on the New Testament. Based on the Version of* 1881. By English and American Scholars and Members of the Revision Committee. Edited by PHILIP SCHAFF, D.D. Vol. I.: The Gospel According to Matthew. Explained by PHILIP SCHAFF, D.D. 16mo, pp. 416. Vol. II.: The Gospel According to Mark. Explained by MATTHEW B. RIDDLE, D.D. 16mo, pp. 243. Vol. III.: The Gospel According to Luke. Explained by MATTHEW B. RIDDLE, D.D. 16mo, pp. 369. Vol. IV.: The Gospel According to John. Explained by WILLIAM MILLIGAN, D.D., and WILLIAM F. MOULTON, D.D. 16mo, pp. 443. Vol. V.: The Acts of the Apostles. Explained by J. S. HOWSON, D.D., and H. D. M. SPENCE, M.A. 16mo, pp. 420. Vol. VI.: The Epistle of Paul to the Romans. Explained by MATTHEW B. RIDDLE, D.D. 16mo, pp. 256. New York: Charles Scribner's Sons.
[10] *History of the United States of America, from the Discovery of the Continent.* By GEORGE BANCROFT. The Author's Last Revision. Volume IV. 8vo, pp. 452. New York: D. Appleton and Co.

[11] *The Complete Works of Samuel Taylor Coleridge.* With an Introductory Essay upon his Philosophical and Theological Opinions. Edited by Professor W. G. T. SHEDD. In Seven Volumes. Vol. VII.: Poetical and Dramatic Works. 12mo, pp. 728. New York: Harper and Brothers.
[12] *The Life and Works of Thomas Guthrie, D.D.* In Eleven Volumes, 12mo. Vols. I. and II.: Autobiography and Memoir, pp. 424 and 494. Vol. III.: The Gospel in Ezekiel, pp. 395. Vol. IV.: Christ the Inheritance of the Saints, pp. 344. Vol. V.: The Parables, pp. 278. Vol. VI.: Out of Harness, pp. 388. Vol. VII.: Speaking to the Heart, pp. 492. Vol. VIII.: Man and the Gospel, pp. 478. Vol. IX.: The Way to Life, pp. 336. Vol. X.: Studies of Character, pp. 436. Vol. XI.: The City: its Sins and Sorrows and Ragged Schools, pp. 364. New York: Robert Carter and Brothers.

logian the Rev. Dr. Guthrie, which constitutes quite a library of Biblical instruction and exposition, as well as of varied and refined literary entertainment. The edition is in eleven handsome volumes, and it comprises one of the most attractive autobiographies in the language, supplemented by an admirably written biography by his sons; a body of sermons which are unsurpassed by those of any modern preacher in eloquence, idiomatic purity of diction, simplicity and directness of style, and rich instructiveness of matter; a series of sketches of Scripture worthies, each of which is a portrait remarkable for its life-likeness and individuality; and a number of narrative, descriptive, and didactic pieces, briefly but graphically depicting some of the most pathetic, most humorous, and most invigorating phases of Scottish life and character. The sermons, which form much the larger part of the eleven volumes, are noteworthy for their force and suggestiveness, and for the earnest persuasiveness of their appeals to the reason and conscience. Strong in their statements of doctrine, bold and vigorous, but at the same time loving, in reproof and admonition, they are entirely free from the hair-splitting and special pleading with which pulpit discourses are too often encumbered, and rendered not only tiresome, but repellent.

SEVERAL recent republications are of such a kind that our readers, especially those who are forming libraries, will doubtless be glad to be apprised of them; but as the most of them have already been noticed in this department of the Magazine upon their original appearance, and besides are too well known to require elaborate notice at this time, we shall announce them by their titles only, as follows: A "people's edition" of Ruskin's works, including thus far his *Sesame and Lillies*,[13] *St. Mark's Rest*,[14] and his Oxford lectures on *The Art of England;*[15] two additional volumes — *Doctor Johns*[16] and *Bound Together*[17]—of the new and complete edition of the writings of Donald G. Mitchell (Ik Marvell); *Matthew Arnold's Collected Poems*,[18] comprising his early and narrative poems, his sonnets, and his lyrical, dramatic, and elegiac poems; a new and cheap, but unabridged, edition of Miss Anne Ayres's ("Sister Anne") affectionate memorial of the

Life and Work of the late Rev. Dr. Muhlenberg,[19] noticed in the Record for August, 1880, upon its original publication by the Messrs. Harper; *Hans Breitmann's Ballads*,[20] by Charles G. Leland; and an exquisitely printed "Parchment Library Edition" of Goldsmith's *Vicar of Wakefield*,[21] with a brief and tasteful preface and interesting illustrative notes by Mr. Austin Dobson.

THE greater number of the novels and tales of the month are by favorite authors, and although they can not be regarded as *chefs-d'œuvre*, they are very attractive specimens of their literary workmanship. Several others are by less practiced and less experienced writers, but yet are written with grace and spirit, and evince commendable narrative and descriptive powers. All are entertaining and wholesome. The list comprises: *The Wizard's Son*,[22] by Mrs. Oliphant; *Jack's Courtship*,[23] by W. Clark Russell; *A Real Queen*,[24] by R. E. Francillon; *The Picture*,[25] by Charles Reade; *Mr. Nobody*,[26] by Mrs. John Kent Spender; a new edition of Captain Marryat's sea tales, *The Pirate* and *The Three Cutters;*[27] *Bethesda*,[28] by Barbara Elbon; *Her Washington Season*,[29] by the author of *Marjorie's Quest; Jack of All Trades: a Matter-of-fact Romance*,[30] by Charles Reade; *The Bowsham Puzzle*,[31] by John Habberton; *Faith Thurston's Work, and How She Did It*,[32] by the author of "The Win and Wear Series"; and *Dr. Barringford's School*,[33] an engaging story for boys, by Henry Ogden.

---

[13] *Sesame and Lillies*. Three Lectures by JOHN RUSKIN. Revised and Enlarged Edition. 12mo, pp. 186. New York: John Wiley and Sons.

[14] *St. Mark's Rest*. The History of Venice. Written for the Help of Travellers who Care for her Monuments. By JOHN RUSKIN. 12mo, pp. 185. New York: John Wiley and Sons.

[15] *The Art of England*. By JOHN RUSKIN. 12mo, pp. 33. New York: John Wiley and Sons.

[16] *Doctor Johns*. Being a Narrative of Certain Events in the Life of an Orthodox Minister of Connecticut. By DONALD G. MITCHELL. 12mo, pp. 431. New York: Charles Scribner's Sons.

[17] *Bound Together*. A Sheaf of Papers. By DONALD G. MITCHELL. 12mo, pp. 291. New York: Charles Scribner's Sons.

[18] *Poems*. By MATTHEW ARNOLD. Two Volumes, 16mo, pp. 272 and 230. New York: Macmillan and Co.

[19] *The Life and Work of William Augustus Muhlenberg*. 12mo, pp. 524. New York: A. D. F. Randolph and Co.

[20] *Hans Breitmann's Ballads*. By CHARLES G. LELAND. Complete. 12mo, pp. 312. Philadelphia: T. B. Peterson and Brothers.

[21] *The Vicar of Wakefield*. By OLIVER GOLDSMITH. With a Preface and Notes by AUSTIN DOBSON. 18mo, pp. 308. New York: D. Appleton and Co.

[22] *The Wizard's Son*. A Novel. By Mrs. OLIPHANT. "Franklin Square Library." 4to, pp. 104. New York: Harper and Brothers.

[23] *Jack's Courtship: a Sailor's Yarn of Love and Courtship*. By W. CLARK RUSSELL. "Franklin Square Library." 4to, pp. 132. New York: Harper and Brothers.

[24] *A Real Queen*. A Novel. By R. E. FRANCILLON. "Franklin Square Library." 4to, pp. 68. New York: Harper and Brothers.

[25] *The Picture*. A Story. By CHARLES READE. 16mo, pp. 48. New York: Harper and Brothers.

[26] *Mr. Nobody*. A Novel. By Mrs. JOHN KENT SPENDER. "Franklin Square Library." 4to, pp. 80. New York: Harper and Brothers.

[27] *The Pirate* and *The Three Cutters*. By Captain MARRYAT, R.N. "Franklin Square Library." 4to, pp. 40. New York: Harper and Brothers.

[28] *Bethesda*. By BARBARA ELBON. 12mo, pp. 312. New York: Macmillan and Co.

[29] *Her Washington Season*. By JEANNIE GOULD LINCOLN. 12mo, pp. 207. Boston: James R. Osgood and Co.

[30] *Jack of All Trades: a Matter-of-fact Romance*. Being a Narrative of the Famous Elephant Djek and her Keeper. By CHARLES READE. 16mo, pp. 49. New York: Harper and Brothers.

[31] *The Bowsham Puzzle*. A Novel. By JOHN HABBERTON. 16mo, pp. 222. New York: Funk and Wagnalls.

[32] *Faith Thurston's Work*. By the author of "The Win and Wear Series." 12mo, pp. 329. New York: Robert Carter and Brothers.

[33] *Dr. Barringford's School; or, The Long Holiday*. By HENRY OGDEN. 16mo, pp. 192. New York: G. P. Putnam's Sons.

Editor's Historical Record.

POLITICAL.

OUR Record is closed on the 17th of April.
—The following bills were passed in Congress: Post-office Appropriation, House, March 18; Deficiency Appropriation, Senate, March 21; joint resolution re-appropriating for the aid of sufferers by the Mississippi River floods the $125,000 not expended on the sufferers by the floods of the Ohio, both Houses, March 26; granting lands to Indians in severalty, Senate, March 26; offering a reward of $25,000 for the discovery of the fate of the Greely expedition, Senate, March 28; Trade Dollar Bill, with amendment striking out the deducting clause, House, April 1; Naval Appropriation, amended, Senate, April 14; Blair Education, appropriating $77,000,000 to be distributed among the States in proportion to their illiteracy on the basis of the census of 1880, the payments of the money to extend over a series of eight years, Senate, April 7; Indian Appropriation, House, April 4.

President Arthur, March 26, sent a special message to Congress urging the appropriation of money to reconstruct the navy.

The House, March 20, unseated Mr. Mayo, Re-adjuster, of Virginia, and gave the place to Mr. Garrison, Democrat.

Hon. A. A. Sargent, Minister to Germany, was offered a transfer to the Russian court, March 26, which he declined.

The bill to extend the period during which whiskey can be kept in bond was defeated by the House, March 27, by a vote of 83 to 185.

The House voted, April 15, by 140 to 138, to consider the Morrison Tariff Bill.

The United States debt was reduced $14,238,324 18 during the month of March.

The New Jersey State Assembly, March 18, rejected the proposed prohibition amendment by a vote of 26 to 30, and on March 31 voted down the Woman's Suffrage Bill by 24 to 27.

The Rhode Island Democrats, March 19, nominated George H. Corliss for Governor. He declined, and Thomas W. Segar was substituted. The Republicans on the following day renominated the present officers, including Governor Bourne. The election, April 2, resulted in a majority of 6289 for the Republican ticket.

The Illinois Republican State Convention met at Peoria, April 16, and nominated for Governor Richard J. Oglesby; Lieutenant-Governor, General J. C. Smith; Secretary of State, H. D. Dement; Auditor, Charles P. Swigart; Treasurer, Jacob Gross; Attorney-General, George Hunt.

A serious riot growing out of the dissatisfaction of the people with a verdict in a murder case was begun in Cincinnati March 28, and lasted three days. Public buildings were burned, and much property was destroyed by the mob. The entire State militia was called

out, and in the conflicts that followed 45 of the people were killed and 138 wounded.

The British House of Commons, March 18, passed the Army Estimates Bill, appropriating £4,230,000.

The British forces defeated the Arabs and burned Tamanieh March 27. On the same day General Graham received orders to return from the Soudan immediately, and on April 1 he sailed with his troops from Suakin for Suez.

The Italian ministry resigned, March 20, because of the smallness of the majority by which Signor Coppino was elected President of the Chamber of Deputies.

An unsuccessful attempt was made, April 13, to assassinate the President of Guatemala. He was only slightly wounded.

The French campaign in Tonquin was terminated, April 13, by the capture of Hong-Hoa.

DISASTERS.

March 29.—Six men killed by the explosion of a nitro-glycerine factory at Thompson's Point, Pennsylvania.

April 1.—Terrific wind-storms in parts of the South and West. The town of Oakville, Indiana, entirely destroyed, and four of the inhabitants killed and fifty wounded.

April 3.—Steamer *Rebecca Everingham* burned on the Chattahoochee River, Alabama, and many lives lost.—Steamer *Daniel Steinmann* wrecked off Sambro Island, Nova Scotia. One hundred and twenty lives lost.

OBITUARY.

March 17.—In London, England, R. H. Horne, aged seventy-seven years.

March 19.—In New York, Madame Anna Bishop, aged seventy years.—In Columbus, Mississippi, Bishop H. H. Kavanaugh, of the Methodist Episcopal Church South, aged eighty-two years.—In Philadelphia, Major-General Godfrey Weitzel, aged forty-nine years.

March 21.—In Boston, Massachusetts, George Fuller, aged sixty-two years.—At Cambridge, Massachusetts, Dr. Ezra Abbot, aged sixty-five years.

March 23.—In New York, John Jay Cisco, aged seventy-eight years.

March 24.—In Paris, François Auguste Marie Mignet, aged eighty-eight years.

March 27.—In New York, Augustus Schell, aged seventy-two years.

March 28.—At Cannes, Prince Leopold. Duke of Albany, youngest son of Queen Victoria, aged thirty-one years.

March 31.—In New York, Frederick Leypoldt, in his forty-ninth year.—In London, Nicholas Trübner, aged sixty-seven years.

April 4.—In Berlin, Gustav Richter, aged sixty-one years.

April 11.—In London, Charles Reade, aged seventy years.

THE great question of the annual migration is upon us. The cyclic philosophers, if there are any, know that civilization moves in a circle, and that the freedom of emancipated culture comes round to the freedom of barbaric life. Originally nomadic, we rove about until circumstances and the accumulation of our possessions compel us to settle down and take root in one place. Then the process of evolution goes on as wealth and uneasiness and dissatisfaction (which are names for modern culture) increase, until we become again in our desires nomadic. The cyclic philosopher, if he exists, says that the instinct for a fixed home is a "middle-class" instinct. The tramps like to roam, and the "higher classes" like also to roam, and to have many places of temporary residence. As we all belong to the higher class in this country, we all like to move about, and we do move according to our several abilities. If we understand the process of evolution on this continent, it was from the nomads to the dwellers in communal houses and villages, like the Pueblos, and then to the possession of separate homes, or, as the Indian philanthropists say now, to the holding of lands in severalty. As we become more highly developed and prosperous, we go back to a sort of communal existence in gigantic boarding-houses (especially in summer) and an association of flats, and those who can do so take a step further, and roam about in Europe, Africa, and Florida. The confessed advantage of a boarding-house and flat is that you can leave it at any time and start on your wanderings with no more preparation than an Indian needs in striking his wigwam, or a Tartar in saddling his horse.

Comparatively few as yet of the very highly civilized can put themselves on this absolutely nomadic basis; but once a year everybody must join in this movement in some way. This is not the dictate of fashion, but the demand of health. Our puny ancestors used to stay at home the year round, except for an occasional family visit, or a modest week or two at some mineral spring, or a sojourn in the neighborhood of an oyster bed. But nobody can live now without an absolute change of air and scene at least twice a year. Even in New England, where there is a change of air every twenty-four hours, and if one will only stay still he will get in the course of the year as many different climates as any human system can digest, there is a semi-annual frenzy for going away from home. Those who have pleasant homes get weary of the routine of comfortable existence and the accumulating burden of an exhaustive modern housekeeping, and long for the meagre accommodations of a gigantic boarding-house in some vast wilderness, or in some caravansary by the sea. It is the communal instinct breaking out again. There are those who say that this is owing to the malaria, that people need to change the kind of malaria, the city sort for the country sort, the sea-side kind for the mountain, and so on. But malaria, which is now nearly co-extensive, and getting to be thought synonymous, with civilization, is not the moving cause. It is the nervous system, which is in the process of evolution round to the old condition in which a man could not keep still. It must be that health demands again an approach to the nomadic state. There are a hundred diseases which wealth allows us to cultivate, besides malaria, that demand a summer and winter change.

As to where we shall go, the Drawer has no advice to give. It may say, however, that it would be well to try to think what the English would do in our circumstances, and then do it. If they would put on thick shoes and short skirts and go climbing about the rocky coast botanizing, that is the thing to do. If they would "ride to hounds" over farms at some fashionable watering-place, why, that would seem to be proper. If they would break wholly away from all chance of a toilet, and go "shooting" in the wilderness or the Rockies, that would be a noble course. If it is "good form" to lead a healthful out-door life, in Heaven's name let us do it, either afoot or a-horseback, in a canoe or on a bicycle.

———

IT is not often that an American is intentionally rude to a foreigner, or that that foreigner, especially when he happens to be one of our British cousins, is successful in returning an unanswerable and unruffled reply. These two things happened concurrently at a club in this city at the recent celebration of Evacuation-day, in commemoration of the final exodus of the British garrison a century before. A young Englishman happens to be seated at breakfast as the procession passes by, and to him enters a convivial young American, who, in a somewhat husky voice, remarks, "I shay, do you know whash thish day we are shelebrating, eh?"

"Yes," said the Briton, calmly, as he scanned his interlocutor through what a novelist would call his unmoved eyeglass; "this was the day when the—ah—the *gentlemen* left New York."

The most patriotic by-standers "could not forbear to cheer."

———

A GOOD story, and one as yet unpublished, was told about Henry Irving, the actor, at a recent dinner of Harvard alumni at Buffalo. When the English actor visited Boston, President and Mrs. Eliot were among the spectators at his first performance, and in order to do due honor to the stranger he was invited out to Harvard, shown all the college lions, and finally entertained at a luncheon to which a select party of distinguished dons were bidden.

"By-the-way, Mr. Irving," said the President, with a praiseworthy desire to open the conversation upon a subject of general interest, "are you a university man?"

"No, sir," was the actor's answer; then, as if he felt that the reply might be taken as in some way implying disrespect for the college, and colleges in general, he added, "but my business manager here is."

HERE is something pleasant and useful for the doctors:

THE FABLE OF THE LEARNED PHYSICIAN.

There once lived in a small village a certain physician who had acquired a reputation for great learning and skill. His practice had been at first confined to the inhabitants of the village and the surrounding districts; but rumors of his peculiar method of treatment, and of some remarkable cures that it had effected, having spread abroad, patients began to come to him from points more and more distant.

This physician employed but three drugs— camomile, sweet-oil, and camphor. These, he maintained, singly, or combined in different proportions, contained all the medicinal virtues, and perhaps a few more besides. The extent of his practice, indeed, may have been due more to the novelty of his treatment than to the number of his cures. For I have noticed that people are commonly eager to believe that the untried will accomplish that in which the tried has failed, and that the greater the seeming improbability is of a new method meeting with favorable results, the greater is the confidence of men in the superior wisdom of its author. However that may be, whether by good luck or by sterling merit, the fame of this physician grew rapidly, as also did his bank account and his hair. During his lifetime he refused to reveal to any one the secret of his success, and how he adapted to the peculiar natures of the thousand and one diseases that beset mankind the few drugs he employed, but after his death the following explanation was found among his papers:

"I make this confession that learned men may not uselessly consume their time in seeking to discover what they imagine to be the hidden properties of camomile, sweet-oil, and camphor. These drugs have, as far as I am aware, no virtues other than those already known to science. Why, then, I confined myself to them in my practice I will briefly explain.

"I started in my profession with no profound knowledge of medicine, and feeling my inability to succeed in a large town, I settled in the small village of F——. My practice here was at first very small; but in the few and ordinary cases which came under my treatment I prescribed much the same as I suppose a more competent physician would have done in my place. But one day the village apothecary came to me and said: 'Doctor, your patients bring me prescriptions which I can not fill from my stock. Now you can make it profitable to me, and I can, I think, make it of advantage to you, if you will not prescribe beyond my limits.' 'Of what, then,' I asked, 'does your stock consist?' He replied, 'Of camomile, sweet-oil, and camphor.' As my means were at that time narrow, and as I was modestly aware of the danger which my patients must incur from my insufficient knowledge of medicine, thinking that I might at once benefit myself and my fellow-men, I acceded to the apothecary's proposal. I have never had reason to regret my action, for at the moment I write I enjoy probably the greatest reputation of any living physician."

This fable teaches us how to make a virtue of necessity.   E. L. THAYER.

THESE two stories are said to be going the rounds in Vermont:

In the days of stage-coaches, when the now thriving town of St. Johnsbury was coming into prominence, awakening the jealousy of rival towns, the stage-driver between St. Johnsbury and Newport was interviewed at the latter place one evening.

"Getting smart up Johnsbury, ain't they?"

"Smart's no name for it," was the reply. "They've built a new hotel up there, and use the old one for a pantry; and they've got a bell in one of the churches so large that it takes four hundred people to hear it; *two hundred can't begin to hear it.*"

The other is that Wendell Phillips was waiting for the train at Essex Junction, where passengers exercised at times great patience. He saw a grave-yard away from the village, near the depot, and very full. He inquired the reason, and a Green Mountaineer calmly informed him *that it was used to bury passengers in who died waiting for the train.*

SOME years ago a stone-mason employed ex-Judge Lee, of the Supreme Bench of Virginia, to write him a deed, and was very greatly surprised when he learned that the price was five dollars. "What, Judge!" he exclaimed, "you surely don't mean to charge me five dollars for that little bit of scribbling, do you?"

"But, Jim," replied the Judge, "you don't appear to understand. Remember I am not charging you for the writing merely—not for the mechanical execution—but for the art of knowing *how* to do it, you see."

This explanation was satisfactory to Jim, and the price was no longer disputed.

Some time after this the Judge had occasion to have a couple of grates set in his residence, and Jim was the man selected to do the work. When he had finished, the Judge inquired the price, and was very promptly informed that it was five dollars. "Five dollars? My goodness! Why, Jim, certainly not five dollars for only a few hours' work? Why, that's enough to—"

"But look here, Judge," interrupted Jim—"look here, now. Remember, I am not charging you for the work merely—not for the mechanical execution—but for the art of knowing *how* to do it, you see."

The joke was too highly appreciated by the Judge to admit of the price being further disputed, and he handed Jim five dollars cheerfully.

SOME time ago, on a very cold and stormy day, an auction sale was held at the New York Custom-house. Among the articles sold were a lot of old doors, bought by a gentleman from Staten Island. Mr. B——, the auctioneer, rather surprised at the purchase, remarked:

"T——, what are you going to do with those doors?"

The quick response was: "Why, Mr. B——, you wouldn't have a man *out of doors* such weather as this!"

ONE AGAINST FIVE.
AN IRISHMAN'S ADVENTURE IN PORTUGAL.

THE sun was sinking over the pretty little town of Setubal, in the west of Portugal, and its last rays lighted up a very stirring and picturesque scene. Along the banks of the stream that ran through the great plain beyond the town there seemed to be a monster picnic going on, and, stranger still, a picnic made up entirely of soldiers. Camp fires were sending up their thin blue smoke into the bright evening sky. Muskets were "stacked" on every side like sheaves of corn, and men in gay uniforms were bustling to and fro, carrying bread and ration beef, hunting for fuel, or fetching water from the river.

But the strangest thing of all was that the men on one side of the stream were all dressed in red, and those on the other side in blue. In fact, the French and English soldiers who had been fighting before Setubal were making friends during a short truce, and having their supper together. The French tried to talk English, the English and Irish to talk French, and many a shout of good-humored laughter arose over each other's mistakes.

A tall, sinewy, bright-eyed "Tipperary boy" —one of the famous Irish Brigade which acquired such a terrible renown in this very war—was dipping his hot face in the stream, when a voice from the opposite bank shouted:

"Hoi! Monsieur Patreek, you come here; I give you some suppare."

"Who's that, annyway, Pat?" asked Patrick's rear-rank man, Denis Moriarty.

"'Who's that,' is it? Sure he's a broth of a boy intirely, whoever he is. 'Twas he that gev me this little remimbrance yisterday" (pointing to a fearful gash in his cheek); "and, by the same token, I wrote my name on that arrum he's got tied up there. Come an, and I'll inthrojuce yez to him."

A very merry party the three made. The French trooper wound up the supper with a French song, and Paddy gave him one in Irish, and they parted the best of friends; but Pat whispered in Moriarty's ear: "It's an illigant supper we've had, Dinny; but thim same chaps will be afther givin' us a hot breakfast in the mornin'."

O'Callaghan's prophecy proved true enough. At daybreak the English outposts were driven in by a large body of French skirmishers, and the battle soon became general along the whole line. The Twenty-eighth were in the thickest of the fight, as usual, and twice repulsed the attack of a French grenadier regiment. As the enemy fell back the second time, the hot Irish blood could stand it no longer, and out rushed the Twenty-eighth men in pursuit, although their officers, seeing the danger, called loudly to them to halt.

But it is no easy matter to stop an Irishman when in chase of an enemy, and the "boys of the ould brigade" followed the pursuit so far that they got scattered, and fell into disorder. At that moment the French dragoons came down upon them like a whirlwind, and Paddy O'Callaghan, after fighting like a hero, and knocking down men right and left, as if he had been at Donnybrook Fair, found himself separated from his comrades, and right in among the enemy.

Just then a riderless horse came flying past, and Pat, making a sudden spring, clutched the reins, and was just going to scramble on its back, when he heard his name called, and looking down, saw at his feet the burly form of Denis Moriarty.

"Are ye hurt, Dinny?" asked O'Callaghan, tenderly.

"They've bruk my arrum, the vagabones!" growled Moriarty, in a voice hoarse with pain. "It's little use I'll be now, at all, at all!"

"But can ye sit a horse, me boy? It's wid yer legs ye do *that*, shure—not wid yer arrums."

"Is it 'sit a horse' ye mane?" rejoined Moriarty, disdainfully. "Faith, thin, jist git me wanst on the baste's back, and av he's as wild as Barney O'Toole's pig, I'll stick on him."

Without another word, Pat lifted his wounded comrade into the saddle, and away went the horse and Denis, who, as he had said, stuck to his seat as if he had been glued.

But Paddy's generous self-devotion seemed likely to cost him dear, for at that instant five of the French dragoons, catching sight of his red jacket, came charging down upon him all at once.

"Five to wan, is it?" muttered Paddy. "Och, it's sartain the thieves have larned their arithmetic, and know that wan Irish boy is as good as five Frinchmin anny day. But ye don't git me so aisy, ye frog-aitin' spalpeens."

With one bound he was behind the trunk of a huge cork-tree that stood near, from which ready-made intrenchment the barrel of his musket poked itself out so threateningly that the Frenchmen pulled up rather hastily.

"What's the matter wid yez?" shouted

O'Callaghan. "Come an, thin, like dacent boys. Don't ye see me here waitin' to spake wid yez?"

One of the dragoons fired his pistol, but the shot only drew a taunting laugh from our hero, while the threatening muzzle fronted them at every turn, face which way they would. Evidently Paddy was master of the situation, and the mischievous twinkle of his blue eyes showed how thoroughly he enjoyed it.

But now the dragoons, enraged at being held at bay so long by one man, divided their forces, two wheeling toward one side of the tree and two toward the other, while the fifth came straight forward. Matters seemed likely to go hard with poor Pat, when suddenly the air was rent with the war-cry of the Irish Brigade, "Faugh-a-ballagh!" (Clear the way), and on came the Twenty-eighth once more, their long line of bayonets glittering through the smoke like sunbeams breaking a mist.

At sight of the coming help Paddy's bold blood was up at once. Out he darted upon his assailants with a flourish of his musket and a real Irish "hurroo," which was sufficient to frighten the whole cavalry of the Imperial Guard.

It *did* scare the horse of the nearest French dragoon, which reared and fell heavily, rider and all. Before the Frenchman could rise again O'Callaghan's foot was on his breast, and held him there "like a dog houldin' a pig by the ear," as Paddy afterward said, till the men of the Twenty-eighth came up and helped him to secure his prisoner.

"Well done, my fine fellow," said the old colonel of the Twenty-eighth, when he heard the story of Pat's exploit. "Here's a guinea for you, and well you've earned it. But why didn't you give those rascals one shot at the last, when you had the chance?"

"Sure for the best of all raisons, yer honor," answered Pat, with a grin; "*there was nothing in the gun, at all, at all.*"

And ever after that day, when any man made a great show of learning upon a subject about which he really knew nothing at all, the officers of the Twenty-eighth used to say that he was like Pat O'Callaghan's musket.

THE Rev. Mr. B——, pastor of a church in ——, Connecticut, told a correspondent this story:

One of the wealthy farmers of his parish had died, leaving behind him an afflicted widow, as he supposed. Circumstances prevented him from seeing her till some weeks had passed, which seeming neglect troubled him exceedingly. At length he called, shrinking from meeting the poor disconsolate woman.

"Madam," he said, "I regret exceedingly that I have not been able to come to you before in your great sorrow, but you have had my warmest sympathy. I trust that your great loss will be more than made up to you by—"

But before he had time to say more she broke in with this exclamation: "Oh, Mr. B——, that would be too much to expect. I've got to bear it as well as I can, but I think I've found a pretty good match already. He isn't quite as big as the other, but maybe he'll do as much work."

Mr. B—— stood aghast. Another husband already! But she went on: "The other used to have balky turns, and wouldn't pull well uphill. I hope this one will be better in that respect."

"Oh, shocking! shocking!" thought Mr. B——. "What a monster!" But she continued: "This one has a much handsomer coat, and some other points superior to the other."

Mr. B—— felt that he must fly from the house, when she added, "I guess I shall have a very fair yoke of oxen again."

What, then, had she been talking about? Why, since her husband's death she had lost one of her oxen, which loss had so effectually obliterated the other from her mind and heart that her husband had passed from the scene entirely, and the ox had taken his place, and this in a few short weeks.

Our poor parson wasted no more sympathy here, but took his leave, disgusted with the world in general, and with widows in particular.

PER ASPERA AD ASTRA.

A CANVAS-BACK duck, rarely roasted, between us;
   A bottle of Chambertin, worthy of praise—
Less noble a wine at our age would bemean us;
   A salad of celery, *en mayonnaise;*
With the oysters we've taken, fresh, cool, and delicious—
   Naught left of them now but a dream and the shells:
No better *souper* e'en Lucullus could wish us.
   Why, even the waiters *must* see we are "swells!"

Your dress was a wonder; your jewels shone finely;
   Your friends in the circle all envied your box.
You tell me that Nilsson sang quite too divinely.
   I know I shall make on that last deal in stocks.
Without waits our footman to call us our carriage—
   How slow he must think us, out there in the cold!
We rode in a hack on the day of our marriage,
   Number two-thirty-six. I was rolling in gold,

For I'd full fifty dollars; and don't you remember
   How we drove down to Taylor's?—a long-cherished dream.
How proudly I ordered—just think, in December—
   Some cakes, and two plates of vanilla ice-cream!
And how we enjoyed it! Your look was the proudest
   Amid the proud beauties; your face the most fair.
I'm rather afraid, too, your laugh was the loudest:
   I know we shocked every one: we didn't care.

Now we'd care a great deal: with two boys in college.
   And daughters, both out, whose sneer makes you wince.
We have tasted the fruit of society knowledge,
   And really have not enjoyed anything since.
Quite finished? Now *don't* wipe your lips with the doyley!
   I'm sure they're not careful at all with the wine—
It hadn't been warmed; and the salad was oily.
   I don't think the duck was *remarkably* fine.

                GEORGE A. BAKER.

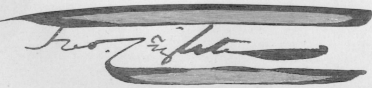

"A DAUGHTER OF THE NILE."—From a Sketch by Sir Frederick Leighton, P.R.A.

HARPER'S
NEW MONTHLY MAGAZINE.

No. CCCCX.—JULY, 1884.—Vol. LXIX.

THE NILE.

A T this moment all eyes are turned eastward, and Egypt has become an object of actual and almost hourly interest. The papers bring us daily all the news that can be collected on the exciting development of events in that hitherto calm and dreamy land. It is not my intention to swell the volume of information which we already possess by any opinions or political prophecies of my own. I only wish to sketch for such of my readers as feel more than a passing interest in the land of Egypt some facts, traditions, and customs which may serve as background to the picture which the present unrolls before us. Owing to my lengthened stay on the shores of the Nile I have had ample opportunity of making observations and studies bearing upon the development of the Egyptian people. When I was a boy, and studying Greek, one of the first sentences I committed to memory was: "Egypt is the gift of the Nile," an opinion expressed by the father of history—Herodotus. Its meaning was at that time in no wise clear to me, and I had no reason then to suppose that fate would put me in the way of testing its truth.

Many a time during the years that I spent in Cairo have I stood on the immense Nile bridge, leading from the Oriental capital to the villages on the western shore of the river and toward the Pyramids, and have brooded over the mysteries of this wonderful and fascinating stream.

In winter and spring, when the waters sink deeper and deeper in their bed, and here and there a sand island appears, the river resembles a weary wanderer who is straining every nerve to reach the longed-for goal. In summer, when the tropical sun sears and scorches all exposed to its rays, it is quite the contrary; then is the time when Father Nile, in proud consciousness of his power and strength, tosses his brown and turbid waves, and hurries on, fierce and grumbling, under the arches of that imposing bridge, threatening to overthrow it, and all else, in his rapid onward course. There are other bridges spanning arms of the Nile further on, but this is the only yoke to which he deigns to bend his broad back while yet an undivided current sweeping onward to the sea.

It is through the Nile, as through an artery, that the body of Egypt draws life and nourishment; where its pulsations cease, death—the desert—begins. The soil is like a sponge, and during the time of the inundation absorbs such quantities of moisture that they suffice for the vegetation of the whole land until a year later, when new floods appear, awaking life, and calling forth an expression of renewed vitality in plants and animals. "First a desert, then a sweet water lake, then a blooming garden," are the words in which Amru, the Mohammedan conqueror of the land, characterizes in short and terse expression its three most salient phases.

At a time when geographical knowledge was in its infancy, Herodotus expressed an opinion, which modern science has confirmed, viz., that not only the Delta, but the whole lower valley of the Nile, had originally been a gulf, filled out gradually by the enormous masses of mud carried along and deposited by the tempestuous river. Nay, more, he even prophesied that, should the river ever change its course, and choose the Red Sea as point of exit, the same phenomenon would be repeated, and in twenty, or even ten, thousand years a new and fruitful continent would be formed where now all is water.

To give an approximate idea of the quantities deposited by the Nile during

THE CITADEL OF CAIRO.

the time of inundation, I will only mention that in a glass of water left standing for an hour, from one to two inches of sediment will be found.

In the immediate vicinity of Cairo are the ruins, scattered over a large space, of the City of the Sun—the "On" of the Bible (Genesis, chap. xli., vs. 45–50). It was the centre of Egyptian science, and has a peculiar interest for us in that Scripture tells us that the wife of Joseph was born here; and here, no doubt, Moses, as the adopted son of an Egyptian princess, became acquainted with the wisdom and learning of that time. One would hardly think it possible, on visiting the spot, that it has once been the scene of so much intellectual life and architectural splendor, for naught remains of the far-famed Egyptian university to speak of its past glory but heaps of débris, interspersed with orange groves surrounded by enormous hedges of cactus. The Nile, during the inundation, presses forward without let or hinderance, and covers with its flood the place where schools, temples, and palaces once stood. There is but one grand and characteristic memento of the past left standing—a huge obelisk, the oldest in all Egypt—a monolith of over one hundred feet in height, erected by the King Userteseu I. in the year 2803 B.C. Of all the family of obelisks which Greek wanderers once saw united here, and which now are scattered all over the world, this one alone is left in solitary grandeur, a fitting tombstone on the grave of the past. This obelisk, at whose base a Joseph and a Moses have wandered, stood before the great Temple of the Sun. But time and the Nile have been busy bedding it deeper and deeper, and full two meters of earth have accumulated at its foot in the more than 2000 years since the ruin of Heliopolis.

One of the peculiarities of the rivers of Africa—this land of mystery, typified by the Sphinx guarding its gates—is that they take the longest possible way to reach the sea. And the Nile is no exception to this rule. Its chief sources, situated the one in the mountains of Abyssinia, the other in the vast lakes of Central Africa, are comparatively near the eastern shore of the continent; and yet, in spite of this, and of the fact that the most southern of its sources takes its start south of the equator, the huge body of water turns northward, and after making a great circuit only reaches the sea at a latitude of thirty-two degrees north. The distance traversed by the Nile on its lower course, where on both sides there is desert, and no tributary whatever, is one of about 800 geographical miles.

The Nile and its inundations could not

be otherwise than a great mystery to the primitive inhabitants of Egypt, who were only acquainted with its lower range, and knew nothing of its sources or tributaries. Even at the time of the Romans, "caput Nile quærere" (seeking the source of the Nile) was a common saying, its meaning being, to try to discover something which was above and beyond the pale of human knowledge or discovery.

Notwithstanding this, there was in ancient times no lack of men who tried to solve the problem, and Herodotus gives us, with more detail than any other ancient writer, the different opinions on the subject which were then current. He stamps as merest legend the conviction entertained by some that the Nile was derived from the oceans surrounding the earth. Another version was that the cold northern winds, which in summer sweep uninterruptedly over the land, checked the flow of the river, and thus caused it to rise and overflow; but this he also stamps as untenable. On the other hand, he as positively rejects the theory held and defended by some few *savants* of the ancient time, especially Anaxagoras, and which we now know to be the true one, viz., that the melting of immense masses of snow accumulated on the mountains in Central Africa caused the Nile to rise. It is, above all, the Blue Nile which, during the rains in Abyssinia, and the time of thawing snow, contributes so largely to swelling the tide. Herodotus, who opposes this theory, says in relation to it: "How is it possible that snow in such quantities should exist in a region where the inhabitants are burned brown by the sun; and where the winds are scorching hot?" He had heard from Egyptian priests that the origin of the Nile was to be found in the deep ravines or chasms called Crophi and Mophi; but the rise and fall of its waters he explained as follows: "In winter, the sun on leaving us takes its course over the earth in more southerly direction. In consequence of this those regions become so intensely hot that the waters of the Nile—only just appearing on the surface of the earth—at once evaporate. When the sun returns to us in summer, and pours its burning rays over our land, those distant countries in Libya are comparatively cool, and the waters of the Nile can, quite unchecked, well up, accumulate, and flow down to us." Thus far

the speculation of the learned. Strongly contrasting with this is the popular tradition concerning the Nile, which, in consequence of its vast influence for good and evil, for plenty or for famine, attributed to

THE OBELISK AT HELIOPOLIS.

it divine power, and gave it a prominent place in the religious ideas and observances of that day—a tradition whose unimpaired transmission is mainly owing to the extreme tenacity with which the Oriental clings to all superstitions connected with his land and people.

The mythology of the ancient Egyp-

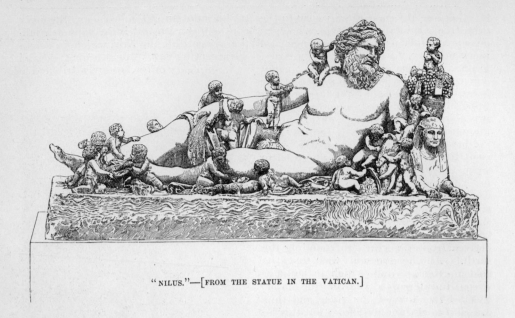

"NILUS."—[FROM THE STATUE IN THE VATICAN.]

tians, revealed to us in the many monuments on which it is recorded, impresses us at first sight as a chaos of color, letter, and design, and one into which the scholars of our time have brought but little order or system, comparatively speaking. It is a curious and interesting fact that this intricate maze of dogmas is reduced to simpler, clearer forms, the older the documents are in which we find its traces. In an extremely ancient sacred scroll, written on papyrus (known as papyrus Briss), we actually find only *one* God mentioned. To those who see in this only a proof of a long prehistoric development of the Egyptian people we will leave this theory, as well as the care of proving it, for as yet it has only been proposed.

It is quite natural that at a time when all manifestations of life, the human as well as the natural, were being deified, this river, representing moisture as a life-giving principle, the cause of all growth, should also be drawn within the magic circle of the deity, and be honored and worshipped as such. Was its appearance in the midst of desert and arid rocks not a miracle? What if not divine influence could be the cause of its yearly growth?

Most of us have no doubt seen pictorial reproductions of those peculiar Egyptian gods, invariably drawn in profile, and utterly without perspective. They are found in Egypt not only on the walls of temples and their gateways, monuments hewn out of the living rock, but also on the inner walls of tombs.

This most peculiar form of imagery has with wonderful tenacity preserved its rigid and inflexible character even at a time when Greek influence on art and religion was strong in Egypt, and when the Ptolemæi, who were desirous of uniting Greek art and beauty with Egyptian wisdom, sat upon the throne.

Among these portraits of their deities we find one—that of a man of greater height and fuller stature than the others—usually painted uniformly red or blue; on his head a wreath of lotus blossoms, in his hands aquatic plants and flowers. This is *the Nile*, the god *Harpi*. A beard gives proof of his manly prowess and strength, and a woman's breasts are symbolical of his nourishing, life-giving qualities.

The Greeks, who strove to clothe all mythological legends in gracious and winning forms, have chosen one far more pleasing than this crude Egyptian image. It is one of the finest specimens of classic sculpture, and such of my readers as have visited the Vatican in Rome will no doubt remember it—a male figure of athletic proportions, in a recumbent position, the left arm resting on a Sphinx. The head is crowned, here also, with aquatic blossoms; in his right hand are sheaves of wheat.

Sixteen graceful cherubs play about him, as symbolical of the sixteen yards of his growth and the universal prosperity caused thereby.

Isis and Osiris were brother and sister, as well as husband and wife—so says the legend—and reigned in prehistoric times in the land of Egypt: wise and gentle in their sway, maintaining peace throughout the land, and much beloved by their subjects. But they had a brother, full of envy and hatred, called Typhon, or Seth, who did not rest till he had murdered Osiris, cut up his body into many parts, and scattered them far and wide. With weeping and wailing Isis went in quest of the remains of her beloved; succeeded in finding all, save one, and gave them fitting burial. Her son, Horus, nurtured with thoughts of revenge, having reached maturity, failed not to seek and, when found, to slay in battle the enemy and murderer of his father. In the world of the immortals, however, Isis and Osiris were once more united, and continued, though invisible, to reign over their devoted subjects.

The manner in which Osiris is most frequently represented is that of King of Hades; the crown of Egypt on his head the scourge and crook in his hand, awaiting, as it were, the souls for judgment. He is monarch of the far west—the land of the dead; the King of Life, whom the souls of the departed must greet on their arrival in his realm with one hundred and twelve names and titles. According to Plutarch, the more intelligent of the priests interpreted this legend in various ways. One of the versions is that Osiris was the type of virtue, which, although often overcome by evil, is still in the end—and most surely in the hereafter—always victorious. But still another and most curious version is this: Osiris was the motive power in all fertilizing moisture, and they did not hesitate to call him plainly—the Nile.

Isis, the receptive, is the earth. Seth was, in their conception, the type of all aridity and dryness, all-scorching, wilting heat, transforming the fertility of the motherly earth (Isis) into a mourning widow; Seth is the wind that blows from the southwest, before whose withering breath all life and moisture disappear. Seth, yellow and reddish in color, comes from the Libyan desert, and resembles the hot sand that the fierce "chamsiu" storms

drive before them in the early spring days, and which is dense and cloud-like, so that it fills the day with gloom, and causes the sun to appear moon-like through the haze.

The course which the Nile takes from the high plateaux of inner Africa to the

BASS-RELIEF OF QUEEN ISIS.
From the Cairo Museum.

lower lands of Egypt is one that leads over rocky terraces, and in that part of its journey, which is called "the Cataracts," it presses forward between opposing rocks and bowlders, causing picturesque waterfalls and rapids. Not till it reaches Assuan is there any calmness or method in the flow, but from this point on the river bears the stamp of a quiet and graceful stream. All "wild oats" are sown, and the Nile enters into the sedate demeanor of a good citizen. Its chief occupations are agriculture, but it disdains not to place its strength at the service of commerce and navigation.

Just before the last rapid, viz., the Pass of Silsileh, the rocky shores approach so

THE ROCK TEMPLES OF SILSILEH.

closely that the Nile, which in some parts of Egypt has a breadth of six thousand feet, in this place is crowded into a space of barely three hundred feet. At this spot were the quarries which furnished the building materials for the majestic temples, and here, too, the adoration of the "god of the Nile" was peculiarly fervent.

On the western rocky projection is a very curious rock temple, and quite near by, in the quarries, are two stone slabs (*stela*) containing the commandment issued by King Rameses II., and renewed by his son Merneptah, and Rameses III., to solemnize on this spot two feasts in honor of the Nile. These inscriptions contain accounts of these festivals, and also a hymn, which was, no doubt, sung on these occasions in adoration of the god Harpi. The moment selected for these festivities was, on the one hand, that at which the Nile in Egypt began to rise; on the other hand, when "the book of the Nile was laid aside," that is, when the feasts which annually accompanied the inundation came to a close.

I have repeatedly conjured up before my mind's eye the picture of that time, when on the heights of Silsileh the priests of the Nile-god, wrapped in gorgeous raiment, with hands upraised, chanted the solemn anthem, while at their feet, in the deep ravine, the Nile rushed tempestuously on toward the thirsting Egyptian plains.

One of the grandest and most wonderful pages of Christian history is that which relates the triumphant march of the Cross through Egypt during the first centuries of our chronology.

The subject so often and justly selected by the Church for artistic representation, the infant Jesus forced to fly from his native land and his persecutors, and seeking shelter in Egypt, offers a parallel to the picture which history gives us of the infant Church, born into life in Bethlehem and on Golgotha, flying from the heights of Judæa and from the persecutions of the "chosen people" into the wastes and deserts of Egypt. The Egyptian religion, which had, till then, invariably conquered all those who had through power of sword swept over the land and possessed it, the Ethiopians, the nomad tribes of the East, the Persians, Greeks, and Romans, and had seen them, one and all, worshipping in its temples—this religion was forced to bow before the image of the Crucified, who, denuded of all outward power and glory, came into their midst. The ancient temples, which for thousands of years had been the nation's sanctuaries, were forsaken; on their ruins, in their vast courts and galleries, at their side, Christian churches sprang up.

And yet Egypt more than any other country showed great readiness in taking into its young Christian life alien elements, which, growing and developing, edge of the sword, threw down the empty forms of doctrine, drove the no longer united brethren into open discord, and in its turn, in place of the Cross, erected the Crescent.

All that remains of this early Christian Church are the Copts of to-day. They resemble the petrified image of spiritual strife long past. Their Christian life now consists in, and is expressed by, a series of purely external and superficial

VIEW OF THE SECOND CATARACT.

could not fail to cause the early decay of Christianity within its gates. Side by side with the adoration of the one true God sprouts, like a luxuriant weed, the adoration of saints, and finds ample nourishment in the traditions of the people. In place of the Serapis priests, who fled from the world and its temptations, came numbers of Christian hermits, soon disciplined and united into orders, to inhabit the Egyptian deserts. A new race of priests, formed and regulated with great accuracy, in accordance with the model of a long-venerated hierarchy, sprang up among those who still called themselves "brethren." Strife of doctrine, whose subtle questions all too soon absorbed the Christian interest, was often fought out with the sword. But Divine punishment was near at hand: Islamism, with the observances, lacking every element of warmth and vitality. And in their life, which bears but too plainly the stamp of long subjection, slavery of spirit has grown habitual. Their services, their small, humble churches and convents, built of clay, were to me always very touching, remembering what they once were, and what they had had to suffer.

It is curious to note how, in spite of such mighty spiritual revolutions, remains of the old heathen belief are to this day found in all classes of the Egyptian population. One finds customs, ideas, and convictions which, notwithstanding Christian and Moslem influence, date back for more than six thousand years. Especially the Nile is at this present day looked upon through the medium of ancient national traditions, and is the ob-

TOMBS OF THE SAINTS.
From a sketch by Sir Frederick Leighton, P.R.A.

ject of a custom which bears the marked traces of heathen ideas and practices.

Such of the "fellahs," or peasants, as have received some little culture know that the waters of the Nile come from the "land of dark men"—from the mountains of Abyssinia. In the year 1874, at the time of the war with Abyssinia, it happened that the Nile was slow to rise, and I have often heard, here and there in the villages, the opinion expressed that "no doubt the King of Dabeseh was revenging himself on the Egyptians by preventing the waters of the Nile from flowing down to them"; or that an ancient threat of Ethiopian kings, *i. e.*, to lead off the Nile before its entrance into Egypt, through a canal into the Red Sea, was being carried out.

But the inhabitants of the more isolated inland villages have not even such lights as these, and should you chance to come across such a fellah crouching at the door of his mud hut, holding his kéf (siesta), and quietly content, with as little mental exertion as possible, smoking his waterpipe, and should you ask him as to his opinion of the Nile and its origin, you would in most cases find that instead of entering upon geographical questions and hypotheses, he would, with a grateful glance toward heaven, answer, simply, "Min Allah!" *i. e.*, from God, or from heaven; and he would no doubt on his side turn questioner, and ask you, "Have you in your country also a Nile?" And great would be his astonishment and surprise on hearing that our vegetation, our crops, and our orchards are nourished by water which falls from the clouds. To him who hardly ever sees rain, and then only in a rare and passing shower, this seems a very precarious form of agriculture.

Nothing is more natural than that the Egyptian peasant, who has never been beyond his own village, and whose conceptions of the world, of men, and things are of the most limited, should, considering that the Nile gives him all he has and all he needs, look upon it as a direct gift of God.

Whether it be that his land is so favorably situated that the Nile flows over it at the time of inundation, or that the water reaches it through artificial irrigation by means of a water-wheel worked by the camel or the oxen of the peasant, or if he be very poor, owning neither camel nor oxen, and obliged to pull up the water in shallow buckets made of reeds, and with his own hand distribute it over his fields, this much is certain, that only in so far as the Nile has blessed his land will his corn or his cotton grow, and the harvest will be in exact proportion to the amount of moisture which the land has received.

And more than this, the Nile gives him so much besides. His hut is built of Nile mud, and thatched with reeds that

HEAD OF A PEASANT.
From a sketch by Sir Frederick Leighton, P.R.A.

grow in the canals; out of Nile clay is the beloved pipe, and also the water jar out of which he drinks (and he drinks incalculable quantities of water); and even for the "tarabooka," the peculiar kind of kettle-drum with which he accompanies all his monotonous songs and religious observances, does the Nile give him the clay. I have just said that the fellah is a great water-drinker, and I may add so are all foreigners in Egypt, for nowhere else that I know of is the water so clear and delicious. This is, no doubt, owing to the constant flowing over a bed of finest sand and loam. Filtered or cooled in a large urn of clay, it becomes perfectly cold, and is very refreshing.

I can well understand that the Bedouin of the desert, who for many months in the year has only briny springs wherewith to slake his thirst, and springs, too, that give but little, knows no greater luxury than to give his fleet camel the rein, and, having reached the green and fertile shores of the Nile, to deeply drink of its pure and limpid waters.

When the canals which furrow the land in every direction, and when the pools which the flood leaves behind it in every hollow and fall of ground, are dried up, when the cisterns grow empty and the women have far to go to fetch the water needed for their household, and are seen in picturesque groups carrying the large earthen jars on head or shoulders back to their humble huts, then is the time when men and animals thirst and yearn for the days when the glad tidings "the Nile is rising" shall meet the ear.

The night of the 17th of June (*i. e.*, the 4th of the Copt or Christian-Egyptian month "Bauneh") is to this day known in popular parlance as "Leilet-en-Mekta" (*i. e.*, the night of the drop). It is a time-honored creed, upheld even now, that during this night a wonderful, mysterious drop from heaven falls into the Nile. The ancient Egyptians believed that it was a tear which Isis wept, and the astrologers of the present time even pretend to calculate with great nicety the exact moment at which this drop is said to fall. Then, far away in the distance where the drop fell, the Nile begins to surge and swell, ever nearer and nearer, and soon the shores are too narrow to hold it.

Many of the inhabitants of Cairo and other towns on the river spend this night on the Nile shores or in adjacent houses or villas of their friends. The women make little rolls of dough, one for each member of the household, and place them on the "terrace," or flat roof, of the house. When the sun rises they go to inspect these rolls. Such as have burst open portend long life, health, and happiness to those whose names they bear; and such as show but small or no signs of development signify the contrary.

When the inundation approaches the capital—usually at the end of June or the beginning of July—the Nile criers (Muna-di-en-Nil) begin their work. These criers are men whose business it is to call out, or rather to recite, before the houses of those who wish it, how much the Nile has risen during the last twenty-four hours. The Oriental does everything, no matter what it is, gravely, slowly, with much dignity and verbosity, and is never chary of his time or breath. Even the form of his greeting in the street is a complicated ceremony of words and motions which usually takes some moments to perform. And in the same way this announcement of the river's rise, which seems to us such a simple matter, is a most serious affair.

The day before the crier begins his task he goes through the streets accompanied by a boy, whose part it is to act as chorus, and to sing the responses at the proper moment. The crier sings:

"God has looked graciously upon the fields."
Response: "Oh! day of glad tidings."
"To-morrow begins the announcement."
Response: "May it be followed by success."

Before the crier proceeds to give the information so much desired, he intones with the boy a lengthy, alternating chant, in which he praises God, implores blessings on the Prophet and all believers, and on the master of the house and all his children. Not until all this has been carefully gone through does he proceed to say, the Nile is risen so many inches.

This ceremony is carried on until the month of September, when the river has reached its culminating point, and the crier, as bringer of such good news, never fails to claim his "baksheesh," sometimes humbly, and sometimes, too, very imperiously.

The reports of these men, who in all Egyptian towns are the ambulant advertisers of the state of the Nile, are not always reliable. This is partly owing to the fact that, with true Oriental indifference, they do not take the trouble to acquire

HEAD OF AN OLD MAN.

From a sketch by Sir Frederick Leighton, P.R.A.

exact information at the only reliable sources, and also that the government intentionally spreads false reports in regard to the advance of the inundation. As the land tax can not be levied on certain large tracts of land until the rise of the Nile shall have reached at least sixteen Egyptian yards, it does not hesitate (a fact that has come within my own experience) to spread false reports; and although the imposition is patent to all, no one dares to raise his voice in remonstrance.

But my readers must not think that exact measurements in this important matter do not exist, or are not to be had. On the contrary, there are most carefully constructed Nile measurers in Cairo, near the First Cataract, and at Khartoom, at the junction of the Blue and the White Nile. The measurer at Cairo is a very remarkable building, erected (as we know with certainty) by the Caliph Motawakil I., A.D. 861, in place of a former measurer destroyed A.D. 716 by the river floods. A detail of peculiar interest, as far as the architecture is concerned, is that here, for the first time, is the Gothic arch employed.

This Nile measurer, called by the Arabs "Mekjas," is situated on the isle of Rhodda, quite near Cairo. It consists of a very deep and carefully constructed well, which is connected with the Nile by a subterranean canal, in consequence of which the height of the water in the well is always in exact accordance with that of the river. In the middle of this well we see an octagon pillar, on which a graduated scale gives us exact information as to the rise of the river. Steps lead down into the well, so that one can at any time reach the water's level and see for one's self. The height considered necessary for a favorable inundation is, in Cairo, eighteen Egyptian yards, or nine and a half meters, over and above the lowest water-mark. But the moment the flood rises above twenty-two yards, it becomes dangerous and devastating.

I wish that my readers might enjoy, what I have often enjoyed, the glorious view, which at the time of the inundation is peculiarly fascinating, from the summit of the mountains which bound the valley of the Nile on the eastern side. Let me try to lead you there, in fancy at least. It is an excursion which amply repays any one who undertakes it.

At other times of the year the valley of the Nile, seen from this height, resembles a green and blooming garden. Waving corn fields, deeply green clover meadows, high-grown Indian corn and beans, sugar-cane and cotton plantations, cover every inch of cultivated ground, interspersed with groups of palm-trees and groves of acacias, in the midst of which the villages nestle. Far away to westward the hills of the Libyan desert frame the picture, and the Pyramids of Ghizeh stand out in bold profile against the sky. If so be that the sun is setting behind them at the time that your eye is resting on this picture, you will enjoy a symphony of color such as once seen is never forgotten. The blue-green tints of the valley meet and blend with the warm browns and ochres of the desert, and through almost purple tints these again are united with and attuned to the deep blue of the sky.

The grand simplicity of subject, combined with the—I might say classic—harmony of lines and the marvellous blending of colors, which go to make up the Egyptian landscape, can not but fascinate every artist; and all who have once seen and studied it are drawn irresistibly again and again to the deeper study of these problems of art. At the moment that I have selected for introducing this picture to my readers, the waters of the Nile, which at other times, hemmed in by the high shores, only resemble a silver ribbon winding in and out among the green fields, and glancing here and there as the sunlight falls upon it—these waters cover all, and the vast plain resembles an extensive lake. The villages, built on more elevated ground, and protected by high dikes, peep out of the vast expanse of water like islands in the sea. The palms, whose bluish-green feathery crowns are already burdened with heavy tassels of dates, red or brown or yellow, are more than halfway up their graceful stems in water. Numberless boats and small craft, with their picturesque lateen-sails, looking like sea-gulls on the wing, skim the water, speeding before the north wind, which at this season blows steadily and strongly, and sends them southward heavily laden with produce of the north, whence they return with cargoes of ivory, ostrich feathers, gum-arabic, and, alas! only too often, with slaves.

This is the time at which, in Cairo, a most curious and interesting fête is celebrated, one which has its origin in a heathen custom, namely, the so-called "break-

THE NILE ABOVE ASSOUAN.

ing through of the Nile," and takes place when the Nile has reached a certain height.

A canal traverses Cairo from east to west. This canal is closed, when the inundation begins, at the junction with the Nile, by a solid and well-made dike, and remains thus closed until the water-mark shall have reached a desired point. The rupture of this dike, which admits the water into the city, is accompanied by festivities in which all classes of the population share.

Already in the afternoon, and still more in the evening, of the day preceding the feast, numbers of dahabeeyahs—a kind of vessel found only on the Nile, and best described as a floating dwelling combin-ing great comfort with ship-like compactness and regard for space—are seen on the Nile approaching the spot where the canal and river meet, and there drop their anchors, while others continue tacking about. Some of these dahabeeyahs are the private property of residents of Cairo, who with their families spend this night on board; others are chartered for the occasion by a party who disperse, as best suits their taste, for the night, some retiring to the divans in the airy saloons, others preferring the deck, with its bright spectacle of illumination on all sides, for in the rigging of all these boats the colored lamps are twinkling and reflecting their light in the water.

One large boat among the many catches the eye in particular; it is that called "Akabeh," by the Arabs—painted in all the colors of the rainbow, its masts and rigging decked with countless lamps and flags. This boat leaves the harbor of Boolak, near Cairo, in the afternoon (and by paying a small sum one can obtain a passage), and sails on till it reaches the isle of Rhodda, quite near to which is the spot at which the festivities of that night are to take place. Here it is made fast by heavy cables, and prepares to remain till the morrow.

On the deck is an awning under which the passengers can wile away, with friendly cigarette and cooling sherbet, the intervening hours. In the imagination of the Egyptians of to-day, this boat represents the splendid vessel on which, in ancient times, the "Bride of the Nile" ("Aruseh"), a maiden, beautiful and of noble birth, was brought annually as a sacrifice to the god, and who, clothed in bridal array, was doomed to a watery grave.

The Arabs believe that Amru, the conqueror of Egypt, found this sacrifice still existing, and that only through Islamism has it been abolished. They say that during the year in which for the first time the sacrifice was wanting the Nile did not rise. On seeing this, Amru had, by the advice of the Caliph Omar, cast a letter into the river—a letter with the following words: "From Omar, the servant of the Lord and sovereign of the faithful, to the Nile of Egypt. If thou flowest of thyself, then cease to flow; but if it be God the Almighty who causes thee to flow, then we implore God the Almighty to let thee flow." And lo! in that same night the Nile rose sixteen yards.

We are more than justified in supposing that this is merely a pious legend— one in which the popular fondness for the wonderful and the tradition of a sacrifice to the Nile have united in glorifying Islam. We have, moreover, very reliable sources of historic information, through which we know that even in the heathen times in Egypt, when the Greeks first came into the land, the Egyptians no longer allowed human sacrifices. We know from a well-authenticated Greek author that the last sacrifice took place at Heliopolis, quite near Cairo, under King Amasis, and that the custom was abolished by him, and in its place a wax figure was annually offered to the Nile.

An Arab scribe states that in Christian times, instead of the yearly sacrifice of a maiden, it consisted in the finger of a mummy laid in a casket, and thus confided to the deep; but one finds it hard to credit such a tale, as it seems almost impossible to suppose that at the time when Christianity took root in Egypt it should have allowed human sacrifice, even in such harmless form, to exist.

Credulous tourists are apt to be told by their guides and dragomans that even to this day the fiction is upheld, and a "grandly attired doll is brought to the altar of sacrifice by the 'Akabeh,' and there, under various ceremonies, given to the river"; but such is not the case. What, however, does take place—and no doubt it points back to very ancient times, when the Egyptian people felt under obligation to give the Nile its best, its blooming, graceful womanhood—is as follows: Some few yards behind the dike already described in the canal through which the water reaches Cairo, the Arabs mould a kind of figure (somewhat resembling the "snow-man" of our school-boy days), and plant corn or clover on the top; this is a practical and prosaic, even if very grotesque, rendering of the old fable, and the Nile, on bursting the dike, has but few strides to make before it encircles this figure (which the Arabs call "el Aruseh," the bride of the Nile), and sweeps it away.

All Orientals, and the Egyptian is no exception to the rule, like to have their merry-makings at night. And they are right. The intense heat of the day is over; the sun, with its rays and its glare, no longer wearies eyes and nerves; the glorious star-lit sky—such a sky as only the far East can show—spreads its canopy over all; a soft, balmy breeze comes gently through the valley, and blows upstream, bringing the cool but never cold atmosphere of the Mediterranean, whose moisture and briny odors have been modified by the long journey it had to make before reaching the inland capital. This is the time, above all others, at which the river and its shores become the scene of animated life. At regular intervals the cannon boom, for without smell of powder, much shouting and screaming, and oft-repeated fire-works the proper holiday mood is wanting. Legions of small boats, like midges glancing over the water, move about in all directions as connecting links

ASSOUAN.

between the large, firmly anchored vessels.

From some one point the sound of the "tarabooka" is heard, and to its monotonous rhythmic accompaniment female singers warble their slow and melancholy ditties, ending generally in a chromatic scale. From another side the sound of castanets meets our ears—a sure sign that here the oft-mentioned and far-famed, though certainly not admirable, dancing-girls are in full performance. Along the shore hundreds of tents are erected, lighted, according to their rank and degree in the social scale, either by most primitive little oil lamps, or, progressing upward, most luxurious colored lanterns. In these booths refreshments of all kinds, but mostly coffee and sherbet, are to be had; and here one finds the sedate and well-to-do paterfamilias and the youthful though independent donkey driver side by side, smoking. The entertainment consists in listening to ballad singers, comic actors, reciters of Koran verses and romances; and all these artists manage to collect an ample public around them, and one which is very simple in tastes and most grateful and appreciative for whatever is offered it. Add to all this, constant, endless screaming and shouting, a maze of human forms ever rolling and unrolling itself, and my readers will be able to form some idea of what are the elements that go to compose every Arab festivity, and so also this "feast of the Nile."

Shortly after midnight the Arabs begin their work at the dike. To the accompaniment of a monotonous strain they dig away valiantly, so that at daybreak only a thin wall of earth remains as partition between them and the mighty flood beyond. At rise of sun the Khedive (viceroy), surrounded by the grandees of his realm, all in uniforms and gold-lace, arrives; he takes his stand in a tent prepared for him, and which commands the best possible view of all that goes on. A secretary takes a place at his side, and is prepared to take notes on this most important act, testifying that the Nile has reached the necessary height for bursting the dike, and for the land-tax on all the fellah to begin its work. This document is sent to Constantinople the moment the festivities are at an end.

A boat with a sharply built bow approaches, and steers straight at the dike, thus breaking through the thin wall of earth, and admitting the flood, which, tumbling and foaming, rushes through the opening, growing wider from minute to minute, and soon the rapid flow of the water has swept away even the last obstacle. Seated in a little boat, which dances on the top of the muddy waves, is the overseer of these earth-works, looking calmly victorious, as, floating onward with the current, he is carried back to the city. Many black and brown individuals hastily divest themselves of their, at best scanty, wardrobe, and jump into the water, swimming about and watching for the moment when the Khedive shall throw a

handful of coin into the river. Formerly these were of gold, then of silver, and
now, alas! are only given in copper. Hardly have the coins flashed in the sunlight
when the swimmers dive after them with
great adroitness, and happy the man who
returns with booty. By the rosy light of
the early morning the last batch of rockets and other fire-works is set off, salvos
of cannon and never-ending shouts and
hurrahs publish far and wide the good
news that the Nile has risen to its full
height.

My readers have kindly followed me on
an imaginary pilgrimage to the most ancient phases of human history, as well as
to the wholly modern times, tracing
through all the veneration, we may say
adoration, which one of the most remarkable nations of the world, in the past as in
the present, has offered to a stream. Not
only the scholars of our day, but every
cultivated person feels an interest in such
questions, and it is particularly Egypt
which has been selected as a frequent subject of study and attention. It is a fascinating problem to seek the source from
which the river of life proceeds, in whose
waters our thirst for knowledge is slaked.
Our civilization rests on the shoulders
of the classic nations, but these, in their
turn, have taken their first lessons of
philosophy, literature, and art from the
Orientals, and especially from the Egyptians.

More and more do our studies tend to
show that *there* was the root of the culture
which bloomed in the classic era. To-day
there are but few traces to be found of
this former grandeur; nothing but colossal ruins, and wastes covered with frag-

ments, speak of the immense work of mind
and as great work of hand which once distinguished this epoch in history.

Any one who has lived in the midst of
Mohammedans, and has had occasion to
study Islamism in all its bearings, can
not, while admitting its power and importance, entertain any doubt of its destroying influence on all culture and
progress. Wheresoever in its triumphal
march it came upon an existing and well-
based civilization, it never failed, vam-
pire-like, to sap its vitality and to absorb its power, and as surely, also, to annihilate its existence in the end. It has
in no wise been able to further or develop
any good or beautiful institution found
blooming on its way. More than one of
our intelligent travellers and scholars,
men who are never disposed to advance
religious points of view in preference to
others, have yet expressed the conviction
that "the land of Egypt" can not rise again
until the Cross be planted where the Crescent now stands.

We Christians can but hope and pray
that, through the present mighty crisis
in the heart of Islam (and especially in
Egypt)—a faith whose political development is identical with its religious—a
day may dawn on which the Egypt that
is now so deeply fallen may "arise and
take a firmer and surer stand" in the
strength of a renewed Christian understanding and renewed Christian life; that
the Nile may become the thoroughfare on
which civilization, bearing onward the
glad tidings of a Saviour of all who have
strayed or are fallen, may bring light into
the inmost recesses of the "Dark Continent."

NEAR ASSOUAN.

THE NATIONAL DEAF-MUTE COLLEGE.

THE SILENT SCHOOLS OF KENDALL GREEN.

THE aim of this article is to sketch faithfully, if briefly, the history of an institution which, æsthetically considered, is the highest expression of a noble philanthropic impulse, yet young among us, and which is, practically viewed, the means of restoring to society many valuable members.

In the year 1855 there appeared in Washington a man professing great zeal in charitable work, who announced his purpose to open a school for the deaf-mute and blind children of the District. Being, like most reformers, as poor in purse as he was rich in promise, he interested several influential patrons, hired a house in the then solitary northwest section of the city, and gathered there all the afflicted children he could find, principally from among the poor classes. He pursued his way undisturbed for some time, but gradually horrible stories grew current about cruelties suffered by those poor little waifs, and the rumor reaching Amos Kendall, who had been deeply interested in the scheme from the first, he went to work to investigate it. His method was very simple—there was no red-tape entanglement about it: he just took a friend with him, went to the house, and finding the door locked, broke it open and walked in. Sterner men than those two kindly visitors would have been moved at the sight before them.

No need to repeat the details. Suffice it to say that the villain who had pretended to protect these unfortunate children had taken advantage of their sightless eyes and dumb lips to subject them to every device of inhumanity. Mr. Kendall's remedy was as practical as his inquiry had been prompt: he took the children to his own home, restored the majority to their parents, and placed the five left on his hands in a little frame house on a two-acre lot, which formed a part of his estate, situated just northeast of the city limits. To assist him in the work he now contemplated, the school having been incorporated by Congress under the name of the Columbia Institution for the Deaf and Dumb and the Blind, he sent for Edward M. Gallaudet, of Hartford, Connecticut, a son of the first American teacher of mutes, and put him in charge. This was in the summer of 1857, and for seven years the work of the young institution was limited to the instruction of children in primary courses. In 1864, under the authority of Congress, given in a special act, the course of study was extended so as to include collegiate branches, and with the active support of

AMOS KENDALL.

Thaddeus Stevens, a separate department was established, which was called the National Deaf-mute College. About the same time the blind, who had hitherto formed part of the community, were removed to the Maryland Blind Asylum, and from that time the establishment at Kendall Green has been identified with deaf-mutes only.

Look at it to-day. Few institutions make such good use of twenty-five years. Remember it began in a two-story frame house on a two-acre lot, and now it is a group of picturesque and stately buildings, surrounded by a fair domain of one hundred acres, standing midway between the pleasant meadows of Maryland and the capital of the nation. It enjoys the rare distinction, too, of being one of the few public works that cost less than the original estimates. The purpose of its foundation seems to touch a chord of universal sympathy, and with rare exceptions no serious opposition has been offered in Congress, while in many cases an examination of the institution has changed prejudice to patronage. Mr. Kendall's benefactions, bestowed during the early years of the work, and before the permanent support of the government had been secured, deserve to be specially noted. And it is to be remembered that his gifts, though small when compared with the sums since ap-

propriated by Congress, were relatively of much greater importance, because they came in "the day of small things."

Besides the frame house and two acres of ground with which the institution began, Mr. Kendall gave a substantial brick building, erected entirely at his own expense in 1859, together with cash donations at different times as special needs arose, making in all a total in value of fifteen thousand dollars. After Mr. Kendall's death, which occurred in 1869, Congress appropriated eighty thousand dollars for the purchase of eighty acres of ground, on which Mr. Kendall's home had been for many years, and to which he had given the name now attaching to the ample and beautiful grounds of the institution.

The college, which has proved to be national in its work as well as in name, has sent out two hundred and sixty young men, apportioned as follows: New England, 47; Middle States, 65; South, 36; West, 111; Ireland, 1. Thirty of these are teachers in deaf-mute institutions, for which work their college training specially fits them; five are connected, as editors, publishers, and contributors, with literature; six are in the civil service, one, who was for eight years a principal examiner in the Patent-office, is now an eminent and successful patent lawyer in Cincinnati; and others are distributed through various professions and trades.

The course of study comprises the higher mathematics; the Latin, French, and German languages; the elements of natural science, including chemistry, botany, astronomy, geology, mineralogy, physiology, and zoology; a full course of English philology and related studies, with ancient and modern history, not omitting proper attention to mental, moral, and political science.

I saw a Latin class not long ago at the college, composed of six good-looking young men — five of them Westerners, parsing one of Cæsar's speeches in Sallust. Each took a word and gave its grammatical character, derivation, and significance so rapidly that the pupils' quick fingers were as marvellous as the teacher's quick eyes. In an adjoining room a preparatory class was reciting a lesson in English grammar, and I doubt if any ten boys, blessed with all their faculties, would have shown such interest in adverbs as these poor fellows did. Every face was alert, every eye was *listening*, every right hand ready to *speak* at a glance from the tutor.

In the infancy of the college, scholarships were endowed by Amos Kendall, George W. Riggs, B. B. French, Charles Knapp, W. W. Corcoran, and Jay Cooke and Co., of Washington, Edson Fessenden and Thomas Smith, of Hartford, William Sprague, of Providence, and George

highly important and interesting division. The instruction given at this stage is the very foundation, the pith, the key, to all future progress. None but the most experienced teachers are assigned to these classes, and, indeed, some principals declare the primary desk to be the post of honor in deaf-mute institutions.

Of every mortal breast, thought is lord. He is born with the body, and lo! speech, his messenger, and hearing, his handmaid-

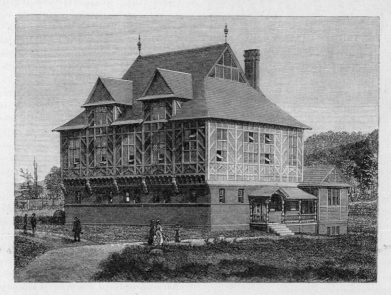

THE GYMNASIUM.

Merriam, of Springfield, Massachusetts. These endowments were only temporary, and the subsequent liberality of Congress filled the place of private generosity. The college library has recently been enriched by a very valuable collection made by Dr. Charles Baker, a distinguished English deaf-mute teacher. Some of the books date back to 1400, and it is one of the largest and best libraries, relating to the education of the deaf, to be found in the world.

The primary school at Kendall Green has an average attendance of fifty scholars. Sometimes men and women of full maturity appear in these classes, but they usually are formed of children ranging from eighteen to eight years of age, there being no advantage gained by sending them very young. Although necessarily subordinate to the college, the school is a

en, arise to do his will. Sight and touch are more humble vassals. Served by each in turn, he emerges from the narrow confines of his individual realm to take his place among his kindred, a link in the shining chain of human sympathy with which God binds the world. Not so with the untaught dumb, for though thought lives in them, it is as a prisoner. While they vainly beat against the cage, without and beyond in the clear daylight the unceasing procession of humanity passes, and if in their weak, imperfect way they recognize among the busy multitude, there a passion that reflects their own, here an emotion they might share, it is but a hint of the divine lesson of life. Beside such they possess nothing, know nothing, hope nothing.

Therefore the first thing to teach a deaf-mute child is that there is community of

CORNER OF TERRACE WALL.

ideas between him and his fellow-beings; the next, to show him how intercourse may be established. He comes to school not only to learn, but to learn *how* to learn. Let us imagine ourselves in the primary class at Kendall Green watching a beginner take his first lesson. The teacher, a lady—for surely nothing but a woman's patience could avail here—calls the boy to her, and shows him some familiar object—say a pen; and when he recognizes it, the first step is made: they both know what it is, and he knows they know it. So far, she has only taught him the object; now she shows him its printed equivalent, PEN. Insensibly trained to memory for shapes, he soon remembers that black lines shaped in that way mean that object. Now, if the object is not present, how can he recall it to her? By spelling p e n on his fingers. So she then teaches him those letters. Next she teaches him to write p e n on the blackboard; and lastly, to substitute for the rude pantomimes

they have both necessarily used up to this time, the sign for *pen*. This is not the work of one lesson, or of one day— far from it; we should be tired looking on long before our little hero gets as far as spelling on his fingers. But gradually, after many delays and innumerable repetitions, so much is secured. New objects are introduced, then their qualities are specified—"big pen," "white cat"; next the action of those objects— "the pen writes," "the cat eats"; and lastly, the various tenses of verbs—always a most tedious process, as it is almost impossible, with such limited means, to present clearly the difference between past, present, and future action. One way of doing this is to teach the pupils to count up to thirty-one—the number of days in a month—and then connect the action with a past, present, or future date. The protean "ough" puzzles them, as does also the use of the same word with different meanings.

Tiresome as the work is, its results appear sooner than one would expect, for the children learn to read, write, and speak (in their language) simultaneously. Little boys who can hardly reach the blackboard write excellent hands, and spell accurately. An exercise among the more advanced scholars which I witnessed required them to write sentences introducing words from the day's lesson. An example of the use of the word "astonished" was amusing: it was, "A boy went to the woods; he astonished some apples on a tree"—meaning he took them by surprise.

Here is a composition exactly as it was written by a boy twelve years old, a member of this class:

"A boy went to the woods. He saw a yellow bird standing on the grass. He want to caught the yellow bird. He put over the bird. The bird would not out. He caught the bird and went away and give for his mother. He tell his mother about the yellow bird. His mother was glad and got the bird and into the cage. Another a yellow bird was glad to meet the bird. Two birds talked about sing sweet. The mother charmed the bird sing. The boy again go to the wood. He saw an old house are weak. He try climbed up. The house with the boy fell to the ground. He soon died on the ground. His mother hoped the boy get the bird. His mother waited. The boy no come it.

His mother to go to the old house. She saw the boy died and she was very cried and hurt in her heart."

It reads like a crude translation. That the house "are weak" and old showed he reasoned, for it is not improbable an *old* house should fall, and the mother being "hurt in her heart" is a little touch that education could hardly improve.

One teacher has kept a record of the odd things the children say, and some entries are funny enough. Here are some of their plurals that make us blush for our illogical language:

Singular.	*Plural.*
Ox	Oxen.
Box	Boxen.
Mouse	Mice.
House	Hice.

A little fellow who lost his hearing from disease remembers a few words; so when he writes on the blackboard c a t, he articulates "pussy," and when v i o l i n, "fiddle." Another time a girl wrote a sketch of Job's history, with the startling information that "the Lord *boiled* him." But the most touching of all is the record of a little fellow who, when asked what George Washington did when his father inquired about the cherry-tree, wrote on the blackboard: "He took his hatchet in his left hand, and told his father he did it."

"Why did he take the hatchet in his left hand?" asked the teacher, surprised at the expression; and the answer came promptly:

"Because he had to use his right hand to tell his father."

The child thought George Washington was deaf and dumb.

When the blind and deaf-mutes were together, the forbearance and sympathy between them were very pretty. "How sad to be blind!" some deaf-mute would spell on his fingers, and perhaps the girl next to him would beg the teacher to give him an easy lesson, "because he is deaf and dumb, you know." The deaf-mutes make an exceptionally happy community, especially at Kendall Green, where the whole regimen of the establishment is home-like, and tends to make the inmates feel like members of one family, rather than two distinct classes of pupils and teachers. As a rule they are robust, and alive to the pleasures of physical exercise. Their base-ball club has a very creditable record, and at a foot-race run some years ago in Washington a Kendall Green Freshman came in second, and would have been first but for some misunderstanding as to the goal. Within two years opportunities for physical development have been greatly increased by the creation of a very complete gymnasium, which has been fitted up under the direction of Dr. D. A. Sargent, well known as the able director of the gymnasium of Harvard. It is interesting to watch the deaf athletes in their recreation hours, some playing games entirely by signal,

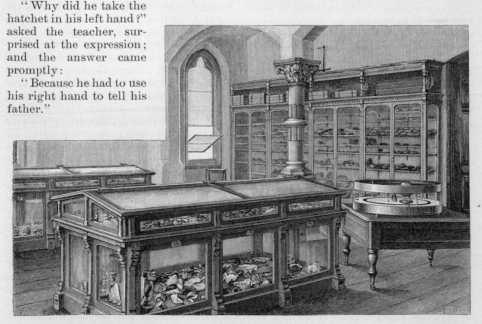

INTERIOR OF MUSEUM.

EDWARD M. GALLAUDET.

others going through the "Lancers," without music, of course, the inexperienced making a deafening noise with tables and chairs and feet.

As a rule the signs imitate so closely the action or object described that they may be readily understood; but there are as many degrees of intelligibility in sign-making as there are in distinctness of speech. "Open the door" is expressed by joining the tips of the fingers, the hands being horizontal, and swinging the right hand outward from the wrist as a door would swing on its hinges; "improvement" is rendered by stretching out the left arm, and climbing up it, as on a ladder, with the right hand. Animals are usually described by some characteristic habit: scratching with two right fingers in the left palm means "hen"; slapping the thigh and snapping the fingers mean "dog." That dear old prayer, "Now I lay me down to sleep," becomes a touching little pantomime from a deaf-mute child; or, again, a fable is rendered by one with such droll actions, such variety of facial expression, such animation, that it is infinitely more interesting than the recitation could ever be. Few people have ever seen so dramatic a representation as "Sheridan's Ride" was made in President Gallaudet's parlor one evening by a Senior. The danger, the alarm, the hurry,

the fear, the snorting of the horse, imitated by his tongue, the clatter of hoofs, imitated by his hands, the booming of cannon, imitated by stamping violently, his eager face, his heaving breast, every limb and feature in significant motion, gave the familiar lines an actuality that was truly wonderful.

Rip Van Winkle's question to his Catskill host suggests itself to visitors of these institutions—"Are there any deaf and dumb girls?"—and not unlike the mountaineer's reply come statistics to show that females constitute a decided minority of the silent community. This flagrant example of the sex's inequality is earnestly commended to the attention of the Woman's Rights Association.

A young Benedictine, the Abbé De l'Épée, first organized a method of instruction for the deaf and dumb. Assuming that pantomime is the natural means of communication for deaf-mutes, he established a sign language by which, and the manual alphabet, they could converse and acquire instruction. This was accomplished in 1760, and with material modifications is known to-day as the "French method." A few years later a German, Heinicke, devised a system which might be briefly described as the opposite of De l'Épée's. Assuming that articulate speech was the natural method of communication for all humanity, and pantomime but an expedient, he devised a method for teaching deaf-mutes articulation by artificial methods, such as manipulating the organs of the throat, and training them to read from the motion of the lips what was said to them. This is known as the "German method." The third, established about the same time by Braidwood, a Scotchman, and known as the "English method," is identical with the German, making therefore virtually but two systems, reviewing which it might be said that while the aim of the German was higher, the benefits of the French must be more general. Schools established on either principle extend all over Europe, from Sweden to Italy, from Great Britain to Russia, and in 1867, desirous to see the practical working of each, President Gallaudet visited thirty-six of these institutions. Nine, embracing about one thousand scholars, were conducted strictly on the French method; eight, embracing about six hundred scholars, on the German method; in the remaining nineteen, embracing about twenty-five hundred scholars, the two methods were combined in different proportions. Mr. Gallaudet's conclusions, set forth in a valuable report, are decidedly in favor of a combined system. The use of the German alone involves excessive labor for both teacher and pupil; in cases of congenital deafness it is useless in a majority of cases; but few of those who pursue it are able to hold free conversation with strangers, and even partial success demands an outlay of time and money few can afford.

The French method, improved by Sicard, was introduced to the United States in 1817 by Dr. Thomas Hopkins Gallaudet, of Hartford, who, with the aid of Clerc, a deaf-mute, established in that city, under private patronage, the first American deaf-mute school. Early in its history it was generously endowed by the national government, and to-day every State in the Union provides for the education of deaf-mutes, the Illinois institution, which has over five hundred scholars, being the largest in the world. In some of the institutions trades are taught, such as cabinet- and shoe-making, tailoring, printing, lithographing, bookbinding, and gardening; and in a few cities rooms in public schools have been devoted to deaf-mutes. The basis of American instruction is the French method, which prevailed exclusively till within the last sixteen years, and the introduction of the German method is regarded by many as experimental.

The French method is retained in the schools at Kendall Green, but articulation and lip-reading are taught in the primary schools, and made use of in the college.

The number of deaf-mutes in the country is about thirty-five thousand, of whom more than seven thousand were under instruction in 1883. Dumbness without deafness is seldom met with except in idiots, but total congenital deafness is invariably accompanied by dumbness. Deafness may be primarily incidental to diseases of the head and ears, fevers, etc., but in three cases out of five it is congenital.

The college at Washington is the only deaf-mute college in the world. Its purpose appeals to all humanity; its success justifies the generosity of the government; its progress reflects high honor on the gentleman identified so intimately with it.

Allied to the philanthropic cause by the example of a noble father, one of its first apostles, and for the sake of a devoted mother, herself a deaf-mute, Edward M. Gallaudet brought to his work the enthusiasm of youth and the incentive of personal interest, and the lapse of time has added the experience he lacked at the outset. From the little frame house with its two acres of ground to the stately buildings which now adorn Kendall Green, for twenty-five years he has watched the institution faithfully, sped its progress, guided its development, controlled it prudently, administered it economically, and inspired it with the high principles of a cultivated Christian gentleman.

PRINCE BISMARCK IN PRIVATE LIFE.

IT is by no means an unlovely characteristic of the men and women of the present day that they wish to know something of that side of the lives of their great contemporaries which is hidden from the public eye, something of their inner life as husbands and fathers, something of their attitude toward religion, science, literature, and art, something of their private tastes and accomplishments, something of them in their capacity as owners of property, and the like. The desire for such information as this looks a little like curiosity. But it is an amiable curiosity, for, as a rule, it is connected with a desire to see one who has been successful in great things, fortunate in small things as well, and happy in his home life. On the other hand, the realization of the wishes of the public in this direction is by no means easy; nor is the problem proposed capable of complete solution as long as the subject which we have to portray still lives among us. Perhaps nobody likes to be analyzed in this direction. Nor do tact and the utmost discretion secure us altogether from disapprobation and reproach when we attempt to follow a contemporary genius or hero into his every-day life, and to exhibit him, as it were, in negligee.

Luther, surrounded by his Katty and his children, and engaged at music or in celebrating the mysteries of the Christ-

PRINCE BISMARCK.

After the photograph by Lesser and Wolf, Berlin.

mas tree, is a picture almost as dear to us as that in which he is seen consigning the papal bull to the flames, or that in which he pleads his cause before the Kaiser and the princes of the empire. How much sympathy is awakened, even out of England, by the picture of blind Milton and his daughters! We follow with the deepest interest the relations between Goethe and the women who wove so much gladness into his web of life. We like to mingle in imagination with the people whom Schiller loved and honored as a husband and a father. Stories which tell of the aged Emperor William's attitude toward his grandchildren and great-grandchildren can always count on grateful recognition. On the other hand, we always miss something about Frederick the Great when we remember that he lived his life without a family, and most of it without a friend. There is something unpleasant, something uncomfortable, something that makes us shiver, about a commanding genius to whom these softer influences are denied. He appears great, indeed, but austere, one-sided, and imperfect, remote from us and cold. It seems as if he lacked his complement, as if his life could not have been happy without this softer side, as if he were deficient in heart, and only the cold, keen, rigorous intellect and the mighty will of the king and the warrior could have ruled in him and spoken through him.

Many of my readers will therefore be glad to learn that the giant spirit who raised the German people from their long abasement, and gave them their place among the nations, in due time, by his choice of a wife, established for himself a happy home, in which his domestic nature has received a manifold and fruitful development, and that he is, after all, not by any means the man of blood and iron which many people suppose him to be. His wife is nine years younger than her husband, and was married to him in 1847. Her maiden name was Johanna von Puttkamer, and she was the daughter of a quiet, godly Pomeranian home, the atmosphere of which was pervaded by the spirit of the Moravian fraternity. That "the mad squire [*Junker*] of Kneiphof," as Bismarck was then called in the gossip of the neighborhood, the future "Iron Chancellor," should have been attracted by, and at the same time should have awakened a warm and lively interest in, a lady whose

first impressions of men and things were received amid such surroundings, need not, after all, create any surprise. Even in those days the period of unrest, storm, and stress had been succeeded by one of calm, and his wildness and love of mischief had given place to self-examination and a longing after higher things. The Princess was strictly and piously brought up; but is of a cheerful and lively disposition, endowed with a considerable amount of mother-wit, keenly sensitive, and possessed of excellent taste. Very musical, and an excellent performer on the piano, she is at the same time a careful and thrifty housewife, and, like the noble ladies of former times, possesses some knowledge of the healing art. During all these years she has shared intelligently her husband's hopes and cares, sometimes even the political ones, as witness the letters published by Hesekiel, written to her when official duties or holiday travels chanced to separate them for a while. In these he addresses her as "My darling" (*mein Herz*), "My best beloved"; he sends her jasmine from Peterhof; he promises her Edelweiss from Gastein. From the royal castle at Ofen he bids her "good-night from far away," and adds, "Where can I have heard the song which has been running through my head all day:

'Over the blue mountains, over the white sea foam,
Come thou, beloved one, come to thy lovely home!'

I wonder who can have sung that to me some time or other in 'auld lang syne.'" Elsewhere he recalls on the sixteenth anniversary of his marriage how it "had brought sunshine into his bachelor life." Over and over again he gives expression to a feeling of homesickness, of longing for her and the children. And in a letter written from Småland he wishes that he had a little castle peopled with those he loved on one of the wood-and-heather-bound lakes of that Swedish province. Many other parts of this correspondence show how dear his wife is to him, and how often he thinks of her. On the other hand, we can infer from several of the letters that the good lady has become deeply imbued with her husband's energetic modes of feeling and of thought.

The Prince has three children—a daughter, the Countess Mary, who was born in 1848, and married about four years ago to Count Rantzau, and two sons, Counts Herbert and William, both of whom are

12*

younger than their sister, and unmarried. The former is in the diplomatic service, and has in his official capacity been attached to several embassies, and recently to that in London. The latter, who bears a strong personal resemblance to his father, has devoted himself to the legal profession, and has been a member of the German Parliament. Both served, at first as privates in the Dragoon Guards, in the last war, during which the Prince evinced much anxiety on their behalf, riding out after them as often as circumstances permitted. Both of them work from time to time in the immediate neighborhood of the Prince, in whose bureau his son-in-law has also found employment. I may mention, too, that the Prince is the happy possessor of grandchildren, fine, sturdy little fellows, the eldest of whom occasionally pays a visit at his grandfather's palace with the cap of the Yellow Cuirassiers on his fair young head.

Prince Bismarck is a deeply religious man. When he began to take an active part in politics, he did so with the conviction that Christianity was a firm bulwark against the revolutionary spirit of the age, and the feeling that, amidst all the storms and troubles by which he was surrounded, in God he had a sure support and a never-failing source of strength and consolation.

In the autumn of 1872, as he was showing me his working-room in Varzin, we happened to approach the enormous fire-place on the right of the entrance from the library. In the centre of the mantelpiece, under the Eagle of the German Empire, is the inscription, "*In trinitate robur*." The history of its origin is as follows: when Bismarck was envoy of the Bund at Frankfort, King Frederick of Denmark bestowed upon him the grand cross of the order of Danebrog. There is a custom according to which the names and arms of the possessors of this decoration are placed in the cathedral at Copenhagen, with a motto which is chosen by the newly elected knight, and which must have a double meaning. "So I invented this one," explained the Prince, "'*In trinitate robur*'—in the trefoil, the clover, and the oak, the ancient coat of arms of our family." "And 'My strength is in the triune God'?" I ventured to guess. "Right! that is what I meant," he said, quietly and earnestly.

Side by side with the religious beliefs of great men we often find something which is described by the enlightened world as superstition, and which, however little it may have its origin in Christianity, has some connection or other with their religion. And of this we find traces in Bismarck.

After the battle of Gravelotte there was some speculation one day at dinner as to what would be the result of a complete conquest of France, and the Chancellor concluded an exposition of his views on the subject with the words: "But we should not speak of the bear-skin before we have shot our bear. I admit that I am superstitious in these matters." Perhaps something crossed his mind about the grudge of the old Greek gods. "There are not thirteen of us for dinner?" inquired his cousin, Count Bismarck-Bohlen, counting the covers one day at Reims. "No; that's right, for the minister has an objection to that." Another time, when there were really thirteen of us at table, I drew the attention of Bucher, who sat beside me, to the fact. But he bade me not to say anything about it, as it would put the chief into low spirits. On the 14th of October, 1870, General Boyer met the Chancellor at Versailles to negotiate on behalf of Bazaine. But Bismarck does not seem to have arranged anything definitely with him on that day. He asked in the bureau what day of the month it was. "The 14th, your Excellency." "The 14th! That was Hochkirch and Jena. No business should be concluded on that day!" Perhaps it occurred to him, too, that this 14th of October was a Friday. In 1852 he writes from Blankenburg to his wife: "I had not as good sport at Letzlingen this time as I had three years ago. It was a Friday!" And in the same year he writes to her from Halle: "I kept cogitating all during the journey yesterday whether, after all, it were not Friday. It was a *dies nefastus* at any rate." In proof of which he goes on to mention a series of small discomforts experienced *en route*, such as an inn infested with bugs, "infamous coffee," Jew peddlers, "some 'princesses' from the *Reezenjasse*," and an obtrusive privy-councillor (*Geheimrath*) who travelled in the same coupé. When the title of "Count" was about to be offered to him, he hesitated for a long time whether or not he should accept it; for he knew that a number of Pomeranian families which had acquired the title had become extinct in a comparatively short space of time. "The country can not afford it," he remarked, when mentioning the matter. On the evening of the 23d of November, 1870, as we were sitting at tea at Versailles, he began to speak about his death, and stated definitely the age to which it was appointed that he should attain, and the year in which it was appointed that he should die. "I know it," he insisted, when I remonstrated with him on the subject; "it is a mystic number." Seven years later, at Varzin, he repeated the same assurance to the narrator of this remarkable circumstance, but added, "God, however, only knows."

Bismarck's love of nature, of the life of the woods and fields, of country sports, and of beautiful landscape, is developed to an unusual degree. He says of himself that he is an enthusiast about nature, and that he loves the sea like a sweetheart. But, more than this, he knows how to reproduce what he sees and feels in charming and characteristic sketches, which often produce on sympathetic natures the effect of little lyric poems. One of his reasons for spending the summer and autumn at Varzin and Friedrichsruhe, and not on his family estate at Schönhausen, is doubtless that at the former places the forest is close to his residence, while at the latter it takes nearly an hour to reach the woods from the mansion-house. In a letter to his sister, dated June, 1854, we find him saying, "I am regularly homesick, and long for the country and the woods and nothing to do, with the appropriate accompaniments of a loving wife and nice well-conducted children." And in August, 1863, he writes to his wife: "I wish some intrigue or other would bring another ministry into power, so that I could honorably turn my back on this never-ceasing ink stream, and live quietly in the country. The restlessness of existence is unbearable. It is no life for an honest country gentleman." Repeatedly during the French war, and subsequently down to the present year, he gave expression to his longing for such a retirement in unmistakable terms. When he is at his Pomeranian home, or his seat in the heart of the Sachsenwald, and his health permits, he never lets a fine day pass without making some excursion into the neighboring beech and fir woods, or to one of the hills and streams which they contain. Many a time, when the dinner hour warned them that it was time to return, he has said to Bucher, who used occasionally to accompany him on these excursions, "Let us go to the top of that hill first; there is a charming view from it." He knows the name of every beautiful tree in the park at Varzin. This is his favorite spot; and sometimes on nights when he can not sleep he walks about it in the moonlight. Unconsciously he carries its image with him wherever he goes; even during the war it was present to him, and he wandered in his dreams among its sunlit trees. The descriptions of scenery, thrown off with a few strokes of the pen, which we find here and there in letters written to his wife and to his sister, are extremely vivid, richly colored, harmonious, and true to nature. Take, for instance, his view from the castle of Ofen of the "dull silvery Danube, and the dark mountains with a pale red background, mountains which became bluer and bluer, and then brownish-red in the light of the evening sun which was setting behind them." I may mention also his lively picture of life on the Hungarian steppes between the Danube and the Theiss, and this description of the wilderness near Tomsjonäs: "Not a town, not a village, far or near, only scattered farms and wooden huts, with patches of barley and potatoes where, here and there, an acre or two of arable land is found among withered trees, pieces of rock, and brambles. Imagine about five hundred square miles of the bleakest country in the neighborhood of Viartlum,* tall heather alternating with short grass and bog, covered in some places to such an extent as to be impassable, in others sparsely and at intervals, with birch-trees, junipers, pine-trees, beeches, oaks, and alders, and the whole strewn with countless stones—some of them enormous blocks as high as a house—and perfumed with wild rosemary and resin, and here and there curiously shaped placid lakes surrounded by woods and heathery hills."

With the characteristics of the Chancellor already described are blended others, such as his love of animals, and his pleasure in the chase, in horse exercise, and in agricultural pursuits. Just as the cornflower (*Kornblume*) is especially dear to the Emperor William, so Bismarck in one

---

* A Pomeranian estate belonging to the Puttkamer family.

of his letters calls the heather "this beloved plant of mine." Once at Versailles he happened to mention the old cowherd Brand, "one of those ancient pieces of furniture" with which, he said, "his youthful memories were inseparably linked"; and he concluded by saying, "I never think of him without at the same time thinking of wild flowers and heather." When he lived at Kneiphof his Danish hound was quite a prominent character in the neighborhood. Four half-tamed young foxes also filled a rôle in his household at the same place. In St. Petersburg their place was taken by young bears, which he used to keep in the room like dogs until they grew up and became dangerous. Hesekiel informs us that "Mischka used suddenly to appear at dinner-time, to the great amusement of the guests, walk quite cleverly round the table between the plates and glasses, snap now and then at the calves of the servants' legs, and slip on the little dinner railway laid down in the dining-room." Sultel, an Ulmer dog presented to him in Munich by Count Holnstein, shared his room at Varzin in 1877; and, with his "wife" Flörchen, was his companion in all his rides and walks until some wandering tramp brutally killed the faithful animal, which the Prince used to feed after dinner with his own hand. Even the jackdaws in the park at Varzin have attracted the attention of the princely friend of the brute creation, and possess a corner of his heart. I have listened with pleasure to his account of how they teach their young to fly, how afterward they introduce them to worm diet on the neighboring coast, and how, like fashionable folk, they spend the winter in town, that is to say, in the towers of Stolpe and Schlawe.

From early youth until about his sixtieth year the Chancellor was an exceptionally good marksman, passionately fond of riding, and an eager and successful sportsman. Lately he has gradually given up one after another of his old tastes and pastimes. When a young man he shot so well with a rifled pistol that he used to knock the heads off the ducks on the pond at Kneiphof. And not less fatal to bird and beast were the fowling-piece and the rifle in his practiced hand. He has acquired a reputation as a sportsman in nearly every country in Europe, and has collected trophies, in the shape of antlers and skins, for his walls and floors,

in his own preserves, in the Taunus Mountains, and in the Ardennes, in the Alps, in Rothschild's park at Ferrières, in the forests of Sweden, and at wolf, stag, and bear hunts in Russia. As a bold and indefatigable horseman, too, Bismarck has performed extraordinary feats, especially in his younger days, when rides of forty or fifty English miles did not seem at all impossible, and were actually accomplished. Even later in life, and years after he became a minister of the crown, he could, when necessary, spend hours in the saddle. During the battle of Königgrätz he was full twelve hours on horseback; and on the day after the battle of Sedan he rode from nine o'clock in the morning until ten o'clock at night. But for the last two years he has not, to my knowledge, mounted a horse. Moreover, he has not always been fortunate in escaping falls. Indeed, he admits himself that he fell with or was thrown by his horse fifty times, at least, in the course of his life, and was sometimes—for example at Varzin, where he broke three ribs—dangerously hurt.

It is a well-known fact that Bismarck, when he was a student at Göttingen and Greifswald, was an excellent fencer, and gave evidence of his prowess in some thirty "duels." And that he was a capable swimmer is proved by his own letters, from which we learn that he undertook swimming excursions in the Rhine at Bingen and in the Danube at Ofen, and still better by an incident which occurred in the year 1844. He was at that time serving as a Landwehr officer with the Stargard Uhlans, and happened to be standing with several of his comrades on the bridge over the Lippehner-See, when he saw his groom Hildebrand, who had ridden one of his horses into the watering-place there, get out of his depth and sink. Bismarck in a moment had off his tunic and his sword, plunged head-foremost into the water, and succeeded in reaching the groom. The latter, however, in his terror grasped his rescuer and drew him under with him. Both were given up for lost, but Bismarck rose to the surface again, and, dragging the lifeless man behind him, swam to the shore, where the groom was soon restored to life.

Emmanuel Kant denounces eloquence as a deceiver who, in matters on which the reason alone ought to decide, unfairly permits the æsthetic feelings to have the casting vote. Goethe, in a letter written from Venice in 1786, calls himself "an enemy of wordiness." Nor is the Chancellor of the German Empire much enamored of the Muse of skillful speech; and she, on the other hand, does not seem, if we may judge from appearances, to be particularly well disposed toward him.

"These eloquent gentlemen" (in the Reichstag), said he to me in February 1870, "are really just like many women who have got small feet, and who wear their boots too tight, and show their feet in order that they may be admired. In the same way, when a man has the misfortune to be an orator, he makes speeches which are too long and too frequent." And at Versailles he told us that "the gift of eloquence has done a great deal of harm in parliamentary life, for every one who thinks he is able to speak must have his say, whether he has anything worth contributing to the discussion or not. There is too much spoken irrelevantly, and too little to the point. Everything has been settled in the party meetings long ago. So when people talk in full Parliament they do it to please the public, and show them what they can do, or still oftener to please the newspapers, which can compliment. The consequence will be that eloquence will come to be looked upon as a public nuisance, and will be punished accordingly, when it is guilty of a long speech." Bismarck, however, possesses much real eloquence, at least in the estimation of those who care to distinguish between the matter and its mere outward form. He is certainly no orator in the ordinary sense of the word. His parliamentary utterances "have hands and feet," as we Germans say. They influence men because they are founded upon solid facts. And we can not help admiring in them his depth and breadth of view. He is too conscientious to beat about the bush with high-sounding but shallow or unmeaning phrases, too truthful to try to produce an effect by a mere exhibition of sophistry, and too thoughtful to care for gratifying his audience by a smoothly flowing stream of words. He suffers, too, from a certain amount of nervousness, is of a warm and rather excitable temperament, and has a voice which, to say the least of it, leaves something to be desired. Even in private conversation, particularly when he is discussing any matter of importance, he can not always express his thoughts quickly and in well-chosen language. On the other hand, he tells a story capitally; and a rich vein of humor, a quick eye for the ridiculous side of men and things, and a gift of quietly ironical yet good-natured description of persons and events, all of which he possesses in no ordinary degree, make him one of the most delightful *raconteurs* I ever heard afford amusement to a social gathering *inter pocula*.

Facility in the acquisition of foreign languages seems to increase as we go from the west to the east of Europe. The French and English generally possess it least, the Poles and Russians most, while we Germans hold a kind of middle position between the two extremes. We find it easy enough to understand a newspaper or a book written in a foreign tongue; but most of us, on the other hand, find considerable difficulty in carrying on a conversation with correctness and fluency in another language; and we have peculiar difficulty in acquiring facility in the use of idioms different from our own. Of course there are exceptions to this general rule; and the Chancellor of the German Empire is a brilliant one. Not only does he speak German without the vestige of a provincial accent, but his French is so pure that even a Genevese, or one of the upper classes in St. Petersburg, could hardly find anything to cavil at. He may claim, too, to be a fair master of English; and he understands enough of Italian to acquaint himself without difficulty with the emanations from the Italian press. He has some knowledge of Polish; and during his residence in St. Petersburg he studied Russian sufficiently to be able to carry on a conversation in that language. The late Emperor Alexander is said to have been deeply impressed when Bismarck replied to a question of his in the Muscovite tongue. This is no easy matter for a German. Gauss, the celebrated mathematician, felt at one time the necessity of doing something to counteract the effect of his purely abstract studies. Two subjects presented themselves to him—the Russian language, and the cumbrous and complicated terminology of the Linnæan system. He determined to learn the latter by heart, and actually succeeded in doing so. The difficulty of conquering the intricacies of Russian was too much for him. The Chancellor is not so strong in ancient as in modern languages. "When I was in the sixth form" (*Primaner*), he said to me at Ferrières, "I could write and speak right good Latin, but I should find difficulty in doing so now, and I have utterly forgotten my Greek."

Historical and geographical studies have always had a special attraction for the Prince, for in them the development of social and political questions may be traced and followed, and dealing as they do with phenomena subject to the law of cause and effect, they supply us with those facts and conditions which enable us, as far as mere human understanding will permit, to prognosticate the future. He is well acquainted with the best-known works on these subjects; and he peruses each new publication with lively interest. Among those which interested him greatly I may mention Taine's excellent *History of the Origin and Progress of the French Revolution*. Among poets he gives the palm to Goethe and Shakespeare. And although he would willingly dispense with a considerable portion of the productions of the former writer, he would be quite content to remain several years on a desert island with the remainder. With Schiller, owing to his strong objection to a pompous and declamatory style, he is less in sympathy; and he considers his glorification of William Tell's legendary deed simply unnatural. Naturally the mass of light literature which has issued of late years from the German press has not interested him much; but he has at least noticed the best-known novels and romances. Modern French and English novelists, especially the former, seem to have attracted more of his attention.

I have seldom heard him speak on any subject relating to art or artists; and his salons at Berlin and Varzin display but a moderate amount of artistic adornment, except in so far as photographs, lithographs, and engravings come within that definition. There were no pictures whatever in his working-room at the latter place in 1877; and his newly erected houses in Pomerania and the Sachsenwald are furnished in the simplest style. Yet I by no means intend to imply that he is destitute of all taste for painting, sculpture, and architecture, but merely that he takes no very particular interest in them. During his residence at Frankfort, at any rate, he associated a great deal with artists and sculptors; and his

criticism on the Brandenburg gate, which he would like to have seen standing by itself, was in the highest degree intelligent.

The Chancellor takes more interest in music, which he learned to appreciate through his intercourse with Kaiserlingk in his student days at Berlin. He is fondest of the classical composers, and among them Beethoven is his favorite. Although he plays no instrument himself, he delights in listening to the performances of others. In a letter to his wife, written in the summer of 1851, he describes himself as "well and cheerful, but with something of melancholy, homesickness, longing for wood, lake, and moor, and you and the children, blended with the sunset and Beethoven." In another letter, dated the 27th of October, 1863, he says to her, "Yesterday I sat alone with Keudell in the blue salon, and he played." Two years later, on the 1st of September, he announces from Baden, "We had a quartette at Count Flemming's with Joachim, who handles his violin in a really masterly manner." At Versailles Herr Von Keudell, the amateur pianist and *Legationsrath*, played soft fantasias for the minister during coffee; and said to me afterward, in reply to my inquiry, if the chief liked music: "Yes, he likes music, although he is not musical himself. You will have noticed, too," he added, "that he sings softly to the music. How soothing it must be to his nerves! They have been sadly tried to-day." Toward the close of the autumn of 1881, just after the election of the opposition candidates, the Prince and I were strolling in the dark about the winding paths in the park behind his palace in Berlin, and were discussing the Liberals in the Reichstag, when the Prince began humming the air of the melancholy student-song, "Wir hatten gebaut ein stättliches Haus," and after a while spoke of Uhland's "Glück von Edenhall," to which he compared the German constitution.

Before the Bohemian war Bismarck laid at stake on one card mighty things, the character of Prussia as one of the great powers, and his own fate. But usually he is neither in this nor in the ordinary sense fond of playing with fate. Unlike other ministers, he has never speculated. Of this he repeatedly, and even as lately as the January of the present year, assured me. Formerly he did not despise a game of cards. On one occasion he actually played whist for seven consecutive hours. The game of hazard also possessed a strong fascination for him for a long time. "But," he observed, as we were speaking of it, "it only interests me when the stakes are high and the pool large, and that does not do for a family man." Nevertheless, as lately as the middle of August, 1865, he took part in a game of *quinze*, but only for diplomatic purposes. "It was when I was arranging the Treaty of Gastein with Blome," he explained, "and although for some time I had quite given up cards, I played so rashly on that occasion that the others were perfectly astounded. But I had a design in doing so. Blome had heard that the game of quinze gave one the best opportunity for the study of character, and he was now trying the experiment with me. I thought it a pity not to let the experiment succeed, so I lost a couple of hundred thalers, which were really expended in his Majesty's service, and ought to have been refunded. For I deceived Blome to such an extent that he fancied I was fool-hardy, and yielded."

As a diplomatist, Bismarck naturally keeps a good table. But he by no means despises simple fare. For instance, he esteems pure Nordhausen rye brandy very highly, and keeps a quantity of it beside the more aristocratic cognac to mature and mellow in his cellar at Schönhausen. Like Frederick the Great, he has a large appetite. But we must take into consideration that, as a rule, he only eats one meal in the day, and that after six o'clock in the evening, and that those who have much brain-work require a great deal of food. He was formerly an inveterate smoker, and once travelled from Cologne to Berlin and smoked all the way "*mit einem Feuer*," *i. e.*, lighting each cigar from the one he had just finished. But after 1870 he gradually gave up cigars, on account of his health, and smoked a long pipe instead; and in 1881 he told me that he had given up smoking altogether, as it no longer agreed with him.

For a good many years—in fact, since his residence in St. Petersburg—the Prince's health has not been particularly good, though his appearance does not generally betray the fact. He suffers frequently from severe and often painful attacks of erysipelas and neuralgia. That he should suffer from nervousness is not at all to be wondered at. For nearly a quarter of a century the most momentous questions in the political history of Germany, with its problems and enigmas, its entanglements, excitements, and dangers, have been worked out in his busy brain, and have all been taken anxiously to heart. In the course of a conversation at table in April, 1878, he called himself "an old man," whereupon the Princess remonstrating with him said, "But you are only just sixty-three." "Yes," he replied, "but I have lived fast, and cash in hand." Then turning to me he added, "By 'cash in hand' I mean that I have always done what I had to do with my whole heart, and I have paid with my health and strength for what I have attained." His chief ailment, besides this nervousness, which takes the form of continual sleeplessness, is a disordered stomach; and he is troubled occasionally with swelling of the veins of the legs. Worry has a particularly prejudicial effect on his health, and the parliamentary factions on the one hand, and the members of certain court circles on the other, take good care that there shall be no lack of this. This was particularly the case during his struggle with the Ultramontanes, and before the outbreak of the Russo-Turkish war, when a well-known noble lady assumed the rôle of an angel of peace, and sought to smooth his path. It may be mentioned in this connection that the Prince's sight is not good for distant objects, but that he does not wear glasses when reading or writing; and that, like all nervous people, he is fond of warm clothing and hot rooms.

The Prince may be described as of a choleric temperament. Anger with him assumes a volcanic aspect, and vents itself in violent outbursts. But the volcano dies out as quickly as it flared up, and there is no thought of malice. Altogether Bismarck possesses a most kindly disposition, which displays itself in acts of compassion and benevolence. He was always kind to the poor. One night at Bar-le-Duc he cut a piece of bread for a hungry sentinel and brought it out to him himself. After the battle of Beaumont he gave some tired and straggling Bavarian soldiers drink from his own flask. He sent cigars to the wounded soldiers at Donchery, and frequently visited the hospital at Versailles, and cheered and saw to the comfort of the sick. If he seems unable to give men credit for unselfish aims, we must remem-

ber that this is the result of a long experience; and the fact that he is strongly inclined to be suspicious and mistrustful
may be explained on the same principle.
Nowhere is there so much intrigue and
falsehood, so much hypocrisy and mean
ambition, as in the diplomatic world and
the circles in which courtiers move. Caution is here the most necessary virtue, and
even those who occupy the loftiest stations
would do well to remember the golden
rule: "Let him that thinketh he standeth
take heed lest he fall."

As Prime Minister of Prussia, Bismarck
has no salary, but as Chancellor of the
German Empire he receives 54,000 marks
($13,500) per annum. The remainder of
his income is derived principally from
landed property, of which he possesses a
considerable quantity. Owing, however,
to the very low prices of grain and timber,
particularly of late years, his receipts from
this source are comparatively small. If
Bismarck were simply a nobleman, or even
a count, he might be considered wealthy,
but for a prince we can only say that he is
moderately well off. Down to 1867 his
only landed property was Schönhausen in
the Altmark, which contains about 2800
acres of generally excellent land. In 1867
he added to this the manor of Varzin in
Hinter Pomerania, which he purchased
with the grant of 400,000 thalers ($288,000)
voted to him by the Landtag. This estate,
to which he subsequently added the properties of Chorow and Sedlitz, now covers
an area of about 30,000 acres. It consists
for the most part, however, of poor land,
some of it being scarcely fit even to grow
firs. After the events of 1870, the Emper-
or, in his capacity as Sovereign Duke of
Lauenburg, presented the Chancellor with
the Sachsenwald, lying in the Schwarzenbeck district not far from Hamburg, and
stretching down to the Elbe. It had previously been crown land, and comprises
an area of about 20,000 acres, covered for
the most part with magnificent beech forests. The Prince has recently added to
this estate, on which there was neither
arable land nor a residence of any sort,
the small properties of Schönau and Silt.
These adjoin the western boundary of
Sachsenwald, and were, by-the-way, by no
means an advantageous purchase. Some
of the timber of the woods at Varzin is
sold to three local paper factories which
are worked by the river Wipper, and that
of the Schwarzenbeck forests is disposed of

to a large powder-mill. Varzin and the
Sachsenwald, as well as Schönhausen,
have the advantage of being close to a
railway, and their products can be brought
readily and cheaply to market. The residences on these three estates are neither
particularly large nor in any way magnificently got up, but they are comfortably
furnished. And Friedrichsruhe, which the
Prince has transformed from a lodging-
house for summer visitors from Hamburg
into a sort of little mansion-house, is, with
its surrounding beech and fir trees and its
winding stream, a really exquisite spot.
The Sachsenwald, with the two estates
which are now united with it, is probably worth about three million marks
($600,000), but the income derived from
it does not much exceed 100,000 marks
($3000) per annum.

The Chancellor understands farming
and forest culture, and has achieved considerable success in the management of
his estate. At Schönhausen he has planted 500 acres, partly with oak, and they are
turning out well. At Varzin he has been
occupied in replanting a large tract of
land which was formerly a beech wood,
and which his predecessor, from a mistaken idea as to the quality of the soil,
had cleared for cultivation. And he has
had fir-trees planted on other parts of the
estate which previously were waste, or
grew only sand-grass and heather. The
six estates which form his little kingdom
in the Pomeranian hill country, and which
consist for the smaller part of arable and
pasture land, have been rendered more
productive by judicious management. A
park has been laid out at Friedrichsruhe,
and the stream which flows through it has
been banked and cleared, and it is now in
contemplation to cut down the oak wood
on the right bank of this stream, and to
plant trees which will be less prejudi-
cially affected by the dampness of the
soil.

These alterations and plans for improvement are all illustrations of the maxim
that "when Nature *will* not, then she
must"—a maxim which, by-the-way, the
Chancellor has many a time put into practice in other spheres, when, as for example, in the working out of his schemes of
economic reform, his path has been crossed either by persons or by things. And
Nature, coerced by clever management
and resolute perseverance, submits and allows herself to be improved.

CAP BLANC, MURRAY BAY.

WHOEVER has made the delightful summer journey from Quebec to the Saguenay can easily remember the zigzag course of the steamer as it cut back and forth across the St. Lawrence. This course was taken to accommodate the host of people who during the hot season flock from Quebec and other cities to the Lower Canadian watering-places.

Perhaps the tourist wondered, as he felt the cool breezes play around him, and recalled the perchance refreshing night he had just spent in Quebec, why Canadians wanted to go to summer resorts. Possibly he turned to a chance acquaintance, throwing upon him the responsibility of solving the problem, and received a reply similar to the one I received years ago to the same question: "Oh, whenever it grows too warm for a polar bear to feel chilly in Quebec, the people go down below." The solution is terse and witty, but hardly gives a correct idea of the Canadian climate. Often in July and August, even over refreshing Quebec, the sun pours down with a fervor which makes the brow of the cliff upon which the old city is built fairly perspire, while at Montreal the mercury boils in its thermometers; and not only does it often boil at Ottawa, but the summer resident (especially of the aristocratic quarter known as Sandy Hill) is fanned occasionally by sultry winds laden with an invisible sand which makes him gladly flee to more inviting quarters.

As he watched party after party of evidently fashionable people disembark at the leading watering-places, he was impressed with the odd fact that one who merely passes up and down the thoroughfare of the St. Lawrence sees absolutely nothing of most of these favorite resorts. The stranger only sees his fellow-traveller, with the air of a man who is doing the correct and respectable thing, step ashore with his wife, children, and nurses, and stowing his party into comfortless-looking vehicles, disappear over a steep and winding road. No outward token of the gayeties toward which he is hastening is given, unless it might be a trim yacht, with quivering pennon at its mast, riding lightly at anchor in the harbor. No magnificent hotels crown the commanding heights, no dashing equipages loiter at the landings.

All this the tourist must have noted as the steamer rounded back into the current, and, with a superabundance of leisure on hand, he thought it over, and about concluded that the Canadian had made a mistake to get off where he did. If he happened to be accustomed to the elegance, richness, and comfort of the ultra-fashionable watering-places of the United States, he would have been fully convinced of this had he landed with him, and learned the simplicity of life in one of the strongholds of Canadian fashion.

Recently I spent some time along the shore of the lower St. Lawrence, drifting in and out of the best known of its summer resorts along with the tide of fashion, receiving impressions which a more inti-

mate acquaintance might have altered, and gathering experiences, agreeable and the reverse, which may interest those whose curiosity has been, as mine was, excited by a passing glimpse of places which their guide-books have described as the Newports and Long Branches of Canada.

Our first stop is made at Baie St. Paul, about sixty miles below Quebec. The magical stamp "fashionable" is not yet unconditionally impressed upon the place, but I feel so sure that it soon will be that I include it among its better-established neighbors. It would be hard to find a lovelier spot in which to spend a quiet summer. Through modern improvements the landing at Baie St. Paul has become a very every-day affair, but five years ago it was an episode in the summer holiday.

The bay offers fine bathing privileges, and the water is quite salty, while the air from the mountains brings health and strength to the dwellers at Baie St. Paul.

At Les Eboulemens, the next stopping-place, an ebullient mass of landscape presents itself. The wharf leads to a narrow opening between disordered rocks and tumbled-up earth. Through it a few quiet-looking pleasure-seekers pass, and are soon lost to sight.

Five hours after leaving Quebec symptoms of an important landing begin to be visible amongst the majority of Canadians on board. These symptoms—such as the collecting of families, shawls, and handkerchiefs to facilitate landing, the arousing to consciousness of the gentleman who has slept peacefully within the cabin as his chosen mode of enjoying scenery, and the closing of the breviary which his priestly neighbor has read indefatigably —the tourist watches with the serenity of the man who knows his baggage is checked for the round trip, and he moves his chair to the land side of the deck, and calmly takes in the grandeur of the hills which rise almost sheer from the water at the wharf of Murray Bay.

During several years' residence in Canada we had heard so much of the delights of life at this the best known of the Quebec watering-places that as we landed there we realized over again almost the bright anticipations of our first ball.

As we dashed off over the stony and dusty road toward the hotel, two miles away, we confessed to ourselves that in scenery nothing different could be desired. To the right the river and bay were always in view, while on the left opened and closed through circling hills vistas of leafy shade and rocky silence. Nature everywhere about us was so sublime that we felt inclined for the moment to quar-

state of mind which calls for a frequent change of raiment, and attempt a whirl of gayety, their failure—at least to the looker-on—is most lamentable. Certainly these do essay, night after night, to bring

POINT À PIC, MURRAY BAY.

rel with the gay world for its invasion. But a short sojourn proved to us that Nature holds her own, for Murray Bay has none of the mad gayety of the fashionable watering-place.

No matter if people go there bent upon being systematically frivolous, Nature takes them in hand and teaches them a perhaps unrealized lesson at every turn. Although a few, strongly tenacious of purpose, try to work themselves into a

into the primitive ball-rooms of the hotels something like the giddy dance; but either because most of the participants are already weary of limb from climbing hills or rowing about the bay, or because pianoforte music, a dearth of young gentlemen, and a not overabundance of coal-oil lamps do not combine readily to form an exhilarating atmosphere, the dance soon languishes. Silence settles down over the house, and by ten or thereabout the most searching grumbler can not find a reason why he should not turn upon his small soft pillow and seek the pleasant land of Nod.

We found our hotel crowded to its utmost capacity—an indication of a popularity which will ever remain a mystery to us. Among the guests there is a certain friendly cheeriness; they all seem to know each other, and they have the manner of people who have taken possession for the summer, and are situated to their satisfaction. There are no costly toilets displayed. The dressing is simple, and entirely appropriate to the place and its requirements, which are rather those of the country town grown into popular favor, and crowded with "summer boarders," than of even the small fashionable resorts of the Western States.

Murray Bay impresses one as being managed on strictly economical principles. Prices are kept down by its habitual visitors, as neither the French nor English Canadians are, as a rule, given to lavish expenditure; consequently it is within the means of many who are obliged to count the cost of their pleasures, and through its lack of luxuries and conveniences it is unlikely to attract foreign sojourners, and the place bids fair to remain the same.

So strongly is the spirit of conservatism intrenched here that the same families come year after year from Quebec, Montreal, and even Toronto, to occupy the same rooms or cottages.

I doubt if for them this orange is ever sucked quite dry, unless it be by the weary chaperon, who has gone conscientiously through her fifty years of Murray Bay. As a girl, this faithful friend has waded through its cold brine, and has fished for smelts from off its piers; as a young woman, she has gone driving in a calèche, or more likely driven it herself; has danced, flirted, and spent her honey-moon there; has brought her rapidly increasing babies to dig in the sand; and finally sits upon one of the breezy galleries and keeps a matronly eye upon her young lady daughters. But even the pangs which usually attend the chaperon are mitigated in her case, for she knows all the frequenters of the place, and has little to fear.

In 1776 there was a prison built here, by order of General Wolfe, and quite a number of American war prisoners were confined in it. A hundred years ago one could have traced the foot-prints of Mars

all the way up to Quebec; but to-day they are quite effaced. The conquered French have taken the conquering English to their hearts and homes with such a readiness that the scales have turned, the old element has completely absorbed the new, and both races have become one. The summer village, made up of hotels and cottages, which accommodates a floating population of about two thousand, lies three miles west of the permanent French village. It has its own little church, in which the Scotch and English congregations worship, having alternate services. Of course all the Catholic visitors find their way to their own church at the French village. Just here I must mention one thing which always impresses the American in Canada, and that is the full attendance at all the churches, and the large proportion of men amongst the worshippers. I do not intend to follow up this observation with any moralizing, or deduce anything from it, though the moment seems so fitting, for I do not find Canadian men holding any loftier views or practicing any more virtues than their cousins across the line.

The drive between the two villages is a delightful one. It skirts around the bay, past Pointe à Gaze, the old Manor-house, over the Murray River, and under the shadow of the grand bluff known as Cap à l'Aigle. I think the greatest charms of Murray Bay are its picturesque walks and drives. The roads in many places are steep and rocky, but horses and vehicles are strong and well adapted to the region, the favorite conveyance being the odd-looking calèche, emigrated from Quebec. It is built to hold two persons and its driver, but it has been seen to hold eight or nine tipsy sailors as it jolted and bounced up the streets of Quebec. It can be hired on most reasonable terms, which vary, however, with your turn for bargaining.

The American always notes with surprise the great proportion of their lives which the Canadians pass in the open air, in winter as well as in summer. They are, as a rule, good walkers, and fond of outdoor pleasures and exercises of all kinds. At Murray Bay, as well as elsewhere, this fondness shows itself, and they make the most of the wild and romantic region in which they are living. After breakfast they wander off in parties up the hills, or to some lovely spot on the bay.

THE CHILDREN'S HOUR.

Frazer Falls and the Chute are within walking distance, being each about five miles from the hotels, while the wonderful Trou is four miles farther off, and is a popular place for picnics. Those who care to try their hand at trout-fishing have every opportunity in Grand Lac, Petit Lac, and Lac Gravel. Sport is to be found, too, amongst the mountain recesses and peaks, for in July the bear wanders about in his search for blueberries, a fruit for which he has a highly developed taste. The caribou makes his appearance in the vicinity as early as September.

In becoming acquainted with Murray Bay the stranger will have his curiosity aroused by the many regularly shaped mounds which he comes upon at a certain elevation above the water. They are really remains of land-slips, and are composed of stratified sand and clay, belonging to the geological formations known as Leda clay and Saxicava sand. They have been rounded off to their present shape by the action of the weather and the receding waters. The whole region is one of deep interest to the geologist or mineralogist, as the Laurentian system contains for them inexhaustible riches.

There are always a few Americans to be found summering here, generally of a class seeking rest and quiet rather than gayety. They certainly do not come for the bathing, as the mere mention of it sets them shivering. Even amongst the Canadians, who can stand such cold baths, I found that bathing was the exception rather than the rule, as most of them seemed to prefer to take their dips in-doors.

The children get over the difficulty of coldness by one of the happy expedients of quick-witted childhood. They appropriate the deep hollows in the great rocks along the beach, which the ebbing tide has left brimful of water, tempered to a pleasant warmth by the sun. In these natural bath-tubs they splash and frolic about to their hearts' content. They patter over the rocks in their bare feet, dripping garments, and high-peaked straw hats, rosy and happy, and are delightfully quaint little pictures.

Almost any afternoon, as you drift about the bay, you are treated to a most bewildering series of mirages, which take all kinds of liberties with the many hills in view. Another experience which you will have whilst rowing is no illusion at all, but undoubted reality, and that is the remarkable changes of temperature as you pass into and out of the varying currents of water and air. One moment you will sit in the perfect enjoyment of a delicious breeze, which does not penetrate with the slightest chill even your thin summer attire. Then, without a moment's warning, a long stroke brings you into a broad band of icy air, which seems to sweep direct from the north pole. You hastily muffle yourself, and a heavy winter shawl will only half warm you.

Cacouna, Murray Bay's fashionable neighbor and rival, is situated on the south bank of the St. Lawrence, about forty miles further down the river. About it the country loses much of the ruggedness of the north shore, the hills being more softly rounded, and clothed with a more generous and summery vegetation.

While the opposite side delights one with the grandeur of its heights and solitudes, it impresses one at the same time with a sense of desolation utterly opposed to all homeliness, and you constantly wonder what could have induced settlements to grow, especially since they are so entirely dependent upon farming industry. But here the farms and the better class of houses, the meadows and waving grain fields, make you feel that summer has not entirely thrown away its time in consenting to visit the land.

This change and much else you have time to note as you drive from the wharf at Rivière du Loup to Cacouna, a distance of five miles.

The Saguenay steamers touch at Rivière du Loup between five and six in the afternoon, and for the drive to Cacouna there could be no more happily chosen hour. The scene on the wharf—which, on account of the tide and level beach, is built fully three-quarters of a mile out into the stream—as you steam up to it is a very lively one. The pier is a rendezvous for the sojourners of the several resorts which cluster about within easy driving or walking distance. Amongst the public conveyances one sees a fair sprinkling of private carriages, wagons, and phaetons, a few horsemen, and a great many pedestrians out for a walk of four or five miles, to get up an appetite for tea, and see the latest arrivals from Quebec.

While the boat remains, all is—I was about to say confusion, but that implies too much the idea of hurry, and one very seldom feels hurried in Canada. The

The drive to Cacouna is a charming one, especially at the hour when the sun is getting ready to sink behind the mountains. Inland, the view extends over the peaceful and softly broken valley of the Loup River, with pleasant-looking hamlets scattered through it, for the elevation upon which you are driving commands a wide range. Your road lies sometimes through "the bush," and sometimes past farms whose great barns would give a Western man an exaggerated idea of the harvests which find their way into

scene rather impresses one as a wave of pleasant excitement flowing in upon this summer life. Warm greetings are exchanged with the new arrivals, or, from wharf to deck, with those going still further down, and there is a good deal of gay banter indulged in between the residents of rival resorts. When the freight is all landed, and the steamer resumes its journey, and final adieux are waved, people and vehicles file off the long wharf, and turn to their various homes.

A CALÈCHE PARTY.

FARM BUILDINGS, CACOUNA.

them. But a more intimate acquaintance with the country develops the fact that it is not the genial climate which fills them, but just the reverse. The farmer here has to provide warm shelter for all his stock during the winter. Sheds and slightly constructed out-buildings do not enter into his calculations; everything must be Northern weather proof, and so the barns are made to do duty for stables as well. Another noticeable feature in the landscape, and one which adds greatly to its picturesqueness, is the windmill with which each farm is provided, and which is made to do much of the heavy work. Then there are the old-fashioned out-ovens, either belonging to each house or built in common by several families, where, winter and summer, the baking is done. And, by-the-way, the baking for a French - Canadian family is not an item to be overlooked; for not only are there usually a goodly number of mouths to fill, but it takes a good deal of bread to fill each, as in none of their tastes do the people show their extraction more strongly than in being bread-eaters.

All of these things we had plenty of time to observe and discuss, since our horse was one of those peculiarly constructed beasts whose mode of locomotion seemed to be up and down rather than onward, and which, in bringing our journey to a close, brought us also into a quandary as to how the feat had been accomplished. But we did not at all mind the slowness of our progress after the clouds in the west began to take on the tints of sunset. They lit up the thirty miles of green water which stretched between us and the other side, forming a bed on which, like cameos, rested the softly modelled islands in the distance; while nearer, the lonely and desolate Pilgrim Isles, a solemn procession turning Gulfward, assumed almost the appearance of merry masqueraders in the bewildering, enchanting light.

We found the principal hotel of the place finely situated upon the brow of a cliff from which a magnificent view is obtained. The beach below it is wide and sandy, and the water being decidedly warmer than at Murray Bay, bathing is here much more indulged in. The beach is reached by pleasant, shady paths, which sidle down the cliff, with acceptable resting-places here and there, for the descent is steep. The first night we spent in Cacouna we were treated to the most brilliant auroral display, this point being far enough north for us to enjoy the phenomenon in all its splendor. The atmosphere here is of a crystal clearness, through which every ray of light, either by night or day, performs its fullest mission.

What the people do with themselves in

Cacouna it is hard for the uninitiated to discover. The hotel was full, and yet the parlors were empty. Upon airy upper galleries and in pleasant nooks of the house you come upon a cluster of ladies sitting, embroidery in hand, chatting the morning away. In the bowling-alley and billiard-room the young ladies were to be found. Out on the lawn the children and their nurses were in force. But what had become of the young ladies who have got beyond billiards and bowling, and not yet reached the tranquillity of the embroidery frame, I shall never know. Neither shall I know where the young gentlemen were. They could not be totally absent, however, since from the conversation of the young ladies I gathered that there was no lack of society. I fancy, though, that gay life centres itself rather at the cottages than in the hotels. Of late years Old Orchard Beach and other American watering-places have proved very attractive to the young Canadians who can treat themselves to the luxury of spending their holidays at a fashionable hotel, and in consequence one is apt to find here only the sons of families occupying summer residences, or such intimate friends as are invited to stay with them. But a few Canadian gentlemen of society proclivities can do valuable duty, as they give themselves up to the good work with a readiness and zeal quite unknown in American life. This especially applies to the "ladies' men" of Lower Canada. They, particularly the French-

Canadian, are perfect specimens in their line. A lady's simplest wish is a law they hold themselves ready to acknowledge and obey. They seem never to have any of

OUT-DOOR OVEN.

those aggravating previous engagements which so often cause the plans of the lady friends to "gang aglee," and they carry out these plans with an enthusiasm which forbids any doubts of their pleasure in them. They are always gay and devoted

SOUVENIR VENDERS.

to all. Usually they do not marry young, but when the important moment comes in which to decide, like Sir Charles Grandison they dispose of themselves "as circumstances render most proper, and bow gracefully upon the hand of the rejected lady and bid her adieu."

Speaking of marriages, it is astonishing how very few inappropriate marriages, viewing the matter in a purely worldly way, take place in Canada. Of course class distinctions are much more sharply defined than in the United States, and, as a rule, people marry within their own classes. Consequently fashionable society is not often shocked by having forced upon it an unacceptable person.

As I was saying, the gay life at Cacouna is rather in the summer homes than in the hotels. There is much visiting between this and the neighboring towns, such as Rivière du Loup, Notre Dame du Portage, Rivière Ouelle, and Kamouraska, and much dancing at the cottages. Then there are picnics and boating, and driving or riding parties. So that while the quiet or the invalid may find Cacouna delightfully tranquil, the butterfly of fashion will also find it delightfully gay.

Of course the sojourner of a few days will feel it incumbent upon him to see as much of the neighborhood as possible, and in strolling about he will come upon various Indian encampments, whose occupants veneer their civilization as much as possible with Indian laziness and unpicturesque dirt. These aborigines live in the ugliest of bark wigwams, by the doors of which the squaws, when not weaving baskets, seem to be either engaged in preparing an untempting mess in a kettle over a smoky fire, or presiding over a chronic washing, which, however, in no wise affects the cleanliness of the family apparel. Amongst the men there appears to be a superfluity of chieftains, who are largely given up to supporting a heavy variety of dignity, and slowly fashioning small canoes, etc., which are sold to their visitors, whom they treat with a snubbing superciliousness. The rising generation, both male and female, gather about strangers with a manner which has the effect of cordiality until it becomes known that their sole object is to solicit pennies, which they propose to earn by shooting them from any given spot in the dust.

Tadoussac, just at the mouth of the Saguenay, has within the last few years made a sudden bound into popular favor. The past season there was an exceptionally gay one. The place has very fair hotel accommodation, and a goodly number of cottages. It has become the chosen resort of some of the most fashionable French families of Quebec, as well as of the quieter people who took possession of the place fifteen or twenty years ago; and a very entertaining, lively society has formed itself in this quaint little nest of a valley amongst the Laurentians.

My first glimpse of Tadoussac, gained from the deck of a rain-washed steamer, was a dismal introduction. It looked like a dreary place to come to, and I thought with pity as well as admiration of those grand old mariners, Jacques Cartier and his followers, who, nearly three hundred and fifty years ago, moored their barks within the bay. I wondered whether their mental vision turned back to the warm, gay land they had left as the cold gray of the landscape broke upon their sight. Whether it did or not, they pressed on, and at this place first landed, in 1535, upon Canadian soil, planted the cross here, and christened the country New France.

But though Tadoussac gave us a chilly welcome, I soon found that when the skies chose to do their part, the place, under a flood of sunshine, could brighten and look beguiling enough, and the broad river could dimple and sparkle with all the grace of a meadow brook.

Jacques Cartier discovered Tadoussac for France, and Lord Dufferin discovered it to fashion. Early during his administration as Governor-General of Canada the Earl of Dufferin built a summer residence here. From that time the place has steadily advanced as a summer resort. Its climate is most healthful; and its wild and magnificent scenery, and the good fishing to be had in the vicinity, make it most attractive to a variety of people, especially as Canadians are very fond of out-door life.

One of the pleasures of which the sojourner at Tadoussac will likely avail himself is that afforded by numerous sailing excursions, lasting sometimes several days, up the Saguenay, and perhaps even up the Sainte Marguerite River, the noble banks of which equal in magnificent

INDIAN BOYS SHOOTING AT PENNIES.

OLD HUDSON BAY COMPANY'S STATION.

grandeur those of the Saguenay itself, into which it empties its waters. This charming trip is denied the usual tourist, as no steamers are run on the Sainte Marguerite. The tiny sail-boats in which these excursions are made must, of course, be well managed, for although the Saguenay has a generally good reputation, it is not a pleasant thing to be caught on its dark waters in a dense fog, as there are often stretches of many miles in length where it is impossible either to anchor or land.

The new element at Tadoussac has settled itself about the crescent-shaped bay, which extends far inland, and offers most excellent bathing. The great white hotel, with all its modern merry-making, throws its shadow over the little two-hundred-year-old chapel of the Jesuits, which stands at the foot of its lawn, still preserved in all the simplicity of its time.

This church was one of the first built in the country, and now in its old age resumes the glory of its youth. Then it had the pride of the pioneer, and now the prestige of the veteran. Standing within its entrance, under the quaint gallery which you can almost touch with your uplifted hand, what a long line of ghosts steal in and out as you look back through the years of its existence! They form a motley procession — travellers, Indians, *habitants*, sailors, hunters, and trappers file past, and bring their woes, as various as themselves, to its altar and confessional. Now and then the ghostly line swerves aside as the patter of high-heeled boots announces the bevy of tourists, which fills for a moment the tiny place with a confusion of neatly fitting fashionable garments, a flash of diamonds on hands clasping guides and note-books, tightly furled veils, and quick, authoritative voices. Then the bevy flits away to look at the old buildings of the Hudson Bay Company near by, or the battery of antiquated four-pounders on the hotel lawn, and the ghosts have the place again to themselves.

Tadoussac has so many natural advantages that it only needs to be properly directed to become the foremost of Canadian watering-places. It starts upon its career —for it is comparatively a young rival to the resorts further up the river—with great promise. And if, as seems the case, it has fallen into the hands of skillful managers, its success is only a question of a few seasons. Its chances for attracting foreign elements to its summer life are good; for although, like its neighboring towns, it hides shyly behind its hills, and so gives but a glimpse of itself to passing boats, still, as all the Saguenay steamers make a halt of several hours at its wharf, the passengers have ample time to see enough of the place to make them want to see more. Tadoussac possesses that most valuable charm, the power to haunt the memory. I am sure that all who have once walked its grassy paths often think of the strange old Northern village. If they loved nature, they carried away with them a picture of clear waters, over which hang gray rocks wreathed with dark evergreens, flaming kalmias, or dainty harebells, and hills swelling away into hills, growing more mysterious as their ranges grow lonelier and more remote. Or, if they love society, they will recall, when the next season comes, the gay, care-free groups they have seen under the trees about the pretty cottages, and the dashing promenades about the hotels, the snatches of conversation, carried on in French or English, which they have caught as picturesque un-American-looking people strolled past them along the rustic road-sides. Tadoussac will haunt them with its quaintness and mystery. They will want to go there again and test their first impressions; and, going, they will be charmed once more with its difference from the other places they have known.

RELIC OF JACQUES CARTIER'S BATTERY.

CHAPTER XIX.

A DAUGHTER OF ENGLAND.

"SWEETHEART WILLIE," she said —and her hand lay lightly on his shoulder, as they were walking through the meadows in the quiet of this warm golden evening—" what mean you to be when you grow up ?"

He thought for a second or two, and then he rather timidly regarded her.

"What would you have me to be, Cousin Judith ?" he said.

"Why, then," said she, "methinks I would have you be part student and part soldier, were it possible, like the gallant Sir Philip Sidney, that Queen Elizabeth said was the jewel of her reign. And yet you know, sweetheart, that we can not all of us be of such great estate. There be those who live at the court, and have wealth and lands, and expeditions given them to fit out, so that they gain fame; that is not the lot of every one, and I know not whether it may be yours— though for brave men there is ever a chance. But this I know I would have you ready to do, whether you be in high position or in low, and that is to fight for England, if needs be, and defend her, and cherish her. Why," she said, "what would you think, now, of one brought up by a gentle mother, one that owes his birth and training to this good mother, and because there is something amiss in the house, and because everything is not to his mind, he ups and says he must go away and forsake her ? Call you that the thought of a loyal son and one that is grateful ? I call it the thought of a pee- vish, froward, fractious child. Because, forsooth, this thing or the other is not to his worship's liking, or all the company not such as he would desire, or others of the family having different opinions—as surely, in God's name, they have a right to have—why, he must needs forsake the mother that bore him, and be off and away to other countries ! Sweetheart Willie, that shall never be your mind, I charge you. No, you shall remain faith- ful to your mother England, that is a dear mother and a good mother, and hath done well by her sons and daughters for many a hundred years; and you shall be proud of her, and ready to fight for her, ay, and to give your life for the love of her, if ever the need should be !"

He was a small lad, but he was sen- sitive and proud-spirited; and he loved dearly this Cousin Judith who had made this appeal to him; so that for a second the blood seemed to forsake his face.

"I am too young as yet to do aught, Cousin Judith," said he, in rather a low voice, for his breath seemed to catch; "but—but when I am become a man I know that there will be one that will sooner die than see any Spaniard or Frenchman seize the country."

"Bravely said, sweetheart, by my life !" she exclaimed (and her approval was very sweet to his ears). "That is the spirit that women's hearts love to hear of, I can tell thee." And she stooped and kissed him in reward. "Hold to that faith. Be not ashamed of your loyalty to your mother England ! Ashamed ? Heaven's mercy ! where is there such another coun- try to be proud of ? And where is there another mother that hath bred such a race of sons ? Why, times without number have I heard my father say that neither Greece, nor Rome, nor Carthage, nor any of them, were such a race of men as these in this small island, nor had done such great things, nor earned so great a fame, in all parts of the world and beyond the seas. And mark you this, too: 'tis the men who are fiercest to fight with men that are the gentlest to women; they make no slaves of their women; they make com- panions of them; and in honoring them they honor themselves, as I reckon. Why, now, could I but remember what my fa- ther hath written about England, 'twould stir your heart, I know; that it would; for you are one of the true stuff, I'll be sworn; and you will grow up to do your duty by your gracious mother England— not to run away from her in peevish dis- content !"

She cast about for some time, her mem- ory, that she could not replenish by any book-reading, being a large and somewhat miscellaneous store-house.

"'Twas after this fashion," said she, "if I remember aright:

'This royal throne of kings, this sceptred isle,
This earth of majesty, this seat of Mars,
This fortress, built by Nature for herself
Against infestion and the hand of war ;
This happy breed of men, this little world,
This precious stone set in the silver sea,
Which serves it in the office of a wall,
Or as a moat defensive to a house,
Against the envy of less happier lands—
This blessed plot, this earth, this realm, this Eng-
   land !'

Mark you that, sweetheart?—is't not a land worth fighting for? Ay, and she hath had sons that could fight for her; and she hath them yet, I dare be sworn, if the need were to arise. And this is what you shall say, Cousin Willie, when you are a man and grown:

'Come the three corners of the world in arms,
And we shall shock them. Naught shall make us
   rue,
If England to itself do rest but true !'"

These quotations were but for the instruction of this small cousin of hers, and yet her own face was proud.

"Shall I be a soldier, then, Cousin Judith?" the boy said. "I am willing enough. I would be what you would wish me to be; and if I went to the wars, you would never have need to be shamed of me."

"That know I right well, sweetheart," said she, and she patted him on the head. "But 'tis not every one's duty to follow that calling. You must wait and judge for yourself. But whatever chances life may bring you, this must you ever remain, if you would have my love, sweetheart, and that I hope you shall have always— you must remain a good and loyal son to your mother England, one not easily discontented with small discomforts, and sent forth in a peevish fit. Where is there a fairer country? Marry, I know of none. Look around—is't not a fair enough country?"

And fair indeed on this quiet evening was that wide stretch of Warwickshire, with its hedges and green meadows, and low-lying wooded hills bathed in the warm sunset light. But it was the presence of Judith that made it all magical and mystical to him. Whatever she regarded with her clear-shining and wondrous eyes was beautiful enough for him—while her hand lay on his shoulder or touched his hair. He was a willing pupil. He drank in those lessons in patriotism: what was it he would not do for his cousin Judith?

What was it he would not believe if it were she who told him, in that strange voice of hers, that thrilled him, and was like music to him, whether she spoke to him in this proud, admonitory way, or was in a teasing mood, or was gentle and affectionate toward him? Yes, this Warwickshire landscape was fair enough, under the calm sunset sky; but he knew not what made it all so mystical and wonderful, and made the far golden clouds seem as the very gateways to heaven.

"Or is there one with a prouder story?" she continued. "Or a land of greater freedom? Why, look at me, now. Here am I, a woman, easily frightened, helpless if there were danger, not able to fight any one. Why, you yourself, Cousin Willie, if you were to draw a dagger on me, I declare to thee I would run and shriek and hide. Well, look at me as I stand here: all the might and majesty of England can not harm me; I am free to go or to stay. What needs one more? None durst put a hand on me. My mind is as free as my footsteps. I may go this way or that as I choose; and no one may command me to believe this, that, or the other. What more? And this security—think you it had not to be fought for?—think you it was not worth the fighting for? Or think you we should forget to give good thanks to the men that faced the Spaniards, and drove them by sea and shore, and kept our England to ourselves? Or think you we should forget our good Queen Bess, that I warrant me had as much spirit as they, and was as much a man as any of them?"

She laughed.

"Perchance you never heard, sweetheart, of the answer that she made to the Spanish ambassador?"

"No, Judith," said he, but something in her manner told him that there had been no cowardice in that answer.

"Well," she said, "I will tell thee the story of what happened at Deptford. And now I bethink me, this must you do, cousin Willie, when you are grown to be a man; and whether you be soldier or sailor, or merchant, or student, 'tis most like that some day or other you will be in London; and then must you not fail to go straightway to Deptford to see the famous ship of Sir Francis Drake lying there. I tell thee, 'twas a goodly thought to place it there; that was like our brave Queen Bess; she would have the youth of

"AND NOW SHE BEGAN READING."—From a Drawing by E. A. Abbey.

[See "Judith Shakespeare," Page 225.]

the country regard with honor the ship that had been all round the world, and chased the Spaniards from every sea. Nay, so bad is my memory that I can not recall the name of the vessel—perchance 'twas the *Judith*—at least I have heard that he had one of that name; but there it lies, to signal the glory of England and the routing of Spain."

"The *Judith?*" said he, with wondering eyes. "Did he name the ship after you, cousin?"

"Bless the lad! All that I am going to tell thee happened ere I was born."

"No matter," said he, stoutly; "the first thing I will ask to see, if ever I get to London, is that very ship."

"Well, then, the story," she continued, shaping the thing in her mind (for being entirely destitute of book-learning, historical incidents were apt to assume a dramatic form in her imagination, and also to lose literal accuracy of outline). "You must know the Spaniards were sore vexed because of the doings of Francis Drake in all parts of the world, for he had plundered and harried them, and burned their ships and their towns, and made the very name of England a terror to them. 'Tis no marvel if they wished to get hold of him; and they declared him to be no better than a pirate; and they would have the Queen—that is, our last Queen—deliver him over to them that they might do with him what they willed. Marry, 'twas a bold demand to make of England! And the Queen, how does she take it, think you?—how is she moved to act in such a pass? Why, she goes down to Deptford, to this very ship that I told thee of—she and all her nobles and ladies, for they would see the famous ship. Then they had dinner on board, as I have heard the story; and the Queen's Majesty asked many particulars of his voyages from Master Drake, and received from him certain jewels as a gift, and was right proud to wear them. Then says she aloud to them all: 'My lords, is this the man the Spaniards would have me give over to them?' Right well she knew he was the man; but that was her way, and she would call the attention of all of them. 'Your Majesty,' they said, ''tis no other.' Then she swore a great oath that the Queen of England knew how to make answer to such a demand. 'Come hither, Master Drake,' says she, in a terrible voice. 'Kneel!' Then he knelt on his knee before her. 'My

lord,' says she to one of the noblemen standing by, 'your sword!' And then, when she had the sword in her hand, she says, in a loud voice, 'My lords, this is the man that Spain would have us give up to her; and this is the answer of England: Arise, Sir Francis!'—and with that she taps him on the shoulder—which is the way of making a knight, Cousin Willie; and I pray you may be brave and valiant, and come to the same dignity, so that all of us here in Stratford shall say, 'There, now, is one that knew how to serve faithfully his fair mother England!' But that was not all, you must know, that happened with regard to Sir Francis Drake. For the Spanish ambassador was wroth with the Queen; ay, and went the length even of speaking with threats. ''Twill come to the cannon,' says he. 'What?' says she, turning upon him. 'Your Majesty,' says he, 'I fear me this matter will come to the cannon.' And guess you her answer?—nay, they say she spoke quite calmly, and regarded him from head to foot, and that if there were anger in her heart there was none in her voice. 'Little man, little man,' says she, 'if I hear any more such words from thee, by God I will clap thee straight into a dungeon!'"

Judith laughed, in a proud kind of way.

"That was the answer that England gave," said she, "and that she is like to give again, if the Don or any other of them would seek to lord it over her."

Three-fourths of these details were of her own invention, or rather—for it is scarcely fair to say that—they had unconsciously grown up in her mind from the small seed of the true story. But little Willie Hart had no distrust of any legend that his cousin Judith might relate to him. Whatever Judith said was true, and also luminous in a strange kind of fashion: something beautiful and full of color, to be thought over and pondered over. And now as they walked along toward the village, idly and lazily enough—for she had no other errand than to fetch back the manuscript that would be lying at the cottage—his eyes were wistful. His fancies were far away. What was it, then, that he was to do for England—that Judith should approve in the after-years? And for how long should he be away—in the Spanish Main, perchance, of which he had heard many stories, or fighting in the lowlands of Holland, or whatever he was called to do—and what was there at the

end? Well, the end that he foresaw
and desired—the reward of all his toil—
was nothing more nor less than this: that
he should be sitting once again in a pew
in Stratford church, on a quiet Sunday
morning, with Judith beside him as of old,
they listening to the singing together. He
did not think of his being grown up, or
that she would be other than she was now.
His mind could form no other or fairer
consummation than that—that would be
for him the final good—to come back to
Stratford town to find Judith as she had
ever been to him, gentle, and kind, and
soft-handed, and ready with a smile from
her beautiful and lustrous eyes.

"Yes, sweetheart Willie," said she, as
they were nearing the cottages, "look at
the quiet that reigns all around, and no
priests of the Inquisition to come dragging
my poor old grandmother from her knitting. What has she to do but look after
the garden, and scold the maid, and fetch
milk for the cat? And all this peace of
the land that we enjoy we may have to
fight for again; and then, if the King's
Majesty calls either for men or for money,
you shall have no word but obedience.
Heard you never of the Scotch knight,
Sir Patrick Spens?—that the Scotch King
would send away to Norroway at an evil
time of the year? Did he grumble? Did
he say his men were ill content to start
at such a time? Nay, as I have heard,
when he read the King's letter the tears
welled in his eyes; but I'll be sworn that
was for the companions he was taking
with him to face the cruel sea.

'The King's daughter from Norroway,
    'Tis we must fetch her home,'

he says; and then they up with their sails,
and set out from the land that they never
were to see more. What of that? They
were brave men; they did what was demanded of them; though the black seas
of the north were too strong for them in
the end. 'Twas a sad tale, in good sooth:

'O lang, lang may the ladies sit,
    Wi' the fans into their hand,
Before they see Sir Patrick Spens
    Come sailing to the strand!

'And lang, lang may the maidens sit,
    Wi' their gold combs in their hair,
All waiting for their ain dear loves,
    For them they'll see nae mair.

'Half owre, half owre to Aberdour,
    'Tis fifty fathoms deep,
And there lies good Sir Patrick Spens
    Wi' the Scots lords at his feet.'

But what then? I tell thee, sweetheart,
any maiden that would be worth the winning would a hundred times liefer wail
for a lover that had died bravely than
welcome him back safe and sound as a
coward. You shall be no coward, I warrant me, when you are grown up to be a
man; and above all, as I say, shall you
be gentle and forgiving with your mother
England, even if your own condition be
not all you wish; and none the less for
that shall you be willing to fight for her
should she be in trouble. Nay, I'll answer for thee, lad: I know thee well."

"But, Judith," said he, "who are they
you speak of, that are discontented, and
would go away and leave the country?"

Well, it is probable she might have
found some embarrassment in answering
this question (if she had been pressed to
name names) but that what she now beheld deprived her of the power of answering altogether. She had come over from
the town with no other thought than to
pay a brief visit to her grandmother, and
fetch back the portion of the play, and
she had not the slightest expectation of
encountering Master Leofric Hope. But
there unmistakably he was, though he did
not see her, for he was standing at the
gate of her grandmother's cottage, and
talking to the old dame, who was on the
other side. There was no pretense of
concealment. Here he was in the public
path, idly chatting, his hand resting on
the gate. And as Judith had her cousin
Willie with her, her first thought was to
hurry away in any direction in order to
escape an interview; but directly she saw
that this was impossible, for her grandmother had descried her, if Leofric Hope
had not. The consequence was that, as
she went forward to the unavoidable meeting, she was not only surprised and a
trifle confused and anxious, but also somewhat and vaguely resentful; for she had
been intending, before seeing him again,
to frame in her mind certain tests which
might remove or confirm one or two suspicions that had caused her disquietude.
And now—and unfairly, as she thought
—she found herself compelled to meet him
without any such legitimate safeguard of
preparation. She had no time to reflect
that it was none of his fault. Why had
not he left the play earlier? she asked herself. Why had not he departed at once?
Why, with all his professions of secrecy,
should he be standing in the open high-

way, carelessly talking? And what was she to say to little Willie Hart that would prevent his carrying back the tale to the school and the town? When she went forward, it was with considerable reluctance; and she had a dim, hurt sense of having been imposed upon, or somehow or another injured.

CHAPTER XX.

VARYING MOODS.

But the strange thing was that the moment he turned and saw her—and the moment she met the quick look of friendliness and frank admiration that came into his face and his eloquent dark eyes—all her misgivings, surmises, suspicions, and half-meditated safeguards instantly vanished. She herself could not have explained it; she only knew that, face to face with him, she had no longer any doubt as to his honesty; and consequently that vague sense of injury vanished also. She had been taken unawares, but she did not mind. Everything, indeed, connected with this young man was of a startling, unusual character; and she was becoming familiar with that, and less resentful at being surprised.

"Ah, fair Mistress Judith," said he, "you come opportunely: I would thank you from the heart for the gracious company I have enjoyed this afternoon through your good-will; in truth, I was loath to part with such sweet friends, and perchance detained them longer than I should."

"I scarce understand you, sir," said she, somewhat bewildered.

"Not the visions that haunt a certain magic island?" said he.

Her face lit up.

"Well, sir?" she asked, with a kind of pride; but at this point her grandmother interposed, and insisted—somewhat to Judith's surprise—that they should come in and sit down, if not in the house, at least in the garden. He seemed willing enough; for without a word he opened the gate to let Judith pass; and then she told him who her cousin was; and in this manner they went up to the little arbor by the hedge.

"Well, good sir, and how liked you the company?" said she, cheerfully, when she had got within and sat down.

Her grandmother had ostensibly taken to her knitting; but she managed all the same to keep a sharp eye on the young man; for she was curious, and wanted to know something further of the parcel that he had left with her. It was not merely hospitality or a freak of courtesy that had caused her to give him this sudden invitation. Her granddaughter Judith was a self-willed wench and mischievous; she would keep an eye on her too; she would learn more of this commerce between her and the young gentleman who had apparently dropped, as it were, from the skies. As for little Willie Hart, he remained outside, regarding the stranger with no great good-will; but perhaps more with wonder than with anger, for he marvelled to hear Judith talk familiarly with this person, of whom he had never heard a word, as though she had known him for years.

"'Tis not for one such as I," said Master Leofric Hope, modestly—and with such a friendly regard toward Judith that she turned away her eyes and kept looking at this and that in the garden—"to speak of the beauties of the work; I can but tell you of the delight I have myself experienced. And yet how can I even do that? How can I make you understand that—or my gratitude either, sweet Mistress Judith—unless you know something of the solitude of the life I am compelled to lead? You would have yourself to live at Bassfield Farm; and watch the monotony of the days there; and be scarcely able to pass the time: then would you know the delight of being introduced to this fair region that your father hath invented, and being permitted to hear those creatures of his imagination speak to each other. Nay, but 'tis beautiful! I am no critical judge; but I swear 'twill charm the town."

"You think so, sir?" said she, eagerly, and for an instant she withdrew her eyes from the contemplation of the flowers. But immediately she altered her tone to one of calm indifference. "My father hath many affairs to engage him, you must understand, good sir; perchance, now, this play is not such as he would have written had he leisure, and—and had he been commanded by the court, and the like. Perchance 'tis too much of the human kind for such purposes?"

"I catch not your meaning, sweet lady," said he.

"I was thinking," said she, calmly, "of

the masques you told us of—at Theobald's and elsewhere—that Master Benjamin Jonson has written, and that they all seem to prize so highly: perchance these were of a finer stuff than my father hath time to think of, being occupied, as it were, with so many cares. 'Tis a rude life, having regard to horses, and lands, and malt, and the rest; and—and the court ladies—they would rather have the gods and goddesses marching in procession, would they not? My father's writing is too much of the common kind, is it not, good sir?—'tis more for the 'prentices, one might say, and such as these?"

He glanced at her. He was not sure of her.

"The King, sweet lady," said he, "is himself learned, and would have the court familiar with the ancient tongues; and for such pageants 'tis no wonder they employ Master Jonson, that is a great scholar. But surely you place not such things—that are but as toys—by the side of your father's plays, that all marvel at, and applaud, and that have driven away all others from our stage?"

"Say you so?" she answered, with the same indifferent demeanor. "Nay, I thought that Master Scoloker—was that his worship's name?—deemed them to be of the vulgar sort. But perchance he was one of the learned ones. The King, they say, is often minded to speak in the Latin. What means he by that, good sir, think you? Hath he not yet had time to learn our English speech?"

"Wench, what would you?" her grandmother interposed, sharply. "Nay, good sir, heed her not; her tongue be an unruly member, and maketh sport of her, as I think; but the wench meaneth no harm."

"The King is proud of his learning, no doubt," said he; and he would probably have gone on to deprecate any comparison between the court masques and her father's plays but that she saw here her opportunity, and interrupted him.

"I know it," she said, "for the letter that the King sent to my father is writ in the Latin."

"Nay, is it so?" said he.

She affected not to observe his surprise.

"'Twas all the same to my father," she continued, calmly, "whether the letter was in one tongue or the other. He hath one book now—how is it called?—'tis a marvellous heap of old stories—the Jests—"

"Not the *Gesta Romanorum?*" he said.

"The same, as I think. Well, he hath one copy that is in English, and of our own time, as I am told; but he hath also another and a very ancient copy, that is in the Latin tongue; and this it is—the Latin one, good sir—that my father is fondest of; and many a piece of merriment he will get out of it, when Julius Shawe is in the house of an evening."

"But the *Gesta* are not jests, good Mistress Judith," said he, looking somewhat puzzled.

"I know not; I but hear them laughing," said she, placidly. "And as for the book itself, all I know of it is the outside; but that is right strange and ancient, and beautiful withal: the back of it white leather stamped with curious devices; and the sides of parchment printed in letters of red and black; and the silver clasps of it with each a boar's head. I have heard say that that is the crest of the Scotch knight that gave the volume to my father when they were all at Aberdeen; 'twas when they made Laurence Fletcher a burgess; and the knight said to my father, 'Good sir, the honor to your comrade is a general one, but I would have you take this book in particular, in the way of thanks and remembrance for your wit and pleasant company'—that, or something like that, said he; and my father is right proud of the book, that is very ancient and precious; and often he will read out of it—though it be in the Latin tongue. Oh, I assure you, sir," she added, with a calm and proud air, "'tis quite the same thing to him. If the King choose to write to him in that tongue, well and good. Marry, now I think of it, I make no doubt that Julius Shawe would lend me the letter, did you care to see it."

He looked up quickly and eagerly.

"Goes your goodness so far, sweet Mistress Judith? Would you do me such a favor and honor?"

"Nay, young sir," the grandmother said, looking up from her knitting, "tempt not the wench; she be too ready to do mad things out of her own mind. And you, grandchild, see you meddle not in your father's affairs."

"Why, grandam," Judith cried, "'tis the common property of Stratford town. Any one that goeth into Julius Shawe's house may see it. And why Julius Shawe's friends only? Beshrew me, there are others who have as good a title to that letter —little as my father valueth it."

"Nay, I will forego the favor," said he at once, "though I owe you none the less thanks, dear lady, for the intention of your kindness. In truth, I know not how to make you sensible of what I already owe you; for, having made acquaintance with those fair creations, how can one but long to hear of what further befell them? My prayer would rather go in that direction—if I might make so bold."

He regarded her now with a timid look. Well, she had not undertaken that he should see the whole of the play, nor had she ever hinted to him of any such possibility; but it had been in her mind, and for the life of her she could not see any harm in this brief loan of it. Harm? Had not even this brief portion of it caused him to think of her father's creations as if they were of a far more marvellous nature than the trumpery court performances that had engrossed his talk when first she met him?

"There might be some difficulty, good sir," said she, "but methinks I could obtain for you the further portions, if my good grandmother here would receive them and hand them to you when occasion served."

"What's that, wench?" her grandmother said, instantly.

"'Tis but a book, good grandam, that I would lend Master Hope to lighten the dullness of his life at the farm withal: you can not have any objection, grandmother?"

"'Tis a new trade to find thee in, wench," said her grandmother. "I'd 'a thought thou wert more like to have secret commerce in laces and silks."

"I am no peddler, good madam," said he, with a smile; "else could I find no pleasanter way of passing the time than in showing to you and your fair granddaughter my store of braveries. Nay, this that I would beg of you is but to keep the book until I have the chance to call for it; and that is a kindness you have already shown in taking charge of the little package I left for Mistress Judith here."

"Well, well, well," said the old dame, "if 'tis anything belonging to her father, see you bring it back, and let not the wench get into trouble."

"I think you may trust me so far, good madam," said he, with such simplicity of courtesy and sincerity that even the old grandmother was satisfied.

In truth she had been regarding the two of them with some sharpness during these few minutes to see if she could detect anything in their manner that might awaken suspicion. There was nothing. No doubt the young gentleman regarded Judith with an undisguised wish to be friendly with her, and say pretty things; but was that to be wondered at? 'Twas not all the lads in Stratford that would be so modest in showing their admiration for a winsome lass. And this book-lending commerce was but natural in the circumstances. She would have been well content to hear that his affairs permitted him to leave the neighborhood, and that would happen in good time; meanwhile there could be no great harm in being civil to so well-behaved a young gentleman. So now, as she had satisfied herself that the leaving of the package meant nothing dark or dangerous, she rose and hobbled away in search of the little maid, to see that some ale were brought out for the refreshment of her visitor.

"Sweetheart Willie," Judith called, "what have you there? Come hither!"

Her small cousin had got hold of the cat, and was vainly endeavoring to teach it to jump over his clasped hands. He took it up in his arms, and brought it with him to the arbor, though he did not look in the direction of the strange gentleman.

"We shall be setting forth for home directly," said she. "Wilt thou not sit down and rest thee?"

"'Tis no such distance, cousin," said he.

He seemed unwilling to come in; he kept stroking the cat, with his head averted. So she went out to him, and put her arm round his neck.

"This, sir," said she, "is my most constant companion, next to Prudence Shawe; I know not to what part of all this neighborhood we have not wandered together. And such eyes he hath for the birds' nests; when I can see naught but a cloud of leaves he will say, why, 'tis so and so, or so and so; and up the tree like a squirrel, and down again with one of the eggs, or perchance a small naked birdling, to show me. But we always put them back, sweetheart, do we not?—we leave no bereft families, or sorrowing mother bird to find an empty nest. We do as we would be done by; and 'tis no harm to them that we should look at the pretty blue eggs, or take out one of the small chicks with its downy feathers and its gaping bill. And for the fishing, too—there be none cleverer at setting a line, as I hear, or more patient in watching: but I like not that pastime, good Cousin Willie, for or soon or late you are certain to fall through the bushes into the river, as happened to Dickie Page last week, and there may not be some one there to haul you out, as they hauled out him."

"And how fares he at the school?" said the young gentleman in the arbor.

"Oh, excellent well, as I am told," said she, "although I be no judge of lessons myself. Marry, I hear good news of his behavior; and if there be a bloody nose now and again, why, a boy that's attacked must hold his own, and give as good as he gets—'twere a marvel else—and 'tis no use making furious over it, for who knows how the quarrel began? Nay, I will give my cousin a character for being as gentle as any, and as reasonable; and if he fought with Master Crutchley's boy, and hit him full sore, I fear, between the eyes—well, having heard something of the matter, I make no doubt it served young Crutchley right, and that elder people should have a care in condemning when they can not know the beginning of the quarrel. Well, now I bethink me, sweetheart, tell me how it began, for that I never heard. How began the quarrel?"

"Nay, 'twas nothing," he said, shamefacedly.

"Nothing? Nay, that I will not believe. I should not wonder now if it were about some little wench. What? Nay, I'll swear it now! 'Twas about the little wench that has come to live at the Vicarage—what's her name?—Minnie, or Winnie?"

"'Twas not, then, Judith," said he. "If you must know, I will tell you; I had liefer say naught about it. But 'twas not the first time he had said so—before all of them—that my uncle was no better than an idle player, that ought to be put in the stocks and whipped."

"Why, now," said she, "to think that the poor lad's nose should be set a-bleeding for nothing more than that!"

"It had been said more than once, Cousin Judith; 'twas time it should end," said he, simply.

At this moment Master Leofric Hope called to him.

"Come hither, my lad," said he. "I would hear how you get on at school."

The small lad turned and regarded him, but did not budge. His demeanor was entirely changed. With Judith he was invariably gentle, submissive, abashed:

now, as he looked at the stranger, he seemed to resent the summons.

"Come hither, my lad."

"Thank you, no, sir," he said; "I would as lief be here."

"Sweetheart, be these your manners?" Judith said.

But the young gentleman only laughed good-naturedly.

"Didst thou find any such speeches in the *Sententiæ Pueriles*?" said he. "They were not there when I was at school."

"When go we back to Stratford, Judith?" said the boy.

"Presently, presently," said she (with some vague impression that she could not well leave until her grandmother's guest showed signs of going also). "See, here is my grandam coming with various things for us; and I warrant me you shall find some gingerbread amongst them."

The old dame and the little maid now came along, bringing with them ale and jugs and spiced bread and what not, which were forthwith put on the small table; and though Judith did not care to partake of these, and was rather wishful to set out homeward again, still, in common courtesy, she was compelled to enter the arbor and sit down. Moreover, Master Hope seemed in no hurry to go. It was a pleasant evening, the heat of the day being over; the skies were clear, fair, and lambent with the declining golden light: why should one hasten away from this quiet bower, in the sweet serenity and silence, with the perfume of roses all around, and scarce a breath of air to stir the leaves? He but played with this slight refection; nevertheless, it was a kind of excuse for the starting of fresh talk; and his talk was interesting and animated. Then he had discovered a sure and easy way of pleasing Judith, and instantly gaining her attention. When he spoke of the doings in London, her father was no longer left out of these: nay, on the contrary, he became a central figure; and she learned more now of the Globe and Blackfriars theatres than ever she had heard in her life before. Nor did she fail to lead him on with questions. Which of her father's friends were most constant attendants at the theatre? Doubtless they had chairs set for them on the stage? Was there any one that her father singled out for especial favor? When they went to the tavern in the evening, what place had her father at the board? Did any of the young lords go with them? How late sat they? Did her father outshine them all with his wit and merriment, or did he sit quiet and amused?—for sometimes it was the one and sometimes the other with him here in Stratford. Did they in London know that he had such a goodly house, and rich lands, and horses? And was there good cooking at the tavern—Portugal dishes and the like? Or perchance (she asked, with an inquiring look from the beautiful, clear eyes) it was rather poor? And the napery, now: it was not always of the cleanest? And instead of neat-handed maids, rude serving-men, tapsters, drawers, and so forth? And the ale —she could be sworn 'twas no better than the Warwickshire ale; no, nor was the claret likely to be better than that brought into the country for the gentlefolk by such noted vintners as Quiney. Her father's lodging—that he said was well enough, as he said everything was well enough, for she had never known him utter a word of discontent with anything that happened to him—perchance 'twas none of the cleanliest? for she had heard that the London housewives were mostly slovens, and would close you doors and windows against the air, so that a countryman going to that town was like to be sickened. And her father—did he ever speak of his family when he was in London? Did they know he had belongings? Nay, she was certain he must have talked to his friends and familiars of little Bess Hall, for how could he help that?

"You forget, sweet Mistress Judith," said he, in his pleasant way, "that I have not the honor of your father's friendship, nor of his acquaintance even, and what I have told you is all of hearsay, save with regard to the theatre, where I have seen him often. And that is the general consent: that this one may have more learning, and that one more sharpness of retort, but that in these encounters he hath a grace and a brilliancy far outvying them all, and, moreover, with such a gentleness as earns him the general good-will. Such is the report of him; I would it had been in my power to speak from my own experience."

"But that time will come, good sir," said she, "and soon, I trust."

"In the mean while," said he, "bethink you what a favor it is that I should be permitted to come into communion with those fair creations of his fancy; and I would remind you once more of your promise, sweet Mistress Judith; and would beseech your good grandmother to take charge of anything you may leave for me. Nay, 'twill be for no longer than an hour or two that I would detain it; but that brief time I would have free from distractions, so that the mind may dwell on the picture. Do I make too bold, sweet lady? Or does your friendship go so far?"

"In truth, sir," she answered, readily, "if I can I will bring you the rest of the play—but perchance in portions, as the occasion serves; 'twere no great harm should you carry away with you some memory of the Duke and his fair daughter on the island."

"The time will pass slowly until I hear more of them," said he.

"And meanwhile, good grandmother," said she, "if you will tell me where I may find the little package, methinks I must be going."

At this he rose.

"I beseech your pardon if I have detained you, sweet lady," said he, with much courtesy.

"Nay, sir, I am indebted to you for welcome news," she answered, "and I would I had longer opportunity of hearing. And what said you—that he outshone them all?—that it was the general consent?"

"Can you doubt it?" he said, gallantly.

"Nay, sir, we of his own household— and his friends in Stratford — we know and see what my father is: so well esteemed, in truth, as Julius Shawe saith, that there is not a man in Warwickshire would cheat him in the selling of a horse, which they are not slow to do, as I hear, with others. But I knew not he had won so wide and general a report in London, where they might know him not so well as we."

"Let me assure you of that, dear lady," he said, "and also that I will not forget to bring or send you the printed tribute to his good qualities that I spoke of, when that I may with safety go to London. 'Tis but a trifle; but it may interest his family; marry, I wonder he hath not himself spoken of it to you."

"He speak of it!" said she, regarding him with some surprise, as if he ought to have known better. "We scarce know aught of what happeneth to him in London. When he comes home to Warwickshire it would seem as if he had forgotten

London and all its affairs, and left them behind for good."

"Left them behind for good, say you, wench?" the old dame grumbled, mostly to herself, as she preceded them down the path. "I would your father had so much sense. What hath he to gain more among the players and dicers and tavern brawlers and that idle crew? Let him bide at home, among respectable folk. Hath he not enough of gear gathered round him, eh? It be high time he slipped loose from those mummers that play to please the cutpurses and their trulls in London. Hath he not enough of gear?"

"What say you, grandmother? You would have my father come away from London and live always in Warwickshire? Well, now, that is nearer than you think, or my guesses are wrong."

But her grandmother had gone into the cottage; and presently she returned with the little package. Then there was a general leave-taking at the gate; and Leofric Hope, after many expressions of his thanks and good-will, set out on his own way, Judith and her cousin taking the path through the meadows.

For some time they walked in silence; then, as soon as the stranger was out of ear-shot, the lad looked up and said,

"Who is that, Judith?"

"Why," said she, lightly, "I scarcely know myself; but that he is in misfortune and hiding, and that he knoweth certain of my father's friends, and that he seems pleased to have a few words with one or other of us to cheer his solitude. You would not begrudge so much, sweetheart? Nay, there is more than that I would have you do: his safety depends on there being no talk about him in the town; and I know you can keep a secret, Cousin Willie; so you must not say a word to any one—whether at school, or at home, or at New Place—of your having seen him. You will do as much for my sake, sweetheart?"

"Yes; but why for your sake, cousin?" said the boy, looking up. "Why should you concern yourself?"

"Nay, call it for anybody's sake, then," said she. "But I would not have him betrayed by any one that I had aught to do with—and least of all by you, sweetheart, that I expect to show nothing but fair and manly parts. Nay, I trust you. You will not blab."

And then, as they walked on, it occurred to her that this young gentleman's secret—if he wished it kept—was becoming somewhat widely extended in his neighborhood. In her own small circle how many already knew of his presence? —her grandmother, Prudence Shawe, herself, Tom Quiney, and now this little Willie Hart. And she could not but remember that not much more than half an hour ago she had seen him at the garden gate, carelessly chatting, and apparently not heeding in the least what passers-by might observe him. But that was always the way: when she left him, when she was with her own thoughts, curious surmises would cross her mind; whereas, when she met him, these were at once discarded. And so she took to arguing with herself as to why she should be so given to do this young man injustice in his absence, when, every time she encountered him face to face she was more than ever convinced of his honesty. Fascination? Well, she liked to hear of London town and the goings on there; and this evening she had been particularly interested in hearing about the Globe Theatre, and the spectators, and the tavern to which her father and his friends repaired for their supper; but surely that would not blind her if she had any reason to think that the young man was other than he represented? And then, again, this evening he had been markedly deferential. There was nothing in his manner of that somewhat too open gallantry he had displayed in the morning when he made his speech about the English roses. Had she not wronged him, then, in imagining even for a moment that he had played a trick upon her in order to make her acquaintance? It is true, she had forgotten to make special remark of his eyes, as to whether they were like those of the wizard; for indeed the suspicion had gone clean out of her mind. But now she tried to recall them; and she could not fairly say to herself that there was a resemblance. Nay, the wizard was a solemn person, who seemed to rebuke her light-heartedness; he spoke gravely and slow; whereas this young man, as any one could see, had a touch of merriment in his eye that was ready to declare itself on further acquaintance, only that his deference kept him subdued, while his talk was light and animated and rapid. No, she would absolve him from this suspicion; and soon, indeed, as she guessed, he would absolve himself by removing from the neighborhood, and probably she would hear no more of him, unless, perchance, he should remember to send her that piece of print concerning her father.

And then her thoughts went far afield. She had heard much of London that evening; and London, in her mind, was chiefly associated with her father's plays, or such as she knew of them; and these again were represented to her by a succession of figures, whose words she thought of, whose faces she saw, when, as now, her fancies were distant. And she was more silent than usual as they went on their way across the meadows, and scarce addressed a word to her companion; insomuch that at last he looked up into her face, and said,

"Judith, why are you so sad this evening?"

"Sad, sweetheart? Surely no," she answered; and she put her hand on his head. "What makes thee think so?"

"Did Dame Hathaway speak harshly to you?" said he. "Methought I heard her say something. Another time I will bid her hold her peace."

"Nay, nay, not so," said she; and as they were now come to a stile, she paused there, and drew the boy toward her.

Not that she was tired; but the evening was so quiet and still, and the whole world seemed falling into a gentle repose. There was not a sound near them; the earth was hushed as it sank to sleep; far away they could hear the voices of children going home with their parents, or the distant barking of a dog. It was late, and yet the skies seemed full of light, and all the objects around them were strangely distinct and vivid. Behind them, the northwestern heavens were of a pale luminous gold; overhead and in front of them, the great vault was of a beautiful lilac-gray, deepening to blue in the sombre east; and into this lambent twilight the great black elms rose in heavy masses. The wide meadows still caught some of the dying radiance; and there was a touch of it on the westward-looking gables of one or two cottages; and then through this softened glow there came a small keen ray of lemon yellow—a light in one of the far-off windows that burned there like a star. So hushed this night was, and so calm and beautiful, that a kind of wistfulness fell over her mind—scarcely sadness, as the boy had imagined—but a dull longing for sympathy, and some

vague wonder as to what her life might be in the years to come.

"Why, sweetheart," said she, absently, and her hand lay affectionately on his shoulder, "as we came along here this evening we were speaking of all that was to happen to you in after-life; and do you never think you would like to have the picture unrolled now, and see for yourself, and have assurance? Does not the mystery of it make you impatient, or restless, or sad—so that you would fain have the years go by quick, and get to the end? Nay, I trow not; the day and the hour are sufficient for thee; and 'tis better so. Keep as thou art, sweetheart, and pay no heed to what may hereafter happen to thee."

"What is't that troubles you, Judith?" said he, with an instinctive sympathy, for there was more in her voice than in her words.

"Why, I know not myself," said she, slowly, and with her eyes fixed vacantly on the darkening landscape. "Nothing, as I reckon. 'Tis but beating one's wings against the invisible to seek to know even to-morrow. And in the further years some will have gone away from Stratford, and some to far countries, and some will be married, and some grown old; but to all the end will be the same; and I dare say now that, hundreds of years hence, other people will be coming to Stratford, and they will go into the church-yard there, and walk about and look at the names—that is, of you and me and all the rest of us—and they will say, 'Poor things, they vexed themselves about very small matters while they were alive, but they are all at peace at last.'"

"But what is it that troubles you, Judith?" said he; for this was an unusual mood with her, who generally was so thoughtless and merry and high-hearted.

"Why, nothing, sweetheart, nothing," said she, seeming to rouse herself. "'Tis the quiet of the night that is so strange, and the darkness coming. Or will there be moonlight? In truth, there must be, and getting near to the full, as I reckon. A night for Jessica! Heard you ever of her, sweetheart?"

"No, Judith."

"Well, she was a fair maiden that lived long ago, somewhere in Italy, as I think. And she ran away with her lover, and was married to him, and was very happy; and all that is now known of her is connected with music and moonlight and an evening such as this. Is not that a fair life to lead after death: to be in all men's thoughts always as a happy bride, on such a still night as this is now? And would you know how her lover spoke to her?— this is what he says:

'How sweet the moonlight sleeps upon this bank!
Here will we sit, and let the sounds of music
Creep to our ears; soft stillness and the night
Become the touches of sweet harmony.
Sit, Jessica: Look, how the floor of heaven
Is thick inlaid with patines of bright gold;
There's not the smallest orb which thou behold'st
But in his motion like an angel sings,
Still quiring to the young-eyed cherubims:
Such harmony is in immortal souls;
But, whilst this muddy vesture of decay
Doth grossly close it in, we can not hear it.—
Come, ho, and wake Diana with a hymn;
With sweetest touches pierce your mistress' ear,
And draw her home with music.'

Is not that a gentle speech? And so shall you speak to your bride, sweetheart, in the years to come, when you have wooed her and won her. And then you will tell her that if she loves you not—ay, and if she loves you not dearly and well—then is she not like one that you knew long ago, and that was your cousin, and her name Judith Shakespeare. Come, sweetheart," said she, and she rose from the stile and took his hand in hers. "Shall I draw thee home? But not with sweet music, for I have not Susan's voice. I would I had, for thy sake."

"You have the prettiest voice in the whole world, Cousin Judith," said he.

And so they walked on and into the town, in silence mostly. The world had grown more solemn now: here and there in the lilac-gray deeps overhead a small silver point began to appear. And sure he was that whatever might happen to him in the years to come, no sweetheart or any other would ever crush out from his affection or from his memory this sweet cousin of his; for him she would always be the one woman, strange and mystical and kind; there never would be any touch like the touch of her hand, so gentle was it as it rested on his hair; and there never would be anything more wonderful and gracious to look forward to than the old and familiar sitting in the church pew by Judith's side, with the breathless fascination of knowing that she was so near, and the thrill of hearing her join (rather timidly, for she was not proud of her voice) in the singing of the choir.

CHAPTER XXI.

A DISCOVERY.

"THAT be so as I tell ye, zur," said Matthew gardener, as he slowly sharpened a long knife on the hone that he held in his hand; "it all cometh of the pampering of queasy stomachs nowadays that can not hold honest food. There be no such folk now as there wur in former days, when men wur hardy, and long-lived, and healthy; and why, zur?—why, but that they wur content wi' plain dishes of pulse or herbs, and for the most worshipful no more than a dish of broth and a piece of good wholesome beef withal. But nowadays, Lord! Lord!—dish after dish, with each his several sauce; and this from Portugal and that from France, so that gluttony shall have its swing, and never a penny be kept for the poor. Nay, I tell ye, zur, rich and poor alike wur stronger and healthier when there wur no such waste in the land; when a man would wear his frieze coat and hosen of the color of the sheep that bore them; and have his shirt of honest hemp or flax, and could sleep well with his head on a block of wood and a sheep-skin thrown o'er it. But nowadays must he have his shirt of fine lawn and needle-work; ay, and his soft pillow to lie on, so that his lily-white body shall come to no scratching; nor will he drink any longer small drink, no, nor water, but heavy ales and rich wines; and all goeth to the belly, and naught to his poorer neighbor. And what cometh of this but tender stomachs, and riot, and waste?—and lucky if Bocardo be not at the end of it all."

As it chanced on this fine morning, Judith's father had strolled along to look at some trained apple-trees at the further end of the garden, and finding goodman Matthew there, and having a mind for idleness, had sat down on a bench to hear what news of the condition of the land Matthew might have to lay before him.

"Nay, but, good Matthew," said he, "if these luxuries work such mischief, 'tis the better surely that the poor have none of them. They, at least, can not have their stomachs ruined with sauces and condiments."

"Lord bless ye, zur," said the ancient, with a wise smile, "'tis not in one way, but in all ways, that the mischief is done; for the poorest, seeing such waste and gluttony everywhere abroad, have no continence of their means, but will spend their last penny on any foolishness. Lord! Lord! they be such poor simple creatures! they that have scarce a rag to their backs will crowd at the mops and fairs, and spend their money—on what? Why, you must ha' witnessed it, zur—the poor fools!—emptying their pouches to see a woman walking on a rope, or a tumbler joining his hands to his heels, or a hen with two heads. The poor simple creatures!—and yet I warrant me they be none so poor but that the rascal doctor can make his money out o' them: 'tis a foine way o' making a fortune that, going vagrom about the country with his draughts and pills—not honest medicines that a body might make out o' wholesome herbs, but nauseous stinking stuff that robs a man of his breath in the very swallowing of it. And the almanac-makers, too—marry, that, now, is another thriving trade!—the searching of stars, and the prophesying of dry or wet weather! Weather? what know they of the weather, the town-bred rogues, that lie and cheat to get at the poor country folks' money? God 'a mercy, a whip to their shoulders would teach them more o' the weather than ever they are like to get out of the stars! And yet the poor fools o' countrymen—that scarce know a B from a battledoor—will sit o' nights puzzling their brains o'er the signs o' the heavens; and no matter what any man with eyes can see for himself—ay, and fifty times surer, as I take it—they will prophesy you a dry month or a wet month, because the almanac saith so; and they will swear to you that Taurus—that is a lion—and the virgin scales have come together, therefore there must be a blight on the pear-trees! Heard you ever the like, zur?—that a man in Lunnon, knowing as much about husbandry and farm-work as a cat knows about quoit-throwing, is to tell me the weather down here in Warwickshire? God help us, they be poor weak creatures that think so; I'd liefer look at the cover of a penny ballad, if I wanted to know when there was to be frost o' nights."

At this juncture the old man grinned, as if some secret joke were tickling his fancy.

"Why, zur," said he, looking up from the hone, "would you believe this, zur—they be such fools that a rogue will sell them a barren cow for a milch cow if he

but put a strange calf to her? 'Tis done, zur—'tis done, I assure ye."

"In truth, a scurvy trick!" Judith's father said. He was idly drawing figures on the ground with a bit of stick he had got hold of. Perhaps he was not listening attentively; but at all events he encouraged Matthew to talk. "But surely with years comes wisdom. The most foolish are not caught twice with such a trick."

"What of that, zur?" answered Matthew. "There be plenty of other fools in the land to make the trade of roguery thrive. 'Tis true that a man may learn by his own experience; but what if he hath a son that be growing up a bigger fool than himself? And that's where 'tis nowadays, zur; there be no waiting and prudence; but every saucy boy must match on to his maid, and marry her ere they have a roof to put over their heads. 'Tis a fine beginning, surely! No waiting, no prudence—as the rich are wasteful and careless, so are the poor heedless of the morrow; and the boy and the wench they must have their cottage at the lane end, run up of elder poles, and forthwith begin the begetting of beggars to swarm over the land. A rare beginning! Body o' me, do they think they can live on nettles and grass, like Nebuchadnezzar?"

And so the old man continued to rail and grumble and bemoan, sometimes with a saturnine grin of satisfaction at his own wit coming over his face; and Judith's father did not seek to controvert; he listened, and drew figures on the ground, and merely put in a word now and again. It was a pleasant morning—fresh, and clear, and sunny; and this town of Stratford was a quiet place at that hour, with the children all at school. Sometimes Judith's father laughed; but he did not argue; and goodman Matthew, having it all his own way, was more than ever convinced not only that he was the one wise man among a generation of fools, but also that he was the only representative and upholder of the Spartan virtues that had characterized his forefathers. It is true that on more than one occasion he had been found somewhat overcome with ale; but this, when he had recovered from his temporary confusion, he declared was entirely due to the rascal brewers of those degenerate days—and especially of Warwickshire—who put all manner of abominations into their huff-cap, so that an honest Worcestershire stomach might easily be caught napping, and take no shame.

And meanwhile what had been happening in another part of the garden? As it chanced, Judith had been sent by her mother to carry to the summer-house a cup of wine and some thin cates; and in doing so she of course saw that both her father and goodman Matthew were at the further end of the garden, and apparently settled there for the time being. The opportunity was too good to be lost. She swiftly went back to the house, secured the portion of the play that was secreted there, and as quickly coming out again, exchanged it for an equal number of new sheets. It was all the work of a couple of minutes; and in another second she was in her own room, ready to put the precious prize into her little cupboard of boxes. And yet she could not forbear turning over the sheets, and examining them curiously, and she was saying to herself: "You cruel writing, to have such secrets, and refuse to give them up! If it were pictures, now, I could make out something with a guess; but all these little marks, so much alike, what can one make of them? —all alike—with here and there a curling, as if my father had been amusing himself —and all so plain and even, too, with never a blot: marry, I marvel he should make the other copy, unless with intent to alter as he writes. And those words with the big letters at the beginning—these be the people's names — Ferdinand, and sweet Miranda, and the Duke, and the ill beast that would harm them all. Why, in Heaven's mercy, was I so fractious? I might even now be learning all the story —here by myself—the only one in the land: I might all by myself know the story that will set the London folk agog in the coming winter. And what a prize were this, now, for Master Ben Jonson! Could one but go to him and say, 'Good sir, here be something better than your masques and mummeries, your Greeks and clouds and long speeches: put your name to it, good sir—nay, my father hath abundant store of such matter, and we in Warwickshire are no niggards—put your name to it, good sir, and you will get the court ladies to say you have risen a step on the ladder, else have they but a strange judgment!' What would the goodman do? Beshrew me, Prudence never told me the name of the play! But let us call it The

Magic Island. The Magic Island, by Master Benjamin Jonson. What would the wits say?"

But here she heard some noise on the stair; so she quickly hid away the treasure in the little drawer, and locked it up safe there until she should have the chance of asking Prudence to read it to her.

That did not happen until nearly nightfall; for Prudence had been away all day helping to put the house straight of a poor woman that was ill and in bed. Moreover, she had been sewing a good deal at the children's clothes and her eyes looked tired—or perhaps it was the wan light that yet lingered in the sky that gave her that expression, the candles not yet being lit. Judith regarded her, and took her hands tenderly, and made her sit down.

"Sweet mouse," said she, "you are wearing yourself out in the service of others; and if you take such little heed of yourself, you will yourself fall ill. And now must I demand of you further labor. Or will it be a refreshment for you after the fatigue of the day? See, I have brought them all with me—the sprite Ariel, and the sweet prince, and Miranda; but in good sooth I will gladly wait for another time if you are tired—"

"Nay, not so, Judith," she answered. "There is nothing I could like better—but for one thing."

"What, then?"

"Mean you to show this also to the young gentleman that is at Bidford?"

"And wherefore not, good Prue? He hath seen so much of the story, 'twere a pity he should not have the rest. And what a small kindness—the loan but for an hour or two; and I need not even see him, for I have but to leave it at my grandmother's cottage. And if you heard what he says of it—and how grateful he is: marry, it all lies in this, sweet Prue, that you have not seen him, else would you be willing enough to do him so small a favor."

By this time Prudence had lit the candles; and presently they made their way upstairs to her own room.

"And surely," said Judith, as her gentle gossip was arranging the manuscript, "the story will all end well, and merrily for the sweet maiden, seeing how powerful her father is? Will he not compel all things to her happiness—he that can raise storms, and that has messengers to fly round the world for him?"

"And yet he spoke but harshly to the young man when last we saw them," Prudence said. "Why, what's this?"

She had run her eye down the first page; and now she began reading:

Enter FERDINAND *bearing a log.*

Ferdinand. There be some sports are painful, and their labor
Delight in them sets off. This my mean task
Would be as heavy to me as odious, but
The mistress which I serve quickens what's dead,
And makes my labors pleasures. Oh, she is
Ten times more gentle than her father's crabbed;
And he's composed of harshness. I must remove
Some thousands of these logs and pile them up,
Upon a sore injunction. My sweet mistress
Weeps when she sees me work; and says such baseness
Had never like executor.

Judith's face had gradually fallen.

"Why, 'tis cruel," said she; "and 'tis cruel of my father to put such pain on the sweet prince, that is so gentle, and so unfortunate withal."

But Prudence continued the reading:

Enter MIRANDA.

Miranda.   Alas, now, pray you,
Work not so hard: I would the lightning had
Burnt up those logs, that you are enjoined to pile!
Pray, set it down and rest you: when this burns,
'Twill weep for having wearied you. My father
Is hard at study; pray, now, rest yourself;
He's safe for these three hours.
Ferdinand.   O most dear mistress,
The sun will set before I shall discharge
What I must strive to do.
Miranda.   If you'll sit down,
I'll bear your logs the while: pray give me that—
I'll carry it to the pile.

At this point Judith's eyes grew proud and grateful (as though Miranda had done some brave thing), but she did not speak.

Ferdinand.   No, precious creature;
I had rather crack my sinews, break my back,
Than you should such dishonor undergo,
While I sit lazy by.
Miranda.   You look wearily.
Ferdinand. No, noble mistress; 'tis fresh morning with me,
When you are by at night. I do beseech you
(Chiefly that I may set it in my prayers),
What is your name?
Miranda.   Miranda.—O my father,
I have broke your hest to say so!
Ferdinand.   Admired Miranda!
Indeed, the top of admiration; worth
What's dearest to the world! Full many a lady
I have eyed with best regard; and many a time

The harmony of their tongues hath into bondage
Brought my too diligent ear: for several virtues
Have I liked several women; never any
With so full soul but some defect in her
Did quarrel with the noblest grace she owed,
And put it to the foil. But you, O you,
So perfect and so peerless, are created
Of every creature's best!
Miranda.   I do not know
One of my sex: no woman's face remember,
Save, from my glass, mine own; nor have I seen
More that I may call men than you, good friend,
And my dear father: how features are abroad,
I am skill-less of; but, by my modesty
(The jewel in my dower), I would not wish
Any companion in the world but you;
Nor can imagination form a shape,
Besides yourself, to like of: But I prattle
Something too wildly, and my father's precepts
I therein do forget.

"Nay, is she not fair and modest!" Judith exclaimed—but apart; and, as the reading proceeded, she began to think of how Master Leofric Hope would regard this maiden. Would he not judge her to be right gentle, and timid, and yet womanly withal, and frank in her confiding? And he—supposing that he were the young prince—what would he think of such a one? Was it too submissive that she should offer to carry the logs? Ought she to so openly confess that she would fain have him to be her companion? And then, as Judith was thus considering, this was what she heard, in Prudence's gentle voice:

Miranda.   Do you love me?
Ferdinand. O heaven, O earth, bear witness to this sound,
And crown what I profess with kind event,
If I speak true; if hollowly, invert
What best is boded me, to mischief! I,
Beyond all limit of what else i' the world,
Do love, prize, honor you.
Miranda.   I am a fool
To weep at what I am glad of.
Ferdinand.   Wherefore weep you?
Miranda. At mine unworthiness, that dare not offer
What I desire to give; and much less take
What I shall die to want: But this is trifling;
And all the more it seeks to hide itself,
The bigger bulk it shows. Hence, bashful cunning!
And prompt me, plain and holy innocence!
I am your wife, if you will marry me;
If not, I'll die your maid: to be your fellow
You may deny me; but I'll be your servant,
Whether you will or no.
Ferdinand.   My mistress, dearest;
And I thus humble ever.
Miranda.   My husband, then?
Ferdinand. Ay, with a heart as willing
As bondage e'er of freedom: here's my hand.
Miranda. And mine, with my heart in't; and now farewell,
Till half an hour hence.
Ferdinand. A thousand thousand!

She clapped her hands and laughed, in delight and triumph.

"Why, sure her father will relent," she cried.

"But, Judith, Judith, stay," Prudence said, quickly, and with scarce less gladness. "'Tis so set down; for this is what her father says:

'So glad of this as they I can not be,
Who are surprised withal; but my rejoicing
At nothing can be more.'

Nay, I take it he will soon explain to us why he was so harsh with the young prince—perchance to try his constancy?"

Well, after that the reading went on as far as the sheets that Judith had brought; but ever her mind was returning to the scene between the two lovers, and speculating as to how Leofric Hope would look upon it. She had no resentment against Ben Jonson now; her heart was full of assurance and triumph, and was therefore generous. Her only vexation was that the night must intervene before there could be a chance of the young London gentleman calling at the cottage; and she looked forward to the possibility of seeing him some time or other with the determination to be more demure than ever. She would not expect him to praise this play. Perchance 'twas good enough for simple Warwickshire folk; but the London wits might consider it of the vulgar kind? And she laughed to herself at thinking how awkward his protests would be if she ventured to hint anything in that direction.

Prudence put the sheets carefully together again.

"Judith, Judith," she said, with a quiet smile, "you lead me far astray. I ought to find such things wicked and horrible to the ear; but perchance 'tis because I know your father, and see him from day to day, that I find them innocent enough. They seem to rest the mind when one is sorrowful."

"Beware of them, good Prue; they are the devil himself come in the guise of an angel to snatch thee away. Nay, but, sweetheart, why should you be sorrowful?"

"There is Martha Hodgson," said she, simply, "and her children, nigh to starving; and I can not ask Julius for more—"

Judith's purse was out in an instant.

"Why," said she, "my father did not use half of what I gave him for the knife he bought at Warwick—marry, I guess he paid for it mostly himself; but what there is here you shall have."

And she emptied the contents on to the table, and pushed them over to her friend.

"You do not grudge it, Judith?" said Prudence. "Nay, I will not ask thee that. Nor can I refuse it either, for the children are in sore want. But why should you not give it to them yourself, Judith?"

"Why?" said Judith, regarding the gentle face with kindly eyes. "Shall I tell thee why, sweetheart? 'Tis but this: that if I were in need, and help to be given me, I would value it thrice as much if it came from your hand. There is a way of doing such things, and you have it: that is all."

"I hear Julius is come in," Prudence said, as she took up the two candles. "Will you go in and speak with him?"

There was some strange hesitation in her manner, and she did not go to the door. She glanced at Judith somewhat timidly. Then she set the candles down again.

"Judith," said she, "your pity is quick, and you are generous and kind; I would you could find it in your heart to extend your kindness."

"How now, good cousin?" Judith said, in amazement. "What's this?"

Prudence glanced at her again, somewhat uneasily, and obviously in great embarrassment.

"You will not take it ill, dear Judith?"

"By my life, I will not! Not from you, dear heart, whatever it be. But what is the dreadful secret?"

"Tom Quiney has spoken to me," she said, diffidently.

Judith eagerly caught both her hands.

"And you! What said you? 'Tis all settled, then!" she exclaimed, almost breathlessly.

"It is as I imagined, Judith," said Prudence, calmly—and she withdrew her hands, with a touch of maidenly pride, perhaps, from what she could not but imagine to be a kind of felicitation. "He hath no fault to find with the country. If he goes away to those lands beyond seas, 'tis merely because you will say no word to hold him back."

"I!" said Judith, impatiently; and then she checked herself. "But you, sweetheart, what said he to you?"

Prudence's cheeks flushed red.

"He would have me intercede for him," she said, timidly.

"Intercede? with whom?"

"Why, you know, Judith; with whom but yourself? Nay, but be patient—have some kindness. The young man opened his heart to me; and I know he is in trouble. 'Twas last night as we were coming home from the lecture; and he would have me wait till he left a message at his door, so that thus we fell behind; and then he told me why it was that Stratford had grown distasteful to him, and not to be borne, and why he was going away. How could I help saying that that would grieve you?—sure I am you can not but be sorry to think of the young man banishing himself from his own people. And he said that I was your nearest friend; and would I speak for him? And I answered that I was all unused to such matters, but that if any pleading of mine would influence you I would right gladly do him that service; and so I would, dear Judith; for how can you bear to think of the youth going away with these godless men, and perchance never to return to his own land, when a word from you would restrain him?"

Judith took both her hands again, and looked with a kindly smile into the timid, pleading eyes.

"And 'tis you, sweet mouse, that come to me with such a prayer? Was there ever so kind a heart? But that is you ever and always—never a thought for yourself, everything for others. And so he had the cruelty to ask you—you—to bring this message?"

"Judith," said the other, with the color coming into her face again, "you force me to speak against my will. Nay, how can I hide from myself, dear friend, that you have plans and wishes—perchance suspicions—with regard to me? And if what I guess be true—if that is your meaning—indeed 'tis all built on a wrong foundation: believe me, Judith, it is so. I would have you assured of it, sweetheart. You know that I like not speaking of such matters; 'tis not seemly and becoming to a maiden; and fain would I have my mind occupied with far other things; but, Judith, this time I must speak plain; and I would have you put away from you all such intentions and surmises—dear heart, you do me wrong!"

"In good sooth, am I all mistaken?" Judith said, glancing keenly at her.

"Do you doubt my word, Judith?" said she.

"And yet," her friend said, as if to herself, and musingly, "there were several occasions: there was the fortune-teller at Hampton Lucy that coupled you, and Quiney seemed right merry withal; and then again when he would have us play kiss-in-the-ring on the evening after Mary Sadler's marriage, and I forbade it chiefly for your sake, sweet mouse, then methought you seemed none overpleased with my interference—"

But here she happened to look at Prudence, and she could not fail to see that the whole subject was infinitely distressing to her. There was a proud, hurt expression on the gentle face, and a red spot burning in each cheek. So Judith took hold of her and kissed her.

"Once and forever, dearest heart," said she, "I banish all such thoughts. And I will make no more plans for thee, nor suspect thee, but let thee go in thine own way, in the paths of charity and goodness. But I mean not to give up thy friendship, sweet Prue; if I can not walk in the same path, at least I may stretch a hand over to thee; and if I but keep so near so true a saint, marry, I shall not go so far wrong."

She took up one of the candles.

"Shall we go down and see Julius?" said she.

"But Tom Quiney, Judith—what shall I say?" Prudence asked, anxiously.

"Why, say nothing, sweetheart," was the immediate answer. "'Twas a shame to burden you with such a task. When he chooses he can at any moment have speech of me, if his worship be not too proud or too suspicious. In Stratford we can all of us speak the English tongue, I hope."

"But, Judith," said the other, slowly and wistfully, "twenty years is a long space for one to be away from his native land."

"Marry is it, sweet mouse," Judith answered, as she opened the door and proceeded to go down the narrow wooden steps. "'Tis a long space indeed, and at the end of it many a thing that seemeth of great import and consequence now will be no better than an old tale, idle and half forgotten."

ROSES AND THE NIGHTINGALE.

IN my garden it is night-time,
But a still time and a bright time,
For the moon rains down her splendor,
　　And my garden feels the wonder
　　Of the spell which it lies under
In that light so soft and tender.

While the moon her watch is keeping
All the blossoms here are sleeping,
And the roses sigh for dreaming
　　Of the bees that love to love them
　　When the warm sun shines above them
And the butterflies pass gleaming.

Could one follow roses' fancies,
When the night the garden trances,
Oh, what fair things we should chance on!
　　For to lilies and to roses,
　　As to us, soft sleep discloses
What the waking may not glance on.

But hark! now across the moonlight,
Through the warmness of the June night,
From the tall trees' listening branches,
　　Comes the sound, sustained and holy,
　　Of the passionate melancholy,
Of a wound which singing stanches.

Oh, the ecstasy of sorrow
Which the music seems to borrow
From the thought of some past lover
　　Who loved vainly all his lifetime,
　　Till death ended peace and strife-time,
And the darkness clothed him over!

Oh, the passionate, sweet singing,
Aching, gushing, throbbing, ringing,
Dying in divine, soft closes,
　　Recommencing, waxing stronger,
　　Sweet notes, ever sweeter, longer,
Till the singing wakes the roses!

Quoth the roses to the singer:
"Oh, thou dearest music-bringer,
Now our sleep so sweetly endeth,
　　Tell us why *thy* song so sad seems,
　　When the air is full of glad dreams,
And the bright moon o'er us bendeth."

Sang the singer to the roses:
"Love for you my song discloses,
Hence the note of grief it borrows."
　　Quoth the roses, "Love means pleasure."
　　Quoth the singer, "Love's best measure
Is its pure attendant sorrows."

CRICKET MATCH AT LORD'S.

HARROW-ON-THE-HILL.

TO a reflective mind London is most delightful at that period of the year when society leaves it. As a rule, the leaders of the gay world pack their trunks for flight almost immediately after the schools' cricket match at Lord's. While the university boat race in early spring may be said to inaugurate the London season, the Eton and Harrow cricket match at Lord's may be said to close it. Eton and Harrow are the two great English schools, as Oxford and Cambridge are the two great universities. The Eton students took with them to the higher colleges the taste for boating which they had acquired on the Thames, and established the sport and pastime of rowing on the Cam and the Isis. Harrow and Eton together emulate in the English meadows the athletic prowess of Oxford and Cambridge on the waters. Eton College was founded by Henry VI. in 1440. John Lyon, a yeoman who was an enthusiastic promoter of the education of youth, established a grammar school at Harrow in 1571, from which sprung the present educational establishment. The old schoolhouse of Harrow bears in its carved panels the names of Sir William Jones, Lord Byron, Sheridan, Shendon, Percival, Peel, Palmerston, among its famous scholars.

Eton is equally well represented in the history of illustrious Englishmen. It is a notable fact that many of the students who have most distinguished themselves in their latter days have been celebrated as boating men and cricketers. During the early days of the schools' match in the classic arena of Lord's ground, in the handsome suburban district of St. John's Wood, only a few hundreds of the wealthy and fashionable friends of the students attended to watch and encourage the sports. To-day "the world of London" attends the match, Belgravia and Mayfair in their drags and coaches, Brompton and Islington in their broughams and hansoms, middle-class London by train and omnibus. The outer circle of the arena is a confused mass of carriages of every description, the drag being most conspicuous. During the interval for refreshment sumptuous luncheons are spread by the servants and retainers of the aristocratic owners of these nineteenth-century chariots. While the match goes on, every incident of the game is watched with scrupulous attention; when the cricketers are resting, a fashionable

THE FOURTH FORM ROOM.

reunion over an *al fresco* luncheon takes place. If it is a fine day, the sight is interesting if not picturesque. The ladies are in their lightest and prettiest costumes; the gentlemen have generally discarded black cloth; the liveries of the servants are bright with many buttons; the silver mountings of coach and carriage flash in the sun; the two blues of the rival schools flutter against the lighter blue of the sky; inside the barricade of carriages thousands of persons are promenading; the grand stands are alive with people coming and going; and then presently the ground is once more cleared for action, everybody gets back to his or her place of observation, and your eye rests upon a green expanse, like an enormous billiard-table, dotted with white-flannelled cricketers. Outside Lord's there is a continual stream of traffic to and fro, coming and going from London; it is regulated by a double line of policemen, who stretch away as far as Baker Street; and in many of the villas round about the grounds private luncheons are spread for friends and visitors. The manager of a London theatre who lives in the shadow of Lord's erects a tent in his garden, where luncheon and dinner are laid for fifty or sixty guests on the two days of the match, which has now become a fashionable festival—the social clasp which binds up for the year the story of the London season.

When society leaves London, as I have already said, then is the great city most delightful to a reflective mind. The parks are rejoicing in their full endowment of autumnal flowers. There is no crowd in the Row. Tradesmen are more than usually polite in response to your business inquiries. You have the run of your club. The attendants are glad to have the monotony of their lives relieved with the incident of serving your dinner. Hansom cabmen will touch their hats to you, and four-wheelers fairly grovel in their politeness. You have become an important person at the West End by the absence of competition.

"By under-ground to Harrow," is the legend that confronts the lingering Londoner at many of the local railway stations of the West End. It is a misnomer. It refers to the extension of London's under-ground system of railway to Harrow;

but from Baker Street, with the exception of two insignificant tunnels, the track runs through open country. Last September, a ticket in one hand, a Byron in the other, and a pleasant companion, I availed myself of the line from Baker Street to the present terminus at the Harewe-atte-Hull of the Saxons. If you want a picturesque illustration of the influence of æstheticism in these practical days, go by the under-ground railway to Harrow. The few silly demonstrations of Bunthornism which have been so quaintly accentuated in *Patience* are only what may be called bubbles on the modern stream of art progress. The advantages of school-of-art culture and the revival of taste are seen not only in the latest forms of domestic decoration, but in many recent efforts in the way of architecture as applied to the commonest purposes. Every railway station or depot at which the train stops by under-ground to Harrow is a red brick picture, a modest adaptation of "Old Kensington" to the most practical purposes. Platforms, waiting-rooms, ticket offices, the buildings generally, are constructed with an eye to beauty as well as usefulness. Bedford Park, Fitzjohn Avenue, and Melbury Road are matched with railway stations on the way to Harrow.

I know London pretty well, and its pleasant spots and historic hunting grounds round about, but I could not last September say with the poet's "Lines on Harrow":

"Again I revisit the hills where we sported,
　　The streams where we swam, and the fields
　　　where we fought;
The school where, loud-warned by the bell, we
　　resorted
　　To pore o'er the precepts by pedagogues
　　　taught."

The new railway station, with its tinted glass and its tiled pavements, is half a mile and more from Harrow, so that the classicality of the little town is not marred by the locomotive. You have quite a long walk up-hill to the steep brow of the church-yard where Byron often wandered

"To catch the last gleam of the sun's setting
　ray."

On one hand your path is bordered by stately trees, through which presently one sees the gables of college and mansion; while on the left green meadows stretch away toward London, until the eye loses them in a hazy outline of oak and elm against a dull, mysterious-looking sky. For three hundred years one of the great public schools of England has held intellectual court on this sloping mount of this ancient Harrow, which had a local habitation and a name before the Norman Conquest.

Does the reader know the cathedral closes of Durham and Worcester and Lin-

HIGH STREET, HARROW.

coln and York? Here and there at Harrow you find yourself recalling bits of those time-honored localities. The houses are not quite wrinkled enough to make the illusion complete; but they have that general air of competence and comfort which characterizes the deaneries and canons' houses of the snug by-ways that belong to cathedral precincts. And what a view there is from the church-yard where Byron pondered with his immortal muse! Four hundred feet high, it commands a magnificent natural panorama, and you may almost be said to stand in the centre of it, as in the artificial panoramas which of late years have become popular in Paris and London. The writer of *The Suburban Homes of London* tells us that from this altitude at Harrow, ten miles from the Marble Arch at Hyde Park, the view toward the east is bounded by the metropolis; that to the south looks on the Crystal Palace and the range of the Surrey Hills; that on the southeast extends from Knockholt Beeches to Shooter's Hill, and across the Thames to the Langdon Hills on the Essex side. "The west and southwest is specially extensive and beautiful from the church-yard, including Windsor Castle and a great part of the counties of Berkshire and Bucks. The north is the least commanding, but singularly rich, including Hampstead, Hendon, and Barnet; but the proximity of the splendid estate of Lord Wolverton at Etonmore interrupts the long range which characterizes every other direction." I confess I could not quite realize all this topographically, neither could I feel that I was within half an hour of the noise and bustle of London. The sylvan plain of a Herefordshire landscape, or a stretch of Worcestershire as seen from the Malvern Hills, could not have seemed further away from the metropolis as I sat near the poet's favorite haunt, while the soft shadows of twilight were gathering about the classic spot, and evening mists made ghostly landscapes and "moving lakes" and mimic waterways in the grassy plain below.

It was twenty years after Byron left Harrow that he wrote to Mr. Murray requesting that the remains of his daughter Allegra might be buried there. "There is," he wrote to Murray, "a spot in the church-yard, near the foot-path on the brow of the hill, looking toward Windsor, and a tomb under a large tree (bearing the name of Peachie or Peachy), where I used to sit for hours and hours when a boy. This was my favorite spot; but as I wish to erect a tablet to her memory, her body had better be deposited in the church." In a note to the fourth canto of "Childe Harold" he says, regarding his leaving Harrow for Cambridge in 1806: "When I first went up to college it was a new and heavy-hearted scene for me. I so much disliked leaving Harrow that, though it was time (I being seventeen), it broke my very rest for the last quarter with counting the days that remained. I always *hated* Harrow till the last year and a half, but then I liked it." In Finden's *Illustrations of the Life and Works of Lord Byron*, published half a century ago, there is an engraving of Harrow from a drawing by Clarkson Stanfield, having for its immediate foreground the tombstone and the poet school-boy, illustrative of the stanza:

> "Again I behold where for hours I have pondered,
> As reclining, at eve, on yon tombstone I lay,
> Or round the steep brow of the church-yard I wandered
> To catch the last gleam of the sun's setting ray."

"Byron's tomb," as it is called, is now incased for safe-keeping in a cage of iron bars, which may preserve it for future generations, but certainly robs it of all picturesqueness to present disciples of the poet.

Under the shadow of the old flint church lies a great colony of the dead, and the living wander curious among the old-fashioned tombstones, or take their summer evening airings on the seats at the northern edge of the church-yard, on the very brow of the hill. Some of the inscriptions are odd indeed, as the following, which commemorates what must have been one of the earliest of railway accidents, for it is dated 1838:

> "Bright rose the morn, and vigorous rose poor *Port;*
> Gay on the *Train* he used his wonted sport:
> Ere noon arrived his mangled form they bore,
> With pain distorted, and o'erwhelmed with gore:
> When evening came to close the fatal day,
> A mutilated corpse the sufferer lay."

The church itself, which is at least seven hundred years old, dominates a wide landscape, and is a part of the familiar view from Hampstead Heath. The shaded roads, the lanes and prescriptive foot-paths all about, are delightful: one can almost reach London by the latter without using the high-roads, albeit at some danger from irate proprietors, very willing to let the

THE KING'S HEAD.

public forget its rights for the score of years necessary to make public ways private property again.

But the glory of Harrow is its school, founded so long ago as 1571 by John Lyon, yeoman. The oldest building is near the church, built in the Tudor style, and rich in reminiscence of the distinguished scholars who are the pride of Harrow. The benches and available wood-work of the fourth-form room—that venerable if not venerated place of learning—bear the marks of many generations of youths determined to carve their names more or less enduringly in the world. But the school has a modern face also, many of its buildings being by Gilbert Scott. The latest of all is the new speech-room, a striking building in red brick, semicircu-lar in form, below the church, near the high-road. To the right of this road stand the college chapel, the Vaughan Library—a memorial of the revered head-master—the master's house, and other school buildings. Passing between them, one comes suddenly out upon a long terrace on the other brow of the hill, at one end of which an old dial counts the sunny hours, and whence is another far and lovely view, the counterpart of that from the church. The master's garden stretches down the hillside in careless, pleasant fashion, as though London and life were of no concern to the sweet idleness of the scholar, while off at the west, Uxbridge way, is a tract of country said to be the most sparsely inhabited in the home counties.

It was at Harrow School that commenced one of the warmest and most lasting friendships Lord Byron ever formed. He saw his old school-fellow Lord Clare in Italy after many years of separation. Says the poet, in his "Detached Thoughts": "I met him in the road between Imola and Bologna, after not having met for eight or nine years. This meeting annihilated, for a moment, all the years between the present time and the days of Harrow. It was a new and inexplicable feeling, like rising from the grave, to me. Clare, too, was much agitated—more in *appearance* than myself, for I could feel his heart beat to his fingers' ends, unless, indeed, it was the pulse of my own which made me think so. We were obliged to part for our different journeys—he for Rome, I for Pisa—but with the promise to meet again in the spring. We were but five minutes together, and on the public road, but I hardly recollect an hour of my existence which could be weighed against them." In *Hours of Idleness* a poem is addressed to Lord Clare which recalls the boyish days of both at Harrow:

"Friend of my youth! when young we roved,
  Like striplings, mutually beloved,
    With friendship's purest glow,
The bliss which winged those rosy hours
Was such as pleasure seldom showers
    On mortals here below."

If one had travelled by steamer and by rail, during many days, to wander in the footsteps of Byron's boyish days, to trace out the spots where he fought the tyrants of his school, played cricket, or indulged his poetic dreams of fame, the pleasures of a Harrow ramble might possibly have been intensified. It would be far more impressive in a London drawing-room to talk of your Byronic reminiscences of Zaragoza, Negropont, Corinth, Verona, Ravenna, than of your excursion from Baker Street to Harrow; and there are many great and wealthy English travellers, who have surveyed mankind from China to Peru, who know nothing of Chertsey meads, Virginia Water, the backwaters of the upper Thames, the haunts about Burnham Beeches, the breezy commons and the shady nooks and corners that lie around London little more than ten miles from town.

Harrow has a history full of antiquarian interest and historic romance. Thomas à Becket held state here, and Wolsey was rector of the parish, and lived in a moated house still to be found by the pedestrian. And, as in other suburban towns and villages about London, the past and the present are pleasantly linked together by a hostelry that seems to belong to the coaching days, and suggests the time when the well-mounted highwayman was a picturesque though dangerous incident of the great roads that lead in and out of the metropolis. There is the swinging sign courting the breeze where probably the cross of the olden times reared aloft its Christian symbol. The inn has a quaint appearance, quietly retiring from the road, its window-panes fairly blinking with geniality. It has a bar redolent of old ale and rum, and a coffee-room where joints of ham and beef, sticks of celery and Gloucestershire cheese, invite the sojourner to physical enjoyment. At the back of the house the old inn has an old-fashioned garden to match its sign, its bar, and its solid English fare. It grows stocks, and daisies, and marigolds, and roses, and "lad's-love," or "old-man"; and beyond the trimmed lawn and the hedge-row that shuts in the flower borders from the grosser forms of vegetation there is a kitchen-garden with apple-trees and asparagus beds and potato patches; and farther away, outside the kitchen-garden, lies that typical English landscape which had so many charms for Byron. Carriers' carts and family carriages and picnic brakes drive up to that inviting way-side inn of suburban London, and foaming tankards are quaffed there by rosy-faced people who look as if they had never seen the great city, though it lies under the mist yonder only a few miles away.

NATURE'S SERIAL STORY.

VIII.

IT is said that there is no heaven anywhere for those incapable of recognizing and enjoying it. Be this as it may, the
month of June is a segment of heaven
annually bestowed on those whose eyes
and ears have been opened to beauty in
sight and sound. Indeed, what sense in
man is not gratified to the point of imaginary perfection during this early frui-
tion of the varied promise of spring?
Even to the sense of touch how exquisite
is the "feel" of the fragrant rose petals,
the soft young foliage that has transformed the world, and the queer downy fledgelings in innumerable nests! To the eye
informed by a heart in love with nature
the longest days of the year are all too
short to note half that exists and takes
place. Who sees and distinguishes the
varied blossoming of the many kinds of
grain and grasses that are waving in every field? And yet here is a beauty as
distinct and delicate as can be found in
some of Mendelssohn's "Songs without
Words"—blossomings so odd, delicate, and
evanescent that they might resemble a
child's dream of a flower. Place them
under a strong glass, and who can fail to
wonder at the miracles of form and color
that are revealed. From these tiny flow-
erets the scale runs upward until it touches the hybrid rose. During this period,
also, many of the forest trees emulate the
wild flowers at their feet until their inflorescence culminates in the white cord-
like fringe that foretells the spiny chestnut burrs.

So much has been written comparing
this exquisite season when spring passes
insensibly into summer with the fulfilled
prophecy of girlhood, that no attempt
shall be made to repeat the simile. Amy's
birthday should have been in May, but it
came early in June. May was still in her
heart, and might linger there indefinitely;
but her mind, her thoughts, kept pace with
nature as unconsciously as the flowers
that bloomed in their season. There were
little remembrances from all the family,
but Webb's gift promised the most pleasure. It was a powerful opera-glass, and
as he handed it to her on the piazza in the
early morning he said:

"Our troupe are all here now, Amy,
and I thought that you would like to see
the singers, and observe their costumes
and expressions. Some birds have a good
deal of expression and a very charming
manner while singing—a manner much
more to my taste than more than one prima
donna that I have heard, although my taste
may be uncultivated. Focus your glass on
that indigo-bird in yonder tree-top. Don't
you see him?—the one that is favoring us
with such a lively strain, beginning with
a repetition of short, sprightly notes. The
glass may enable you to see his markings
accurately."

"Oh, what an exquisite glossy blue!
and it grows so deep and rich about the
head, throat, and breast! How plainly I
can see him, even to the black velvet under his eyes! There is brown on his
wings, too. Why, I can look right into
his little throat, and almost imagine I see
the notes he is flinging abroad so vivaciously. I can even make out his claws
closed on a twig, and the dew on the
leaves around him is like pearls. Truly, Webb, you were inspired when you
thought of this gift."

"Yes," he replied, quietly, looking
much pleased, however, "with a very
honest wish to add to your enjoyment of
the summer. I must confess, too, that I
had one thought at least for myself. You
have described the indigo-bird far more accurately than I could have done, although
I have seen it every summer as long as I
can remember. You have taught me to
see; why should I not help you to see
more when I can do it so easily? My
thought was that you would lend me the
glass occasionally, so that I might try to
keep pace with you. I've been using the
microscope too much—prying into nature,
as Burt would say, with the spirit of an
anatomist."

"I shall value the glass a great deal
more if you share it with me," she said,
simply, with a sincere, direct gaze into his
eyes; "and be assured, Webb," she added,
earnestly, "you are helping me more than
I can help you. I'm not an artist, and
never can be, but if I were I should want
something more than mere surface, however beautiful it might be. Think of it,
Webb, I'm eighteen to-day, and I know
so little! You always make me feel that
there is so much to learn, and, what is

WATCHING THE SWARM.

more, that it is worth knowing. You should have been a teacher, for you would make the children feel, when learning their lessons, as Alf does when after game. How well nature bears close scrutiny!" she added, sweeping the scene with her glass. "I can go every day now on an exploring expedition. But there is the breakfast bell."

Mr. Clifford came in a little late, rubbing his hands felicitously, as he said:

"I have just come from the apiary, and think we shall have another swarm to-day.

'A swarm of bees in June
Is worth a silver spoon.'

If one comes out to-day, and we hive it safely, we shall call it yours, and you shall have the honey."

"How much you are all doing to sweeten my life!" she said, laughing; "but I never expected the present of a swarm of bees. I assure you it is a gift that you will have to keep for me, and yet I should like to see how the bees swarm, and how you hive them. Would it be safe? I've heard that bees are so wise, and know when people are afraid of them."

"You can fix yourself up with a thick veil and a pair of gloves so that there will be no danger, and your swarm of bees, when once in the hive, will take care of themselves, and help take care of you. That's the beauty of bee-culture."

"Our bees are literally in clover this year," Leonard remarked. "That heavy coating of wood-ashes that I gave to a half-acre near the apiary proved most effective, and the plot now looks as if a flurry of snow had passed over it, the white clover blossoms are so thick. That is something I could never understand, Webb. Wood-ashes will always bring white clover. It's hard to believe that it all comes from seed dormant in the ground."

"Well, it does," was the reply.

"A great many think that the ashes simply produce conditions in the soil which generate the clover."

"Out of nothing? That would not be simple at all, and if any one could prove it he would make a sensation in the scientific world."

"Now, Len, here's your chance," laughed Burt. "Just imagine what a halo of glory you would get by setting the scientific world agape with wonder!"

15*

"I could make the scientific world gape in a much easier way," Leonard replied, dryly. "Well, Amy, if you are as fond of honey as I am, you will think a swarm of bees a very nice present. Fancy buckwheat cakes eaten with honey made from buckwheat blossoms! There's a conjunction that gives to winter an unflagging charm. If the old Hebrews felt as I do, a land flowing with milk and honey must have been very alluring. Such a land the valley of the Hudson certainly is. It's one of the finest grass regions of the world, and grass means milk; and the extensive raspberry fields along its banks mean honey. White clover is all very well, but I've noticed that when the raspberry bushes are in bloom they are alive with bees."

"Well," said Mr. Clifford, "I shall look after the apiary to-day. That's good lazy work for an old man. You can help me watch at a safe distance, Amy, and protected as I said, if they swarm. It wouldn't be well for you to go too near the hives at first, you know," he added, in laughing gallantry, "for they might mistake you for a flower. They are so well acquainted with me that I raise neither expectations nor fears. You needn't come out before ten o'clock, for they don't swarm until toward mid-day."

With shy steps, and well protected, Amy approached the apiary, near which the old gentleman was sitting in placid fearlessness under the shade of a maple, the honey of whose spring blossoms was already in the hive. For a time she kept at a most respectful distance, but, as the bees did not notice her, she at last drew nearer, and removed her veil, and with the aid of her glass saw the indefatigable workers coming in and going out with such celerity that they seemed to be assuring each other that there were tons of honey now to be had for the gathering. The bees grew into large insects under her powerful lenses, and their forms and movements were very distinct. Suddenly from the entrance of one hive near Mr. Clifford, which she happened to be covering with her glass, she saw pouring out a perfect torrent of bees. She started back in affright, but Mr. Clifford told her to stand still, and she noted that he quietly kept his seat, while following through his gold-rimmed spectacles the swirling, swaying stream that rushed into the upper air. The combined hum smote the ear with its intensity. Each bee was describing circles with almost the swiftness of light, and there were such numbers that they formed a nebulous living mass. Involuntarily she crouched down in the grass. In a few moments, however, she saw the swarm draw together and cluster like a great black ball on a bough of a small pear-tree. The queen had alighted, and all her subjects gathered around her.

"Ah," chuckled the old gentleman, rising quietly, "they couldn't have been more sensible if they had been human—not half so sensible in that case, perhaps. I think you will have your swarm now without doubt. That's the beauty of these Italian bees when they are kept pure. They are so quiet and sensible. Come away now, until I return prepared to hive them."

The young girl obeyed with alacrity, and was almost trembling with excitement, to which fear as well as the novelty of the scene contributed not a little. Mr. Clifford soon returned, well protected and prepared for his work. Taking an empty hive, he placed it on the ground in a secluded spot, and laid before its entrances a broad, smooth board. Then holding a large tin pan in his left hand, he mounted a step-ladder, and gently brushed the bees into it as if they had been inanimate things. A sheet had first been spread beneath the pear-tree to catch those that did not fall into the pan. Touched thus gently and carefully, the immense vitality of the swarm remained dormant; but a rough, sudden movement would have transformed it instantly into a vengeful cloud of insects, each animated by the one impulse to use its stiletto. Coming down from the ladder, he turned the pan toward Amy, and with her glass she saw that it was nearly half full of a crawling, seething mass that fairly made her shudder. But much experience rendered the old gentleman confident, and he only smiled as he carried the pan of bees to the empty hive, and poured them out on the board before it. The sheet was next gathered up and placed near the hive also, and then the old gentleman backed slowly and quietly away until he had joined Amy, to whom he said, " My part of the work is now done, and I think we shall soon see them enter the hive." He was right, for within twenty minutes every bee had disappeared within the new domicile. "To-night I will place the hive on the platform with the others, and to-morrow your bees will be at work for you, Amy. I don't wonder you are so interested, for of all insects I think bees take the palm. It is possible that the swarm may not fancy their new quarters, and come out again, but it is not probable. Screened by this bush, you can watch in perfect safety"; and he left her well content, with her glass fixed on the apiary.

Burt had expended more on his present for Amy than had any of the family, and, while it had been acknowledged most cordially, he was a little disappointed that his choice had not been so happy as Webb's. Therefore after dinner he said: "I feel almost envious. I wish I could give you a great deal of pleasure also to-day. How would you like to go in a row-boat to Constitution Island, and make that visit to Miss Warner of which we spoke last winter? It's warm, but not sultry, and we would keep in the shadow of the mountains most of the way down."

She hesitated a moment.

"Don't be afraid, Amy," he said, in a low tone.

"I'll go with you," she assented, cordially, " and I can not think of anything that would make my birthday more complete."

"I'll be ready in an hour," he said, flushing with pleasure, and he went up to his room two steps at a time.

Burt's mental processes during the past few weeks were characteristic, and would have amused Amy had she been fully aware of them. As Webb surmised, his fever had to run its course, but after its crisis had passed he rapidly grew rational. Moreover, in his mother, and indeed in Amy herself, he had the best of physicians. At first he was very penitent, and not a little chagrined at his course. As days went by, however, and it was not referred to by word or sign on the part of the family, his nervous apprehension passed away. He thought he detected a peculiar twinkle in Leonard's eyes occasionally, but it might have resulted from other causes. Still Amy did the most to re-assure him both consciously and unconsciously. As she said, she took him at his word, and being unembarrassed by any feeling of her own, found it easy to act like a sister toward him. This naturally put him at his ease. In her floral expeditions with Johnnie, however, and her birdnestings with Alf, wherein no birds were robbed, she unconsciously did more to reconcile him to the necessity of waiting than could hours of argument from even his mother. She thus proved to him that he had spoken much too soon — that she was not ready for his ill-chosen, passionate words, which had wounded instead of firing her heart as he had intended they should. He now berated his stupidity, but consoled himself with the thought that love is always a little blind. He saw that she liked Webb exceedingly, and enjoyed talking with him, but he now was no longer disposed to be jealous. She ever seemed to be asking questions like an intelligent child. "Why shouldn't she like Webb?" he thought. "He is one of the best fellows in the world, and she has found out that he's a walking encyclopædia of out-door lore."

Burt was not one to be depressed or to remain in the valley of humiliation very long. After a week or two a slight feeling of superiority began to assert itself. Amy was not only too young to understand him, but also, perhaps, to appreciate him. He believed that he knew more than one pretty girl to whom he would not have spoken as he had in vain. Some day the scales would fall from Amy's eyes. He could well afford to wait until they did, and he threw back his handsome head at the thought, and an exultant flash came into his blue eyes. Oh, he would be faithful, he would be magnanimous, and he also admitted to himself that he would be very glad and grateful; but he would be very patient, perhaps a little too much so to suit her. Since he had been told to "wait," he would wait until her awakening heart constrained her to give unequivocal signs of readiness to surrender.

Thus his thoughts ran on while he was busy about the farm, or galloping over the country on business or pleasure. After the corn-planting and the rush of work in May was over, he had given himself a week's outing among the trout streams of Ulster County, and had returned with his equanimity quite restored. To assure Amy of this, and that she had nothing more to fear, but everything to gain, was one of his motives in asking her to take the long sail that afternoon. He succeeded so well that a smile of very genuine satisfaction hovered about her lips more than once. She enjoyed the expedition exceedingly. She was grateful for the kind reception given her by the authors who had done much to sweeten and purify the world's thought. She was charmed with the superb scenery as on

their return they glided along in the shadows of Cro'nest, whose sides seemed lined with a choir of wood and veery thrushes and other wild songsters. At last they evoked the spirit of music in her. She took an oar with Burt, and they pulled, sang, and laughed together like careless, happy children. Yet more than once she shyly glanced at him, and queried, Could his flushed and mirthful face be that of the passionate lover and blighted youth of scarce a month since? Burt said something droll, and her laugh raised a musical echo against the steep rocks near. His wit was not its cause, but her own thought: "My plea was that I was too young; he is very young too."

As they neared the point of Storm King the evening boat, the *Mary Powell*, swept toward them with scarcely more apparent effort than that of a swan. A few moments later their skiff was dancing over the swells, Amy waving her handkerchief, and the good-natured pilot awakening a hundred echoes by his steam-whistle of responsive courtesy.

They were at home in time for supper, and here another delicious surprise awaited Amy. Johnnie and Alf felt that they should do something in honor of the day. From a sunny hill-side they had gleaned a gill of wild strawberries, and Webb had found that the heat of the day had so far developed half a dozen Jacqueminot rosebuds that they were ready for gathering. These with their fragrance and beauty were beside her plate in dainty arrangement. They seemed to give the complete and final touch to the day already replete with joy and kindness, and happy, grateful tears rushed into the young girl's eyes. Dashing them brusquely away, she said: "I can't tell you all what I feel, and I won't try. I want you to know, however," she added, smilingly, while her lips quivered, "that I am very much at home."

Burt was in exuberant spirits, for Amy had told him that she had enjoyed every moment of the afternoon. This had been most evident, and the young fellow congratulated himself. He could keep his word, he could be so jolly a companion as to leave nothing to be desired, and waiting, after all, would not be a martyrdom. His mood unloosed his tongue and made him eloquent as he described his experiences in trout-fishing. His words were so simple and vivid that he made his listeners hear the cool splash and see the foam of the mountain brooks. They saw the shimmer of the speckled beauties as they leaped for the fly, and felt the tingle of the rod as the line suddenly tightened, and heard the hum of the reel as the fish darted away in imagined safety. Burt saw his vantage—was not Amy listening with intent eyes and glowing cheeks?—and he kept the little group in suspense almost as long as it took him to play, land, and kill a three-pound trout, the chief trophy of his excursion.

Webb was unusually silent, and was conscious of a depression for which he could not account. All was turning out better than he had predicted. The relations between Burt and Amy were not only "serene," but were apparently becoming decidedly blissful. The young girl was enthusiastic over her enjoyment of the afternoon; there were no more delicately veiled defensive tactics against Burt, and now her face was full of frank admiration of his skill as an angler and of interest in the wild scenes described. Burt had spent more time in society than over his books while at college, and was a fluent, easy talker. Webb felt that he suffered in contrast, that he was grave, heavy, dull, and old—no fit companion for the girl whose laughing eyes so often rested on his brother's face and responded to his mirth. Perhaps Burt would not have long to wait; perhaps his rash, passionate words had already given to Amy's girlish unconsciousness the shock that had destroyed it, and she was learning that she was a woman who could return love for love. Well, granting this, was it not just what they were all expecting? "But the change is coming too soon," he complained to himself. "I wish she could keep her gentle, lovable, yet unapproachable May-day grace a little longer. Then she was like the wind-flower, which the eyes can linger upon, but which fades almost the moment it is grasped. It made her so different from other girls of her age. It identified her with the elusive spirit of nature, whose beauty entrances one, but search and wander where we will, nothing can be found that is distinctly and tangibly ours or any one's. Amy, belonging definitely to any one, would lose half her charm."

Webb saw and heard all that passed, but in a minor key thoughts like these were forming themselves, with little vo-lition on his part, and were symptoms which as yet he did not understand. In an interval of mirth Johnnie heard footsteps on the piazza, and darting out, caught a glimpse of Mr. Alvord's retreating form. He had come on some errand, and seeing the group at the supper table, had yielded to the impulse to depart unrecognized. This the little girl would by no means permit. Since Easter an odd friendship had sprung up between her and the lonely man, and she had become almost his sole visitor. She now called after him, and in a moment was at his side. "Why are you going away?" she said. "You must not go till I show you my garden."

Maggie joined them, for he deeply enlisted her sympathy, and she wished to make it clear by her manner that the tie between him and the child had her approval. "Yes, indeed, Mr. Alvord," she said, "you must let Johnnie show you her garden, and especially her pansies."

"Heart's-ease is another name for the flower, I believe," he replied, with the glimmer of a smile. "In that case Johnnie should be called Pansy. I thank you, Mrs. Clifford, that you are willing to trust your child to a stranger. We had a lovely ramble the other day, and she said that you told her she might go with me."

"I'm only too glad that you find Johnnie an agreeable little neighbor," Maggie began. "Indeed, we all feel so neighborly that we hope you will soon cease to think of yourself as a stranger." But here impatient Johnnie dragged him off to see her garden, and his close and appreciative attention to all she said and showed to him won the child's heart anew. Amy soon joined them, and said:

"Mr. Alvord, I wish your congratulations also. I'm eighteen to-day."

He turned and looked at her so wistfully for a moment that her eyes fell. "I do congratulate you," he said, in a low, deep voice. "If I had my choice between all the world and your age, I'd rather be eighteen again. May your brow always be as serene as it is to-night, Miss Amy!" His eyes passed swiftly from the elder to the younger girl, the one almost as young at heart and fully as innocent as the other, and then he spoke abruptly: "Good-by, Johnnie. I wish to see your father a moment on some business;" and he walked rapidly away. By the time they reached the house he had gone. Amy felt that with the night a darker shadow had fallen upon her happy day. The deep sadness of a wounded spirit touched her own, she scarcely knew why. It was but the law of her unwarped, unselfish nature. Even as a happy girl she could not pass by, uncaring, on the other side. She felt that she would like to talk with Webb, as she always did when anything troubled her; but he, touched with something of Burt's old restlessness, had rambled away in the moonlight, notwithstanding the fatigues of the day. Therefore she went to the piano and sang for the old people some of the quaint songs of which she knew they were fond. Burt sat smoking and listening on the piazza in immeasurable content.

To Mrs. Clifford the month of June brought the halcyon days of the year. The warm sunshine revived her, the sub-acid of the strawberry seemed to furnish the very tonic she needed, and the beauty that abounded on every side, and that was daily brought to her couch, conferred a happiness that few could understand. Long years of weakness, in which only her mind could be active, had developed in the invalid a refinement scarcely possible to those who must daily meet the practical questions of life, and whose more robust natures could enjoy the material side of existence. It was not strange, therefore, that country life had matured her native love of flowers into almost a passion, which culminated in her intense enjoyment of the rose in all its varieties. The family, aware of this marked preference, rarely left her without these flowers at any season; but in June her eyes feasted on their varied forms and colors, and she distinguished between her favorites with all the zest and accuracy which a connoisseur of wines ever brought to bear upon their delicate bouquet. With eyes shut she could name from its perfume almost any rose with which she was familiar. Therefore in all the flower beds and borders roses abounded, especially the old-fashioned kinds, which are again finding a place in florists' catalogues. Originally led by love for his mother, Webb, years since, had begun to give attention to the queen of flowers. He soon found, however, that the words of an English writer are true, "He who would have beautiful roses in his garden must have them first in his heart," and there with queenly power they soon enthroned themselves. In one corner of the garden, which was protected on the north and west by a high stone wall, where the soil was warm, loamy, and well drained, he made a little rosery. He bought treatises on the flower, and when he heard of or saw a variety that was particularly fine, he added it to his collection.

On the third morning after her birthday Amy came down very early. The bird symphony had penetrated her open windows with such a jubilant resonance that she had been awakened almost with the dawn. The air was so cool and exhilarating, and there was such a wealth of dewy beauty on every side, that she yielded to the impulse to go out and enjoy the most delightful hour of the day. To her surprise she saw Webb going down the path leading to the garden. "What's on your conscience," she cried, "that you can't sleep?"

"What's on yours?" he retorted.

"The shame of leaving so many mornings like this unseen and not enjoyed. I mean to repent and mend my ways from this time forth; that is, if I wake up. Can I go with you?"

"What a droll question!" he replied, in laughing invitation.

"Well, I did not know," she said, joining him, "but that you were going to visit that *sanctum sanctorum* of yours."

"I am. Your virtue of early rising is about to be rewarded. You know when some great personage is to be specially honored, he is given the freedom of a city or library, etc. I shall now give you the freedom of my rosery for the rest of the summer, and from this time till frost you can always find roses for your belt. I meant to do this on your birthday, but the buds were not sufficiently forward this backward season."

"I'm not a great personage."

"No, thanks, you're not. You are only our Amy."

"I'm content. Oh, Webb, what miracles have you been working here!" she exclaimed, as she passed through some screening shrubbery and looked upon a plot given up wholly to roses, many of which were open, more in the phase of exquisite buds, while the majority were still closely wrapped in their green calyxes.

"No miracle at all. I've only assisted nature a little. At the same time let me assure you that this small place is like a picture-gallery, and that there is a chance here for as nice discrimination as there would be in a cabinet full of art. There are few duplicate roses in this place, and I have been years in selecting and winnowing this collection. They are all named varieties, labelled in my mind. I love them too well, and am too familiar with them, to hang disfiguring bits of wood upon them. One might as well label his friends. Each one has been chosen and kept because of some individual point of excellence, and you can gradually learn to recognize these characteristics, just as mother does. This plot here is filled with hardy hybrid perpetuals, and that with tender tea-roses that require very different treatment. Here is a moss that will also bloom in the autumn. It has a sounding name—*Soupert-et-notting*—but it is worthy of any name. Though not so mossy as some others, look at its fine form and beautiful rose-color. Only one or two are out yet, but in a week this bush will be a thing of beauty that one would certainly wish might last forever. Try its fragrance. Nothing surpasses it unless it is La France over there."

She inhaled the exquisite perfume in long breaths, and then looked around at the budding beauty on every side, even to the stone walls that were covered with climbing varieties.

"Well, Webb," she said, laughing, "I can not think of anything lacking in my morning's experience. I was wakened by the song of birds. You have revealed to me the mystery of your sanctum, and that alone, you know, would be happiness to the feminine soul. You have also introduced me to dozens of your sweethearts, for you look at each rose as Burt does at the pretty girls he meets. You have shown me your budding rosery in the dewy morning, and that was appropriate too. Every one of your pets was gemmed and jewelled for the occasion, and unrivalled musicians, cleverly concealed in the trees near, have filled every moment with melody. What more could I ask? But where are you going with that basket?"

"To gather strawberries for breakfast. There are enough ripe this morning. You gather roses in the other basket. Why not have them for breakfast also?"

"Why indeed, since it would seem that there are to be thousands here and elsewhere in the garden! Fresh roses and strawberries for breakfast—that's country life to perfection. Good-by."

He went away as if in a dream, and his heart almost ached with a tension of feeling that he could not define. It seemed to him the culmination of all that he had loved and enjoyed. His rosery had been complete at this season the year before, but now that Amy had entered it, the roses that she had touched, admired, and kissed with lips that vied with their petals grew tenfold more beautiful, and the spot seemed sacred to her alone. He could never enter it again without thinking of her and seeing her lithe form bending to favorites which hitherto he had only associated with his mother.

He brought the strawberries to Amy in the breakfast-room, and stood near while she and Johnnie hulled them. He saw the roses arranged by his mother's plate in such nice harmony that one color did not destroy another. He replied to her mirthful words and rallyings, scarcely knowing what he said, so deep was the feeling that oppressed him, so strong was his love for that sweet sister who had come into his life and made it ideally perfect. She appreciated what he had loved so fully, her very presence had ever kindled his spirit, and while eager to learn and easily taught, how truly she was teaching him a philosophy of life that seemed divine! What more could he desire? The day passed in a confused maze of thought and happiness, so strange and absorbing that he dared not speak lest he should waken as from a dream. The girl had grown so beautiful to him that he scarcely wished ed to look at her, and hastened through his meals that he might be alone with his thoughts. The sun had sunk, and the moon was well over the eastern mountains, before he visited the rosery. Amy was there, and she greeted him with a pretty petulance because he had not come before. Then in sudden compunction she asked:

"Don't you feel well, Webb? You have been so quiet since we were here this morning! Perhaps you are sorry you let me into this charmed seclusion."

"No, Amy, I am not," he said, with an impetuosity very unusual in him. "You should know me better than even to imagine such a thing."

Before he could say anything more, Burt's mellow voice rang out, "Amy!"

"Oh, I half forgot; I promised to take a drive with Burt this evening. Forgive me, Webb," she added, gently; "I only spoke in sport. I do know you too well to imagine I am unwelcome here. No one ever had a kinder or more patient brother than you have been to me;" and she clasped her hands upon his arm, and looked up into his face with frank affection.

His arm trembled under her touch, and he felt that he must be alone. In his usual quiet tones, however, he was able to say: "You, rather, must forgive me that I spoke so hastily. No; I'm not ill, but very tired. A good night's rest will bring me around. Go and enjoy your drive to the utmost."

"Webb, you work too hard," she said, earnestly. "But Burt is calling—"

"Yes; do not keep him waiting; and think of me," he added, laughing, "as too weary for moonlight, roses, or anything but prosaic sleep. June is all very well, but it brings a pile of work to a fellow like me."

"Oh, Webb, what a clod-hopper you're trying to make yourself out to be! Well, 'Sleep, sleep'—I can't think of the rest of the quotation. Good-by.—Yes, I'm coming!" rang out her clear voice; and, with a smiling glance backward, she hastened away.

From the shrubbery he watched her pass up the wide garden path, the moonlight giving an ethereal beauty to her slight form with its white, close drapery. Then, deeply troubled, he threw himself on a rustic seat near the wall and buried his face in his hands. It was all growing too clear to him now, and he found himself face to face with the conviction that Amy was no longer his sister, but the woman he loved. The deep-hidden current of feeling that had been gathering volume for months at last flashed out into the light, and there could be no more disguise. The explanation of her power over him was now given to his deepest consciousness. By some law of his nature, when she spoke he had ever listened; whatever she said and did had been invested with a nameless charm. Day after day they had been together, and their lives had harmonized like two chords that blend in one sweet sound. He had never had a sister, and his growing interest in Amy had seemed the most natural thing in the world; that Burt should love her, equally natural—to fall in love was almost a habit with the mercurial young fellow when thrown into the society of a pretty girl—and he had felt that he should be only too glad that his brother had at last fixed his thoughts on one who would not be a stranger to them. He now remembered that while all this had been satisfactory to reason, his heart for a long time had been uttering its low, half-conscious protest. Now he knew why. The events of this long day had revealed him unto himself, because he was ripe for the knowledge.

His nature had its hard, practical, business side, but he had never been content with questions of mere profit and loss. He not only had wanted the corn, but the secret of the corn's growth and existence. To search into Nature's hidden life, so that he could see through her outward forms the mechanism back of all, and trace endless diversity to simple inexorable laws, had been his pride and the promised solace of his life. His love of the rose had been to him what it is to many another hard-working man and woman—recreation, a habit, something for which he had developed the taste and feeling of a connoisseur. It had had no appreciable influence on the current of his thoughts. Amy's coming, however, had awakened the poetic side of his temperament, and while this had taken nothing from the old, it had changed everything. Before, his life had been like nature in winter, when all things are in hard, definite outline. The feeling which she had inspired brought the transforming flowers and foliage. It was an immense addition to that which already existed, and which formed the foundation for it. For a long time he had exulted in this inflorescence of his life, as it were, and was more than content. He did not know that the spirit gifted even unconsciously with the power thus to develop his own nature must soon become to him more than a cause of an effect, more than a sister upon whom he could look with as tranquil eyes and even pulse in youth as in frosty age. But now he knew it with the absolute certainty that was characteristic of his mind when once it grasped a truth. The voice of Burt calling "Amy," after the experiences of the day, had been like a shaft of light, and everything was instantly revealed. For her sake more than his own he had exerted himself to the utmost to conceal the truth of that moment of bitter consciousness. He trembled as he thought of his blind, impetuous words and her look of surprise; he grew cold with dread as he remembered how easily he might have betrayed himself.

And now what should he do? what could he do but hide the truth with sleepless vigilance? He could not become his brother's rival. In the eyes of Amy and all the family Burt was her acknowledged suitor, who, having been brought to reason, was acting most rationally and honorably. Whether Amy was learning to love him or not made no difference. If she, growing conscious of her womanhood, was turning her thoughts to Burt as the one who had first sought her, and who was now cheerfully waiting until the look of shy choice and appeal came into her eyes, he could not seek to thrust his younger brother aside. If the illustration of the rose which she had forced into unnatural bloom was still true of her heart, he would be false to her and himself, as well as to Burt, should he seek her in the guise of a lover. He had felt that it was almost sacrilege to disturb her May-like girlhood; that this child of nature should be left wholly to nature's impulses and to nature's hour for awakening.

"If it only could have been, how rich and full life would be!" he thought. "We were in sympathy at almost every point. When shall I forget the hour we spent here this morning! How can I hide all this from her, and seem merely her quiet elderly brother? How can I meet her here to-morrow morning, and in the witchery of summer evenings, and still speak in measured tones, and look at her as I would at Johnnie? The thing is impossible until I have gained a stronger self-control. I must go away for a day or two, and I will. When I return, neither Burt nor Amy shall have cause to complain;" and he strode away.

The evening mail brought an excuse. A firm to whom the Cliffords had been sending part of their produce had not given full satisfaction, and Webb announced his intention of going to the city in the morning to investigate matters. His father and Leonard approved of his purpose, and when he added that he might stay in town for two or three days, that he felt the need of a little change and rest before haying and harvest began, they all expressed their approval still more heartily.

The night was so beautiful that Burt prolonged his drive. The witchery of the romantic scenery through which he and Amy passed, and the loveliness of her profile in the pale light, almost broke down his resolution, and once, in accents much too tender, he said, "Oh, Amy, I am so happy when with you!"

"I'm happy with you also," she replied, in brusque tones, "now that you have become so sensible."

He took the hint, and said, emphatically: "Don't you ever be apprehensive or nervous when with me. I'll wait, and be 'sensible,' as you express it, till I'm gray."

Her laugh rang out merrily, but she made no other reply. He was a little nettled, and mentally vowed a constancy that would one day make her regret that laugh.

Webb had retired when Amy returned, and she learned of his plans from Maggie. "It's just the best thing he can do," she said, earnestly. "Webb's been overworking, and he needs and deserves a little rest."

In the morning he seemed so busy with his preparations that he had scarcely time to give her more than a genial off-hand greeting.

"Oh, Webb, I shall miss you so much!" she said, in parting, and her look was very kind and wistful. He did not trust himself to speak, but gave her a humorous and what seemed to her a half-incredulous smile. He puzzled her, and she thought about him and his manner of the previous day and evening not a little. With her sensitive nature, she could not approach so near the mystery that he was striving to conceal without being vaguely impressed that there was something unusual about him. The following day, however, brought a cheerful, business-like letter to his father, which was read at the dinner table. He had straightened out matters in town, and seemed to be enjoying himself. She more than once admitted that she did miss him as she would not any other member of the household. But her out-door life was very full. By the aid of her glass she made the intimate acquaintance of her favorite songsters. Every day she took Mrs. Clifford in her garden chair to the rosery, and proposed through her instruction to give Webb a surprise when he returned. She would prove to him that she could name his pets from their fragrance, form, and color as well as he himself.

A PASTORAL.

Burt did his best to keep things lively, and a few days after Webb's departure, said: "I've heard that there is to be a sham battle at West Point this afternoon. Suppose we go and see it?"

The heavy guns from the river batteries had been awakening deep echoes among the mountains every afternoon for some time past, reminding the Cliffords that the June examinations were taking place at the Military Academy, and that there was much of interest occurring near them. Amy not only assented to Burt's proposition, but Leonard also resolved to go and take Maggie and the children. In the afternoon a steam-yacht bore them and many other excursionists to their destination, and they were soon skirting the grassy plain on which the military evolutions were to take place.

The scene was full of novelty and interest for Amy. Thousands of people were there, representing every walk and condition of life. Plain farmers with their wives and children, awkward country fellows with their sweethearts, dapper clerks with bleached hands and faces, were passing to and fro among ladies in Parisian toilets and with the unmistakable air of the metropolis. There were officers with stars upon their shoulders, and others, quite as important in their bearing, decorated with the single bar of a second lieutenant. Plain-looking men were pointed out as Senators, and elegantly dressed men were seen to be nobodies at a glance. Scarcely a type was wanting among those who came to see how the nation's wards were drilled and prepared to defend the nation's honor and maintain peace at the point of the bayonet. On the piazzas of the officers' quarters were groups of favored people whose relations or distinguished claims were such as to give them this advantage over those who must stand where they could to see the pageant. The cadets in their gray uniforms were conspicuously absent, but the band was upon the plain discoursing lively music. From the inclosure within the barracks came the long roll of a drum, and all eyes turned thitherward expectantly. Soon from under the arched sally-port two companies of cadets were seen issuing on the double-quick. They crossed the plain with the perfect time and precision of a single mechanism, and passed down into a depression of the ground toward the river. After an interval the other two companies came out in like manner, and halted on the plain within a few hundred yards of this depression, their bayonets scintillating in the cloudless afternoon sun. Both parties were accompanied by mounted cadet officers. The body on the plain threw out pickets, stacked arms, and lounged at their ease. Suddenly a shot was fired to the eastward, then another, and in that direction the pickets were seen running in. With marvellous celerity the loungers on the plain seized their muskets, formed ranks, and faced toward the point from which the attack was threatened. A skirmish line was thrown out, and this soon met a similar line advancing from the depression, sloping eastward. Behind the skirmishers came a compact line of battle, and it advanced steadily until within fair musket range, when the firing became general. While the attacking party appeared to fight resolutely, it was soon observed that they made no further effort to advance, but sought only to occupy the attention of the party to which they were opposed.

The Cliffords stood on the northwestern edge of the plain, near the statue of General Sedgwick, and from this point they could also see what was occurring in the depression toward the river. "Turn, Amy, quick, and see what's coming," cried Burt. Stealing up the hill-side in solid column was another body of cadets. A moment later they passed near on the double-quick, went into battle formation on the run, and with loud shouts charged the flank and rear of the cadets on the plain, who from the first had sustained the attack. These seemed thrown into confusion, for they were now between two fires. After a moment of apparent indecision they gave way rapidly in seeming defeat and rout, and the two attacking parties drew together in pursuit. When they had united, the pursued, who a moment before had seemed a crowd of fugitives, became almost instantly a steady line of battle. The order, "Charge!" rang out, and, with fixed bayonets, they rushed upon their assailants, and steadily drove them back over the plain, and down into their original position. It was all carried out with a fair degree of life-like reality. The "sing" of minie bullets was absent, but abundance of noise and sulphurous smoke can be made with blank cartridges; and as the party attacked plucked victory from seeming defeat, the people's acclamations were loud and long.

At this point the horse of one of the cadet officers became unmanageable. They had all observed him during the battle, admiring the manner with which he rode and restrained the vicious brute, but at last the animal's excitement or fear became so great that he rushed toward the crowded sidewalk and road in front of the officers' quarters. The people gave way to right and left. Burt had scarcely time to do more than encircle Amy with his arm and sweep her out of the path of the terrified beast. The cadet made heroic efforts, until it was evident that the horse would dash into the iron fence beyond the road, and then the young fellow was off and on his feet with the agility of a cat, but he still maintained his hold upon the bridle. A second later there was a heavy thud heard above the screams of women and children and the shouts of those vociferating advice. The horse fell heavily in his recoil from the fence, and in a moment or two was led limping and crest-fallen away, while the cadet quietly returned to his comrades on the plain. Johnnie and little Ned were crying from fright, and both Amy and Maggie were pale and nervous; therefore Leonard led the way out of the crowd. From a more distant point they saw the party beneath the hill rally for a final and united charge, which this time proved successful, and the companies on the plain, after a stubborn resistance, were driven back to the barracks, and through the sally-port, followed by their opponents. The clouds of smoke rolled away, the band struck up a lively air, and the lines of people broke up into groups and streamed in all directions. Leonard decided that it would be best for them to return by the evening boat, and not wait for parade, since the little yacht would certainly be overcrowded at a later hour.

The first one on the *Powell* to greet them was Webb returning from the city. Amy thought he looked so thin as to appear almost haggard, but he seemed in the best of spirits, and professed to feel well and rested. She half imagined that she missed a certain gentleness in his words and manner toward her, but when he heard how nearly she had been trampled upon, she was abundantly satisfied by his look of deep affection and solicitude as he said: "Heaven bless your strong, ready arm, Burt!" "O that it had been mine!" was his inward thought. He masked his feeling so well, however, that all perplexity passed from her mind. She was eager to visit the rosery with him, and when there he praised her quickly acquired skill with such sincerity that her face flushed with pleasure. No one seemed to enjoy the late but ample supper more than he, or to make greater havoc in the well-heaped dish of strawberries. "I tasted none like these in New York," he said. "After all, give me this old-fashioned kind. We've tried many varieties, but the Triomphe de Gand proves the most satisfactory, if one will give it the attention it deserves. The fruit ripens early and lasts till late. It is firm and good even in cool wet weather, and positively delicious after a sunny day like this."

"I agree with you, Webb," said his mother, smiling. "It's the best of all the kinds we've had, except, perhaps, the President Wilder, but that doesn't bear well in our garden."

"Well, mother," he replied, with a laugh, "the best is good enough for you. I have a row of Wilders, however, for your especial benefit; but they're late, you know."

The next morning he went into the haying with as much apparent zest as Leonard. They began with red-top clover. The growth had been so heavy that in many places it had "lodged," or fallen, and it had to be cut with scythes. Later on the mowing-machine would be used in the timothy fields and meadows. Amy from her open window watched him as he steadily bent to the work, and she inhaled with pleasure the odors from the bleeding clover, for it was the custom of the Cliffords to cut their grasses early, while full of the native juices. Rakes followed the scythes speedily, and the clover was piled up into compact little heaps, or "cocks," to sweat out its moisture rather than yield it to the direct rays of the sun.

"Oh dear!" said Amy, at the dinner table, "my bees won't fare so well, now that you are cutting down so much of their pasture."

"Red clover affords no pasturage for honey-bees," said Webb, laughing. "How easily he seems to laugh of late!" Amy thought. "They can't reach the honey in the long tube-like blossoms. Here the bumble-bees have everything their way, and get it all except what is sipped by the humming-birds, with their long beaks, as they feed on the minute insects within the flowers. I've heard the question, Of what use are bumble-bees?—I like to say *bumble* best, as I did when a boy. Well, I've been told that in Australia they could not raise red clover without this insect, which, passing from flower to flower, carries the fertilizing pollen. The rats there and the field-mice were so abundant that they destroyed these bees, which, as you know, make their nests on the ground, and so they had to import cats in order to give the bumble-bees and red clover a chance for life. There is always trouble in nature unless an equilibrium is kept up. Much as I dislike cats, I must admit that they have contributed much toward the prosperity of an incipient empire."

All through the afternoon the musical sound of whetting the scythes with the rifle rang out from time to time, and in the evening Leonard said, "If this warm dry weather holds till to-morrow night, we shall get in our clover in perfect condition."

On the afternoon of the following day the two-horse wagon, surmounted by the hay-rack, went into the barn again and again with its fragrant burden; but at last Amy was aroused from her book by a heavy jar of thunder. Going to a window facing the west, she saw a threatening cloud that every moment loomed vaster and darker. The great vapory heads tipped with light towered rapidly, until at last the sun passed into a sudden eclipse that was so deep as to create almost a twilight. As the cloud approached, there was a low, distant, continuous sound, quite distinct from nearer and heavier peals, that after brief and briefer intervals followed the lightning gleams athwart the gloom. She saw that the haymakers were gathering the last of the clover, and raking, pitching, and loading with breathless haste, their forms looking almost shadowy in the distance and the dim light. Their task was nearly completed, and the horses' heads were turned barnward, when a flash of blinding intensity came with an instantaneous crash, that roared away to the eastward with deep reverberations. Amy shuddered, and covered her face with her hands. When she looked again, the clover field and all that it contained seemed annihilated. The air was thick with dust, straws, twigs, and foliage torn away, and the gust passed over the house with a howl of fury scarcely less appalling than the thunder-peal had been. Trembling, and almost faint with fear,

THE LAST LOAD.

she strained her eyes toward the point where she had last seen Webb loading the rick. The murky obscurity lightened up a little, and in a moment or two she saw him whipping the horses into a gallop. The doors of the barn stood open, and the rest of the workers had taken a cross-cut toward it, while Mr. Clifford was on the piazza shouting for them to hurry. Great drops splashed against the window-panes, and the heavy, monotonous sound of the coming torrent seemed to approach like the rush of a locomotive. Webb, with the last load, is wheeling to the entrance of the barn. A second later, and the horses' feet resound on the planks of the floor. Then all is hidden, and the rain pours against the window like a cataract. In swift alternation of feeling she clapped her hands in applause, and ran down to meet Mr. Clifford, who with much effort was shutting the door against the gale. When he turned he rubbed his hands and laughed as he said, "Well, I never saw Webb chased so sharply by a thunder-shower before; but he won the race, and the clover's safe."

The storm soon thundered away to parts unknown, the setting sun spanned its retreating murkiness with a magnificent bow, long before the rain ceased the birds were exulting in jubilant chorus, and the air grew still and cool and fragrant. When at last the full moon rose over the Beacon Mountains there was not a cloud above the horizon, and Nature in her June-clad loveliness was like a radiant beauty lost in reverie.

THE PROFESSIONAL BEAUTIES OF THE LAST CENTURY.

ABOUT the year 1751 a little print was issued by Messrs. Sayer and Co., and sold in their shop in the Strand. It is apparently engraved from a miniature, and bears the name of "Boitard." Probably it was intended for what was then called a "watch paper"—that is to say, the portrait of some fair one made of the shape and size to wear inside the lid of the "warming-pans" of the period. This little print represents the head of a young lady, with a small mouth and bright eye, wearing a coquettish velvet hat daintily poised on one side of her simple coiffure, and it bears the inscription, "The celebrated Miss Gunning."

The medallion has little or no merit of its own. It is badly drawn and badly engraved, and if we had no ampler means of forming a judgment on the fashionable beauty, we might infer that the taste of our own day is of a higher order in female loveliness. But fortunately there are more adequate records of the distinguished belle, both from the brush and the pen of the period, and the curious little print should be regarded less as a veracious representation of the features that won such universal admiration than as the proof that notoriety could be as easily won in days when the art of photography was unknown as in a time when the portraits of distinguished fair ones can be purchased with a couple of shillings from the window of any print-shop in Regent Street or Piccadilly.

The worship of beauty has never been quite extinct in any nation or at any period, and although the loveliest women need certainly not be the most notorious, a careful study of history would probably show us that from the time of Helen of Troy to our own day the "professional beauty" has always existed in everything save in name.

Elizabeth Gunning and her elder and lovelier sister Maria were the daughters of John Gunning, Esq., of Castle Coote, Roscommon, in Connaught. The family was of good English extraction, and dated back to the early part of the sixteenth century. It was not until the reign of James I. that a branch of it had settled in Ireland, and from that time its resources appear gradually to have dwindled, until in the time of this John Gunning it had become so impoverished as to be quite unable to keep up the style of the gentry to which it belonged, so that the girls, who afterward filled the highest positions in the land, enjoyed only such rudiments of an education as their mother could spare time from household duties to give them; and in an age when it was thought absolutely necessary for every woman who hoped to enter into society to learn "manners" and "deportment" as an art, these luckless damsels were left to run wild among the moors and bogs of a country so bleak and desolate that it gave rise to the saying, "to hell or to Connaught." Echoes of the gay doings at Dublin under the rule

ELIZABETH GUNNING, DUCHESS OF HAMILTON AND BRANDON AND DUCHESS OF ARGYLE.
From the painting by C. Read.

of Chesterfield came feebly, however, even to the remoteness of Roscommon, and the mother, who had been used, as the daughter of a Viscount Mayo, to see something of the world in her own girlhood, pined to watch the beauties which she saw daily unfolding beneath the healthy country breezes growing to maturity unheeded.

Though she seems to have been of a gentle and retiring disposition, since, even in the gay vortex where she was afterward chaperon, she appears never to have provoked any further remark than that "she was a lady of elegant figure," Mrs. Gunning had nevertheless sufficient ambition to determine her to stretch a point that she might try the effect of her daughters' budding charms in a wider sphere. Accordingly, just as Chesterfield finished his luxurious reign, and Earl Harrington, arriving at the Castle, announced a grand ball to the neighborhood, Mrs. Gunning scraped together the last resources of the unfortunate family, and removed her four daughters and son (John Gunning, afterward famous at Bunker Hill) with all possible speed to the capital.

Maria was at this time in her sixteenth,

Elizabeth only in her fifteenth, year, and of the two younger girls one died as a child about this time, or shortly afterward, and the other, though she served as the third in the group that was known as "the three Graces," never reached notoriety, but was content, at a later date, to bestow her simple charms upon an Irish squire in her own rank of life: in his keeping we will leave her.

When the Gunnings removed to Dublin, tradition has it that they were so poor that Miss Bellamy, the actress—then performing in the city—heard of the family as in such distress, with the bailiffs in the house, that, with the usual good-nature of her profession, she relieved their wants, and even assisted them to throw some of their small valuables out of the window of the house, in Great Britain Street, to be caught by her man below. The ambitious mother seems to have had no means of introducing her daughters into the magic circle where her maternal pride hoped they would outshine all rivals. She seems even so far to have despaired of attaining her end as to have seriously thought of placing her girls upon the stage, and, presumably with this intent, obtained access to Sheridan, who was then managing the Dublin theatre. This acquaintance was the means of their introduction to one who was to be even more instrumental in their triumph. Margaret Woffington, the darling of London audiences, had returned for a while to the Dublin public that she had been used to fascinate as a little child, when she danced upon the tight-rope in Madame Violante's booth.

Enthroned at the "Beef Steak Club," in Dublin, by Sheridan, she at the same time so captivated the Lord Lieutenant that, it was said, she ruled the Castle just as she ruled the greenroom. Whether this be so or not, it appears to be certain that, either through Mrs. Woffington or through Sheridan himself, the girls obtained that invitation to the grand ball at the Castle which was the beginning of their good luck. The actress ransacked her own store of dresses to supply the deficiencies of her new friends' slender wardrobe, and, with her usual sweet and affectionate tact, persuaded them to make use of what suited them best among her garments, that they might appear to the best advantage before the Dublin court.

The triumph of the two sisters at the great ball at Dublin Castle far exceeded

the boldest prophecies that had been made for them. Fascinatingly coy, with all the timidity of untutored country lasses, yet bold at the same time with all the daring of their perfect simplicity, artlessly captivating by the ingenuous ardor of their enthusiasm for the gay sight in which they found themselves for the first time, the dazzling loveliness of the little unknown nobodies won an easy victory over the long-established glory of Mrs. Madden (Lady Ely), the popular Irish toast, and even deposed from her throne the lovely hostess of the evening, handsome Lady Caroline Petersham, the bride of Earl Harrington's eldest son. Lady Caroline had been one of the "Beauty Fitzroys," and had been a reigning belle in town before her marriage.

" Where Fitzroy moves, resplendent, fair,
So warm her bloom, sublime her air,
Her ebon tresses formed to grace
And heighten while they shade her face,"

Walpole had said of her in his poem on "The Beauties." Through the gorgeous ball and supper rooms, so lavishly decorated by Chesterfield in his day, where "candles glowed behind transparent paintings, and flutes played unseen, and fountains flowed with lavender-water," the stately hostess must have glided to receive, amongst others, the two unknown misses who were to pale her own lustre. Luckily for them, Lady Caroline, judging from numerous mentions of her in Walpole's letters, appears to have been as generous and unselfish as she was handsome.

In spite of their raw freshness, the Connaught damsels won admirers on every side by their rare beauty, and kept them, strange to say, by their very innocence of artifice, by their unsophisticated enthusiasms, and —though none are prophets in their own country—even by their good-natured Irishisms. The wits of the court were charmed with such lovely and good-humored butts for their jokes, and the lucky maidens went home with their heads turned by such a signal triumph, and boasting one friend at least, if not more, who would help them in the dangerous future. For the début at Dublin Castle was but the match that was required to set fire to the train. The loveliness of these two extremely youthful and naïve damsels made such a stir in this comparatively provincial society that Mrs. Gunning was determined to strain every nerve that they might try their fortunes on the only real stage of adventure. By means partly of loans,

MARIA GUNNING, COUNTESS OF COVENTRY.
From the painting by C. Read.

wrung here and there from friends nearly as poor as herself, and partly of a fund of one hundred and fifty pounds a year granted to her for some inexplicable reason by the Irish establishment, the devoted mother succeeded at last in landing her beauties safe and sound within the new arena.

It was in the autumn of 1750, when Maria was but eighteen, Elizabeth barely seventeen years of age, that the two sisters first made their *entrée* among the fashionables of London society. They were at that time tall, slim girls, upright as river reeds, and just as graceful; already conspicuous for the seductive fascination of figure and gait for which they were even more specially noted than for beauty of feature, and for the brilliant delicacy of complexion, bred in the damp breezes and healthy out-door life of their native bogs. Maria, the elder, who must already have had within her the seeds of the fatal disease that was to kill her before she was ten years older—Maria, perhaps, held the palm. She was a shade taller than Elizabeth, and rumor affirms that her foot and hand were smaller, but apparently the chief difference consisted in the greater sweetness of the expression. Dr. Carlyle, however, swears that the younger sister was by far the handsomer of the two; and high-minded old Mrs. Delany, in a letter where she deplores with her usual strictness the "want of discretion" of the two damsels, insists that, in spite of the great beauty of the elder, she had "a silly look about the mouth," proof of a disposition which, in spite of its gentle amiability, seems always to have been sorely weak and vacillating, while "Betty Gunning," on the other hand, had the name of "a fine spirit." Judging from the various portraits and miniatures extant of the two famous belles, we are inclined to think that if there was indeed anything to choose between the two, Maria had the more delicate features, the softer dimples, the more melting eye, the serener smile, and Elizabeth the archer glance, the more spirited carriage of the head, the more coquettishly pouting lips. The maidens, however, had much in common in their loveliness: the exquisitely modelled oval contour of the face, the delicate nostrils, the slender bridge of the nose, the dimples beside the mouth, the full curved lips, and particularly the long, almond-shaped, sleepy eyes, the finely pencilled eyebrows, the clear low foreheads, the gracefully shaped heads—so much better displayed by the simple mode of dressing the hair smoothly drawn back from the temples than by the subsequent extravagant fashions of high heads and stiff rolls of cushioned hair that disfigured the ladies of 1773 and after.

When the two Irish belles first made their appearance in the metropolis, the world of fashion was just in the state to mould out of such excellent materials the characters called "professional" and (according to a characteristic historian of those times) "standard" beauties. The life of the last century, as it is presented to us by its most faithful chroniclers, was in every way a fit and flattering frame for such figures. A gay and easy freedom of intercourse; a devotion to the outward modes and manners of life, in which we are nowadays afraid to be held as conspicuous as our Continental neighbors; a taste for open-air amusements and out-door display, to which our insular climate seems of late to offer an insuperable objection as opposed to that of a country that we can discern with the naked eye from our shores; a care—bred of greater leisure, but carried almost to excess—for

the dainty and becoming in furniture, equipage, dress, and every kind of offset to human perfection—all these things went far to cultivate a soil fit for the nurture of the exotic called "the professional beauty."

Folk lived before the world, and the world was the world of the upper ten, into which none who were not of it dared to intrude. It would not seem that even the great literary and artistic men of the age, Gray, Gibbon, Johnson, Fielding, Richardson, Sterne, Smollett, Swift, Goldsmith, Sheridan, and in art, Hogarth, Romney, Sir Joshua Reynolds, Barry, Gainsborough, and others, were lionized then as they would be now, although probably there was never a time when the gatherings of wits and connoisseurs at Dr. Johnson's, Mrs. Cholmondeley's, Mrs. Thrale's, and other recognized rendezvous of the "Blues," as well as at Sir Joshua's studio, and at the well-known Dilettanti Club, were as brilliant as they were then. This exclusiveness of the aristocracy is no doubt partly accounted for by the fact that, except in the case of Gainsborough, and chiefly of Sir Joshua Reynolds, who became the fashionable portrait painter of the day, most of these great men—Hogarth in his pictures, and the novelists and playwrights in their books—far too accurately mirrored the vices and vulgarities of the age to be acceptable to those who moulded it.

But when the Gunnings came to London, *Evelina* was not yet published, and Sheridan's mirrors of fashion were yet to be held up to the world. The winter of 1750–51 was a dull time in politics, as it was in art and letters, and had the *beau monde* wanted else to amuse it than the account of its own successes and scandals, it would not have found much to gratify it.

At the time of which we are writing a woman walked daily in St. James's Park with her set of gallants, just as she rides or drives now in the Row, and it was just as correct to make a party at a tea garden as it is now to go to a private kettledrum, or to walk in the Zoo on Sundays. In 1750 Vauxhall and Ranelagh—the two fashionable Cremornes of the last century—spread their gay fronts of lamp-lit trees to the river, and were at the zenith of their success. Walpole refers to the latter as so much in vogue that it took twenty-five minutes of waiting in the rank before a carriage could "set down" at the

16*

door, and speaks of the crush as a nuisance upon an occasion when the Prince of Wales had given a silver cup to be rowed for, which took everybody upon the Thames, and was followed by a great ball at the Carlton House. And though the method of conducting these entertainments would not always appear to have been of the most correct, the company that attended them was always distinguished. The Princess Emily herself used to go to Ranelagh, and Walpole describes "Madame l'Ambassadrice de Venise in a green sack, with a straw hat, and attended by my Lady Trawley and the Misses Molyneux," being fêted at Vauxhall by the Prince of Wales "in a new sky-blue watered tabby-coat with gold button-holes, and a magnificent gold-fringed waistcoat." No doubt these great folks were wont to behave a little more quietly at such public rendezvous than jolly Lady Caroline Petersham and her set, though "Beauty Fitzroy" was the leader of fashion since her return from the gay doings at Dublin Castle, where her father-in-law had succeeded Chesterfield in the government of Ireland.

Upon this society the two adventuresses were to burst like meteors, quickly becoming, from poor nobodies, the very kernel of its interests, and leaders of its fashions. Brave, bold, beautiful, with everything to win and nothing to lose, it was not perhaps so wonderful that, in such an age of display and easy adulation, they should have made their way even into the sacred circle of titled people, to which they did not by rights belong; but it *was* wonderful, it was even marvellous, that they should have become, as they did, the very idols of the mob itself, so that at last, history swears, it was not safe for them to walk abroad unguarded. Far beyond anything which they achieved in the capital of their own country was this strange triumph that came to bloom as it were in a single night, and something —may we not fancy it ?—after the following fashion.

The scene is at Ranelagh, upon the occasion of one of the numerous masquerades that Walpole describes as taking place there. For though, in the March of this year, Frederick, Prince of Wales, had died, leaving those eight children, of whom the eldest was to come to his grandfather's throne as George III., masquerades and assemblies were in no wise stopped in the capital. In the month of May

"there was," says Walpole, "what was called a masquerade in the Venetian manner at Ranelagh: it had nothing Venetian in it, but was by far the best understood and the prettiest spectacle I ever saw: nothing in a fairy tale ever surpassed it. One of the proprietors, who is a German, and belongs to the court, got my Lady Yarmouth" (Sophia de Walmoden, the King's mistress) "to persuade the King to order it. It began at three o'clock, and, about five, people of fashion began to go. "When you entered you found the whole garden filled with masks, and spread with tents. In one quarter was a May-pole dressed with garlands (for it was in the month of May). People danced round it to a tabor and pipe and rustic music, all masked, as were all the various bands of music that were disposed in various parts of the garden; some like huntsmen with French horns, some like peasants, and a troop of Harlequins and Scaramouches in the little open temple on the mount. On the canal was a sort of gondola, adorned with flags and streamers and filled with music, rowing about. All round the outside of the amphitheatre were shops filled with Dresden china, japan, etc., and all the shop-keepers in mask. The amphitheatre was illuminated, and in the middle was a circular bower, composed of all kinds of firs in tubs, from twenty to thirty feet high; under them orange-trees with small lamps in each orange, and below them all sorts of the finest auriculas in pots, and festoons of natural flowers hanging from tree to tree. There were booths for tea and wine, gaming tables and dancing, and about two thousand persons. The King was well disguised in an old-fashioned English habit, and much pleased with somebody who desired him to hold their cups as they were drinking tea. The Duke of Cumberland had a dress of the same kind, but was so immensely corpulent that he looked like Cacofogo, the drunken Captain, in *Rule a Wife*. The Duchess of Richmond was a Lady Mayoress in the time of James I.; and Lord Delawarr, Queen Elizabeth's porter, from a picture in the guard-chamber at Kensington: they were admirable masks. Lord Rochford, Miss Evelyn, pretty Miss Bishop" (described on another occasion as one of Sir Cecil Bishop's crowd of beauty daughters), "Lady Stafford, and Mrs. Pitt were in vast beauty, particularly the latter, who had a red veil, which made her look gloriously handsome. Mr. Conway was Don Quixote, and the finest figure I ever saw. Miss Chudleigh, the King's favorite maid of honor, was Iphigenia, but her dress was so remarkable that the maids of honor (though not of maids the strictest) would not speak to her." How gay the scene is! Where folks are not strictly in fancy costume, but have only donned the mask to obtain an admission, gay flowered sacques abound looped over bright petticoats, and worn over the enormous hoops that were still in fashion this year, and which it required all the skill of a navigator to pilot safely about in the crowd. The women's shoulders rise bare out of the smooth edge of the low bodies, hemmed perhaps with pearls, but unfinished by lace or ruffle. Where the sacques are not worn the full brocade skirts are trimmed with wide lace flounces that repeat themselves in enormous frills at the elbows; and beneath the point of the long stiff bodice which Walpole deplores coming into fashion in 1745, a costly lace apron falls sometimes from the waist to the feet; the hair is smoothly drawn back from the temples, adorned perhaps with a single star or spray of diamonds, or a simple string of pearls, for the hideous fashion of high cushioned heads has not yet come in. And the men do not fear to vie also with so much gorgeous display. Their coats too are made of lovely flowered brocades that would stand alone with their own richness; their waistcoats are of cut velvet, their exquisitely fitting knee-breeches of lovely flowered satins; their high-heeled shoes are adorned with huge paste buckles, and priceless lace ruffles hang at their wrists and from the throats of their fine lawn shirts; their fingers are covered with handsome rings, and their watch chains sparkle with jewels; their hair is elaborately dressed, and their smart court hats are tucked away under their arms, that they may the better bring their feet together and make the obsequious bow of the period, or tap their jewelled snuff-boxes as they pay their court to the ladies. Surely the word fop must have been invented in such an age! "Lovely Mrs. Pitt" is there, sister to Sir Richard Atkins. She is, perhaps, of all the belles the popular favorite this year. She was mobbed in the Park last week, and that is a great sign of success in those times, and insures attention at the next assembly. But, alas! she is

madly in love with her husband, and that is a poor recommendation to social favor. There is beautiful Lady Mary Capel,

"In whose smiling, bounteous look
Rich autumn's goddess is mistook";

and there sweet Caroline Campbell, Countess of Aylesbury, "mild as a summer sea, serene," sweeps softly across the grass. Who are those two pretty, slim girls yonder in the shade? The warm spring sunshine flickers still, and lamps will not be lit yet awhile. They are the two Misses Evelyn, rivals of the "pretty Bishops"; and she who comes something haughtily past them is that "majestic Juno" Miss Lepelle Hervey, who, in spite of her beauty, Walpole vows is a thought masculine. The celebrated beauty Peggy Banks is there, perhaps with my Lady Lincoln for chaperon; and the Duchess of Bridgewater has brought her charming daughter, Lady Di Egerton. Peggy Banks is one of the Duke of Cumberland's many flames, and it is maybe at her side that he spends his time to-night; for the "Royals" have no compunction in showing their preferences openly. The King himself gave a ball t'other night for Miss Chudleigh at Vauxhall, and he walks around with her this evening in the dress described, and presently even "believes himself to be so much in love with her that he gives her a fairing for her watch at one of the booths, which must have cost him thirty-five guineas—actually disbursed from his own privy purse, and not charged on the civil list! I hope," adds Walpole, in cynical comment upon the well-known parsimoniousness of King George II., "some future Howe or Holinshed will acquaint posterity that thirty-five guineas was an immense sum in those days."

A little while ago, when the Duke of Cumberland was in his full zenith of popularity from the victory of Culloden, he gave Peggy Banks a ball—as it was the custom for gallants to do in those days—at Vauxhall. Walpole saw them get into their barges at Whitehall, and heard the City Companies, who had been up the river "swan-hopping," strike up the national anthem to him as they came by. The duke was near being drowned from the enthusiasm of the people, and had to retreat into the ball-room, where "five and twenty hundred people" were waiting for him. But the ball to Peggy Banks was only given "to pique my Lady Rochford for the Prince of Hesse," says Walpole. Perhaps there is a show of jealousy between the two beauties to-night at Ranelagh, and Lady Rochford—"with whom all the Royals have been in love"—is more majestic than ever in her stately fairness. Here, maybe, comes our old friend, bright, brilliant Lady Caroline Petersham, laughing and flirting as she unfurls her great fan, and bravely sprinkling her broad fun among the company, regardless of the sharper arrows of such recognized wits as the Viscountess Townshend, mother of the well-known Charles, or of Lady Gower, Lady Walpole, and Mrs. Selwyn, all of whom are busy exchanging witticisms with Chesterfield and Bolingbroke and George Selwyn, and perhaps with Horace Walpole himself. They are not sparing of their victims, but then nobody dares be thin-skinned. No doubt they have no compunction in making fun of Lady Caroline's blunter darts for the sake of an extra *bon mot* of their own, but happily she is both too good-natured and too sure of her own conquests to mind. In and out among the booths or around the brightly lighted amphitheatre more gay folks wander in knots. She who was pretty Fanny Macartney, and is now the wife of Fulke Greville, Esq., stands talking with Horace Walpole. The young bride, however happy she may be in her newly found bliss, can still spare time for a blush and a smile and a pretty stare for an old friend. The polished man of the world is habited with an elegance that is far too distinguished to err on the side of vulgar gaudiness, even in those days of extravagant luxury; his finely chiselled features are set for once to a tune that is not cynical, as he stands in the presence of a "divinity," and idly toying with his jewelled snuff-box, forges his daintiest compliments in praise of the last and most becoming of gowns. Hard by is haughty Lady Ann Dawson, from whom Sir Joshua Reynolds is soon afterward to paint his lovely picture of the crescent-crowned Diana; and there, under a tree, gay Harry Vane whispers venturesome stories to little Miss Ashe. Brightly painted and gilded chairs, inclosing more unknown fair ones, are borne to the door every minute; the press is so great at the gate that it is impossible for coaches to set down without an affray.

As the tardy May daylight begins to lengthen at last into gloaming, and booths and tents and gaming tables glow with brilliant light, a whisper runs around among those sacred few who always know the last thing in gossip and scandal, and folk ask themselves where are the two sisters the renown of whose rare beauty has penetrated even from the Dublin court across the water. Some one tells of two tall figures of wondrous grace that have been seen here and there in the garden, and some one else of beautiful golden brown tresses seen above temples of ivory whiteness, of arched lips smiling beneath the edge of the mask, of bright eyes, of tiny feet peeping from beneath the ample skirts, of rippling laughter and silvery voices, and Lady Caroline Petersham's friends press around her to ask for details about her new *protégées*.

Of the men, the fops are languidly curious, the enthusiasts begin to have their curiosity inflamed; of the women, not one but is eager to know the worst, and not a few think it safer to begin depreciating mildly already. But the moment for unmasking arrives at last; the worst fears and the best hopes are realized at once—the interlopers are a success. There is no describing how or why: merit alone will not insure it, for society is so capricious. But silently the conviction comes home to all those who are in the secrets of its ways—the Gunnings are to be the new belles of the season. There is a subtle sinking in the hearts of all the vain women who fear rivals; and in the breasts of the two girls whose faces must be their fortunes who shall say that there is not a silent thrill of wild exultation?

The evening grows into night, and the night wears away into morning, and the two misses make many admirers and many foes, and a fair sprinkling of friends. Indeed, excepting those women who are jealous of new candidates to their title of beauties, every one likes the "wild Irish girls." The fops like them because of their countrified and undisguised love of a beau's fine coat and manners; the wits like them because of their fresh appreciation of the time-worn old jokes and puns; every one likes them because of their rare loveliness and grace. Nothing was wanting but that they should be received into the magic circle of the "first set," and that their good friend Lady Caroline Petersham, herself its queen, has achieved for them. Since she has held out her hand to them, every door will be opened; it is not to be only a "first ball success"; their triumph is complete, their careers are made. Little do any present imagine, envious as are the women, admiring as are the men, what the two "Irish adventurers" are going to achieve. For at that very ball, perhaps, there is one walking sedately among the gay guests who is to have no mean influence on the life of one of the sisters. He is not a very brave or gallant or handsome swain, he is "a grave young lord, of the remains of the patriot breed," and he rather disapproves of the merry doings of his age, and will not admire the white and carmine with which the pretty ladies think it necessary to touch up their beauty. Perhaps that is one reason why he is captivated to-night by this fresh loveliness that has not hitherto been tempted into spoiling nature's work. We fancy we see him there, standing silently by, as fresh introductions crowd upon the two beauties. He is afraid to come forward; he is afraid to venture into the ranks of the light adulators who surround the new divinity; he even thinks maybe that the divinity smiles too contentedly at the foolish flatteries that flit around her, shows too plainly her pleasure at wicked Lord March's compliments and cynical George Selwyn's patronage; but the net is about him, nevertheless, out of whose toils he is not to escape.

The next day, perhaps, when the fashionable hour comes round for the gay folk to show their pretty plumage by sunlight in the Park and the Mall, amorous swains of the night before are seen loitering with well-feigned carelessness at the corners of alleys and beneath the becoming shade of spreading trees, eager for another sight of the Cinderellas that have fired their imagination. And so deftly do the untutored lasses manage their affairs that before a month is over it has become the mode to waylay them in the Mall, to track them around the Park, until the police have to be in attendance when the sisters go to fit on shoes in St. James Street, and thoroughfares are crowded half a mile down when it is known they are visiting at some house in the vicinity. "They can't walk in the Park or go to Vauxhall," Walpole says, "but such mobs follow them that they are generally driven away." Who cares though this unbounded notoriety be fraught now and then with some small inconvenience? "The other day," writes Walpole, "they went to see Hampton Court. As they were going into

the Beauty Room another company arrived. The housekeeper said, 'This way, ladies; here are the beauties.'" Though he goes on to declare that "the Gunnings flew into a passion, and asked her what she meant, and said that they had come to see the palace, not to be showed as a sight themselves," may we not take leave to wonder whether they were not also a little pleased at the success?

Gayly the two celebrities run their round of dissipations and amusements. First there is the presentation at court on a Sunday in December—as we learn from *Faulkner's Dublin Journal*, which also tells us that Drawing-rooms on a Sunday were then no rare occurrence—and this passport is enough to admit them to every kind of entertainment. We may follow them, in full dress, with patches and powder and lace and jewels—gifts of admiring gallants—to fashionable assemblies, balls, and masquerades; we may fancy them parading up and down the Mall in short hoop-skirts and lace flounces, and dainty high-heeled shoes, and coquettish lace caps, and looped Leghorn hats; we may watch them exchanging civilities with some perfumed beau from the windows of their dainty chairs at the Park gates; we may note them at merry Lady Caroline's Vauxhall "tea-fights," and rowdy tavern supper parties with fashionable dandies after the play. Their pretty faces are everywhere to be seen, listening with well-moderated interest to the somewhat coarse fun of Kitty Clive or Mrs. Pritchard in the *Beggar's Opera*, laughing at Margaret Woffington as Lady Betty Modish, at Garrick as Fribble in *A Miss in her Teens*, or as Benedick to Mrs. Pritchard's charming Beatrice—better than all, trembling at him as King Lear or Hamlet, and weeping at his sufferings as young Belmont, in that fashionable play of Moore's called *The Foundling*, where the distresses of the poor betrayed heroine were so ably played by Mrs. Cibber. They have their little court of elegant beaux around them, who, with jewelled snuff-boxes and unimpeachable manners, make love in the boxes for all the world as Barry does upon the stage.

Merrily the season rattles along, and merrily the belles pick their way through it. In spite of my Lord March's ill-natured innuendoes with regard to Maria and the Scotch earl, they hold their own, too, on the dangerous quicksands of society, and bravely scorn all small-fry in the hope of the highest prizes. Yet many a time must their hearts have fluttered uneasily behind their gallant unconcern, as their first season bids fair to hand them to its doors unwed; for, in spite of their popular success, even Maria has not yet been able quite to land that "grave young lord" about whom there have been so many unkind sneers. Undauntedly they pursue their prey to the gay round of watering-place duties at Bath, and deftly lead gallants on to madness with the coquettish head-gear and fascinating deshabille of the pump-room, but only to be obliged to return once more to work again in London with the New-Year of 1752. Now, however, their triumph is close at hand. Wrapped around in warm quilted satin pelisses and rich furs that set off the dazzling whiteness of their complexions, their tiny hands hidden away in huge muffs, and their tiny feet shod in golden-heeled shoes, the belles take up their stand once more in the Park, and make up their parties for Ranelagh, and engage their partners for balls and assemblies. Who is this who attends Elizabeth to her chair with such obsequious devotion? He is the scion of a great and ancient race, and many in the world of fashion look eagerly to his great marriage—though, to be sure, he is not one of whose love any woman need be proud. He has been jilted by the fast maid of honor Miss Chudleigh, afterward Duchess of Kingston, about whom there is one day to be a lawsuit for bigamy, and folks say he will run no risk of such a fate again where he pleases to set his heart. He is a man of parts, and might have done something in his day if he had not led a life which by this time has "equally damaged his person and his fortune."

Nevertheless, he is a great "catch" still, and the ambitious heart of Elizabeth Gunning must have beat indeed the other night at my Lord Chesterfield's brilliant assembly, "made to show his magnificent house!" For "the Duke of Hamilton," says Walpole, "having already fallen in love with her six weeks ago at a masquerade, made such violent love to her tonight at one end of the room, while he was playing at pharaoh at the other, that he saw neither the bank nor his own cards, which were of three hundred each, and soon lost a thousand." That is a fortnight ago now, and the passion has

not yet cooled. Those who watched them this morning in the Park begin to be sadly afraid that the duke will make a fool of himself. By to-morrow, at the same hour, they will be saying that he *has* made a fool of himself. For this very night, while her mother and sister are at Bedford House, Elizabeth Gunning is alone with her impetuous suitor, and makes him "so impatient," Walpole tells us, "that he sent for a parson. The doctor refused to perform the ceremony without a license or ring; the duke swore he would send for the archbishop. At last they were married with a ring of the bed-curtain at half an hour after twelve at night, at Mayfair Chapel." No wonder that "the Scotch are enraged and the women mad that so much beauty has had its effect." The poor daughter of an Irish squire is to hold such state that she will "walk in to dinner before her guests," and be Lady of the Bed-chamber to good Queen Charlotte; she will become the mother of two Dukes of Hamilton, and live to be made a baroness in her own right, and to unite, by her second marriage, the two great houses of Hamilton and Argyll, becoming the mother of two dukes of the latter title also. No wonder that "in Ireland the peasant women greet you with 'The luck of the Gunnings attend you!'" For now that an example has been set, that more diffident and "grave young lord," the Earl of Coventry, takes his courage in his hand and determines to wed the elder sister. In March, 1752, we hear of their both being presented under their new titles, and learn that the excitement about them has by no means abated because of their rare good fortune, and that "even the noble mob in the drawing-room clambered upon chairs and tables to look at them, and that there are mobs at their doors to see them get into their chairs," while "people go early to get places at the theatres when it is known they will be there." By the May of that year we may imagine the ambitious mother, content at last with her daughters' achievements, quietly wending her way home again to the desolate Irish moor after having dispatched her darlings to their several castles.

She hears that "seven hundred people sat up all night in and about an inn in Yorkshire to see the Duchess of Hamilton get into her post-chaise next morning"; and she learns with satisfaction that her darlings still vie in the public interest even with the old Duchess of Devonshire's last charming vulgarity, and with the thrilling details of the execution of two murderesses, Misses Blandy and Jeffries, of whom witty Lady Gower said that "since the two misses were hanged, and the other two misses married, there was nothing at all talked of."

Presently the public papers tell her how "a shoemaker at Worcester, the county town for the earl's seat, gained two guineas and a half by showing a shoe he was making for the countess at a penny apiece"; and then she follows her dear Maria's success in Paris, when, in the July of the same year, she goes there with Lady Caroline Petersham. No doubt the fond parent is scarce of the opinion of those who affirm that Lady Coventry "did no execution," and was even outshone by pretty Mrs. Pitt, who took a box opposite hers at her début at the Paris Opera, while even the "travelled English allow that there is a Madame De Brionne handsomer." She probably sympathized deeply with her poor child for being placed at "such a terrible disadvantage" by the "prudery" of her "dear Cov," who "will not suffer her to wear any red or powder." One of the fair Maria's non-admirers was even condescendingly sorry "that, added to her extreme silliness, ignorance of the world and of the French language, she had that perpetual drawback on her beauty." So scrupulous was "dear Cov" on this point that he chased his wife round the table before a party of sixteen persons on one occasion, and scrubbed off with a napkin the "little red she had stolen on." To be sure, as Chesterfield, writing soon afterward to Dayrolles, affirms, "she did not want it," and the poisonous white which she did manage to steal on soon "ruined both her natural complexion and her teeth," and even engendered, tradition has it, the fatal disease which finally killed her in the flower of her youth. Yet she only followed the mad fashion of her time, and it was rather hard her lord should mortify her so for a little piece of natural vanity. According to Chesterfield, he "used her so brutally in Paris that he made her cry more than once in public," and on one occasion obliged her to "ask for a fan back again which she had civilly given to the Maréchale De Lowenthal, and send an old one in its place, because the presented one had been a marriage gift from himself."

If these statements are correct, she certainly had not a husband of worldly knowledge sufficient to cover her own ignorance, and it is little wonder she used to complain of him in a childish kind of way, inquiring openly why "her lord treated her so ill when he loved her so, and had been so good as to marry her without a shilling." Glad indeed must the mother have been when her treasure was safe back in England, where everything she did and said and wore won unmitigated applause, where witty George Selwyn himself had a fondness for so lovely a simpleton, and would advise her and shield her and warn her, as he did once, that a "birth-night dress" covered with large silver coins might make her look "like change for a guinea." At home even the old King so easily condoned the offenses of such a beautiful face that he would laughingly tell the story of how my Lady Coventry had deplored to him that "the only sight she had not yet seen was a coronation." But no doubt these little peccadilloes — mere specks on the sun, after all—did not reach the mother's ears any more than the inevitable little social scandals could penetrate such complete solitude as the lonely precincts of Castle Coote. For there were "scandals" whispered about the beauties. Even Walpole descends to repeating one about my Lady Coventry and Bolingbroke, nephew of the great earl, though he will not swear to its authenticity: "T'other night at the masquerade the King sent for Lady Coventry to dance," he says, "and I believe if he had offered her a boon, she would have asked for the head of St. John." The innamorati were, however, both short of their twentieth year, and something must be forgiven to an untutored girl who is made a lady of quality in her teens.

At all events, in spite of any little whispered tales, Lady Coventry continued to be as great a favorite as ever. Walpole may hint at her beauty being impaired by illness, and at her having a great rival in a certain Miss Wynne, but the truth remains that in 1755 even he swears "she looked better than ever" at one of the masquerades, while we find a tale alleging that an American lady accosted her as she removed her mask at a ball, and, courtesying to her after the manner of the day, said, with feeling, "Madam, I have crossed the Atlantic to see you, and I am not disappointed." Mobs still followed the sisters' steps, and dressmakers copied their costumes; and yet, if we may believe an old lady's verdict, these were not always in the height of fashion, for Lady Coventry at least seems to have had good taste enough to ignore modes that were ungraceful. "Yesterday," writes old Mrs. Delany, "the duchess brought Lady Coventry to feast me, and a feast she was. She has a thousand airs, but with a sort of innocence that diverts one. Her dress was a black silk sack made for a large hoop, which she wore without any, so that it trailed a yard on the ground; she had a cobweb laced handkerchief, a pink satin long cloke lined with ermine mixed with squirrel-skins. On her head a French cap, that just covered the top of it, of blond, standing up in the form of a butterfly with the wings not quite extended; frilled sort of lappets crossed under her chin, and tied with pink ribbon—a head-dress that would have charmed a shepherd! She has a thousand dimples and prettinesses in her cheeks; her eyes a little drooping at the corners, but very fine for all that."

What a sweet picture! And here is another, none the less fascinating. The scene is Walpole's castle of Strawberry Hill; the company the serenely beautiful Caroline Campbell, Countess of Aylesbury, no less perfect in her mature charms than her lovely daughter, the Duchess of Richmond, who stands beside her; Elizabeth Gunning, Duchess of Hamilton, and Maria Gunning, Countess of Coventry, each at the ripest moment of her matchless beauty. Who could desire a fairer sight than to watch these lounge upon the great terrace, watching the sunset as they sip their coffee and fan themselves languidly with their great fans? Walpole certainly did not, and swears he will tell the younger generation how much handsomer the women of his time were, when he could muster four such faces at a sitting, and could frankly tell that one who was a mother that she was as handsome as her own daughter. Sir Joshua Reynolds should have been there to see such a picture; but unfortunately, among the many and many exquisite records of fair women that he has left us—the mother and daughter of this group among them—we have to regret that his brush had not yet attained its highest skill before the Gunnings' beauty was at the waning, and that the portraits he has left were scarce-

ly true emblems of that extraordinary loveliness.

Other artists, Cotes and Reade and Latour and others, set down those rare features for posterity both in miniature and on canvas, the picture of the two sisters washing and ironing, by Moreland, being perhaps the popular favorite; but no one with Sir Joshua's genius ever, so far as we can learn, attempted the task, and he came to it too late. For we find that the duchess and her sister did not sit to the great painter until the year 1759—at the same time that he was also painting the two great rival courtesans, beautiful Kitty Fisher and bewitching Nelly O'Brien—and alas by this time the beauty of Lady Coventry, at least, must have already borne terrible signs of the advancing end. She saw her sister a widow and a bride once more, when Betty refused the Duke of Bridgewater to make that Campbell match which Walpole vows was "the prettiest in the world," though *he* would have been afraid to be the husband of a Gunning, lest he should be "hustled out of the world to make room for another adventure." Maria was even "in all her former beauty" at the time, but it was but a last flicker. When that royal coronation took place which she had so earnestly wished to see, the poor "standard beauty" lay on a bed whence she was never to rise again. Would that she had followed her strict lord's wishes a little more faithfully, and had shown as good taste in the matter of painting her face as in that of discarding the hideous fashion of hoops! If tradition is to be believed, the disease bred of Irish fogs might thus have been kept under. Be that as it may, poor foolish, good-natured, beautiful Maria is dying. Other beauties — the coronation beauties — are growing up in her place, and she will soon be forgotten. There is sad, pensive Lady Bolingbroke, whose husband has deserted her for the famous Miss O'Brien, and her sister, Lady Pembroke, "the picture of majestic modesty"; there is Elizabeth Gunning, Duchess of Hamilton, now a baroness in her own right, and the wife of Jack Campbell, and soon to be Duchess of Argyll and Lady of the Bed-chamber to the new Queen; there is splendid Lady Kildare, and "a pretty Lady Sutherland, and a perfect beauty, an Irish Miss Smith" (afterward Lady Llandaff); "lovely Mrs. Pitt" has returned from Italy, too, and is holding her own again; and there is

MARIA WALPOLE.—FROM THE PAINTING BY SIR JOSHUA REYNOLDS.
Photographed by the Autotype Company, London.

bright, witty little Lady Essex, Prince Edward's love, like a rich, dark damask rose, with her cherry lips and melting eyes. She, poor soul, has but little hope left either, for not long after this she is to die of "a bad kind of throat," following the fairer queen of belles where beauty is of no account. The Duchess of Rutland is at the height of her success; so are the Duchess of Richmond and that other most distinguished and graceful of duchesses, with "far more dignity and address" than the Duchess of Hamilton, "one of our first great ladies," the *spirituelle* Duchess of Grafton. Then there are the bridemaids to good plain little Queen Charlotte, who can not have chosen them as foils to an ugliness of which a courtier was heard to say later that, "thank God, the bloom of it was wearing off!" Lady Sarah Lenox, afterward Lady Sarah Bunbury, Lady Susan Strangways, Lady Caroline Russell, afterward Duchess of Marlborough, Lady Elizabeth Keppel, afterward Marchioness of Tavistock, and many of the other bridemaids, were all among Sir Joshua Reynolds's favorite sitters, although perhaps the two countesses are constantly mentioned together, and are quoted as being mobbed while walking in the Park in June, 1759. Speaking of his beautiful niece, Walpole declares, "She is beauty

MRS. BOUVERIE AND MRS. CREWE.—FROM THE PAINTING BY SIR JOSHUA REYNOLDS.
Photographed by the Autotype Company, London.

one of the loveliest models he ever had was the beautiful Maria Walpole, Countess of Waldegrave, who could not at that time be admitted at court.

Some ten years afterward this beautiful and gifted woman won for herself the affections of the royal family, to which she was reluctantly admitted because of her secret marriage with the Duke of Gloucester, the King's brother. At this time, however, she had not yet risen to such high dignity, for it was before her first husband died of the terrible smallpox through which she nursed him so heroically, and she was only Maria, Countess of Waldegrave, "one of the loveliest women of her time," and evidently one of the most intimate friends of the poor belle into whose shoes she was to step, for

itself; her face bloom, eyes, teeth, hair, and person, all perfect"; and describing her again, "in a white silver gown," at her own wedding, he particularizes these charms as "warm complexion tending to brown, fine eyes, brown hair, fine teeth, and infinite wit and vivacity"; while on another occasion he speaks of her tall and graceful figure. The portraits of her show the keen eyes, arched mouth, slightly Roman nose, and rich hair growing low on the forehead, sometimes turned back beneath a coiffure *à la* Mary Stuart; but in Sir Joshua's lovely portrait of her with her child we find the gentle modesty which her uncle eulogizes as the "sweetest delicacy in the world" dwelt upon with greater emphasis than the more queenly side of the character, while the shade of the hair in-

EMMA LYON, LADY HAMILTON.
From the painting by George Romney.

clines more to golden than Walpole would lead us to suppose—a detail borne out by the fact that a "lock of delicate golden brown hair" was found many years after in Sir Joshua's pocket-book, with a ticket bearing the name of Maria, Countess of Waldegrave. This little anecdote proves the affection with which the great man regarded his lovely sitter, of whom he always spoke in terms of the highest praise. And if anything were needed to justify Walpole's evident partiality in the appreciation of his niece's beauty, it would be this homage of one who knew and painted all the fairest women of his day in every class of society, not to dwell upon the fact that it was left to the illegitimate daughter of a poor seamstress to become a royal princess and mother to children of the blood.

Such, then, were the new belles who were springing up, as it were, around the death-bed of her who could once have held a candle to them all. When the royal pageant was in course of preparation in which, if fate had willed it, she would have held so proud a place, "poor Lady Coventry was concluding her short race, with the same attention to her looks" which she had displayed throughout her lifetime. "She lay," says Walpole, "constantly on a couch, with a pocket-glass in her hand, and when that told her how great the change was, she took to her bed, and, the last fortnight, had no light in her room but the lamp of a tea-kettle, and at last took things in through the curtains of her bed without suffering them to be undrawn. The mob, who never quitted curiosity about her, went, to the number of ten thousand, only to see her coffin. If she had lived to ninety, like Helen, I believe they would have thought her wrinkles deserved an epic poem. Poor thing! how far from ninety! she was not twenty-eight!"

Strange as is the flight of the Gunnings' career, the romance of Emma Lyon's is a hundredfold more marvellous. Born of peasant parents, brought up in the most abject poverty by a widowed mother, deprived of the means of the commonest education, and placed, at the age of fourteen years, as nursery-maid in a physician's family, this wonderful girl found the means of instructing herself at least in the more superficial branches of a lady's education. She cultivated the rare gift of a musical voice with which nature had endowed her, and after going through the various vicissitudes of reigning as the petted favorite of two gentlemen of good position, consecutively shining as the most graceful of horsewomen upon the valuable mounts of Sir Harry Featherstonhaugh in the county of Sussex, figuring in the nude as an illustration of the beauty of health in the show of a quack-doctor, posing to the painter George Romney for all his most beautiful pictures, she positively succeeded in duping a gentleman of the name of Greville into believing her an innocent little seamstress, and accepted his offer of educating her to be a worthy companion of his cultured existence.

And so fitly did he form and tutor that gifted nature that as years ripened the girlish loveliness into womanly grace and beauty, the native genius of a most receptive mind was developed so well in every direction that the laborer's daughter became a lady able to compete with the shrewdest intellects in the land. Nor was her education neglected in the more special departments of her own rare musical and dramatic gifts. One evening Ranelagh—the scene of so many strange conquests and wonderful pictures — was convulsed as it had perhaps never been before, even in the days of its favorite belle, the lovely and simple Maria.

There had been beauties since her day. Lovely, witty Mrs. Crewe—Fanny Macartney's daughter—and her inseparable friend pretty Mrs. Bouverie, in the days when "True blue and Mrs. Crewe" had been the great Whig toast for the charming Whig canvasser; the beautiful and distinguished Duchess of Buccleugh, with her oval face and sad eyes; and the Marchioness of Tavistock, whom Sir Joshua has struck so statelily for us upon his canvas ; gentle Mrs. Brinsley Sheridan, with her long throat and clear-cut features, and those plaintive dark eyes that we always seem to see turned to heaven, as in his picture of her as St. Cecilia playing the organ. These—not to speak of handsome Miss Pelham, the painter's pet, of "poor Perdita" (Mrs. Robinson), beloved of the Prince of Wales, and even of "that artful coquette with amorous eyes and eyelashes a yard long," Anne Luttrell (Mrs. Horton), who bewitched the King's brother into marrying her—all have flitted across the stage of Ranelagh, but none have taken it by storm as it was taken that evening when Mr. Greville brought an unknown belle into its precincts.

Later on, after her separation from Mr. Greville, Emma Lyon was married to Sir William Hamilton, his Majesty's ambassador at Naples. For a short year society shut its eyes to whispered tales, and welcomed the fair one to its arms, that her matchless beauty, her rare dramatic and musical gifts, her winning and distinguished manners, might draw admiring and curious crowds to their assemblies.

All the belles of the season were eclipsed for the moment. Lady Cadogan's pert prettiness made no way, and even the brilliant Duchess of Devonshire herself had, we may fancy, to give way for a short space to this turbulent rush of wonderful notoriety; while as for the fashionable scandals of the hour, such as the Prince of Wale's secret marriage with comely Mrs. Fitzherbert, they were fairly smothered by this far more marvellous *mésalliance*. But the new belle was fortunately not to risk living through her success into the cold region of bad memories revived that lay beyond. Little more than a year after her marriage Lady Hamilton returned to Naples, laden with the "lamentations of fashionable life," and with her departure ends our consideration of her as a society belle. Of her strange and uncanny friend-

MRS. BRINSLEY SHERIDAN AS ST. CECILIA.—FROM THE PAINTING BY SIR JOSHUA REYNOLDS.
Photographed by the Autotype Company, London.

ship with the Queen of Naples, of her un-deniable influence on the politics of the Neapolitan court, of the services she is supposed to have rendered to the English nation by her efforts to assist Lord Nelson's enterprises, and last, but not least, of her romantic amours with the great ad-miral, and the almost magical fascination which she exercised upon him, we have little to do, for they are matters of history and not of society talk. A few years after Lord Nelson's death Lady Hamilton herself died at Calais, whither she had fled from her London creditors.

AT THE NARROWS.

Fort Lafayette.

APPROACHES TO NEW YORK.

I.—BY THE SEA.

THOSE who have approached New York by the sea need not be told that the harbor of New York is exceedingly beautiful. It has also other advantages. It is not separated from the ocean by a long river like the Thames, nor by an island wall like Ireland, as Liverpool is, and while the Atlantic beats up to the very entrance, the turbulence of the sea is shut out by a circle of hills which form a basin large enough to shelter all the fleets of the world. The conformation of the estuary lends itself to a system of fortification which in the event of war could be made impregnable; the bar admits vessels of the largest draught at all seasons; the shoals are in a measure permanent, and do not harass the mariner by the gradual changes which in some harbors necessitate the discovery of new passages; the currents are not strong or treacherous, and the beacons, lights, and buoys are numerous and distinct. The many captains to whom I have spoken at various times in reference to New York Harbor have all praised it for its capacity, safety, and ease of access. If it has any disadvantages, they are such as result from the far-reaching corruption and incompetency of the municipal government.

The bluffs of the Highlands and the sandy spit of the Hook are passed; then the quiet embouchure of Raritan Bay, with fleets of fishing-boats. On one side Staten Island, hilly, and green to the water's edge, bends to meet the opposite shore, and where the distance between them is

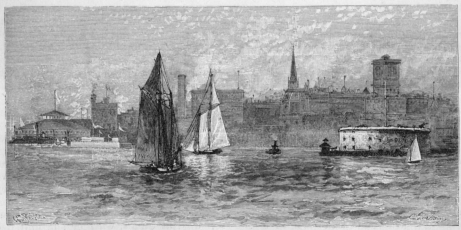

Castle Garden.

VIEW OF NEW YORK FROM BELOW GOVERNOR'S ISLAND.

EASTERN STEAMERS ROUNDING THROGG'S NECK.

least stand Fort Richmond and Fort Hamilton, which together could hurl such fire upon an invader as would cripple him at the portals of the city.

Just beyond the Narrows (as the passage between the forts is called) the two shores curve further apart, forming the upper bay, at the head of which the city lies. A blue haze wreathes itself around Staten Island, upon the heights of which are villas that, from a distance at least, appear tasteful and attractive. The Long Island shore, losing the white, barren, sandy aspect it has outside the Narrows, becomes woody and fertile. The water is a clear green, and even the vessels have a holiday cleanness novel to the emigrant, who, before he reaches Castle Garden, is charmed by the little he sees of his future home.

If we should say there are safe moorings for nearly all the navies of the world, our readers would still be unable to comprehend the vast space available in the harbor. Measurements are more explicit. The Hudson or North River washes thirteen miles of the city's shore-line, every foot of which may be made available for vessels of the greatest tonnage; the East River washes nine and a quarter miles, most of which may also be made available to vessels of all classes; and the Harlem River has an available frontage of two and a quarter miles. The area of the Hudson and East rivers immediately opposite the city which is available for anchorage is thirteen and a half square miles, the anchorage of the upper bay is fourteen square miles, and that of the lower bay eighty-eight square miles. Thus, besides twenty-four and a half miles of wharfage, we have over one hundred and fifteen square miles so safe that the gale would need to be of uncommon force which could drag a ship whose anchor had been cast upon any spot of this wide area.

II.—BY THE SOUND.

But the channels through the bays are not the only inlet from the sea to the city, though all vessels of the greatest burden select them. Another approach is by the way of Long Island Sound, which is stirred by a hurrying fleet of smaller traders, both sail and steam.

The Sound itself is wide and deep enough for any vessels, and though the waves run high after prolonged storms,

Long Island is interposed between it and the ocean. On both sides of it there are fashionable summer resorts, quiet old fishing villages with primitive inhabitants, and long expanses of prosperous farmland. In the summer weather its banks blend the charms of the country and the shore. From a stretch of pasturage or the porch of a farm-house we look down upon a motionless schooner with brown sails, or a snowy yacht so airy and phantomlike that she appears to be hung in a mirage.

At the southwestern extremity the Sound becomes a narrow strait with low grassy banks. There are boat-houses at the water's edge, and trim little cat-boats and sloops are moored to private wharves. Straggling little canals lead off into the sedge, which ripples in the wind; and along here, toward five o'clock in the afternoon, is a sight which can not be seen anywhere else in the world. Between the low banks, and towering above them, come the steamers which connect at New London, Stonington, Providence, and Fall River with the railway for Boston, their colors streaming, and the passengers promenading to the music of their string bands. These vessels are the principal feature of travel on the Sound, and in size and luxury of appointments they are superior to all others. They rival in size and surpass in beauty ocean steamers, and their brilliant whiteness and gay flags are reflected in the water, which swells and dashes in big waves on the shore as they pass. Another fleet comes from the opposite direction in the morning; and standing at the bow of one of these as we round Throgg's Neck and Fort Schuyler, we may briefly end our survey of the second approach to New York from the sea. We pass Ward's and Randall's islands with their enormous red brick charities; the Harlem curves off to the northwest; and here, where that river and the Sound join the East River, a strong current shows the former site of Hell Gate. Now our course is almost due south down the East River, which for nearly half a mile is divided into two channels by Blackwell's Island, with its work-houses, hospitals, and prisons; then the stream widens from an eighth of a mile or less to a mile, and the view on both sides includes the half-hidden streets, the close buildings, and the roofy wilderness of the metropolis. Soon the boat passes under the wide span of the Brooklyn Bridge, and, rounding the Battery, reaches its pier on the Hudson River.

III.—BY RAIL AND FERRY FROM THE WEST.

Whoever has approached the city as a stranger must remember the experience of some emotion which is revived, in memory at least, as often as he retraces the path. The character of the emotion is determined by the object which brings the pilgrim hither; it may be hope, apprehension, or delight; and the quiet observer may see all of these at work among the passengers on a train that has come a long distance toward New York. After leaving Trenton, which, though it is some fifty miles from this city, is an outpost of it in the idea of those who have travelled a thousand miles, the stations and the villages become more and more frequent; the road widens, and has four tracks, and we are constantly meeting other trains. Big signs confront us with offers of desirable building sites, and we see gangs of workmen putting up new villas and laying open new streets. New Brunswick, Elizabeth, and Newark are left behind, and then the landscape changes. The suburban cottage with its garden and orchard and suggestiveness of tranquil domesticity, the plenteous farm-lands, the growing little towns with the chiming of the trowels, are absent, and instead we see a great flat wilderness of brownish-green marshes, stagnant but for the train, which, if we could stand away from it and watch, would appear like some long black monster hurrying through the desert. The Passaic River flows alongside the tracks for some distance, and winds off into Newark Bay; we are carried over the Hackensack on a high bridge, which gently sways under the weight upon it. At times a wonderful light dwells on the dull green sedge of the marshes, which at sunset glows with crimson fires that give it a grandeur many artists have found out. At the edge of the marshes we are whirled through another village, and thence the railway is in a deep rock cutting, with a sharp curve that suddenly brings you into Jersey City, through which we are carried between two rows of shops and dwellings, with only a low fence on each side to separate the track from the street. A quick transfer is made to the ferry-boats which are in waiting, partings are said, a gong is struck, and in ten minutes more we

West Shore Railroad.　　　Brooklyn Bridge.　　VIEW OF NEW YORK FROM WEEHAWKEN HEIGHTS, NEW JERSEY.　　Del. and Lac. R.R., Erie R.R., Pa. R.R., and Cent. R.R. of N. J.

APPROACH TO NEW YORK BY THE HUDSON.

stand in a crowd of solicitous hack-drivers and expressmen on the New York side.

The tonnage of the ferry-boats now in use varies from seven hundred and twenty-five to one thousand and twenty-two, the value of each of them is over one hundred thousand dollars, and the computed horse-power of one is seven hundred and twenty-five. Unlike the English ferry-boats, which are ocean steamers in miniature, these are a type by themselves; their hulls support a huge deck overhanging the water, and stout enough to resist all sorts of "bumps"; in the centre is a roadway divided into two parts by the narrow space required for the walking-beam which drives the side-wheels; and on either side is a long, covered cabin for foot-passengers. The deck is rounded at both ends, and as the boat reaches her landing "end on," it fits closely into the "slip." It is as though a section of roadway shuttled to and fro between the shores; and the living freight loads and unloads itself down the "bridge," or tidal float, on the one side, and up that on the other, with surprising facility. Some of these ferry-boats, as the *Maryland*, which makes the journey around New York, from the Jersey to the Harlem shore, are fitted with rails, and can take a whole railway train at a load.

The Pennsylvania is only one of a number of great roads which reach the metropolis by means of ferries from the New Jersey side of the river. The New Jersey Central crosses Newark Bay on a viaduct of pile-work nearly two miles long; the Erie Railway enters Jersey City over salt-meadows adjoining those crossed by the Pennsylvania road; the Delaware and Lackawanna comes through the sylvan valleys of the Orange Mountains, and also runs across the meadows parallel with the Pennsylvania; the new West Shore line accords with its name by following the west bank of the Hudson from Albany to its terminus at Weehawken, nearly oppo-

site Forty-second Street; and still other suburban lines make the New Jersey shore, as seen from the heights of Wee-hawken, a very gridiron of rails.

IV.—BY THE HUDSON RIVER.

But the approach most famed for its picturesqueness—famed, indeed, the world over—is that from the north by the Hudson River. The summer traveller reaching Albany from Montreal or Saratoga has choice of three routes—the New York Central and Hudson River Railroad, hugging the shore at the water level on the east side, in its day one of the greatest feats of railroad engineering; the new "West Shore" line, already referred to, which runs now inland through pleasant rural landscape, now close by the water's side, or on the edge of a height that gives fine outlook over the rolling stream below—each a part of great routes from the West; and, finest of all, by Albany "day boat" or "night boat," both of them superb specimens of river craft, not unlike the Sound steamers. The "day boat" leaves Albany about eight, and reaches New York, a hundred and fifty miles distant, before six, making landings here and there. The passage through the Highlands is reached at West Point, where, between Storm King and Anthony's Nose, the great river, narrowed and deepened, breaks its way through a spur of the Appalachian chain of mountains. Below here the river widens into the calm expanse of the Tappan Sea, and thence to New York the east-side hills are crowned with the finest villas that the metropolis can show, while villages and minor cities nestle at the river's edge or climb half-way up the hills. The Palisades come in sight at last—the long bare face of mountain-wall that seems set to confine the great river in its due course —and soon we pass the picturesque north end of Manhattan Island, and catch our first glimpse of the great city.

V.—BY THE GRAND CENTRAL SYSTEM.

The only approach to New York which avoids the ferries is that by the railways which, reaching the island by the bridge over the Harlem River, land their passengers at the Grand Central Depot. These include the Hudson River Railroad, which leaves the banks of the river at the entrance to Spuyten Duyvil Creek, where (though a branch still borders the river down to Sixty-eighth Street) the main line diverges, and passes under High Bridge, that splendid piece of masonry by which the Croton Aqueduct is carried over the

precludes the possibility of collisions, except through the failure of the signaling machinery or the carelessness of those in charge, but also, it seems to us, embodies, with a force that can not fail to excite wonder, the highest results attained in mechanical science. Electricity, captive and subject to an ivory disk not larger than the tip of a lady's finger, conveys by semaphore the invisible, inaudible, and unmistakable messages that need no transcription, and that control the movements of hundreds of trains rushing to and from the city in a chain which with a few connections

Hudson River Railroad.

HIGH BRIDGE.

Harlem River; the Harlem, which comes from the north over the hills of Westchester; and the New Haven, which, passing the pretty suburban towns of Connecticut, connects Boston and the rest of New England with New York. The Hudson River, the New Haven, and the Harlem meet at a point some five miles above Forty-second Street, and enter the city on the same tracks. From the Harlem River to One-hundred-and-sixteenth Street the tracks, four in number, are carried through a sunken cut, thence to Ninety-eighth Street they are on a viaduct; thence to Fifty-third Street they are in a tunnel, and thence they are again in a sunken cut until they emerge into the station yard. The viaduct, tunnel, and the walls of the cuts are substantially built of masonry, and this approach is by far the most convenient of all. All trains are operated by the block system, which in its perfection not only

would be endless—control them not merely by indicating to the engineers what it is proper to do, but more effectually by making it impossible for the engineers to do otherwise, except in the face of extreme peril.

The mainspring of the system is in an octagonal observatory, not much larger than the clock at the other end, projecting from the northern wall of the Grand Central Depot at a dizzy height from the floor—a position which commands a view of the interior and the tracks outside, and at a glance seems inaccessible, though in fact it is easily reached from the offices in the western wing of the building.

Come with us up here, reader, or if the narrow gallery which we have to trace is at an elevation greater than your nerves are equal to, picture the place from these details. A box inconveniently small for three persons, with a glass inclosure, revealing on one side the depot partly filled with cars, and on the other side the tracks converging into the deep cutting that leads northward: the depot is very quiet, and a few knots of manikins are discussing Lilliputian affairs on the platforms, while others, quite unconscious that we are watching them, are gathering up their skirts and packages and hurrying into the cars. The furniture of our lookout consists of a chair, a desk, a table, a clock, and what an organist would call a "bank" of ivory keys about the size of the chips used in games of cards, besides which there are a few wires secured to the walls and bells. You now have an account of all the visible apparatus with which the electrician in the signal-box is provided, and by which he regulates the arrival and departure of over one hundred and fifty trains daily.

The train in the depot which the people are entering is the 2.20 P.M. to New Haven. At two o'clock the electrician depresses one of the keys, which are divided into three sets, one set, classified X, for Harlem trains, another, classified Y, for New Haven trains, and the third, classified Z, for Hudson River trains. Each key has engraved upon it a word indicating its purpose, and that just touched in the Y set opens the doors leading from the New Haven waiting-rooms to the New Haven platform. The corresponding key in the X set would open the doors of the Harlem waiting-rooms, and that in the Z set the Hudson River waiting-rooms. Only passengers holding tickets and the officials are admitted to the platforms, and even the former are excluded until twenty minutes before the departure of the train. From two o'clock, when the doors are opened, until "two-fifteen" the "two-twenty" train gradually fills without confusion, and the electrician then depresses another key in the Y set, which warns tardy passengers that they have only five minutes to spare before the departure of the train, and also intimates to the baggage men that they are to stop checking baggage. Precisely at "two-twenty," the advertised time of departure, another key is touched, which closes the door leading from the waiting-room, and thirty seconds are allowed to enable those who have just entered upon the platform to board the train. At the end of these moments of grace, during which the knots of talkers break up and the stragglers enter the cars, the dispatcher, as the electrician is technically called, puts his finger upon a fourth key, that sounds a bell attached to a pillar by which a locomotive is standing outside the depot; and at this signal the locomotive backs in, and, when it is coupled to the foremost car, glides off with the train with the extremest smoothness. Observe that during the five or six seconds spent in coupling, the locomotive is not wholly within the depot; the smokestack is kept outside the wall, for the managers are careful of the fresh blue and gray paint with which the interior of the building is decorated.

Trains, like ships, are cast in the feminine gender by their operators, and the moment the "two-twenty" is started, the dispatcher telegraphs by an ordinary instrument the number of cars *she* includes to the signal-man at the junction above Mott Haven, that the latter official may see that no cars have been inadvertently left behind, and at the same time he depresses another of the small ivory keys, which "blocks" the railway from the "cross-over" at Fifty-third Street to the depot. A word of explanation is necessary here. The outgoing trains leave the depot and proceed as far as the "cross-over" on the western tracks, when they are thrown over to the eastern tracks; similarly the incoming trains approach the city on the western track until they reach the "cross-over," which throws them to the eastern track, the change being necessitated by the fact that the depot must be approached from the eastern side. Now the key which the dispatcher touches as the "two-twenty" leaves the depot sets all the signals in positions and colors which forbid any train to pass the "cross-over" until she is clear of it, and a bell rings continually with great liveliness in the dispatcher's lookout; but as she clears it the bell ceases, and she touches a track instrument which automatically reverses all the signals, and shows that the line is open for other trains. A track instrument is a very simple-looking contrivance—a slender iron shaft like a small street hydrant, placed a few inches from the rail, but the momentary pressure a wire connecting with it receives from the passage of the train causes it to change the color of all the lamps used in signaling between the depot and the "cross-over" at night, and all the daylight marks used for the same purpose, by a magic which eclipses the cleverest feats of Heller. Before our cicerone has finished his explanation a "pinging" bell is heard, announcing that the "two-twenty" has passed Seventy-second Street; and by this time another train is made up, and the electrician is repeating his previous performance on the ivory keys. The position of the dispatcher is a most responsible one, requiring the greatest caution and an intense degree of application. Until the "two-twenty" clears Seventy-second Street the track is blocked between that point and Fifty-third Street, but is open between Fifty-third and the depot; then the section between Seventy-second and Fifty-third is opened, and that between Seventy-second and Ninety-sixth is blocked. Meanwhile an incoming train signals itself to the dispatcher by a track instrument at Sixty-third Street; a minute later it is at the "cross-over," and the dispatcher, by touching another of the ivory keys, gives it a flying switch into the depot; that is to say, the locomotive is uncoupled from the cars, and they are thrown on one track, while it is thrown over to another.

The depot and all the plant between Forty-second Street and the junction above Mott Haven are used in common, as we have said, by the Harlem, the Hudson River, and the New Haven companies, which are separately and proportionately assessed by a distinct corporation known as the Grand Central. The Grand Central owns and operates the depot and all the tracks to the junction, and employs its own servants. The depot is the finest in America, and has few equals in Europe. It covers two blocks, and is spanned by a graceful arch of iron and glass, painted with delicate shades of blue and gray; instead of being the nerve-torturing Babel that some depots are, it is clean, cheerful, and orderly, the locomotives not being admitted until the minute of departure, and all persons except passengers and officials being excluded.

Here our account must end. The approaches to New York, as one thinks of them at his desk, seem like a heroic frieze, with multitudes of living figures coming and going in an interminable procession, the knight, the priest, the merchant, and the warrior—seekers after fortune and fortune's complement, fame; some to win both, others neither; and as we contemplate the variety of mankind and the diversity of motive which the procession suggests, the mechanical details sink into insignificance.

"OLD HICKORY."

DR. VON HOLST, the most philosophic of historians, when he passes from the period of John Quincy Adams to that of his successor, is reluctantly compelled to leave the realm of pure history for that of biography, and to entitle a chapter "The Reign of Andrew Jackson." This change of treatment could, indeed, hardly be helped. Under Adams all was impersonal, methodical, a government of laws and not of men. With an individuality quite as strong as that of Jackson— as the whole nation learned ere his life ended—it had yet been the training of his earlier career to suppress himself, and be simply a perfect official. His policy aided the vast progress of the nation, but won no credit by the process. Men saw with wonder the westward march of an expanding people, but forgot to notice the sedate, passionless, orderly administration that held the door open, and kept the peace for all. In studying the time of Adams, we think of the nation; in observing that of Jackson, we think of Jackson himself.

In him we see the first popular favorite of a nation now well out of leading-strings, and particularly bent on going alone. By so much as he differed from Adams, by so much the people liked him better. His conquests had been those of war, always more dazzling than those of peace; his temperament was of fire, always more attractive than one of marble. He was helped by what he had done, and by what he had not done. Even his absence of diplomatic training was almost counted for a virtue, because all this training was then necessarily European, and the demand had ripened for a purely American product.

It had been quite essential to the self-respect of the new republic, at the outset, that it should have at its head men who had coped with European statesmen on their own soil and not been discomfited. This was the case with each of the early successors of Washington, and in view of his manifest superiority this advantage was not needed. Perhaps it was in a different way a sign of self-respect that the new

ANDREW JACKSON.
Engraved by G. Kruell from the lithograph by La Fosse, copyrighted by M. Knoedler and Co.

republic should at last turn from this tradition, and take boldly from the ranks a strong and ill-trained leader, to whom all European precedent—and, indeed, all other precedent—counted for nothing. In Jackson, moreover, there first appeared upon our national stage the since familiar figure of the self-made man. Other Presidents had sprung from a modest origin, but nobody had made an especial point of it. Nobody had urged Washington for office because he had been a surveyor's lad; nobody had voted for Adams merely because stately old ladies designated him as "that cobbler's son." But when Jackson came into office the people had just had almost a surfeit of regular training in their Chief Magistrates. There was a certain zest in the thought of a change, and the nation certainly had it.

It must be remembered that Jackson was in many ways far above the successive modern imitators who have posed in his image. He was narrow, ignorant, violent, unreasonable; he punished his enemies and rewarded his friends. But he was, on the other hand—and his worst opponents hardly denied it—chaste, honest, truthful, and sincere. It was not commonly charged upon him that he enriched himself at the public expense, or that he deliberately invented falsehoods. And as he was for a time more bitterly hated than any one who ever occupied his high office, we may be very sure that these things would have been charged had it been possible. In this respect the contrast was enormous between Jackson and his imitators, and it explains his prolonged influence. He never was found out or exposed before the world, because there was nothing to detect or unveil; his merits and demerits were as visible as his long, narrow, firmly set features, or as the old military stock that encircled his neck. There he was, always fully revealed; everybody could see him; the people might take him or leave him—and they never left him.

Moreover, there was after the eight years of Monroe and the four years of Adams an immense popular demand for something piquant and even amusing, and this quality they always had from Jackson. There was nothing in the least melodramatic about him; he never posed or attitudinized — it would have required too much patience; but he was always piquant. There was formerly a good deal of discussion as to who wrote the once famous "Jack Downing" letters, but we might almost say that they wrote themselves. Nobody was ever less of a humorist than Andrew Jackson, and it was therefore the more essential that he should be the cause of humor in others. It was simply inevitable that during his progresses through the country there should be some amusing shadow evoked, some Yankee parody of the man, such as came from two or three quarters under the name of Jack Downing. The various records of Monroe's famous tours are as tame as the speeches which these expeditions brought forth, and John Quincy Adams never made any popular demonstrations to chronicle; but wherever Jackson went there went the other Jack, the crude first-fruits of what is now known through the world as "American humors." Jack Downing was Mark Twain and Hosea Biglow and Artemus Ward in one. The impetuous President enraged many and delighted many, but it is something to know that under him a serious people first found that it knew how to laugh.

The very extreme, the perfectly needless extreme, of political foreboding that marked the advent of Jackson furnished a background of lurid solemnity for all this light comedy. Samuel Breck records in his diary that he conversed with Daniel Webster in Philadelphia, March 24, 1827, upon the prospects of the government. "Sir," said Mr. Webster, "if General Jackson is elected, the government of our country will be overthrown; the judiciary will be destroyed; Mr. Justice Johnson will be made Chief Justice in the room of Mr. Marshall, who must soon retire, and then in half an hour Mr. Justice Washington and Mr. Justice Story will resign. A majority will be left with Mr. Johnson, and every constitutional decision hitherto made will be reversed." As a matter of fact, none of these results followed. Mr. Justice Johnson never became Chief Justice; Mr. Marshall retained that office till his death in 1835; Story and Washington also died in office; the judiciary was not overthrown, nor the government destroyed. But the very ecstasy of these fears stimulated the excitement of the public mind. No matter how extravagant the supporters of Jackson might be, they could hardly go farther in that direction than did the Websters in the other.

But it was not the fault of the Jackson

DANIEL WEBSTER.

From the painting by G. P. A. Healy.

party if anybody went beyond them in exaggeration. An English traveller, William E. Alexander, going in a stage-coach from Baltimore to Washington in 1831, records the exuberant conversation of six editors, with whom he was shut up for hours. "The gentlemen of the press," he says, "talked of 'going the whole hog' for one another, of being 'up to the hub' (nave) for General Jackson, who was 'all brimstone but the head, and that was aquafortis,' and swore if any one abused him he ought to be 'set straddle on an iceberg, and shot through with a streak of lightning.'" Somewhere between the dignified despair of Daniel Webster and the adulatory slang of these gentry we must look for the actual truth about Jackson's administration. The fears of the statesman were not wholly groundless, for it is always hard to count in advance upon the tendency of high office to make men more reasonable. The enthusiasm of the editors had a certain foundation; at any rate it was a part of their profession to like stirring times, and they had now the promise of them. After four years of Adams, preceded by eight years of Monroe, any party of editors in America, assembled in a stage-coach, would have showered epithets of endearment on the man who gave such promise in the way of lively items. No acute journalist could help seeing that a man had a career before him who was called "Old Hickory" by three-quarters of the nation, and who made "Hurrah for Jackson!" a cry so potent that it had the force of a popular decree.

There was, indeed, unbounded room for popular enthusiasm in the review of Jackson's early career. Born in such obscurity that it is doubtful to this day whether he was born in South Carolina, as he himself claimed, or on the North Carolina side of the line, as Mr. Parton thinks, he had a childhood of poverty and ignorance. He was taken prisoner as a mere boy during the Revolution, and could never forget that he had been wounded by a British officer whose boots he had refused to brush. Afterward, in a frontier community, he was successively farmer, shop-keeper, law student, lawyer, district attorney, judge, and Congressman, being first Representative from Tennessee, and then Senator, and all before the age of thirty-one. In Congress Albert Gallatin describes him as "a tall, lank, uncouth-looking personage, with long locks of hair hanging over his brows

and face, and a queue down his back tied in an eel-skin; his dress singular, his manners and deportment those of a backwoodsman." He remained, however, but a year or two in all at Philadelphia—then the seat of national government—and afterward became a planter in Tennessee, fought duels, subdued Tecumseh and the Creek Indians, winning finally the great opportunity of his life by being made a Major-General in the United States army on May 31, 1814. He now had his old captors, the British, with whom to deal, and entered into the work with a relish. By way of preliminary he took Pensacola, without any definite authority, from the Spaniards, to whom it belonged, and the English whom they harbored; and then turned, without orders, without support, and without supplies, to undertake the defense of New Orleans.

Important as was this city, and plain as it was that the British threatened it, the national authorities had done nothing to defend it. The impression prevailed at Washington that it must already have been taken, but that the President would not let it be known. The Washington *Republican* of January 17, 1815, said, "That Mr. Madison will find it convenient and will finally determine to abandon the State of Louisiana we have not a doubt." A New York newspaper of January 30, quoted in Mr. Andrew Stevenson's eulogy on Jackson, said, "It is the general opinion here that the city of New Orleans must fall." Apparently but one thing averted its fall—the energy and will of Andrew Jackson. On his own responsibility he declared martial law, impressed soldiers, seized powder and supplies, built fortifications of cotton bales, if nothing else came to hand. When the news of the battle of New Orleans came to the seat of government it was almost too bewildering for belief. The British veterans of the Peninsular war, whose march wherever they had landed had heretofore seemed a holiday parade, were repulsed in a manner so astounding that their loss was more than two thousand, while that of the Americans was but thirteen. By a single stroke the national self-respect was restored; and Henry Clay, at Paris, said, "Now I can go to England without mortification."

All these things must be taken into account in estimating what Dr. Von Holst calls "the reign of Andrew Jackson."

After this climax of military success he was for a time employed on frontier service, again went to Florida to fight Englishmen and Spaniards, practically conquering that region in a few months, but this time with an overwhelming force. Already his impetuosity had proved to have a troublesome side to it; he had violated neutral territory, had hung two Indians without justification, and had put to death, with no authority, two Englishmen, Ambrister and Arbuthnot. These irregularities did not harm him in the judgment of his admirers; they seemed in the line of his character, and helped more than they hurt him. In the winter of 1823–4 he was again chosen a Senator from Tennessee. Thenceforth he was in the field as a candidate for the Presidency, with two things to aid him—his own immense popularity and a friend. This friend was one William B. Lewis, a man in whom all the skillful arts of the modern wire-puller seemed to be born full-grown.

There was at that time (1824) no real division in parties. The Federalists had been effectually put down, and every man who aspired to office claimed to be Democratic-Republican. Nominations were irregularly made, sometimes by a Congressional caucus, sometimes by State Legislatures. Tennessee, and afterward Pennsylvania, nominated Jackson. When it came to the vote, he proved to be by all odds the popular candidate. Professor W. G. Sumner, counting up the vote of the people, finds 155,800 votes for Jackson, 105,300 for Adams, 44,200 for Crawford, 46,000 for Clay. Even with this strong popular vote before it, the House of Representatives, balloting by States, elected on the first trial John Quincy Adams. Seldom in our history has the cup of power come so near to the lips of a candidate and been dashed away again. Yet nothing is surer in a republic than a certain swing of the pendulum, afterward, in favor of any candidate to whom a special injustice has been done, and in the case of a popular favorite like Jackson this might have been foreseen to be irresistible. His election four years later was almost a foregone conclusion, but, as if to make it wholly sure, there came up the rumor of a "corrupt bargain" between the successful candidate and Mr. Clay, whose forces had indeed joined with those of Mr. Adams to make a majority. For General Jackson there could be nothing more fortunate.

The mere ghost of a corrupt bargain is worth many thousand votes to the lucky man who conjures up the ghost.

When it came the turn of the Adams party to be defeated, in 1828, they attributed this result partly to the depravity of the human heart, partly to the tricks of Jackson, and partly to the unfortunate temperament of Mr. Adams. The day after a candidate is beaten everybody knows why it was, and says it was just what any one might have foreseen. Ezekiel Webster, writing from New Hampshire, laid the result chiefly on the candidate, whom everybody disliked, and who would persist in leaving his bitter opponents in office. The people, he said, "always supported his cause from a cold sense of duty, and not from any liking of the man. We soon satisfy ourselves," he added, "that we have discharged our duty to the cause of any man when we do not entertain for him one personal kind feeling, nor can not, unless we disembowel ourselves, like a trussed turkey, of all that is human within us." There is, indeed, no doubt that Mr. Adams helped on his own defeat, both by his defects, and by what would now be considered his virtues. The trouble, however, lay further back. Ezekiel Webster thought that "if there had been at the head of affairs a man of popular character, like Mr. Clay, or any man whom we were not compelled by our natures, instinct, and fixed fate to dislike, the result would have been different." But we can now see that all this would really have made no difference at all. Had Mr. Adams been personally the most attractive of men, instead of being a conscientious iceberg, the same result would have followed, the people would have felt that Jackson's turn had come, and the demand for the "old ticket" would have been irresistible.

Accordingly, the next election, that of 1828, was easily settled. Jackson had 178 electoral votes; Adams but 83—more than two to one. Adams had not an electoral vote south of the Potomac or west of the Alleghanies, though Daniel Webster, writing to Jeremiah Mason, had predicted that he would carry six Western and Southern States. In Georgia no Adams ticket was even nominated, he being there unpopular for one of his best acts—the protection of the Cherokees. On the other hand, but one Jackson elector was chosen from New England, and he by less than two hundred majority. This was in the Maine district that included Bowdoin College, and I have heard from an old friend of mine the tale how he, being then a student at Bowdoin, tolled the college bell at midnight to express the shame of the students, although the elector thus chosen (Judge Preble) was the own uncle of this volunteer sexton. It would have required many college bells to announce the general wrath of New England, which was not diminished by the fact that Mr. Calhoun, another Southerner, was chosen Vice-President over Richard Rush. To be sure, Mr. Calhoun had filled the same office under John Quincy Adams, but then there was a Northern man for President. For the first time the lines seemed distinctly drawn for the coming sectional antagonism.

But even this important fact was really quite subordinate, for the time being, in men's minds. The opposition to Jackson, like his popularity, was personal. It was not a mere party matter. The older statesmen distrusted him, without much regard to their political opinions. When Monroe asked Jefferson in 1818 if it would not be well to give Jackson the embassy to Russia, Jefferson utterly disapproved it. "He would breed you a quarrel," he said, "before he had been there a month." At a later period Jefferson said to Daniel Webster: "I feel much alarmed at the prospect of seeing General Jackson President. He is one of the most unfit men I know of for such a place. He has had very little respect for laws or constitutions, and is, in fact, an able military chief. His passions are terrible. When I was President of the Senate he was a Senator, and he could never speak on account of the rashness of his feelings. I have seen him attempt it repeatedly, and as often choke with rage. His passions are no doubt cooler now; he has been much tried since I knew him; but he is a dangerous man." And dangerous indeed the public office-holders soon found him. As has been already seen, a large part of those who had held office under Adams were already partisans of Jackson; but the rest soon discovered that a changed policy had come in. Between March 4, 1829, and March 22, 1830, 491 postmasters and 230 other officers were removed, making, as it was thought, with their subordinates, at least two thousand changes. Mr. Sumner well points out that it is unfair to charge

this, as we often do, solely upon Jackson. Crawford, as has already been seen, prepared the way for the practice; it had been perfected in the local politics of New York and Pennsylvania. It was simply a disease which the nation must undergo— must ultimately overthrow, indeed, unless overthrown by it; but it will always be identified, by coincidence of time at least, with the Presidency of Andrew Jackson. If not the father of the evil, he will always stand in history as its godfather.

It is a curious fact in political history that a public man is almost always, to a certain extent, truthfully criticised by the party opposed to him. His opponents may exaggerate, they may distort, but the instinct of the people—or even of any large portion of the people—generally goes to the right point, and finds out the weak spot. Jackson was as vehemently attacked as Jefferson, and by the same class of people, but the points of the criticism were wholly different. Those who had habitually denounced Jefferson for being timid in action were equally hard on Jackson for brimming over with superfluous courage, and being ready to slap every one in the face. The discrimination of charges was just. A merely vague and blundering assailant would have been just as likely to call Jackson a coward and Jefferson a fire-eater, which would have been absurd. The summing up of the Federalist William Sullivan, written in 1834, was not so very far from the sober judgment of posterity. "Andrew Jackson.... is a sort of *lusus reipublicæ*, held by no rules or laws, and who honestly believes his sycophants that he was born to command. With a head and heart not better than Thomas Jefferson had, but freed from the inconvenience of that gentleman's constitutional timidity, and familiar with the sword, he has disclosed the real purpose of the American people in fighting the battles of the Revolution and establishing a national republic, viz., that the will of Andrew Jackson shall be the law and only law of the republic."

Really General Jackson himself would not have so very much objected to this estimate could he have had patience to read it. He was singularly free from hypocrisy or concealment, was not much of a talker, and took very little trouble to invent fine names for what he did. But on another point where he was as sharply criticised he was very vulnerable; like most ignorant and self-willed men, he was easily managed by those who understood him. Here again was an illustration of the discernment of even vehement enemies. Nobody charged Jefferson with being over-influenced by a set of inferior men, though all the opposition charged Jackson with it. The reason was that it was true, and during the greater part of his two administrations there was constant talk of what Webster called the "cabinet improper," as distinct from the cabinet proper—what was known in popular phrase as the "kitchen cabinet." Here again came in the felicity of Jack Downing's portraiture. The familiarity with which this imaginary ally pulled off the President's boots or wore his old clothes hardly surpassed the undignified attitudes popularly attributed to Swartwout and Hill and Van Buren.

On the day of his inauguration the President was received in Washington with an ardor that might have turned a more modest head. On the day when the new administration began (March 4, 1829), Daniel Webster wrote to his sister-in-law, with whom he had left his children that winter: "To-day we have had the inauguration. A monstrous crowd of people is in the city. I never saw anything like it before. Persons have come five hundred miles to see General Jackson, and they really seem to think that the country is rescued from some frightful danger." It is difficult now to see what this peril was supposed to be; but we know that the charges of monarchical tendency made against John Adams had been renewed against his son—a renewal that seems absurd in case of a man so scrupulously republican that he would not use a seal ring, and so unambitious that he always sighed after the quieter walks of literature. Equally absurd was the charge of extravagance against a man who kept the White House in better order than his predecessor on less than half the appropriation—an economy wholly counterbalanced in some minds by the fact that he had put in a billiard table. But however all this may have been, the fact is certain that no President had yet entered the White House amid such choruses of delight; nor did it happen again until Jackson's pupil, Van Buren, yielded, amid equal popular enthusiam, to another military hero, Harrison.

For the social life of Washington the President had one advantage which was altogether unexpected, and seemed difficult of explanation by anything in his earlier career. He had at his command the most courteous and agreeable manners. Even before the election of Adams, Daniel Webster had written to his brother: "General Jackson's manners are better than those of any of the candidates. He is grave, mild, and reserved. My wife is for him decidedly." And long after, when the President was to pass in review before those who were perhaps his most implacable opponents, the ladies of Boston, we have the testimony of the late Josiah Quincy, in his *Figures from the Past*, that the personal bearing of this obnoxious official was most unwillingly approved. Mr. Quincy was detailed by Governor Lincoln, on whose military staff he was, to attend President Jackson everywhere when visiting Boston in 1833; and this narrator testifies that, with every prejudice against Jackson, he found him essentially "a knightly personage—prejudiced, narrow, mistaken on many points, it might be, but vigorously a gentleman in his high sense of honor and in the natural straightforward courtesies which are easily distinguished from the veneer of policy." Sitting erect on his horse, a thin stiff type of military strength, he carried with him in the streets a bearing of such dignity that staid old Bostonians who had refused even to look upon him from their windows would finally be coaxed into taking one peep, and would then hurriedly bring forward their little daughters to wave their handkerchiefs. He wrought, Mr. Quincy declares, "a mysterious charm upon old and young"; showed, although in feeble health, a great consideration for others; and was in private a really agreeable companion. It appears from these reminiscences that the President was not merely the cause of wit in others, but now and then appreciated it himself, and that he used to listen with delight to the reading of the "Jack Downing" letters, laughing heartily sometimes, and declaring: "The Vice-President must have written that. Depend upon it, Jack Downing is only Van Buren in masquerade." It is a curious fact that the satirist is already the better remembered of the two, although Van Buren was in his day so powerful as to preside over the official patronage of the nation, and to be called the "Little Magician."

But whatever personal attractions of manner President Jackson may have had, he threw away his social leadership at Washington by a single act of what may have been misapplied chivalry. This act was what Mr. Morse has tersely called "the importation of Mrs. Eaton's visiting list into the politics and government of the country." It was the nearest approach yet made under our masculine political institutions to those eminent scandals which constitute the minor material of court historians in Europe. The heroine of the comedy, considered merely as Peggy O'Neil, daughter of a Washington innkeeper—or as Mrs. Timberlake, the wife of a naval purser who had committed suicide because of strong drink—might have seemed more like a personage out of one of Fielding's novels than as a feature in the history of an administration; but when fate made her Mrs. Secretary Eaton she became one who could disturb cabinets and annihilate long friendships. It was not merely out of regard for her personal wrongs that all this took place, but there was a long history behind it. There had been a little irregularity about President Jackson's own marriage. He had espoused his wife after a supposed divorce from a previous husband; and when the divorce really took place the ceremony had to be repeated. Moreover, as the divorce itself had originally been based on some scandal about Jackson, he was left in a state of violent sensitiveness on the whole matrimonial question. Mrs. Eaton had nothing in the world to do with all this, but she got the benefit of it. The mere fact that she to whom the President had good-naturedly nodded as Peggy O'Neil had been censured by his own officials, after she had become the wife of one of them, was enough to enrage him, and he doubtless looked across the fire-place at the excellent Mrs. Jackson—a plain, estimable backwoodswoman, who sat smoking her corn-cob pipe in the opposite corner—and swore to himself, and very probably aloud, that Peggy O'Neil should be sustained.

For once he overestimated his powers. He had conquered Indian tribes, and checked the army of Great Britain, but the ladies of Washington society were too much for him. Every member of his cabinet expressed the utmost approval of his position, but they said with one accord that those matters must be left to their wives. Mrs. Donelson, his own niece—that is, the wife of his nephew, and the lady who received company for him at the White House—would not receive Mrs. Eaton, and was sent back to Tennessee. Mrs. Calhoun, the wife of the Vice-President, took the same attitude, and ruined thereby her husband's political prospects, Mr. Calhoun being utterly superseded in the President's good graces by Mr. Van Buren, who, being a widower, could pay attention to the offending fair one without let or hinderance. Through his influence Baron Krudener, the Russian Minister, and Mr. Vaughan, the British Minister, both bachelors, gave entertainments at which "Bellona," as the newspapers afterward called the lady, from her influence in creating strife, was present. It did no good; every dance in which she stood up to take part was, in the words of a Washington letter-writer, "instantly dissolved into its original elements," and though she was placed at the head of the supper table, every lady present ignored her very existence. Thus the amenities of Van Buren were as powerless as the anger of Jackson; but the astute Secretary won the President's heart, and with it that of his whole immediate circle—cabinet proper and cabinet improper. It was one of the things that turned the scale between Calhoun and Van Buren, putting the New York "magician" in line for the Presidential succession; and in this way Peggy O'Neil had an appreciable influence on the political history of the nation. It was fortunate that she did not also lead to foreign embroilments, for the wife of the Dutch Minister once refused to sit next to her at a public entertainment, upon which the President threatened to demand the Minister's recall. All this time Jackson himself remained utterly free from scandal, nor did his enemies commonly charge him with anything beyond ill-timed quixotism. But it shows how feminine influence creeps inside of all political barriers, and recalls Charles Churchill's couplet:

"Women, who've oft as sovereigns graced the land,
But never governed well at second-hand."

The two acts with which the administration of President Jackson will be longest identified are his dealings with South Carolina in respect to nullification, and his long warfare with the United States Bank. The first brought the New England States back to him, and the second took them away again. He perhaps won rather more applause than he merited by the one act, and more condemnation than was just for the other. Let us first consider the matter of nullification. When various Southern States—Georgia at first, not South Carolina, taking the lead—had quarrelled with the tariff of 1828, and openly threatened to set it aside, they evidently hoped for the co-operation of the President; or at least for that silent acquiescence he had shown when Georgia had been almost equally turbulent on the Indian question, and he would not interfere, as his predecessor had done, to protect the treaty rights of the Indian tribes. The whole South was therefore startled when he gave at a banquet on Jefferson's birthday (April 13, 1830) a toast that now seems commonplace—"The Federal Union; it must be preserved." But this was not all; when the time came he took vigorous, if not altogether consistent, steps to preserve it.

When, in November, 1832, South Carolina for the first time officially voted that certain tariff acts were null and void in that State, the gauntlet of defiance was fairly thrown down, and Jackson took it up. He sent General Scott to take command at Charleston, with troops near by, and two gun-boats at hand; he issued a dignified proclamation, written by Livingston (December 10, 1832), which pronounced the act of South Carolina contradictory to the Constitution, unauthorized by it, and destructive of its aims. So far, so good; but unfortunately the President had, the week before (December 4, 1832), sent a tariff message to Congress, of which John Quincy Adams wrote, "It goes far to dissolve the Union into its original elements, and is in substance a complete surrender into the hands of the nullifiers of South Carolina." Then came Mr. Clay's compromise tariff of 1833, following in part the line indicated by this message, and achieving, as Mr. Calhoun said, a victory for nullification—leaving the matter a drawn game, at any rate. The action of Jackson thus accompanied settled nothing; it was like valiantly ordering a burglar out of your house with a pistol, and adding the suggestion that he will find a portion of the family silver on the hall table, ready packed for his use, as he goes out.

Nevertheless, the burglar was gone for the moment, and the President had the credit of it. He had already been re-elected by an overwhelming majority in November, 1832, receiving 219 electoral votes, and Clay 49, while Floyd had the 11 votes of South Carolina (which still chose electors by its Legislature—a practice now abandoned), and Wirt the 7 of Vermont. Van Buren was chosen Vice-President, being nominated in place of Calhoun by the Democratic National Convention, which now for the first time came into operation. The President was now at his high-water mark of popularity—always a dangerous time for a public man. His vehement nature accepted his re-election as a proof that he was right in everything, and he grew more self-confident than ever. More imperiously than ever, he ordered about friends and opponents, and his friends repaid it by guiding his affairs, unconsciously to himself. Meantime he was encountering another enemy of greater power, because more silent, than Southern nullification, and he was drifting on to his final contest with the United States Bank.

Sydney Smith says that every Englishman feels himself able, without instruction, to drive a pony-chaise, conduct a small farm, and edit a newspaper. The average American assumes, in addition to all this, that he is competent to manage a bank. President Jackson claimed for himself in this respect no more than his fellows; the difference was in strength of will and in possession of power. A man so ignorant that a member of his own family, according to Mr. Trist, used to say that the General did not believe the world was round, might easily convince himself that he knew all about banking. As he had besides all this very keen observation and great intuitive judgment of character, he was probably right in his point of attack. There is little doubt that the bank of the United States, under Nicholas Biddle, concentrated in itself an enormous power; and it spent in four years, by confession of its directors, $58,000 in what they called "self-defense" against "politicians." When on July 10, 1832, General Jackson, in a message supposed to have been inspired by Amos Kendall, vetoed the bill renewing the charter of the bank, he performed an act of courage, taking counsel with his instincts. But when in the year following he performed the act known as the "removal of the deposits," or, in other words, caused the public money to be no longer deposited in the National Bank and its twenty-five branches, but in a variety of State banks instead, then he took counsel of his ignorance.

The act originally creating the bank had, indeed, given the Secretary of the Treasury authority to remove these deposits at any time, he afterward giving to Congress his reasons. The President had in vain urged Congress to order the removal; that body declined. He had in vain urged the Secretary of the Treasury to remove them, and on his refusing, had displaced the official himself. The President at last found a Secretary of the Treasury (Roger B. Taney) to order the removal, or rather cessation, of deposits. The consequence, immediate or remote, was an immense galvanizing into existence of State banks, and ultimately a vast increase of paper money. The Sub-Treasury system had not then been thought of; there was no proper place of deposit for the public funds; their possession was a direct stimulus to speculation; and the President's cure was worse than the disease. All the vast inflation of 1835 and 1836 and the business collapse of 1837 were due to the fact not merely that Andrew Jackson brought all his violent and persistent will to bear against the United States Bank, but that when he got the power into his own hands he did not know what to do with it. Not one of his biographers—hardly even a bigoted admirer, so far as I know—now claims that his course in this respect was anything but a mistake. "No monster bank," says Professor W. G. Sumner, "under the most malicious management, could have produced as much havoc, either political or financial, as this system produced while it lasted." If the bank was, as is now generally admitted, a dangerous institution, Jackson was in the right to resist it; he was right even in disregarding the enormous flood of petitions that poured in to its support. But to oppose a dangerous bank does not necessarily make one an expert in banking. The utmost that can be said in favor of his action is that the calamitous results showed the great power of the institution he overthrew, and that if he had let it alone the final result might have been as bad.

Two new States were added to the Union in President Jackson's time—Arkansas (1836) and Michigan (1837). The population of the United States in 1830 had risen to nearly thirteen millions (12,866,020).

There was no foreign war during his administration, although one with France was barely averted, and no domestic contest except the second Seminole war against the Florida Indians—a contest in which these combatants held their ground so well, under the half-breed chief Osceola, that he himself was only captured by the violation of a flag of truce, and that even to this day, as the Indian Commissioners tell us, some three hundred of the tribe remain in Florida. The war being equally carried on against fugitive slaves called Maroons, who had intermarried with the Indians, did something to prepare the public mind for a new agitation which was to remould American political parties, and to modify the Constitution of the nation.

It must be remembered that the very air began to be filled in Jackson's time with rumors of insurrections and uprisings in different parts of the world. The French revolution of the Three Days had roused all the American people to sympathy, and called forth especial enthusiasm in such cities as Baltimore, Richmond, and Charleston. The Polish revolution had excited universal interest, and John Randolph had said, "The Greeks are at your doors." All these things were being discussed at every dinner table, and the debates in Virginia as to the necessity of restricting the growing intelligence of the slaves had added to the agitation. In the session of 1829–30 a bill had passed the Virginia Assembly by one majority, and had failed in the Senate, prohibiting slaves from being taught to read or write; and the next year it had passed almost unanimously. There had been, about the same time, alarms of insurrection in North Carolina, so that a party of slaves were attacked and killed by the inhabitants of Newbern; alarms in Maryland, so that fifty blacks had been imprisoned on the Eastern Shore; alarms in Louisiana, so that re-enforcements of troops had been ordered to Baton Rouge; and a traveller had written even from Richmond, Virginia, on the 12th of February, that there were constant fears of insurrections and special patrols. Then came the insurrection of Nat Turner in Virginia—an uprising described minutely by myself elsewhere; the remarkable inflammatory pamphlet called "Walker's Appeal," by a Northern colored man—a piece of writing surpassed in lurid power by nothing in the literature of the

French Revolution; and, more potent than either or both of these, the appearance of the first number of the *Liberator* in Boston. When Garrison wrote, "I am in earnest, I will not equivocate, I will not excuse, I will not retreat a single inch, and I will be heard," Andrew Jackson for once met a will firmer than his own, because more steadfast, and moved by a loftier purpose. Thenceforth, for nearly half a century, the history of the nation was the history of the great antislavery contest.

The administration of Jackson will thus be most remarkable, after all, not because of any triumph of his will, but because of something that arose in spite of it—an agitation so far opposed to his wishes, in fact, that he wished for the passage of a law excluding antislavery publications from the mails. It was an agita-

tion destined to draw new lines, establish new standards, and create new reputations; and it is to be remembered that the Democratic President did not abhor it more, on the one side, than did his fiercest Federalist opponents on the other. The Federalist William Sullivan, at the close of his *Familiar Letters on Public Characters*, after exhausting language to depict the outrages committed by President Jackson, points out as equally objectionable the rising antislavery movement, and predicts that, if it has its full course, " even an Andrew Jackson may be a blessing." But of the wholly new series of events which were to date from that agitation neither Sullivan nor Jackson had so much as a glimpse. This series of papers may well close, for the present, with the dawn of that great agitation.

MY BULL-CALF.

I AM an animal painter, and although I am not well known to fame, I have painted a good many pictures, most of which may now be seen on the walls of my studio. In justice to myself I must say that the critics of the art exhibitions and those persons competent to judge who have visited my studio have spoken in praise of my pictures, and have given me a good place among the younger artists of the country; sometimes, indeed, they have said things about the suggested sentiment of some of my work which I am too modest here to repeat. But in spite of this commendation, which I labor hard to deserve, there has been no great demand for my paintings.

A facetious brother artist once attempted to explain the slowness of my sales. "You see," said he, "that painting changes the nature of its subjects. In real life animals frequently go off very rapidly, but when they are painted they don't."

The same gentleman also made a good deal of fun of one of my first paintings— a dead lion. This animal had died in a menagerie in the city, and having heard of his decease, I bought his remains for five dollars, and after dark I conveyed them to my studio in a wheelbarrow. I was quite young and enthusiastic then, and as the animal had apparently died of a consumption, he was not very heavy. I worked day and night at a life-size (so to

speak) portrait of the beast, and it was agreed by all who saw it that I succeeded very well. But no one seemed inclined in the slightest degree to buy the picture. "What you are waiting for," said my facetious friend, "is the visit of a live ass. When he comes along he will buy that thing, and make your fortune."

My latest work was a life-size picture of a bull-calf. Some time before, I determined to devote myself to cattle painting, and had bought a cow for a model. This I did because I found it difficult to have control over the cows of other people. I live a short distance out of town, and while the farmers thereabout were very willing that I should go into the field and sketch their cows, they would not allow me to pen one of them up in a confined space where I could study her form and features without following her, easel and material in hand, over a wide and sometimes marshy pasture. My cow proved a very valuable possession. I rented a small grassy field for her, and put up a cheap and comfortable shed in one corner of it. I sold her milk to the good lady with whom I lived, and my model cow paid all her expenses, attendance included. She was a gentle creature, and becoming accustomed to my presence, would generally remain in one position for a long time, and when I stirred her up would readily assume some other attitude of repose. I did not always copy her exactly. Sometimes I gave her one color and sometimes another, and sometimes several blended; at one time I gave her horns, and at another none; and in this way I frequently made a herd of her, scattering her over a verdant mead. I did not always even paint her as a cow. With a different head and branching horns, a longer neck, a thinner body, a shorter tail, and longer legs, she made an excellent stag, the life-like poses which I was enabled to get giving the real value to the picture. Once I painted her as a sphinx, her body couched in the conventional way, with claws at the ends of the legs instead of hoofs, and a little altered in contour, making an admirable study; and there was an expression in her eye, as she meditatively crunched a cabbage leaf, which made me give it to the woman's head that I placed upon her. "What a far-off, prophetic look it has!" said one who stood before the picture when it was finished. "It seems to gaze across the sands of Egypt, and to see things thousands of years ahead. If you could fix up a little bit of sunset in the distance, with some red and yellow clouds in the shape of the flag of England, the symbolized sentiment would be quite perfect."

The bull-calf which afterward served as my model was the son of my cow. When he was old enough to go about by himself and eat hay and grass, I sold his mother at a good profit, and retained him as a model, and the life-size picture of him, on which I worked for a long time, was my masterpiece. When it was nearly finished I brought it to my studio, and there day after day I touched and retouched it, often thinking it finished, but always finding, when I went home and looked at my calf, that there was something of life and truth in the real animal which I had not given to the picture, and which I afterward strove to suggest, if not to copy.

I had a friend who occupied a studio in the same building, and who took a great interest in the portrait of my bull-calf. The specialty of this artist was quiet landscape and flowers, and we had frequently gone into the country and sketched together, the one drawing the cattle, and the other the field in which they roved. One day we stood before my almost completed work.

"What a spirited and life-like air he has!" remarked my companion. "He looks as if he was just about to hunch up his back, give a couple of awkward skips, and then butt at us. I really feel like shutting the door, when I come in, for fear he should jump down and run away. You are going to brighten up the foreground a little, are you not?"

"Yes," I answered; "and what it needs is a modest cluster of daisies in this corner. Won't you paint them in for me? You can do it so much better than I can!"

"No," she answered; "I positively will not. No one but yourself should touch it. It is your very best work, and it should be all your picture."

In the course of my life I had not had, or at least I believed that I had not had, many of those pieces of good fortune which people call "opportunities." Now here was one, and I determined to seize it. "Why can it not be *our* picture?" I asked.

She looked up at me with a quick glance, which seemed to say, "What! are you about to speak at last?"

In ten minutes all had been said, and we were engaged to be married.

Our studios were opposite each other, separated by a wide hall, and it had been our custom, when one went to luncheon, for the other to sit with open door, so that visitors to the absent one might be seen and attended to. Emma generally lunched at a quiet restaurant near by, much frequented by ladies, and where an occasional male visitor might be seen, and to this place I also went as soon as she came back. I knew her favorite little table in the corner, and I always tried to occupy the place she had just vacated. But to-day we determined to lock our studio doors, and lunch together. There was really very little reason to expect a visitor. The waiter who attended to our wants was a quiet colored man, with white hair and whiskers, and an expression of kindly observation on his sable countenance. He arranged our table with much care, and listened to our orders with a deference I had not noticed before; but perhaps he always waited thus on ladies. While we were eating he retired to a little distance, and stood regarding us with an interested but not too intent attention. We had so often eaten at the same table, but never before at the same time.

When we returned we went first to my studio, and when we opened the door the bull-calf seemed to smile. We both noticed it.

"There is something in the way he looks

at us," said Emma, "that reminds me of our old waiter."

"Strange," I replied. "I noticed that myself."

Again I urged her to make the daisies for me, but she still refused.

"No," she said. "It is your picture, and you must not be unable to say that you did it all yourself. And, besides, if I were to put in any daisies, your calf is so natural that he would snip them off. I will not have my daisies snipped off, even by that handsome creature."

She looked up, as she said this, with a smile as bright and fresh as any daisy, and I— But never mind.

The next day we went again together to the restaurant, and the kindly observation deepened on the face of the waiter. When he had arranged with unusual nicety the little table service, he placed before Emma a wine-glass containing a button-hole bouquet. When we were leaving he detained me a moment, and said, in a low voice,

"After this, sir, if you would first order your beef for one with two plates, and then order the lady's chicken and salad for one with two plates, you would each have some beef and some chicken. It wouldn't cost any more, sir, and 'twould make more of a *menu*."

"'After this!'" I mentally repeated, as I gratefully put my hand in my pocket. If that old waiter had been an artist, what a gift his powers of observation would have been to him!

We agreed that we would be married in the early autumn, for truly there was little reason for delay. "It has been so many, many months," I said, "since I declared to myself that I would never marry any one but you that I really consider that I have been engaged to you for a very long time."

"I may as well admit that something of the same kind has passed through my mind. It is no harm to tell you so now, and it will make more of a *menu*."

If my calf really cared to snip daisies, he must have envied me then.

There was no impediment to our early marriage except the fact that neither of us had any money.

"What you must do," said Emma, "is to finish your picture and sell it. You must stop looking at the calf you have at home. Of course he is growing every day, and new beauties are coming out on him all the time. You can not expect to

have his picture keep pace with his development. After a while you will have to give him horns, and make him larger."

"The model is bigger now than the picture," I said; "and I must take your advice, and stop looking at him. If I don't, his portrait will never be done."

I would not put any flowers in the foreground, for, if I did so, I was sure they would look as if they had been picked out of a lady's bonnet. After what I had seen Emma do, I knew I could not paint daisies and buttercups. I put in some pale mullein leaves, and a point of rock which caught the light, and when this was done I determined to call the picture finished.

"What are you going to ask for it?" asked Emma.

"I had thought of a thousand dollars. Don't you consider that is a reasonable price?"

"I think it is a very low price," she answered, "considering the size of the picture and the admirable way in which it is painted. I imagine it is seldom that a picture like that is offered at a thousand dollars; but, as you want to sell it very much, I suppose it will be well not to ask any more."

"I do want very much to sell it," I said, giving her hand a squeeze which she understood.

I had also made up my mind in regard to the mode of disposing of the picture. Some weeks before, an artist friend in Boston had written to me that a well-known picture-dealer would open in that city early in September an art establishment particularly for the sale of pictures on commission, and that he would inaugurate his enterprise with an exhibition of paintings, which he wished to make as extensive and attractive as possible.

"If you have anything good, finished in time," wrote my friend, "I think you will do well to send it to Schemroth. He knows your work, and, if I mistake not, bought one of your pictures when he was in business in New York. I doubt if he has many animal subjects, and he wants variety. He says he is going to make his exhibition one of the art features of the season."

Emma agreed with me that I could not do better than send my picture to Schemroth. He was an enterprising man, and would be certain to do everything he could to attract attention to his exhibition, and she felt sure that if the art public of Boston had a good opportunity of seeing my picture it would certainly be sold.

The painting was carefully packed, and sent to Boston, in care of my friend there, who shortly afterward wrote me that Schemroth liked it, and had given it a good place in his gallery, which would open in a day or two. My studio looked very bare and empty after the departure of my spirited bull-calf, so long my daily companion; but my mind was so occupied with the consideration of the important event which was to follow his sale that I did not miss him as much as I would otherwise have done. Emma and I talked a good deal about the best way of beginning our married life, and I was much in favor of a trip to Europe; but in regard to this she did not agree with me.

"A thousand dollars," she said, "would not go far for such a purpose. The steamer tickets would cost us about a hundred dollars apiece, and that would be four hundred dollars to go and come back. Then you certainly ought to keep a hundred dollars for your own use before you start, and that would only leave five hundred dollars with which to go to Paris and Rome and Dresden. If we did less than that, it would be hardly worth while to go at all. And five hundred dollars would not begin to be enough for two people."

I was obliged to admit that she was correct, and the European trip was given up. "My idea is," said Emma, "that we ought to take the money and furnish a house with it. That will be a good practical beginning, and after a while, when we have painted a few more pictures, we can go to Europe. You could keep a hundred dollars for your own use; we could put aside two hundred for rainy days or whatever kind of weather it may be when money is needed and there is none coming in, and then with seven hundred dollars we could buy enough furniture and other things to begin housekeeping in a small way. By this plan, you see, sir, your beautiful calf would give us an excellent start in life."

This proposition needed no discussion. Before she had half finished speaking I was convinced that nothing could be more sensible and delightful. "We must look for a house immediately," I said. "It won't do to put off that part of the business. We should know where we are going to live, so that when we are ready to buy the furniture there need be no delay."

Good fortunes as well as misfortunes sometimes object to coming singly; and just at this time I heard of something which was certainly a piece of rare good luck to a young couple contemplating matrimony. A gentleman named Osburn, who lived near my country home, with whom I had become well acquainted, and to whom I had confided the important news of my engagement, met me on the train a day or two after Emma and I had agreed upon the furniture project, and told me that if I intended to go to housekeeping he thought he could offer me a desirable opportunity. "My wife and I," he said, "wish very much to travel for a year or two, and the time has now arrived when we can do it, if we can dispose of our household effects, and get some one to take our house, on which we have a lease. Now if you are going to marry, and care for a place like ours, it might be worth your while to consider the question of taking it and buying our furniture. We will sell everything just as it is, excepting, of course, the books and such small articles as have a personal value, and you can walk right in and begin housekeeping at once. Everything was new two years ago, and you know my wife is a very careful housekeeper. The house is small and very simply furnished, and I have no doubt you would want to add all sorts of things, but at first you wouldn't really need anything that you wouldn't find there. We wish to dispose of the whole establishment—linen, china, silver (it's only plated, but it's very good), kitchen utensils, garden tools, a lot of fine poultry, a dog, a cat—everything, in fact, excepting the few articles I spoke of. What do you say?"

"Say!" I exclaimed; "there is nothing to say, except that I should be perfectly delighted to take the place off your hands if I could afford it; but I am afraid your price would be above my means. I suppose you would want to sell all or nothing?"

"Oh yes," said Mr. Osburn; "it would not pay us to sell out piecemeal, and we do not wish to let the house to any one who will not buy the furniture. If you think the proposition worth considering, my wife and I will make an estimate of what we consider the effects worth, and let you know."

I told him I should be very glad indeed to know, and he said I should hear from him in a day or two.

When I told Emma of this, and described to her the Osburns' house, with its neat and comfortable furniture, its æsthetic wall-paper, its convenient and airy rooms, its well-kept garden and little lawn, its handsome barn and poultry-house, the wide pasture field belonging to it, the little patch of woodland at the upper end, the neatness and order of everything about the place; and all this at a very moderate rental, with a lease that had several years to run, she agreed with me that while it would be perfectly delightful to take this ready-made home off the Osburns' hands, there was no reason for us to hope that we should be able to do it. We should have to be content with something far less complete and perfect than this.

Two days after, I received a note from Osburn. "We have carefully considered the present value of our possessions," he said, "with an especial view of making it an object to you to buy them as a whole. Everything is in good order, but as we have had two years' use of the articles, we have considered that fact in making an estimate of what we think we ought to receive for them. After going over the matter several times we have determined to offer you the furniture and other things of which I spoke to you for seven hundred and fifty dollars."

"Why," cried Emma, as she read this letter over my shoulder (for I had taken it into her studio before I opened it), "that is only fifty dollars more than we had appropriated!"

"But we won't stop for that," I exclaimed.

"Stop!" she said, as with sparkling eyes and glowing cheeks she took both my hands in her own—regardless of the fact that she already held a brush heavily charged with Vandyck brown—"I should think not."

To work any more then was impossible for either of us. That afternoon we shut up both our studios, and went out to look at the paradise which had been offered us. Mr. Osburn had not yet come home, but his wife took great pleasure in making Emma's acquaintance and in showing us over the house and grounds. We found everything better of its kind, better adapted to the place in which it was, better suited to our every purpose, and altogether ever so much more desirable, than we had thought. I never saw Emma so enthusiastic. Even the picture of my bull-calf had not moved her thus. If the price had not been fixed beforehand, our delighted satisfaction would have been very impolitic. When Mr. Osburn returned I told him without hesitation that I would accept his offer. I think that he and his wife were almost as much pleased as we were. They had set their hearts on an extended tour in the South and far West. The lady's health demanded this, and her husband had found that he could now so arrange his business as to unite travel with profit; but it would have been impossible, as he afterward told me, for him to adopt this new mode of life without first disposing of his furniture and household goods. Ready money, I fancy, was not abundant with him.

When we took leave of the Osburns four people in very high spirits stood shaking hands in the porch of the pretty house in which we had decided to make our home. There was an extraordinarily good point in this extraordinary piece of good fortune which had befallen us. If the Osburns had wished to settle the business with us at once it would, of course, have been impossible for us to do our part, but it would be at least six weeks before they intended to give up their house, and in that time we felt quite sure that my picture would be sold. But although we could take no actual steps toward making our arrangements for housekeeping, there was nothing to prevent our thinking and talking about them, and planning what was to be done; and this occupied a great deal of our time, much to the detriment, I am sure, of our daily work. We were always finding new good points in the matter.

"The only things about the Osburn house that I don't like," said Emma, "are the pictures and the bric-à-brac. Now these are the things that they want to keep, and if we are well off in any way, it is in pictures, and we can just take some of the paintings we have on hand, and a lot of our large engravings, and have them framed, and with that old armor and brass and china which you have collected, and which an animal painter doesn't want in his studio anyway, we can make our house look just lovely. I have collected too, and I have a good many nice things in my room which you have never seen."

"The house is a good one now," I exclaimed, "but it will look like another place when you and I get into it. And there is another thing that I have been thinking about. Of course I'll take my calf over there the first thing, and he will get a great deal better eating in that meadow than he has now. But he won't be the only animal we will have. I intend to have a little model farm; that is to say, a farm on which we will keep models. Of course we will have a cow, and she will not only give us milk and butter, but I can paint her. There is a fine little barn and stable on the place, but Osburn says he never thought he ought to keep a horse, because the house is only five minutes from the station, and it would be a piece of sheer extravagance for him to have a horse just to drive about after he came home at night. But it wouldn't be extravagant in me; it would be actual economy. I ought to paint horses, and to do so properly and economically I should own one. And so with all sorts of animals. If I buy a fine dog or a beautiful cat, it will actually be money in my pocket."

"That is true," said Emma; "but you mustn't bring any wild animals there until they are so dead that you can wheel them home in a wheelbarrow. It will be perfectly delightful to have a horse, and, as I intend to paint birds as well as flowers, I can begin on the hens and little chickens and the ducks; and the sparrows and robins, if I can make them tame enough for me to sketch them."

"Yes," I exclaimed, "and you can paint the wild flowers in your own field; and we'll raise splendid Jacqueminot roses, and the hybrid tea, and other fine kinds; and we'll fix up a room for them in the winter, so that you can always have flowers for models at whatever stage you want them."

In the weeks that followed we paid several visits to the Osburns by their invitation, during which the husband explained to me the management of the celery beds, and many of his out-door improvements, while the wife had some long conversations with Emma about her household arrangements.

As the time approached when the Osburns wished to give up their house, Emma and I became very anxious to hear from Boston. I had written to my friend there explaining the situation, and he had prom-

ised to attend to the matter, and see that Schemroth communicated with me as soon as the picture was sold; so there was nothing to do but wait. I frequently met Mr. Osburn on the train, and I began to feel, as the time passed on, that I ought to be able to say something to him about concluding our bargain.

Of course he must have his preparations to make, and he would not wish to delay them too long. Although there was no real reason for it, as we assured ourselves over and over, both Emma and I began to be very uneasy, and we sometimes even regretted that we had accepted Mr. Osburn's offer. If we had not complicated the affair in this way we could have calmly waited until the picture was sold, and have then done what seemed to us best. There was no probability that we would have met with so good an opportunity of going to housekeeping, but we should have been independent and easy in our minds. But now we were neither. The plans and prospects of others depended upon us, and our uneasiness and anxiety increased every day. I disliked to meet Mr. Osburn, and every morning hoped that he would not be on the train. Never did I await the arrival of the mails with more anxiety and impatience.

One day, as Emma and I were returning from luncheon, the janitor of the building met us at the door. "A box came for you, sir, by express," he said. "I paid two dollars and twenty cents on it. It is up in your room."

I said nothing, but put my hand in my pocket. I began to count the money in my pocket-book, but my hand shook, and I dropped a quarter of a dollar on the floor, which rolled off to some distance. As the janitor went to pick it up, Emma approached me, and I noticed that she was very pale.

"If you haven't enough," she said, "I have some change with me."

I needed seventy cents to make up the sum, and Emma gave it to me. And then, without a word, we went upstairs. We did not hurry, but it was the first time, I think, that I ever became out of breath in going up those stairs. The moment we looked at the box we knew. The picture had been sent back.

I gazed at it blankly, reading over and over the painted address.

"Perhaps you had better open it," said

Emma, in a very low voice. "It may not be—"

As quickly as I could I took off the centre board. The bull-calf, with a melancholy greeting in his eyes, looked out upon us. Then Emma sat down upon the nearest chair and burst into tears, and I drew near to comfort her.

Half an hour later I had taken the picture from the box, which I carefully searched. "Do you know," I cried, a sudden anger taking the place of the deadened sensation of my heart, "that this is an outrageous insult? He should have written to me before he sent it back; but to return it, without a word or line of any kind, is simply brutal."

I said a great deal more than this. I was very angry. I would write to Schemroth, and let him know what I thought of this. Emma now endeavored to soothe my passion, and urged me not to do anything in a moment of excitement which might injure me in a business point of view. I did not promise forbearance, but suddenly exclaimed: "And then there is Osburn! He must be told. It will be a hard, hard thing to do! They will both be terribly disappointed. It will break up all their plans."

"I have thought about the Osburns," said Emma, coming close to me, and putting her hands upon my arm, "and I will tell you what we will do. I will go and see Mrs. Osburn. That will be much better than for you to see her husband. She will not be angry, and I can explain everything to her so that she will understand."

"No, my dear," said I; "that will not do. I shall not suffer you to bear what must be the very heaviest brunt of this trouble. In a case like this it is the duty of the man to put himself forward. I must go immediately and see Osburn at his office before he starts for home."

"I wish you would not," she said, earnestly. "Of course the man ought to take the lead in most things, but there may be times when it will be easier and better for the wife to go first."

The moment she said these words she blushed, and I snatched her into my arms. The wife! If those rich lovers of art had only known what they might have made of this dear girl by buying my picture, it would never have come back to me.

But time was flying, and if I was to see Osburn at his office, I must hurry. The thing was hard enough to do, as it was, and I did not feel that I could have the heart to tell the story in the presence of his wife.

"If he is very much troubled," said Emma, "and says anything to you which you do not like, you will not let him make you angry, will you?"

"Oh no," said I; "I am not so unreasonable as that. I have so much pity for him that he may say to me what he pleases. I will bear it all."

"I am very sorry for you," said Emma, looking up at me, "and I do wish you would let me see Mrs. Osburn."

But I was firm in my resolution not to shift this very unpleasant duty upon Emma, and in a few minutes I had started down-town. When I reached Mr. Osburn's place of business I found that he had gone home, although it was several hours earlier than his usual time of leaving. "He had something he wanted to attend to at his house," said one of the clerks.

This was a great disappointment to me, for now I would be obliged to go to see him that evening, and most probably to tell him the bad news in the presence of his wife. I did not fully appreciate until now how much easier it would have been to talk to him at his desk in the city. As I walked toward the Osburns' house just after dark that evening I could scarcely believe that I was going to the place which I had lately visited with such delight. Emma and I had fallen into the way of already considering the house and grounds as our own, and as I opened the gate I remembered how we had stood there while I told her about some improvements I intended to make in said gate, so that the weight and chain would never fail to latch it. And now it made no difference to me whether the gate latched or not. And the flower borders, too, on each side of the path! How Emma had talked to me, when we had walked far enough away, so as to be sure not to hurt Mrs. Osburn's feelings, of what she intended to do in those borders! It all seemed to me like visiting the grave of a home. But I walked steadily up to the house. The parlor shutters were wide open, and the room was brightly lighted, so that I could see plainly what was passing within. There was an air of disorder about the pretty room. Mr. Osburn, in his shirt sleeves, was on a step-ladder taking down a picture from the wall, while his wife stood below ready to receive it. All the other pictures—the portraits of their parents and the chromos which Emma and I thought so little of, but which they valued so highly—had been already taken down. These, with various little articles of ornament and use, valuable to them on account of association with some dear friend or some dear time, were the things which they intended to reserve; and it was plain that it was to take down and pack up these that Mr. Osburn had come home early that day. It was now only four days from the date he had fixed for surrendering the house to me, and he was working hard to have everything ready for us. He knew very well that Emma and I had arranged that we would be quietly married as soon as the house should be ours, and that in this charming home, all ready to our hands, we would immediately begin our married life. How earnestly and honestly they were doing their part!

I do not think I am a coward, but as I stood and gazed at these two I felt that it would be simply impossible for me to walk into that room and tell them that they might hang up their pictures again and unpack their bric-à-brac, and that they were not going to take the pleasant journeys they had planned, until they had found some other person, more able to keep to his word than I was, who should take their house and buy their goods.

No, I could not do it. I would go home and write to Osburn. I did not feel that this was as manly a course as to speak to him face to face, but I could not speak to him now. As I was about to turn away, Osburn got down from the ladder, and they both looked around the room. Their faces wore an expression of pleasant satisfaction at the conclusion of their task, but mingled, I truly believe, with a feeling of regret that they should leave to us such bare walls. How Emma and I had talked of what we intended to do with those walls! How I had drawn little sketches of them, and how we had planned and arranged for every space!

I hurried home, wrote a note, and tore it up. I wrote another, but that too did not properly express the situation. It was late, and I could do no more. I would write in the morning, take the letter into town and show it to Emma, and then send it to Osburn at the office.

The next day Emma was in my studio reading the disgraceful confession I had written, when the janitor came in, and handed me a letter.

"It is from Osburn," I exclaimed, glancing at the address, as the man closed the door behind him. "I know his handwriting. Now this is too bad. If Schemroth had only treated me with decent politeness I could have seen Osburn, or have written to him, before he felt himself obliged to remind me that the time had come for me to attend to my part of the contract."

"But you must not allow yourself to be so disturbed," said Emma. "You don't know what he has written."

"That is the only thing he could write about," said I, bitterly, as I opened the letter. "It is very humiliating."

We read the note together. It was very brief, and ran thus:

"DEAR SIR,—I have a customer who is willing to buy your picture, but he is dissatisfied with the foreground. If you will put in some daisies or other field flowers to brighten it up and throw the animal a little back, he will take it. I can ask him enough to cover your price and my commission. As I am sure you will make the alterations, I will forward the picture to you immediately.

"Yours truly,   L. SCHEMROTH."

The letter was dated four days previously.

We looked at each other, unable to speak. Our great cloud had turned completely over, and its lining dazzled us. We found words very soon, but I will not repeat them here. We could have fallen down and worshipped our painted calf.

"And now, my darling," I cried, "will you put the daisies in our picture?"

"Indeed will I," she said. And away she ran for her paints and brushes.

The rest of that afternoon she steadily painted, while I sat beside her, watching every touch of her brush.

"This daisy," she said, as she finished the first one, "is to make you happy, and the next one will be for myself; then I will paint two more for Mr. and Mrs. Osburn, and you must not fail to go and tell them to-night that you will settle up our business in a very short time; and I will paint a small daisy for Mr. Schemroth, and if he hadn't forgotten to mail his letter when it was written I would have made his daisy bigger."

The picture soon went back to Boston, and the original of it now spends most of his time looking over the fence of his pasture into the pretty yard of the house where the Osburns used to live, and hoping that some one will come and give him some cabbage leaves. If he could see all that there is to be seen he would see that the parlor of that house is hung with the spoils from the studios of two artists, that there is a room in the second story, with a northern light, in which flowers grow on canvas as beautifully as they grow in the fields and garden, and where a large picture is steadily progressing in which he figures as "The Coming Monarch." He would also see, far away on the Pacific shore, another couple whom he has helped to make happy; and if he could cast his eyes Bostonward he would see, every now and then, Mr. Schemroth writing to me to know when I could send him other animal pictures, and assuring me that he can find ready and profitable sale for all that I can paint. And, best of all, he could see, every day, Emma painting daisies into my life.

BEEF.

FROM THE RANGE TO THE SHAMBLES.

AN establishment in Chicago which combines the operations of "shipping" and of "canning" beef has a slaughtering capacity of 400,000 head annually. When we add to this the requirements of other similar although smaller concerns, and the large number shipped eastward on the hoof, we have a grand total of not far from 2,500,000 head marketed in the city of Chicago alone. To meet this unceasing and regular demand there must be an unfailing source of supply somewhere in reserve from which an average daily quota can be expected. Whence does it come? Let the five great trunk lines which have their termini on the borders of Lake Michigan answer. Like the outstretched fingers of a hand, they meet in the central palm, Chicago. All from the West, but from the extreme northern and southern portions, Texas representing the latter, and the utmost limits of Montana the former. Ten thousand miles of rail at least are occupied in the transit.

Twenty years ago the pseudonym of a "Texas ranger" conveyed to the mind all that was rough and lawless in the uncivilized border white man. Tall, raw-boned, long-armed, with broad sombrero hat, and wild and unkempt locks and visage, he was at once the representative of the State and the terror of the newly arrived emigrant seeking a home in the wilderness. To-day some of his characteristics have descended to the native steer, and the broad-horned, lank-sided, long-legged bovine ranger of the prairies has usurped the title and the place of his *possibly* more human prede-cessor. To each class of these native Texans are we indebted for much of the stock which is now covering the immense grass-producing regions of the broad Northwest. With the great annual cattle drives which start from the arid plains of the Red River and the Pecos comes the wild cow-boy, with his six-shooter on his hip and his leathern girdle bristling with the little metal cylinders. The cool breezes from the snow-clad peaks of "the Rockies" temper somewhat his heated blood, and the semblance of law and order growing out of the necessity for a better protection of life and property, which is now pretty well inaugurated in the northern Territories, has already had its effect in modifying his reckless disregard of any restraint not imposed by himself.

Change of temperature and of climate has likewise produced a marked impression upon the Texas steer, after being for a few years transplanted to a more temperate zone. The nutritious grasses of Wyoming and Montana, combined with the fresh and vigorous air, give even to the beef of a southern-bred bovine an improved flavor and quality; while the great attention recently paid by stock-growers to the introduction of the best-blooded animals has already been instrumental in raising the grade of entire herds now roaming over the northern ranges. No beef-producing Territories have a higher reputation than those above-named in the markets of the Lake City, and while in the Eastern towns the indiscriminate title of "Chicago beef" is given to all passing

.through its slaughter-houses, yet the expert buyer knows full well from what source to seek for his choicest supplies.

There are many Eastern housekeepers who profess a great aversion to what they are pleased to designate as "Western beef," not knowing, or perhaps not caring to know, that the very finest corn-fed animals in the world come from the broad and fertile prairies which have been subdued into bearing the richest grasses and the most abundant fat-producing cereals in the country.

The great reservoir from which has been drawn the bulk of the cattle which are now becoming so abundant in all our Western Territories is the State of Texas. In 1870 one-seventh of the horned cattle in the United States was found within its borders, and it outnumbered the aggregate of those of all the other States and Territories west of the Missouri, California and the Pacific coast included. This ratio was slightly changed by the statistics of 1880, the State representing somewhat less than one-eighth of the whole number, while it still contained more than all the others mentioned above. From this source of supply has been drawn the great bulk of the range cattle now to be found on the public lands east of the Rocky Mountains—an industry which has grown to huge proportions, and yet dating back in these States and Territories a few years only. As an evidence of this we note that in 1870 the number given for Montana, Wyoming, and Colorado was a little less than 280,000. Ten years later Wyoming alone equalled this, while the three together aggregated nearly 800,000. We do not doubt that an accurate census taken to-day would more than double these figures.

To Texas, then, we must still look for the supply from which to draw recruits to further develop the capabilities of the northern ranges. Like the tide of immigration which is daily landing thousands of foreigners on the shores of the New World, more than equalling the relative birth increase, so the annual cattle drive from Texas must yet be the base of supplies for all the country north.

Said one of the "kings" who holds his court on the broad ranges of the great plains to a friend spending a few weeks at Little Rock, Arkansas, partly for recreation, but more particularly to gather information concerning the cattle business

of the Southwest: "If you are inclined to invest in cattle, and want to move cautiously in an enterprise in which at present you have no experience, buy steers." On this hint I acted, and while I drop the personal in what I may have to say in the remainder of this article, the facts as stated are the result of somewhat definite knowledge in the premises.

There are several ways of becoming interested in the cattle business on a northern range. One may commence by buying out a small herd, with the ranch and primitive equipments which accompany it, and with this nucleus build up by natural increase and additional purchases from time to time. To do this the owner must have had some experience in the business, or have secured the services of a competent foreman, or, better, both. Or, again, one may contract in Texas during the winter for a given number of one or two year old steers, to be delivered on a certain range in Wyoming or Montana the coming summer. Having previously made an arrangement for their herding for two or more years, for which he pays annually one dollar per head, including all expenses, all he has to do is to await their arrival about midsummer, see them counted and branded, and then turn them loose upon the range. Or, thirdly, he may become a stockholder in one of the organized gigantic companies already existing, in which case he will probably pay full value for his shares, and if the present high prices of beef cattle continue, will receive fair dividends for his investment. In this latter case he may remain in the business ten years, and if at the end of that time the herd should fail to count out one-half of the original number, he would no more know what had become of them than a director of a broken bank would know where to look for its missing capital.

If the second method is adopted, in accordance with the advice given above, we will suppose a purchase made in Texas, say the 1st of February, of two thousand steers, one-half to be yearlings, and the other half two-year-olds, to be delivered on a range in Wyoming the following summer. These would be well bought at fifteen and eighteen dollars a head respectively, and then only as part of a larger drive of perhaps ten or twelve thousand going through to the same locality. About one-third cash will be paid at the signing of the contract, an equal amount when the cattle are started on the trail early in April, and the balance when they are delivered on the range. Of course in a transaction of this character responsible parties must be dealt with, but most of the larger herders are "princes" in fortune as well as "kings" in the business, and are men of honor, having a reputation to maintain.

With the early starting of the grass in the spring the cattle are on the trail. They have the road brand by which the present owner is known, and are headed northward for their new and distant home. A thousand miles they will travel before they reach their destination, and in the windings of the road, and in the course which many a wayward steer will take, no doubt much more. If all goes well, and no mishaps occur, the end may be reached in three months' time, or about the middle of July. In the hands of a careful foreman they will come through with but little loss in flesh and numbers.

The word "drive" is a misnomer as applied to the trail. It is exactly this which should *not* be done. Cattle once gathered, and headed in the direction of their long journey, should be allowed to "drift" rather than be urged. Walking as they feed, they will accomplish their twelve or fifteen miles a day with but little exertion to themselves, and with very much less care and anxiety on the part of the herder. This remark is especially applicable to the handling of beef herds, and to "through" Texans likewise, with the qualification that there are "drags" to every herd which need urging to keep them up to the mark; and it is among these last that the losses, if any, occur. All excitement of the animals is to be avoided, and the dangers of a stampede are lessened in proportion as the cattle are handled with gentleness and discretion. When a panic does arise, it is then that the cow-boy himself must be equal to the situation, and ride fearlessly to turn the flank of the flying beasts. No fear of a charge of the long horns must then affect him, but putting his "broncho" on his mettle, he must ride hard and ride long until the column is headed and the herd once more brought into line. A successful stampede within a hundred miles of the starting-point may result in the return of the animals to their native heath, or, farther on, to their being scattered abroad upon the plains, not all to be found for weeks, if ever.

There are several distinct trails across the plains, and the pathways are as distinctly marked as a road could be, pressed by the hoofs of thousands for years past.

The essentials of grass and water are to be considered in a region none too well supplied with these requisites, and the possibilities of fencing and occupation in districts which are being rapidly redeemed from their original state. The raids of hostile Indians no longer enter into the question, and the chances are that the full quota of the winter's purchase will be safely delivered on the range within a few days of the expected time. If this is not later than the first of August, the new arrivals will have ample time to become wonted to their new home, and to settle down in a peaceful frame of mind, taking on all the flesh possible before the advent of the wintry blasts. The count and the branding over, the cattle are distributed upon the range, and told to shift for themselves. If the grass is well cured and abundant, they will get in fine condition in three months' time, and be well able to stand the severe cold to follow. If, on the other hand, they do not reach their destination until late in the fall, they are quite apt to be thin in flesh, and if a severe winter comes on, much loss will ensue. It is in such cases that the large percentage of loss is reported in the returns after a period of heavy storms. Ten per cent., or even more, of loss may have to be charged against a herd of "through" cattle in this condition, while two per cent. will fully cover the loss on a well-located range occupied by cattle which have been on the same a year or more. As previously stated, the expense of herding a "bunch" of cattle is one dollar per head annually, which includes all charges after they are turned loose upon the range until they are delivered as "beeves" at the nearest railroad shipping point. If the owner is wise, he will not allow a hoof to be gathered until it has been two years wintered. The temptation is great, when prices are high and cattle are in good demand, to ship steers that have been only one year upon the range. This is a mistake, as the second year is the one that tells both in the weight and quality of the beef; and as to age, no steer reaches maturity until he is four years old. High rates, however, have induced many shipments during the past two years, and the gathering of beeves has been much closer than formerly. Now for the results of this business, the most simple, easily managed, and conducted with less chance of loss than in any department of the cattle business:

Purchase—

1000 head of yearling Texas steers, to be delivered on a northern range, at $15 each	$15,000
1000 head of two-year-olds, at $18 each	18,000
	$33,000
Branding same, say	250
Two years' herding, at $1 each per year	4,000
	$37,250
At the end of second year sell 750 head of the older lot, which will then be four years old, to be delivered at the railroad shipping station, at $33 per head..	$24,750
1250 will then be left to be herded one year, at $1 each	1,250
	$38,500
At the end of third year sell the balance of first lot, which will then be five years old, viz., 200 head (allowing five per cent. for losses), at $36 per head......	7,200
Also 500 head of the younger lot, then four years old, at $33 ...	16,500
	$48,450
Cost of herding the balance one year	$500
At the end of fourth year sell remainder of herd, which will then be five years old; after deducting ten per cent. for missing and losses, will leave 400 head, at $36 per head........	14,400
Add to cost for taxes and incidentals.....................	850
Total product of sales	$62,850
Total cost and expenses....	$39,850
Profit at end of four years—nearly sixty per cent.	23,000
	$62,850

The drawback to investments of this character is the fact that constant renewals must be made by purchase, or the business will soon run itself out. With the rapid advance which has taken place in the value of Texas cattle during the past few years, and the possible falling off in the price of beef, which is already apparent, as compared with the prices of 1882, it may happen that the balance-sheet for the next period may not present as attractive an array of figures. It is fair to state, however, that much higher profits have been realized during the past, when purchases were made fully forty per cent. below the prices named above. It is within the writer's knowledge that a profit of one hundred per

cent. has been realized within three years from the time of the original investment.

The result of the first year's sale will no doubt have the effect of stimulating the somewhat timid operator into becoming interested in a permanent herd. He already begins to think that he knows something about cattle, and talks learnedly to those who are still more novices than himself of ranges and ranches, corrals and round-ups, brands and branding, although he has probably never been within a thousand miles of either. It is comparatively an easy and comfortable thing to sit in an Eastern counting-house and figure up on a sheet of paper the cost of a herd, and the increase and profits after a five or six years' outlay. It is a very different thing to ride the range day after day for three or four months, in snow and rain and mud, or in the dust and heat, or, worse still, to face the blizzard of an almost arctic winter, when the thermometer ranges 20° to 40° below zero, and the wind blows a gale at fifty miles an hour. That cattle live and even flourish in such a climate, with no shelter to cover them, and with no food but the standing grass of last summer's growth, is one of the mysteries of the business. But the argument is a good one that where the buffalo has found a home and a living for a thousand years, more or less, there may cattle likewise profitably range. At any rate experience has proved it, and herds now numbering hundreds of thousands peacefully graze where less than ten years since wild Indians hunted the buffalo, or murdered the white man whenever a convenient opportunity offered.

As a matter of interest to those who are studying the pecuniary results set forth in this article, I will give the figures as written out by an experienced cattle man in one of our Eastern counting-houses during the winter of 1880–81, the object being to show what would be the result of an investment of about $50,000 at prices as they stood at that time.

1881. Put on the range 2000 cows, 140 bulls, and 1000 one and two year old steers; cost, $57,000.
1882. Will brand 250 steer calves and 250 heifer calves.
1883. Will brand 700 steer calves and 700 heifer calves.
1884. Will brand 700 steer calves and 700 heifer calves.
1885. Will brand 800 steer calves and 800 heifer calves.

1886. Will brand 1000 steer calves and 1000 heifer calves.

1887. Will brand 1300 steer calves and 1300 heifer calves.

Total increase, 4750 head each of steers and heifers, the heifer calves of 1882, 1883, and 1884 raising progeny during the three following years.

Inventory at the end of six years:

1650 three, four, and five year old steers, average value $30 each	$49,500
800 two years old, at $22 each	17,600
1000 one year old, at $15 each	15,000
1300 calves, at $10 each	13,000
2450 cows and heifers, at $20 each	49,000
1000 yearling heifers, at $15 each	15,000
1300 calves (heifers), at $10 each	13,000
1000 steers (original purchase), at $30 each	30,000
2000 cows (original purchase)	40,000
140 bulls	5,600
	$247,700

Ranch expenses, first two years	$6,000	
Ranch expenses, third and fourth years	8,000	
Ranch expenses, fifth and sixth years	10,000	
Add twenty per cent. of the gross amount for losses during six years	49,540	73,540
Net value of herd at the end of six years		$174,160

In explanation of the above estimate and figures we observe that the calf product from a given number of cows on a northern range is estimated at seventy per cent., varying somewhat as the winter and spring may be severe or mild. The ranch expenses may seem small, and we think they are perhaps rather understated, but it must be remembered that the outfit for the business is of the most rude and primitive description. A cow-boy scorns a tent, and will roll himself in his blanket and sleep under the open canopy of heaven, often during the entire round of seasons. If timber can be had within fifteen or twenty miles, a few hundred dollars will build the necessary pens or "corrals," and the "shack" or ranch itself is a one-story log structure of two or three rooms, seldom consisting of anything more than an earth floor and a mud roof. Until within the last year horses have been comparatively cheap, a good saddle and bridle often costing more than the animal itself. Tin plates and cups, iron forks and spoons, with a wagon sheet for a table-cloth and the ground for a table, complete the outfit for the *regular* meals. But oftentimes even these are a luxury, as frequently the cow-boy is in the saddle twelve to fourteen hours on a stretch, with a bite from hand to mouth, caught at odd intervals, as his only sustenance.

As the allowance of twenty per cent. on the gross inventory for losses during the period of six years is a large one—and few Wyoming or Montana men would be willing to admit any such discount in selling or inventorying a herd—that sum will easily cover taxes, and any increase in the running of the ranch not included in the estimate under that head. On the other hand, present values would largely increase the prices set opposite the different grades given above. While some classes have risen more than others, we could easily add twenty per cent. to the gross footings of the entire list, a corresponding increase, of course, being charged upon the original purchase.

When this estimate and these figures were made, barely three years ago, an investment of $50,000 was considered a very respectable amount with which to start a cattle company. To-day the concentration of smaller interests, coupled with the introduction of a large amount of English capital, has had the effect to consolidate and build up many large corporations. Firms representing a million of money are no longer rare, and some companies are found whose stock ledger foots up double that sum.

In the statement already given of the herding of two thousand steers, the returns are estimated upon a sale to dealers at the railroad shipping station. But it often happens, and indeed it is more usual, for the owner to take his beeves directly through to the Chicago stock-yards, and market them himself. If there is a profit to the buyer, there is also one to the owner, and if he has the time and the ability, he may as well reap the same himself. Supposing him to drive five hundred head, he will require for their transportation twenty-four cars; these the Union or the Northern Pacific Company will furnish at from one hundred to one hundred and fifty dollars per car, according to the distance travelled. Stock pens for feeding and watering are found at convenient intervals along the line of the roads; for the animals have to be properly cared for during their long and weary journey, and even with the best attention considerable shrinkage is inevitable. The owner spends his days and nights in the caboose with his rough assistants, and it is questionable whether he is much more comfortable than the beasts huddled into the crowded cars ahead of him.

Cattle trains arrive in Chicago early in the morning. They are unloaded, the cattle are classified and entered upon the stock-yard books in the name of the consignee, and after they are fed and watered in their respective pens, are ready for the inspection of the buyer. The owner then steps aside, and the commission man takes his place. The selling and the buying are not transactions which occupy a great deal of time. Both classes are experienced in their business, which is often conducted on horseback, the purchaser riding back and forth, and looking over the pens from his favorable point of observation. It is not unusual for a bargain to be struck, the cattle weighed, the accounts adjusted, a check given for the amount, and all before eleven o'clock in the morning of the day of arrival. It rarely happens that any considerable number are carried over into the next day; the law of supply and demand works in this, as in many other classes of business, with great regularity. This remark applies more particularly to the receipts of the day; for it is an unquestioned fact that, owing to the immensely increased facilities for canning beef, and the great perfection arrived at in the matter of shipping dressed quarters, the business has assumed proportions not dreamed of ten years since, and the general market has advanced in consequence. Our "cowman" having concluded his business, can sit down quietly to a comfortable dinner at the Transit House, with his check for $15,000 or $20,000 in his pocket, make his bank deposit afterward, and take the evening train back to the ranch, without having even spent a night in the city.

Let us now see what becomes of the cattle as they pass into the hands of the butcher. This term is also somewhat of a "misnomer" when applied to the present system of dressing beef, but we will let it stand, for the want of a more intelligible designation. There are two distinct departments in the large establishments of the day, viz., the "shipping" and the "canning." Into the former come the choice corn-fed animals from the great cereal districts of what can hardly now be called the "far West," as well as the best "grass" cattle which have had the run of the summer ranges. The latter receives most of the "through Texans," the old cows, and the "scrubs" and "culls" from the better lots. The process of slaughtering each is substantially the same up to a certain point, where the inferior quality passes from the killing to the canning house.

As we come within the gate we reach first the outer inclosure or pen, where may be gathered one hundred head of choice "shippers." They come in quietly and without excitement, and in a few minutes perhaps one-third of them are driven into a narrow alleyway adjoining the single pens, where each one is in a few minutes to meet his death. This part of the yard is boarded up with heavy plank about six or seven feet high, and open at the top, along which we walk on a single plank running from end to end. As an animal is wanted, a slide door opens, and he passes into the pen nearest him. Here he stands, unconscious of the fate that awaits him, and that his executioner is at that moment loading the fatal weapon above his head. A few seconds later and a mild-looking man with a short carbine in his hand drops the muzzle to a point in the centre of the forehead, just below the horns, and pulls the trigger. The steer falls without a struggle or a groan, and he passes on to the next, taking the life of half a dozen in a couple of minutes, more or less. The door at the other end of the pen is raised, a hooking chain passed around the neck, and the animal is drawn out upon a broad platform about fourteen feet wide, at the bottom of which runs a shallow trough to catch the blood. Suspended by the hind-feet, the sticking-knife completes the bleeding process, and then two men step forward and disconnect the head. Four follow, stripping down the hide, two others, in the mean while, taking off the feet. Sawing the breast and haunch bones is the next operation, and then the carcass is hoisted preparatory to taking out the inwards. This accomplished, a number are detailed to do the trimming, cleaning, and turning to account every scrap and particle connected with the animal, so that nothing is wasted, down to the horns and hoofs. While these several operations are in progress the carcass has been moving along a distance of some two hundred feet, being attached to a track overhead. The men at work maintain their relative positions as one after another of the carcasses come before them, and in the brief space of fourteen minutes from the time of the fatal shot the animal is hung up, "drawn and quartered," and then left to cool in the chill-room for forty-eight hours preparatory to shipping. Twenty different processes take place in the course of the fourteen minutes aforesaid, and ninety men are engaged in it. The average weight of this class of cattle, as brought into the slaughter-house, is 1250 pounds, and during the summer season five hundred head are killed daily in the nine hours allotted to the work.

Perhaps the most satisfactory part of the operations we have witnessed is the scrupulous cleanliness observed throughout. The pure creamy fat and dark rich red meat attest the perfection and purity attained, which the most expert stall-man in Fulton Market can not excel. Next comes the shipping of the quarters, and here science comes to the aid of mechanical skill with the most perfect adaptation of a means to the end. It does not seem possible to improve the "refrigerator" cars as now built and used. We will assist in the loading of one, and see how it is done.

The car stands alongside of the platform at the extreme end of the building; the cooled meat, hanging in rows, is in the adjoining apartment. Once more the sides run along upon a track; the forequarters, partially severed from the hind, are ready to be cut loose as they are carried into the car. Here rows of hooks extend crosswise just below the roof. In one end are hung the hind-quarters, and in the other the fore, suspended about a foot from the floor; a sufficient space is left underneath, which is utilized to the full extent for shipping boxes of sausage-meat. The ice compartment is in the forward end, and is filled from above and from the outside. The sides of the car are double; a cool current of air passes around but not through the apartment where the meat is hung. With a proper watching of the ice-box, which is filled from time to time during the journey, the temperature will not vary over four degrees, and the meat, while never allowed to freeze, is chilled to the proper point for preservation. Shipped in this way, it will keep for weeks, and be improved by the process. Perfect system, order, and scrupulous cleanliness have brought this mode of transporting beef to perfection, and the day is not distant when the moving of cattle long journeys by rail will give place to the practice of dressed beef shipping,

slaughter-houses springing up on the line of the road a thousand miles westward to meet the cattle as they come in on the trail.

The canning and packing department is another branch of the business entirely distinct from that of shipping. Up to a certain point the process is substantially the same, until it comes to cutting up the quarters into suitable pieces for these uses. Here division of labor takes complete possession of the work, and it is carried to the perfection of economy. A man will stand by the hour giving but a single turn to his knife, which separates a joint. But one portion of the carcass comes upon his block. His work is done with unerring accuracy, but he does this, and this only. A hundred others are on the same floor with him, each doing what may seem a trifling portion of the work, but before the carcass, which came in on one side in quarters, leaves the room, it is entirely bereft of bones, and then wheeled away in small pieces ready for the curing and the canning. It is marvellous with what rapidity "boned ox" can be made ready for the table. We are not prepared to say that it will ever find its way on the *menu* of a Delmonico supper alongside of a turkey rival, nor can we say that we should care to give it a place on even an ordinary bill of fare. We should taboo it, however, only on the ground that it is made up of the inferior parts of poorly fattened animals, or of the "lean and ill-favored kine" of the stock-yards.

While walking through one of the latter one day in May last we noticed a pen of gaunt, raw-boned "through Texans," and turning to our companion said, "What are those cattle doing here? there certainly can be no market for them." Much to my surprise, he replied, "They will go off quicker than a better lot; the canners will pick them up at once." And so it proved, for they were driven away before a splendid pen of corn-fed "Iowas" near by had found a purchaser. Aside from the facts here stated, there is nothing repulsive or objectionable in the matter of canned beef.

The average weight of the class of animals used for "mess" and "canning" is 950 pounds, and 800 head are daily disposed of in this way. If necessities of trade call for a large proportion of barrelled beef, then the carcasses are mostly cut with reference to this demand. In this case the division is made into the various pieces here named, many of which are familiar to household providers, viz., loins, ribs, mess, plates, chucks, rolls, rumps, hams, shoulders, tenderloins, striploins, sirloins, butts, rump butts, strips, rounds, and canning beef. "Extra mess" is composed of chucks, plates, rumps, and flanks, and the time of curing is twenty-four days. All hams are cut into three pieces, or "one set"; time of curing, sixty days. Plates are cut into five pieces. Loins, ribs, and shoulders are also sold to the city butchers. "Prime" tallow is made from the kidney and caul fat only, while "regular" tallow is made from the other fat, bones, and trimmings. Glue factories and fertilizing establishments use up the bones and refuse, and the hides find their way to the tanneries. Not a scrap of the animal is wasted, or fails to yield some revenue to the buyer.

To show the immense nature of the business now centring in Chicago, and the increase which has taken place in the last ten years, we give the statistics as furnished by the reports of the Union Stockyard and Transit Company. Five railroads leading into Chicago brought, in the year 1883, 1,512,212 head; the receipts from all other sources were 366,732—making a total of 1,878,944. The receipts for the year 1873 were 761,428; so that the business has more than doubled itself during ten years past. The largest receipts on any one day during that period was on November 15, 1882, being 12,076. The largest for one week was on that ending October 20, 1883, being 52,192, while that of the same month gave 217,791. The total valuation of stock of all kinds received during the year 1873 was $91,321,162, while for 1883 it was $201,252,772. A record so remarkable of the growth of a single industry is indeed a marvellous one. But who shall say what the next decade may bring forth?

Before closing this article let me give a few words of suggestion and advice to those who wish to become thoroughly posted either in the cattle business or in the empires over which it is conducted, for such they are in extent and territory, if not in name. Not all the articles and books that have been written will suffice to convey a clear idea of the wonderful country which extends for 200 miles north and south and west of the one-hundredth meridian of longitude. Personal inspection and experience will alone satisfy.

A brief summary of camp life on the range during the summers of 1882 and 1883 may be of benefit to those who are to follow, and of some interest to those who remain at home. The line of railroad travel across the continent is familiar to many; the experience on the stage routes, which extend for hundreds of miles far away into the interior of the Territories, is known to but few. Before leaving home you have, no doubt, taken some pains to look up your destination and the means of reaching the same, and have possibly become possessed of a handbill which gives the information that a line of "four-horse Concord coaches" has been established, leaving tri-weekly, and making the distance, it may be, of 400 miles in six days, or in half the time in case of night travel. When speaking of a Concord coach one not unusually has in view a White Mountain outfit, and looks out on leaving the train for the familiar equipage. Vain delusion! A low, two-seated, canvas-covered, mud-stained, or alkali-dusted vehicle stands near the platform, under the flapping curtains of which we crawl, if fortunate enough to have secured a seat several days in advance; otherwise one may have to stay over two or four days, as the case may be, waiting for the same. And here for a little practical advice as to personal luggage. You may have been beguiled on leaving home into taking a trunk, and this may be well, as part of the journey is to be within the limits of civilization; but leave it behind at the railway station, and in it all linen of every description, except handkerchiefs and a few towels. "Boiled shirts" are not admissible on the plains, and collars and cuffs are an unheard-of luxury. Wear coarse, second-hand, *thick* clothing and flannel shirts. Put as few necessaries as possible into a stout valise, not omitting a small supply of medicines most likely to be needed when you are fifty miles from the nearest doctor. Carry a pair of the *best* and *heaviest* blankets to be had, a pair of boots, a rubber pillow, and a "slicker," all tied up with a cord into as compact a bundle as possible: weight and space are both to be considered when on the stage or riding the range.

I was told on leaving the East that after the 1st of June we should have almost cloudless skies, with possibly now and then a light shower. Whereas the facts are that it rained more or less every day for three weeks, and we were more than once encamped beside raging torrents, waiting for the subsidence of the waters. Therefore do not be beguiled into leaving "slicker," overcoat, or boots behind, as when it rains it rains hard, and when it is muddy the mud is deep and tenacious beyond expression. I had taken the precaution when journeying through Wyoming in 1882 to leave my gold watch at home, and take a cheap silver one, also to carry as little ready money as possible. No "road agents" had been seen on the line for over two years, and I had not hesitated to say, in consequence, that one was in much more danger of being robbed in the streets of New York than on the plains of Wyoming. This year, although equally fortunate over stage routes in Montana, yet I had hardly reached home when, on the same line taken by me from Helena to Deer Lodge, two cases of "holding up of hands" occurred in the passes of the mountains, and the passengers were relieved of all their available assets. That such unpleasant episodes may have still more disagreeable incidents was shown by one of our fellow-travellers of last season, who pointed to a scar on the lobe of one ear caused by a road agent's bullet, who mistook his motion in pulling on a boot, as the stage was stopped by the robbers, and fired without delay.

Strictly speaking, there are no roads on the great plains. Certain well-defined trails there are, which can not be mistaken, and as there is very little limit to the area of freedom, as soon as one track becomes rough and cut up by travel another alongside takes its place. There are places where no road in Central Park can excel the smooth, hard surface of a track across the prairie, while again there are passes over the mountains and through deep cañons which would exhaust a descriptive vocabulary. Bridges are an exceptional convenience, and streams are forded with safety or with doubtful results, as the weather of twenty-four hours previous often determines. A sudden shower in the mountains, or a day or two of hot sun melting the snows, will send down a raging torrent with very little warning. A variation of two feet in a night is not unusual, and I have sat beside a rapidly running stream more than once, with a stick planted in the edge of the current, anxiously noting the number of inches rise or fall, and predicating thereon the chances of crossing

during the day. Many narrow escapes have been had and some fatal accidents have occurred in these wild streams of the West. We crossed one roaring little run in Wyoming six times in as many miles, the water coming into the bottom of the coach every time. The sensation is not a pleasant one, when the possibility of an upset in the middle of a stream is considered, especially in a current running six or eight miles an hour.

But it will not do to be too critical while travelling through this primitive country. It is barely seven years since the Custer massacre, when central Wyoming and Montana were given over to roving bands of red men. It is none too safe even now from the revolvers of the road agents. Be satisfied, therefore, if your slumbers are comparatively safe, even if not altogether undisturbed, and take your rations, which are fair if not luxurious, seasoned with the appetite which travel and the breezy air of these elevated plains are sure to give. You may not always have butter for your bread or milk for your coffee, notwithstanding that thousands of cows are roaming within a few miles of you. But one gets used to almost anything when necessity compels.

If we are to ride a range for a few weeks to get some insight into the cattle business, we will join an outfit, and take what experience comes in our way. First in importance is to secure a good saddle. Much of our comfort and ability to endure depends upon this. One day's ride upon an ill-fitting, badly constructed saddle may send a man into "the hospital"—*i. e.*, the camp wagon—at the outset. This provided, we will take our choice of fifty horses, more or less, belonging to the ranch, and there is a choice, although the animals are plenty enough. If we should chance to select "a bucker," the probabilities are that we will come to grief, and bite the dust before many hours are past. An experienced cow-boy will keep his seat, and the animal soon knows that he has found his master. But he also is quite well aware when a "tenderfoot" bestrides him, and he will carry him as far as "his own sweet will" inclines him, and no farther.

The Texas ponies are small, tough, and unkempt in appearance. Seldom groomed, shod, or stabled, they run loose until wanted for the saddle or the harness, when they are driven in from the range to the pen. Picking up their own living on grass only, they can not stand the hard work of grain-fed animals; consequently two or three sets must be provided. Each is ridden in turn until exhausted, when another lot takes its place. For this reason at least double the number of horses in daily use must be kept on hand during the season of the round-ups.

A couple of horses are placed at our command, and having secured a well-fitted saddle, we are ready for business. This means riding twenty, thirty, or forty miles a day, according to circumstances, starting with the rising sun, perhaps reaching some ranch at noon, or giving a rendezvous for the wagon with the commissary stores. At night we look out for wood and water as prime requisites for a camping ground. These are not so readily at hand as may be imagined in a region proverbially treeless, and where alkali is the basis of most of the water deposits. They are found, however, and we pitch our tent, making it secure by banking against the insidious draughts in the low temperature of summer nights in this elevated region. Blankets are unrolled, and we proceed to make our beds, having previously spread a canvas over the damp or dusty earth, as the case may be. Others are cutting wood, mixing bread, frying bacon, or making coffee, as called upon by the chief cook. The welcome cry, "To supper!" soon brings hungry men to their hams around the improvised table. A smoke by the camp fire concludes the day, and exhausted nature generally seeks repose ere twilight has fairly faded from the western sky. A cow-boy seldom indulges in the luxury of a tent, but with his saddle for a pillow, and a soft hollow in the ground for a cot, rolls himself up in a blanket, and takes the stars for his canopy.

The limits of a range may be twenty-five or thirty miles square, or it may be twice the distance in one direction, as the size of the herd or the different sections occupied may determine. Cattle turned out in a region well supplied with water, and where hills and broken country form a natural boundary, will not often "drift" a very great distance, except in the case of prolonged and severe winter storms. When these occur, natural instinct seems to come to the aid of the beasts, and they move before the gale in search of bare ground and better grass. If they find it, all is well; if not, the weak ones must succumb, and losses take place according to the depth of snow and the period which it remains upon the ground. Cold weather is not so much dreaded by cattle men as a deep fall of snow without wind. Twenty below zero in the dry air of the plains does not carry with it the same intensity as a like temperature on our Eastern coast; and although many calves are seen with frozen ears and tails, attesting the severity of the cold, yet they come through all right if they are old enough to run by the mother's side.

If an Eastern man wonders, when first discussing the cattle business, how the animals are ever found after being turned loose upon the limitless prairies, it is an equal mystery to him, while riding the ranges, to know on what they manage to subsist. To the unpracticed eye a full-grown steer would apparently starve to death in a week, while the facts are that he is growing fatter every day, and in a moderate winter will even hold his own during the entire season. There is no such thing as a *sod* known upon the plains, and the general outlook is that of bare ground rather than of grass. Yet what there is is nutritious beyond the comprehension of one brought up in a region where rain and not dry weather is supposed to be required for the development of grass.

I say this with a qualification, for early rains are desirable to start the growth in the spring. After that, the less moisture the better, as the grass cures like standing hay; and cattle do their own foraging with much better success than an Eastern farmer can put his hay under cover and feed it out to his stock in the winter.

The limits of this article will not permit a farther insight into the details of the working of a range. Let him who seeks to know it better leave the fox-hunters of Newport to chase one poor frightened Reynard, whose hounding to death seems to be considered a great achievement, and come out upon the breezy plains where the buffalo still roams, and into the region of the big-horn and the elk—game worth the seeing and the killing; let him camp, hunt, and fish under the shadow of the mighty mountains which form the backbone of the continent, and he will take in a good deal more stock of health, wealth, and knowledge than he will get on the velvety lawns of tennis, or riding the little circuit of the polo grounds.

"THAR'S Mis' Bliss's pieces in the brown kaliker bag, an' thar's Mis' Bennet's pieces in the bed-tickin' bag," said she, surveying the two bags leaning against her kitchen wall complacently. "I'll get a dollar for both of them quilts, an' thar'll be two dollars. I've got a dollar an' sixty-three cents on hand now, an' thar's plenty of meal an' merlasses, an' some salt fish an' pertaters in the house. I'll get along middlin' well, I reckon. Thar ain't no call fer me to worry. I'll red up the house a leetle now, an' then I'll begin on Mis' Bliss's pieces."

The *house* was an infinitesimal affair, containing only two rooms besides the tiny lean-to which served as wood-shed. It stood far enough back from the road for a pretentious mansion, and there was one curious feature about it—not a door or window was there in front, only a blank, unbroken wall. Strangers passing by used to stare wonderingly at it sometimes, but it was explained easily enough. Old Simeon Patch, years ago, when the longing for a home of his own had grown strong in his heart, and he had only a few hundred dollars saved from his hard earnings to invest in one, had wisely done the best he could with what he had.

Not much remained to spend on the house after the spacious lot was paid for, so he resolved to build as much house as he could with his money, and complete it when better days should come.

This tiny edifice was in reality simply the L of a goodly two-story house which had existed only in the fond and faithful fancies of Simeon Patch and his wife. That blank front wall was designed to be joined to the projected main building; so of course there was no need of doors or windows. Simeon Patch came of a hard-working, honest race, whose pride it had been to keep out of debt, and he was a true child of his ancestors. Not a dollar would he spend that was not in his hand; a mortgaged house was his horror. So he paid cash for every blade of grass on his lot of land, and every nail in his bit of a house, and settled down patiently in it until he should grub together enough more to buy a few additional boards and shingles, and pay the money down.

That time never came: he died in the course of a few years, after a lingering illness, and only had enough saved to pay his doctor's bill and funeral expenses, and leave his wife and daughter entirely without debt in their little fragment of a house on the big sorry lot of land.

There they had lived, mother and daughter, earning and saving in various little petty ways, keeping their heads sturdily above-water, and holding the dreaded mortgage resolutely off the house for many years. Then the mother died, and the daughter, Martha Patch, took up the little homely struggle alone. She was over seventy now, a small, slender old woman, as straight as a rail, with sharp black eyes, and a quick toss of her head when she spoke. She did odd housewifely jobs for the neighbors, wove rag carpets, pieced bed-quilts, braided rugs, etc., and contrived to supply all her simple wants.

This evening, after she had finished putting her house to rights, she fell to investigating the contents of the bags which two of the neighbors had brought in the night before, with orders for quilts, much to her delight.

"Mis' Bliss has got proper harnsome pieces," said she—"proper harnsome; they'll make a good-lookin' quilt. Mis' Bennet's is good too, but they ain't quite ekal to Mis' Bliss's. I reckon some of 'em's old."

She began spreading some of the largest, prettiest pieces on her white-scoured table. "Thar," said she, gazing at one admiringly, "that jest takes my eye; them leetle pink roses is pretty, an' no mistake. I reckon that's French caliker. Thar's some big pieces too. Lor, what bag did I take 'em out on! It must hev been Mis' Bliss's. I mustn't git 'em mixed."

She cut out some squares, and sat down by the window in a low wooden rocking-chair to sew. This window did not have a very pleasant outlook. The house was situated so far back from the road that it commanded only a rear view of the adjoining one. It was a great cross to Martha Patch. She was one of those women who like to see everything that is going on outside, and who often have excuse enough in the fact that so little is going on with them.

"It's a great diversion," she used to say, in her snapping way, which was more nervous than ill-natured, bobbing her head violently at the same time—"a very great diversion to see Mr. Peters's cows goin' in an' out of the barn day arter day; an' that's about all I do see—never git a sight of the folks goin' to meetin' nor nothin'."

The lack of a front window was a continual source of grief to her.

"When the minister's prayin' for the widders an' orphans, he'd better make mention of one more," said she, once, "an' that's women without front winders."

She and her mother had planned to save money enough to have one some day, but they had never been able to bring it about. A window commanding a view of the street and the passers-by would have been a great source of comfort to the poor old woman, sitting and sewing as she did day in and day out. As it was, the few objects of interest which did come within her vision she seized upon eagerly, and made much of. There were some children who, on their way from school, could make a short-cut through her yard, and reach home quicker. She watched for them every day, and if they did not appear quite as soon as usual she would grow uneasy, and eye the clock, and mutter to herself, "I wonder where them Mosely children can be?" When they came she watched their progress with sharp attention, and thought them over for an hour afterward. Not a bird which passed her window escaped her notice. This innocent old gossip fed her mind upon their small domestic affairs in lieu of larger ones. To-day she often paused between her stitches to gaze absorbedly at a yellow-bird vibrating nervously round the branches of a young tree opposite. It was early spring, and the branches were all of a light green foam.

"That's the same yaller-bird I saw yesterday, I do b'lieve," said she. "I recken he's goin' to build a nest in that ellum."

Lately she had been watching the progress of the grass gradually springing up all over the yard. One spot where it grew much greener than elsewhere her mind dwelt upon curiously.

"I can't make out," she said to a neighbor, "whether that 'ere spot is greener than the rest because the sun shines brightly thar, or because somethin's buried thar."

She toiled steadily on the patchwork quilts. At the end of a fortnight they were nearly completed. She hurried on the last one one forenoon thinking she would carry them both to their owners that afternoon and get her pay. She did not stop for any dinner.

Spreading them out for one last look before rolling them up in bundles she caught her breath hastily.

"What hev I done?" said she. "Massy sakes! I hevn't gone an' put Mis' Bliss's caliker with the leetle pink roses on't in Mis' Bennet's quilt! I hev, jest as sure as preachin'! What shell I do?"

The poor old soul stood staring at the quilts in pitiful dismay. "A hull fortnit's work," she muttered. "What shell I do? Them pink roses is the prettiest caliker in the hull lot. Mis' Bliss will be mad if they air in Mis' Bennet's quilt. She won't say nothin', an' she'll pay me, but she'll feel it inside, an' it won't be doin' the squar' thing by her. No; if I'm goin' to airn money I'll airn it."

Martha Patch gave her head a jerk. The spirit which animated her father when he went to housekeeping in a piece of a house without any front window blazed up within her. She made herself a cup of tea, then sat deliberately down by the window to rip the quilts to pieces. It had to be done pretty thoroughly on account of her admiration for the pink calico, and the quantity of it—it figured in nearly every square. "I wish I hed a front winder to set to while I'm doin' on't," said she; but she patiently plied her scissors till dusk, only stopping for a short survey of the Mosely children. After days of steady work the pieces were put together again, this time the pink rose calico in Mrs. Bliss's quilt. Martha Patch rolled the quilts up with a sigh of relief, and a sense of virtuous triumph.

"I'll sort over the pieces that's left in the bags," said she, "then I'll take 'em over an' git my pay. I'm gittin' pretty short of vittles."

She began pulling the pieces out of the bed-ticking bag, laying them on her lap, and smoothing them out, preparatory to doing them up in a neat tight roll to take home—she was very methodical about everything she did. Suddenly she turned pale, and stared wildly at a tiny scrap of calico which she had just fished out of the bag.

"Massy sakes!" she cried; "it ain't, is it?" She clutched Mrs. Bliss's quilt from the table, and laid the bit of calico beside the pink rose squares.

"It's jest the same thing," she groaned, "an' it came out on Mis' Bennet's bag. Dear me suz! dear me suz!"

She dropped helplessly into her chair

by the window, still holding the quilt and the tell-tale scrap of calico, and gazed out in a bewildered sort of way. Her poor old eyes looked dim and weak with tears.

"Thar's the Mosely children comin'," she said—"happy little gals, laughin' an' hollerin', goin' home to their mother to git a good dinner. Me a-settin' here's a lesson they ain't larned in their books yit; hope to goodness they never will; hope they won't ever hev to piece quilts fur a livin', without any front winder to set to. Thar's a dandelion blown out on that green spot. Reckon thar *is* somethin' buried thar. Lordy massy! *hev* I got to rip them two quilts to pieces agin an' sew 'em over?"

Finally she resolved to carry a bit of the pink rose calico over to Mrs. Bennet's, and find out, without betraying the dilemma she was in, if it was really hers.

Her poor old knees fairly shook under her when she entered Mrs. Bennet's sitting-room.

"Why, yes, Miss Patch, it's mine," said Mrs. Bennet, in response to her agitated question. "Hattie had a dress like it, don't you remember? There was a lot of new pieces left, and I thought they would work into a quilt nice. But, for pity's sake, Martha, what is the matter? You look just as white as a sheet. You ain't sick, are you?"

"No," said Martha, with a feeble toss of her head, to keep up the deception; "I ain't sick, only kinder all gone with the warm weather. I reckon I'll hev to fix me up some thoroughwort tea. Thoroughwort's a great strengthener."

"I would," said Mrs. Bennet, sympathizingly; "and don't you work too hard on that quilt; I ain't in a bit of a hurry for it. I sha'n't want it before next winter anyway. I only thought I'd like to have it pieced and ready."

"I reckon I can't get it done afore another fortni't," said Martha, trembling.

"I don't care if you don't get it done for the next three months. Don't go yet, Martha; you 'ain't rested a minute, and it's a pretty long walk. Don't you want a bite of something before you go? Have a piece of cake? You look real faint."

"No, thanky," said Martha, and departed in spite of all friendly entreaties to tarry. Mrs. Bennet watched her moving slowly down the road, still holding the little pink calico rag in her brown withered fingers.

"Martha Patch is failing; she ain't near so straight as she was," remarked Mrs. Bennet. "She looks real bent over to-day."

The little wiry springiness was, indeed, gone from her gait as she crept slowly along the sweet country road, and there was a helpless droop in her thin narrow shoulders. It was a beautiful spring day; the fruit trees were all in blossom. There were more orchards than houses on the way, and more blooming trees to pass than people.

Martha looked up at the white branches as she passed under them. "I kin smell the apple-blows," said she, "but somehow the goodness is all gone out on 'em. I'd jest as soon smell cabbage. Oh, dear me suz, kin I ever do them quilts over agin?"

When she got home, however, she rallied a little. There was a nervous force about this old woman which was not easily overcome even by an accumulation of misfortunes. She might bend a good deal, but she was almost sure to spring back again. She took off her hood and shawl, and straightened herself up. "Thar's no use puttin' it off; it's got to be done. I'll hev them quilts right ef it kills me!"

She tied on a purple calico apron and sat down at the window again, with a quilt and the scissors. Out came the pink roses. There she sat through the long afternoon, cutting the stitches which she had so laboriously put in—a little, defiant old figure, its head, with a flat black lace cap on it, bobbing up and down in time with its hands. There were some purple bows on the cap, and they fluttered; quite a little wind blew in at the window.

The eight-day clock on the mantel ticked peacefully. It was a queer old timepiece, which had belonged to her grandmother Patch. A painting of a quaint female with puffed hair and a bunch of roses adorned the front of it under the dial-plate. It was flanked on either side by tall green vases.

There was a dull-colored rag carpet of Martha's own manufacture on the floor of the room. Some wooden chairs stood around stiffly; an old yellow map of Massachusetts and a portrait of George Washington hung on the walls. There was not a speck of dust anywhere, nor any disorder. Neatness was one of the chiefest comforts of Martha's life. Putting and keeping things in order was one of the interests which enlivened her dullness and made the world attractive to her.

The poor soul sat at the window, bending over the quilt, till dusk, and she sat there bending over the quilt till dusk many a day after.

It is a hard question to decide whether there was any real merit in such finely strained honesty, or whether it was merely a case of morbid conscientiousness. Perhaps the old woman, inheriting very likely her father's scruples, had had them so intensified by age and childishness that they had become a little off the bias of reason.

Be that as it may, she thought it was the right course for her to make the quilts over, and thinking so, it was all that she could do. She could never have been satisfied otherwise. It took her a considerable time longer to finish the quilts again, and this time she began to suffer from other causes than mere fatigue. Her stock of provisions commenced to run low, and her money was gone. At last she had nothing but a few potatoes in the house to eat. She contrived to dig some dandelion greens once or twice; these with the potatoes were all her diet. There was really no necessity for such a state of things : she was surrounded by kindly, well-to-do people, who would have gone without themselves rather than have let her suffer. But she had always been very reticent about her needs, and felt great pride about accepting anything which she did not pay for.

But she struggled along until the quilts were done, and no one knew. She set the last stitch quite late one evening; then she spread the quilts out and surveyed them. "Thar they air now, all right," said she; "the pink roses is in Mis' Bennet's, an' I 'ain't cheated nobody out on their caliker, an' I've airned my money. I'll take 'em hum in the mornin', an' then I'll buy somethin' to eat. I begin to feel a dreadful sinkin' at my stummuck."

She locked up the house carefully—she always felt a great responsibility when she had people's work on hand—and went to bed.

Next morning she woke up so faint and dizzy that she hardly knew herself. She crawled out into the kitchen, and sank down on the floor. She could not move another step.

"Lor sakes!" she moaned, "I reckon I'm 'bout done to!"

The quilts lay near her on the table; she stared up at them with feeble complacency. "Ef I'm goin' to die, I'm glad I got them quilts done right fust. Massy, how sinkin' I do feel! I wish I had a cup of tea."

There she lay, and the beautiful spring morning wore on. The sun shone in at the window, and moved nearer and nearer, till finally she lay in a sunbeam, a poor, shrivelled, little old woman, whose resolute spirit had nearly been her death, in her scant night-gown and ruffled cap, a little shawl falling from her shoulders. She did not feel ill, only absolutely too weak and helpless to move. Her mind was just as active as ever, and her black eyes peered sharply out of her pinched face. She kept making efforts to rise, but she could not stir.

"Lor sakes!" she snapped out at length, "how long *hev* I got to lay here! I'm mad!"

She saw some dust on the black paint of a chair which stood in the sun, and she eyed that distressfully.

"Jest look at that dust on the runs of that cheer!" she muttered. "What if anybody come in! I wonder if I can't reach it!"

The chair was near her, and she managed to stretch out her limp old hand and rub the dust off the rounds. Then she let it sink down, panting.

"I wonder ef I *ain't* goin' to die," she gasped. "I wonder ef I'm prepared. I never took nothin' that shouldn't belong to me that I knows on. Oh, dear me suz, I wish somebody would come!"

When her strained ears did catch the sound of footsteps outside, a sudden resolve sprang up in her heart.

"I won't let on to nobody how I've made them quilts over, an' how I hevn't hed enough to eat—I won't."

When the door was tried she called out feebly, "Who is thar?"

The voice of Mrs. Peters, her next-door neighbor, came back in response: "It's me. What's the matter, Marthy?"

"I'm kinder used up; don' know how you'll git in; I can't git to the door to unlock it to save my life."

"Can't I get in at the window?"

"Mebbe you kin."

Mrs. Peters was a long-limbed, spare woman, and she got in through the window with considerable ease, it being quite low from the ground.

She turned pale when she saw Martha lying on the floor. "Why, Marthy, what is the matter? How long have you been laying there?"

"Ever since I got up. I was kinder dizzy, an' hed a dreadful sinkin' feelin'. It ain't much, I reckon. Ef I could hev a cup of tea it would set me right up. Thar's a spoonful left in the pantry. Ef you jist put a few kindlin's in the stove, Mis' Peters, an' set in the kettle an' make me a cup, I could git up, I know. I've got to go an' kerry them quilts hum to Mis' Bliss an' Mis' Bennet."

"I don't believe but what you've got all tired out over the quilts. You've been working too hard."

"No, I 'ain't, Mis' Peters; it's nothin' but play piecin' quilts. All I mind is not havin' a front winder to set to while I'm doin' on't."

Mrs. Peters was a quiet, sensible woman of few words; she insisted upon carrying Martha into the bedroom and putting her comfortably to bed. It was easily done, she was muscular, and the old woman a very light weight. Then she went into the pantry. She was beginning to suspect the state of affairs, and her suspicions were strengthened when she saw the bare shelves. She started the fire, put on the tea-kettle, and then slipped across the yard to her own house for further re-enforcements.

Pretty soon Martha was drinking her cup of tea and eating her toast and a dropped egg. She had taken the food with some reluctance, half starved as she was. Finally she gave in—the sight of it was too much for her. "Well, I will borry it, Mis' Peters," said she; "an' I'll pay you jest as soon as I kin git up."

After she had eaten she felt stronger. Mrs. Peters had hard work to keep her quiet till afternoon; then she would get up and carry the quilts home. The two ladies were profuse in praises. Martha, proud and smiling. Mrs. Bennet noticed the pink roses at once. "How pretty that calico did work in," she remarked.

"Yes," assented Martha, between an inclination to chuckle and to cry.

"Ef I ain't thankful I did them quilts over," thought she, creeping slowly homeward, her hard-earned two dollars knotted into a corner of her handkerchief for security.

About sunset, Mrs. Peters came in again. "Marthy," she said, after a while, "Sam says he's out of work just now, and he'll cut through a front window for you. He's got some old sash and glass that's been laying round in the barn ever since I can remember. It 'll be a real charity for you to take it off his hands, and he'll like to do it. Sam's as uneasy as a fish out of water when he hasn't got any work."

Martha eyed her suspiciously. "Thanky; but I don't want nothin' done that I can't pay for," said she, with a stiff toss of her head.

"It would be pay enough just letting Sam do it, Marthy; but, if you really feel set about it, I've got some sheets that need turning. You can do them some time this summer, and that will pay us for all it's worth."

The black eyes looked at her sharply. "Air you sure?"

"Yes; it's fully as much as it's worth," said Mrs. Peters. "I'm most afraid it's more. There's four sheets, and putting in a window is nothing more than putting in a patch—the old stuff ain't worth anything."

When Martha fully realized that she was going to have a front window, and that her pride might suffer it to be given to her and yet receive no insult, she was as delighted as a child.

"Lor sakes!" said she, "jest to think that I shall have a front winder to set to! I wish mother could ha' lived to see it. Mebbe you kinder wonder at it, Mis' Peters—you've allers hed front winders; but you haven't any idea what a great thing it seems to me. It kinder makes me feel younger. Thar's the Mosely children; they're 'bout all I've ever seen pass *this* winder, Mis' Peters. Jest see that green spot out thar; it's been greener than the rest of the yard all the spring, an' now thar's lots of dandelions blowed out on it, an' some clover. I b'lieve the sun shines more on it, somehow. Lor me, to think I'm going to hev a front winder!"

"Sarah was in this afternoon," said Mrs. Peters, further (Sarah was her married daughter), "and she says she wants some braided rugs right away. She'll send the rags over by Willie to-morrow."

"You don't say so! Well I'll be glad to do it; an' thar's one thing 'bout it, Mis' Peters—mebbe you'll think it queer for me to say so, but I'm kinder thankful it's rugs she wants. I'm kinder sick of bed-quilts somehow."

Editor's Easy Chair.

THE musical season that closed in New York with May-day was the most memorable in the annals of the city, and was unequalled in any other city in the world. The chief singers of the two great schools, that of Germany and of Italy, were singing in New York at the same time—Materna and Patti and Nilsson and Gerster and Scalchi and Winkelmann and Campanini and Scaria, and all of them admirably supported. There was the usual enthusiasm over the exquisite vocalization and coquetry of the Italian *prime donne*, who warbled the old familiar music with the old familiar grace and skill and charm, and the young people of to-day renewed the spectacle of the youth of their parents, and enjoyed with a freshness of delight a pleasure which was old half a century ago—old and forever new — not the pleasure of listening to sweet music only, but that of listening to it with sympathetic ears, and with hearts that make a sweeter music with each other.

But the great novelty and the greatest delight were the Wagner concerts in the new Metropolitan Opera-house. A magnificent chorus filled the depth of the stage upon ascending seats, and a great orchestra occupied the front of the stage, and with the three singers selected by Wagner as the especial vocal interpreters of his music, and all directed by Theodore Thomas, they revealed the scope and character of the Wagner music as never before has it been displayed in this country. It was, indeed, a concert presentation of music which is composed for a peculiarly spectacular opera. But it is not easy to understand why the supernatural spectacle would not imperil the impression of the music, which can better supply to the imagination the due suggestion of supernatural or unusual effects than any stage machinery can represent them to the eye. No one who heard Materna in the music of the self-immolation of Brünnhilde, especially on the last evening of the first series of the concerts in Boston, could have wished for any stage properties to deepen the majestic effect, or have felt it to be a misfortune that the music was presented without scenic accessories.

The scheme of the concerts embraced scenes from all the chief works of Wagner, and certainly the selections from the *Tristan und Isolde* tried to the utmost the attention of those who, without technical musical training, were disposed to appreciate and enjoy. Had the entertainment been a feast of wine, it could be said truly that the *Tristan und Isolde* was the very driest brand offered to the consumer. The patient listener who said that it was like swaying to and fro in the monotonous swell of the ocean, and the other who held that it was a gray cloud broken at long intervals and showing the radiant blue sky for a tantalizing instant through the rifts, both expressed the bewildered anticipation of something in-

definably striking and imminent which, just about to be disclosed, did not quite appear. But the climbers of the awful Alpine heights on which the edelweiss blooms are few. For the multitude the charms of the lower slopes suffice, and the selections from the *Flying Dutchman*, the *Tannhäuser*, the *Meistersinger*, the *Lohengrin*, the *Götterdämmerung, Walküre*, and *Siegfried* were all more accessible to the average climber than the perpendicular cliffs of *Parsifal* and *Tristan und Isolde*.

These concerts have removed all doubt, if any doubt still lingered, that, whatever may be true of Wagner's theories—and the theories of great artists are not always their best performances—he has contributed much to the accumulated stores of memorable music, while in interpreting his music Madame Materna and Mr. Winkelmann and Mr. Scaria have renewed the best traditions of "the grand manner" in a wholly new form. Madame Materna's ample and delightful voice, her grandeur of method, and her simple dignity of presence contrast charmingly with the arch prettiness of the usual *prima donna ;* and her great scene, to which we have alluded, Brünnhilde's self-immolation—following the Dead March of Siegfried, one of the most powerful and impressive of orchestral compositions—was a scene to be paralleled only in the memory of those who can recall Pasta in her great moments, or who, like the Easy Chair, seeing her only after the failure of her voice, and long after her retirement from the stage, yet saw the magnificence of the manner and felt her fame to be justified.

With Madame Materna's noble impression must be recalled the manly vigor and artistic sentiment and skill of her associates, Mr. Winkelmann, the tenor, and Mr. Scaria, the bass. In both it was a *vox sana in corpore sano.* There was no prettiness, no sentimentality, no grimace, but the honest and adequate singing of music which is not designed to exalt the singer, but to subordinate his part to a general effect. This, indeed, must be something of a trial for the singer who desires to emphasize himself, and to be personally and rapturously applauded. But the vast audiences which attended the concerts, the intelligent eagerness, and the enthusiasm at the end, especially in Boston and in Brooklyn—which would have been no less in New York if the wretched acoustic defects of the Metropolitan Opera-house had not robbed the singers of some of their due by robbing the audience of the fullness of enjoyment—must have assured the trio that they had not crossed the sea in vain, and that they had given our musical taste a standard which no exquisite vocalist of the tum-titum school can hope to satisfy.

And no one concerned in this musical triumph was more earnestly and gratefully cheered, and cheered again and again, than the masterly conductor and director, who has done more than any other individual for the progress and development of the musical taste of this country—Theodore Thomas. His activity and achievement are extraordinary, and two of his enterprises of the winter are as worthy of remembrance as this culminating success of the Wagner concerts. We mean his concerts for children, and the series of free concerts for the people. The interested, intelligent, and enthusiastic throngs which attended the latter, and their hearty enjoyment of the works of the best composers, show that the higher the genius and the truer the art, the more universal is the popular enjoyment. It is not the praise of the connoisseur which is most precious to the artist, but the delight of the people in his best endeavor.

Mr. Henry Irving and Miss Ellen Terry, with their admirable company, have gone home to England, but will return in the autumn, so pleasant and so profitable have they found their American tour to be. The secret of Mr. Irving's success is an open one. It is the result of doing everything well. His career is a verification of the old wisdom, that whatever is worth doing at all, is worth doing well. He has evidently a strong taste for the stage, and the instinct of the actor. Yet he has serious natural difficulties to encounter, and he has not, like Garrick and Edmund Kean, great genius. Nevertheless he played for six months in all parts of the country with extraordinary success, and for every character that he represented there are enthusiastic admirers, and no actor of his time has done so much to improve the acting of plays. And how has he done it?

It will not be denied that if Mr. Irving had played with no other stage accessories and scenery than those of the Elizabethan stage and those amid which Garrick appeared, or with the kind of support upon which the elder Booth was used to rely, he could hardly have acquired his great reputation as the head of the contemporary English stage. That is largely due to his apprehension that no person, of whatever genius or however accomplished, can alone present a play adequately. Acting is a mimetic art, and everything concerned in the representation must have a certain proportion to everything else, and a certain relation of resemblance to the scenes represented.

The most satisfactory and adequate interpretation of a play of Shakespeare that the Easy Chair ever enjoyed until it saw Mr. Irving's *Merchant of Venice* was a reading of *As You Like It* by Mrs. Kemble. The scene was left to the imagination, but by ingenious modifications of the voice, assisted by the hearer's knowledge of the play, all the characters were satisfactory, and their speech had the unity and harmony with which it was conceived and written. Many of the characters, of course, are rustic and rude. But the play is in every part, those characters included, a work of art, and every part, and consequent-

ly the whole, can be represented only by artists. A boor can not play a boor, because he can not play at all. But a consummate artist can play a boor as he can play a king or a poet. Mrs. Kemble presented Audrey perfectly because she so exquisitely rendered Rosalind.

This is the theory of Mr. Irving's management, and this largely explains the success of his career. Symmetry of representation is his aim, and to this symmetry the careful treatment of every detail of scene and action is indispensable. This has been for a long time the tendency of the English stage. Charles Kean and Macready lavished great care upon the production of certain plays, but they both lacked the comprehension, perception, and skill which distinguish Mr. Irving. The same general spirit has been long observable also in some of our own theatres, and whoever saw the recent performance of *A Scrap of Paper* at Wallack's saw a charming little play as neatly and adequately performed as the vaudevilles in which Rose Chéri used to play at the Paris Variétés.

The new Wallack's is a pretty little theatre, not too large for complete enjoyment; and the value of the thoroughness and proportion of which we have spoken is very evident in the Wallack representations. The play in which Mr. Wallack returned to his stage this season, *A Scrap of Paper*, is an adaptation from Jules Sardou; and its airy nothingness, a gossamer web in which human moths of several kinds are entangled, and from which they all happily escape, is most felicitously treated. The success of the play depends wholly upon the light touch, the precision, and brisk gayety with which it is acted, and all these were supplied at Wallack's. Mr. Wallack himself finds in it one of his peculiar parts, a man of the world, idle, blasé, good-natured, clever, and ready to fence with Fortune in any form in which she may present herself. His complete mastery of his happy talent was never more conspicuous, and except that he is no longer in his first youth, there is probably no more elegant light comedian upon the English stage.

There is undoubtedly a certain mannerism in his acting, that is to say, a quality which is peculiar to himself. But he has avoided the tendency to extravagant emphasis of his peculiarity, which is the besetting peril of an actor. The worldly ease and grace and gayety of an amiable lounger, who has little faith in anything but self-indulgence, and who takes everything with humorous badinage or with mere conventional warmth of feeling, could not be better done. The art is so complete that the simplicity and naturalness seem to be the absolute want of art, and the tyro might easily believe, as he sits in the parquet and watches the effortless play, that he could do it instantly and quite as well. But how many such finished and charming comedians does he know?

In this little play Mr. Wallack was admirably

supported by Miss Helen Russell, upon whom much of the chief action devolved, and it was delightful also to see again the perennial youth, Mr. Gilbert. It is under such auspices of clever play, careful mounting in every detail, and admirable acting at every point, that the theatre is the most charming of relaxations. It is Mr. Irving's principle applied to light comedy that makes Wallack's Theatre and similar theatres so attractive; and sitting in the comfortable house and watching the bright play, the pleased spectator recalls the hard, narrow, backless benches in the pit of the old Park and of the London theatres of Charles Lamb's and Hazlitt's day, and wishes that those adepts in theatre-going and those experts in plays could but return for one happy evening to see a play at Wallack's, and gossip about it before they vanished.

At every public amusement such as those of which we have been speaking an Easy Chair or any other spectator naturally observes the audience as well as the actors or singers, and as naturally such spectators mark with sorrow the youth or maid who either does not know or who disregards the common law of good conduct to which everybody submits himself when he makes one of an audience. There was no more excellent or refreshing incident of its kind during the last winter than the rising of a gentleman in the parquet of the Metropolitan Opera-house, while the performance was proceeding, to request some people in the boxes, who were talking audibly, to hush.

The offenders in the box were probably inhabitants of some frontier village where guests at the taverns slam the doors, and help themselves to butter at the common table with their own knives, and giggle in church, and wear jewelry at breakfast, and are unused to finger-bowls. But the ignorance of the manners of refined society upon the part of those who occupy a box at the opera can not be allowed to disturb an audience; and very possibly in this instance the offenders were as well-meaning as they were ignorant: they did not intend to annoy, but only did not know how to behave under the circumstances, and were perhaps—at least let us hope so—very grateful to the friendly mentor who reproved them. Let us also hope—as the good minister said to his pompous brother clergyman who could not find a front seat, and who was obliged to retire to the rear—that it may be sanctified to the good folks, who hereafter should never venture into well-bred society without ascertaining in advance how they should behave.

When it was proposed, upon the coming of the Princess Louise to Canada, to establish a kind of royal court, a worthy master of the dance at once issued proposals to teach the nobility and gentry how to conduct themselves at a presentation, how to walk backward with an ample train without tumbling into it or over it, and how to bow profoundly without being entangled and overthrown by a dress sword between the legs. The behavior of queer people—of course from the remote frontier villages—in the opera boxes suggests that an academy of polite conduct might be advantageously opened in the immediate vicinity of the opera-houses. Or the actual offense during a performance might be charitably condoned by the audience if, upon proper rebuke from the parquet or some other box, a placard should be instantly displayed from the offending box with the legend, "Just from Poker Flat," or, "From Dead Man's Gulch."

At a recent concert in the suburbs of the city a young man brought a chair and placed it in the aisle beside the seat of a young woman, and as the music began, so did the conversation. It was at once evident that the indulgent parents of the young people had thoughtlessly permitted them to come out without their nurses. As children are not allowed to go alone on the street until they can walk, so they should not be allowed to go alone to concerts or to the theatre until they have learned how to behave. An American audience is the best-natured audience in the world. It will be bullied and annoyed and maltreated in every way without remonstrance. But, like all weakness, this kind of submission is punished by annoyance of many kinds, and the hearty applause which greeted the voice at the Metropolitan Opera-house which rebuked the frontier people in the box shows how gladly an audience hails its deliverer.

Such conduct as the disturbance of an entire audience by tattle in a box suggests a gloomy view of the domestic interior of the tattlers. The boorishness which does not hesitate, either from ignorance or willfulness, to annoy a whole audience, must be formidable at home. The domestic vulgarity which is indicated by chattering in church or in any throng of listeners is mournful to contemplate. Does yonder woman in the box, feathered and furbelowed and diamonded, who chuckles and tattles to the man beside her, come down to breakfast in brocade, and fling the toast, if it is burned, at the waiter's head? Does that pretty young lady who disturbs without a thought a hundred listeners promenade the Avenue in white satin slippers, and wear ruby rings over the fingers of her gloves? There is, indeed, no other connection between the performances than that of a total want of a sense of propriety. It is not a high crime to wear white satin shoes in the street, nor to correct a waiter with a piece of toast—no, nor to disturb your neighbors at the play. It is only bad manners and vulgarity.

And whether or not a censor arises in the parquet, or a neighbor cries "Hush!" or a whole group of annoyed auditors frown, the offenders in the boxes, or wherever they may be, may know that the verdict upon their conduct is unanimous. They are instantly found guilty of gross vulgarity and bad manners, without the least recommendation to mercy, and with the fervent desire of all well-behaved persons that they will promptly return to Poker Flat, or Dead Man's Gulch, or other wilderness, where they evidently belong.

SIXTY years ago Wendell Phillips and Lothrop Motley and "Tom Appleton" were boys of the same neighborhood in Boston, playing together upon the Common and Beacon Hill. They entered college together, and Phillips and Motley were chums. The three classmates were constantly associated, and were of an equal brilliancy of talent and of an apparent equal promise. Appleton, who was the last survivor, used to tell of the gay afternoons when they draped themselves in coats and cloaks of many colors, and with flowing wit and fancy improvised plays "in which the conversation was not bad." The young men graduated together, and together studied law. But none of them cared for the profession or practiced it. Two of them became famous; the third, with all the rich temperament of genius, of an unsurpassed social charm, and of a mind so nimble and incisive, and a wit so shrewd and sparkling, and an intellectual and æsthetic sympathy so generous, that the wonder of his friends always was how a genius so fine had no adequate and permanent expression—the third was not famous, although with the gifts that make fame.

Phillips took his solitary and splendid way as the great orator of emancipation; Motley lived in Europe devoted to historical study; and Appleton, as long ago the Easy Chair elsewhere called him, the gentleman of two hemispheres, lived much abroad and at home, and gave full play to that genius for society, that taste for letters and art, in devotion to which his life was passed. Yet he was proud, with a certain tenderness, of his old comrades. From Phillips his conservative temper and strong convictions and traditions separated him, so that they seldom met. But he recalled with unfailing delight the earlier day, and owned the charm of his friend's character and the power of his genius. With Motley his personal relations were always maintained, and it was fine to see the ardor with which in Newport, many years ago, just before Motley's first history was published, he burst into a friend's room, his face glowing, his voice earnest, and the whole man delighted, as he said: "Motley has written the history of the Dutch Republic. I've been reading the proofsheets, and, by Jove! Motley has done it at last!"

Appleton always quoted with glee Motley's famous saying in college, that he could spare the necessaries but not the luxuries of life, and with the luxuries he was himself always surrounded. He was a gentleman of leisure, familiar with the best books, a skillful ama-

teur in painting, of a highly educated taste in beauty, blending the most manly vigor of character and a virile mind with the most delicate and just appreciation of whatever is rare and exquisite in every form of art. His estimate of men was singularly shrewd, and his cosmopolitan nature opened to him a most extensive and various range of acquaintance. To his conservative temperament traditions that have lost their charm for many others had an enduring attraction, but not to the exclusion of enjoyment of the later innovation and the new suggestion.

At his funeral the hymn was sung,

> "The saints above and those below
> But one communion make."

—"No saint," said Mr. Brooke Herford, in his tenderly felicitous address, and certainly that is not the word for him. Sybarite might seem to some a fitter word, but it carries a sense of effeminacy, of enervating self-indulgence, which the brisk and breezy manliness of "Tom Appleton" instantly repelled. No man knew better than he what "Ik Marvel" long ago called the uses of beauty, and in his intelligent care for every enterprise of that kind in Boston he was its faithful minister. It is painful to think what might not be officially done in deforming cities and public buildings with execrable works except for the active influence in every community of men like Mr. Appleton, who speak upon such subjects with authority. Much, indeed, is done in that kind which artistically is both grotesque and outrageous. But it is what is not done that we owe to the taste and intelligence of a few men. Mr. Appleton doubtless smiled at his classmate Phillips's sparkling gibes at the public statues in Boston, but his method of dealing with the subject was different.

It is, however, in no public service, nor in any book that he published, nor in any picture that he painted, that the genius and the true impression of this rare and charming man are to be sought. He has left no monument but a memory. Nothing that he did was an adequate expression of himself; and his personal contact and his marvellous play of conversation were only glimmering revelations of a rare and generous genius which some inexplicable and untoward fate withheld from fitting utterance. His conversation, indeed, in its glancing play of insight, wit, thought, and poetic beauty, was unsurpassed, but also inexpressible. The famous great talkers, Macaulay, Sydney Smith, Carlyle, harangued the company; Coleridge, as Carlyle describes him, and as Charles Lamb humorously asserted, preached. In Appleton's talk there was nothing of this tone. It was an airy comment, a gay monologue, so sparkling, so original, so striking, so imaginative, so unique, that the listener seemed to see the seething and simmering brain of a poet creating. But he was evanescent and elusive. Some few of his teeming myriads of "good things" are remembered as rounded and complete *mots*. But for the most part the impression was not to be justified by any distinct recollection. The captivated listener could only say, as Jefferson said of Patrick Henry, "It was inconceivably eloquent, but I can not recall a single word."

But the singularly alert mind and brilliant tongue did not assert themselves at the expense of the loving and liberal heart. Never was there a mean thought or ungenerous word. Sharp censure often and unquailing criticism you might have heard from him, but all was frank, open, honorable, gentlemanly. He held his opinions strongly, but he had that perfection of good-breeding which avoids long and strident argument. Instinctively he apprehended the scope and kind of difference, and the possibility of mutual understanding or agreement. Genius, talent, taste, sincerity, in every degree, he knew at sight and generously admired, quite capable of complete and friendly sympathy with some interests and tendencies in the same person whose other views he might not share.

Yet the endeavor to describe a nature and power so delightful, but which left no explanation of itself except in the undying friendly impression, is useless. Like a beautiful day long gone, like a lovely scene remembered in youth, the tone of a voice now silent, the bloom of a fruit, the perfume of a flower, all vanished, the genius and personality of "Tom Appleton"—for so was he universally known—must remain a tradition. The charm will be known by others only in the warmth with which his friends remember him, and the kindly affection with which they speak of him. The places which they knew with him—Nahant, Newport, Cambridge—are henceforth forever invested with

"The tender grace of a day that is dead."

And now that he is gone, the melancholy that breathes through his verse will seem more than ever to be the unconscious sigh of a sweet and noble and unrepining nature, to which, with all its affluent humor and unequalled colloquial power, commensurate and enduring expression was denied.

Editor's Literary Record.

PHILOLOGISTS and scholars generally will be profoundly interested in *A New English Dictionary on Historical Principles*,[1] which has been in course of preparation for more than a quarter of a century, and of which the first part, comprising entries from A to Ant, has now just issued from the Clarendon Press at Oxford. The work has been prepared mainly from materials collected for the purpose by the Philological Society of Great Britain, under the competent editorial supervision of its president, James A. H. Murray, LL.D., and some conception of its extent may be formed when we say that when at his death, in 1843, Dr. Noah Webster ceased from his life-long labors on his great American Dictionary, he had traced to their source, defined, and embodied in its vocabulary about 80,000 words; that in the latest revised and enlarged edition of the work, edited by Dr. Goodrich and President Porter, the vocabulary was increased to 114,000 words; and that the work now under notice when complete will contain 187,792 main entries, and will comprise, with the subsidiary words explained and words referred to their synonyms by cross-reference, 231,115 entries. Or if we confine our attention to the part of the work now completed and published, we find that the principal words treated in it in separate articles are 6797 (of which 4799 are current and 1998 obsolete); that the compounds explained under the principal words are 570; and that the words with cross-reference and defining synonym are 998—a total of 8365 words, as against 4162 words in the corresponding portion of Webster's Unabridged Dictionary and Supplement, including all the above classes.

From first to last, the work of collecting the materials for this great undertaking—consisting of typical quotations severally from all the great English writers, from all the chief writers on special subjects, from all writers before the sixteenth century, and from as many as possible of the more important writers of later times—has occupied about 1300 readers in the United Kingdom, in the United States, and in the British colonies, the work of the readers in this country, many hundred in number, having been organized by and prosecuted under the superintendence of Professor F. A. March, of Lafayette College. This large corps of readers was further supplemented and assisted by many distinguished scholars in Germany, Holland, Denmark, and Sweden, with the result that, by this co-operation of literary effort, up to the present time about three and a half millions of quotations have been amassed, collected from above five thousand authors of all periods. Moreover, independently of the 1300 readers above mentioned, more than thirty sub-editors have been engaged on individual letters or sections, and the editor-in-chief has been in continual correspondence and consultation with eminent specialists on various

---

[1] *A New English Dictionary on Historical Principles.* Founded mainly on the Materials Collected by the Philological Society. Edited by JAMES A. H. MURRAY, LL.D., President of the Philological Society. With the Assistance of many Scholars and Men of Science. Part I., A–Ant. Royal 4to, pp. 352. Oxford : The Clarendon Press. London : Henry Frowde.

points, literary, critical, philological, phonological, bibliographical, historical, scientific, and technical. The list of scholars who have assisted in the preparation of the work in all these departments is an imposing one, embracing some of the most distinguished names in Europe and America, and is a guarantee of the thoroughness and exhaustive learning with which the work has been and will continue to be prosecuted. The size of the page of the work is the same as that of the great French dictionary of M. Littré, some of whose features have been adopted, while in other important particulars there have been departures from it—especially in the breaking up of the articles into paragraphs, in the typographical distinction between explanations and quotations, and in the prominence given to the dates of quotations—which will be recognized by scholars as manifest improvements upon the work of the eminent French lexicographer. The amount of labor that may be expended upon a work, and the number and eminence of the scholars who may contribute materials for it, are, however, secondary considerations, since despite all this it may be practically valueless. But the facts that no labor has been spared upon the work before us, and that the entire English-speaking world and its lingual cognates have been made tributary to its completeness and accuracy, furnish strong *prima facie* evidence in its favor; and the severest and most critical inspection of the work itself, so far as it has progressed, both as relates to its general plan and the details of its execution, will place its value and importance beyond any reasonable question.

The aim of this new dictionary is to furnish an adequate account of the origin, history, and meaning of every English word now in general use, or known to have been in use at any period during the last seven hundred years— that is to say, from the very beginnings of the English language, as represented in its literature and in public and private manuscripts. In prosecution of this aim it shows how, when, in what shape, and with what signification each individual word became English; what developments of form, pronunciation, and meaning it has since undergone; which of its original uses and forms have in the process of time become obsolete, and which still survive; and what new uses have arisen, by what processes, and when. Further, it illustrates and establishes all these facts by quotations ranging from the first-known to the latest occurrence of the word, each word being thus made to exhibit its own history and transitions of form and meaning. And, finally, it treats the etymology of each word on the basis of historical fact, and in accordance with the methods and results of modern philosophical science. The vocabulary is classified as *Main Words*, including under this head all single words, radical or derivative, and all their compound words and phrases which, for any reason, are of suffi-

cient importance to deserve separate treatment; *Subordinate Words*, or those which include variant or obsolete forms of main words, and words of bad formation, of doubtful existence, and of alleged use; and *Combinations*, or all collocations of simple words, whether they are formally connected by the hyphen or virtually by the unity of their signification. The treatment of each *Main Word* comprises: (1.) The *identification*, which includes the usual or typical spelling, the pronunciation and its fluctuations and diversities, the grammatical designation, the *status* of the word, whether it be obsolete, archaic, colloquial, dialectical, etc.; its earlier forms and spellings, and the inflections. (2.) The *morphology*, or form history, comprising the derivation or actual etymological origin of each word; its subsequent form history whensoever it presents special features of importance, such as phonetic change, contraction, corruption, perversion, etc.; and a body of miscellaneous facts illustrative of the history of each word, its phonetic descent, adoption, age, obsolesence, revival, refashioning, change of pronunciation, and confusion with other words. (3.) The *signification*, including under this division explanations of words that have only one invariable meaning; of those which have acquired a long and intricate series of meanings, as the primitive sense was gradually extended to include allied or associated ideas, or was transferred to figurative and analogical uses; and of those which have obsolete or catachrestic senses. And (4.) *illustrative quotations*, showing by citations from books, documentary archives, and other manuscripts the forms and uses of each word, its age, and its various senses, arranged chronologically, so as to give at least one quotation for each century, with the original spelling preserved (save contractions, italics, and erratic capitals), as forming an essential part of the history of the language. This imperfect outline will convey some idea, though a faint one, of the wealth of valuable information respecting the history and philology of the English tongue—the mutations, permutations, and transitions that have attended and contributed to its growth and development—which has been condensed within the pages of this work. It is scarcely needful to say that it is not suited for popular use, and can not be expected to come in competition with, much less to supplant, the great dictionaries of Webster and Worcester as an every-day library companion or book of reference. It is essentially a work for scholars, who will prize it for its vast accumulation of valuable materials, for the novelty and originality of its methods, and for the consummate learning and ability with which the history of each word that has ever lived in our literature is traced from its first appearance until the present day.

THERE is no grander figure in English history, and none that is more pitiable, than that of Lord Bacon; and by whomsoever it may be recorded, whether by eulogists or censors, there is no life whose story is sadder, or abounds in contrasts so amazing and humiliating. No man has ever lived who had loftier or nobler aims, none whose aims were more beggarly and grovelling. His own advancement by every shift, and at the cost of the grossest subserviency and the most ignoble cringing, ran parallel in his mind with the prosecution of a succession of works as grand and as influential as any that have occupied the mind of man; and he stands before the ages a perpetual monument of the humiliating truth that the most brilliant parts, the richest intellectual endowments, the profoundest and most varied knowledge, and the most consummate wisdom are compatible with a low and time-serving morality and acts of unpardonable baseness. The sad story[2] of this grand life, with its wonderful achievement and pitiable wreck, is told with judicial candor, with all the tenderness and commiseration that are compatible with justice, and with all the sympathy and admiration that great genius inevitably inspires, even when it is companioned and dwarfed by great errors and imperfections, by the Rev. R. W. Church, the accomplished Dean of St. Paul's, London, in the latest volume of the "English Men of Letters" series. Having before him all that has been written in defense or censure, Mr. Church's full and impartial summing up of the argument, based upon the unquestionable facts of Bacon's life and career, presents the final conclusion that will be accepted by the judgment of the majority of fair and considerate men—neither too merciful nor too inexorable to the great Englishman's defects as a man; doing full justice to his virtues; awarding a just meed to his abilities and accomplishments as a lawyer, judge, statesman, author, and philosopher; recording the events and doings of his life with fullness and dignity; and estimating, analyzing, and summarizing his imperishable writings with admirable clearness and discretion.

THE sixty-six years of the life of the late Frederick Denison Maurice spanned an eventful period in the history of England and of the Established Church; and of the many eminent men who exerted an influence in shaping the great changes, for better or worse, that occurred in church and state during that period, none was a more assiduous, a more unobtrusive, and, in a certain line, a more potential factor than he. A deep and original thinker, an indefatigable worker, an able and ready writer, an eloquent speaker, an earnest advocate of every reform that commanded the assent of his conscience, a devoted but not a subservient son of the Church of England, an unselfish and unflagging friend of the work-

ing-man, and a persistent and courageous laborer for his education and social and industrial betterment, he was emphatically an educator and stirrer-up of thought. His magnetic and pervasive influence penetrated almost every ramification of English society, and even where it did not effect a permanent lodgment that was productive of results, it commanded attention and respect, and sensibly softened the asperity of opposition. His son, Frederick Maurice, has given to the world the record of this active, symmetrical, and influential life in a memoir which he appropriately styles *The Life of Frederick Denison Maurice, Chiefly Told in his own Letters*.[3] A part of the memoir is autobiographic, but, as the title intimates, Mr. Maurice's letters and correspondence form a substantive part of the biography. No letter is given except for the purpose of adding something to the story of the life and of the movements with which Mr. Maurice was identified, either as to facts, or as to the development of thought and character; and only wherever information has seemed necessary, in order to round the continuity of the narrative and to connect the intervals between the letters, has the son intruded his own words upon the relation. Whether it be regarded as the record of the life of a penetrating and original thinker living in an age of great spiritual and material unrest and evolution, or as a contribution to the inner history of English ecclesiastical, political, and industrial life for the forty years prior to 1872, the memoir is one of great and sustained interest, and is especially full of attraction for those whose religious and theological views are based upon the principles of the Church of England. Aside from its historical value in these respects, the work is deeply interesting for the near personal glimpses it gives of many of the greatest Englishmen of the period, and of the part they bore in its mental, moral, social, religious, and political activities. Among others who are thus brought prominently and often familiarly into view are Carlyle, Gladstone, Sir T. Acland, Bishops Wilberforce and Trench, Tennyson, John Sterling, Cardinal Newman, John Stuart Mill, the brothers Hare, Charles Kingsley, Hartley Coleridge, the Chevalier Bunsen, and many others. The large body of letters which form the basis of the memoir are not only among the most perfect of their kind for the grace and ease of their style, but they touch upon many deep problems of faith, morals, and practical politics with an earnestness that is contagious, and a spiritual intensity and an eagerness for the truth that are profoundly impressive.

Memories of Rufus Choate[4] is the title of a se-

[2] *Bacon.* By R. W. CHURCH, Dean of St. Paul's. "English Men of Letters" Series. 16mo, pp. 214. New York: Harper and Brothers.

[3] *The Life of Frederick Denison Maurice, Chiefly Told in his own Letters.* Edited by his Son, FREDERICK MAURICE. In Two Volumes, 8vo, pp. 552 and 712. With Portraits. New York: Charles Scribner's Sons.
[4] *Memories of Rufus Choate.* With some Consideration of his Studies, Methods, and Opinions, and of his

ries of admirable papers, by Judge Joseph Neilson, of this State, comprising his recollections of the personal traits and characteristics of Mr. Choate, and of incidents in his professional and public career, which were originally printed in the *Law Journal*, but have since been revised and enlarged and materially re-enforced by anecdotal, biographical, and illustrative recollections supplied by other survivors who were the professional associates, companions, and friends of the great New England orator and lawyer. In addition to these pleasing reminiscences, Judge Neilson and his correspondents engage in the deeper subject of the consideration of Mr. Choate's studies and opinions, his style as a writer and speaker, his professional methods, the quality of his intellect, and his peculiar gifts as an orator, an advocate, and a dialectician—with the result of a life-like delineation of the man in all the relations of life, exhibiting the practical, the poetical, the earnest, the loyal, and the reverential traits of character which he revealed in his daily and professional life, in his family, and in the companionship of his friends and intimates. Among the distinguished men who have assisted Judge Neilson in depicting the salient features of Mr. Choate's character, and in recalling interesting incidents in his life, are Mr. Joshua Van Cott, Rev. Drs. Putnam, Storrs, and Hitchcock, the late Senator Carpenter, Judges Strong and Fancher, the late James T. Fields, Professors Washburn and Sanborn, William W. Story, and the late George P. Marsh. The volume is a welcome supplement to the excellent *Life of Choate* published several years ago, and written by President Brown, of Hamilton College.

"WORK and wages" are words which ordinarily portend hard reading on a dry subject. Considered as a branch of political economy, and discussed abstractly in that relation, the prognostic would inevitably be borne out by the reality. But if considered historically, the subject becomes not only luminous of interest, but rich in entertainment to the general reader, while at the same time he may almost insensibly imbibe a large fund of valuable information that lies at the very root of an important branch of political economy, and be thus enabled to comprehend much that now seems shrouded in clouds and darkness. The subject has been treated in this way by Professor James E. Thorold Rogers, formerly Professor of Political Economy in King's College, London, and at present a member of the House of Commons, in a compact volume entitled *Six Centuries of Work and Wages*.[5] In this volume he gives a complete history of labor and wages for the whole of the six centuries which inter-

vene between the time (about 1259) at which the first information begins and that at which our present experience concludes. Its earlier chapters are introductory to the specific historical inquiry, and are devoted to a sketch of early English society up to and during the latter half of the thirteenth century; and they also deal with the pursuits of Englishmen from the Norman Conquest to that day, especially as relates to that particular pursuit, agriculture, which in the thirteenth century had become the business of the vast majority of the people of England, and which was prosecuted on land divided in nearly equal moieties between manorial lands and tenants at fixed rents with permanent holdings. The author then turns his attention to life in the towns; the processes by which trade was carried on in town and country; the classes who made up mediæval society, and their methods of trade, travel, transportation, and intercommunication; the products of the several geographical divisions of England, and the prices paid in each for land, rent, wages, and articles of food and use, as compared with prices at various periods down to the present day. The remainder of the work deals with great particularity upon the history of labor and wages from the accession of Edward the First to the present century, including a sketch of the rise and progress of the various industries, a general history of agriculture, and such particulars in the political history of England as are germane to the main topic of inquiry. The subjects specially treated, in the order of their historical and chronological development, are the influence exerted upon labor and wages by the king and his extraordinary revenues, by famine and the plague, and by discontent, combination, and insurrection; and their discussion also comprises a survey of the landlord's remedies; of the development of taxation; of the condition of labor and wages in the fifteenth century, and the kinds of labor that prevailed; of the state of the clergy till the Reformation, and their relation to the fruits of labor and wages; and of the wages of labor after the rise in prices—this last inquiry embodying a view of wages, first, from 1495 to 1725, then from 1725 to 1750, again from 1750 to 1770, and finally in the dear years from 1780 to 1820, and at the great rise in 1853, and also including some interesting observations on trades-unions. In other chapters accounts are given of the English poor-law, of English husbandry from the period of the rise of prices, of agriculture and agricultural wages in the eighteenth century, and of wages in the present century. The work concludes with a thoughtful survey of the present situation of labor and wages, the attitude of labor to capital and *vice versa*, and a statement of the remedies for existing evils which have suggested themselves to Professor Rogers as the result of his investigations and observation. The work supplies in great and carefully collected detail a chapter of history

Style as a Speaker and Writer. By JOSEPH NEILSON. 8vo, pp. 460. Boston: Houghton, Mifflin, and Co.
[5] *Six Centuries of Work and Wages.* The History of English Labor. By JAMES E. THOROLD ROGERS, M.P. 8vo, pp. 591. New York: G. P. Putnam's Sons.

on a subject of immediate and transcendent importance, which is usually treated most inadequately or entirely ignored by historians; and in connection therewith it presents a great number of vivid pictures of social and industrial life in England, extending through six centuries, among all classes, in every department of business or industry, and in nearly every phase of England's rural, urban, and sylvan conditions. There is nothing in Macaulay more graphic and picturesque than several of Professor Rogers's chapters delineating the social and industrial features of England in the early centuries covered by his volume, and there are numerous extended passages which surpass anything that Macaulay has written in substantial present interest, though it must be conceded that they by no means rival the ornateness of Macaulay's style, the splendor of his rhetoric, or the rhythmical cadence of his periods.

Mrs. FRANCES L. MACE has a just conception of the dignity of the poet's calling. Whether her theme be lofty or lowly, familiar or impassioned, she rigorously refrains from an indulgence in those smart conceits, flippant levities, and jaunty efflorescences of wit with which—copying the bad example of the degenerate poets of the Restoration and of the reign of Anne and the first George—not a few of our contemporary poets deface their lighter verse, and which they not infrequently admit into their graver efforts. We shall look in vain through Mrs. Mace's *Legends, Lyrics, and Sonnets*[6] for an exhibition of these trivialities and disfigurements. Always profoundly in earnest, always reverent, and always restrained by good taste, her verse, as relates to its matter, is characterized by delicacy and refinement combined with strength, and glows with a vivid but chastened imagination, so that it is impossible to read any one of her poems without experiencing that sense of exaltation which inevitably accompanies our contact with a work of true genius. Nor are the form and structure of her verse unworthy of its matter, and whether it be narrative or legendary, lyrical, descriptive, or emotional, they are always finely adjusted to the sentiment, and evince in every line and stanza a patient and honest effort to attain a high standard of technical excellence. Several of her poems are remarkable for their sustained imaginative effects, notably the noble legends in which she pictures the cause and origin of Israfil's mission as the Angel of Death, and in which she lifts the veil from those material and soulless forms which peopled the world during the dawn of creation, but vanished into "dim obstruction" upon the genesis of man. Besides these lofty and extended efforts there are a score of other poems in the just published collection of her poetical writings which are scarcely less remarkable for the exceeding grace and delicacy of their thought and expression, the rich picturesqueness of their descriptions, and the tenderness, gladness, hopefulness, and sensitiveness to all forms of beauty with which they are tremulous. Among these may be instanced the fine lyrics entitled, "Easter Morning," "Arcadia," "Greenwood Greetings," and "The First Robin," and her finished sonnets inscribed "Orient to Occident," "Occident to Orient," "The Seven Days" (figuring the seven days of the week), and "St. Cecilia." Each of these is exquisite in its kind, and has the "true accent that comes only from a poet's lips," of which she herself speaks in one of her noblest lyrics.

IF the matter of Miss Wheeler's *Poems of Passion*[7] were equal to their manner, a distinguished place might be augured for her among our coming poets. She has an enviable gift for weaving fluent and musical verse, and it is evident that her loyalty to art will not suffer her to remain satisfied with mere correctness, but will operate as a perpetual stimulus to greater perfection in structural harmony and variety. Her vocabulary is limited, but her choice of words is singularly apt, and her epithets, turns of expression, and collocations of phrases are generally happy and original, and are oftentimes richly laden with suggestive or picturesque meanings. The great defects of her style are due to her extreme volubility, and her constant intrusion upon her verse of riddling and staccato-like questions, which break its continuity and impair its clearness as well as its force and elegance. These abated—and it should be said that in many of her poems, especially her sonnets, they are not visible—Miss Wheeler's style is suggestive of large possibilities. Of her matter we must speak with more reserve. Her imagination is quick, versatile, and virile, but it is limited in its range, and its flights are not exalted. Her conception of the passion of love is intense but narrow, and neither true nor elevating; her ideals, though far from being lascivious, are carnal and sensual; the love that she pictures is not pure, constant, true, and ennobling, but is mere amorousness, hot while it lasts, but inconstant, and flavored with a spice of license. While these are the characteristics of the greater portion of the poems in the volume before us, it is only just to say that in several of her lyrics and most of her sonnets she rises to a higher and more spiritual level, and celebrates the influences of the master-passion with great power and tenderness, and also with entire purity.

PROFESSOR NOURSE, of the United States navy, has prepared, chiefly from official sources,

6 *Legends, Lyrics, and Sonnets.* By FRANCES L. MACE. 16mo, pp. 192. Boston; Cupples, Upham, and Co.

7 *Poems of Passion.* By ELLA WHEELER. Sq. 16mo, pp. 160. Chicago: Belford, Clarke, and Co.

an account of *American Explorations in the Ice Zones*,[8] which is designed to accredit the work of American explorers in a manner sufficiently popular to satisfy the needs of youthful readers, but yet with a due regard to the claims of science. He has very properly prefaced his record of the labors of our own countrymen in recent times by a brief epitome of the various voyages made by eminent navigators in search of a northwest passage, from the discovery of America, and of the new way to India by the Cape of Good Hope, to the present century, including the voyages of Frobisher, the Cabots, Chancellor, Davis, Baffin, Phipps, Anson, and Sir John Franklin. He then gives more extended but still condensed sketches of the voyages and explorations of De Haven, Dr. Kane, the late Admiral Rodgers, and Dr. Hayes, the three expeditions of Captain Hall, the remarkable sledge journey of three thousand miles by Lieutenant Schwatka, the cruise and loss of the *Jeannette*, the relief expedition sent out for De Long by the Treasury Department under Captain Hooper and by the Navy Department under Lieutenant Berry. To these is added a notice of the first expedition sent out by the United States for scientific purposes, being that of 1838–42 to the antarctic regions, under Lieutenant Wilkes, and the volume closes with a statement of the positions and objects of the arctic observers under the United States Signal Service. The compilation comprises the instructions under which our various commanders acted, a statement of the results accomplished in each instance, and a connected and authentic narrative of the incidents and events of each expedition. The work embodies a record that reflects honor upon our country, and is a very convenient reference-summary for all who are interested in this field of scientific investigation and adventure.

It is seldom that we have found in more pretentious books so much solid food for reflection and so much of valuable counsel and suggestion as we have found in an unassuming little volume entitled *Mothers in Council*,[9] ostensibly, and perhaps really, proceeding from the informal gathering of certain mothers in a Virginia county in what they term " mothers' meetings," and in which they read and discussed original or selected observations on such practical subjects as the management and the social, moral, and intellectual education and training of children, the selection and treatment of servants, the care of a household, and the oversight of the domestic economies and amenities that appertain thereto, the selection and use of books for children, the question of amusements and Sunday occupa-

tions, of dietetics, clothing, hygiene, and manifold other equally practical subjects, each of which is treated from diverse points of view, with the earnestness and sincerity of purpose that we should naturally look for in a council of intelligent and thoughtful mothers, and with an unwonted degree of thoroughness, independence, and wisdom. The little book is a treasury of helpful and suggestive thought, readily applicable in every family, upon themes of immediate practical importance, which are hourly pressing themselves upon the attention of those who have the care and nurture of children and the domestic government of our households.

WHILE it is undoubtedly true that common-sense and good taste lie at the basis of the manners and usages of polite society, and that no very serious infractions of its canons will happen where these co-exist, it is no less true that all are not born with an intuitive knowledge of the minutiæ of these usages any more than they are born with an intuitive knowledge of orthography or geography. It is further true that even the most practiced men and women of the world are occasionally liable to solecisms in politeness, just as the most accomplished scholar may contract the habit of lapsing into occasional improprieties of speech and pronunciation. It may be—nay, it is—as great a mark of ill-breeding to "make eyes" in society at one's little short-comings or improprieties, or to make an ostentatious parade of our own superiority in the social observances, as it is to invite attention to a slip in grammar or pronunciation, and to parade our own superior accuracy in such matters. In either case, genuine good-breeding—which, as we have said, has its basis in good sense and good taste, and, we may add, in that fine urbanity which has its spring in a tenderness for the feelings of others—would take no notice, would seem unconscious. But still we must take the world as we find it, and if we would escape ridicule and inconvenient mistakes, we must constantly revise our manners by the code that is in vogue, so as to conform to the prevailing usage. And although we should scarcely go so far as to declare that one might as well be "out of the world as out of fashion," yet when we consider that polite society is as certainly as the rest of the world making improvements on the old methods, which are often substantial additions to comfort, or convenience, or enjoyment, we are impelled to ask, Where is the sense in holding out against the new mode, and in making ourselves conspicuous and perhaps uncomfortable by so doing? Indeed, is there not something that is contrary to that true delicacy which is of the essence of good-breeding in flaunting our old-fashioned ways in the face of the new ones that have become customary? Montaigne has wisely said in one of his delightful essays that "the knowledge of courtesy and manners is a

[8] *American Explorations in the Ice Zones.* Prepared Chiefly from Official Sources. By Professor J. E. NOURSE, U.S.N. Illustrated. 8vo, pp. 578. Boston: D. Lothrop and Co.
[9] *Mothers in Council.* 16mo, pp. 194. New York: Harper and Brothers.

very necessary study," that "fashion is like grace and beauty," and that "while a wise man ought to withdraw and retire his soul from the crowd, and there keep it at liberty and in power to judge freely of things, yet he should absolutely follow and conform himself to the fashion of the times." There is sound common-sense and true worldly wisdom in this counsel of the shrewd Frenchman. And if our readers, alike those who are only a little "rusty" in the new usages and those who are just beginning to learn the alphabet of social etiquette, are inclined to follow it, we know of no guide which may be more satisfactorily consulted than an eminently sensible and very comprehensive little volume on *Manners and Social Usages*,[10] which has been prepared by Mrs. Sherwood, in which she describes the ceremonies that prevail and the etiquette that is observed in the polite society of to-day, and also gives the reasons for them, with the tact and refinement of a true gentlewoman. Her convenient and tasteful little manual covers the entire round of social observances, requirements, and proprieties; and it may be consulted with the certainty of finding all that is necessary to enable those who have a reasonable share of intelligence so to acquit themselves as to avoid those compromising blunders and improprieties which are regarded by the fashionable world as only less unpardonable than crimes.

It might be very naturally inferred from its title that Mr. George Alfred Townsend's romance, *The Entailed Hat*,[11] belongs to the class of popular wonder-stories such as have been written by Hans Christian Andersen, the brothers Grimm, and others, in which the legends and traditions of folk and fairy lore are reproduced for the amusement of young people. But the perusal of a few only of its pages will suffice to disabuse the mind of the reader of any such impression. It is true that an "entailed hat"—which had been preserved from generation to generation, as an heirloom of their ancestors and a memento of their departed greatness, by the family of one of the chief actors in the story, and which finally came into his possession as its head and representative, the sole legacy of his impoverished father—plays a conspicuous and even a weird part in the drama that is unfolded. But it possesses no magical properties, and figures merely as one of the stage effects or accessories by which the peculiar idiosyncrasies and the mental, moral, and physical characteristics of its modern owner and wearer are made to appear more pronounced, more grotesque and incongruous, more violently in contrast with his social surroundings, and the man himself more impos-

sible as a successful suitor for the respect and affection of a beautiful and cultivated woman. The scene of the story is laid in one of the counties of the Eastern Shore of Maryland, which a little over half a century ago was the headquarters of an organized band of thieves, robbers, murderers, and kidnappers, under the leadership of a bold, astute, and desperately wicked woman; and the narrator depicts with great vividness the system of kidnapping and its attendant villainies and horrors as it then existed, and of which the Eastern Shore was one of the most convenient centres. This, however, is but one of the aspects of the story. Another object which the author has held steadily in view, and which is illustrated with genuine but crude power, is to delineate the contrasts that existed between the old patrician families of Maryland and Virginia, descendants of the dissolute favorites of Charles II. and James II., who originally and for many generations absorbed the wealth and social distinction of the province, but at the time of the opening of the tale had begun to show signs of impoverishment and decay, and the plebeian laborers and foresters who constituted the body of the people. These classes and the conflicts of interest and mutations of fortune which they experienced are typically represented by two principal actors—Judge Custis, the last male descendant of the family of whom Martha Custis, the wife of Washington, was a member, and Meshach Milburn, a descendant of the Jacob Millborne, son-in-law of Governor Leisler of New York, who, with his father-in-law, was illegally executed in 1690 on a plea of high treason and felony, but whose sentence and attainder were afterward reversed by William III. Judge Custis is made to reflect the virtues and vices of the Cavalier stock, while Milburn reflects the directly opposite Puritan traits of character, and in addition is made to appear odd and grotesque to the verge of the ridiculous by persistently wearing the ancient and dilapidated hat of his forefathers on all holidays, high days, and notable occasions, and is otherwise rendered unpleasant, if not exactly odious, by his hard, grasping, miserly, and capable business methods, his utter indifference to the opinions of others, and his apparently cold, unemotional, and unloving nature. The elegant and polished descendant of the Cavaliers wastes his substance in expensive living, in the race for social and political distinction, and in large business enterprises for which he has no aptitudes. The hard and ungainly descendant of the old Puritan stock is constantly accumulating wealth and influence by parsimony, prudence, and keen far-sightedness, and is silently and unobtrusively embarking in broad and comprehensive business undertakings. In a pinch of necessity the judge, having sunk his wife's trust-money in one of his unsuccessful enterprises, applies to Milburn for a loan, and upon its being granted, repeats his applications until all his property

[10] *Manners and Social Usages.* By Mrs. JOHN SHERWOOD. 16mo, pp. 325. New York: Harper and Brothers.

[11] *The Entailed Hat; or, Patty Cannon's Times.* A Romance. By GEORGE ALFRED TOWNSEND ("Gath"). 16mo, pp. 565. New York: Harper and Brothers.

is in the grasp of his creditor, together with the evidence of transactions which must forever blast his reputation if they are exposed. While events were shaping in this wise, the daughter of Judge Custis had grown up from beautiful childhood to still more beautiful womanhood; and besides being endowed with every captivating grace of mind and person, was the possessor of rare force of character conjoined with the utmost gentleness of disposition and manners. She had first attracted the attention of Milburn when she was a child of seven or eight, by a characteristic act that he never forgot. As he was passing along the street, shunned and derided by his fellow-townsmen, his grotesque hat and his uncouth appearance generally were hailed with scoffs and jeers by the children of the place, with the exception of the judge's beautiful daughter. Instead of joining in the derision that her companions showered upon the attire and appearance of the descendant of the Round-heads, she was moved by a touch of divine pity for his isolation and friendlessness, and to his great surprise offered him a flower with words of gracious and kindly sympathy. This trifling act aroused a feeling of profound gratitude in the heart of the cold, hard man, and was the active cause of his favorable response to her embarrassed father's repeated applications for large pecuniary loans. As the years rolled on, and the girl ripened into a beautiful and accomplished woman, Milburn's gratitude insensibly ripened into passionate love, which at first and for a long while manifested itself by silent and distant adoration. Under the influence of the divine passion, and the sense of his own unworthiness which it inspired, Milburn devoted himself with all the concentrated energy of his nature to the refinement of his speech and manners, the cultivation of his great native powers of intellect, and the exercise of carefully concealed acts of benevolence, while at the same time he redoubled his exertions for the accumulation of wealth and power. So that at length, when the crisis arrived in the affairs of the judge, and bankruptcy and shameful exposure impended, Milburn was able to offer to stand between him and financial and social ruin. But the offer was coupled with the condition that the judge's favorite and accomplished daughter should become his wife. Naturally the proposition was abhorrent to the judge, who at first stormed and raved over it, but took no steps—and indeed was powerless to take any—to avert it. Meantime the judge's unhappiness, his growing addiction to strong drink, and the distress resulting from his business embarrassments had not escaped the keen and loving eyes of his child; but the extent of the complications that environed him, and their terrible contingencies, were first revealed to her by Milburn, accompanied by the offer to extricate her father from them, and its astounding condition. Vesta was not absolutely fancy-

free, neither was she unequivocally in love with any one, and the startling proposition was at first received by her with astonishment not unmixed with repugnance. But the delicacy and chivalry of Milburn, the unexpected revelation to her of his great natural powers and genuine worth, and the impending ruin and disgrace of her father, determined her to accept it. In handling this portion of his romance—so that the true nobility of Milburn is made apparent beneath the husk of his grotesque and unconventional garb and of his unprepossessing general exterior, and wins in a natural manner upon the respect and esteem of the fastidious and beautiful woman, and so also that her grand act of self-sacrifice is robbed of any semblance of mere mercenariness—Mr. Townsend has manifested the skill of a true artist. Equally delicate and artistic is the development of the drama in which he depicts the growth in the mind of the daughter of the feeling of genuine wifely pride and love. On this main stem sundry other episodes are grafted, some of them cleverly and skillfully, and others coarsely and clumsily wrought. Mr. Townsend is a ruthless iconoclast of the reputations and character of the patrician families of Virginia and Maryland, and with a zest that may be only characterized as brutal does his best to shatter the traditional reverence that is entertained for many of the most illustrious names. Of this there is an excess in the story—an excess likewise in the scenes of blood and violence with which it is studded, and which reduce portions of his otherwise powerful and inthralling tale to the level of a highly seasoned dime novel.

THE remaining works of fiction that merit notice are *The Man She Cared For*,[12] by F. W. Robinson; *An Old Man's Love*,[13] by Anthony Trollope; *Good Stories of Man and Other Animals*,[14] by Charles Reade; *A Grave-yard Flower*,[15] by Wilhelmine von Hillern; *Archibald Malmaison*,[16] by Julian Hawthorne; *Thörns in Your Sides*,[17] by Harriette A. Keyser; three volumes of *Stories by American Authors*,[18] originally published in sundry of our monthly periodicals; and a cheap illustrated edition of Mr. Roe's *The Opening of a Chestnut Burr*.[19]

[12] *The Man She Cared For.* A Novel. By F. W. Robinson. "Franklin Square Library." 4to, pp. 74. New York: Harper and Brothers.
[13] *An Old Man's Love.* A Novel. By Anthony Trollope. "Franklin Square Library." 4to, pp. 40. New York: Harper and Brothers.
[14] *Good Stories of Man and Other Animals.* By Charles Reade. "Franklin Square Library." 4to, pp. 69. New York: Harper and Brothers.
[15] *A Grave-yard Flower.* By Wilhelmine von Hillern. Translated by Clara Bell. 18mo, pp. 160. New York: William S. Gottsberger.
[16] *Archibald Malmaison.* By Julian Hawthorne. 16mo, pp. 126. New York: Funk and Wagnalls.
[17] *Thorns in Your Sides.* By Harriette A. Keyser. 16mo, pp. 238. New York: G. P. Putnam's Sons.
[18] *Stories by American Authors.* Vols. I., II., and III. 16mo, pp. 177, 198, and 190. New York: Charles Scribner's Sons.
[19] *The Opening of a Chestnut Burr.* By E. P. Roe. Paper, 4to, pp. 88. New York: Dodd, Mead, and Co.

Editor's Historical Record.

POLITICAL.

OUR Record is closed on the 14th of May. —In Congress the following bills were passed: Post-office Appropriation, $49,750,400, Senate, April 18; to establish a Bureau of Labor Statistics, House, April 19; to provide a uniform system of bankruptcy, Senate, April 21; to increase the pension list, House, April 21; to create a Bureau of Navigation, House, April 21; Pension Appropriation, House, April 22; Shipping Bill, with amendment making it lawful for any citizen of the United States to import iron and steel steam-ships of not less than 4000 tons free, and entitling such vessels to American registry, provided they are owned exclusively by Americans, and not to be employed in the coastwise trade, House, April 26, and amended and passed by Senate, May 8; pleuro-pneumonia, Senate, April 27; to secure stricter enforcement of the anti-Chinese law, House, May 3; to appropriate $1,000,000 for New Orleans Exhibition, House, May 8; to place General Grant on the retired list, Senate, May 13; Indian Appropriation, Senate, May 13; to provide a civil government for Alaska, House, May 13.

The Morrison tariff bill was defeated in the House, May 6, by a vote of 159 to 155. Of the ayes, 118 were Republicans and 41 Democrats; and of the nays, 151 Democrats and 4 Republicans.

The following nominations were made by State Conventions: Tennessee Republican, April 17, Judge Frank T. Reid, for Governor, by acclamation; New York Republican, April 23, Hon. Charles Andrews (Republican) and Hon. Charles A. Rapallo (Democrat), for Judges of Court of Appeals (present incumbents); Ohio Republican, April 23, J. S. Robinson, Secretary of State, and Chief Justice W. W. Johnson, Judge of Supreme Court; Maine Republican, April 30, renominated Governor Robie.

The Louisiana State election, April 22, resulted in the choice of S. D. McEnery, Democrat, for Governor, by a majority of 50,000.

An attempt in the British House of Commons, May 13, to censure the Gladstone ministry for not taking measures to rescue General Gordon failed by a vote of 275 to 303.

France and China have made a treaty of peace. China engages to recognize the present and any future treaties that may be made between France and Anam. In view of the conciliatory attitude taken by China, and the patriotic wisdom of Li Hung Chang, France abandons all claim to indemnity for the losses sustained during the troubles between the two nations. China consents to freedom of trade between Anam, France, and China, for the establishment of which a treaty of commerce will shortly be concluded.

The election for members of the Spanish Chamber of Deputies resulted in the choice of 334 Conservatives, including 20 Ultramontanes.

Two thousand men, women, and children, many of them refugees from Khartoom, were massacred by the Arabs in Shendy.

DISASTERS.

April 18.—Collision in mid-ocean between steamer *State of Florida* and bark *Ponema*. Both vessels lost and 135 persons drowned.

April 21.—Five persons killed and one hundred injured during a fire and panic in a circus building in Bucharest.

April 27.—More than forty persons killed by the falling of a train of cars into the river near Ciudad Real, Spain.

April 28.—French banker *Paquebot* run down and sunk by Norwegian bark *Venus*. Twelve men drowned.

April 29.—Fourteen inmates of Van Buren County poor-house, near Hartford, Michigan, burned to death.—Explosion of powder-magazines of San Antonio, near Havana. Twenty-one persons killed and many wounded.

Late in April and early in May extensive forest fires in New York, New Jersey, and Pennsylvania, burning several villages and many square miles of timber land. A number of persons perished in the flames.

OBITUARY.

April 17.—In New York, Thomas G. Appleton, of Boston, aged seventy-two years.

April 22.—In New York, Alvin J. Johnson, aged fifty-seven years.

April 24.—In Paris, France, Maria Taglioni, the famous dancer, aged eighty years.

April 25.—In New York, Dr. Willard Parker, in his eighty-fourth year.—In New York, General Emerson Opdycke, aged fifty-four years.—In Newark, New Jersey, ex-Governor Marcus L. Ward, aged seventy-one years.

April 27.—At Irvington, New Jersey, Dr. Sandford B. Hunt, editor of the Newark *Advertiser*, aged fifty-eight years.

April 29.—At Brighton, England, Sir Michael Costa, aged seventy-four years.

May 2.—At Brighton, England, Henry (Chevalier) Wikoff, aged seventy-four years.

May 4.—At Prague, Bohemia, ex-Empress Anna, in her eighty-first year.

May 6.—In Philadelphia, Dr. Samuel D. Gross, aged seventy-nine years.

May 7.—In Norwich, Connecticut, John F. Slater, aged sixty-nine years.

May 8.—In London, Judah P. Benjamin, aged seventy-three years.

May 11.—In Constantinople, Midhat Pasha, aged sixty-two years.

May 12.—At Nantucket, Massachusetts, Charles O'Conor, aged eighty years.

May 13.—In Chicago, Cyrus H. McCormick, aged seventy-five years.

WHAT *is* the matter with the human race? What obliquity is it that induces people to tell lies out of which they can get no possible benefit? Are the majority of people consciously unveracious, or are they really the dupes of their senses? "I said in my *wrath* all men are liars." Perhaps he might have said it coolly and with scientific precision. Perhaps it is a question of physiology rather than of morals. The human frame is acknowledged to be a wonderful piece of mechanism. The Psalmist admired it, but it puzzled him. If he had been a scientist he would have been able to give physiological reasons for the opinion that there is not one perfect man—no, not one. Scarcely a perfect woman. It is known that two people do not see the same thing alike, and consequently they describe it differently. They do not hear the same statement alike, and they always repeat it with variations. Of all witnesses the eye is the least trustworthy. It appears to be the most subject to delusions. There is a reason for this. No two persons have eyes alike. The two eyes in one head are seldom alike; if they match in color, they are different in form, different in focus. Not one eye in ten millions is in a normal, perfect condition. The focus is either behind the retina or in front of it, and the eye is either near-sighted or far-sighted. What can be expected of such an imperfect organ in the way of correct observation? It appears to be still worse with the ear. It is at best a crooked organ, and nearly everything that passes through it gets a twist. And these two defective machines are allied with probably the most deceitful little member that ever was—the tongue. The effort of the tongue to put into sound and speech the so-called impressions obtained through the complicated mechanism of the eye and the ear is a ludicrous failure. Any one who is familiar with a court of justice or neighborhood talk knows that. And owing to the sympathy of one part of the body with another, the thumb and the fore and middle fingers (which hold the pen) become infected. The substitution of the inflexible stylographic pen for the flowing quill and the flexible steel it was thought would tend to remedy this defect. But this obstacle in the way of writing does not check the tendency to prevaricate any more than stuttering does in the case of the tongue; and it is just as difficult for a stutterer to speak the truth as for a glib-tongued person. The consequence of this infection of the pen-fingers is that what is not strictly true now and then creeps into print. People are beginning to find out this physical defect, and many persons now will not believe what they read in a newspaper any more than if it were told them by an intimate friend. But they read it and repeat it; and owing to the eye defects before spoken of, they scarcely ever repeat it as it is printed. So we all become involved in a congeries of misrepresentation. The Drawer need not point out that the remedy for all this is the production of a physically perfect man.

The Drawer, which sits at the receipt of stories, has occasion to muse much upon the fallibility of human testimony. Do the men and women who send it stories which are as old as Solon, and declare that the incidents related occurred in their own observation and experience, *know* that there is another world? Sisters and brothers, why are we made thus? You remember the story told years ago about Henry Ward Beecher. More than one person, attendants upon Mr. Beecher's church, known to be persons of character and veracity, told the writer of this paragraph, and declared that they told the exact truth, that one hot Sunday morning Mr. Beecher ascended his pulpit, wiping his face, and when he stood up to preach began with this sentence: "It is as hot as h–ll—was the remark I heard coming in at the door." This was vouched for by several trustworthy persons who heard Mr. Beecher say it. And yet Mr. Beecher never made any remark in the pulpit like that. He assured the writer of this paragraph that he never said anything like it; and his denial was unnecessary, for the story is a very old one, and is related of Robert Hall, among others. It might have been told of a priest of Jupiter, who made that remark on ascending the steps of the temple at Rome, if the popular notion of the temperature of Hades had been in Rome what it is in Brooklyn of h–ll. Sisters and brothers, what induced you to tell that story about Beecher?

Take another case. There is a story about a wedding trip that has been knocking about the country for some time. We have tried to keep it out of the Drawer, but it is of no use to kick against it any longer. It was first told to the Drawer editor in October, 1883, by a clergyman of strict temperance principles and high character—in fact, a total abstainer—who had it from a friend of his, first hand, who had just returned from the West. This friend, mind you, saw and heard what he related, and he was a person of undoubted veracity, though perhaps as an abstainer, when travelling, not so total as the clergyman. It was, in brief, to this effect. In the car on a train from Toledo to Chicago was a man who sat alone, looking absently out of the window, and appearing dejected. During the passage an accident happened to a newsboy, and the generous passengers passed round the hat for him. The solitary man alone of all the carful refused to contribute anything, not even a quarter. Somebody remarked audibly upon his stinginess, when he turned round and said: "Gentlemen, it may appear strange to you that

I give nothing; but I haven't a cent of money. The fact is, I was married yesterday, and I am on my wedding trip, and I hadn't money enough to bring my wife along."

In December following the editor of the Drawer was seated with two other gentlemen in a library in New York. One of them said: "I heard a good story the other day from a friend of mine who has just returned from Europe. Going down the Danube from Pesth last summer, he noticed on the steamboat a melancholy-looking man, who did not appear to care much for the scenery, but leaned over the guards and vacantly regarded the river. Falling into conversation with him, he ascertained that the man was a Prussian. Remarking that the journey did not seem to interest him, the Prussian said: 'No; I'm rather lonesome. The truth is, I'm on my wedding tour, and I could not afford to bring my wife.'"

The editor of the Drawer said that it was a good story, and that he began to think it was true, as it was confirmed by so many independent witnesses. Thereupon he took from his pocket a letter which he had received that morning from Paris. In it the writer, a gentleman of culture and travel, said that a curious incident happened to *him* last summer. He and his wife were on a Rhine steamer, when they noticed a melancholy passenger whom all the beauties of the scenery failed to rouse from his dejection. He was an object of interest to them all the morning, and at length the wife's sympathy was so much excited that she proposed to go and speak to the melancholy stranger, and find out the cause of his sadness. The husband said that would be a foolish thing to do, and she might get into trouble. But the wife insisted (for though American women have little curiosity, they have warm hearts), and crossed over to where the stranger stood, and accosted him, and they engaged in conversation. In a few moments the lady returned, laughing. "What is it?" asked the husband. "Why, the man is a South German. He says that he is on his wedding trip, and couldn't afford to bring his wife."

The editor then related the original true story as it was told him by the T. A. clergyman. So it appeared, on unimpeachable testimony, that the same strange incident happened in the experience of three persons the same year—one near Chicago, one on the Rhine, the other on the Danube. Did it happen to any one of these veracious people? When the editor had raised this question, the third member of the party, who had been silent and had not interfered with the story in any way, said: "I can tell you the real original of that story. Several years ago, in a well-known wholesale house in this city, an old bachelor book-keeper, who had been many years with the firm, suddenly announced that he was to be married. The partners gave him a week's holiday, and his fellow-clerks raised a little purse and presented it to pay the expenses of his

wedding trip. A couple of days afterward one of the members of the firm went down to Newport, and there, lounging about the Ocean House, and apparently enjoying himself immensely, he saw his recently married old bookkeeper, but alone. "Where's your wife?" "She's at home." "But I thought you had money given you for a wedding trip?" "So I did, but I didn't understand that it was intended to include her."

Now we are not saying that this is an unwise way of taking what is really one of the most perilous journeys in life, a wedding tour. But what could have induced all these different respectable people to appropriate this particular instance to their own personal observation? It sometimes seems as if people are not what they should be.

_____

MANY years ago—in fact, back in the thirties—Dr. Grant, of Enfield, whose reputation as a physician in Connecticut is still in memory of the first rank after years of retirement from practice, was travelling in South Carolina, his native State, going by stage from Savannah to Augusta. At a certain stopping-place it was found that there were more passengers than the stage could carry, and an extra was ordered for the accommodation of five passengers. These passengers were John Forsyth, of Georgia, John Branch, Postmaster-General, George McDuffie, of South Carolina, Dr. Grant, and an unknown gentleman. The party soon became talkative, and by degrees all knew who each one was, with the exception of the one silent stranger. As the stage creaked along, the attention of Dr. Grant, who was a lad at that date, was attracted by a little dog following the stage, which reminded him of one described by Washington Irving in *Astoria*, which he had just been reading. He was laughing quietly to himself, when one of the gentlemen insisted that he should tell them the cause of his amusement, that they might join in the fun. Dr. Grant said, "That little dog reminds me of Washington Irving's dog, whose skin was so tight that it drew up his hind-legs."

This led to a talk about Irving, in which all joined except the unknown man. One of the gentlemen then appealed to him, and asked if he did not think Irving one of our wittiest and most delightful writers. The person appealed to replied that he could not say that he did. The gentlemen all expressed their astonishment, and one of them persisted in demanding why he did not agree with the others in their admiration of the favorite author.

"Have you ever read any of his works?" they asked.

"Yes," was the reply.

"Well, don't you think the *Sketch-Book* one of the most beautiful specimens of English which our country has produced?"

"Well, no," the unknown replied; "I cannot say that I see anything remarkable in it."

"Well," said the other, "then you must be

Washington Irving himself, for no one else could resist the humor and pathos of his pen."

The unknown colored to the roots of his hair, but made no reply, and his tormentor continued:

"Come, tell us the truth; are *you* not Washington Irving himself?"

The poor man at last blushingly confessed that he was, and then followed a general introducing and hand-shaking, and a delightful and never-to-be-forgotten stage-ride.

THE BATHER.

I LIST to the patter of waves,
  I list to her laugh of glee,
And dream about beauteous coral caves
  And sirens beneath the sea.

I imagine I see her put,
  In a manner free and bold,
In the ocean her dainty sandaled foot,
  To see if the water's cold.

I dream of her shimmering hair,
  And her little snowy hand,
And the half-forgotten, free-from-care,
  Dear hours spent on the strand.

Once more I lead her about
  In the tossing, foamy main.
   *   *   *   *   *
But my vision is quickly put to rout,
  And my bosom filled with pain,

As I wake to the merry cries,
  All coming with wondrous vim
From the bath-room, and I realize
  They're washing my brother Jim.
                    R. K. MUNKITTRICK.

THE following letter is published in the interest of insurance companies, since it is said that laughter lengthens life.

" *Mr.* —— ——, *Vice-President of the* —— ——
  Life-insurance Company :

"DEAR SIR,—I am in receipt of a postal card advising me that my next annual premium (policy No. 43,369) is $147 04. Thereby I am reminded that the life-insurance business, as managed by your company, is, like the providence of God, past finding out. I began paying $80 cash and $52 note on this policy in 1867, and it seemed on these terms an inexpensive luxury. It would have been if I had died. Unhappily I survived, and now for ten years I have been struggling as much to keep the policy as myself alive. But the appetite of this policy, I observe, *does* grow by what it feeds on, and the danger is that it will shortly exceed in its demands my ability to provide for it, and I shall see it die on my hands.

"The steady and constant increase in the amount of the premium on this policy began to excite my curiosity, not to say my admiration, several years ago. The agent to whom I applied for enlightenment (I have passed through the hands of five or six, each of whom has amassed a fortune and retired) so overwhelmed me with mathematics of the most mixed and abstruse character that I fell back from the investigation greatly humiliated at my own ignorance, and profoundly impressed with the reasons of the company—or the agent; I could not tell which.

"I think I realize, and hope I appreciate gratefully, the beneficent operation of this steady progression in the cost of the policy. It makes one contemplate death with resignation, and look upon that consummation as devoutly to be wished for—to checkmate the company. Did you ever think how Booth or McCullough might improve Hamlet's soliloquy and thrill an admiring audience by just holding up one of your life-insurance policies at the words ' *There's* the respect that makes calamity of *so long* life' ?

"But I fear I trespass on your time. Is it true that insurance officials, notwithstanding the meagreness of their salaries, are overworked ? I will come at once to business. I need not trace the steady increase in these premiums. Sufficient that last year I paid $142 75, and this year you call for $147 04, upon a policy the annual premium on which was $132 ten years ago. At this rate of increase, and my discouragingly sound health, I can not undertake to compete with the company. I am aware, of course, that a policy-holder who has paid ten annual premiums can hardly expect the consideration due one who, not being insured, seeks information. Being a fish *in the basket*, I do not expect the consideration due one *in the sea*. And yet I *would* like to know whether policy No. 43,369 has any surrender value. I am already in possession of a considerable accumulation of tracts, pamphlets, circulars, almanacs, calendars, and extracts from religious newspapers which afford abundant knowledge as to the facilities and methods of getting *into* life-insurance. But what I now seek is information as to how to get *out*.

"Pardon me if I have used too great familiarity in addressing a man whose acquaintance with logarithms, mortality tables, and the differential calculus entitles him to the *name* of benefactor and the *salary* of an actuary. I am not ignorant of what is due the representative of $27,000,000 —if these be the figures— of assets. I address you because your name appears on the seductive postal card which invites me to add $147 04 to these twenty-seven millions. I presume you are no stranger to the complaints of disappointed policy-holders, and it is not impossible that you dismiss them all without consideration. But there *may* be *some one* in your employ who can show me the cheapest way out. Will you please refer me to him, that I may present my policy and receipts and things, with the conundrum which once staggered the intelligence of Daniel Webster—'What is all this worth?' But then Webster knew scarcely anything of life-insurance."

THE life of a minister is not so prosaic and uneventful as many imagine; on the contrary, he often has many pleasant, though not altogether pious, experiences. A rising young minister of the Methodist Church relates the following as an actual experience which he had not long ago:

There was an Irishman, whose name we will call Michael, who was very sick. The doctor had given up all hopes of his recovery, and the wife was informed of the sad end soon to come. She took it very philosophically, and in her conversations with Michael everything was arranged, even to the funeral service. It seems he had no coat suitable to be laid out in, and with his consent it was decided to have the tailor make him a garment at once. This was done.

In a short time Michael died, and the funeral day arrived. The minister had come to speak of the good qualities of poor Michael, and to comfort the hearts of the sorrowful. Everything was ready, but there was a delay, evidently caused by the non-appearance of some important mourner. Finally the man who had general charge of the funeral, getting impatient, called up the stairs: "Tommy! Tommy! come down. They're waitin' fur ye."

The person addressed thrust his bushy head past the door, and concealed the rest of his person. Tommy's face was full of anxiety as he replied to the inquiry and said, "I can't—I can't."

"But ye must come," said the man at the foot of the stairs; "the funeral is waitin', and ye must walk wid the widder."

"But I can't," shouted Tommy, more earnestly than before. "I can't; the corpse has got me coat on."

"Och! man, what do ye mane?" said the man. "Ye must come down anyhow and walk wid the widder. Put on the corpse's coat, and come down."

In a few moments Tommy appeared with the corpse's coat on. It was too long, and too large in every way. The sleeves extended over his skinny hands, and as he slowly descended the stairs he was occupied in trying to roll them up. It gave him a most ridiculous appearance, and as Tommy took his place beside the widow a suppressed smile was visible on every countenance. The minister could hardly restrain himself from laughter. The service, however, proceeded, and the coffin was soon carried out and placed in the hearse, followed by the minister, Tommy with the widow, and the friends. The procession was on the point of starting, when suddenly Tommy began jumping up and down, and, with his arms flying, shouted: "Shtop! shtop! The corpse has got me money and me spectacles in me coat. Give me the money and the spectacles."

All the money Tommy had was locked up with the corpse. It would not do for him to lose it, and make this unnecessary sacrifice. Nothing would do now but to restore the personal effects to Tommy. The coffin was carried back into the house, and the corpse removed. The coat was taken off and given to Tommy, who immediately took off the one belonging to the corpse, and put on his own with a degree of alacrity that was delightful to behold. Tommy found his money and his spectacles all right, and seemed quite contented. The coat made by the tailor was put on the corpse, which was then replaced in the coffin and the hearse. The humor of the situation was fully appreciated, and no less by the widow than the minister; for when she let down her veil and looked up, her face was full of smiles as she said, "I was just thinkin' what a foine time Michael was havin' in Tommy's coat, wid his pockets filled wid money and a pair of spectacles."

GRANDMOTHER BROWN.

Dear Grandmother Brown
Lived in Cranberrytown,
And a kindly old woman was she;
There was no one so bad,
Either lassie or lad,
But some good in the same she could see.

One June afternoon
Mistress Polly Muldoon
Ran in for that moment that ends
In an hour or more,
And did naught but talk o'er
The short-comings of neighbors and friends.

But in vain did she scold
About young folks and old,
Only patient excuses she heard,
Till at last she cried out,
"You would speak, I've no doubt,
For old Satan himself a good word."

Then said Grandmother Brown,
Of Cranberrytown,
"Well, whatever his failin's may be,
I don't think we could find
Many people who mind
Their own business as closely as he."

MARGARET EYTINGE.

THE following modest request was recently made of the Mayor of a large city not a thousand miles distant. It certainly evinces great confidence in the willingness of the person addressed to answer any query the writer might feel inclined to propound, as well as great liberality of heart.

GIRARD, TRUMBULL Co., Jan. 30, '84.

Mayor of the City of —— :

DEER SUR,—Sume time a gow, with in 2 to 4 years, their was a Claim brought and Sute commenced by the Stork Heirs against youre city to recouver of youre city the Heirship of the Stork Heirs known as the Noah Stork Esstake if i am not misstakined in the givven Name of the Man to whom this esstake descended from of Course you must be famillier with the facts in the Cais thoug I may ere in a minute way the Sute has terminated and what i wish to learn from you is when the Sute Commenced and who was *leading Manager* as plaintiff and when Judgment was took against your city and fer how much and before what Judg and what Court and whare the Court was held and who did the monney gow in to the hands of and *what was the names of the jurymen* was their or who was the administrator of the esstake and whether the monney has been divided and how much their was if eny and between how many Heirs it went and *if you know* what is the names of the Heirs that received the monney and how much it ammounted to to them a piece. Will you give me this infirmation in hast as fer as possible.

—. ——.

P.S.— *Will go snacks* if you can get my sheer fer me.

A GRADUATE of the Sheffield Scientific School, who was greatly interested in botany, once spent a winter in Western Connecticut, where he boarded with a clergyman's family. The minister's little daughter, an inquisitive child of six years, accompanied the botanist in all his rambles, until one day when he scandalized her almost into hysterics by saying that "a *blasted* woodpecker" had destroyed the bark of a rare and beautiful tree. After hearing him use this shocking expression, Margery flatly refused to bear him company. She explained that "blasted" was "a wicked swear word," and that she "could not possibly love a blaspheming swearer."

As spring approached, the botanist daily brought home plants and lichens for analysis. These seemed very ugly to the eyes of our little critic. One day she overcame the reserve she had maintained ever since discovering his enormous wickedness, and asked him if he considered "those weeds" were pretty. He declared they were beautiful.

"If you call *those* beautiful," she said, loftily, "I don't know what you would have called my calla lily. It was *lovely*. But it died last fall just because it was *blasphemed* by Jack Frost." She was too consistent to say it had been *blasted*.

WITH the institution of "side judges" residents at this end of the State have been made most familiar in recent years through a flagrant failure of justice in Brooklyn, where the small-fry politicians holding those positions overruled the judge, and the author of a murderous assault, inspired by political motives, escaped with a nominal fine. A good old judge in Western New York, now gone over to the majority, a man of a goodly carriage, and corpulent, and also addicted to sack, used to feel a professional contempt for these "associates" which he did not always conceal. On one memorable occasion his honor had been dining deeply, and when the afternoon session of the court opened was decidedly incapable of holding the balance of justice—or anything else—with a steady hand. He was sufficiently aware of his condition to adjourn the court and send for his carriage, to which, as he tossed to larboard, tossed to starboard, fearfully, while descending from the bench, his two colleagues kindly escorted him. It was not an easy task to boost a jurist of so much helpless avoirdupois in through the carriage door, but the task was accomplished successfully, to the great relief of all parties.

"Thank you, gentlemen—thank you," hoarsely murmured the judge, adding, as he sank back upon his seat, "*Now* I know what a mershful Provinsh created shide judgesh for!"

CHIEF JUSTICE CARTTER, of the District of Columbia, who, by-the-way, is credited with the remark that the inhabitants of the District have only once been formally recognized in an official document—viz., when President Taylor spoke of "all the world, and the rest of mankind"—when he was a young lawyer, made a severe and successful hit at the expense of the dude of the period, which is worth recording: An honest farmer was driving along the road in a heavy wagon laden with material destined for the compost heap, when he ran into or was run into by a light wagon driven by a youth of *ton*. The frailer vehicle was instantly wrecked, and its enraged proprietor brought suit to recover its value. Mr. Cartter, then a young lawyer, appeared for the defense, and in opening his case won it by an unhallowed inspiration. (N.B.—It was a jury of horny-handed agriculturists, naturally prejudiced against a plaintiff who lisped and parted his hair in the middle.) "Your honor, and gentlemen of the jury," he said, "the facts in this case are simply these: My client, the defendant, an honest and substantial farmer, a member of the great and virtuous class upon which," etc., "was proceeding along the road in a wagon filled with manure, when, by accident, it came into collision with the vehicle of the defendant—*similarly laden.*"

WE have received the following note from the author of "The Drainage of the Everglades," published in the March number of this Magazine:

KISSIMMEE CITY, ORANGE Co., FLA., *April* 25, 1884.
Editor of Harper's Magazine:
DEAR SIR,—Upon a more careful review of the letter of the Secretary of War, Ex. Doc. No. 189, First Session, Forty-seventh Congress, and other reports not then before me, I find that in my essay on "The Drainage of the Everglades," published in the March number of *Harper's Magazine,* I failed to give proper credit to General Q. A. Gillmore for his valuable study of the watershed and soil of the Kissimmee Valley. Had it been intentional, *Harper's* would be the last magazine to permit a contributor to abuse his privilege. Perhaps the editor and the writer alone know how difficult it is, in an essay of that kind, to compile the facts, compare them with one's own observations, and then adjust them to the economy of space necessary to the magazine. It is a matter of no moment to an engineer of national reputation, like General Gillmore, that an essayist failed to give him that credit due to his careful analytic study of South Florida, though it is mortifying to the latter to feel that he has given occasion for complaint. The courtesy of friends in Washington, D. C., through the War Department, enables me to know how very valuable and interesting to us are the thorough and masterly reports of General Gillmore.

Very respectfully, WILL WALLACE HARNEY.

"A PRELUDE."—FROM THE PAINTING BY T. W. DEWING, OWNED BY C. T. BARNEY, ESQ.

HARPER'S
NEW MONTHLY MAGAZINE.

No. CCCCXI.—AUGUST, 1884.—Vol. LXIX.

ARTIST STROLLS IN HOLLAND.

Fifth Paper.

IT has always seemed to me a most deliberate and cold-blooded proceeding, at best of times, to set out on a pleasure journey alone by one's self (a sentiment in which many a lone lorn wife of many a galivanting husband will only too readily concur, without doubt); but on that particularly damp and drizzly night in October when I, sad and solitary, sank into a cold corner seat of the Queensborough train for the Flushing boat, and heard the sharp patter of rain as we slid out of the station drive against the pane, and saw the ghostly shreds of steam scud by, it added awfully to the loneliness and depression, and seemed more cold and deliberate than usual. It had all been so deliberately planned—this little trip—between my pleasant sketching companion of last year and myself! There were to be no false starts, no chasing of the wild-goose vainly all over the "Land of Cuyp," *this* time. Maps had been studied, all sorts of information bearing on the country had been got at and carefully stored up, and, after all, this was the upshot! The pleasant friend was obliged to go sooner, and I could only go later, than we intended, and the only balm and consolation we could offer to each other was the chance of meeting blithely in some weedy town, *somewhere* on the damp surface of the Low Countries.

I have already given a slight "impressionist" sketch of the first view of Holland at early morn from the steamer's deck. There was no healthy impulse to repeat the picture with a slightly altered background of gray mizzle on that particular morning; in fact, there was not much to see except the dim damp outlines of the Flushing landing-place when I came on deck.

Familiarity with the Dutch language to the extent of a dozen or two words gave me a certain feeling of calm security through the various little ordeals of the custom-house, and I soon found myself on the train bound for the good old town of Middelburg.

It was a pet part of the new plan to begin Holland again where we left off so grudgingly. We had only a mere glimpse of the quaint old capital of this island of Walcheren when we were hurried away, but vowing to return on the first opportunity.

The distance between Flushing and Middelburg is so short that notwithstanding a longish wait at the station and a most deliberate express train—when once started—it was still early morning when we arrived at our destination. I say *we*, as there was seemingly another blinking passenger besides myself that descended, but he disappeared so suddenly into the misty air that he must have been a ghost. I was left alone to the well-meant but utterly foggy attentions of a dazed youth, who appeared to be ticket-taker, porter, and station-master in one. The only visible conveyance to take me to the hotel was a man with a weird elongated wheelbarrow.

Stay! there was even a choice between the man with the wheelbarrow and a long, frail, sketchy youth, who offered to carry the things on his back. He seemed to have grown up overnight like some pale stalk of rank asparagus, and be in danger of cracking in two if bent under the burden of a travelling bag. I took the wheelbarrow man, as I had not the heart to try any experiments on the youth. So, failing as porter, he offered himself as guide. I was obliged to discourage even this ambi-

AN EARLY SKETCH.
From drawing by George H. Boughton.

tion in him, although it went against me, he looked so pathetic, and eager to earn the breakfast that his weedy constitution stood so much in need of. Failing as guide, he became a hopeful follower, and shambled on after us at a respectful distance. He kept reminding me of poor Smike, with the cuffs of his faded outgrown jacket half up to his elbows, and his well-patched trousers half up to his knees. He saw us well up to the hotel door, and had evidently, like "Melancholy" in his own case, "marked me for his own."

When we could prevail on the rosy young giantess to stop splashing and squirting water over the fan-light of the hotel door a moment, so that we might enter, I found a tolerably cheery welcome. There was a moment's shade of gloom when I declined to take any more breakfast. There had been a kind of one on the boat, and a further trifling with one at the station; a third one would have been mere vanity. So, not to lose time, or happy chance, or the misty morning effects, I soon arranged hotel matters, and turned out again into the chill air. Smike was waiting for me, pathetic and eager. He kindly pointed out the very obvious Town-hall, and remarked, "Museum." If I could

have spoken Dutch fluently, I should probably have spoken it harshly to that weedy lad, but the moment's hesitation about terms sufficiently abusive gave me time to reflect. Why should I discourage the only evidence of enterprise that seemed to be awake in the place? He was, furthermore, picturesque and quaint, and the very twin brother of the poor drudge over whom so many bitter boyish tears were shed when *Nickleby* was read for the first time—yea, even the tenth time! This Smike was evidently no great linguist; he had small English, and less French, and but hazy German. But why not—he looked long-suffering and defenseless—why not try some elementary Dutch on him? Poor boy, he seemed delighted with it, and understood it nearly as well as I did myself. And I, guessing at the probable replies to my own observations, could frequently understand him.

We would go, then, and see the Abbey. That venerable pile at best of times is slightly shut in, and naturally somewhat damp, mouldy, and depressed; but on this chill October morning, with the great gaunt trees weeping tears of thick dew over the bed of dead leaves that strewed the soppy ground, reeking with stale miasma, it was far, far from cheerful. Artistic or antiquarian enthusiasm needs much pumping to insure a warm or steady flow on such a morning. Poor Smike left all such pumping to me; he was gradually turning a delicate mauve tint with cold and damp and long-deferred hope. There is a fairish hotel in part of the tory is the sad and stormy history of most abbeys. I should like to write a little more of it than I have space to give—all the little I can remember or turn to—but the temptation to keep on would be dangerous: better not begin. It was getting chilly, or rather it was getting more and

PART OF ABBEY, MIDDELBURG.
From drawing by J. E. Rogers.

Abbey building, but it is rather shaded, and haunted with the reek of rotting leaves on wet autumnal days. (I much preferred the "Doelan," in the fine open square.) There are government offices and schools, a church or two, and various other institutions within the precincts of the fine old rambling pile, which must have covered more ground than the Abbey of Westminster at one time. Its his- more so. Smike was turning from a tint of watery pink to the off-white of a farthing dip, and his teeth were all a-chatter.

"This will do for the first entertainment," I managed to convey to him. "Not a bit of it," he contrived to reply. He was bent on showing me the "Park," and so *much* bent that I did not like to suddenly turn him the other way, for fear of seeing him crack in twain. The Park was not far, so I let him lead the way. It was not far enough, in fact. I should have liked to have walked off the chill of the Abbey: it was only like stepping out of an ice-house into a cold bath. The ornamental waters were further enriched by a thick litter of fallen leaves upon their emerald mat of duck-weed. It seemed like a long stretch of Persian carpet of simple and severe design. The weeping-willows dripped their pendent switches dejectedly over the chilly ooze. The morning dew lay in thick beads on everything; it even seemed to bead the surface of the fat, rich water. I need not say that there was not a living thing, not even a duck or frog, enjoying that rank, lush paradise. Neither did we venture much further than the gate. One glance at the cindery path littered with drenched leaves and twigs, one peep at the dripping willows, would suffice as well as a wilderness of such moist joys. Even Smike appeared to be taken aback—he had probably never seen it before under such a depressing aspect—and almost apologized for intruding on its bath of dew and fog. "We will go back now to the market-place."

He offered no objection, merely drew my attention to a long green-mouldy colonnade that we were passing, deserted by human shape, strewn with wetter, rottener, and bigger leaves than we had yet seen, festooned with beaded spider webs, just glistening in the now appearing sun. This institution was the "Bourse" (*Beurs*, Dutch), or Merchants' Exchange. Business was evidently rather torpid, if not dead and gone altogether.

"Business *bad*?" I managed to express to my guide. He smiled a wan smile, and waved his pallid finger sadly, and said something which I took to be a Dutch equivalent for the "last ditch," or something as hopeless. I could now see the pinnacled tower of the Town-hall shining afar, and hear the sweet low wrangle of its archaic chimes. So I dismissed Smike with an odd assortment of brasses, nickels, coppers, and other specimens of small Dutch currency. He radiated enormously in broadest smiles, and hied him off to breakfast as fast as he could shuffle. Our conversation had begun to lag. He began to suspect that I didn't know the proper answers any more to my own questions. And as for being able to guess any chance observation of his own, I was rather losing ground than improving in my

"shots." I even think that when we parted in view of that guiding tower we were equally glad to be rid of each other. I did not need him, as I could easily sight the lofty spire when I wished to return to the hotel. There is a very curious old sixteenth-century house with richly carved front, showing in a series of tablets in marble the manner and mystery of stone-working—quarrying, shipping, cutting, building, and so forth. I did not know the way to it, nor did I care to ask, preferring to amuse myself with trying to find it by wandering off in the direction I thought it ought to be. I knew that it was called the "Steen Huis," if I wanted to ask at any time, and with a vague recollection of having seen a photograph of it (to identify it by when I saw it), I thought I would let it discover itself.

After much meandering up and down and around, now forgetting, now remembering my vague quest, I came suddenly upon it. It was like seeing an old friend someway, and yet I had never seen it before in the concrete. There had been a wholesale tampering with the lower story; it was no longer in the stone tablet trade, but given over to dealings in sailors' clothing, marine stores, and bunting generally. The preserved part of the front is well worthy of study, or at least inspection, as an example of the stone fronts of its period. It is one of the best specimens of its class that I have seen in the Netherlands.

Of all towns in Holland, I think (after seeing about fifty) Middelburg about the most peculiarly representative and Dutch. It has in it the most charming examples of architecture and costume that one could wish to see. It is quaint and original, clean to a degree, and not too dead and gone; in fact, on a market-day, it is for the time being about as lively and stirring a place as one could happen on; and they do say that on the occasion of the annual kermesse, which lasts about a week, the great market-place at night, when the fun is wildest, is no faint hint of those far more ancient and more nether regions *en fête*. So much of an affair is it here that they talk of the past one for six months, and prepare for the next one the rest of the year.

In passing along some of the silent, well-swept quays under the tall trees, one is struck by the number of well-to-do and even stately residences, seemingly the homes of the descendants of the "merchant princes" who made their fortunes here when Middelburg had a commerce to boast of. There were no finer docks and waterways in all the country; but, alas! fickle Commerce one fine day found other

Middelburg was only sleeping—it was a very long Rip Van Winkle drowse—there was still strong life somewhere dormant. It woke to energy and action again some fifteen years ago. When its old neighbor and rival, Flushing, began its splendid

PUMP IN THE QUADRANGLE OF THE ABBEY, MIDDELBURG.
From drawing by E. A. Abbey.

harbors. The big ships sailed away one by one into the "Eternal Whither," and came back no more. The docks and basins took on the scum of idleness, busy ship-yards grew silent, and the half-finished hulks rotted where they stood. 'Tis the fate of many once thriving towns. But

new harbors and docks and station, high hopes were held that the new life-blood let into Flushing would revive the entire island of Walcheren. Middelburg "shook itself together" for the long-looked-for return of prosperity. New docks, canals, and basins were made, big enough to float the vast commerce she wished to see again bustling about her long-deserted quays.

But, sad to say, after much outlay of money and labor, after grand opening ceremonies, and much kermessing, coy commerce came not, to any great extent, to gladden the souls of the good burghers either of Flushing or Middelburg. Let us say, rather, that for many years it did not come. Just lately there is a better show of shipping at both places. "Time was" when this same Middelburg was the richest, proudest, and most powerful city in the Netherlands. Its most prosperous times were during the fourteenth and fifteenth centuries, when all the wines of France and Spain that came not only for the entire country, but for towns along the Rhine far into Germany, had first to pay duty here. There exist still many relics of this powerful "octroi." There is still the "Rouenische Kade," where the wine galleons of Rouen disgorged their cargoes and their heavy customs duties. The wool-staplers of England and Scotland had also rich and powerful houses here, and at Veere, near by, under the protection of the Duke of Burgundy, who married a daughter of James I. of Scotland.

Now a great assistance to any one's enjoyment of this charming old town is to "get up" just a little of its past history before coming to it. Havard* tells one just enough; that is, one who merely wishes to visit the place as a rambler, and not as a student of history. As for my own duty to my readers, I am sure that they would much sooner follow me as a simple wandering sketcher than as a more wandering and sketchy historian. I know that the history of Zeeland is as tempting as a fairy tale—so enchanting that if once I began, there would be no stopping me.

Take this same isle of Walcheren, for instance, just for a wee bit. Before the Romans came to civilize it by fire and sword and slavery, the country was overrun by wandering tribes of Gauls. It was one dense forest, of such depths of tangle and despair that it was known for centuries by the equivalent of "La Forêt sans Pitié." What a background for the imagination to fill in with wild pictures! What sirens rise up as one goes on! What temptation to weave in the thin gold threads of the sad history of Jacqueline of Bavaria! She was more of a mar-

tyr than a heroine; more of a Fair Rosamond than a Joan of Arc. Her memory is still a poem to the good folks of Zeeland. One moment's turning aside, and I should forget the things I came to see and sketch—"The Things of To-Day."

How happy we three were last year, when our only historians were Motley (whom we knew only "by sight") and Jacob, whom, if we took at all, it was with cellars full of salt. It was still early forenoon, and I was wandering loose and free down and around crooked and devious streets, and under archways into *culs-de-sacs*, and out of them into wherever the picturesque led me—making my way back to the market-place. When I wished to make sure of my Town-hall weather-cock, I had only to wait for an intersection of a few streets or canals, and it would show itself. And as its silvery *carillon* rang out some small tinkle every seven minutes, one could not well get out of ear-shot if it should happen to get lost to view. There were lots of the picturesque country people about the streets, and as I followed stray groups, sketching as I walked, I was led rather a dance. I generally found, however, that no matter how often I lost sight of the Town-hall, I could always—and did often without wishing—get back to the Abbey. This began to bother me finally, for when I had fairly started for my Town-hall once or twice, and losing sight of my spire through winding narrow short-cuts, I had found myself back again every time to my starting-point at the Abbey. I began to say, "Confound this tiresome old relic of antiquity! it seems to be a loadstone."

As all roads lead to Rome, so did they here all tend to this one spot. There was at first only a small circular chapel built, and then the great Abbey gradually grew around it, the village grew around that, and the city finally grew around all with its walls and ramparts. The streets mostly diverge from the great central church; others seem to wind themselves spirally about it, as if planned by some old monkish humorist to prevent the people straying from the fold, even if they wished to. I think I had that special bit of street plan well into my understanding before I got out of that merry-go-round of the Sacred Precincts. There was no lost time, however. It is mostly all fish that comes into the sketcher's net. The Town-hall looks all the better if it has a foreground of the

---

* In *The Heart of Holland.*

picturesque market-day people. By the time I arrived there the picture was complete, even to an effect of golden sunlight struggling through the haze of the cool October forenoon. Market-day is generally a holiday as well in Holland. On the slightest pretext out come all the antique finery and all the family jewels, and they wear them in profusion, men, women, and children, in Zeeland. They pile on the entire hoard, on nearly every salient part of their person. The dress of the Zeelanders is by far the most complete and elaborate of any part of Holland. It is rarely nowadays that the men resist the inroads of modern fashion, but here they keep strictly to the costume of their forefathers.

Still, if you take the *ensemble* of the male "get up," it is rather mixed in periods and styles. The hat—one shape of it especially (there are three varieties) with the universal cut of hair and the closely shaven face, has a purely fifteenth-century effect. Such a number did I meet that reminded me of the portraits of the eleventh Louis of France, or certain heads in Van Eyck's pictures! The shirt collars, often embroidered with black lines, and fastened with large gold button links, are fifteenth century also. The jacket seems to be a survival of the jerkin of two centuries later. The velvet knee-breeches are evidently a century later still, as the shoes are. The silver buckles on the nether garments are often chased richly; while as for the four great silver waist buttons, or rather plates, that half encircle the belt, embellished often with Scriptural subjects in *repoussé*, there is a vague sort of impression that they must have survived since the wandering Gauls overran the islands of Zeeland. The other style of nether garment is short, wide, flowing velvet trousers. On both these there is the same profusion of silver plate, and both styles have on either side, back of the hip, a deep narrow pocket. Exactly where the wild Texan Ranger secludes his revolver, the Zeelander carries his brace of sheath-knives. They are about the size and shape and usefulness of the sort of knife that one takes to a good-sized ham. The handles are often of richly chased silver, or the more modest box-wood carved in quaint old design. These murderous implements, I need not say, are carried more to complete the costume of the country than for actual service, though they

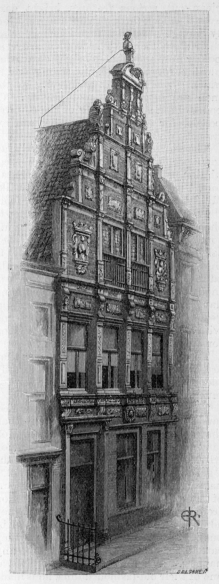

HOUSE OF THE GOLDEN SUN, MIDDELBURG.
From drawing by J. E. Rogers.

do say that every proper Zeelander knows well how to use them in case of need. We all know how unhappy the most amiable full-dressed Highlander would be without a few dirks about his girdle, and at least one handy in his garter. So doth the genial Zeeland peasant sport his pair of carvers, not necessarily to use on a friend, but rather on his bread and cheese.

The men are a strongly built race, with clean-cut, serious features, bright dark eyes that look through you, and yet kindly enough natured I found them, for all their stern looks. The women are very bonny now and then—a bright, clear complexion, rosy and fresh and strong, and as much given to smiles and levity as the men are to grimness and gravity. Of course I am still speaking of the country people, for even the peasantry are extremely well-to-do.

The towns-people are like nearly all town people the world over—just one regulation pattern, as if clad by the same tailors, "as per sample." But in towns like Middelburg the servants are often from the country round about, and they keep to their costume religiously. I was buying some gold head-gear here such as they sell to the country girls, and wishing to find out how it went on, the jeweller called in his servant from her window splashing, who took off her own corkscrews and dangling disks of gold—much more gorgeous than those I was bargaining for—and with a certain air of condescension tried on for me my simpler arrangement.

The children are too delightful, as they are, when quite correct, dressed exactly like their elders, and the effect is often too much for gravity.

The "attitude," so to speak, of the Zeelander is more dignified—proud even—than that of the natives in most parts of Holland; in fact, I doubt if in all Europe you will find people with more of the air of the "grand seigneur" about them. In fact, I have heard that the air of repose about some of the old Dutch towns is not stagnation from their point of view; it is what they admire. They don't wish to bustle, or be bustled about. They are all as rich as they care to be, and they don't want to be any happier. When a stray tourist arrives at one of their old-fashioned inns, he is made to feel that he is only entertained as a favor; they don't really *want* him.

In Middelburg, however, there is a certain movement that looks like a lingering love of trade. The shops are numerous and good—most of them, as usual, for the sale of finery and confectionery.

There was a constant fascination in and about the old Town-hall for me. The outside is very perfect, from door-scraper to the gold weather-cock. Built by a Burgundian architect in 1468, it is more French than Flemish or Dutch in character. At the butchers' stalls in one corner of the building the set-out of the meat, the chopping blocks and hooks, and the general arrangements of the place give one a perfect picture of the shambles and fleshers' stalls of the late fifteenth century. The inside of the building, I grieve to say, has not *quite* escaped the demon of modern improvement. The fine old Council-chamber, however, has been preserved pretty much in its original form. They do say that the sketch for the council-chamber scene in *The Bells*, as played at the Lyceum, was taken from this very quaint old room. Holland is very rich in old council-chambers, and there are few finer than this and the one at Veere —or rather than the Veere one was before they took down the bronze hands. There is a most interesting museum in this Middelburg Town-hall, filling several rooms, mostly with objects connected with the history of Zeeland. There are, among other things, the grand old feasting batteries of the various guilds and corporations: tankards and beakers and dishes of gold and silver; plates and trenchers of pewter and quaint old Delft; goblets of glass of Venice and Bohemia; corporation seals, medals, and badges; flags, banners, and pennons; warlike weapons of every period; old instruments of music; books, parchments, and views of old towns; plans and maps; pictures of pageants and ceremonies, many of them showing by-gone festivals at this same old burg. But most interesting to us were the several fine old guild and corporation pictures, some on the same scale and in manner of treatment as those that Frans Hals and Van der Helst painted so gloriously years after these were done. These have a certain charm of grim sincerity and *naïveté* which the others, with all their magisterial grandeur, lack. The portraits of the leading worthies in the guilds of Wine Coopers and Wine Merchants are most vigorous, and "personal" in the last degree to every defect or merit of the originals.

To entirely enjoy the grand corporation and guild portraiture of Rembrandt, Hals, and Van der Helst the art student should see these curiously fine examples of an earlier and kindred school. This was my second visit to them, and they seemed even better than at first, when we all but screamed with joy at our discovery. I also remember how Jacob came down to solid facts at once, while our delight was still gushing, by assuring us that though that grand old race of wine merchants and their monopolies had gone, there was still here and there splendid old Burgundy in

Ingenious old boy! The thought of him at that moment suggested "Why not?" I was getting rather depressed; I felt that somehow I had the whole weight

TOWN-HALL, VEERE.
From drawing by J. E. Rogers.

Middelburg—to keep up the tradition of some of the ancient houses. "Well, if you carry some of dot old wine droo de church-yard at night, you not pe zafe; de spooks get out of deir grave and follow you."

of the fallen fortunes of Zeeland on my soul; that I *ought* to be able to suggest some scheme that would bring back its former grandeur, and was either a fool or a craven for not setting about it at once.

VEERE, ISLAND OF WALCHEREN.
From drawing by E. A. Abbey.

Even when the polite custodian offered to show me the dungeon and the various instruments of mediæval torture — rack, wheel, thumb-screw, and spiked collar— even offering to show me how they worked (without the victim, naturally), my mind was far away. I knew Jacob's address. "No, thank you; no more rack or thumb-screw to-day. How far is the telegraph office? Round the corner? Good-morning." And in five minutes I had wired to that faithful henchman of last year to meet me by next train from Amsterdam.

At the hotel, when I turned in for luncheon, I found Jacob's reply beside my plate. He would be with me by the night train. I felt a certain load off my mind. At early morn I had almost decided to do Holland this time without him; but, as incident after incident of the Faithful One's usefulness and cheery qualities came to my mind, I could not resist him.

Dutch is such an awful language to be left all earthly alone with! You can never believe that the people are likely to understand the hideous gurgles and croaks you are preparing back of your throat just before you utter them. And yet, if they would not try to disguise the spelling, there is much that is good English about the Dutch language, especially the Frisian variety. It was a gushing scene, our meeting at the windy railway station near to midnight. There was such effusion of greeting, such display of "fatted calf" at supper afterward, that the won-

dering natives must have thought that I was in some manner celebrating the return of a prodigal father or uncle.

"I was yoost at de delekraf office by de 'otel wiz a barty of dourist going to zee de windmills of Zaandam. Zo I 'ands ofer de barty to a vriendt, and I zay to myzalif, 'You may all go to Yaricho!' and puts some cloze in my pag, and I yumps in de drain, and here I am! We have a good time again, I bets to myzalif as I comes along."

I then unfolded to Jacob my little idea, which was to take a trap in the morning, and drive as far as we could around the sea edge of the island, if the day promised to be fine—rainy days to be kept for in-door exploring. The morrow was a perfect thing of its kind—a hazy, cool October morning. The trap, a towering landau, with a strong team and rueful driver, was soon ready, and we were rattling over the long stretch of well-paved brick road toward Veere. The whole face of nature had a wet, shiny look, as if it had been drenched down, Dutch fashion, with plentiful buckets of water overnight.

The landscape stretched before us, steaming and glistening in the morning sun. I tried to interest Jacob in effects of misty sunrise. "Oh, dot's de *doo*—dot is not rain last night. De doo she is varry strong here. Dot shows a good deal of ague about, dose doo." I then tried to lure Jacob into statistics—the relative amount of ague to the square Dutchman, etc.; but that wary worthy so mixed his figures with saving "exceptions"—viz., schnapps and smoking as preventives—that we came to no conclusion, except that were it not for schnapps and maag-bitter the average Zeelander would be shaken off the face of the islands. Beguiling the time with much information that "went into one ear and out of the other," we soon came to Veere. We drove to a small, neat, anxious inn, with the very un-Dutch name of the Hotel Rolandi. They seemed much more pleased to see us than the Tower Inn landlady last year, who did not care to take us, as we were "strangers." We strolled on to the Town-hall, and saw the newly arranged museum in it. A gaunt, bare upper room, well meant enough, the whole thing, on the part of the Burgomaster and Council, but what demon of bad taste possessed them to denude the fine old Council-chamber of many objects that made it unique of its kind in Europe? The bronze fists were taken down from the chimney breast, where they had hung for centuries as a warning to traitors, and were ticketed away in a glass show case, with stupid odds and ends lying about them, spread out flat on the rawest of white paper. The Council-chamber was not to be seen, as the Council was in session. I lost all interest in the rest of the treasures. Even the great gold cup palled upon me. To do the place justice, however, the Town-hall is still worth seeing, all the same.

The sapient Council seems to have taken the old town in hand too, and furbished it up for stray visitors. The streets looked cleaner, the houses more cheerful, and the cobwebby little shops seemed to have a fresh supply of tinned mysteries from Chicago. Here, now, is a town with a history to wring tears. Some centuries ago it was called Kamp-veer, being then the ferrying-place to an opposite town of importance called Kampen. But one awful night Kampen disappeared entirely from the face of the earth, and simply "slumped," as they say in the far West, beneath the waters and mud that ingulfed it. There being no longer any Kampen to ferry to, this town was then called merely Veere, and as the situation was good for trade, though of treacherous foundation otherwise, it grew and grew, rich and prosperous and famous. It even used to pitch-battle with Middelburg in good mediæval fashion over certain rights to tolls and customs. At one time there

were two great sea towers (the one remaining being the lesser), and a goodly portion of the trading part of the town was across the harbor, about the great tower. One wild night of tempest and earthquake shook the island again, and when morning broke there was no opposite tower to be seen, nor sister town, nor towns-people; the muddy sea swirled about over all as if they had never been. No wonder that the remaining portion of the town took a discouraged view of the situation, and moved themselves to a land of greater stability! This cruel chapter is even more complete in the history of many of the lost towns and islands of Holland.

On some of the very old maps there are places marked down where towns flourished of some importance, there are roads traced through prosperous lands, there are islands named, and that is all that remains of them, this trace on the maps and the mentions in old chronicles. The sea on one tempestuous night or another has swept all beneath its waters. It gives one a feeling even to-day of a shiftless foothold when wandering over what remains of Zeeland. It is a long time ago. But if history takes to repeating itself, one feels most cheerful here who reads the least of the sea's doings in ages gone by. We found little of fresh interest in Veere, and with some small feeling of misgiving appropriate to the locality, we bade adieu to a place of such shaky antecedents.

Skirting along the dikes, we had a good opportunity of seeing some of the incessant toil, some of the constant engineering and battling with the sea, to keep it at anything like a safe distance. The dikes about this island are perhaps the finest, the most constantly guarded, in all the country. The dike-workers are a distinct class, a guild, in fact, jealous of their craft and its rights and privileges. It is not the first-comer who may be a regular dike-worker, even if he should wish to be. We saw great gangs of them going from point to point with pick and shovel, ever on the lookout for weak spots in the great embankment, ever refacing it with miles of concrete, and strengthening every point with strong groins running into the sea.

It was almost pathetic to note with what solicitude every blade of the binding bent-grass was coaxed to grow. Every little tuft was watched and tended as if it was some choice tulip. The top of the dike formed a level, firm road, stretching away for miles. The sea looked so mild and gray and innocent as it gently lapped the edges of the mighty barriers that it seemed an effort to fancy it an enemy capable of mischief. The breezes were simply delicious and fresh, coming over the wide North Sea. Inland, the scenery was flat and grim and serious. Farmsteads in the far distance looked green and fat enough. Sheep and kine were plentiful about the rich fields. Just over the edge of the dikes were the little scattered hamlets of the fisher people and the polder-men; the dike-workers lived more of a roving life, camping out here and there as their work called them from one point to another. Sometimes the wind had blown up and the seas tossed up great long meandering mounds of sand, helping to back and strengthen the dikes. On these billowy hillocks the grass was carefully planted in little regular tufts, and stunted pines were set wherever the tempest would spare them to grow. All sorts of binding vegetation were carefully protected. The very children knew enough to let it alone. Just before reaching Domburg one drives through the domain of Westhoeven and past the old château. The building dates back, parts of it, to the fifteenth century, but it has all been so restored and villafied that it might be anything. Oak-panelled rooms have been painted, and others depanelled, and papered with French arsenical papers; French windows have been cut in down to the ground. It was unoccupied, and we got permission to go over it. What a place it must have been before the restorer and villa-fier came! It was bright and open and airy, but crude, to set one's teeth on edge. The last of its race of occupants had given it up, and it was to have been pulled down to save property tax. Some kind, enthusiastic lady, with the money to indulge the whim, bought it for a song to save it, if only as a relic. The whole place has been made damp and dank, like too many places, not only in Holland, but elsewhere, by overwhelming it with dense lofty trees. There was no chance for the free air and sun to warm the damp out of it, and let the fresh free air put life into it. If the lady be wise she will cut down most of the trees for timber, and make the house habitable. The old gardener who showed the place seemed tumbling to pieces with ague. If he had been soaked all

night in the slimy green water of the moat, he could not have looked more damp and clammy. It was a relief to get out of the dense chill park into the breezy sunshine again.

After a short drive we come upon the fashionable sea-side resort of Domburg, where we stopped for luncheon. It is here that in the season one will find the *élite* of Zeeland. We found nobody whatever, as the season had just closed. The air seems magnificent, and the sea pure and uncontaminated with the sewage from the little village. The scenery is very severe and simple, mostly sand dunes, with sparse tufts of bent-grass, and little nooks of stunted, shrivelled, inland-blown trees.

We stopped to rest the horse and refresh our melancholy driver at West Kapelle. It was here that we noticed the greatest number of dike-workers and polder-men, and it is just about here that the whole science is at its best development; so that if any one should feel an interest in this one peculiar expression of Dutch genius, this is the favored spot. The sketching is well worth while. It is stern and serious enough in all conscience; there is little frivolity of archaic costume about these sea-tanned dike-men, or even their womenkind or children. The archaism in dress is only among the well-to-do rustics. The road between West Kapelle and Zoutland keeps more down behind the dikes, along the country roads, past farmsteads, and through grazing lands. The sheep seem to be more of the black-faced, smaller breed than one finds farther north. The villagers are neat and tidy enough, but there is always a curious mixture of the fishing and farming element in them. We stopped again at Zoutland, and climbed to the top of the dunes to look about us and sniff the sea-breeze. Down far below us lay the village—so far that had the waters swept over the rim of the sandy dike, the sea would have only reached its level when it played about the tail of the weather-cock on the gray old church tower. There are watchers ever on the lookout, day and night, calm and storm. No wonder that the set, anxious look one sees on every face, that seems to be born with every babe, should be the only characteristic expression one remarks among the people here!

When the watchers of the dikes see danger, the alarm-bell is rung, and every

VILLAGE BEHIND THE DIKES.
From drawing by G. H. Boughton.

soul either flies to the dikes for safety, or to help the gangs of workers to stop the threatened breach. All was calm enough at that moment, the tide was far out, and yet the village seemed far below its level. The cottage window lights were twinkling in the gloom, as evening was just coming on. The church bell was tolling for evening service, and the warm glow of sunset just touched the top of its tower. Through the tall lancet windows one could see a flush of warm lamp-light within. All sounds and sights were of peace and calm, and yet there somehow came upon the imagination the grim reverse of the picture: the clanging alarm-bell, the hurrying to and fro, the wild fight for safety from the mad, hungry sea. We were feeling deadly oppressed by the prevailing seriousness of the place. Jacob was no relief; his most cheerful theme was still fever and ague. He drew bright pictures of most enchanting regions in Holland and elsewhere to lure me away. I must admit that the air was chill and damp as we drove home in the gloom, and that "de doo" was falling heavily, and that the sea mist would drift past us in damp ghostly shreds when we passed a depression in the dunes. How damp and cheerless the houses, even the best of them, looked in the soppy hollows where the lush meadows were richest! The hay-

ricks seemed like great toadstools. There was a cold, soaked look and feel to everything. We blessed our thick ulsters, and cheered ourselves with thoughts of a good warm supper. The mention of hot supper was the only theme that brought a passing smile to Jacob's damp visage, and he translated the idea to the damp, silent driver, who translated it to the team by a liberal application of whip-lash, which soon, but not a moment too soon, brought us to the pleasant reality. "By Chove, we are well out of dot akue," said the Faithful One, as he sat him down to the promised "fat of the land."

The next day we went to Goes by rail. As an introduction to a romantic mediæval town a modern railway station is about the most illusion-dispersing form possible. One should enter over an ancient bridge or under the arch of an old water-gate; anything is better than giving up the same form of ticket to be snipped by a station-master in the same dress that one finds everywhere; and then to go up an arid cindery road, past the toadstool growth of pot-houses and restaurants that crop up round every railway station! I was tempted to shut my eyes and give my hand to Jacob, and say, "Lead me past all these utilities of our glorious Present to the old church in the market square, and when we are well

WEST KAPELLE.
From drawing by J. E. Rogers.

within its portals I will look about me."
As it was, I did nothing of the kind. I
had still my solemn duty toward the well-
meaning fiend, who will exact, to the last
dead cat in the gutter, "the things I ought
to see about me." So I made mental
notes of the sodden little drinking booths,
with their soppy gardens surrounded with
weedy moats, the necks of broken bottles
jagging through the duck-weed and floating débris of paper bun-bags and orange
peel, besides other nameless filth I did not
linger to define. I saw a great modern
iron building that houses a horde of agricultural implements, mowers and threshers and reapers. I even went with the
worldly-minded Jacob to have a nearer
view of them. It was with pride that I
pointed out to him that they came from
the United States mostly, especially those
painted a very raw blue or eye-peeling
red. I got so lost in contemplation of
their limb-amputating charms that we almost left a few fingers behind in seeing
how they worked. The old church and
square came afterward, as it might to the
gaze of the average modern-minded Cook's
tripper; they looked out of date and paralyzed. After so many mowing-machines
I fancied myself in some back street of
Chicago.

There are many quaint old houses here,
but none so good as at Middelburg. There
is a queer little house near the fish-market,
with a big gold mermaid for a weather-
cock, that is rather amusing. The shipping in the docks and the distant river
craft were very well worth while to the
sketcher. We were passing a row of very
old almshouses, with carven gateway,
showing old figures in sixteenth-century
costume. Venturing in the court-yard to
look about us, we noticed an old well with
rather an insisted-on inscription in staring
letters.

"What does it say, Jacob ?"

"It say dot dis well-water is not so very
good, dot you better be careful how you
drink him."

"That's curious."

"Not at all. Much better warn the
people; den dey don't get ill. Now here is
another well" (and sure enough this pump
was placarded even more prominently
than the well); "dis pump she zay dot
you must not drink de water at all; she is
only fit to wash de floors wiz."

Jacob was not content; he must satisfy
himself and me by finding out all about
it. So, boldly knocking at one of the
doors, he inquired of the quaint old black-
and-white-clad crone who came out all
about the water. She gave the well and
pump a shocking character, and said that
they had to get all their drinking water
from afar, etc., and presently asked us in
to see her little abode. In a few minutes
we were as chatty and as much at home
as if we were paying a long-expected afternoon call. It was an almshouse for old

ladies in reduced circumstances. It was about three hundred and fifty years old or so. They had to pay a very small sum for maintenance; it was not entire-

on our having some tea, which rite and ceremony was duly performed, as it always is in Holland, with much warmth and cordiality. Meanwhile the fact of

CHÂTEAU OF WESTHOEVEN.
From drawing by J. E. Rogers.

ly a charity; there was much liberty of coming and going, etc. She was not entirely alone in the world, but had one son, a sailor, which accounted for the carved whales' teeth and the bits of strange pottery. I think Jacob managed to find out somebody she knew, and to know them also—anyhow, we soon got on most friendly terms. She would insist

the old lady having strange visitors to tea spread rapidly over the institution. First of all a small child came to the door and looked in, and then a little girl came for the child, and lingered long too, with wide-eyed interest, and then the child was suddenly dragged away, and in a few minutes there seemed to be a procession gradually passing of all the old women in the

SUNDAY MORNING IN ZEELAND.
From drawing by G. H. Boughton.

place. They first of all sauntered carelessly by, staring in very hard, and then
one more bold stopped to ask some needless question, and all the others closed in
about the door to hear the reply. Our ancient dame was not to be imposed upon
with indiscreet interest in us, or our tea.
So she soon, very soon, sent the party
about their affairs, and shut the door. We
finished our afternoon call in peace, and
pleasant and queer it all was. The old
lady was really loath to take the silver
Jacob tendered on my part to get more
tea for us some time.

We had a good hour to spare at the railway station, having, through lingering
over our tea, missed our train. It was no
unlucky miss for me, however. We took
a favorable table in the little coffee-room,
and ordered up simple refreshments we
did not need, so as to keep the place. The
buxom waiter-girl was fresh from the country, and brave in big gold pendant and
necklace, and bristling with tremendous
corkscrews and dangling squares of gold
by the side of each wicked brown eye.
Jacob detained her in various ways until
I had sketched her. She was rather joked
by the severe, unpicturesque, middle-aged
lady behind the bar, until she showed
her the goodly silver coin that Jacob rewarded her with in answer to my sign to
him. Jacob enjoyed this paying out for
me; it gave him a certain lordly air, as if
he had me in his retinue at so much a
month. He enjoyed the day so much, in
fact, that he quite forgot about the dangers
of the dread ague. "To-morrow we will
go to Katwyk-by-the-Sea, Jacob: there is
no ague there: so, 'if you're waking, call
me early.'" The Faithful knew not his
"May Queen," and only answered, "Oh,
you petter let me yoost look out de train
first in my 'dime-daple'."

SOME WORK OF THE "ASSOCIATED ARTISTS."

THE wave of popular decorative art has broken over us and receded. With it have gone the sticks and straws of incompetency. Away floats many a fond illusion of whilom artists, who have reluctantly lived to see their blurred ideals piled high on the cupboard shelf, or bestowed upon the married maid-servant intending housekeeping. Torn from the pedestal where so long it stood upon one weary leg, the immemorial stork has gone down the stream in company with sunflowers and apple blossoms in every stage of experimental presentment.

In plain words, the decorative "craze" has had its day. Amateurs no longer creep in where artists dare not tread. The legitimate adorners of our homes breathe a long sigh of relief. The field is theirs. What happily remain with us of the stimulating period just past are a more enlightened taste in all these matters and a more impartial understanding of æsthetic law. Stripped though they are of home-made faience and pre-Raphaelite crewel-work, our houses bear internal evidence of a hundred decorative fancies, well imagined and fitly applied. To know how to adjust the things we have is of far greater value than to know how to yearn for those we have not. This naturally applies to those who have followed, as a fashion, what they style "decorative art." To the earnest workers, especially among women, what a boon has it not been? Of the various schools established in New York, beginning with the noble Society of Decorative Art, all have been successfully and honorably maintained, while to reckon up the benefits they have conferred upon the self-helpers of our country at large would be a task of magnitude. The roots of every one of these large establishments where the decorations of life are considered to the exclusion of its necessaries, strike deep and far into the soil fed by our national industries.

A few years ago a little band of artists of New York, headed by Mr. Louis C. Tiffany, determined to inaugurate a new era in house decoration, where each member of the advisory firm should be a specialist of skill and ripe culture. This was done; and the results they have brought about may, without exaggeration, be called the first-fruits of the American Renaissance. Very little was attempted by the association to secure the attention of the public that throngs and wonders. Their work, principally executed to beautify certain elaborate interiors, has been hurried by the owners from work-room or atelier into jealous seclusion as soon as it was finished. The curtain for the Madison Square Theatre, decorations for the beautiful interior of the Church of the Divine Paternity, for the Union Club House, and for the picturesque Veterans' Room of the Seventh Regiment Armory, were almost the only exhibits of their industry known to New York until the exhibition of embroideries in the Loan Collection of December, 1883, held in aid of the Pedestal Fund for Bartholdi's Statue of Liberty. Then was displayed a series of bold and original needle-woven tapestries, before which the artist world paused to do homage, as the most decided advance in needle-work known to the century. Of this tapestry a full description will be given farther on. Since the earlier work mentioned the artists have been enabled, by repeated efforts in combinations, through advanced skill on the part of their workpeople, and with successful development of native industries, to show continual progress in all these departments. In their hands wood, metals, glass, mother-of-pearl, gold and silver, canvas, silk, serge, "cloth o' gold and cloth o' frieze," dyes and pigments, threads of silk and gold and wool, have been alternately treated to the action of tool, brush, or needle, and dismissed bearing unmistakable evidence of their artistic birth-place.

In this development of combined industries it was soon found that the department of tapestries and embroideries had assumed a character of distinct national and commercial importance, requiring for development certain conditions materially hindered by an association for the production only of combined forms of decorative work. After three years of co-operative study and fruitful experiment it was decided, therefore, to detach this department of artistic needle-work, allowing it to convene a new group of artists having taste and gifts especially adapted to its growth. The original scheme of the enterprise was continued under the name of Louis C. Tiffany and Co., its offshoot retaining the impersonal title of Associated Artists as better suited to the requirement of an enterprise under feminine control. Of these artists themselves it is permitted me to say little. That the association is directed and inspired by Mrs. Wheeler, Miss Dora Wheeler, and Miss Rosina Emmet is to Americans an earnest of the results attainable, as well as an explanation of those attained. And it is pleasant to record here a tribute to the progressive excellence of the designs furnished by Miss Ida Clark, formerly a pupil, and now an active worker in the councils of the Associated Artists.

It is in the blending of art and manufacturing industry that we Americans are vitally interested, and we shall now see how far into this fresh field the footsteps of a few brave women have led the way. One who is fortunate enough to possess an open sesame to the modest dark green portal in East Twenty-third Street behind which the Associated Artists conjure into

over like honest Autolycus with his inkles, caddisses, cambrics, lawns, "as they were gods or goddesses"—it will be a satisfaction to the unsympathizing to hear the practical side of this enthusiasm.

Remembering the gallant struggle made, during the last twenty years especially, by the silk weavers of the United States, who have tried in the face of so many obstacles to obtain for their products footing with imported goods, it is pleasant to record to their honor an unqualified success. One of the first problems the Associated Artists set themselves to encounter was how to lighten the cost and extend the variety of silk and woollen stuffs. American women have as a rule withheld their patronage from American silks; but it is safe to say that any one examining the recent products of Connecticut and New Jersey looms, woven to the order of the Associated Artists, after designs furnished by

BORDER OF WEAVING DESIGN FOR PALACE CAR CURTAINS.

existence so many marvels will at the outset be forcibly struck by the fact of the growth in American taste making such an establishment not only possible, but remunerative. Here, under Mrs. Wheeler's inspiring rule, are produced the beautiful pieces of embroidery of which this paper designs to treat. To describe the furniture, inlay-work, ceilings, wall-papers, panellings, parquetry floors, and glass mosaics originating in the fertile brain of Mr. Tiffany and his coadjutors in the ateliers of Fourth Avenue close by would be a chapter apart.

Now that the reign of stuffs has asserted itself in our homes—when we sigh before a yard of imperial yellow damask, and caress a bit of plush as a lover might the cheek of his fair one, singing them

them, will go away repenting past omissions, and zealous of future purchase. These fabrics include filmy "India" silks, silk sail cloths of great lustre and durability, silk canvases, and damasks like those in which Paul Veronese clothed his golden blondes.

For hangings of all kinds, and for "picture" dresses, these materials are not to be surpassed. The designs where a pattern is employed are admirable, and the tints supplied range from silver white to amber, gold, and orange, from blush pink to copper and pomegranate, with many greens and blues, in some cases intermingled, as in the gown bestowed on Enid by Earl Doorm.

"Where, like a shoaling sea, the lovely blue
  Played into green."

THE DESIGNING-ROOM.

Not satisfied, however, with producing stuffs to exchange for the plentiful shekels of American plutocracy, the artists have wisely carried their experiments into the region of cheap materials. One result is a fabric of raw silk, serving to utilize the waste of costlier webs, and dyed in the skein, in varied tints of the same color, giving it when woven all the effect of the Eastern hand-dyed, hand-woven stuffs so much admired. This is sold at a very moderate price. Chintzes and cottons receive as much care in the design as their expensive brocades, and Kentucky jean or denim has been known to take upon itself the semblance of Oriental drapery for wall or door. A sort of dado of this homely dark blue stuff (so familiar to the eyes of Southern or of Western people in the common garments of their negro population) has been decorated with interlaced rings of chestnut plush, a space on the wall above covered with blue and white striped awning stuff, and the frieze painted in reds and pinks above. Always design is studied with reference to use. A woven stuff designed by Miss Ida Clark for the hangings of a palace car has for its pattern a peal of bells, scattered as if driven by the wind, with a border of coupled car wheels, and drifting smoke between.

Thus it will be seen that the æsthetic housekeeper ambitious to adorn her room of state, the modest mother of a household who can spare this much and no more for a thing of beauty in her home, and the embroiderer seeking fresh fields for the vagaries of her needle, need no more look to sources over sea for their material.

Embroidery silk, to take the place of filoselle, is another industry of this busy hive. Brilliant as floss, it is expected that in time this silk will cost less than imported filoselle.

To properly classify the methods of embroidery used by the Associated Artists I have no hesitation in placing at the head of the list a needle-woven tapestry illustrating a distinctly new departure in decorative needle-work, which will probably take the name of the originator, and be known to collectors of the future as the Wheeler tapestry. A brief history of this work, secured to Mrs. Wheeler by letters patent both in America and England, may prove of interest to my readers.

For some years past Mrs. Wheeler has been experimenting in varieties of stitches applied to varieties in material, while aiming to produce an embroidered surface which should possess all the softness of painting in water-colors, yet have the enduring quality of ancient hand-wrought tapestries. To find a suitable ground for such work proved her main difficulty, and it was only while standing by the Jacquard loom one day watching the progress of a bit of silk-weaving to her order, that she observed one portion of the design suggesting the very arrangement of threads so long desired. A discarded remnant of imperfect texture was found having the idea still better carried out for her purpose. This was made to serve as a model for the new silk canvas, which was promptly put under way.

The result is a stuff woven of three shades of color (as, for instance, in the olive canvas, black, light green, and dark green), having a raw silk back, with silk warp and face. It resembles, in effect, "laid-work," or "couching," as seen in the grounds of so many old embroideries, as well as that variety of decoration recently revived under the name of "Queen Anne's darned-work." Next followed a series of experiments in stitches to preserve the elasticity of the textile, while allowing the introduction of additional warp threads without changing the plane of the surface.

The method of working this tapestry finally adopted may be best understood by calling to mind the much-neglected domestic art of stocking darning, which,

in these days of machine-made hosiery, has been tossed into the waste-basket of oblivion. This homely stitch is still seen in some Turkish embroideries, and was once made famous by old Flemish workers, as well as by those of Italy and Germany. In the Wheeler tapestry the darned threads are carried across either the woof or warp of the ground according to the desired effect of texture, and are *not* crossed by a returning thread, as in ordinary basket darning. When finished it is difficult even for a practiced eye to discern how they have apparently become incorporated with the stuff. The impression gained is that of a vignette, where the atmosphere fades into the ground tint of the stuff. In many cases the last range of stitches is supplied by using the ravelled silk of the original material.

The general effect of color aimed at in these needle-work pictures is flat, but the artist who continually oversees them while under the worker's hand can not resist a suggestion of light or shadow here and there, a deepening of tone in the hollow of plait or fold, a loving touch of the brush, as it were, supplying the gradations of tint that transform a lifeless surface of needle-work into a spirited portrayal, as by pigments, of some form of natural beauty. What will no doubt recommend it to the artistic amateur is that there are no fixed rules for the stitches to be taken. Wherever, by changing the direction of them, a good effect can be rendered, it is done unhesitatingly. But, at the same time, experienced workers will see how impossible would be the undertaking of such a labor as one of these tapestries without constant supervision from the eye of a trained artist.

After the design is sketched upon the canvas, a strong outline in silks is supplied, unlike that made with the brush in china painting in that it precedes instead of finishing the work. The worker is supplied with a carefully colored sketch of the subject, and some idea of the labor necessary to complete a piece of this tapestry may be gained from the fact that the "atmosphere" alone, surrounding a breezy nymph now being clothed with substance upon the frame, will require to perfect it fully four months' time of a steady work-woman.

The most conspicuous achievement in hand-wrought tapestry yet sent out by the Associated Artists, and certainly the most

TAPESTRY FROM DESIGN BY MISS DORA WHEELER.

important order in needle-work ever executed in this country, is the Vanderbilt set of wall-hangings already alluded to as having excited favorable notice in the recent Loan Collection at the Academy of Design. These tapestries, eleven in number, were executed after designs from Miss Dora Wheeler, representing phases of life in its holiday aspect. They include groups of dancing figures; an Undine seated beneath the curve of a wave holding a shell, from which drop garnered pearls; her comrade, a creature of the air, summoning birds, which come swiftly at her call;

nymphs with musical instruments; amorini swinging upon ropes of roses, or playing at hide-and-seek amid flowers; together with a design full of poetic beauty, entitled "The Birth of Psyche."

To supplement these tapestries are portières and window curtains of a pale greenish-white satin, with underlet appliqués of other pale-hued silks, conveying to the surface a peculiar opaline effect. Over this is embroidered a prodigal variety of roses dropping from the stems in their plenitude of bloom and color. Most of these roses are drawn from sketches made while

DESIGNING FROM A FISH.

the overlapping plumage of a bird.

This brilliant use of roses in their natural shape and color naturally suggests the much discussed question of conventionalizing flower forms for the purposes of ornamental design. In the practice of this association a plant rarely has to be twisted or perverted from the lines of beauty conferred on it by nature. When it is desired to decorate a given surface, the flower or plant chosen is found to be one entirely in harmony with its surroundings. It is placed finally only after consideration of it in all its relations to texture, color, and ultimate purpose.

The same nice care follows the piece of embroidery to its destination in the home. And in this connection I may quote some recent sayings of a distinguished art critic regarding the achievements of the association: "Their exhibition has a distinct importance in the development of decorative art, which, if we ever have it fitly applied to our domestic arrangements, must be indigenous. The conditions of life and light, manner of living and housing ourselves, differ so widely from the corresponding conditions in any other country that they can never be adequately met except by a decoration which grows up to them and fits them. It is easy to understand that what suits perfectly the gray and lightless sky

on a winter journey in the South, and are pleasant chronicles of life in the bowery haunts of the Carolinas and of Florida. The work bestowed on them is no artistic sleight of hand, where the needle flies, Atalanta-like, across the plain, but is the perfection of close embroidery, the old *opus plumarium*, or feather-stitch, resembling

of England, and the comparative gloom of its in-doors, or the system of furnishing which accords properly with French social and domestic surroundings, will jar with ours. When the American decorator finds his tone and style, and the women of our cultivated society learn that what is 'kill-bilt, the Associated Artists have completed several other important examples of the Wheeler tapestry. A set of wall panels and window curtains wrought in opalescent tints for a London drawing-room were lately shown, before being packed for shipment, to a few appreciative friends.

EMBROIDERED PORTIÈRE IN FLEUR-DE-LIS.

ing' on the boulevards is garish on Broadway, we shall have made the first step in an escape from artistic provincialism. The Associated Artists are helping us to this much-to-be-desired end."

Apart from the now famous tapestries embroidered for Mr. Cornelius Vander-A large hanging, arranged from Le Roux's painting of the "Arena" by Miss Ida Clark, was exhibited at the Loan Collection; and there is now in process of completion at the rooms a charming curtain, designed by Miss Rosina Emmet, having for subject the figure of Ruth carrying a sheaf of

PORTIÈRE OF VETERANS' ROOM IN SEVENTH
REGIMENT ARMORY.

wheat beneath her arm. The color of the drapery in this example is extremely subtle, and the hand is tempted to pass caressingly over its graceful folds before doubting Thomas can be made fairly to believe that needle, not brush, has brought to pass this wonder. Another delightful example is a study by Miss Dora Wheeler of a nymph and Cupid at a fountain, charming alike in design and color.

In the department of appliqué embroidery the Associated Artists have originated many interesting pieces of work. One of their earliest efforts was a portière for the Veterans' Room of the Seventh Regiment Armory, made of dull Japanese brocade, bordered with plush representing leopardskin. Upon the main space of the curtain are worked square appliqués of velvet, each one embodying some design suggesting the days of knighthood and romantic warfare. The intermediate spaces of the brocade are covered with overlapping rings of steel, to represent a coat of mail.

For the solace of those pathetic wanderers from home compelled to seek the shelter of a club-house, the artists have invented more than one noteworthy piece of decorative embroidery. Among those at the Union League is a large curtain for the library window. This is made of cloth of gold, and is framed in massive plush. Upon the central panel is embroidered a net, in whose meshes are entangled fish with jewelled scales. At intervals the stuff is cut from beneath the fish, leaving, when the curtain hangs against the light, the effect of an illuminated transparency.

A favorite bit of embroidery is known as "The Sermon." On a curtain of ordinary brown holland appear appliqué disks containing groups of field flowers, bees, or butterflies, with connecting traceries of silk thread. It was devised as a reminder no less than a proof of the fact that true art in needle-work depends not upon stuffs and mere externals, but upon the worker's artistic intuition. This delicate admonition is enforced by the materials employed to produce this pleasing result in decoration, none of them soaring beyond the ranks of ordinary use, or exceeding the possibilities of the humblest worker.

Thus it will be seen that although appliqué-work in the original form is classed among the antiquities of needle lore, the Associated Artists have contrived to throw around it a mantle of originality. In every case their aim has been so to bring together differing shades and differing textures that the result might be a scale of color otherwise unattainable. Even the same tones of the same color have

worker a distinguishing characteristic of their productions.

An attractive corner in the rooms of the association is that occupied by the ancient dower chests, now made to serve for

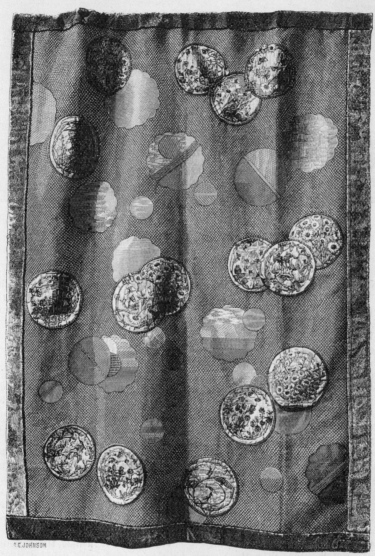

"THE SERMON."

been made to produce a difference in tint through the combination of varying textures.

And so, in other branches of needlework, the artists have continually striven to make the development of color schemes depending upon the inspiration of the

storing hoards of thin stuffs used for lighter draperies.

These diaphanous materials seem peculiarly in harmony with poetical designs for outline tracery, and are intended to be hung against the light, upon the glass of vestibule door or drawing-room window.

ENTRANCE TO BOSTON HARBOR.

THE GATEWAY OF BOSTON.

WHEN you go to sea from New York, the uninterrupted expanse of the bay is opened to you soon after you leave the wharf, and the channel lies across the middle of it in a nearly straight line. The spaciousness of the harbor is revealed at a glance; the few small islands, like Governor's and Bedloe's, are close to the extremity of the city, and when they are passed the course is clear to the Narrows, where the wooded and villa-dotted shores come so nearly together that a little more stretching would unite them, and make a circular lake with no other outlets to the sea than the East River and Long Island Sound and the Kill von Kull.

The gap in the shores is so narrow, indeed, that any hostile craft would be completely at the mercy of the forts, through the embrasures of which black-nosed cannon can be seen projecting on both sides, and it would not be more than the work of an hour to lay across from side to side such a barrier of torpedoes as would scatter an invader as chaff before the wind, though all the guns should be silent.

From the Narrows you pass down the lower bay, the open expanse of which is also unbroken, except by the two small artificial islands of the quarantine station, and at a little distance from the tropical-looking spit of cedar-tufted white sand which curves out at Sandy Hook the great ship channel debouches in the blue water of the Atlantic.

When you go to sea from Boston, you of course miss the activity of traffic and the picturesque variety of floating things, under steam and sail, which may be seen in New York, for the commerce of Boston is only a trifle compared with that of the metropolis. But you miss more than these the clear, unobstructed reach of water.

Measured by its coast-line, Boston Harbor is probably larger than the upper bay of New York, and the effusive local pride, caring less for accuracy than for the poetical suggestiveness of the comparison, has likened it to that rhetorically serviceable city, Venice.

Writing of it in 1634, the author of *New England Prospects* said of it: "It is a safe and pleasant Harbour within, having but one common and safe entrance, and that not very broad, there scarce being roome for 3 ships to come in board and board at the same time; but being once within, there is anchorage for 500 ships. This Harbour is made by a great company of Ilands, whose high cliffs shoulder out the boisterous seas, yet may easily deceive any unskillfull Pilote; presenting many faire openings and broad sounds, which afford too shallow waters for any ships, though navigable for Boates and small pinnaces."

The islands are not picturesque or interesting, however; had they cliffs, or woods, or cultivated shores, we should not regret the way they deprive Boston Harbor of the splendid unobstructed prospect which New York has. But most of them are arid and treeless and unadorned, except (if these can be regarded as ornaments) by the buildings of the charitable and reformatory institutions of the city, the station of the quarantine officers, and the depot of light-house supplies.

Some of them are low and sloping; others present sandy escarpments, fluted by the washings of the rain, and protected from what Thoreau calls the "nibbling" of the waves only by a low granite sea-wall. Before the walls were put up the sea had eaten up several without showing any appeasement of appetite, leaving nothing of them undevoured but a shoal like that which has a black sepulchral memorial in the beacon known in local tradition as Nix's Mate.

The beacon marks the sunken ruin of an island upon which pirates were gibbeted in the days when the black flag and the skull and cross-bones were accounted no less among the terrors of the sea than the hurricane. Nix was murdered by his mate, and when the latter was executed he protested his innocence, and prophetically declared that in proof of it the island would disappear.

As we go to sea we wind down past these islands and vestiges of islands through a narrow but deep channel. The craft we see are mostly coasters, of which as many as three hundred are sometimes gathered together waiting for the wind; the transatlantic traffic is represented by the weekly Cunarder and the tremendous Liverpool cattle steamers; a bark alive with walnut-skinned passengers is towed up, inward bound from the Azores, and we may catch the redolence of a Gloucester fishing schooner, with a contented crew busying about her scaly and dripping deck. Large ships are not very frequent, but occasionally an East Indiaman recalls to us that former glory of the harbor when Boston had a large share of the grandest commerce of the world, and her

SPEARING SCULPIN IN BOSTON HARBOR.

wharves were filled with Yankee ships, manned by Yankee crews—officers from Harvard and seamen from the Cape.

Getting farther down the harbor, we catch over the slopes of the islands object in view is Fort Warren, which, with its silent armament and flaming banner, stands at the very edge of the channel. Looking back to the city, we find that it has almost dissolved in a mixture

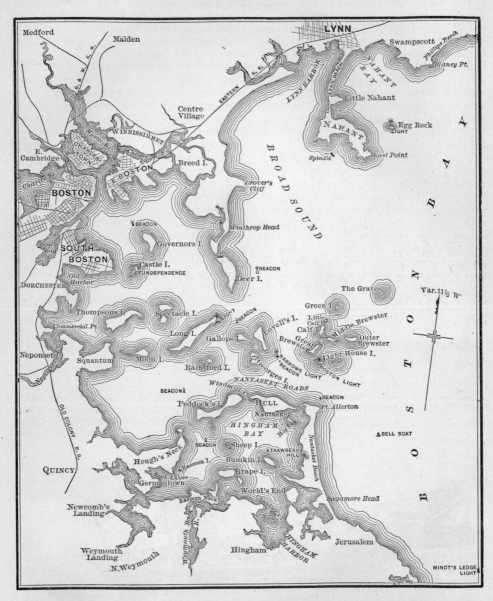

BOSTON BAY AND HARBOR.

glimpses of a southward range of hills steeped in a restful blue haze, and sprinkled with villages; we pass a solitary lobster-man tipping his dory over to the gunwale as he hands in his pots, and the next of purple and gray, through which the gilt on the State-house dome burns like the sun going down in a murky cloud; and now, turning by a squat screw-pile light-house, which looks like an enormous

BUG LIGHT—ENTRANCE TO NARROWS.

tarantula, and is known to mariners as "the Bug," we have a straight course of about a mile to the mouth of the harbor.

Here all disparagement of Boston in comparison with New York must cease. The entrance to the great ship channel of the latter port is fully twenty-three miles out at sea, and vessels of large draught are exposed to the unchecked force of the Atlantic while they are waiting for the tide. In Boston the bar is within the harbor, and if any waiting is necessary, it is only in the case of vessels of unusual size, and they can anchor, secure from the storm, under the headlands and within the breakwater which nature has erected across the entrance.

Unlike New York, Boston Harbor has no outer bay; it is an indentation with a narrow mouth in the sweeping curve of Massachusetts Bay, and it has no straggling estuary, so that, once out of it, a ship is at sea, and once within it, she is safe, and Boreas may puff his cheeks till they crack without hurting her.

Sloops and schooners can find their way into the harbor through a northerly passage called Broad Sound, but for larger vessels the only entrance is that of which we have spoken. It is scarcely more than a mile wide. At one side of it some pale yellow bluffs, deeply grooved by the rain, shoot up perpendicularly to a breezy houseless plateau, the advantages of which were recognized in Revolutionary times, as a series of old redoubts testify. At the seaward extremity these bluffs terminate in Point Allerton, and on the south they slope easily down to the slab-like crescent of Nantasket Beach, with its reproductions of Coney Island architecture and Coney Island diversions. At the other side a group of islands form that natural breakwater to which allusion has been made, shouldering out the boisterous seas as described by the

THE HERRING FLEET OFF GREAT BREWSTER.

PAINTING LOBSTER BUOYS.

author of *New England Prospects*, and although the islands within the harbor add little to its attractiveness, these are memorably picturesque in a wild and rugged way. Eight of them are high enough out of the water to be habitable, and the group includes the Shag Rocks and the Graves, which the sea keeps for its own. The largest is the Great Brewster, which is sandy and barren, facing the sea with a yellow escarpment like the bluffs on the opposite shore; the others are masses of rock of irregular outline, which were probably shoved out into their present position by an ancient glacier, and though they have arable surfaces, there are few points in their circumference at which a landing can be effected. These are the Middle Brewster, the Outer Brewster, the Little Brewster, Green Island, Calf Island, and Little Calf Island. The Little Brewster is the site of the graceful white pillar of Boston Light, which marks the entrance of the harbor for inward-bound mariners, and its only occupants are the keepers with their wives and children. The rest of the group are uninhabited during the greater part of the year, except by a few lobster-men, who have yielded nothing of their primitive simplicity to modern influences, and seem to be unconscious of the city which frets and toils so near them, though, if they cared to think of it, a purplish-gray cloud would reveal its proximity by day, and a dome of pale light by night.

Along the coast, both north and south, the summer boarder and the revelling excursionist have full sway; big hotels vying with those at Rockaway and Manhattan Beach have been built for them, and after dark the summer sky is set ablaze by the sheaves of rockets exploded for their amusement. But the Brewsters and their sister islands have been left happily alone. No ferry or telegraph links them with the mainland, and no wharf is there to make landing easy. The only way by which they can be reached is in a private boat, and when the easterly gales are blowing, flinging the surf over the Graves and the Shag Rocks, and dashing the spray as high as the top of the Middle Brewster, nothing can approach or leave them, and the isolation is complete.

The summer brings only three additions to the winter population—a lawyer, a banker, and a marine artist, who are variously benefited or become benefactors through the seclusion. The lawyer is entirely out of the reach of litigious clients, who, if he were accessible to carry out their impulses, would precipitate themselves into actions, from which they refrain after the calmer consideration which his absence allows. He tells how one of these once called at his office to have a deed prepared which, if it had been executed, would have caused a loss of fifty thousand dollars; but instead of being in his office he was down at the Brewsters, drinking in ozone—which, except tea, coffee, and lemonade, is the only thing ever drank there—and before he returned to town his client had abandoned the proposed transaction, having perceived the folly of it. The islands may therefore be said to make a benefactor of the lawyer by keeping him out of the way of reckless clients, and by frustrating unnecessary litigation.

The banker can add nothing to his obnoxious millions while sojourning upon them, and from the point of view of those cheerful philosophers who console themselves for the lack of wealth by stigmatizing it as an evil, he is benefited. But the debt of the marine artist to the islands exceeds that of either of the others, for during the few months he is among them they supply him with more than enough material to occupy him all the rest of the year.

Nature is less variable in her external appearances on land than on the sea, which on a gray day does not seem to be the same element as that which effervesces and sparkles when the sun is shining; the transition from light to shadow affects not merely the color, but the form and substance, and the billows of emerald become with a change of cloud inert ridges of lead.

CANAL, OUTER BREWSTER.

No place could be better than the islands for observing these variations, and very soon after the artist takes possession for the summer the rude boards of the studio walls are hidden under the sketches pinned to them of the sea in all its moods—now broken and ragged, its blackish-green having the sinister effect of some concealed tragedy as sunrise puts a red wedge under

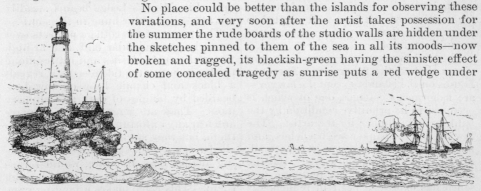

BOSTON LIGHT-HOUSE.

"MUSIC AT THE LIGHT."

the inky clouds which droop along the eastern horizon; now blue and flashing with a jocund brilliancy, the vessels scooping their way through it with a conscious sportiveness; and then pallid and vague, a phantom sea with ghostly ships.

The reference to the rude boards of the studio walls ought, perhaps, to be explained. The isolation of the Brewsters entails upon those who enjoy it the sacrifice of some conveniences, and compels the utilization of many little things which would be disregarded elsewhere. The studio was a cow shed originally, but with a great window cut in its northern side, opening up the Atlantic and the eastern shore as far as Gloucester, it is so well adapted to its new uses that its prosaic antecedents are unthought of.

The life of the summer visitors is as simple as that of the fishermen. The only houses on the islands, except the lawyer's, are fishermen's cottages, one of which is occupied in its primitive condition by the banker, and another by the artist. The lawyer and the banker are bachelors, and may be seen, frying-pan in hand, attending to their own simple wants. But the artist is married, and the feminine presence has expressed itself in refinements which, in contrast with the meagre estab-

lishments of the celibates, put the latter on the plane of savages. Her cottage has been transformed by dull red and dark green paint, and the addition of a piazza and hooded dormers, into a cozy little Queen Anne house, and when she comes at the beginning of summer a dory loaded with household luxuries is towed after her. It is usually found, after the difficult landing has been made, that the piano has shipped some water; but when it has been pumped out and oiled it serves well enough to cheer up the evening after the lamps have been lit within, and Boston Light can be seen flashing across the channel, while Minot's Ledge beams steadily out at sea like a star hung in the south.

The piazza of the cottage projects over a nearly perpendicular cliff, and at high water the surf splashes and rattles along the base; but as the tide recedes it reveals a black and chaotic heap of bowlders, bearded by tangles of dark and slippery moss. These are jagged enough to pierce and tear any unfortunate ship driven upon them, but they stretch out to a long bevelled ridge with a sharp edge, which, being higher than they are, would scrape her bottom out before she could reach them. This ridge makes a landing practicable at the Middle Brewster.

The Outer Brewster stands outside the rest of the group, and is more rugged than any of them. It has been so gashed and hacked at by disrupting forces that its scars have become weapons of reprisal, in the manner that a whipped and overdriven mortal himself becomes a scourge when ill treatment obliterates his humanity. More plainly than if she had used any alphabetical language, Nature has written over these cliffs, "No landing here." The bristling rocks vaguely remind us of the regulation position of infantry prepared to receive cavalry, when the foot-soldiers crouch down under their own upright bayonets, which are as a spiked wall to the advancing riders.

But in the northern side of the island there is a cove, and in the hope of making this accessible as a harbor of refuge an attempt was made some years ago to cut through the rocks which barred the entrance. A canal of considerable length was excavated, but the work has never been finished. No ship would dare to steer in a gale for portals so narrow and so beset with snares.

The Outer Brewster is not only the wildest in form, but also the richest in color. Great masses of golden-brown sea-weed droop along the water's edge, and above this tremulous fringe the rocks are of varied shades of red. Higher up they are a grayish-green and purple, and in the places which the surf can not reach grass thrives, adding the brilliance of its verdure to the other colors. Though the largest of the islands contains only twenty-five acres, there are pastoral little hollows in some of them where the sea is out of sight, and for all we can see we might be in some upland valley. Cattle are grazing in the tall grass among the bowlders, and the fishermen have built hanging gardens of vegetables upon the step-ladders of rock. But on the calmest days, in the centremost part of the islands, one can always hear the gurgle of the water in the steep-walled caves; odors are blown from the tangles of kelp and moss which tingle in the nostrils as no land-born breeze ever does, and the whistling-buoy off the Graves is never silent; even when the sea is without a ripple the buoy utters its admonition in a voice of pain, like a tormented spirit murmuring against an irrevocable judgment.

From Telegraph Hill, near the old earthworks on the sandy cliffs which bound the opposite side of the entrance to the

RESCUE OF THE CREW OF THE "FANNY PIKE."

The King of Calf Island

harbor, we can see all the islands at once. It was from this elevation that the villagers of Hull saw the smoke and heard the roar of the cannon in the bloody engagement between the *Chesapeake* and the *Shannon;* and here now, with windows that look far out to sea, is a little signal-box in which a vigilant watcher with a spy-glass telegraphs all arrivals to the city. From this hill the Brewsters seem to be a mere group of bowlders scattered by a giant hand; but they are so distributed that they form a wall across the harbor, and leave, as we have said, only a narrow gateway for ships of large tonnage. The shallow passage called Broad Sound is open to the northward, but it resembles the back door of a gentleman's residence, and is only used by such petty craft as steamers from the provinces and coastwise sloops and schooners, while all the more distinguished visitors come in by the main channel between Telegraph Hill and the Little Brewster, or Lighthouse Island.

The Boston Light is at the very entrance to the channel, and the white shaft towers up from its foundations in the reddish-brown rock of the little island like a saint in the desert. Its rays are visible sixteen miles away—one flash every thirty seconds, and with the twin lights of Thatcher's Island in the northeast and Minot's Ledge to the southward—an American Eddystone, pillared in the sea—it defines the position of the harbor to the approaching mariner.

There has been a light here since 1715, for the "generall benifit to Trade," but the present tower was built in 1783, after the destruction of the original building by the British as they passed out of the harbor. It has been frequently strengthened and altered, and is now in excellent condition. The walls are six feet thick at the base and four feet at the top. The lantern is nearly one hundred feet above the ground, and is nearly ten feet in diameter. In this glass house a man can stand upright, and in the centre of it the illuminating apparatus revolves, emitting its penetrating flashes at intervals of thirty seconds. Under the tower there is a steam fog-horn, which splits the air with stentorian warnings when the weather is thick, and between the harsh trumpetings of this instrument the ear catches the moaning of the whistling-buoy anchored off the Graves, and the tolling of the bell-buoy which floats over the perilous Harding's Ledge.

But the custodians of the light have their Lares and Penates enshrined in the comfortable house which is connected with the tower by a covered passage; and when the curtains are drawn over the windows it is cheerful in there, even though the channel is choked with ice, and the winds blow as if they would rock the pillar with its six-foot walls off its foundations. Music exerts its soothing spell through the medium of an accordion, played by Assistant-keeper Gorham; and sometimes, when the family join voices in "Hold the Fort" or "The Sweet By-and-By," Keeper Bates, carried away with rapture, urgently cries, "B'ar down thar, Edward; b'ar down on that instrument!" as if the accordion were the pump of a sinking ship, and salvation depended on the vigor of the performer.

The keepers occasionally have more exciting work to do than trimming their lamps and rubbing the moisture off the panes of glass in the lantern. Bates is possessor of the Humane Society's medal. He does not wear it on his breast, as bicycle-riders and roller-skaters wear their trophies; it is stowed away somewhere in a drawer, and he does not care to talk about it. It is, however, a memento of the time when the *Fanny Pike*, of Calais, was wrecked on the Shag Rocks, the ledge which extends seaward from the point of the Little Brewster. She struck and went to pieces during a very heavy northeasterly snow-storm, and, reckless of the tremendous sea, Bates put off in a small boat to rescue her crew, all of whom he saved, with the aid of Assistant-keeper Bailey and Charles Pochaska, a young fisherman belonging to the Middle Brewster.

The occupants of the other islands are lobster-men, chief among them being old Turner, who from time immemorial has hauled his pots in the waters surrounding the Brewsters. The islands seem enchained by the buoys which mark the spots where their traps are sunk for the voracious crustacean of the dragonish shape, and no object is seen more frequently than the solitary lobster-man making his rounds in his dory to see what spoils the sea has brought him. He takes with him a basket or a keg filled with sculpin, that hideous and marrowless fish, which is only good for bait, and he has so schooled himself to acquiesce in the unalterable that no curse escapes him when, after laborious hauling, he brings the dripping snare to the surface empty; nor, on the other hand, does he give utterance to any feeling of pleasure when the cage-like pot is seen to be full of prisoners as it is dragged over the tipping gunwale. I do not imagine that old Turner ever smiles; his deep-lined visage is puckered with seriousness, and though he is not talkative, an unexplained pathos speaks out of his eyes, which are screened from the forehead by a bristling pair of brows. He has been so saturated with salt-water for nearly fourscore years that he has a half-pickled appearance, and his beard and the curly locks which still flourish, though bleached by age and exposure, are always wet with brine.

In autumn the surrounding waters are brisk with herring, and for a few weeks the denizens of the islands can find occupation with the motley fleet which comes to catch them. This helps them a little; and now and then they have a chance to earn something more by piloting out of her difficulties some vessel which has been caught in the mazes of the rocks.

Winter smites the Brewsters severely; but we prefer that our parting glance at them should reveal them as they appear on a calm summer evening, when they are masses of purple on a golden sea, and the dying light in the west is reflected so brilliantly in the east that it seems to be a promise of perpetual day.

ON CALF ISLAND.

TRANSCRIPTS FROM NATURE.

XI.

SUNSET IN THE NORTH BEHIND PINES.

AGAINST the steel-blue sky the pines
　　Stand outlined, dark and weird and tall;
　　Low down, beyond, the sun's red ball
Between their forest pillars shines;
The sunset sky their boughs enfold
Gleams as in some cathedral old;

Beyond the pillared nave, o'erhead,
A window flames with mystic red.

XII.

DRAGON-FLIES.

Blue as though fallen from the skies,
　　The pool dreams in the gorse-clad heath;
　　The yellow newts dart swift beneath;
Above, the wheeling dragon-flies
Flash in their shining coats of mail,
Or with spread wings slow float or sail

Through the windless air: live gems they seem,
That late in the earth's bowels did gleam.

XIII.

APPROACHING SKYE, FROM THE NORTH.

The sweeping seas with foam are white.
　　The Isle of Mist before us lies,
　　Pale as the blue of morning skies
Ere quickened by the sun's full might.
Lo! there Dunvegan's crags; and there
Macleod's Maids, delicately fair;

And, shadowed faint in harebell blue,
The dim Cuchullins haunt our view.

XIV.

MOONLESS NIGHT OFF SKYE.—AUGUST.

The heavens with sprinkled star-dust hang
　　Above the phosphorescent sea,
　　Where swim medusæ luminously,
Live-purple, green. The casual clang
Of swaying chains within the boat
The silence only breaks, save note

Of passing gull, or the dull sound
Where whales blow o'er yon herring ground.

IN THE FENS.—SUMMER.

Broad, deep, and still the salt creeks twisting flow
Between the long green flats, where to and fro
The water-weeds wave sluggishly, and where
Amid the beds of flag the shy coot's lair
Is hidden, and the wild-ducks swim unseen;
And in the stagnant pools, o'ergrown with green
And vegetable slime, the water-rats
Swarm thick; and in the lower flats
And salter oozing tide whole clouds of shrimps
Flicker and vanish, and in one short glimpse
The flounders dart from sight in troubled sand.
And far across the wide expanse of land
Miraculously green the pastures reach,
O'er which the plovers call and curlews screech
In the fresh wind, and the fat oxen low
Hock-deep within the grasses, where these grow
Cool, rich, with green and purple seeded plumes,
Sweet-smelling; where the samphire blooms,
And the sea-poppies wave, and the wild thyme;
And where the sheep bells make a pleasant rhyme
All day; and underneath the fresh blue sky
The fledgeling sea-birds learn to wheel and fly.

SUNSET IN THE NORTH BEHIND PINES.

ANTELOPE HUNTING IN MONTANA.

OF all the numerous species of large game to be found in the far West, there is none whose pursuit furnishes grander sport to the expert rifleman than the antelope (*Atilocapra americana*). His habitat being the high open plains, he may be hunted on horseback, and with a much greater degree of comfort than may the deer, elk, bear, and other species which inhabit the wooded or mountainous districts. His keen eyesight, his fine sense of smell, his intense fear of his natural enemy, man, however, render him the most difficult of all game animals to approach, and he must indeed be a skillful hunter who can get within easy rifle range of the antelope, unless he happens to have the circumstances of wind and lie of ground peculiarly in his favor. When the game is first sighted, even though it be one, two, or three miles away, you must either dismount and picket your horse, or find cover in some *coulee* or draw, where you can ride entirely out of sight of the quarry. But even under such favorable circumstances it is not well to attempt to ride very near them. Their sense of hearing is also very acute, and should your horse's hoof or shoe strike a loose rock, or should he snort or neigh, the game is likely to catch the sound while you are yet entirely out of sight and far away, and when you finally creep cautiously to the top of the ridge from which you expect a favorable shot, you may find the game placidly looking for you from the top of another ridge a mile or two farther away.

But we will hope that you are to have better luck than this. To start with, we will presume that you are an expert rifleman; that you are in the habit of making good scores at the butts; that at 800, 900, and 1000 yards you frequently score 200 to 210 out of a possible 225 points. We will also suppose that you are a hunter of some experience; that you have at least killed a good many deer in the States, but that this is your first trip to the plains. You have learned to estimate distances, however, even in this rare atmosphere, and possess good judgment as to windage. You have brought your Creedmoor rifle along, divested, of course, of its Venier sight, wind-gauge, and spirit-level, and in their places you have fitted a Beach combination front sight and Lyman rear sight. Besides these you have the ordinary open-step sight attached to the barrel just in front of the action. This is not the best arm for antelope hunting; a Winchester Express with the same sights would be much better; but this will answer very well.

We camped last night on the bank of a clear, rapid stream that gurgles down from the mountain, and this morning are up long before daylight, have eaten our breakfasts, saddled our horses, and just as the gray of dawn begins to show over the low, flat prairie to the east of us we mount, and are ready for the start. The wind is from the northeast. That suits us very well, for in that direction, about a mile away, there are some low foot-hills that skirt the valley in which we are camped. In or just beyond these we are very likely to find antelope, and they will probably be coming toward the creek this morning for water.

We put spurs to our horses and gallop away. A brisk and exhilarating ride of ten minutes brings us to the foot-hills, and then we rein up, and ride slowly and cautiously to near the top of the first one. Here we dismount, and, picketing our ponies, we crawl slowly and carefully to the apex. By this time it is almost fully daylight. We remove our hats, and peer cautiously through the short, scattering grass on the brow of the hill.

Do you see anything?

No; nothing but prairie and grass.

No? Hold! What are those small, gray objects away off yonder to the left? I think I saw one of them move. And now, as the light grows stronger, I can see white patches on them. Yes, they are antelope. They are busily feeding, and we may raise our heads slightly and get a more favorable view. One, two, three—there are five of them—two bucks, a doe, and two kids. And you will observe that they are nearly in the centre of a broad stretch of table-land.

"But," you say, "may we not wait here a little while until they come nearer to us?"

Hardly. You see they are intent on getting their breakfast. There is a heavy frost on the grass, which moistens it sufficiently for present purposes, and it may be an hour or more before they will start for water. It won't pay us to wait so long, for we shall most likely find others within that time that we can get within range of without waiting for them. So you may as well try them from here.

Now your experience at the butts may serve you a good turn. After taking a careful look over the ground, you estimate the distance at 850 yards, and setting up your Beach front and Lyman rear sights, you make the necessary elevation. There is a brisk wind blowing from the right, and you think it necessary to hold off about three feet. We are now both lying prone upon the ground. You face the game, and support your rifle at your shoulder by resting your elbows on the ground. The sun is now shining brightly, and you take careful aim at that old buck that stands out there at the left. At the report of your rifle a cloud of dust rises from a point about a hundred yards this side of him, and a little to the left, showing that you have underestimated both the distance and the force of the wind—things that even an old hunter is liable to do occasionally.

AN EARLY MORNING CALL.

We both lie close, and the animals have not yet seen us. They make a few jumps, and stop all in a bunch. The cross-wind and long distance prevent them from knowing to a certainty where the report comes from, and they don't like to run just yet, lest they may run toward the danger instead of away from it. You make another half-point of elevation, hold a little farther away to the right, and try them again. This time the dirt rises about twenty feet beyond them, and they jump in every direction. That was certainly a close call, and the bullet evidently whistled uncomfortably close to several of them. They are now thoroughly frightened. You insert another cartridge, hurriedly draw a bead on the largest buck again, and fire. You break dirt just beyond him, and we can't tell for the life of us how or on which side of him your bullet passed. It is astonishing how much vacant space there is round an antelope, anyway. This time they go, sure. They have located the puff of smoke, and are gone with the speed of the wind away to the west. But don't be discouraged, my friend. You did some clever shooting, some *very* clever shooting, and a little practice of that kind will enable you to score before night.

We go back to our horses, mount, and gallop away again across the table-land. A ride of another mile brings us to the northern margin of this plateau, and to a more broken country. Here we dismount and picket our horses again. We ascend a high butte, and from the top of it we can see three more antelope, about a mile to the north of us; but this time they are in a hilly, broken country, and the wind is coming directly from them to us. We shall be able to get a shot at them at short range. So we cautiously back down out of sight, and then begins the tedious process of stalking them. We walk briskly along around the foot of a hill for a quarter of a mile, to where it makes a turn that would carry us too far out of our course. We must cross this hill, and after looking carefully at the shape and location of it, we at last find a low point in it where by lying flat down we can crawl over it without revealing ourselves to the game. It is a most tedious and painful piece of work, for the ground is almost covered with cactus and sharp flinty rocks, and our hands and knees are terribly lacerated. But every rose has its thorn, and nearly every kind of sport has something unpleasant connected with it occasionally; and our reward, if we get it, will be worth the pain it costs us. With such reflections and comments, and with frequent longing looks at the game, we kill time till at last the critical part of our work is done, and we can arise and descend in a comfortable but cautious walk into another draw.

This we follow for about two hundred yards, until we think we are about as near our quarry as we can get. We turn to the right, cautiously ascend the hill, remove our hats, and peer over, and there, sure enough, are our antelope quietly grazing, utterly oblivious to the danger that threatens them. They have not seen, heard, or scented us; so we have ample time to plan an attack. You take the standing shot at the buck, and together we will try and take care of the two does afterward. At this short distance you don't care for the peep and globe sights, and wisely decide to use the plain open ones. This time you simply kneel, and then edge up until you can get a good clear aim over the apex of the ridge in this position. The buck stands broadside to you, and at the crack of your rifle springs into the air, and falls all in a heap, pierced through the heart.

And now for the two does. They are flying over the level stretch of prairie with the speed of an arrow, and are almost out of sure range now. You turn loose on that one on the right, and I will look after the one on the left. Our rifles crack together, and little clouds of dust rising just beyond tell us that, though we have both missed, we have made close calls. I put in about three shots to your one, owing to my rifle being a repeater, while you must load yours at each shot. At my fourth shot my left-fielder doubles up and goes down with a broken neck; and although you have fairly "set the ground afire"—to use a Western phrase—around your right-fielder, you have not had the good fortune to stop her, and she is now out of sight behind a low ridge.

But you have the better animal of the two, and have had sport enough for the first morning. We will take the entrails out of these two, lash them across our

23*

horses behind our saddles, go to camp, and rest through the heat of the day; for this September sun beams down with great power in mid-day, even though the nights are cool and frosty.

And now, as we have quite a long ride to camp, and as we are to pass over a rather monotonous prairie country *en route*, I will give you a point or two on flagging antelope, as we ride along, that may be useful to you at some time. Fine sport may frequently be enjoyed in this way. If you can find a band that have not been hunted much, and are not familiar with the wiles of the white man, you will have little trouble in decoying them within rifle range by displaying to them almost any brightly colored object. They have as much curiosity as a woman, and will run into all kinds of danger to investigate any strange object they may discover. They have been known to follow an emigrant or freight wagon with a white cover several miles, and the Indian often brings them within reach of his arrow or bullet by standing in plain view wrapped in his red blanket. A piece of bright tin or a mirror answers the same purpose on a clear day. Almost any conspicuous or strange-looking object will attract them; but the most convenient as well as the most reliable at all times is a little bright red flag.

In the fall of 1881 I was riding down the Yellowstone River in company with my friends Huffman and Conley, on our return from a hunting expedition to the Big Horn Mountains. While passing over a piece of high table-land overlooking a portion of the valleys of the Yellowstone River and Big Porcupine Creek we met a couple of hunters, who told us that a large herd of buffaloes were grazing on the Big Porcupine about fifteen miles from us; and knowing that antelope are nearly always found hanging on the outskirts of every herd of buffaloes, we at once began to scan the country with our glasses in search of them. We were soon rewarded by seeing a number of small white specks on the dead grass away up the Porcupine that seemed to be moving. We rode toward them at a lively gait for perhaps a mile, and stopped to look again. From this point we could easily identify them, although they still seemed to be about the size of jack-rabbits. We again put spurs to our horses, and rode rapidly to within a mile of them, when we picketed our animals in a low swale, took out our "antelope flag"—a piece of scarlet-colored calico about half a yard square—attached it to the end of my wiping stick, and were ready to interview the antelopes.

I crawled to the top of a ridge within plain view of the game, and planted the flag. The breeze spread it out, kept it fluttering, and it soon attracted their attention. This bit of colored rag excited their curiosity to a degree that rendered them restive, anxious, uneasy, and they seemed at once to be seized with an insatiable desire to find out what it was. Huffman went to the top of another ridge to my right, and some distance in advance, and Conley crawled into a hollow on the left, so that we three formed a half-circle, into which we intended, if possible, to decoy the game.

When they first discovered our flag they moved rapidly toward it, sometimes breaking into a trot. But when they had covered about half the distance between us and their starting-point they began to grow suspicious, and stopped. They circled around, turned back, and walked a few steps, then paused and looked back at the, to them, mysterious apparition. But they could not resist its magic influence. Again they turned and came toward us, stopped, and gazed curiously at it. The old buck that led the herd stamped impatiently, as if annoyed at his inability to solve the mystery. They walked cautiously toward us again down an incline into a valley which took them out of sight of the flag.

This, of course, rendered them still more impatient, and when they reached the top of the next ridge they were running. But as soon as the leader caught sight of the flag again he stopped, as did the others in turn when they came in sight of it. They were not more than a hundred yards from me, and were still nearer to my friends. There were seven in the band—two bucks, three does, and two kids. Their position was everything we could wish, and though we might possibly have brought them a few yards nearer, there was a possibility of their scenting us even across the wind, which, of course, we had arranged to have in our favor, and I decided that rather than run the risk of this and the consequent stampede, I would open on them where they were. It had been arranged that I was to begin the entertainment, and drawing a fine bead on the white breast

of the old buck, I pulled. Huffman's and Conley's rifles paid their compliments to the pretty visitors at almost the same instant, and for about thirty seconds thereafter we fanned them about as vigorously as ever a herd was fanned under similar circumstances. The air was full of leaden missiles, and the dry dust raised under and around the fleeing quarry. Clouds of smoke hung over us, and the distant hills echoed the music of our artillery, until the last white rump disappeared among the cottonwoods on the river-bank. When the smoke of battle cleared away, and we looked over the field, we found that we had not burned our powder in vain. Five of the little fellows, two bucks and three does, had fallen victims to their curiosity. The two fawns had, strangely enough, escaped, probably because they, being so much smaller than their parents, were less exposed.

I once saw a coyote sneak from behind a hill toward a herd of antelope. Instantly there was a grand rush of all the adult members of the band, male and female, toward the intruder, and when they had gotten in front of the kids they stopped, with bristles erect, ears thrown forward, and heads lowered, presenting a most warlike and belligerent appearance. The coyote, when he saw himself confronted with this solid phalanx, suddenly stopped, eyed his opponents for a few moments, and then, apparently overawed at the superiority of numbers and warlike attitude of his intended prey, slunk reluctantly away in search of some weaker victim. When he was well out of sight, the older members of the band turned to their young, caressed them and resumed their grazing.

The speed of the antelope is probably not excelled by that of any other animal in this country, wild or domestic, except the greyhound, and in fact it is only the finest and fleetest of these that can pull down an antelope in a fair race.

In the little village of Garfield, Kansas, there lived a man some years ago—the proprietor of a hotel—who had two pet antelopes. The village dogs had several times chased them, but had always been distanced. One day a Mexican came to town who had with him two large, handsome greyhounds. Immediately on riding up to the hotel he saw the antelopes in the yard, and told the proprietor, gruffly, that he had better put "them critters" in the corral, or his dogs would kill them. The proprietor said he guessed the "critters" were able to take care of themselves, especially if the dogs did not spring upon them unawares. This aroused the Mexican's ire, and he promptly offered to wager a goodly sum that his dogs would pull down one or both of the antelopes within a mile. The challenge was accepted, the stakes deposited, and the antelopes turned into the street, and the "greaser" told his dogs to "take 'em."

The dogs sprang at the antelopes, but the latter had soon reached a vacant lot across the street. They started off down the river. For a distance of four miles the river-bottom was an open prairie, and as level as a floor. As the quartette sped over this grand natural race-course, the whole populace of the town turned out *en masse* to see the race. Men and boys shouted, and ladies waved their handkerchiefs. Betting was rife, the natives offering two to one on the antelopes, the Mexican and the few other strangers in town being eager takers. It was nip and tuck, neither animals gaining nor losing perceptibly, and when at last the four went round a bend in the river four miles away, and were hidden by a bluff, the game was, as nearly as could be seen by the aid of good field-glasses, just about the same distance ahead of the dogs as when they left town.

Some hours later the dogs returned, so tired they could scarcely walk. The Mexican eagerly looked for hair on their teeth, and although he could find none, was confident that his dogs had killed the antelopes. A mounted expedition to search for the carcasses and settle the question was agreed upon, but as it was too near night to start when the dogs returned, it was arranged to go in the morning. But when the parties got up the next morning they found the antelopes quietly grazing in the hotel yard. The Mexican left town in disgust, followed by his lame, sore-footed dogs, and muttering that he "never seed no varmints run like them things did."

The antelope, one of the brightest and most graceful and beautiful of all our Western game animals, is fast disappearing from our broad plains, owing to the ceaseless slaughter of it that is carried on by "skin hunters," Indians, "foreign noblemen," and others who come to this country year after year and spend the entire summer in hunting. Thousands of them are killed every summer by this latter class, and left to rot where they fall, not a pound of meat, a skin, or even a head being taken from them. I have seen with my own eyes this butchery carried on for years past, and know whereof I speak.

Nearly all the Territories have stringent laws intended to prohibit this class of slaughter, but in these sparsely settled countries the provisions for enforcing them are so meagre that these men violate them day after day and year after year with impunity. This is one of the instances in which prohibition does not prohibit. And what I have said of the antelope is true of all the large game of the great West. The buffalo, elk, deer, mountain-sheep, etc., are being slaughtered by the thousands every year—tenfold faster than the natural increase. And the time is near, *very* near, when all these noble species will be extinct. The sportsman or naturalist who desires to preserve a skin or head of any of them must procure it very soon or he will not be able to get it at all.

THE MANOR-HOUSE OF KERSUEL.

I.—THE SHAPE.

THE sky is a dull gray, so low that the mass of heavy cloud seems as if it might touch the chimneys of the old manor-house; yet a keen wind is blowing, a wind which rushes along the galleries at the back of the manor-house, and shakes both the narrow casements of the lower gallery and the circular lights in the gallery overhead. The blasts are so violent that it seems as if the small diamond-shaped panes might soon be whirled out of their leadings into the river below. The old house is built at the end of a lofty ridge, so that the ascent to it is gradual from the far-off road; but the descent to the river in the deep wooded valley in the rear is precipitous, and makes a natural defense. The house, though fortified in front, and boasting an overgrown moat and draw-bridge and a rusty portcullis, is only defended behind by the absence of doors or any openings in its massive old wall. There are no windows till you reach the galleries outside the bedrooms of the second and third floors.

Even these windows are small and infrequent, and the light fades quickly in this dull February weather, so that the long low gallery is dreary and gloomy; it has not even the sullen flow of the dark river to break its stillness; only now and then the hoot of an owl sounds in the lofts overhead. At the farthest end is a door with a flight of steps leading to it. This door opens suddenly, and a girl, wrapped in a cloak, with a hood pulled over her face, comes down the steps, and hurries rapidly along the gallery till she has passed the last door leading into it; then she goes down two more steps at its farther end on to a square stair-head at the top of the great staircase, which does not go beyond this floor: the upper gallery is reached by spiral flights of stone steps in the curious little tourelles at the angles of the old house.

As the girl steps out on to the broad landing, a bat skims across it, and almost touches her cheek.

"Ah!" and with a shriek of dismay she flies down the rickety, uneven steps, crosses the huge earthen-floored hall, and vanishes through a door below the staircase leading to the numerous passages at the back of the house.

It leads, too, by a passage on one side, into the garden on the terrace that borders the steep hill; but before she can reach the end of the passage which intervenes between the hall and this side entrance her way is stopped.

A short, square-faced woman stands fingering her many-striped apron; she wears a black gown, the armholes of which are bordered with broad black velvet, a cap of plain white muslin, which frames in a sunburned face with sad blue eyes, and then hangs down behind in two broad white tails. When the girl reaches her she smiles, and stands aside to let her pass.

"Oh, Marguerite, I have been so frightened! A bat flew nearly in my face!"

"A bat! Is that all? You looked so scared, Ma'm'selle Geneviève, that I did not know what you might not have been seeing!"

Geneviève shivers, and then looks over her shoulder. "Marguerite! as if this house were not dismal enough in itself! This is the third time you have hinted at apparitions, and yet you vowed to me that there is not one room haunted in the

house. However, I have no faith in such nonsense."

Marguerite looks uneasy. She stuffs both hands into the large pockets in front of her apron. "Come into the kitchen, mademoiselle, and see the fish that Louis has just brought in; you have not seen such big ones since you came home. Come, mademoiselle."

Marguerite waddles down a side-turning out of the passage, and Geneviève follows into a long low room with a rack overhead, in which are bacon and skins of lard, a good store of herbs and cheese, and at one end a pile of freshly made galettes. On the table below is an open basket half full of brown speckled trout.

"Yes, they are fine"—but Geneviève speaks as if she is thinking of something else. Then going close to the open hearth, she bent down and warmed her hands at the cheerful blaze of the fagots piled up between huge dogs. "Oh, Marguerite," she says, "I am so weary of this winter life! I begin to hate Kersuel."

The woman's sad face seems to grow sadder and longer. "Mademoiselle must try against such feelings," she says, solemnly; "for she will always have to live at Kersuel."

Geneviève shakes her head with so much energy that the hood falls back and shows her face. It is very remarkable there is beauty in it, but the first thought it suggests is that it is different from any other face, there is in it so much delicacy of outline, so much power of expression; the skin is clear and colorless, except that the temples show a creamy white where the soft dark brown hair leaves them; but the fine well-marked eyebrows and large deep-colored eyes are full of life and feeling. The eyes are indefinable—gray and green and brown and yellow, all mellowed into a tender velvet-like lustre that has no dry hardness in it; the brilliancy is liquid, softened by long dark lashes. Now, as she looks at Marguerite, there is protest in them and in every line of the expressive face.

"You are quite wrong. Grandmother will not stay here next winter; she will have got well, and then she will go to Paris again, and the old house will be shut up for the winter. It is a dear old place in the summer, but I had no notion it was so wretched in winter: it is only fit for bats and rats now. You have the best of it here"—the girl is looking at the huge carved oak wardrobe on one side, and the box bedstead fixed into the wall opposite. "This is cozy enough; but those rooms upstairs are so eerie when it gets dark"—she shivers. "I hate that gallery."

"Mademoiselle must learn to love the old place; she used to be happy here, and it is always to be her home. Madame has said to me, Mademoiselle Geneviève will live and die at Kersuel."

Geneviève stamps her foot—for Marguerite's face is full of reproof—and then she dances round the kitchen table. "You are such an old goose! you never reflect. Of course I used to like Kersuel; I liked the convent well enough, but I liked holidays better; and I only came to Kersuel for holidays, and remember I was only here in summer-time. You know very well that this is grandmother's first winter in the old place."

Marguerite shakes her head. "Pardon, mademoiselle. Long ago, when madame was young, she and Monsieur De Kersuel spent more than one winter here. And Monsieur Georges too, for that matter."

A faint color flickers into the girl's face. "You have told me that before, Marguerite. It appears to me that Monsieur Georges must be very old, if he was here so long ago."

Marguerite looks stiff and sad again. "No, mademoiselle, Monsieur Georges is not so old. He is many years younger than madame."

Geneviève's dark eyes are fixed on the old servant, but she is not thinking of her. Marguerite has been her nurse ever since she came an orphan baby to Kersuel, and she is accustomed to tyrannize over the old woman.

"Marguerite," she says, suddenly, "because you knew me when I was a baby you think I am a child still. Now open your eyes, old woman, and look at me well. I am quite grown up, and I insist on knowing the exact age of Monsieur Georges."

Marguerite looked still more sad. "I will tell mademoiselle, because she will soon judge for herself. Monsieur Georges is fifty years old. Yesterday Madame told me that many weeks ago, when first she became ill, she sent for Monsieur Kersuel: he will soon be here. This has made me very sad."

"You are always sad, you dear old thing!"

She kissed first one, then the other, sunburned cheek. "But why are you specially sad about Monsieur Georges's arrival? —it is my affair, not yours."

Color flashed into Marguerite's blue eyes, and across her sunburned cheeks.

"It is mademoiselle who does not think now," she said. "Does she think that madame would ask her nephew to take so long and expensive a journey unless she felt it was necessary he should come and see her—necessary at least that he should be here?" She sighed and put her apron to her eyes.

Geneviève stood in shocked silence, she turned very pale, and her lips trembled.

"For Heaven's sake, Marguerite, speak plainly. Can you mean that my darling grandmother is dangerously ill, and that —that she sends for this man to— Oh, Marguerite, you can not have known this all this time, and not have told me!"

The old servant has left off wiping her eyes. "I have known it more than a month, but madame did not wish mademoiselle to know, and she will be angry if she hears that I have told."

"She will never know that, but who said my grandmother is so very ill? Oh, Marguerite, the doctors are often wrong." And all the while she says this, hints and convictions are thronging to be listened to by the unwilling mind of Geneviève. How changed she found her grandmother when she arrived just before Christmas; and did she not look mournful when she said, "I shall never see Paris again!"

"Her complaint is mortal, mademoiselle, and she knows it; but she has said to me, 'Do not tell the child, Marguerite; her bright face does me so much good, I could not bear to see a cloud on it.'"

Marguerite wipes her eyes again.

Geneviève does not cry; her heart feels like a great lump, as if it must choke her; she does not speak.

"Yes, yes," the old servant says. "It was just in gray weather like this that Monsieur Kersuel passed away. Madame was in the gallery, but she did not think of his death till she got the warning."

"Marguerite!" the girl speaks, solemnly. "What is this warning? You have spoken of it before, but I would never listen. Tell me, does it really come when a Kersuel dies, or is it a fable?"

Marguerite shrugs her shoulders. "Is it likely that I should repeat fables to mademoiselle at such a time as this? I must go to my mistress now, mademoiselle. She will not pass away till the warning has been sent; and"—her voice sinks to a whisper— "it will be sent to you, mademoiselle: the shape can only be seen by one of the Kersuel blood!"

II.—AN APPARITION.

Marguerite departed, leaving the young lady standing by herself beside the broad, open hearth.

Geneviève was full of awe. She had jested secretly at the old servant's superstition; but this was a new idea, and she could not manage to laugh at it. She looked round, and she thought the kitchen was, after all, not so cozy as she had fancied it. The corners farthest from the fire were very shadowy in the waning light, and that huge wardrobe looked full of mystery; so did the closely drawn curtains of the bedstead in the wall, and the carved oak chest beneath it, for all the world like the tomb of Ginevra.

"The garden is the only place fit to stay in." The girl pulled her hood over her head, and made her way through the passages to the terraced garden.

Three grassed banks, one above another, separated the garden plots and the clumps of shrubs behind them, and this division made the garden seem larger than it really was. Perhaps because in her summer holidays she had chiefly lived out-of-doors, Geneviève loved this garden, and spent all her spare moments there. In one corner, near a flight of steps which led down to the bottom of the steep hill, and made a short way from the house to the high-road, was a summer-house—desolate enough now that the roses and clematis that made its summer loveliness were leafless; but an evergreen honeysuckle still spread a sort of screen on one side, and the stone bench and table were always there. Geneviève walked up and down the edge of the terrace till she was tired of the view into the valley, and then she came and rested herself on the stone bench.

"Fifty years old," she said to herself; and then it seemed wicked to dwell on such a thought. Could Marguerite have spoken truly, and was her grandmother dying?

Geneviève's heart ached.

Every complaining thought, every petulant word she had spoken to her, came back and weighed like lead on the girl's heart. They were not many, but just now, in sight of the parting so soon to come, Geneviève felt that she would give all that could be asked of her to atone for them, to blot them out from the memory of her grandmother.

How little the young know of a parent's love till they too become parents! How true it is that no child can ever measure the endurance and forbearance of a mother's love!

Madame Kersuel, lying now on a couch in her own room, and hearing from Marguerite how Geneviève shrank from the dullness of the old house, sighed softly to herself. "I have been selfish to bring the sweet child here at this time; I could have died in Paris."

If her grandmother had been well, Geneviève would not have so dreaded the dark hours at the old manor-house. By nature she was brave and light-hearted; but though she loved Madame De Kersuel, there was little intimacy between them. The old lady was very old for her age, and her lameness had always kept her much in-doors, even in those summer holidays which the girl had spent in rambling about at her own sweet will in the garden and wood on the side of the valley. Still, now, as she seated herself in the old summer-house, Geneviève thought this might have been different; she might have staid in-doors more; she might have read and sung more to her grandmother.

"And instead," she sobbed, "I thought of my own enjoyment. Oh, if she will only get well, I will try to be so different!"

Her grandmother had thought Kersuel too dull a house to bring up this bright-eyed child in, and in those days she and her husband only lived half the year in the old manor-house; so Geneviève's real home had been the convent at Quimperlé. Her winter holidays had been spent busily there with the kind, cheerful sisters and companions of her own age, and it had been a delightful change to come to Kersuel in summer-time, when the garden was full of flowers and fruit. More than once Marguerite had spoken to Geneviève of Monsieur Georges—a nephew of the late Monsieur Kersuel. He was heir to the property, and would succeed to it on the death of her grandmother; but he lived far away in the West Indies.

Once Marguerite had said that he was to be the husband of Geneviève, but the merry girl had treated this as a joke, and when, later on, she had asked questions, Marguerite answered that in her own good time madame would explain her intentions.

Geneviève is only eighteen, and until the dark weather came she was not afraid of the shadowy corners and gloomy galleries of Kersuel. She is so gay and so young, and she has always had such perfect health, that her nerves are in good order. Hitherto she has lived in the present. At the convent, time was taken up by study or cheerful recreation; there was no leisure for thinking. Life to this happy-tempered girl had been like a summer sky.

But almost ever since her return home —for she said good-by to the convent at Christmas—Madame De Kersuel has been ailing, and for these last two weeks has lived entirely in her own rooms. Geneviève is left to herself, and perforce must spend much of her time in-doors. The snow lies so thickly on the hill and the drifts are so deep in the valley that she rarely stirs beyond the garden, and the garden, small as it is, is Geneviève's only happiness. In-doors the long dark afternoons and the weird stillness of the winter evenings give Geneviève more thinking time than she cares for. The garden is a most blessed refuge.

"There is no furniture to creak here," she says; "no dim corners where something seems always to move just when I am not looking. I could not stay at Kersuel if it were not for the garden."

But even in the garden she gets plenty of thinking time, for she is fearless of the cold; and as she sits there, well wrapped in her hood and cloak an hour or more at a time, she has now and then asked herself what is the future shaped out for her.

One day her grandmother said, "You will always live at Kersuel, Geneviève;" and yet Monsieur Georges, she well knows, is heir to the old manor.

She has been content to dream in a passive, quiescent way about this, but to-day Marguerite's words let in light on her unformed vision. While she stood with her deep, thoughtful eyes fixed on Marguerite she was making a picture of Monsieur Georges—a stiff, middle-aged man, ugly perhaps, certainly cold and severe as her grandfather was—and she was to be his wife, bound to him forever, bound never to leave him or the gloomy old house, to

beat her heart out here in wild, rebellious thoughts. A quite new tumult of feeling stirred in the girl's heart; she would hate to be the wife of any one, and give up her freedom of action; but if this Monsieur Georges were really so old, she would rather fling herself down into the ravine and drown herself in the dark river than be mistress of Kersuel.

But Marguerite's last tidings filled the girl's heart and banished all feelings except sorrow; and she had sat sobbing a long time before she grew calm; then she sat thinking. Marguerite was only a servant, and servants were always ignorant, however good they might be. She could not talk to Madame De Kersuel about her illness, but she might ask the doctor, if only she could get to speak to the doctor apart from Marguerite; but that seemed impossible.

If Monsieur Georges came she might question him; but she could not bear to think of his arrival. It was not only that she shrank from him because he was to be her husband, but it seemed to the girl that his coming was connected with her grandmother's death, and that one hinged on the other.

Death—the word seemed awful to Geneviève—the unusual fears which had been gathering strength day by day, shapeless and nerveless, seemed to surround her now, and close her in their clammy, trembling ranks. They drove out for the time even love.

The living part of her grandmother, the warm heart and tenderness that Geneviève had clung to, had disappeared, and she could only picture a rigid form lying on a bed, covered, and yet too surely showing what it was. She covered her face with her hands, and then she tried to fight against her fear. Marguerite had said, "She will not pass away till the warning has been sent. It will be sent to you, mademoiselle." Geneviève shuddered as she realized the words. Then the intensity of her fear seemed to end it. She lifted her head, and opened her eyes. She would not be such a coward; she would conquer this vain terror.

"I will go in and have candles," she said. "Darkness makes all this worse; and to-morrow I will waylay the doctor on his road, and he shall tell me the truth about my grandmother. I do not believe about the *shape*. There are no such appearances. They are only traditions which live on in the tales of peasants and servants like Marguerite."

She shivered. But Marguerite said that Madame De Kersuel had seen it before her husband died.

"Yes, but if Marguerite is wrong on one point, she may be on another. She may have fancied or dreamed it, as she sits alone in that eerie work-room of hers," the girl said; for Marguerite had a little sewing-room in one of the staircase turrets in a lonely part of the house. "She is there now, I dare say," and she looked up at the narrow slit that made a window in the tower.

While she looked up she saw how the light had faded out of the sky. It was growing too late to be out, and she drew her hood closer. Suddenly a figure stood near her, not close, but near enough for her to see that the face was like that of her grandmother's picture. The figure stood an instant gazing at her, and then it faded out of sight. Geneviève gasped for breath; a thick horror seized her and held her fast, and she became unconscious.

It was quite dark when Geneviève opened her eyes. She felt stiff and numbed with cold, and she was lying on the ground beside the stone seat of the arbor. She got up with difficulty. Had she been missed? This was her first thought; the next was one of shuddering dread; and with a violent effort she fled into the house as if she were pursued.

She hurried upstairs and along the dark gallery, which a feeble oil lamp, burning on one of the window-ledges, seemed to make yet more gloomy; but when she reached her room, and lit the candles on her dressing-table from the blazing fire on the hearth, her recollections returned, and she understood the meaning of what had happened. She threw off her cloak, and going back along the gallery, she knocked at the door of the little antechamber which shut off her grandmother's rooms from the rest of the house. The door was opened by the young maid Françoise. She put up her fingers, and said "Hush!" very softly.

"How is my grandmother?" said Geneviève. "I want to see Marguerite."

The girl came out into the gallery and closed the door behind her.

"Marguerite has been to look for you, mademoiselle, and I was to ask you not to go in, for madame is sleeping sweetly, and Marguerite is asleep too, I think, beside her. Does mademoiselle know how late it is?"

Geneviève turned away with a feeling of relief. Her grandmother must be better if she was quietly asleep. She tried to think that the warning had been a creation of her fancy.

III.—A MEETING.

It is a bright summer morning—early summer, before the tender green of the beech leaves lose their delicate silken fringe, and showers of gold blossoms still gleam against dark laburnum branches. Bright sunshine gilds the river Ellé as it washes the feet of the little gardens behind some tall old stone houses at Quimperlé. One of these houses is very quaint. It belongs to the Procureur de la République, and has once been a place of importance. Its old stone walls, stained green and brown with age and weather, are partly covered by green climbing plants. There is an outer and an inner entrance door, and both these are cased with iron, and are studded with ponderous nails, and the old green stone staircase leading up from the hall looks as if it belonged to some ancient stronghold rather than to a peaceful dwelling-house; but the group coming down the old staircase dispels all gloomy fancies. First comes a fair, plump young matron, leading by the hand a lovely cherub-faced miniature of herself, and behind the mother and her child is Geneviève Plouré, her bright face bent in almost adoring contemplation of the bonny sunburned baby she is carrying.

"Make haste, make haste, Mimi," says the young mother, "or Aunt Geneviève will jump over us." And the rosy prattling lips repeated, with a sort of wondering glee, "Aunt Geneviève jump over Mimi!"

There is really no relationship, but this loving old school-fellow of Geneviève's had taught her little girl to call her dear friend "Aunt Geneviève" when the girl came to her after Madame De Kersuel's death. Her friend's kindness and the delight afforded by the two children had done much in these three months to cheer Geneviève's spirits. Then there was Monsieur Agier, who teased and rallied her into playful arguments; but he was now away in Paris, and the two ladies were left to the society of each other. To-day they were going to the fête of St. Berlaize, a few miles distant from Quimperlé.

"We have really no time to lose," Madame Agier said, "if we are to get to this fair in good time, and as Charles is not with us, I do not care to stay there late."

It was a charming drive, partly beside the river, and Madame Agier, exhilarated by the sunshine and the loveliness of the scene around her, chatted as they drove along the pleasant shaded road. Now she pointed out a clump of tall king-ferns growing in the river, now she told Geneviève some of the many quaint legends of the picturesque region; but she had all the talk to herself, and at last she too lay back silent in the carriage, and admired the ever-changing beauty of the sparkling river.

Geneviève could not talk. She had had a letter from Marguerite that morning, telling her that Monsieur De Kersuel's arrival was again postponed, and ever since she had not found a moment's time for thought. She was free for some time longer, but that idea was not the one that chiefly engrossed her.

On the morning after that strange warning her grandmother had sent for Geneviève. She had spoken seriously to her on the subject of Monsieur Georges. She told Geneviève that the marriage had been arranged by her grandfather, and that no other provision had been made for her. "Georges is a good, kind man," Madame De Kersuel said, "and he will make you happy one way or another." She had waited for the girl to speak, and then, as Geneviève remained silent, she added: "I am glad you make no objections, dear child; you have made me very happy. Now you may go, my dear obedient Geneviève." And then Madame De Kersuel had closed her eyes, exhausted, and a strange gray shade had passed over her face. The little sentence of protest which Geneviève had been framing died away in terror; she dared not think of what might be about to happen. She ran to fetch Marguerite, but when the woman reached her mistress's bedside she wrung her hands.

"Go away, Ma'm'selle Geneviève," she whispered. "I must be left alone with madame."

Geneviève never saw her grandmother again. Next day she learned that all was over, and that Madame De Kersuel had passed away in the night; and then she had fallen ill herself, and Madame Agier had come and fetched her away for change of scene. Geneviève felt that she was bound to marry Monsieur Kersuel. It would be terrible to break a promise claimed by the dead.

Geneviève shivered as if she were once more in the old manor-house and saw the ghostly shape. She had no one to advise her. Madame Agier was kind and loving, but she was wanting in judgment about her own affairs, and Geneviève knew that her secret would not be safe with her. She did not believe that any one except Marguerite knew that she was promised. Madame Agier knew nothing about the Kersuels or their affairs. She had never even asked the girl where her future home would be, and Geneviève had tried to forget her sorrow and her perplexed future in playing with Baby and Mimi. She had plenty of courage. She felt that she must decide for herself. She could not marry a man so much older than herself. At last light came into her perplexed brain. Why should she not tell Monsieur Georges the truth, and ask him to release her from her promise? "Surely the man will not be an old tyrant; he will let me off," she said. But he might not release her. She knew she could not be made to marry against her will; but if Monsieur Georges refused, then she could never marry any one.

"That will not be a hardship"—the girl's bright spirits came back—"if I can find myself a home. Perhaps Lucie will let me live here always, and teach Mimi."

For some time now the road had been full of carts, some drawn by two horses, some by only a small pony, but all full of men, women, and children, dressed in their best, with broad-leaved hats and silver buckles, or snowy caps, showing that beneath them the heads were bound with blue and silver or scarlet and gold ribbons. They overtook men and women driving before them cattle and pigs. There was no noise or outcry, except from the pigs. All the faces were grave even to sadness.

At last they came to a lane leading to the scene of the fête. This was almost impassable, for the high banks on each side, and the close growth of the chestnut branches that stretched over it from one side to the other, excluded air, and as much rain had lately fallen, the ground was wet and heavy, and the traffic of so many feet and of the animals had churned the earth into mud, and the vehicles had left deep ruts filled with water. It was so difficult to keep the carriage wheels from going into these that their driver went at a foot-pace. All at once the horse stopped, shied, and down went a wheel into a rut ten inches deep.

The driver uttered a volley of oaths, and got rebuked by an old farmer, who, in a cream-colored flannel coat and three or four waistcoats, sat on the top of one of the banks, watching the busy, animated scene. The driver turned round, his eyes sparkling with anger, and pointed out with his whip the cause of the accident. A smart young Breton, dressed in jacket and trousers of cream-colored flannel, his waistcoat trimmed with rows of black velvet and silver buttons, and the black velvet streamers of his broad flapping felt hat fastened round its low crown with a big silver buckle, had tied his horse to a tree on one side of the lane, and stood plaiting its long chestnut tail, which stretched about two feet from its body, and formed a barrier across the road.

As it was a part of the ceremony of the day to present the beasts as well as their owners in their best array to the saint, the young Breton was considered to be merely doing his duty, and, without disturbing himself, he just glanced over the top of the high white collar which reached his ears and told the driver to have patience.

" The road was not made only for you," he said.

Madame Agier laughed. "He does not know Alexis," she said; "he never was patient in his life, I am sure; but unless we make up our minds to walk through this mud, Geneviève, we shall see nothing of the fête."

"I do not mind mud," the girl said; and she opened the door of the carriage.

No one came forward to help them. Indeed, there seemed to be only peasants in the crowd streaming down to the old church, which stood in a sort of green glade surrounded by chestnut-trees at the bottom of the lane.

"I can go no farther," said Madame Agier; "my feet stick fast in this heavy clay."

Just then there stepped forth from the party-colored crowd of peasants a gentleman. Geneviève was behind her friend, and she did not see his face; she heard a very pleasant voice say:

"If you will take my arm, madame, I can take you a short-cut through the field."

Geneviève was wondering who he could be, and from whence he had, as if by magic, sprung. Just then Madame Agier said something about her friend, and he turned his head.

For a moment Geneviève stood still, puzzled. Where had she seen that face before? And then the cold thrill that made her feel as if a chill wind were passing over her helped her to remember: it was like the face of the shape she had seen in the garden at Kersuel. Geneviève looked round her; it seemed as if she must be dreaming. No; behind her was the crowd of vehicles, with drivers urging their straining horses on through the mud, and in front was the dandy young farmer still plaiting the bright yellow tail of his horse; beyond were groups of men gathered round one of their fellows who, swathed in a dirty blanket, was being shaved; others standing by waited their turn, it being customary to let the beard grow some weeks before the festival, and then to be shaven clean in honor of the day. A man was beating a drum close beside; another was hawking about gaudy pictures of the saint, with a hymn underneath it, the verses of which he yelled out in a hoarse voice. No; Geneviève saw that unless she wanted to be parted from her companions, she must follow them quickly through a little gate in the low wall which surrounded the church. Inside the gate was a dry path leading round the back of the church to the chestnut-shaded glade in which the fair was held. Here all was bustle and movement. Except some sieve-sellers, who loudly extolled their wares, piled up in huge heaps beside them, the chief part of the buying and selling was at provision stalls and under tents where huge casks of cider, crowned with green boughs, had been tapped. The smell of the various stews dispensed in earthenware mugs was not very savory, and Madame Agier gathered up her dress carefully, for men, women, and children sat about on the grass eating and drinking. Among them was an old man bending over a frying-pan full of sardines, which he held over a pile of red-hot charcoal. Everywhere in this pleasant chestnut grove the crowd seemed given up to enjoyment and refreshment; they did not even stare at the two ladies as they passed.

"This is rather rough walking for you," the stranger said to Madame Agier; "and I fear before long the crowd will be noisier than it is now; the cider will have its effect."

He pointed to the entrance of a long low tent; a narrow table ran from one open end to the other, with benches on each side, and these were filled with men and women, while the table was covered with jugs and glasses full of cider.

"I should like to stay and see the angel come down," said Geneviève. She had never seen so large a crowd before, and she was excited by the novelty of the scene. The stranger was certainly no phantom; he was good-looking and young, and there was an infectious merriment in his laugh which made her feel ashamed of the fancied likeness she had seen to the face of the apparition at Kersuel.

He turned to her at once when she spoke. "If madame"—he bowed to Madame Agier—"will permit me to take care of you, I think you will be able to see the descent of the angel."

He had a charming voice, and his eyes were full of expression. Geneviève had thought she detested blue eyes: her grandfather had had blue eyes, and it seemed to her that they belonged exclusively to cross old men; perhaps they looked more pleasant shining down on her from under bright golden curly hair: she could not tell; but while she stood listening to him, it seemed to her as if there was no such thing as sorrow or perplexity: life was as radiant as the sunshine that streamed down in burning patches on the grass whenever it found a space between the leaves. Madame Agier was never very wise, and to-day she was so exhilarated by the excitement of the scene around her that she walked on beside Geneviève and the stranger, amused with his evident admiration of her charming friend, and never troubling herself to wonder what her husband would have thought of this sudden acquaintance with a man entirely unknown to her. She had been thinking of Geneviève's future lately, and how important it was that she should marry; and she thought, in her happy, careless fashion, that if this gentleman was rich, he would make a very nice husband for her dear friend.

All at once there was a stir in the crowd, it swayed backward, and presently there was a forward movement and a vio-lent rush to the front, which but for the stranger's care would have carried the two ladies with it. Drawing them quickly on one side, he led them up the grassed hill on the side of the glade opposite the church, whence they could look down on the struggling crowd below circling round a huge pile of fagots at some little distance from the church. All at once a gun was fired; down came a little angel from the steeple, and set light to the bonfire, and the crowd shrieked and yelled and stared as first one and then another of the crackers fixed above the fagots exploded as the blaze reached them. The uproar was deafening.

"We certainly could not have staid here alone," said Madame Agier. "You are very kind, monsieur, and take so much trouble about us! You are willing to go now, are you not, Geneviève?"

It was the first time she had called the girl by her name, and the stranger seemed struck by it.

"It is you, madame," he said, "who have been so kind as to accept my services. Can I help you toward home? My name is Jean Dupuy, and I am going to Quimperlé."

Madame Agier looked radiant.

"You must come with us, then," she said; "we also are going home to Quimperlé. Do you know my husband, Monsieur Agier, the Procureur de la République? He is in Paris just now. This is my friend Mademoiselle De Plouré."

Monsieur Dupuy made a low bow to Geneviève, and then he gave her a long, wistful look, which carried her back once more to that weird night in the garden at Kersuel. She felt herself grow pale.

"Mademoiselle is, I fear, very tired," said Monsieur Dupuy. "The church must now be empty. We can make our way there behind the crowd, and you will have the kindness to wait there while I seek for your coachman."

IV.—AN UNEXPECTED PROPOSAL.

It is one of those mornings of early summer when the month seems to have gone astray, and to have wandered into the glow of autumn, or at least into the fullness of summer heats; there is no lingering chill; the leaves hang motionless on the trees across the river; and yet, though the air is full of languid sweetness, the scents which lade it are rather those of changeful June than of glowing

July; the low hedge over which Geneviève leans as she looks at the river sends up a delicate fragrance of wild-rose blossoms, and from the garden behind there comes a mingling of pleasant odors with the sweet country scent, suggestive of newly mown fields, while a breath from the east seems to flit over the little space from the plot of white pinks under the windows.

Madame Agier has gone on business to a farm-house which her husband owns among the hills, and she has taken the children and their nurse. Geneviève is glad to be alone. This week has been filled with so many new feelings and pleasures that it is a delicious luxury to stand now and then plucking the leaves off the hedge, thinking over all that has happened, trying to call up again the delightful sensations that have awakened in her while she has stood here talking to Monsieur Dupuy, or sat with him just within the long open windows yonder.

For Monsieur Dupuy has come nearly every day to the old stone house. He borrowed a book, and had to return it; then he brought a song which Geneviève wished to hear, and sang it while she listened; and all this while Madame Agier had said softly to herself, "He is just suited to Geneviève." She had to play the accompaniment to his song. Oh yes, she felt that she could do this, but as she said, shyly too, it only gives Geneviève a better chance of listening; but the latter took up a book and read—a most unusual occupation—or else she became absorbed in music during Monsieur Dupuy's visits; and once when the young pair had strolled out through the window into the garden, Madame Agier had buried herself in her book, and pretended when they came in again that she had not missed them.

Geneviève had lived in a dream of bliss. Every day there had been Monsieur Dupuy's visit to look forward to, and every day some words which she had specially meant to say had been forgotten, and now how should she get through the time until she saw him again? She had not talked to him of her old life; there had been nothing to remind her of Kersuel or of Monsieur Georges; she had gone out of herself and of the dull chrysalis old life into this new winged existence full of never-ending joy. And now he was gone away for some days. Yesterday he had said at parting,

"It may be a week before I see you again: I have to take a journey."

Madame Agier saw clearly into her friend's heart, but she was discreet enough to refrain from comment. She had loved her husband before she married him, and although this was unusual, she did not see why Geneviève should not do as she had done. There could be no doubt about Monsieur Dupuy's feelings, and directly Charles came home she should get him to find out whether this lover was rich enough to marry Geneviève.

The girl could have staid for hours leaning against the fence, her dark eyes bent on the river; now and then a faint flush rose on her clear, colorless skin, and the red lips smiled.

A trim Breton maid wearing a white muslin cap pointed at the top, and finished behind the head with large wings, came across the garden.

"There is a gentleman asking for mademoiselle."

Geneviève started. "You had better say your mistress is out," she said. "Is it a stranger?"

"Yes, mademoiselle; but when I told him that, he said he did not want Madame Agier; he said he was the man of business of Madame Kersuel, and that he must speak to Mademoiselle Geneviève de Plouré. He is old, mademoiselle," the woman added.

Geneviève felt chilled. The present slipped away from her; she was once more in the old weird manor-house, and once more she pictured Monsieur Georges beside her.

"You had better ask him to come here," she said, for it seemed to her that the delicious sunshine around was a help against the gloomy memories of Kersuel.

The maid came back, followed by a small man in a hat much too large for his square gray head. His hair was long, and his whole appearance untidy, yet with an attempt at smartness evidenced by a bright yellow neck-tie and a green waistcoat; he also wore small gold rings in his ears.

He made a low bow when he came up to Geneviève.

"You do not remember me, mademoiselle; but I have often seen you when you were a child staying with my esteemed old friend Madame De Kersuel."

Geneviève held out her hand. The past came back in a sudden wave of recollection, and she recognized the lawyer's quaint, kindly face.

"You are Monsieur Maugin," she said; "and you brought me once a box of sugar-plums. Yes, I remember you."

"Well, then, mademoiselle, shall we go in and sit down? My business is long, and is rather private, and I am not fond of discussing affairs in the open air." He turned and led the way to the window.

A horrible feeling of bondage crept over Geneviève, and Marguerite's words came back: "Mademoiselle will live and die at Kersuel." She gave a frightened glance at the old lawyer. He was smiling kindly at her, but there was a meaning twinkle in his eyes.

"Mademoiselle"—he waited till they were seated in the drawing-room—"I presume that you know the provisions made for you under the will of your deceased grandfather?"

Geneviève bent her head.

"It appears"—Monsieur Maugin looked at a paper he held in his hand, and then coughed—"that a few days before her death Madame De Kersuel learned of the serious illness of Monsieur Georges Kersuel, and the determination he had expressed to transfer the right of marrying Mademoiselle Geneviève de Plouré to his brother." He glanced at Geneviève, for she had started at the mention of Monsieur Georges. "Since then Monsieur Georges has died; and his brother, who is also his heir, has arrived at Kersuel; and before he enters on the possession of the old manor-house and the estates thereto belonging, he requests permission to wait upon you, and to arrange preliminaries."

He was stopped. Geneviève's cheeks burned crimson, and her eyes were full of angry light.

"I am not a chair or a table, monsieur, to be transferred in this way from one man to another. Why, I had not even consented to marry Monsieur Georges."

"I understood that you had made no objection." Monsieur Maugin's face had lengthened, and there was a deep furrow down the middle of his forehead.

There was a pause. Geneviève's heart beat so fast that it seemed to choke her. And yet she must speak; she could not again suffer her silence to be taken for consent.

"I could not have married Monsieur Georges," she said, feeling all at once so shy and foolish under the lawyer's grave

eyes that she was tempted to run away. "And so, monsieur," she went on, lamely, "there is no use in my seeing his brother. We had better remain strangers."

Monsieur Maugin smiled; then he took a pinch of snuff, and leaned back in his chair.

"It is quite natural that this change of persons comes on you at first with a kind of shock, dear young lady; but remember it is no uncommon thing that is asked of you. On the contrary, my client goes so far as to ask for an interview before he considers himself your betrothed husband."

Geneviève was smarting with impatience. She felt stung.

"Please to make him understand, monsieur, that I thank him for the honor he intends to offer, but that it is not in my power to accept it."

She rose, for she considered the matter ended; but Monsieur Maugin kept his seat.

"Not in your power!" He raised his eyebrows till his forehead was ridged with curved lines. "I can not see the objection that can be brought against a gentleman completely unknown to you. Why should you not see him? Do not be in such a hurry, mademoiselle. I will come to-morrow for your answer. Remember, if you please, that the original promise is of long standing, that you have never repudiated it, and that my client can, if he so pleases, refuse to release you."

The room grew dark to Geneviève; a cloud came between her and all the sunshine that had poured in just now through the muslin curtains. She shivered as if she were in the bat-haunted gallery of Kersuel.

"Monsieur," she said, sadly, "your client must do as he pleases. I can only give the same answer. I will not be passed on like a bit of old furniture."

The lawyer waited, frowning till his eyes were scarcely to be seen.

"Is this to be considered your final answer?" he said.

Geneviève bowed her head in reply.

"Well, then," he said, "have you any wish to revisit Kersuel before its new owner takes possession? Old Marguerite said you had gone away so hurriedly that you had left many of your effects behind."

"I should like to go for a day or two," she said, timidly, "but—"

"But you do not wish to see my client. Have no fear, mademoiselle; my client is a gentleman; he will be absent a week longer, and he will prolong his absence if you wish to stay longer at Kersuel."

"He is very kind"—Geneviève felt deeply ungrateful to her rejected suitor— "but in a couple of days I can do all I have to do at the old place."

The lawyer took another pinch of snuff. Then he rose from his chair, and made her a low bow.

"I do not quite see how you mean to live, mademoiselle," he said. "There is no other provision made for you."

"I am not afraid, monsieur." But her voice sounded sad and dreary. The lawyer bowed again, and when the door closed on him, Geneviève sank on the floor and cried bitterly.

V.—WITH THE BATS.

Geneviève's two days at Kersuel had lengthened out to a fortnight. On her arrival she found Marguerite ill in bed, with no one but a rough country girl to nurse her. Geneviève sent for the doctor, and then she wrote to Monsieur Maugin, and asked leave to stay and nurse her dear old friend. The permission came in a most courteous message from the new owner of Kersuel. Mademoiselle De Plouré was to stay as long as she pleased at the old house. Geneviève shrank into herself when she remembered that she was the guest of the man she had refused to marry; but at least she was safe from his presence. He was sure not to come to Kersuel till his housekeeper was well, and able to prepare for his reception.

The lawyer told Geneviève in his letter that the house would have to be set in order before his client took possession of it.

It seemed to the girl that the old house was even drearier than she had thought it in her grandmother's lifetime. Marguerite had been ailing for some time before Geneviève's arrival, and unable to do much work, and long cobwebs hung from the ceilings, and clouded the corners of the unused rooms. A smell of mouldering damp pervaded the long gallery, and the bats haunted it more than ever.

The girl's spirits drooped. It seemed as if sickness and sadness were inseparable from the old manor-house. Would Marguerite die here? she wondered. She had not known how strong her love for her old nurse was till this dread of losing her came. The rough servant-girl Barba came from North Brittany, and Geneviève could not understand her dialect well enough to talk to her. She rarely wandered about the garden as she used to do, and she never went beyond it; she could not leave her patient.

"She is all I have left of grandmother," she said.

She thought it was the gloom of the old house which thus depressed her, for all joy seemed to have faded from her life. Madame Agier wrote bright, chatty little notes, but Geneviève looked vainly in them for the name of Monsieur Dupuy; he was never mentioned. Madame Agier spoke of her husband's return, but the burden of every letter was how much Mimi and the baby missed their dear Aunt Geneviève.

"He said he would come back in a week," said Geneviève; and then her cheeks burned.

She had known Monsieur Dupuy only a fortnight, and yet it seemed as if all the rest of her life would be flavorless and colorless unless she saw him again. He could not be her friend in the way that Lucie Agier was, and yet Geneviève knew that she cared much more for Monsieur Dupuy than she did for Madame Agier.

"It is only because he is so wise and clever. I can look up to him," she sighed. She had been foolish enough to think that Monsieur Dupuy really cared for her friendship, and instead he had only considered her a pleasant chance acquaintance. She should probably never see him again.

To-day Marguerite was better; she was to sit up a little while, and Geneviève was now on her way to the old woman's room. It was on the upper story, leading from the yet more gloomy second-floor gallery, only lighted by small round windows set few and far between. Here the plaster had peeled off in huge patches from the low, damp wall, and cobwebs festooned the discolored ceiling.

Marguerite was sitting up in an easy-chair beside the fire-place when Geneviève came in. She looked very pale and worn, but she smiled at the sight of her young mistress.

Geneviève knelt down before the blazing logs which partially lit up the gloomy room, and began to warm her hands.

"Although it is summer weather, your fire is a welcome sight," she said. "How do you feel, dear Marguerite?"

Her old nurse had been studying the girl's face as she knelt in the fire-light.

"I am better, dear child, and I shall soon be well; but it is you who look ill, Mademoiselle Geneviève; you are thin, and your eyes are heavy. What ails you, dear heart?"

"I"—but Geneviève shrank from the old woman's gaze, and bent over the fire—"I am quite well. I have felt anxious about you, but that is over now. You are going to get well directly."

Marguerite did not answer. She was not, however, satisfied. She lay back in her chair, half closing her pale blue eyes.

"Mademoiselle has been very happy at Quimperlé?" she said.

"Oh yes; I told you so;" and then Geneviève sighed.

"Does Madame Agier live quietly, or does she have many visitors? I have heard nothing about your doings, Mademoiselle Geneviève."

"Oh, we have not done much sightseeing. I have been to Quimper, and to Carnac and Ouray, and we went to a fête at St. Blaize. I liked that."

The nurse, keeping her eyes fixed on the well-shaped head bent over the fire—she could not see her face—saw the girl's ear and neck redden suddenly at these words.

"Did Monsieur Agier go with you, mademoiselle? Pardon me, but a fair is not a place to which young ladies can go alone," said Marguerite, severely.

"No, Monsieur Agier did not go with us; a friend took care of us."

Marguerite was burning with curiosity, but she did not know how to shape her next question. There was a pause. Geneviève struck the log with the poker, and watched the bright sparks fly up the broad chimney shaft.

"Mademoiselle does not say if she has been seeing much company," Marguerite said.

"Not lately; Madame Agier does not receive much in her husband's absence. We had two or three visitors; that was all."

"Were they gentlemen, mademoiselle—young gentlemen?" persisted Marguerite.

Geneviève got up from her knees, and began to smooth her hair from off her face. She thought her old nurse had grown inquisitive.

"There were two old gentlemen and one young one," she said, repressively. "But, dear Marguerite, you are talking too much; you must be getting tired. Let me help you to bed again." She spoke lovingly,

and the old woman kissed the soft hand that rested on her chair.

"I will go to bed, dear Mademoiselle Geneviève; but first will you tell me if you are going to marry the brother of Monsieur Georges?"

"I am not going to marry any one," said Geneviève, hotly. "I prefer to live single. There is no use in worrying me, Marguerite; I shall only get cross. Monsieur Georges and his brother seem to have been a pair of old managers; please do not talk any more about them."

"Pardon, mademoiselle; I will not talk; but I must tell you that the brother is not old."

Geneviève stared at her. "How do you know? You have not seen him. Monsieur Maugin told me his client had not been to Kersuel since it had become his property."

"No, mademoiselle, he has not been here."

"Come—never mind him. I must put you to bed," the girl said.

And soon Marguerite was safe in bed again, and Geneviève went away down the dark gallery, wishing she had brought a lamp with her, the tower staircase was so very dark, only lighted by slits, as it went down in a spiral to the bottom of one of the corner towers.

"Barba! Barba!" Geneviève's voice sounded hollow in the still darkness of the passage that led to the kitchen. There was no answer, and pushing open the door, Geneviève saw that the long dark kitchen was empty. The fire had burned so low on the hearth that Barba must have been some time absent.

Geneviève went in, and groped in a dark corner till she found a huge pair of bellows; with these she soon roused up the smouldering logs. Then she went in search of Barba. A country-woman of Barba's kept the lodge at the entrance gates of the old manor-house, and Geneviève guessed that she should find the careless damsel chattering there.

It was much lighter out-of-doors, and before she got as far as the lodge she saw Barba flying along in such haste that she held her cap on with one hand. Her rosy face grew pale at the sight of Mademoiselle De Plouré.

"Oh, Barba," Geneviève said, gravely, "you have almost let the fire out, and Marguerite is ready for her supper."

Barba fled forward to the house, and

Geneviève went slowly after her, thinking over her old nurse's questions. She went into the old hall, and then going to the kitchen door, she gave the penitent Barba instructions about Marguerite's supper. Then, as there was still half an hour of daylight left, she took her way along the gloomy passages to the garden.

She had not spent much time here since her return to Kersuel; the deserted look of the garden saddened her. It was difficult to believe that three months could so completely have wrecked all that remained of order in the deserted place. There were flowers because the sweet blossoms opened whether they were cared for or not, but tall lilies lay prostrate, hiding their silver-white faces on the weed-grown earth, while a mass of the white cluster rose which high winds had dragged away from the summer-house grovelled on the grass-plot before it. The grass had grown tall and rank, and the unpruned vine had flung out lovely but wild luxuriant wreaths across the slate-strewn garden path. The air was much warmer out here than in the damp, unused house, but Geneviève shivered as she stood looking at the desolation.

She paced up and down, musing over Marguerite's words. She thought, of the two, she would have preferred Monsieur Georges to his brother: it must be easier to be the wife of an old man one did not care for than of a young one.

"A young man would expect to be loved, an old one would be grateful for friendship," she said to herself.

A warm, blinding blush rose to her temples. She was asking herself, or rather the question came without her aid, why should she not marry the owner of Kersuel? There was a surging tumult, a rush of new incomprehensible feeling, and she could not tell whence it had sprung. For very shame she hid her face between her hands. At that moment she realized with a sort of shame that she was no longer heart free, that her heart was bound by an invisible chain to one who perhaps had forgotten that he had ever seen her.

It was a terrible moment. At the convent there had been little time to talk of love, and Geneviève, even in her objections to Monsieur Georges, had only shrunk from his age and probable dullness; no romantic ideas of love had associated themselves in her mind with the idea of marriage. She felt herself disgraced, and she could not tell how this new feeling had

come to her, for Monsieur Dupuy had said nothing that he might not have said to Madame Agier herself; and yet no one had looked at her as he had done.

"I will go in," she said; "there is something eerie in this summer-house. I shall be less miserable in-doors."

But the thought of Monsieur Dupuy followed her as she groped her way along the gloomy gallery to her own room; perhaps she had never heeded the weird stillness so little, or the bats as they broke into it with their whirr past her face; she could think only of Jean Dupuy, and that she should never see him again.

The wind howled and blustered through the night, and Geneviève got little sleep. She tossed about, fancying all sorts of impossibilities. It seemed to her at last that she must leave Kersuel as soon as possible. Nowhere else could she find so much solitude to feed these idle fancies.

VI.—CONCLUSION.

It is nearly a week since the stormy night which tore down the vine from the summer-house, and flung some of the old chimneys on to the grass-grown drive in front of the old manor-house. Marguerite is so much better that when Geneviève wrote to Monsieur Maugin to tell him of the mischief worked by the wind, she announced her intention of going back to Quimperlé.

She has written to Madame Agier too, asking her to come and fetch her away, and the day has come for her departure. She is quite ready: she has only to say a last good-by to Marguerite; and she goes first into one deserted room, and then into another, saying a last adieu to all. It seems hard that this new owner of Kersuel, who never even saw her grandmother, should have the picture Geneviève loves.

"Very likely he will never glance at it," she says, as she goes out to take her last look at the garden.

The summer-house seems transformed; it stands bare, its moss-grown, crumbling stone-work fully revealed, while at its base lie the tangled and broken vine wreaths.

Geneviève can not tell why she feels so sad; she is sorry to leave Marguerite, but the old house is a dread and a terror to her. Yet as she sits down on the cracked stone bench she begins to cry bitterly.

Once more there are steps coming up the hill-side, and when the sound of them reaches Geneviève, she starts with frightened eyes. A few moments more, and Jean Dupuy stands beside her.

"You here, mademoiselle!" he says; and then he stands holding her hand in his, looking intently at her.

Geneviève draws away her hand.

"I am going away, monsieur. Madame Agier is coming for me. She will be here very soon." Then, as he does not speak, she goes on: "Ah, you do not know. This used to be my old home, and when I have said adieu to it I shall never see it again."

"And this causes your sorrow?" He looked tenderly at her reddened eyelids. "I thought—that is, I had been told—that you were the future mistress of Kersuel. Is it not so?"

"No, monsieur."

"Indeed? Your dislike to the new owner is then so decided? You will pardon me for speaking thus freely, but Monsieur Maugin is an old friend of mine, and so is his client."

Geneviève felt stung; a great bitterness swept over her. "Are you sent here, monsieur," she said, haughtily, "to plead for Monsieur De Kersuel?"

Jean Dupuy kept his eyes from her face. "I did not say so, mademoiselle; but yet I care so much for his happiness and for yours that I long to ask you why you refuse even to see him."

Geneviève was so wrought up that she scarcely knew what she said. Her love was flung back at her. This man had sought her friendship from the first only on behalf of his friend.

"Why should I see him, monsieur?"

"Because he loves you, mademoiselle. No mere sense of duty binds him to fulfill his part in this contract. Will you not hear him plead his own cause once"—he stopped; Geneviève stood still, but she had turned her head; he could not see her tell-tale face—"unless, indeed," Monsieur Dupuy went on, "he comes too late—to—to win your love." He moved a few paces, and he saw how deeply she was blushing. "Geneviève," he whispered, "will you not listen to him? He is speaking to you now."

She started; her downcast eyes opened widely, with a mixture of fear and wonder in their gaze. "You!" she said, incredulously. "How can you be Monsieur De Kersuel?"

"I am Georges's half-brother only," he said; "but he has made me his heir, provided I take the name of his property. But now—"

Geneviève interrupted him. "Why did you not tell me this at first?" she said. "Why did you not say, 'I am your cousin'?"

Monsieur De Kersuel (for he had taken the necessary steps for a change of name) took her hand tenderly. "Did you not tell Monsieur Maugin you could not be treated as if you were a chair or a table" —he smiled at her—"and can you not understand that I guessed at your feelings, and felt too that I must see this wife who had been assigned to me whether she willed it or not?"

Geneviève looked foolish. "And now that you have seen her"—she said, with an attempt at her old playfulness.

Jean kissed the hand he held. "I have nothing to say," he answered, gravely; "my fate is in your hands, Geneviève."

Even now he did not believe she loved him; her playful tone jarred on his eager love. But at her silence he looked up, met the timid eyes raised to his, brimming with liquid sweetness, and he was answered.

"I know where I have seen you now," she whispered; "you are the shape that so terrified me before my grandmother died."

For her lover had related to her how his brother had sent him as ambassador to Madame De Kersuel, feeling himself too old and infirm to take so long a journey, or to marry so young a wife. His brother's death had recalled him at once to Jamaica, and when he first met Geneviève he had only just arrived for the second time in Brittany.

They were roused from that most exquisite hour, the hour that follows the owning of true love—by the sound of Madame Agier's carriage wheels.

"Come to Madame Agier," the girl said; "you must tell her, while I go to Marguerite."

Madame Agier was triumphant; her husband had blamed her imprudence, till he heard the name of her visitor, and then he had bade her keep silence, as he knew all about the new owner of Kersuel.

"I shall always call you the shape," Madame Agier said to Jean as he told his story; "and I am not sure that I forgive you for robbing Mimi and Baby of their sweet Aunt Geneviève."

THE American boy ought always to have a smack of Columbus about him: he should pine to be a discoverer, and explore strange countries. And the first and perhaps the most interesting country that he explores is the one which is bounded by his own jacket and trousers. At any rate, until he learns something about that, he is not likely to prosper much in his subsequent expeditions. These arms and legs, this back and chest, what a continent they are! to become an active and law-abiding citizen of which is to possess a passport and a letter of credit to all nations, not to mention transport, van-guard and rear-guard, and physician. A boy who can run a mile, skin the cat, and put up his muscle (the last two are technical expressions which the boy will understand) is a boy with a future before him. He may not discuss celestial mechanics, but he can make himself useful nearer home. Let us not enter here upon that famous inquiry whether a hard biceps is a symptom of a fine brain. There is no reason why it should not be; but for my part I am disposed to hope that it may turn out a symptom of plain common-sense. Our brains are quite fine enough: in certain parts of New England they have reached a degree of tenuity beyond which they can not go and hold together. But nothing comes of it except refinement, which, as history and our innate knowledge of human nature tell us, is not only the last step away from savagery, but the next step before it. It is no matter about us who are going out with the present dispensation; but the men of the twentieth century, if they are going to be anything, must be creative rather than critical: they must have strength rather than refinement; and one would sooner fancy them developing new muscles, or, at any rate, new hearts, than new evolutions of the cerebrum.

Bodily exercises imply society and a social disposition; for if a solitary person, like Robinson Crusoe or Enoch Arden, were to be found daily practicing with the bars and rings, we should suspect him, not of social, but of ominously selfish and morbid tendencies. The pleasure of being strong lies in the fact that others are strong around us, thereby furnishing us with companionship and competition, which are the fuel of life. Health is, or should be, incidental to this pleasure; that is to say, I question the propriety of making health the deliberate object of exercise. Let it come if it will; but it will come none the slower if you forbear to be on the watch for it. To make yourself strong for the sake of your private health is the analogue of obeying the decalogue for the sake of your private crown; there is something unpleasantly unsympathetic about it. But be strong simply because mankind at large will be better if all men become physically more efficient, and the other blessings shall be added to you. Moreover, apart from the stimulus of example and fellowship, it is doubtful whether one man in twenty will take the trouble regularly to exert himself. Unless there be some motive outside himself he will soon cease to think it worth while. Dr. Winship used to say that he never would have made himself the man he was but for the purpose he had formed to thrash a certain offensive upper-class man in college; and Mr. William Blaikie began his athletic career an apparently hopeless consumptive. Dr. Winship lifted three thousand pounds, and Mr. Blaikie pulled stroke of the Harvard crew in their great race with Yale; but it would be useless to tell me that the desire to thrash a man or to heal a diseased lung had more than the minutest share in bringing these results about. If it had not been for the gymnasium, with its jolly society of zealous and emulous young gymnasts, Winship would never have lifted his own weight, and Blaikie would have been, at best, a valetudinarian. The fame of the Olympic and Isthmian games still echoes in our ears; but it was not the games that made Greece go to see them; it was Greece going to see them that made the games. In the same way I have noticed that the university crews of Oxford and Cambridge, for example, profess to be superbly indifferent as to whether the British public on the day of the race lines the river-bank from Putney to Mortlake; indeed, they have lately undertaken to intimate that they would prefer to have the public keep away. But no one knows better than they themselves that, were the public some day to take them at their word, not only would the crews never find the energy to get themselves into condition, but, were that difficulty overcome, they would never find it in their hearts to pull further than

Hammersmith Bridge, near which there is a very good ale-house. I do not wish, however, to run this theory into the ground; I only wish to indicate that athletics are essentially a popular pursuit, conducive to good citizenship, and the cultivation of which, therefore, good citizenship should imply. To say that athletics may be overdone is nothing to the purpose; the Pharisees overdid virtue, and thereby became obnoxious to a rebuke which will last them to the end of time, but no one pretends that virtue is not a good thing, if pursued in a proper spirit. There is rivalry in athletics, of course, but much less of petty jealousy than an outsider would suppose; not nearly so much, for example, as subsists between eminent astronomers in quest of a comet, or fashionable ladies in search of a new sensation. It is a great, healthy sort of freemasonry. The pride of an athlete is largely an impersonal pride; so that when the champion runner in America hears that the champion runner in England has lowered the record for a mile, he feels almost as glad as if he had done it himself, though that will not prevent him, of course, from himself straightway setting to work to lower that lowest, not so much for his own glory as for the credit of running in the abstract. In short, if mankind would only realize the same fellowship in their minds and hearts that they feel in their arms and legs, the Millennium would be nearer.

Nothing could be more humane and amiable than the frank respect that boys feel for one another's prowess. The present writer, looking far back into the dim past, sees a group of boy friends in a famous Continental city, who entertained small reverence for the Coliseum or St. Peter's, but much for that one of their number who could "jump leap-frog" over a higher stone post than any of his companions. We may say that these boys abused or neglected their opportunities; but this would be to take a low and illiberal view of the matter. A generous emotion is not the less generous because its object does not possess conventional dignity. Any curmudgeon can admire the Coliseum, or profess to do so; but to admire an achievement which is beyond your own capacity is characteristic of true Christian charity. These boys knew how difficult it was to jump over a high stone post, because they had tried it, and when

the champion boy overcame the post which had baffled all the rest, the latter rejoiced in the triumph of that physical nature which they all alike shared and understood. It was a triumph for them all, and one invincible post the less. On the other hand, the champion was not unduly uplifted in spirit, for he remembered that he would never be able to get the better of the column in the Forum, and he reflected that there might be other boys in other cities who could beat him by as much as he beat the others.

In later years—not much later—there was a boy at school who had the reputation of being a good runner. Every morning he would arise betimes, and run round the two-mile square before breakfast. Occasionally some of us would attempt to accompany him on his journey, but we generally found it inconvenient to press him too hard. There was a point in the second mile where the beauty of repose seemed more desirable than any activity. But because we could not catch him, did we revile him or ostracize him? By no means. He was the pride and darling of the school. He could do better than any of us what each of us could do in his own degree, and therefore we all felt our repute illuminated by his prowess. At last there came a day when a famous Indian runner arrived among us, and challenged the best man in town to contend against him. We allowed that the Indian was doubtless very fleet, but we would have been ashamed not to believe that our champion could beat him. To be sure, he was but sixteen, and had never run in a race, whereas the Indian had outstripped a thousand competitors. But no matter; the school freely intrusted its honor to its representative, and he freely though modestly accepted the trust. But when the rosy-cheeked boy and the lean and sinewy red man took their places side by side at the mark, we realized what we had let ourselves in for, and some of us, perhaps, felt uncomfortable. Off they started, the Indian with an appalling whoop and curvet, our man with the same business-like steadiness as if he were taking his customary morning constitutional. The course was half a mile, and return. Away they went up the long straight road overshadowed by elm and willow; and when they reached the old red bridge, near the further end, our straining eyes seemed to see that the Indian's foot was the first to sound upon its planks. Not very much the first, though. Now they had crossed the bridge, and had gained the turning post, and they turned about together, but which turned first we could not tell. Down they came on the homestretch; but now it was seen that one was leaving the other rapidly astern, and that the race was already won and lost. And our hearts sank in our bosoms, and we scarcely cared to look any longer, for we thought that it was impossible the famous Indian should be so easily defeated by a boy. But as the winner drew swiftly near, some one yelled out, "Look, fellows! it's Jim!" and behold! amidst an uproar of joy and astonishment impossible to describe, in raced our champion, with a fine glow and a modest grin upon his countenance, and as he crossed the line, fifty yards the winner, said, pantingly and deprecatingly, "Thunder, fellows!—why, any one of you could have beaten him!" Time, 4.40.

I maintain that such things as this incline us to love our neighbor rather than ourselves, without mentioning incidental advantages. Moreover, looking at it for a moment from the other side, I know of nothing that affords a man in his after-life more innocent and solid satisfaction than the recollection of his youthful feats of strength. There they are, concrete and undeniable achievements, brought about by his unaided prowess, and eloquent, to those who know how to judge, of his patience, persistence, and pluck. For no memorable athletic triumph was ever won without a long previous discipline of effort and self-denial. They are wholesome and worthy triumphs, and, once more, they are beyond most others free from envy. For I may be as strong as Hercules, and yet, unless I embrace the calling of Mr. Sullivan, no one will be the worse, but only the better, for it. But if I attain eminence as a writer of dime novels, say, or as a lawyer or railroad owner, then I am constantly liable to be treading on some other person's toes. And can you not imagine a man, toward the close of a long life, not all of it wisely spent or successful, looking back gloomily over the past, until at length a recollection brightens his eye, and he exclaims, more cheerfully, "Well, anyhow, I won that race for Harvard!" He was a better man both for the race and for the memory of it.

Since Harvard has been mentioned, I may as well observe that when I attempted to connect myself with that institution there was one person appertaining to it of whom I often thought with awe and reverent curiosity. The fame of him preceded by several months my actual introduction to him, so that my imagination had time to picture him in all manner of portentous guises. Who was this mighty being? Was it President Hill? Was it Jones, the ubiquitous and incalculable individual who always turned up where no student expected him to be? Was it Dr. Peabody, whose innocent inquiry, "What *is* ethics?" had deaded so many a promising but ill-performing student? Was it that terrific old Athenian, Professor Sophocles, concerning whom so many blood-curdling anecdotes were rife? No, it was none of these. The gentleman to whom I refer was an under-graduate, and at that period a Sophomore. He was commonly spoken of as "Bill Blaikie," and his claim to my reverence lay in the fact that he was the typical strong man of the college. I doubt whether I should have had the perseverance to wriggle my way through the examinations for admission had I not been constantly stimulated by the reflection that Bill Blaikie was (to my mind) the central fact of the university.

My boyish studies had made me familiar with Spenser's "Faerie Queene," with King Arthur and his Round Table, and in general with all the knights and giants of mediæval romance; and I therefore had plenty of heroic types at command by which to prefigure this college Titan. But a week or more of my Freshman existence passed by without my seeing him, though by no means without my asking and hearing about him. Then one sunny morning there was a knock at my door, and in walked a broad-shouldered, brown-bearded personage, with a burly gait, a deep bluff voice, and a strong, good-humored countenance. My prophetic soul divined him before he announced his name—it was Blaikie himself. He was dressed in a suit of rough, light-colored tweed, with a soft hat of the same material on his head. My eyes perused him anxiously from top to toe, and my heart was satisfied. Even as he was, and not otherwise, would I have wished him to be. He was not a disappointment; and during the many years of our friendship since that day I have never known him fail to come up to expectation.

His visit on that occasion was, I believe, to procure my subscription to the boat club; and I need not say that, had Blaikie asked it of me, I would gladly have subscribed half my allowance for moral pocket-handkerchiefs for the Patagonians. That boat club was the more or less direct occasion of our association together during our college residence; and though perhaps it helped to cost me my sheep-skin, I am not yet regenerated from my impression that I made, upon the whole, the wiser choice. I speak, of course, for myself alone; and as Blaikie got his degree, the boat club probably had less to do with my catastrophe than I flattered myself with imagining. In the evenings it was my delight to go down to the gymnasium and see Blaikie put up the big dumb-bell, and to listen to his discourses upon matters of muscular interest. Somehow or other he always seemed to know more about these things than any of us; and he was inspired by a strenuous missionary spirit, persuasive enough almost to make an oarsman out of a humpback, or a sprint-runner out of a cripple. And I am glad to see that in these later years the missionary spirit has not deserted him, but has, on the contrary, become incarnate in two admirable and most practical little books, of which the American public have already evinced their very substantial appreciation.

I have, perhaps, alluded to this friend of mine with more freedom than strict etiquette allows; but it was in the way of illustrating my belief that young men can not make one another's acquaintance upon a sounder and more natural ground than is afforded by their muscles. Boys and youths have no intellectual pursuits (as a general thing) wherein they can mutually sympathize, yet they are thrown much in one another's company, and feel the need of some subject of common interest. Some seek it in swell clothes; some in late hours and tobacco; some in secret societies; but the gymnasium, the ball ground, and the river are the least artificial, the healthiest, and the most profitable bases of association. The friendships made there are cordial friendships, full of mutual respect and honorable reminiscences, and they last a long time. The building up of the muscles and that of genial comradeship go on *pari passu*. And when, in after-years, we meet again and grasp hands, we smile to feel that the bone

and sinew have lost but little of their early vigor. A dumb-bell will serve just as well as an earthquake to bring two honest fellows together; but in these latitudes there are happily more dumb-bells than earthquakes; and since honest fellowship is, after all, the best result of earthly existence, let us cultivate the dumb-bell.

Possibly, indeed, there is little necessity at this day to preach the gospel of athletics. Athletic associations crop up everywhere, and the newspapers are full of base-ball and rowing. Nevertheless, an idealist might still find something to wish for. The peril of all muscular cultivation is professionalism. Of all unproductive industries, professional athleticism seems to me the least reasonable. What reasonable motive is there for getting strong muscles if not to aid a man in rendering himself useful to society? Whether he avail himself of them directly to hew timber, or indirectly to counteract the exhaustion of brain-work, matters not; but he can have no justification for getting them and then putting them up for sale. Our college boys, no doubt, have no idea of doing that; but they had better neither be that ill-odored rose nor be near it. We used to train ourselves in my day, and were often absurdly mistaken in our methods no doubt, and now and again lost a race by it possibly; but men who do not row for money are not afraid to lose a race if they have done their best. And it is wonderful how soon vulgarity and uncleanness creep in when boys begin to think more of winning than of the means by which they win. I wish, for my part, that our college and intercollegiate contests were more varied, and that so much was not made to depend on any particular event. Our gymnasiums have become schools of specialists; they seldom graduate a finished athlete such as they might easily make in four years out of any average man. Let us take a lesson from the Isthmian games, and try to evolve champions who shall be best at all points. And as for society, perhaps it will reflect that it can hardly, as a body, do anything better for the rising generation than to raise these boyish sports into something really dignified and respectable. Blackguards are always ready to rush in where angels will not take the trouble to be present; and brutality can be banished from our palæstræ just as easily as from our drawing-rooms, and by precisely the same means.

LIKE "all Gaul," the United States is divisible into three parts—the Atlantic slope, the Pacific coast, and the Great Basin. All of the waters resulting from rain-fall or the melting of the snows on the mountains in the Great Basin can find no outlet to the ocean, but must either disappear in desert sands or drain into the Great Salt Lake.

The fame of this large body of "noxious and extremely salt" water penetrated southward to the early Spanish explorers, and the French from the Northwest got near enough to it a century ago to hear of its magnitude and peculiarities. It is put down, therefore, in maps made toward the end of the last century as much by guess as maps of twenty years ago contained the lakes of Central Africa in problematic positions. When the trappers of the fur companies began to overrun the Rocky Mountains, Utah was invaded, and the beautiful valleys of the northern Wahsatch became favorite wintering places. From any of these peaks the lake would be visible, but it is not known that before 1825 any white man had reached its shore. It was not until Captain Bonneville had come back from oblivion to the eyes of a surprised world, and Washington Irving had written his travels, in 1837, that we knew anything definitely about this inland salt sea, and could place it on a map correctly. It is a great pity that the good and proper name Lake Bonneville has been lost in the prosaic name it now bears, and will probably forever retain; but a just attempt to restore it has been made by Major Powell's survey. The present lake is only a remnant of a more ancient and larger body of water, whose bounds can now be easily traced in the horizontal benches along the base of the mountains.

Stimulated by Irving's book, emigration immediately began overland to Oregon. In 1842 and 1843, General Fremont piloted his celebrated expedition through the mountains and made a boat trip on the lake, although at that time it was not the property of the United States, but belonged to Mexico.

Utah and its lake were well known to geographers when the Mormon Church, expelled from Illinois, driven out of Missouri, and persecuted to the point of death in Iowa, decided to abandon their beautiful Nauvoo, and betake themselves not only to the far West, but outside of the lines of a country whose people and government they hated.

Days counted themselves into weeks, and weeks made months, and months followed one another from early spring into midsummer, and still the emigrants, likening themselves to Israel in the wilderness, kept their faces westward. On the 24th of July, 1847, the head of the advance train, winding its way down through the last tortuous little ravine in the western foot-hills of the Wahsatch, looked out on that great basin—miles of sage-green velvety slopes sweeping down on every side from the bristling mountain rim to the azure surface of the tossing salt sea.

Brigham Young, their leader, told them that here the Lord commanded a halt, and directed that His tabernacle should be set up. This sounded well, and perhaps the majority believed; but Young knew well enough that beyond lay the lifeless alkali deserts, and that this spot was the very last upon which his band of faithful emigrants could be colonized with any hope for the future.

But the camp was not made on the borders of the Great Salt Lake, nor is the present city in proximity to it. It is almost twenty miles away in a straight line, and just at the base of the range. Indeed, it is only from the "bench" that the lake can be seen at all from within the city limits, and then it appears only as a line of distinct color between the dusty olive of the hither plain and the vague blue of the further hills.

Among the first things that Brigham Young ordered done after his pioneers had come into the valley was to survey a site for the future city. This was done on a generous scale. The streets are a hundred and thirty feet wide, run true to the points of the compass, and cross one another at right angles. Each square contains ten acres, so that when of an evening you walk "around the block," just to smoke a post-prandial cigarette, you will tramp exactly half a mile. A square of nine blocks was made to constitute a "ward," of which the city now has twenty-four, each ward being presided over by a bishop of the Church, who, however, was more a temporal than a spiritual head in those first days, deciding all small cases in dispute, when there was no appeal, nor desire for one, from ecclesiastical decisions to civil judgment. This ward classification is one that even yet enters largely into the social constitution of the city, which is thus a sort of federation of bishops' wards, each inclined to be clannish.

The pioneers divided each ten-acre square into eight household lots, giving every man an acre and a quarter, and half the people corner lots. The result has followed that these have been divided and subdivided, to suit individual wants and notions, until many of the houses stand right in the heart of the block, behind those fronting on the street, and are approached by alleys, many of which are bordered by a double row of thrifty Lombardy poplars. Regularity and perhaps convenience are sacrificed by this, but picturesqueness is gained.

The next necessity was a regular water supply, for rain can not be expected here between May and October. Down out of Emigration Cañon, through which the trail passed from the East, comes a creek to empty itself into the Jordan, which latter stream connects Lake Utah and Great Salt Lake, just as its namesake of the Holy Land links together Gennesaret and the Dead Sea. It was simply a matter of ditching from a high level, and making subsidiary canals, to bring the snow-fed water of this city creek in never-failing plenty wherever it was desired. The combined labor of the pioneers, who all worked pretty much in common at first, accomplished this primitive irrigation very speedily, so that within a few days a great many seeds had been put in the ground.

The emigrants, however, did not stop with the planting of vegetables and a little grain. They at once began a nursery of fruit trees, while shade and ornament were not forgotten. Making it the duty of every citizen to plant seeds of Eastern shade trees, or set out saplings brought from the hills, on both sides of every thoroughfare, the public looked to their preservation by making broad, deep gutters along each curbing. Now those saplings of acacia, poplar, cottonwood, mulberry, box-elder, honey-locust, and maple have grown into wide-spreading and lofty trees that canopy with grateful foliage every avenue outside the business centre; and down those gutters flow rippling, sparkling streams of water, clear as their snowy fountains, and dashing over their beds of mossy pebbles with all the glee of native brooks.

Formerly this water alone was available for domestic purposes and drinking as well as for irrigation, and even yet the poorer part of the population dip it up for daily service. But the introduction of pipes has superseded this old way. The hydrant water, however, comes from the same sources as the ditches, and is really no better, since it is unfiltered. For table use, therefore, the water that has been drawn from very deep wells is preferred by every one.

But in spite of the copious water supply arranged for by the founders, and recently largely increased by a canal leading from Lake Utah, Salt Lake City is in summer the dustiest town I ever saw or heard of. This blinding, all-pervading dust forms the only serious objection I can bring against the town as a pleasant place to live in.

The houses built by the first settlers were mainly log cabins. Some few of these are yet to be found hidden away in orchards. The Spanish adobe house of dried mud was also a favorite, and has continued so to the present, though instead of almost shapeless chunks of mud, plastered in Mexican fashion, regular unburned bricks are made by machinery. These adobes are twice the size of ordinary bricks, and the wall into which they are formed is made twice as thick as one of burned bricks would be. Of course this material lends itself readily to any style of architecture, and many of the elaborate buildings as well as cheap cottages are made of it, the soft gray tint of the adobe reminding one of the cream-colored walls of Milwaukee. Generally, however, the adobe is overlaid by a stucco, which is tinted. Low houses with abundant piazzas are the most common type in the older part of the town, and over these so many vines will be trained and so much foliage cluster that one can hardly say of what material the structure itself is formed. The residences more recently built have a more Eastern and conventional aspect, and some are very imposing; but big or little, old or new, it is rare to find a home not ensconced—almost buried—in trees and shrubs and climbing plants, while smooth, rich lawns greet the eye everywhere in town, in brilliant contrast to the bleak, bare hills towering overhead just without the city. As for flowers, no town East or West cultivates them more universally and assiduously.

Salt Lake City, then, is beautiful—a paradise in comparison with the buffalo plains or the stony gulches in which the great majority of Rocky Mountain towns must needs be set.

The suburbs, except toward the rocky uplands northward, grade off into farms quite imperceptibly, the streets continuing straight out into country roads between dense jungles of sunflowers—glorious walls of gold edged with green and touched with innumerable dots of maroon. And in these suburbs you may find some of the quaintest, most idyllic homes. One such, for example, stands down in the third ward. The house is hardly bigger than a good-sized room, and is entered through a queer narrow cowled doorway. The second story is hardly half as large as the lower one, leaving a slanting roof between, and a picturesque hedge and fence inclose the whole. This would be striking enough alone for its shape; but every two weeks the whole adobe and stucco affair is whitewashed from roof-tree to foundation, until it gleams like a fresh snow-bank against the grape-vines that creep around its angles, and the poplars and maples that photograph their boughs in shadow upon its spotless sides. But to set it off the better, the owner paints his small window-sashes bright yellow, his casings the reddest of red, and his sills and shutters and door panels vivid green. If the whole affair had just been handed out of a Dutch toy shop, it could not be more fantastic and childishly pretty.

One would think that with its dry and clear air, with an elevation of 4600 feet, with breezes sweeping down from a range of mountains where the snow is always to be seen, or across a broad and purifying lake, and with so much dry earth at hand to be used as a ready antiseptic, this locality ought to be as healthy as any on the face of the earth. So, with any care, it would be; but such care seems not to be taken, and there are few cities showing a larger death-rate among children. The bleak and desolate cemetery upon the wind-swept bench is a perfect Golgotha of infants' graves—a pitiful army of victims to diphtheria.

For this condition of things, and for much ill health among adults, there is no excuse. Even chills and fever are gaining a foot-hold where they should most easily be kept at a distance; but, strangely, all the malarial diseases seem more malignant and prevalent upon the bench than down in the lower part of the city, probably owing to the fact that the nightly draught of air down out of the cañons strikes the lower end of the city with more briskness, sweeping away what noxious gases may arise.

The climate of Salt Lake Valley is about what one might expect: in winter, much snow, and steady, intense, but dry cold; in summer, prolonged but dry heat. The sun blazes down day after day through a cloudless atmosphere, and burns like fire when its direct rays strike. The hot breath of the valley pours up when there is any wind from the southward, and one nearly suffocates. Yet perspiration does not flow copiously even under exertion, and the heat is not debilitating, for the moment you get into the shade you are comfortable. All day the earth sends upward volumes of heated air, but at night, striking the snow-banks on the neighboring peaks, the air rapidly chills and drops down to revive us, making sleep a luxury.

For their summer vacation, when they take any, the citizens can choose between the mountains and the Great Salt Lake, and generally end by going to both. The lake, indeed, is constantly visited. A narrow-gauge railway, aimed at Nevada, has got as far as the lake shore, and trains run out and back morning and evening, stopping long enough to give passengers time for a bath. The fare for the round trip (twenty miles each way) is only fifty cents. At the landings, in addition to bathing arrangements, there are dancing pavilions, and excursions often go out in the evening, returning by a special train in the morning.

On special occasions, such as Pioneer-day (July 24), when the Mormons celebrate their first entrance to the valley, great crowds of Saints, with all the wives and innumerable little ones, pack the open Coney-Island-like excursion cars, throng at the water-side, and spread their luncheons on the long tables under the bough-covered booths which give the only protection against the sun. Unfortunately it is impossible to make trees grow on the borders of the lake—the water and soil are too bitterly salt; moreover, there is no fresh-water in the rocky hills that tower straight up from the beach, and any irrigation is thus denied the would-be forest-

EAST SIDE OF SALT LAKE CITY.

er. Lack of shade seems to make little difference with the bathers, however. They go in under the noonday blaze, and say their bare heads suffer no discomfort, and children and horses rush about apparently as energetic as in October. While the danger of sun-stroke somehow seems very small, the lake is a treacherous water for swimmers. The great density of its waters sustains you so that you float easily, but swimming ahead is very hard work. Moreover, fatal consequences are likely to ensue if any of the brine is swallowed; it not only chokes, but is described as fairly burning the tissues of the throat and lungs, producing death almost as surely as the breathing of flame. Of course this occurs only in exceptional cases, but some lives are thus destroyed each summer, and many persons suffer extremely from a single accidental swallow.

The powerful effect of this water is not surprising when one remembers that the proportion of saline matter in it is six times as great as the percentage of the ocean, and almost equal to that of the Dead Sea, though Lake Urumiyah, in Persia, is reputed to contain water of a third greater density yet. This density is due mainly to common salt held in solution; but there are various other ingredients. In Great Salt Lake, for example, only 0.52 per cent. of magnesia exists, the Dead Sea having 7.82 per cent.; and of lime Salt Lake holds 1.80 per cent., while the Dead Sea contains only a third as much. The waters seem utterly lifeless, yet the innumerable gulls and pelicans there must find something to live upon. Walking on the shore in midsummer, you are surrounded by clouds of little sand-fleas (*Artemia salina*), which quickly drive you away, and wherever the muddy shores are exposed to the sun a sulphurous stench arises which is nauseating. Salt is made in great quantities in summer by the simple process of damming small bays and letting the inclosed water evaporate, leaving a crust of crystallized salt behind. Several thousands of tons are exported annually, and great quantities used at home in chlorodizing ores.

I think few persons realize how wonderfully, strangely beautiful this inland saline sea is. Under the sunlight its wide surface gives the eye such a mass of brilliant color as is rarely seen in the temperate zone. Over against the horizon it is almost black, then ultramarine, then glowing Prussian blue, or here and there, close by, variegated with patches of green and the soft skyey tone of the turquoise. Gaz-

lights are blotted out in the uniform immaculate indigo which slowly solidifies heights and depths into a single grand silhouette of the whole Wahsatch.

Watching these changing and lovely exhibitions of lavish color, feeling the

BATHING RESORT ON THE LAKE.

ing straight down off the end of the pier, or from the rough little steamboat, which is now degraded to do duty at its moorings as a restaurant, you learn that the water is transparent as glass, and the ripple marks on the bluish-white sand are visible at a great depth.

If the lake were in a plain (remembering the total absence of forest or greensward), doubtless this richness of color would not suffice to produce the effect of beauty, but on every side stand lofty mountains. They seem to rise from the very margin to their riven, bare, and pinnacle-studded crests, where the snow lies in shaded patches. Some of these ranges are a score of miles beyond the further beach, others close by, a few completely surrounded by the water—mere islands; but every group has its own color, from the snuff-brown earthen hue of the nearer slopes to the blue and misty ranges far away. In the noonday blaze of the vertical sun, or when at dawn its rays glint upon them, their prominences stand out distinctly, and streaks of shadow mark each of the great cañons separating neighboring peaks; but at night, or when the sun loses its angle of advantage, these high

freshening and medicinal breeze, hearkening to the gentle lapping of the wavelets, one can choose many a poetic name and foreign latitude to fit the scene, and easily forget that he is in Utah, until his eye catches the sage-brush.

The mountain trip is of quite different character, and can be made by choosing any one of half a dozen cañons, into which miners long ago led the way. The favorite is the beautiful American Fork Cañon, in reaching which you have the advantage of a railway for the greater part of the distance. A fortnight's camping and trout-fishing in the mountains once a year is considered indispensable to health and happiness by most families.

At the very first, one square of the city was set apart, as the "Temple Block," for holy use. This was intended to be not only the spiritual but the geographical centre of the city (for in spite of their present claims the founders certainly had no idea that so great a town as this would ever arise here), and all the streets are named from this point out—First South, First West, and so on, oddly reversing the ordinary style of designation.

On this ten-acre lot the Mormons held

their first worship; here was built the small building now known as the Endowment House; here, later on, the combined voluntary labor of the members of the Church erected the first Tabernacle; and here were laid the foundations of the Temple, wherein (it is promised) Jesus Christ shall appear bodily to the faithful as soon as it is completed.

This Temple is to be a tall, many-turreted building of white granite, brought from Little Cottonwood Cañon — famous as the locality of the Emma Mine — where it is split from enormous detached fragments that have fallen from the cliffs. It is almost as white and crystalline as marble, and unexcelled as material for an imposing structure. Until the very recent extension of the Denver and Rio Grande Railway into the cañon, all this stone was brought to the city by bullock teams, but now the railway tracks run from the quarries into the Temple yard.

The Temple was contrived and sketched out by Brigham Young. The style is one unknown to architectural schools, I think, but more nearly resembles the Gothic than any other. The structure is of Cyclopean strength; its base, far below the surface, is sixteen feet in thickness, decreasing to nine feet in thickness at the surface. One course of the basement stones stands in the shape of a series of solid reversed arches. Above, the walls rise nearly seven feet in thickness to the present height of eighty feet, which is nearly to where the roof begins.

A BALCONY.

There is no hollowness, or "filling," or brick-work — nothing but solid chiselled granite through and through, not only the outer walls, but in the partitions, the ceilings, and the stairways. The window openings are like the embrasures of a fort, and the heavily walled compartments of the basement suggest the direst dungeons.

RESIDENCE OF BRIGHAM YOUNG.

JOHN TAYLOR.

All the externals of the building have a religious significance. For instance, near the ground are a series of great bosses, upon which are to be carved maps of various regions of the world—and there will be room for a full atlas. Between the windows of the first and second stories similar bosses express eight phases of the moon, while a row of great stone suns is placed between the windows of the second and third tiers, and a star is chiselled upon the key-stone of every arch. When by-and-by the New-Zealander visits the ruins of Salt Lake City, he will be justified, I should say, in concluding the Mormons to have been sun-worshippers or astrologers, or both. President Taylor told me Brigham Young's intention was that the building should last a thousand years.

This enormous Temple is not intended as a place of worship, but as a sacred edifice within which various ceremonies of consecration, marriage, etc., shall be performed that are now celebrated in the Endowment House. For this purpose the whole building is cut up into little cloister-like rooms. The houses for public worship are the Tabernacle, and a handsome granite building, more civic than ecclesiastical in appearance, which occupies one corner of the Temple Square. In the interior this building is arranged with galleries, tiers of pulpits, and organs just like the Tabernacle, but in a much finer style, and it is used for Quorum meetings, evening sessions, and winter services.

What has been the cost of the Temple, which during thirty years has been rearing before the eyes of the towns-people, is a subject of natural curiosity, and one hears many rumors of how many millions supposed to have been expended upon it have really gone into the pockets of a few dignitaries of the Church. These rumors arise, no doubt, from the difficulty of understanding how men formerly poor are now rich, although they have been engaged in none of the ordinary methods of acquiring even a competence. I have the word of President Taylor, however, that the total cost has been, in round numbers, two millions of dollars, nine-tenths of which is accounted for as cash. It is supposed that three years more time and another million dollars will complete it. It is doubtful whether there is in the United States another public building so massive and genuine.

Across the street, just east of the Temple block, Brigham Young took possession of another whole square for himself, erecting at the end nearest the Temple a series

A SUBURBAN COTTAGE.

of store-houses for the reception of tithing levied upon all members of the Church. At the other end were his residences—the "Lion" and "Bee-hive" houses, where he guarded his wives terrestrial and celestial; and behind them the vast stables and corrals where he kept his hundreds of horses and mules, and the sires of his flocks and

manded the building of a general fortification around the whole young city—a "Spanish" wall of mud, which has now disappeared, saving a few remnants. Similarly the high walls have been replaced by fences, except that one which still protects the Temple and Young's house.   The first Tabernacle was built by contributions of

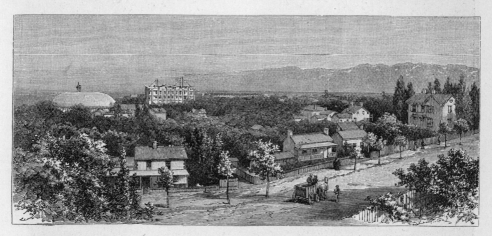

THE TABERNACLE AND TEMPLE.

herds.   Here too were the Church offices— the *sanctum sanctorum* of the Prophet of the Church on Earth of Jesus Christ of Latter-day Saints, the head-quarters of the military and civil ruler of the community, the Court of the High Judge of Zion, beyond whom there was no appeal, and the counting-house of the divinely appointed leader.

Mud and cobble-stones were cheaper than fence timber; the Canaanitish tribes, viz., Pah-Utes, Shoshones, Uintahs, etc., were thievish and belligerent, and, worst of all, unrighteous dwellers in Babylon were beginning to approach and inquire curiously into the ways and means of Mormondom.   So walls sprang up in every direction.   Not low picturesque stone fences with angular shadows and many-colored slabs and an embroidery of vines and lichens trailing pleasantly across them, but hideous forts of mud around every lot —walls ten to twenty feet high, supported by round bulging bastions at the corners, and guarded by prison-like gates at the entrances.   Brigham Young's property in particular looked like a Moorish fortress. Not content with this, the President com-

manual labor for the most part, and was early completed.   It had a general resemblance to the present structure, and was of great size.   Interiorly it is said to have been exceedingly plain, but to have held a very fine organ.   Only a few years elapsed, however, before the construction of the present larger edifice was begun.

The form of the Tabernacle is elliptical, and its roof an elliptical dome, arching everywhere from the eaves to the ridge, and supported upon a series of heavy stone piers, the shortest span between which is 172 feet.   As their height is only about twenty feet, and the height of the arched roof much less than a hundred feet, the Tabernacle from without gives you the impression of an enormous building more than half buried.   From the general level of the city it is almost impossible to obtain the smallest glimpse of it, either because of the trees or of the great wall behind which it is hid, and in order to get any notion of its size, you must climb to some eminence like the northern bench, where you can look down upon its huge fungus-like form. Elevate it sixty feet, or set it on a hill, and, perfectly fitting Utah scenery in its severe-

OLD MILL, AMERICAN FORK CAÑON.

days at two o'clock in the afternoon. The Saints assemble not only from the city, but from all the country round, and many vehicles of all sorts are left standing in the neighborhood. The centre of the church fills rapidly with women, while men predominate in the side rows of seats. There are seats for thirteen thousand persons in the amphitheatre and gallery, and many more crowd in at some of the great conferences. A broad gallery closes around at the front, where the choir sit in two wings, facing each

ly simple outlines, it would be as grand in its place as the Parthenon at Athens.

Service in the Tabernacle is held on Sun-

other, the men on one side and the women opposite. The space between is filled by three long crimson-cushioned pulpit desks, in each of which twenty speakers or so can sit at once, each rank overlooking the heads of the one beneath. The highest was designed for the president and his two counsellors; the second one for the twelve apostles, and the lowest for the bishops, but I believe the order is not very rigidly observed.

The acoustic properties of the house are almost perfect. A former deficiency of light has been overcome by the use of electricity; and the chilling bareness of the huge whitewashed vault is relieved by hangings of evergreen and flowers made of tissue-paper, the effect of which is very good indeed.

Every Sunday the sacrament is administered, the table loaded with the baskets of bread and tankards of water occupying a dais at the foot of the pulpits. Gradually a number of bishops take their places behind this table, and watch the congregation gather, people coming in through the dozen or more side doors as though the Tabernacle was a huge sponge absorbing the population of the Territory. Mingling with the rest come many strangers, bringing the latest tailoring and millinery, and these strangers are always conducted to seats down in front, where they can be addressed effectively in a body. At one door stands a huge cask of cold water, with several tin cups handy, and nearly all stop to drink as they come in. Later you will see tin pails holding a quart or more, and having handles on both sides, circulating through the audience, and refilled from time to time by small Ganymedes running about in chip hats and well-starched pinafores. Precisely at two o'clock the great organ sends forth its melodious summons, and the noise of busy voices — the hum of the veritable honey-bees of Deseret in their home hive —is hushed. A hymn is announced (by some brother in a business coat whom you will meet in trade to-morrow, perhaps), and sung by the choir, for though the tune may be one of the old familiar ones, the audience does not join in the singing.

The music of the Tabernacle has a great reputation in the West, and it would hardly be fair to decry it because it does not come up to a New York performance. It is conspicuously good for the material at hand and the locality. The organ, a handsome instrument, nearly as large as the great organ in the Boston Music Hall, is not so readily discounted, however, and is played with much skill, to the constant delight of the people.

After the singing comes a long prayer by some layman-priest, and a hymn, during the singing of which eight bishops break the slices of bread into morsels. Then, while the bread is being passed through the audience to the communicants—everybody, old and young, partaking—President Taylor or some other dignitary reads a chapter from the Bible, usually from Revelation, and makes extempore remarks upon it. Sometimes the Hon. George Q. Cannon, the most eminent of the Mormon leaders, occupies the pulpit.

It is three o'clock before the bread and water have been partaken of by all, and fully four by the time the preacher has ceased, the bishop pronounced the benediction, and the congregation is dismissed. As the people scatter about the great dusty yard, picking their way among the blocks of stone awaiting their place in the Temple, one sees how largely foreigners they are, the predominant nationalities being British and Scandinavian. Their peasantry, too, is unmistakably stamped upon their faces, though they have exchanged their foreign characteristics for a rusticity of the American type. Among the most prominent of the Mormon apostles are Orson Pratt, the most distinguished scholar and writer in the sect, and Joseph F. Smith, a nephew of the original Prophet and founder of Mormonism.

In Salt Lake City there are four separate sections of society which react upon one another. First, the adherents of the Mormon Church—the Saints; second, those who never have been nor will be Mormons—the Gentiles; third, the seceders from the Mormon Church; and fourth, the renegades and irresponsible of all parties, for whom has been adopted the Californian word hoodlum. This classification makes queer bedfellows: the Jew finds himself a Gentile, and the Roman Catholic becomes a Protestant, making common cause with Calvinism against the hierarchy of the Tabernacle. The result, of course, is that each section keeps pretty well to itself, and is likely to despise the others.

A few women of Salt Lake, years ago, formed a mutual-improvement club, having for its object a uniform course of reading. Now there are two flourishing ladies' literary societies, which are of far more significance here as centres of a healthy intellectual and social existence and progress than they would be in any other com-

GEORGE Q. CANNON.

munity. Most of their members are also members of the Anti-polygamy Society, which publishes a monthly journal, *The Standard*, under the editorship of Mrs. Jennie A. Froiseth.

The McKenzie Reform Club, established under Gentile auspices for the suppression of intemperance, has prospered so that it has erected the handsome building known as the Walker Opera-house, which cost nearly $75,000. The corner-stone was laid with much ceremony early in August of 1881.

Mormons are publicly very sociable, and remarkably peaceable. In their various ward meeting-houses—for each bishop's ward has an assembly-room—are held at frequent intervals during the colder half of the year assemblies where dancing is the main object, and where it is indulged without stint. Gentiles are occasionally invited. These dances (and all other Mormon festivities) are opened and closed by prayer.

The Salt-Lakers are also diligent musicians. From the great organ in the Taber-

nacle down to a jew's-harp, everybody handles some sort of musical instrument, or sings, and the music shops of the city seem about as brisk as any places on the street. You will hear singing all the time, and in all localities. This has been encouraged by the Church, as has also been the dramatic taste of the people, who very early organized a company of actors, and long ago built the great theatre which is a prominent feature of the city. For a long time only "home talent" graced its boards, but since the railway gave easy access, every company of actors that crosses the continent stops here, and some great names have been among those who have played in this temple of histrionics. Among the local celebrities in the theatrical line were several members of the family of Brigham Young, and one of his daughters is yet "on the boards," in San Francisco.

The annals of this theatre, perhaps, afford quite as good a gauge of the change which has taken place in Salt Lake City during the last twenty years as any other one thing in town. At first, as I have said, it was wholly supported by the local company of amateurs, and patronized in a most unconventional way by the simple Mormons in their sun-bonnets, who came with their whole families. The floor of the theatre in those days was reserved to the Saints; Jews, Gentiles, and other "dwellers in Babylon" sat in the first gallery. The audience now does not noticeably differ from that of any Eastern theatre, and the new opera-house is one of the handsomest in the Union.

Concerning the sociability among Mormon families in a private way, an outsider can only know by report. It is said to be small. The interchanges of calls and the forms of neighborly etiquette prevailing in ordinary society are little practiced. Even in the case of the wealthy, social visiting is said to be infrequent.

The private home routine of a polygamous family is a matter upon which so much curiosity is constantly expressed by my acquaintances that I venture to say here what little I know; but the reader must remember that less than ten per cent. of the voting Mormon population of Utah are polygamists.

The polygamist, as a rule, has accumulated some property and owns a house

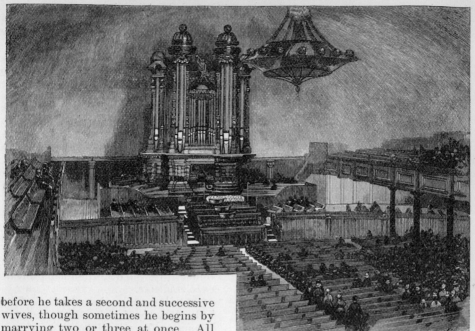

PULPITS AND ORGAN IN THE TABERNACLE.

before he takes a second and successive wives, though sometimes he begins by marrying two or three at once. All of these marriages, however, except the first, are made secretly by the Church, and no record of them is accessible.

In the city, at least, it is seldom that the different wives share the same quarters. In the country this is not so uncommon, but the natural unpleasantness follows in most cases. The general method is to have a large house, the main part of which, perhaps, is occupied by the first wife, and wings or additions by the successive candidates for marital honors. These large, straggling, hotel-like houses are common in Salt Lake City, and mark a difference between it and a town of small houses like Cheyenne and most other Western villages. In many cases, however, the husband sets up his wives in separate homes, either side by side or in different parts of the city. In any case each has her own kitchen-garden, etc. I have in mind a wealthy dignitary of the Church whom you might easily have mistaken for the late Peter Cooper, and who is possessed of seven wives. Each of these women has some farming and garden ground of her own, and all are greatly devoted to rearing bees. With the help of their grown children they each raise a large amount of produce and honey annually. The husband acts as their agent. He hives their swarms of bees, and charges them for it; he renders special aid when called upon, and is paid for it; he sells their crops and honey when it is ready,

and credits each wife with her due share. Most of them live in suites of apartments under the roof of his great house in town, but the first wife has a beautiful farm of her own a little out of the city, to which she and her children have retired, to end their days in peaceful independence.

The way in which this old gentleman has always arranged his domestic life is reported to be thus: He had certain rooms in his house where he kept his bed, his wardrobe, his books, and saw any visitors who called upon him. Here he was a bachelor, and here he staid every other day and night. On alternate days and nights he was the guest of one or another of his wives in regular rotation, devoting the one day (in this case fortnightly) which was hers diligently to her society. Of course this routine was not invariable, but for the most part it was regularly followed.

In respect to the general morals of the community, it may be said that they are simply those of any old and well-regulated town East or West. If as a Western city it differs from an Eastern town of similar size, it is merely in classification, not degree. Anything like open violence is extremely rare ; ladies walk the streets at night unmolested; and burglary is almost

JOSEPH F. SMITH.

unknown. Thievery, however, is common enough, and a large police force is needed. Gambling is wholly "on the sly." In the matter of liquor-drinking, a great change has recently come about. For many years after the foundation of the city Brigham Young rigidly excluded all liquors, and even as late as a dozen years ago only two or three bars met the patronage of ten or fifteen thousand people. Whatever else they might be, the President evidently intended his people should not become drunkards. Now, however, local breweries turn out great quantities of lager-beer; every hotel and nearly every restaurant has its bar, while dozens of liquor saloons exist, some managed by Mormons.

Observance of Sunday used to be very rigid and sanctimonious, and even now it is far more strict than in most cities west of the Missouri; for in California, as in New Orleans, Sunday is mainly devoted to recreation, the theatres are opened, and pleasure excursions of all sorts are encouraged. Denver is dropping into this way somewhat also, while as for Santa Fe, Cheyenne, and Helena, they never had any principle at all so far as the Sabbath was concerned. With the growth of Salt Lake City this worldly influence is more and more apparent, and the trains to the bathing re-

sorts are never so crowded as on Sundays. To be sure, it is the plebeian element which goes, for the most part; but the patricians stay at home more as a matter of taste than righteousness, for you will see them playing croquet in the orchard, and hear them singing decidedly secular songs around the household piano in the evening. Undoubtedly there are many conscientious to "keep the Sabbath holy"; but what I mean to say is that the City of the Saints is little better than its neighbors in this particular form of religious observance.

So far as my own observation went, the condition of Salt Lake City did not seem at all superior to other well-settled towns of its size either East or West as regards that special kind of immorality which Mormonism professes to eradicate.

Of the arrests made annually in Salt Lake City, by far the larger number belong to the non-Mormon minority. Many of the culprits, however, are not residents of the city, but are a part of the floating crowd of miserable and dissolute men that infest every Western city. The Gentiles of the city probably enjoy themselves more than they would if they could run off to a great town in an hour,

ORSON PRATT.

and were not necessarily so self-centred as the isolation of the locality compels them to be. It is a society made up of the families of successful merchants and mining men, of clergymen and teachers, of the officers of the army stationed at Camp Doug-long produced pretty well up to their several capacities. There must, then, be an increased area of plantation if there is to be a greater supply; but examination proves that it is probably impossible to bring under cultivation a hundred thousand acres

A TYPICAL MORMON FAMILY.

las, and the representatives of the government in the judicial and other Territorial offices. This composition, it will be seen, presupposes considerable intelligence and culture, the effect of which is plainly to be seen in their homes.

Utah has always been pre-eminently an agricultural district. Out of her 150,000 people probably 120,000 are now farming or stock-raising in some capacity or other. When you look down the valley from the city your eye takes in a wide view of fields and orchards and meadows, green with the most luxuriant growth, and marked off by rows of stately trees or patches of young woodland. All these farms are small holdings, and though cultivated by no means scientifically, have

more of land in the whole Territory. Leaving out the cactus plains of the south, the bleak plateaus east of the Wahsatch, the saline deserts on the western border, and the volcanic sands which run down from Idaho, nearly all the rest of the Territory where water is accessible has already been taken up. It must be remembered that all the agriculture of Utah is by artificial irrigation. Every mountain cañon discharges a stream fed by the melting snows of the heights. This stream is dammed, its waters led along the "benches" beneath the foot-hills in great ditches, and thence distributed through slender conduits to each man's land. The sources of the water are held to be public property, and many questions of law are more and more becoming involved in the consideration of the rights and responsibilities of the public in relation to its water supply.

The important fact in this connection is that the limit of otherwise arable land is not so soon to be reached as that of irrigation. The Mormon leaders recognize this, and are continually sending colonies of new-comers away into neighboring Territories to establish themselves. The present waste of water may be largely saved, and more economical methods of farming introduced, but Utah can hardly expect to do more than double her present agricultural population. This class, however, will be able to produce far more than would be needed for their own consumption. That is done now, and the export of all sorts of grain, fruit, and produce is large, and is constantly increasing.

To something more than agriculture, then, which in the opinion of the first settlers was their stronghold, must Utah and her metropolis look for future growth. The Mormon leaders, and particularly Brigham Young, always opposed any attempt at a development of the mineral resources of the Territory, though it is said that he informed himself as thoroughly as he could upon their character and value. He forbade all mining to his devotees, and would have closed the mountains to Gentile prospectors if he had been able. So far as a desire existed to avoid the evils of a placer-working excitement, drawing hither a horde of ruffianly gold-seekers, this course was commendable. But as years went on it was seen by the shrewder heads among the Mormons themselves that this abstinence from mining was harmful. There was no cash in the Territory, and none to be got. If a surplus of grain was raised, or more of any sort of goods manufactured than could be used at home, there was no sale for it, since at that time the market was so far away, and transportation was so deficient and expensive, that no profits could possibly be made. Business was almost wholly by barter, and payments for everything had to be by exchange. A man who took his family to the theatre wheeled his admission fee with him in the shape of a barrel or two of potatoes, and a young man would go to a dance with his girl on one arm, and a bunch of turnips on the other with which to buy his ticket. The Gentiles soon began to bring in coin, but the relief was gradual and inadequate.

Finally, about fifteen years ago, it was publicly argued by some bold minds, in the face of the Church, and to their own discomfort, that the only things Utah had which she could send out against competition were gold and silver. When from preaching they began to practice, and such men as the Walker brothers encouraged outside capital to join them in developing silver ledges in the Wahsatch, then Salt Lake City began to rouse herself. Potatoes and carrots and adobes disappeared as currency, and coin and greenbacks enlivened trade, which conformed more and more to the ordinary methods of American commerce.

One perfectly legitimate means taken for monopoly of trade was the establishment, twenty-five years ago, of Zion's Co-operative Mercantile Institution. In the early days it was exceedingly difficult for country shop-keepers to maintain supplies, when everything had to be hauled by teams from the Missouri River, and extortionate prices would be demanded for staples when, as frequently happened, some petty dealer would get a "corner" in them. The design of this establishment was to furnish goods of every sort known to merchants out of one central depot in Salt Lake City, under control of the Church, and partly owned by it. This was a joint-stock "co-operative" affair, however, and the capital was nearly a million dollars. The people were commanded from the pulpit to trade there, but they would have done so anyhow, for the "co-op," as it is called, was able to reduce and equalize prices very greatly. Branches were established in Ogden, Logan, and Soda Springs, and a warehouse built in Provo. These and other additions were rapid. The central sales-rooms in this city now occupy a four-story brick building three hundred and eighteen feet long by ninety-seven feet wide, where every species of merchandise is to be found. In other quarters are a drug-store, a shoe factory (supplied by its own tanneries, and running one hundred and twenty-five machines propelled by steam), and a manufactory for canvas "overall" clothing. Altogether about two hundred and fifty persons are employed, working at reasonable hours and reasonable pay. The stock, which originally was widely scattered in small lots, has been concentrated for the most part in the hands of a few astute men, who are credited with large

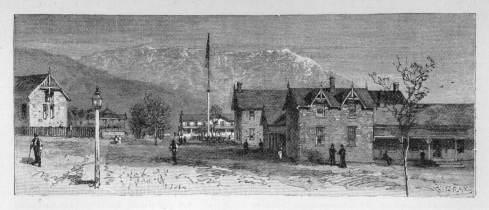

CAMP DOUGLAS.

profits. There is an air of great prosperity about the institution, whose business is stated to reach five millions of dollars annually, derived almost wholly from Utah and Southern Idaho.

Though this concern had a practical monopoly at first, as soon as the railways came to Salt Lake individual merchants could sell goods about as cheap, and opposition arose. Then the power of the Church was brought directly to bear to crush competition.

For example, the four Walker brothers, sons of a Mormon father, were engaged in trade, and were getting rich, having surmounted obstacles fatal to lesser strength. Brigham Young, in the height of his pride and power, chose to insist that their tithe offerings were not large enough, and to demand a large amount of cash additional—$30,000, it is reported, at one fell swoop. Instead of a check he received a refusal. Instantly relays of Saints were established to stand in front of the Walkers' shop, and report for condemnation every Mormon who traded there. Nevertheless the Walker brothers survived, and are to-day probably the most powerful mercantile firm in Utah.

Brigham Young's attitude led to a schism in the Church, and a small but far-reaching rebellion among some of his most trusted followers.

The leaders of this movement were W. S. Godbe, H. W. Lawrence, and E. L. T. Harrison, and they had plenty of encouragement. Through the pages of the *Utah Magazine* they declared that Young was not a dictator over their temporal as well as spiritual life, that commerce should be left to its own laws, that Utah's prosperity lay in the development of her mines, that

the United States was above the Church in civil matters, and that the priesthood should confine itself to its proper function —that of spiritual guidance. They were expelled from the Church, which did all it could to ruin their business. All they asked was independence and religious liberty to worship God in the same forms that Brigham Young professed to enjoy and to enjoin; but that autocrat would brook no opposition to his infallibility. Nevertheless, the Godbe movement was of lasting strength, and through it Salt Lake City took an important step toward the freedom and prosperity of the present.

The policy, or at any rate the action, of the Church has changed greatly since Young's death. Everybody now buys in the best market, modern manners in all the walks of life are cultivated, better schools are being established among both Mormons and Gentiles, and the best newspapers are patronized no matter what their creed.

The Church is as ambitious as ever, and taking advantage of the general indifference to its movements, is steadily aggressive through all its missionary channels. If it has grown weaker among its earliest adherents and in its first stronghold, it is growing stronger through new accessions, and in other Territories is quietly laying the foundations of future political power.

Salt Lake City is one of the points in the United States that all tourists think should not be missed. It is one of the certain stopping points in the programme of the globe-trotter. Consequently the city is always full of strangers, and various excursion facilities have grown up and flourished almost wholly by patronage of sight-seers. Hotels are well supported, too, and consequently are unusually good. A few days after the arrival at San Francisco of each steamer from the other side of the Pacific there is a special flux of visitors. Then it is highly entertaining to sit in the long, Southern-like, acacia-shaded veranda of the Continental and watch the omnibuses unload their foreign travellers, with heaps of queer-looking luggage bearing marks affixed in Yokohama or Melbourne, and concealing a stratification of labels that would read right around the world. This tourist business is of value to the city, and is becoming more noticeable than ever now that a second line of railway, the Denver and Rio Grande, has been opened between this city and the East. Heretofore the only railway communication had been by the Union Pacific at Ogden, the Utah Central connecting Salt Lake City with that town. The famous narrow-gauge railway of Colorado, however, pushed its line through the southern passes of the Rockies, and made a rival connection with the Central Pacific at Ogden. This diverted at once so large a body of travellers who were anxious to avail themselves of the opportunity to see the marvellous scenery of the interior Rocky Mountains that the old line was obliged to bestir itself.

The competition in the transportation of farm products, ores, and merchandise also caused a very considerable diminution in rates of freight, and has been a stimulus to all business in eastern Utah. Grain and potatoes, hitherto fed to the hogs or not harvested, found a quick market at advanced rates. The new road made accessible new coal mines also, and cheapened fuel and coke, while important concessions were made to those who wished to send their ores to Denver, Pueblo, or eastward, or to bring Colorado ores, for the advantage of the smelters, here. The building of the western end of the Denver and Rio Grande was done almost wholly by Mormons, and great sums of money have been expended here, so that cash has been abundant, trade and building brisk, and the increase of population in and about the city very rapid. The census of 1880 gave the city only a little over 20,000; she now has close upon 25,000. At the same time the rise of large towns in Montana, the opening of railway outlets in the north, and eastern demands have made unlooked-for drafts upon the cattle herds and the farms of the whole region. The result has followed in Salt Lake that the cost of living has advanced nearly fifty per cent. in two or three years.

GRAVE OF BRIGHAM YOUNG.

CHAPTER XXII.

PORTENTS.

IT was somewhat hard on little Bess Hall that her aunt Judith was determined she should grow up as fearless as she herself was, and had, indeed, charged herself with this branch of her niece's education. The child, it is true, was not more timid than others of her age, and could face with fair equanimity beggars, school-boys, cows, geese, and other dangerous creatures; while as for ghosts, goblins, and similar nocturnal terrors, Judith had settled all that side of the question by informing the maids of both families, in the plainest language, that any one of them found even mentioning such things to this niece of hers would be instantaneously and without ceremony shot forth from the house. But beyond and above all this Judith expected too much, and would flout and scold when Bess Hall declined to perform the impossible, and would threaten to go away and get a small boy out of the school to become her playmate in future. At this moment, for example, she was standing at the foot of the staircase in Dr. Hall's house. She had come round to carry off her niece for the day, and she had dressed her up like a small queen, and now she would have her descend the wide and handsome staircase in noble state and unaided. Bess Hall, who had no ambition to play the part of a queen, but had, on the other hand, a wholesome and instinctive fear of breaking her neck, now stood on the landing, helpless amid all her finery, and looking down at her aunt in a beseeching sort of way.

"I shall tumble down, Aunt Judith; I know I shall," said she, and budge she would not.

"Tumble down, little stupid! Why, what should make you tumble down? Are you going forever to be a baby? Any baby can crawl down-stairs by holding on to the balusters."

"I know I shall tumble down, Aunt Judith—and then I shall cry."

But even this threat was of no avail.

"Come along, little goose; 'tis easy enough when you try it. Do you think I have dressed you up as a grown woman to see you crawl like a baby? A fine woman—you! Come along, I say!"

But this lesson, happily for the half-frightened pupil, was abruptly brought to an end. Judith was standing with her face to the staircase, and her back to the central hall and the outer door, so that she could not see any one entering, and indeed the first intimation she had of the approach of a stranger was a voice behind her:

"Be gentle with the child, Judith."

And then she knew that she was caught. For some little time back she had very cleverly managed to evade the good parson, or at least to secure the safety of company when she saw him approach. But this time she was as helpless as little Bess herself. Dr. Hall was away from home; Judith's sister was ill of a cold, and in bed; there was no one in the house, besides the servants, but herself. The only thing she could do was to go up to the landing, swing her niece on to her shoulder, and say to Master Walter that they were going round to New Place, for that Susan was ill in bed, and unable to look after the child.

"I will walk with you as far," said he, calmly, and, indeed, as if it were rather an act of condescension on his part.

She set out with no good-will. She expected that he would argue, and she had an uncomfortable suspicion that he would get the best of it. And if she had once or twice rather wildly thought that in order to get rid of all perplexities, and in order to please all the people around her, she would in the end allow Master Walter Blaise to win her over into becoming his wife, still she felt that the time was not yet. She would have the choosing of it for herself. And why should she be driven into a corner prematurely? Why be made to confess that her brain could not save her? She wanted peace. She wanted to play with Bess Hall, or to walk through the meadows with Willie Hart, teaching him what to think of England. She did not want to be confronted with clear, cold eyes, and arguments like steel, and the awful prospect of having to labor in the vineyard through the long, long, gray, and distant years. She grew to think it was scarcely fair of her father to hand her over. He at least might have been on her side. But he seemed as willing as any that she should go away among the

AN UNWELCOME VISITOR.—[SEE PAGE 415.]

saints, and forsake forever (as it seemed to her) the beautiful, free, and clear-colored life that she had been well content to live.

And then, all of a sudden, it flashed upon her mind that she was a player's daughter, and a kind of flame went to her face.

"I pray you, good Master Blaise," said she, with a lofty and gracious courtesy, "bethink you, ere you give us your company through the town."

"What mean you, Judith?" said he, in some amazement.

"Do you forget, then, that I am the daughter of a player?—and this his granddaughter?" said she.

"In truth, I know not what you mean, Judith," he exclaimed.

"Why," said she, "may not the good people who are the saints of the earth wonder to see you consort with such as we?—or, rather, with one such as I, who am impenitent, and take no shame that my father is a player—nay, God's my witness, I am wicked enough to be proud of it, and I care not who knows it, and they that hope to have me change my thoughts on that matter will have no lack of waiting."

Well, it was a fair challenge; and he answered it frankly, and with such a reasonableness and charity of speech that, despite herself, she could not but admit that she was pleased, and also, perhaps, just a little bit grateful. He would not set up to be any man's judge, he said; nor was he a Pharisee; the Master that he served was no respecter of persons— He had welcomed all when He was upon the earth—and it behooved His followers to beware of pride and the setting up of distinctions; if there was any house in the town that earned the respect of all, it was New Place; he could only speak of her father as he found him, here, in his own family, among his own friends—and what that was all men knew; and so forth. He spoke well, and modestly; and Judith was so pleased to hear what he said of her father that she forgot to ask whether all this was quite consistent with his usual denunciations of plays and players, his dire prophecy as to the fate of those who were not of the saints, and his sharp dividing and shutting off of these. He did not persecute her at all. There was no argument. What he was mostly anxious about was that she should not tire herself with carrying Bess Hall on her shoulder.

"Nay, good sir," said she, quite pleasantly, "'tis a trick my father taught me; and the child is but a feather-weight."

He looked at her—so handsome and buxom, and full of life and courage; her eyes lustrous, the rose-leaf tint of health in her cheeks; and always at the corner of her mouth what could only be called a disposition to smile, as if the world suited her fairly well, and that she was ready at any moment to laugh her thanks.

"There be many, Judith," said he, "who might envy you your health and good spirits."

"When I lose them, 'twill be time enough to lament them," said she, complacently.

"The hour that is passing seems all in all to you; and who can wonder at it?" he continued. "Pray Heaven your carelessness of the morrow have reason in it! But all are not so minded. There be strange tidings in the land."

"Indeed, sir; and to what end?" said she.

"I know not whether these rumors have reached your house," he said, "but never at any time I have read of have men's minds been so disturbed—with a restlessness and apprehension of something being about to happen. And what marvel! The strange things that have been seen and heard of throughout the world of late—meteors, and earthquakes, and visions of armies fighting in the heavens. Even so was Armageddon to be foreshadowed. Nay, I will be honest with you, Judith, and say that it is not clear to my own mind that the great day of the Lord is at hand; but many think so; and one man's reading of the Book of Revelation is but a small matter to set against so wide a belief. Heard you not of the vision that came to the young girl at Chipping Camden last Monday?"

"Indeed, no, good sir."

"I marvel that Prudence has not heard of it, for all men are speaking of it. 'Twas in this way, as I hear. The maiden is one of rare piety and grace, given to fasting, and nightly vigils, and searching of the heart. 'Twas on the night of Sunday last —or perchance toward Monday morning —that she was awakened out of her sleep by finding her room full of light; and looking out of the window she beheld in the darkness a figure of resplendent radiance—shining like the sun, as she said, only clear white, and shedding rays around; and the figure approached the window, and regarded her; and she dropped on her knees in wonder and fear, and bowed her head and worshipped. And as she did so, she heard a voice say to her: 'Watch and pray: Behold, I come quickly.' And she durst not raise her head, as she says, being overcome with fear and joy. But the light slowly faded from the room; and when at last she rose she saw something afar off in the sky, that was now grown dark again. And ever since she has been trembling with the excitement of it, and will take no food; but from time to time she cries in a loud voice, 'Lord Jesus, come quickly! Lord Jesus, come quickly!' Many have gone to see her, as I hear, and from all parts of the country; but she heeds them not; she is intent with her prayers; and her eyes, the people say, look as if they had been dazzled with a great light, and are dazed and strange. Nay, 'tis but one of many things that are murmured abroad at present; for there have been signs in the heavens seen in sundry places, and visions, and men's minds grow anxious."

"And what think you yourself, good sir? You are one that should know."

"I?" said he. "Nay, I am far too humble a worker to take upon myself the saying ay or no at such a time; I can but watch and pray and wait. But is it not strange to think that we here at this moment, walking along this street in Stratford, might within some measurable space—say, a year, or half a dozen years or so—that we might be walking by the pure river of water that John saw flowing from the throne of God and of the Lamb? Do you not remember how the early Christians, with such a possibility before their eyes, drew nearer to each other, as it were, and rejoiced together, parting with all their possessions, and living in common, so that the poorest were even as the rich? 'Twas no terror that overtook them, but a happiness; and they drew themselves apart from the world, and lived in their own community, praying with each other, and aiding each other. 'All that believed,' the Bible tells us, 'were in one place, and had all things common. And they sold their possessions and goods, and parted them to all men, as every one had need. And they continued daily in the Temple, and, breaking bread at home, did eat their meat together with gladness and singleness of heart, praising God, and had

favor with all the people; and the Lord added to the Church from day to day such as should be saved.' Such a state of spiritual brotherhood and exaltation may come among us once more; methinks I see the symptoms of its approach even now. Blessed are they who will be in that communion with a pure soul and a humble mind, for the Lord will be with them as their guide, though the waters should arise and overflow, or fire consume the earth."

"Yes, but, good sir," said she, "when the early Christians you speak of thought the world was near to an end they were mistaken. And these, now, of our day—"

"Whatever is prophesied must come to pass," said he, "or soon or late, though it is possible for our poor human judgment to err as to the time. But surely we ought to be prepared; and what preparation, think you, is sufficient for so great and awful a change? Joy there may be in the trivial things of this world—in the vanities of the hour, that pass away and are forgotten; but what are these things to those whose heart is set on the New Jerusalem—the shining city? The voice that John heard proclaimed no lie: 'twas the voice of the Lord of heaven and earth —a promise to them that wait and watch for his coming. 'And God shall wipe away all tears from their eyes; and there shall be no more death, neither sorrow, neither crying, neither shall there be any more pain, for the first things are passed. .... And there shall be no more curse; but the throne of God and of the Lamb shall be in it, and His servants shall serve Him. And they shall see His face, and His name shall be in their foreheads. And there shall be no night there; and they need no candle, neither light of the sun, for the Lord God giveth them light, and they shall reign for evermore.'"

She sighed.

"'Tis too wonderful a thing for poor sinful creatures to expect," she said.

But by this time they were at the house, and he could not say anything further to her; indeed, when he proposed that she should come into the sitting-room, and that he would read to her a description of the glories of the New Jerusalem, out of the Book of Revelation, she excused herself by saying that she must carry Bess Hall to see her father. So he went in and sat down, waiting for Judith's mother to be sent for; while aunt and niece went out and through the back yard to the garden.

"Bess," said Judith, on the way, "heardst thou aught of a white figure?"

"No, Judith," said the child, who had been engaged all the way in examining the prettinesses of her aunt's velvet cap, and ruff, and what not.

"That is well," said she.

When she got into the garden, she could see that goodman Matthew eyed their approach with little favor—for Bess Hall, when her grandfather had charge of her, was allowed to tear flowers, and walk over beds, or do anything she choose; but Judith did not mind that much. On the other hand, she would not go deliberately and disturb her father. She would give him his choice—to come forth or not as he pleased. And so, quite noiselessly, and at a little distance off, she passed the summer-house. There was no sign. Accordingly, she went on idly to the further end of the garden, and would doubtless have remained there (rather than return within-doors) amusing the child somehow, but that the next minute her father appeared.

"Come hither, Bess! Come hither, wench!" he called.

Nay, he came to meet them; and as he lifted the child down from Judith's shoulder, something—perhaps it was the touch of the sunlight on the soft brown of her short curls—seemed to attract his notice.

"Why, wench," said he to Judith, "methinks your hair grows prettier every day. And yet you keep it overshort—yes, 'tis overshort—would you have them think you a boy?"

"I would I were a man," said she, glancing at him rather timidly.

"How, then? What, now?"

"For then," said she, "might I help you in your work, so please you, sir."

He laughed, and said:

"My work? What know you of that, wench?"

The blood rushed to her face.

"Nay, sir, I but meant the work of the fields—in going about with the bailiff and the like. The maids say you were abroad at five this morning."

"Well, is't not the pleasantest time of the day in this hot weather?" he said—and he seemed amused by her interference.

"But why should you give yourself so many cares, good father?" she made bold to say (for she had been meditating the saying of it for many a day back). "You that have great fame, and land, and wealth. We would fain see you rest a little more, father; and 'tis all the harder to us that we can give you no help, being but women-folk."

There was something in the tone of her voice—or perhaps in her eyes—that conveyed more than her words. He put his hand on her head.

"You are a good lass," said he. "And listen. You can do something for me that is of far more value to me than any help in any kind of work: nay, I tell thee 'tis of greater value to me than all of my work; and 'tis this: keep you a merry heart, wench—let me see your face right merry and cheerful as you go about—that is what you can do for me; I would have you ever as you are now, as bright and glad as a summer day."

"'Tis an easy task, sir, so long as you are content to be pleased with me," she managed to answer; and then little Bess Hall—who could not understand why she should have been so long left unnoticed—began to scramble up his knees, and was at last transferred to his arms.

Judith's heart was beating somewhat quickly—with a kind of pride and gladness that was very near bringing tears to her eyes; but, of course, that was out of the question, seeing that he had enjoined her to be cheerful. And so she forced herself to say, with an odd kind of smile,

"I pray you, sir, may I remain with you for a space—if Bess and I trouble you not?"

"Surely," said he, regarding her; "but what is it, then?"

"Why," said she, pulling herself together, "good Master Blaise is within-doors, and his last belief is enough to frighten a poor maiden—let alone this small child. He says the world is nigh unto its end."

"Nay, I have heard of some such talk being abroad," said he, "among the country folk. But why should that frighten thee? Even were it true, we can make it nor better nor worse."

"Only this, father," said she, and she looked at him with the large, clear-shining gray eyes no longer near to tears, but rather suggesting some dark mystery of humor, "that if the end of the world be so nigh at hand, 'twould be an idle thing for the good parson to think of taking him a wife."

"I ask for no secrets, wench," her father said, as he sat little Bess Hall on the branch of an apple-tree.

"Nay, sir, he but said that as many were of opinion that something dreadful was about to happen, we should all of us draw nearer together. That is well, and to be understanded; but if the world be about to end for all of us, surely 'twere a strange thing that any of us should think of taking husband or wife."

"I'll meddle not," her father said. "Go thine own ways. I have heard thou hast led more than one honest lad in Stratford a madcap dance. Take heed; take heed—as thy grandmother saith—lest thou outwear their patience."

And then something—she could scarce tell what—came into her head: some wild wish that he would remain always there at Stratford: would she not right willingly discard all further thoughts of lovers or sweethearts if only he would speak to her sometimes as he had just been speaking; and approve of her hair; and perchance let her become somewhat more of a companion to him? But she durst not venture to say so much. She only said, very modestly and timidly,

"I am content to be as I am, sir, if you are content that I should bide with you."

"Content?" said he, with a laugh that had no unkindness in it. "Content that thou shouldst bide with us? Keep that pretty face of thine merry and glad, good lass—and have no fear."

CHAPTER XXIII.

A LETTER.

WHEN she should get back from Master Leofric Hope the last portion of the yet unnamed play, there remained (as she considered) but one thing more—to show him the letter written by the King to her father, so that when the skies should clear over the young gentleman's head, and he be permitted to return among his friends and acquaintances, he might have something else occasionally to talk of than Ben Jonson and his masques and his favor at court. Nor had she any difficulty in procuring the letter; for Prudence was distinctly of opinion that by right it belonged to Judith, who had coveted it from the beginning. However, Judith only now wanted the loan of it for a day

or two, until, in her wanderings, she might encounter Master Hope.

That opportunity soon arrived; for whether it was that the young gentleman kept a sharp lookout for her, or whether she was able to make a shrewd guess as to his probable whereabouts at certain hours of the day, she had scarcely ever failed to meet him when she went over to Shottery for the successive installments of the play that he had left for her there. On this occasion she had found the last of these awaiting her at the cottage; and when she had put it into her velvet satchel, and bade good-by to her grandmother, she set out for home with a pretty clear foreknowledge that sooner or later the young gentleman would appear. Was it not his duty?—to say what he thought of all this romance that he had been allowed to see; and to thank her; and say farewell? For she had a vague impression that she had done as much as could reasonably be expected of her in the way of cheering the solitude of one in misfortune: and she had gathered, moreover, that he was likely soon to leave the neighborhood. But she would not have him go without seeing the King's letter.

Well, when he stepped forth from behind some trees, she was not surprised; and even the Don had grown accustomed to these sudden appearances.

"Give ye good-day, sweet lady," said he.

"And to you, sir," she said. "I thank you for your care in leaving me these pages; I would not have had any harm come to them, even though my father will in time throw them away."

"And my thanks to you, sweet Mistress Judith," said he—"how can I express them?"—and therewith he entered upon such a eulogy of the story he had just been reading as she was not likely to hear from any Stratford-born acquaintance. Indeed, he spoke well, and with obvious sincerity; and although she had intended to receive these praises with indifference (as though the play were but a trifle that her father had thrown off easily amid the pressure of other labors), she did not quite succeed. There was a kind of triumph in her eyes; her face was glad and proud; when he quoted a bit of one of Ariel's songs, she laughed lightly.

"He is a clever musician, that merry imp, is he not?" said she.

"I would I had such a magic-working

spirit to serve me," said he, looking at her. "One could shape one's own course then. 'Under the blossom that hangs on the bough,' would be my motto; there would be no going back to London or any other town. And what think you: might he not find out for me some sweet Miranda? —not that I am worthy of such a prize, or could do aught to deserve her, except in my duty and humble service to her. The Miranda, I think, could be found," he said, glancing timidly at her; "nay, I swear I know myself where to find just such a beautiful and gentle maiden; but where is the Ariel that would charm her heart and incline her to pity and kindness?"

"Here, sir," said she, quickly, "is the letter I said I would bring you, that the King wrote to my father."

He did not look at the blue velvet satchel; he looked at her—perhaps to see whether he had gone too far. But she did not show any signs of confusion or resentment; at all events she pretended not to be conscious; and, for one thing, her eyes were lowered, for the satchel seemed for a second or so difficult to open. Then she brought forth the letter.

"Perchance you can tell me the English of it, good sir?" said she. "'Tis some time since Master Blaise read it for us, and I would hear it again."

"Nay, I fear my Latin will scarce go so far," said he—"'tis but little practice in it I have had since my school-days; but I will try to make out the sense of it."

She carefully opened the large folded sheet of paper, and handed it to him. This was what he found before him:

"JACOBUS D. G. Rex Anglorum et Scotorum poetæ nostro fideli et bene dilecto GULIELMO SHAKESPEARE, S. P. D.

"Cum nuper apud Londinium commorati comœdiam tuam nobis inductam spectâssemus, de manu viri probi Eugenii Collins fabulæ libro accepto, operam dedimus ut eam diligenter perlegeremus. Subtilissima illa quidem, multisque ingenii luminibus et artis, multis etiam animi oblectamentis, excogitata, nimis tamen accommodata ad cacchinationem movendam vulgi imperiti, politioris humanitatis expertis. Quod vero ad opera tua futura attinet, amicissime te admonemus ut multa commentatione et meditatione exemplaria verses antistitum illorum artis comœdicæ, Menandri scilicet Atheniensis et Plauti et Terentii Romani, qui minus vulgi plausum captabant quam vitiis tanquam flagellis castigandis studebant. Qui optimi erant arte et summa honestate et utilitate, qualem te etiam esse volumus; virtutum artium et exercitationum doctores, atque illustrium illorum a Deo ad populum regendum præpositorum adminicula. Quibus fac ne te minorem præstes; neque tibi nec familiaribus tuis unquam deerimus quin, quum fiat occasio, munere regali fungamur. Te interea Deus opt. max. feliciter sospitet.

"Datum ex regia nostra apud Greenwich X. Kal. Jun."

He began his translation easily:

"'To our trusty and well-beloved poet, William Shakespeare: Health and greeting.'" But then he began to stammer. "'When formerly—when recently—tarrying in London—thy comedy—thy comedy'—nay, fair Mistress Judith, I beseech your pardon; I am grown more rusty than I thought, and would not destroy your patience. Perchance, now, you would extend your favor once more, and let me have the letter home with me, so that I might spell it out in school-boy fashion?"

She hesitated; but only for a second.

"Nay, good sir, I dare not. These sheets of the play were thrown aside, and so far of little account; but this—if aught were to come amiss to this letter, how should I regard myself? If my father value it but slightly, there be others who think more of it; and—and they have intrusted it to me; I would not have it go out of my own keeping, so please you, and pardon me."

It was clear that she did not like to refuse this favor to so courteous and grateful a young gentleman. However, her face instantly brightened.

"But I am in no hurry, good sir," said she. "Why should you not sit you on the stile there, and take time to master the letter, while I gather some wild flowers for my father? In truth, I am in no hurry; and I would fain have you know what the King wrote."

"I would I were a school-boy again for five minutes," said he, with a laugh; but he went obediently to the stile, and sat down, and proceeded to pore over the contents of the letter.

And then she wandered off by herself (so as to leave him quite undisturbed), and began to gather here and there a wild rose from the hedge, or a piece of meadow-sweet from the bank beneath, or a bit of yarrow from among the grass. It was a still, clear, quiet day, with some rainy clouds in the sky; and beyond these, near to the horizon, broad silver shafts of sun-light striking down on the woods and the distant hills. It looked as if a kind of mid-day sleep had fallen over the earth; there was scarce a sound; the birds were silent; and there was not even enough wind to make a stirring through the wide fields of wheat or in the elms. The nose-gay grew apace, though she went about her work idly—kneeling here and stretch-ing a hand there; and always she kept away from him, and would not even look in his direction; for she was determined that he should have ample leisure to make out the sense of the letter, of which she had but a vague recollection, only that she knew it was complimentary.

Even when he rose and came toward her she pretended not to notice. She would show him she was in no hurry. She was plucking the heads of red clover, and suck-ing them to get at the honey; or she was adding a buttercup or two to her nosegay; or she was carelessly humming to herself:

" O stay and hear; your true love's coming,
That can sing both high and low."

"Well, now, Mistress Judith," said he, with an air of apology, "methinks I have got at the meaning of it, however imper-fectly; and your father might well be proud of such a commendation from so high a source—the King, as every one knows, being a learned man, and skilled in the arts. And I have not heard that he has written to any other of the poets of our day—"

"No, sir?" said she, quickly. "Not to Master Jonson?"

"Not that I am aware of, sweet lady," said he, "though he hath sometimes mes-sages to send, as you may suppose, by one coming from the court. And I marvel not that your father should put store by this letter that speaks well of his work—"

"Your pardon, good sir, but 'tis not so," said Judith, calmly. "Doubtless if the King commend my father's writing, that showeth that his Majesty is skilled and learned, as you say; and my father was no doubt pleased enough—as who would not be?—by such a mark of honor; but as for setting great value on it, I assure you

he did not: nay, he gave it to Julius Shawe. And will you read it, good sir?—I remem-ber me there was something in it about the ancients."

"'Tis but a rough guess that I can make," said he, regarding the paper. "But it seems that the King had received at the hands of one Eugene Collins the book of a comedy of your father's that had been presented before his Majesty when he was recently in London. And very diligently, he says, he has read through the same; and finds it right subtly conceived, with many beau-ties and delights, and such ornaments as are to be approved by an ingenious mind. It is true his Majesty hints that there may be parts of the play more calculated than might be to move the laughter of the vul-gar; but you would not have a critic have nothing but praise?—and the King's praise is high indeed. And then he goes on to say that as regards your father's future work, he would in the most friendly man-ner admonish him to study the great mas-ters of the comic art; that is, Menander the Athenian, and the Romans Plautus and Te-rentius, who—who—what says the King? —less studied to capture the applause of the vulgar than to lash the vices of the day as with whips. And these he highly commends as being of great service to the state; and would have your father be the like: teachers of virtue, and also props and aids to those whom God hath placed to rule over the people. He would have your fa-ther be among these public benefactors; and then he adds that, when occasion serves, he will not fail to extend his royal favor to your father and his associates; and so commends him to the protection of God. Nay, 'tis a right friendly letter; there is none in the land that would not be proud of it; 'tis not every day nor with every one that King James would take such trouble and play the part of tutor."

He handed her the letter, and she pro-ceeded to fold it up carefully again and put it in her satchel. She said nothing, but she hoped that these phrases of com-mendation would remain fixed in his mind when that he was returned to Lon-don.

And then there was a moment of em-barrassment—or at least of constraint. He had never been so near the town with her before (for his praise of her father's comedy, as they walked together, had taken some time) and there before them were the orchards and mud walls, and, further off, the spire of the church among the trees. She did not like to bid him go, and he seemed loath to say farewell, he probably having some dim notion that, now he had seen the end of the play and also this letter, there might be some difficulty in finding an excuse for another meeting.

"When do you return to London?" said she, for the sake of saying something. "Or may you return? I hope, good sir, your prospects are showing brighter; it must be hard for one of your years to pass the time in idleness."

"The time that I have spent in these parts," said he, "has been far more pleasant and joyful to me than I could have imagined—you may easily guess why, dear Mistress Judith. And now, when there is some prospect of my being able to go, I like it not; so many sweet hours have been passed here, the very fields and meadows around have acquired a charm—"

"Nay, but, good sir," said she, a little breathlessly, "at your time of life you would not waste the days in idleness."

"In truth it has been a gracious idleness!" he exclaimed.

"At your time of life," she repeated, quickly, "why, to be shut up in a farm—"

"The Prince Ferdinand," said he, "though I would not compare myself with him, found the time pass pleasantly and sweetly enough, as I reckon, though he was shut up in a cave. But then there was the fair Miranda to be his companion. There is no Ariel to work such a charm for me, else do you think I could ever bring myself to leave so enchanting a neighborhood?"

"Good sir," said she (in some anxiety to get away), "I may not ask the reason of your being in hiding, though I wish you well, and would fain hear there was no further occasion for it. And I trust there may be none when next you come to Warwickshire, and that those of our household who have a better right to speak for it than I, will have the chance of entertaining you. And now I would bid you farewell."

"No, dear Judith!" he exclaimed, with a kind of entreaty in his voice. "Not altogether? Why, look at the day!—would you have me say farewell to you on such a day of gloom and cloud? Surely you will let me take away a brighter picture of you, and Warwick-

shire, and of our brief meetings in these quiet spots—if go I must. In truth I know not what may happen to me; I would speak plainer; but I am no free agent; I can but beg of you to judge me charitably, if ever you hear aught of me—"

And here he stopped abruptly and paused, considering, and obviously irresolute and perplexed.

"Why," said he at length, and almost to himself—"why should I go away at all? I will carry logs—if needs be—or anything. Why should I go?"

She knew instantly what he meant; and knew, also, that it was high time for her to escape from so perilous a situation.

"I pray you pardon me, good sir; but I must go. Come, Don."

"But one more meeting, sweet Mistress Judith," he pleaded, "on a fairer day than this—you will grant as much?"

"I may not promise," said she; "but indeed I leave with you my good wishes; and so, farewell!"

"God shield you, dearest lady," said he, bowing low; "you leave with me also a memory of your kindness that will remain in my heart."

Well, there was no doubt that she felt very much relieved when she had left him and was nearing the town; and yet she had a kind of pity for him too, as she thought of his going away by himself to that lonely farm: one so gentle, and so grateful for company, being shut up there on this gloomy day. Whereas she was going back to a cheerful house; Prudence was coming round to spend the afternoon with them, and help to mark the new napery; and then in the evening the whole of them, her father included, were going to sup at Dr. Hall's, who had purchased a dishful of ancient coins in one of his peregrinations, and would have them come and examine them. Perhaps, after all, that reference to Miranda was not meant to apply to her. It was but natural he should speak of Miranda, having just finished the play. And carrying logs: he could not mean carrying logs for her father; that would be a foolish jest. No, no; he would remain at the farm and spend the time as best he could; and then, when this cloud blew over, he would return to London, and carry with him (as she hoped) some discreet rumor of the new work of her father's that he had praised so highly, and perchance some mention of the compliments paid by the King; and if, in course of time, the young gentleman should make his way back to Stratford again, and come to see them at New Place, and if his pleasant manner and courtesy proved to be quite irresistible, so that she had to allow the wizard's prophecy to come true in spite of herself, why, then, it was the hand of fate, and none of her doing, and she would have to accept her destiny with as good a grace as might be.

As she was going into the town she met Tom Quiney. He was on the other side of the roadway, and after one swift glance at her, he lowered his eyes, and would have passed on without speaking. And then it suddenly occurred to her that she would put her pride in her pocket. She knew quite well that her maidenly dignity had been wounded by his suspicions, and that she ought to let him go his own way if he chose. But, on the other hand (and this she did not know), there was in her nature an odd element of what might be called boyish generosity—of frankness and common-sense and good comradeship. And these two had been very stanch comrades in former days, each being in a curious manner the protector of the other; for while she many a time came to his aid —being a trifle older than he, and always ready with her quick feminine wit and ingenuity when they were both of them likely to get into trouble—he, on his side, was her shield and bold champion by reason of his superior stature and his strength, and his terrible courage in face of bulls or barking dogs and the like. For the moment she only thought of him as her old companion; and she was a good-natured kind of creature, and frank and boyish in her ways, and so she stepped across the road, though there was some mud about.

"Why can't we be friends?" said she.

"You have enough of other friends," said he.

It was a rebuff; but still—she would keep down her girlish pride.

"I hope you are not going away from the country?" said she.

He did not meet her look; his eyes were fixed on the ground.

"What is there to keep me in it?" was his answer.

"Why, what is there to keep any of us in it?" she said. "Heaven's mercy, if we were all to run away when we found something or another not quite to our liking, what a fine thing that would be! Nay, I hope there is no truth in it," she continued, looking at him, and not without some memories of their escapades together when they were boy and girl. "'Twould grieve many—indeed it would. I pray you think better of it. If for no other, for my sake: we used to be better friends."

There were two figures now approaching.

"Oh, here come Widow Clemms and her daughter," she said; "a rare couple. 'Twill be meat and drink to them to carry back a story. No matter. Now, fare you well; but pray think better of it; there be many that would grieve if you went away."

He stole a look at her as she passed on: perhaps there was a trifle more than usual of color in her radiant and sunny face, because of the approach of the two women. It was a lingering kind of look that he sent after her; and then he, too, turned and went on his way—cursing the parson.

CHAPTER XXIV.
A VISITOR.

MASTER LEOFRIC HOPE, on leaving Judith, returned to the farm, but not to the solitude that had awakened her commiseration. When he entered his room, which was at the back of the house, and facing the southern horizon (that alone showed some streaks of sunlight on this gloomy day), he found a stranger there— and a stranger who had evidently some notion of making himself comfortable, for he had opened the window, and was now sitting on the sill, and had just begun to smoke his pipe. His hat, his sword, and sword-belt he had flung on the table.

For a second the proper owner of the apartment knew not who this new tenant might be—he being dark against the light; but the next second he had recognized him, and that with no good grace.

"What the devil brings you here?" said he, sulkily.

"A hearty welcome, truly!" the other said, with much complacency. "After all my vexation in finding thee out! A goodly welcome for an old friend! But no matter, Jack—come, hast naught to offer one to drink? I have ridden from

Banbury this morning; and the plague take me if I had not enough trouble ere I found the hare in her form. But 'tis snug—'tis snug. The place likes me; though I thought by now you might have company, and entered with care. Come, man, be more friendly! Will you not ask me to sit? Must I call the landlady—or the farmer's wife—myself, and beg for a cup of something on so hot a day? Where be your manners, Gentleman Jack?"

"What the devil brings you into Warwickshire?" the other repeated, as he threw his hat on the table, and dropped into a chair, and stretched out his legs, without a further look at his companion.

"Nay, 'tis what the devil keeps thee here—that is the graver question—though I know the answer right well. Come, Jack, be reasonable! 'Tis for thy good I have sought thee out. What, man, would you ruin us both?—for I tell thee, the end is pressing and near."

Seeing that his unwilling host would not even turn his eyes toward him, he got down from the window-sill, and came along to the table, and took a chair. He was a short, stout young man, of puffy face and red hair, good-natured in look, but with a curious glaze in his light blue-gray eyes that told of the tavern and himself being pretty close companions. His dress had some show of ornament about it, though it was rather travel-stained and shabby; he wore jewelled rings in his ears; and the handkerchief which he somewhat ostentatiously displayed, if the linen might have been whiter, was elaborately embroidered with thread of Coventry blue. For the rest, he spoke pleasantly and good-humoredly, and was obviously determined not to take offense at his anything but hearty reception.

"Hoy-day," said he, with a laugh, "what a bother I had with the good dame here, that would scarce let me come in! For how knew I what name you might be dancing your latest galliard in?—not plain Jack Orridge, I'll be bound!—what is't, your worship?—or your lordship, perchance?—nay, but a lord would look best in the eyes of a daughter of Will Shakespeare, that loveth to have trumpets and drums going, and dukes and princes stalking across his boards. But 'fore Heaven, now, Jack," said he, interrupting himself, and sending an appealing look round the room, "have you naught to drink in the house? Came you ever to my lodging and found such scurvy entertainment?"

The reluctant host left the apartment for a second or two, and presently returned, followed by the farmer's wife, who placed on the table a jug of small beer, and some bread and cheese. The bread and cheese did not find much favor with the new-comer, but he drank a large horn of the beer, and took to his pipe again.

"Come, Jack, be friendly," said he; "'tis for thine own good I have sought thee out."

"I would you would mind your own business," the other said, with a sullen frown remaining on his face.

"Mine and yours are one, as I take it, good coz," his companion said, coolly; and then he added, in a more friendly way: "Come, come, man, you know we must sink or swim together. And sinking it will be, if you give not up this madcap chase. Nay, you carry the jest too far, *mon ami*. 'Twas a right merry tale at the beginning—the sham wizard, and your coquetting with Will Shakespeare's daughter to while away the time; 'twas a prank would make them roar at the Cranes in the Vintry; and right well done, I doubt not—for, in truth, if you were not such a gallant gentleman, you might win to a place in the theatres as well as any of them; but to come back here again—to hide yourself away again—and when I tell you they will no longer forbear, but will clap thee into jail if they have not their uttermost penny—why, 'tis pure moonshine madness to risk so much for a jest!"

"I tell thee 'tis no jest at all!" the other said, angrily. "In Heaven's name, what brought you here?"

"Am I to have no care of myself, then, that am your surety, and have their threats from hour to hour?"

He laughed in a stupid kind of way, and filled out some more beer and drank it off thirstily.

"We had a merry night, last night, at Banbury," said he. "I must pluck a hair of the same wolf to-day. And what say you? No jest? Nay, you look sour enough to be virtuous, by my life, or to get into a pulpit and preach a sermon against fayles and tick-tack, as wiles of the devil. No jest? Have you been overthrown at last—by a country wench? Must you take to the plough, and grow turnips? Why, I should as soon expect to see Gentleman Jack consort with the Finsbury archers, or go a-ducking to Islington ponds! Our Gentleman Jack a farmer! The price of wheat, goodman Dickon?—how fatten your pigs?—will the fine weather last, think you? Have done with this foolery, man! If all comes to the worst, 'twere better we should take to the road, you and I, and snip a purse when chance might serve."

"You?" said his companion, with only half-concealed contempt. "The first click of a pistol would find you behind a hedge."

"Why, old lad," said the other (who did not seem to have heard that remark, during his pouring out of another hornful of beer), "I know you better than you know yourself. This time, you say, 'tis serious—ay, but how many times before hast thou said the same? And ever the wench is the fairest of her kind, and a queen! For how long?—a fortnight!—perchance three weeks. Oh, the wonder of her! And 'tis all a love-worship; and the praising of her hands and ankles; and Tom Morley's ditty about a lover and his lass,

'That through the green corn fields did pass
    In the pretty spring-time,
        Ring-a-ding-ding!'

Ay, for a fortnight; and then Gentleman Jack discovers that some wench of the Bankside hath brighter eyes and freer favors than the country beauty, and you hear no more of him until he has ne'er a penny left, and comes begging his friends to be surety for him, or to write to his grandam at Oxford, saying how virtuous a youth he is, and in how sad a plight. Good Lord, that were an end!—should you have to go back to the old dame at last, and become tapster—no more acting of your lordship and worship—what ho, there! thou lazy knave, a flask of Rhenish, and put speed into thy rascal heels!"

The cloud on his companion's face had been darkening.

"Peace, drunken fool!" he muttered—but between his teeth, for he did not seem to wish to anger this stranger.

"Come, come, man," the other said, jovially, "unwitch thee! unwitch thee! Fetch back thy senses. What?—wouldst thou become a jest and by-word for every tavern table between the Temple and the Tower? Nay, I can not believe it of thee, Jack. Serious? Ay, as you have been

twenty times before. Lord, what a foot and ankle!—and she the queen o' the world—the rose and crown and queen o' the world—and the sighing o' moonlight nights—

    ' Mignonne, tant je vous aime,
        Mais vous ne m'aimez pas'—

and we are all to be virtuous and live cleanly for the rest of our lives; but the next time you see Gentleman Jack, lo, you, now!—'tis at the Bear-house; his pockets lined with angels wrung from old Ely of Queenhithe; and as for his company—Lord! Lord! And as it hath been before, so 'twill be again, as said Solomon the wise man; only that this time—mark you now, Jack—this time it were well if you came to your senses at once; for I tell thee that Ely and the rest of them have lost all patience, and they know this much of thy Stratford doings, that if they can not exactly name thy whereabout, they can come within a stone's-cast of thee. And if I come to warn thee—as is the office of a true friend and an old companion—why shouldst thou sit there with a sulky face, man? Did I ever treat thee so in Fetter Lane?"

While he had been talking, a savory odor had begun to steal into the apartment, and presently the farmer's wife appeared, and proceeded to spread the cloth for dinner. Her lodger had given no orders; but she had taken his return as sufficient signal, and naturally she assumed that his friend would dine with him. Accordingly, in due course, there was placed on the board a smoking dish of cow-heel and bacon, with abundance of ale and other garnishings; and as this fare seemed more tempting to the new-comer than the bread and cheese, he needed no pressing to draw his chair to the table. It was not a sumptuous feast; but it had a beneficial effect on both of them—sobering the one, and rendering the other somewhat more placable. Master Leofric Hope—as he had styled himself—was still in a measure taciturn; but his guest—whose name, it appeared, was Francis Lloyd—had ceased his uncomfortable banter; and indeed all his talk now was of the charms and wealth of a certain widow who lived in a house near to Gray's Inn, on the road to Hampstead. He had been asked to dine with the widow; and he gave a magniloquent description of the state she kept—of her serving-men, and her furniture, and her plate, and the manner in which she entertained her friends.

"And why was I," said he—"why was poor Frank Lloyd—that could scarce get the wherewithal to pay for a rose for his ear—why was he picked out for so great a favor? Why, but that he was known to be a friend of handsome Jack Orridge. 'Where be your friend Master Orridge, now?' she says, for she hath sometimes a country trick in her speech, hath the good lady. 'Business, madam—affairs of great import,' I say to her, 'keep him still in the country.' Would I tell her the wolves were waiting to rend you should you be heard of anywhere within London city? 'Handsome Jack, they call him, is't not so?' says she. Would I tell her thou wert called 'Gentleman Jack?' as if thou hadst but slim right to the title. Then says she to one of the servants, 'Fill the gentleman's cup.' Lord, Jack, what a sherris that was!—'twas meat and drink; a thing to put marrow in your bones—cool and clear it was, and rich withal—cool on the tongue and warm in the stomach. 'Fore Heaven, Jack, if thou hast not ever a cup of that wine ready for me when I visit thee, I will say thou hast no more gratitude than a toad. And then says she to all the company (raising her glass the while), 'Absent friends'; but she nods and smiles to me, as one would say: 'We know whom we mean; we know.' Lord, that sherris, Jack! I have the taste of it in my mouth now; I dream o' nights there is a jug of it by me."

"Dreaming or waking, there is little else in thy head," said the other; "nor in thy stomach, either."

"Is it a bargain, Jack?" he said, looking up from his plate and regarding his companion with a fixed look.

"A bargain?"

"I tell thee 'tis the only thing will save us now." This Frank Lloyd said with more seriousness than he had hitherto shown. "Heavens, man, you must cease this idling; I tell thee they are not in the frame for further delay. 'Tis the Widow Becket or the King's highway, one or t'other, if you would remain a free man; and as for the highway, why, 'tis an uncertain trade, and I know that Gentleman Jack is no lover of broken heads. What else would you? Live on in a hole like this? Nay, but they would not suffer you. I tell you they are ready to hunt you out at this present moment. Go be-

yond seas? Ay, and forsake the merry nights at the Cranes and the Silver Hind? When thy old grandam is driven out of all patience, and will not even forth with a couple of shillings to buy you wine and radish for your breakfast, 'tis a bad case. Wouldst go down to Oxford and become tapster?—Gentleman Jack, that all of them think hath fine fat acres in the west country, and a line of ancestors reaching back to Noah the sailor or Adam gardener. Come, man, unwitch thee! Collect thy senses. If this sorry jest of thine be growing serious—and I confess I had some thought of it, when you would draw on Harry Condell for the mere naming of the wench's name—then, o' Heaven's name, come away and get thee out of such foolery! I tell thee thou art getting near an end, o' one way or another; and wouldst thou have me broken too, that have ever helped thee, and shared my last penny with thee?"

"Broken?" said his friend, with a laugh. "If there be any in the country more broken than you and I are at this moment, Frank, I wish them luck of their fortunes. But still there is somewhat for you. You have not pawned those jewels in your ears yet. And your horse—you rode hither, said you not?—well, I trust it is a goodly beast, for it may have to save thee from starvation ere long."

"Nay, ask me not how I came by the creature," said he, "but 'tis not mine, I assure ye."

"Whose, then?"

Master Frank Lloyd shrugged his shoulders.

"If you can not guess my errand," said he, "you can not guess who equipped me."

"Nay," said his friend, who was now in a much better humor, "read me no riddles, Frank. I would fain know who knew thee so little as to lend thee a horse and see thee ride forth with it. Who was't, Frank?"

His companion looked up and regarded him.

"The Widow Becket," he answered, coolly.

"What?" said the other, laughing. "Art thou so far in the good dame's graces, and yet would have me go to London and marry her?"

"'Tis no laughing matter, Master Jack, as you may find out ere long," the other said. "The good lady lent me the horse, 'tis true; else how could I have come all the way into Warwickshire?—ay, and lent me an angel or two to appease the villain landlords.. I tell thee she is as bountiful as the day. Lord, what a house!—I'll take my oath that Master Butler hath a good fat capon and a bottle of claret each evening for his supper—if he have not, his face belieth him. And think you she would be niggard with Handsome Jack? Nay, but a gentleman must have his friends; ay, and his suppers at the tavern, when the play is over; and store of pieces in his purse to make you good company. Why, man, thy fame would spread through the Blackfriars, I warrant you: where is the hostess that would not simper and ogle and court'sy to Gentleman Jack, when that he came among them, slapping the purse in his pouch?"

"'Tis a fair picture," his friend said. "Thy wits have been sharpened by thy long ride, Frank. And think you the buxom widow would consent, were one to make bold and ask her? Nay, nay; 'tis thy dire need hath driven thee to this excess of fancy."

For answer Master Lloyd proceeded to bring forth a small box, which he opened, and took therefrom a finger ring. It was a man's ring, of massive setting; the stone of a deep blood red, and graven with an intaglio of a Roman bust. He pushed it across the table.

"The horse was lent," said he, darkly. "That—if it please you—you may keep and wear."

"What mean you?" Leofric Hope said, in some surprise.

"'I name no thing, and I mean no thing,'" said he, quoting a phrase from a popular ballad. "If you understand not, 'tis a pity. I may not speak more plainly. But bethink you that poor Frank Lloyd was not likely to have the means of purchasing thee such a pretty toy, much as he would like to please his old friend. Nay, canst thou not see, Jack? 'Tis a message, man! More I may not say. Take it and wear it, good lad; and come back boldly to London; and we will face the harpies, and live as free men, ere a fortnight be over. What?—must I speak? Nay, an' you understand not, I will tell no more."

He understood well enough; and he sat for a second or two moodily regarding the ring; but he did not take it up. Then he rose from the table, and began to walk up and down the room.

"Frank," said he, "couldst thou but see this wench—"

"Nay, nay, spare me the catalogue," his friend answered, quickly. "I heard thee declare that Ben Jonson had no words to say how fair she was: would you better his description and overmaster him? And fair or not fair, 'tis all the same with thee; any petticoat can bewitch thee out of thy senses: Black Almaine or New Almaine may be the tune, but 'tis ever the same dance; and such a heaving of sighs and despair!—

'Thy gown was of the grassy green,
    Thy sleeves of satin hanging by;
Which made thee be our harvest queen—
    And yet thou wouldst not love me.'

'Tis a pleasant pastime, friend Jack; but there comes an end. I know not which be the worse, wenches or usurers, for landing a poor lad in jail; but both together, Jack—and that is thy case—they are not like to let thee escape. 'Tis not to every one in such a plight there cometh a talisman like that pretty toy there: beshrew me, what a thing it is in this world to have a goodly presence!"

He now rose from the table and went to the door, and called aloud for some one to bring him a light. When that was brought, and his pipe set going, he sat him down on the bench by the empty fire-place, for the seat seemed comfortable, and there he smoked with much content, while his friend continued to pace up and down the apartment, meditating over his own situation, and seemingly not over well pleased with the survey.

Presently something in one of the pigeon-holes over the fire-place attracted the attention of the visitor; and having nothing better to do (for he would leave his friend time to ponder over what he had said), he rose and pulled forth a little bundle of sheets of paper that opened in his hand as he sat down again.

"What's this, Jack?" said he. "Hast become playwright? Surely all of this preachment is not in praise of the fair damsel's eyebrows?"

His friend turned round; saw what he had got hold of, and laughed.

"That, now," said he, "were something to puzzle the wits with, were one free to go to London. I had some such jest in mind; but perchance 'twas more of idleness that made me copy out the play."

"'Tis not yours, then? Whose?" said Master Frank Lloyd, looking over the pages with some curiosity.

"Whose? Why, 'tis by one Will Shakespeare, that you may have heard of. Would it not puzzle them, Frank? Were it not a good jest, now, to lay it before some learned critic and ask his worship's opinion? Or to read it at the Silver Hind as of thy writing? Would not Dame Margery weep with joy? Out upon the Mermaid!—have we not poets of our own?"

He had drawn near, and was looking down at the sheets that his friend was examining.

"I tell thee this, Jack," the latter said, in his cool way, "there is more than a jest to be got out of a play by Will Shakespeare. Would not the booksellers give us the price of a couple of nags for it if we were pressed so far?"

"Mind thine own business, fool!" was the angry rejoinder; and ere he knew what had happened his hands were empty.

And at that same moment, away over there in Stratford town, Judith was in the garden, trying to teach little Bess Hall to dance, and merrily laughing the while. And when the dancing lesson was over she would try a singing lesson; and now the child was on Judith's shoulder, and had hold of her bonny sun-brown curls.

"Well done, Bess; well done! Now again—

'The hunt is up—the hunt is up—
Awake, my lady dear!
O a morn in spring is the sweetest thing
Cometh in all the year!'

Well done indeed! Will not my father praise thee, lass; and what more wouldst thou have for all thy pains?"

FROM THE MOUNTAIN-TOP.

DEAR World, looking down from the highest of heights that my feet can attain,
I see not the smoke of your cities, the dust of your highway and plain;
Over all your dull moors and morasses a veil the blue atmosphere folds,
And you might be made wholly of mountains for aught that my vision beholds.

Dear World, I look down, and am grateful that so we all sometimes may stand
Above our own every-day level, and know that our nature is grand
In its possible glory of climbing; in the hill-tops that beckon and bend
So close over every mortal he scarcely can choose but ascend.

Though here, O my World, we miss something—the sweet multitudinous sound
Of leaves in the forest a-flutter, of rivulets lisping around,
The smell of wild pastures in blossom, of fresh earth upturned by the plough—
The uplands and all the green hill-sides lead the way to the mountain's brow.

One world; there is no separation; the same earth above and below;
Up here is the river's cloud-cradle; down there is its fullness and flow;
My voice joins the voice of your millions who upward in weariness grope,
And the hills bear the burden to heaven—humanity's anguish and hope!

Dear World, lying quiet and lovely in a shimmer of gossamer haze,
Beneath the soft films of your mantle I can feel your heart beat as I gaze;
I know you by what you aspire to, by the look that on no face can be
Save in moments of high consecration; you are showing your true self to me.

Dear World, I behold but your largeness; I forget that aught petty or mean
Ever marred the vast sphere of your beauty, over which as a lover I lean;
And not by our flaws will God judge us; His love keeps our noblest in sight:
Dear World, our low life sinks behind us; we look up to His infinite height!

THE GREAT HALL OF WILLIAM RUFUS.

I.

WILLIAM RUFUS once built himself a great banqueting hall.

When he ascended the throne of his father, William the Conqueror, two royal palaces came into his hands, which were destined to play a conspicuous part in the future history of England. They were both on the north side of the Thames. One was just outside the walled city of London, and stood directly upon the water's edge. The other was several miles further up the river, on a low meadow island, which lay quite secluded, close under the well-wooded river-shore. The crooked stream made one of its abrupt curves midway between them, in this instance as sharp as a right angle, so that, in ascending it from London, the battlements of the one had long gone out of sight before the turrets of the other came into view. The city palace was really part of a castle which had been built on the foundation of an old Roman citadel. The country palace was almost the wing of a monastery, which had risen on the site of an ancient Saxon church. When Rufus arrived on the scene the castellated palace was new and still unfinished, just as it had been left by the Conqueror; but the monastic establishment—palace, convent, and abbey in a single pile—stood complete, just as it had been built by the Conqueror's predecessor.

He determined to distinguish himself upon both of them, and he did, but in the diverse fashion which might have been expected from the two opposite sides of his character. William Rufus is generally most vividly remembered on account of his fatal adventure with an arrow in the New Forest, but his best claim to present recollection lies in the two very striking additions which he made to these royal edifices, both of which additions are extant, and one of which—the one we are now interested in—met with quite as accidental an experience as the arrow, in glancing from the direction of its immediate aim, and thereby doing excellent service to the state. The arrow went to the

EDITOR'S NOTE.—The Magazine is indebted to the courtesy of George Scharf, Esq., Keeper of the National Portrait Gallery, London, for assistance in selecting the most authentic and characteristic portraits of English historical personages for the illustration of this article.

heart of but one tyrant; the Hall knocked over a whole dynasty of such.

Rufus first took hold of the unfinished fortress with all the military vigor which was his wont, completing the circuits of its walls, building a huge council-chamber, and carrying up the great white tower whose image is still reflected in the bosom of the Thames. But what interests us especially now is the nature of the "improvement" which this reckless and notorious personage thought it desirable to make in its monastic companion on the island up the river.

As we may well suppose, the associations and traditions of this meadow isle were rather too holy to be much to his taste. It had been the seat of a church for three or four hundred years. Not very long before, King Edgar and the famous Dunstan had turned the church into a Benedictine monastery, and enriched it with lands and gold. King Canute, when he came along, had shown a grave and good disposition by making it his royal abode, and putting himself and his courtiers on the best of terms with the abbot and monks. All of these facts, together with some superstitions, working a divine enthusiasm into St. Edward's soul, led him to decide that this should be the site of the grandest minster which England had ever seen, dedicated, like its predecessor, to St. Peter.

Canute's palace having been burned down, the Confessor built another in its place. Before this, however, he had razed the old monastery to the ground, and began that great minster the memories of whose magnificence continue to this day. He devoted to it a tenth of all his substance. When finished, it stood up a stupendous Norman pile, looking as if one of the great Continental abbeys had been taken up bodily and set down on English soil. The rude and heavy Saxon churches retired into insignificance before its massive semicircular arcades, its great square bell towers, its rich carvings, and its stained windows. As to the palace, which stood between its eastern apse and the main channel of the river, we know not how it appeared, except that it must have partaken somewhat of the same style under a castellated form. Fitz-Stephen, a hundred years after, speaks of it as "exalting its head and stretching wide—an incomparable structure, furnished with bastions and a breastwork."

It was very natural in the Conqueror, with his claim to the throne under the will of the Confessor, to feel at home under the familiar Norman pile, and to decide that this should be the place where he would establish his court and receive the fealty of his subjects.

But a change came over all of the Confessor's and much of the Conqueror's dream when William Rufus took up his quarters here. This sovereign, instead of devoting one-tenth of all his substance to the Church, would have taken all its tenths from it if he could. Instead, also, of giving his attention to the civil duties of his post, conciliating his new subjects, and prudently administering the laws, he employed his leisure, when not quarreling with somebody, in the wildest festivity and profligacy which his royal prerogatives could open a field for. The abbot and monks hard by stood aghast, and so did after a while the archbishops and bishops all over the kingdom, for besides this devil's dance under their very noses, he laid his rapacious hand, without stint and everywhere, on their sacred funds. He did not shrink from taking even their golden shrines and silver chalices. Religion was a scorn to him, and the monks a derision.

After a while the building fever set in with him again. He had reared a tower, known to this day as "The Tower," in the other palace: what should he have here? He evidently scouted the whole concern as it stood, and projected a brand-new palace on the grandest possible scale. It was to cover the green meadows and gardens on the north of the present one, and put the Abbey out of sight behind it to any one coming up the river. What would be more consistent with his character than that he should build a banqueting hall! The Confessor had begun with a church. But now the Church itself should blush for what he was going to put up on this holy ground. He determined to make it a rival also to the Abbey both in size and splendor. None of the records intimate that he set about it exactly with such a purpose, but the event justifies the surmise.

A banqueting hall in itself was nothing new or out of keeping. Every baronial castle had one. This old palace had a large one. Such an apartment was often useful as a hall of business. But Rufus never dreamed of public business on the Conqueror's scale. He had a magnificent soul, but it ran all into a hunger for glory and a thirst for pleasure. Before his new temple of Bacchus and Venus—for it was nothing more—the old Abbey, having reddened to the ears for shame, was next to turn pale with indignation. Through the open windows of the Hall the chanting monks should hear the outbursts of royal revelry and voices in ribald song. No greater congregation should the abbot get into the one than the king would put into the other.

As we say, the event gives color to this suggestion. The building was fully two hundred and forty feet long, nearly seventy feet wide, and proportionately high. Whether in derision, or only to follow the Angevine fashion of the time, its style was ecclesiastical: a noble nave divided by heavy round columns from long-drawn aisles on either side. With dimensions so close upon those of the Abbey as it then was, its first aspect must have been that of a church on a cathedral scale. It was enough to make the Confessor turn in his shrine.

Turlogh O'Brien, King of Ireland, getting wind of this great project of a palace, sent over a fine present of oak from the oak forests of Shillelagh. The generous Irishman would have held his hand if he had known that Rufus, not long before, had been taking a look at his own dominions, from a rock on the coast of Wales, with the shout, "That country shall be mine! my ships shall bridge across that sea!" This was an ominous interchange, in view of the way in which the shillelagh has played its part over the heads of British counsels ever since.

At the end of two years, in 1099, Rufus returned from Normandy to find his Hall ready for his inspection. He strode into it with a throng of steel-clad barons at his heels. To his nobles its size was stupendous. Their own halls were but closets beside it. Some of them exclaimed that "it was too large; larger than it should have been." But the king declared that "it was not half so large as it should have been, and that it was only a bedchamber in comparison with the building he intended to make."

Before we go on, the reader must form an idea of how this remarkable edifice stood in relation to the architectural group at that time presented to the eye. It will help him in imagining the scenes which afterward took place within and around it. If he will place himself at the north—that is, down the river, as it happened to flow just here—he will have the Abbey extending westward on the right, and the old palace in a cluster on the left, with an inclosed quadrangle, partly wall, partly cloister, connecting them. The Great Hall of William Rufus stands forward of these, its front gable facing him, and its rear gable abutting partly upon the palace, partly upon this palace yard. It is therefore at right angles with the Abbey. Rufus has laid out in front of it a new quadrangle, around which the new palace buildings are to rise. Other buildings did, in the course of ages, gather about it, but not those of his palace. Yet now, after the lapse of nearly eight centuries, this open space in front of the Hall is still called "the *New* Palace Yard."

The red-haired monarch held only one banquet in his new Hall. He kept his Whit-Sunday festival in it, not, one might be sure, in the Abbey. We may imagine his convivial court and retainers in full and multitudinous session round groaning boards, loaded heavily with gigantic joints, after the barbaric Norse fashion, flowing with whole casks of wine, but the courtiers themselves costumed after the pink of Norman refinement, in long robes and trailing mantles, long hair curled with hot irons, and long-peaked shoes turned up like rams' horns, carousing, trolling drinking songs, listening to jesters and troubadours, gambling, quarreling, and what not!

Very soon after that, while his eyes and cheeks were aflame with the wine-cup, but while also in pursuit of a more manly banquet under the rafters of the New Forest, the arrow of Sir Walter Tirrel laid him dead under a greenwood tree, and what was left of him was marched, to the tune of the Church, though to the scandal of the time, into the consecrated precincts of Winchester Abbey, the tower of which very properly toppled over upon him soon afterward. He and King Canute now share the same stone coffin. Their bones are strange bedfellows.

II.

His brother and successor, Henry the First, found his hands full. The year 1100 opened a new era, not only in Eng-

land, but in the Great Hall. The tables were now to be laid for the long historic banquet of the state: the tables of eight centuries, thronged by the figures of thirty generations! Rufus had builded better than he knew.

Had Rufus and his brother Henry been rolled into one, the Conqueror would have come again. But the heritage of his powerful nature had been divided between them, and now, for the first time since his death, his prudence, foresight, and wisdom in civil administration were to appear.

The ship of state at that time was a crank-sided concern, trying to keep its balance as well as to make headway in a channel made treacherous and tumultuous by two opposing tides: the spirit of Norman baronism on one side, and the spirit of Anglo-Saxon freedom on the other. Rufus had plunged through the difficulty in the spirit of his celebrated saying, when once crossing to Normandy in a storm, "Kings never drown!" Henry took the helm at the moment of impending shipwreck, and by one adroit turn in his course saved both his throne and his people. He married Edith, the fair Saxon descendant of Alfred. Then the vessel righted itself. It was safe from his barons.

What a banquet was now held at her coronation and marriage festival in the Hall! for virtually the whole Saxon people sat down to it. "Never," says Palgrave, "since the battle of Hastings had there been such a joyous day as when Queen Maud [her Norman name], the descendant of Alfred, was crowned in the Abbey and feasted in the Great Hall." By the Norman nobles "the marriage was regarded," says Macaulay, "as a marriage between a white planter and a quadroon girl would now be regarded in Virginia." But "Godric," as they called the king, and "Godiva," as they called the queen, presided that day at a marriage feast which united his house with the English people forever.

The centuries began in round numbers—November 11, 1100—on that auspicious eve. The Saxons who crowded the vast hall, and looked into Edith's fair face beneath its cloud of golden hair, saw perhaps only the triumph of her race in her place on the dais beside her Norman lord. They saw Alfred, "the darling of England," again on the throne, and his blood again descending through the line of their future kings. Hardly deeper than this could

WILLIAM RUFUS, AND COINS OF HIS REIGN.
After Vertue's engraving.

have been the insight of the popular heart, and its reading of the auspice.

But Edith had come with the atmosphere of destiny around her. She had come from the court of the "murdered Duncan." She was the daughter of his son Malcolm Canmore, who himself had been restored to the crown on the "Stone of Fate" at Scone—the stone which bore a prophecy yet to be fulfilled in the throne and constitution of England; and in her appearance here, even as a princess of Scotland, she was an unrecognized daughter of destiny. She had brought with her the first influx of that Celtic blood which in five hundred years was to place a predicted Scottish monarch on the English throne. How much also was there unrecognized in her *then*, as the daughter of England, that we are *now* able to discern! —we who can read the presages of her appearing there in the light of events that have come. She brought with her, in bringing her race with her, the spirit and power as well as the memory of the ancient *Witena-gemôt*, the representative body which had "elected" kings, and without which kings could not reign. She brought with her, too, the spirit and power as well as the memory of an ideal king, who

had lived for the elevation of his people, in the closest ministration to their wants, who had saved them by the principles he had implanted among them, who had inspired them with a reverence for the *Law*. All this was mystically written on that sweet, devout face, because it was written in the fact that she was there. The Norman was slowly to retire; the Saxon was inevitably to rule. The coronation banquet of Edith, Queen of England, was a banquet of consequences and prophecies for England. It was a forecast of the coronation of the people!

III.

Fifty-four years from that day, Henry the Second, the son of Edith-Maud's daughter, by Earl Geoffrey Plantagenet, sat on that marble seat at his own coronation banquet, the first undisputed master of the realm.

Now blood was to tell. The Conqueror and King Alfred had not both come into the heart and brain of this leonine young monarch for naught. He wrought a metamorphosis in his kingdom which wrought a metamorphosis also in the Hall. A wassail-bowl before now has been turned into a font; so Rufus's banqueting Hall was

HENRY II.
From the effigy at Fontevrault.

turned, at the word of the king, into a consecrated Chamber of Justice. It was the reflection within its walls of the reign of law in the realm.

This fact revives the reminiscence of the primitive palace Hall, when it was the admitted extension of the palace peopleward, the gate at which the people entered into the presence of the king, to find him either at the head of the table to which he had invited them, or, what was more usually the case, on the seat of judgment, administering the law to them. One of the most ancient pictures we have of an early English king is as a judge, the head of a supreme tribunal, in the act of ex-

tending his power to reach the necessities of his subjects. And one of the sublimest ideals that we have of the English sovereign to-day is that he virtually sits upon every judgment-seat in his kingdom. Hence the word "court" has long dissociated itself from the king's palace, and now designates everywhere both a hall of justice and him who presides in it. It is the glamour of this name which at this point we see gathering about the Great Hall of William Rufus: the "court," in the sense which even republics can understand, had now begun to crystallize within these walls. Here the Roman code which the Normans brought over, here the Saxon principles to which the people clung, were to blend themselves more and more together in age after age, for here Henry the Second laid the foundations, in a distributive system of courts, of that science of jurisprudence whose practical superstructure became afterward so inwrought with the building that the name "Westminster Hall" grew into a popular name for the law itself.

The courts were still ambulatory, following the king wherever he journeyed in the kingdom, and were not permanently fixed in the Hall until several reigns later, but their places had been taken, and we shall not be anticipating any important details if we give at this point Palgrave's picture of the interior.

"The edifice and the tribunals," he says, "gave a reflected importance to and upon each other.... Upon the high dais stood the table of marble stone; here at the foot of the monarch sat the chancellor and his clerks when the seal was opened, and the public function annexed to the highest emblem of judicial authority, the sovereign's symbolical representation, was performed. Here, also, in the earliest period did the king in person, or those judges who held their places before the king himself, exercise the supreme criminal judicature. Even after all the changes in our jurisprudence there are still purposes for which the Chancery and the King's Bench are one.

"At the entrance of the Hall, on the left side, you passed the Exchequer. You may yet see over the doorway the grotesque effigies of the teller, with the quaint verses in which his duty is described. On the right are the judges of the Common Pleas. They were not fixed in the Hall until the promulgation of Magna Charta;

but Rufus first provided the habitation for them, to which they had become accustomed."

It indicates what a vast volume of space William Rufus had unwittingly provided when these four great courts could take up each its assigned position, and inclose itself behind a balustrade or seat itself upon a platform, and yet trench no more upon the roominess of the apartment as a royal banqueting room or public meeting hall than so many chancels or chapels could abridge the uses of a cathedral. It will now be necessary for the reader to carry them in his mind in any subsequent depiction of the place, most especially the two inclosures which occupied the upper end—the Court of Chancery on his right, the Court of King's Bench on his left. This arrangement, by which all four courts were in session under the same roof and in sight of one another, continued until the coronation of George the Fourth, when the Hall was cleared for the most splendid and costly banquet ever held in it—a banquet in the blaze of which all its ancient uses of every kind came to an end.

How familiar names go back to material circumstances! The "court," as we have seen, to the king's palace; the "King's Bench," to the marble slab, three feet wide and nineteen feet long, which was then raised on a conspicuous platform, but which now lies buried under the pavement beneath; the "Chancery," to the crossed timber-work, or lattice—*cancelli*—which from time immemorial had sought to guard from intrusion its sacred precinct; the "Exchequer," to the table covered with checkered work, on which the officers received and counted the revenues of the kingdom; the "Common Pleas," to the fact that a tribunal was first seen in the Hall where the "Commons" might bring their own controversies for adjustment—a court which has been well called "the most steady pillar of the kingdom's franchises."

What scenes, too, now fill the imagination as we look from this point down the vista of ages under the dark roof of Rufus's Hall! The group of scarlet and ermined judges, grandly bewigged, assembling in pomp or sitting in grave mystery and dignity before the eyes of the crowds also gathered here. The majesty of royalty itself is not greater than that of these, "their majesties" of the law. Here the scales of justice are held up, and here they tremble in all those passing centuries.

Here the hearts of generation after generation also tremble as they watch those exquisite balances on which hang life or death, property, security, or good name. Here even the destinies of the nation tremble between the weight of crowns and sceptres on the one hand, and the weight of a people's happiness and wealth on the other.

What a bench of chancellors and chief justices, too, is ranged along that southern wall! Gascoigne, and More, and Bacon, and Camden, and Holt, and Coke, and Mansfield, and Thurlow, and Eldon—we have not room to name them all.

Let us return now to Henry the Second, engaged in the supreme and characteristic conflict of his reign—a conflict which shook England—as he reached out his

RICHARD I.
From the effigy at Rouen, copied from "Archeologia" by permission of the Society of Antiquaries, London.

RICHARD II.
After Hollar.

taries of the realm on either side of him. Becket will not come, and afterward excommunicates the bishops who do. The time for bringing in the boar's head arrives. The usual flourish of trumpets is heard, loud and prolonged as it advances. To the astonishment of all, King Henry is seen in the procession, bearing the great dish, like a servitor, to the royal seat, and kneeling as he presents it to his royal son! The grand king has thrown his heart into the symbolic act; but that highly distinguished young man shows the quality of his character—the quality that led him to hold on fiercely to his crown and robes long after the ceremony was over—by lifting his head most magnificently on high, and looking around even "more stately than is his wont."

"Be glad, my good son!" exclaims the overwhelmed Archbishop of York: "there is not another prince in the world that hath such another server at his table!"

"Why dost marvel at that?" replies the

sceptre to enforce his great decree that all men should be equal before the law. The proud priest Becket resists the ordinance which would bring even the criminals of the Church under these secular courts in the Hall. Much of the battle is fought upon this very spot. The king is victorious, but he has reason to fear a clap of papal thunder which may shake the new fabric of his throne.

Now comes a banquet as solemn in its meaning to him, under its convivial forms, as a rite of the Church. In it all his solicitude concentrates itself, and produces a scene of self-abnegation as touching as it must have been remarkable to see. In order to provide against a possible decline of loyalty to himself in case the papal excommunication should fall upon his own person, he crowns his son Henry in the Abbey, and gathers his prelates, nobles, and people to the coronation banquet in the Hall. The young man sits under the "cloth of estate," with the high digni-

EDWARD I. ON THE GREAT SEAL.

THE CORONATION CHAIR.

From photograph by F. York, London.

precious youth. "My father, in doing it, thinketh it not more than becometh him, he, being born of princely blood only on the mother's side, served me that am a king born, having both a king to my father and a queen to my mother!" In oth-

IV.

But nineteen years after that day, September 3, 1189, Richard the First, the brother between them, who did his full share with the others in breaking his father's heart, holds a gorgeous banquet in the

PARLIAMENT OF EDWARD I.

er words, the son of an earl might well wait on the son of a king!—a remark worthy of the eldest brother of John. Happily this King Henry did not live.

Out of this banquet and coronation came the assassination of Becket, for it was his excommunication of the prelates which afterward excited the rage of the king.

Hall on his coronation day. His father now serves *him* by being out of the way.

The rude magnificence of the scene comes back to us in *Ivanhoe*, not so much in the story as in the general picture there given of the period. The new-made monarch, after a most royal consecration in the Abbey, now sits in the brilliantly

FLIGHT OF THE HORSES.
From drawing by H. M. Paget.

lighted Hall, amid all the prelates, barons, and nobles of his kingdom. The description by Sir Walter Scott will bring back to us the rich and costly dresses in which they appeared on such occasions. The scene at the evening meal in the mansion of Cedric the Saxon need only be imagined, on a more gorgeous scale, to revive the spectacle of that night: the table along the high dais at the upper end, covered with scarlet cloth, loaded with the choicest viands of the feast, its silver cups and flagons glittering under the light thrown from silver candelabra set with waxen torches; the scarlet canopy overhead emblazoned with the royal arms; the walls hung with rich tapestries; the floor of the dais covered with carpets, the remainder of the Hall with green rushes; the long and thronged tables extending laterally down the Hall in vistas before the king, who, repeating the lion visage inherited from his father, fills the eye at the centre in his high chair of state, with his greater prelates and barons in carved oaken chairs below him on either side. We hear also how the chief citizens of London served him in his cellar, the chief citizens of Winchester in his kitchen, and the greatest of the earls about his person.

But there was a banquet also of blood, into which this banquet ran, that has made the scene memorable to this day. Scott has woven the spirit of it into his famous romance, but the characteristic event took place here. The Jews had been warned off the premises by especial decree, for fear of their "enchantments." But they were slow to believe that their "disabilities" went so far as this. The good Rufus had never displayed any such weakness. He had liked them so well as they were that he would not even let them become Christians. The more they were Jews, the more welcome they were. How now should the coming hero of the Crusades, who was hurrying up this very coronation in order to be off to "the sepulchre in stubborn Jewry"—how should he distinguish himself without their shekels? Had he not said that he would sell London itself to the highest bidder? So Isaac of York, or a relation of his, and many well-lined brethren of the Hebrew persuasion, incredulous of any such antipathy in the royal heart, covertly mingled with the torch-lit crowd in the New Palace Yard, concealing the whole apparatus of their magical arts, namely, gifts of gold, silver, and precious stones, under the folds of their ample gabardines. They succeeded in getting inside the triple Norman doors before they were detected. We may be sure that the time they had chosen was *after* the boar's head had gone up to the king, with its usual flourish of trumpets, and upon the intruders. There was a dreadful scuffle on the threshold, somewhat stifled, however, lest the king should hear. The crowd outside—burghers, yeomanry, and Saxon churls—rose from their cakes and ale to take part in it. What the Lords

THE GREAT ROOF.
From drawing by H. Hawley.

the odor of swine's flesh had also gone up to the roof in the fumes of the wine, which had now begun to flow more freely than ever. The carousing was at its height. In another moment they would have wrapped their spells about the king, when all at once the pious Templar Sir Brian de Bois Guilbert, and the gentle Reginald Front de Bœuf, or, if not precisely they, some of that kind, horrified at the sight of the yellow faces at the door, leaped from their places and threw themselves had thus begun, the Commons undertook to finish; Gurth laid on with his cudgel, and Wamba with a gammon of bacon. The king shouted from within, "What is all this noise to-day?" The door-keeper answered, "Nothing; only the boys rejoice, and are merry at heart"—for which mendacious statement to the really disappointed Crusader he was afterward dragged to death at the tails of horses. Whence some might conclude that Isaac of York was wise in insisting upon plying his "enchantments." But what began that night as an enraged expulsion from the doorway of the Hall, ended in a massacre and pillage of the wretched people all over the kingdom.

It was many a day thereafter before the realm of England could get the vapors of this vague fear of "enchantments" out of its head. And it required a long steelyard of no less than six hundred and seventy years before the sliding weight of justice could notch itself far enough along to lift away the dead-weight of that bloody day from the doorway of Westminster Hall. But when that hour arrived, the richest Jew in England, the greatest money-lender of Europe, walked unchallenged across that self-same threshold, across the very area where Richard and his barons had held their feast, to take his seat at the higher table of the House of Commons, though *not* "on the true faith of a Christian."

V.

We make a long step now, over the reign of John, into the closing years of Henry the Third. We look for the massive old Abbey of the Confessor; it has gone. But another, of lighter, richer, more beautiful design, is rising in its place. Pointed arches—no longer heavy round ones. The new minster is to cover, also, a greater space. But after thirty years only the choir and transepts are finished. There is no great nave, as yet, trending westward. Still Henry has opened it with imposing ceremonies, and resepulchred the Confessor's bones in a gorgeous shrine. The gray old Hall has almost a shabby aspect now, under the tall, majestic, cream-colored torso of an abbey which looks clear over its head down the river. But the compensation is to come. A very mountain of the nation's treasure had been melted into that mass of richly sculptured stone. Bad enough had it been to see the court run down with foreign adventurers, to hear a polyglot of alien tongues all round the palace, to be taxed for endless banquets and pageants, for jesters and mummers, for painters and troubadours. But the cost of these had been nothing to what the Abbey had swallowed up. The king, who had not a spark of royal spirit in him, had stooped to any meanness in order to provide himself with funds. Soft and flabby enough as a man, he proved a very sponge as a builder, and sucked church and state and people dry that he

might pour the wealth of the kingdom over the Abbey walls. The now humiliated Hall, after watching it all during these many years, was curiously driven at last into developing a mind of its own. It turned out to be a democratic mind—a new experience for a royal hall.

These following three incidents will show that the now excited old Hall is getting its sluggish faculties together. The king is brought down on his marrowbones before it, first by the people, next by the prelates, last by the barons.

London at that time was a thriving commercial city, driving a brisk trade up and down the Channel, and away round into the Mediterranean. Its merchants had grown so big that Henry ill-naturedly twitted them with trying to be barons. Their wealth made them a rich prey for him whenever there was a money crisis at court. Their pride, too, was something he liked to cut down. It was the age of fairs—huge mercantile encampments, held occasionally in different parts of the country, by bishops and other local authorities, as a way of adding to their revenues. The king proposed to hold what he called a "St. Edward's Fair" in the meadows around his palace. He first issued a decree prohibiting all other fairs in the kingdom. Then he turned upon London, and ordered its merchants literally "to shut up shop." All its traffic must cease during the two weeks of this royal sale. The traffic, therefore, suddenly ceased, but, at his further command, broke out in a huge and brilliant encampment all round him at Westminster. Its tents and pavilions, filled with the rich merchandise of the city, rolled in billows along the river-bank, and back around the Abbey and the Hall. All might have gone merrily still, if not for the merchants, for his Majesty. But Father Thames rose in dudgeon and an inundation. The clouds also poured down water. The meadows became a marsh, the tents went down, the merchandise was ruined, and the merchants maddened. It did not soften their tempers to know that the royal spite had brought them to this, as well as the royal will.

It is seldom we get in one package such a neat piece of tyranny as this with such consequences upon the mind of the tyrant. It will stand for a specimen. When the Londoners at last, through this and a great deal more like it, had been wrought up to the highest pitch of exasperation,

27*

the great Hall was called to his help by the equally frightened and disappointed king. He sent for the citizens to come down with their wives and families, even to their boys of twelve years old, in order that he might try the effect of an apology with tears. And he did stand up before a crowd of thousands of them—"the short, stout, ungainly old man with the blinking left eye"—and "humbly, and as if with rising tears," entreated their forgiveness for "his anger, malevolence, and rancor toward them."

But now for the next scene, three years after. His bishops had lost confidence in his repeated promises to keep inviolate the charters of John. He was again in desperate need of money, and, in order to get a grant from their revenues, offered to take a form of oath which confessed that his royal word was worthless.

The ceremony to which he submitted was as appalling as it was humiliating. It took place deep in the night, when the Hall was wrapped in darkness. All the prelates entered in procession, with the Archbishop of Canterbury at their head, and each bore a lighted taper in his hand. The barons stood looking on in the gloom. A taper was offered to the king, but he excused himself, as "he was no priest," but, to prove his sincerity, "he would keep his hand upon his breast during the proceedings." The charters of King John were now read aloud. Then in solemn tones the archbishop pronounced the anathema, invoking the curse of Heaven upon those persons who in future should violate the two charters now confirmed by the king. Suddenly the Hall was in darkness. Every light had been extinguished, and thrown "stinking and smoking upon the ground." Then again was heard the voice of the archbishop uttering the dire malediction that the souls of every one who infringed the charters "might thus be extinguished, and stink and smoke in hell!" The ceremony was thought to be over, when the king broke the dead stillness by voluntarily saying, "So, may God help me, I will inviolably observe all these things, as I am a man and a Christian, a knight and a crowned and anointed king."

How well he kept the oath is shown by what followed five years after, on the 2d of May, 1258.

The great council of the barons was to meet, but when they had assembled it was, by preconcert, in full armor. The stone floor rang with their iron tread. They held their drawn swords in their hands—a kind of tapers that would not go out. When the king and the other counsellors appeared, they sheathed their weapons or laid them aside. It was an act of respect, but the clash of steel resounded through the hall. The emphasis with which the blades went home showed that they might be forth-coming again. The king started back in alarm, exclaiming: "What means this? Am I a prisoner?"

"No, sir," said the violent Roger Bigod; "but your foreign favorites and your prodigality have brought misery upon this realm. Wherefore we demand that the powers of government be delegated to a committee of the bishops and barons, who may correct abuses and enact good laws."

This high-tempered noble had been the first to speak, but the real leader of the formidable league was the king's own brother-in-law, Simon de Montfort, Earl of Leicester—the idol of the people and the terror of the king. He opened the memorable debate. The meeting closed with the appointment of the commission, with De Montfort at the head of it. It was the first roll of thunder which betokened the coming storm. It ushered in a civil war. The swords of the barons did spring from their scabbards again, and not only the king, but Prince Edward, his son, were prisoners. Then, seven years from that day, a Parliament met in this self-same Hall of William Rufus, in which, for the first time, representatives of the people, knights, citizens, and burghers, sat and deliberated with the barons, bishops, and abbots. *The House of Commons was born!*

VI.

Nine years after—August 9, 1274—Edward the First, just returned from the Crusades, having been crowned in the Abbey, held his banquet in the Hall. Eleanor, the devoted wife who had sucked the Saracen's poison from his wound, sat by his side. The Hall could not contain the hospitalities of this coronation. It was to be a banquet of the people as well as of the nobles: rich and poor, high and low, were alike made welcome at the gates of Westminster. Great temporary halls were built, supplied by kitchens in the open air. Innumerable leaden caldrons poured forth their steam and savory odors for fifteen days. Droves of oxen, sheep, and swine were paddocked close by, as on a modern market day when a city is to be fed. White wine and red flowed like water through conduits close by. On the very spot where St. Margaret's Church now stands, a vast stable was built for the gorgeously caparisoned steeds on which the barons and prelates, with their richly attired retinues, had likewise come to the coronation.

On the first day of the banquet, Alexander the Third of Scotland, a baron also of England, rode up to the door of the Hall, attended by one hundred of his knights. As they sprang to the ground, their chargers, with all their gorgeous housings, were allowed to dash away whithersoever they would, and into the possession of any who could catch them. No sooner had this, the head of the arriving cavalcade, vanished in such an astonishing style, than the king's nephew, the Earl of Cornwall, closed the gap with another glittering train of one hundred knights, and the same scene was enacted again. Then followed the Earl of Gloucester, after him the Earl of Pembroke, after him the Earl of Warrenne, each in the midst of a dazzling retinue of knights, when three hundred horses more were successively set loose. In a few moments the whole five hundred were careering away down the streets and over the fields, with an excited multitude in a mad chase after them.

After this lordly exhibition of pride, and of rather reckless good-will to the people—reckless as to who were to be run over, and who were to be made happy by these benefits—the sumptuous king of the north, with these equally sumptuous earls, and the whole five hundred knights, went into the Hall, moving in stately procession to the upper end, amid as stately a ceremony of reception as such a costly entrance deserved. The Scottish king had come from his palace down the river—since famous as Scotland Yard—for which and his other possessions in England he had done homage to the English king. He was in an acquiescent mood to anything reasonable that might be desired, and it was therefore so contrived that he sat under Edward's thumb on the right. There had been great hopes that Llewellyn of Wales might also arrive, and sit under his thumb on the left. But the wary Welshman was suspicious, and would not come. Hence this symmetrical as well as significant arrangement was spoiled.

Things went very well with the constitution, but not with the union, under Edward. He did noble work with the legislature, bringing it into very much the form it has to-day. The lines of his policy, so far, were all statesman-like, and ran deep into the future. But when he put his hand on the lines which tended to union, he seemed to touch the electric threads of fate. Wales yielded; but Scotland appeared to be charged with the very genius of a destiny which foiled him at every turn. The "Hammer of the Scots" hammered the nation out of all apparent existence, and yet it instantly sprang into more vigorous life than ever. The blows he struck on those chords of fate awoke all the minstrelsy of the border for four hundred years to come. But they awoke first the pibroch of William Wallace, and with it a spirit and power in that people—and in all people thereafter—to a depth which never had been stirred before.

A strange humor was it in Edward—looking like a fatality in his own nature—which led him to defy even the very voice of prophecy, and place the "Stone of Destiny" in the Abbey of Westminster, within the very oaken chair which was to be the coronation throne of every sovereign of England thenceforth. For wherever that stone should be found, so its ancient inscription ran, the all-potential force of Scotland should be felt. Little did Edward dream, when he thus enthroned the stone, that a Scottish king should legally sit upon it within three hundred years, under the two nations' unanimous acclaim! Little did he dream that in a century more a constitution should rise out of this self-same popular spirit he now evoked, so interwoven by the reciprocal working of one people upon the other that their union should come in the institutional blending of both!

And as little did he dream that he was to receive in his own person the first shock of this fated and recoiling influence of Scotland upon his throne. He received that shock in Westminster Hall. When he put forth his hand to tax the people in order to sustain his wars, he overstrained the charter of King John. Then his barons and the people rose. It was a prerogative he would not yield. But when Wallace had hurled his armies out of the Highlands, and he found himself on the verge also of a civil war, his spirit gave way—or rather his good sense came to the rescue — under the onset of the popular feeling. He bowed to the will of the nation. It was a memorable day for England when its greatest, wisest, proudest, most patriotic prince stood before those assembled thousands on a scaffold in front of the Hall of Rufus, the tallest man in his dominions, and "every inch a king," his heroic frame trembling in the agony of his pride, his brave voice breaking as he spoke, and the tears rolling down his noble, indomitable face. But it was the son of Alfred who stood there, as well as the son of the Conqueror, the first Norman king with a Saxon name, the first also with an English spirit, admitting to the people, but in no craven impulse like his father, that he had done them wrong, and promising them amends! Out of the sincere emotion of that hour came the signature to the statute of the confirmation of the charters. "The greatest of the distinctions between a limited and despotic monarchy" was established. After this the Commons of England alone were to raise the supplies which should sustain the power of the crown.

What a picturesque *finale* to all this is now given us in the great Hall! It comes to us tartaned with the romance of Miss Porter's *Scottish Chiefs*. The heroic Wallace, after eight years' warfare in his native mountains with all the power which Edward could put forth; Wallace, once the "Protector" of Scotland, still the idol of its people, the noblest and foremost of all its chieftains, whose name was to ring in both legend and song through the heart of his nation for generations to come; Wallace, the yellow-haired giant, whose two-handed claymore had flashed on loch-side and hill-side for the independence and freedom of his country — was brought down from his prison in Dumbarton Castle, and crowned in mockery with a garland of oak leaves as "a king of outlaws and robbers," was dragged into Westminster Hall, and arraigned before the judges of Edward as a traitor to the English crown. The mockery which crowned him with such a title was only equalled by the mockery which tried him on such a charge. "Traitor I could never be," was his true and bold answer, "for I was not a subject to King Edward."

It was on August 23, 1305, that he went forth from that door—the door of liberty itself to-day—condemned to suffer all the horrible barbarities of a traitor's death, a sacrifice to the very fatality which was to be the life and glory of Scotland. At that door he was tied down to a hurdle, and taken to the elms of Smithfield to be hanged; but the decree of the bar within, which placed his head on London Bridge, and sent his quartered body to Newcastle, Berwick, Perth, and Aberdeen, did its fateful work in rousing his countrymen again, even as one man, to place the crown on the head of Robert Bruce, as king of a united and independent Scotland.

VII.

We should be emptying a full budget indeed if we attempted to recount all the memorable scenes which took place in the great Hall of William Rufus. We have thus far selected, as we went along, only those which had an especial historical significance or romantic interest; scenes also which awakened some characteristic of their time.

We now pass over the reign of Edward the Second, and pause for a moment to look about us in the reign of Edward the Third. There have been great changes in both the Palace and the Abbey. The latter has been completed to the end of the nave; but there has been attached to the palace a chapel of such exquisite architecture, so enriched with houses and lands, so equipped with its own chapter and clergy, that the Abbey has become jealous of the beauty and dignity which the royal hands have given it. It is the chapel of St. Stephen's, as brilliant within, at the time we are speaking of, as the Sainte Chapelle in Paris is to-day with the glory of polychromatic decoration and the splendor of stained windows. Not for a long time yet are its sculptures and paintings to be boarded over, as they were in Edward the Sixth's day, in order to make it the famous council hall of the House of Commons. It stands, like the Abbey, at right angles with the Hall, but running just the other way, toward the river, with the northern corner of its western gable touching the southeastern corner of the Hall. The square quadrangle of its cloisters now fills the space under the east wall of the Hall, between it and the Thames. St. Margaret's also has risen under the shadow of the Abbey, and a crowd of other buildings besides—walls, gate-houses, almonries, towers—an enormous pile, with the Abbey for its apex.

Parliament has been divided into its two Houses, the House of Lords meeting in one of the great chambers of the palace, the House of Commons in the octagonal chapter-house of the Abbey. It is to meet, however, now and then, and especially on extra-legislative occasions, in the great Hall. The courts, which are more than ever fixed there, have undergone a great and significant change in one respect. The pleas are no longer made in Norman French, but "pleaded, showed, defended, answered, debated, and judged in the English tongue." The law itself has also been so improved that we have the authority of Sir Matthew Hale for saying that it is now approaching its meridian.

Under Edward the military spirit has been so roused in the nation that chivalry rises to its highest perfection in his reign; and yet, even while the spectacles of the joust and tournament are carried to a pitch of splendor never before witnessed, the very earliest distinction of chivalry, the soldier on horseback, is losing itself in the new glory and importance which the yeomanry of England have won in the battles of Crécy and Poitiers. The bowman has become as formidable as the knight. But the noble and gentle virtues of chivalry are now emulated in England as never before: its courtesy, and its honor, as well as its devotion to truth and to duty. We are now to witness a scene in which the Hall flings open its doors for a most royal expression of the new spirit which has seized the time.

King John of France has been taken prisoner at the battle of Poitiers, after fighting desperately, and all alone, except for the presence of his youngest boy, Philip the Bold, then only fourteen years old. The boy's cries still come down to us from the bloody field, as the enemy struck at his dismounted father from every side: "Father, ware right! father, ware left!" The gallant king did not yield until he had secured his delivery to the Prince of Wales. Poitiers was a second Crécy in the deep mortification to France of being a defeat by inferior numbers. The Black Prince was the hero of both. He took the king and Prince Philip into his tent, serving them at table with his own hands, with the most touching demonstrations of sympathy and respect, and promising to the king such manifestations of regard from his father as could not but result in the kindest friendship between them. In the course of time (May 24, 1356) the French king and his son were brought to London. It turned out as the prince had promised. Their arrival was like the triumphal entrance of a victor. The whole city, at Edward's desire, came out to do them honor. The windows and arches across the streets were hung with carpets, tapestries, plate, and glittering armor. The trades filled the avenues with their pageantry. King John, in royal apparel, and mounted on a beautiful cream-colored charger, rode in front, while the Black Prince rode behind him, like an attendant, on a little black hackney. A cavalcade of a thousand citizens, sent by King Edward, met them near London and conducted them to Westminster, where, at high noon, they dismounted at the doors of the Hall, after having been nine hours on the way through the great concourse of the people. King Edward sat on his throne, surrounded by his prelates and barons. As soon as the doors were thrown open and the French king appeared, "he descended from the royal seat, embraced him with tokens of respectful attention, and, leading him to partake of a magnificent banquet, entertained him in his palace for some time as his guest."

VIII.

Twenty years after this—the Black Prince, "that young Mars of men," having died in the palace before his father—a beautiful boy, scarcely more than ten years old, was helped, half fainting, up the steps of his grandfather's throne by the great bishops and nobles of the realm, amid the splendors of such a coronation as even England had never seen. The brilliant complexion and golden hair of Richard the Second would alone have proclaimed him as the son of "England's idol," the hero of Crécy and Poitiers. Time, also, was to show how much he had inherited of his father's gallant and imperious spirit. It was a pity that his Plantagenet blood received the overheating it did amid the blaze of these few hours. His barons and people, in fear of ambitious John of Gaunt, had got up this magnificent exhibition of regal glory, from the Tower to the Abbey and from the Abbey to the Hall—even to a shower of coronets and crests from the child's fingers upon the heads of a crowd of new-made earls and knights, bent in homage before him at the banquet—in order to seal by one overwhelming demonstration his supreme right to the throne. Strange had it been if all this had not, as it did, put the seal also of an indelible determination to rule on the impressible wax of the boy's now thoroughly overstimulated nature—a determination which afterward obliged the same barons and people to put his Great Seal out of sight.

Even the rampant chivalry of Edward, which in him had gone into the Order of the Garter and the Round Table at Windsor, was now made to cap this pageantry at Westminster in an empty spectacle which, if we may judge from its repetition at every coronation since, to that of George the Fourth, must have made a great sensation at the time, even when a man in armor was not such a curiosity as now.

Sir John Dymoke, whose family had held some especial privilege of service near the royal person since the Conqueror's day, having now established his right over all claimants to this one, came forward at the banquet in a style which, very far from intentionally, made chivalry appear what it actually was in that shape—more pretty to look at than powerful. As the "champion of England" he took "the best charger, save one, in the king's stables," and "the best suit of armor, save one, in the royal armory," and, decked out in this regal panoply, presented himself at the entrance to the Hall while the banquet was in progress. Before the winding horn of his heralds, and with a great flourish of clarions and trumpets, the doors flew wide open, and he rode in, with his spear-bearer on his right, and his shield-bearer on his left, to the centre of the room, where he drew up his steed, while the heralds announced, after another flourish of brass instruments, that he, "John Dymoke, knight, etc., was ready to do battle with his body against any one who should gainsay the right of Richard the Second to the throne," etc., when, clash! clang! down went his steel gauntlet upon the floor. Which safe proceeding, in that presence, was concluded by a herald taking up the gage and giving it back to him.

The poor champion doubtless did it very well at the time, but there has crept down in an old chronicle a bit of gossip which, if known at the moment, would have made him appear even more unreal than he was. It seems that he had been

ignominiously overthrown that very afternoon by a hand unfriendly to the honor he had gained. He had presented himself at the Abbey door by mistake, and, as it happened, just as a number of nobles were coming out bearing the young king in a faint, after the exhausting services of the coronation. They were headed by Harry Hotspur's uncle as Earl Marshal, who, springing into his saddle, was ordering everybody out of the way, when the apparition of the champion with his supporters startled his eyes—perhaps his risibles, if any such thing were possible in his grim countenance. He took poor Dymoke down from his high horse at once, by asking "what he was doing there," and then telling him "to wait until the king sat down to dinner," adding, with derisive courtesy, that in the mean time he "had better disarm himself, and take his rest and ease awhile." The formidable but now flustered figure, doubtless with a wry face and hot blush behind his closed visor, beat a retreat before this malicious assault into some proper hiding, where he abode in his discomfiture as he best could until the right moment for ventilating his valor had come. The entrance of the champion at subsequent coronation banquets seldom escaped, as we shall take care to note in one or two instances, some such grotesque incongruity to mitigate the terror of his appearing.

The reign of Richard was, in both the banqueting and building line, the reign of Rufus over again. But he out-Heroded Herod in the scale of his household. He had ten thousand servants wearing his livery, of whom three hundred were cooks. He had at times ten thousand guests at his table, overflowing the Hall into the palace chambers and both palace yards. He kept in his pay four thousand good Cheshire archers, who were in constant attendance about his person, ready to defend the imperious and extravagant course it was his will to pursue. Like his grandfather, from whom he inherited his taste for chivalry, he did not rely so much on his mail-clad gentry, when it came to the point, as upon those mercenary yeoman bowmen. The "champion" was for ornament, not use. So long as he held this formidable body-guard in hand, no man, be he baron or burgher, dared open his mouth—except to eat. This was always in order.

Richard felt that he must have the honor of vastly improving Rufus's banqueting hall. There was a curious coincidence of dates which could hardly have been designed; it was in 1097 that Rufus began to put up the Hall. It was in 1397 —exactly three hundred years later—that Richard undertook to put it up two feet higher. Pretty much all that he did to it was involved in this increased elevation of its walls: with due reverence for his model, he thought the other dimensions unsurpassable. Not a stone was unnecessarily removed, but the Norman style was stripped naked and rubbed down for the Gothic vesture which was to bring it into harmony with the brilliant Abbey on one side and the beauteous St. Stephen's on the other. The greatest achievement of his restoration was the magnificent new roof which the old 'walls were given the honor to sustain; but as the two rows of pillars were removed in order to make the interior one vast nave, twenty-six mighty shoulders in the form of corbels, of richly sculptured Caen stone, were furnished the walls within, and a number of flying-buttresses were made to press to their support on either side without. A casing of stone outside, a foot and a half thick, also covered the rubble and grout work of Rufus, to make sure that it should not be crushed by the extraordinary burden which Richard designed to put upon it.

This roof, when it was in place, became the wonder of Europe. It is the astonishment of architects to this hour. It was made to span the whole volume of space below by a single spring from wall to wall throughout the whole two hundred and forty feet, supported not only by the buttressed walls, but by certain inherent elements of strength developed by the interlocking of its timbers on geometrical principles. Its peak is ninety-two feet above the pavement. The old oak of Shillelagh was wrought in with a whole forest of Normandy chestnut, and this amazing piece of joiner-work still hangs in mid-air as solidly as it did five hundred years ago. Its intricate massiveness is made to look light and alive by sculptured angels under the hammer-beams, flying horizontally out, head to head, from both sides of the Hall, each bearing in his hands a shield turned toward the face of the spectator below, with the arms alternately of Richard and Edward the Confessor. The stone moulding or stringcourse that runs round the room still pre-

serves the white hart couchant, the favorite device of the banqueting king.

The other striking addition to the building, made necessary by the now lofty pointed gable, was a pair of square, massive, embattled towers projecting from the corners of the front. These were pierced with pointed windows—characteristic of the whole Hall now—beneath which were niches with carved canopies of stone. In these were a series of statues of the kings of England, standing in rows above each other. In the carved spandrels of the magnificent porch, which displaced the Norman triple entrance, were sculptured the arms of both the Confessor and Richard. The anchorite Edward would never have so locked arms with him in life.

While the workmen were crowding over the scaffolds, and swinging the mighty crane which let down the prodigious fabric of each rafter into its sockets, the king called a Parliament in order to make another ostentatious exhibition of his power. He called it in the open air, in a temporary building of wood, roofed with tiles, erected in the great quadrangle of Rufus, in front of the Hall. This building was open on all sides, "that all men should see and hear what was both said and done." His four thousand archers compassed it about, "with their bows bent and arrows notched in their hands, always ready to shoot." A lofty throne had been prepared, on which he sat, crowned and robed and holding the sceptre. The spectacle and proceedings together—the trial of certain lords—showed how completely, at the moment, Parliament was at his feet, and how "the authority of the crown had superseded every principle of the constitution."

He sandwiched the daily sessions of this court between as many evening banquets, at which ten thousand guests made the welkin ring with noisy revelry. But now, as it proved, he had strained his own bow too far. His high-strung despotism broke in his hands, and turned aside. The banished son of John of Gaunt landed from the Continent at this opportune instant, to recover his own unjustly confiscated estates, and found himself very willingly swept into the new marble chair of the Hall by the estates of the realm.

Richard, like Rufus, had held but one festival in his redecorated banqueting room, and in a few months lay dead in

Pontefract Castle. The great Hall passed again, as before, into a new era. The courts resumed their places. The grave transactions and royal festivals of the realm took up their order. A history now opens within it even more rich in scenes—events so representative of the spirit of their time that, like its new roof, they interlock themselves at last into a self-sustaining constitution, resting on the self-same ancient walls of the kingdom, but no longer dependent on the interior support of kings, because buttressed from without by the whole strength of the people.

RICHFIELD SPRINGS.

IT must be acknowledged that American watering-places do not lead the world. We are, in fact, in this respect far behind our European cousins. Natural sanitary centres abound among us, but their mineral waters and other remedial influences have received but little careful consideration. Probably a large majority of the European spas have the advantage of governmental support, by which their proper maintenance and improvement are insured. The development of our springs is accomplished by private enterprise in the face of State and communal indifference; and this management lacks that liberality which is engendered by community of interest. In Germany and France few remedial agents are more carefully studied and highly esteemed than natural spring waters. Here we employ them empirically, if at all, and are skeptical as to their value. We fail to appreciate the benefit gained or the danger incurred by their proper or improper administration. There is not, to my knowledge, in all New York State a sanitary resort at any of our many watering-places where accurate records are kept of the number and kind of cases treated, where the methods and effects of treatment are noted, and the results of experience tabulated for reference. The medical profession is greatly to blame. Among our medical schools balneology as a subject of systematic study is entirely neglected. It has no place in the various curricula, and in the text-books is slighted or ridiculed. Hence among physicians as among the laity, in respect to the relative therapeutic merits of our springs, there exists that gross ignorance which accounts for the hap-hazard way in which mineral waters are prescribed by our doctors and taken by their patients. This practice is attended by great danger. Health and disease are so akin, and our physical natures are so dissimilar, that the same cold baths that cure an Augustus may prove fatal to a Marcellus. Ill-advised invalids go the rounds of our springs, and only discover when too late that an aggravation of their disease is the result of their health-seeking efforts.

"So from that spring whence comfort seemed to come,
  Discomfort swells."

An accurate knowledge of the chemical constitution and the therapeutic value of mineral waters is essential to their rational employment. The medical faculty appreciate this fact; for their own sake and the good of the public they ought invariably to act thereupon. The State, being naturally interested in the development of all its resources, can, not unlikely, be influenced to encourage, through its indefatigable "Board of Health," any reasonable plan for the scientific investigation and improvement of its mineral springs. Could this be done, we would obtain a guide to our water-cures invaluable both to physician and patient.

Within the boundaries of New York State there are, with but few exceptions, examples of all the different varieties of springs. They appear in nearly every county, and emerge from almost every species of rock. Among them the sulphur springs greatly preponderate. Many are utilized to a greater or less degree in the treatment of disease. To one who visits any one of these so-called sanitaria the thought is apt to occur, how vastly superior the natural are to the artificial attractions, and yet how dependent the former are upon the latter for facilities for practical usefulness! From a medical stand-point the results attained at none of these localities have been entirely satisfactory. Approaching more closely than any other to our notion of a sanitary watering-place is Richfield Springs—its natural attractions being inferior to few, and its artificial surroundings vastly superior to most. Richfield has long enjoyed a very considerable popularity as a summer resort. During the winter it is a dull little village of about twelve hundred inhabitants; in the summer it becomes a gay little town of twenty-five hundred or three thousand people. Its location in the northwest portion of Otsego County, high up among the hills between the Mohawk and Susquehanna valleys, its facilities for easy drainage and water supply, the great variety and picturesque nature of its scenery, are natural features of this resort hardly secondary in importance to its salubrious climate and healing waters. To these have been added good accommodations for man and beast which few of our large cities can equal, and a bill of health so clean as to put most of our village sanitary bureaus to the blush.

To many a traveller the greatest charm of Richfield is the spirit of generous hospitality and good fellowship with which he is received at hotel and cottage, and made welcome in-doors and out by a choice company of delightful people.

During the season of 1882 the number of visitors was from ten to twelve thousand. Seventy per cent. are pleasure-seekers, who drink the water or take the baths as a matter of experiment, or because it is perhaps the correct thing to do. Five or ten per cent. of the visitors are really invalids, whose sole object in coming is to try the water-cure under the best obtainable advice. Most of these frequent the smaller hotels and cottages, although some prefer the gay life and excitement of the large hotels. They may be seen frequently during the day, usually early in the morning or late in the forenoon, waiting their turn at the spring to get their prescribed portion of cold or warmed sulphur water. Some only drink the water, taking from one to twelve or more glasses each day, but the majority take a course of from ten to twenty-five warm or hot baths as well. From one to seven baths a week are administered, according to the effect produced or desired. After the course is completed, the patients either continue with the internal use of the water alone, or are advised to leave the springs for a while, and return later in that or during the next season. Then bathers are counselled to rest awhile after bathing, eat plain food at regular set hours, go to bed early, rise early, and take plenty of light exercise.

Those who are the most susceptible to the beneficial influences of treatment are those who are most in sympathy with their surroundings. This point deserves special consideration in the treatment of rheumatics, who so largely preponderate among the invalided visitors at our sulphur springs. Your rheumatic patient is essentially a nervous one; he is keenly alive to every external influence. Pure air is as much more relished by him when inhaled amid scenes of natural beauty as is a good meal when tastefully served. He, to the utmost, feels the good effect of a judicious change in climate and in all his household, business, and social relations. Is his home life monotonously tiresome, he requires something stimulating; is it full of excitement, he needs sedative influences. The dull life and the gay each is benefited, the one by a touch of color, the other by a bit of gray.

In relation to a health resort, we must remember that the good effects of air and water may be neutralized in the case of many by a dreary monotony of scenery and unattractive environments, food, and company. Success waits upon any watering-place at which artificial attractions are disposed and conducted so as to develop and utilize natural resources in accordance with good taste and the general requirements of the invalid. It is this happy combination of effects that proves the good fortune of Richfield.

There is one artificial attraction at Richfield that appeals to all of us as of the utmost importance: I mean good drainage. Its present system of water supply and sewerage is not perfect, but is surprisingly satisfactory. Fresh spring water is supplied to hotels, cottages, and many of the village houses; provision is made for the rapid carrying off of surface water and all forms of sewage; no unclean beasts are allowed within the village borders during the warm season, and the suggestions made by the State Board of Health are carried out in every way practicable to promote the salubrity of the township and the health of its inhabitants.

Many people ascribe the benefit they receive at Richfield to the change in climate. A climate that is varied by the regular succession of seasonable climatic changes is the most consonant with perfect development. A seasonable change of climate may act both as a prophylactic and a curative remedy. Either the new order of things is more compatible with the state of one's system, a lurking diathesis is suppressed or subdued by necessary changes in the mode of living, or, under new influences, our old diseases become more amenable to previously disappointing remedies. The climate of Richfield affects visitors at once—inducing some to depart, but more to remain. The mean temperature of spring is calculated to be 40° F., of summer, 68° F., of autumn, 50° F., and of winter, 23° F., making the mean of the year about 45° F. Thus the temperature is low, and though on rare occasions in summer the mercury rises above 90° F., it remains at that point but a very short time during mid-day; the nights are almost invariably cool, and frequently necessitate the use of blankets in midsummer. The barometric mean is estimated at about 28½ inches; the air is dry, pure, sweet, and exhilarating; electrical disturbances are not infrequent; sunshine predominates greatly over shadow; and the prevailing winds are westerly and southwesterly, following along up the course of the Susquehanna River, which has its source in several of the small lakes in the vicinity. The village is 1300 feet above sea-level, and is surrounded by hills rising 300 or 400 feet above the plain. The soil is sandy, with a slight admixture of clay, and the adjacent country-side is parcelled out into trim farms, with here and there a patch of woodland. Thus we have virtually a mountainous climate characterized by pure, cool, dry air. The changes in the temperature are sometimes sudden and great, but, owing to the elevation, this variability is not so trying to delicate constitutions as it would be on the sea-coast, while to the more robust it acts as a stimulant.

From one high point—"Rum Hill"— there may be seen the waters of five lakes, two of these, Otsego and Canaderaga, being pretentious both in size and beauty. The ground is fertile, its nature being particularly adapted to the cultivation of the hop vine, and yields a generous return to labor. The purity of the atmosphere, which reminds one of the Adirondacks, is insured by the elevation and character of the soil and surrounding country, and the electrical and other changes to which the air is subject. Therapeutically, certain general principles may be enunciated. Among the great classes of catarrhal, pulmonary, and rheumatic dis-

eases which seem to be subject to similar meteorological laws, the dry and bracing air of our hilly interiors is best adapted to ultra-susceptible and nervo-sanguineous subjects; the insensitive and phlegmatic do better in the more stimulating air of the sea, and, as a rule, the dweller at the sea-coast finds greater relief among the hills than those coming from the far interior. This is well illustrated at Richfield, which enjoys its greatest popularity among people who live along the Atlantic sea-board. But among these the recent convalescent from an acute disease may find the change too radical, unless his muscular tone is so far restored as to respond freely to the stimulus of the hill air which invites him to exercise. He whose heart is better than his legs needs the serenity of mind and repose of body which are nowhere so readily attained as upon the open sea. The overworked brain and unstrung nerve are refreshed and invigorated among the hills; but he whose malady is of a serious organic nature is chilled and depressed, and had best remain away. It is, however, to the great army of the bilious that this climate is of the most value. Here they find in the "keen and eager" air a stimulant to all their vital energies, which stirs up their portal circulation, and thereby removes the digestive disturbances consequent upon passive congestion.

The greatest, though apparently not the most highly prized, attraction at Richfield is the sulphur water. The springs are numerous, and although it is not quite true that "within this mile break forth a thousand springs," yet it is true that within a radius of a mile there are about a score. Of this water much is said, something is known, and a good deal is imagined. It is called a sulphur water on account of its strong impregnation with sulphuretted hydrogen. It probably ascends from a great depth, and obtains its many mineral ingredients from the various strata of rock and the soil through which it percolates. Like most all sulphuretted waters, those of Richfield are nominally classed as thermal waters, since the temperature, 48° F., is several degrees higher than the mean of temperature of the village.

The exact chemical constitution of the water has of late been made the subject of investigation, and at the instance of I. K. Proctor, Esq., a new and important analysis has been made. The water tested is from what is known as the Great White Sulphur Spring. It is not probable that there exists any very essential difference in the composition of the water as derived from the various springs in the immediate vicinity.

Many of the ingredients are common to many mineral waters, the difference in their relative proportion and association with other minerals accounting for their various effects.

No one element is thought to be characteristic of the Richfield water, nor does the combination altogether account for its efficacy in a certain class of cases. Wherein lies its special therapeutic power is a matter of speculation. One learned gentleman will tell you that the sulphuretted hydrogen acts as an antidote to the rheumatic poison; a second believes that the minerals are associated in just the right proportion to stimulate digestion and assimilation, and promote all the necessary alterative changes necessary to limber up a stiff joint or clear out a torpid liver; a third pins his faith to the well-known anti-malarial influence of sulphur; and so on. They agree about as well as the learned usually do. However, inexplicable as it may be, the good results of treatment in *properly selected cases* can not be denied. In this all-important selection, too, personal experience is, and must remain, a great guide; and I do not undervalue it when saying that, being re-enforced by a complete knowledge of the water, it is far less fallible.

All sulphur waters, hot or cold, are undoubtedly especially useful in rheumatic diseases, and in nervous complaints that are dependent upon, or more or less closely allied to, the rheumatic diathesis. As Ferguson sings of his favorite "Caller Water,"

> "Though joints be stiff as any rung,
> Your pith wi' pain be sairly dung,
> Be you in caller water flung
>   Out o'er the lugs,
> 'Twill make ye supple, swack, and young,
>   Withouten drugs."

In similar cases our sulphur water is equally efficacious, and though it is difficult to understand its *modus operandi*, a possible or partial explanation may be given. Such cases are almost invariably dependent upon or complicated by some form of that peculiar concatenation of disagreeable symptoms called "biliousness," the pathology of which can no more read-

ily be described than by saying that it is a state of congestion, more generally passive than active, affecting all or a part of the great digestive organs. People who suffer from this malady are not partial to water; they drink, in fact, but little; and in consequence of this abstemiousness, or because of intemperance in the use of various substitutes, their blood becomes "too thick," as it is popularly termed. Set all these people to drinking freely of pure Croton or any other indifferent water, let them take it hot or cold, before, during, or after meals, as they prefer, and ninety-nine out of every one hundred is benefited by the process. According as one is a sanitarian, a chemist, or a malarialist will he give the credit to the hygienic, the solvent, or the antiseptic properties of *aqua pura*.

In some way water as water is a useful remedy. It promotes both the processes of growth and decay, and is to be used as a stimulant to one or the other, or both, in order to maintain the normal equilibrium and restore it when lost. The quantity administered should be proportionate to the strength of the patient.

Besides the medicinal effect of water, there is also to be considered its hygienic influence. The skin does not receive the amount of attention which it deserves by reason of its complex relations to the economy as an organ of secretion, excretion, respiration, and absorption, and as a covering and protection to the rest of the body. Cleanliness, though ranking high as a virtue and a conservator of individual health, is neglected, or at least not cultivated, by many of the godly as well as of the ungodly.

This is true to a great extent among the young. Instead of the bath being considered as much of a comfort as a good table and an easy bed, to be enjoyed every day, it is regarded quite too generally as a troublesome necessity to be endured as seldom as common decency will permit. The face and hands, being exposed to public gaze, are cleansed each day, but the rest of the surface of the body is frequently allowed to act as a sort of receiver-general for all the filth that tries to get both in and out of the body for a week's time. When the great washing and soaking does occur—generally Saturday night or Sunday morning, the effect of the necessary prolonged immersion in hot soapy water is oftentimes so startling and unpleasant that the natural repugnance of the victim to the bath is apt to be increased by a prejudice that his system is constitutionally intolerant of water. Can it be a matter of wonder that a course of baths, one every day or two for three or four weeks, should benefit people of this state of mind and body? The frequent and judicious application of water, followed by brisk rubbing or massage, stimulates the integument to increased activity, and, *pari passu*, promotes the vitality of all the underlying structures. This effect is, no doubt, increased by the presence in the water of organic and mineral agents whose medicinal influence acts directly upon local and reflexively upon constitutional disorders.

The chemical analysis of the Richfield water, as made by Professor C. F. Chandler, Ph.D., is as follows:

ANALYSIS.

One United States gallon of 231 cubic inches contains:

	Grains.
Hydrosulphate of sodium	1.7189
" " calcium	0.0908
Sulphate of lime	112.3379
" " potash	1,6656
" " strontium	0.0105
" " barium	trace.
" " magnesia	5.1498
Hydrosulphite of soda	0.3801
Bicarbonate of magnesia	31.7403
" " iron	trace.
Phosphate of lime	0.0067
Chloride of sodium	0.5249
" " lithium	0.0165
Alumina	trace.
Silica	0.6415
Total	154.2835

Sulphuretted hydrogen...14.206 cubic inches.

The reaction of the water is alkaline. This fact is important in estimating the relative value of its various features, inasmuch as the alkalies are deservedly popular as medicinal agents. This alkalinity is due to the presence of sodium, potassium, and lithium. Whatever the definition of their effect, antacid, alterative, or specific, it is certain that many diseases dependent upon hepatic engorgement or the rheumatic diathesis are relieved by the administration of alkalies. Alkalies are important as natural elements of the body. They enter actively into the composition of the blood and bile, the saliva and pancreatic juice, and consequently need to be maintained in proper proportion in order that the various functions of digestion may be regularly and healthfully per-

formed. In disease such drugs may be considered natural remedies. It is to the alkalinity of the Carlsbad waters that their success is in great part attributable; and there is a suggestion as to the relationship of various diseases contained in the exaggerated statement that these waters are equally efficacious in biliousness, lithæmia, and diabetes.

Filtering up through deep strata of calcareous formations, the Richfield water contains so large a per cent. of lime that it may well be called a calcic-sulphur water. This mineral, while rendering the water unpleasant for the toilet, and somewhat indigestible, forms the basis of an extensive and varied therapeutic action. In disorders of digestion and nutrition, and in conditions of retarded or defective ossification consequent upon a scrofulous or tuberculous cachexy in the young or old, the various salts of lime are very valuable natural medicinal agents. Chemically they exercise antacid and anti-fermentative properties, mechanically they supply a deficiency existing in the system, and dynamically they stimulate the powers of assimilation.

The next most noticeable mineral ingredient is magnesium, which exists both as a bicarbonate and sulphate. The latter is the well known Epsom salt. Magnesium has but slight action upon the liver, its chief influence being exerted upon the intestinal tract, and medicinally it is peculiarly useful in rheumatic and other disturbances attended by undue acidity of the digestive secretions.

Sodium combined with sulphur and chlorine is also present. Sodium exists normally in the bile as an essential element in that vastly important secretion of the liver. This fact aids us to understand the efficacy of the water in bilious disorders, in plethora, in dyspepsia accompanied by uric acid gravel, and in some forms of the gouty disease. The alkaline and irritant action of sodium also enhances the value of the water in a large proportion of simple skin diseases.

Potash and lithium are principally useful in the water as alkalies, and the influence of the minute proportions of alumina, iron, barium, and strontium, though perhaps not inconsiderable, must remain hypothetical.

Perhaps the most important element is the sulphuretted hydrogen gas, whose suggestive flavor and volcanic odor have given the water its classification. In its concentrated form it is totally irrespirable, but a poisonous dose may be beneficially taken medicinally if largely diluted, as in this water. It then takes rank as a more or less energetic stimulant, acting promptly upon both blood and nerve. Its therapeutic effects in rheumatic and scrofulous disorders are due rather to its stimulating action upon nutritive functions than to any inherent power as a specific. Under its influence the various vital processes are facilitated, good is more easily absorbed and evil more readily eliminated, health encouraged, and disease controlled.

Carbonic acid gas is present in combination. As the water escapes from the spring, this gas dissolves its chemical associations, and bubbles up to the surface. It is exceedingly common in mineral waters, and plays an important rôle. Chemically it prevents the precipitation of various minerals, and medicinally it exerts a stimulating influence, both local and general, upon the nervous system, so that water made effervescent by it is pleasanter and more healthful for the bath, and more palatable and digestible as a drink.

Some of the other springs furnish water containing a greater proportion of iron, magnesium, and so on, and thus indicate their special adaptation to appropriate cases. These springs, though little used at present, need only to be developed to rival the "White Sulphur."

The value of these many chemical ingredients in combination is difficult to estimate, and is therefore oftentimes unduly depreciated, especially by that class of egoists who love to parade before the world as apostles of skepticism.

Our analysis of the water helps us to understand the results of clinical experience. The drugs most prominent in this water are those whose influence upon the organism is manifested chiefly in disturbances of the digestive tract, including stomach, liver, and intestines; and these same drugs in solution as a mineral water are found to be chiefly indicated in those subacute and chronic rheumatic, nervous, and skin disorders which are consequent upon or associated with disorders of digestion. In other words, by reason of its influence over the processes of digestion, this water is a remedy for those diseases which bear a rather definite relation to an irregular performance of those processes. The closer the relation, the more useful the wa-

ter. Thus, while including a large class, we must exclude an equal number, whose sufferings are the result of a diseased action in organs not specially interested in nutrition. Thus some forms of rheumatism and gout may be traced to a nervous origin; a large number of nervous conditions are miasmatic, and many skin diseases are purely local. I will not say that some of these cases are not much relieved by the use of the Richfield water, but that it is not especially indicated, and that the results are in general unsatisfactory.

Chronic rheumatism, particularly that form in which the muscles and nerves rather than the joints are the chief sufferers, responds readily to treatment as applied at Richfield. In a less degree, also, success is attained in rheumatic gout, especially if it be ingrafted upon a scrofulous cachexy; and the same is true of various neuralgias, rheumatic and malarial. In the most of these cases the water may profitably be used internally and externally.

Among skin diseases, those that are simple, non-malignant, or specific, such as eczema and acne, boils, old wounds, and indolent ulcers, are oftentimes cured, while the obstinate psoriasis and lichen are as often greatly benefited. The warm baths alone are sufficient, as a rule, but if symptoms of bilious indigestion are prominent, I would advise the moderate drinking of the water as well.

Sulphur-water treatment is highly vaunted in paralysis, but is only applicable in those cases that result from defective nutrition, especially when engendered by a gouty or rheumatic disposition. If the cause be some spinal or cerebral lesion, more harm than good is likely to ensue. In nerve disturbances dependent upon lead-poisoning, no other method of treatment can be more successfully applied.

I can not speak so favorably of the results of treatment as applied to catarrhal diseases. But there are forms of nasal, pharyngeal, laryngeal, and bronchial catarrh characterized by anæmia of the mucous membrane resulting from a malarial or rheumatic habit. Such cases are amenable to the stimulating influence of the waters; and the same is true, under similar conditions, of dyspepsia and chronic diarrhœa. Generally those catarrhs that are congestive, and attended by profuse mucous discharges, are only benefited when the water produces a laxative effect upon the intestinal tract.

Irritable conditions of the stomach, duodenum, and liver, induced by irregular or intemperate habits in eating or drinking, and the many nerve disturbances secondary thereto, are almost invariably ameliorated. Gall stones are unaffected.

In diabetes, in inflammation of the kidney, and in phthisis this water is inappropriate, and very little is to be expected from its use in uterine diseases, unless symptoms of a gouty or rheumatic constitution co-exist.

In all cases the waters should be used cautiously. Excellent medical advice may be obtained of the resident physicians, whose constant experience with the water makes them expert in its use.

As drugs are often observed to lose their effect upon the system, and their intermittent rather than continuous exhibition is attended by the most gratifying results, so, in regard to mineral waters, I am inclined to think that the biennial visitor to our health resorts is apt to derive more benefit than the regular *habitué*. I have also observed that after visiting the springs the benefit received may be developed, fostered, and fixed by free exposure to the strongly stimulating air of the sea, after which one may wisely return to the hills. Arising from this observation is the custom of many to spend the early summer season in the highlands, and reserve the sea-shore or a sea trip till later, and *vice versa*.

Though so well prepared to minister to the wants of a large class of invalids, Richfield is in great need of a thoroughly equipped and properly conducted sanitarium, in which guests can not only receive the best of advice, but be encouraged and assisted in acting thereon, and where the severest tests can be applied to the water and climate systems of cure for the benefit of patients present and to come. There is a good prospect that ere long such an institution will be established, and provided with every convenience for a winter residence. Many visitors find it desirable to remain late in the season; and in appropriate cases a sojourn at the springs during the cold season may well prove advantageous.

At present, also, the bathing facilities are deficient and unattractive. The rows of cell-like bath apartments remind one of the whited sepulchre, and instead of presenting every possible allurement, are so plain and primitive in their appointments as to repel one. Immediately after bathing one ought, by rights, to rest in comfort, be exposed to air whose temperature is carefully regulated, and be surrounded by influences calculated to promote repose of mind and serenity of heart. To supply this want a plan is projected to erect an elaborate establishment that will rival any to be seen abroad, and furnish every appliance for the satisfaction of the physician and the comfort of the bather.

It is to be hoped that the authorities of Richfield will grow in grace and wisdom, and that the spirit of enterprise manifested by them in the adornment of their charge thus far may grow with its growth, until its streets shall be immaculate, its walks without a flaw, its water supply inexhaustible, and its drainage perfect; until all its waste places shall be recovered, its water-courses improved, and its crooked places made straight. Plans for a public park ought to engage their early attention, and the erection of a building for public consort would naturally follow.

It has recently been said of Saratoga that it is a resort for fashionable people, instead of a fashionable resort for invalids, and that it has not maintained its deserved reputation as a remedial watering-place. Richfield, I think, tends in the same direction; but if she will but make her springs the centre of attraction, and round about them carry out all improvements suggested by wisdom and good taste, she may hope for a future justifying her name, and rival Saratoga, not perhaps as a centre of summer fashion, but as a sanitary resort for both the gay votaries of fashion and the dejected victims of a morbid civilization. Of the many other sulphur springs in the State, those at Clifton, Avon, and Sharon are the most prominent. These waters, while strongly resembling those of Richfield in their impregnation with sulphuretted hydrogen and the presence of lime salts, differ from them and from each other in some important particulars. More exhaustive analyses, especially of the Clifton and Avon waters, are very much needed.

The Clifton water contains a much larger proportion of the laxatives sulphates of magnesium and sodium than that of Richfield or Sharon, though not so much as that of Avon, and much more of the chlorides than Richfield or Sharon, though no more than Avon. It therefore is applicable to a similar class of diseases as the Richfield water, with this general qualification, that it is especially indicated in gouty, rheumatic, or scrofulous cases characterized by congestion of the mucous passages, with a tendency to copious discharges therefrom.

The waters of Avon are undoubtedly of very fine quality. They are more laxative, and, owing to the presence of a smaller amount of lime, are less indigestible, than any of the others; they are as useful in general rheumatic disorders as any, and of scarcely less value in catarrhal complications than the Clifton water; while in scrofulous conditions they have a special remedial value, dependent perhaps upon the iodine they contain.

The Sharon water is the weakest of all medicinally, though it contains as much lime as that of Richfield. Its most important ingredient is the sulphate of magnesium, and this, together with smaller proportions of the chlorides, produces a resemblance to the Clifton waters and to the Virginia "White Sulphur" water, and renders its use appropriate in similar cases, but more especially in those in which a less energetic medicinal action is desirable.

Irrespective of their waters, these resorts present many attractive features.

Clifton Springs has its well-established sanitarium open the entire year, where everything is pervaded by a religious atmosphere, and nothing done except upon business principles. Here facilities are offered for a perfectly quiet and regular life,

and for the systematic application of sulphur-water treatment, alone and in combination with various other methods of cure. Some of the house regulations seem rather oppressive to the invalid who desires to enliven the monotony incident to life in a water-cure by unrestrained indulgence in social pleasures, but are not at all unpleasant to those who find enjoyment in the religious performance of duty. Capable physicians are in constant attendance.

At Avon the best results are not attained, for want of disinterested management of the spring property. Yet many a rheumatic veteran can recall pleasant recollections of the home-like hostelries, the unconventional society, and wholesome waters that have made the resort popular for many years; and when he feels twinges of his faithful enemy, will think longingly of the beautiful Genesee Valley. There are here two water-cure establishments, under competent medical direction, that furnish limited but very comfortable accommodations and well-arranged therapeutic appliances for the visiting invalid.

The springs of Sharon are beautifully situated in the hill country of Schoharie County, nine miles distant from, and nine hundred feet above, the Mohawk Valley, and twenty-two miles east of Richfield.

Some of the other sulphur waters in our State, of which I can not speak, may before long demand our earnest consideration, but at present, for want of a proper scientific basis for popular interest, their usefulness is necessarily, though unfortunately, circumscribed.

THE GARDEN OF FAME.

"The garden-land of fame lies between Walhalla and the sea."—*Scandinavian Poet.*

WOULDST thou walk in the garden of fame,
    Wouldst thou taste of the fruits that grow
In alleys where grapes hang low,
    In fields that are never the same?

By the feet of the awful sea
    Alone canst thou reach those flowers,
And sit in the shaded bowers,
    Calm home of the bird and the bee.

No pathway, no compass, can lead;
    Alone must thou find the shore,
Alone through the fret and the roar
    Where the mailèd waters tread.

But he who would cling to a spar,
    Or hold by a knotted rope,
And laugh in his secret hope,
    Nor question his way of a star,

May be saved by a master hand,
    And fast to the shore may hold;
He may see the apples of gold;
    He may wander indeed on that strand.

But when the days are fulfilled,
    And the master's feet are led
Where only the gods may tread,
    And whither the gods have willed,

Then he who clung to the keel,
    Nor worshipped in labor and love,
Nor yearned for the apples, nor strove
    With a yearning the lover must feel,

Sees the waves of oblivion rise,
    And gather to drag him down,
While the face of the east wears a frown,
    And are vanished the god-like eyes.

WHO remembers when his childhood ceased? Who can name the hour when buoyant, thoughtless, half-reckless youth felt the first sobering touch of manhood, or recall the day when he passed over the summit of his life, and faced the long decline of age? As imperceptibly do the seasons blend when one passes and merges into another. There were traces of summer in May, lingering evidences of spring far into June, and even in sultry July came days in which the wind in the groves and the chirp of insects at night foretold the autumn.

The morning that followed the thundershower was one of warm, serene beauty. The artillery of heaven had done no apparent injury. A rock may have been riven in the mountains, a lonely tree splintered, but homes were safe, the warm earth was watered, and the air purified. With the dawn, Amy's bees were out at work, gleaning the last sweets from the white clover that was on the wane, from the flowers of the garden, field, and forest. The rosery yielded no honey: the queen of flowers is visited by no bees. The sweet-brier, or eglantine, belonging to this family is an exception, however, and if the sweets of these wild roses could be harvested, an Ariel would not ask for daintier sustenance.

White and delicate pink hues characterize the flowers of early spring. In June the wild blossoms emulate the skies, and blue predominates. In July and August many of the more sensitive in Flora's train blush crimson under the direct gaze of the sun. Yellow hues hold their own throughout the year, from the dandelions that first star the fields to the golden-rod that flames until quenched by frost and late autumn storms.

During the latter part of June the annual roses of the garden were in all stages and conditions. Beautiful buds could be gleaned among the developing seed receptacles and matured flowers that were casting their petals on every breeze. The thrips and the disgusting rose-bug were also making havoc here and there. But an untiring vigilance watched over the rosery. Morning, noon, and evening Webb cut away the fading roses; and Amy soon learned to aid him, for she saw that his mind was bent on maintaining the roses in this little nook at the highest attainable point of perfection. It is astonishing how greatly nature can be assisted and directed by a little skilled labor at the right time. Left to themselves, the superb varieties in the rosery would have spent the remainder of the summer and autumn chiefly in the development of seed-vessels, and in resting after their first bloom. But the pruning-knife had been too busy among them, and the thoroughly fertilized soil sent up supplies that must be disposed of. As soon as the bushes had given what may be termed their first annual bloom they were cut back half-way to the ground, and dormant buds were thus forced into immediate growth. Meanwhile the new shoots that in spring had started from the roots were already loaded with buds, and so by a little management and attention the bloom would be maintained until frosty nights should bring the sleep of winter. No rose-bug escaped Webb's vigilant search, and the foliage was so often sprayed by a garden syringe with an infusion of white hellebore that thrips and slugs met their deserved fate before they had done any injury. Thus for Mrs. Clifford and Amy was maintained a supply of these exquisite flowers, which in a measure became a part of their daily food.

Nature was culminating. On every side was the fulfillment of its innumerable promises. The bluebird, with the softness of June in his notes, had told his love amid the snows and gales of March, and now, with unabated constancy, and with all a father's solicitude, he was caring for his third nestful of fledgelings. Young orioles were essaying flight from their wind-rocked cradles on the outer boughs of the elms. Phœbe-birds, with nests beneath bridges over running streams, had nevertheless the skill to land their young on the banks. Nature was like a vast nursery, and from gardens, lawns, fields, and forest the cries and calls of feathered infancy were heard all day, and sometimes in the darkness, as owls, hawks, and other night prowlers added to the fearful sum of the world's tragedies. The cat-birds, that had built in some shrubbery near the house, had by the last

AMONG THE ROSES.

of June done much to gain Amy's good-will and respect. As their domestic character and operations could easily be observed, she had visited them almost daily from the time they had laid the dry twig and leafy foundation of their nest until its lining of fine dry grasses was completed. She had found that, although inclined to mock and gibe at outsiders, they were loyal and affectionate to each other. In their home-building, in the incubation of the deep bluish-green eggs, and in the care of the young, now almost ready to fly, they had been mutually helpful and considerate, fearless and even fierce in attacking all who approached too near their domicile. To Amy and her daily visits they had become quite reconciled, even as she had grown interested in them in spite of a certain lack of the high breeding which characterized the thrushes and other favorites.

"My better acquaintance with them," she said one evening to Dr. Marvin, who with his wife had stopped at the Cliffords' in passing, "has taught me a lesson. I think I'm too much inclined to sweeping censure on the exhibition of a few disagreeable traits. I've learned that the gossips in yonder bushes have some excellent qualities, and I suppose you find that this is true of the gossips among your patients."

"Yes," replied the doctor, laughing. "But the human gossips draw the more largely on one's charity; and if you knew how many pestiferous slugs and insects your neighbors in the shrubbery have already destroyed, the human genus of gossip would suffer still more in comparison."

That Amy had become so interested in these out-of-door neighbors turned out to their infinite advantage, for one morning their excited cries of alarm secured her attention. Hastening to the locality of their nest, she looked upon a scene that chilled the blood in her own veins. A huge black-snake suspended his weight along the branches of the shrubbery with entire confidence and ease, and was in the act of swallowing a fledgeling that, even as Amy looked, sent out its last despairing peep. The parent birds were frantic with terror, and their anguish and fearless efforts to save their young redeemed them forever in Amy's eyes.

"Webb!" she cried, since, for some reason, he ever came first to her mind in an emergency. It so happened that he had just come from the hay field to rest awhile and prepare for dinner. In a moment he was at her side, and followed with hasty glance her pointing finger.

"Come away, Amy," he said, as he looked at her pale face and dilated eyes. "I do not wish you to witness a scene like that;" and almost by force he drew her to the piazza. In a moment he was out with a breech-loading gun, and as the smoke of the discharge lifted, she saw a writhing sinuous form fall heavily to the earth. After a brief inspection Webb came toward her in smiling assurance, saying: "The wretch got only one of the little family. Four birds are left. There, now, don't feel so badly. You have saved a home from utter desolation. That surely will be a pleasant thing to remember."

"What could I have done if you had not come?"

"I don't like to think of what you might have done—emulated the mother bird, perhaps, and flown at the enemy."

"I did not know you were near when I called your name," she said. "It was entirely instinctive on my part; and I believe," she added, musingly, looking with a child's directness into his eyes, "that one's instincts are usually right; don't you?"

He turned away to hide the feeling of intense pleasure caused by her words, but only said, in a low voice, "I hope I may never fail you, Amy, when you turn to me for help." Then he added, quickly, as if hastening away from delicate ground: "While those large black-snakes are not poisonous, they are ugly customers sometimes. I have read of an instance in which a boy put his hand into the hole of a tree where there had been a bluebird's nest, and touched the cold scales of one of these snakes. The boy took to his heels, with the snake after him, and what would have happened it is hard to say had not a man plowing near come to the rescue with a heavy ox-whip. What I should fear most in your case would be a nervous shock had the snake even approached you, for you looked as if you had inherited from Mother Eve an unusual degree of hate for the reptile."

The report of the gun had attracted Alf and others to the scene. Amy, with a look of smiling confidence, said: "Perhaps you have rescued me as well as the birds. I can't believe, though, that such a looking creature could have tempted Eve to either good or evil;" and she entered the house, leaving him in almost a friendly mood toward the cause of the catbirds' woe.

Alf exulted over the slain destroyer, and even Johnnie felt no compunction at the violent termination of its life. The former with much sportsman-like importance measured it, and at the dinner table announced its length to be a little over four feet.

"By-the-way," said Webb, "your adventure, Amy, reminds me of one of the finest descriptions I ever read;" and jumping up, he obtained from the library Burroughs's account of a like scene and rescue. "I will just give you some glimpses of the picture," he said, reading the following sentences: "'Three or four yards from me was the nest, beneath which, in long festoons, rested a huge black-snake. I can conceive of nothing more overpoweringly terrible to an unsuspecting family of birds than the sudden appearance above their domicile of the head and neck of this arch-enemy. One thinks of the great myth, of the tempter and the cause of all our

woe, and wonders if the Arch-One is
not playing off some of his pranks before him. Whether we call it snake
or devil matters little. I could but
admire his terrible beauty, however,
his black shining folds, his easy gliding movement, head erect, eyes glistening, tongue playing like subtle
flame, and the invisible means of his
almost winged locomotion. Presently, as he came gliding down the slender body of a leaning alder, his atten-

A STEALTHY FOE.

tion was attracted by a slight movement of my arm; eying me an instant with that crouching, utter, motionless gaze which I believe only snakes and devils can assume, he turned quickly,'" etc.

Amy shuddered, and Mrs. Clifford looked a little troubled that the scene in Eden should be spoken of as merely a "myth." When she was a child, *Paradise Lost* had been her story-book, and the stories had become real to her. Burt, however, not to be outdone, recalled his classics.

"By-the-way," he said, "I can almost parallel your description from the Iliad of Homer. I won't pretend that I can give you the Greek, and no doubt it would be Greek to you. I'll get even with you, Webb, however, and read an extract from Pope's translation," and he also made an excursion to the library. Returning, he said, "Don't ask me for the connection," and read:

"'Straight to the tree his sanguine spires he roll'd,
And curl'd around in many a winding fold.
The topmost branch a mother-bird possess'd;
Eight callow infants filled the mossy nest;
Herself the ninth: the serpent as he hung
Stretched his black jaws, and crashed the crying
young;
While hovering near, with miserable moan,
The drooping mother wail'd her children gone.
The mother last, as round the nest she flew,
Seiz'd by the beating wing, the monster slew.'"

"Bravo!" cried Leonard. "I am now quite reconciled to your four years at college. Heretofore I had thought you had passed through it as Shadrach, Meshach, and Abednego passed through the fiery furnace, without even the smell of fire upon their garments, but I now at last detect a genuine Greek aroma."

"I think Burt's quotation very pat," said Amy, "and I could not have believed that anything written so long ago would apply so marvellously to what I have seen to-day."

"Marvellously pat indeed," said Leonard. "And since your quotation has led to such a nice little pat on your classical back, Burt, you must feel repaid for your long burning of the midnight oil."

Burt flushed slightly, but he turned Leonard's shafts with smiling assurance, and said: "Amply repaid. I have ever had an abiding confidence that my education would be of use to me at some time."

The long days grew hot, and often sultry, but the season brought unremitting toil. The click of the mowing-machine, softened by distance, came from field after field.

As the grain in the rye grew plump and heavy, the heads drooped more and more, and changed from a pale yellow to the golden hue that announced the hour of harvest. In smooth and level fields the reaping-machine also lightened and expedited labor, but there was one upland slope that was too rough for anything except the old-fashioned cradle. On a breezy afternoon Amy went out to sketch the harvesters, and from the shade of an adjacent tree to listen to the rhythmical rush and rustle as the blade passed through the hollow stalks, and the cradle dropped the gathered wealth in uniform lines. Almost immediately the prostrate grain was transformed into tightly girthed sheaves. How black Abram's great paw looked as he twisted a wisp of straw, bound together the yellow stalks, and tucked under the end of his improvised rope!

Webb was leading the reapers, and they had to step quickly to keep pace with him. As Amy appeared upon the scene he had done no more than doff and wave his hat to her, but as the men circled round the field near her again, she saw that her acquaintance of the mountain cabin was manfully bringing up the rear. Every time before Lumley stooped to the sweep of his cradle she saw that he stole a glance toward her, and she recognized him with cordial good-will. He too doffed his hat in grateful homage, and as he paused a moment in his honest toil, and stood erect, he unconsciously asserted the manhood that she had restored to him. She caught his attitude, and he was the subject of her sketch. Rude and simple though it was, it would ever recall to her a pleasant picture—the diminishing area of standing rye, golden in the afternoon sunshine, with light billows running over it before the breeze, Webb leading with the strong assured progress that would ever characterize his steps through life, and poor Lumley, who had been wronged by generations that had passed away, as well as by his own evil, following in an honest emulation which she had evoked.

As far as possible the prudent Leonard, who was commander-in-chief of the harvest campaign, had made everything snug before the Fourth of July, which Alf ushered in with untimely patriotic fervor. Almost before the first bird had taken its head from under its wing to look for the dawn, he had fired a salute from a

THE BILLOWY FIELD.

little brass cannon. Not very long afterward the mountains up and down the river were echoing with the thunder of the guns at West Point and Newburgh. The day bade fair to justify its proverbial character for sultriness. Even in the early morning the air was languid and the heat oppressive. The sun was but a few hours high before the song of the birds almost ceased, with the exception of the somewhat sleepy whistling of the orioles. They are half-tropical in nature as well as plumage, and their manner during the heat of the day is like that of languid Southern beauties. They kept flitting here and there through their leafy retirement in a mild form of restlessness, exchanging soft notes—pretty nonsense, no doubt—which often terminated abruptly, as if they had not energy enough to complete the brief strain attempted.

Alf with his Chinese crackers and his cannon, and Johnnie and Ned with their torpedoes, kept things lively during the forenoon, but their elders were disposed to lounge and rest. The cherry-trees, laden with black and white ox-hearts, were visited. One of the former variety was fairly sombre with the abundance of its dark-hued fruit, and Amy's red lips grew purple as Burt threw her down the largest and ripest from the topmost boughs. Webb, carrying a little basket lined with grape-vine leaves, gleaned the long row of Antwerp raspberries. The first that ripen of this kind are the finest and most delicious, and their strong aroma announced his approach long before he reached the house. His favorite Triomphe de Gand strawberries, that had supplied the table three weeks before, were still yielding a fair amount of fruit, and his mother was never without her dainty dish of pale red berries, to which the sun had been adding sweetening with the advancing season until nature's combination left nothing to be desired.

By noon the heat was oppressive, and Alf and Ned were rolling on the grass under a tree, quite satiated for a time with two elements of a boy's elysium, firecrackers and cherries. The family gathered in the wide hall, through the open doors of which was a slight draught of air. All had donned their coolest costumes, and their talk was quite as languid as the occasional notes and chirpings of the birds without. Amy was reading a magazine in a very desultory way, her eyelids drooping over every page before it was finished, Webb and Burt admiring the exquisite hues that the heat brought into her face and the soft lustre of her eyes. Old Mr. Clifford nodded over his newspaper until his spectacles clattered to the floor, at which they all laughed and asked for the news. His invalid wife lay upon the sofa in dreamy, painless repose. To her the time was like a long quiet nooning by the way-side of life, with all her loved band around her, and her large dark eyes rested on one and another in loving, lingering glances— each so different yet each so dear! Sensible Leonard was losing no time, but was audibly resting in a great wooden rocking-chair at the farther end of the hall. Maggie only, the presiding genius of the household, was not wilted by the heat. She flitted in and out occasionally, looking almost girlish in her white wrapper. She had the art of keeping house, of banishing dust and disorder without becoming an embodiment of dishevelled disorder herself. No matter what she was doing, she always appeared trim and neat, and in the lover-like expression of her husband's eyes, as they often followed her, she had her reward. She was not deceived by the semi-torpid condition of the household, and knew well what would be expected in a Fourth-of-July dinner. Nor was she disappointed. The tinkle of the bell at two o'clock awakened unusual animation, and then she had her triumph.

Leonard beamed upon a hind-quarter of lamb roasted to the nicest turn of brownness. A great dish of champion-of-England pease, that supreme product of the kitchen-garden, was one of the time-honored adjuncts, while new potatoes, dug for the first time that day, had half thrown off their mottled jackets in readiness for the feast. Nature had been Maggie's handmaid in spreading that table, and art, with its culinary mysteries and combinations, was conspicuously absent. If Eve had had a kitchen range and the Garden of Eden to draw upon, Adam could scarcely have fared better than the Clifford household that day. The dishes heaped with strawberries, raspberries, cherries, and white grape-currants that had been gathered with the dew upon them might well tempt the most *blasé* resident of a town to man's primal calling.

Before they reached their iced tea, which on this hot day took the place of coffee, there was a jar of thunder on the air.

"I knew it would come," said old Mr. Clifford. "We shall have a cool night, after all."

"A Fourth rarely passes without showers," Leonard remarked. "That's why I was so strenuous about getting all our grass and grain that was down under cover yesterday."

"You are not the only prudent one," Maggie added, complacently. "I've made my currant jelly, and it jellied beautifully: it always does if I make it before the Fourth and the showers that come about this time. It's queer, but a rain on the currants after they are fairly ripe almost spoils them for jelly."

The anticipations raised by the extreme sultriness were fulfilled at first only in part. Instead of a heavy shower accompanied by violent gusts, there was a succession of tropical and vertical down-pourings, with now and then a sharp flash and a rattling peal, but usually a heavy monotone of thunder from bolts flying in the distance. One great cloud did not sweep across the sky like a concentrated charge, leaving all clear behind it, as is so often the case, but as if from an immense reserve Nature appeared to send out her vapory forces by battalions. Instead of the long siesta which she had promised herself, Amy spent the afternoon in watching the cloud scenery. A few miles southwest of the house was a prominent highland that happened to be in the direct line of the successive showers. This formed a sort of gauge of their advance. A cloud would loom up behind it, darken it, obscure it until it faded out even as a shadow; then the nearer spurs of the mountains would be blotted out, and in eight or ten minutes even the barn and the adjacent groves would be but dim outlines through the myriad rain-drops. The cloud would soon be well to the eastward, the dim landscape take form and distinctness, and the distant highland appear again, only to be ob-

The family applauded from the piazza. Leonard and his father, remembering the hay and grain already stored in the barn, congratulated each other that the recent showers had prevented all danger from sparks.

After the last rocket had run its brief, fiery course, Alf and Johnnie were well content to go with Webb, Burt, and Amy to an upper room whose windows looked out on Newburgh Bay and to the westward. Near and far, from their own and

CLOUDING UP.

scured in like manner within the next half-hour. It was as if invisible and Titanic gardeners were stepping across the country with their watering-pots.

Burt and Webb sat near Amy at the open window, the former chatting easily, and often gayly. Webb, with his deep-set eyes fixed on the clouds, was comparatively silent. At last he rose somewhat abruptly, and was not seen again until evening, when he seemed to be in unusually good spirits. As the dusk deepened he aided Alf and Johnnie in making the finest possible display of their fire-works, and for half an hour the excitement was intense.

the opposite side of the river, rockets were flaming into the sky, and Roman candles sending up their globes of fire. But Nature was having a celebration of her own, which so far surpassed anything terrestrial that it soon won their entire attention. A great black cloud that hung darkly in the west was the background for the electric pyrotechnics. Against this obscurity the lightning played almost every freak imaginable. At one moment there would be an immense illumination, and the opaque cloud would become vivid gold. Again, across its blackness a dozen fiery rills of light would burn their way in zig-

"HE NEVER FORGOT THE PICTURE SHE MADE UNDER THE RUSTIC ARCHWAY."—[SEE PAGE 459.]

zag channels, and not infrequently a forked bolt would blaze earthward. Accompanying these vivid and central effects were constant illuminations of sheet-lightning all round the horizon, and the night promised to be a carnival of thunder-showers throughout the land. The extreme heat continued, and was rendered far more oppressive by the humidity of the air.

The awful grandeur of the cloud scenery at last so oppressed Amy that she sought relief in Maggie's lighted room. As we have already seen, her sensitive organization was peculiarly affected by an atmosphere highly charged with electricity. She was not re-assured, for Leonard inadvertently remarked that it would take "a rousing old-fashioned storm to cool and clear the air."

"Why, Amy," exclaimed Maggie, "how pale you are! and your eyes shine as if some of the lightning had got into them."

"I wish it was morning," said the girl. "Such a sight oppresses me like a great foreboding of evil;" and, with a restlessness she could not control, she went down to Mrs. Clifford's room. She found Mr. Clifford fanning the invalid, who was almost faint from the heat. Amy took his place, and soon had the pleasure of seeing her charge drop off into quiet slumber. As Mr. Clifford was very weary also, Amy left them to their rest, and went to the sitting-room, where Webb was read-

ing. Burt had fallen asleep on the lounge in the hall. Leonard's prediction promised to come true. The thunder muttered nearer and nearer, but it was a sullen, slow, remorseless approach through the absolute silence and darkness without, and therefore was tenfold more trying to one nervously apprehensive than a swift, gusty storm would have been in broad day.

Webb looked up and greeted her with a smile. His lamp was shaded, and the room shadowy, so that he did not note that Amy was troubled and depressed. "Shall I read to you?" he asked. "I am running over Hawthorne's *English Note-Books* again."

"Yes," she said, in a low voice; and she sat down with her back to the windows, through which shone momentarily the glare of the coming tempest. He had not read a page before a long, sullen peal rolled across the entire arc of the sky. "Webb," faltered Amy, and she rose and took an irresolute step toward him.

His preoccupation was gone instantly. Never had he heard sweeter music than that low appeal, to which the deep echoes in the mountains formed a strange accompaniment. He stepped to her side, took her hand, and found it cold and trembling. Drawing her within the radiance of the lamp, he saw how pale she was, and that her eyes were dilated with nervous dread.

"Webb," she began again, "do you—do you think there is danger?"

"No, Amy," he said, gently; "there is no danger for you in God's universe."

"Oh, that frightful glare!" and she buried her face on his shoulder. "Webb," she whispered, "won't you stay up till the storm is over? And you won't think me weak or silly either, will you? Indeed I can't help it. I wish I had a little of your courage and strength."

"I like you best as you are," he said; "and all my strength is yours when you need it. I understand you, Amy, and well know you can not help this nervous dread. I saw how these electrical storms affected you last February, and such experiences are not rare with finely organized natures. See, I can explain it all with my matter-of-fact philosophy. But, believe me, there is no danger. Certainly I will stay with you. What would I not do for you?" he could not help adding.

She looked at him affectionately as she said, with a child's unconscious frankness: "I don't know why it is, but I always feel safe when with you. I often used to wish that I had a brother, and imagine what he would be to me; but I never dreamed that a brother could be so much to me as you are. Oh, Webb!" and she almost clung to him, as the heavy thunder pealed nearer than before.

Involuntarily he encircled her with his arm, and drew her nearer to him in the impulse of protection. She felt his arm tremble, and wholly misinterpreted the cause. Springing aloof, she clasped her hands, and looked around almost wildly. "Oh, Webb!" she cried, "there is danger. Even you tremble."

Webb was human, and had nerves also, but all the thunder that ever roared could not affect them so powerfully as Amy's head bowed upon his shoulder, and the appealing words of her absolute trust. He mastered himself instantly, however, for he saw that he must be strong and calm in order to sustain the trembling girl through one of nature's most awful moods. She was equally sensitive to the smiling beauty and the wrath of the great mother. The latter phase was much the same to her as if a loved face should suddenly become black with reckless passion. He took both her hands in a firm grasp, and said: "Amy, I am not afraid, and you must not be. You can do much toward self-control. Come," he added, in tones

almost authoritative, "sit here by me, and give me your hand. I shall read to you in a voice as quiet and steady as you ever heard me use."

She obeyed, and he kept his word. His strong, even grasp re-assured her in a way that excited her wonder, and the nervous paroxysm of fear began to pass away. While she did not comprehend what he read, his tones and expression had their influence. His voice, however, was soon drowned by the howling of the tempest as it rushed upon them. He felt her hand tremble again, and saw her look apprehensively toward the windows.

"Amy," he said, and in smiling confidence he fixed his eyes on hers and held them.

The crisis of the storm was indeed terrific. The house rocked in the furious blasts. The uproar without was frightful, suggesting that the Evil One was in very truth the "prince of the power of the air," and that he was abroad with all his legions. Amy trembled violently, but Webb's hand and eyes held hers. "Courage!" he said, cheerily; "the storm is passing."

A wan, grateful smile glimmered for a moment on her pale face, and then her expression passed into one of horror. With a cry that was lost in a deafening crash, she sprang into his arms. Even Webb was almost stunned and blinded for a moment. Then he heard rapid steps. Burt at last had been aroused from the slumber of youth, and, fortunately for his peace, rushed first into his mother's room. Webb thought Amy had fainted, and he laid her gently on the lounge. "Don't leave me," she gasped, faintly.

"Amy," he said, earnestly, "I assure you that all danger is now over. As I told you once before, the centre of the storm has passed. You know I never deceived you."

Maggie and Burt now came running in, and Webb said: "Amy has had a faint turn. I will get her a glass of water."

This revived her speedily, but the truth of Webb's words proved more efficacious. The gale was sweeping the storm from the sky. The swish of the torrents mattered little, for the thunder peals died away steadily to the eastward. Amy made a great effort to rally, for she felt ashamed of her weakness, and feared that the others would not interpret her as charitably as Webb had done. In a few minutes he smilingly withdrew, and went out on the rear porch with Leonard, whence they anxiously scanned the barn and out-buildings. These were evidently safe, wherever the bolt had fallen, and it must have struck near. In half an hour there was a line of stars along the western horizon, and soon the repose within the old house was as deep as that of nature without.

Webb only was sleepless. He sat at his open window and saw the clouds roll away. But he felt that a cloud deeper and murkier than any that had ever blackened the sky hung over his life. He knew too well why his arm had trembled when for a moment it encircled Amy. The deepest and strongest impulse of his soul was to protect her, and her instinctive appeal to him had raised a tempest in his heart as wild as that which had raged without. He felt that he could not yield her to another, not even to his brother. Nature itself pointed her to him. It was to him she turned and clung in her fears. And yet she had not even dreamed of his untold wealth of love, and probably never would suspect it. He could not reveal it—indeed, it must be the struggle of his life to hide it—and she, while loving him as a brother, might easily drift into an engagement and marriage with Burt. Could he be patient, and wear a smiling mask through it all? That tropical night and its experiences taught him anew that he had a human heart with all its passionate cravings. When he came down from his long vigil on the following morning his brow was as serene as the scene without. Amy gave him a grateful and significant smile, and he smiled back so naturally that observant Burt, who had been a little uneasy over the events of the previous night, was wholly relieved from anxiety. They had scarcely seated themselves at the breakfast table before Alf came running in, and said that an elm not a hundred yards from the house had been splintered from the topmost branch to the roots. All except Mrs. Clifford went out to look at the smitten tree, and they gazed with awe at the deep furrow ploughed in the blackened wood.

"It will live," said Webb, quietly, as he turned away; "it will probably live out its natural life."

Amy, in her deep sympathy, looked after him curiously. There was something in his tone and manner which suggested a meaning beyond his words. Not

infrequently he had puzzled her of late, and this added to her interest in him. She understood Burt thoroughly.

Good old Mr. Clifford saw in the shattered tree only reasons for profound thankfulness, and words of Christian gratitude rose to his lips.

The July sun speedily drank up the superabundant moisture, and the farm operations went on with expedition. The corn grew green and strong, and its leaves stretched up to Abram's shoulder as he ran the cultivator through it for the last time. The moist sultriness of the Fourth finished the ox-heart cherries. They decayed at once, to Alf's great regret. "That is the trouble with certain varieties of cherries," Webb remarked. "One shower will often spoil the entire crop even before it is ripe." But it so happened that there were several trees of native or ungrafted fruit on the place, and these supplied the children and the birds for many days thereafter. The robins never ceased gorging themselves. Indeed, they were degenerating into shameless *gourmands*, and losing the grace of song, as were also the bobolinks in the meadows. Already there was a perceptible decline in the morning and evening minstrelsy of all the birds, and with the exception of calls and twitterings, they grew more and more silent through the mid-day heat. With the white bloom of the chestnut-trees the last trace of spring passed away. Summer reached its supreme culmination, and days that would not be amiss at the equator were often followed by nights of breathless sultriness. Early in the month haying and harvest were over, and the last load that came down the lane to the barn was ornamented with green boughs, and hailed with acclamations by the farm hands, to whom a generous supper was given, and something substantial also to take home to their families.

As the necessity for prompt action and severe labor passed, the Cliffords proved that their rural life was not one of plodding, unredeemed toil. For the next few weeks Nature would give them a partial respite. She would finish much of the work which they had begun. The corn would mature, the oats ripen, without further intervention on their part. By slow but sure alchemy the fierce suns would change the acid and bitter juices in the apples, peaches, plums, and pears into nectar. Already Alf was revelling in the harvest apples, which, under Maggie's culinary magic, might tempt an ascetic to surfeit.

While Burt had manfully done his part in the harvest field, he had not made as long hours as the others, and now was quite inclined to enjoy to the utmost a season of comparative leisure. He was much with Amy, and she took pleasure in his society, for, as she characterized his manner in her thoughts, he had grown very sensible. He had accepted the situation, and he gave himself not a little credit for his philosophical patience. He regarded himself as committed to a deep and politic plan, in which, however, there was no unworthy guile. He would make himself essential to Amy's happiness. He would be so quietly and naturally devoted to her that she would gradually come to look forward to a closer union as a matter of course. His fleet horse Thunder was his great ally, and in the long twilight evenings they explored the country roads far and near. When the early mornings were not too warm they rowed upon the river, or went up the Moodna Creek for water-lilies, which at that hour floated upon the surface with their white petals all expanded—beautiful emblems of natures essentially good. From mud and slime they developed purity and fragrance. He was also teaching Amy to be an expert horsewoman, and they promised themselves many a long ride when autumn coolness should make such exercise more agreeable.

Burt was a little surprised at his tranquil enjoyment of all this companionship, but nevertheless prided himself upon it. He was not so mercurial and impetuous as the others had believed him to be, but was capable of a steady and undemonstrative devotion. Amy was worth winning at any cost, and he proposed to lay such a patient siege that she could not fail of being his. Indeed, with a disposition toward a little retaliation, he designed to carry his patience so far as to wait until he had seen more than once an expression in her eyes that invited warmer words and manner. But he had to admit that time was passing and that no such expression appeared. This piqued him a little, and he felt that he was not appreciated. The impression grew upon him that she was very young, unaccountably young for one of her years. She enjoyed his bright talk and merry ways with much the same spirit that Alf's boyish exuberance called

forth. She had the natural love of all young, healthful natures for pleasure and change, and she unconsciously acted toward him as if he were a kind, jolly brother who was doing much to give spice and variety to her life. At the same time her unawakened heart was disposed to take his view of the future. Why should she not marry him after her girlhood had passed? All the family wished and expected it, and surely she liked him exceedingly. But it would be time enough for such thoughts years hence. He had the leisure and self-control for good-comradeship, and without questionings she enjoyed it. Her life was almost as free from care as that of the young birds that had begun their existence in June.

Only Webb perplexed and troubled her a little. At this season, when even Leonard indulged in not a little leisure and rest, he was busy and preoccupied. She could not say that he avoided her, and yet it seemed to happen that they were not much together. "I fear I'm too young and girlish to be a companion for him," she sighed. "His manner is just as kind and gentle, but he treats me as if I were his very little sister. I don't seem to have the power to interest him that I once had. I wish I knew enough to talk to him as he would like." And she stealthily tried to read some of the scientific books that she saw him poring over.

He, poor fellow, was engaged in the most difficult task ever given to man—the ruling of his own spirit. He saw her sisterly solicitude and good-will, but could not respond in a manner as natural as her own. This was beyond human capability. His best resource was the comparative solitude of constant occupation. He was growing doubtful, however, as to the result of his struggle, while Amy was daily becoming more lovely in his eyes. Her English life had not destroyed the native talent of an American girl to make herself attractive. She knew instinctively how to dress, how to enhance the charms of which nature had not been chary, and Webb's philosophy and science were no defense against her winsomeness. In her changeful eyes lurked spells too mighty for him. Men of his caste rarely succumb to a learned and aggressive woman. They require intelligence, but it is a feminine intelligence, which supplements their own, and is not akin to it. Webb saw in Amy all that his heart craved, and he believed that he also saw her fulfilling Burt's hopes. She seemed to be gradually learning that the light-hearted brother could bring into her life all the sunshine and happiness she could desire. Webb depreciated himself, and believed that he was too grave and dull to win in any event more than the affection which she would naturally feel for an elder brother, and this she already bestowed upon him frankly and unstintedly. Burt took the same view, and was usually complacency itself, although a week seemed a long time to him, and he sometimes felt that he ought to be making more progress. But he had no misgivings. He would be faithful for years, and Amy could not fail to reward such constancy.

Not only had the little rustic cottages which had been placed on poles here and there about the Clifford dwelling, and the empty tomato cans which Alf, at Dr. Marvin's suggestion, had fastened in the trees, been occupied by wrens and bluebirds, but larger homes had been taken for the summer by migrants from the city. Among these was a Mr. Hargrove, a wealthy gentleman, who had rented a pretty villa on the banks of the Hudson a mile or two away. Burt, with all his proposed life-long constancy, had speedily discovered that Mr. Hargrove had a very pretty daughter. Of course he was quite indifferent to the fact, but he could no more meet a girl like Gertrude Hargrove and be unobservant than could Amy pass a new and rare wild flower with unregarding eyes. Miss Hargrove was not a wild flower, however. She was a product of city life, and was perfectly aware of her unusual and exotic beauty. Admiring eyes had followed her even from childhood, and no one better than she knew her power. Her head had been quite turned by flattery, but there was a saving clause in her nature—her heart. She was a belle, but not a cold-blooded coquette. Admiration was like sunshine—a matter of course. She had always been accustomed to it, as she had been to wealth, and neither had spoiled her. Beneath all that was artificial, all that fashion prescribed and society had taught, was the essential womanhood which alone can win and retain a true man's homage. For reasons just the reverse of those which explained Amy's indisposition to sentiment, she also had been kept fancy-free. Seclusion and the companionship of her father, who had been an invalid in his later years, had kept the former a child in many respects, at a time when Miss Hargrove had her train of admirers. The city belle enjoyed the train very much, but showed no disposition to permit any one of its constituents to monopolize her. Indeed, their very numbers had been her safety. Her attention had been divided and distracted by a score of aspirants, and while in her girlish eyes some found more favor than others, she was inclined to laughing criticism of them all. They amused her immensely, and she puzzled them. Her dark and almost velvety black eyes, and the rich color that came and went beneath her clear brunette complexion, suggested a nature that was not cold and unresponsive, yet many who would gladly win the heiress for her own sake found her as elusive as only a woman of perfect tact and self-possession can be. She had no vulgar ambition to count her victims who had committed themselves in words. With her keen intuition and abundant experience she recognized the first glance that was warmer than mere friendliness, and this was all the committal she wished for. She loved the admiration of men, but was too good-hearted a girl to wish to make them cynics in regard to women. She also had the sense to know that it is a miserable triumph to lure a man to the declaration of a supreme regard, and then in one moment change it into contempt. While, therefore, she had refused many an offer, no one had been humiliated, no one had been made to feel that he had been unworthily trifled with. Thus she retained the respect and good-will of those to whom she might easily have become the embodiment of all that was false and heartless. She had welcomed the comparative seclusion of the villa on the Hudson, for, although not yet twenty, she was growing rather weary of society and its exactions. Its pleasures had been tasted too often; its burdens were beginning to be felt. She was a good horsewoman, and was learning, under the instruction of a younger brother, to row as easily and gracefully on the river as she danced in the ball-room, and she found the former recreation more satisfactory from its very novelty.

Burt was well aware of these out-of-door accomplishments. Any one inclined to rural pleasures won his attention at once; and Miss Hargrove, as she occasionally trotted smartly by him, or skimmed near on the waters of the Hudson, was a figure to win from his eyes more than a careless glance. Thus far he had observed her critically, and he found little to disapprove. She also was observing him, and was quite as well endowed as he with the power of forming a correct judgment. Men of almost every description had sought her smiles, but he did not suffer by comparison. His tall, lithe figure was instinct with manly grace. There was a fascinating trace of reckless boldness in his blue eyes. He rode like a centaur, and at will made his light boat, in which Amy was usually seated, cut through the water with spray flying from its prow. In Miss Hargrove's present mood for rural life she wished for his acquaintance, and was a little piqued that he had not sought hers, since her father had opened the way.

Mr. Hargrove, soon after his arrival in the neighborhood, had had business transactions with the Cliffords, and had learned enough about them to awaken a desire for social relations, and he had courteously expressed his wishes. Maggie and Amy had fully intended compliance, but the harvest had come, time had passed, and the initial call had not been made. Leonard was averse to such formalities, and, for reasons already explained, Burt and Webb were in no mood for them. They would not have failed in neighborliness much longer, however, and a call was proposed for the first comparatively cool day. A little incident now occurred which quite broke the ice, and also somewhat disturbed Burt's serenity. Amy was not feeling very well, and he had gone out alone for a ride on his superb black horse Thunder. After riding a few miles in a shady road, where the willows interlaced their branches overhead in a long Gothic-like arch, he saw Miss Hargrove, mounted also, coming slowly toward him. He never forgot the picture she made under the rustic archway. Her fine horse was pacing along with a stately tread, his neck curved under the restraining bit, while she was evidently amusing herself by talking, for the want of a better companion, to an immense Newfoundland dog that was trotting at her side, and looking up to her in intelligent appreciation. Thus in her preoccupation Burt was permitted to draw comparatively near, but as soon as she observed him it was evidently her intention to pass rapidly. As she gave her horse the rein and he leaped forward, she clutched his mane, and by a word brought him to a stand-still. Burt saw the trouble at once, for the girth of her saddle had broken, and hung loosely down. Only by prompt action and good horsemanship had she kept her seat, and now was quite helpless, for if she attempted to dismount, the heavy saddle would turn, with unknown and awkward results. She had recognized Burt, and knew that he was a gentleman; therefore she patted her horse and quieted him, while the young man came promptly to her assistance. He, secretly exulting over the promise of an adventure, said, suavely, as he lifted his hat,

"Miss Hargrove, will you permit me to aid you?"

"Certainly," she replied, smiling so pleasantly that the words did not seem ungracious; "I have no other resource."

He bowed, leaped lightly to the ground, and fastened his horse by the road-side; then came forward without the least embarrassment. "Your saddle-girth has broken," he said. "I fear you must dismount. Shall I lift you off? You maintained your seat admirably, but a very slight movement on your part will cause the saddle to turn."

"I know that," she replied, laughing. "Helplessness is always awkward. I am only too anxious to reach ground in safety," and she dropped the reins and reached out her hands.

"Your horse is too high for you to dismount in that way," he said, quietly, "and the saddle might fall after you and hurt you. Pardon me," and he encircled her with his right arm and lifted her gently off.

She blushed like the western sky, but he was so grave and apparently solicitous, and his words had made his course seem so essential, that she could not take offense. Indeed, he was now giving his whole attention to the broken girth, and she could only await the result of his examination.

"I think I can mend it with a strap from my bridle so that it will hold until you get home," he said; "but I am sorry to say that I can not make it very secure. Will you hold your horse a moment?"

"I am indebted to Mr. Clifford, I think?" she began, hesitatingly.

"I am Mr. Clifford, and, believe me, I am wholly at your service. If you had not been so good a horsewoman you might have met with a very serious accident."

"More thanks are due to you, I imagine," she replied; "though I suppose I could have got off in some way."

"There would have been no trouble in your getting off," he said, with one of his frank, contagious smiles; "but then your horse might have got away, or you would have had to lead him some distance at least. Perhaps it was well that the girth gave way when it did, for it would have broken in a few moments more in any event. Therefore I hope you will tolerate one not wholly unknown to you, and permit me to be of service."

"Indeed I have only cause for thanks. I have interfered with your ride, and am putting you to trouble."

"I was only riding for pleasure, and as yet you have had all the trouble."

She did not look excessively annoyed, and in truth was enjoying the adventure quite as much as he was, but she only said: "You have the finest horse there I ever saw. How I should like to ride him!"

"I fear he would be ungallant. He has never been ridden by a lady."

"I should not be afraid as long as the saddle remained firm. What is his name?"

"Thunder." At the sound of his name the beautiful animal arched his neck and whinnied. "There, be quiet, old fellow, and speak when you are spoken to," Burt said. "He is comparatively gentle with me, but uncontrollable by others. I have now done my best, Miss Hargrove, and I think you may mount in safety if you are willing to walk your horse quietly home. But I truly think I ought to accompany you, and I will do so gladly, with your permission."

"But it seems asking a great deal of—"

"Of a stranger? I wish I knew how to bring about a formal introduction. I have met your father. Will you not in the emergency defer the introduction until we arrive at your home?"

"I think we may as well dispense with it altogether," she said, laughing. "It would be too hollow a formality after the hour we must spend together, since you think so slow a pace is essential to safety. Events, not we, are to blame for all failures in etiquette."

"I was coming to call upon you this very week with the ladies of our house," he began.

"Indeed!" she said, lifting her eyebrows.

"I assure you of the truth of what I say," he continued, earnestly, turning his handsome eyes to hers. Then, throwing his head back a little proudly, he added, "Miss Hargrove, you must know that we are farmers, and midsummer brings the harvest and unwonted labors."

With a slight piquant imitation of his manner she said: "My father, you must know, Mr. Clifford, is a merchant. Is not that an equally respectable calling?"

"Some people regard it as far more so."

"Some people are very silly. There is no higher rank than that of a gentleman, Mr. Clifford."

He took off his hat, and said, laughingly: "I hope it is not presumption to imagine a slight personal bearing in your remark. At least let me prove that I have some claim to the title by seeing you safely home. Will you mount? Put your foot in my hand, and bear your whole weight upon it, and none upon the saddle."

"You don't know how heavy I am."

"No, but I know I can lift you. Try."

Without the least effort she found herself in the saddle. "How strong you are!" she said.

"Yes," he replied, laughing. "I developed my muscle, if not my brains, at college."

In a moment he vaulted lightly upon his horse, that reared proudly, but, at a word from his master, arched his neck and paced as quietly as Miss Hargrove's better-trained animal. Burt's laugh would have thawed Mrs. Grundy's very self. He was so vital with youth and vigor, and his flow of spirits so irresistible, that Miss Hargrove found her own nerves tingling with pleasure. The episode was novel, unexpected, and promised so much for the future that in her delightful excitement she cast conventionality to the winds, and yielded to his sportive mood. They had not gone a mile together before one would have thought they had been acquainted for years. Burt's frank face was like the open page of a book, and the experienced society girl saw nothing in it but abounding good-nature, and an enjoyment as genuine as her own. She was on the alert for traces of provincialism and rusticity, but was agreeably disappointed at their absence. He certainly was unmarked, and to her taste unmarred, by the artificial mode of the day, but there was nothing under-bred in his manner or language. He rather fulfilled her ideal of the light-hearted student who had brought away the air of the university without being oppressed by its learning. She saw with a curious little blending of pique and pleasure that he was not in the least afraid of her, and that, while claiming to be simply a farmer, he unconsciously asserted by every word and glance that he was her equal. She had the penetration to recognize from the start that she could not patronize him in the slightest degree, that he was as high-spirited as he was frank and easy in manner, and she could well imagine that his mirthful eyes would flash with anger on slight provocation. She had never met just such a type before, and every moment found her more and more interested and amused.

It must be admitted that his sensations kept pace with hers. Many had found Miss Hargrove's eyes singularly effective under ordinary circumstances, but now her mood gave them an unwonted lustre and power. Her color was high, her talk animated and piquant. Even an enemy, had she one, would have been forced to admit that she was dazzlingly beautiful, and inflammable Burt could not be indifferent to her charms. He knew that he was not, but complacently assured himself that he was a good judge in such matters.

Mr. Hargrove met them at the door, and his daughter laughingly told him of her mishap. There was evidently the utmost confidence between the two. He met her in like spirit with her own, and interpreted her unspoken wishes by so cordially pressing Burt to remain to dinner that he was almost constrained to yield. "You will be too late for your own evening meal," he said, "and your kindness to my daughter would be ill requited, and our reputation for hospitality would suffer, should we let you depart without taking salt with us. After all, Mr. Clifford, we are neighbors. Why should there be any formality?"

Burt was the last one to have any scruples on such grounds, and he resolved to have his "lark" out, as he mentally characterized it. Mr. Hargrove had been something of a sportsman in his earlier days, and the young fellow's talk was as interesting to him as it had been to his daughter. Fred, her younger brother, was quite captivated, and elegant Mrs. Hargrove, like her daughter, watched in vain for mannerisms to criticise in the breezy youth. The evening was half gone before Burt galloped homeward, smiling broadly to himself at the adventure.

His absence had caused little remark in the family. It had been taken for granted that he was at Dr. Marvin's, or the parsonage, for the young fellow was a great favorite with their pastor. When he entered the sitting-room, however, there was a suppressed excitement in his manner which suggested an unusual experience. He was not slow in relating all that had happened, for the thought had occurred to him that it might be good policy to awaken a little jealousy in Amy. In this effort he was obliged to admit to himself that he failed signally. Even Webb's searching eyes could not detect a trace of pique. She only seemed very much amused, and was laughingly profuse in her congratulations to Burt. Moreover, she was genuinely interested in Miss Hargrove, and eager to make her acquaintance. "If she is as nice as you say, Burt," she concluded, "she would make a pleasant addition to our little excursions and pleasure parties. Perhaps she's old and bright enough to talk to Webb, and draw him out of his learned preoccupation," she added, with a shy glance toward the one who was growing too remote from her daily life.

Even his bronzed face flushed, but he said, with a laugh: "She is evidently much too bright for me, and would soon regard me as insufferably stupid. I have never found much favor with city dames, or with dames of any description, for that matter."

"So much the worse for the dames, then," she replied, with a piquant nod at him.

"Little sisters are apt to be partial judges—at least one is," he said, smilingly, as he left the room. As he walked out in the moonlight he thought: "There was not a trace of jealousy in her face. Well, why should there be? Burt's perfect frankness was enough to prevent anything of the kind. If there had been cause for jealousy, he would have been reticent. Besides, Amy is too high-toned to yield readily to this vice, and Burt can never be such an idiot as to endanger his prospects."

A scheme, however, was maturing in Burt's busy brain that night which he thought would be a master-stroke of policy. He was quite aware of the good impression that he had made on Miss Hargrove, and he determined that Amy's wishes should be carried out in a sufficient degree at least to prove to her that a city belle would not be wholly indifferent to his attentions. "I'll teach the coy little beauty that others are not so blind as she is, and I imagine that with Miss Hargrove's aid I can disturb her serenity a little before many weeks pass."

But a few days elapsed before Mr. Clifford, with Burt, Maggie, and Amy, made the call which would naturally inaugurate an exchange of social visits. Mr. Hargrove was especially interested in the old gentleman, and they were speedily deep in rural affairs. Maggie was a little reserved at first with Mrs. Hargrove, but the latter, with all her stateliness, was a zealous housekeeper, and so the two ladies were soon *en rapport*.

The young people adjourned to the piazza, and their merry laughter and animated talk proved that if there had been any constraint it was vanishing rapidly. Amy was naturally a little shy at first, but Miss Hargrove had the tact to speedily put her guests at ease. She proposed to have a good time during the remainder of the summer, and saw in Burt a means to that end, while she instinctively felt that she must propitiate Amy in order to accomplish her purpose. Therefore she was disposed to pay a little court to her on general principles. She had learned that the young girl was a ward of Mr. Clifford's. What Burt was to Amy she did not know, but was sure she could soon find out, and his manner had not led to the belief that he was a committed and acknowledged lover. She made no discoveries, however, for he was not one to display a real preference in public, and, indeed, in accordance with his scheme, she received his most marked attentions. Amy also both baffled and interested her. She could not immediately accept this genuine child of nature, and Amy's very simplicity was puzzling. It might be the perfection of well-bred reserve, such complete art as to appear artless. Miss Hargrove had been in society too long to take anything impulsively on trust. Still she was charmed with the young girl, and Amy was also genuinely pleased with her new acquaintance. Before they parted a horseback ride was arranged, at Burt's suggestion, for the next afternoon. This was followed by visits that soon lost all formality, boat-

ing on the river, other rides, drives, and excursions to points of interest throughout the region. Webb was occasionally led to participate in these, but he usually had some excuse for remaining at home. He also was a new type to Miss Hargrove, "indigenous to the soil," she smilingly said to herself, "and a fine growth too. With his grave face and ways he makes a splendid contrast to his brother." She found him too reticent for good-fellowship, and he gave her the impression also that he knew too much about that which was remote from her life and interests. At the same time, with her riper experience, she speedily divined his secret, to which Amy was blind. "He could almost say his prayers to Amy," she thought, as she returned after an evening spent at the Cliffords', "and she doesn't know it."

With all his frankness, Burt's relations to Amy still baffled her. She sometimes thought she saw his eyes following the young girl with lover-like fondness, and she also thought that he was a little more pronounced in his attentions to her in Amy's absence. Acquaintanceship ripened into intimacy as plants matured under the waning suns of July, and the girls often spent the night together. Amy was soon beguiled into giving her brief, simple history, omitting of course all reference to Burt's passionate declaration and his subsequent expectations. As far as she herself was concerned, she had no experiences of this character to relate, and her nature was much too fine to gossip about Burt. Miss Hargrove soon accepted Amy's perfect simplicity as a charming fact, and while the young girl had all the refinement and intelligence of her city friend, the absence of certain phases of experience made her companionship all the more fascinating and refreshing. It was seen that she had grown thus far in secluded and sheltered nooks of the world, and the ignorance that resulted was like morning dew upon a flower. Of one thing her friend thought herself assured—Burt had never touched Amy's heart, and she was as unconscious of herself as of Webb's well-hidden devotion. The Clifford family interested Miss Gertrude exceedingly, and her innate goodness of heart was proved by the fact that she soon became a favorite with Mr. and Mrs. Clifford. She never came to the house without bringing flowers to the latter—not only beautiful exotics from the florists', but wreaths of clematis, bunches of meadow-rue from her rambles, and water-lilies and cardinal-flowers from boating excursions up the Moodna Creek—and the secluded invalid enjoyed her brilliant beauty and piquant ways as if she were a rare flower herself.

Burt had entered on his scheme with the deepest interest and with confident expectations. As time passed, however, he found that he could not pique Amy in the slightest degree; that she rather regarded his interest in Miss Hargrove as the most natural thing in the world, because she was so interesting. Therefore he at last just let himself drift, and was content with the fact that the summer was passing delightfully. That Miss Hargrove's dark eyes sometimes quickened his pulse strangely did not trouble him: it had often been quickened before. When they were alone, and she sang to him in her rich contralto, and he at her request added his musical tenor, it seemed perfectly natural that he should bend over her toward the notes in a way that was not the result of near-sightedness. Burt was amenable to other attractions than that of gravitation.

Webb was the only one not blind to the drift of events. While he forbore by word or sign to interfere, he felt that new elements were entering into the problem of the future. He drove the farm and garden work along with a tireless energy, against which even Leonard remonstrated. But Webb knew that his most wholesome antidote for suspense and trouble was work, and good for all would come of his remedy. He toiled long hours in the oat harvest. He sowed seed which promised a thousand bushels of turnips. Land foul with weeds, or only half subdued, he sowed with that best of scavenger crops, buckwheat, which was to be ploughed under as soon as in blossom. The vegetable and fruit gardens gave him much occupation also, and the table fairly groaned under the overabundant supply, while Abram was almost daily dispatched to the landing or to neighboring markets with loads of various produce. His rosery, however, seemed to afford him his chief recreation, and a place of rest, and the roses in Amy's belt were the envy and wonder of all who saw them. His mother sometimes looked at him curiously, as he still brought to her the finest specimens, and one day she said: "Webb, I never knew even you to be so tireless before. You are growing very thin, and you are certainly going beyond your strength, and—forgive me—you seem restlessly active. Have you any trouble in which mother can help you?"

"You always help me, mother," he said, gently; "but I have no trouble that requires your or any one's attention. I like to be busy, and there is much to do. I am getting the work well along, so that I can take a trip in August, and not leave too much for Leonard to look after."

August came, and with it the promise of drought, but he and his elder brother had provided against it. The young trees had been well mulched while the ground was moist, and deep, thorough cultivation rendered the crops safe unless the rainless period should be of long duration.

Already in the rustling foliage there were whisperings of autumn. The nights grew longer, and were filled with the sounds of insect life. The robins disappeared from about the house, and were haunting distant groves, becoming as wild as they had formerly been domestic. The season of bird song was over for the year. The orioles whistled in a languid and desultory way occasionally, and the smaller warblers sometimes gave utterance to defective strains, but the leaders of the feathered chorus, the thrushes, were silent. The flower beds flamed with geraniums and salvias, and were gay with gladioli, while Amy and Mrs. Clifford exulted in the extent and variety of their finely quilled and rose-like asters and dahlias. The foliage of the trees had gained its darkest hues, and the days passed, one so like another that it would seem that Nature was taking a summer siesta.

MONTEREY BAY.

The black ducks fly across the sky
    In level line,
The great white gulls the ether ply
    With wings ashine.
Now high, now low, they come and go
    'Twixt sky and sea;
They cleave the air, no bondage know,
    So wild and free.
The black ducks fly in level line,
The white gulls soar with wings ashine.

The water raves in darksome caves
    With moan and sigh,
But out in the light the mighty waves
    With joy dash high.
On sea and shore, while the waters roar,
    Bright shines the sun.
The west winds blow and the white gulls soar,
    And one by one
The black ducks fly in level line,
The wild waves roll with crests ashine.

ALL three were '78 men. It was just after Commencement. Dinsmore and Ross had been down on a flying visit —not so very flying either, for they staid a fortnight—to Cushing, at his father's country-seat on the Charles. It is altogether doubtful if three fellows ever had such a good time before. In the prime of youth and health, just through with that long four-years' grind over at Cambridge; sheep-skins all snugly tucked away in their trunks, the big load of pedagogic authority suddenly lifted from their shoulders, it is no wonder that the sky seemed a net-work of rainbows, and that sunrise and sunset glowed all round the horizon.

Those two bright weeks at the Cushings' had flown like magic to all four. For Stanley was counted in; she made the fourth, and had been in the thick and thin of all the glad hurly-burly. Brother Dick's guests were always her guests, and so she went along—in the saddle, on the river, on the tramp—always one of the party, vigor and courage outweighing the objection of petticoats.

Besides, Dinsmore and Ross were old acquaintances; that is, they had been home with Dick a good many times during his college course, to dine, or sup, or lodge, and thus she had often seen them. Why, yes, seen them, it may be said, as she had seen the swallows flitting through the air, or the passing clouds that shadowed her sunny pathway.

Wrapped in sweet matin unconsciousness, she was heart and soul intent on the fun alone, and never troubled her head with any nice analysis of her two guests.

Perhaps a careful diagnosis of her heart might have brought to light an unrecognized subconsciousness that Ross was forever staring at her with his wistful brown eyes, or continually contriving that they two should be thrown together. She seemed not to object to this, but none the less showed in various little ways, all too evident to poor Ross, that she would have considered it "twice as much fun" to make a ring, and have in Dick and Dinsmore.

Blissfully ignorant, however, of the havoc she was daily making of poor Ross's peace of mind, of the rapture caused by her slightest favor, of the wretchedness by her least neglect, she went gayly on her way,

"In maiden meditation, fancy-free,"

and wrought by mere simple impartiality and indifference all the harm that ensues from the most consummate coquetry.

The morning they went away she chanced to be on the piazza romping with the dogs, tousling a big St. Bernard, while a jealous little black-and-tan stood by vainly waiting to be noticed. Flushed with the exercise, her hair blown about by the morning breeze, she looked, with her tall, willowy figure, like a very Diana as she rose from her crouching position and came gracefully forward to shake hands when they appeared with their traps. Perhaps it was the tumult of leave-taking that rendered her blind and deaf to the almost painful significancy of Ross's manner. At any rate she sent them both off with the same friendly smile and an equally hearty hand-shake, saying, frankly, "Dick and I shall miss you ever so much."

Nor did it seem to occur to her as being of the slightest consequence that she happened to give the rose from her belt to Dinsmore, who, being the last to step into the carriage, had seen and asked for it.

Dick had the reins, and drove them to the station at a humming pace. In ten minutes more they were aboard the train whirling off to Boston.

Dinsmore and Ross were all the better companions for being as unlike as light and darkness. It was the old theory of contrasts. Dinsmore, born of bony, bilious New England stock, was yet like a "sport" of some far-descending Visigoth strain, big, broad-shouldered, with vigorous blunt features, close-clipped tawny hair, and a ruddy complexion—a magnificent animal. With a mind, moreover, as healthy as his body, not handicapped with overmuch wit, sentiment, or imagination, with clear ideas untainted by originality, with convictions halting conveniently in the wake of probation, with excellent reasons for the faith that was in him—reasons none the less good that they had been discovered by somebody else—he was of the stuff whence comes the world's practical leadership, a man who at fifty would ripen into a bank president or an effective Governor of the Commonwealth.

Ross was at the antipodes of all this. Far less striking in looks, he was in reality far more handsome. His slight graceful figure, clear olive tints, exquisite aquiline features, were barely saved from effeminacy by a virile look of power that shot from his eyes like a javelin, and told of sub-lying moral force. His facial lines were all downward, as though gravity had got the better of levitation. Hope and mirth, too, were evidently angel visitors in a breast where conscience was the reigning despot. Conscientiousness, indeed, bristled all over him, from his well-brushed hat to his methodical shoe-strings. He took life *au grand sérieux*. Brooding care spread wide her wings over the pettiest detail of existence, till as nice attention was bestowed upon the tying of a cravat as the writing of an essay.

It was something less than a week after their return to town that the two friends were invited to a yachting party down the harbor. Among the ladies on board was a certain Miss Bromfield, with whom Dinsmore was slightly acquainted, and to whom he duly presented Ross. As everybody in Boston is related, it was no great surprise when Miss Bromfield proved to be an aunt of Stanley Cushing, and the conversation naturally turned upon their late visit, of which the young men gave an enthusiastic account.

"Oh yes," said Miss Bromfield, innocently, "I have a letter from Stanley telling all about it. I quite envied you."

Miss Bromfield was experienced socially, and eventually proved to be the life of the party. She was an oldish young lady, spare in figure, with a look of much energy and intelligence. She had excellent manners, an unusual facility of expression, and, as it gradually appeared, was somewhat formidably informed. Happily, however, she was adroit enough to dissemble her information, and let it straggle out suggestively in a way that disarmed criticism and captured respect.

Miss Bromfield had what she gracefully called "a silly, idle fondness" for riddles, enigmas, macaronic verse, and the like verbal trifles. She had made a collection of these, at once extensive and select. She had all the celebrated anonymous riddles, all the unanswerable riddles, all the riddles made by famous men or on famous occasions and events, and a store of others especially curious, clever, or difficult.

Not unnaturally, therefore, as they were sailing up the harbor on their homeward way, the outspread city with its myriad steeples, turrets, and towers lying before them bathed in the dusky golden twilight,

the gilded dome of the State-house showing dark against the brighter yellow of the clouds, and away to the left the tender blue of the Milton Hills deepening to indigo in the fading light. Miss Bromfield, with a voice and manner nicely accommodated to the moment, restored the flagging conversation by propounding a riddle. The riddle, which was received with the grave and becoming attention due to its origin, oddly enough furnished the motive for this little narrative, through some slight badinage that passed between Dinsmore and Ross, resulting in a wager as to who should first solve it.

Miss Bromfield sanctioned the wager, and invested it with a momentous interest to the disputants by announcing that she was about to visit the Cushings, and that whichever of them should first send her the true solution should straightway be rewarded by an invitation to their delightful retreat upon the Charles.

"This is a very famous riddle," continued Miss Bromfield, taking out her pencil, and tearing in two the back of an old letter. "It is too long to remember, and so I will write it for you. It is said to have been given"—she went on busily writing on the blank side of her bits of paper as she talked—"by Aspasia to Pericles, by Cleopatra to Antony, by Elizabeth to Essex, and in modern times by Eugénie to Louis Napoleon. What truth there may be in these various stories, or in what language the original version appeared, I do not know. I merely tell you the tradition to give you a passing hint as to the character of the riddle. But here at last it is for you," she concluded, handing a fragment of the torn letter to each of the young men; "and now you must guess it without any more hints or suggestions, which, if you do," she added, as the yacht rounded beautifully up to the wharf, "I shall set you down among the very clever heads."

The young men had no time to read what had been written, but hastily thrust the bits of paper in their pockets, and helped the ladies to disembark. Upon the wharf they separated, each taking the most convenient route home.

Dinsmore lived in Boston, while Ross's home was in New York. The latter, however, was spending a few days at the Parker House, whither, accordingly, the two went to dine, and afterward adjourned to smoke and talk in Ross's room. Here, after a random chat upon various topics, Dinsmore suddenly bethought him of the riddle, and drew it laughingly from his pocket, predicting that he should win the wager.

Ross duly produced his own copy, and they proceeded to read it aloud, pondering and criticising it line by line, with many facetious comments. In the midst of this idle banter Ross chanced to turn over his scrap of paper and glance carelessly at the other side. In an instant he was struck dumb; his face changed; to Dinsmore's jocularity he henceforth returned no answer save now and then an absent monosyllable. He became more and more distraught, till Dinsmore demanded an explanation.

"What's the matter?"

"Matter?"

"Yes; what the deuce makes you so glum?"

"Nothing."

"Pooh! out with it. What ails you?"

"I'm out of sorts; don't want to talk. Guess you'd better go home."

"Sha'n't do it. Go home, indeed! What confounded megrim has seized you? You're bilious; ate too much dinner. Throw away your cigar, and send for a glass of Vichy."

"No, no; it's only I don't want to talk."

"Well, hold your tongue, then."

"I want to be alone, I tell you," exclaimed Ross, with rising impatience.

"Fudge! Get on your hat, and let's go to the theatre. You're a little seasick after knocking around all day on the water; that's it."

"It's nothing of the sort. Look here, Dins. We agreed to waive ceremony and all sorts of fiddle-faddle long ago. You know I love you; but—"

"Oh, bosh!"

"Very well. If you insist on staying here, why, stay, of course; but," continued Ross, rising and taking his hat, "you must excuse me."

"Here! here! hold on! I'm not going to drive a man out of his own room. You must be sick, or you wouldn't be so savage. Bile does upset a man deucedly, I know," continued Dinsmore, rising and tranquilly lighting a fresh cigar preparatory to taking his leave. "You'd better turn in as soon as I go, and put a mustard plaster on your liver. Ta, ta. Shall I send you a sawbones?"

"No."

As soon as his companion's footsteps had died away in the hall, Ross jumped up and locked the door; then drawing forth once more the piece of paper from his pocket, and ignoring now the historic puzzle of Miss Bromfield, he addressed himself with intent and harrowed countenance to the more absorbing riddle contained in these few broken lines upon the other side:

"The two young
arrived last week,
Dick's college friends,
One was a big noble fellow,
I fell in love with at on
The other little wretch,
I could not bear; he
and perfectly insignificant.
was glad to get rid of him.
come to see us while the
            "Your affect
                "STANLEY

It will easily be surmised what interpretation the sensitive Ross put upon these few elliptical sentences, and the effect may as readily be imagined. No further word was needed to his keen susceptibilities. His jealous temper seized upon patent probability as damning proof. Again and again he conned the little fragment of paper with intense and painful anxiety; but no, the conviction was as irresistible as it was crushing. All his hopes had been in vain, his delicate attentions distasteful, his presence obnoxious, and his very person derided.

Even to the respectable human pachyderm such a discovery might well have proved a shock; to Ross it was a knockdown blow, all the more terrible for being the first of the sort he had ever received. He sat for a long time, apparently stupefied, staring at the fatal scrap of paper. At length, starting to his feet, he paced the floor hurriedly for a few moments, consulted his watch, packed his trunk with feverish haste, called a carriage, and driving to the station, took the night train for New York.

Dinsmore was greatly astonished the next day to receive the following telegram:

"Came home last night. Forgive my running away. It was necessary. Can not explain now. Start for Europe Tuesday. Good-by!"

This was all quite incomprehensible to

Dinsmore. It was unlike Ross, who had never shown himself capricious. They had planned going abroad together in the fall. Dinsmore wrote directly, remonstrating against the breach of their agreement. He received no answer. Presently he saw Ross's name in the passenger list of the next Cunarder.

Up and down Europe like an uneasy spirit wandered hapless Ross week after week and month after month, staring with absent eyes at scenes and objects which to his unpossessed fancy would have been invested with a thousand charms, gazing unmoved at the wonders of art which otherwise would have aroused his æsthetic nature to wonder and veneration. Hither and thither in dreary, aimless course he overran the Continent, shunning notice, avoiding friends, repelling sympathy, vainly trying to escape from the dark shadow that sat perched upon his saddle croup. At length, late in the fall, more by chance than design, he found himself in Rome, where, going to his banker's one day, he received the following letter from Dinsmore. It was already more than a month old, having followed him about from place to place.

"BOSTON, *September* 1, 1878.

"WELL, OLD PILGRIM,—Where are you now? Have you got over your sulks yet? or was it a touch of downright lunacy you had, which has developed into violence, and brought you before this, deservedly enough, to a mad-house? Have you ever coolly considered the shabby way in which you gave me the slip? Come, make a clean breast of it, what did you mean, anyway? In the old times you wouldn't have treated a respectable dog so. But never mind. I forgive you. You were always walking on imaginary nettles, getting struck by air-drawn daggers, or stung by metaphysical wasps. But, deuce take you, it's time you begged my pardon, all the same; so come down now, like a man, and say you're sorry and ashamed of yourself.

"While you've been loafing about on the Continent, moping and getting demoralized, I've gone into business—got a good chance, and snapped it up as a cock-robin does an angle-worm. You see, the governor has some interest with those big Lowell fellows, and so succeeded in tucking me into a snug little vacancy in one of the mills, where I am now cotton-bat-tening. It's a big thing, I can tell you, having something to do, and you feel mighty respectable going home at night tired with a hard day's work. Have let my whiskers grow, given up all arts and graces, forsworn womankind—no, not quite that either. By-the-bye, let me tell you. You remember Miss Bromfield and her famous riddle? Well, what do you think?—I got that riddle—'pon my honor actually solved it; never did such a thing before in my life. 'Twas good too—deuced good. Have it in my desk now. Will slip it in this letter to remind you, and show how clever I was. Well, of course I won the wager. Remember the wager? Send me the box of cigars, then, you rascal. None of those wretched foreign cigars; real Havanas, mind you. But to come back to the riddle. Of course I lost no time in notifying Miss Bromfield. She was as good as her word, and I was invited straightway to the Cushings', where I had the jolliest week imaginable. Dick pretended he missed you, and Miss Stanley asked after you ever so sweetly. Jove! she's a lovely girl, and improves immensely on acquaintance. But, come, now, here's an olive branch for you, four long full pages. You deserve a thrashing rather than any such Christian conduct, but I was brought up on the beatitudes, and am magnanimous by instinct, as you know.
"Yours, DINS."

Ross read this letter with very mixed and tumultuous emotions. To the natural delight which shone in his eyes at sight of the well-known handwriting succeeded a look of pain, followed by an expression of suppressed bitterness as he approached the end. He sat musing for a long time with the open sheet in his hand. At length, recovering himself, he was about putting it back in the envelope, when he noted in the latter a small slip of paper. He drew it forth mechanically, and recognized the counterpart of his own copy of the hated riddle in the all too familiar handwriting of Miss Bromfield. With a half-repressed exclamation he tossed it impatiently to the floor, and seizing his hat, went out for a walk.

In the midst of his promenade, as he was listlessly making his way along the busy, bustling Corso, thronged with people waiting for some gala procession, he suddenly stopped as if he had been shot, turned like a flash, and hurried with breathless pace back to his lodgings. He burst open the door, rushed into the room, and looked anxiously about the floor. There lay the little slip of paper still undisturbed. With trembling hands he picked it up, hastily unfolded it, took from his pocket-book the carefully preserved corresponding fragment, adjusted the indentures, and eagerly scanned the completed page.

For a moment the blood rushed in a torrent to his face, and big drops of perspiration stood like beads upon his forehead. Then he became pale, and sank limply into his chair, with a long-drawn sigh of mingled pain and relief. These were the few innocent words that caused his emotion:

> pets papa promised
> the same evening as
> sent on approval.
> a St. Bernard, whom
> ce, and decided to keep.
> a black-and-tan,
> was a snarling cur,
> I sent him back, and
> Do hurry and
> fine weather lasts.
> ionate niece,
> CUSHING."*

Half the night Ross paced his chamber floor, recovering from the sudden revulsion of feeling caused by his discovery. Recognizing his own folly and precipitancy, deprecating all his ungenerous thoughts of Dinsmore, certain passages in whose letter, however, awakened fresh alarm, blushing with mortification at the thought of accounting to his friends for his strange behavior, yet sustained by a new sweet hope that the future might hold a solace for all past suffering and present shame, he at length with trembling eagerness addressed himself to action. Hastily packing his things and taking leave of his few friends, he left Rome the next day for London, whither, after a journey of ten days, he duly arrived. His English friends hardly knew him: the color had returned to his cheek, the sparkle to his eye—nay, he had actually gained flesh on his way from Rome. Some necessary business detained him for a few days in London; it was, indeed, two weeks before the vessel sailed in which he had taken passage for home. At length all prepara-

---

* Join the above to the fragment on page 466, to get the complete sense.

tions were made. He was just upon the eve of starting, when, on making a final visit to his banker's one morning, he was handed a second letter from Dinsmore. This time he beheld the bold, well-known handwriting with unqualified delight. He seized the letter with eagerness, a smile of anticipation parted his lips, his eyes glistened with old-time tenderness, as he tore it open upon the spot and read as follows:

"BOSTON, *October* 15, 1878.

"MY DEAR ROSY,—Why haven't you answered my letter, eh? Why haven't you done anything that was fair and square and amicable? Have I no rights that a white man is bound to respect? or have you ceased to call yourself a white man, you sallow wretch? Never mind; here goes, all the same. I will do my duty; I will go on heaping coals of fire upon your head, comforting myself with the reflection that whatever you may or may not *say*, you must *feel* ashamed of yourself. Hang it, man, won't it do when I say I forgive you? I could forgive anybody now. I'm in such a glorious, all-embracing, melting mood that I can even say the Lord's Prayer with fervor. I used to kick a little over that clause about the trespasses, but now I not only forgive my enemies, I wish them joy, ten strikes, double sixes, and all sorts of bounty. I'm light-headed; I jump over tables from morning till night; I sing myself hoarse; I grin like a Cheshire cat; and it really seems as if nothing but going up in a balloon would relieve my ecstatics.

"What's the matter? That's what I am going to tell you. Do you remember the riddle?—'that everlasting riddle,' you will say; but don't asperse it; it's been the making of me. I have adopted the answer to it as my life's motto. You have the answer, of course, before this. If not, behold in me, perched upon my present pinnacle of happiness, its living exemplification. The answer is 'Success,' and I have succeeded. God bless the riddle! God bless Miss Bromfield! *I am engaged to be married to her niece.*"

Ross stopped. A thunder-bolt could not have more quickly, more thoroughly arrested every function of his being, every movement of muscle, nerve, or pulse. It was death in life. A moment before, his eager eyes had been dancing from line to line adown the page, discounting with joyous confidence the grateful news of every coming sentence. Now a mist rolled before him, the ground rose under his feet, the room, the city, the world of things, whirled about him. In the dizzy confusion he had but one thought, he saw but one thing—that fatal line glowing in letters of fire upon his retina.

A sudden draught from the opening door, the sharp voice of a new-comer asking about some detail of business, at length aroused him. His eyes were still riveted to the page. Mechanically he read the next sentences:

"Do not be alarmed. It is not your precious Stanley Cushing. Miss Bromfield is rich; she has other nieces, and I have captured the queen of them all. Come home and see. Come home and envy me. Come home and be best man at the approaching nuptials of your faithful old DINS."

The world has long sought an antidote to seasickness. The search may now end. The remedy is found. It is sublimation. Let any man or woman embark upon the wildest seas that ever tossed, in the mood with which Ross set foot upon ship, and Neptune's rage will prove innocuous. To this day he has no remembrance of a single detail of what he afterward learned was a boisterous voyage. He landed in New York. He went straight to Boston. He brushed off the dust of travel at his old haunt, the Parker House, and hurried down to see D— No, not Dinsmore. We grieve to say the ingrate again neglected his old friend, and made his first call on Dick Cushing.

Dick was the same hearty creature in the counting-room that he had been aforetime in college. He fell upon his old classmate, shook his arm nearly out of joint, hurried him off to the club for a smoke and a chat, and later carried him thence home to dinner. Marvellous was Ross's submissiveness under all this hospitable violence; marvellous, too, how entirely he seemed to have recovered from the hurry and fluster that had possessed him ever since he left home.

The Cushings had come to town for the winter. They had a comfortable house in the Back Bay, and as the two friends made their way thither against a bleak November wind, Dick poured into ears that became every moment deafer and deafer a store of pleasant gossip about all their old classmates.

"Why, Mr. Ross, is it really you? We thought you were never coming back."

Heavens! was this vision of loveliness Stanley?—this tall figure rising from the midst of an elegant confusion of books and bric-à-brac as they entered the library. Was she, could she, still be free? Was that faint little flush that crept over her face at sight of him due only to surprise? Was there any especial significancy in her first unstudied greeting?

These are questions of vital interest to the querist—questions which he evidently finds it not quite easy to answer; for after a prolonged visit of several weeks in Boston, he comes all the way back from New York to renew the study every Sunday through the winter.

But patience is a wondrous touch-stone. It may be safe to say that no human fortress is impregnable to its magic siege. Of what avail it was in the present instance may be sufficiently indicated by a little conversation that occurred in the library just after the Christmas holiday. The subject of Ross's late trip to Europe was under discussion—a subject, be it said, that came upon the carpet not entirely by accident.

"But how ever came you to go off in that strange way? Everybody thought you were crazy."

"So I was."

"What do you mean?"

"Shall I tell you the truth?"

"Yes, if it isn't a secret."

"It has been a secret, but I don't want it to be a secret any longer," said Ross, with glowing eyes, as he drew forth his pocket-book and took therefrom two folded slips of paper, which he duly proceeded to unfold. "A secret which I have been ashamed to acknowledge to any one but you."

"How do I deserve such honor?"

"It was partly your fault."

"Mine!"

"Yes. Do you remember this?" he asked, holding out the first scrap of paper.

"Why, this is my writing. What is it about? I can't remember. It wasn't written to you. How came it torn? How very odd! Where is the rest of it?"

"Here."

"Oh, I see; it was to Aunt Kate. Where did you get it?"

"Miss Bromfield gave it to us. She

wrote this riddle in duplicate upon the other side—see?—and gave one to Dinsmore. This is the piece she gave me. It was just after our visit, you remember. Read it."

"But this is only half. I can not make anything out of this."

"Try."

"What? Why, Mr. Ross, you didn't—you couldn't surely think—"

Raising her eyes with a quick look of intelligence, the speaker paused, flushing deeply. After a moment her companion completed the sentence. He went on earnestly, ardently, eloquently, and completed a good many more, of a purport needless to be told, during which flush succeeded flush upon the fair, ingenuous face before him, till at length all other emotions were merged in a tremulous look of happiness quite indescribable.

It might have been an hour afterward that Dick came striding into the room, booted and spurred, to get Ross to go for a ride.

"What's all this?" he asked, poking about some scraps of paper on the floor with his riding-whip.

"Only a riddle!" said his sister, quickly gathering the fragments up in her hand.

Editor's Easy Chair.

A NATIONAL nominating Convention is one of the most interesting spectacles in this country of mass-meetings. It is a signal illustration of the simple methods of popular government, and it is, of course, unparalleled by any assembly in any other country, for nowhere else does the selection of the depositary of the chief executive power proceed directly from the delegates of the people. The two Conventions which assembled in Chicago during the early summer represented the ten millions of voters who will elect the President.

The great party council called the Convention has succeeded the old Congressional caucus, which until sixty years ago nominated the Presidential candidates. When communication over the great territory of the country was difficult, it was a natural and convenient method of selecting candidates that members of Congress of the same party should meet and name the candidate. It was very easy and convenient, but obviously it was the work of a very indirect representation of the preferences of the people, and it was a blending of the two powers which the Constitution carefully separates—the executive and the legislative. The last of the Congressional caucuses was held in 1824, by the friends of Mr. Crawford. Very few members attended, and the nomination had no moral force. The contest of that year was personal. The election was decided by the House of Representatives, and happily in favor of the best man—John Quincy Adams.

In 1828 the national nominations were made by the State Legislatures or by common consent, as in the earliest elections. The national nominating Conventions first assembled in 1831 and 1832, when the National Republicans, the Democrats, and the Anti-Masons all held Conventions in Baltimore for the election of 1832. Henry Clay, Jackson, and Wirt were the candidates. The system of Conventions has continued since that time, and there is no prospect of a change. The Democrats in recent years have adopted a rule which requires that the nomination must be made by a vote of two-thirds of the members elected to the Convention, and the Republicans, by requiring the district delegates to be elected in their districts, and thereby breaking up the practice of central instruction and a unit rule, have made the Convention more truly the representative of the party. This plan has the merit of revealing the real spirit of the party in its personal preferences for the nomination. In this way it shows the actual character of the party, and how closely it adheres to its traditional impulse and principle, and how far it strays from it.

Of late years the Conventions have assembled in enormous buildings designed for industrial exhibitions. This practice results in an immense popular assembly, amid which the Convention itself is comparatively lost. In the Chicago Conventions of this year the nominating body was composed of something more than eight hundred persons in a multitude of fifteen or twenty thousand. The vast crowd is swayed by excited feeling, and the storms of tempestuous and prolonged applause inevitably influence the Convention.

The "supreme moment" in a National Convention is that of the sudden and instinctive perception of the multitude that a nomination is about to be made. This perception may be due to the withdrawal of a candidate, and the transfer of his solid vote to another, or to a simultaneous turning toward a "dark horse," or to any other significant event. But the effect is extraordinary. The excitement is universal and intense. The Convention is on its feet. The galleries are strained to hear and to see. There is dead silence to hear a certain vote. There are roars and a tornado of acclamation when it is announced. A profound hush follows. The decisive instant has arrived. A vote is declared which carries the whole vote beyond the majority point, and the nomination is actually made. The shout that greets it is indescribable. The shout is jubilantly renewed and prolonged. It rolls and lifts like the ocean surf in a storm, and culminates and breaks in a mighty tenth wave of cheers and cries. The voting proceeds. There is universal change to the side that has won of the vote that has held out for another candidate. There is no change of that which has held fast to another cause as well as candidate. That vote holds fast to the end. The formal announcement of the nomination is made. The formal motion of unanimity is declared adopted amidst universal uproar. The thunder of cannon shakes the great building in Chicago. The electric wire at the same moment whispers the nomination to Katahdin and the Golden Gate and all the continent between, and the twenty-second Presidential campaign has begun.

NEW YORK is fast wiping away the reproach that she cares little for her own history. In many ways that history is supremely interesting. It was the Empire State of the Indian Confederation before it was that of the American Union, and the legends of the Long House of the Iroquois are the most commanding of the Indian traditions. In that Long House what thriving and beautiful cities now stand and prosper and extend—cities of yesterday, but already homes of plenty, of intelligence, of refinement, of all the virtues and the energy that make great communities! Indeed, it is in contemplating that series of inland cities which stretches from the Hudson to Lake Erie that the name of the Empire State is justified and its power and ascendency are explained.

It was by a happy fortune that in one of those cities lived the most learned student of the old Iroquois Confederation, Lewis H. Morgan; and greatly must that accomplished scholar have been missed at the late celebration by the city of Rochester of the fiftieth anniversary of its incorporation. Yet nothing was wanting in historic narrative and eloquent speech worthily to commemorate the event, and to describe vividly the simple miracle of the rise and growth of the city of the Genesee. The historical address by Mr. Charles E. Fitch was a masterly grouping of the significant progressive events of the growth of the city with that skillful blending of local details and noted names which is indispensable in such a discourse, and which gives a special interest to the story.

When the century began, although the famous expedition to found Marietta had reached the Ohio, the western frontier of the United States was drawn practically at the Genesee River. Through the woods of central New York the long procession of emigrant wagons which Leutze has commemorated in his picture in the Capitol had already begun to pass—the long procession which carried New England into New York and beyond—and was not to pause until it had carried it to the Pacific Ocean. It passed no fairer or more fertile region than that of the valley of the Genesee, and yet at what point upon the river the mill, the mart, the gathering settlement, the prosperous and stately city of the future was to be, no pioneer was shrewd enough to see, until Nathaniel Rochester, born in Virginia, and subsequently a citizen of North Carolina and of Maryland, came, in 1808, to western New York. The impulse of his emigration from Maryland, Mr. Fitch tells us, was his hatred of slavery. "Thus Rochester, which the Chrysostom of the colored race was afterward to make his home, and from which New York's most philosophic statesman was to announce the 'irrepressible conflict,' is, through the resolution of its founder, most honorably identified with the revival of antislavery sentiment in America."

Colonel Rochester built his mill, and Rochester began. It was peopled in great part by New-Englanders, and the orator gladly owns the sturdy industry, the "faculty," the skill, the strong character, and, above all, the steady moral impulse, which the Puritan stock contributed to the little village. They built upon "the town meeting, the spelling-book, and the Bible," and they built for the future. Step by step the historian unrolls the development of the mill into the village, the town, the city. Seventy years ago Rochester had a population of one hundred and fifty persons. It was an outpost in the forest, as far removed almost from the Rochester of to-day as Boston from its earliest settlement, and yet of that little forest village there is still a survivor in the person of Mrs. Abelard Reynolds. It was not until 1819 that the village was called simply Rochester. The next year it had fifteen hundred people and a cotton mill. The stage-coach brought the mail and wound its horn along the lake, and the Erie Canal was to pass through Rochester. Already the town was laid out in streets, but happily it escaped the devastating classical dictionary of good old Surveyor-General Simeon De Witt, who caught western New York at a defenseless moment, and tattooed its surface ineradicably with Greek and Roman names.

In 1827 there were eight thousand people in Rochester, and among her citizens were men famous in the State and country, the fathers of whom any city might be proud. In 1834, the year which the celebration recalled, Colonel Rochester was still living. There were banks, newspapers, lines of coaches and packets, an academy, and ten hotels. The city proceeds to elect a Mayor, and although party politics really have no more to do with municipal government than with the conduct of a manufacturing corporation, the new Whig party carries the day, and an excellent Mayor is chosen. In his inaugural address he said that men who had levelled the forest to clear a site on which to build the city sat with him at the council board of the city. Mrs. Abelard Reynolds saw it a little village of one hundred and fifty persons hidden in the forest of central New York. She sees it to-day a city of a hundred thousand inhabitants — the fourth city in New York, the twenty-first in the United States.

How natural was the eloquent congratulation of Rochester on her semi-centennial day! How proudly she called the roll of her sons, who, in serving in many ways the common interests of the country, shed lustre upon their civic mother's name! Such days, dawning upon the restless hurry of our money-getting life, upon our pursuit of low aims and deliberate renunciation of lofty and generous ideals, upon our forgetfulness that in a higher than Poor Richard's sense honesty is the best policy, break like a benediction. In recalling the fathers Rochester strengthens her moral fibre, and her loyalty to that principle without which civil prosperity is an illusion.

———

THERE is no more beautiful and impressive passage in the New Testament than that which contrasts the Pharisee thanking God that he is not as other men are and the Publican who asks mercy as a sinner. But there is no passage, also, which has been more ingeniously perverted, and it is exceedingly amusing to hear Jeremy Diddler or Robert Macaire or Dick Turpin railing at honest and industrious men as Pharisees because they prefer honesty and industry to knavery.

The taste for honesty and sobriety seems natural and simple enough, and the qualities themselves quite as valuable as those of Diddler, or even of Jonathan Wild the Great. But Jonathan will have none of them. They are Pharisaic impertinences. They are impracticable and visionary speculations, which assume heaven while yet we stand upon the green earth; and Mr. Wild, who assures us that he does not desire to pass himself off as better than other men, declares, with the noble candor which distinguishes him, that simple, downright dishonesty is good enough for him. He does not, indeed, choose that precise word, but he conveys that precise idea.

'Tis a good trick, and it is generally sure of applause. But it is only another version of a familiar maxim, that when you have no argument, you must abuse the plaintiff's attorney. As a matter of fact, your client did steal the handkerchief, or forge the name, or fire the barn. But I ask you, gentlemen of the jury— you may well say—and I appeal to all good citizens, is not this ostentation of superior virtue, this fine air of moral indignation toward my client simply because he happened to slip his hand into the wrong pocket, a little suspicious? Are we angels? I ask your honor is this work-a-day world the celestial seat and the Mount of Vision, and is a man so very

much better than his fellows merely because he rolls up his sanctimonious eyes with the Pharisee and thanks God that he is holier than other men? Nay, gentlemen, have we not in this sublime and immortal parable a Divine warning against this Phariseeism which denounces the slides and slips of our common frail humanity? I ask you, gentlemen, by your verdict not to place a premium upon that most odious of all repulsive arrogancies—Phariseeism.

But it is upon the political platform that the gibes and sneers at Phariseeism are intended to be most stinging. The Honorable Jonathan Wild the Great comes out strong, as his henchmen truly declare, against his political opponents. With one vast comprehensive sneer he brands them as Pharisees, as if he were snorting consuming fire. It is not surprising, because they have had their eye upon Jonathan. They have seen him in bad company. They have caught him "conveying" public treasure. They know all about him, and he knows that they know all about him. He called himself Tweed, and he made a mesh of statutes to legalize robbery. But how good he was to the poor! How he distributed coal to the chilly! How he planted pinks and daisies in the City Hall Park, and made the Battery to bloom as the rose! How he received wedding gifts for his daughter from our best citizens; and how generously they subscribed to erect his statue to commemorate that bright flower of the State! And now a sneaking, mousing gang of would-be archangels prate about common honesty, and demand that public hands shall be clean hands! Fellow-citizens, Jonathan Wild is a man of the people. He doesn't pretend to be higher and purer and better than other men. He didn't graduate at a college, indeed, and he never read the Iliad in the original Greek. No, fellow-citizens, there is no cambric handkerchief and oh-de-cologne about him. He is just one of the boys. He whoops it up with the plain people, and, thank God, whatever he is, he is not a Pharisee.

The argument is ingenious. It does not deny that he is a thief. It only insists that those who assert it are Pharisees—and Pharisees are so odious that it is much better to scoff at them than to punish Mr. Wild. There was a good old countryman who had been early taught to take men as they are, which means to consider them liars and rascals. One day a neighbor remarked to him that he thought that the old man had lost the money with which he bought voters, because, he said, while they take your money, the other side take their votes. "The deuce they do!" said the old countryman. "Yes," said the other; "and you will find, in the long-run, that political honesty is the best political policy." "You think so, do you?" was the reply. "Well, do you know that you're a blanked metaphysical Pharisee?"

It is obvious that when the advocacy of

common honesty in any relation of life is savagely and scornfully decried as Phariseeism, it is because somebody's withers are wrung. It is a plea of guilty. It is the cry of Squeers when the picture of Dotheboys Hall was displayed to the world: "I didn't do it." If a man demands honesty in politics, and it is retorted, "You're a Pharisee," it is because the dishonesty can not be denied or disproved, and the retort is therefore a summons to all honest men to look out for thieves.

To deride the demand for decency is to concede that anything but indecency is impracticable. If it is only Pharisees who insist that sugar shall not be sanded, that milk shall not be swill-fed, that coffee shall not be chiccory, that nutmegs shall not be wood, that cloth shall not be shoddy, that employés of the government shall not be forced to pay for their places, that public officers shall be honest, and that government shall not be venal, it is pleasant to think how many intelligent, upright, industrious, and practical Americans belong to that sect.

THE financial flurry of the spring, which was almost a panic, and which made Wall Street a striking scene of confusion and excitement, soon passed away, but it left much meditation behind. Its most important service was the warning furnished by the sudden vivid glimpse of the methods to which the reckless eagerness of money-getting resorts. The banking house and the bank whose failure precipitated the alarm were apparently entirely under the control of a few persons who were practically gamblers and swindlers, and who played with the good names of their associates, and with the money of honest people.

The fascination of the game was shown in the course of the men who put a certain sum into the wheel, presently received it doubled in profits, and then returned it to be doubled again. It is hardly conceivable that such men supposed the profits to be honest, but so long as the profits were paid they did not choose to inquire, and if a suspicion crossed their minds that the risk was enormous, the fact of previous success, and the hope of escape which always resistlessly allures the gambler, drew them on.

The result and the disclosure are naturally disturbing. How much more of this swindling is there which will suddenly appear in the same way? is the inevitable question, and the uncertain feeling produces a paralysis of enterprise. It is true that the old proverbs assure us that all is fair in business and politics, and that custom-house morality is not exactly that of the Sermon on the Mount, and that the buyer must beware, which means that the seller will try to cheat him. It is true that excellent men are often described as too honest for their own good, and yet it is truer than all the rest that the great commercial transactions of the world are founded upon good

faith. Credit is the basis of trade, and credit is confidence in honesty.

Moreover, such crimes as those of Ferdinand Ward, while they spring often from depravity, are oftener the result of mere weakness of character. Thackeray in many of his minor sketches constantly draws the portrait of the man and woman whose means are not equal to the style of living which they desire; and they desire it not for itself, but only because others have it. They are not strong and steady enough to be content with that which they can command and afford, and the means to secure the other must somehow be obtained. Thackeray puts the fact in the simplest and most amusing form. The young couple must give a dinner, and instead of the joint of lamb and the glass of beer which is the only repast to which they have the moral right to invite a friend—if, indeed, the beer may be morally permitted—they must needs prepare a feast which they can not honorably afford, and for the sole reason that other people who can afford it give such feasts.

It is this doing a little more, or a great deal more, than the doer can honestly afford, which leads to the swindles of Wall Street. Living in a house too expensive for his means, maintaining it accordingly, dressing as his richer neighbors dress, doing in all things as they do—it is this weak compliance which is hidden in the fine houses, and drives to the Park in the fine equipages, which presently ends in Ludlow Street Jail and hopeless disgrace. Yet it is the poorest kind of competition, because the little imitator might see even with his dull eyes that there must always be a few persons who can "do the thing" better than all the rest, and without feeling it. The bullfrog may swell until he bursts, but he can not rival the ox.

This is the tendency which all sensible people—and a great many otherwise sensible people are swept away by it—ought quietly to resist. The power of individual example is immense, but it is often underestimated by the individual. "My vote is of no consequence, but, since you wish it, I will vote," said a man to his neighbor, and the right candidate was elected by a majority of one. The family which in the midst of a saturnalia of luxury and extravagance refuses to take part in it, and holds to a simple, moderate, temperate way, is diminishing the supply of Ferdinand Wards and Wall Street panics.

Undoubtedly a foolish expense and extravagance is the vice of our society. It is a vice which spreads. It degrades character and corrupts conduct, and its consequences are historically seen in the decadence of old Rome and the French Revolution. The remedy is not chiefly nor primarily in law, but in the individual will. If every man will take care of himself, the community will be taken care of. The financial flurries and panics are writings upon the wall. If a select company should assemble in Newport during this pleasant summer, and repairing to the cliff, should engage in a competition to determine which of them could throw at once the most money farthest into the sea, they would justly be supposed to be a company of lunatics who had escaped from Utica or Somerville.

Yet a philosopher who strolls the cliffs avers that there is such a company, and that they are engaged in that very enterprise, and he adds that in any country such a company is the dangerous class, because they stimulate the riot of selfish extravagance which all sensible people condemn.

THE summer brings the college Commencement, and although the story of the festival properly fills much space in the press, it is not because of the multitude of graduates. The number of annual graduates is but in the ratio of one to about twenty-five hundred of the population. Half a century ago it was about one to two thousand. During that time the population has increased fourfold, the colleges threefold, the aggregate number of students twofold. These figures, which we owe to President Barnard, of Columbia College, are susceptible of various explanations. But it will be found—and it is a pleasant fact to remember in the Commencement season—that the colleges still maintain their influence in the leadership of the country.

There is an occasional gibe at college-bred men as if they were too fine for practical service in affairs. But the fact is that they have had a powerful and controlling part in such service. The New England emigration, which was the most momentous in history and the most influential in early American affairs, was led by college men. The most powerful Revolutionary leaders were college men. The chiefs of the Constitutional Convention of 1787 were college men. The party captains and political champions during the constitutional century have been, in most effective part, college men. It is not weakness nor an impracticable tendency which breeds in the mind of the poor country boy the desire to go to college. On the contrary, it is the instinct of conscious power seeking to strengthen itself, and such boys have come to stand among great Americans.

The colonial colleges were few and small, but the best of them did their work well. New York was a little late in founding a college. But the New-Yorker who first distinctly hinted at independence, and clearly stated the central argument of the Revolution, John Morin Scott, was a son of Yale, and the Revolutionary fathers of New York, John Jay, the Livingstons, Gouverneur Morris, and many another, were of Columbia College. Indeed, when President Cooper, of Columbia, who

had been brought from England to preside over the college, took up the Tory cudgels to discipline New-Yorkers, they were knocked out of his hands by a doughty antagonist in a work of anonymity, who proved to be Alexander Hamilton, one of his own pupils.

The college does not guarantee to every graduate all the virtues and moral graces, nor all knowledge and wisdom, nor genius and statesmanship and common-sense. Neither can the common school or the academy do this, nor the counting-room, nor the workshop, nor the caucus. But experience shows that the youths who earnestly desire the knowledge and the training which the college supplies are those who become men that the country wants. To like to read good books, to associate with generous and enlightened persons, to be frugal and temperate and cleanly of life, are evidences of tendencies and tastes which every parent hails in his child with delight. In like manner the taste and the desire for college education are proofs of the qualities which have been of the highest public service.

Of course every private business and every public department is full of the most honorable and efficient men who are not college-bred, and their number is so great that there is sometimes a disposition to think that the college is a dilettant retreat, and an enervating rather than a strengthening influence. But this impression is, as we have said, historically inaccurate, and no college man, whether he be Freshman or Senior or graduate, need doubt that he belongs to a company which has furnished the most efficient and illustrious leaders at every period of the national life.

The legend of Dartmouth College, the eighth college founded in this country, was *Vox clamantis in deserto.* Upon the sequestered shores of the Upper Connecticut in 1769 a college devoted to the higher education, in a region which was still at close quarters with a rigorous climate and the hard necessities of a frontier, might well call itself a voice crying in the wilderness. But the impulse which founded and sustained it, the feeling which bred in the heart of Daniel Webster's father the purpose to send his son to the college, and which in the son's breast nourished the desire to go—this loyalty to knowledge as a source of power, and to intellectual training as the means of its effective exercise, is one of the profound instincts of human nature.

So, as the happy college days end, and, amid music and congratulations, and hopes and prayers, and smiles and tears, the graduate receives his degree, the generous youth will feel that it not only certifies an achievement, but imposes a duty. On every diploma is written invisibly what his inward eye plainly reads, *Noblesse oblige.*

THERE is no period in the history of the Roman Empire that is more deserving of the study of men of modern times than that which witnessed the rule of the two Antonines. Aside from the interest that attaches to the personal character of the men whose virtues and abilities have made the name resplendent, aside also from the great historical fact that it was during their lives, when the glory and power of Rome had seemingly reached the highest pitch of grandeur, that the seeds of disintegration and decay, previously sown by the policy of universal conquest which alike swayed the republic and the early empire, first began to germinate and to assume menacing proportions, it was under their benignant imperial rule, more especially under that of the last and greatest of the name, that those great legislative and administrative reforms were devised which placed justice within the reach of citizens of every class in all parts of the empire, which introduced principles of equity into its interpretation and application, which mitigated the cruel severity of penalties, which enforced the obligation of contracts, gave security to property and rendered its transmission easy, regulated inheritance, elevated the plane of woman, encouraged and dignified marriage, and conserved the personal rights, interests, and liberties of the individual, particularly of the feebler classes, such as women, children, minors, slaves, and debtors—reforms that were far in advance of the age, and that continue to exert a powerful influence upon us of this late generation, and, in fact, form the basis of a large body of the civil and common law of our own day. The brilliant outline of the age of the Antonines contained in the first three chapters of Gibbon's great work is doubtless familiar to most intelligent readers, but with all its minuteness Gibbon's masterly sketch is yet lacking in many details that are essential to a full comprehension of the infinity and the extent of the reforms for which we are indebted to Marcus Aurelius, and to a complete conception of his life and character. Nor has there been heretofore any single work in the English language which deals either with the man or his influence upon the institutions and events of his age with the continuity and comprehensiveness that they deserve. What has been possible to be known of the great pagan philosopher, statesman, legislator, and ruler must have been derived from a great variety of scattered works not generally accessible or intelligible even to scholars, and many of which preserve, amidst a mass of rhetoric, sentiment, and controversy, here and there a sparkle of important fact so colored by passion or prejudice or prepossession as to be almost indistinguishable except to the eye of a practiced scholar. To sift all the writings bearing upon the man and his times, to produce a clear and well-defined portrait of the individual and a connected abstract of the age, so as to arrive at a just estimate of each and a just perception of the interaction of the one upon the other, is the difficult and interesting task that was set for himself by an American scholar, Mr. Paul Barron Watson, and which has been executed by him with signal ability in a monograph on the *Character and Times of Marcus Aurelius Antoninus*,[1] just published by the Messrs. Harper. The work bears witness throughout to the author's large and diligent research, and to his intelligent comparison and candid valuation of authorities. He has been equally unsparing of his pains to verify facts and to dissipate fable and conjecture; and his industry in search and collation is matched by the fullness and precision with which he has traced the impress made by the emperor at every stage of his career upon the body of the law of his time, and, through the legislation which had its source in his imperial will, upon its moral and social well-being also. While prosecuting a study of personal character which is made highly attractive by grace of style and vividness of portraiture, and while analyzing with nice discrimination the intellectual and moral equipment and the writings of his great subject, Mr. Watson carries on concurrently therewith a comprehensive historical survey which embraces a near view of the entire structure of the empire, so that no essential detail is omitted that is requisite to cast light upon its spirit and tendencies. In his generous enthusiasm for the character of Marcus Aurelius, and in his warm admiration of his wisdom, justice, and humanity, of his severity to himself and his indulgent consideration for the imperfections of others, we think, however, that Mr. Watson glosses over the emperor's unquestionable weaknesses. He is silent concerning the artful and designing men who, taking advantage of his unsuspecting goodness of heart, humoring his bent for learning and the stoical philosophy, and pretending to a purity that they did not possess and a disdain for the good things of the world that they did not feel, made him their dupe, and, as Gibbon tersely remarks, "approached his person in the disguise of philosophic sanctity, and acquired riches and honors by affecting to despise them." He also palliates, or extenuates by his silence, the emperor's excessive indulgence to his lascivious and unfaithful wife, the Empress Faustina, and to his profligate and inhuman son—an indulgence in both cases which, as Gibbon justly declares, "exceeded the bounds of private virtue, and became a public injury by the example and consequences of their vices, while in the case of the son [the infamous Commodus] it operated

[1] *Marcus Aurelius Antoninus.* By PAUL BARRON WATSON. 8vo, pp. 338. New York: Harper and Brothers.

to sacrifice the happiness of millions to a fond partiality for a worthless boy." In like manner, in his generally excellent and convincing chapter on the attitude of the emperor toward Christianity, Mr. Watson, while dissipating at once and forever some superstitious fables that were formerly credited by the early Christian apologists, exaggerates the extent of the heretical and undervalues that of the genuine Christianity with which the emperor was brought face to face. Heresy was undoubtedly rife in the times of Marcus Aurelius, but it was far from universal, and it is impossible to believe that a scholar as diligent and a philosopher as intelligent and enterprising as he should not have come into contact with and have been impressed by "the plain and simple doctrines which were taught by Jesus." That he had been so impressed, perhaps unconsciously, may be fairly inferred from the peculiar nature of his virtues, which were far in advance of those of the rest of the heathen world, and find their counterpart only in the practice and example of the early Christians. This inference is further sustained by numerous passages in his writings, which are sometimes a diluted version and at other times a surprisingly clear echo of the familiar tones of the Gospel. With these reservations, we give our hearty commendation to Mr. Watson's able and profoundly interesting volume, and to predict that it will take an honorable place among the standard works of Roman history.

THE predominant feeling that we experience while reading Mr. Hubert H. Bancroft's *History of California*[2] is one of commingled amazement and bewilderment. We are amazed at the extent of his researches, the magnitude of the task he has performed, and the indomitable energy and patient industry with which he has prosecuted both; and we are bewildered and perplexed by the immense mass of materials —"wood, hay, stubble," with the scant gleam here and there in the promiscuous aggregate of "gold, silver, and precious stones"—which he has emptied into his capacious volume. He has gathered together an overwhelming array of names, dates, and facts, of petty incidents and colorless and fruitless occurrences, mingled with others of larger proportions and greater significance, bearing with equal minuteness alike upon every trivial and every considerable event that happened in California from its first discovery and occupation in 1542 until its more complete colonial organization and development in 1800. He has exercised the same unwearying diligence in collating the insignificant and the weighty particulars of its history, and in dislodging them from their countless obscure retreats and hiding-places in books, pamphlets, manuscripts,

and official archives; has brought the same painstaking industry, clear-sighted accuracy, and tireless precision to bear upon their verification and authentication; and has arranged them in the same orderly and monotonous sequence. The volume will prove a rich repository of valuable material for the use of the future historian.

SIX or seven years ago the world was admitted to a closer and more familiar knowledge of Prince Bismarck than had been previously accorded, through the medium of a memoir by Dr. Moritz Busch, entitled *Bismarck in the Franco-German War,* in which the great Chancellor was exhibited as well in his unguarded moments and hours of relaxation as when he was under the strain of official duty during the critical periods and sudden emergencies of that eventful campaign. A confidential member of Bismarck's literary bureau, and his trusted personal friend, Dr. Busch enjoyed unusual opportunities for observing the character and actions of his chief, and for gauging his mind and penetrating his motives; and his memoir, though frequently and very obviously colored by his prepossessions, embodied a graphic and life-like portraiture of the man, and a profoundly interesting presentment of the masterful and imperious policy of the statesman, throughout the brief but momentous duel which levelled the Second Empire in the dust, and confirmed and consolidated the unity of the German Empire. The same facile and vigorous pen has now been employed upon another memoir, *Our Chancellor,*[3] in which a larger and more expanded view is afforded of the character of Bismarck—his personal traits and characteristics, his moral and intellectual equipment, his social bearing and his religious tendencies—and especially and most fully of his attitude and governing principles as a legislator, diplomatist, statesman, and prime minister, covering his life from the outset of his public career until the present hour. Although Dr. Busch assumes an air of judicial gravity and candor, he is never entirely impartial. His judgments and estimates of the character, actions, motives, and political principles of his chief are those of a passionate but thoroughly honest admirer and advocate. None the less, however, is his delineation of the man and his career singularly able, presenting and defending the extremest doctrines of kingly prerogative and rule with an audacity that propitiates while it amazes the reader who has been nurtured under the free institutions of England and the United States.

A TRUER and purer interest than that which usually attaches to memoirs of noble or princely personages invests the Biographical Sketch

[2] *History of the Pacific States of North America.* By HUBERT HOME BANCROFT. Vol. XIII. California—1542 to 1800. Vol. I. 8vo, pp. 744. San Francisco: A. L. Bancroft and Co.

[3] *Our Chancellor.* Sketches for a Historical Picture. By MORITZ BUSCH. Translated by WILLIAM BEATTY-KINGSTON. Two Volumes in One. 12mo, pp. 407 and 303. New York: Charles Scribner's Sons.

and Letters[4] of the late Princess Alice, recently published in this country and England in a translation from the German original. For it is not only the record of the life of a princess, admitting us to near and familiar views of one of a class whose exceptional rank and station always actively engage curiosity, but also, and above all, it is the memorial of a pure, thoughtful, and singularly earnest yet gentle woman; of one of those rare women by whom the world is occasionally blessed and beautified, whose simple and unaffected virtues, whose depth of affection, sincerity, and singleness of purpose, steadfastness of character, and active and practical human sympathies, are infinitely more durable and worthier of contemplation than any mere accidents of birth and title. In a loving and chastely written preface the Princess Christian, between whose character and that of her sister there are many and striking points of resemblance, gives an account of the motives that led to the memoir, from which we learn that the preparation of the biographical portion was intrusted to the Rev. Dr. Sell, a clergyman of Darmstadt, who was personally known to the Princess Alice, was intimately associated with her in some of her enterprises for the alleviation of human suffering and deprivation, and who had had every opportunity to study the many beautiful features of her character. Dr. Sell has wisely confined himself to the delineation of the purely personal and domestic side of the Princess Alice's life, omitting, except incidentally, any exposition of her opinions on public and political affairs; and in order that he might have it in his power to perfect the picture of her every-day life, Queen Victoria selected for his guidance and placed at his disposal a large number of her daughter's letters, which he has judiciously incorporated in the memoir in connection with a biographical sketch so arranged under distinctive periods as to display the growth and manifestations of the Princess's character at different portions of her life, severally in her childhood and girlhood, in her new home as a youthful and loving bride, at home and at work as matron, wife, mother, daughter, and philanthropist, and, later on, under the stress of domestic cares, trials, and afflictions. The memoir is one of great interest, by turns gay, serious, and tearful, admitting us to an inside view alike of the joys that irradiate and the troubles, perplexities, trials, cares, and griefs that beset the path of princes as well as of common mortals, and at the same time furnishing a wholesome study of gracious and noble womanhood.

The Duke of Argyll, whose able and learned work, *The Reign of Law*, was received with great favor on its publication some years ago, now gives us, in *The Unity of Nature*,[5] an extension of the same line of thought to the ideas which are alike fundamental to all religions and inseparable from the facts of nature. In opposition to the materialistic and agnostic theories of some of the evolutionists, the writer discerns everywhere in the phenomena of matter, of animal instinct, of human faculties, knowledge, and history, and of religious influences, a unity of plan which reveals unmistakably the power and wisdom of an intelligent Creator and providential Ruler. The chapter, in especial, on a Divine prescience as reflected in the wonderful instincts of the lower animals, and in the truth-apprehending intuitions of man, is as exceptionally beautiful as it is original and deeply suggestive. The history of our race, as far as it can be traced in any direction, betrays, the author thinks, an evolution *downward* rather than upward. "The religion of savages, like their other peculiarities, is the result of this kind of evolution." The most ancient records of the Aryan language, which Professor Max Müller considers five thousand years old, show purer and higher religious conceptions than any found in that tongue of recent date. So, also, "the first beginnings of human speech must have had their origin in powers of the highest order,......while the first use of fire, and the discovery of the methods by which it can be kindled, the domestication of wild animals, and, above all, the processes by which the various cereals were first developed out of some of the wild grasses—these are all discoveries with which in ingenuity and importance no subsequent discoveries may compare." Indeed, the Duke concludes that it is simply inconceivable, in the light of all the facts, that the first man should have been a savage or a beast. The treatise evinces an easy familiarity with literature, science, and theology, as well as with the current discussions of evolution by Darwin, Haeckel, Spencer, Tyndall, and others, and it abounds in passages of far-reaching thought most eloquently expressed. Nor is it lacking in evidences of much patient and independent observation of natural phenomena. However greatly any reader may dissent from the conclusions of this masterful work, he will be obliged to admit that it embodies a deal of knowledge put in a fresh and stimulating way.

It has been reserved for a layman, Dr. William H. Thomson, Professor of Materia Medica in the University of New York, in a volume entitled *The Great Argument, or Jesus Christ in the Old Testament*,[6] to make one of the most valuable contributions to Biblical exegesis and criticism, and to religious thought generally, that this abnormally active era of religious in-

---

[4] *Alice, Grand Duchess of Hesse, Princess of Great Britain and Ireland*. Biographical Sketch and Letters. With Portraits. 12mo, pp. 415. New York: G. P. Putnam's Sons.

[5] *The Unity of Nature*. By the Duke of Argyll. 8vo, pp. 571. New York: G. P. Putnam's Sons.
[6] *The Great Argument; or, Jesus Christ in the Old Testament*. By William H. Thomson, M.D. Crown 8vo, pp. 480. New York: Harper and Brothers.

quiry and discussion has yet produced. Recognizing the fundamental fact that if the writings of the Old Testament be not genuine their testimony is unreliable, and that to establish their genuineness is an essential preliminary to an attempt to trace the stream of Messianic prophecy from its source to its close in the Old Testament canon, before undertaking to show that Christ was the fulfillment of all prophecy, and to mark out the lines of what he justly denominates the great argument, Dr. Thomson first institutes an exhaustive examination, which is prosecuted with exemplary candor combined with great learning and cogency of reasoning, of the evidence that these writings are genuine in the fullest and strictest sense of the term; and he demonstrates their authenticity by subjecting them to the same severe critical tests that are applied to all other literary and historical productions, supplemented and corroborated by other evidence which is intrinsic and *sui generis*. He then enters upon a close examination, pursued under specific heads in separate chapters, of all the passages in the Old Testament which relate to the Messiah, traces their relations link by link, interprets and applies their meanings, and shows that each added prediction presupposed and includes all that go before; that all are definitely linked together, and specialize the line of fulfillment; that the prophets gave witness to the advent of Christ, foretelling in many ways not only the coming, but also its manner, time, and object, until not a fact about Him which had relation to that object was without its corresponding prophecy; that the life of Christ, in all its singular fullness of event, purpose, and results, having been thus really written beforehand in the Hebrew scriptures, the truth of the Gospel is rendered indisputable; and finally, that each distinctive doctrine in the New Testament relative to the person and character of Jesus being found in the long antecedent sacred scriptures also, and there foretold with the most perfect completeness and unmistakableness of intention, the truth of Christianity is thus established beyond a reasonable doubt from the Jewish books of the Old Testament. In his exposition of the Old Testament writings Dr. Thomson rejects the narrow literalism which some exegetes have insisted upon, considering that it tends to empty the prophecies of much of their profoundest and most precious meanings, and to render some of the simplest statements and descriptions of the Old Testament dark and inscrutable. He has, however, no sympathy with the rationalistic methods of interpretation that have carried some theological writers to the verge of skepticism, and his work throughout is noteworthy for its reverent and devout spirit. Among the most interesting features of the volume are its many apposite illustrations drawn from the East as it exists to-day, of Scriptural terms, expressions, modes of thought and language, and descriptions of places, manners, and customs.

DR. GEORGE R. CROOKS and Bishop Hurst are furnishing a "Biblical and Theological Library" which will be in harmony with the doctrinal standards of the Methodist Episcopal Church, and yet acceptable to all evangelical Christians. The second volume in the series is an able and comprehensive treatise on *Biblical Hermeneutics*,[7] by Milton S. Terry, D.D. . The key-note of this valuable contribution to the science of interpretation lies in the author's method of discovering the grammatico-historical sense of the sacred writer, as unveiled by the laws of grammar and the facts of history—the only safe method of interpretation—as distinguished from the allegorical, mystical, naturalistic, mythical, etc., which have been more or less productive of error. In the first part of the treatise Dr. Terry compares the Bible with other sacred books, treats of the languages in which it is composed, of the principles of criticism, of inspiration, and of the qualifications of an interpreter. The second part, after reviewing the different methods of interpretation, shows how to ascertain the *usus loquendi* of the sacred writers; what aid can be derived from considering the context, scope, plan, and from a comparison of parallel passages; how figurative language is to be handled; unfolds the characteristics of fables, riddles, and enigmas; dwells at length upon the principles to be applied to the parables, allegories, proverbs, and gnomic poetry, types, symbols, dreams, and prophecies. Nor does the author fail to deal fairly with the alleged discrepancies of the Scriptures and the contributions of science, as well as with the doctrinal and practical use of the Bible. Indeed this portion and some others, such as his essays on the parables and eschatology, lie, strictly speaking, outside of his theme, and yet they are so rich, so discriminating and just, that we readily overlook his violation of unity in the pleasure experienced from his admirable views of truth. The third division of the treatise traces the history of exegesis through its chronological stages—the ancient Jewish, the Rabbinical, the Early Christian, the Patristic, that of the Middle Ages, of the Reformation, and of the more recent centuries down to the present time. On the subject of inspiration, which is now so prominently up for discussion, Dr. Terry holds that "a particular Divine providence secured the composition of the Scriptures in the language and form in which we possess them." Again he says, "We see no good reason for denying the Divine guidance to all parts and forms of the records"; and yet he thinks the statement that the sun and moon stood still at the command of Joshua, though it appears to the plain reader as much a matter of fact as any other part

[7] *Biblical Hermeneutics.* A Treatise on the Interpretation of the Old and New Testaments. By MILTON S. TERRY, S.T.D. Being Vol. II. of the "Library of Biblical and Theological Literature." Edited by GEORGE R. CROOKS, D.D., and JOHN F. HURST, D.D. 8vo, pp. 781. New York: Phillips and Hunt.

of the narrative, is no more to be understood literally than we are to infer that the stars actually fought, or that the mountains melted, or that Lebanon skipped. In his view the millennium is now in progress; every element of truth and righteousness has been gaining prominence and control in the laws of nations since Christ came; and he charges the Chiliasts with error in making His coming a yet future event. But we can not attempt further to note Dr. Terry's special interpretations. His principles generally are certainly sober, well digested, and ought to be fruitful of much good theology in their application. The book is a credit to his Church as well as himself, and will probably be accepted as one of the best on the subjects of which it treats.

WITH the exception of Dr. Staunton's *Dictionary of the Church*, which covered only a limited field, and has been long out of print, there has been no single handy volume to which members of the Protestant Episcopal Church could refer for full and accurate information respecting the organization, constitution, nature, and government of their Church, its ritual, discipline, ordinances, and history, the origin and meaning of its symbols, forms, institutions, vestments, doctrines, ecclesiastical and ecclesiological terms, and innumerable other particulars that are of interest to churchmen. This want is now supplied by an elaborate and well-digested *Church Cyclopædia*,[8] designed especially for the use of the laity of the Protestant Episcopal Church in this country, which has been prepared under the editorial supervision of the Rev. A. A. Benton, Professor of Mathematics in Delaware College, assisted by writers of varying shades of opinion, whom he has called to his aid as collaborateurs from among the bishops, presbyters, and laymen of the Church, so as to express the views of no particular school or party, but as far as possible to reflect the many-sidedness of the Church's views on practical questions of ritual, practice, discipline, history, and doctrine. The work has been executed with equal discretion and learning. Each of its titles bears evidence to the careful and precise scholarship of its writer, and the complete work contains in a condensed and handy form for quick reference a great variety of facts and information concerning the Church and its institutions, and all that appertains to both, not generally easily accessible to the laity, or, indeed, to the clergy.

Contrary Winds, and Other Sermons,[9] is the title of a new volume of sermons by the Rev. Dr. Taylor, of the Broadway Tabernacle in this city, which have the great merit of addressing themselves in a practical and familiar way, and with remarkable variety and aptness of illustration, to convince those who are not yet experimental Christians of the importance to their well-being of their adoption of the principles and doctrines of Holy Scripture, and to encourage and assist those who have already chosen the better part in their efforts for continuous and larger growth in spiritual life. Although these sermons touch upon themes that are of great interest to all men, it is evident that their special and paramount aim is to arrest the attention and fix the thoughts of adult minds, and to impress business men and those who are engrossed in practical affairs with the reasonableness of religion and the beauty of holiness of life. The manliness and frankness with which the preacher presents the great lessons, truths, warnings, and consolations of the Bible, his freedom from cant and casuistry and hair-splitting subtleties in his exposition and application of the Scripture, and the wealth, simplicity, and pertinence of his allusions and illustrations drawn from or bearing upon homely, practical, and every-day affairs —from art, business, politics, social conditions, and contemporaneous history — appeal persuasively and impressively to the intellects of those who plume themselves upon their hard common-sense, and at the same time the earnest spirituality that pervades all his arguments and invitations, and the fervid eloquence and ripe wisdom with which he enforces it, must find its way to the heart.

THERE is much more than poetic promise— there is also the evidence that promise has ripened into performance, and prophecy into fulfillment—in the modest sheaf of poems that Dr. S. Weir Mitchell has garnered with a frugal hand into his dainty little volume, *The Hill of Stones, and Other Poems*.[10] Evidently Dr. Mitchell's poetic style has been materially influenced by, if, indeed, it has not been directly modelled after, that of Tennyson. In especial his blank verse compositions, though having the stamp of a distinct individuality, and far removed from being mere imitations of the manner or echoes of the spirit and sentiments of Tennyson, are often strongly suggestive of "The Princess" in their turns of thought and expression, in their scrupulous attention to verbal niceties and felicities, and in their use of archaisms and of figures and trains of thought which have a dual meaning. Dr. Mitchell does not attempt any prolonged or ambitious flights, but those that he essays are so vigorous, and indicate such a reserve of strength and quiet

[8] *The Church Cyclopædia.* A Dictionary of Church Doctrine, History, Organization, and Ritual. Containing Original Articles on Special Topics, written expressly for the Work by Bishops, Presbyters, and Laymen. Designed especially for the Use of the Laity of the Protestant Episcopal Church in the United States. Edited by Rev. A. A. BENTON, M.A. 8vo, pp. 809. Philadelphia: L. R. Hamersly and Co.

[9] *Contrary Winds, and Other Sermons.* By WILLIAM M. TAYLOR, D.D., LL.D. 12mo, pp. 372. New York: A. C. Armstrong and Son.

[10] *The Hill of Stones, and Other Poems.* By S. WEIR MITCHELL, M.D. 18mo, pp. 98. Boston: Houghton, Mifflin, and Co.

husbandry of power, as to give assurance that it is in him to rise to loftier heights than any he has yet undertaken. Few of our poets have penetrated as closely as he to the heart of Nature. Lovingly and vigilantly observant of her, and of her moods and haunts in wood and field, in farm and orchard, in marsh and meadow, on lake and river, in the "forest primeval" and beside the "ever-sounding and mysterious sea," he has descried her manifold changeful beauties with a poet's eye, has surprised many of her most cherished and most coyly guarded secrets with a poet's unerring instinct, and has woven his discoveries into picture-bearing verse with a poet's taste and skill. There is very little of what may be termed dead wood in any of his poems. He has not hesitated to follow the pen with the pruning-knife, and to lop off all useless and superfluous verbiage; and as a result, in all his poems an unusual number of lines, phrases, and extended passages gleam upon us which are not only chaste and elegant, but are eminently quotable, and effect a permanent lodgment in the memory. If this were a review instead of a notice, it might be easy to establish the truth of what has been said by a liberal citation of lines and passages that have most impressed us, more particularly in the delicious summer pastoral entitled "Wind and Sea," the spirited forest idyl picturing the wilds of Elk County, and the glowing lyrics grouped under the head of "Camp-fire Lyrics"; but as that course is inadmissible, we shall be content merely briefly to refer those who love and are ready to extend a cordial welcome to good poetry to Dr. Mitchell's unobtrusive but sterling little volume.

Our Famous Women[11] is the title which the publishers, with rather questionable taste, have given to an otherwise attractive and meritorious volume. It comprises thirty brief and well-executed biographical sketches of as many well-known American writers, artists, educators, philanthropists, etc., of the gentler sex, prepared by twenty of their country-women who belong to the sisterhood of literature, and it is illustrated with a number of excellent full-page portraits, engraved from photographs taken expressly for the work. The biographical sketches are earnest, discriminating, and heartily sympathetic, and display, as woman only can when woman is her subject, a subtle insight of those delicate but strong traits of female character which are woman's chiefest ornament. Among the sketches are memoirs of Miss Alcott, by Mrs. Moulton; of Catherine E. Beecher and Mrs. A. D. T. Whitney, by Mrs. Stowe; of Rose Terry

Cooke, Clara Louise Kellogg, Mrs. Moulton, and Miss Mary L. Booth, by Harriet Prescott Spofford; of Marian Harland (Mrs. Terhune) and Margaret Fuller, by Kate Sanborn; of Mrs. Mary Mapes Dodge, by Lucia G. Runkle; of Maria Mitchell, by Julia Ward Howe; of Lydia Maria Child, by Susan Coolidge; of Mrs. Stowe and Mrs. Spofford, by Rose Terry Cooke; and of Lucy Larcom, Clara Barton, Lucretia Mott, Elizabeth Prentiss, Susan B. Anthony, Mrs. Stanton, Miss Phelps, Mary Clemmer, Charlotte Cushman, and Mrs. Burnett, by other equally capable and appreciative writers. The work is sold only by subscription.

———

CONSIDERED from a purely literary standpoint, Mr. Hatton's report of *Mr. Henry Irving's Impressions of America*[12] is a nondescript, but if regarded as the shrewd advertising device of an enterprising manager, intent upon wooing the attention of the public, and making the popular pulse beat high, it is intelligible, and not much unlike similar devices with which Mr. Barnum has made us familiar. Mr. Hatton has executed his part of the performance admirably, as he always does; but with all his tact and art as a writer he has found it impossible to hide the plain business purpose that has obviously inspired the glib outpourings of his friend and principal, and of which it were an insult to his intelligence to suppose him unconscious. There is much in the volume that is amusing, some clever things are said, some entertaining anecdotes and interesting incidents are related, but, on the whole, it causes a sense of satiety. We suffer from a surfeit of blarney—of praise showered without stint *upon* Mr. Irving, and of praise showered back again *by* him with compound interest. In such a desert of sugared compliments a dash of tart criticism, or even of sharp and biting satire, would be as refreshing as a spring in the wilderness.

———

THE exciting events that have recently occurred, or are now on the eve of transpiring, in Egypt and the Soudan, invest with considerable interest a volume by General Loring, entitled *A Confederate Soldier in Egypt*.[13] General Loring is an ex-Confederate officer who was for ten years in the service of the Khedive of Egypt, with the rank of Féreek Pasha and General. During that time he had unusual opportunities for informing himself as to the plans and purposes of the Khedives, and as to the character of the Egyptians of all classes, to study the resources and institutions of the country, and to observe the political and social influences that made an impression upon it.

———

[11] *Our Famous Women*. Comprising the Lives and Deeds of American Women who have Distinguished themselves in Literature, Science, Art, Music, and the Drama, or are Famous as Heroines, Patriots, Educators, Physicians, etc. With Numerous Incidents, Anecdotes, and Personal Experiences. Superbly Illustrated. 8vo, pp. 715. Hartford: A. D. Worthington and Co.

[12] *Henry Irving's Impressions of America*. Narrated in a Series of Sketches, Chronicles, and Conversations. By JOSEPH HATTON. 16mo, pp. 474. Boston: James R. Osgood and Co.

[13] *A Confederate Soldier in Egypt*. By W. W. LORING, Late Colonel in the United States Army, Major-General in the Confederate Service, General in the Army of the Khedive of Egypt, etc. 8vo, pp. 450. New York: Dodd, Mead, and Co.

After a succinct outline of such of the social, political, and religious history of Egypt as he deems a necessary preliminary for a comprehension of the events that occurred there during his term of service, and that are now happening, General Loring gives the results of his personal observations with great clearness and minuteness, in connection with a narrative of his official services in Egypt proper, and in the campaign against Abyssinia, in which he participated, in 1875. In the course of his narrative he deals in detail with the political and military incidents that signalized the administrations of the last six rulers of Egypt, depicts their persons and delineates their character, describes their foreign and domestic policies and complications, and their attitude toward the body of the people, dilates indignantly upon what he emphasizes as "the selfish and cruel policy of France and England" (especially of the latter) toward Egypt, and traces the antecedents and recent exploits of El Mahdi, both as a prophet and as a military and political leader. In addition General Loring introduces a brief summary of recent explorations and discoveries in Africa, a *résumé* of the causes that influenced Mehemet Ali and his successors to attempt the extension of the area of their empire, and an account of their efforts in this direction, and of the political and financial embarrassments that ensued. The volume comprises, with much matter that is already well known, and which has been gleaned at second-hand from the works of other writers, much fresh and original information concerning the geography and topography of the present scene of military operations, some sharp and vigorous reflections and criticisms upon the Egyptian policy of France and England, and some grave and thoughtful forecasts of the future of Egypt.

NEARLY forty years ago the writer of this notice became the owner of Haswell's *Mechanics' and Engineers' Pocket-Book of Tables*,[14] etc., then in its first edition, in the form of a thin volume of 284 pages; and he still retains a lively recollection of his sense of obligation to its author for the large body of precise and reliable practical information of which it was the repository. Since then this excellent handbook has been consulted with similar feelings of gratitude, in its various editions, by thousands of mechanics and engineers, young and old, to whom it has been an indispensable companion, until now it has reached its forty-fifth edition, and has grown from the thin pamphlet of 1843 to the dimensions of a generous book of 922 pages, its old matter entirely revised, amended, and reconstructed so as to adapt it to the needs of the present day, and its value increased by the extension of its tables of areas and circumferences of circles, weights of metals, balls, tubes, pipes, etc., and by the addition of a large amount of new and valuable matter upon mechanical and physical subjects in every department.

IT is seldom that any previous month has witnessed the publication of so many novels, none of which rises greatly, if any, above the level of mediocrity. Even Mr. Blackmore, the prince of story-tellers, has been affected by the prevalent influenza. His new novel, *The Remarkable History of Sir Thomas Upmore*,[15] is not merely lamentably inferior to its predecessors, but is unworthy of his genius, and of his taste and skill as an artist, and will be the occasion of keen disappointment to his numerous admirers. The same criticism applies, though less unreservedly, perhaps, to Mr. Hale's *The Fortunes of Rachel*,[16] Mr. Russell's *John Holdsworth*,[17] and Mr. Crawford's *A Roman Singer*,[18] each of which betrays a manifest falling off in quality as compared with the previous productions of their authors. Of the remaining novels the least insipid are Mr. Grant's *An Average Man*;[19] May Crommelin's *In the West Countree*;[20] Mr. Newell's (Orpheus C. Kerr) *There Was Once a Man*;[21] Miss Townsend's *But a Philistine*;[22] *A Palace Prison*,[23] by an anonymous author; *At Daybreak*,[24] by A. Stirling; *Eustis*,[25] by Robert A. Boit; *A Midsummer Madness*,[26] by Ellen O. Kirk; *Barbara Thayer*,[27] by Mrs. Annie J. Miller; and *Clytia*,[28] by George Taylor.

[14] *Mechanics' and Engineers' Pocket-Book of Tables, Rules, and Formulas pertaining to Mechanics, Mathematics, and Physics; including Areas, Squares, Cubes, and Roots, etc.; Logarithms, Hydraulics, Hydrodynamics, Steam and the Steam-Engine, Naval Architecture, Masonry, Steam Vessels, Mills, etc.; Limes, Mortars, Cements, etc.; Orthography of Technical Words and Terms, etc.* Forty-fifth Edition. By CHARLES H. HASWELL, Civil, Marine, and Mechanical Engineer, etc. 16mo, pp. 922. New York: Harper and Brothers.

[15] *The Remarkable History of Sir Thomas Upmore, Bart., M.P. Formerly known as Tommy Upmore.* By R. D. BLACKMORE. 16mo, pp. 255. New York: Harper and Brothers.
The Same. "Franklin Square Library." 4to, pp. 63. New York: Harper and Brothers.
[16] *The Fortunes of Rachel.* By EDWARD E. HALE. 12mo, pp. 221. New York: Funk and Wagnalls.
[17] *John Holdsworth, Chief Mate.* A Novel. By W. CLARK RUSSELL. "Franklin Square Library." 4to, pp. 53. New York: Harper and Brothers.
[18] *A Roman Singer.* By F. MARION CRAWFORD. 16mo, pp. 318. Boston: Houghton, Mifflin, and Co.
[19] *An Average Man.* By ROBERT GRANT. 16mo, pp. 300. Boston: James R. Osgood and Co.
[20] *In the West Countree.* A Novel. By MAY CROMMELIN. "Franklin Square Library." 4to, pp. 54. New York: Harper and Brothers.
[21] *There Was Once a Man.* By R. H. NEWELL (Orpheus C. Kerr). 16mo, pp. 526. New York: Fords, Howard, and Hulbert.
[22] *But a Philistine.* By VIRGINIA F. TOWNSEND. 12mo, pp. 328. Boston: Lee and Shepard.
[23] *A Palace Prison; or, The Past and the Present.* 16mo, pp. 342. New York: Fords, Howard, and Hulbert.
[24] *At Daybreak.* A Novel. By A. STIRLING. 16mo, pp. 316. Boston: James R. Osgood and Co.
[25] *Eustis.* A Novel. By ROBERT APTHORP BOIT. 12mo, pp. 360. Boston: James R. Osgood and Co.
[26] *A Midsummer Madness.* By ELLEN OLNEY KIRK. 16mo, pp. 395. Boston: James R. Osgood and Co.
[27] *Barbara Thayer: Her Glorious Career.* A Novel. By ANNIE JENNESS MILLER. 16mo, pp. 180. Boston: Lee and Shepard.
[28] *Clytia.* A Romance of the Sixteenth Century. By GEORGE TAYLOR. Translated by MARY J. SAFFORD. 16mo, pp. 364. New York: William S. Gottsberger.

Editor's Historical Record.

POLITICAL.

OUR Record is closed on the 18th of June. —The Republican National Convention was held at Chicago, opening June 3. General John B. Henderson, of Missouri, was chosen permanent chairman. On the 6th, Hon. James G. Blaine, of Maine, was nominated for President on the fourth ballot, and Hon. John A. Logan, of Illinois, for Vice-President, without opposition. The ballots for President were as follows: *First*—Whole number of votes cast, 818; necessary to a choice, 410; for James G. Blaine, of Maine, 334½; for Chester A. Arthur, of New York, 278; for George F. Edmunds, of Vermont, 93; for John A. Logan, of Illinois, 63½; for John Sherman, of Ohio, 30; for Joseph R. Hawley, of Connecticut, 13; for Robert T. Lincoln, of Illinois, 4; for William T. Sherman, of Missouri, 2. *Second*—Whole number of votes cast, 818; necessary to a choice, 410; Blaine, 349; Arthur, 276; Edmunds, 85; Logan, 61; Sherman, 28; Hawley, 13; Lincoln, 4; William T. Sherman, 2. *Third*—Whole number of votes cast, 819; necessary to a choice, 410; Blaine, 375; Arthur, 274; Edmunds, 69; Logan, 53; Sherman, 25; Hawley, 13; Lincoln, 8; William T. Sherman, 2. *Fourth* — Whole number of votes cast, 813; necessary to a choice, 407; Blaine, 541; Arthur, 207; Edmunds, 41; Logan, 7; Hawley, 15; Lincoln, 2. The nomination was then made unanimous.

The following bills were passed in Congress: Appropriating $1,000,000 for the New Orleans Centennial Exposition, Senate, May 15; Consular and Diplomatic Appropriation, House, May 19, Senate, June 12; Army Appropriation, House, May 19; Agricultural Appropriation, Senate, May 20; Mr. Aldrich's substitute for Labor Statistics Bill, Senate, May 23; for relief of sufferers by Mississippi floods, House, $100,000, May 27, Senate, $40,000, May 29; reducing postage on newspapers to one cent for four ounces, Senate, June 2 (subsequently signed by the President); prohibiting Chinese subjects from importing opium into the United States, Senate, June 2; Legislative Appropriation, House, June 2; River and Harbor Appropriation (after striking out the Hennepin Canal clause), House, June 12; Deficiency Appropriation, House, June 17.

The House of Representatives, May 19, by a vote of 52 to 179, rejected the bill to reduce the duty on works of art of American and foreign artists from thirty to ten per cent. *ad valorem.*

The National Greenback Convention met at Indianapolis, May 29, and nominated for President General B. F. Butler, of Massachusetts; for Vice-President, A. M. West, of Mississippi.

The Vermont Greenback State Convention met at Waterbury, May 15, and nominated for Governor Samuel Soule, of Fairfield; Lieutenant-Governor, M. C. Bailey, of Newbury.

The Vermont Democratic State Convention,

June 5, nominated P. W. Redington for Governor.

The Maine Democratic State Convention, June 17, nominated John B. Redman for Governor.

The new treaty between France and Anam has been signed. By its terms the provinces of Bin-thuan and Than-goa are restored to Anam. A customs system similar to that in force in Cochin-China is established. A French military occupation of all strategic points in Anam and Tonquin may be effected if necessary. A permanent French garrison will hold a portion of the citadel of Hué, capital of Anam.

Egyptian advices of June 14 confirm the news of the capture of Berber by the rebels, May 23, and the massacre of the garrison of 1500 men and of 2000 of the population.

DISASTERS.

May 14.—Fourteen men killed by collision of freight and gravel trains on the Baltimore and Ohio Railroad, near Connellsville.

May 19.—Earthquake on the island of Kishur, near the mouth of the Persian Gulf. Twelve villages destroyed and two hundred persons killed.

May 23.—Loss of the French brig *Senorine*, off the Great Banks, with fifty-three passengers and a crew of nine.

June 1.—Eleven men drowned in a flood caused by a cloud-burst, in camp on Frenchman's Creek, Colorado.

June 10.—Schooner *Six Brothers* and fourteen men lost off Newfoundland.—Eleven men drowned at Thompson's Falls, Montana.

June 16.—News from Greenland of the loss of the Danish brig *Elena* and ten of her crew.

June 17.—Two Americans and twelve Mexicans killed in a railroad accident in New Laredo.

OBITUARY.

May 19.—At Pegli, Italy, Sam Ward, aged seventy-one years.

May 21.—In New York city, Ex-Judge Joseph S. Bosworth, aged seventy-seven years.

May 22.—At Evona, New Jersey, Ex-Judge W. R. Beebe, aged sixty-eight years.

May 29.—In London, England, Sir Henry Bartle Edward Frere, aged sixty-nine years.

May 31.—In this city, Bishop Benjamin Bosworth Smith, of Kentucky, aged ninety years.

June 1. — In this city, General Mansfield Lovell, aged sixty-two years.

June 7.—In this city, James Watson Webb, aged eighty-two years.

June 8.—In this city, Noah Haynes Swayne, ex-Justice of the United States Supreme Court, in his eightieth year.

June 11.—In Reading, Pennsylvania, Ex-Congressman Hiester Clymer, in his fifty-seventh year.

IN America, more than anywhere else in the world, it is the women who determine what the society recreation for the month of August shall be. In England the men are to a certain extent independent, if not rebellious. They go into far countries to shoot; they stalk the moors for small game; they ride to hounds; they get away for long walking tours and mountain climbing. They control to a considerable extent their own sports and recreations. If the women want their company, the women must put on thick shoes, and be prepared for tramping, even for scaling mountains; they must be mounted for the "meet," and assume an interest, if they do not feel it, in dogs and horses, and a little knowledge of manly slang, delicately spoken, is not amiss. The summer recreation in America has, if one may say so without offense, the feminine tone, where it is not anglicized. The women commonly decide what the outing shall be; they declare for the sea or the mountains, for Newport, or the White Sulphur, or Bar Harbor, or Saratoga, or the strictly bucolic and restful, not to say tame, existence of the farm-house. The men may think they decide all these matters, but wherever they go the recreations are really set to the feminine standard. At least nearly all the amusements are such as the sexes can join in; and I suppose that the advocates of co-education can show that this is for the benefit of both, that the manly roughness is refined, and the womanly gentleness gains in spirit. The gospel of the time certainly is that it is not good for man to be alone. He can not be alone if he wants to, and it is depraved in him to want to. Woman orders society, and the recreations of society seem to be taking more and more the tone of her nature. The sexes meet upon neutral ground— say upon that of lawn tennis—where the masculine energy is put in harness, and the feminine energy is allowed free expansion. The process of refinement and civilization goes on year by year, and in due time American men will become the gentlest and most docile in all history. Perhaps few of them can yet stand the succession of two seasons of gayety —the Newport, for instance, following immediately the one in New York—and follow the fiddle and the beckoning plume the year round, without any relaxation into the natural savage life of man, but they can be trained to it. As for the American women, there are none others anywhere who have so much endurance —until after marriage.

The American men, indeed, have a reputation to sustain. American men—so the legend runs now in all the feminine world of England, France, Italy, and Germany—make the best husbands in the world. To this pitch of enviable fame have they come by a century of tutelage, by a strict attention to business, and

a meek surrender of all direction of social matters. Loss of power is amply compensated by this universal good esteem in which they are held. But this commendable behavior of theirs may be only a sign, it ought to be said, of a still deeper change in female temper. We are not certain, indeed, whether the change is in women or in the way men regard them, but there is an apparent change. Nothing was more common in the sixteenth century than a "scolding woman," and the scolding woman had not disappeared in this country till after the Declaration of Independence—some even survived that. The evidence of this does not rest upon tradition. The literature and the laws are full of it. Laws had to be framed with severe penalties to protect men from the "common scold"; and these penalties were often inflicted, one of the most effective of them being the "ducking-chair," which in many cases was the only one that could check the wagging of a virulent tongue. Nothing is commoner in the ballad literature of the sixteenth century than the complaints of the railing of the scold and the shrew, and the devices for taming them were as ingenious as they were brutal. Either the literature of the time is an awful libel, or scolding women were so numerous as to be a great feature of the age; scolding was as prominent as begging, and the scolding wife as common as the tipsy husband. The philosopher wants to know whether it is the temper of women which has changed, since it is a fact that the "common scold" has practically disappeared from modern life (there used to be women whom even the sheriff was afraid of), is no more a *pièce de résistance* of literature, and has not to be legislated against, or whether the apparent difference is only a change in man's attitude toward the sex. Some students of sociology think that man's submission has wrought the transformation, and that women appear to be more sweet and amiable now they have their way unruffled. It is a very delicate question, and one that would not be raised here except in the interest of science. For the disappearance of traits in human nature is as useful a study as the elimination of useless members or the development of new organs in our evolution. Nobody except the sociologist can say what the disappearance of the "common scold" has to do with man's position in the modern recreations of society; the business of this department is to collect facts, not to co-ordinate them.

A VERY neat *mot* is credited to Judge Grover, in a tilt at the bar with Judge Peck. The latter had delivered a particularly rasping speech, to which the former felt compelled to reply in kind.

"Your honor," he said, "it rained last night, and this morning, when I took my course across the fields, at almost every step I came upon some slimy, venomous creature that had issued from its hiding-place. Snails, toads, frogs, lizards, worms, snakes, vipers, adders—every description of loathsome reptile was to be seen, crawling, filled with venom, and yet, your honor, though there seemed so many of them, all of them put together would not have made up a Peck!"

"OLE MARSTER."

('FO' DE WAH.)

Ole Marster comin' fru de bars—
  Don't you hear dat horse a-snortin'?
Shuv dem marbuls in yer pocket;
  Shet up, and hishe dat torkin'.
Drap dat hoe agin dem 'taters;
  Horsewhip mighty coolin':
Ole Marster sorter cur'us
  When he ketch de nigger foolin'.

Hi, looker yonder, Ephrum;
  B'l'eve he gone down in de medder;
Jes fotch dem marbuls out agin;
  We'll hev a game togedder.
Wish I was white fokes,
  Eatin' sweet cake an' muffin,
A-bossin' ub de niggers,
  Ridin' roun', an' doin' nuffin.

Ole Marster ride de blooded horse;
  Got plenty in de stable;
Bit an' sturrups shinin'
  Like silber on de table.
Ride ober to de odder place,
  Pocket full ub money;
Arter 'while he come back home,
  An' buck dat peach an' honey.

Ole fiel' lark sing pooty chune;
  Ebery Sunday mornin'
Br'er Ambrose at de meetin'-house,
  To gib de niggers warnin'.
Ole Marster at de big chu'ch,
  Wid de 'ligious an' de sinner;
An' den he fotch de preacher
  An' all de people home to dinner.

Ole Marster got a heap ub lan',
  An' money widout figgers;
Ole fiel' full ub sheep an' thing,
  An' quarter full ub niggers.
He treat de black fokes mighty well,
  'Pears like 'tis in he nacher;
Oberseer play de debil, dough,
  When he at de Legislacher.

Ole Marster war de high black hat,
  An' standin'-up shut coller:
Shuv dem marbuls in yer pocket—
  Dat de oberseer holler.
Don't you hear him 'hind de 'backer-house?
  Cowhide soon be rulin';
Oberseer mighty quar'lsome
  When he ketch de nigger foolin'.

                                    W. P. CARTER.

THE Irish beggars who meet passengers at Queenstown often give as much as they get. A persistent old woman stood on the gang-plank, to whom a waggish passenger held up a gold coin. Advancing with a face suffused with devout thankfulness, she cried out, "May the blessings of Heaven follow ye all your days." The man (who was certainly cruel) put the gold in his pocket, when, with a change of expression to rage, the old woman instantly finished her sentence with, "And never overtake ye, ye dirty spalpeen!"

HOW HE SAVED HIS BACON.

IN a town of Western Pennsylvania Rev. George Washington Spooner is well known as an occasional dispenser of the Gospel to his colored brethren. Of late years, however, he has had such a reputation for intemperance and dishonesty that few hearers can be found for his eloquent discourses upon the joys of heaven.

Several winters ago he was walking along a main street when his attention was attracted to a wagon near by. It was driven by a farmer who had sold his entire load of pigs, with one exception; and, as it was growing late, he was anxious to dispose of the defunct porker. He readily closed in with Mr. Spooner's offer to purchase it, and asked where it should be delivered.

"Well, now, you jis go down dat way two squars, and den turn up Huckleberry Alley, and de fourth house is mine. I can't go back wid you, 'cause I's gwine on a 'portant errand; but you jis lay de pork on de table, and wait dar till I come to pay you. My old gran'mudder's sick in bed. You tell her I tole you to wait fur me."

The unsuspecting wagoner drove to the place as directed.

Meanwhile the dusky reverend had slipped across by a "short-cut," donned a night-cap, and lay in bed awaiting his arrival.

The knock at the door was answered by a feeble "Come in." Entering, he saw the supposed grandmother, who asked, "Who are you?"

"Your grandson told me to wait here until he comes to pay me for some pork he bought. I'll lay it on the table."

"Well, sah, do look if he's a-comin'. He went fur de doctor fur me, an' I's feelin' mighty bad. Oh dear! Oh me! How I's a-sufferin'!"

"What is the matter with you?" asked the farmer, pitying the old woman's moans.

"Oh, de doctor says I'll git over it. It's jist *a light touch ob de small-pox.*"

Out of the door shot the frightened countryman, caring not that his pork was left behind him, and not pausing until he was out of the infected locality.

A few moments afterward the quondam small-pox patient arose, viewed the porker with a chuckle of delight, and said, "De small-pox a mighty good ting in a 'mergency."

                                    JUDITH EYRE.

MANY years ago in Cliff Street, New York, lived a man named Woolley, a deacon in St. George's Church. His servants had the habit of emptying the ashes and cinders from his house into the street just before the door, where a heap accumulated, much to the annoyance of the neighbors. One day a wag who lived next door hit upon a neat device by which the nuisance was abated. He planted a stick in the heap which bore a placard inscribed with these words in large letters: "Here lie the ashes of Deacon Woolley."

THERE was a very stout and haughty volunteer general in the Southern army who had contrived to make himself hated by his men, one of whom took occasion to revenge himself as follows. The general, who was extremely vain of his appearance and horsemanship, dissatisfied with his own horse, secured a large, showy chestnut (the property of a baker in a neighboring town), which he rode for the first time on the occasion of a grand review of the army by the commander-in-chief. His enemy heard of the transaction from the garrulous baker, and an inspiration came to him. On the day in question the soldiers were drawn up, the general came curveting and caracoling down the line, his immense frame squeezed into the newest, tightest, most gorgeous uniform that ever field-officer sported, conscious of the eyes of his chief, and rejoicing to run his course, when out stepped his enemy and shouted, "Bread!" with a voice like a bassoon. The horse, recognizing the familiar summons, stopped short, and presently his rider was sprawling in the dust before his command, the most absurd figure in the world.

THE following bit of wit upon the part of a North Carolina girl comes to us from the Greenbrier White Sulphur Springs, the fashionable Virginia watering-place:

Among the regular *habitués* is Colonel B——, a well-preserved, handsome old beau of uncertain age. His society record is brilliant, and though he has raised many hopes, yet season after season has ended and the colonel has yielded his liberty to none. His special strength is pride of family, boasting as he does, in season and out of season, not only the bluest South Carolina blood, but the most direct Huguenot descent.

During the past summer there appeared, flitting about the broad piazzas and through the long drawing-room, a bright, dashing girl from the "Land of the Sky." The colonel, as usual, began the scheme of monopoly, and the ambitious young belle seemed nothing loath to accord to him the coveted position as chief of staff. It began to be whispered about that the colonel was really in earnest for once in his life. Those who knew him best and watched him closest were sure that he was on the eve of a victory. His gait was more martial, his manner more lofty, than ever before, and the poor ancestral Huguenots were dragged to the front without mercy.

Unfortunately a bit of eavesdropping in the dim star-lighted seclusion of what the colonel thought to be a deserted corner of the piazza told the story of such woful discomfiture that

he fled the place within twenty-four hours afterward. He had evidently proposed in his most pompous and condescending manner, and had heard with amazement a quiet negative from the young lady's lips.

"But, I think—I am sure," said the colonel, hardly able to control his indignant pride, "you do not understand, you do not appreciate, miss, the honor that has been conferred upon you, that you so lightly decline. I am a Huguenot of South Carolina!"

"Ah, colonel, it is you who forget," said Miss ——, with her most roguish smile. "You do not appreciate the honor to which you aspire. I am a *Lightwood Knot of North Carolina!*"

CANDOR.

O SWEET, refreshing innocence of youth!
　I was aged five, of fair, cherubic grace;
She five-and-thirty; and, to tell the truth,
　There *was* no beauty in her shrewd, kind face.

And yet, one afternoon, when on her knee
　I sat and talked, tired out at last with play,
She asked me if I did not think that she
　Was handsome like my pretty sister May.

"Oh, Miss Janet!" I cried, "you can't *think* so!
　You're nothing like so beautiful as she.
But then I love you; and you're *nice*, you know;
　So *I* don't mind!" I added, soothingly.

"Well, Arthur, you are frank! But tell me why—
　I'm rather like your sister, I should say.
She has red cheeks, blue eyes; and so have I:
　Why am I not as beautiful as May?"

"Oh, but you're not; indeed you're not!" I said.
　"You're thin and freckled. And your eyes *are* blue,
But *different*. Besides, your hair is red;
　And—and you're kind of girlish-looking, too."

"Girlish? And can it be that I have wrung
　A compliment from you at last? I see!
I am not *handsome*, but I'm *fresh* and *young*.
　Girlish, indeed! Well, this is flattery."

"Oh no!" I shouted, much perplexed in mind;
　"It isn't that. It's girlish like Christine,
And Bridget—oh, you know—the *other* kind;
　It's—why, it's *servant-girlishness* I mean!"
　　　　　　　　　　ROBERTSON TROWBRIDGE.

THE following anecdote will be appreciated by military readers:

In the cavalry service it frequently happens that, by reason of death, desertion, and discharge, the number of men in a troop is less than the number of horses on hand. A troop captain, not long since, had occasion to send up a requisition for ordnance stores, including, among other things, "sixty-five nose-bags."

After the usual long interval this requisition was duly returned from San Antonio, with the indorsement: "Respectfully returned to Captain —— ——, —th Cavalry. The returns of his troop show that he has only *fifty-four* men, and explanation is desired as to why he requires *sixty-five* nose-bags."

The captain's explanation was as follows:

"Respectfully returned. The nose-bags are required for my *horses*, and not for the *men*."

This illustrates that careful and economical attention with which the Ordnance Department looks to the issue of government stores, which has given it such popularity among the soldiers of the army.

It is needless to say that the following "medical advice" is "sifted" out of Texas:

Mr. Walcott is a gentleman who has been in bad health for some time, so he consulted with a prominent Austin physician, who told him he must travel for his health.

"I have neither the money nor the inclination to travel," replied Walcott.

"Well, I'll tell you what to do," suggested the medical adviser. "You are employed in a bank. All in the world you will have to do will be to steal about $10,000, and you will have both the inclination and the money to travel."

ERMINIE.

With music most emotional
I wooed the icy Erminie,
And chose the most devotional
Of Italy and Germany;
But music had no charms for her,
At least where I had part,
For no pathetic strains could stir
Her feelings or her heart.

In pansies and in violets
And all heart-flowers that grow,
In rondeaux and in triolets,
My love I've tried to show.
But e'en the garden's sweetest tongue,
Alas! she would not hear,
And all the loving songs I've sung
Fell on a careless ear.

No matter how importunate,
I could not win the fair,
Until, at last—how fortunate!—
My uncle made me heir.
I laid my riches at her feet,
Flashed diamonds in her eyes:
The maiden cold grew fond and sweet;
Through gold I won the prize.

GEORGE BIRDSEYE.

AN OLD-TIME PREACHER.

"Seventy years ago there lived, or rather sojourned, in Erie County, New York, one Elder Le Sieur, a Baptist preacher, who, without knowing it, was a kind of John Baptist of the Hard-shell branch of that persuasion. Nothing but his name indicated his French origin, he being, in fact, rather a shiftless Yankee. In his day he was as well if not as widely known as his fellow-preacher Lorenzo Dow. He carried with him wherever he went a strong and unfailing appetite, and an equally strong and unfailing aversion to any kind of work by which it might have been satisfied. Much experience had made him sage, and although he might often be seen stopping for a mid-day luncheon at a laborer's cottage on Saturdays, he always drew up at some sub-stantial farm-house in time for supper, and to have the news go round that Elder Le Sieur would 'preach' on Sunday. In those far-off, delightful days the good people were glad of any reason for coming together. A husking or a horse-race, a prayer-meeting or a 'preaching,' where there would be something to hear or something to say, something to eat or something to drink, was always welcome. The 'elder' was always sure of a congregation; the hearers were always certain to be amused, if not edified. If he had any wit of his own, he was quite unconscious of it, yet gave abundant cause for merriment and wit in others. One summer Saturday he rode into the yard of my father's house and down to the barn, with which and the whereabout of the oats bin he was as familiar as if he had made them, and returned to the house just as my mother drew from the old brick oven an immense pan of pork and beans, intended for the Sunday dinner of the family and any others who might 'drop in' at meal-time. It was a dish the traditions of which my mother had brought, if not from Boston, at least from as good a place—her far-off home in Sheffield, Berkshire, next farm to the Sedgwicks'. Beautifully browned, a little island of pork resting on a leguminous sea, it had been softly simmering since the taking out of the bread at ten o'clock in the morning. Only the gentle 'Elia' could have spoken properly of the 'delicious crackling'; only a woman born and bred in New England could have prepared the dish in its perfection. The 'elder' eyed the pan with such looks of longing as Richard gave the venison pasty after the preliminary pease in the cell of the jolly friar, and, as the event proved, mentally made a careful note of its whereabouts.

"The next morning the 'elder' partook of a hearty breakfast, and at half after ten was ready for the sermon. Placing a small table, on which was a Bible and hymn-book, in front of the cupboard which contained the precious pan, he made a short prayer, and then chose and read to the hearers the longest hymn he could find, and added, 'While the brethren and sisters sing this hymn, your elder will refresh himself.' Opening the door of the closet, he drew the pan forward, and with the help of a knife, which he was never without, helped himself abundantly throughout the singing. My mother told me the people sang the hymn from beginning to end without a smile on any face. A congregation that could do the like in these days would be a sight to see.

"After an absence from home once of several weeks, the 'elder' learned that a young girl in whom he felt greatly interested had died and been buried. In his next discourse he spoke of her with much feeling, and, with eyes full of tears, said: 'Poor child! she is dead, and gone to heaven. I should have gone to see her before this time if I could have got a one-horse wagon.'"

AN IDEAL HEAD.
Engraved by W. B. Closson, from the painting by George Fuller, A.N.A.

HARPER'S
NEW MONTHLY MAGAZINE.

No. CCCCXII.—SEPTEMBER, 1884.—Vol. LXIX.

A RUN ASHORE AT QUEENSTOWN.

QUEENSTOWN is full of interest. It is the entrance for many Americans to Europe, the point of their initiation into scenes read of and mentally pictured, but yet to be tried by the light of personal experience. It is the first page of the book of foreign travel, and it is often the last of the same volume—a place of meeting and farewell, where the ocean voyage practically begins and ends. Those who have friends bound to Europe look for its name with much anxiety in the telegraphic columns of their newspapers, and they are relieved by seeing among the marine news the brief paragraph which tells them in formal words like these that the steamer for which they have been hoping has reached her destination:

"QUEENSTOWN, *Thursday.*—The steamer *Servia* arrived here this morning, and having landed all mails and some passengers, proceeded for Liverpool immediately."

On board the ship herself this famous port of call is also the subject of much speculation, and the probabilities as to when it will be reached occupy no small part of the abundant leisure of the voyage. A miniature chart of the North Atlantic on a scale so diminished that a pen line of an inch indicates three or four hundred miles is hung in the companionway, and from day to day the vessel's course and position are marked upon it. It is taken away from its place into the chief officer's room for a few minutes at noon, and when it is replaced a crowd of passengers surround the little frame in which it is hung, and are grateful for the pledge which the extremity of the ink line, with its note of latitude and longitude, gives that they are somewhere and not nowhere, as the similarity of the view day after day would lead them to think. The line has its beginning at Sandy Hook; thence (at certain seasons) it is drawn due east about

an inch, and from this point it works in a curve, inclining to the south as it approaches the irregular shape of the Irish coast near Cape Clear. It is when it is within an inch or two of Cape Clear that Queenstown becomes a more engrossing topic than ever, and not the day but the hour of arrival is now spoken of with a confidence which has dismissed any fears or doubts there may have been at the outset of the voyage. The novels and games which have engaged the passengers previously are abandoned. The saloon tables are littered with stationery, and the general occupation is epistolary. No one is unexcited by the prospect save a few used-up travellers who are too familiar with Queenstown to care in the least about it; but to most of those on board the place means many things: it is land again, and brings them once more in communication with home; it opens new scenes and awakens new emotions, and through it old associations are renewed and new relations established.

The land is perhaps sighted in the early morning—a gray upheaval scarcely distinguishable among the moist and billowy clouds which hang on the faint horizon. Very pale and cold are the sunrises on this southern coast, though full of wild and unusual color. The water holds on its surface deep greens, warm browns, and a purple over which a translucent white seems to have been washed. The heavily gray masses conceal the sky, but as they break and unfold they reluctantly permit a cheerless light to fall upon the sea. Long before the solid cliffs are visible the vapor shapes itself into a phantasmal coast, which seems more real to the inexperienced eye than the land when it appears; and if you stood up on the bridge of the steamer on one of these white mornings you would likely not recognize the

A COTTAGE ON THE QUEENSTOWN ROAD.

hills of Kerry when they first revealed themselves in the indistinct distance to the sharp eyes of the watch. From the lofty bridge the whole length of the ship is visible, and at four in the morning, though land is so near, the long decks have not one passenger upon them. The hills of the mountainous county in which Ireland ends have extricated themselves from the clouds, and instead of gray they appear softly blue before the sleepers are stirring; but by seven o'clock many of the ports are thrown open, and many eyes are looking out of the small circular apertures in the vessel's side to see the expected land.

Then, until Queenstown is reached, there is more animation than at any other time during the voyage. Flags are flying from each mast and astern; the decks are holy-stoned to a creamy whiteness; the officers wear their best uniforms, with the newest of gold-lace, and the passengers have discarded the loose and *négligé* costumes of the voyage for the more precise and elegant attire of the shore. The transformations in dress are so complete that one's most intimate acquaintances are not immediately recognizable. The soft Tweed hat and helmet, and the loose, copious ulsters, are packed up somewhere in the rolls of shawls and rugs which the stewards are bringing up from the cabins, and those who have worn them have adopted closer-fitting garments and the uncomfortable "stove-pipes" of civilization.

But what is the land like at which most of the passengers are looking with wistful

eyes and many surmises? One of the first points sighted is Crookhaven, a telegraph station from which the arrival of the ship is telegraphed over both continents, and a few miles east of this is the island of Cape Clear and the rock of Fastnet, on which one of the most useful lights is pillared. The distance from Fastnet to Queenstown is about seventy-five miles, and between them the coast is broken by many bays and perilous headlands which jut out from the cliffs. The cliffs are lofty and savage, and in contrast with their brown escarpment the sea fringes their bases with a long line of white surf, which is high enough to be visible many miles away when the Atlantic is calmest, and which, when a gale is blowing, is uplifted half-way to their tops. The land above the cliffs is drowsy and vacant, a moist green in color, sad in its effect, with few other signs of life upon it than the dots of white where a small village lies under the pale blue streak of its own smoke, and the tower and inclosing walls of a light-house. The white of the cottages and the light-house looks the whiter from the darkness of the rocks, and the cloudiness which shuts out the sun or admits it in misty beams. The feeling inspired is one of desolation. An uncompanionable maiden or youth may yield to this, and sigh responsively to this piteous-looking land; but most of the passengers find too much to do to let the scene, which soon becomes tiresome, absorb them. There are good-byes to be said to those who are going ashore at Queenstown, and telegrams and letters to be written for dispatch at that port; the purser has to be consulted on the times of trains, the selection of routes and hotels, and on a variety of encyclopædical questions with which that useful officer is expected to be acquainted. About four hours after passing Fastnet the steamer is abreast of a bolder promontory than any: it is the Old Head of Kinsale, and in the distance, over the port bow, another promontory is seen. This is Roche's Point, at the entrance to Queenstown Harbor, and standing off it is the tender which is to take ashore the mails and the passengers who are not going on to Liverpool.

Perhaps it will be well to say just here what the uses of Queenstown are to the transatlantic steamers, and what their relations are with it. All the mail steamers between New York, Boston, and Philadelphia and Liverpool call at it both on their way from America to England and from England to America. They deliver the American mails there, and receive the English mails. The distance from Queenstown to Liverpool is two hundred and forty miles, and the steamers usually take from seventeen to twenty hours in making it. The time is occasionally increased by from one to nine hours through detentions caused by the insufficiency of water at the Liverpool bar. But by the mail service *via* Dublin and Holyhead the time occupied between Queenstown and London, two hundred and one miles farther than Liverpool, is only nineteen hours; and thus it is possible for a mail to be delivered in London before the steamer which brought it to Queenstown has entered the Mersey. The service is by train to Cork and Dublin; thence by extraordinarily powerful Channel steamers across the Irish Sea to Holyhead, on the Welsh coast, and from Holyhead to the metropolis by fast trains, which cover the distance, two hundred and sixty miles, in six hours and forty minutes. In coming to America the steamers are required to wait at Queenstown for the mail leaving London at nine o'clock in the evening of the day on which they sail from Liverpool. In other words, supposing that one of them left the latter port at noon on Saturday, she would be in Queenstown early on Sunday morning, and would anchor there until the arrival of the train which left London nine hours

after she left Liverpool, and which would be due in Queenstown at about three o'clock on Sunday afternoon. The mail is not the only thing benefited. A hurried business man gains a whole working day on shore by using the mail route to Queenstown, and the steamers themselves find that a

A QUEENSTOWN PEDDLER.

convenient port for the embarkation of the large number of emigrants coming from Ireland. The passengers who embark at Liverpool usually have enough time ashore at Queenstown, while their steamers are waiting for the mail, to see the beautiful harbor, the river Lee, Cork, and even to kiss the Blarney Stone, and for those who are bound to Europe it is the best starting-point for the tour of Killarney. To such an extent are Americans seen in it, and to such an extent do they patronize its hotels, its shops, its hawkers, and its beggars, that it seems like an American possession, and the American flag, throwing out its crimson bars, looks quite at home on the roof of the consulate, which is embanked high on one of the white terraces of the town.

But let us return to our steamer off the Old Head of Kinsale, on her way to Liverpool. The tender lying to off the port bow is the *Lord Bandon*, the *Mount Etna*, or the *Jackal*, and when we are within half a mile of her the engines are have been living on the Eden isle of their all-absorbing passion, and propose to take that unreal estate on shore with the rest of their baggage. Except to them there

BLARNEY CASTLE.

slowed, and then stopped, to allow her to come alongside. There is a hush and a straining of sight among the passengers as she approaches. A few of them expect friends to meet them; all of them are deeply interested. She breaks the eight-day spell of the voyage, and reopens communication with the larger world, and solves the little social knot which the isolation of the voyage has tied. The firmness and greenness of the land are not more welcome than the new and unfamiliar faces, except to the bridal pair who is a sense of release, and we at once begin to feel a greater fullness of space than the immensity of mid-ocean has ever impressed upon us. The spell is indeed broken and the knot untied. Scarcely is the gang-plank out when a vender of newspapers is distributing the New York *Herald* and the London *Times*. There is a flutter of excitement over a weather-stained leather dispatch bag which a man from the shore delivers to the purser. That gentleman is uncivilly mobbed by the passengers in their anxiety to get at the contents. The little circular plate to the lock focuses their attention, and for a moment, while the key is inserted, every face is fixed in suspense. A bundle of letters and telegrams is brought out and distributed; then the mob disperses to read what it has received in quiet corners, while the few disappointed ones who have received nothing mournfully try to interest themselves in what is going on upon the deck. In the mean time the mails have been put on board the tender, and the passengers are warned by bells and whistles to follow them. This is speedily done, and the great ship, which looks nobler at the end of the voyage than when she started, is hailed with cheers, which are answered with three hoarse blasts from her fog-horn. She bears off to the northeast, and the tender makes for Roche's Point, within the shelter of which she soon is.

Queenstown Harbor is not unlike that of New York. As the Narrows protect the latter, Roche's Point and its opposite headland are so close together that they shut out the storms from the former, and keep the water within it smooth when that outside is raging. The circular bay, with its islands and hilly shores, is also a duplicate of what may be seen in the neighborhood of Staten Island. At the mouth the land is craggy, and the heights are fortified, but farther in the foliage is profuse. There is anchorage for thousands of ships, and a sufficient depth of water to admit the largest at all states of the tide.

At the head of the bay, in an almost straight line from the Point, is the town, built in terraces, one above the other, on a wooded and heathery bluff. The houses are nearly all white and square and uniform in feature. Their color and the frequent green which surrounds them give them a tropical resemblance, especially, as is not often the case, when the sun lights them up and distills all sorts of rainbow tints from the atmosphere, which is usually soft, but gray and dispiriting. On a clear and placid summer day Queenstown Harbor is as beautiful as anything that can be imagined. The foliage has a soft and cloudy depth, and the water is a still pool of emerald. Every object is refined and idealized, every color harmonized. The substantial things themselves seem as beautifully phantasmal as their minute reflections.

At the foot of the cliff and along the quays is a street of shops and taverns, most of them aiming for patronage at tourists, emigrants, and seamen. The higher terraces are principally dwellings, and the higher they are, the better is the class to which they belong. On the ridge above all the others are two or three houses which may be called palaces without extravagance of phrase. Though the interests of Queenstown are not much varied, and social complications are scarcely to be expected from them, the lines of caste and rank are drawn with English precision. Primarily the chief interest of Queenstown is as a port of call. Like Falmouth, which is similarly situated on the southern coast of England, it is made for by many ships consigned to order, or, in other words, sent here that the choice of a port of delivery may be governed by the condition

STREET VIEW IN QUEENSTOWN.

LAKES OF KILLARNEY.

of the market, and ships in ballast from abroad, which can be ordered from here to that point where the most favorable terms for carrying a cargo are procurable.

The captain whose vessel is lying in the harbor waiting orders is one of the constituent figures of Queenstown—a comfortable person, with a complexion of copper bronze and a marked steadiness of eye, and a simplicity and brevity of manner. One degree above him is the ship agent, who also is a comfortable person, with a villa on the heathery bluff, set in its own grounds, and commanding a view of the mirror-like bay—a cozy habitation, full of the spoils of travel, in which he gives little dinners, celebrated by libations as deep as they were in country houses twenty years ago. This is the great ship agent, whose argosies, "with portly sail, like signiors and rich burghers of the flood, do overpeer the petty traffickers." The agent of "the petty traffickers" also has a house somewhere on the hill, and a little office, filled with charts and maps and pictures of ships, in the street by the waterside. Another element is contributed by the officers of the garrison and the officers of the Board of Trade, whose duty lies with the outgoing ships; and the salubrity of its climate brings a small number of invalid

visitors to it, especially consumptives and sufferers from nervous debility. The dominant person in this little society is the admiral of the port, and not to know him is to be unknown—at least in fashionable eyes. An obsolete old war ship is moored in the harbor, and though it is nominally a guardship, its principal use is as a vessel on which the admiral can fly his flag. Practically he might fly his flag with no less effectiveness from any pole on land, but that would be an infringement of naval usages, and the harmless old frigate is maintained, with a crew of two hundred or more men, to fulfill a tradition. Besides flying his flag, the admiral has one or two other duties to perform. Now and then one of the enormous armored ships calls at Queenstown, or a great white transport comes into the harbor to carry troops away from this inactive little station to the Cape or India, and as soon as she is moored a ladder is lowered down her side, and the captain in full uniform enters a boat which bears him away to the admiral to report, and the admiral receives him with gratifying blandness. The functions of the admiral are almost entirely ornamental, and around him clusters an acquiescent little court, with many naval and military courtiers. A few yachtsmen, whose bird-like vessels add to the beauty of the harbor, are also present in the summer season, and sometimes there is the special correspondent of an important newspaper waiting to beguile some distinguished traveller by sea into an "interview." These dissimilar elements find a point of contact in the Club, which adheres to many of the rules under which it was formed in 1720, and is the oldest of all yacht clubs. A writer in 1748 thus describes one of its customs to the Admiralty: "I shall now acquaint

Sea, once a year, in a Number of little Vessels which for painting and gilding exceed the King's Yacht at Greenwich and Deptford. Their Admiral, who is annually elected, and hoists his Flag on board his little Vessel, leads the Van, and receives the honours of the Flag. The rest of the fleet fall in their proper stations, and keep their line in the same manner as the King's Ships. This Fleet is attended with a prodigious Number of Boats, which with their colors flying, Drums beating, and Trumpets sounding, forms one of the most agreeable and splendid Sights your Lordships can conceive." Some of the rules are very odd. They direct, among other things, that "no admiral do bring more than two Dishes of Meat for the Entertainment of the Club"; that "no ad-

THE TOURISTS' CAR.

your Lordships with a ceremony they have at Cork. It is somewhat like that of the Doge of Venice's wedding the Sea. A set of worthy Gentlemen who have formed themselves into a body, which they call the Water Club, proceed a few leagues out to

miral do presume to bring more than two Dozen of Wine to his Treat, for it has always been deemed a Breach of the ancient Rules and Constitutions of the Club, except when my Lords the Judges are invited"; that "no captain do bring any

WATER-FALL AT GLENGARIFF.

stranger to the Club, unless they should lie at the Captain's House the Night before: this order not to extend to the admiral, who has a right to invite whom he pleases"; and that "no long tail Wigs, large Sleeves, or Ruffles be worn by any Member at the Club."

Though the club is less restrictive now, and is a very pleasant little house of entertainment, it is not enough to beguile all the spare time which the men have, and one hears many complaints of *ennui* among those who are fixtures. Queenstown is dull, and to an active temperament the torpor of its ways soon becomes execrable. The passengers of the ocean steamers ripple the surface for a few hours, but the moment they are gone the place relapses into its usual and oppressive quietude.

As soon as an American steamer is telegraphed it is known among the thatched cottages on the hill-side through some rapid but mysterious agency, and long before the tender comes in from Roche's Point a voluble and excited rabble of hawkers, beggars, and carmen gathers on the quays. When the passenger lands he is confused by the chorus of importunities to buy and to give. Each carman pretends to believe that he has been especially selected, and waves his whip and arms frantically at the supposititious hirer: "Very well, yer haner; this kyer, yer haner; I'm waiting for yer haner"—though the person addressed has not signified any intention of riding. Unless he mounts one of the shabby jaunting-cars, however, he will not find it easy to extricate himself from the beleaguering mendicants, who surround him and follow him with propitiatory blessings, which are showered upon him with rapid and indistinct reiteration. There are old women with long black cloaks falling from the shoulders to the feet, and square caps which envelop the whole of the back and crown of the head, surrounding the face with a clean white frill, who have grapes and other fruit to sell at five times their value. There are hawkers of lace, shillalahs, bog-oak, pictures, and sprigs of the shamrock—everything at unscrupulous prices. There is an unblushing fluency of lying, flattery, and humbug, and when the crowd is evaded without purchases the blessings are quickly turned into muttered curses. The Englishmen who have to run this blockade scowl at the nuisance, and do not disguise their annoyance with it; but the Americans treat it as capital fun, and buy and give with a reckless liberality which has made many of the peddlers rich, and begging a lucrative profession.

The run ashore at Queenstown depends for what it embraces on the time which the passengers have; but the westward-bound steamers are usually in the harbor long enough, waiting for the mails, to enable them to go up the river to Cork and kiss the Blarney Stone. The "sweetness" of Cork has been sung by one of its melodious sons in easily remembered lines, but its beauty was surely in the glamour cast upon it by his own fondness. The stranger wanders its streets and quays in vain to find a confirmation of Father Prout's musical verses. What he sees is a city of small size, which reminds him somehow of inky-sleeved and dissolute Captain Shandon penning the prospectus of the *Pall Mall Gazette* in the Fleet Prison. W. Maginn, the original of that famous picture of Thackeray's, was a native of Cork. So, too, was Francis Mahony, the gifted humorist who has sent the music of the Shandon Bells all round the world.

Cork, as the second city of Ireland, is of no little commercial importance, and though its streets are untidy and its architecture is uninteresting, the scenery above it and below it is exceedingly beautiful. From the wide and deep harbor of Queenstown the Lee winds up to it, in an almost straight course, between verdant hills, with many comfortable villages and luxurious residences upon them, and several quiet little watering-places along the grassy shore. The distance is eleven miles, and the channel has a depth of ten feet at low water. Above Cork the river greatly

resembles the Thames in the neighborhood of Henley. It flows placidly through fragrant meadows, with willows drooping over it, and here and there inclosing it. The banks here are low and firm, and the hills are distant, so that long reaches of the stream are open to the view. The scene has the highly cultivated character of the best of English landscape.

This is the way to Blarney, which is five miles from Cork, and there is the stone of talismanic eloquence, one of the greatest of the many humbugs in Ireland. Blarney itself is a thriving manufacturing village which produces excellent cloth, and the castle is a picturesque ruin, once the stronghold of the Earls of Clancarty. The origin of the magic power ascribed to the stone is not known, but whoever kisses it acquires, in the language of one version of the legend, "the gift of gentle insinuating speech, with soft talk in all its ramifications, whether employed in vows light as air, such as lead captive the female heart, or elaborate mystifications of a grosser grain, such as may do for the House of Commons." This magniloquence is of a piece with the description Father Prout gave Sir Walter Scott, who made a pilgrimage to Blarney in 1825. "You behold, Sir Walter, the most valuable remnant of Ireland's ancient glory, the most precious lot of her Phœnician inheritance. Possessed of this treasure, she may well be designated

'First flower of the earth, and first gem of the sea,'

for neither the musical stone of Memnon that so 'sweetly played in tune,' nor the oracular stone of Delphi, nor the lapidary talisman of the Lydian Gyges, nor the colossal granite shaped into a Sphinx in Upper Egypt, nor Stonehenge, nor the Pelasgic walls of Palestrina, offer so many attractions. The long-sought *lapis philosophorum*, compared with this jewel, dwindles into insignificance; nay, the savory fragment which was substituted for the infant Jupiter when Saturn had the mania for devouring his children; the Luxor obelisk; the treaty stone of Limerick, with all its historic endearments; the zodiacal monument of Denderah, with all its astronomic importance; the Elgin marbles, with all their sculptured, the Arundelian, with all their lettered, riches—can not for a moment stand in competition with the Blarney block. What stone in the world save this alone can communicate to the tongue that suavity of speech and that splendid

TORC LAKE, FROM BRICKEEN BRIDGE.

effrontery so necessary to get through life?"

The authentic stone can only be reached by a perilous suspension from the top of the castle tower; but the more sensible visitors satisfy any ambition they may have to add unconscionable garrulity to their other vices by touching a less horrifying part of the masonry with their lips. After the osculation a rapid journey must be made to the harbor. The mails will be on board the tender, and the beggars and peddlers crying for patronage with increasing urgency. An hour later, Queenstown will be behind, and from the quiet headlands a long black shape, emitting an endless chain of smoke, will be seen silently gliding into the sunset.

The greatest pleasure of the run ashore is when the passenger lands from an inward-bound steamer, and has time to visit Glengariff and Killarney. There are some disadvantages connected with this excursion. The rain is as wearily persistent as the sunshine is infrequent. The mountains are nearly always in a gray retirement. The rains and mists are not so objectionable, however, that the splendor of scenery will not atone for them. What detracts from the tour most is the miserable comprehensiveness of the beggars, who from end to end of the journey follow the visitor with dogged perseverance, and chase him for miles and miles—barefooted women, shock-headed children, and even able-bodied men whose appearance is far from that of destitution. He can never be alone, never for a moment left to the quiet enjoyment of what he has come to see. Every cottage on the way sends out after him a rosy-faced and well-fed crowd of beggars, who will not take the most absolute refusal nor the most savage rebuke, and who keep at his heels until another cottage is reached, when they give up the chase to the emissaries of that, who continue it until they reach their limit, where they leave their next neighbor to sustain the agony. There is a deliberate intention to weary him into surrender, and surrender increases rather than diminishes the plague. Killarney can only be half enjoyed under these circumstances, but it is so lovely that the pleasure which can be derived from it is great, despite the many annoyances.

All natural beauties are embraced in this region; not one form, but all forms—mountains and lakes; gaunt hills and delightful valleys; the amplest fertility and the most unconquerable barrenness; the bleakest uplands, and glens and lanes in which everything is green. History, tradition, and poetry increase the charm which Nature herself possesses. Scarcely a spot is unstoried; scarcely a spot unsung, or unclaimed by fable.

There are two ways of approaching the lakes, and that which includes Glengariff is the better. The train leaves the traveller at Bantry, a little town on a magnificent bay which sweeps in from the Atlantic between jutting and rocky shores, and carries its brine in a deep flood at least seven miles inland. Bantry is the terminus of the railway, and thence the way is by car along the edge of the bay, which is now on a level with the road, and then far down at the foot of the bowlder-strewn slopes.

At the head of the bay, under the shadow of clustered mountains, is Glengariff. When it is discovered from a height the scene is one of sterile and tawny-colored splendor. The water spreading out to its gates is encircled by savage mountains; the rocks are bare and brown; the sky is cold. There is no promise of the fragrance and juicy verdure, the melting mood in which nature is found at a lower elevation; and as from the top of the hill we go down into an ever-increasing luxuriance of green of varying shades, from the solemn dark of the fir to the transparence and luminousness of banks of ferns, winding into tunnels of foliage, mixed with which is the blazing fruit of the mountain ash, and the fire-drops of the fuchsias, it seems like penetrating the outer brusqueness of one who at heart is full of gentleness. The cordiality of nature is expressed in elastic turf, springing softly under the pressure of the foot, in the moist exuberance of the verdure, in the sound of many rills which gush out from and between the rocks, in the strength and brilliance of scores of flowers, and in the languishing mildness of the air. The very hedges, as dense and as trim as the hawthorn of English fields, are compact masses of blossom, and the vines clamber up above the window-sills to the roofs, enmeshing every stone in their tenacious threads. The mountains that from above look shaggy and awful are quieting in their influence down here, and the salt-water bay with its woody islands is like a calm inland lake. One or two houses and two hotels of uncommon excellence are built in this happy spot, and the climate is so genial that they are occupied all the year round.

Winding away from Glengariff again, of which Thackeray, Macaulay, Froude, Lever, and many more writers have sung the praises—their testimony being hung in a printed form on the walls of all the bedrooms—the fertility is succeeded, as the mountains are ascended, by wild, stony pastures, deserted farms, sad moorlands, and craggy ridges, and for nearly forty miles these are the characteristics of the scenery. Great long rocky valleys are revealed, shut in by lofty mountains, and entered by dark and forbidding ravines, and the predominant color is a russet brown, or, in the farthest distance, a stormy blue. In one of these valleys, looking small, bleak, and wild, the three lakes of Killarney are at first seen from the summit of the Kenmare Road, a distance at which all their less austere beauties are hidden; but, as in approaching Glengariff, the way descends from sterile uplands into a maze of foliage, and overhead and at both sides crops up the luscious green entanglement. The drive down from the police barracks to the untidy little town, a large part of whose population lives on the alms of summer visitors, is along a smooth and clean road. On one hand is a precipitous mountain slope completely covered with grasses, mosses, ferns, and shrubs, and in all that high embankment soaring up many hundred feet not one gray rock nor one black patch of earth is without its crown of green. On the other hand is a magnificent demesne of pasture and woodland opening out into vistas of the placid lakes, with their many islets, and the shadowy forms of the opposite mountains springing into the clouds.

It is impossible to imagine a fuller loveliness than that of Killarney. To-day we strike out between the immense walls of Dunloe Gap, where the mountains almost clasp one another overhead, and the bluish-gray rocks bear all the evidences of their fierce origin, and the spent force of immemorial ages. Up this way there are Acherontic pools whose unrippled waters are dyed black by the surrounding fields of peat, and spongy bogs treacherously covered with pallid and feeble grasses, whose nature is forever sullen and threatening. To-morrow we loiter under the arbutus groves and by the white ruins of sweet Innisfallen, or tread through the vacant chambers of old Ross Castle, or conjure up the past out of the picturesque decay of Muckross Abbey. One hour we may be amid an uncompromising sterility, and the next imprisoned in a tropical prodigality of leafage, where the Torc water-fall leaps seventy feet down a precipice; one hour in the cool shadows of the Colleen Bawn caves, or calling echoes from the towering bluff of the Eagle's Nest,

COLLEEN BAWN CAVES.

or swiftly shooting down the race under the old weir bridge, and next lying idly in the pasturage of the Earl of Kenmare's demesne, and watching a scene of pastoral contentment which seems to belong to another world than the Gap of Dunloe.

So varied is the interest and so many are the beauties of Killarney that the run ashore at Queenstown will be a memorable experience if it include this incomparable pleasure-ground. It was so much to me that I begin to forget and forgive the pertinacity of the beggars and the cunning and servility of the guides.

WHEAT FIELDS OF THE COLUMBIA.

I.—EAST OF THE MOUNTAINS.

A GLANCE at the map will remind the reader that Oregon and Washington Territory are divided into eastern and western halves by the Cascade Mountains. The western side of this "divide" is called the Coast, and the people who live there speak of the other side as the country "east of the mountains." This general phrase has now come to have specific application to the basin of the Columbia, a plateau region drained by the middle part of that great stream and its tributaries from the westward, such as the Yakima and Okanagon, and the lower part of the Snake River. To understand this thoroughly the reader in the Atlantic States should consult some modern map of this northwestern corner of the Union, whose features have only recently been accurately known and cartographed.

Until some of the projected railways through passes of the Cascades shall have made an appearance outside of surveyors' note-books, the only avenue from the coast to the plains or plateaus east of the mountains is the Columbia River.

Half a century has not yet gone by since a canoe trip of two weeks' duration was accounted good progress from Fort Vancouver to the Dalles, much time being lost in making the long portage at the Cascades, and in laboriously dragging the emptied canoe along the edge of the boiling rapids to the slack-water above. Thirty years ago small stern-wheeled steamboats began to run from Portland to the Cascades. There passengers and freight were transported by a wooden tramway to the other steamboats that carried them up to the Dalles, where a second portage was necessary. The next advance was the replacing of the old tramway by a railroad, and later by the construction of a railway from the Dalles to Walla Walla.

All this river traffic was in the hands of the Oregon Railway and Navigation Company, which was rivalled at its ocean end by the Pacific Steam-ship Company, running boats between Portland and San Francisco, and eastwardly by the pretensions, if not the actual presence, of the Northern Pacific. Within the past few years, however, great changes have occurred. Seeing the advantage that might follow a union of these local interests in east and west of the mountains, acts in unison. There are now, therefore, a continuous railway from Portland, Oregon, to Minnesota; a line southward from the Columbia to Baker City, Oregon, to meet the road proceeding westward from Granger, Wyoming; and several short "feeders" extended into the agricultural region where the great Snake River approaches the Columbia. Portland and San Francisco are connected by the Ore-

IN THE ENGINE-ROOM OF THE "WIDE WEST."

transportation and developement with the transcontinental line of the Northern Pacific, which his genius was carrying to a successful completion, Mr. Henry Villard, of New York, secured control and substantial coalition of the ocean-going business of the Pacific Steam-ship Company, the river traffic and detached railways of the Oregon Railway and Navigation Company, and of the rights and introductory construction of the Northern Pacific Company at this end. It happens at present, therefore, that the whole transportation system of Oregon and Washington, both gon and California Railway, traversing the long hollows between the Coast Range and the Sierra Nevada. To these should be added a fourth means of ingress to the public lands of the Columbia Basin—the ocean steamers on the Pacific, since thus will come many travellers from Europe, viâ the Atlantic steamers to Aspinwall and across the Isthmus.

It was my fortune recently to make a trip through this basin, with good opportunities to examine what the region contained attractive to emigrants, and I have thought my experiences worth the telling.

II.—AROUND WALLA WALLA.

Among the earlier immigrants into Oregon, thirty years ago, a few halted on the eastern skirts of the "blue hills" that had so long guided them across the wearisome plains. When a settlement became fixed there, the Indians massacred it, and war began. The government established a military post amid the sands of Wallula, but soon moved it a dozen miles up the Walla Walla River to a beautiful site among rolling green prairies, where it exists to-day as one of the pleasantest of all our army posts. Under this protection it rapidly grew up a community of farmers, tilling the valleys and creek-bottoms, scattering more widely with increasing numbers and assured safety, until now a district is covered by civilization stretching irregularly from the Columbia River southward to Pendleton, thence eastward along the base of the Blue Mountains to Lewiston, Idaho. This tract lies wholly south of the Snake River, partly in Oregon and partly in Washington Territory. It is a hundred miles long by an average of perhaps forty miles in breadth, and contains not far from 25,000 people. In addition, to the southward, there are the fertile Wallowa and the Grande Ronde valleys of Oregon, lying within circling spurs of the Blue Mountains; and also the long strip of arable country between the Blue Mountains and the Cascade Range, through which flow John Day's and the Des Chutes rivers. I do not know how many thousands of acres or square miles of cultivable soil these separate and hill-bordered patches would make if united; but two or three Atlantic States could be made up out of them without any trouble.

Down across the upper portion of the Blue Mountains, from Umatilla *via* Pendleton and the Grande Ronde, there is a railway which gives access to all the western part of this region, and furnishes a quick outlet for its products both eastward and westward. Elsewhere ingress is had by the railway from Portland to Walla Walla, and thence by branches to Dixie, to Dayton, and across to the Snake River at Riparia, whence steamboats ascend to Lewiston, Idaho, while stages run across the country in all directions to remote settlements.

The whole of this great track, though nowhere flat, is comparatively level, except where it reaches up into the foot-hills, or is crossed by long ridges, like that between Walla Walla and Dayton. The first settlers took the bottom-lands because they held their greenness longest and were easiest of cultivation. The streams here and there showed old beaver-dams, and were bordered by broad thickets of willows and cottonwoods convenient to "slash." The older farms are in such localities. Before long, however, adventurous spirits, finding that irrigation was unnecessary, made experiments in planting upon the round tops of the hills, whose yellow backs lay hot under the sun between the river copses and the mountain woods. The tufaceous soil turned up by the plough was dark and rich, and the yield outranked the best acres along the creek-side. The hills were many and high, sufficing for all the wants of the scant population during many years, so that the wide level benches that lay between the foot-hills and the prairies—middle lands, light-soiled, dry, and dusty, covered with sorry bunch-grass and sad rabbit-weed—were neglected, and came to be considered worthless, and were to be had almost for the asking.

One day about seven years ago a young man came into Walla Walla driving all his wealth in the shape of a span of horses and an old wagon. A day or two later he was busy hauling flour to Wallula, which he continued until he had saved a little money and won a little credit. Walla Walla stands some miles out in the plain, and none of its plentiful shade trees grew there naturally. Seeing the demand for fire-wood in the village, he built a small flume from the nearest wooded foot-hill, and brought down cord-wood or small timbers more cheaply than they could be drawn by horses. The profits of this, together with his practice as a physician, in which respect he had now had time to prove himself, made enough money to enable him to try an experiment in agriculture, namely, the cultivation of the intermediate bench lands. Taking up 160 acres, he sowed wheat, and his success was so encouraging that he enlarged his operations until his crop of 1881 was no less than 80,000 bushels from 2000 acres of despised "rabbit-weed"—an average of forty bushels to the acre. This experiment has shown that the benches are nearly, if not quite, as good as the uplands or creek-bottoms. The average crop of the best uplands, taking a long series of years togeth-

VIEW ON THE COLUMBIA RIVER.

er, is thirty bushels. This is of wheat, scarcely anything else being raised, not for lack of ability—oats and potatoes are especially successful—but because there is so much more ready money in wheat, for which there is always a market. Here, too, the dangers attending so exclusive a method of farming are lessened, for there has never yet been a failure of crops at Walla Walla, though absence of rain now and then shortens the yield to half its proper amount. So strong is the soil, also, that any manuring is not yet thought of, and one farm was pointed out to me where for eighteen successive years good crops had been produced. The farmers, nevertheless, are more and more generally adopting the "summer fallow" plan as a precaution against too great depletion of their soil. Another bit of economy is the use of "headers" rather than the ordinary mowers and reapers, the long stubble remaining after the harvest being burned, and thus returning to the soil in ashes the greater part of the minerals drawn into the straw during the previous half-year. Unfortunately, however, there is a large class of ignorant and shiftless farmers, "old-timers" for the most part, who are heedless of these far-seeing precautions.

What I have said applies to the whole region between the Blue Mountains and the dry plateaus that begin at the Idaho line.

Besides Walla Walla, there are half a dozen thriving, progressive farming centres, all connected by railway or stage lines, having the telegraph, a daily mail, local newspapers, and other appurtenances of civilization. The heavy storms of midwinter, mantling the face of the earth in snow four or five feet deep, and sinking the mercury away below zero for weeks together, isolate these communities sometimes, but not for protracted intervals.

III.—UP SNAKE RIVER.

The railway from Walla Walla struck Snake River about ninety miles above its mouth, at a station called Riparia, but known to the people of the region as Texas Ferry. The station and steamboat landing consisted here, as elsewhere in this region, of an immense wharf-boat or covered scow moored at the shore. Beside it a railway track ran upon a long incline down to the very lowest water mark, so that as the river sank or rose, and the boat's level altered accordingly, freight-cars would still stand even with her deck. The steamer proved to be a large, handsome craft, receiving a cargo of merchandise for the country stores, supplies of bran and such feed for cattle, and much agricultural machinery. It was a very hot day, but a breeze coming down the cañon made the sheltered upper deck a comfortable place to sit and watch the clever way in which the men handled the bulky freight in the narrow limits of the forward gangway.

This used to be the crossing-place for all the lower Palouse region, and the ferry did a good business, but now it is of small consequence. It consisted of a wire rope stretched across the river over a tripod on each bank high enough to keep it out of the way of the steamboats. Suspended to this wire by two pulleys, the small flat-bottomed ferry-boat ran across by the force of the current, the right sheer being obtained by a windlass in the boat, which lengthened or shortened the guy-ropes at the will of the ferryman. This proved to be the type of all the ferries.

The shores are lava hills that rise steeply from the water—so steeply that here no room is left for a cattle trail or beach. Maroon-red level cliff ledges, broken through by angular ravines, and connected, one terrace above the other, by grass-grown slopes or a natural riprapping of fallen fragments, stand with faces almost vertical for two or three hundred feet above the river, and then round off into golden-edged domes of sun-ripened turf. Everything in this deep river gorge appears as dry and useless as possible, but wheat is growing right on the brow of those bluffs, where the soil is rich, though the crops are always exposed to suffer from drought.

We cast loose and began our voyage up-stream soon after noon.

The first landing was a curious sight. The cutting away of the bluff by a water gully had formed a bar of sand and gravel, and ploughed out a passage up to the table-land. The nose of the steamer—a flat-bottomed, run-on-a-heavy-dew style of boat—was pushed right up on the beach, whereupon the current quickly drifted her stern inshore, and the plank was run out. A small shed stood near the margin, in which some bags of salt were stored; otherwise every kind of freight, boxes, bales, barrels, packages of furniture, sacks of meal, crates of wooden

ware, and the brilliant red wheels and wood-work of threshers and other machinery, all in pieces, lay scattered higgledy-piggledy, and half buried in the sand. Gradually these things would be carted back to their owners over the hills. Meanwhile the weather was to be trusted, and nobody would disturb them.

This landing was named New York Bar by a company who once proposed to go into placer-mining here, but the diggings were soon abandoned to the patient Chinamen, who are only too glad to be let peacefully alone with second pick at anything. We could see them working as we passed, half a dozen or so, hard to distinguish from the bowlders among which they delved. There is gold to be taken out of all the gravel banks and island bars along the whole river, and also down the Columbia.

So the afternoon wore on, the sun blazing down, the scenery repeating itself exactly as we turned each bend in this truly snake-like river—long, level, red-brown escarpments like ruined walls fallen forward here and there under the pressure of the bulging earth behind, or rounded bluffs, whose gleaming yellow intensified the clear azure of the filtered sky, crowned with massive fortifications and pillared domes of lava, whose rifts and shadows were painted in ultramarine and indigo. Thus the view was limited between high horizons scarcely a mile apart, while the river filled the bottom of the winding cañon.

At Penewawa the stage road crosses from Colfax to Dayton and Walla Walla, following up the long dry bed of Dead Man's Hollow. This ferry, like the others, made a great deal of money before the Northern Pacific Railway turned all the merchandise from this route. Here were two or three extremely fine orchards, and pleasant homes surrounded by trees and gardens, for which they were indebted to a spring near the top of the hill.

Recent farming on the highlands of the Snake has proved very successful. Meanwhile the plateaus are devoted to stock-raising and sheep-herding, affording fine pasturage. The bottoms are utilized in growing wheat, which is cut and stacked for hay, little timothy being sowed here. This wheat hay is to be fed in the snowy winter to the sheep.

The breezy evening found us at Almota, a village with shops and hotels, and a wharf which is the landing-place for the large farming district about Moscow and westward. There is a government weather station here, and two youths were exchanging wig-wag practice with signal-flags across the river.

the dews out. The life they lived was far more comfortless and savage and isolated than that of the Indian on the opposite bank, who had his family, his horses, and his neighbors always with him, and who no doubt enjoys himself, according to his

THE FERRY.

In this neighborhood, again, were to be seen colonies of Chinese washing gold out of the gravelly shores of the river. Their houses were little holes dug in the bank, and roofed with just enough poles and brush to sustain a layer of earth and keep

lights, from Easter to Christmas, enduring the bad season of midwinter as best he can.

It was utter night when we cast off from the last landing at Granite Point, and passed under the black frown of the preci-

DALLES OF THE COLUMBIA.

pice. The water swishing by the prow flashed a moment in the yellow glare of our low head-light, and swept back into the velvety, noiseless gloom behind. No wind made moans or music through the wire cordage of the steamer's upper works, and the stillness of sleep settled upon the boat as I smoked my last warm pipeful in the pilot-house, studying

> "the deep sapphire overhead,
> Distinct with vivid stars inlaid."

After this, cool oblivion, and an awaking in the bright morning at Lewiston, at the junction of the Snake and Clearwater rivers.

IV.—ACROSS THE PALOUSE.

The agricultural region north of the Snake River is known as the Palouse country, or simply as the Palouse, after the name of its central river. Stages traverse it, carrying the mail in several directions, and I chose the route from Lewiston to Cheney, a station on the Northern Pacific Railway, the direction being due north, and right along the boundary between Washington and Idaho.

Five o'clock in the morning was the hour for starting, the vehicle proving to be an open two-seated and badly used-up buckboard. With great joy I saw a trio of the mangiest of "bagmen" drive away in the opposite direction, and found that my companion was to be a young Californian, acting as advance agent for The Man Mystery—a magician, contortionist, etc., who was making a tour of the region, "his wonders to perform" before the excited frontiersmen. Driving to the brink of the Clearwater, whose current is blue, while that of the Snake is yellow, we shouted to the ferryman opposite, who calmly finished his breakfast, and then leisurely steered us across by means of his wire-suspended flat-boat. He had eighteen dogs, all of which, "without distinction of race, color, or previous condition," came down to welcome our bark with theirs.

Here, too, stood a tall, sunburned maiden, straight as a wheat stalk. She had just alighted from a big black horse, and now climbed up beside the driver, who evidently considered us two passengers in the low seat behind entirely unnecessary to his happiness. Her costume was well adapted to her journey—a broad-brimmed and badly cracked chip hat, a double-caped water-proof, rusty with sunshine and dust, two green Balmoral skirts, and (outside the water-proof cloak) a riding-skirt of faded alpaca, which, when she took her seat on the buckboard, she wrapped around her waist like a sash. That she had a better hat, however, was manifest by the shape of a parcel carefully carried in her lap.

glowed, under the beams of the rising sun, with broad color—a mingled tone of the yellow of straw and the grayish-green of hay, with cobalt lying solid in the angular masses of shadow near at hand, or washed evenly and almost impalpably over the misty background. It soon appeared that our new passenger was a school-mistress, and wished she were back in California, not liking Idaho. The advance agent and she discovered they had acquaintances in common in the Sacramento Valley,

INDIAN HORSE-TRADER.

Before us loomed a hill that it would require two and a half hours to climb, in order to get up to the plateau level, so deep was the river-bed sunken. The road wound here and there, wherever the grade was best. Expanding before us as we went higher and higher, all the landscape

and were soon very talkative together, whereupon the driver became sulky, and devoted himself to giving me geographical information, none of which was new.

The deep ravine in the bare and gravelly bluff along which we were climbing was covered with hundreds of narrow sheep paths, dividing the face of the hill into a multitude of minute terraces. On our side we could hardly trace these through the weeds, though at a distance they were as plain as the lines of shingling on a roof. Great flocks of sheep passing back and forth in spring and again in the autumn, between their high summer pastures and the sheltered fields along the river, keep these tiny trails well trodden.

As the summit approached, a vast scene was spread before us,

"grassy, wild, and bare,
Wide, wild, and open to the air."

At the base of the bluff the two rivers came down to join currents, and break through the jagged indigo of the cañon just visible at the right. In the south some mountain silhouettes were painted faintly on the far horizon, and right underneath us the orchards and white houses of Lewiston and the green meadows along the Clearwater formed bright notes in the landscape. All the rest was a treeless plateau, but a plateau through which the water had cut tortuous and confluent lines of drainage, beginning far back as mere pencil scratches, like the outermost twigs of a tree, and uniting into deeper and deeper channels, until the great gulches opened into the river gorge. All these rivulets, brooks, and winding river-courses were now dry and brown, with sere grass to their very beds, and between them lay rounded ridges like well-shaven lawns, as smooth and close-cropped and tawny as a pig's back. We were 1800 feet above the town, the school-mistress said, and only now could we begin to appreciate how deeply sunken, broad, and forcible a stream was this great river of the Snake. Its course could be traced for a score of miles—a vast cliff-guarded chasm ploughed far through the basalts that here and there protruded from underneath their thick blanket of soil and herbage. I have said ploughed, but that is only partially true, for one could easily see how the edges of the bluffs along each side of both the Snake and the Clearwater were higher than the general level of the plateaus back of them, showing that subterranean forces had forced the earth's crust apart along this line, furnishing an irregular drainage channel, to which all Idaho contributes.

Walking slowly up the long hill in the freshness of the morning, and much of the time in the shade, there had been little discomfort; but here on the summit began the "heat and burden of the day." The sun blazed down straight from the cloudless vault, and was reflected back from an unbounded area of seared plain. The light soil, powdered by incessant travel and prolonged drought, was kicked into a dense cloud, hiding the horses' feet, and poured off the wheels into our faces and over our clothes. The glib tongue of the school-mistress was kept fast shut in her mouth, which she dared not open in the blinding dust, and the driver substituted touches of his whip-lash for speech in addressing his team.

The people of this neighborhood were largely Norwegians, most of whom had previously dwelt somewhere else on the Pacific coast. Their houses were chiefly built of logs, which they had hauled ten or twenty miles from the hills, and the walls inclined inward somewhat, as I have seen represented in pictures of settlements. There was not the least appearance of an attempt to be *nice* about any of the houses, and almost no bushes or trees were set out. As the small, comfortless school building came into view on a distant eminence, the school-mistress began to talk about the difficulties of her position.

"Most of my pupils are as old as I am, and it is hard to behave like a teacher with them. And stupid? Lordy!"

I could see by the way her two hands went up that their dullness was immeasurable by words.

"I guess some of 'em are pretty smart in their own lingo; but all they want of our teaching is just enough to read a little and make change. As soon as these boys get grown, you see, they're going away off a thousand miles or so, buy some land, and go to farming, just as their fathers did. They don't need much savvey for that."

Nobody was to be seen around the hot little log school-house, the windows of which were boarded up, showing how the boys had smashed the glass. It looked pretty lonely for the young woman, who waved us good-by with her big hat as we came to the crest of the next hill. The driver was much affected. "I wouldn't mind goin' to school myself this afternoon," he sighed. "I think, if I were to try, I could make it interesting for the teacher."

"WE'LL WHOOP 'ER UP FOR THE PROFESSOR."

Arrived at Moscow for dinner, we looked very much like darkies or coal-heavers. Moscow is a lively little town, doing a large trade with the farmers.

The advance agent thought this town, having so large a tributary population, would be a good place for his man, and so he "billed" it, which I learn is the proper expression for posting announcements and arranging the preliminaries of any exhibition. A lounger at the hotel took vast interest in the proceedings, and promised him a big house, as though he "carried the county in his breeches pocket," like a politician.

"We 'ain't had a show since 'way back, and every feller that can raise the bullion 'll come, and bring his girl. Better not have any reserved seats. Charge everybody four bits straight, and the kids two bits. That 'll fetch 'em. Don't you fret. We'll whoop 'er up for the Professor."

The same endless succession of rolling hills, farm-covered as far as the eye could reach, continued all the way to the Palouse River—a distance from Lewiston given as forty-five miles; but that is measured in an air line simply by counting the section lines. The road always takes two sides of a triangle, either in going over a hill or around a farm, so that it is much longer in fact, the hot sun and stifling dust not tending to shorten our estimate.

At Palouse City we spent the night. The town is on the river, here a small, swift stream running through a thin growth of yellow pines. The water-power has caused two saw-mills to be built, to which logs are rafted down, and on the steep sides of the ravine a rough village of a hundred people or so has grown up, forming a supply point for the neighborhood. It has dawned upon them, however, that the rugged little cañon is no place for the town, so they are picking it up bodily and moving a mile down the creek to where it may stand on a level. Colfax, a village of considerable size, not far away, had been burned just before my visit, and it was expected that the dwellers there would not rebuild, but would come and start afresh at this new town, or else at Endicott. It never occurred to any of these persons that there was any sentiment to hinder their pulling up stakes and moving a town about in this fashion. The whole country is merely laid off in squares. States, counties, towns, farms, are all run by surveyors' lines. Nothing has been brought about by a course of events, or is determined by the natural boundaries of big-tree, stream, or hill range, as is pleasantly the case in the father-land. Hence there is no character in any district or piece of real estate, nor more hold upon a man's affection than in any other quarter section he might "take up." It is not *home* at all. No-

body has been born, or died, or married there; the owner has not planted hopes along with his orchard, and therefore has none to uproot in the abandonment of his trees. All that sort of thing is yet to come, and it costs him and his family no more pangs to pack up and go where they think they can do a little better than it does a hunter to move his nightly lodge as he follows the game.

Between Palouse City and the railway occurs the same wide expanse of rolling fertile hills and valleys, everywhere dotted with farms. Various small streams, the largest of which is Hangman's Creek, exist, and it is said that springs are abundant throughout the whole region, and good wells easily obtained.

Hangman's Creek is not at all as forbidding as its name, winding its way cheerily through willowy and flower-strewn banks. In 1857 the trees along its banks a little lower down were decorated with the bodies of several ringleaders of a murderous revolt on the part of the Spokane Indians, to whom General Wright administered a defeat so severe and so well merited that this tribe has been most polite and friendly to the whites ever since. The name of the pleasant creek perpetuates this execution, which in Idaho phrase was a "hanging-bee."

Two villages north of the Palouse were passed through—Farrington and Spangle—which have a dozen stores and various workshops each, and look forward to a long continuance of their rapid growth. The heaviest establishment in all these villages is the warehouse of the man who sells agricultural implements. These farms—a few of which exceed a thousand acres—require the use of machinery, and every farmer is discontented unless he owns a complete set, with all the latest improvements. This is expensive, for here machinery costs fully twice its price in the Eastern States. It is seldom that the farmer can pay more than a fraction of the cost; but the dealer gives him credit, takes a mortgage on the farm, and charges him one to two per cent. a month interest. The farmers don't deserve their good wagons and implements, even on these ruinous terms, for I saw them, in many instances, left out-of-doors to crack and rust.

The methods of farming show nothing extraordinary except, perhaps, the cultivation of wheat for hay, to which end almost the entire crop has been consigned

"BEEF À LA MODE!"

FALLS OF THE SPOKANE.

hitherto. Timothy, clover, and alfalfa do well, but have been cultivated very sparingly. The principal crop until recently was flax—the wild plant is plentiful all about these hills—the yield of which would average about fourteen bushels to the acre. It was profitable because of the saving in freight compared with a cargo of grain of equal value. Now, however, the farmers are turning their attention more to wheat and oats; not much barley is raised. The average yield per acre of these grains is very large compared with the East, though by no means reaching the extravagant estimates often published, nor am I judging from the present year,

which is one of unusual drought, the total yield of the region not being expected to more than equal last year's crop, in spite of the increased acreage. Drought is the great enemy the farmer has to dread, but no irrigation is considered necessary, and probably lack of grain is to be looked for no more here than in the Prairie States.

Stock-raising was profitable to the first comers, but the rapid filling up and fencing in of the country has limited the possibilities of this. One does not see many cattle, therefore, and fewer horses than formerly, though every farmer has a small band, which are disposed of to drovers, who sell them again to the herdsmen of

Wyoming and Colorado, to be used up and mercifully shot after a year or two of cattle-chasing. In the horse and cattle business, but especially the former, the farmers have keen competitors in the Nez Percé Indians, who raise great numbers of ponies, which they sell not only to the cattle men, but also to the Northern Indians—Spokanes, Cœur d'Alenes, Crees, and Flat-heads—who are less favorably situated for horse-breeding. These Indian ponies, and the half-breed scrub stock raised by the white men as well, go by the name of "Kyuses"—derived from a tribe of Indians in northern California with whom the pioneers first began to trade in horseflesh. They are tough, active, often speedy little brutes, but as full of tricks and deviltry as their homely skins will hold.

V.—THE SPOKANE REGION.

The sand and lava along the banks of the Columbia River extend northeastward from the Dalles in a triangular tongue of desert penetrating almost to Cœur d'Alene Lake. Its scenery, as viewed from the car window, is perfectly described by Bret Harte's familiar stanza:

"Just take a look about you: alkali, rock, and sage,
Sage and rock and alkali—ain't it a pretty page?
Sun in the east at mornin', sun in the west at night,
And the shadow of this yere station the only thing moves in sight."

Through this desolation the Northern Pacific Railway, with incredible hardship to its engineers and workmen, has constructed its main line, following an ancient water-course, called the Great Coulé. There is no station better than a switch and a telegraph office for two hundred and fifty miles, or all the way from the Dalles to the Spokane Valley. The situation was told very well by an old gentleman as the car drew up at a station consisting of a section-house and a big sign-board, when he said, "The people here get just two drinks of water a day, one when the train goes up, and the other when it comes down."

Nevertheless, in spite of this cheerless aspect of affairs, the sage-brush plains that lie on top of the bluffs bordering the railway are very rich, and beyond them bunch-grass uplands of scarcely less fertility stretch northward and southward (as we have already seen), and are contin-

ued west of the Columbia in the vastly useful valleys and grazing plateaus of the Yakima, and the other drainage slopes of the Cascade Range. All these uplands are being settled upon with amazing rapidity, and are to be yet more eagerly appropriated when the railway connections heretofore explained have made them readily accessible. At Sprague the shops of the Pacific division are established, and a considerable town has sprung up, to which much farm trade will presently go, in addition to the support of the railway mechanics.

At present, however, the next station northeast of Sprague has great advantages. This is Cheney, just now the largest and most active village in eastern Washington.

Cheney was the terminus of my Palouse stage trip, and my first impression of the town was that it was the scene of a military funeral. Getting nearer, the truth appeared. The nucleus of a band was playing before a theatre door, the brazen character of the performance appearing more in the temerity of the musicians than in the nature of their instruments. To make up for this deficiency, tones of thunder were being struck from a big bass-drum by a sad-spirited German, and it was this I had mistaken for the minute-guns of my funeral. Several times the music seemed about to break down, and the musicians to turn and flee; but the big drum kept thundering on to keep their courage up, and the little snare-drum trotted bravely along at the heels of the humming and banging as a sort of rear-guard to force into the thin ranks any cowardly or straggling notes that might fall behind.

I thought the deepest misery of tavern life had been sounded at Walla Walla and Palouse City; but, bless you! I was inexperienced. The "gentlemanly clerk" of the Cheney hotel was a homicide not only under conviction, but actually undergoing a year's sentence, and he went up to the jail to sleep every night, carrying the key to his cell in his pocket. The crockery was the most valuable of bric-à-brac, if cracks are a criterion. The waiters were assorted into three nationalities and two colors, to suit every taste, and were obliging enough to sit beside you at the table and entertain you with enlivening conversation if their duties were slack for a moment. The bill of fare was gorgeously adorned with Egyptian scenery composed by the job-printer

32*

out of material kindly furnished by the type-foundry, and contained line after line of French dishes that complimented the erudition of the cooly cook far more than his ability when they presented themselves.

"Beef *à la mode!*" one traveller was heard to exclaim. "I suppose that means 'after a fashion.'"

A very bad fashion.

When I wanted to go to bed I was conducted to a house some distance away, and shown to a little doorless cell upstairs, built of new lumber, out of which the resin was exuding in big drops and trickling streams. The total furniture consisted of three nails, a tin candlestick, and a rough bedstead on which was laid an inch or so of hay in a sack, and two army blankets. A series of these balsamic cells was occupied at a dollar a night each by men very glad to get any place to lie down.

> "Weariness
> Can snore upon the flint, when resty sloth
> Finds the down pillow hard."

A pair of stentor-voiced minstrels going through a long repertory for the benefit of a contiguous beer saloon, in which "Rock of Ages" came next to "Patrick, mind the Baby," and "Annie Laurie" found herself in close pursuit of "Biddy McGee," made no hurtful impression upon my drowsy ears. It did wake me up, however, when at midnight one lodger who had left his bed for five minutes in search of a drink —of water, he said, but that is doubtful— came back to find a stranger between his warm blankets. Naturally a row ensued, but nobody was killed; and presently the sunshine of another day came streaming through the horizontal cracks in the wall and the vertical cracks in the partition, dividing the gloom of my cell into hundreds of cubes of gleaming dust-motes.

Cheney possesses several hundred people, all of whom are enterprising and busy. Two years ago there was not a vestige of a town. Now it is the chief place for business "in the upper country," except Spokane Falls; is building brick stores, churches, a big new hotel, has a large academy, and is selling town lots at big prices. That it will have long and steady life, I have no doubt; whether its ambition of becoming the metropolis of the region is to be realized, remains to be seen. As yet it is new and rough to the last degree.

At Spokane Falls is Liberty Hall.

"That is your room," said our host, opening a door into a cool, prettily furnished chamber, domestic enough either to make us homesick or cure us of it, as the effect happened to be—"That is your room ; make the most of it. We don't get up till we get ready, but there is a good restaurant, where you can get your breakfast. For luncheon you will always find trifles in the cupboard"—and with that he led to the darkened dining-room—"and beer or claret in this refrigerator. Help yourself. We dine at five o'clock, but you needn't worry about any spike-tailed coat or clerical tie."

So the jolly days went by in the luxurious idleness of rest, and in picking up loose ends of work that had trailed behind our rapid transit—went by in strong hot blaze at noonday, and in breezy coolness after sunset. Then in the comfort of hammocks and easy-chairs, under the influence of good tobacco and merry company, we heard much about the attractions of Spokane Falls, and believed it all, because we wished to. We learned what a bright little town was growing up there, and that a very excellent class of people were choosing it for their home; how it had none of the signs of the rough, temporary "camp," but was destined to grow solidly and prettily into the most important and most desirable town in the whole region. Why this confidence? was the question asked and discussed. Because of the vast fertile plains north and south of it, which are being settled with great rapidity, and will send it a large portion of their trade; because of the loveliness of its site; because of its healthfulness and comfortable climate, especially in winter; because its interests are already in the hands of enterprising and intelligent people; but chiefly on account of the inducements which it offers to manufacturers.

The Spokane River at the falls comes sweeping down, a clear, full-bodied, powerful stream more than a hundred feet wide, and it goes crashing in a short series of magnificent cascades down three ledges, measuring together 150 feet. Few cataracts in the wide world are more splendid in their snowy, tumultuous beauty than this—a glory no device of men can ever destroy, as has been done at St. Anthony. But the grand picture of the falls is not the claim they make upon us for prophecy; it is the power in this swift and easily harnessed water to turn mill-wheels. At Spokane Falls will rise the manufacturing town that the wide farming population of the plateaus of the Columbia and Spokane must soon make necessary, and about it will cluster the most solidly constituted and agreeable society to be found "east of the mountains."

THE HERO OF THE TOWER.

Long time ago, when Austria was young,
There came a herald to Vienna's gates,
Bidding the city fling them open wide
Upon a certain day; for then the king
Would enter, with his shining retinue.

Forthwith the busy streets were pleasure-paths;
And that which seemed but now a field of toil,
With weeds of turbulence and tricky greed,
Flashed into gardens blooming full of flowers.
Beauty blushed deeper, now the rising sun
Of royalty upon it was to shine;
Wealth cast its nets of tinsel and of gold
To catch the kingly eye; and wisdom merged
Itself into the terms of an address,
Which the old Mayor sat up nights to learn
(A needy poet wrote the same for him).
No maiden fluttered through the narrow streets
That pondered not what ribbons she should wear;
No window on the long procession's route
But had its tenants long engaged ahead.

But the old sexton of St. Joseph's Church
Moped dull and sulky through the smiling crowd,
A blot upon the city's pleasure-page.
"What runs wrong with you, uncle?" was the cry—
"You who have been the very youngest boy
Of all the old men that the city had,
Who loved processions more than perquisites,
And rolled a gala day beneath your tongue—
What rheumatism has turned that temper lame?
Speak up, and make your inward burden ours."

The old man slowly walked until he came
Unto the market-place, then feebly stopped,
As if to talk; and a crowd gathered soon,
As men will when a man has things to say.
And thus he spoke: "For fifty years and more
I have been sexton of St. Joseph's Church.
St. Joseph's would have fared ill but for me.
And though my friend the priest may smile at this,
And wink at you an unbelieving eye,

My office shines in heaven as well as his.
Although it was not mine to make the church
Godly, I kept it clean, and that stands next.
If I have broke one circle of my sphere,
Let some one with straight finger trace it out.

"And no procession in these fifty years
Has marched the streets with aught like kingly tread,
But on the summit of St. Joseph's spire
I stood erect and waved a welcome-flag,
With scanty resting-place beneath my feet,
And the wild breezes clutching at my beard.
It took some nerve to stand so near to heaven
And fling abroad its colors. Try it, priest.

"But I am old; most of my manhood's fire
Is choked in cold white ashes; and my nerves
Tremble in every zephyr like the leaves.
What can I do?—the flag must not be missed
From the cathedral's summit. I've no son,
Or he should bear the banner, or my curse.
I have a daughter: she shall wave the flag!

"And this is how my girl shall wave the flag.
Ten suitors has she; and the valiant one
Who, strong of heart and will, can climb that perch,
And do what I so many times have done,
Shall take her hand from mine at his descent.
Speak up, Vienna lads! and recollect
How much of loveliness faint heart e'er won."

Then there was clamor in the callow breasts
Of the Vienna youth; for she was far
The sweetest blossom of that city's vines.
Many a youngster's eye climbed furtively
Where the frail spire-tip trembled in the breeze,
Then wandered to the cot wherein she dwelt;
But none spoke up, till Gabriel Petersheim,
Whose ear this proclamation strange had reached,
Came rushing through the crowd, and boldly said:

"I am your daughter's suitor, and the one
She truly loves; but scarce can gain a smile
Until I win her father's heart as well;
And you, old man, have frowned on me, and said

I was too young, too frivolous, too wild,
And had not manhood worthy of her hand.
Mark me to-morrow as I mount yon spire,
And mention, when I bring the flag to you,
Whether 'twas ever waved more gloriously."

And thus the old man answered: "Climb
    your way;
And if a senseful breeze should push you off,
And break that raw and somewhat worthless
    neck,
I can not greatly mourn; but climb your way,
And you shall have the girl if you succeed."

High on the giddy pinnacle next day
Waited the youth; but not till evening's sun
Marched from the western gates, that tardy
    king
Rode past the church. And though young
    Gabriel's nerves
Were weakened by fatigue and want of food,
He pleased the people's and the monarch's
    eye,
And flashed a deeper thrill of love through
    one
Who turned her sweet face often up to him,
And whose true heart stood with him on the
    tower.

Now, when the kingly pageant all had
    passed,
He folded up the flag, and with proud smiles
And prouder heart prepared him to descend.
But the small trap-door through which he had
    crept
Had by some rival's hand been barred! and he,
With but a hand-breadth's space where he
    might cling,
Was left alone to live there, or to die.

Guessing the truth, or shadow of the truth,
He smiled at first, and said: "Well, let them
    voice
Their jealousy by such a paltry trick!
They laugh an hour; my laugh will longer be!
Their joke will soon be dead, and I released."
But an hour, and two others, slowly came,
And then he murmured: "This is no boy's
    sport;
It is a silent signal, which means 'Death!'"

He shouted, but no answer came to him,
Not even an echo, on that lofty perch.
He waved his hands in mute entreaty, but
The darkness crept between him and his
    friends.

A half-hour seemed an age, and still he
    clung.
He looked down at the myriad city lights,
Twinkling like stars upon a lowlier sky,
And prayed: "O blessèd city of my birth,

In which full many I love, and one o'er-well,
Or I should not be feebly clinging here,
Is there not 'mongst those thousands one kind
    heart
To help me? or must I come back to you
Crashing my way through grim, untimely
    death?"
Rich sounds of mirth came faintly—but no
    help.

Another hour went by, and still he clung.
He braced himself against the rising breeze,
And wrapped the flag around his shivering
    form,
And thus he prayed unto the merry winds:
"O breeze, you bear no tales of truer love
Than I can give you at this lonely height!
Tell but my danger to the heart I serve,
And she will never rest till I am free!"
The winds pressed hard against him as he
    clung,
And well-nigh wrenched him from that scanty
    hold,
But made no answer to the piteous plea.

Hour after hour went by, and still he held—
Weak, dizzy, reeling—to his narrow perch.
It was a clear and queenly summer night;
And every star seemed hanging from the sky,
As if 'twere bending down to look at him.
And thus he prayed to the far-shining stars:
"O million worlds, peopled perhaps like this,
Can you not see me, clinging helpless here?
Can you not flash a message to some eye,
Or throw your influence on some friendly
    brain
To rescue me?" A million sweet-eyed stars
Gave smiles to the beseecher, but no help.

And so the long procession of the night
Marched slowly by, and each scarce hour was
    hailed
By the great clock beneath; and still he clung
Unto the frail preserver of his life,
And held, not for his life, but for his love—
Held while the spiteful breezes wrenched at
    him;
Held while the chills of midnight crept through
    him;
While Hope and Fear made him their battle-
    ground,
And ravaged fiercely through his heart and
    brain.
He moaned, he wept, he prayed again; he
    prayed—
Grown desperate and half-raving in his woe—
To everything in earth, or air, or sky:
To the fair streets, now still and silent grown;
To the cold roofs, now stretched 'twixt him
    and help;
To the dumb, distant hills that heedless slept;
To the white clouds that slowly fluttered past;

To his lost mother in the sky above;
And then he prayed to God.

                  About that time
The maiden dreamed she saw her lover, faint,
Clinging for life; and with a scream uprose,
And rushed to the old sexton's yielding door,
Granting no peace to him until he ran
To find the truth, and give the boy release.

  An hour ere sunrise he came feebly down,
Grasping the flag, and claiming his fair prize.
But what a wreck to win a blooming girl!
His cheeks were wrinkled, and of yellow hue,
His eyes were sunken, and his curling hair
Gleamed white as snow upon the distant Alps.

But the young maiden clasped his weary head
In her white arms, and soothed him like a child;
And said, "You lived a life of woe for me
Up on the spire, and now look old enough
Even to please my father; but soon I
Will nurse you back into your youth again."

And soon the tower bells sung his wedding song.
The old-young man was happy; and they both,
Cheered by the well-earned bounty of the king,
Lived many years within Vienna's gates.

GEORGE FULLER.

THE death of George Fuller occurred in the most interesting period of his artistic career. He had developed his method of painting so far as to be able to express with much more accuracy than at any previous stage of his progress that peculiar effect of light and atmosphere which excited his imagination and tempted his brush; he had attained a skill in rendering the finest qualities of expression in the human face which has not been equalled in the history of art in this country. He was one of the few painters of modern times who have kept young in art while they have advanced in years. At his death the conditions of progress were apparently as vital and as sound in him as in any youth who thumbs his first palette. Like Corot, he developed slowly and ripened late in life; like Millet, his love for art and his singleness of purpose only strengthened as he grew older; like all great painters, his art was his life, and strongly reflected his personality. To fully understand Fuller as a painter it is necessary to keep in mind the conditions under which he pursued his profession. If we take into consideration his surroundings, if we properly gauge the influences to which he was subjected, then much that seems hesitating and uncertain in his methods will be accounted for as necessary phases of his development, and we shall gain a more just estimate of his strength as a painter and his character as a man. It was a common remark among his friends that in any other country he would long ago have been honored as a master in the profession. It is undoubtedly true that in a community where artists, as a class, have more popular distinction than they have here, Fuller would have found at a much earlier point in his career an appreciative audience, and he would have had a wider influence with his art than he has had. Not that every painter of marked individuality is speedily recognized even in the novelty-hunting French artistic circles, but the quality of human interest and the personal charm in Fuller's work are too eloquent not to have been deeply felt in any society susceptible to artistic impressions. The individuality of his work, though intense, was never revolutionary in character. It did not oblige the spectator to lay aside all previous predilections, and to try to analyze the charm of the new creations. It did not attempt the glorification of the humble and the uncouth, nor deal with any problems beyond the scope of the observer gifted with ordinary intelligence. His art was grounded in the poetry of every-day life. It was not based upon any peculiarities of social condition, and it made no appeal for recognition through the dramatic emotions. He has built his own temple out of fine materials, and it is because he has chosen the rarest textures from among the mass of superficially attractive material ready to his hand that his individuality deserves such honor.

Fuller passed his early life in a New England village. To any one who has experienced the artistic dearth and desolation of the American country town remote from a commercial centre, this fact is a significant one. Most painters readily trace the beginning of their artistic impulse to childish impressions, and in countries where the churches and the public buildings popularize the art of an old civilization the taste for art is insensibly fostered and is naturally developed. It is an impossibility in most European countries for a youth to receive a good education and reach man's estate without ever having been brought in contact with a single serious work of art. Here it has been not only a possible, but even a common, experience. At the time when Fuller began his art education the foundation of that irregular system of art schools which has overspread the country since the Centennial Exhibition was not even thought of, and whatever training he had in the rudiments of his profession was at the best but meagre and insufficient. A short trip abroad helped in a measure to supply the deficiency of instruction at home, but, unlike most Americans who pursue their studies abroad, he did not identify himself with any of the schools then in vogue. He is known to have been much impressed by the old masters, and particularly, perhaps, by the works of Correggio, whose delicacy of sentiment and refinement of color appealed to his feelings more than the stronger and more masculine productions of other Italian painters. But he revered all the old masters with an intensity of feeling almost amounting to worship, and when he came home after a study of them he was so filled with the spirit of the large purpose of their art that the influence never left him.

During the period of his residence in New York he received but slender encouragement. The circle of art-lovers was then very small, and the interest manifested in the productions of local artists was comparatively insignificant. Fuller had, besides, none of the pushing qualities which were often necessary to secure recognition. But in all probability, notwithstanding the unpretentious character of the work he then produced, he would have made himself a place as a portrait painter if he had stuck to his easel, and had persistently pursued his studies. He, however, after a short stay in the metropolis, gave up his studio, betook himself to his native town, and devoted the larger part of his time and attention to farming. It is a mistake to suppose that he was influenced to take this step solely by the want of success he met with in New York. He was not making money, it is true, but he would probably have continued the fight if the death of his father had not happened at that time. He felt called to return to his country home to endeavor to fill the responsible place of head of the family and manager of the farm. It was an act so characteristic of the man that we can not criticise the motives of it, although we must regret the cause of the apparent desertion of his profession. One of the articles of his creed was that an artist should first of all be a man. His life shows how well he acted up to this principle. In sacrificing his own immediate interests for the good of others he was satisfied that he performed his first duty, and we find him directing the operations of a country farm with the same enthusiasm that he carried on a studio.

The facility with which he exchanged the brush for the plough-handle is essentially characteristic of a typical American. It is a common reproach to our mechanics that they are jacks of all trades; to our doctors that they are surgeons, physicians, and professors at the same time; to the members of the legal profession that they are solicitors, lawyers, and politicians in one. It seems to be a condition of our civilization that we shall be able to do more than one thing, be it well or ill. Indeed, specialties in professions are with us quite a recent innovation. This state of things is, I believe, partly the heritage of our early struggles in the settlement and civilization of the country, the remote echo of that personal independence and self-reliance which the necessities of existence developed in our ancestors. But Puritans and pioneers, however useful they may have been in founding the institutions which make the country what it is, are not harmonious factors in the development of an art-loving community. This fatal facility for acquiring a trade or a profession, this adaptability to circumstances, is one of the greatest drawbacks to the production of serious, thoughtful, intense work in any sphere of life. This same facility is also the cause of that superficiality of acquirement which is the well-merited reproach to the artistic profession in this country. The glamour of skillful technique and the temptation of easy production preoccupy the attention of the artist, and confine his thoughts to the narrow limits of his immediate occupation. This preoccupation leaves him without impulse or inclination to pursue those collateral branches of study which are quite as necessary to the full development of the artist as are others which relate directly to the production of pictures. But while this facility, if undirected, is unfavorable to the productions of great works of any kind, and especially of imaginative works, it may be turned into the strongest element of real success by making use of it as a means, and not relying on it as an end. Fuller did exactly this, although it cost him great and continuous effort. He, improbable as it would seem from an examination of his later and finished works, had a good share of the innate Yankee skill in the use of materials. Precision of touch and a rigid method of treatment, amounting almost to conventionality, are seen in some of his earlier works, and may be sometimes traced even in his late productions. But he regarded facility as a jeopardy to all good art, and despising the qualities obtained by manual skill and adroitness, he was satisfied only with the exhaustive results which follow intense study and severe labor.

Although his sojourn of fifteen of the best years of his life on a country farm would appear to have been fatal to his progress in art, yet, on the contrary, it doubtless had a beneficial effect on him. He did not by any means wholly throw up his chosen work, although the duties of a farmer's life prevented any continuous application to painting. It was during this sojourn in the country that he was able to accomplish what perhaps would have been impossible if he had depended on his painting for his support— the development of a method by which he could express his appreciation of the charm in mysterious effect of light, and his acute sense of beauty of form.

He painted many landscapes, a number of beautiful heads, and was evidently occupied with the study of certain effects and compositions which afterward appeared in completed pictures. Naturally enough, his isolation only served to crystallize his ideas of art in general. Quite outside the influence of the different schools which have dragged our artists and our public hither and thither, he went on in his own way, and put his own personality in his works. It is very interesting to trace the effect on his art of this intimate study of nature. He was evidently more vividly impressed by the quality of sunlight than by anything else, and in his successive attempts to realize this impression upon canvas he gradually left behind altogether the rigid treatment which was the residual of his early training, and sought more and more to give the truth of effect without regard to how this truth was obtained. The quality of solidity and relief, which was a strong element in his early work, now became modified, and was sometimes almost lost in the endeavor to secure more subtle truths. We thus find during his country life a constant and distinct progression toward refinement. If he had not had this opportunity for self-development, it is difficult to surmise the direction which his progress would have taken, because his extreme sensitiveness to impressions would undoubtedly have insensibly directed his endeavor to meet the demands of recognized taste.

When he appeared in public for the second time, about eight years ago, he came forward with a method, a way of looking at nature, an intention, entirely his own, no more to be copied or to be imitated than any strongly individual painter who has preceded him. In the first place, he showed himself a colorist; not an adjuster of brilliant harmonies, nor an inventor of startling contrasts, but a colorist in the best sense of the term, finding beauty of color in the commonest material, selecting combinations sober in tone, but rich and full in quality. He was never satisfied with an accidental suggestion of color, and rarely stopped short of a complete rendering of the quality he sought. In the second place, he showed himself a draughtsman, for he preserved all the large lines of the forms, while sacrificing the minor details to the beauty of the whole. Lastly, he showed himself an imaginative painter, for he rejected all facts which interfered with his rendering of the impression he had in his mind. The soul of his art was selection. His common remark was that art is cosmopolitan, that neither school nor nationality should govern an artist in his work, but his own choice of what is beautiful in nature should be his school. In the works of the old masters he found the doctrine fully exemplified. Each of them, he reasoned, chose what most attracted him, and clung to that as the only thing worth painting. His method of painting was directed by this conviction, which the long opportunity for quiet study and contemplation of nature strengthened and fixed in his mind. He loved in a landscape that quality of sunlight which unites all objects in a warm glow, softens the lines, fills the shadows with mysterious forms, and glorifies the earth with palpitating color. For him there was no immediate foreground: he chose an effect which carried the composition far beyond the frame. He did not consider it worth while to attempt to represent the commonplace actuality of foreground objects, for that diverted the attention from the charm of the effect. He painted his landscapes with the same exalted feelings that possess one at the sight of the glories of a sunset or the loveliness of an Indian summer day.

He argued and proved by his work that in the presence of a sublime effect all detail which does not emphasize a great fact is overlooked or forgotten. He threw over his landscapes an atmosphere which gave them a bewitching charm of mystery, and concealed none of the beauty of line or the contrast of masses. His figures have the same warm glow thrown about them which covers the landscape in which they stand. They thus become a part of the harmonious whole, retire from the first plane, and lose the gross and commonplace aspect of foreground objects. From the persistency with which Fuller studied this peculiar effect he was, of course, often charged with affectation. The same charge is always made against a painter who diligently pursues a favorite theme. Corot's effects have been both sneered at and accepted. Fuller chose another and equally attractive effect of light, and studied it with an astonishingly parallel result. Take for a good example of figures and landscape the "Turkey Pasture in Kentucky." No one would think of calling this a realistic landscape, because we have, by common usage, confined that adjective to the description of the representation of the most commonplace objects of nature. But, at the same time, no one familiar with the country can look at this picture without experiencing the glow of the delightful memory of some similar effect. The broad, broken field dotted with figures, and the dark masses of the birds with burnished backs, the distant, irregular silhouette of trees against the sky, the sky itself feathery and soft in

texture, and over all that pervading and harmonizing veil of rich but softened sunlight, suggesting not only the heat but the hum of a summer day, when all the insect world is busy, and the earth seems to open its pores and store up the warmth of the sunlight and the wealth of its color. The same principles which governed his selection of effect of light directed his choice of type and expression in his heads. He placed before him an urchin from the street. If there was a suggestion of refinement in the type of face or in the expression, Fuller caught it and put it down. He never painted a brutal head. If he saw brutality, he did not like it, and would not represent it. He believed the province of art was to call attention to the beauties of nature, not to insist upon the defects, the deformities, and the vulgarities of man or landscape. His street urchin on canvas remains a street urchin still, but he has a gentle expression, such as will sometimes be caught on the veriest of vagabonds, and the sunburned skin affords an opportunity for rich and glowing color, not an excuse for the imitation of the repulsive condition of human flesh. In his studies of girlhood Fuller has fixed the loveliest expression of innocence and happiness that has ever been put on canvas. In his idealized heads he has created a type of beauty thoroughly natural in its character and individual in its style, and one which will live as a representative impression of the feminine beauty of the present day. In this type he has combined the choice elements of innocence and simplicity of character, and has given us a refined and sweet country maiden, full of health and youthful vigor, and rich in the promise of perfect womanhood.

"Winifred Dysart" will always remain in the mind of every one who has felt the graceful charm of her presence as a unique type of the loveliness of maidenhood. The picture is simplicity itself. The life-size figure of a girl, with her arms hanging by her side, stands in a spacious landscape facing the spectator. Not even the suggestion of an incident gives interest to the subject. In the bewitching sweetness of the face, in the girlish grace of the figure, and in the wonderful delicacy of the color there is united such elements of real beauty and such a wealth of artistic expression that the spectator is first attracted, then absorbed and elevated, by its contemplation. Common realism, even in its

GEORGE FULLER.

greatest perfection, has no such power to invest its creations with personal interest and impressiveness. In "Winifred Dysart," Fuller has succeeded in rendering much of the strength of his own impression, and thus through his work he is able to communicate some of the contagion of his own appreciation of beauty. In other pictures he has given much of the same quality of loveliness, but in none has he reached the height of expression which is found in "Winifred Dysart." In his latest work, "Arethusa," he has extended to the female figure the same sense of perfection of form and refinement of color which he has striven for in his heads. No more chaste and poetical rendering of the figure has been seen in modern times.

Fuller doubtless often failed with his portraits to satisfy the requirements of ordinary portraiture, because he could not be content with the superficial imitation of flesh, feature, or textures. What he attempted and usually succeeded in doing was to represent his sitters under the best aspect which his observation and imagination suggested. Of absolute realism in his portraits there is little; of accurate imitation of the details of form and color there is also little; but there is, what is very much better, a masterly generalization of the characteristic traits of the sitter. A portrait which has this quality is not less an accurate representation because it happens not to be a commonplace one. It is this quality which has made the portraits of the old masters live as models for all future painters, and it is the lack of this which makes the ordinary portrait no more valuable as a likeness than the photograph.

I have said enough to show what a broad purpose Fuller had in his art, and I have given a hint of the strength of the personality he put into everything he touched. Of course he could not have arrived at his way of looking at the large facts of nature unless he had cultivated his mind by the study of the world outside the narrow workshop where material imitation is often the sole end. He was familiar with all subjects which furnish food for a vigorous intellect. From history, religion, politics, and social science he always derived support for the principles which governed his painting, as they did his life, and he had a way of generalizing on the questions of the day which is remembered by his friends as a prominent feature in his familiar conversation.

It will be readily understood why he never took any pupils, nor made any decided attempts to influence the production of art in the community in which he lived. His way of working could not be imparted with profit to the student, because it was suited to the temperament of the master alone. The one lesson he felt impelled to teach was the great lesson of choice, and this he could best show in his own works. The only painter who has been of late years closely associated with Fuller is Mr. J. J. Enneking, of Boston, and in their friendship there was as much of the relation of master and pupil as was possible to one of Fuller's ideas in art. Although he did not have the enthusiastic and admiring circle of students around him that the late William M. Hunt had, Fuller's influence was far from insignificant. He had a conspicuous following of the younger men in the profession, who gave him what was denied by his

contemporaries in years—membership in their artistic organization, and an honored place in the annual exhibition. To them must be given the credit of recognizing the vital qualities of his work.

It is impossible to adequately represent Fuller's pictures through the medium of engraving, but Mr. Closson, whose long intimacy with the artist has made him familiar with his methods, has interpreted several of the paintings as perfectly as the material will allow. The charm of line and the mystery of the effect are there, but of course the great beauty and delicacy of the color can not be more than suggested. It may not be out of place to add, in closing, that Fuller's method of flesh-painting, the peculiarity of which consisted largely in the harmonizing of textures and tones by the use of the brush-handle, was not by any means confined to him, although he has made more frequent use of it than any one else. His ordinary mode of procedure in the case of a portrait was to make a realistic study during the sitting, and after the sitter went away to eliminate all the unnecessary details, and refine the form and color. As may be seen by an examination of the work of his life, he found it as easy to make the commonplace realistic study as any one else. This study he considered but the means toward producing the end he had in view; that is, the realization of the high ideas he cherished.

The lesson of Fuller's life is just what we need now. We are in the secondary stage of artistic development in this country. We are painting the surface of things. Our portraits are commonly masks, our pictures deal with textures and forms. The higher fields of expression, of composition, of beauty in art, are seldom occupied. It is natural that this should be so. It has been so in the history of every country where art is not indigenous, and we can not expect to do better, with all our education, our wealth, and our facilities for travel, than to hasten the progression of the different stages through which we must arrive at an appreciation and a cultivation of the highest in art. Fuller was the forerunner of a new tendency in our art, which is as sure to continue as our progress in art is certain. He has turned our attention from bric-à-brac, from pots and pans, from beggars and rags, and has made us look for the nobler facts in nature. To have done this is to have lived to some purpose.

ZEELAND FISHERMAN.

a light, flourishy, courtly touch that takes one back to the time of powdered wigs, and of patches deftly placed near dimples and at outer corners of roguish eyes, of jewelled snuff-boxes and Sedan-chairs, and the loftiest of high-heeled brocade shoes. Yet there is much that is modern and Parisian. There is also a good fair bit that was built when the Dutch had an architecture of their own, when they were making glorious chapters of history, when their flags were flying in every clime, and they were good hard hitters by sea and land.

The vague excitement-hunting, mere sight-seeing tourist could "do" the Hague and all about it in a good long heart-breaking day, and forget all about it before the next morning, and be ready again for a similar dose; but to those who have an interest in matters of Dutch history, its art, or its past,

THE Hague is an excellent "foot-hold" or starting-point for many places of interest lying thereabout, both landward and seaward. In itself it is one of the most charming of all the towns in the Low Countries. It has all the fresh, brisk air of a sea-port, without quite so many of the serious and substantial odors of harbor mud at low tide that one gets so often in a sea-port town.

There is also a quaint, genial air of court gentility still lingering about its many palatial residences. It is easy to see that at one time its dream, its ideal, was Versailles. Not any vain attempt to outshine its queenly splendors is evident; but over much that remains of the best part of the Hague of the eighteenth century—which is a very prominent part indeed—there is

or its picturesque, prosperous present, the Hague would afford pleasant exploring ground for a week or more. Even the artist, *working* at Scheveningen, would perhaps *live* cheaper and more pleasantly at the Hague—only a few minutes off by train. Scheveningen is all very well when one has a "purpose," and does not mind expense and discomfort in pursuit of it; but if the sketcher wishes to exist in quiet and comparative economy, or even if he wishes his money's worth of luxury, the Hague itself is the best place to stay at. At least such is my experience. Not far from Scheveningen by the coast—six miles, about—is Katwyk, the smaller sister fisher village, and growing up to be a fashionable sea-side resort, and putting on all the airs (of gorged and

KATWYK.

bewildered drainage among others) of the elder place. Wishing to see all the Dutch sea-side resorts I could comfortably, we planned an early day at Katwyk. The quickest, cheapest, and easiest way from the Hague was by rail to Leyden, and then by tram a couple of miles or so. This, however, was much too easy and popular for us; we must needs do something difficult and roundabout in order to be out of the common. Taking the tram to Scheveningen, and another good look at the mass of saline picturesqueness thereabout, for purposes of comparison, seemed an idea; anyhow, we did it, and also I a sketch or two "while handy by." Jacob was then sent in quest of a trap to drive us on to Katwyk along the coast road. In an evil moment, however, came *another* idea to Jacob. Why not go by the Prince's Wood? It was a little farther, but it was through such a lovely shady park, and it would be a relief after so much sea and town, and all the rest of it. Good! the Prince's Wood be it. A park, or a wood, or a straggling scrubby forest, is considered a great treat always in Holland. The trap was soon at hand, with a serious, sad-eyed driver and a hangdog, fly-tormented horse. The Prince's Wood, I am bound to say, had a cool and soothing effect after the glare of the white sand and white cottages; but as we wended our way under the dense over-arching boughs the air began to strike more and more chill, and the odor of the thick mat of rotting leaves all about became more pungent and wearisome. I began to long for the free air again.

It was a blessed relief to come to a quiet shady village, with a quiet little inn, fair in the warm sunlight. The horse was rested, and we were cheered and comforted by a frugal lunch, indeed, but it seemed a regal repast, and unlooked-for in that solitude. There was more Prince's Wood still to do, but luckily there was at this point a choice of roads. I need not say that we chose the other way round. It was only half shaded; the dense trees followed us on one side with their chill shadows and their acrid autumnal odors, but overhead was the fair sky; and on the other hand we could see, stretching far away over the interminable net-work of little rush-fringed water-courses cutting about the broad emerald meadows, the high grassy dikes that kept back the brown waves of the North Sea. We could see the flapping pennons of the fisher-boats on the strand, and we could scent from afar the air tingling with ozone. The saline whiffs got stronger, but even when mingled with dashes of peat reek, and tarry smoke from boat-menders' fires, with a few pungent fish-curing odors blended artfully now and then, it was fragrant perfume after the grave-like damps of that depressing grove. Katwyk has the same exhilarating air and movement as Scheveningen. One is lifted over its breezy dunes as if with winged feet. There is a mad impulse to catch one of the tanned fish-girls around her ample waist and have a wild, careering waltz across the level sands. Katwyk is much more quiet and retired than her neighbor, while

"You must pay him for his back journey all de same," suggested the literal-minded Jacob.

"With all the joy imaginable, so long as he takes me not with him."

The tram ride between Katwyk and Leyden was a pleasant little run. It was a relief to have it as a change. We were rather a merry party on the tram. Some Leyden students had been taking a few friends to the sea, and they had evidently improved the occasion by appropriate libations to Neptune and Aphrodite in bumpers of "the rosy." They sang—uproariously they sang—and the song of the Dutch student is no feeble piping. The platform of

INNER KATWYK.

for artistic purposes I think it has many advantages. There is more variety of landscape line in its environs, and quite near lies the village of Katwyk-*Within*, full of picturesque material. In fact, I found it of more interest to *me* than Katwyk-on-Sea. Jacob began to remind me that we must not linger too long, as there was the return drive to Scheveningen. Wild horses would not have got me home by way of that dark Prince's Wood again. So I sang blithely, to the Faithful One's astonishment,

"We will kick the sad driver, and let him go free,
   And sing *hey* for the bonnets of Bonny Dundee!"

the tram was rather a nice place to stand on, and even to sketch a few flying forms from. We lingered for a few minutes at Inner Katwyk, and I could see that the place was rich in material for the painter. Mentally resolving to return on the morrow, I began at once to sketch a much-bepatched native. With every chance to have ruined himself by howling discords of color, in the variety he had about him, I could not help regarding him as a harmonious success. His garments would have been a study of *tone*. He was a living, loafing symphony in browns and grays. Even his ruddy bronze face and his warm sandy hair were in perfect harmony with his clothes. His position was so comfortable to him, with his hands jammed well down his deep pockets, that he did not budge until I had booked him; and then, just as the car went rattling off, I cut the leaf from the solid block to put it in the pocket. Away it went, with a puff of wind. He saw the flying leaf coming toward him, and quicker than I thought him capable of moving, he caught it, and ran after the car to give it to me. He soon saw that it was himself that he was bringing. He must have counted the patches, as the likeness was not elaborate. He trotted beside the car for some distance, roaring with glee at his "take off." He was joined by two or three other loafers, who also laughed. There was a slight chance of its coming to grief in the tussle to see it at one time. However, I finally got it again all safe, and the good-natured original got some coin that seemed to delight him more than his sketch.

The next day we returned to Katwyk-Within, and found it even better than it promised from the tram platform the day before. There is a widish river running through the village. On one side is a tree-shaded promenade, with quaint old residences standing back from the road behind garden walls. On the other side of the stream are red-roofed cottages with little gardens and orchards, and brick walls sloping down to the water's edge. There were women busy washing at the brink, beating the clothes with many a noisy spat of their flat paddles, the rattling clack of their merry chatter and laughter keeping time. Children were playing in the boats with their own tiny craft, generally the toy boats would be one of their own wooden shoes, or *klumpen*, with a little stick stuck through a paper sail. The whole scene was full of ever-changing bits of form and color. It was not so enticing to sketch as it was to watch it. There was a stalwart young woman hanging clothes on a line, and every movement displayed rugged grace and strength. She might have inspired a wholesome-minded, realistic sculptor with many of her unconscious poses. I watched her every movement until she exhausted her basket, and then I watched for her to come again. The river was not very wide, and I could see perfectly; and, which was only natural, I could *be* seen in my watching; and then began a skirmishing fire of such light

"chaff" as the fraternity who wash their own and other peoples' soiled linen in public know how to indulge in. Poor Jacob, who could understand it, for his sins was fain to blush at times. He fairly chuckled and gurgled with enjoyment over some of the richly seasoned jokes they pelted us with. When my statuesque hanger-out returned to her work with a fresh basket, she was made aware of her being sketched. It made all the difference in the world. She was conscious and restrained, and not overpleased. The rural policeman then favored us with his society, as a change. The line of washers screamed with delight at first, as it seemed quite on the cards that we might be led off in custody. He had no such idea, however, that big, mild functionary. When he saw the sketching, the latent art instinct of his nature was awakened. He would gladly have sat with us and even protected us from gibe all afternoon if I had only gone on with drawing the women at the washing. He and Jacob soon struck upon a chord of mutual sympathy. Jacob must have discovered, as usual, that they were distant relations in some way. They fed each other on snuff, and sneezed and snorted in grand concert. It was like oil on the waters, this fraternity between them. The washers turned to other matters of nearer interest, and my "hanger-out" came back to the attitudes of simple unconsciousness again. The policeman told us of a good place to lunch, not at the inn—that would be too dear—but at the grocer's, in a quiet, friendly way. I did not care for this idea at first, but there was the charm of novelty about it, after all. It was so long since I had gone to a village grocer's for lunch that I wished to renew my impressions. Having secured us for his friend, the policeman moved off, and I firmly believe he was good enough to advise the grocer of our coming. There was a beam of welcome on his face that could never have come unaware. We were soon seated in his own little back parlor, and through the open door leading into the snuggest and brightest little Dutch kitchen we could presently hear the sizzling of our cutlets. There was a welcome odor with the frying, as it helped to neutralize a powerful fragrance of crude petroleum that filled the place.

In Holland they simply revel in all the varieties of things that can be made from

HANGING OUT CLOTHES.

that wonderful but penetrating and pungent article. I think the fire was made from it; the knives and forks were cleaned with it. The grocer himself had taken some of it for his cold, and the apprentice, who was also waiter, had copiously anointed his shiny head with it. They don't seek to disguise it in Katwyk with pretty names of vaseline, but they take it as it is, and love it for itself. I thought at one time of leaving the scene of novelty, with whatever other charms there might be in store for us, and going off to the inn. But that would be a confession of tenderness of the "oil-factory" nerves, as the old lady said. So looking only on the bright and shiny side of the scene, I waited for further delights. The petroleum made no difference to Jacob; I doubt if he smelled it at all. It was a favorite theme of his in conversation. If he could introduce it *once*, it was as hard to get rid of as its clinging flavor. Petroleum stores were favorite objects in nature with him; he always pointed them out to me with great relish, until I positively forbade him to do it any more. He would even then forget himself sometimes, and begin with a flourish: "Do you zee dose large building wiz de helevators on de outzide?" "Yes; well, go on." He would then remember. "Oh, well—never mind. No; I dinks she is not de houze I mean. I s'pects dot is only one of dose petroleum sdores." He would thus manage to point it out, after all, without appearing to. Now I was wondering how he enjoyed the full blast of the article that wreathed about us on every side. We opened the window giving on the street. This was a relief and amusement. The friendly policeman came and stood outside, and took a lively interest in our repast when it came; he even suggested a salad which the old grocer was famous for. I declined for various reasons, principally because I felt sure that it would be mixed with vaseline and vinegar. The policeman called our attention particularly to the pepper as being the best he ever tasted. He was evidently bent on our making a good meal of it, as we never dusted on enough to please him. Jacob told him that we would offer him beer, but dare not while on duty. He said nothing, but looked sad and thoughtful. The policeman was joined by several other worthy citizens, who staid by until the repast was over. A small but ribald boy, however, who wished to while away a fragment of

his spare time at our window, was sent off about his not very urgent business promptly by our friendly protector. After all, it was some fun. I know several simple natures who would have enjoyed it with me enormously.

We then bade adieu to our fragrant grocery, to our confiding policeman, to our string of washers still laving their linen in the sudsy stream, getting a few parting shots of chaff from them as we went by. It was all in fun, and the ringing chorus of laughter that went up showed that the joke struck *them*, though we went lightly by unscathed. It is a grand thing not to understand too much of a *tongue*— even that of a Dutch laundress.

The Faithful One had often tried to arouse in me an interest in a certain sleepy old town called Oudewater—personally dear to him from tender associations. "It wos dere I go for my onnymoon. Heer Gott, wot larks we 'ave!" He did say how many years ago, but I forget. However, this particular Sunday was the anniversary of that larky event.

"Suppose, then, we go to Oudewater on a little modest celebration of the happy day? Would that suit you, Jacob?" It suited us both so well that in ten minutes we were on our way to the station. The idea was to take the train to Gouda, and then get a trap to carry us the rest of the way. From the Hague to Gouda— even under the softening effects of a golden scumble of October haze—the scenery was not of a kind to be cheered or gilded into the slightest interest. It had the flat, endless, monotonous repetitions of a common pattern on a roll of cheap wall-paper. Lines of toy-like windmills at even distances, rows of spindly poplars all out of the same toy box, speckless little white cottages, so many to the mile, and even the cows and geese were littered carefully about in exact ratio to the other pretty little things.

The little ditches were as straight as the ruled lines on a sheet of writing-paper. It was so very odd that I could not help jotting down some of the more rigid patterns of the landscape as they unrolled before our window. With the exception of a few way-side stations there was not a break in the "design" until we reached Gouda. As we decided to put off our look at this place until our return from Oudewater, Jacob was sent in quest of a

nice open trap. I could amuse myself on the old bridge until he came. He gave me a good long wait, and finally came upon the scene with a neat, new, highly varnished little close brougham. Seeing my look of dismay, he proceeded to explain. It was Sunday, it was a fine day, and every other thing was let. "Never mind, Jacob; this is your own celebration; so you shall go in proper style." I thrust him in, and turned the door on him, and mounted up beside the coachman. There was no end of protesting on Jacob's part, but he finally accepted the position cheerfully, and I hope he enjoyed it. The driver was deeply amused at the move, which puzzled him fearfully as well; but we soon forgot all about Jacob in his tank, and launched out into a very mixed and dislocated conversation. He would try bad English on me, and I would pay him back in worse Dutch; and when our talk got hopelessly involved, Jacob would kindly lean out of the carriage window and undo the conversational tangle.

The road ran most of the way on the top of a high dike, and beside the road and dike ran a placid little stream, that was now a river, now a canal, now a mill-pond; or it would lose itself in great pools and marshes among sandy flats, and then pull itself into a stream-like shape again, and go on as before, first one side of the dike and then the other, in the most wayward and un-Dutch-like manner. There were constant changes of the character of the scenery about it, funny little ferries now and then, and quaint little boats and bridges. There was plenty of characteristic figures, too, lolling over the bridges, smoking and chatting to other picturesque but podgy figures in the boats; curly blue smoke, too, everywhere, peat reek from the red chimneys of the fat and placid farmsteads nestled away among the apple and cherry trees, wreaths and puffs of pungent fat cigars from the idling figures.

It seemed a plodding, happy land on every side, where it was nearly always Sunday or fête-day afternoon. Rich, succulent fields of pasturage, where the drowsiest and sleekest cows and the fleeciest of pink-eyed sheep fairly waded about in the cloying grasses. The grain ricks seemed bursting with fullness, the orchards were laden down with apples, rosy, golden, and russet, and the air was filled with their fragrance. Great rich mellow pears were bearing down the looped branches of the long avenues of espaliers. Every inch of the "well-larded earth" seemed to be under the most loving and elaborate cultivation. Small wonder that the farm-houses looked pictures of home contentment; that the porches and arbors were overrun with vine and flower; that the garden paths were lined out with great splashes of color in masses of dahlia and hollyhock and aster; that the great brass door-knockers and the gilded weather-cocks filled the sunshine with tinges of glinting gold! The apples had their rosy hues repeated in ripe pippin-like cheeks of the tow-headed children rolling about in the orchards, and the glints of gold were reflected back from the massive ornaments of the Sunday-clad people at every turn, so that there was no lack of opulent Rubens-like color to gladden the soul of the lover of a full, rich picture. Although the men as a rule were arrayed in shiny black "store clothes," they compensated nobly to the general color scheme by wearing such startling scarfs of "Magenta," and "Solferino" hues, singly and in combination, that their massive rings and pins paled into half-tones beside them. The womenkind did not, either, put on much "blare" of color in their dress material. The correct form seemed *amplitude*. Skirt on skirt, "until it took the shape, fold after fold, of mountain" and of minor haystack. I have seen other women-folk of Holland who made rather a parade of their wealth of piled-on petticoats, but I fancy the best of them would have felt rather slim and poor beside these rotund maids and matrons. What airing of fine Brussels lace, too, on gold-bedizened cap, on gold-bangled sleeve, and jewel-clasped collar and frill! "And some had got rings upon every finger, and on some fingers they had got three," like Lord Bateman's bride. There was color enough, too, of the positive and eye-searing sort in cap strings and pinner. And how they seemed to enjoy their own and each others' magnificence of attire and ample spread of sail and beam! wandering about hand in hand, champing the rosy apple, or absorbing the melting pear. It seemed a vale of health, too, as well as wealth: nowhere had I seen such brilliant fresh complexions, such cheeks of peach (and peony) and cream, such bright-gleaming, kindly eyes. They had not the hale, bronzed look of the sea-side Dutch, but they were

GATHERING CABBAGES.

seemingly just as strong and hearty. It was our driver's own province, and he was delighted with our rather frank and free admiration of his fair country-women. We passed through several spick-and-span villages—one down by the water-side, with some very good sketching about it, I should say. I could have told more about it if it had not been for our driver's consuming vanity. He loved to rattle furiously over the little cobble-paved streets with much too much crack of whip, and effort to witch the gaping rustics with noble drivership. It was only a fleeting vision of neat little brick houses, with gleaming windows, and doors polished like coach panels, and curly iron-work in the shape of dates and monograms embellishing the gable fronts, sloping cellar doors to most of them, where the happy rotund urchins could slide down all day long; speckless pavements of mottled brick, laid herring-bone-wise; a glimpse only of a tobacconist's shop, with priceless old Delft and Japan jars for the holding of snuff in the window; then past a little chemist's, with a golden mortar and pestle outside as a sign, and another big golden-*looking* one, with scales and weights of the same burnished metal, and more jars containing spices from the Indies inside the shop; pendent bunches of dried herbs hung from the ceiling.

We soon got through that small "dorp" at the lively pace we were displaying. Scared mothers ran out and rescued wandering babes, and blessed us both loud and deep; dogs flew after us; chickens, ducks, and geese flew cackling before us. But for all our whip-snapping and prancing and dust, I don't fancy we made much impression on the groups of sleek, stolid villagers, who, with rich green cigars, and hands deep in pockets, smoked calmly and grinned broadly—that sort of expansive, many-sided smile that may be complimentary or it may *not*, so wanting is it in decision of character.

We reached Oudewater just in time to order lunch and to take a preliminary stroll while it was being prepared. I naturally expected a choice *menu* in the very centre of that land of plenty. Not a bit of it. Our choice at the choice inn was the choice of Hobson—the inevitable veal steak, fried potatoes, pickled cabbage, and Dutch cheese. Of course if we chose to wait some hours they could get us a fowl or duck, but the fatted calf was the only thing in the larder.

It was not much of a *menu* to celebrate the wedding feast, but I did not care particularly. I left the problem "how to get more" to Jacob, and he gave it up, and consoled himself by remembering that the original "onny-moon" festival consisted largely of "weal and bickles and dings," and this was a happy coincidence, after all. The sights of Oudewater were soon seen, and we were soon out into the free air again, and back-tracking to Gouda over the breezy high-road. The drive was charming, although it was only

the reverse way of seeing the same scenes of the morning.

We were in Gouda again in time to see a little of the place, and to go over the cathedral, famed principally for its stained glass.

Gouda itself, as a town, is rather interesting, quite good enough to while away an odd day in, if the sketcher happens to find himself at the Hague. Altogether, the day had been a most pleasant one, and though the towns and villages I had heard of disappointed me, the ones unknown to me were pleasant surprises. In considering the lay of the land from the map I fancied that there ought to be some good material on the southern shores of the Zuider Zee where it trends round toward Amsterdam. I liked the look of Muiden, Naarden, and the little villages thereabout (as they took their spots on the map, that was all), and Jacob, being appealed to, confirmed the guess that there was a chance for "skitses" in abundance. And as I wished to go to Zandvoort, I could see Haarlem again on the way.

So then let us go on to Amsterdam as a centre. There is one advantage in Holland: it is not a vast empire, and one can soon get from place to place of interest, as they all lie tolerably near together. Amsterdam has so much in it to interest and amuse one, an artist especially, that he need never feel injured if he has to see it again and again. On the morning after our arrival we took advantage of the splendid weather for our investigation of Muiden.

What a queer, delicious little old Zuider Zee port Muiden turned out to be—far, far beyond my hopes of it! It is a straggling old place, evidently of some importance in days gone by, still flourishing, however, and full of life and movement. There is a broad eccentric river dividing it and interlacing it, making it into bridge-connected islands, filling its tree-shaded streets and wharves with river-side folk, and the water-ways with broad-hulled Zuider Zee shipping. The gayly painted and gilded, carved, and brass-enriched sterns of the various craft gave forth glowing spots of color. The haze of the October afternoon took an extra scumble from the peat reek of galley fire and shore kitchen, and blended—in all and sundry of the local colors, harsh or harmonious—into one pleasant bit of gleaming tone. The quays were border-

CASTLE OF MUIDEN.

ed by avenues of trees, and the fat yellow tints of autumn mingle and blend or stand brightly out in spots of trembling gold against the meshes of interwoven masts and rigging, of brown sails and gay flutter of pennon, of lines of many-tinted garments hung out to flap themselves dry in the soft air. If any one loves what is called "a play of color," let him happen in Muiden on some such October afternoon. There are piles of purple and tender green cabbages, mounds of red and gold cheeses, bags of dusty meal, and kettles and pots of black-brown tar and pitch, heaps of newly kippered sails and cordage, and against and among all this array of foreground and background objects can be seen examples of all the queerly rigged sailor people of the North Sea ports. The women take no small part in this moving play of light, shade, color, and sound. The feminine notes ring out clear and free in the universal chaff and chatter, and the "Yo heave O!" of the sailors. (The Dutch seaman's equivalent, however, for our "Heave O!" is far more of an agonizing bellow.) The little water-side taverns, with shady skittle grounds and arbors, had changed so little since the days of Ostade and Jan Steen that either worthy might have sat down to work without a sigh of regret. There was the same noisy

click and clatter of balls and pins, the same groups at play or looking on, smoking and quaffing tankards of ale, or sipping little glasses of schnapps. There were Jan Steen's rosy, buxom, obliging handmaidens, with close-fitting white caps and tabbed jackets, short skirts and buckled shoes, threading their way wherever thirst raged direst with their tall beakers of beaded ale. I could watch the festive Dutch sailor play skittles with the inebriate boor, and even wish there might be another Jan Steen to arise and paint them as they are, just to show them, if nothing else, what amusing but sad boors they can make of themselves. It was only a step from beer and skittles to a little shaded court, so neat and clean, the windows so sparkling, the tiles and bricks so immaculate, the white walls so dazzling, the knockers and doors so burnished, that I felt old Pieter de Hoogh must have incanted some spell over the place to keep it forever fresh and sunny.

Look which way you please, up or down the busy river-side street, it was teeming with life and movement—not the roaring racket and din of a Thames-side street, with its struggling masses of carts and drays and its bellowing draymen; it was a movement as gentle and placid as the tide running down the broad muddy stream. Look across the slow-moving river, filled with slow-trailing, brown-sailed craft, at the clanging ship-yards on the other shore. What tangles of masts and spars and ropes crossing and bewildering themselves from the vessels tilted over at every angle to suit the calker's need! What spots of color in the sea-worn old hulls! How the red flame under the seething caldrons of tar and pitch lick and dart from under the black sides of great iron pots! How the smoke and steam swirl about in wreaths and clouds, and the little busy figures of the calkers and riggers run here and there like ants! Even their distant shouts and laughter, and choice sea-faring Dutch, culled from profane authors, can be heard, as in a distant dream, mingled with the faintly echoed clack of the calking mallet, or the rhythmic beat of the hammer on the blazing iron sending out showers of sparks in the ruddy glow of the blacksmiths' shops. The music of toil seems to have a kindred sympathy with the pictures of toil, seen through the shifting veils of mists across the water.

Looking toward the Zuider Zee, one sees the square outlines of the slot or castle of Muiden. The whole subject—towers, sea, and surroundings—"compose" so pictorially from that point of view that one feels rather as if it was too much of a good thing—too like a "sweetly pretty" chromo on the top of a plum box. This strikes one all the more if it be a dry purple haze and melting colors. Nearer by, the square weather-scarred old walls are rugged enough, and when one can take note of the dreadfully modern windows that are stuck too liberally about it, and the various other improvements that have broken out all over it like a sad distemper, the "Slot Muiden" is ugly enough to satisfy the most exacting realist of the new school.

In spring, when the fruit bloom is out, I should think the country about Muiden would sing with color, there are so many gardens. And then when that pearly haze that hangs about the Zuider Zee should conspire to mingle with the other tones and tints, I fancy that the effect would be entirely "precious," to borrow the happy slang of the amateur. I found Muiden so fascinating that I went several times to it, sometimes spending the day, other times an hour or so, going to or from neighboring places.

If, while at Amsterdam, the visitor intends to devote part of a day to the inevitable Zaandam, it would be as well to eke out the entire day by going on to Zandvoort-on-Sea, and getting a blow of the fine North Sea breeze, and at the same time a little idea of a favorite Dutch watering-place well worth seeing. The sketcher will find far more to interest him at the former place, however. In fact, weeks might be spent there with pleasure and advantage if a note or sketch book forms part of one's outfit. The sight-seeing tourist will easily knock off both places in a short day, and sigh for a few more villages to conquer. Zandvoort, being the bathing, breathing, and "gambolling place" of Amsterdam and Rotterdam, and their neighboring towns, is no small, retiring, or modest affair. When the visitor comes by train into its vast and elaborate railway station of red and yellow intercomplicated brick and stone work, the first impression is that he has arrived at a chief town in Opera-comique Land. One passes, after the first surprise, not always pleasant, that these chattering, clattering fisher girls, so very decorative in costume on the station platform, are not, after all, part of a *corps de ballet*, on along an avenue of bazar-like shops, containing all those enticing things that people with restless money boring holes in their pockets love to invest in the moment they see them, such as huge carven meerschaum pipes and cigar tubes. Venus, rising from the ocean, yet innocent of the thrill of nicotine, was a favorite design on these works of art. For the spendthrift and prodigal the Venus was full-figured, and in other respects exhausted the powers of the limner. For the more modest purse and person the Venus was more fragmentary and natural: heads, busts, arms with showy bracelets on, and legs with high-heeled Paris boots to meet the thirst for realism, strongly *prononcé* in Dutch sea-side towns. Huge windows full of the most glaring ties and scarfs, and handkerchiefs of every hue and style of decoration, with borders of every sportive thing, from ballet girls to butterflies. There was not, in all that long line of glittering shops, a single thing of common, low-minded utility. There was one shop of chromos and photographs of the professional beauty of every clime; before its unblushing windows (outside) was a surging crowd nearly all day long. Inside the shop, never a soul but a dark, brooding, lone female, a prey to *ennui* and thoughts of coming bankruptcy. There was little or no crowd in any other part of the arcade, and as this did not seem a very paying one, perhaps it was just as well for the others. The fact was coming sadly home to most of the wearied shop-keepers in that draughty arcade, the gay season was nearly over and gone. We passed on through the covered way to a vast echoing restaurant. How empty it looked, with its spare tables and chairs piled away in one corner—literally in hundreds!

There is generally a spasmodic revival of business on Saturdays at these places, and as we happened to be there on that day we were not entirely alone. The few specimen waiters about were of the frizzed-hair, black-jacketed, white-aproned, correct boulevard type. The *menu* and the prices thereon were also boulevard with a vengeance. Never mind! we will now wander forth and see what there may be to note in this land of Offenbachanalia. Scene first, a wilderness of blown sand, tacked lightly down with sparse threads of wiry grass to whatever solid foundation there may be for this part of watery Holland. A strip of vexed gray sea beyond. A crowd of bathing-hut frames piled under shelter, except just a very few left out for the Saturday visitor. A rim of red roofs and crazy chimneys of fisher huts just peeping over the edge of the sandy dunes. A few fisher people, with idle hands in wide pockets, staring at the sea, at each other, and at the stranger most of all. Along the newly embanked road (or perhaps they call it a boulevard) were irregular masses of florid-looking villas — mushroom things that seemed to have come up overnight. They were all more or less empty, having most of them pleading appeals to the passing stranger to come and hire or buy them. They looked a better speculation for the builder than for the buyer. There were several hand-organs playing at once, a couple in view, and the rest in the air somewhere. This was the *mise en scène* of the operatic-looking place as we first caught sight of it. But as no smiling troop of fisher maidens, with wax-work eyes and complexions, and clock-work movements, came bounding forward to twittering music, expressive of their robust calling, Jacob and I took the stage and had our little scenes all to ourselves. It was early in the

day for the gay *mondains* of Amsterdam to arrive (goodness be thanked!). So we turned our attention to the fisher folk, mostly the younger fry thereof ; and I need not say that the entire community turned its undivided attention to us the moment I began to sketch them. There was one small girl, with a very large healthy baby, who took a great deal of manœuvring and dodging to circumvent and bring to book. Her notion was, seemingly, that by bringing that baby to bear upon me like a battering-ram she would finally succeed in getting a sight at what I was doing. I had only to keep well faced to the pair, noting down their little ways, and sketching furiously meanwhile. When they came too near I would make believe to tickle the baby with light prods of the pencil butt, or else seriously take the two, and speaking to them in good round English, set them back to a convenient spot, and proceed with my notes again as fast as I could. I tried a sort of mild mesmerism on them by endeavoring to "fix them with a glittering eye," but either the eye didn't glitter as it ought, or else they were slow in fixing. Jacob and the mamma were laughing and enjoying our little *contredanse*, and were not disposed to help a bit. However, my little partners were soon sufficiently noted down, and then there was the usual reward of small coin, evidently quite unexpected, for there was an extra caper and a whoop of delight, and a disappearance from the scene to tell the other small fry of the place, who soon came in noisy droves to see if there was to be any more fun. I think that on the same terms I could have danced away and off with the entire infant population of Zandvoort, like another "Pied Piper of Hamelin." After a few more notes we came away; there was not much more to do in a sketchy way. The men-folk were all off fishing, and most of the womenkind were at Amsterdam market, making the place unearthly with their strident yells.

While waiting at the highly decorated railway station for our return train to town, there arrived the late afternoon train from Amsterdam. It was positively running over with these very blooming, picturesque, and pungent goddesses of the fish creel, whose absence as spots of color and high-pitched efforts of sound we had all day missed from the breezy sands of Zandvoort. How that very lively train-

ACROSS THE SANDY DUNES.

ful of fisher-damsels seemed to fill the great echoing station at once with life and animation! As the train came slowly rumbling in, all that could manage to squeeze their rosy but weather-beaten countenances out of the car window did so, and they also waved wild recognitions right and left, and laughed and sang and whooped at the highest capacities of their healthy lungs. Before the train had half stopped they were skipping down with loud impact of wooden *klumpen* upon the platform; and then slinging their empty scale-spangled creels over their shoulders with a round, free-handed swirl, regardless of how near the banging baskets might shave the heads of the by-standers, they clattered out of the place, leaving a certain sense of displacement and change of atmospheric conditions, as if there had been a slight visitation of a saline whirlwind. There was no sort of evidence of fatigue after their hard day's work; with such a free lilt in their stride they looked as if they could vault a six-barred gate, *klumpen* and all. I followed the crowd to the open, and saw them form into small chummy groups, and straggle homeward over the brow of the sandy dunes. I had no time to sketch them very elaborately, but I just made a note of the picture they seemed to streel into. Their gold-pinned lace caps with a high fore-and-aft cocked straw hat atop, the brown empty creels over their shoulders, the short skirts fluttering in the wind, the dark blue stockings, in white wooden shoon plodding or prancing through the sand, and all standing clear against the pale late afternoon sky. Every movement had some grace or strength or character as they went, as if blown by the breeze across the plains of blown sand and stunted grass, to their homes behind the dike in the little sandy rift.

UNCHANGED.

THE same to thee, though years of pain
  May leave their trace on cheek or brow,
And hopeless tears, in silence shed,
  May dim the smiles that glad thee now.

Time's unrelenting hand may grasp
  Each charm that other friends most prize,
Yet leave untouched this heart of Love,
  That makes me lovely to thine eyes.

NATURE'S SERIAL STORY.

X.

A DAY in August can be as depressing as a typical one in May is inspiring, or in June entrancing. As the season advanced, nature appeared to be growing languid and faint. There was neither cloud by day nor dew at night. The sun burned rather than vivified the earth, and the grass and herbage withered and shrivelled before its unobstructed rays. The foliage along the road-sides grew dun-colored from the dust, and those who rode or drove on thoroughfares were stifled by the irritating clouds that rose on the slightest provocation. Pleasure could be found only on the unfrequented lanes that led to the mountains or ran along their bases. Even there trees that drew their sustenance from soil spread thinly on the rocks were seen to be dying, their leaves not flushing with autumnal tints, but hanging limp and bleached, as if they had exhaled their vital juices. The moss beneath them, that had been softer to the tread than a Persian rug, crumbled into powder under the foot. Alf went to gather huckleberries, but, except in moist and swampy places, found them shrivelled on the bushes. Even the corn leaves began to roll on the uplands, and Leonard shook his head despondingly. Webb's anxieties, however, were of a far deeper character, and he was philosophical enough to average the year's income. If the cows came home hungry from their pasture, there was abundance of hay and green-corn fodder to carry them through until the skies should become more propitious. Besides, there was an unfailing spring upon the place, and from this a large cask on wheels was often filled, and was then drawn by one of the quiet farm-horses to the best of the flower beds, the young trees, and to such products of the garden as would repay for the expenditure of time and labor. The ground was never sprinkled so that the morning sun of the following day would drink up the moisture, but so deluged that the watering would answer for several days. The grape-vine is a plant that can endure an unusual degree of drought, and the fruit will be all the earlier and sweeter for it. The clusters of the earlier varieties were already beginning to color, and the season insured the perfect ripening of those fine old kinds, the Isabella and Catawba, that too often are frost-bitten before they become fit for the table.

"It seems to me," Leonard remarked at the dinner table one day, "that droughts are steadily growing more serious and frequent."

"They are," replied his father. "While I remember a few in early life that were more prolonged than any we have had of late years, they must have resulted from exceptional causes, for we usually had an abundance of rain, and did not suffer as we do now from violent alternations of weather. There was one year when there was scarcely a drop of rain throughout the summer. Potatoes planted in the late spring were found in the autumn dry and unsprouted. But such seasons were exceedingly rare, and now droughts are the rule."

"And the people are chiefly to blame for them," said Webb. "We are suffering from the law of heredity. Our forefathers were compelled to fell the trees to make room for the plough, and now one of the strongest impulses of the average American is to cut down a tree. Our forests, on which a moist climate so largely depends, are treated as if they incumbered the ground. The smoke that we are breathing proves that fires are ravaging to the north and west of us. They should be permitted no more than a fire in the heart of a city. The future of the country depends upon the people becoming sane on this subject. If we will send to the Legislature pot-house politicians who are chiefly interested in keeping up a supply of liquor instead of water, they should be provided with a little primer giving the condition of lands denuded of their forests."

"Bravo, Webb!" cried Burt; "we must send you to the Legislature."

"How is the evil to be prevented?" Leonard asked.

"Primarily by instruction and the formation of public opinion. The influence of trees on the climate should be taught in all our schools as thoroughly as the multiplication table. The national and State governments would then be compelled to look beyond the next election, and to appoint foresters who would

have the same power to call out the people to extinguish a forest fire that the sheriff has to collect his *posse* to put down
mob violence. In the long-run fire departments in our forest tracts would be
more useful than the same in cities, for,
after all, cities depend upon the country
and its productiveness. The owners of
woodland should be taught the folly of
cutting everything before them, and of
leaving the refuse brush to become like
tinder. The smaller growth should be
left to mature, and the brush piled and
burned in a way that does not involve the
destruction of every sprout and sapling
over wide areas."

Events furnished a practical commentary on Webb's words. Miss Hargrove
had come over to spend the night with
Amy, and to try some fine old English
glees that she had obtained from her city
home. They had just adjourned from the
supper table to the piazza when Lumley
appeared, hat in hand. He said that a
fire had broken out on a tract adjoining
that belonging to the Cliffords. "City
chaps was up there gunning out o' season,"
Lumley explained, "and wads from their
guns must 'a started it."

As there was much wood ranked on the
Clifford tract, the matter was serious.
Abram and other farm hands were summoned, and the brothers acted as did the
minute-men in the Revolution when the enemy appeared in their vicinity. The young
men excused themselves, and there were
bustle and confusion. Burt, with a flannel blouse belted tightly around his waist,
soon dashed up to the front piazza on his
horse, and flourishing a rake, said, laughingly, "I don't look much like a knight
sallying forth to battle, do I?"

"You look as if you could be one if the
occasion arose," Miss Hargrove replied.

During the half-jesting badinage that
followed, Amy stole away. Behind the
house Webb was preparing to mount,
when a light hand fell on his shoulder.
"You will be careful?" said Amy, appealingly. "You don't seem to spare yourself in anything. I dread to have you go
up into those darkening mountains."

"Why, Amy," he replied, laughing,
"one would think I was going to fight
Indians, and you feared for my scalp."

"I am not so young and blind but that
I can see that you are quietly half-reckless with yourself," she replied; and her
tone indicated that she was a little hurt.

"I pledge you my word that I will not
be reckless to-night; and, after all, this is
but disagreeable humdrum work that we
often have to do. Don't worry, little sister. Burt will be there to watch over me,
you know," he added. "By-the-way,
where is he? It's time we were off."

"Oh, he's talking romantic nonsense to
Miss Hargrove. He won't hurt himself.
I wish I was as sure of you, and I wish I
had more influence over you. I'm not
such a very little sister, even if I don't
know enough to talk to you as you would
like;" and she left him abruptly.

He mastered a powerful impulse to
spring from his horse and call her back.
A moment's thought taught him, however,
that he could not trust himself then to say
a word, and he rode rapidly away. Burt
soon overtook him, and their ride was
comparatively silent, for each was busy
with his own thoughts.

Amy went to the piano, and played
softly until summoned without by an excited exclamation from her friend. A line
of fire was creeping toward them around
a lofty highland, and it grew each moment more and more distinct. "Oh, I
know from its position that it's drawing
near our tract," cried Amy. "If it is so
bright to us at this distance, it must be almost terrible to those near by. I suppose
they are all up there just in front of it,
and Burt is so reckless." She was about to
say Webb, but, because of some unrecognized impulse, she did not. The utterance
of Burt's name, however, was not lost on
Miss Hargrove.

For a long time the girls watched the
scene with awe, and each in imagination
saw an athletic figure begrimed with
smoke, and sending out grotesque shadows into the obscurity, as the destroying
element was met and fought in ways unknown to them, but which, they felt sure,
involved danger. Miss Hargrove feared
that they both had the same form in mind.
She was not a girl to remain long unconscious of her heart's inclinations, and she
knew that Burt Clifford had quickened
her pulses as no man had ever done before. This very fact made her less judicial, less keen, in her insight. If he was
so attractive to her, could Amy be indifferent to him after months of companionship? She had thought that she understood Amy thoroughly, but was beginning to lose faith in her impression.
While in some respects Amy was still a

child, there were quiet depths in her nature of which the young girl herself was but half conscious. She often lapsed into long reveries. Webb's course troubled her. Never had he been more fraternal in his manner, but apparently she was losing her power to interest him, to lure him away from the material side of life. "I can't keep pace with him," she sighed; "and now that he has learned all about my little range of thoughts and knowledge, he finds that I can be scarcely more to him than Johnnie, whom he pets in much the same spirit that he does me, and then goes to his work or books and forgets us both. He could help me so much, if he only thought it worth his while! I'm sure I'm not contented to be ignorant, and many of the things that he knows so much about interest me most."

Thus each girl was busy with her thoughts as they sat in the warm summer night and watched the vivid line draw nearer. Mr. Clifford and Maggie came out from time to time, and were evidently disturbed by the unchecked progress of the fire. Alf had gone with his father, and anything like a conflagration so terrified Johnnie that she dared not leave her mother's lighted room.

Suddenly the approaching line grew dim, was broken, and before very long even the last red glow disappeared utterly. "Ah," said Mr. Clifford, rubbing his hands, "they have got the fire under, and I don't believe it reached our tract."

In little more than half an hour a swift gallop was heard, and Burt soon appeared in the light of the late-rising moon. "It's all out," he exclaimed. "Leonard and Webb propose remaining an hour or two longer, to see that it does not break out again. There's no need of their doing so, for Lumley promised to watch till morning. I'm not fit to be seen. If you'll wait till I put on a little of the aspect of a white man, I'll join you." He had been conscious of a feverish impatience to get back to the ladies, having carefully, even in his thoughts, employed the plural, and he had feared that they might have retired.

Miss Hargrove exclaimed: "How absurd! You wish to go and divest yourself of all picturesqueness! I've seen well-dressed men before, and would much prefer that you should join us as you are. We can then imagine that you are a bandit or a frontiersman, and that your rake was a rifle, which you had used against the Indians. We are impatient to have you tell us how you fought the fire."

He gave but scant attention to Thunder that night, and soon stepped out on the moon-lighted piazza, his tall, fine figure outlined to perfection in his close-fitting costume.

"You will, indeed, need all your imagination to make anything of our task to-night," he said. "Fighting a mountain fire is the most prosaic of hard work. Suppose the line of fire coming down toward me from where you are sitting." As yet unknown to him, a certain subtle flame was originating in that direction. "We simply begin well in advance of it, so that we may have time to rake a space, extending along the whole front of the fire, clear of leaves and rubbish, and as far as possible to hollow out with hoes a trench through this space. Thus, when the fire comes to this cleared space, there is nothing to burn, and it goes out for want of fuel. Of course it's rough work, and it must be done rapidly, but you can see that all the heroic elements which you may have associated with our expedition are utterly lacking."

"Well, no matter. Amy and I have had our little romance, and have imagined you charging the line of fire in imminent danger of being strangled with smoke, if nothing worse."

Amy soon heard Maggie bustling about, preparing a midnight lunch for those who would come home hungry as well as weary, and she said that she would go and try to help. To Burt this seemed sufficient reason for her absence, but Miss Hargrove thought, "Perhaps she saw that his eyes were fixed chiefly on me as he gave his description. I wish I knew just how she feels toward him!"

But the temptation to remain in the witching moonlight was too strong to be resisted. His mellow tones were a music that she had never heard before, and her eyes grew lustrous with suppressed feeling, and a happiness to which she was not sure she was entitled. The spell of her beauty was on him also, and the moments flew by unheeded, until Amy was heard playing and singing softly to herself. "She does not join us again!" was Miss Hargrove's mental comment, and with not a little compunction she rose and went into the parlor. Burt lighted a cigar, in the hope that the girls would again join him, but Leonard, Webb, and Alf returned sooner than they were expected, and all speedily sat down to their unseasonable repast. To Amy's surprise, Webb was the liveliest of the party; but he looked gaunt from fatigue—so worn, indeed, that he reminded her of the time when he had returned from Burt's rescue. But there was no such episode as had then occurred before they parted for the night, and to this she now looked back wistfully. He rose before the others, pleaded fatigue, and went to his room.

They all gathered at a late breakfast, and the surface current of family and social life sparkled as if there were no hidden depths and secret thoughts. Amy's manner was not cold toward Webb, but her pride was touched, and her feelings were a little hurt. While disposed to blame herself only that she had not the power to interest him and secure his companionship, as in the past, it was not in human nature to receive with indifference such an apparent hint that he was far beyond her. "It would be more generous in Webb to help than to ignore me because I know so little," she thought. "Very well: I can have a good time with Burt and Gertrude until Webb gets over his hurry and preoccupation;" and with a slight spirit of retaliation she acted as if she thoroughly enjoyed Burt's lively talk.

The young fellow soon made a proposition that caused a general and breezy excitement. "There never was a better time than this for camping out," he said. "The ground is dry, and there is scarcely any dew. I can get two large wall tents. Suppose we go up and spend a few days on our mountain tract? Maggie could chaperon the party, and I've no doubt that Dr. and Mrs. Marvin would join us."

The discussion of the project grew lively. Maggie was inclined to demur. How could she leave the old people and her housekeeping? Mr. and Mrs. Clifford, however, became the strongest advocates of the scheme. They could get along with the servants, they said, and a little outing would do Maggie good. Leonard, who had listened in comparative silence, brought his wife to a decision by saying: "You had better go, Maggie. You will have all the housekeeping you want on the mountain, and I will go back and forth every day and see that all's right. It's not as if you were beyond the reach of home, for you could be here in an hour were there need. Come, now, make up your mind for a regular lark. It will do you good."

The children were wild with delight at the prospect, and Miss Hargrove and Amy scarcely less pleased. The latter had furtively watched Webb, who at first could not disguise a little perplexity and trouble at the prospect. But he had thought rapidly, and felt that a refusal to be one of the party might cause embarrassing surmises. Therefore he also soon became zealous in his advocacy of the plan. He felt that circumstances were changing and controlling his action. He had fully resolved on an absence of some weeks, but the prolonged drought and the danger it involved made it seem wrong for him to leave home until rain insured safety. Moreover, he believed that he detected symptoms in Burt which, with his knowledge of his brother, led to hopes that he could not banish. An occasional expression in Miss Hargrove's dark eyes, also, did not tend to lessen these hopes. After all, Miss Hargrove, perhaps, would suit him far better than Amy. They are both fond of excitement and society. Why can't we all be happy? At least, if the way were clear, I would try as no man ever tried to win Amy, and I should be no worse off than I am if I failed in the attempt."

These musings were rather remote from his practical words, for he had taken pains to give the impression that their woodland would be far safer for the proposed expedition, and Amy had said, a little satirically, "We are now sure of Webb, since he can combine so much business with pleasure."

He only smiled back in an inscrutable way.

Musk-melons formed one of their breakfast dishes, and Miss Hargrove remarked, "Papa has been exceedingly annoyed by having some of his finest ones stolen."

Burt began laughing, and said: "He should imitate my tactics. Ours were stolen last year, and as they approached maturity, some time since, I put up a notice in large black letters, 'Thieves, take warning: be careful not to steal the poisoned melons.' Hearing a dog bark one night about a week ago, I took a revolver and went out. The moonlight was clear, and there, reading the notice, was a group of ragamuffin boys. Stealing up near them, behind some shrubbery, I fired my pistol in the air, and they fairly tumbled over each other in their haste to escape. We've had no trouble since, I can assure you. I'll drive you home this morning, and, with your father's permission, will put up a similar notice in your garden. We also must make our arrangements for camping promptly. This weather can't last much longer. It surely will not if our mountain experience makes us wish it would;" and full of his projects, he hastened to harness Thunder to his light top-wagon.

He might have taken the two-seated carriage, and asked Amy to accompany them, but it had not occurred to him to do so, especially as he intended to drive on rapidly to Newburgh to make arrangements for the tents. She felt a little slighted and neglected, and Miss Hargrove saw that she did, but thought that any suggestion of a different arrangement might lead to embarrassment. She began to think that the camping experience would make everything clearer. At any rate, it promised so much unhackneyed pleasure that she resolved to make the most of it, and then decide upon her course. She was politic, and cautioned Burt to say nothing about it until she had first seen her father, for she was not certain how her stately and conventional mother would regard the affair. She pounced upon Mr. Hargrove in his library, and he knew from her preliminary caresses that some unusual favor was to be asked for.

"Come," he said, "you wily little strategist, what do you want now? Half of my kingdom?"

She explained rather incoherently.

His answer was unexpected, for he asked, "Is Mr. Burt Clifford in the parlor?"

"No," she replied, faintly; "he's on the piazza." Then, with unusual animation, she began about the melons. Her father's face softened, and he looked at her a little humorously, for her flushed, handsome face would disarm a Puritan.

"You are seeing a great deal of this young Mr. Clifford," he said.

Her color deepened, and she began, hastily, "Oh, well, papa, I've seen a good deal of a great many gentlemen."

"Come, come, Trurie"—his pet name for her—"no disguises with me. Your old father is not so blind as you think, and I've not lived to my time of life in ignorance of the truth that prevention is better than cure. Whether you are aware of it or not, your eyes have revealed to me a growing interest in Mr. Clifford."

She hid her face upon his shoulder.

"He is a comparatively poor man, I suppose, and while I think him a fine fellow, I've seen in him no great aptness for business. If I saw that he was no more to you than others who have sought your favor, I would not say a word, Trurie, for when you are indifferent you are abundantly able to take care of yourself. I've been expecting this. I knew you would in time meet some one who would have the power to do more than amuse you, and my love, darling, is too deep and vigilant to be blind until it is too late to see. You are merely interested in Mr. Clifford now. You might become more than interested during an experience like the one proposed."

"If I should, papa, am I so poor that I have not even the privilege of a village girl who can follow her heart?"

"My advice would be," he replied, gently, "that you guide yourself by both reason and your heart. This is our secret council-chamber, and one is speaking to you who has no thought but for your lasting happiness."

She took a chair near him, and looked into his eyes as she said, thoughtfully and gravely: "I should be both silly and unnatural did I not recognize your motive and love. I know I am not a child any longer, and should have no excuse for any school-girl or romantic folly. You have always had my confidence; you would have had it in this case as soon as there was anything to tell. I scarcely understand myself as yet, but must admit that I am more interested in Mr. Clifford than in any man I ever met, and, as you said, I also have not reached my time of life without knowing what this may lead to. You married mamma when she was younger than I, and you too, papa, were 'a comparatively poor man' at the time. I have thought a great deal about it. I know all that wealth and fashionable society can give me, and I tell you honestly, papa, I would rather be the happy wife that Maggie Clifford is than marry any millionaire in New York. There is no need, however, for such serious talk, for there is nothing yet beyond congenial companionship, and— Well," she added, hastily, in memory of Amy, "I don't believe anything will come of it. But I want to go on this expedition. There will probably be two married ladies in the party, and so I don't see that even mamma can object. Rest assured I shall never become engaged to any one without your consent; that is," she added, with another of her irresistible caresses, "unless you are very unreasonable, and I become very old."

"Very well, Trurie, you shall go, with your mother's consent, and I think I can insure that. As you say, you are no longer a child." And his thought was, I have seen enough of life to know that it is best not to be too arbitrary in such matters. After a moment he added, gravely, "You say you have thought. Think a great deal more before you take any steps which may involve all your future."

Burt was growing uneasy on the piazza, and feared that Miss Hargrove might not obtain the consent that she had counted on so confidently. He was a little surprised also to find how the glamour faded out of his anticipations at the thought of her absence, but explained his feeling by saying to himself, "She is so bright and full of life, and has so fine a voice, that we should miss her sadly." He was greatly relieved, therefore, when Mr. Hargrove came out and greeted him courteously. Gertrude had been rendered too conscious by her recent interview to accompany her father, but she soon appeared, and no one could have imagined that Burt was more to her than an agreeable acquaintance. Mrs. Hargrove gave a reluctant consent, and it was soon settled that they should try to get off on the following afternoon. Burt also included in the invitation young Fred Hargrove, and then drove away elated.

At the dinner table he announced his success in procuring the tents, and his intention of going for them in the afternoon. At the same time he exhorted Leonard and Maggie to prepare provisions adequate to mountain appetites, adding, "Webb, I suppose, will be too busy to do more than join us at the last moment."

Webb said nothing, but disappeared after dinner. As he was at supper as usual, no questions were asked. Before it was light the next morning Amy thought she heard steps on the stairs, and the rear hall door shut softly. When finally awaking she was not sure but that her impression was a dream. As she came down to breakfast Burt greeted her with dismay.

"The tents, which I put on the back piazza, are gone," he said.

"Where is Webb?" was her quick response.

No one had seen him, and it was soon learned that a horse and a strong wagon were also missing.

"Ah, Burt," cried Amy, laughing, "rest assured Webb has stolen a march on you, and taken his own way of retaliation for what you said at the dinner table yesterday. He was away all the afternoon, too. I believe he has chosen a camping ground, and the tents are standing on it."

"He should have remembered that others might have some choice in the matter," was the discontented reply.

"If Webb has chosen the camping ground, you will all be pleased with it," said his mother, quietly. "I think he is merely trying to give a pleasant surprise."

He soon appeared, and explained that with Lumley's help he had made some preparations, since any suitable place with water near, from which there was a fine outlook, would have seemed very rough and uninviting to the ladies unless more work was done than could be accomplished in the afternoon of their arrival.

"Now I think that is very thoughtful of you, Webb," said Amy. "The steps I heard last night were not a dream. At what unearthly hour did you start?"

"Was I so heavy-footed as to disturb you?"

"Oh, no, Webb," she said, with a look of comic distress, in which there was also a little reproach; "it's not your feet that disturb me, but your head. You have stuffed it so full of learning that I am depressed by the emptiness of mine."

He laughed as he replied, "I hope all your troubles may be quite as imaginary." Then he requested Leonard to spend the morning in helping Maggie, who would know best what was needed for even mountain housekeeping, and that he would see to farm matters, and join them early in the evening. The peaches were ripening, and Amy from her window saw that he was taking from the trees all fit for market; also that Abram, under his direction, was busy with the watering cart. "Words can not impose upon me," she thought, a little bitterly. "He knows how I long for his companionship, and it's not a little thing to be made to feel that I am scarcely better qualified for it than Johnnie."

Burt galloped over to Dr. Marvin's, who promised to join them, with his wife, on the following day. He had a tent which he had occasionally used in his ornithological pursuits.

At two in the afternoon a merry party started for the hills. All the vehicles on the farm had been impressed into the service to bring up the party, with chairs, cooking utensils, provisions, bedding, etc. When they reached the ground that Webb had selected, even Burt admitted his pleased surprise. The outlook over the distant river and a wide area of country dotted with villages was superb, while to the camp a home-like look had already been given, and the ladies, with many mental encomiums, saw how secluded and inviting an aspect had been imparted to their especial abode. As they came on the scene Lumley was finishing the construction of a dense screen of evergreen boughs which surrounded the canvas to the doorway. Not far away an iron pot was slung on cross-sticks in gypsy style, and it was flanked by rock-work fire-places which Maggie declared were almost equal to a kitchen range. The men's tent was pitched at easy calling distance, and, like that of the ladies, was surrounded by a thick growth of trees, whose shade would be grateful. A little space had been cleared between the two tents for a leaf-canopied dining hall, and a table of boards improvised. The ground, as far as possible, had been cleared of loose stones and rubbish. Around the fire-place mossy rocks abounded, and were well adapted for picturesque groupings. What touched Amy most was a little flower bed made of the rich black mould of decayed leaves, in which were some of her favorite flowers, well watered. They did not suggest indifference on the part of Webb. About fifty feet from the tents the mountain shelf sloped off abruptly, and gave the magnificent view that has been mentioned. Even Burt saw how much had been gained by Webb's forethought, and frankly acknowledged it. As it was, they had no more than time to complete the arrangements for the night before the sun's level rays lighted up a scene that was full of joyous activity and bustle. The children's happy voices made the echoes ring, and Fred Hargrove, notwithstanding his city antecedents, yielded with delight to the love of primitive life that exists in every boy's heart. Although he was a few years older than Alf, they had become friendly rivals as incipient sportsmen and naturalists. Amy felt that she was coming close to nature's heart, and the novelty of it all was scarcely less exciting to her than to Johnnie. To little Ned it was a place of wonder and enchantment, and he kept them all in a mild state of terror by his exploring expeditions. At last his father threatened to take him home, and with this awful punishment before his eyes he put his thumb in his mouth, perched upon a rock, and philosophically watched the preparations for supper. Maggie, however, was the presiding genius of the occasion, and she looked like the light-hearted girl that Leonard had wooed more than a dozen years before. She ordered him around, jested with him, and laughed at him in such a lively way that Burt declared that she was proving herself unfit for the duties of chaperon by getting up a flirtation with her husband. Meanwhile, under her supervision, order was evoked from chaos, and appetizing odors arose from the fire-place.

Miss Hargrove admitted to herself that in all the past she had never known such hours of keen enjoyment, and she was bent on proving that, although a city-bred girl, she could take her part in the work as well as the fun. Nor were her spirits dampened by the fact that Burt was often at her side and that Amy did not appear to care. The latter, however, was becoming aware of his deepening interest in her brilliant friend. As yet she was not sure whether it was more than a good-natured and hospitable effort to make one so recently a stranger at home with them, or a new lapse on his part into a condition of ever-enduring love and constancy, and the smile that followed the thought was not flattering to Burt.

A little before supper was ready Maggie asked him to get a pail of water.

"Come, Miss Gertrude," he said, "and I'll show you the Continental spring at which the Revolutionary soldiers drank more than a hundred years ago;" and she tripped away with him, nothing loath. As they re-appeared, flushed and laughing, carrying the pail between them, Amy trilled out,

"Jack and Jill came up the hill."

A moment later Webb followed them, on horseback, and was greeted with acclamations and overwhelmed with compliments. Miss Hargrove was only too glad of the diversion from herself, for Amy's words had made her absurdly conscious, for a society girl.

They feasted through the long twilight.

Never had green corn, roasted in its husks on the coals, tasted so delicious, and never before were peaches and cream so ambrosial. Amy made it her care that poor Lumley should feast also, but the smile with which she served him was the sustenance he most craved. Then, as the evening breeze grew chilly, and the night darkened, lanterns were hung in the trees, the fire was replenished, and they sat down the merriest of merry parties. Even Webb had vowed that he would ignore the past and the future, and make the most of that camp fire by the way-side of life. It must be admitted, however, that his discovery of Burt and Miss Hargrove alone at the spring had much to do with his resolution. Stories and songs succeeded each other, until Ned was asleep in Maggie's arms, and Johnnie nodding at her side. In reaction from the excitements and fatigues of the day, they all early sought the rest which is never found in such perfection as in a mountain camp. Hemlock boughs formed the mattresses on which their blankets were spread, and soon there were no sounds except the strident chirpings of insects and the calls of night birds.

There was one perturbed spirit, however, and at last Burt stole out and sat over the dying fire. When the mind is ready for impressions, a very little thing will produce them vividly, and Amy's snatch of song about "Jack and Jill" had awakened Burt at last to a consciousness that he might be carrying his attentions to Miss Hargrove too far, in view of his vows and inexorable purpose of constancy. He assured himself that his only object was to have a good time, and enjoy the charming society of his new acquaintance. Of course he was in love with Amy, and she was all that he could desire. Perhaps he had pursued the wrong tactics. Girls even like Amy were not so unsophisticated as they appeared to be, and he felt that he was profoundly experienced in such questions, if in nothing else. Had not her pride been touched? and would not his evident admiration for Miss Hargrove lead the former to believe that he was mercurial and not to be depended upon? He had to admit to himself that some experiences in the past had tended to give him this reputation. "I was only a boy then," he muttered, with a stern compression of the lips. "I'll prove that I am a man now;" and having made this sub-

lime resolution, he slept the sleep of the just.

All who have known the freshness, the elasticity, the mental and physical vigor, with which one springs from a bed of boughs, will envy the camping party's awakening on the following morning. Webb resolved to remain and watch the drift of events. Burt, however, began to show himself a skillful diplomatist. He felt that perhaps he had checked himself barely in time to retrieve his fortunes and character with Amy, but he was too adroit to permit any marked change to appear in his manner and action. He said to himself that he cordially liked and admired Miss Hargrove, but he believed that she had enjoyed not a few flirtations, and was not averse to the addition of another to the list. Even his self-complacency had not led him to think that she regarded him in any other light than that of a very agreeable and useful summer friend. He had seen enough of society to be aware that such temporary friendships often border closely on the sentimental and yet with no apparent trace remaining in after-years. To Amy, however, such affairs would not appear in the same light as they might to Miss Hargrove, and he felt that he had gone far enough. But not for the world would he be guilty of *gaucherie*, of neglecting Miss Hargrove for ostentatious devotion to Amy. Indeed, he was more pronounced in his admiration than ever, but in many little and unobtrusive ways he tried to prove to Amy that she had his deeper thoughts. She, however, was not at this time disposed to dwell upon the subject. His manner merely tended to confirm the view that he, like herself, regarded Miss Hargrove as a charming addition to their circle, and proposed that she should enjoy herself thoroughly while with them. Webb was more like the brother she wished him to be than he had been for a long time. The little flower bed was an abiding re-assurance, and so the present contained all that she desired.

This was not true of either Webb or Miss Hargrove. The former, however, did not lose heart. He thought he knew Burt too well to give up hope yet. The latter, with all her experience, was puzzled. She speedily became conscious of the absence of a certain warmth and genuineness in Burt's manner and words. The thermometer is not so sensitive to heat and cold as the intuition of a girl like Miss Hargrove

AT THE CONTINENTAL SPRING.

to the mental attitude of an admirer, but no one could better hide her thoughts and feelings than she when once upon her guard.

The few remaining days of August passed, and September came, bringing little suggestion of autumn rains or coolness. Dr. and Mrs. Marvin had joined them, and the former's interest in every wild creature in the woods became infectious. Alf and Fred were his ardent disciples, and he rarely found an indifferent listener in Amy. The heat of the day was given up to the fashioning of alpenstocks and reading, and the morning and late afternoons to excursions. In one of these they had sat down to rest near an immense decaying tree that was hollow in parts, and full of holes from the topmost shattered branches to the ground.

"That," said the doctor, "might fitly be called an old tenement-house. You have no idea how many and various creatures may have found a home in it."

He was immediately urged to enumerate its possible inhabitants in the past, present, and future.

The doctor, pleased with the conceit of regarding the decaying tree as an old tenement, began with animation: "All three of the squirrels of this region have undoubtedly dwelt in it. I scarcely need to do more than mention the well-known saucy red or fox squirrel, whose delight is mischief. By-the-way, we have at home two tame robins that were tumbled out of their nest before they could fly by one of these ruthless practical jokers. The birds come in and out of the house like members of the family. The graceful gray squirrel is scarcely less familiar than the red one. He makes a lively pet, and we have all seen him turning the wheel attached to his cage. The curious little flying-squirrel, however, is a stranger even to those to whom he may be a near neighbor, for the reason that his habits are chiefly nocturnal. He ventures out occasionally on a cloudy day, but is shy and retiring. Thoreau relates an interesting experience with one. He captured it in a decayed hemlock stump, wherein it had a little nest of leaves, bits of bark, and pine needles. It bit viciously at first, and uttered a few 'dry shrieks,' but he carried it home. After it had been in his room a few hours it reluctantly allowed its soft fur to be stroked. He says it has 'very large, prominent black eyes,

which give it an innocent look. In color it was a chestnut ash, inclining to fawn, slightly browned, and white beneath. The under edge of his wings(?) tinged yellow, the upper dark, perhaps black.' He put it into a barrel, and fed it with an apple and shag-bark hickory-nuts. The next morning he carried it back and placed it on the stump from which it had been taken, and it ran up a sapling, from which it skimmed away to a large maple nine feet distant, whose trunk it struck about four feet from the ground. This tree it ascended thirty feet on the opposite side from Thoreau, then coming into view, it eyed its quondam captor for a moment or two as much as to say, 'good-by.' Then away it went, first raising its head as if choosing its objective point. Thoreau says its progress is more like that of a bird than he had been led to believe from naturalists' accounts, or than he could have imagined possible in a quadruped. Its flight was not a regular descent on a given line. It veered to right and left, avoiding obstructions, passed through branches of trees, and flew horizontally part of the way, landing on the ground at last over fifty-one feet from the foot of the tree from which it sprang. After its leap, however, it can not renew its impetus in the air, but must alight and start again. It appears to sail and steer much like a hawk when the latter does not flap its wings. The little striped chipmunk no doubt has heaped up its store of nuts in the hole there that opens from the ground into the tree, and the pretty white-footed mouse, with its large eyes and ears, has had its apartment in the decayed recesses that exist in the worm-eaten roots.

"Opossums and raccoons are well-known denizens of trees, and both furnish famous country sports, especially in the South. ''Possum up de gum-tree, 'coony in de hollow,' is a line from a negro ditty that touches a deep chord in the African heart. The former is found not infrequently in this region, but the Hudson seems to be the eastern boundary of its habitat."

"I took two from a tree in one night," Burt remarked.

"The raccoon's haunts, however, extend far to the northward, and it is abundant in the regions bordering on the Adirondacks, though not common in the dense pine woods of the interior. They are omnivorous creatures, and often rob nests of eggs and young birds, for they are expert climbers. They are fond of nuts and fruits, and especially of corn when in the condition of a milky pulp. Nor does poultry come amiss. They are also eager fishermen, although they are unable to pursue their prey under water like the otter and mink.

"Two other interesting animals may have lived in that tree, the lesser weasel, and his sanguinary cousin the ermine, or large weasel. Both are brown after the snow finally disappears, and both turn white with the first snow-storm."

"Now you are romancing, doctor," cried Miss Hargrove.

"Yes," added Leonard; "tell us that you have caught a weasel asleep, and we will at least look

moles, shrews, and insects, and does not attack larger animals or poultry. It is so exceedingly lithe and slender that its prey has no chance to escape. Where a mouse or a mole can go it can go also, and if out-run in the field, it follows the scent of its game like a hound, and is as relentless as fate in its pursuit.

"In its next of kin, the ermine, or

THOREAU'S PET.

credulous, but this turning white with the first snow, and brown as soon as the snow is gone, is a little off color."

"It's true, nevertheless," maintained the doctor, "although I have seen no satis-factory explanation of the changes. It's a provision of nature to enable these ani-mals to pursue their prey or escape from their enemies with the greater ease. Na-ture appears to have been very partial to weasels. They not only make their nests in hollow trees, but in the sides of banks. Were it not for its habit of destroying the eggs and young of birds, the lesser weasel might be regarded as a wholly useful crea-ture, for it devours innumerable mice,

large weasel, we have perhaps the most cruel and blood-thirsty animal in exist-ence. Its instinct to kill is so strong that, were it possible, it would destroy the means of its subsistence. It would leave none of its varied prey alive. The lion, and even the man-eating tiger, when gorged, are inert and quiet. They kill no more than they want for a meal; but the ermine will attack a poultry-yard, satiate itself with the brains of the fowls or by sucking their blood, and then, out of 'pure cussedness,' will kill all the rest within reach. Fifty chickens have been destroyed in a night by one of these remorseless lit-tle beasts. It makes fearful ravages among grouse, rabbits, and hares. It is the mythical vampire embodied. It is not very much larger than the lesser weasel, and has the same long, lithe, slender body and neck. A gray squirrel would look bulky beside one, but in indomitable courage and pitiless ferocity I do not think it has an equal. Only lack of material or bodily fatigue suspends its bloody work, and its life is one long career of carnage. It has a terrific set of teeth, which are worked by most powerful muscles. Dr. Coues, an eminent naturalist, has given a graphic account of him. His words, as I remember them, are a true portrait of a murderer. 'His forehead is low, and nose sharp; his eyes are small, penetrating, cunning, and glitter with an angry green light. His fierce face surmounts a body extraordinarily wiry, lithe, and muscular, which ends in a singularly long slender neck that can be lifted at right angles with the body. When he is looking around, his neck stretched up, his flat triangular head bent forward, swaying to and fro, we have the image of a serpent.'

"This is a true picture of the ermine when excited or angry; when at rest, and in certain conditions of his fur, there are few more beautiful, harmless, innocent-looking creatures. Let one of the animals on which he preys approach, however, and instantly he becomes a fiend. In the economy of nature he often serves a very useful purpose. In many regions field-mice are destructive. The ermine is their deadliest foe. A rat will fight a man if cornered, but it gives up at once in abject terror when confronted by the large weasel. This archenemy has a pride in his hunting, and when taking up his quarters in a barn will collect in one place all the rats and mice he kills. Sometimes a hundred or more have been found together as the result of two or three nights' work. The ermine hunts, however, both by day and night, and climbs trees with great facility. He is by no means shy, and one has been known to try to kill chickens in a coop when a man

DISREPUTABLE TENANTS.

was standing near him. Hunger was not his motive, for he had destroyed dozens of fowls the night before. The ermine has been used successfully as a ferret. Having first filed the creature's teeth down, so that it could not kill the game, a hole for high-holders' eggs, and a big black-snake ran down my back, but not inside of my coat, however."

"Please say nothing more about snakes," cried Amy; and she rose decisively, adding, in a low tone: "Come,

WOODPECKERS AT HOME.

a gentleman secured twelve live rabbits in one forenoon. But it's getting late, and time we started tentward, and yet I'm not through even the list of quadrupeds that may have dwelt in our old tenement. There are four species of bats to be mentioned, besides moles and shrews that would burrow in its roots if they are as hollow as the branches. Including the owls, wrens, and woodpeckers, there are thirteen species of birds that would live in a tree like that, not to speak of tree-toads, salamanders, brown tree-lizards, insects and slugs innumerable, and black-snakes—"

"Snakes?" interrupted Burt, incredulously.

"Yes, snakes. I once put my hand in

Gertrude, let us go. The tenants of the old tree that we've heard about may be very interesting to naturalists, but some of them are not to my taste."

The days passed, and the novelty of their mountain life began to wane a little. There were agreeable episodes, as, for instance, visits from Mr. Clifford, Mr. Hargrove, and the Rev. Mr. Barkdale, who were entertained in royal style; but, after all, the camping experience was not apparently fulfilling the hopes of two of the party. Webb's doubt and suspense had only been increased, and Miss Hargrove was compelled to admit to herself that her father's fears were not groundless. She was the life of the party, and yet she was not at rest. Even in her dreams there was a minor key of trouble and dread. The past few weeks were bringing a revelation. She had read novels innumerable; she had received tender confidences from friends. Love had been declared to her, and she had seen its eloquent pleading in more than one face; but she acknowledged that she had never known the meaning of the word until without her volition her own heart revealed to her the mystery. Reason and will might control her action, but she could no more divert her thoughts from Burt Clifford than a flower can turn from the sun. His mirthful blue eyes, and spirited ways and words, set all her nerves tingling with a delicious exhilaration which she could neither analyze nor control. In brief, the time that her father foresaw had come; the man had appeared who could do more than amuse; her whole nature had made its choice. She could go back to the city, and still in semblance be the beautiful and brilliant girl that she had been; but she knew that in all the future few waking hours would pass without her thoughts reverting to that little mountain terrace, its gleaming canvas, its gypsy-like fire, with a tall lithe form often reclining at her feet beside it.

The camping party came very near breaking up in a horrible tragedy. The day was growing warm, and they were returning from a rather extended excursion, straggling along a steep wood road that was partially overgrown with bushes. Burt had been a little more attentive to Miss Hargrove than usual, but was now at Amy's side with his ready laugh and jest. Dr. Marvin was in the rear, peering about, as usual, for some object of interest to a naturalist. Miss Hargrove, so far from succumbing to the increasing heat, was reluctant to return, and seemed possessed with what might be almost termed a nervous activity. She had been the most indefatigable climber of the party, and on their return had often diverged from the path to gather a fern or some other sylvan trifle. At one point the ascending path formed an angle with a ledge of rock that made a little platform. At the farther end of this she saw a flower, and she went to gather it. A moment or two later Burt and Amy heard her scream, and the sound of her voice seemed almost beneath them. Grasping his alpenstock firmly, Burt sprang through the intervening copse, and witnessed a scene that

he never forgot, though he paused not a second in his horror. Even as he rushed toward her a huge rattlesnake was sending forth the "long, loud, stinging whirr" which, as Dr. Holmes says, is "the dreadful sound that nothing which breathes can hear unmoved." Miss Hargrove was looking down upon it, stupefied, paralyzed with terror. Already the reptile was coiling its thick body for the deadly stroke, when Burt's stock fell upon its neck and laid it writhing at the girl's feet. With a flying leap from the rock above he landed on the venomous head, and crushed it with his heel. He had scarcely time to catch Miss Hargrove when she became apparently a lifeless burden in his arms.

Dr. Marvin now reached him, and after a glance at the scene, exclaimed, "Great God! Burt, she was not bitten?"

"No; but let us get away from here. Where there's one of these devils there is usually another not far off;" and they carried the unconscious girl swiftly toward the camp, which fortunately was not far away, all the others following with dread and anxiety in their faces.

Dr. Marvin's and Maggie's efforts soon revived Miss Hargrove, but she had evidently received a very severe nervous shock. When at last Burt was permitted to see her, she gave him her hand with such a look of gratitude, and something more which she could not then disguise, that his heart began to beat strangely fast. He was so confused that he could only stammer some incoherent words of congratulation; but he half-consciously gave her hand a pressure that left the most delicious pain the young girl had ever known. He was deeply excited, for he had taken a tremendous risk in springing upon a creature that can strike its crooked fangs through the thick leather of a boot, as a New York physician once learned at the cost of his life, when he carelessly sought to rouse with his foot a caged reptile of this kind.

Miss Hargrove had ceased to be a charming summer acquaintance to Burt. She was the woman at whose side he had stood in the presence of death.

Before their mid-day repast was ready a rumble of wagons was heard coming up the mountain, and Webb soon appeared. "The barometer is falling rapidly," he said, "and father agrees with me that it will be safer for you all to return at once."

CAUGHT NAPPING.

He found ready acquiescence, for after the event of the morning the ladies were in haste to depart. Lumley, who had come up with Webb, was sent to take the rattles from the snake, and the men drew apart, with Alf and Fred, to discuss the adventure, for it was tacitly agreed that it was not best to talk about snakes to those whose nerves were already unstrung at the thought of such fearful neighbors. Dr. Marvin would have gone with Lumley had not his wife interposed. As it was, he had much to say concerning the habits and character of the reptiles, and told many thrilling stories about them, to which the boys listened with awe.

DISCONTENT.

I.

THE BRIER ROSE.

I CLING to the garden wall
  Outside, where the grasses grow;
Where the tall weeds flaunt in the sun,
  And the yellow mulleins blow.
The dock and the thistle crowd
  Close to my shrinking feet,
And the gypsy yarrow shares
  My cup and the food I eat.

The rude winds toss my hair,
  The wild rains beat me down,
The way-side dust lies white
  And thick on my leafy crown.
I can not keep my robes
  From wanton fingers free,
And the veriest beggar dares
  To stop and gaze at me.

Sometimes I climb and climb
  To the top of the garden wall,
And I see her where she stands,
  Stately and fair and tall—
My sister, the red, red Rose,
  My sister, the royal one,
The fairest flower that blows
  Under the summer sun!

What wonder that she is fair?
  What wonder that she is sweet?
The treasures of earth and air
  Lie at her dainty feet;
The choicest fare is hers,
  Her cup is brimmed with wine;
Rich are her emerald robes,
  And her bed is soft and fine.

She need not lift her head
  Even to sip the dew;
No rude touch makes her shrink
  The whole long summer through.
Her servants do her will;
  They come at her beck and call.
Oh, rare is life in my lady's bowers
  Inside of the garden wall!

II.

THE GARDEN ROSE.

The garden path runs east,
  And the garden path runs west;
There's a tree by the garden gate,
  And a little bird in a nest.
It sings and sings and sings!
  Does the bird, I wonder, know
How, over the garden wall,
  The bright days come and go?

The garden path runs north,
  And the garden path runs south;
The brown bee hums in the sun,
  And kisses the lily's mouth;
But it flies away ere long
  To the birch-tree, dark and tall.
What do you find, O brown bee,
  Over the garden wall?

With ruff and farthingale,
  Under the gardener's eye,
In trimmest guise I stand—
  Oh, who so fine as I?
But even the light wind knows
  That it may not play with me,
Nor touch my beautiful lips
  With a wild caress and free.

Oh, straight is the garden path,
  And smooth is the garden bed,
Where never an idle weed
  Dares lift its careless head.
But I know outside the wall
  They gather, a merry throng;
They dance and flutter and sing,
  And I listen all day long.

The Brier Rose swings outside;
  Sometimes she climbs so high
I can see her sweet pink face
  Against the blue of the sky.
What wonder that she is fair,
  Whom no strait bonds enthrall?
Oh, rare is life to the Brier Rose,
  Outside of the garden wall!

TROUVILLE.

TROUVILLE has arrived at that melancholy period when it has a reputation to sustain. In its early days its spontaneity and joyful flow of spirits were the distilled essence of all that was gayest and most piquant in Parisian life. These are now exhausted. But *noblesse oblige*. Trouville must still appear nonchalant, reckless, and extravagant. It must put on smiles to conceal its yawns, for there on the beach sits the *bourgeoisie* in provincial toilets and open-eyed expectation, fully in the faith it is seeing "the hig lef," to quote *Figaro*'s English, as she is spoke, and on that faith Trouville is now sustained. Nothing can be more tedious than the affectation of frivolity after the mood has passed, and the piper is standing outside waiting to be paid. If Trouville had been content to sit down, like Houlgate, in quiet domesticity, and cultivate its gardens, or to have simply remained artistic, like Étretat, it might enjoy a quiet decline in years, instead of this feverish, nervous existence it must continue or lose its grip.

The glamour of literature, the magic of art, first brought this village of fishers into notice. Alexandre Dumas, Isabey, and Charles Mozin divide the right of discovery. The French artist is the most serious man of his generation, but in summer, in spite of himself, he is amusing.

Did you ever see a hen, having scratched up a nice fat worm, chased by the rest of the barn-yard until, in breathless despair, she dropped it, and the rest gobbled it up? That hen is the unhappy French artist. His *flair* for suitable material is keener than that of the industrious hen. But he has no sooner set up his easel than all the world follows him, overruns and transforms the locality, and he throws down his brushes and runs away in disgust. The French artists made Trouville; they discovered Étretat; they retired to Pont-Aven, and there now a large hotel has been built, and the tourist is *en route*.

There certainly could be no more fitting place for travel and recreation than Normandy, nor is there a better part of Normandy than the coast between Honfleur and Cabourg. It is hard to say anything kind of the English Channel, that source of unspeakable woe and unthinkable misery. To do so implies virtue so great that it almost allows for the commission of some little sin—the usual fibs about the charms of life at Trouville, for example. But two nations as opulent as England and France can well afford to share between them such a breeder of skies, of templed clouds, of magical colors, of mists which softly descend like a veil from heaven, and shroud the earth in mystery, through which phantom sails go to and fro. This coast was one of Daubigny's haunts, and it is easy to see whence came his skies. Le Havre (the harbor) is but the mouth of the Seine; but the bay is a never-ending panorama of beauty.

The shore is its fitting mate. It rises not too abruptly in terraces of verdure up to the lofty heights of Les Tremonts. These terraces characterize the coast. The landscape is beautiful in its essential features, but its charm lies in its human aspect. The cool slopes of the orchards, the sheep nibbling in the open pastures, the thatched roofs with their fringes of flags and mosses glowing like gold in the sunlight, the wind-blown poplars standing in rows like overgrown school-boys, the highways perfect in construction between hedge-rows and beneath arching trees, and into which cool pathways lead, impenetrable to the sun—these all bring warmth to the heart and light to the eyes as can never the majesty of the Alps or the wonders of the Yellowstone.

Trouville has but little in common with such scenes as these. A Coney Island in a summer sea would make its appropriate setting. The landscape has a heart; the town has only a feather-head, fitted for smiles, sunshine, and thoughtless gayety.

In painters' talk, the architecture of Trouville does not compose well. Each villa and maisonnette is a caprice in brick and stone. The Salon of Trouville, by which name the Casino is known, stands first, with its circular colonnade and wings, in form suggesting the Trocadéro. It is alive with color. It is built of alternate blocks of yellow and red bricks. A striped pavilion is raised on the parapet for the music on sunny days. Large umbrellas, red, yellow, and blue, like gaudy mushrooms, are planted on the outer edge. From the roof the flags of France hospitably inclose those of America, England, and Russia, which the breeze from the Channel keeps constantly afloat. The Casino itself quivers with life.

The sea suggests much of the ornament of the villas. Large panels of mosaic adorn the façades, on which dolphins and mermaids sport on gold grounds. Shells and sea-weeds in colored reliefs form friezes. Good taste is not always shown in the decorations. Pretentious villas display plaques wherever space offers, and recall oil-cloth factories ingeniously displaying their wares. But in the *ensemble* they contribute to the life, gayety,

and unrest which distinguish Trouville, and take their proper place. Other houses assume distinctive styles. The Chalet Persan, the home of the Princesse de Sagan, is a mass of arabesques, with indented arches picked out in color. The Maison Normande, its neighbor, with its solid and sombre pointed towers, accents the line. But its size, which is small to daintiness, keeps it playful. Then there are the great hotels, the Roches Noires and Hôtel de Paris, in which during the height of the season he who enters leaves all his wealth behind.

In front extends the beach, a dazzling strip of sand, soft and fine enough for a baby's tender foot. It dips so gently that low tide leaves a vast pleasure-ground, soon covered with children, dogs, and gay groups. This magnificent sweep of beach extends almost unbroken from Trouville to Cherbourg.

In the background villas half hidden in foliage crest the terraces. A Frenchman spends three-quarters of his life on a boulevard, but he surrounds his home even in the country with high walls and impenetrable hedges. Within are smoothly shaven lawns, ribbon beds of flowers, kiosks, Chinese pagodas, and all those adornments of the landscape that with us only fulfill part of their mission until they have caught the eye and admiration of the wayfaring man.

At Trouville everybody lives out-of-doors. The routine of the day is as regular as that of a boarding-school, and everybody falls in with much less rebellion. By ten o'clock all the world is abroad; perhaps earlier, if the tide intimates. However, at Trouville the tide, elsewhere so inexorable, seems to bend to the caprices of the whimsical world of pleasure and fashion. One may bathe any time, but the bathing hour, the rendezvous, is at high tide.

Like everything at Trouville, the bathing is minutely prescribed. There is, of course, a bureau. Nothing takes place without a bureau. A Frenchman cast adrift on an uninhabited isle would pick himself up and go to find the bureau. At the bureau the tickets are bought. This is a business negotiation of some moment and minutes. Fifty centimes will get a bath *simple*. How little that means I do not know. A franc will secure a bath and a cabin attached; two francs, a bath *de luxe*. Then follow the details—so much for a costume, so much for towels,

THE BATHING HOUR.

so much for *cache-tête*, so much for *spa-drilles*, and a handful of colored tickets. The mistress of the robes makes the affair more formidable. There seems to be in France a race of elderly becapped women that wait on all the impatient moments of life. One finds them in theatres and at bathing bureaus. They move slowly and talk fast. The alien and stranger would rather they moved fast and talked slowly. The exchange of printed cards and clothing being effected, the bathing is free.

There is a colony of bath-houses and a suburb of ambulant cabins drawn by stout Norman horses. Two cables divide the bathing grounds into three parts. These are allotted to the *dames seules*, families, and men, which everywhere in France make the three grand divisions of the human race. In the central space every day the grand levée is held by the brink of the water at the bathing-house. To reach this the shortest route is through the space belonging to the *dames seules*. Across this also is a plank, and a plank through this sand has something of the value of a plank to a tired swimmer in deep water. Naturally this path is constantly taken, notwithstanding the warning "*C'est défendu*," which is intended to protect this sacred inclosure. A further security is an old man with a baton, who alone is supposed to see the unprotected nymphs skipping to and fro across the sands.

Unless a man is accustomed to fine distinctions, if he wishes to enjoy the spectacle in the water, he enters this way. He possibly sees with some amusement this aged man in the centre performing a sort of war-dance, brandishing his stick, and uttering wild cries. Innocently and curiously he comes nearer; then suddenly turns and flees, chased by the enraged elderly, and has darted under the rope, impelled by the instinct of self-preservation, but without consciousness of his crime.

Only the wall through which Pyramus and Thisbe exchanged vows that merry night was more impenetrable than the screen which these cables afford. However, everybody seems to be satisfied with the protection they give. The single women sport freely on their side of the rope, and, if they choose, can wander at will. The assorted families occupy the centre, husbands and brothers being freely admitted. Across the third rope men bathe in the briefest of calicoes, and women

cling to their side of the rope in clusters of all ages. All is in perfect propriety, since all is prescribed.

For an artistic people, as are the French, the costumes are surprisingly hideous. The hybrid that the bureau furnishes is a short basque, with long trousers of the columnar order, and reaching to the ankle. An oil-skin cap and a pair of *spadrilles* complete the costume. The material of the dress is so flimsy that the skirt of the basque as soon as it touches the water lies up over the back, and remains there. The *costumes particuliers* have more rows of faded galloon, and are more lavishly ornamented with buttons; but neither of these tends to keeping down the basque skirt. Fancy, in the midst of these nondescript, uncouth forms, a pretty American girl in a blue blouse, short knickerbockers, and skirt reaching to the knee, a red sash bound around her waist, and her hair in a red turban. At first red stockings completed her costume; but as these were regarded from a moral rather than artistic stand-point, and her immodest modesty a matter of comment, she discarded them for Amelias.

For weeks before the season every one is begged, through the newspapers, not to go "*au bord de la mer sans Amelia.*" The advertisement is effective. Every one takes not only Amelia, but Amelias—linen gaiters, the fronts cut out, and lacing across the foot to the ankle. These, except the peignoir, are the only attractive part of the French costume. The peignoir is not obligatory, as at many French places; but it should be, since it is capable of graceful draping, and conceals the uncouth objects beneath until the water kindly hides them.

The arrangements for safety and comfort of bathers are perfect. In front of each division is a life-boat manned by a sailor. Steps hang from the stern into the water. The boat is the goal of the swimmers, who cumber the steps, and dripping creatures fringe its edges. The red-shirted baigneurs, burned to bronze, take each one in turn, and give a lesson in swimming, handling deftly the French matron, who overflows, so to speak, in a bathing costume, and is as shapeless as a porpoise. The baigneurs have histories and pedigrees and reputations which make them specially desirable, like famous guides in the Alps or on the plains. Women become hysterical in the water, and

FLOATING.

rend the air with shrill cries. It is the baigneur who looks after their nerves, and discovers the insidious chill. He takes you by the shoulder and pushes you toward shore. Halting on the brink, he seizes a wooden pail of water and dashes it violently on the back several times, for there is not enough surf at Trouville to produce sufficient reaction. Wrapped in peignoir, the bather runs to the cabin, where the hot foot-bath is waiting to send the blood like a race-horse through the veins. One leaves the cabin with renewed sense of the joy of existence. But while the bathing is thus agreeable and salutary, nowhere is it more devoid of piquant interest.

The gregariousness of Trouville breaks out three times a day. By ten o'clock everybody is abroad, wending his way through the Rue de Paris, where eccentric costumes in the windows, Norman jewelry, bric-à-brac shops newly stocked from Paris, but to be regarded as freshly gleaned from Calvados, and the toothsome *pâtisserie* beguile the eye. The sand of the beach beyond the tide, which twice a day reduces it to submission, riots high and dry to the garden walls. Bridging this impassable gulf is a wide deal walk extending from the pier to the *roches noires*. This from ten to twelve is the grand promenade. This walk is the arena of Trouville. Here its most athletic sport takes place—the promenade in tight shoes and high heels. No other nation can so walk with lightness, elegance, and grace in tight shoes.

But brilliant and exhilarating as is the pageant, the promenade belongs to the individual. The unwritten laws of Trouville are so strictly defined that they allow the largest license. If this is paradoxical, it is because France to an Anglo-Saxon is a paradox. Paris is France, and Trouville a sublimated Paris. Here one

THE PROMENADE.

realizes the elasticity of good taste. The boundaries are removed out of sight. The *toilettes inédites*—to use the suggestive French phrase—that flutter through the crowd embody many a daring caprice; but while they attract, they never offend. Dandies in white flannel *à l'anglais* wind their way through the crowd to discover a face beneath a bewildering parasol, and women hasten their steps to catch the tantalizing secret of a bit of drapery. The men do not dress well, even when they try, but the cheerful wave of the long ends of their polka-dotted cravats, and expressions of lively good-nature, make them more interesting than the stout English yachtsmen, immaculately clad, who mingle in the crowd. To one who knows the composition of this animated brilliant procession it has a keener interest. Trouville is common ground. Dan-

dies, princesses, men of letters, actresses, journalists—all that floating populace lying so lightly on the surface of Parisian life is to be found here. The provinces, and the opulent trades-people of the cities, swell the crowd ; and now an English matron and her brood go by to recall the fact that life is real, life is earnest.

By twelve o'clock the sandy plain lies deserted. Eleven o'clock is the breakfast hour as officially announced. The mechanical accuracy with which the butcher cuts the meat according to the cloth induces promptness at table. Moreover, one's love of order hesitates to disturb the symmetry of *table d'hôte* by eating with a spoon when the *entrées* are served. It is amusing to see people who come late make up time, impelled by a consciousness they have not analyzed, and restrained only by the difficulty of extricating

François or Alphonse from the routine in which he is involved.

The beach on a fine sunny afternoon at low tide is one of the most charming and characteristic scenes of Trouville. It lies like a vast plain diversified by shining pools and slender rills. The sand dries quickly, and soon the most aristocratic boot can tread it fearlessly. The low levels become croquet grounds, occupied by many groups. Athletics are not cultivated at Trouville, but nothing could be less athletic than croquet as played on the *plage*. The fashionable costumes of the promenade are not constructed to allow for free movement of the arms. Even the men, whose hands are carefully gloved, hold their mallets in both hands, and distribute the motion as carefully as possible, lest it prove too violent.

Amateur shrimpers saunter gayly along, with trousers rolled above the knee, and nets picturesquely swung. Toward the water's edge groups wander, dropping sous into the palm of the fisher-boy who has bridged the little streams. Afar the lithe form of some swimmer skims like a Greek runner across the sandy plain, and plunges into the surf. It is the happy hour of children and dogs. The dogs at Trouville are among the pleasantest acquaintances one meets.

At four o'clock the scene is at its height. From under the picturesque tent on the esplanade of the Casino the strains of music float, and surging about it is the gay, vivacious, well-dressed crowd. One feels that sense of the elegant enjoyment of the pleasures of life which is so characteristic of the French, and which

AMATEUR SHRIMPERS.

we vainly strive to catch. Although the Casino is the centre of life, Trouville is too heterogeneous to make it the background of society. There is more freemasonry among the children. Between eight and nine is the daily *bal d'enfant*. It is not as pretty a term as our "children's hour," but is a much more simple and child-like hour of diversion. The children are not the gay little butterflies as to toilet that one sees in our great summer hotels. Many still wear the blue skirts and jerseys in which they have played all day in the sand, and dance in their rubber-soled shoes. But all the forms are observed. The differentiation begins early. The boy babies are led up to the girl babies, and that fine flower of drawing-room manner which comes to such perfection in France gets its first favoring start. It is charming to see with these first tender efforts at gallantry such unconsciousness, such freedom from affectation. In boys of eight and nine this protecting ball-room regard is almost a travesty of their maturer years, they dance much better than their elders, having the advantage of modern training, which even in France has been profoundly influenced by a nation now recognized as producing the best drawing-room dancers in the world, but which it would be more modest not to name.

Across the corridor in the reading-room is a long table. In the centre is a dial, with needles like a compass; on the baize is a diagram laid off into small sections, in which are pictures of different animals. It is a game called the mascotte, an aristocratic form of roulette. On the pictures lie shining gold pieces. The ball is surging about the table. Mademoiselle Rouge et Noir, who has just come in, elbows Mademoiselle Haute Noblesse. The game is at its height. We have touched the pulse of Trouville. The gaming is the only vital thing.

It is of the most trivial sort, for the world is not admitted to those inner rooms sacred to the *cercle* where baccarat and higher games of cards are played. The Salle des Petits Jeux, where chances only are sold, is the only sort of gaming permissible in France. But it is enough. The *Course à Salon*—the *petits chevaux* and the little *courriers*—hold a charm with which nothing else at Trouville can compete. The one verb which is conjugated most often throughout all its moods and tenses is *gagner*.

There is quiet about the table of the couriers. Scarcely a sound is heard but the "Nolez" of the starter, which is his own peculiar way of saying *roulez*. It is curious to look down the row of hands setting the men in place. It is Trouville in a glance. Here are the brawny hand of the comfortable tradesman, the long slender fingers of the man of leisure, the glove stretched on the pudgy hand of the fat bourgeois, the tender fingers of a child scarcely able to reach the little figure, the white bejewelled hand of a dandy, and the faultlessly gloved hand of the young woman who has come in alone, and oblivious of everything but her game. She is lucky, for the silver and gold pile up in front of her.

Around the *petits chevaux*, at the other end of the room, the crowd surges and the noise waxes loud and louder. The table is placed between two rows of raised seats

intended for the players. But the game has extended out beyond, and ranks deep in the crowd. The table is divided into concentric circles. In each of these a horse with mounted jockey runs. The horses are set in motion by a lever, and the speed is arranged by the distance of the circle from the centre. The chances are sold for one and two francs each on the horses, one horse always being reserved for the table. The horse stopping nearest the goal is the winner. As the speed slackens the excitement begins. The estimable mother of five children whom we meet often at *table d'hôte* rises in her seat with cries of delight or disappointment. Other doubtless estimable mothers and fathers also rise and express their various emotions. The last horse stops; the money is distributed. "Ah! Angèle has won twenty francs," our friend exclaims, with joy; and Angèle—a little lame fellow of nine—takes his money with a pleased blush, as if he had received a prize at Sunday-school. The game begins again. At twelve the room is closed, and as the hour approaches, the heat and noise wax fiercer. A second table is started. The eager crowd buy right and left from both tables. The chances are exhausted. Premiums are offered, bidding begins, and men and women buy, sell, and compete against one another with loud tones and excited gestures. The craze is at its height. We mount the highest rank of benches and look over the crowd. An English boy, with a female relative on each side of him, sits where we have seen him all evening. A pile of money is heaped before him; but he leans back in a half-dazed state, as if unconscious of what is going on about him. All ranks and conditions are in the heated, seething mass below us. There is but one level. This is, after all, the true democracy.

There is one noteworthy fact. There are scarcely any young girls at Trouville. It is the paradise of children, but there is no such equipment of youth and beauty as one finds at the White Sulphur Springs or at Newport. It takes much charm from the place, for there is nothing so beautiful as youth. But there is nothing one could do with young girls at Trouville, but to give them a daily dip in the salt-water, and then send them toward the hills well guarded, and safely mounted on donkeys, to come home tired and sigh for bed.

TABLE OF THE COURRIERS AT THE CASINO.

The excursions are many and delightful. Down the Villersville road, past the picturesque eerie in which Mr. Homer Martin, the painter, lives, is the old Criqueboeuf church, half hidden in ivy. A cordon of white umbrellas surrounds it, under each an artist helping to prepare the annual crop for the next Salon, where with great regularity it is to be found. Beyond is Pennepied and the old manor-house where Mr. W. J. Hennessy, the artist, has found an idyllic home. Beyond the village of Longues is the château of Bonneville, with its old ivy-wreathed ogives and historic dungeon, which long ago served the purposes of Robert the Devil, the father of William the Conqueror. It is a wise country that in early years invests in a hero. In Calvados Guillaume le Conquérant is a permanent source of revenue. We follow his trail with enthusiasm, which is never an economical gratification. Dives, the port from which William sailed, is now swept inland by the sands, and Cabourg taken its place. The road to Dives leads through Villers, a commercial town that has built a casino, perched among the rocks a number of ornate villas, and set up in recent years as a watering-place under the name of Villers-sur-Mer. From Villers to Houlgate the drive leads inland between magnificent châteaux, thatched cottages, and Normandy farm-yards, each vying with the other in picturesqueness.

It is but a short distance from Dives to Cabourg. We drive under arching elms, and would fancy we are in a New England village but that the streets are filled with the noisy followers of the races. The races, like a peripatetic circus, are on the road, and from Cabourg they are due at Trouville. They mark there the climax of the season. Properly they belong to Deauville, and are the legacy of its creator, the late Duc de Morny. In the Place du Morny stands the pedestal, with its inscription, which once held the statue of the founder and patron saint of Deauville. The republic has now deposed the statue; it is reposing somewhere, its sacred nose in the dust, waiting until some future *régime* shall reinstate it.

The town is built on the low land made by the tides across the River Touque from Trouville. The well-built basin pierces it, filled with its forest of masts. The railway station is there, and its manifest destiny is to be a manufacturing and commercial town. This Deauville does not admit. It is the summer resort of the most exclusive of the French aristocracy. There is a bridge near the station, but the short-cut is by the *bac* (the ferry), with its facetious rowers. Deauville seems to have been built all at once, and out of ham sandwiches, for these its alternate red and yellow blocks resemble. The villas are pretentious, but dull. That of the Duc de Morny is low, with classic columns, and adorned with busts. It might pass for some small sequestered library, but never for the abode of the gay pleasurer.

AT THE RACE-COURSE.

NATIVES.

The race-course is a low grassy plain, left to its own luxuriance, for the horses run on the turf. The *pesage* is like a vast pleasure-ground, with walks, trees, and ornamental buildings. The grand stand is on a slight elevation, and casts its shadow on the green slope below. But more beautiful than all is the picture in front of the gray cliffs beyond the Touque, and the Church of Our Lady of Victory piercing the summer sky.

The gay crowds gather. The scene in the *pesage* is charming. The slope below is dotted with brilliant groups; the grand dames hold court on the grass, and athwart them pass a priest and two young boys clinging to his hands. There are some eccentric toilets. Mimic yachts careen on the woollen waves of a gray dress. On a blue nuns' veiling a Noah's ark procession march around the over-skirt in lighter blue defined with gold. On another, cocks' heads embroidered in brilliant colors seem just ready to crow. But these are the exceptions, and freshness the rule.

A shout goes up. The eager horses are bounding to the start. The flag drops. They are off, weaving a ribbon of color about the course. Everybody is on his feet, and shrill shrieks rend the air. A gentleman near, who has vindicated his faith in Tabarka, rises to heights of exaltation and sinks into gulfs of despair at alternate intervals. He climbs on the rail and hangs to a slender support, and shouts "À la tête, Tabarka!" like a last confidential message. Tabarka goes promptly to the head. But the race is decided off, and his lip quivers with undisguised emotion. There is the usual hasty masculine dispersion to the book-makers. A curious anomaly is again presented. Women in America have not been unknown to buy pools, but it is usually done under the tutelage of the other sex. At Trouville they seemed to manage their own affairs. The wives of the followers of the stable bought, talked, and quarrelled in loud tones, presenting an unseemly spectacle.

But the crowds are not large. It is only the last and greatest disappointment of the season. The illustrated papers continue to rehearse its frequent scenes. But they have not taken place. Their pencils report them from force of habit only.

The red flag drops for the last time. The races are run. The yachts spread their sails, and float out of the basin and away. We find time to go to assist at the *quête* at Our Lady of Victory. The orchestra in the nave plays the *entr'acte* from *Traviata*, and a prima donna in the organ-loft sings Bruga's serenade off the key. The princesses and countesses take up the offerings. By all these tokens the gay season is over, the last diversions are reached. Lord Rivers and the Salvation Army arrive. We take the boat for Havre, and with a trembling effort, not wholly due to emotion, take our last look at the fair, foolish little town glowing in the distance.

TRANSCRIPTS FROM NATURE.

XV.—A DESOLATE COAST.

A LONG gray coast, where the green waves
  Roll ever with the self-same boom
  Of sorrow weary with its doom.
The storm-reared sea-birds from the caves
Flit like lost souls, with wailing cries,
Beneath the desolate gray skies.

At times the wild wind blows, and rain
Swirls down; then all is gray again.

XVI.—CULVERS AND CURLEWS AT DUSK.

The soft-aired gloaming, purple-hued,
  Throbs with the beat of winnowing wings,
  And with a wailing music rings;
The culvers speed to yonder wood,

Wing-weary, yet with eager flight.
Silence is now the name of night,

Save when a startled curlew's cry
Ruffles the hushed monotony.

XVII.—SUNRISE IN THE ANTARCTIC OCEAN.

Bleak, desolate, the twilight gray,
  The weary leaden-colored sea,
  The spectral icebergs silently
Strange voyaging. But, lo! the day
Leaps from the east with sudden might,
And all the sea is travelling light.

Each iceberg by the morning kissed
Turns ruby, emerald, amethyst.

A SEA-GARDEN.

Far down in the green depths I see below
The long sea-grasses waving to and fro
With sleepy motion, pliant to the tide
That stealthily steals shoreward from the wide
Deep sea beyond. Here silver-fishes gleam,
And vanish quite, or, stationary, seem
Poised like a cloudlet in a liquid sky,
And clear medusæ swim past silently,
Like ocean orchids, while, with motions strange,
Crabs hither and thither through the sea-weeds range.
A lithe brown eel winds in and out, scarce known
From twisting wrack, and like a wave-worn stone
The flat sole rests upon a patch of sand;
And on the weedy rocks, by no winds fanned,
But soothed by under-currents, red and white
The sea-flowers, the anemones, make bright
These songless groves, which only hear the sighs
Of tides at flow and ebb, or the sharp cries
Of wind-lashed waves when breaking, when a storm
Drives shoreward surging billows multiform,
Or the long moan reverberant from the sea
When dreaming of wrath past or yet to be.

FOREST SILENCE.

XVIII.—FOREST SILENCE.

There is a soft green darkness round,
  Wherein the noon sleeps hushed and still;
  Only a little hidden rill
Moves murmuring through mossy ground;
The doves are silent, and the bees
Hum here no more; the green-branched trees

Are moveless in the windless air,
And silence broodeth everywhere.

XIX.—SUNSET OFF MULL.

All heaven is aglow with flame,
  With bars of molten gold between,
  And narrow streaks of shining green
That long-drawn banks of purple frame.
Inland, a carmine glory dreams;
Seaward, a crimson splendor streams;

And pure and white in the flushed sky
Full Hesper throbs deliciously.

CHAPTER XXV.

AN APPEAL.

GREAT changes were in store. To begin with, there were rumors of her father being about to return to London. Then Dr. Hall was summoned away into Worcestershire by a great lady living there, who was continually fancying herself at the brink of death, and manifesting on such occasions a terror not at all in consonance with her professed assurance that she was going to a happier sphere. As it was possible that Dr. Hall would seize this opportunity to pay several other professional visits in the neighboring county, it was proposed that Susan and her daughter should come for a while to New Place, and that Judith should at the same time go and stay with her grandmother at Shottery, to cheer the old dame somewhat. And so it happened, on this July morning, that Judith's mother having gone round to see her elder daughter about all these arrangements, Judith found herself not only alone in the house, but, as rarely chanced, with nothing to do.

She tried to extract some music from her sister's lute, but that was a failure; she tried half a dozen other things; and then it occurred to her—for the morning was fine and clear, and she was fond of the meadows and of open air and sunlight —that she would walk round to the grammar school and beg for a half-holiday for Willie Hart. He, as well as Bess Hall, was under her tuition; and there were things she could teach him of quite as much value (as she considered) as anything to be learned at a desk. At the same time, before going to meet the staring eyes of all those boys, she thought she might as well repair to her own room and smarten up her attire—even to the extent, perhaps, of putting on her gray beaver hat with the row of brass beads.

That was not at all necessary. Nothing of the kind was needful to make Judith Shakespeare attractive and fascinating and wonderful to that crowd of lads. The fact was, the whole school of them were more or less secretly in love with her; and this, so far from procuring Willie Hart such bumps and thrashings as he might have received from a solitary rival, gained for him, on the contrary, a mysterious favor and good-will that showed itself in a hundred subtle ways. For he was in a measure the dispenser of Judith's patronage. When he was walking along the street with her he would tell her the name of this one or that of his companions (in case she had forgotten), and she would stop and speak to him kindly, and hope he was getting on well with his tasks. Also the other lads, on the strength of Willie Hart's intermediation, would now make bold to say, with great politeness, "Give ye good-morrow, Mistress Judith," when they met her, and sometimes she would pause for a moment and chat with one of them, and make some inquiries of him as to whether her cousin did not occasionally need a little help in his lessons from the bigger boys. Then there was a kind of fury of assistance instantly promised; and the youth would again remember his good manners, and bid her formally farewell, and go on his way, with his heart and his cheeks alike afire, and his brain gone a-dancing. Even that dread being, the head-master, had no frown for her when she went boldly up to his desk, in the very middle of the day's duties, to demand some favor. Nay, he would rather detain her with a little pleasant conversation, and would at times become almost facetious (at sight of which the spirits of the whole school rose into a seventh heaven of equanimity). And always she got what she wanted; and generally, before leaving, she would give one glance down the rows of oaken benches, singling out her friends here and there, and, alas! not thinking at all of the deadly wounds she was thus dealing with those lustrous and shining eyes.

Well, on this morning she had no difficulty in rescuing her cousin from the dull captivity of the school-room; and hand in hand they went along and down to the river-side and to the meadows there. But seemingly she had no wish to get much farther from the town; for the truth was that she lacked assurance as yet that Master Leofric Hope had left that neighborhood; and she was distinctly of a mind to avoid all further communications with him until, if ever, he should be able to come forward openly and declare himself to the small world in which she lived. Accordingly she did not lead Willie Hart far along the river-side path; they rather kept to seeking about the banks and hedge-rows for wild flowers— the pink and white bells of the bind-weed she was mostly after, and these did not abound there—until at last they came to a stile; and there she sat down, and would have her cousin sit beside her, so that she should give him some further schooling as to all that he was to do and think and be in the coming years. She had far other things than Lilly's Grammar to teach him. The Sententiæ Pueriles contained no instructions as to how, for example, a modest and well-conducted youth should approach his love-maiden to discover whether her heart was well inclined toward him. And although her timid-eyed pupil seemed to take but little interest in the fair creature that was thus being provided for him in the future, and was far more anxious to know how he was to win Judith's approval, either now or then, still he listened contentedly enough, for Judith's voice was soft and musical. Nay, he put that imaginary person out of his mind altogether. It was Judith, and Judith alone, whom he saw in these forecasts. Would he have any other supplant her in his dreams and visions of what was to be? This world around him—the smooth-flowing Avon, the wooded banks, the wide white skies, the meadows and fields and low-lying hills: was not she the very spirit and central life and light of all these? Without her, what would these be?—dead things; the mystery and wonder gone out of them; a world in darkness. But he could not think of that; the world he looked forward to was filled with light, for Judith was there, the touch of her hand as gentle as ever, her eyes still as kind.

"So must you be accomplished at all points, sweetheart," she was continuing, "that you shame her not in any company, whatever the kind of it may be. If they be grave, and speak of the affairs of the realm, then must you know how the country is governed, as becomes a man (though, being a woman, alack! I can not help you there), and you must have opinions about what is best for England, and be ready to uphold them, too. Then, if the company be of a gayer kind, again you shall not shame her, but take part in all the merriment; and if there be dancing, you shall not go to the door, and

hang about like a booby; you must know the new dances, every one; for would you have your sweetheart dance with others, and you standing by? That were a spite, I take it, for both of you!—nay, would not the wench be angry to be so used? Let me see, now—what is the name of it? —the one that is danced to the tune of 'The Merchant's Daughter went over the Field'?—have I shown you that, sweetheart?"

"I know not, Cousin Judith," said he.

"Come, then," said she, blithely; and she took him by the hand and placed him opposite her in the meadow. "Look you, now, the four at the top cross hands —so (you must imagine the other two, sweetheart); and all go round once—so; and then they change hands, and go back the other way—so; and then each takes his own partner, and away they go round the circle, and back to their place. Is it not simple, cousin? Come, now, let us try properly."

And so they began again; and for music she lightly hummed a verse of a song that was commonly sung to the same tune:

> Maid, will you love me, yes or no?
> Tell me the truth, and let me go.

"The other hand, Willie—quick!"

> It can be no less than a sinful deed
> (Trust me truly)
> To linger a lover that looks to speed
> (In due time duly).

"Why, is it not simple!" she said, laughing. "But, now, instead of crossing hands, I think it far the prettier way that they should hold their hands up together—so: shall we try it, sweetheart?"

And then she had to sing another verse of the ballad:

> Consider, sweet, what sighs and sobs
> Do nip my heart with cruel throbs,
> And all, my dear, for the love of you
> (Trust me truly);
> But I hope that you will some mercy show
> (In due time duly).

"And then," she continued, when they had finished that laughing rehearsal, "should the fiddles begin to squeal and screech—which is as much as to say, 'Now, all of you, kiss your partners!'— then shall you not bounce forward and seize the wench by the neck, as if you were a ploughboy besotted with ale, and have her hate thee for destroying her head-gear and her hair. No, you shall come forward in this manner, as if to do her great courtesy, and you shall take her hand and bend one knee—and make partly a jest of it, but not altogether a jest—and then you shall kiss her hand, and rise and retire. Think you the maiden will not be proud that you have shown her so much honor and respect in public? —ay, and when she and you are thereafter together, by yourselves, I doubt not but that she may be willing to make up to you for your forbearance and courteous treatment of her. Marry, with that I have naught to do; 'tis as the heart of the wench may happen to be inclined; though you may trust me she will be well content that you show her other than alehouse manners; and if 'tis but a matter of a kiss that you forego, because you would pay her courtesy in public, why, then, as I say, she may make that up to thee, or she is no woman else. I wonder, now, what the Bonnybel will be like—or tall, or dark, or fair—"

"I wish never to see her, Judith," said he, simply.

However, there was to be no further discussion of this matter, nor yet greensward rehearsals of dancing; for they now descried coming to them the little maid who waited on Judith's grandmother. She seemed in a hurry, and had a basket over her arm.

"How now, little Cicely?" Judith said, as she drew near.

"I have sought you everywhere, so please you, Mistress Judith," the little maid said, breathlessly, "for I was coming in to the town—on some errands—and —and I met the stranger gentleman that came once or twice to the house—and— and he would have me carry a message to you—"

"Prithee, good lass," said Judith, instantly, and with much composure, "go thy way back home. I wish for no message."

"He seemed in sore distress," the little maid said, diffidently.

"How, then? Did a gentleman of his tall inches seek help from such a mite as thou?"

"He would fain see you, sweet mistress, and but for a moment," the girl answered, being evidently desirous of getting the burden of the message off her mind. "He bid me say he would be in the lane going to Bidford, or thereabout, for the next hour or two, and would crave a word with you—out of charity, the gen-

tleman said, or something of the like— and that it might be the last chance of seeing you ere he goes, and that I was to give his message to you very secretly."

Well, she scarcely knew what to do. At their last interview he had pleaded for another opportunity of saying farewell to her, and she had not definitely refused; but, on the other hand, she would much rather have seen nothing further of him in these present circumstances. His half-reckless references to Prince Ferdinand undergoing any kind of hardship for the sake of winning the fair Miranda were of a dangerous cast. She did not wish to meet him on that ground at all, even to have her suspicions removed. But if he were really in distress? And this his last day in the neighborhood? It seemed a small matter to grant.

"What say you, Cousin Willie?" said she, good-naturedly. "Shall we go and see what the gentleman would have of us? I can not, unless with thee as my shield and champion."

"If you wish it, Cousin Judith," said he: what would he not do that she wished?

"And Cicely—shall we all go?"

"Nay, so please you, Mistress Judith," the girl said; "I have to go back for my errands. I have been running everywhere to seek you."

"Then, Willie, come along," said she, lightly. "We must get across the fields to the Evesham road."

And so the apple-cheeked little maiden trudged back to the town with her basket, while Judith and her companion went on their way across the meadows. There was a kind of good-humored indifference in her consent, though she felt anxious that the interview should be as brief as possible. She had had more time of late to think over all the events that had recently happened—startling events enough in so quiet and even a life; and occasionally she bethought her of the wizard, and of the odd coincidence of her meeting this young gentleman at the very spot that had been named. She had tried to laugh aside certain recurrent doubts and surmises, and was only partially successful. And she had a vivid recollection of the relief she had experienced when their last interview came to an end.

"You must gather me some flowers, sweetheart," said she, while I am speaking to this gentleman; perchance he may have something to say of his own private affairs."

"I will go on to your grandmother's garden," said he, "if you wish it, Cousin Judith, and get you the flowers there."

"Indeed, no," she answered, patting him on the shoulder. "Would you leave me without my champion? Nay, but if you stand aside a little, that the gentleman may speak in confidence, if that be his pleasure, surely that will be enough."

They had scarcely entered the lane when he made his appearance, and the moment she set eyes on him she saw that something had happened. His face seemed haggard and anxious—nay, his very manner was changed: where was the elaborate courtesy with which he had been wont to approach her?

"Judith," said he, hurriedly, "I must risk all now. I must speak plain. I—I scarce hoped you would give me the chance."

But she was in no alarm.

"Now, sweetheart," said she, calmly, to the little lad, "you may get me the flowers; and if you find any more of the bind-weed bells and the St. John's wort, so much the better."

Then she turned to Master Leofric Hope.

"I trust you have had no ill news," said she, but in a kind way.

"Indeed, I have. Well, I know not which way to take it," he said, in a sort of desperate fashion. "It might be good news. But I am hard pressed; 'twill be sink or swim with me presently. Well, there is one way of safety open to me: 'tis for you to say whether I shall take it or not."

"I, sir?" she said; and she was so startled that she almost recoiled a step.

"Nay, but first I must make a confession," said he, quickly, "whatever comes of it. Think of me what you will, I will tell you the truth. Shall I beg for your forgiveness beforehand?"

He was regarding her earnestly and anxiously, and there was nothing but kindness and a dim expression of concern in the honest, frank face and in the beautiful eyes.

"No, I will not," he said. "Doubtless you will be angry, and with just cause; and you will go away. Well, this is the truth. The devils of usurers were after me; I had some friends not far from here; I escaped to them; and they sought out

this hiding for me. Then I had heard of you—you will not forgive me, but this is the truth—I had heard of your beauty; and Satan himself put it into my head that I must see you. I thought it would be a pastime, to while away this cursed hiding, if I could get to know you without discovering myself. I sent you a message. I was myself the wizard. Heaven is my witness that when I saw you at the corner of the field up there, and heard you speak, and looked on your gracious and gentle ways, remorse went to my heart; but how could I forego seeking to see you again? It was a stupid jest. It was begun in thoughtlessness; but now the truth is before you: I was myself the wizard; and—and my name is not Leofric Hope, but John Orridge—a worthless poor devil that is ashamed to stand before you."

Well, the color had mounted to her face; for she saw clearly the invidious position that this confession had placed her in; but she was far less startled than he had expected. She had already regarded this trick as a possible thing, and she had also fully considered what she ought to do in such circumstances. Now, when the circumstances were actually laid before her, she made no display of wounded pride, or of indignant anger, or anything of the kind.

"I pray you," said she, with a perfect and simple dignity, "pass from that. I had no such firm belief in the wizard's prophecies. I took you as you represented yourself to be, a stranger, met by chance, one who was known to my father's friends, and who was in misfortune; and if I have done aught beyond what I should have done in such a pass, I trust you will put it down to our country manners, that are perchance less guarded than those of the town."

For an instant—there was not the slightest doubt of it—actual tears stood in the young man's eyes.

"By heavens," he exclaimed, "I think you must be the noblest creature God ever made! You do not drive me away in scorn; you have no reproaches? And I—to be standing here—telling you such a tale—"

"I pray you, sir, pass from that," said she. "What of your own fortunes? You are quitting the neighborhood?"

"But how can you believe me in anything, since you know how I have deceived you?" said he, as if he could not understand how she should make no sign of her displeasure.

"'Twas but a jest, as you say," she answered, good-naturedly, but still with a trifle of reserve. "And no harm has come of it. I would leave it aside, good sir."

"Harm?" said he, regarding her with a kind of anxious timidity. "That may or may not be, sweet lady, as time will show. If I dared but speak to you—well, bethink you of my meeting you here from day to day, in these quiet retreats, and seeing such a sweetness and beauty and womanliness as I have never met in the world before—such a wonder of gentleness and kindness—"

"I would ask you to spare me these compliments," said she, simply. "I thought 'twas some serious matter you had in hand."

"Serious enough, i' faith!" he said, in an altered tone, as if she had recalled him to a sense of the position in which he stood. "But there is the one way out of it, after all. I can sell my life away for money to pacify those fiends; nay, besides that, I should live in abundance, doubtless, and be esteemed a most fortunate gentleman, and one to be envied. A gilded prison-house and slavery; but what would the fools think of that if they saw me with a good fat purse at the tavern?"

Again he regarded her.

"There is another way yet, however, if I must needs trouble you, dear Mistress Judith, with my poor affairs. What if I were to break with that accursed London altogether, and go off and fight my way in another country, as many a better man hath done? ay, and there be still one or two left who would help me to escape if they saw me on the way to reform, as they would call it. And what would I not do in that way—ay, or in any way—if I could hope for a certain prize to be won at the end of it all?"

"And that, good sir?"

"That," said he, watching her face— "the reward that would be enough and more than enough for all I might suffer would be just this—to find Judith Shakespeare coming to meet me in this very lane."

"Oh, no, sir," was her immediate and incoherent exclamation; and then she promptly pulled herself together, and said, with some touch of pride: "Indeed, good sir, you talk wildly. I scarce understand how you can be in such grave trouble."

"Then," said he, and he was rather pale, and spoke slowly, "it would be no manner of use for any poor Ferdinand of these our own days to go bearing logs or suffering any hardships that might arise? There would be no Miranda waiting for him, after all?"

She colored deeply; she could not affect to misunderstand the repeated allusion; and all she had in her mind now was to leave him and get away from him, and yet without unkindness or anger.

"Good sir," said she, with such equanimity as she could muster, "if that be your meaning—if that be why you wished to see me again—and no mere continuance of an idle jest, plain speech will best serve our turn. I trust no graver matters occupy your mind; as for this, you must put that away. It was with no thought of any such thing that I—that I met you once or twice, and—and lent you such reading as might pass the time for you. And perchance I was too free in that, and in my craving to hear of my father and his friends in London, and the rest. But what you say now, if I understand you aright—well, I had no thought of any such thing. Indeed, good sir, if I have done wrong in listening to you about my father's friends, 'twas in the hope that soon or late you would continue the tale in my father's house. But now—what you say—bids me to leave you—and yet in no anger—for in truth I wish you well."

She gave him her hand, and he held it for a moment.

"Is this your last word, Judith?" said he.

"Yes, yes, indeed," she answered, rather breathlessly and earnestly. "I may not see you again. I pray Heaven your troubles may soon be over; and perchance you may meet my father in London, and become one of his friends; then might I hear of your better fortunes. 'Twould be welcome news, believe me. And now fare you well."

He stooped to touch her hand with his lips; but he said not a word; and she turned away without raising her eyes. He stood there, motionless and silent, watching her and the little boy as they walked along the lane toward the village —regarding them in an absent kind of way, and yet with no great expression of sadness or hopelessness in his face. Then he turned and made for the highway to

Bidford; and he was saying to himself as he went along:

"Well, there goes one chance in life, for good or ill. And what if I had been more persistent? What if she had consented, or even half consented, or said that in the future I might come back with some small modicum of hope? Nay: the devil only knows where I should get logs to carry for the winning of so fair a reward. Frank Lloyd is right. My case is too desperate. So fare you well, sweet maiden; keep you to your quiet meadows and your wooded lanes: and the clown that will marry you will give you a happier life than ever you could have had with Jack Orridge and his broken fortunes."

Indeed, he seemed in no downcast mood. As he walked along the highway he was absently watching the people in the distant fields, or idly whistling the tune of "Calen o Custure me." But by-and-by, as he drew near the farm, his face assumed a more sombre look; and when, coming still nearer, he saw Frank Lloyd calmly standing at the door of the stables, smoking his pipe, there was a sullen frown on his forehead that did not promise well for the cheerfulness of that journey to London which Master Lloyd had sworn he would not undertake until his friend was ready to accompany him.

CHAPTER XXVI.

TO LONDON TOWN.

But that was not the departure for London which was soon to bring Judith a great heaviness of heart, and cause many a bitter fit of crying when that she was lying awake o' nights. She would rather have let all her lovers go, and welcome, a hundred times over. But, as the days passed, it became more and more evident, from certain preparations, that her father was about to leave Stratford for the south, and finally the very moment was fixed. Judith strove to keep a merry face (for so she had been bid), but again and again she was on the point of going to him and falling on her knees and begging him to remain with them. She knew that he would laugh at her; but did he quite know what going away from them meant? And the use of it? Had they not abundance? Still, she was afraid of being chid for meddling in matters beyond her; and so she went about her duties with as much cheerfulness as she could assume; though, when in secret conclave with Prudence, and talking of this, and what the house would be like when he was gone, quiet tears would steal down her face in the dusk.

To suit the convenience of one or two neighbors, who were also going to London, the day of departure had been postponed; but at last the fatal morning arrived. Judith, from an early hour, was on the watch, trying to get some opportunity of saying good-by to her father by herself (and not before all the strangers who would soon be gathering together), but always she was defeated, for he was busy in-doors with many things, and every one was lending a helping hand. Moreover, she was in an excited and trembling state; and more than once she had to steal away to her chamber and bathe her eyes with water lest that they should tell any tale when he regarded her. But the climax of her misfortunes was this. When the hour for leaving was drawing nigh she heard him go out and into the garden, doubtless with the intention of locking up the cupboard in the summer-house; and so she presently and swiftly stole out after him, thinking that now would be her chance. Alas! the instant she had passed through the back-court door she saw that Matthew gardener had forestalled her; and not only that, but he had brought a visitor with him—the master constable, Grandfather Jeremy, whom she knew well. Anger filled her heart; but there was no time to stand on her dignity. She would not retire from the field. She walked forward boldly, and stood by her father's side, as much as to say: "Well, this is my place. What do you want? Why this intrusion at such a time?"

Grandfather Jeremy was a little, thin, round-shouldered ancient, with long, straggling gray hair, and small, shrewd, ferret-like eyes that kept nervously glancing from Judith's father to goodman Matthew, who had obviously introduced him on this occasion. Indeed, the saturnine visage of the gardener was overspread with a complacent grin, as though he were saying, "Look you there, zur, there be a rare vool." Judith's father, on the other hand, showed no impatience over this interruption; he kept waiting for the old man to recover his power of speech.

"Well, now, master constable, what would you?" he said, gently.

"Why can't 'ee tell his worship, Jeremy?" Matthew gardener said, in his superior and facetious fashion. "Passion o' me, man, thy tongue will wag fast enough at Mother Tooley's ale-house."

"It wur a contrevarsie, so please your worship," the ancient constable said, but with a kind of vacant stare, as if he were half lost in looking back into his memory.

"Ay, and with whom?" said Judith's father, to help him along.

"With my poor old woman, so please your worship. She be a poor, mean creature in your honor's eyes, I make no doubt; but she hath wisdom, she hath, and a strength in contrevarsie past most. Lord, Lord, why be I standing here now—and holding your worship—and your worship's time and necessities—but that she saith, 'Jeremy, put thy better leg avore;' 'speak out,' saith she; ''twur as good for thee as a half-ox in a pie, or a score of angels in thy pouch.' 'Speak out,' she saith, 'and be not afraid, Jeremy.'"

"But, master constable," said Judith's father, "if your good dame be such a Mary Ambree in argument, she should have furnished you with fewer words and more matter. What would you?"

"Nay, zur, I be as bold as most," said the constable, pulling up his courage, and also elevating his head somewhat with an air of authority. "I can raise hue and cry in the hundred, that can I; and if the watch bring me a rogue, he shall lie by the heels, or I am no true man. But Lord, zur, have pity on a poor man that be put forward to speak for a disputation. When they wur talking of it at furst, your worship—this one and the other, and all of them to once—and would have me go forward to speak for them, 'Zure,' says I, 'I would as lief go to a bride-ale with my legs swaddled in wisps as go avore Mahster Shaksper without a power o' voine words.' But Joan, she saith, 'Jeremy, fear no man, howsoever great, for there be but the one Lord over us all; perzent thyself like a true countryman and an honest officer; take thy courage with thee,' saith she; 'and remember thou speakest vor thy friends as well as vor thyself. 'Tis a right good worshipful gentleman,' she saith, meaning yourself, sweet Mahster Shaksper; 'and will a not give us a share?'"

"In Heaven's name, man," said Judith's father, laughing, "what would you? Had Joan no clearer message to give you?"

"I but speak her words, so please your worship," said the ancient constable, with the air of one desperately trying to recall a lesson that had been taught him. "And all of them—they wur zaying as how she hath a power o' wisdom—and, 'Jeremy,' she saith, 'be not overbold with the worthy gentleman; 'tis but a share; and he be a right worthy and civil gentleman; speak him fair, Jeremy,' she saith, 'and put thy better leg avore, and acquit thee as a man. Nay, be bold,' she saith, 'and think of thy vriends, that be waiting without for an answer. Think of them, Jeremy,' she saith, 'if thy speech fail thee. 'Tis but a share; 'tis but a share; and he a right worshipful and civil gentleman.'"

Judith's father glanced at the sun-dial on the gable of the barn.

"My good friend," said he, "I hear that your wife Joan is ailing; 'tis through no lack of breath, I warrant me. An you come not to the point forthwith, I must be gone. What would you? Or what would your good dame have of me?—for there we shall get to it more quickly."

"So please you, zur," said Matthew, with his complacent grin, "the matter be like this, now: this worthy master constable and his comrades of the watch, they wur laying their heads together like; and they have heard say that you have written of them, and taken of their wisdom the couple o' nights they wur brought in to supper; and they see as how you have grown rich, so please you, zur, with such writing—"

"A vast o' money—a vast o' money and lands," the other murmured.

"And now, zur, they would make bold to ask for their share, for the help that they have given you. Nay, zur," continued Matthew gardener, who was proud of the ease with which he could put into words the inarticulate desires of this good constable, "be not angry with worthy Jeremy; he but speaketh for the others, and for his wife Joan too, that be as full of courage as any of them, and would have come to your worship but that she be sore troubled with an ague. Lord, zur, I know not how much the worthy gentlemen want. Perchance good Jeremy would be content wi' the barn and the store of malt in the malt-house—"

At this the small deep eyes of the ancient began to twinkle nervously; and he glanced in an anxious way from one to the other.

"And the watch, now," continued Matthew, grinning, and regarding the old constable: "why, zur, they be poor men; 'twould go well with them to divide amongst them the store of good wine in the cellar, and perchance also the leather hangings that be so much talked of in the town. But hark you, good Jeremy, remember this, now—that whoever hath the garden and orchard fall to his lot must pay me my wages, else 'tis no bargain."

For the first time in her life Judith saw her father in a passion of anger. His color did not change; but there was a strange look about his mouth, and his eyes blazed.

"Thou cursed fool," he said to the gardener, "'tis thou hast led these poor men into this folly." And then he turned to the bewildered constable, and took him by the arm. "Come, good friend," said he, in a kindly way, "come into the house and I will explain these matters to thee. Thou hast been misled by that impudent knave—by my life, I will settle that score with him ere long; and in truth the aid that you and your comrades have given me is chiefly that we have passed a pleasant evening or two together, and been merry or wise as occasion offered. And I would have you spend such another to-night among yourselves, leaving the charges at the ale-house to me; and for the present, if I may not divide my store of wine among you, 'tis no reason why you and I should not have a parting cup ere I put hand to bridle—"

That was all that Judith heard; and then she turned to the ancient wise man and said, coolly,

"Were I in thy place, good Matthew, I would get me out of this garden, and out of Stratford town too, ere my father come back." And Matthew was too frightened to answer her.

The outcome of all this, however, was that Judith's father did not return to the garden; and when she went into the house she found that he had taken such time to explain to Jeremy constable how small a share in his writings had been contributed by these good people that certain of the members of the expedition bound for London had already arrived. Indeed, their horses and attendants were at the door; and all and everything was in such a state of confusion and uproar that Judith saw clearly she had no chance of saying a quiet good-by to her father all by herself. But was she to be again balked by goodman Matthew? She thought not. She slipped away by the back door and disappeared.

There was quite a little crowd gathered to see the cavalcade move off. Dr. Hall was not there, but Tom Quiney was— bringing with him as a parting gift for Judith's father a handsome riding-whip; and the worthy Parson Blaise had also appeared, though there was no opportunity for his professional services amid so much bustle. And then there were handshakings and kissings and farewells; and Judith's father was just about to put his foot in the stirrup, when Susanna called out:

"But where is Judith? Is she not coming to say good-by to my father?"

Then there were calls for Judith, here, there, and everywhere, but no answer; and her mother was angry that the girl should detain all this assemblage. But her father, not having mounted, went rapidly through the house, and just opened the door leading into the garden. The briefest glance showed him that the mastiff was gone. Then he hurried back.

"'Tis all well, good mother," said he, as he got into the saddle. "I shall see the wench ere I go far. I know her tricks."

So the company moved away from the house, and through the streets, and down to Clopton's bridge. Once over the bridge, they struck to the right, taking the Oxford road by Shipston and Enstone; and ere they had gone far along the highway, Judith's father, who seemed less to join in the general hilarity and high spirits of the setting out than to be keeping a watch around, perceived something in the distance—at a corner where there was a high bank behind some trees—that caused him to laugh slightly, and to himself. When they were come near this corner the figure that had been on the sky-line had disappeared; but down by the road-side was Judith herself, looking very tremulous and ashamed as all these people came along, and the great Don standing by her. Her father, who had some knowledge of her ways, bade them all ride on, and then he turned his horse, and sprang down from the saddle.

"Well, wench," said he, and he took her by the shoulders, "what brings you here?"

In answer she could only burst into tears, and hide her face in his breast.

"Why, lass," said he, "what is a journey to London? And have you not enough left to comfort you? Have you not sweethearts a plenty?"

But she could not speak; she only sobbed and sobbed.

"Come, come, lass, I must be going," said he, stroking the soft brown hair. "Cheer up. Wouldst thou spoil the prettiest eyes in Warwickshire? Nay, an thou have not a right merry and beaming face when I am come again, I will call thee no daughter of mine."

Then she raised her head—for still she could not speak—and he kissed her.

"Heaven's blessings on thee, good wench! I think 'tis the last time I shall ever have the courage to leave thee. Fare you well, sweetheart; keep your eyes bright and your face happy—to draw me home again."

Then she kissed him on each cheek, and he got into the saddle and rode on. She climbed up to the top of the bank, and watched him and his companions while they were still in sight, and then she turned to go slowly homeward.

And it seemed to her, when she came in view of Stratford, and looked down on the wide meadows and the placid river and the silent homesteads, that a sort of winter had already fallen over the land. That long summer had been very beautiful to her—full of sunlight and color and the scent of flowers; but now a kind of winter was come, and a sadness and loneliness; and the days and days that would follow each other seemed to have no longer any life in them.

CHAPTER XXVII.
EVIL TIDINGS.

But a far sharper winter than any she had thought of was now about to come upon her, and this was how it befell:

After the departure of her father, good Master Walter Blaise became more and more the guide and counsellor of these women-folk; and indeed New Place was now given over to meetings for prayer and worship, and was also become the head-quarters in the town for the entertainment of travelling preachers, and for the institution of all kinds of pious and chari-table undertakings. There was little else for the occupants of it to do: the head of the house was in London; Judith was at Shottery with her grandmother; Susanna was relieved from much of her own domestic cares by the absence of her husband in Worcestershire; and the bailiff looked after all matters pertaining to the farm. Indeed, so constant were these informal services and ministerings to pious travellers that Julius Shawe (though not himself much given in that direction, and perhaps mostly to please his sister) felt bound to interfere and offer to open his house on occasion, or pay part of the charges incurred through this kindly hospitality. Nay, he went privately to Master Blaise and threw out some vague hints as to the doubtful propriety of allowing a wife, in the absence of her husband, to be so ready with her charity. Now Master Blaise was an honest and straightforward man, and he met this charge boldly and openly. He begged of Master Shawe to come to New Place that very afternoon, when two or three of the neighbors were to assemble to hear him lecture; and both Prudence and her brother went. But before the lecture, the parson observed that he had had a case of conscience put before him—as to the giving of alms and charity, by whom, for whom, and on whose authority—which he would not himself decide. The whole matter, he observed, had been pronounced upon in the holiday lectures of that famous divine Master William Perkins, who was now gone to his eternal reward; these lectures having recently been given to the world by the aid of one Thomas Pickering, of Emmanuel College, Cambridge. And very soon it appeared, as the young parson read from the little parchment-covered book, that the passages he quoted had been carefully chosen and were singularly pertinent. For after a discourse on the duty of alms-giving, as enjoined by Scripture (and it was pointed out that Christ himself had lived on alms—"not by begging, as the Papists affirm, but by the voluntary ministration and contribution of some to whom he preached"), Master Blaise read on, with an occasional glance at Julius Shawe: "'It may be asked whether the wife may give alms without the consent of her husband, considering that she is in subjection to another, and therefore all that she hath is another's, and not her own. *Answer.* The wife may give alms of some things, but with these cautions: as, first, she may give of those goods that she hath excepted from marriage. Secondly, she may give of those things which are common to them both, provided it be with the husband's consent, at least general and implicit. Thirdly, she may not give without or against the consent of her husband. And the reason is, because both the law of nature and the word of God command her obedience to her husband in all things. If it be alleged that Joanna, the wife of Chuza, Herod's steward, with others, did minister to Christ of their goods (Luke, viii. 3), I answer: It is to be presumed that it was not done without all consent. Again, if it be said that Abigail brought a present to David for the relief of him and his young men, whereof she made not Nabal, her husband, acquainted (1 Sam., xxv. 19), I answer, it is true, but mark the reason. Nabal was generally of a churlish and unmerciful disposition, whereupon he was altogether unwilling to yield relief to any, in how great necessity soever; whence it was that he railed on the young men that came to him, and drove them away, ver. 14. Again, he was a foolish man, and given to drunkenness, so as he was not fit to govern his house or to dispense his alms. Besides, that Abigail was a woman of great wisdom in all her actions, and that which she now did was to save Nabal's and her own life—yea, the lives of his whole family; for the case was desperate, and all that they had were in present hazard. The example, therefore, is no warrant for any woman to give alms, unless it be in the like case.' " And then he summed up in a few words, saying, in effect, that as regards the question which had been put before him, it was for the wife to say whether she had her husband's general and implied consent to her pious expenditure, and to rule her accordingly.

This completely and forever shut Julius Shawe's mouth. For he knew, and they all knew, that Judith's father was well content that any preachers or divines coming to the house should be generously received; while he on his part claimed a like privilege in the entertainment of any vagrant person or persons (especially if they were making a shift to live by their wits) whom he might chance to meet. Strict economy in all other things was the rule of the household; in the matter of hospitality the limits were wide. And if Judith's mother half guessed, and if Su-

sanna Hall shrewdly perceived, why this topic had been introduced, and why Julius Shawe had been asked to attend the lecture, the subject was one that brought no sting to their conscience. If the whole question rested on the general and implied consent of the husband, Judith's mother had naught to tax herself with.

After that there was no further remonstrance (of however gentle and underhand a kind) on the part of Julius Shawe; and more and more did Parson Blaise become the guide, instructor, and mainstay of the household. They were women-folk, some of them timid, all of them pious, and they experienced a sense of comfort and safety in submitting to his spiritual domination. As for his disinterestedness, there could be no doubt of that; for now Judith was away at Shottery, and he could no longer pay court to her in that authoritative fashion of his. It seemed as if he were quite content to be with these others, bringing them the news of the day, especially as regarded the religious dissensions that were everywhere abroad, arranging for the welcoming of this or that faithful teacher on his way through the country, getting up meetings for prayer and profitable discourse in the afternoon, or sitting quietly with them in the evening while they went on with their tasks of dressmaking or embroidery.

And so it came about that Master Walter was in the house one morning—they were seated at dinner, indeed, and Prudence was also of the company—when a letter was brought in and handed to Judith's mother. It was an unusual thing; and all saw by the look of it that it was from London; and all were eager for the news, the good parson as well as any. There was not a word said as Judith's mother, with fingers that trembled a little from mere anticipation, opened the large sheet, and began to read to herself across the closely written lines. And then, as they waited, anxious for the last bit of tidings about the King or the Parliament or what not, they could not fail to observe a look of alarm come into the reader's face.

"Oh, Susan," she said, in a way that startled them, "what is this?"

She read on, breathless and stunned, her face grown quite pale now; and at last she stretched out her shaking hand with the letter in it.

"Susan, Susan, take it. I can not understand it. I can not read more. Oh, Susan, what has the girl done?"

And she turned aside her chair, and began to cry stealthily: she was not a strong-nerved woman, and she had gathered but a vague impression that something terrible and irrevocable had occurred.

Susan was alarmed, no doubt; but she had plenty of self-command. She took the letter, and proceeded as swiftly as she could to get at the contents of it. Then she looked up in a frightened way at the parson, as if to judge in her own mind as to how far he should be trusted in this matter. And then she turned to the letter again—in a kind of despair.

"Mother," said she at last, "I understand no more than yourself what should be done. To think that all this should have been going on, and we knowing naught of it! But you see what my father wants; that is the first thing. Who is to go to Judith?"

At the mere mention of Judith's name a flash of dismay went to Prudence's heart. She knew that something must have happened; she at once bethought her of Judith's interviews with the person in hiding; and she was conscious of her own guilty connivance and secrecy; so that the blood rushed to her face, and she sat there dreading to know what was coming.

"Mother," Susan said again, and rather breathlessly, "do you not think, in such a pass, we might beg Master Blaise to give us of his advice? The Doctor being from home, who else is there?"

"Nay, if I can be of any service to you or yours, good Mistress Hall, I pray you have no scruple in commanding me," said the parson—with his clear and keen gray eyes calmly waiting for information.

Judith's mother was understood to give her consent; and then Susan (after a moment's painful hesitation) took up the letter.

"Indeed, good sir," said she, with an embarrassment that she rarely showed, "you will see there is reason for our perplexity, and—and I pray you be not too prompt to think ill of my sister. Perchance there may be explanations, or the story wrongly reported. In good truth, sir, my father writes in no such passion of anger as another might in such a pass, though 'tis but natural he should be sorely troubled and vexed."

Again she hesitated, being somewhat unnerved and bewildered by what she had just been reading. She was trying to recall things, to measure possibilities, to overcome her amazement, all at once. And then she knew that the parson was coolly regarding her, and she strove to collect her wits.

"This, good sir, is the manner of it," said she, in as calm a way as she could assume, "that my father and his associates have but recently made a discovery that concerns them much, and is even a disaster to them; 'tis no less than that a copy of my father's last-written play—the very one, indeed, that he finished ere leaving Stratford—hath lately been sold, they scarce know by whom as yet, to a certain bookseller in London, and that the bookseller is either about to print it and sell it, or threatens to do so. They all of them, my father says, are grievously annoyed by this, for that the publishing of the play will satisfy many who will read it at home instead of coming to the theatre, and that thus the interests of himself and his associates will suffer gravely. I am sorry, good sir, to trouble you with such matters," she added, with a glance of apology, "but they come more near home to us than you might think."

"I have offered to you my service in all things—that befit my office," said Master Walter, but with a certain reserve, as if he did not quite like the course that matters were taking.

"And then," continued Susan, glancing at the writing before her, "my father says that they were much perplexed (having no right at law to stop such a publication), and made inquiries as to how any such copy could have found its way into the bookseller's hands; whereupon he discovered that which hath grieved him far more than the trouble about the play. Prudence, you are her nearest gossip; it can not be true!" she exclaimed; and she turned to the young maiden, whose face was no longer pale and thoughtful, but rose-colored with shame and alarm. "For he says 'tis a story that is now everywhere abroad in London—and a laugh and a jest at the taverns—how that one Jack Orridge came down to Warwickshire, and made believe to be a wizard, and cozened Judith—Judith, Prudence, our Judith!—heard ye ever the like?—into a secret love affair; and that she gave him a copy of the play as one of her favors—"

"Truly, now, that is false on the face of

it," said Master Blaise, appositely. "That is a tale told by some one who knows not that Judith hath no skill of writing."

"Oh, 'tis too bewildering!" Susan said, as she turned again to the letter in a kind of despair. "But to have such a story going about London — about Judith — about my sister Judith — how can you wonder that my father should write in haste and in anger? That she should meet this young man day after day at a farm-house near to Bidford, and in secret, and listen to his stories of the court, believing him to be a worthy gentleman in misfortune! A worthy gentleman truly! —to come and make sport of a poor country maiden, and teach her to deceive her father and all of us, not one of us knowing—not one—"

"Susan! Susan!" Prudence cried, in an agony of grief, "'tis not as you think. 'Tis not as it is written there. I will confess the truth. I myself knew of the young man being in the neighborhood, and how he came to be acquainted with Judith. And she never was at any farm-house to meet him, that I know well, but —but he was alone, and in trouble, he said, and she was sorry for him, and durst not speak to any one but me. Nay, if there be aught wrong, 'twas none of her doing, that I know: as to the copy of the play, I am ignorant; but 'twas none of her doing. Susan, you think too harshly—indeed you do."

"Sweetheart, I think not harshly," said the other, in a bewildered way. "I but tell the story as I find it."

"'Tis not true, then. On her part, at least, there was no whit of any secret love affair, as I know right well," said Prudence, with a vehemence near to tears.

"I but tell thee the story as my father heard it. Poor wench, whatever wrong she may have done, I have no word against her," Judith's sister said.

"I pray you continue," interposed Master Blaise, with his eyes calmly fixed on the letter; he had scarcely uttered a word.

"Oh, my father goes on to say that this Orridge—this person representing himself as familiar with the court, and the great nobles, and the like—is none other than the illegitimate son of an Oxfordshire gentleman who became over well acquaint with the daughter of an innkeeper in Oxford town; that the father meant to bring up the lad, and did give him some smattering of education, but died; that ever

since he hath been dependent on his grandmother, a widow, who still keeps the inn; and that he hath lived his life in London in any sort of company he could impose upon by reason of his fine manners. These particulars, my father says, he hath had from Ben Jonson, that seems to know something of the young man, and maintains that he is not so much vicious or ill-disposed as reckless and idle, and that he is as likely as not to end his days with a noose round his neck. This, saith my father, is all that he can learn, and he would have us question Judith as to the truth of the story, and as to how the copy of the play was made, and whether 'twas this same Orridge that carried it to London. And all this he would have inquired into at once, for his associates and himself are in great straits because of this matter, and have urgent need to know as much as can be known. Then there is this further writing toward the end—'I can not explain all to thee at this time; but 'tis so that we have no remedy against the rascal publisher. Even if they do not register at the Stationers' Company, they but offend the Company; and the only punishment that might at the best befall them would be his Grace of Canterbury so far misliking the play as to cause it to be burned—a punishment that would fall heavier on us, I take it, than on them; and that is in no case to be anticipated.'"

"I can not understand these matters, good sir," Judith's mother said, drying her eyes. "'Tis my poor wench that I think of. I know she meant no harm— whatever comes of it. And she is so gentle and so proud-spirited that a word of rebuke from her father will drive her out of her reason. That she should have fallen into such trouble, poor wench! poor wench!—and you, Prudence, that was ever her intimate, and seeing her in such a coil—that you should not have told us of it!"

Prudence sat silent under this reproach: she knew not how to defend herself. Perhaps she did not care, for all her thoughts were about Judith.

"Saw you ever the young man?" Susan said, scarcely concealing her curiosity.

"Nay, not I," was Prudence's answer. "But your grandmother hath seen him, and that several times."

"My grandmother!" she exclaimed.

"For he used to call at the cottage," said Prudence, "and pass an hour or two

—being in hiding, as he said, and glad to have a little company. And he greatly pleased the old dame, as I have heard, because of his gracious courtesy and good-breeding; and when they believed him to be in sad trouble, and pitied him, who would be the first to speak and denounce a stranger so helpless? Nay, I know that I have erred. Had I had more courage I should have come to you, Susan, and begged you to draw Judith away from any further communication with the young man; but I—I know not how it came about; she hath such a winning and overpersuading way, and is herself so fearless."

"A handsome youth, perchance?" said Susan, who seemed to wish to know more about this escapade of her sister's.

"Right handsome, as I have heard; and of great courtesy and gentle manners," Prudence answered. "But well I know what it was that led Judith to hold communication with him after she would fain have had that broken off." And then Prudence, with such detail as was within her knowledge, explained how Judith had come to think that the young stranger talked overmuch of Ben Jonson, and was anxious to show that her father could write as well as he (or better, as she considered). And then came the story of the lending of the sheets of the play, and Prudence had to confess how that she had been Judith's accomplice on many a former occasion in purloining and studying the treasures laid by in the summer-house. She told all that she knew openly and simply and frankly; and if she was in distress, it was with no thought of herself; it was in thinking of her dear friend and companion away over there at Shottery, who was all in ignorance of what was about to befall her.

Then the three women, being somewhat recovered from their first dismay, but still helpless and bewildered, and not knowing what to do, turned to the parson. He had sat calm and collected, silent for the most part, and reading in between the lines of the story his own interpretation. Perhaps, also, he had been considering other possibilities—as to the chances that such an occasion offered for gathering back to the fold an errant lamb.

"What your father wants done, that is the first thing, sweetheart," Judith's mother said, in a tremulous and dazed kind of fashion. "As to the poor wench, we will see about her afterward. And not a harsh word will I send her; she will have punishment enough to bear—poor lass! poor lass! So heedless and so headstrong she hath been always, but always the quickest to suffer if a word were spoken to her; and now if this story be put about, how will she hold up her head—she that was so proud? But what your father wants done, Susan, that is the first thing—that is the first thing. See what you can do to answer the letter as he wishes: you are quicker to understand such things than I."

And then the parson spoke, in his clear, incisive, and authoritative way:

"Good madam, 'tis little I know of these matters in London; but if you would have Judith questioned—and that might be somewhat painful to any one of her relatives—I will go and see her for you, if you think fit. If she have been the victim of knavish designs, 'twill be easy for her to acquit herself; carelessness, perchance, may be the only charge to be brought against her. And as I gather from Prudence that the sheets of manuscript lent to the young man were in his possession for a certain time, I make no doubt that the copy—if it came from this neighborhood at all—was made by himself on those occasions, and that she had no hand in the mischief, save in overtrusting a stranger. Doubtless your husband, good madam, is desirous of having clear and accurate statements on these and other points; whereas, if you, or Mistress Hall, or even Prudence there, were to go and see Judith, natural affection and sympathy might blunt the edge of your inquiries. You would be so anxious to excuse (and who would not, in your place?) that the very information asked for by your husband would be lost sight of. Therefore I am willing to do as you think fitting. I may not say that my office lends any special sanction to such a duty, for this is but a worldly matter; but friendship hath its obligations; and if I can be of service to you, good Mistress Shakespeare, 'tis far from repaying what I owe of godly society and companionship to you and yours. These be rather affairs for men to deal with than for women, who know less of the ways of the world; and I take it that Judith, when she is made aware of her father's wishes, will have no hesitation in meeting me with frankness and sincerity."

It was this faculty of his of speaking clearly and well and to the point that in a large measure gave him such an ascendency over those women; he seemed always to see a straight path before him; to have confidence in himself, and a courage to lead the way.

"Good sir, if you would have so much kindness," Judith's mother said. "Truly, you offer us help and guidance in a dire necessity. And if you will tell her what it is her father wishes to know, be sure that will be enough; the wench will answer you, have no fear, good sir."

Then Susan said, when he was about to go:

"Worthy sir, you need not say to her all that you have heard concerning the young man. I would liefer know what she herself thought of him; and how they came together; and how he grew to be on such friendly terms with her. For hith-erto she hath been so sparing of her favor; though many have wished her to change her name for theirs; but always the wench hath kept roving eyes. Handsome was he, Prudence? And of gentle manners, said you? Nay, I warrant me 'twas something far from the common that led Judith such a dance."

But Prudence, when he was leaving, stole out after him; and when he was at the door, she put her hand on his arm. He turned, and saw that the tears were running down her face.

"Be kind to Judith," she said—not heeding that he saw her tears, and still clinging to his arm; "be kind to Judith, from my heart I beg it of you—I pray you be kind and gentle with her, good Master Blaise; for indeed she is like an own sister to me."

SPOKEN AFTER SORROW.

I KNOW of something sweeter than the chime
    Of fairy bells that run
Down mellow winds; oh, fairer than the time
You sing about, in happy, broken rhyme,
    Of butterflies and sun.
But oh, as many fabled leagues away
As the To-morrow, when the east breaks gray,
Is this which lies, somewhere most still and far,
Between the sunset and the dawn's last star,
    And known as Yesterday.

I know of something better, dearer too,
    Than this first rose you hold,
All sweet with June, and dainty with the dew,
The summer's golden promise breathing through
    Its white leaves' tender fold;
Oh, fairer, when the late winds, gathering slow
Behind the night, shall, moaning sad and low
Across the world, make all its music dumb.
Oh, dearer than the earliest rose to come,
    Will be the last to go.

I know of something sadder than this nest
    Of broken eggs you bring,
With such sweet trouble stirring at your breast
For love undone: the mother bird's unrest,
    That yesterday could sing.
My little child, too grieved to want my kiss,
Do I forget the sweetness they will miss
Who built the home? My heart with yours makes moan;
But oh, that nest from which the birds have flown
    Is sadder far than this.

A CLOUD ON THE HONEY-MOON.

A COMEDY IN ONE ACT.

CHARACTERS:

MR. RICHARD PEDDER.   MRS. RICHARD PEDDER.
JOHN, *a Waiter.*

SCENE.

A private parlor in a hotel in the White Mountains. French window at back, opening on piazza, shows view of Mount Washington in the distance. Door to sleeping-room, Right. Door to corridor of hotel, Left. Usual furniture of parlor, with table set for breakfast.

John (discovered looking at bill of fare, which has been marked). Broiled trout, spring chicken, and ham omelet. Um! He's getting particular about his food. That's a sign they've been married more than a week. If he stays out the honey-moon here, he'll swear at the cook. They all do. The cook's a kind of safety-valve that lets out the steam when the matrimonial kettle gets too hot. Well, I'll order the stuff.   [*Goes left.*

Enter Mr. Pedder *from door R.*

Mr. P. Any letters this morning, John?
John. I'll ask, sir.
Mr. P. Thank you. And breakfast as soon as possible.
John. Won't be ten minutes, sir.
[*Goes out.*

Mr. P. (walking about). How hungry I am! Couldn't eat much of that supper last night. Perhaps the head cook doesn't condescend to look after the late meals. Hope my wife won't keep me waiting for breakfast. "My wife" sounds well, doesn't it? Gives a man a sense of dignity and comfort to have a wife. And she's such a darling, is Ellen! If it weren't for thinking of poor little Lulu, there wouldn't be the faintest cloud on my happiness.

Enter John *with letter.*

John. Only one letter, sir, for you, sir.
[*Mr. P. takes letter ; John goes out.*
Mr. P. (sitting, looks at letter). From George. He promised to write soon. What's he got to say? [*Reads.*] "Dear Dick,—Hope the honey-moon is proving all that the poets describe it to be." [*Speaks.*] You can just bet it is, old boy. [*Reads.*] "The city is beastly dull; nothing decent at the theatres, and nearly all the nice girls out of town." [*Speaks.*] And I've got the nicest here. [*Reads.*] "I must except the Tomlinsons, on whom I called yesterday to fulfill my promise to you to see how Lulu was getting on." [*Speaks.*] Dear old Lulu! [*Reads.*] "I

saw only Miss Tomlinson and Lulu. Miss Tomlinson inquired kindly after you, and Lulu was very affectionate in her greeting. Poor little thing! it does seem hard you had to give her up." [*Speaks.*] It was tough! [*Reads.*] "Perhaps Mrs. Pedder's prejudices may not prove so strong as you think, and you may yet all three be good friends. Having duly reported, I don't think there's any more to tell you. May join Vaughan on his yacht. He has written to me twice. With kindest regards to the bride, yours, George Hammond."

Mr. P. (folding up letter). One can always rely on George. Glad he's seen Lulu. Better not let my wife read this. She wouldn't like what he says about her prejudices. [*Puts letter in pocket.*] I hear her dress rustling.

Enter Mrs. Pedder *in pretty morning dress.*

Mrs. P. Here I am, dear.
Mr. P. And very charming you look, too.
Mrs. P. (turning round so that he can see all the dress). I thought you would like it. Isn't the looping back of the skirt pretty? I haven't kept you waiting, have I?
Mr. P. No; he hasn't brought breakfast yet.
Mrs. P. (going to window). It's a lovely morning; we must go for a walk directly after breakfast. There's that fast-looking widow going horseback-riding.
Mr. P. (advancing toward window). Do you mean the big brunette?
Mrs. P. (stopping him). You needn't go and stare at her. You did enough of that last evening at the hop.
Mr. P. Why, my love, I scarcely glanced at her.
Mrs. P. Well, there was no occasion to glance at all.
Mr. P. If it weren't too ridiculous, I should think you were a little bit jealous.
Mrs. P. Jealous of that great Amazon, who carries a dog under her arm! You know how I hate horsy and "doggy" women. I'd as soon carry about an alligator as a dog.
Mr. P. (soothingly). Yes, dear, I know.

Enter John *with breakfast things, including kettle with spirit-lamp lighted.* Mr. *and* Mrs. P. *sit, and begin eating.*

Mr. P. This trout is dried up too much.

Mrs. P. I am sure, Dick dear, I don't see anything the matter with it.

John (aside). I thought he was due.

Mr. P. I'm glad you can eat it; I can't. Change my plate, John.

Mrs. P. No letters for me this morning, John?

John. No, mum. Only one for Mr. Pedder. [*He goes out with plates.*

Mr. P. (aside). Why the deuce couldn't he simply say "no"? [*Aloud.*] Just a few lines from Hammond, dear. He sends his kindest regards to you.

Mrs. P. Much obliged to him. I like George Hammond best of all your friends I have met.

Mr. P. I'm very glad you do, for he's the best I have. I want you to make him feel at home in our crib, when we get back to the city.

Mrs. P. I'll try, Dick. [*Holding out sugar bowl.*] Does my dicky-bird want a piece more sugar?

Mr. P. No, thank you. [*Aside.*] I wish she'd drop that canary racket.

Mrs. P. What does Mr. Hammond write about?

Mr. P. Oh! nothing in particular. Only wrote because he promised. Sends a little club gossip, and says he may go yachting.

Mrs. P. Can I read his letter? I'd like to see exactly what he says about me.

Mr. P. All right, dear; I'll show it you some time. But I want you now to get ready for a walk. [*Rises.*

Mrs. P. You're in a great hurry this morning. Are you sure you're not dying to catch sight of that widow on horseback?

Mr. P. The widow be—married again!

Mrs. P. (coming to him). Oh, Dick, you say that as if you thought it would be a punishment.

Mr. P. Perhaps it would be, to *her* husband.

Mrs. P. (anxiously). But *you* don't think so?

Mr. P. How can I tell anything about it? I don't know her or her intended victim.

Mrs. P. You know that isn't what I meant, Dick. *You* don't find marriage a punishment?

Mr. P. How can I, when I have married a girl I love so much?

Mrs. P. The only one you have ever really loved?

Mr. P. Haven't I told you so, a hundred times?

Mrs. P. Well, tell it again. I can't hear it too often.

Mr. P. (kissing her). The only one I have really loved. Now, while you put on your things, I'll have a smoke. [*Takes out a cigar and looks in match-safe.*] No matches again! I believe this case must leak.

Mrs. P. There's a light under the kettle, Dick. But please go outside to smoke.

Mr. P. All right. [*He takes out some letters from his pocket, and tears a piece off one to make a lighter; walks to table, lights cigar, and in putting letters back drops one without noticing he has done so.*] I'll go out on the balcony. Bring my hat and gloves, dear, when you're ready; and don't be long.

[*He goes out through window.*

Mrs. P. I wish tobacco smoke didn't make me cough so. I hope I shall get used to it, for Dick's sake. Dear Dick, how good he is! [*Sees letter.*] Why, he's dropped one of his letters. [*Picks it up, and sees signature.*] "George Hammond." That's the one he received this morning. He said I might read it. [*Begins to read.*] "Dear Dick." [*Speaks.*] I don't like any one else calling Dick, "Dick." I wonder if he couldn't get them to call him Richard? [*Reads.*] "Hope the honey-moon is proving all the poets describe it to be." [*Speaks.*] Of course it is, and sweeter, too. Such perfect happiness is beyond the expression of mere words. [*Reads.*] "The city is beastly—" [*Speaks.*] What a horrid word! [*Reads on.*]—"dull; nothing decent at the theatres, and nearly all the nice girls out of town." [*Speaks reflectively, and with a self-satisfied tone.*] Yes, I suppose they are. [*Reads.*] "I must except the Tomlinsons, on whom I called to-day—" [*Speaks.*] Dick never mentioned them; I wonder why he didn't? [*Reads.*]—"to fulfill my promise to you to see how Lulu was getting on." [*Speaks.*] Who is Lulu Tomlinson, and why should Dick want to know how she is getting on? Perhaps Tomlinson has married a friend of Dick's; but even then I don't see why he should take so much interest in her. [*Reads.*] "I saw only Miss Tomlinson and Lulu. Miss Tomlinson inquired kindly after you, and Lulu was very affectionate in her greeting." [*Speaks.*] Perhaps Lulu is going to marry George Hammond. [*Reads.*] "Poor little thing! It does seem hard you had to give her up." [*Speaks.*] Oh! Dick has been in love with Lulu. And how often has he sworn that I was the only woman he had ever really loved! And I—I believed him, fool that I was! I feel that all my faith is shattered. So this Mr. Hammond has been helping Dick to deceive me. I never could bear him, anyway. [*Reads.*] "Perhaps Mrs. Pedder's prejudices—" [*Speaks.*] My prejudices! Go on, Mr. Hammond—go on. I always thought you were sly and fast. What more does the wretch say? [*Reads.*] —"may not prove so strong as you think; and you may yet all three be good friends." [*Speaks.*] Very likely, very likely indeed, Mr. George Hammond. Friends with a forward minx like this Lulu, who, I am sure, was much more to blame than Richard. He has cruelly deceived me, though. If he had only told me the truth, I might have forgiven him. [*Gets up and walks about.*] But now—now I can never trust him again. And all for a girl who was ready to give his friend an affectionate greeting. A pretty friend, this man whom I was to make feel at home! Home! I shall never have a home now. [*Looks at letter again.*] "With kindest regards to the bride." [*Speaks.*] The hypocrite! How I hate him! And as for this Lulu, what can I do? Let me think. Oh, if mamma were only here to advise me!

Enter Mr. P. *through window.*

Mr. P. Not dressed yet, dear?

Mrs. P. (*hiding letter, and struggling to appear calm*). No.

Mr. P. Why not?

Mrs. P. I am not going out. I have a headache.

Mr. P. Your eyes look red. I'm so sorry, dear! [*Coming closer.*] Can I get you anything?

Mrs. P. (*shrinking back*). No. Don't touch me.

Mr. P. What *is* the matter?

Mrs. P. Oh, nothing. Only my heart is broken.

Mr. P. What nonsense! What has broken it?

Mrs. P. It may be nonsense to you, *sir*, but it is death to me. I have discovered your cruel perfidy.

Mr. P. (*amazed*). My perfidy! [*Aside.*] What in thunder is she driving at?

Mrs. P. Yes. You need not affect innocence. I have proof of one case, but I dare say it is only one of hundreds. Oh!

to think that I should have married such a Don Juan!

Mr. P. Will you please explain what you are talking about?

Mrs. P. (*sobbing*). Not ten minutes ago you told me that I was the only woman you had ever really loved.

Mr. P. And I tell you so once more.

Mrs. P. Don't! *don't!!* DON'T!!! Do not, Mr. Pedder, shatter any lingering remnant of faith I may have. Do not heap perjury on perjury.

Mr. P. (*aside*). "Mr. Pedder!" It's serious. [*Aloud.*] My dear, you are using very strong words.

Mrs. P. I have heard of your loves, and the false stories you have told others—the affections you have wronged—the hearts you have betrayed. And I—I, who was ready to worship you, am to be rewarded with the worn-out feelings of a rake. Oh! it is a bitter awakening from my dream!

Mr. P. If you will drop your tragic vein, and tell me what's the matter, I shall, no doubt, be able to explain it. I can see that some one has been trying to make mischief between us. Who is the liar?—the false friend? Tell me, that I may prove myself innocent.

Mrs. P. You brazen it out boldly, sir, but your acting does not impose on me. I have proofs—the best of proofs.

Mr. P. Then show them to me—tell me what they are. I can not answer an accusation that is so vague.

Mrs. P. You could not answer it if I demeaned myself by stating it in the clearest words.

Mr. P. Ellen, is this the faith and trust you promised me at the altar?

Mrs. P. Do you dare to speak to me of faith and trust? You, who are false and disloyal.

Mr. P. If you won't tell me, you won't; but I'll be hanged if I know what all this is about.

Mrs. P. Go on, sir, go on. Use bad language if you want to. You don't respect me, but you can't impose on me. Had you confessed all, and trusted to my love, I might have forgiven you; but your shameless protestations of ignorance and innocence show me what I have to expect in the future. I am going to my room, sir, and I beg you will not disturb me. [*Goes to door.*] If you want amusement this morning, sir, you can think of Lulu Tomlinson.

[*She enters room and slams door.*

Mr. P. (*alone*). Whe-e-e-w! Lulu Tomlinson! [*Takes letters from his pocket, and looks them over.*] By Jove! I've dropped George's, and she's read it! And she thinks Lulu is a girl! [*Laughs.*] That's the best joke I ever heard. Come to think of it, his phrases were rather ambiguous. Poor Ellen! it is really too bad she should have been so worried. But *I* was worried too. I began to get in no end of a fright. I couldn't for the life of me imagine which of my flirtations she had dropped on. It all comes of this ridiculous notion of a wife wanting to be the only woman her husband has ever loved. The only way to get that would be to marry a boy baby; and then, if the baby could speak, she'd find she had a predecessor in the nurse. Now Ellen was inclined to be jealous of that widow. I shall have to give her a little lesson. [*Goes to door, opens it a little, and calls.*] Mrs. Pedder!

Mrs. P.'s voice. I asked you to respect my grief.

Mr. P. (*in calmly dignified tones*). I am aware how cruelly you have misjudged me. I can not rest quietly under a false and wicked aspersion. It will be well for the future happiness of both of us that you come here and listen to me.

Mrs. P.'s voice. I have proofs.

Mr. P. Proofs that I shall demolish.

Enter Mrs. P.

Mrs. P. I shall be only too delighted if you can.

Mr. P. Kindly take a seat. Thank you. When you left me, just now, you hurled at me the name Lulu Tomlinson. What would you say if I were to assure you that there is no such person?

Mrs. P. (*rising*). Oh, Dick darling, isn't there really?

Mr. P. Oblige me, Mrs. Pedder, by remaining seated.

Mrs. P. (*sitting*). Don't call me Mrs. Pedder, Dick.

Mr. P. Madam, just now, on a groundless suspicion, you called me Mr. Pedder once, and sir five times. Had you told me all, and trusted to my love, I might have forgiven your want of faith — the faith that you promised me at the altar. [*Hides face in handkerchief.*]

Mrs. P. Oh, but, Dick, I didn't really mean it! I never really doubted you.

Mr. P. Madam, your acting does not impose on me. Your anger was too natural to have been assumed.

Mrs. P. Don't, Dick, don't! I can't stand it. But you haven't explained it all yet.

Mr. P. I should have, had you not interrupted me. You found a letter I dropped, and you immediately proceeded to read it.

Mrs. P. I saw it was from Mr. Hammond, and you said I might read it.

Mr. P. When I showed it to you. But, Mrs. —

Mrs. P. Don't, Dick, don't! If you call me Mrs. Pedder again, I shall break my heart.

Mr. P. Your distrust has almost broken mine. You found in that letter a reference to Miss Tomlinson and Lulu, and immediately jumped to the conclusion that Lulu was a girl to whom I had behaved like a villain.

Mrs. P. And isn't she a girl?

Mr. P. No; Lulu is a dog.

Mrs. P. A dog!

Mr. P. A terrier of pure Skye breed.

Mrs. P. (*rising*). Oh, Dick, how foolish I have been!

Mr. P. Don't touch me: hear me out. The first time I met you, you happened to mention your peculiar dislike to dogs. I fell in love with you that evening; so I determined not to spoil my chances by speaking of Lulu or letting you see her. When you accepted me, the Tomlinsons kindly took charge of Lulu, with the understanding that if I didn't claim her in six months, she was to be theirs.

Mrs. P. (*kneeling before him*). Oh, Dick, how wickedly suspicious I have been! Can you ever forgive me?

Mr. P. My dear, I'll try, if you will promise never to be jealous again.

Mrs. P. Never, Dick dear, never!

Mr. P. You see that, however strong appearances may be, they are not proofs.

Mrs. P. No, Dick, no. I will never suspect you again; and I'll never read any of your letters—unless you give them to me.

Mr. P. That's my own trustful darling again! [*They embrace.*

Mrs. P. Dick, I believe I love you more than ever, though I didn't think that was possible. And, oh! Dick dear, you may send for Lulu if you like.

Mr. P. But you can't bear dogs.

Mrs. P. Lulu can't be like any other dog. I know I shall love her for your sake. Besides, I don't want that Miss Tomlinson to have anything that belonged to you.

THE WARRIOR'S QUEST.

A WARRIOR rode upon a quest
　　For deeds to crown a noble name,
And give to her whom he loved best
　　Not only love, but fame.
Where'er the storm of war might drift,
　　Its din to him was music rare;
Nor e'er did smoke of battle lift
　　But he was there.

Of him the lands afar had heard;
　　His prowess lived in many a song;
His name became a household word—
　　The Righter of the Wrong.
The years like moments sped away,
　　While onward still some vision lured,
And calm within his bosom lay
　　His love assured.

But the sweet lady for whose sake
　　The warrior rode upon his quest
Found the years long to watch and wake
　　For tidings east or west;
And oft she sat within her bower
　　Silent and sad as day grew dim,
And oft she climbed the lofty tower
　　To watch for him.

"O love," she sighed, "since life is sweet,
　　Since life is brief, why seek so long
For gifts to lay before my feet?
　　Thou doest love a wrong.
I can not ride from east to west
　　To meet thee in the battle's fray,
But I must bear an aching breast
　　From day to day."

Homeward at length the warrior turned,
　　Sated with victory, and full fain
To tell the love that once more burned
　　Into a cherished pain.
His glorious steed with trappings gay
　　Bore him right proudly, and his train
Of gallant knights far stretched that day
　　Across the plain.

But as they neared the castle walls
　　Where dwelt the lady of his love,
What sight upon their joyance falls,
　　What sound their fear doth move?
A funeral train from out the gate
　　To tolling bells is slowly led:
Glory and love have come too late—
　　They greet the dead.

HENRY IV.
From painting in Windsor Castle.

THE GREAT HALL OF WILLIAM RUFUS.

IX.

IT was on the 30th of September, 1399, when the great Hall took the new departure, indicated in the last chapter, at the meeting of the barons. Three centuries before (1099), Rufus, fresh from a military expedition, had come clanking into it with his iron-clad barons to have a look at the new banqueting room where they expected to have many a royal feast. Now the barons came into it again, but in no such devil-may-care style. They assembled with grave ceremony, and with graver faces, in robes of state, not in armor, with no king at the head of them, but led by the mitred prelates of the realm, not to inspect the Hall, however gloriously restored, but to take account of the kingdom, and to set up a new throne.

This latter they had already literally done, for they had caused a new marble chair to be set upon the high dais, under a sumptuously trimmed canopy of state, between the Court of King's Bench on its right and the High Court of Chancery on its left. There was now no king to occupy it, and they had come to make one. As it stood there it was a symbol both of a vacancy and an innovation.

At this moment Richard the Second was occupying one of the unregal apartments in the other palace of William Rufus, the Tower, at London.

When Edward the Second had been deposed, seventy-two years before, within these very walls, it had been amid the vociferations and curses of the populace, in the hurry and passion of the vassals themselves, and the tumult had ceased only when Edward, his son, was brought forward and proclaimed in his stead. But now, when no such alternative presents itself, and a greater opportunity is offered, everything is done decently and in order. The great Hall had not been the seat of the law during these two centuries and a half since Henry the Second's day for nothing. The legal atmosphere of the place

RICHARD III.
From painting in National Portrait Gallery.

There was no president. It was only yesterday that the king had resigned. The Archbishop of York now rose and read his renunciation. The Archbishop of Canterbury put the question of its acceptance. It was answered in the affirmative, the multitude cheering as each member signified his assent. After this the coronation oath was read, as a preliminary to thirty-three articles of impeachment, which were now presented. They were a strange foreshadowing of the impeachment of still another king, who should be arraigned for trial here in about two hundred and fifty years. They charged him with despotism, dissembling, and inconstancy. No one questioned them. Then the sentence of deposition was solemnly pronounced by eight commissioners. The kingdom was vacant.

was breathed into the proceedings, and at every stage they showed the inspiration of the minds which had been trained in this the ancient homestead of the courts. When finished, their work was as elaborate as the new rafters over their heads, and as substantial as yonder marble seat. Hence a constitutional precedent was established which was never to be removed, however much it was destined to be agitated. A king not of the lineal order, but of the ancient royal stock, might be *chosen* if the vassals of the crown were so inclined.

Shakespeare has made the scene in the Hall both a tumultuous and a pathetic one, introducing Richard himself, but we will give it as it actually occurred. Close under the shadow of the empty throne sat the mitred prelates. Behind them, on one side, sat the Lords, and somewhat further back, on the other, the Commons. The remainder of the Hall, below the bar, was densely crowded by the people. The Duke of Lancaster, who had arrived in London some weeks before, with sixty thousand men, amid the rejoicings of the populace, sat in his proper place among the peers.

Amid the hush of the breathless interval which now ensued, the Duke of Lancaster, Henry of Bolingbroke, rose in his place. He made the sign of the cross upon his forehead and breast, and approaching the empty throne, thus challenged the realm and the crown:

"In the name of Fader, Son, and Holy Ghost, I, Henry of Lancaster, chalenge this Rewme of Ynglonde, and the Crown, with all the members and the appurtenances; als I that am descendit, be right line of the blode, coming fro the gude lord Henry therde," etc. He then held up his hand, showing a signet ring which Richard had delivered to him the day before. Not a whisper was heard denying the validity of the claim, but its validity lay not in what he had declared, but in the silence around him, which gave consent to what he had done. The two archbishops gave voice to the silence by coming toward him and leading him up to the throne. He knelt upon its steps for a few moments as in silent prayer. When he arose they placed him upon it, and then the acclamations of the multitude

SELF-INAUGURATION OF RICHARD III.
From drawing by E. F. Brewtnall.

burst forth. The primate next addressed the assembly, congratulating them upon the advancing prosperity of the realm, and then the new-made king briefly thanked them for the decision to which they had come. Henry the Fourth held his throne by a Parliamentary revolution.

But, as we know, neither he nor his successors continued to hold it without contention. There was shortly a scene in

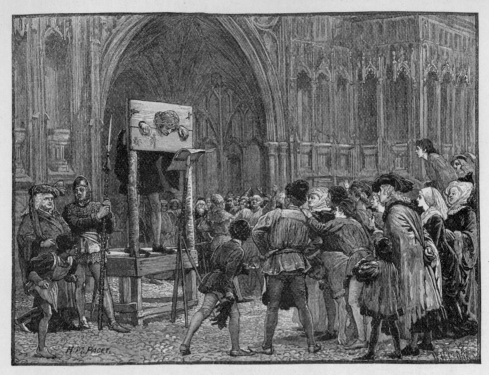

PERKIN WARBECK IN THE PILLORY.
From drawing by H. M. Paget.

Parliament which rang ominously of the coming wars of the Roses. There was an angry debate between two barons over a question of treason toward both the late and the present king. They fiercely called each other liar and traitor. The excitement spread among the other nobles, and upward of twenty gauntlets were dashed upon the stone floor as pledges of challenge or defense. This took place only nineteen days after the coronation banquet, at which the champion of England, armed *cap-a-pie*, and mounted on a barbed steed with crimson housings, had pranced about the Hall and flung down his gage in something less than half a dozen places. But here was the real thing now, in these as yet invisibly red and white roses of steel scattered on the pavement. The king was equal to the occasion, however, as he always was, and by "his address" allayed the storm. Shakespeare depicts this stirring scene in his *Richard the Second* out of time, but in its proper place, Westminster Hall.

We hasten on over the splendid reign of Henry the Fifth, the imbecile but bloody reign of Henry the Sixth, and the bloody but not imbecile reign of Edward the Fourth, to find the Hall in a bad way, swinging into the hands of a ruffianly Rufus again. In this abrupt transition we only avail ourselves of the dramatic liberty of compressing time for want of space. We pause at a scene which it would never do to pass over, especially as it gathers into itself the total result, so far, of the omitted period. Behold now the bright, consummate flower of the wars of the Roses!

X.

Enter Richard the Third. It is June 26, 1483. The white rose of York is red with the blood of that June. The "protector" has been proclaimed king. The nobles and bishops and people fill the great Hall. He enters with a gorgeous retinue, and mounts the dais. Thus brightly does he emerge from the foul plot which he has hatched out of his brother's death. He has used the name of his nephew to build himself up to this. In a council held yonder in Rufus's Tower, to prepare for his nephew's coronation, he has just stricken down the last of the loyal group, in striking off the head of Hastings upon a log in the Tower green. "He would not to dinner before he saw his head off." The princes are in the Tower, destined to be smothered. This much will do for what has taken place on his vigorous right hand. On his withered left is Elizabeth Woodville, the mother of the princes, in the "sanctuary" of the Abbey, sitting "alone in the rushes, all dismayed and desolate"; and the coronation is at hand wherein the very damask and satin and velvet and cloth of gold made ready to give splendor to Edward the Fifth is to be wrought up for his own pageant in the Abbey, and his own banquet in the Hall.

The head of the house of York conducts himself here rather differently from the head of the house of Lancaster. He does not challenge the crown before the marble chair, but moves off to the right, and seats himself on the long marble slab of the King's Bench. There he opens his bloody lips, scarce wiped from the dinner over Hastings's head, and declares that he will take upon him the crown "in that place, there where the king himself sitteth and ministereth the law, because he considered that it was the chiefest duty of a king to minister the laws." Now he proceeds to wave his winsome wand over the nobles, the merchants, the artificers,

and all kinds of men, "but especially the lawyers of this realm." Last of all, to fascinate the public heart by one more dramatic stroke, he sets forth the great

HENRY VIII.—After Holbein.

evil of discord and the great good of concord and unity, and makes the magnanimous proclamation that he puts out of his own mind all enmities, and does now and here pardon all offenses committed against him.

There was at that moment a man appropriately named Fog, "whom he had

CARDINAL WOLSEY.—After Houbraken.

long deadly hated," and who had sought refuge in the sanctuary of the Abbey for fear of him. Richard now ordered him to be brought before him. Then "in sight of all he took him by the hand," and the common people entered into the fog of the whole humbug—but, says the chronicler, "wise men tooke it for vanitie."

We do not care to stay at the coronation, nor to look in at the coronation banquet, even to see the champion in *white armor*, on his horse trapped with white silk, throw down his gage for the last of the Plantagenets. History has long ago picked up that lily-white gauntlet of York, and tilted the blackest of ink on both the king and the occasion.

XI.

On a certain day in Henry the Seventh's reign, in the autumn of 1498, thirteen years

after Richard's death, a hooting crowd fills New Palace Yard to look and jeer at a rather royal appearing young man who is in the stocks in front of the entrance to the Hall. He bears the handsome, gallant features of Edward the Fourth. He is engaged alternately in cursing his fate and in reading his confession. He has been figuring extensively of late as an apparition of one of the princes of the Tower—not a dramatic ghost, this time, making things comfortable for Henry of Richmond on the eve of Bosworth Field, but giving him the nightmare, long after that victory, as a claimant to the crown then lost and won. The fellow now confesses that he is not little Richard of York, but plain Perkin Warbeck, whose pretensions only have been smothered. On the next day he will be "set upon a like scaffold in Cheape," where he will go through the same interesting ceremony. There we leave him, and the king whom he has disturbed, to enter the Hall.

If we would find anything there especially worth recording we must suppose that something like nineteen years have slipped by as we cross the threshold. It

This is the second or third time it has escaped. The palace will be repaired, not for the king, but for the Parliament, which has a proper disinclination to leave the historic ground. The fact is now destined to make these precincts more memorable than ever.

EDWARD STAFFORD, DUKE OF BUCKINGHAM.
After painting owned by the Marquis of Bath.

will then be the eighth year of Henry the Eighth. Unless we have a great taste for pageantry—there has been an inordinate amount of *that*—we are content to let all this time pass. If the reader is fond of going to a fire, we might say that there has been a rather ruinous conflagration in the palace, and the king has removed his quarters elsewhere. Henceforth its glory departs as a royal habitation. But some of the ancient chambers remain intact, and the old Hall stands secure, good for many an extraordinary scene to come.

Henry the Eighth, as the conundrum has it, was more than a wonder. He was a Tudor, a curious dynastical, if not botanical, product of the Red Rose of Lancaster and the White Rose of York. At the moment we come to him he is full blown on the Welsh stem to which he owes his name. Red, however, predominates. Every petal of him makes a leaf in the history of despotism, and the odor of him is even worse now than it was then. Rufus's Hall came very naturally and conveniently to be the conservatory

ANNE BOLEYN.—After Holbein.

best liveries," and a number of court ladies, the big and burly, but richly robed and rubicund, young king occupies the central place under the cloth of estate. But a figure more vivid than all fairly lights up the stage. It is the master of ceremonies, Cardinal Wolsey, arrayed from hat to shoes in pontifical scarlet, "*ego et Rex meus*," officiating! He has so contrived it that no less than three resplendent queens shall be also on hand—Katharine of Aragon, Margaret of Scotland, and Mary of France.

On the floor below are arraigned no fewer than four hundred and eighty men and eleven women, bound together by ropes, and standing in their shirts. They seem to be condemned to death already, for a halter is dangling from the neck of every one of them. It looks all the worse for them to know that ten pairs of gallows, set upon wheels, have been erected in different parts of the city. This is to be the tragical ending of a May-day jollification. It had begun with a garlanded May-pole, and it was to conclude with this little forest of gibbets; for out of the festival had come a riot, and out of the riot an insurrection. In the absence of the modern Metropolitan Police, in the absence of any provision at all, in fact, by the city authorities, the lieutenant of the Tower had been obliged at last to quiet the city by opening his ordnance upon it. No wonder that the matter had come to the king's ears after that! Now nothing less than a trial of all concerned, in Westminster Hall, and before the king's majesty himself, would give stunning effect to another discharge, namely, of the insurgents themselves. Mercy had been resolved upon as good policy, but it was to come in a most frightful way. So we have our tableau—a fierce king under his canopy, ermined judges and robed nobles looking on sternly, the Lord Mayor and aldermen in anxious suspense, court ladies shedding tears, and down on the floor below them the poor, pallid apprentices, blue to the lips with terror, and the populace beyond the bar in hushed horror awaiting the apparently sure issue of it all!

The cardinal appears to be the most bloody-minded man on the stage. He first rates the city fathers for their negligence, and then turns upon the criminals, denouncing their conduct, and showing

in which he bloomed with such bloody effect. The courts still sat there, but he sat on the courts. The work of Henry the Second and of the whole Plantagenet era was now almost undone.

As might be supposed, this Henry of a different plant was inclined on especial occasions to take the judgment-seat himself. We will begin with one of these, and end with another.

As we enter the Hall, at 9 A.M. on May 13, 1517, it is to catch sight of him at such a business, and it looks at first very bad for the criminals; but, as it happens, he is under the clement control of another personage who is only externally red.

Henry was always ready for a court masque, and enjoyed dramatic surprises. His adroit chancellor had first risen into favor, and had often since brought about a desired end, through the royal taste for such things. This scene, we may be sure, was all got up by him. From our end of the Hall it looks like a tableau.

Amid the brilliant group, on the high dais, of dukes, earls, and other lords of the king's council, the Lord Mayor, aldermen, and chief citizens of London, "in their

them how richly they deserved death. They cry out to the king, "Mercy!—gracious lord, mercy!" The three queens throw themselves on their knees before him, and plead that they may be forgiven. Henry keeps their majesties in that one whips off his rope, and up go the nearly five hundred slip-nooses fifty feet or so in the air toward the great roof. The gallows turns into a May-pole once more, the merriest of whose dances is the last.

SIR THOMAS MORE.——After Holbein.

position a long while. The nobles, too, bending their knees, entreat for their release. The ferment is working well. At last also the red cardinal, having been appealed to by the king, recommends their pardon. The poor wretches give a scream of surprise and delight. Every Four years afterward the cardinal does not appear in a so merciful light, and Henry is allowed to get his first taste of blood. When his vengeance lights, without much cause, on the Duke of Buckingham, "the bounteous Buckingham, mirror of all courtesy," the lineal descendant

EDWARD VI.

it was here that the anger of his king first flashed vividly upon him in the writ which deposed him; more cruel to him at the moment than the axe of the Tower had been to Buckingham when its fatal edge was turned toward *him*, under this very roof, as Norfolk sentenced him to death.

He was accustomed to spend his mornings in the Hall, coming to the Chancery attended by great pomp and state from York Place, the archiepiscopal palace on the river shore below, which the king was afterward to wrest from him and make the palace of Whitehall. It was when Michaelmas term commenced, October 9, 1529, that his gilded barge brought him from this princely residence to sit in the Court of Chancery for the last time. The intimation of his disgrace fell upon him there as suddenly as a stroke of paralysis. He was riven in two; office, rank, wealth, state, power—all that had given him consequence—were gone at once, and he was "left naked to his enemies." When the Great Seal had fallen from his hands as chancellor, when the King's Bench, on the other side of the Hall, had stripped him of houses, lands, and jewelled plate, a thousand boats gathered on the Thames to see his once proud barge pass out of sight forever.

Shakespeare has made Wolsey utter the simple fact when he thus speaks of Anne Boleyn:

"There was the weight that pulled me down! O,
     Cromwell,
The king has gone beyond me: all my glories
In that one woman I have lost forever."

She is the next personage who now most fills the eye in Westminster Hall. Before the beauty of "that one woman," not only the glories of Wolsey have faded away, but the Queen of England has been dethroned! Who else is to fall before it? What else is to come because of it? Bishop Fisher is to fall. Sir Thomas More is to fall. The whole realm is to turn as on another centre, break loose from the fastenings of ages, reverse all its traditions, enter a new era! The Church of Rome shall depart, her bishops shall be dis-

of Edward the Third, distinguished on the Field of the Cloth of Gold, the last hereditary High Constable of England, Wolsey is felt to be at the bottom of it; at any rate, not at the top, as he might have been. The great trial of the duke before his peers, and its consequences upon Wolsey, form the burden of the opening scenes in Shakespeare's *Henry the Eighth*.

1 *Gent.* Whither away so fast?
2 *Gent.*   O—God save you!
Even to the Hall, to hear what shall become
Of the great Duke of Buckingham.
1 *Gent.*   I'll save you
That labor, sir. All's now done, but the ceremony
Of bringing back the prisoner. . . .
When he was brought again to the bar—to hear
His knell rung out, his judgment—he was stirr'd
With such an agony, he sweat extremely,
And something spoke in choler, ill, and hasty:
But he fell to himself again, and, sweetly,
In all the rest show'd a most noble patience. . . .
2 *Gent.* The cardinal is at the end of this.
1 *Gent.*   'Tis likely,
By all conjectures.

The play concludes with the fall of Wolsey himself. Shakespeare does not allude to the Hall as the scene of his agony when the announcement came, but

placed, her monasteries shall be dissolved. "The king has gone beyond her," and himself become head of the Church. As with her great cardinal—the reflection of royal barge, and takes her place again on the high dais, under the cloth of state, "dressed in purple velvet, furred with ermine, her hair escaping loose under a

PHILIP AND MARY.
From a gold medallion by Trezzo.

her pomp and of her secular assumption —"all her glories in that one woman she has lost forever!"

The Tower, the Abbey, and the Hall, each in turn is made to minister to the new queen. From the Tower she comes, amid the booming of its guns, into the decorated, crowded streets, seated, says Froude, "in a white chariot drawn by two palfreys in white damask which swept the ground, a golden canopy borne above it, making music with silver bells. . . . There she sat, dressed in white tissue robes, her fair hair flowing loose over her shoulders, and her temples circled with a light coronet of gold and diamonds, most beautiful, loveliest, most favored perhaps, as she seemed at that hour, of all England's daughters."

On reaching the Hall she is borne in a litter into the midst of it, when she alights and ascends the stairs to the high dais, where a rich banquet of viands, spices, and wines lies spread before her. She sends them down to her ladies, and after they had drank to her, she gracefully thanks them all, the ladies and the lords, for their attendance on her.

That night she sleeps in Wolsey's former palace, and the next morning, Whit-Sunday, 1533, returns to the Hall in the

wreath of diamonds." The same brilliant assemblage of robed nobles and mitred prelates is in waiting before her. A railed passageway, laid with carpet, starts from the entrance, and makes the circuit of the Abbey to its western gates. When all is ready, "the blazing trail of splendor" is resumed as she moves out under her canopy.

In the Abbey she

"opposes freely
The beauty of her person to the people,
    . . . .which when the people
Had the full view of, such a noise arose
As the shrouds make at sea in a stiff tempest,
As loud, and to as many tunes: hats, cloaks
(Doublets, I think), flew up."

Then in the Hall again that night she sits at the coronation banquet, amid such splendors as no Queen of England before had ever known. The delighted king, who still keeps himself invisible amid it all, seated in a closet framed into an east window from the adjoining cloister of St. Stephen's, gazes enraptured at the spectacle of her beauty, receiving the homage of the kingdom.

2 *Gent.* Heaven bless thee!
Thou hast the sweetest face I ever look'd on.
Sir, as I have a soul, she is an angel.
Our king has all the Indies in his arms.

The coming reign of Elizabeth, with all its completed issues of this time, is at this moment lying beneath her heart! And yet in three years, almost to a day, that fair, proud head with all its wealth of hanging hair is to fall into a pool of its own blood beside the fatal block in the Tower. So she completes the circuit of her destiny, weaving first the Tower and the Hall, then the Abbey and the Hall, and now at last the Tower again, into the historic drama of her young, eventful life.

Two years after this, as an Irish way of keeping a foot-hold in England, the Pope sent to John Fisher, Bishop of Rochester, a cardinal's hat. The brave old man had opposed the divorce of the late queen and the king's assumption of spiritual suprem-acy. Thereupon Henry swore that he should have no head to put in it. The legal mechanism of the Hall was accordingly put in motion—it was a guillotine arrange-ment all through the Tudor dynasty, obe-diently worked by the judges, and the axe of the Tower came chopping down as often as the sovereign willed—and the venerable white head was swept as neatly off as the circumstances required. The atrocity made a sensation in Europe and in the late Universal Church. But it was a hor-ror which passed with the epoch. There was another impending, which, when it fell, and cut short a life as precious to the world as to the realm, seemed to bereave all mankind for all time. The bloody king will never get over what he deter-mined upon now. He struck a teeming brain and a noble heart out of life, as well as cleaved off a head, when he stretched Sir Thomas More upon his red and swift legal process in Westminster Hall.

"The greatest Englishman of his day," "the philosopher of the *Utopia*, the friend of Erasmus, whose life was of blameless beauty, whose genius was cultivated to the highest attainable perfection," "the cham-pion of Parliamentary freedom," had sat as chancellor in Wolsey's seat. He had not affected the pomp of his predecessor; he had not made the Hall brilliant with his retainers as he entered and took his lordly place. Yet the pomp of the king-dom had enveloped him; the rich scarlet robe of the office had enwrapped his per-son whenever he appeared beneath the deep arch of the great entrance, and the Mace and the Seal had been carried be-fore him as he walked the whole length of the Hall, leading the robed procession of those who gave splendor and dignity to the high court which sat upon the plat-form, behind the *cancelli* in yonder south-west corner. What a reverse has been wrought by time and tyranny now! He enters beneath the arch on that hot sum-mer morning, July 1, 1535, tottering with the fatigue of a long and dusty walk from the Tower, tottering also with the weak-ness of a year's confinement there. The bright, erect, alert presence has gone. His face is pallid, his brown locks are touched with gray, his form is bowed. Only the brilliant sparkle of his eye remains, and the benignant look which neither the in-gratitude of his king nor the treachery of his accusers could drive from his counte-nance. He enters, clad in a coarse wool-len gown, leaning upon a stick, feebly keeping pace with the axe of the Tower as it is borne in front of him, to stand before the very bar at which he had so recently presided, to be arraigned before Audley, his new successor, and the whole bench of the Special Commission, to an-swer a charge of high treason. The great chancellor is to furnish his own scarlet for the ceremony now begun. The er-mine of his innocence and uprightness already composes the inner lining of his crime.

The engine of this Lord's anointed, though running now with stolen papal oil—for Henry was head of the Church—had many a hitch before it could bring the final catastrophe to bear. Respect for the illustrious prisoner repeatedly clogged its wheels. The summary process with Bishop Fisher, which, as it is recorded, reads like two or three sudden jerks— "Pleads not guilty—Venue awarded— Verdict, guilty"—is now prolonged by the judges themselves pleading with the prisoner to change his resolution. Seated in the chair which out of charity had been brought him, he steadfastly but respectful-ly declines. First, the indictment was read. Then the Lord Chancellor rose, tell-ing him "it was not yet too late to ask for mercy, which his Majesty desired to show."

"My lord," More replied, "I have great cause to thank your honor for your court-esy, but I beseech Almighty God that I may continue in the mind that I am in through His grace unto death."

The machine was obliged to work. The sentence was pronounced in the usual form. But even here reluctance hung upon its word. It should be decapitation

QUEEN ELIZABETH.
From painting owned by the Duke of Portland.

pure and simple; no disembowelling, no dismembering; none of the final grinding up and ignominious mutilation which followed the fall of the axe. And this was told the prisoner as "a special instance of the royal clemency."

The man who could at the very last wittily remove his beard from beneath the executioner's blow, "because *it* had committed no treason," was equal now to the sarcasm veiled in pleasantry, which veiled, in its turn, his most Christian contempt for his Majesty: "God forbid that the king should show any more such mercy unto any of my friends, and God bless all my posterity from such pardons."

Even while the court was concluding its session, and the procession was forming to lead back the "traitor," the machine stood still an instant once again. "The commissioners," says Froude, "once more adjured him to have pity on himself, and offered to reopen the court if he would reconsider his resolution. More smiled, and replied only a few words of graceful farewell."

It was but a few hours after the clang behind him of the Traitor's Gate that the axe fell, and the signal went to Henry and Anne Boleyn that Sir Thomas More was dead. They were playing at the game of tables. Anne was standing by the king's chair. Henry's face darkened as he turned and looked up at his new queen. "Thou art the cause of this man's death!" muttered this royal son of Adam, and in less than eleven months from that hour he swept off her head also.

XII.

In the early part of Edward the Sixth's reign, the exquisite St. Stephen's Chapel— of whose interior splendor we have already spoken, and which, it will be remembered, stood in the rear of the Hall, running eastward toward the Thames from its southeast corner—was wainscoted over so thoroughly that its sculptures, paintings, gorgeous gilding, and elegant tracery were totally forgotten until the beginning of the present century. It became the new council hall of the House of Commons, which now abandoned the Chapter-House of the Abbey, where it had met since the days of Edward the Third. From that day to this "St. Stephen's" has been an expression for the Commons, as "St. James's" for the court, and "Westminster Hall" for the law. The famous chapel in which such a glorious era of the British constitution was soon to open stood above the vaulted arches of a lower and older chapel called the Crypt, and was therefore a story higher than the floor of the Hall, from which in after-years it was chiefly reached by a flight of stairs from a passage-way between the Court of Chancery and the Court of King's Bench. This middle door, high up in the gable, and close under the great window, was not cut through until the trial of Lord Stafford, on which occasion it was made the door of entrance for the Lords and Commons. There were other doors of communication, however, and the Hall now became one of the approaches to the Parliament Chamber, and far more frequently than we shall have time to mention entered into the sphere and the proceedings of the House of Commons. But this connection between them must now be borne in mind.

We might be tempted—if we had not so much more to relate which stands in greater proportion to the present day—to linger over the momentous trial of the Earl of Somerset, the Protector of Edward the Sixth, "the fatal ending of a struggle between two political rivals which in this day would have ended in a change of ministry." For the same reason we can not stop and look into the Hall during the arraignment of the Duke of Northumberland and other nobles concerned in the elevation of Lady Jane Grey to the throne, bringing up all that pathetic tragedy afterward enacted at Whitehall and in the Tower.

We must pause, however, at one significant scene in the reign of Mary, and at still another in the reign of Elizabeth, about which not a little romance has gathered.

The scene in Mary's reign is no less than the gorgeous and imposing ceremonial in which the kingdom was switched back again into the dominion of the Pope of Rome—a curious correspondence, indeed, with her father's late doings in the venerable old Hall. It took place on November 30, 1554. The would-be King of England on this occasion was no less a personage than that devoted son of the Church, Philip the Second of Spain. Think of *him* on the rostrum of Westminster Hall, with the possibility of the Invincible Armada in his black eyes, if this occasion should be of none effect! It was the feast of St. Andrew, the festival, also, of Philip's highest order, the Golden Fleece. The high mass of the order was sung in the Abbey in the presence of the king and his six hundred courtiers, "dressed in their court costumes of white velvet striped with red, which they had not worn since their first entrance into England." The Knights of the Garter sat with them, decorated with their badges and collars. Now came the final and yet grander ceremony. Transfer the whole splendid array from the nave of the Abbey into the body of the Hall. The triumphant but most amiable cardinal had not attended the mass, but had reserved himself at Lambeth, across the river, in order to make his presence, at this instant, of greater effect. Now he came over in great state, and "there," says Stanley, "in the fast waning light of that November evening, took place the solemn reconciliation of the English Church and nation with the See of Rome, so enthusiastically received at the time, so totally reversed within the next few years, so vainly re-attempted since."

Passing over the whole length of Elizabeth's reign, and its divers trials for high treason, we pause for a single moment at the memorable arraignment of the Earl of Essex, which occurred so near its close, and with which that close is so strangely interwoven. The trial is memorable not only in itself and its romantic interest, but especially, as we think, because the portrait of Elizabeth is so vividly painted upon it, and the character also of the Earl of Essex, the so-called traitor, or Francis Bacon, his most strenuous accuser? Essex had been his friend, his benefactor; he had fought with his enemies to procure him honorable and lucrative appointments; he had even given him an estate, and loaded him with obligations—and there at the bar was Bacon outdoing even the bitter Coke in the unscrupulous urgency and brilliancy of his arguments against him. They were addressed to the

ROBERT DEVEREUX, EARL OF ESSEX.
From painting in National Portrait Gallery.

"greatest, wisest, meanest of mankind" begins to appear in it. The handsome, chivalrous, but scatter-brained Essex, the favorite of the queen, and the delight of the people, but a failure with both, has yet the historic strength to bring with him to the front both Elizabeth Tudor and Francis Bacon.

And who now is most on trial in the Hall before the tribunal of posterity, the weak side of the queen's character, to her pride, to her jealousy, to everything in her which might disincline her to grant a pardon.

Bacon had then already written the *Essays* which prophesied his fame; he now exhibited the character which as surely predicted his fall. That sorry scene is now awaiting us in the near future of Westminster Hall.

CHARLES READE.
From the painting bequeathed by Mr. Reade to Messrs. Harper and Brothers.

CHARLES READE:
A PERSONAL REMINISCENCE.

19 ALBERT GATE, Knightsbridge, London, is one of a row of old-fashioned houses facing southward across a cab-rank to the opening of Sloane Street, and northward to the ride in Hyde Park. It is rather a gloomy-looking dwelling, with a narrow slip of garden in front, and a longer and broader slip in the rear; but within it has cozy possibilities, and from the garden in the rear one can watch the long procession of fashion coming and going any afternoon during the season. Along the piece of wall beneath the front railing there used to run, painted in huge white letters, the curious inscription:

NABOTH'S VINEYARD,

the name given to the house (when its very existence was threatened by a bill surreptitiously smuggled into Parliament) by its owner, Charles Reade.

Here for many years Charles Reade

lived, studied, wrote, and entertained the few friends he loved. Dreary and mean as the place looked from without, it was pleasant enough inside, the pleasantest room of all being the big study, or literary workshop, in the rear, carpeted, and full of great mirrors reaching from floor to ceiling, in front of which were India-rubber trees in pots; adorned with two or three paintings (the most noticeable, at a cursory glance, one of a *pierrot* rescuing an infant from a fire), scarlet curtains, and pieces of marquetry; and opening through glass doors on the quiet back garden. At a large writing-table close to the fire-place and facing the window sat the famous novelist, with great books of memoranda at his feet, and by his side plated buckets brimming with correspondence. It was here, too, that he generally dined, or held high wassail on festive occasions; and light and cheery it was indeed when the curtains were drawn, and the innumerable wax candles, used in lieu of lamps or gas, were burning on every point of vantage. From this *sanctum sanctorum* went forth the copious correspondence, the fulminations against injustice, the epistolary diatribes, which made the name of Charles Reade a household word. The stranger, entering it in fear and trembling, and expecting perhaps to find a truculent and savage figure, was soon relieved on perceiving a loosely clad and mild-mannered elderly gentleman, with soft brown ox-like eyes, gray hair, and a placid smile, ever eager to help him if he had a grievance, and ready to advise him, in any case, with old-fashioned kindness and courtly grace. But if the new-comer were a friend, one of the initiated, the brown eyes would become beaming, the smile merry, and the gentle host would show himself as what he was in reality—a man with the great heart and simple tastes of a school-boy, ripe for any sport that was innocent and merry, and content "to fleet the time carelessly, as they did in the golden world." He would refresh himself, too, like a school-boy, with cakes of all kinds, cocoa-nuts, and sweet confections manufactured by Duclos. "Charles," his loving housekeeper would cry, "leave those sweets alone—you'll make yourself ill." "Quite right, Seymour," he would reply, munching a *bonbon* with infinite relish; "take them away." He had not even arrived at the point of culture, or indigestion,

which desiderates dry champagne, but was quite a young lady in his appreciation of saccharine vintages. He abominated tobacco. His idea of an orgy was a feast of sugar-plums. His ideal of feminine perfection was a fresh young English girl. One of his favorites, known to him and others as "The Queen of Connaught," complained to him on a certain occasion that the sun was spoiling her complexion. "Not at all, my dear," he answered; "you look like *a nice ripe pear*."

As I think of him now, when the grave has just closed over him, and when he has done forever with all the misconceptions of the world, what lingers with me most is the picture of him in these simple and child-like moods. His sweetness of disposition, his kindly frankness, his love of all that is sunny and innocent in human nature, his utter absence of literary arrogance, were qualities peculiar to him, and unique in a generation of shams and pretenses. He had little or no interest in mere literature or merely literary people, but his fascination for all forms of genuine life, from the highest to the lowest, was deep and abiding. What he sought invariably to get out of a man was, not what he fancied or what he dreamed, but what he *knew*. Supremely veracious and sincere himself, he hated falsehood and insincerity in others, and that soft brown eye of his was lynx-like in detecting a prig or a bore. It was easy enough to tell when he *was* bored: he bottled himself up, so to speak, and presented a countenance of serene yet dogged vacuity; and I have known him to sit thus, to all intents and purposes dumb as a mole and deaf as a post, for a whole evening together. I am afraid I must add that this demeanor invariably thawed before a pretty face. Under *that* charm all his ice melted, and he showed himself as he was—delightful, a gray-haired boy.

The occasion of our first meeting was peculiarly interesting to me. A near relation of mine, Miss Harriet Jay, then a very young girl in her teens, had published an anonymous novel, *The Queen of Connaught*, which had been attributed in many quarters to no less a person than Charles Reade himself. Far from resenting the blunder, and quick to perceive the fruit of genuine and unique experience, Charles Reade had evinced the greatest curiosity concerning the real author; and so it came about that an introduction took place at the rooms of a genial actor and manager, and a life-long friend of Reade's, Mr. John Coleman. It was a merry meeting, the first of many, and from that time forth the young authoress and the famous author were close friends. A little later, when we proposed to dramatize *The Queen of Connaught* for the Olympic Theatre, Charles Reade informed us that he had once conceived the idea of doing it himself, and showed us, pasted in one of his enormous Indexes, a long review which he had cut from the *Spectator*, and indorsed in his own handwriting with these words, "Good for a play." When our manuscript was ready, and accepted at the theatre, we took it down to "Naboth's Vineyard" and read it to Naboth; and I well remember how, at a certain situation in the fourth act, he leaped to his feet, clapped his hands, and insisted on "toasting" that situation in a bumper of champagne. Nor was this all. When the rehearsals began he came down to the theatre more than once, and gave us the benefit of his advice and great experience, even to the extent of personally rehearsing a "terrific struggle" between the hero and the villain of the piece. The piece ran over a couple of months, and was succeeded by a drama of his own, *The Scuttled Ship*.

Something may be said here, not inappropriately, of his connection with the stage. Dramatic writing was his hobby; he loved it with all his heart and soul; and he loved it none the less because he was again and again defeated in his efforts to attain success. It was George Eliot's ambition to be recognized as a poet; it was Charles Reade's to triumph as a dramatist. In neither case was the wish completely granted. When the drama of *Never too Late to Mend* was first produced, it was a comparative failure, and it was only in after-years that it became successful, and repaid its author for the labor and anxiety bestowed upon it. When Reade essayed theatrical management for the purpose of bringing out his own pieces, he invariably lost large sums of money. His one great financial success came late in life, in *Drink*, a free adaptation of *L'Assommoir;* and so little was this success anticipated that a couple of days before the production, when I called upon him, he prophesied the dreariest of failures. "Yes, Charles," echoed Mrs. Seymour, who was sitting by, "I wish to

Heaven you had never touched *the thing*." When the night of production came, his faithful friend and housekeeper was too unwell to be present. Before the curtain rose I met him in the theatre lobby. He was walking wearily, looking very worn and old, and when I wished his new venture "godspeed" he shook his head sadly. "Seymour is too ill to come. It is the only 'first night' of mine at which she has not been present; so I don't look for good luck, and indeed I don't much care." Contrary to all expectations, *Drink* made an instantaneous popular success; but, alas! it brought little or no joy to its adapter, for the illness of his faithful adviser and companion was only the beginning of the end.

The reader of *Harper's Magazine*, though familiar with the name and works of Reade, may require to be reminded that he lived and died a bachelor, and that the Mrs. Seymour of whom I have more than once spoken was his housekeeper for many years. When he began to write plays she was a popular actress, and thus they were brought together; and presently he went to reside with her, her husband (who was then living), and two other friends and lodgers. Gradually the little circle thinned; its members died off one by one, till Mrs. Seymour, a widow, was left to keep house for only one survivor, Charles Reade. Their relationship, from first to last, was one of pure and sacred friendship, and the world would be better, in my opinion, if such friendships were more common. Bright, intelligent, noble-minded, and generous to a fault, Laura Seymour deserved every word of the passionate eulogy which Charles Reade composed upon her death, and had engraved upon her tombstone. She was a little woman, bright-eyed, vivacious, and altogether charming. In all literary matters she was his first adviser and final court of appeal; but, like himself, she was very impulsive, and occasionally wrong-headed. She had the best and finest of all virtues —charity. Wherever there was poverty and suffering, her purse was as open as her heart. She loved dumb animals, dogs especially. In the pleasant days that are gone I used to drive down to Albert Gate a certain Pickwickian pony of mine, christened Jack. On his first appearance at the gate, nothing would content the good Seymour but that I should take him out of the trap, release him of his harness, and escort him *through the house* to the back garden. "Poor fellow!" she cried; "do bring him in, and let him graze on the lawn." This would hardly have done, as Jack was a soft sybarite already, and too plump, moreover, to get through the lobby without accidents. Mrs. Seymour relieved her kind heart by sending him out some cakes and bread, to which he was very partial; and ever after that day, when Jack pulled up at the Vineyard, be sure he had his treat of something nice, given by that kindly and gentle hand.

In his personal habits Reade was exceedingly eccentric. For example, he had a mania for buying all sorts of flotsam and jetsam, with the idea that they might "come in useful." On one occasion he purchased a stuffed horse's head, thinking he might utilize it in one of his plays, and placed it in his lumber-room, where it soon became moth-eaten. On another, he invested in a large number of knives and forks, which he secreted away, thinking to produce them afterward triumphantly. "Seymour," he explained to a confidant, "thinks of giving a party; so I've purchased this cutlery in case she may *run short*." He was troubled with corns, and wore enormous boots. We found him one morning with a whole waste-paper basket full of new boots, which he had ordered wholesale, after a pattern that took his fancy. His gingham umbrella would have delighted Mrs. Gamp. Altogether, his whims and oddities were a constant care to Mrs. Seymour, who rallied him mercilessly about them. In his play of *Jealousy*, produced at the Olympic Theatre, there was a scene where one of the actresses, supposed to be a *danseuse*, had to hide behind a very high screen. "Do you think, my dear," he said to the actress rehearsing the part, "you could show the agility of the *danseuse* by lifting your foot and letting foot and ankle pass in sight of the audience, close to the top of the screen?" but this bit of gymnastics was declined as simply impossible. "Then, my dear, we'll have a *false leg* made, and at the proper moment you will work it, gracefully and rapidly, as I shall direct." It is scarcely necessary to add that this realistic notion was not carried out.

I am disposed to think that Mrs. Seymour's influence had much to do in sweetening and softening the character of Charles Reade; that it was altogether a benign and beautiful influence, to which the world, however indirectly, owes much. A photograph of Reade, taken when he was about five-and-thirty, shows a sternness of outline and truculence of expression which afterward completely changed; it represents, indeed, a face of extraordinary power, but no gentleness. Another photograph in my possession, taken at Margate in 1878, pictures the same face, softened by the touch of time; the face of a "benevolent imbecile," he himself playfully calls it in a brief note upon the back. I have no doubt whatever that his benevolence was greatly fostered by his warm-hearted companion; but be that as it may, he was, when I knew him, the gentlest of men—like our friend Boanerges, all fire and thunder in the pulpit, all kindliness and sweetness at his own fireside. The fact is, his style was a thorough-bred, and often ran away with him, or, when he sought to drive it mildly, kicked the subject to pieces. He was the Boythorn of literature, only the big speeches and terrible invectives were not spoken, but set down on paper. Yet he looked on human nature with the eye of a lover. He too had a passion for dumb animals. Not long before his death he filled the garden with tame hares. A noble deed stirred him like a trumpet; great as his hate for wrong-doing, was his compassion for suffering. Over and above all was his natural piety, which bound his days each to each as with a chain of gold.

In these days of problem-guessing, when the simple religion of our fathers is put aside and labelled "anthropomorphic," when the mathematician is rampant, and the gigman ostentatiously spells God with a little "g," it was refreshing to meet with a man who found the old-fashioned creed all-sufficing. Perhaps Charles Reade's intellect was not speculative, perhaps it had exhausted all its speculation in the "*Sturm und Drang*" period of early youth; but whether or not, his latter mood was one of untroubled faith in an All-Wise and All-Merciful Father. He believed in science, as all sane men do, but he clung to religion, as all wise men must. He was not, until the very last, a church-goer, and he had no regard for dogmas, however domineering; but he was deeply and unobtrusively pious in his heart of hearts. Remembering what he was throughout all his days, I think that last epitaph of his, composed for his grave-stone when he already felt the finger of Death upon him, one of the most touching things that have ever been written by a strong man. It was as follows:

HERE LIE,
BY THE SIDE OF HIS BELOVED FRIEND,
THE MORTAL REMAINS OF
CHARLES READE,
DRAMATIST, NOVELIST, AND JOURNALIST.

HIS LAST WORDS TO MANKIND
ARE ON THIS STONE.

I hope for a resurrection, not from any power in nature, but from the will of the Lord God Omnipotent, who made nature and me. He created man out of nothing, which nature could not. He can restore man from the dust, which nature can not.

And I hope for holiness and happiness in a future life, not for anything I have said or done in this body, but from the merits and mediation of Jesus Christ.

He has promised his intercession to all who seek it, and he will not break his word: that intercession, once granted, can not be rejected: for he is God, and his merits infinite: a man's sins are but human and finite.

"Him that cometh to me, I will in no wise cast out." "If any man sin, we have an advocate with the Father, Jesus Christ the Righteous; and he is the propitiation for our sins."

It is doubtful if any other living man could have composed the above, clear and commonplace as it may sound ; it has all the wisdom of supreme simplicity, all the science of perfect expression.

Charles Reade's literary life embraces a period of little more than thirty years. When we first met, in 1876, I was years younger than he had been when he published his first book. "I envy you, Buchanan," he once said to me; "you might lie by and rest silent for ten long years, and still have a glorious time of work before you." His conviction was that a literary man, especially a novelist, was scarcely ripe enough for important utterance before he reached the forties. I cited the cases of certain famous poets. "Oh, that is different," he replied, with his sly smile; "poetry requires neither knowledge nor experience, you know—it is nonsense pure and simple." Yet the *great* poets, he continued, were qualified by gray hairs: Homer, Dante, Shakespeare, Milton, had a long foreground of life for their masterpieces. Speaking generally, he shared Carlyle's prejudice about verse-poetry. Of all the modern singers, Scott was his favorite, "because he could tell a great story." Of course my friend's poetical

tastes were old-fashioned, and his canons in criticism not far in advance of those of Dr. Johnson, whom, by-the-way, he particularly admired. There is something to be said, however, even for his point of view. Modern verse-writers have alienated the public, because they have imitated the Eastern Spinning Dervish, lost in rapt contemplation of his own navel, or inner consciousness, forgetting life with all its endless humors, its pathos, and its infinite variety of theme.

He was a great reader of novels, blue-books, and the newspapers. Of criticism he had the same opinion as George Henry Lewes, who once wrote : "The good effected by criticism is infinitesimal, the evil incalculable." It was quite natural, therefore, that such a man should be the target for all sorts of attacks. The general idea of him is that he was morbidly sensitive in such matters. He was nothing of the kind; but he was pugnacious, and when roused, dearly loved to flourish the shillalah. Of course he did not always see the joke when his good name was filched away, his character maligned, and his patient work undervalued, as very often happened. Yet, like all strong fighting men, he was magnanimous. I know of one instance where the widow of a literary opponent—a man who had assaulted him very cruelly—reaped the full measure of his forgiveness, and his charity. He was, as we all know, litigious, less because of any infirmity of temper than because he was a brilliant lawyer and advocate, invariably successful in conducting his own cases. He was proud, and justly proud, of his power as a publicist and journalist, for on more than one occasion his pen had opened the prison door, and his voice appalled the soul of an unjust judge. The good he did in this way lives after him; the world is freer, justice is more alert, innocence feels safer, through the sunlight reflected back on our jurisprudence from the mirror of Charles Reade.

The death of Mrs. Seymour, which took place not long after the production of *Drink* at the Princess's Theatre, was a blow from which he never entirely rallied. I was in Ireland at the time, and when I came to London the funeral was over, and Reade was alone in the desolate house. Never shall I forget his look as he sat, a broken man, at the writing-table, surrounded by likenesses, paintings and colored photographs, of his beloved friend.

In all of them, however unfaithful to the original, he found something that suggested her loving face. He could talk of nothing, think of nothing, but her whom he had lost. His grief was pitiful to witness. In his desolation his godson, Mr. Liston, himself a man of scholarship and fine attainments, came to live with and comfort him, doing a thousand gracious things, working with him, reading with him, to help him in his great trouble. But it soon became clear that to reside permanently in the old house was to keep the wound green and open, and as speedily as possible he removed to Shepherd's Bush, taking a small house next door to the one occupied by his brother. He still continued, however, to visit 19 Albert Gate for a few hours every day, though his most frequent pilgrimage was to the quiet churchyard at Willesden, where Laura Seymour was lying. He eased his overladen heart in constant charities done in *her* name; found out her pensioners, of whom there were many, and helped them for her sake. Whenever he gave a gift of money it was given "from Laura Seymour and Charles Reade." She was with him in the spirit still, helping him as of old, and sanctifying his life. As time wore on he recovered a little of his old power of work, but his power of human enjoyment was gone forever. "I have done with this world," he said. He lived to write another novel and to produce another play (written in collaboration with Mr. Henry Pettitt), but in both cases it was clear that the busy hand had lost its cunning. In the winter of 1883 he went to Cannes, where he finished his last novel, *A Perilous Secret*. With the hand of Death upon him, he struggled homeward, fluttered as far as Calais, where he rested, moribund, arrived finally at Shepherd's Bush, wrecked in mind and body, and there, within a few days, painlessly passed away, in the seventieth year of his age.

It was a dark, showery day in April last when they carried him to his last resting-place, beside his life-long companion, in Willesden church-yard. Only a few mourners were gathered round the grave, but those few loved him, and were deeply moved. His only surviving brother, his godson Mr. Liston, his old friend John Coleman, with whom he had had many a dramatic experience, and Davenport Coleman, attached and faithful in death as in life, were among the number; there, too,

was George Augustus Sala, who never wrote ungenerously of any man, and whose name is a synonym for good-fellowship and kindliness of heart. As we stood and listened to the beautiful burial service (old-fashioned, in the fashion of the loveliness that is stronger than death), and saw the flower-covered coffin lowered into the grave, the sun shone out in answer to the words of immortal promise, and the light sparkled on the trees, and the world brightened as for resurrection. "O grave, where is thy victory! O death, where is thy sting!" It was the last scene of a noble play, the end of a beautiful and honorable life. When we turned away and left him, we seemed to hear a voice crying, "Well done, thou good and faithful servant," for truly he had earned his rest.

In one of the most charming of his *Roundabout Papers*, which opens with a description of a London suburb very early in the morning, Thackeray took occasion to remark that his readers would no doubt wonder that he was awake at so early an hour. "The fact is," he explained, "I have never been able to sleep since the *Saturday Review* said I was no gentleman." This delicious piece of humor was vividly recalled to my mind by some of the obituary comments on the novelist just departed. He, good man, slept soundly enough, never again to be baited by the Bottoms of contemporary criticism, and it would have disturbed his equanimity little to have read, even during his lifetime, that he was neither a "gentleman" nor a "genius." To us who knew him, who perceived both his gentleness and his genius, who mourned in him the last of a race of literary giants, and who believe that his name is written on the rock, and must endure, it was nevertheless somewhat painful to perceive that the stupidity which pursued him during his lifetime had little or no respect for his memory even while it was yet green;

"For o'er him, ere he scarce be cold,
    Begin the scandal and the cry."

The scandal of a slipshod criticism, the cry of all the purblind talents, which was summed up with painful directness in some verses contributed by Mr. William Archer to the *Pall Mall Gazette*—verses as remarkable, I am bound to say, for their old-fashioned literary power as for their obliquity of literary vision. In Mr. Archer's estimate, or epitaph, Charles Reade was a genius *manqué*—

"A Quixote full of fire misplaced,
　A social savior run to waste. . . .
Unskilled to reach the root of things,
He spent his strength on bickerings;
In controversies small and great
Would dogmatize and fulminate,
Till 'Hold, enough!' the people cried,
Converted—to the other side!. . . .
For, gauge his merit as you will,
'Tis 'manner makes the classic' still,
And he who rests in silence here
Was but a copious pamphleteer."

Fortunately this sweeping censure trenches on matter of fact, and can so far be met by an appeal to popular experience. Is it true, then, that on all or any of the great topics handled by Charles Reade the public sided against him? or is it true, on the other hand, that he really did convert the public to his own side, and so redress innumerable wrongs? The answer may be given without hesitation. On the question of prison reform, of the lunacy laws, of copyright in plays and books, of criminal procedure, he appealed to the great English people, and invariably triumphed. But the works in which he made his immortal appeals are not pamphlets; they are masterpieces of realistic imagination. It is as true to say of him that he was only a "copious pamphleteer" as it was to say of Thackeray that he was no gentleman, of Dickens that he was only a cockney humorist, of Shelley that he was merely a transcendentalist, of Wordsworth that he had no "form," and of Shakespeare that he had no "style," all which weighty assertions have been made within man's memory by the criticism that is contemporary, or by the perversity which is "not for an age, but for all time."

To tell the truth, Charles Reade knew little of that art which is called "humor-ing one's reputation," and which in our England has enabled little men to sit in the great places, and mediocre men to reap the honors of ephemeral godhead. A little talent, a great deal of reticence, a spice of coterie glory, *plus* a large amount of public ignorance, soon constitute a bogus reputation, which resembles the bogus residences run up by speculative builders, where everything is perfectly finished to the eye, in admirable taste and temper, but where nothing, in the long-run, will stand wind and water. The "manners make the classic," says Mr. Archer, and the manners decidedly make the bogus reputation. From the time of Ben Jonson to that of Pope, from the time of Pope to that of Samuel Johnson, from the time of Johnson to that of Crabbe and Gifford, your bogus reputation has flourished exceedingly for a little season, to slip down ultimately upon sandy foundations.

But when all is said and done, the style is the man, and by it the man lives or dies. Because the style or manners of Charles Reade, projected into books, preserves for us one of the most lovable and love-compelling personalities of this or any time, we who knew the master can smile at the mistakes of the literary critic and the epitaph-writer, and safely leave the verdict to a near or remote posterity. For the rest, it is not my present office to criticise, or even to protest. I have merely set down, to the best of my ability, a few personal sketches of the man in his habit as he lived. I know him to have been good and great. A man of genius, a true servant of the public, a faithful friend, and a humble Christian, he leaves a precious memory, and works which the world will not willingly let die.

THE WAYFARERS.

Young man with the keen blue eyes,
　　Clear and bold,
　Why, as thou dost fare,
　　With so searching air
Scannest thou each face thou dost behold,
Each small flower, faint-colored like the skies,
　Growing by the way? Why gazest thou
　　O'er the round hill's brow?

"Ah, in every bearded face,
　　Looking deep,
　My heart's friend seek I;
　　In each maiden shy
My heart's dearest, dreamed upon in sleep;
And in each fair flower a hope I trace;
And the hill may hide the flashing sea
　　That doth call to me!"

Old man with the pale blue eyes,
　　Mild and clear,
　Why, as thou dost fare,
　　With that pondering air,
Into passing faces dost thou peer?
Why dost pause where dim like autumn skies
　Starry asters grow? Why gazest thou
　　O'er the round hill's brow?

"Ah, from each gray-bearded face
　　Would I know
　What that heart hath found;
　　And in youths that bound
See a youth that vanished long ago;
In each flower a memory can I trace;
O'er the hill the green, still place may be
　　That doth wait for me."

"SAY, Josiah, let's get up a fam'ly gath-erin', same as other folks do."

"I'd like to see a Hopson gatherin'! Folks would say 'twas an ant-hill on a bender, Ozias. We're all too little. 'Twon't do to make our short-comin's public, as you may say."

"Well, I'd ruther be little and good than be an Irish giant. I don't never hanker after betweenness. It goes quite a ways to be somethin' nobody else is. Now there's them Schuylers, the grandees over to New-ton. They do say—and I guess it's so—that they're always a-talkin' pompious about the 'Schuyler nub,' a kind of a bunion like that grows on to the outside of their hands. Why, they think the world on't, because the Schuylers all hev hed it as long as the memory of man endureth not to the contrary. I'd jest as lives be little as have a nub."

"Do tell! Well, Ozy, folks is folksy, ain't they? Come to think on't, there's a tribe over to Still River they call the Sandy Steeles, all of 'em red-heads. It's pop'lar to call 'em sandy, but you could warm your hands real well, the coldest day in winter, to any crop amongst 'em. Carrots a'n't no-where; it's coals."

"Anyhow, 'Siah, if we are little, we're spry, and that's half the battle. Moreover, there haven't none of us been hanged, nor put into States-prison, nor yet see the in-side of no jail."

"Not yet," said Josiah.

Ozias turned and looked at him with a twinkle in his deep-set eye.

"Expectin' on't, be ye?"

Josiah laughed.

"I don't know as I be; but life's chock-full of onexpectedness. There! there's the meetin' bell. Come over to-night, will ye, after sundown. We'll talk this here matter over deliberate then. The idee kinder takes hold of me."

"Yes, I'll drop in. 'Mandy 'll be real willin' to get rid of me for a spell. Ye see, Obed's first wife's boy's to home, and it seems as though he was a-thinkin' about sparkin' my girl. I don't know. It's pe-cooliar, anyway, how quick girls gets to be women-folks. I never see the beat on't. 'Tis snip, snap, so to speak. Makes me think of Priest Hawes's favoright hymn, or one line on't, that he used to come down on real sollum:

"'The creturs—look, how old they grow!'"

"Hope you don't foller that kotation out entire," said Josiah, "next line bein',

"'And wait their fiery doom.'"

Ozias looked at him with a face of the demurest fun.

"Come along," he said. "'Mandy's fel-ler ain't one of the Still River Steeles."

Josiah tried to solemnize his face, but barely succeeded, as they entered the church door.

Hop Meadow was a little village in one of our New England States, lying in a tiny green valley shut in by low rolling hills, patched here and there with yellow grain fields, squares of waving grass, or crimson clover fragrant as the breath of Eden; and threaded by a big noisy brook that pursued its joyful way to the great river rolling but a mile or two beyond the valley, yet quite out of sight of its inhab-itants. In this fertile and sunny spot, when New England was first settled, An-drew Hopson, yeoman, from Kent, Old England, had staked out his share of land, and built his hut; he had married, short-ly after, his second cousin, and in due time a goodly family of ten children gathered about them. Cousins, too, came over and settled beside Andrew, and more distant relatives were gradually persuaded to find homes in the new country; so, partly for the sake of the numerous Hopsons, and partly in memory of the goodly Kentish hop fields which they hoped one day to emulate, the village was called Hop Mea-dow. It was a peculiarity of the Hopson family that almost without exception its members were small in body. Not a man, for years after their emigration, as for un-known years before it, reached a height of over five feet two; most of them ig-nored the inches; and here and there a real dwarf carried the family specialty to excess.

But if nature had given them little bod-ily presence, they all had keen wits, humor, good temper, and good principles—except exceptions.

Josiah and Ozias were Hopsons by name, but there were Browns among the cousinry, and here and there a Hopson girl had married "outside," and brought her tall husband home to Thanksgiving occasionally, half proud and half ashamed of him. There was a tradition in the family that the first Hopson, that Andrew who put up his log hut in the sunny intervale beside Bright Brook, had left Old England quite as much from pique as principle. He had become a Puritan, no doubt from deep conviction, but there was only the parish church for him to worship in, and the old rector was a stanch adherent of Church and King. When Parson Vivyan heard of the emigrating seceders of Leyden he felt afraid that Andrew Hopson might cast in his lot with those fanatics; and having a kindly feeling for the small yeoman, whom he had christened, and hoped to marry, he exhorted him in season and out of season on the folly of such rebellion against King and Church. Andrew resented the interference, for he had neither thought nor talked of leaving his goodly farm; and he grew tired, too, of the parson's one theme of conversation; so he evaded him everywhere, and showed all the quick wit of his race in those evasions; like a drop of mercury he departed from under Mr. Vivyan's touch and was off; so that worthy man took unworthy advantage of his position and preached a long sermon on the text, "The conies are a feeble folk, and dwell in the clefts of the rock," in which discourse he took occasion to set out with humiliating detail what would naturally be the fate of a poor little creature like the cony if it forsook its home and friends in the rocks that sheltered it, and went out to wandering and strife with wolves and foxes.

The natural history was correct, but the application was so pointed, when Parson Vivyan drew out at length the analogy, and portrayed the fate of the man unfitted by nature for wars and hardships who should leave his neighbors and his native land for the sake of a misguided and heretical opinion, that not even the proverbial good-nature of the Hopsons could abide it.

Andrew took fire at once. He made immediate preparation to sell his farm—a hereditary freehold—and having obtained Prudence's consent to follow him when he should have a home prepared for her, he gathered his household goods together and set sail for the New World, where, as he expressed himself to Parson Vivyan, "there be no prelatical priests to vex the soul, nor yet the ungodly kingdom of a carnal king."

That Sunday evening on which our story opens, a bright June moon-lit night,

Ozias, avoiding the youth who came slowly and slyly to the front door, which stood hospitably open, with evident intent of "sparking," betook himself to Josiah's house, and perfected the plan for a Hopson reunion.

There were many letters to write, for the tribe had branched far, if sparsely. There were two Browns in Ohio and three Hopsons in Illinois, and then three generations ago a certain Mark Hopson had settled on a stony piece of land in Vermont, to dig and sell iron, and called the village which sprung up about his furnace Hopyard; but so unfit was the name when that cleft in the hills became strewed with slag heaps, and overshadowed with black smoke, that a scoffing stranger had said in the tavern one night, "Better call it the Devil's Hopyard, I should say." This ill name had fastened itself firmly on the little cluster of houses, and though the Hopsons themselves swarmed therein, and looked like a troop of gnomes whenever there was a run of iron, and they skipped about the moulding beds in the lurid firelight, yet outsiders were shy of settling there, and told quaint stories of the tiny tribe who occupied the land, and delved, smelted, and hauled pig-iron with an energy that seemed to make up for strength.

It was currently reported that in the early days of the Devil's Hopyard a tin-peddler from "below" stumbled on this small village, and trying to catch some of the little people for purposes of exhibition, chased a dozen of them into the bung-hole of an empty barrel, and triumphantly proceeded to stop up the aperture and secure his prize; but while he pounded at the bung the agile creatures made their escape through the spigot-hole, and derided him with shrill laughter and mocking gestures from the top of a barn, whither they had climbed on a wild grape-vine. Peddler or not, there was plenty of Hopsons there now; and then there was Pamela Bunnell in remote parts of Iowa, who had married out of the clan; and Ozias Brown, who had settled in Pennsylvania; and Marinus Hopson, on Cape Cod; and Tertius Hopson, in Quebec; and more, whom time forbids me to chronicle, but who all received an invitation to this Hopson gathering; and almost all meant to come.

Then began a stir in Hop Meadow. There was a big tent to be hired and pitched on the green—an even bit of turf with some fine elms about it, right in front of the church—and there were spare rooms to clean and dust; and the whole tavern was engaged to afford lodgings if private rooms overflowed; and such baking, boiling, stewing, frying, and other culinary performances set in that one would have thought the ten lost tribes of Israel, all in a famished condition, were coming for a month's stay, and needed unlimited pie, cake, poultry, and pickles — except that there were hams, boiled, roasted, and chopped or sliced for sandwiches, prominent in every house, and hams are pork! In all these preparations nobody was more busied than Prudence Hopson, Widow Polly Hopson's daughter and only child. Bezaleel Hopson, her father, had kept the "store" in Hop Meadow forty years, when he died, and having married late in life, left behind him this little five-year-old daughter, and plenty of "means" to console his wailing widow, who was an "outsider," and perhaps attracted her fat and jolly husband by her extreme difference from any of his kindred.

Paulina Flower had been pretty in a certain way: long curling yellow hair, limp and flabby even in its trailing ringlets, languishing blue eyes, a white skin, narrow, low forehead, and long chin seemed to express and adorn her manners and customs with peculiar fitness.

Nobody but the Hopsons would ever have called her Polly; to "her folks" she was "Pawliny," nothing less; but Bezaleel couldn't stand three syllables, so he had followed the custom of his race, and tried to make the best of his wife's melancholy while he lived.

"She beats all," said Ozias to Josiah, his cousin and special crony. "I never see a woman who likes to howl so well in my life; she's forever a-spillin' salt-water. She'd oughter keep clus to a pork barrel, so's to save brine. I b'lieve she'd set down an' cry to the heavenly gates, ef ever she got there, to think the' wa'n't a fiery chari't sent down to fetch her."

"Well," answered the more slow-minded Josiah, "some folks is made so; nothin' suits 'em, never. Their eggs gets addled second day out, and if they haven't really got a thing to cry for, they'll do it a-puppus. She's one o' them that likes to cry jest as well as you do to larf, Ozy. It a'n't real comfortin' to other folks to see 'em, and I will say I've hankered some to give Polly a hidin'; 'twould do her solid good

ter have somethin' real to cry for. But you can't tune another man's wife no-how."

"That's so," sadly responded Ozias.

But Prudence—"little Prudy," as everybody called her, borrowing her title from the most utterly delightful children's books ever written—was a thorough Hopson.

When her father died she was but five years old, and though she mourned him heartily and sincerely, it was as children mourn, with brief tears and tender remembrance, but a blessed incompetence of understanding what loss, death, separation, really mean. She saw her mother no more, if no less, tearful; she could not be more doleful and forlorn under any loss than she had been in the daily fashion of her life; and Prudy was as different from Polly as was possible—a gay, sparkling, happy creature, everybody's pet and darling. If she had lost one father, she had twenty uncles and cousins ready to protect and indulge her, and she grew up to womanhood as nearly spoiled as her sweet, honest nature would allow. But who ever was proof against those beautiful brown eyes, red and saucy lips, that tossing, wavy, shining hair, never in order, but never anything but exquisite in its dark shadows and golden lights?

Who could resist that coaxing, caressing, beguiling voice—that voice that could soften with pity and sparkle with mischief? Who did not clamor for the help of those deft and taper fingers that were always ready and able to do whatever was asked of them? It was Prudy who came to the front now in all the adornments of preparation. She made the long wreaths of ground pine and coral pine for festooning the tent and the church, and fastened them up under knots of golden-rod and bosses of purple aster, for the Hopson gathering was early in September. She arranged the baskets of fruit that adorned the table, so that pink and purple and amber grapes lay heaped together on vine leaves, and the profusion of green and gold pears was set off with the earliest scarlet foliage of the maple and deep maroon of lingering beet leaves.

She made the wonderful ornaments of stars and roses and architectural devices that would have adorned the countless pies had not the oven baked them out of all shape. And it was Prudy who manufactured the whitest silver cake and the clearest jelly that made contrast of ivory and ruby beside the grosser aliments of cold ham and roast turkey.

Her mother looked on and shook her melancholy head when Prudy dragged that unwilling parent to see what had been done.

"Yes, I dare say; it's pretty, I suppose. But, oh, I can't help a-mournin' to think how that your pa would ha' relished it. This world's a fleetin' show, Prudence. Ef you'd ha' ben through what I have you wouldn't take no great of int'rest in these triflin' things."

Prudy laughed; her father had been dead a thousand years—to her; and her mother's melancholy moans had no more significance to her than the wind in the spout.

"Well, mammy, they're pretty, anyway, and I expect most of these things will be a fleetin' show when a crowd of hungry Hopsons get hold of 'em. Who's coming to our house to stay ?—do you know yet ?"

"I should ha' liked to have Pamely Bunnell and her boy, but she was bespoke by Ozias's folks. I used to know her some before I was married, for she married Bunnell when he lived to our place, and while she lived here a spell I come here to visit, and then I see your pa. Oh, I remember of it well, the fust time I see him; 'twas to a meetin' of the sons an' daughters of Massachusetts. Josiah he'd put it in the paper that 'all who are or were born in Massachusetts is expected to attend th' annooal meetin' in Clark Hall.' You see, Josiah's wife she come from Hingham; and well do I rec'lect he got up that evenin' and said the 'highest "gaol" of his ambition hed always been to marry a Massachusetts girl.' Some didn't really understand what he meant, but Pamely she said he'd got the wrong word; Josiah's a little mixy, always an' forever was and will be; and your pa he bu'st out laughin' behind me, and I looked round and see him. He hadn't no business there, only 't he provided the provisions, and he'd jest fetched in a pot of pickles 't somebody 'd forgot, and— Oh! I've kinder run off from Pamely. Well, I can't hev her: she writ to Ozias for to have her place in his house. I s'pose 'tis more cherk up there than 'tis to a solitary widder's like me. One that's seen so much 'fliction and is so cast down into the valley of mournin' as I be a'n't

good company. And jest my luck!—me that never could abide children—they've sent Marinus's people to us—seven small children, and she's weakly. Oh land! how be I to bear it ?"

Prudy laughed again; she couldn't help it; the idea of seven children secretly delighted her sunshiny soul. What romps they would have! What corn-poppings! —she would rub up the old warming-pan to-day; and there were five kittens in the barn!

Polly did not betray her own secret hopes to her daughter. Like many languid, selfish, sloppy, mournful people, she had a certain cunning or slyness, which tended to amuse her—and sometimes other people—when it did not vex them! She had purposely delayed asking Pamela Bunnell, who was a widow with one son, to her house, lest the son should take a fancy to Prudy.

Mrs. Polly did not intend to lose her girl if she could help it: no servant could or would so neatly curl her lank ringlets, that, threaded with the gray of forty-nine years, still dropped absurdly down her back; nor would any other woman wait on her so handily and cheerfully on the frequent days when she chose to keep her bed, and must be fed with the daintiest morsels that Prudy knew just how to prepare.

To be sure, Hopson Bunnell, Pamela's boy, was "well spoke of" by such of the clan as had heard of him, and had some property of his own, besides a reversion of the great prairie farm his mother superintended with all the energy and skill a bigger woman could have brought to bear on the premises; but for all this Mrs. Polly cared nothing. Her listless self-absorption would have come between Prudy and the best match possible, so she had never asked Pamela—who expected it of her—to come to her house, but had gently hinted to the Reception Committee of the occasion that she could take a large family if they were mostly children, and could be crowded two or three in a chamber. Prudy had her own intimate friend, of course, in the village, for though there were but few young girls in Hop Meadow, the Hopsons having a way of marrying young, there were a few, and Lizzy Brown was the best and prettiest, next to Prudy—a sober, steady, discreet maiden, with brown hair and blue eyes, who looked at Prudence as a robin might at an oriole, but did not treat her at all as the one bird treats the other, but held her in all adoration, and served her with earnest affection.

At last the day of the Hopson reunion arrived—one of those soft, golden, gorgeous days in autumn when the air is quiet, the heavens serene, and the earth steeped in dreams and rainbows; but the Hopsons were not still; not at all. They swarmed like troops of good-sized fairies through the wide streets, laughing, shaking hands, chattering, singing, full of welcome and cheer—slight, airy girls; rounder but still tidy matrons, with dolls of babies in their arms; fat little men, laughing and joking with every new-comer—the only woful face being Mrs. Polly's; while Prudy, in the daintiest white gown, with a big bunch of red late roses at her belt, was threading the crowd everywhere, marshalling the guests to their several lodgings, smiling at every child, coquetting with every old man, and turning a bewitching cold shoulder on the youths who buzzed about her like contending bumble-bees on a Canada thistle, prickliest and most delicate of its tribe.

But one of the race, Pamela's boy, towered far above the rest, to his own disgust and their amusement. Hopson Bunnell was all of six feet in his stockings, powerful, athletic, and handsome, with dark keen eyes, firm lips, a shock of deep brown curls, and a silky beard of darkness that showed well against the cool healthiness of his smooth if sunburned skin.

"I know he's awful tall," said Pamela, deprecatingly, to Ozias, "and I've set my heart on his marryin' one of our folks. Seems as though Providence interfered serious with my plans. The' ain't no girls anywhere near to us, and them that's nearest, Hopson don't seem to fellowship; but I never seemed to sense his tallness as I do now, 'mongst the rest of us."

"Well," answered Ozias, "'tain't always best to make no great of plans about folks's marryin'; they gener'lly do as they darn please about that, I've observed. Providence hes got severial other things to do, I guess, than makin' matches. I'm a free-will Baptist, so fur as that comes in, now I tell ye."

"Oh my!" exclaimed Pamela. "I don't expect to settle nothing, nor I haven't said a word to Hopson, you better believe. I was only speakin' of it to you, Ozy, out of the fullness of my heart, as you may say, accordin' to Scripter."

"Well, I sha'n't tell; and 'tain't best to put a finger into sech pies. Natur is pecooliar, Pamely; you can't never tell how it 'll work; so I calc'late always to leave out the bung for fear of a bu'st. There's my 'Mandy, now. Mariar bein' dead ever sence the girl was ten year old, I've been consider'ble pestered what *to* do with her; but fin'lly I *con*cluded to see 't she read the Bible right along and said her prayers punctooal, and then I let her went. She had her ups an' downs, but she's come up about as good as the average; and now she's got to keepin' company with a pretty clever feller, and she'll be off my mind afore long."

Hopson Bunnell, all unconscious of his mother's wish in his behalf, was meantime enjoying himself mightily; he recovered from his awkwardness very fast, turning the laugh on his kindred in various ways, and dangling after Prudy like an amiable giant in the toils of a fairy queen. She seemed to this tall, handsome fellow something daintier than a flower, and more bewitching than a bird; he never tired of seeing that graceful little figure waiting on the tables, coaxing the old men with dainty morsels, filling the boys with good things, hollow though they were "down to their boots," as she declared, being unused to boys; or playing with the little girls, who all adored her. But to Hopson himself Prudy was the most malicious elf! Nobody teased him as she did; nobody could.

"Cousin Hopson," she said to him, the day after the feast—for though almost all the rest had gone, a few of the more distant remained to extend a visit they had come so far to make—"Cousin Hopson, will you please to do something for me?"

"I *guess* I will," alertly answered Hopson, bewitched with the sweet, shy voice.

"Just hand me down one of them stars to put in my hair, will you?" and Prudy vanished with a peal of mocking mirth, echoed by a cackle of fat laughter from Tertius Hopson, the Quebec cousin, a very jolly, rosy, stout old bachelor, looking for all the world like a Sir Toby jug.

"She beats all," said Tertius. "I never see a hum-bird fuller o' buzz than little Prudy."

Hopson bit his lips. "I'll be even with her," he said to himself; so that very evening, as some of the clan gathered round a tiny open fire in Ozias's kitchen, rather for companionship than cold, the young farmer said to Prudy: "You oughter to be put to use, Prudy. I'd like to buy ye up for a mantel-shelf figure; you're just big enough."

"I a'n't for sale," snapped Prudy.

"Why, you'd do first-rate; them things are all the go, and you're the exact size."

So saying, he stooped, and before Prudy knew what had happened, two strong hands grasped her tiny waist, and she was swung up like a feather by those mighty arms, and set on the broad oaken shelf among the flat-irons, candlesticks, and other miscellaneous articles thereon; while Hopson, retreating a step, looked her in the face, and a roar of laughter from Tertius, Ozias, 'Mandy, Josiah, and the rest completed her discomfiture. Prudy colored scarlet, her eyes flashed, and one little fist clinched instinctively; the other hand held fast to the shelf.

"Cousin 'Zias, take me down," she called out, imperatively.

"Bless your soul, Prudy! I ain't big enough."

"Get a chair."

"Why, folks is settin' on 'em, every one," and Ozias looked round with an air of innocent dismay that renewed the laughter.

"I'll take ye down, Prudy, if you'll say 'please,' like a good baby," calmly remarked Hopson.

Prudy choked. "I'll stay here all night first," she snapped.

"Well, 'tis jest as I said now. You do make about as good-lookin' a figure for a mantel as ever was."

"Take me down!" shrieked Prudy.

But oh, how pretty she was up there! Dresden could not match with her costliest figurines the delicate creature in her china-blue gown (a sudden chill having come after the September heats had made woollen garments comfortable), falling in soft dim folds just to the smallest shoes that ever a Hopson even could wear, her white throat set off by carnation ribbons under the lace frill, and another bow of that tender, vivid color in her waving, shining hair, her eyes sparkling, her red lips apart, and her cheeks rosier than her ribbons. Hopson Bunnell could have looked at her forever, but he did not say so. "Say 'please' now—real pretty," was all he did say, unconsciously drawing nearer to the lovely little creature.

Prudy was quick-witted; she controlled her rage a moment. "W-e-ll"—reluc-

tantly—"I don' know but I'd whisper it, rather'n stay up here all night."

Luckless man! He drew near to catch the precious whisper, but as he turned his ear, Prudy's hand descended on his brown cheek with a resounding slap that left a print of five little fingers impressed thereon visibly for at least an hour; but, alas! in avenging herself Prudy lost her balance, and Hopson caught her fairly in his arms, and kissed the lovely, indignant face before he really knew what he was doing.

"'A kiss for a blow, always bestow,'" cackled Tertius. And everybody roared again, except Prudy, who dropped to the floor, burst into tears, and fled.

Hopson was really ashamed of himself, but it did seem to him as if his head whirled; a sense of wild bliss ran in all his veins; he knew well that he had taken an unfair advantage of Prudy, but so reckless was his delight that he was not a bit repentant.

However, he had to repent next day. Prudy turned into a perfect snow-ball whenever he came near her. It took a week of abasement and apologies to put them on the old footing (externally) again. Could he tell, poor fellow, being only a man, how Prudy secretly exulted in the apology she professed to despise?—i. e., "You were so sweet and so pretty, I couldn't help it, Prudy."

How was he to know that these words rung in her ears like a song of joy day and night, or that in the once still depths of her heart Prudy recognized a sweet perturbation that dated from the second she was held in those powerful arms, close against a manly, throbbing heart?

But nobody could be cross in this clear autumnal weather, with gay leaves beginning to illuminate the woods, daily parties to hunt for gentian blossoms, to gather "wintergreen plums," to heap up red and golden apples under the orchard boughs, or clamber after fragrant wild grapes on the hill-sides. Hopson grew deeper in love with every new day, and Prudy fought more feebly against the chains that seemed daily to imprison her will and her thoughts. Perhaps the course of true love might for once have run smooth but for that unruly member that spoils most of our plans in this world, and brings to naught the best intentions and the sincerest good-will. Tertius Hopson still lingered in Hop Meadow, as well as Pamela Bunnell and her son. Tertius was living in Quebec "on his means," as we Yankees phrase it. He had made some money there in trade, and settled down to enjoy it in a sort of selfish fashion that was not natural to his jolly, kindly disposition.

He had never known how close and pleasant are the ties of kindred till now; he seemed at last to have got home; here was the stir, the interest, the sweetness of a daily intercourse hitherto denied him, and it seemed to warm and rejuvenate his life, to quicken his pulses, to brighten his ideas; he loved it; he could not tear himself away; and above all things he loved to "bother" Polly Hopson. Whenever she sighed, he smiled, broad and beaming as the harvest-moon; whenever she bewailed herself, he laughed; when she wept, as now and then she did weep over the departed Bezaleel, he would deliberately sit down and sing to her all the queer old songs he had learned in the "old country," as he persisted in calling Quebec, till the Meadow boys learned by heart "The Leather Bottell," "The British Grenadiers," "Hunting the Hare," "Lasses and Lads," and sundry other rollicking ditties which once delighted the ears of our forefathers across the water, and have in them still a ringing, hearty smack of country squiredom and rural sports. At first Polly was outraged; her chin fell half an inch, and her curls frayed out of curliness with the solemn shakes of her head and the dampness of her tears; but she endured from helplessness, and began at last to smile wintrily and forbearingly on the unconquerable jollity of the man whom at first she mildly contemned. It threatened to be the old story of "first endure, then pity, then embrace"; and, as usual, outsiders saw most of the game.

Ozias and Josiah, after their custom, sat in conclave upon the matter. They had just set the cidar mill going, which they owned in common, and perched themselves on a cart neap, where they could "chirk up the hoss," which revolved with the beam of the press, and yet indulge in that gossip which delighted their souls, combining business with pleasure.

"Say," began Josiah, "haven't you sorter surmised, Ozy, that Tertius favors Hop Meadow for a residin'-place, so to speak?"

"Well, I hev," Ozias answered, "and I shouldn't be no more'n surprised ef that he settled down here after a spell; he's lonesome up to Quebec, I expect. There arn't nothin' like your own folks, after all, when you're gettin' along in years; the' don't nobody else sorter seem to belong t' ye."

"It does make a sight of difference," replied the moralizing Josiah. "When one's young, and havin' their monsterious days, it don't make no great of difference where they be, nor what they're a-doin' of; but come to git rheumatiz onto a feller, and hev the grinders cease because they are few, as Scripter tells, why, you begin to be everlastin' thankful that there's a house 'n' home for ye, and a woman to cook your vittles."

"That's so, Josh, and that's why I'm a-goin' to hev 'Mandy and her feller settle down along with me when they get married. She'll hev the farm when

'The end o' my nose
An' the tips o' my toes
Is turned up to the roots of the daisies,'

as the song-book says; and she might as well stop to hum and look after me as to go further and fare worse. But seems to me kinder as if Tertius was slyin' round Polly, if you'll b'lieve it."

"Heavens to Betsey!" gasped Josiah. "That old feller?"

"Well, I never see the time, Josh, 't a man was too old to git married—nor a woman nuther, for that matter. It's everlastin' queer, surely, for him to take a likin' to Polly. I'd as lieves hang on to a wet dish-rag as her, when all's said an' done, but 'many men of many minds,' as the sayin' goes, and if she's to his'n, why, I don't make nor meddle with 'em. She's got a good place for to take him into."

"Yes; that's suthin. He's got means, I s'pose, but it's kind o' lonesome to live the way he does up to Quebec, a-lodgin', as he calls it, and to be took down with the sarcastic rheumatiz as he was, an'—"

"Land sakes! what's that?" asked Ozias.

"Well, I don't reelly know; I b'lieve it's principally confined to one leg, an' starts pretty high up, but that's what he called it, anyway; mabbe 'tis the English name on't; but it's real severe, now I tell ye; he said it made him holler like a loon."

"Polly can cry for somethin' then," dryly remarked Ozias.

"And I sorter surmise, Ozy, that Pamely's boy is a-hankerin' after little Prudy."

"Well, I've had my idees sot that way too. He's a clever feller as ever was; but I should hate to lose little Prudy. Darn the cretur! a'n't there nobody else to Hop Meadow he could set his eyes onto but her?"

"I'd like to know who else," answered Josiah. "'Mandy's spoke for, as well you know; and I have heered lately that Lizzy Brown is promised to Marinus's nevy down to Cape Cod; he's mate to a three-master, so they tell, and is off on a voyage jest now, so they don't talk on't, but it's so. Marinus has kep' his mouth shut. He's a kind of a dumb, oyster cretur." (Poor "mixy" Josiah meant "austere.")

"Nat'ral for him to keep his mouth shut," put in Ozias; "they gener'lly do."

Josiah stared, but serenely went on. "But he did allow 'twas so to Aunt Nancy, an' she up an' told my wife, so ye see the' ain't reelly nobody but little Prudy to hev."

"Hobson's choice for him, ain't it? Hullo, young feller! Speak of a donkey 'n' you see an ear direct;" for here Hopson Bunnell stalked into the cider-mill shed, his handsome face warm with exercise, and his eyes softened and deepened by his unspoken thoughts.

"We was just a-talkin' about you," explained Josiah.

"And Cousin 'Zias had to call me a donkey. Now is that friendly?" laughed Pamela's boy.

"There's worse critters than donkeys," blandly answered Ozias; "but I was only a-usin' the term proverbially, as it were, or was, or might be. Fact is, my eyes is gettin' open to your designs, sir, and I was kind of dammin' in a genteel way about your carryin' off little Prudy to Iowy, when she's the one we all set by like our eyes, and I was askin', in a general manner, ef there wasn't no other Hopson girl you could have took up with besides her; and Josiah said the' wa'n't; the rest was all bespoke; an' I said 'twas Hobson's choice with ye."

Pamely's boy flushed to his dark curls, his head was lifted as if some proud delight lay on a height that he could see, but no other, and his voice rang out in subdued yet clear cadence as he answered:

"There isn't another girl, outside of Hop Meadow neither, Ozias; there ain't in the world. There's nobody for me but little Prudy. You was right one way; she's Hopson's choice, and no other."

Unlucky mother-tongue! why are *b* and *p* so near alike in our queer old language that the distinction between them is almost inexpressible by human lips? As luck would have it, Prudy and Lizzy Brown had privately stolen up to the cider press, thinking it deserted, to indulge in the surreptitious but dear delight of sucking sweet new cider through a straw. They were old and demure enough to be ashamed of the trick if any one saw them, but the rich fruity beverage was delicious to their girlish memories, and slyly they stole out to indulge in the tipple, carrying gold-bright straws in their hands, and came up behind the shed just in time to hear Hopson's declaration.

Prudy's face flamed, the tender visions that had dwelt in her dumb heart and softened her cool brown eyes were struck by the lurid light of sudden fury, and fled away: she grasped Lizzy's arm with a vise-like grip.

"Come right away," she whispered; and fleet as a silent pair of goblins they left the green yard where the shed stood, and disappeared down a narrow lane that led to Josiah's barn.

Prudy rushed into that friendly shelter, banged the door behind her, relaxed her hold of Lizzy, and sitting down promptly on a wheelbarrow, cried with rage.

"Why, Prudy," said the gentle Elizabeth, "what in the world's the matter?"

"Didn't you he-he-hear him?—the awful, horrid, mean thing," sobbed Prudy.

"Hear who, dear?"

"Why, that great, horrid Hopson Bunnell. Didn't you hear him—I'm sure he spoke out loud enough—say that he'd got to marry me: 'twas Hobson's choice and no other?"

Prudy did extend the facts a little, it is true; she didn't mean to l—extend them, but she gave the idea as she took it in, just as the rest of us poor mortals do, without a thought that any other construction than her own could be put upon the words, or that she had confounded those confounded letters—forgive the phrase, dear reader; they continually exasperate me—*b* and *p*.

"No, I didn't hear him," condoled Lizzy. "Poor dear Prudy, did he say such a mean thing? Well, never mind, dear, that don't make it so; you know you haven't got to take him. You don't like him."

Prudy reared her dishevelled little head from the side of the wheelbarrow, like a snake about to strike.

"You goose!" she said. "I *do* like him. Oh dear! oh dear! Lizzy Brown, I'll kill you if you ever tell. But I do. I can't help it, and, oh!—and—and I thought he liked me first, or I never—oh!—oh!—"

Here a flood of tears literally drowned her voice, and in Lizzy's soft eyes tears shone with sympathetic brightness. She sat down by Prudy, and began to sob too.

"And he—oh, Liz!—he kissed me once, and now he says 'twas Hobson's choice. I'd just like to shoot him."

Prudy started suddenly, and the wheelbarrow, overloaded with grief and girls, as suddenly tipped over, leaving girls and grief in a heap on the barn floor. This was too much for Prudy. Blinded with hay seed, damp with tears, choked with hysteric laughter, it was a good hour before Lizzy could calm her or restore her to her proper aspect, and make her consent to go home quietly, though with burning vengeance in her heart.

Poor Hopson! the world was hollow now, and his doll stuffed with bran. If he didn't want to go into a convent, he did want to go back to Iowa, and yet Prudy controlled him like a Fate, and kept him miserable, abject, and longing in Hop Meadow, growing thin, pale, and silent, after the approved hang-dog fashion of unhappy lovers who are tacitly allowed to flaunt their wretchedness all abroad—probably because it is so transitory.

Polly sighed and wept; Tertius laughed and sung more than ever. Changeful as the aptest specimen of her sex, she now earnestly desired that Prudy should marry and leave her to Tertius, for Polly had at last consented to try another Hopson—"try" in more senses than one—and much she feared that Prudy would send "Pamely's boy" home in despair.

Pamela, too, was distressed to the heart with her boy's misery. She dared not try to console him, for on her feeblest attempt to break the ice he would turn on his heel and leave her. At last she brought her trouble to Ozias, with whom she had been brought up, and whom she regarded as a brother.

"Say, Ozy, what *do* you suppose ails Hopson? He don't never eat a meal of vittles; jest picks a mouthful, as you may see, not enough for a chippin'-bird. And he's a-grievin' in'ardly the whole time: I know he is, for he don't sleep nights, and he a'n't no fatter'n a hen's forehead. He's wastin' away, dyin' by inches, I do believe."

"Well, Pamely, he'll be quite a spell dyin', then, if that's a comfort to ye: there's consider'ble many inches *to* Hopson."

"Oh-zias, I b'lieve you'd laugh ef I was a-dyin'!" indignantly snapped Pamela.

"Mabbe I should. I don't love to cry before folks; but really now, Pamely, I b'lieve what ails Hopson is that little witch of a Prudy; he's most amazin' sot on her, and she won't so much as look at him. I'm free to confess I thought she liked him for a spell; but, Lord! what can a feller find out about women-folks? They're spryer, an' cuter, an' sinfuler, an' more pernickity 'n a fire-hang-bird! I don't see into it."

"Oh dear! what shall I do?" sighed Pamela, despairingly.

"Don't do nothin'! I'll see to it. It's one of them cases where somebody's got to speak in meetin', an' when there's a woman to pay, it's a sight better to ketch a-holt of her with a strong hand, same as I used ter squeeze grasshoppers when I was a boy, and hold her still till she tells. I'll tackle Miss Prudy myself, for the thing's got to be did: this hangin' on by the eyelids ain't nateral nor pleasin'. You keep still." Pamela was used to the masterful ways of Ozias, so she took to her rocker and her knitting, wiped a few mild tears from her kind old eyes, and waited for events.

Ozias, well aware of Prudy's haunts, followed the path by the side of Bright Brook down to a cluster of shag-bark walnut-trees on a meadow that belonged to Bezaleel's farm; he knew she had gone there nutting, and meeting the doleful Hopson on his way, remarked, curtly, "Young feller, I want you should happen down this road in twenty minutes: don't make it longer."

Hopson stared.

"Come, now; do as I tell you: you'll be glad on't."

"I'll come if you want me," was the listless answer.

Ozias found Prudy doing anything but nutting; her basket was on the ground empty, all about her lay husks and nuts that the keen wind of November had thrown down, but she left them to lie there. Her shawl was drawn over her head, her head leaned against a mighty tree, and she was crying fast and silently, when Ozias jumped over the fence. She tried to tie on her hat, but Ozias sat down beside her and took her two hands fast in his.

"Prudy," he said, "I've got a word to say to ye: why on the face of the airth *air* you treatin' Pamely's boy the way you be?"

"I ain't," said Prudy, irrelevantly and femininely.

Ozias went on, regardless of her futile remark: "He's a-actin' like a born fool, jest because you won't not so much as look at him. He thinks the sun rises an' sets in your face, an'—"

"He don't either," broke in Prudy, "an' you know he don't."

"I know he does. He don't nyther eat nor sleep for thinkin' of ye. The great, strong, hulkin' feller acts like a sick chicken. Now what's to pay?"

"Hm?" sniffed Prudy, her color rising and her eyes flashing. "I guess he's found out I ain't Hobson's choice for him, not noway."

"Whew!" whistled Ozias. "Who told you he thought you was?"

"Nobody. I heard him say so—and you was sittin' by and heard him too—in the cider-mill shed, that time—"

"Well, if ever I did!" and Ozias laughed till the woods about them rang again. Prudy grew furious. Ozias stopped when he heard her angry sobs, and called out,

"Hopson Bunnell, step over that air five-rail fence, and come here."

Prudy struggled to escape, but Ozias held her tight. He had reckoned well on Hopson's overpunctuality, and the tall fellow vaulted over the rails at his call.

"Say, Prudy here was behind the shed that day me an' Josiah was a-pesterin' you about sparkin' of her. Now you tell what you said."

"I? I was sort of riled at your sayin' that she was Hobson's choice, and I spoke up and said 'twa'n't so; she was Hopson's choice. And so she is, and will be for evermore, whether she cares a cent about it or not."

At the strong ring of that voice Prudy felt her very heart thrill, and Ozias, with preternatural wisdom, let go her hands, as he said: "I've always heered that two was company and three was none, and I'm a-goin' to put the hearsay into expec-r'ence direckly; but it's also a fact that two is better witness than one, and I hereby say and *de*clare, a-holdin' up my right hand to wit, that this here mortal long Bunnell feller did say jest what he says he said, that the aforesaid Prudy was, out of all Hop Medder, and the hull creation besides, Hopson's choice. And I swan to man I b'lieve she is!" he added, looking abroad at the shag-barks as he saw Prudy run into Hopson's arms, and kindly left the two to their own company, whistling as he went, but not for want of thought.

THE RESERVOIR SYSTEM.

IN the heart of northern Minnesota, about seventy miles distant from Lake Itasca, are to be found the beginnings of a work whose exact counterpart the world has never seen. The idea of the reservoir system, as applied to the improvement of river navigation, belongs originally, perhaps, neither to this country nor to this century. The practical application of it is to be credited to American engineering science and American daring. When the experiment—if that can be called an experiment for the success of which the best engineers of the country have put their professional reputation in bond—shall have been completed in these northern solitudes, and when the volume of water passing down the Upper Mississippi can, within certain limits, be regulated by a few touches upon a telegraphic transmitter in Washington, man will have made one more of nature's forces partially subject to his will.

The idea of reservoirs on the head-waters of the Mississippi was conceived many years ago. There is even a tradition that Nicollet took an interest in the subject, and such a project might well have commended itself to his bold imagination. But the first examination known to have been made of the sources with a view to reservoirs is of recent date. It was undertaken by Mr. Cook, of Minneapolis, under the direction of General G. K. Warren, then stationed at St. Paul. The examination, but a hasty one at best, was made as part of a plan for the preservation of the Falls of St. Anthony, it being thought at that critical period in the history of the falls that danger to them would be lessened and the work of improvement facilitated by withholding a part of the water of freshets in reservoirs. The result of this cursory examination was to determine that there were no insuperable natural obstacles to the construction of reservoirs. General Warren, however, was impressed with the wider view of the matter, and concluded that reservoirs might be made to benefit the river lower down. Recommendations to this effect are to be found in his report of 1870, as well as in an exhaustive document on the Fox and Wisconsin rivers. In 1873–4 Colonel F. U. Farquhar made extensive surveys of the lakes at the head-waters of the Mississippi, and reported decidedly in favor of reservoirs. The government had by this time become alive to the importance of the subject, and in 1878 Major Charles J. Allen was directed to examine the matter in detail, make the necessary preliminary surveys, and exhaust the subject of the feasibility of the proposed reservoirs. Upon his hearty concurrence in the views of other engineers, and relying upon his important independent investigations, the government then decided to make the attempt. Congress appropriated sums sufficient to begin the undertaking by the construction

of an experimental reservoir as a practical test. As soon as the money became available and the necessary settlements with the Indians were completed, work was begun. It has since gone steadily forward, under the direction and according to the plans of Major Allen, to whom so much of the present promise of the enterprise is due.

The reservoir system contemplates the erection of five dams on the Mississippi River proper in its upper course, one on each of two of its earliest tributaries, and others on the head-waters of the St. Croix, Chippewa, and Wisconsin. Surveys for those on the last-named rivers have been made, but work upon them will probably be deferred until those on the parent stream have been put in operation. The theory is that in these immense dams the surplus waters of the rivers can be retained in the spring and fall, and released during the summer in sufficient quantity to secure a fair stage of water in the navigable channel of the river every day through the dry season. The necessity for regular channel improvement, by the removal of snags and bars and the construction of jetties and wing-dams, will by no means be obviated. The reservoirs are only to provide enough water to fill that channel when unobstructed.

To understand the probabilities of a successful application of this system, a glance at the topography of the surrounding country is necessary. The Upper Mississippi presents a strange likeness in miniature to the lower sec-

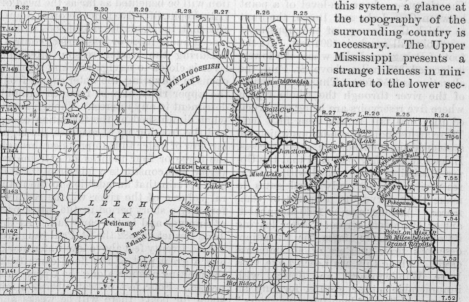

MAP OF RESERVOIR REGION.

tion of the river. The wild region in which it has its origin lies just south of the water-shed of the northern boundary, and in the heart of the lake district of Minnesota. Instead of mile posts there are mile ponds, and the traveller through the wilderness records the progress of his journey by "three-mile lake," "five-mile lake," or "ten-mile lake," the numbers having reference, not to size, but to distance from some given point. In the low and swampy ground about these lakes, an elevation of more than twenty or thirty feet is an exception. Almost all of them have feeders and outlets, but the slope is too gradual to give more than a placid flow. The lakes are only expansions of streams, which are threads connecting a rosary of lakes. The Upper Mississippi shares this general character. Itasca, Cass, and Winibigoshish lakes form, in order, parts of the Mississippi proper. Into and out of them the river, even here a respectable-sized stream, steals quietly, and between and below them it winds for the most part through tamarack swamps and fields of wild rice, with a course as sinuous as in the canebrakes of Louisiana. It is quite as possible to lose one's self in "sloughs" five hundred miles north of St. Paul as in the bayous of the lower river. The Father of Waters changes his skies, but not his character. The sluggish current is too nearly imperceptible to guide the doubter. The elevation above sea-level of a point between Cass Lake and Itasca, the limit to which the flowage of the uppermost reservoir will reach, is 1304 feet. At the foot of Pokegama Falls, where the lowest is located, 350 miles above St. Paul, the elevation is 1255 feet. Thus in the course of the river through the whole region where five reservoirs are being constructed the total fall is less than fifty feet. These are the natural conditions which the system demands as indispensable to success. Indeed, it may fairly be said that the Upper Mississippi is furnished with natural reservoirs, needing only flood-gates to make them serve the purposes of commerce. As long ago as 1860 an inhabitant of Minnesota wrote: "After leaving its source in Lake Itasca, the Mississippi describes three-quarters of an immense circle. Along this are Leech Lake, Cass Lake, Winibigoshish, and Itasca, with innumerable minor groups, forming an immense system of lacustrine reservoirs." It has been intended to locate the dams

at or near the outlet of the larger lakes, so that by a slight elevation a large amount of water may be retained. The whole work is above the reach of navigation, nor is the character of the country such that commerce would ever need to seek this portion of the stream. The contrast between the head-waters of the Mississippi and those of most European or, indeed, American streams is as great as that between a mountain torrent and a canal. The situations of the dams to be built, beginning with that nearest to the river's source, are at the outlet of Lake Winibigoshish, 110 miles north and west of Duluth, and 200 miles north of St. Paul; at the outlet of Leech Lake, one of the largest sheets of water in northern Minnesota; at the outlet of Mud Lake, through which Leech Lake River flows on its way to the Mississippi; below the mouth of Vermilion River; and at Pokegama Falls. Pine River flows into the Mississippi some distance below Pokegama, and Gull River flows first into the Crow Wing River and thence into the Mississippi below Brainerd. Both of these streams are to be dammed. These seven reservoirs constitute the system proper. If they do all that is promised for them, innumerable smaller streams will be put in durance.

The advocates of the reservoir system claim that, by the construction of these works on the Upper Mississippi, navigation will be benefited as far as the head of Lake Pepin, fifty-five miles below St. Paul, and that, incidentally, river floods will be placed under more or less perfect control.

During the winter season, after the river is closed to navigation, and before it opens in the spring, the water supply from the upper river may be retained without detriment to any interest. Though somewhat diminished by the formation of ice and the freezing up of marshes, the regular flow of water thus imprisoned through the three or four months of extreme severity will constitute a fair supply. It is also certain that an addition to the natural volume of the river will be required for only a short period in the latter part of summer and in the early fall. At the June freshet of 1882 the St. Paul gauge recorded twenty feet above low-water mark, and a great part of the flood came from the melting of snow along the Upper Minnesota. Four feet of water being a fair stage for boats, there will be weeks and even months of the summer when nearly the whole supply tributary to the reservoirs can be stored up, not only without injury, but to the great benefit of the river valley, by lessening the volume of disastrous floods. On an outside calculation, if the reservoirs can furnish water for one hundred days in the year, it will be all that is desirable even in the driest season. A river requiring more would be scarcely worth improving at all. It will take from fifteen to twenty days after the flood-gates of the dams are opened for the water to reach St. Paul, the head of navigation. The reservoirs will seldom, if ever, have to be opened in the interest of navigation earlier than July 1. From April 15 to July 1 it is estimated from careful measurements that not less than 41,751,903,840 cubic feet of water passes the Falls of Pokegama, the point where the lowest of the five reservoirs on the Mississippi proper is located. The reservoirs, if operated in the interest of navigation only, would never be opened after November 1. If the entire flow from November 1 to April 15 be added, the quantity will be augmented by about 7,344,000,000 cubic feet, which can be retained outside of the season of navigation. This addition brings the whole supply available during any season between the latest assignable date for closing the reservoirs in the fall and the earliest for their opening in the spring—two dates which will never both have to be adopted in practice in the same season—up to 49,095,903,840 cubic feet for the five upper reservoirs only. From the two reservoirs on Gull Lake River and Pine River, emptying into the Mississippi below the point of the preceding observations, enough more will be supplied to make the aggregate available for use by the 1st of July, 55,795,903,840 cubic feet for the seven reservoirs above St. Paul. This quantity, if all used in the interest of navigation, can be released, and it is expected to release it, during the low-water months of July, August, September, and October. This is the result of a calculation based on the most conservative hypothesis, and therefore an actual minimum.

Suppose, now, the gates to be opened on the 1st of July, and to remain open for 100 days—the longest period that could possibly be necessary—what volume of water could be added to the river? A discharge of 6400 cubic feet per second would amount in 100 days to a total of 55,296,000,000 cubic feet. It is therefore claimed that, under the most adverse conditions supposable, the seven Upper Mississippi reservoirs are capable of adding 6400 cubic feet per second to the volume of the stream. Figures, however, are abstractions. What does this mean to the Mississippi River, and to those who use it as an avenue of commerce? When the river is at its lowest stage at St. Paul, the discharge is not less than 5800 cubic feet per second. If the addition calculated can be secured, it will more than double the volume of the river, allowance having been made for evaporation and absorption in so far as they can be computed. As to the utility of such a change, Major Allen in one of his reports very justly says, "The stream must be despicable whose navigation could not be assisted by doubling its lowest water volume." And in arriving at a definite conclusion as to the depth of channel thus secured, he says: "If we take for a discharge of 12,200 cubic feet, the mean velocity at three feet, and width at 1000 feet, we have, assuming the area of cross section to be a rectangle, a depth of about four feet. But the cross section of a stream flowing through a sandy bed does not approach the rectangular; it varies, sometimes approaching the parabolic and sometimes the triangular. The height of a triangle having a base of 1000 feet and area of 4000 square feet would be eight feet. It would certainly be within safe limits to say that, supposing the width of water surface to be as much as 1500 feet, the ruling depth for a flow of 12,200 feet per second would be at the least four feet."

Here, then, we arrive at a clear idea of what the reservoir system proposes to do, and how it proposes to do it. It promises, with what prospect of success its own figures must witness, to gather up the supply of water now running to waste and increasing the devastative power of floods, together with the excess of the spring and fall discharge; to impound it until the stream becomes so low that navigation will shortly be impeded, and then to release it in such measured quantities as will maintain a minimum depth of four feet in the channel at the head of navigation the year round, with corresponding benefit to the river as far as the point where it broadens out into Lake Pepin. With the opening to settlement of millions of acres in the Northwest, and the increasing urgency which their cultivation will lend to the question of transportation to the sea-board, this is no inconsiderable promise. The total estimated cost of the seven dams is $558,135. Such is the practical aspect of the work to which the nation, through Congress, has given its support. We will now leave the field of reasoning for the field of labor.

To reach Lake Winibigoshish, the location of the first of the reservoirs, one must make a three days' journey from St. Paul into the wilderness. A six hours' ride over the Northern Pacific sets the traveller down at the little town of Brainerd; then there is a long ride of sixty-five miles to Leech Lake. The remainder of the journey is by canoe.

At the eastern extremity of Winibigoshish a small bay turns abruptly to the south; and from its lowest point issue, in their sluggish course, the waters of the Mississippi. This is the location selected for the construction of the first of the proposed system of reservoirs. It was thought best, for several reasons, to begin the work here. This embankment is higher than any of the others, the elevation of the reservoir's surface above the present level of the lake being fourteen feet. The engineering difficulties are greater than will be encountered elsewhere. The capacity of the reservoir, which will drain an area of more than fourteen hundred square miles, is amply sufficient to test the truth of the theory that the volume of a river may be regulated with precision by artificial means. It is not to be expected that any material benefit to navigation will result from this single reservoir; but if its effects upon the river equal or exceed those foreshown by the reports of engineers, then the value of the reservoir system as a whole will have been demonstrated to the senses.

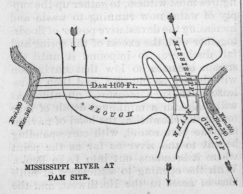

MISSISSIPPI RIVER AT
DAM SITE.

The dam site at Winibigoshish seems to have been expressly designed by nature for the location of such a work. About half a mile below the outlet of the lake rise two bold elevations on opposite sides of the wide marsh through which the river slowly oozes. They form natural continuations of any dike placed between them, and remove all danger of wash-outs at the extremities of the dam. The space of eleven hundred feet clear from one end to the other is converted into a great wall of timber-work, clay, sand, and stone. Work was begun by the building of a series of coffer-dams.

It must be borne in mind, in considering the construction of the dam proper, that those in charge of the work are limited in plan and execution by the resources at their command. Congress has thus far appropriated $525,000 to cover the cost of plant, material, and labor. Hence there will be found here no massive walls of masonry stretching from shore to shore, such as the word "reservoir" might suggest to one familiar with the works of that name on some of which Great Britain has spent hundreds of thousands of pounds. Primarily the reservoir dams are earth embankments, with the additions necessary to prevent percolation. Nor, in the opinion of many competent to judge, will they be on this account the more subject to accident or the less enduring.

The complete embankment, rising to a height of six feet above the water-line of the wasteway, will be 120 feet wide on an average at the base, and ten feet wide at the top, with a slope of one on two. It consists of several parts. In the centre is a diaphragm of timbers six inches in thickness, bedded in the hard blue clay which underlies the whole river-bottom at varying depths below the surface, and rising two feet above the reservoir when filled. This diaphragm is inclosed on both sides in a clay puddle wall, six feet in thickness at the top, with a slope of six on one to the clay foundation below. Within the coffer-dams a space of fifteen feet in width is excavated to a short depth below the surface of the blue clay stratum. In this the timbers of the diaphragm are firmly fixed, and the puddle wall is so thoroughly amalgamated with the native clay that the whole forms an impervious layer, fifteen feet wide at the base and six feet at the top, which extends four feet above the high-water line of the reservoir. This is

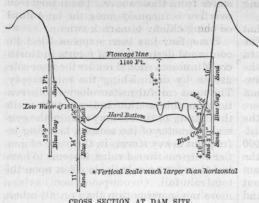

CROSS SECTION AT DAM SITE.

quantity of water that could possibly reach the dam at any season, can be discharged. Directly above these, which are placed with the upper surface on a level with the low-water line of the reservoir, is a wasteway 140 feet in length, over which the surplus water can pour should the supply exceed the capacity of the dam. Ample protection against the undermining action of the eddy is placed in the rear. This timber section of the dam is most interesting and important. A reservoir where the releasing is as carefully looked after as the retaining of the water, and is managed on as grand a scale, is elsewhere practically unknown.

the real retaining wall of the dam. The remainder is added chiefly to give an immovable weight and solidity to the structure, that it may be able to resist both the enormous pressure of more than 15,400 square feet of water surface, and the action of waves with a sweep of miles behind them. Outside of the puddle wall the embankment is chiefly sand and the natural earth foundation. Its base is bounded by continuous lines of sheet piling, and when completed it will be covered with clay, gravel, and sod to the depth of two feet. The face slope from the bottom of the reservoir to the top of the embankment, and the rear to about four feet above low-water line, are riprapped with stone. That end of the dam which fronts the natural channel of the river is devoted

Such are some features of this important work, constructed in a wilderness farther from St. Paul in point of time than St. Paul is from New York. Every piece of machinery, every tool, every pound of supplies, and nearly all the workmen employed have been transported more than one hundred miles over roads which were in great part laid out for the purpose. It has required rare courage and executive ability to compel success from such hostile conditions. Everything had in it some element that could not be accurately calculated in advance. Estimates were pretty sure to be inaccurate, and a great part of the work is so entirely without precedent that only its development could indicate what would be required. Consequently the contract system was abandon-

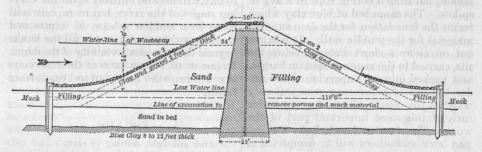

CROSS SECTION OF RESERVOIR EMBANKMENT.

to the works necessary to regulate the outflow of water. Twenty-four sluices, controlled by flood-gates, are constructed through a mass of crib timber-work resting on a pile foundation. These supply the means of exit. Through them 12,000 cubic feet per second, or nearly twice the

ed at the outset. The management of practical details has been confided to Mr. Charles Wanzer, assistant of engineers, the presiding genius of active work at Winibigoshish. He has been obliged to superintend everything in person, and to decide the multitudes of unforeseen questions which are constantly presenting themselves.

It was not until January 9, 1882, that the work was actually commenced. The remainder of the winter was devoted largely to preparing for activity in the spring. A heavy boiler for a steam saw-mill, and tons of supplies that could not possibly have been carried by boat, were hauled through the woods and over the frozen surface of the lakes. A busy little saw-mill, capable of cutting 25,000 feet of lumber per day, was built on the river between the lake and the dam site. The timber for the work, about 1,750,000 feet of magnificent white and Norway pine, was cut on the borders of the lake, from land belonging to the Chippewa reservation. Ten buildings, to be used as quarters for men and teams, were erected, 250 tons of ice were stored, and everything was placed on a working basis. Since then there has been no intermission of labor. The government owns a small steamer on the lake. It is 115 feet over all, and among the excellent services which it has rendered are the towing of 1,450,000 feet of logs an average distance of ten miles across the lake, and the transportation of 525 cubic yards of rock, for masonry-work and riprapping, on barges built upon the location for that purpose. Two steam pile-drivers, also built upon the location, have been in constant use; and it requires an effort of the imagination to conceive of a bustling workshop, such as this, more than one hundred miles, not from a lemon, but from a coil of rope or a keg of spikes. The same bed of blue clay which forms the foundation for the dam supplies material for the puddle wall. It is taken out on shore a short distance below the site, carried to the required spot on barges, and packed into an impervious mass under the eye of a foreman who jealously watches the construction of every cubic inch of this most important part of the work. The dam at Leech Lake was begun later, and others will be completed as rapidly as possible.

The reservoirs will not be, when completed, so many isolated dams, but will form a connected system. The water from the other four on the Upper Mississippi must pass through the one located at Pokegama Falls. It will therefore act to some extent as a distributing reservoir, being the first to be called on in time of need; and it, in turn, will replenish its stores from those above. The injury from overflow is inconsiderable, the land flooded being chiefly tamarack swamp.

Some fear has been expressed lest the continued destruction of forests in Northern Minnesota should render the reservoirs useless by diminishing the rain supply. The most careful meteorological observations in this section indicate that while the cutting of timber may change the general character of the seasons, bringing infrequent heavy storms in the place of gentler long-continued rains, it seems to have had thus far no calculable effect upon the total rain-fall. On one point there has been more misapprehension than on all others combined. It has been asserted frequently that the sudden release of water from the reservoirs, and the consequent rise of the Mississippi, will be a source of constant perplexity and even danger to those engaged in river industries; and that the increased evaporation and absorption over the larger water area thus created will upset all calculations. Were any such thing as a sudden influx of water contemplated or possible, this would doubtless be true. But the practical operation of the reservoirs is intended to be simply as follows: When the upper river gauges show a daily fall of water, and it is evident that in two or three weeks the depth of channel near the head of navigation will be less than four feet, an order will be telegraphed to those operating the dams to release enough water to keep the river at that stage. The number of sluices to be opened from day to day will depend entirely upon the varying stages of the river, but in no case will there be a sudden release of imprisoned water in volume sufficient to fill the banks beyond the immediate vicinity of the dams. In one word, the purpose of the reservoirs is not to raise the river, but to keep it from falling.

ESCAPE.

Airy and light, drifting so slow,
  Drifting softly, I see
Coming through air the feathery snow
  Of the milk-weed unto me.
Scarcely I feel its touch so light;
  See, 'tis wafted away;
Grasp it I can not in its flight;
  'Tis far on the wind at play.

Like to a love which the heart doth know
  Within itself to be,
Swiftly cold reason pursues, and lo!
Love flutters his wings and is free.

OUR ANNIE.

WHEN Johnny brought her cloak or her dinner to the factory door, he always left them for "our Annie," and his confidence in the efficacy of the pronoun and his contempt for any other appellation caused his name for her to follow her even inside the door, where it clung to her, and invested her with an affectionate distinction in a place where the strictest justice is meted out by popular opinion, and that opinion never too modest to make its verdict public.

There were some among us who thought her worthy of the name of heroine as well, though when she came to be compared with the accepted standard in literature, the divergence was so wide that her title was clearly open to dispute.

She was not beautiful, to begin with; hers was a quiet face, dark eyed and shy, and not one to impress an observer unless it had been seen upon an occasion when struggling hate and victorious love transfigured it, and such occasions are rare in a lifetime. As a rule, the heroines who wander somewhat inanely on from preface to finis have but one occupation, that of love-making, and this excludes all others. They toil not, neither do they spin, nor take any thought for raiment. Clothes, becoming and imperishable, grow upon them. They go through fire and flood, mire and snow, with no disfigurement of scorching or bedrabbling, or they

> "Sit in splendor, like the sun,
> Shining with nothing at all to do."

If by any miracle a venturous author makes his heroine labor for her dress and shoes, with what a flourish of trumpets is that fact proclaimed, and with what special providences he surrounds her, that this monotonous business known as "earning a living" may not be painfully prolonged! In a late case an unfortunate young lady made a few æsthetic bonnets, but wealthy friends and a lordly lover hovered near to see that she did not overtax herself, and to protest at intervals against her doing anything whatever. Not so with our Annie. From the hardest of mattresses she rose singing in the morning, and, rain or shine, trudged to her work, returning long after the sun had set. Of her and thousands like her it was sternly written from eternity that "one who can not work in this universe can

not get existed in it," and it was her specific business to keep herself, and certain others dependent upon her, alive, which she did by the labor of her hands, wealth and nobility, as lookers-on, being conspicuously absent.

Notwithstanding which she was busy and light-hearted as any chirping sparrow —that despised bird, in common with her class, being taxed with many vices, but never with sulkiness or laziness. Her shoes would wear out, to her sorrow, and her dress fray at the seams; worse than that, when spring rains poured down upon her, it was not without reason Johnny teasingly sung,

> "Jenny's a' wat, poor body,
> Jenny's seldom dry;
> She draiglet a' her petticoatie
> Comin' thro' the rye. "

She hated a wet and ravelled skirt, and to keep her dress of gray wool neat at the bottom, she cut it off whenever it began to sprout into ragged threads; but it needed the pruning process so often that if it did not, like the dress of the ballet-dancer, begin too late, it must certainly, like that, have ended too soon, had she not taken the precaution to piece it at the top. Therefore in external decoration the statuesque heroines of fiction left little Annie far behind, and in this respect quite hopeless of ever overtaking them. Their draperies float or cling, and the plainest fall gracefully in simple folds to their feet, but when were they ever pieced at the top to eke them out ?

As quite a secondary, if not accidental consideration, Annie "kept company" with Tom, who stood at his table and cut by thousands the shirts she made by dozens. She must have made them all the same, whoever held the keen knife, the price of them being highly necessary to her getting existed. For her this world's business consisted first in living; after that, in loving. He was like the sugar in her tea or the butter on her bread, not absolutely necessary, but very pleasant withal, and not to be relinquished without a pang. His tenderness flavored a life that must have been either flat or bitter without him, but which, with him, was not only endurable, but hopeful, contented, and sometimes blissfully happy. There was neither romance, nor rivalry, nor mystery in an affair so commonplace. Tom was "our Annie's steady company," and all the factory had, for two years, quietly accepted and understood the situation. Their attachment was like the constant flame of a burning lamp, rather than the wild, irregular glitter of love's phosphorescent light; some day they were to be married, and waited only, as such lovers do, for a favoring opportunity. Meanwhile she was satisfied with the daily nod and smile she looked for and received as she passed the cutter's table. She could even be proud of Tom; he was not only strong and handsome, but ambitious, master of his trade, and bound to make money by it. When he was head cutter, and the old folks comfortably settled, when Johnny was big enough to take the burden from her shoulders, then she might begin to think of her simple trousseau. With such thoughts to speed her fingers, she would sing softly to herself, and her cup of joy seemed too full to keep without sharing. There was something more than generous in the manner of her diffusing so small a sunbeam of happiness to her right hand and to her left. She befriended a new worker, forlorn, homesick, and discouraged, with a kindly grace that sprung from her own glad heart, and imparted to her in a few days all those secrets whereby labor might be saved, and which it had taken her some years of toil to discover. When the crusty foreman of the pressers would no longer grant the privilege of making tea upon the laundry stove, our Annie found a way. Down upon her knees she went, and patiently boiled her water on a hot flat-iron, and shared her cupful with a comrade, and Hebe's immortal bosom never thrilled with more delight, hearing Olympian praises of her nectar, than did Annie when there was a gathering of the clans, a rise in hot irons, and the corner in boiling water being broken, little clouds of fragrant steam arose once more to that black and sooty heaven, the factory ceiling. When grimy and fatal oil spots, almost as tragic in their consequences as that "damned spot" which would not "out" for all the perfumed washings and invocations of Lady Macbeth, scared some poor timid worker with their ruinous ugliness, Annie would leave her seat, and with a drop of cold water and her magical touch restore the snowy whiteness of the fabric. When a neighbor's scissors grew dull, and funds for sharpening were low,

she gave them an edge upon the neck of a glass bottle, counting her time well spent for a grateful "Oh, thank you!" and her needles, her oil, her soap to smooth a stubborn seam, or to hide the lime in weighted muslins, were ever at the service of others, who were not slow to avail themselves of her liberality. With a pieceworker, time is literally money, and though the power of fifty horses drove the wheels, it would have taken a concentration of selfishness not possessed by Annie to see any one, unaided, trying vainly to make living wages on shirts at fifty cents a dozen. To a more worldly-minded worker, who chided her good-nature, and reminded her of her own loss, she replied, "But, dear heart, you don't want a voice from heaven or handwriting on the wall to tell you what to do, when there's something to be done and nobody by but yourself to do it!"—a homely paraphrase of the noble maxim, Do the duty that lies nearest.

There was nothing in her akin to the priest or Levite who merely looked on or passed by; she had the sociable Samaritan way of crossing over and giving her two pence unsolicited; and in the exclusive society of the other world—more exclusive and more just, perhaps, than this— little Annie and that good man may stand side by side with other kindly company whose merits have been overlooked or underrated.

It seemed impossible for harm to befall one so gentle and so safe in her obscurity. That heaven's lightning should fell a heaven-defying tree or tower is in the course of nature; but that it should descend merely to root up and blast a simple violet, or strike a wild bird dead in ruthless violence, appeared to us who saw it like blindest fate or bitterest chance.

One frosty winter's morning a stranger came into the factory to work. Her white and awkward fingers fumbling nervously with the bands, her softer voice and finer dress, marked one who had descended a step or two to walk upon our level. A fierce tempest it must have been that drove her from *her* world down to this, so poor, so bare, so grinding. No nobleman sighed nor wealthy friend protested in her case, nor were there, apparently, any æsthetic bonnets to be made. Silent but assiduous, she took her place, and whatever she thought of the poor company in which she found herself, she breathed no word of it aloud. The absence of a lordly lover may have sealed her lips, for she never declared loudly of us, as did the bonnet-maker, that we were guilty of a newly discovered sin, exclusiveness being new to us, at all events.

"They are poor silly things, most of them, and as full of prejudice and exclusiveness as any one," she avers. "I've never seen distinctions in society so awful as the distinctions between shop-girls and parlor-girls. I supposed once that all work-people were on a level, but really I had no idea of inequality till I came down to them."

Little Annie knew nothing of the criticisms flung at her class by one not born to labor, if there are any such, and had she known it, she would never in consequence have bidden Alice keep her distance. She might have wondered greatly, as some of us did, what occupation "a parlor-girl" followed, that a chasm so awful yawned between her and a shop-girl; but factory-girls are on a plane still lower, perhaps, and as they live and eat and work together from dawn till dark, draw only one distinction, the natural one between vice and virtue, and recognize but one inequality, that which gives a skillful worker the advantage over one less deft. The stranger sat by Annie, whose dark eyes saw with instant pity how sorrowful and ill at ease she looked, and knowing every turn in labor's long lane, she would not see her go astray. Sympathy delicately expressed by encouraging smiles and a helpful hand soon won her confidence, and in a few weeks Annie was the acknowledged protector and friend of one her senior by a year at least. As one who nurses some poor transplanted flower sees it at last upon a sunny morning raise its drooping head and turn its leaves to the light, and knows that it will root and bloom, so Alice's self-appointed guardian rejoiced when she lifted her blue eyes to look around, and counted her work at the day's end, and gayly smiled to find the count so creditable.

"I shall really be able to pay my way," she cried, and, as an after-thought, "many thanks to you," while Annie told her how she might do better on the morrow, not dreaming that there are plants which twine and hug, and with their parasitic breath and clinging arms kill the brave sapling that nourishes them; and so, as in the nurse's tale, they gaed, and they gaed,

till spring-time came again, and with the awakening buds and blossoms bitter wisdom came to one at least.

When Tom had looked, through the long winter hours, where duty and inclination bade him, to the face of his sweetheart, he saw the stranger's shy sweet glances, and slowly became aware that he looked twice as often as before; and if he did, he asked himself, who was to blame for it? He had not walked into temptation nor courted it; it met him suddenly with his feet set in honor's path, and assailed him there unarmed and unprepared. He *could* not look at Annie and not see Alice; he could not but compare this delicate porcelain with the coarser ware which fate had assigned to his lot. He was ambitious of the best in all things, in his work and in his ways, and so, in love, his virtue had a fatal leaning toward vice. He saw a woman of finer mould than the woman who was waiting his word, and saw, too, that she recognized and approved of his ambition, could help him, being a step above him, as Annie never could, and be a credit to him. If she held him bound —well, he had made a fatal mistake for himself; but if she held him to it, he would not swerve from the fulfillment of a plain duty; he had no more intention of defrauding little Annie than he had of turning soldier or sailor, or otherwise changing his trade. Until the day when Annie herself saw the thoughts of his inmost soul laid bare by an accident that he had no power to avert, he kept his secret, or thought he kept it, as well as is in the power of man to keep such a secret, which at best is not very well.

Was it by coincidence merely, or was it by design, that one day, when they were all free at dinner hour to draw new breath or stretch their cramped limbs, a merry singer gayly sung her "Courage Song," low at first, and then louder, with her bright eyes fixed on Annie?

"And if heaven, bending over,
   Should turn black instead of blue,
If my own, my *own* true-lover
   Should prove false instead of true,
Do you think for the untrue one I would cry?
No; I'd laugh and get a new one—that would I!"

"I hate that song," cried Annie; "it has a broken heart in it."

"What would *you* do, then?" asked the singer, while her companions glanced compassionately at Annie. "You can't die just because you want to, you know."

"Then I would live to weary Heaven for justice," she said, with sudden fire, and rose to resume her work, wondering somewhat at the earnest eyes that looked into hers, but more at Alice's averted face, crimson to the forehead. Days after, when the very air seemed to bring her ill omens, she thought of it. In a path where the roses of love and pleasure grow thick on every side a wayward hand reaching over might pluck a bud or two and the loss remain unnoticed, but in a life that is barren and desolate except for the greenness of a single cherished plant, the jealous eye detects every change, and after some months of painful doubting, Annie found that the blossoms she loved were strangely blighted; not in a single night, but slowly, surely, as if the secret dews that nourished them were gradually withheld; their perfume and their color went, and all their ancient sweetness, and as they dropped their dry leaves one by one through her trembling fingers, she knew that they were dead. Then the sun vanished, and the heavens frowned like brazen walls, from which she hid her face in terror, mourning like the Arabian emir of old, "Wherefore is light given unto him that is in misery, and life unto the bitter of soul; which long for death, but it cometh not, and dig for it more than for hid treasures; which rejoice exceedingly and are glad when they can find the grave?" Wandering bewildered in a darkened land, like one in an evil dream, she could not but know who had stolen her lover from her, and it was in those days that she took to discussing theological questions in her own mind with unwonted vehemence as she stitched, not that they were a diversion or recreation, but only because she could not help it. *Was* there a heaven? and when one had by martyrdom won an entrance, would its strange unwelcome aspect and cold spirituality be any compensation for the familiar joys of the dear old earth so reluctantly resigned? She was amazed to find that, even with death possible, the paradise of the blessed was nothing to her, any more than Italy or Spain might be; she had no longing to see *them*, nor to be thrust into heaven against her will. Was there a hell, then, and eternal punishment for false friends and deceitful lovers? and was it wicked to be glad? She was shocked to find that she was fast growing wicked in the hard certainty that God would

punish all falsehood and deceit, and that it was any comfort to think so. The poor little violet whose leaves had reached up toward the sky, drawn thither by love's soft sunlight, had still its dark root in the black earth, and if Annie again turned heavenward, it was, as she said, to weary the saints for justice. Did God mean to punish her by so sore a trial? Like righteous Job, she felt she had not merited her suffering; that it was not the natural consequence of her own acts, but a frightful calamity that had befallen her, and she prayed that she might die. Then, in the fierce reaction of jealous passion, she hoped that they might be punished for their perfidy, not hereafter, but here, where she could see and know; and still the everlasting wheels whirled around as she stitched, and her whole life whirled round with them. That one prayer, at least, God put into her power to fulfill, or leave unfulfilled, for herself.

She still wore upon her finger the circlet of gold that Tom had placed there; and though they were estranged—that was undeniable—they had not quarreled, nor spoken the words which must part them. *That* he would never do, she was sure; but she would prove it, for the strain of suspense was greater than she could bear. Alice, glancing sideways, measured her with the bonnet-maker's measure, which may, from her level, be correct. They *are* poor silly things most of them, this one especially so—poor, for she lost her lover, silly, in that she had not chosen a truer friend; but Alice never dreamed of the storm raging beneath that calm exterior; nor did Tom, who wondered at her tameness; while *she*, under her eyelids, saw, and felt too, his bright, flashing, cruel knife crunching and dividing with unerring certainty from morning till night, till it seemed as if her heart lay bare beneath the stroke. She would not stay to be tortured so; she would end it *now*.

Rising from her seat, she folded the work she had finished, and carried it to be inspected; she must pass Tom's table on her way to the room below, and she had resolved to lay the ring before him without a word: she could not breathe till that was done. But some one stood in her path. Lifting her eyes, she saw Alice, whom she had not missed from her side. Though her back was turned, Annie could see the flush on her fair cheek, her pretty, shy face raised to his, while she waited for the bands he was cutting. They did not notice her, nor even see her as she passed, crying aloud in her soul for vengeance upon them, while Heaven listened and answered her prayer. She loitered by the inspector's desk, and returned with leisurely step, carrying her new work in her arms: she had slipped the ring from her finger, and wrapped it in a scrap of clean muslin; the little package burned her palm: she could not go back to her seat with her purpose unaccomplished. Lingering by the door, she looked within. How absorbed they were! She waited with as much patience as her sorely tried soul could summon, for he could not cut bands forever, though he evidently prolonged the task to its utmost extent; nor could Alice tarry many minutes more, for all her dainty counting them, and taking them up one by one with her white and slender fingers, and doubting that she had enough until he counted them again. Annie lost not a glance nor a smile; she would, woman-like, have gleaned them all though purgatorial pains were in them; and so they stood, unconscious of the flashing eyes that watched them.

Could she ever forget those minutes which seemed unending, or the long room photographed forever on her memory? Shining beneath his table, the swiftly revolving shaft gleamed in the waning light, twisting noiselessly, like a mighty snake in pain, turning, now visible, now in shadow, as it had turned for years before. Close to the floor, and projecting beyond the end of the table, the treacherous rod spun round till the air was blurred with its motion, as it had spun harmless for months. Once they had imprisoned it in a box, which, carelessly broken, had never been replaced. No one could be caught by it, or fail to see it, who walked toward it, for its draught alone was warning to one who approached it, and who ever walked backward in a place like that?

Alice, perfidious Alice! Moving as if to depart, she saw—they both saw—the pale face, the bended brows, the disquieting eyes flashing upon them in astonished observation, and startled into guilty recoil, she took that one step backward. Something in that dreadful look reminded her of death and judgment; while Annie, in mental misery, was madly demanding of her own soul, "And does the Lord command us to forgive *our* enemies while He burns His?"

Then for answer she saw her enemy sway and totter, pulled backward toward the shaft, heard her sharp cry, and understood. The deadly draught had caught but a wandering thread of her flounce, then the dress itself, and fast in a gigantic embrace, from which neither her own strength nor Tom's could release her, they writhed together, while her shrieks paralyzed those who, having lost presence of mind, were powerless to assist her. He had sprung to her at her first cry, knife in hand, but in her unreasoning terror she threw herself upon him, pinioned his arms, and clung to him, though he shouted and entreated in agony, "For your life, for your life, Alice, let me go!"

She heard nothing, saw nothing; her head was on his breast, her arms around him, and the knife fell from his grasp. Of no avail to brace himself against the table, and hold her till the muscles stood out upon his skin like whip-cords, his one-man power against that of fifty horses—which dragged them to the floor, had them down upon their knees, will grind them to powder unless some angel intervene. She who stood in the doorway, looking with horror upon her answered prayer, saw in his face the love he felt for Alice above the agony of his struggling, and it has not flashed into any mind but hers—*hers*—in all that confused and flying crowd, the one thing that will save them. *Had* she prayed for vengeance? With tenfold vehemence she cries aloud, "Now God forgive me!" and looks about her. They have shouted to each other, the lookers-on, to stop the engine; but it is in the basement, and there is now but the twinkling of an eye, an inappreciable fragment of time, between life and a most dreadful death. A woman has but two weapons, the use of which comes to her as naturally as if she had been born with them in her hands. One is her scissors, the other her broom. With the first she does all her carpentering; with the other she goes forth to warfare or defense; and a broom now stood beside little Annie at the doorway, where a careless sweeper had left it. The broad belt of the engine was directly over her head, whirling upon its wheel. With the end of the handle of her improvised weapon she took unerring aim, and flung off the belt, and with the consistency of her sex, having cried to the heavens for justice, would none of it when offered, but turned aside into a corner, and wept with gratitude for their deliverance.

Nay, more: with trembling hands she wrapped her own cloak around the shoulders of her enemy, whose dress was but a rope of twisted rags; with her own handkerchief she bathed the pale forehead of the foe she had rescued from the jaws of death, bruised and bleeding, sick and faint with the shock, but otherwise unharmed, and held her in her arms till they brought a carriage in which to send her home, then relinquished her place to him whose right no one disputed, and the factory knew Alice no more.

Close by his knife she found her ring, and in the silence of her own home she wrapped it anew, and sent it to them, and took up her life, desolate indeed, its one flower having perished, but not barren of humbler blooming, sweet and comforting in after-days. The tenderest consideration, the most affectionate solicitude, and the unfailing kindness of her companions were Annie's, though life had changed, and she with it. We who knew her well loved her well, and saw in her dark eyes a something that was better than beauty, while looking on her patient forehead we felt it better a thousandfold to be Abel than Cain.

And they pass backward and forward, at dawn and at dusk, by thousands, such girls, each with her own heart and her own story; "but," saith Æsculapius, in quiet scorn, "they are as much alike as if a grain of corn that had been ground and bolted had tried to individualize itself by a special narrative."

Which sounds as if the learned doctor and the casual maker of æsthetic bonnets had shaken hands, and agreed upon it that no good thing could come out of Nazareth.

BROOK FARM.

Down the long road, bent and brown,
    Youth, that dearly loves a vision,
    Ventures to the gate Elysian,
As a pilgrim from the town.

Coming not so late, so far,
    Rocks and birches! for your story;
    Not to prate on vanished glory
Where of old was quenched a star;

Where of old, in lapse of toil,
    Time but mocked a prayer pathetic;
    Where the flower of good prophetic
Starved in our New England soil.

Ah! to Youth with radiant eyes,
    For whom grief is not, nor daunting,
    Lost glad voices still are chanting
'Neath those unremaining skies,

Still the dreams of fellowship
    Beat their wings of aspiration;
    And a smile of soft elation
Trembles from its haughty lip

If another dare deride
    Hopes heroic snapped and parted,
    Disillusion so high-hearted
All success is mean beside.

Editor's Easy Chair.

THE Easy Chair has more than once alluded to Charles Fenno Hoffman, one of the chief figures in the "Knickerbocker literature" of forty years ago, and the founder of the *Knickerbocker Magazine*. The felicitous phrase Knickerbocker literature was first used in the *Nation* by Mr. Denny, an admirably accomplished writer, who gave it a satirical turn as describing a kind of cockney or local and ephemeral literature, and his article had the tone of the Boston sexton who politely informed the stranger seeking a pew in the church for the afternoon service that it was hardly worth his while to go in—"excellent man, sir, but no talents; a New York man, sir."

But while many of the noted writers in the Knickerbocker circle of half a century since are no longer famous nor even much known to the New York readers of to-day, yet the great Knickerbocker names are great still, and Irving, Cooper, Bryant, and perhaps Halleck, although Halleck is fading, still hold the place they held with our fathers. Willis is probably rapidly passing out of the public mind, and the loiterers at Newport and Saratoga, at Nahant, Long Branch, Rockaway, and Long Beach, scarcely know the name of Philip Slingsby, or the other gay little "society" sketches of Willis. The misfortune of his fate was twofold, that he was tempted to turn his bright talent into ready money, and that he did it. His gayety and his graceful fluency made him the first of our proper "magazinists." He had the lightness and ease of touch which are traditionally characteristic of the distinctive writer for the magazines, and whose success contradicts the old saying that easy writing is hard reading. But Willis's ease became at last a mannerism, and a certain tone of affectation and apparent insincerity crept over his page.

This, however, was rather unjust to the author. Willis was essentially an amiable man, and he was early flattered and successful. He loved ease and luxury, and he listened too fondly to the sirens. He was a man of the boudoir and the drawing-room, trained in the Byronic tradition, and with no very lofty sense of the duty and responsibility of the literary life. He wrote enormously. His name was the synonym of a certain clever grace and audacity. But how many of the younger readers of the Easy Chair have read the *Pencillings by the Way*, or *Letters from under a Bridge*, or even the Scriptural poems which were once thought to be so beautiful?

Hoffman was a year older than Willis, and he belonged to the same Knickerbocker group. Willis came from Boston, but Hoffman was of an old Knickerbocker family. Willis had a certain European tone and character, but Hoffman was completely American. Willis died seventeen years ago, when he was sixty years old. Hoffman died the other day at the insane retreat in Pennsylvania where he had been secluded for more than thirty years— so absolutely secluded, indeed, that Bartlett's book of *Familiar Quotations* records him as dying in 1850. Hoffman's books, like Willis's, are read no more, and his name survives only in his familiar song, "Sparkling and bright." That alone will give his name yet a longer date than Willis's, and the sad story of his life will be long tenderly told in our American literary biography.

Those who still recall his manly figure, and his fresh, breezy, gay manner, will remember the sense of profuse vitality with which he impressed those who saw him. He was a lover of the woods and waters, a natural sportsman, and this taste is reflected in his tales and sketches. His poems, as is always true of a great multitude of poems in every period, were echoes of the greater poets of his time. But they show his poetic feeling and facility, and a certain heartiness of nature which was his characteristic quality. The mental calamity which arrested his career, and practically ended his life nearly forty years ago, was not the only sorrow which this brave and generous man endured. As a boy of eleven a sore misfortune befell him in the loss of a leg. The circumstances of this event have not been very clearly understood, and the kindness of a relative of Mr. Hoffman enables the Easy Chair to put them here upon permanent record.

An old letter of his mother's, dated in New York on the 4th of December, 1817, and written to a sister in Paris, tells the story. The letter is well preserved, and it is written in the clear and firm hand which was characteristic of the writing of that day:

"I was very much gratified by your letter handed me by Mr. Gouverneur, and have thus long been prevented from acknowledging it by one of the greatest afflictions I have yet sustained, which has occupied me wholly for the last six weeks.

"Charles came from Morristown to spend his fall vacation with us; and the day of his arrival, toward the close of it, he was down on the rocks watching the steam ferry-boat, and as it came up he jumped on board and had a ride up to the wharf. This he had done several times, and thought to take one more ride ere he went home to dinner. But alas! the boat came up faster than was expected, and in the act of jumping his right leg was caught, and so shockingly mangled as to require immediate amputation. Mr. and Mrs. Verplanck were dining with us, and two gentlemen from the country, when the news was brought. What could exceed the shock we experienced to have so promising and active a boy go out in the morning in the full possession of all bodily blessings, brought home before evening a cripple for life, and from the want of a little prudence! These reflections overwhelmed me for a time, and I could not reflect upon the mercy of the Providence which had spared his life and endued him with fortitude much beyond his years to sustain this sad loss, and even to smile amidst his pains to hear us who were sorrowing over him. But it consoles me to see that if he was a child in getting into trouble, he has been a man in bearing it. He has been down-stairs this morning for the first time; he moves about very actively upon a pair of crutches.".....

The mother and the son are both gone, but it is not possible to hold the yellowing paper and to read the sad little story without pain. At seventy-seven the poet walked alone in the rural neighborhood of Harrisburg, pleased to hear the sounds and to see the sights of the fields and the woods, harmless and murmuring to himself. But for more than thirty years he had had no actual human companionship. The generation to which he belonged had passed away, and to the new generation his name was unknown. That solitary figure, wandering by the streams and standing under the trees, recalls the pensive music of Wordsworth's "Ruth":

> "That oaten pipe of hers is mute,
> Or thrown away; but with a flute
> Her loneliness she cheers;
> This flute, made of a hemlock stalk,
> At evening, in his homeward walk,
> The Quantock woodman hears.
>
> "I too have passed her on the hills,
> Setting her little water-mills
> By spouts and fountains wild—
> Such small machinery as she turned,
> Ere she had wept, ere she had mourned,
> A young and happy child."

ONE of the pleasantest glimpses into the world of thought and feeling of another time is that which is opened by a scrap-book of the verses which in that time pleased an intelligent and cultivated literary taste. There is a fashion in literary expression as in everything else, and in nothing is the mysterious "spirit of the age" more evident than in the changes of that fashion from time to time. There is no more pathetic scene in Thackeray than that of Colonel Newcome sitting and gazing at the picture and trying to understand his son. He is conscious that his son's standards and ideas and sympathies are different from his own, and that somehow he is wronged when the child of his love, the bone of his bone and the flesh of his flesh, is severed from him by a power that he can not comprehend.

The worship of Byron by the young men and women of his time is half inexplicable to their children. But the poet in whom the children delight, Tennyson, or Browning, or whomsoever he may be, is equally strange to the taste of the parent. Let any man of these closing years of the century look over the "extract book" of any man of its earlier years, and it will have what we call the quaintness—that is, the remoteness and strangeness—of another age. In the same way the old music books which the daughter inherits from the mother are curious and interesting to her because of the difference from her own. They imply to her taste an Arcadian simplicity. What a small and innocent world it must have been when a young lady at the piano sang "I see them on their winding way," or "Brignal banks are wild and fair"!

But for that very reason, how pleasant a glimpse of another world it is! We call it another, but we juggle ourselves. Verona was a very different town from New York. But the world of Romeo and Juliet was precisely the world of the young people in New York who were betrothed yesterday. The same hopes, passions, and feelings which swell the bosom of the singer of the *Lohengrin* music of to-day filled the heart of the young man or woman who sang "Robin Adair" and "Auld Robin Gray" fifty years ago. It is only the phrase and the fashion, not the thing itself, that has changed. It is not another world, after all, that the old scrap-books recall. As we grow older, those older figures which seemed to the young mind so grave and wise, so always mature and beyond the reach of romantic feeling, are softened in the light of the perception that they were but ourselves, and that the songs they sang breathed a wild and ardent passion which our own does not surpass.

Such an old scrap-book, gathering songs and verses for more than fifty years, has just been privately printed, and it is a book of singular value and interest, because it is a perfectly genuine accumulation of the favorites of all that time, selected by sincere poetic feeling and a generous manly taste full of tenderness, but wholly free from morbid tendency. It contains very many—no book could contain all—of the poems and songs that were heard during that time in refined and cultivated homes in which refinement and cultivation had not smothered the love of roaming by sea and land, of every kind of sport, of games, and adventure, and vigorous out-door life of every kind, so that it is a striking revelation of the best American domestic life of the last half-century.

As it comes down to this time it covers the whole period of the war, and many a song which was universally familiar twenty years ago, and whose melody the bands and the hand-organs still recall, is retained here, and presently may not be easily found elsewhere. The collection is fitly called *An Old Scrap-Book*, and it is printed for distribution among personal friends; and as those friends turn the pages and linger long and long over verses which are inwrought with their own associations, and have become intimate parts of their own lives, they will see visions of an enchanted island, lovely in itself, and rich with traditions of generous hospitality, of woodland walks and rides and sea-side musings, of the hunt of the red deer, of yachts coming and going, of famous people—visions of an island life of the utmost simplicity and refinement and cultivation, and of every resource—home of the young and happy, of the mature and wise—the scene of a thousand joys unfading in memory :

"Such jests that, drained of every joke,
  The very bank of language broke;
Such deeds that Laughter nearly died
  With stitches in his belted side;
While Time, caught fast in pleasure's chain,
  His double goblet snapped in twain,
  And stood with half in either hand,
  Both brimming full—but not of sand !"

as the Autocrat sang long ago, himself one of the most welcome of guests and sparkling of revellers in the charmed and charming circle which *An Old Scrap-Book* recalls.

THERE was recently a curious and interesting revelation of the life of the professional literary man of the day in the preface to *Echoes for the Year* 1883, by George Augustus Sala, and in a sketch of M. Blowitz, the Paris correspondent of the London *Times*, who is undoubtedly, as the caption of the sketch describes him, "the most famous and influential of foreign correspondents." Mr. Sala has been long known. He was first distinguished as a writer in *Household Words* during its palmiest day under the editorship of Dickens, and his *Journey due North* was a very brilliant piece of work.

Since those days, and indeed during a career of more than five-and-thirty years, as he says, Mr. Sala has been one of the most devoted and industrious of professional literary men—men who live by their literary labor. He distinguishes, however, between literary and journalistic work. Yet he also states that his thirty books had been previously published in a newspaper or a magazine; and the volume to which his interesting statement is the preface is a collection of weekly articles of gossiping comment upon passing affairs which are published in the *Illustrated London News*. The books, he says, were written even more hurriedly than his regular newspaper articles, either editorial or epistolary, because many of the letters were written in foreign countries, before the correspondent was tied to the wire, and when he had leisure to look about him and to confer with himself.

But when the journalist is at home, and to the functions of a writer of leading articles adds those of a reviewer, an art critic, a dramatic critic, and a scribbler of gossip, besides other miscellaneous work, then everything, except the leading article, is necessarily hurried. Mr. Sala says that this article must be deliberately planned, carefully thought out, and written with the greatest care and attention. It fills but little more than a column of largish type, and does not occupy more than two hours in actual writing, but at least three hours in deliberation and planning; and then, he adds, ruefully, in the course of twenty-four hours it is completely forgotten. Mr. Sala says that he has written some seven thousand of these ephemeral essays, and now that he is growing old he thinks, with some bitterness, that if remembered at all, it will not be by this

careful work to which he has devoted all his ability and knowledge, but only as a writer of desultory essays, and sketches of travel, and "a mass of bald chat," and four bad novels. In writing the last he says that often, as he has been scribbling copy for the printer's boy clamorous in the passage, he has forgotten the very names of his characters.

This is a confession in singular contrast with that of the haunting reality to their creators of the characters of Thackeray and Dickens, and it shows that the novels of the moment are written as they are read, without any firm intellectual or artistic grasp, and only to prick and please a half-morbid palate. Every day when he is in England Sala says that he works at his trade of journalist for many hours, and it brings him a queer recompense in the letters of an army of correspondents all over the globe, who besiege him with questions to be answered in the *Echoes;* and not in letters and questions only, but in gifts of potatoes, and Indian corn, and Kentish butter, apple jam, and gingerbread nuts, and one good soul proposed to send some conger-eel, which happily miscarried. He begs, however, that such proofs of kindly regard may be discontinued, and desires under no circumstances to receive "packages of what the Americans term 'projuce.'"

There is a tone of sadness and weary dissatisfaction and regret in this story. But there is a striking contrast to it in the account of M. Blowitz, which recalls Dumas's *Monte Cristo* and Disraeli's novels. The description of his rooms would have done credit to Lord Beaconsfield. The photographs of Albert Edward, Thiers, etc., and the "*souvenir affectueux*" from Queen Isabella of Spain, and the other souvenir "from the frailest body to the finest mind," a stroke of Sara Bernhardt's, might have fallen out of *Lothair* or *Endymion*. M. Blowitz is described as an Austrian *Slav*, of a singularly checkered career, and had made a special study of European politics, and commended himself in correspondence to M. Thiers so warmly that M. Thiers, as President, promised him the consulate at Riga. But during the delay he was asked to replace temporarily the Versailles correspondent of the *Times*, and his service was so satisfactory that in 1871, just as his commission as consul was about to be signed, he was offered and accepted the post of assistant correspondent to Mr. Laurence Oliphant, then chief correspondent of the *Times* at Paris; and he succeeded to the chief place in 1875.

As Mr. Sala has written seven thousand newspaper articles, M. Blowitz has written more than three thousand columns of the *Times*. He has talked freely, and as a kind of public character, with half the sovereigns and statesmen in Europe, has received twenty-two decorations from all kinds of princes and potentates, and in 1878 he was promoted officer of the Legion of Honor for "services rendered to peace during the Congress." It is his pride never to have reported a conversation without authority, and never to have attacked a public man without warning him; and he was never approached with a bribe but once, and that was by a woman when he was exposing Monaco, the paradise of gamblers. M. Blowitz has all the personal attributes which Vivian Grey admired. He has a good appetite and sound digestion. He sleeps like a soldier, anywhere and at any time. He works with a type-writer, and lives as he pleases, enjoys life, and is writing his memoirs.

This story is in a very different key from that of Mr. Sala's preface. His has the seriousness of the English genius—although we believe he is not wholly English—and that of M. Blowitz the air of European adroitness. Much of the English force lies in the fact that it does take life earnestly and gravely, and not as a game. This is precisely the difference in the impression of Mr. Gladstone and of Lord Beaconsfield—

"The hand that rounded Peter's dome,
And groined the aisles of Christian Rome,
Wrought in a sad sincerity;
Himself from God he could not free."

This is true of Michael Angelo; it is peculiarly true of the great Englishmen; and it is the secret of England as a power in civilization.

The weariness and the half-disappointment which are perceptible in Mr. Sala's preface are natural, but they might be relieved somewhat by the reflection that the service of the professional man of letters or of the journalist, when it is honestly and adequately done, is a genuine service, and quite worth doing. It may not be a work of genius, and, as he says, it may be forgotten at the end of twenty-four hours. But in a time of universal reading, when something, good or bad, will be read, when public questions will be discussed, when books and pictures will be criticised, and passing events will be described and improved, surely the talent that discusses and criticises and describes with sincerity, felicity, and good-humor, with courage and wholesome vigor, bringing everything to the standard of good morals and generous principle, is a talent to be respected, and whose work in the world is not less valuable than that of the honest clerk or mechanic, or merchant or professional man.

It may not be the work of genius, as we say, for that is the infrequent work in any department of human activity. Addison and Steele, men of genius though they were, were but newspaper men, and they wrote with Mr. Sala's purpose, to entertain the reader. Had their essays lacked the especial charm which makes them immortal, still the pleasure that such writing gives would have been its own reason and justification. The long series of other essays of the same school, the *Connoisseur*, the *Lounger*, and the rest, are not, like the *Tatler* and *Spectator*, signalized by the genius of an acknowledged master, and they are now seldom read. But the good service of their writers is undeniable, and none of them need have sighed to think that in a few years their names would have vanished and their essays be forgotten.

The hack writer, as he is called, is sometimes mentioned in a deprecatory tone as if he were a useless and not quite respectable character. But it would be as reasonable to speak in the same tone of a book-keeper or a carpenter. They are all men who follow a calling which is useful to society, and they are to be blamed only if they are unfaithful in it. If the book-keeper or the carpenter slurs and neglects his work—in a word, if he cheats—he may be turned over to the scorner; and if the hack writer does likewise, he may be justly left to the same fate. But Charles Lamb writing an essay of Elia or posting the books of the India House was doing the same thing, so far as the essential respectability of the work was concerned. His industry in the one branch merely served the India Company for the time, while in the other it is a perennial delight to thousands.

For the comfort of every honest hack writer and professional man of letters there are two familiar passages from two famous English poets which should be always remembered. George Herbert says:

"A servant with this clause
Makes drudgery divine:
Who sweeps a room as for Thy laws
Makes that and th' action fine."

And Wordsworth, with similar feeling:

"Small service is true service while it lasts;
Of all thy friends, though humble, scorn not one:
The daisy, by the shadow that it casts,
Protects the lingering dew-drop from the sun."

ALTHOUGH the centennial commemoration at Newburgh on the Hudson last autumn, and the imposing celebration of Evacuation-day in the city of New York in a drenching storm, which yet could not diminish the patriotic feeling of the day, seemed to close the series of such observances, yet this year is the centenary of an event of another kind which is most interesting in the annals of New York. A hundred years ago King's College became Columbia College, and the University of the State of New York was founded. The university was expected to gather itself about Columbia College, and the Board of Regents was established as its governing body. The board "has had perpetual succession" for a century, and it is one of the most ancient official bodies in the State. But its action is so quiet that its service is generally unnoted, and often unknown.

The peculiar relation between Columbia College and the Regents was dissolved by the act of 1787, revising the original act of 1784, and the story of Columbia is told in President Moore's annals, and in the commemorative address of Mr. Jay, and in the discourses of other eminent "Columbians," and it is, of course, distinct from that of the university. But what and where is the university, and what do the Regents do? is a question which is often heard, and which is not always clearly answered. One reason of this inadequate response is that the university is not a building nor a group of buildings, but a system. Alexander Hamilton submitted the bill which provided for its organization, and the bill was undoubtedly prepared by him. It comprehended and designed a complete scheme of education, in which the higher schools were to consist of all the colleges that might arise in the State, and which were to be placed under the authoritative control of the board. This plan, however, has been modified, and the independence and individuality of the different colleges have been carefully maintained.

This was natural, because they are all private foundations. The Legislature has authorized the board to charter colleges, and to revoke charters in the event of failure to comply with the conditions, and it requires an annual report of their condition to be made by the colleges to the board, and every year, under the auspices of the Regents, a convocation, or assembly of college faculties and of teachers of academies, is held at Albany, which secures the opportunity of personal knowledge and intercourse to the whole body of such teachers in the State, and the advantage, also, of a comparison of experience in methods of instruction and in every question of education which would interest such a body. The proceedings consist of the reading of papers and of discussions, and at the close of the sessions, which continue usually for three days, honorary degrees of the higher grade are conferred by authority of the Regents. Examinations are also held by the Regents, and their certificate of proper success in the examinations admits the student to any college in the State which is under their visitation.

The Regents have a more authoritative control of the academies, conducting an immense and elaborate system of examinations, according to the results of which they distribute the State aid to academies, and they provide for the maintenance in certain academies of teachers or normal classes, in which teachers are fitted for the common schools. The Regents are also trustees of the State Library and of the State Museum of Natural History, and are charged also with other similar responsibilities. For this immense and varied service, which is of the highest importance, the Regents receive only their actual expenses, and the vast detail of the work is accomplished at an annual expense to the State of about nine thousand dollars. It may be fairly doubted whether there is any State service at once so important, so efficient, and so economical.

The misapprehension in regard to the university and the Regents arises from the name. The Regents are humorously held to be kings of Brentford or Barataria, monarchs of a nonexistent realm; instead of which their realm is most tangible and substantial, and their sway one of enormous care and responsibility. The details of the labor, of course, fall upon the office at Albany, and they are discharged with an intelligence, an industry, and a success which might well stimulate the admiration and emulation of all other public offices.

It was natural that the centenary of such an institution, the establishment of which marks the beginning of a complete system of education in the State of New York, should be celebrated with much quiet congratulation and wholly without ostentation, according to the tradition of the board. Many of the most distinguished collegiate and academic teachers in the State assembled, and besides the usual essays and debates, there were papers of specific reference to the centenary, among which a detailed and chronological history of the university and its functions, by Dr. Hough, was exceedingly valuable. The great public advantage of the occasion was the presentation to the people of the State of a clearer view of the history and the significance of the university, and perhaps of a refreshing glimpse of the possibility of transacting a great public work most efficiently and economically without a suspicion of mere political interference.

Editor's Literary Record.

HITHERTO English readers have not had access to any work in the vernacular which gives a full and exhaustive history of the Thirty Years' War. Schiller's history, a translation of which by the Rev. A. J. W. Morrison was published over thirty years ago in "Bohn's Standard Library," is a delightful work, considered from a purely literary standpoint, and some of its portraitures of men and descriptions of critical or momentous epochs, incidents, and events are brilliant specimens of his matchless powers of delineation; but, taken as a whole, it has little historical value at this day, and, with occasional exceptions, gives only a superficial view of the political, diplomatic, and military complications which attended the eventful and protracted conflict in the German states and throughout the entire Continent. Gardiner's history, published in 1874, in the excellent series of "Epochs of History" edited by Mr. Morris, is a masterly historical sketch, bringing clearly into view all the shifting scenes in the terrible drama, with their political, religious, and dynastic accompaniments and consequences, giving special prominence to its most influential or decisive turning-points, and their influence upon the growth of religious toleration, and affording an insight into the character, thoughts, feelings, and motives of the Catholic princes, as exhibited by their own correspondence. Able and original, however, as is this thoroughly trustworthy work, it makes no pretensions to be aught more than an epitome, and in its extreme condensation it necessarily passes cursorily or silently over many interesting and highly important connecting links and illustrative details. Nevertheless, it supplies in very brief and convenient form all, perhaps, that the great majority of English readers will consider to be of grave historical interest. It is well known, also, that Mr. Motley contemplated the preparation of a history of the Thirty Years' War, or, as he termed it, " that fight of demons which we call the Thirty Years' War," and that his *Life of John Barneveld* was intended as the connecting link between it and his previous histories, *The Dutch Republic* and *The United Netherlands*. Unfortunately his life closed before his meditated life's work was finished, and his history of the Thirty Years' War was left unwritten, although we have glimpses of the bold and incisive manner in which he would have treated the subject in the eleventh and twelfth chapters, and especially in the thirteenth chapter, of his *Life of Barneveld*, where he describes the real commencement of the war, the causes that led to it, and the actors who precipitated it. During nearly twenty years of industrious study and research, Professor Gindely, who fills the chair of German History in the University of Prague, has been engaged upon an elaborate history of this great conflict, of which at the present date only four volumes have been completed, covering the period from 1612 to 1623, and the volumes covering the remainder of the war, from 1623 to 1648, are in course of preparation. When it is considered that the war really began in 1618, and that his completed volumes travel leisurely over the six preceding years, when the causes were being developed or were actively at work which led to the war, and as leisurely, also, over the first five preparatory years or stages of the war, every step in its progress being fortified with citations from or full-text republications of original documents, the extent to which this great work must reach before the last of the twenty-five years is recorded, which closed the war in 1648, may be easily conjectured. Fortunately Professor Gindely has been prevailed upon by his publisher, pending the completion of this larger history, to put the result of his studies and researches into a form better suited to the wants of the great majority of readers, and he has compressed all the matter of the larger history, suppressing only the full text of the documentary evidence, within the bounds of two convenient octavo volumes,[1] which cover the entire period from the fateful 23d of May, 1618, when the Austrian stadtholders and their secretary, who bore to Prague the royal letters of Ferdinand revoking all religious rights of Protestants, were hurled out of the window of the Council Chamber by the Bohemian magnates, and the war was begun that had been so long impending, until the conclusion of peace by the Treaty of Westphalia, more than thirty years later, on the 24th of October, 1648. This smaller work has been admirably translated in this country, under an arrangement with and with the full sanction of the author and his German publishers, by Mr. Andrew Ten Brook, formerly Professor of Mental Philosophy in the University of Michigan. Mr. Ten Brook has also enriched it by an able introductory chapter, containing a large amount of information of great value to American readers, explanatory of the intricacies of the politics of the German Empire and its subdivisions in the first quarter of the seventeenth century, and by a thoughtful concluding essay, in which he indicates the place that the Thirty Years' War occupies in the world's progressive course of education. Professor Gindely's narrative is exceedingly minute, without being prolix, and very graphic, although it lacks the richness of coloring and the brilliant rhetoric that we find in Macaulay or Motley. Characters and events, battles and campaigns, the conflicts of creeds and policies, the intrigues of statesmen and diplomatists, the jarring interests of the German states, the perfidies and rivalries of princes, the rapacity and treason of generals, the subservience of ministers, and the almost universal atrophy of patriotism are described; an interminable procession of kings, palatines, electors, margraves, warriors, statesmen, diplomatists, and ecclesiastics is deployed; the infinite entanglements of German relations are displayed; the sufferings of an impoverished people are depicted; and every step in the dreadful conflict is followed with painstaking accuracy and the keenest interest. His style is simple, perspicuous, and dignified; his collation of facts is astonishingly full, and their arrangement masterly; his analysis and interpretation of political and military events and of religious and civil occurrences are clear and eminently candid and philosophic; and his judgments of the men, the times, and the principles and objects contended for are uniformly calm, impartial, and free from any coloring of prejudice or prepossession. His work deserves to take not merely a high, but the first, rank in literature as the fullest and most authentic history that has yet been written of the most stupendous war which has ever lacerated Christendom, and which, in the name

[1] *History of the Thirty Years' War.* By ANTON GINDELY. Translated by ANDREW TEN BROOK. Complete in Two Volumes, 8vo, pp. 456 and 457. With Twenty-eight Illustrations and Two Maps. New York: G. P. Putnam's Sons.

and under the pretense of religion, set at naught every precept of its Divine Author. In reality the religion that was announced by the one side and the other as its motive was merely a cloak to cover or afford a pretext for the ambitious aims of rapacious and remorseless men, whose sole object was to increase their possessions and augment their power. Neither Protestant nor Romanist will be able to find any ground for self-gratulation in Professor Gindely's able and severely dispassionate work, so far as the chief actors in the war are concerned, not even excepting the comparatively pure and noble-minded Swedish hero, Gustavus Adolphus. Both sides were intolerant, cruel, selfish, and dominated by the lust of conquest and acquisition. Neither had any true conception of civil and religious liberty, nor any real sympathy for it. Yet they wrought better than they knew, since the Thirty Years' War was doubtless the last great and formal struggle the world will ever witness having for its object the annihilation of man's personality, and the subjection of all religious thought to the arbitrary rule of an artificial civil and ecclesiastical system.

THE alarming increase of the various forms of mental disease, which has been stimulated of late years by the strain and excitements of modern civilization, has had the effect of concentrating the attention of observant physicians and psychologists upon the special investigation of the phenomena, causes, nature, and treatment of insanity and the allied nervous diseases, and also upon the extent and limitations of the moral and legal responsibility of those who are afflicted with them. The investigation has resulted in a large accumulation of material bearing usefully and practically upon the subject. In the number of this Magazine for October last, a synoptical outline was given of an important *Treatise on Insanity*, by Dr. Hammond; and we have now to invite attention, but necessarily very briefly and imperfectly, to another equally important related work, by Dr. Edward C. Mann, entitled *A Manual of Psychological Medicine and Allied Nervous Diseases*,[2] premising, before entering upon our notice of the last-named volume, that the two treatises, read in connection, are practically exhaustive of the authoritative ascertained knowledge upon the subject of cerebral or mental disease, and contain in systematized form the results of the prolonged and minute research of all the most recent investigators, brought down to the latest date, and verified and supplemented by the observation and ex-

perience of two of the most eminent specialists among them. Dr. Mann's manual bears upon every page the impress of sterling good sense, and a perfect freedom from all doubtful or crotchety speculations. This feature, in connection with its other merits, invests it with a substantial practical value to students of medicine and practicing physicians, and indeed it has been expressly designed by the author to meet the wants of those general practitioners who are obliged in the course of their practice to deal with diseases of every kind, and who must necessarily often encounter, perhaps in their incipient and avertible forms, some one or other of the largely increasing number and variety of diseases that affect the brain and produce partial and temporary or total and permanent insanity. His work is a complete and methodical treatise and manual on diseases of the mind, and treats of their predisposing and exciting causes; their detection, prevention, alleviation, or cure; their medico-legal aspects and relations, and the care and custody of those who are under their influence. It embodies a large mass of material for the guidance of the general practitioner, by means of which he may be assisted to detect insanity in its incipient stages, and in its concealed or simulated forms, as well as in its more marked acute and chronic manifestations. Cases are reported of almost every form of insanity, and accounts are given of the phenomena that attended each, and of the treatment that was found to be successful or the reverse, derived not only from the record of well-authenticated instances reported by eminent specialists, but also from the author's own experience and observation, and the experience and observation of his medical friends and coadjutors, at the bedside of the patients. In the same way the author discusses the allied nervous diseases now so rife in our country, and whose tendency is to develop into insanity; describes their causes and indicates the best methods for their prevention; particularizes instances of the manner in which nearly every form of this class of disease has been successfully dealt with; and prescribes the treatment by which its tendency to develop into insanity may be lessened, arrested, or averted. In connection with the consideration of the purely medical aspects of mental disease, Dr. Mann introduces at appropriate stages in his treatise elaborate essays on the medical jurisprudence of insanity, on the legal consequences of its different varieties, on the duties of medical practitioners when consulted concerning the mental condition of a patient, on the office and duties of experts, and the weight of expert testimony in criminal trials where insanity is alleged as a defense, and on the moral and legal responsibility of persons laboring under any of the forms of mental disease with respect to the commission of crimes or the fulfillment of civil contracts. Dr. Mann has incorporated in his valuable and comprehensive treatise a co-

---

[2] *A Manual of Psychological Medicine and Allied Nervous Diseases.* Containing the Description, Etiology, Diagnosis, Prognosis, Pathology, and Treatment of Insanity. With especial reference to the Clinical Features of Mental Disease and the Allied Neuroses, and its Medico-legal Aspects, etc. By EDWARD C. MANN, M.D., Member of the New York Medico-legal Society, etc. With Phototype Plates and other Illustrations. 8vo, pp. 699. Philadelphia: P. Blakiston, Son, and Co.

pious store of information relative to the increasing prevalence of insanity in the Middle States, and the causes that contribute to it, and some thoughtful suggestions indicating the necessity for such a revised codification of the law relative to insanity as shall recognize the existence of mental disease in its various degrees, and its influence on conduct and moral responsibility. In a valuable appendix a compendious *résumé* is given of the treatment of the insane, accompanied by prescriptions which have been found efficacious in Dr. Mann's practice; and also a carefully prepared abstract of the laws relating to the care and custody of the insane in the various States of the Union, alphabetically arranged according to the States, the latter having been compiled expressly for the work by the author's brother, Mr. William J. Mann, of the New York bar. The volume is an ample repository of facts and information, serviceable alike to the medical and legal practitioner, the jurist, and those who have charge of institutions for the insane, covering as it does the entire field of the diagnosis, care, custody, and treatment of mental disease, and of the medical jurisprudence of insanity.

IF the perils which beset our Ship of State are as numerous, as imminent, and as real as they have been represented to be by numerous critics and croakers, alarmists and malcontents, and even by timid or nervous or downhearted patriots, its course is destined to be a short one, and to terminate with a tragic catastrophe. What with the spectres they have evoked of disunion, disintegration, State sovereignty, mobocracy, plutocracy, aristocracy, communism, monarchy, and the strife between labor and capital, there would seem to be no safety for the republic, and, to imitate their own turgid and inflated phrases, it must either drift on treacherous shoals and sands, be dashed against gigantic rocks and icebergs, be dismantled by terrific gales and tempests, be ingulfed in irresistible whirlpools and cloudbursts, or founder in mid-ocean through the agency of its own internal forces, which, escaping all control, shall become the blind elements of promiscuous ruin. Fortunately these bodements are for the most part imaginary or greatly exaggerated. We have been familiar with them from the earliest hours of the old Confederation and of the Federal union; and yet, under Providence, the good sense, self-control, and patriotism of the great body of the people, and the strength and elasticity of our institutions, have carried us safely through every peril that has been presaged, as well as through the perils that have burst upon us without any warning.

Of course nations, like individuals, must be exposed to danger, and must suffer from disease and natural imperfection. This is a condition of all things human or of human contrivance. But in neither case is it wise, and

in the case of one's own nation it is not patriotic, to gaze so intently and exclusively upon perils and imperfections as to accept the one as inevitable, and the other as irremediable, and to become blind to the fact that they are only the occasional, as they are the inevitable, conditions of every strong and healthful life, and do not constitute its prevalent normal state. Nevertheless it were scarcely less unwise or unpatriotic to shut our eyes to the dangers that beset the nation, or to the imperfections in our institutions and political conditions which may cause these dangers to become actively potent and formidable. And although its author is often extravagant in his statements and assumptions, and arrives at conclusions which are chimerical, we have rarely met with a volume which presents some of these dangers more clearly or more forcibly than they are presented in a treatise by Mr. Henry C. Lockwood, entitled, *The Abolition of the Presidency*.[3] Mr. Lockwood is at great pains to establish the following positions: That many incongruities and imperfections exist and are intrinsic to our system of government; that while we claim to be republican in form, we are in reality monarchical in respect to the powers conferred upon and exercised by the President and Senate; that the system of checks and balances in our constitution is an attempt to create a sovereignty, without permitting it to become apparent, by the formation of three co-ordinate and co-equal powers in the same government; that it has often occurred since our existence as a nation that the Executive has thrown down these divisions, and virtually achieved his own sovereignty; that the executive office and power are in organized conflict with the other two branches; that the evils of the Presidential system have within them the potency of danger to the public weal; and finally, that if we would preserve the essence and spirit of American liberty we must remedy these grave defects by the abolition of the Presidency, and the substitution for our present form of government of a system that shall be more truly in conformity with the idea of a republic.

In a number of preliminary chapters, leading up to the statement of the precise remedy that he proposes, Mr. Lockwood recapitulates the monarchical powers exercised by the President—powers greater than those exercised by any limited monarch, and only less than absolute—as exhibited by his independence of the will of Congress in the matter of the execution of the laws it may enact, and by his exercise of the veto; by the dangerous powers placed in his hands as commander-in-chief of the army and navy, by means of which the country may be plunged into war, at home or abroad, by his sole will, without the authority of Congress, and even in opposition to its will;

[3] *The Abolition of the Presidency.* By HENRY C. LOCKWOOD, of the New York Bar. 8vo, pp. 332. New York: R. Worthington.

by his extraordinary powers in the matter of reprieves and pardons, in the negotiation of treaties and alliances, in appointing to and removing from office, and in the recognition of State governments—all of which, Mr. Lockwood contends, are powers that belong to a monarch, not to the executive officer of a representative government, who should merely execute the will of the people as manifested by the laws of Congress—and tend inevitably to the institution at some time of a personal government under some ambitious incumbent of the Presidency. Mr. Lockwood would therefore abolish the office which combines in itself all these dangerous powers, so full of menace to popular liberty and of invitation to the establishment of a dynastic government, and he proposes the substitution in its stead of the following changes: That the supreme power of making and executing the laws of the United States shall be vested in a Congress consisting of one body and elected by the people, which body shall be the final judge of its own powers, subject, however, to the right of a creature of its own making, denominated an Executive Council, to dissolve or prorogue it, and to take an appeal to the people upon a framed issue; that Congress shall appoint this Executive Council, which shall consist of officers analogous to the present heads of departments forming "the cabinet," each of whom shall be at the head of his respective department, shall prescribe regulations thereunder not inconsistent with law, and shall be subject to removal by Congress whensoever he fails properly to perform the duties imposed upon him by law, or may resign at his own pleasure, and all of whom must either resign or appeal to the people if the policy determined upon by the Council meets with the disapproval of Congress. The plan further proposes that if the Council submit to a decision of Congress adverse to its policy, or be defeated by the popular vote on an appeal being taken from Congress to the people, then a new Council shall be appointed by Congress; but if, on the other hand, the Council be sustained by the people, the old members shall still continue in power despite the disapproval of that particular policy by Congress. According to Mr. Lockwood's scheme, the Secretary of State would be the chairman of the Council, with authority to convene it at any time he should elect, or, upon his refusal or neglect to do so, it would be convened upon the request of a majority of its members. The ordinary proceedings of the meetings of the Council for mutual instruction, counsel, or advice would be secret; but in case the Council should be defeated in Congress, it would have the power to order the dissolution of that body, in which event all motions, decisions, and speeches made or proceedings had must be public. The members of the Council would be entitled to seats in Congress, and would have the right to debate and to initiate legislation. Each or all

of them would be subject to be called before Congress to answer questions or give information. When Congress is not in session the Council would perform every act necessary to execute the laws and to carry on the affairs of government. During a recess of Congress, whensoever one-half of its members shall jointly or separately request the Secretary of State to convene it, he shall issue a proclamation calling it together. And, finally, Mr. Lockwood proposes that the judicial power of the United States shall be limited and confined to defining, expounding, interpreting, and explaining the laws and intent of Congress, and be shorn of its present sovereign power of finally determining the meaning and operation of our fundamental law, of which Congress alone shall be the judge.

Mr. Lockwood's treatise is very suggestive. He points out forcibly and sensibly many defects that should be remedied, and many dangers and frictions that should be lessened or removed. But he is better as a critic and stronger as a political iconoclast than as an architect of a system of government. His plan of a shadowy Congress clothed with indefinite power to make laws and determine their constitutionality, yet liable at any moment to be dispersed and dissolved at the will of its own monstrous progeny, the Executive Council, is at once cumbrous, utopian, incredibly weak, and infinitely more full of dangerous possibilities than anything in our present system. The corruption and agitation that now centre every four years upon the election of a President would be concentrated with tenfold force and greater frequency upon the election of members of Congress, and upon appeals taken from Congress to the people by the Council, and would ultimately come to have a direct reference to the composition of the Council or its maintenance in power. The Council itself would be a cumbrous Executive, incapable of quick action in an emergency, unless, as is almost certain, it should fall under the domination of the superior intellect and stronger will of one or two of its members; and instead of the imaginary danger of an ambitious President with an eye fixed on monarchy, we should have the ever-present and real menace of an ambitious and hydra-headed Council gravitating toward the monopoly of the supreme power. We incline to the opinion that the people of the United States will decide that they would "rather bear the ills we have than fly to others that we know not of." The ills investing our present scheme of government are definite and ascertained, while those that invest Mr. Lockwood's scheme are indefinite, unascertained, and charged with possibilities that no line can fathom.

———

A NATURAL and very general interest is taken in biographies of parents whose sons have become greatly distinguished, more especially in those which trace genius, talents, or virtues of great men and women to their origin in the character of their mothers. And although a critical investigation would undoubtedly disclose the fact that the parents of great men are not always endowed with any special traits of greatness, and, further, that the great qualities of men and women of transcendent abilities are not invariably transmitted to their descendants, yet it can scarcely be questioned that the influence of heredity is not confined to the physical frame, where, as is universally conceded, it manifests itself most unmistakably, but is equally potent in the transmission of moral and intellectual qualities. Aside from the scientific interest that attaches to the study of the operation of this interesting physiological fact, as revealed by biographies of the mothers of great men, and aside also from the mere pleasure and curiosity that are ministered to by such biographies, they are rich in wholesome incitements and encouragements to woman, must impress her with a profounder sense of her responsibilities, and stimulate her to the cultivation of her moral and intellectual nature to the utmost, in the consciousness that whatever lifts her to a higher plane must also elevate and ennoble the race. Very hearty, therefore, is the welcome we extend to a series of excellent brief sketches of *The Mothers of Great Men and Women, and Some Wives of Great Men,*[4] by Mrs. Laura C. Holloway, in which, among others, are given outlines of the lives and characters of the mothers of Washington, Napoleon, St. Augustine, the Wesleys, the Napiers, the Gracchi, Sheridan, Madame De Staël, Carlyle, John Quincy Adams, and "Stonewall" Jackson, and of the wives of Lord Russell (the heroic and brilliant Lady Mary), Milton, Dr. Johnson, Lord Beaconsfield, and others. The sketches are skillful and sympathetic as portraitures, and trustworthy as compilations.

ALTHOUGH the military operations of General Burgoyne have been diligently studied and fully described by capable writers, what we know concerning them has been chiefly derived from American authorities, and much has been left untold that relates to the *personnel* of the British army, the plans and intentions of its commanders, and the details of numerous minor but yet not unimportant movements which they projected during the campaign that resulted in the capitulation at Saratoga. Considerable light has been thrown upon the general events of the campaign and upon many interesting lesser passages in it by the publication, under the patient and exhaustive editorship of General Horatio Rogers, of the *Journal and Orderly Books*[5] of Lieuten-

ant James M. Hadden, of the British Royal Artillery, who served first under Sir Guy Carleton in Canada, and afterward under Generals Phillips and Burgoyne in New York, from the early summer of 1776 till the surrender of Burgoyne in the autumn of 1777. These are printed *verbatim* from original manuscript memorandum-books in Lieutenant Hadden's handwriting, that were formerly in the possession of William Cobbett, from whom they passed through several other hands, until they finally reached this country, and were purchased by the editor, General Rogers. After fully satisfying himself of their genuineness, and being convinced of their great value as original contemporaneous evidence by a close examination of them and of the carefully prepared accompanying maps, plans, and sketches, General Rogers determined upon their publication in permanent form as a contribution to the history of an important episode in the Revolutionary War, which would clear up some doubtful and controverted points involving dates and facts, and impart fuller and clearer information concerning many interesting passages and incidents that attended the movements of Burgoyne's forces and the engagements in which they, or portions of them, participated. Not content with performing this part of his task with scrupulous fidelity, General Rogers has added materially to the value and interest of the original documents by contributing an admirably written explanatory chapter, in which he has embodied a large amount of interesting materials, comprising, among other matter, a biographical sketch of Lieutenant Hadden, a large number of brief outline sketches of Burgoyne and other eminent or active British officers referred to in Lieutenant Hadden's manuscript, a historical account of the organization, composition, and services of the regiments composing the army of Burgoyne, and a fund of varied information bearing closely or remotely upon the campaign which resulted so disastrously to the British arms in this country. Besides, General Rogers has enriched nearly every page of his reproduction of this interesting relic by an immense number of well-digested foot-notes, historical, biographical, and explanatory of incidents and movements referred to in the original text, or having even a possible and contingent bearing upon them; and he has also gathered into a capacious appendix of more than two hundred pages a copious array of biographical, military, and historical ana, illustrative of some of the operations of the war, and outlining the lives and services of meritorious soldiers and officers in both armies. The volume is overclosely edited, but for that very reason it will be specially prized by historical students.

4 *The Mothers of Great Men and Women, and Some Wives of Great Men.* By LAURA C. HOLLOWAY. Illustrated. 8vo, pp. 647. New York : Funk and Wagnalls.
5 *Hadden's Journal and Orderly Books.* A Journal kept in Canada and upon Burgoyne's Campaign in 1776 and 1777 by Lieutenant James M. Hadden, Royal Artillery. Also Orders kept by him and issued by Sir

Guy Carleton, Lieutenant-General, John Burgoyne, and Major-General William Phillips in 1776, 1777, and 1778. With an Explanatory Chapter and Notes by HORATIO ROGERS. 4to, pp. 581. Albany : Joel Munson's Sons.

A VOLUME that will be regarded with special interest by students of political economy, and those who are giving attention to the history of the currency and of banking and finance in the United States, has been prepared by the Hon. John Jay Knox,[6] formerly of the Treasury Department, in which he presents in brief compass a history of the various issues of paper money by the government, including an account of the emissions of paper money by the colonies, of the causes that led to them, the methods that were pursued to force the notes into circulation, and the circumstances that led to their depreciation. Separate chapters are devoted to a historical summary of the legislation relative to paper money at various periods, and to a description of the nature of the loans negotiated and the notes issued, comprising historical sketches of the paper money authorized by the Continental Congress, of the action in the Federal Convention when the subject of the emission of bills of credit was under consideration, of the Treasury notes respectively authorized in the war of 1812, during the financial crisis of 1837, in the Mexican war, during the administration of Mr. Buchanan, and in the period of the civil war, and including an account of the silver dollar and the silver certificates. Specific chapters are also devoted to the history of the legal tender cases in the Supreme Court of the United States, and of the distribution of the surplus in 1837, and the legislation that preceded it. In an appendix Mr. Knox prints the full text of the recent legal tender decision of the Supreme Court, together with the full text of Justice Field's dissenting opinion. This bare outline of the subjects treated in Mr. Knox's able and useful volume affords but a slight idea of the wealth of historical facts, dates, and information, and of the sound financial doctrines, that is embodied in the luminous essays that form its brief and comprehensive chapters.

MR. PARKE GODWIN has completed his fine edition of the *Life and Works of William Cullen Bryant*[7] by the reproduction, in two elegant octavo volumes, of a selection from Mr. Bryant's prose works, including some of his essays, tales, orations, letters, sketches of travel, addresses, and editorial comments, criticisms, and opinions. Mr. Bryant's reputation as a prose writer, though respectable, was greatly inferior to that which he deservedly enjoyed as a poet. Nevertheless, he is always genial, instructive, and elevating. The instinctive delicacy and refinement that pervade all his prose writings, combined with their vigorous manliness, their purity of thought and diction, and their clear and equable common-sense, will insure them a permanent place in our best, most wholesome, and most invigorating literature.

EVERY good working library must be made up largely of books of reference. To be able to consult instantly and with confidence various sources of information is the supreme joy of the student. Doubtless it was to minister to such a feeling that Drs. George R. Crooks and John F. Hurst prepared their *Theological Encyclopædia and Methodology.*[8] The basis of their work is the excellent volume of Dr. Karl Hagenbach, so long the eminent Professor of Theology in the University of Basel, but they have enlarged and supplemented it with a copious bibliography of English and American authorities in the various departments, with an appendix of great value, and with a list of the histories of Christian Churches in the United States. Methodology is defined, after Harless, to be " the regulative conclusions from the principles and historical character of a science which are requisite for the process of appropriation"—a definition which, it must be admitted, is sufficiently enigmatical and abstract, but which becomes clearer through the explanations of the context. The first part of the work is a general encyclopædia, which treats of the relation of theology to science, to art, to philology, philosophy, ethics, logic, etc. It also exhibits the leading tendencies of theological thought in the Early Church in the Middle Ages, among the Reformers, and in the seventeenth and eighteenth centuries, as well as the new direction it has recently received in England and America. The second part, or special theological encyclopædia, discusses the ideas, scope, literature, etc., of theology, in its exegesis, in its history as developed into a system, and in its practical bearings. A vast variety of carefully sifted knowledge on manifold topics is summed in about six hundred pages, designed to afford a useful hand-book and guide to the scholar's inquiries. The catalogues of the literature of the various departments added by the American editors, while of course not complete, are yet full enough to prove of great help to most investigators.

A DICTIONARY of geography and gazetteer of the world that is compressed into a single handy duodecimo volume, which is not too bulky for a satchel, and yet affords full, specific, and accurate information, must be considered an invaluable item in the equipment of a traveller or of a home library. Such a work we have found the *Globe Pronouncing Gazetteer*

---

[6] *United States Notes.* A History of the Various Issues of Paper Money by the Government of the United States, etc. By JOHN JAY KNOX. 8vo, pp. 250. New York: Charles Scribner's Sons.

[7] *The Life and Works of William Cullen Bryant.* Vols. V. and VI. Prose Writings of William C. Bryant. Edited by PARKE GODWIN. Volume I.: Essays, Tales, and Orations. Volume II.: Travels, Addresses, and Comments. 8vo, pp. 431 and 425. New York: D. Appleton and Co.

[8] *Theological Encyclopædia and Methodology.* On the Basis of Hagenbach. By GEORGE R. CROOKS, D.D., and JOHN F. HURST, D.D. 8vo, pp. 610. New York: Phillips and Hunt.

of the World[9] to be. Its descriptive, geographical, and statistical departments are sufficiently full to cover all ordinary general needs for popular use or ready reference, and are uniformly accurate. They embrace compact accounts of the various countries of the world, their physical aspects and political subdivisions, and the location, population, and characteristic features and industries of their principal towns. And in addition the pronunciation is given of geographical names, and in most cases the meaning and etymology of the name forms are supplied. It is also accompanied by convenient and generally excellent maps of all the chief countries.

IF there were no other evidence that the Psalms of David (as they are popularly designated) are inspired than that which is afforded by the fact that no maltreatment of translation in prose or verse to which they have been subjected has quenched their marvellous spiritual power or destroyed their rich poetry, it would be well-nigh conclusive. No other literary work has been put to so great a variety of severe tests, and none has triumphed so signally over the poverty, the ignorance, the misconception, and the prosaic commonplace of its translators. The baldest and crudest version that has ever appeared has preserved something of the grandeur, the beauty, the melody, and the transfiguring power and spirit of the original. Probably, however, the most crucial test to which these incomparable hymns have ever been subjected is that to which they are now being put by Biblical scholars, who bring to the task an amount of philological learning that has never before been approached, and, we may add, an absence of poetic taste and genius that is unparalleled. The latest translation[10] is one that has been made by the Rev. T. K. Cheyne, an English scholar and clergyman, and again the royal singer emerges triumphant from the crucible; and we may now conclude that nothing that man may do can rob his precious lyrics of their poetry and inspiration. Although we may miss some beautiful figures from Mr. Cheyne's translation, or find some favorite or familiar thought incrusted with pedantic literalism, instances of this kind are comparatively few, and the work as a whole remains with its beauty unimpaired. Read in connection with the text of the Accepted Version of the Bible, or with the exquisitely beautiful version in the Book of Common Prayer, Mr. Cheyne's translation will be found a suggestive and instructive commentary. If it obscures some beauties, it reveals many new ones of a high order.

WHILE the movement inland of towns, cities, populous communities, and the nervous activities and accompaniments of our artificial society, have driven the more restless of the old settlers and pioneers of our Western plains and lowlands still farther west, where they form the fluttering outer fringe of our advancing civilization, the dwellers in our midland mountains have escaped the inundation, and still remain in their hilly fastnesses comparatively untouched and unaffected by the wave of progress. In Virginia, North Carolina, northern Georgia and Alabama, and Tennessee the ridges and declivities of the Appalachian range are still peopled by a primitive folk who retain the dialect and the simple and uncouth ways of their forefathers, together with their dress, occupations, and forms of intercourse, their inartificial and rough-and-ready vices and virtues, their quick responsiveness to passion and emotion, and their full share of that human nature which makes all men kin. With the keen instinct of a true artist Mr. Charles E. Craddock has chosen these mountaineers for study and illustration, and in a collection of vigorous stories, entitled *In the Tennessee Mountains*,[11] he graphically depicts their life and manners, their impulses and emotions, their joys, sorrows, triumphs, and tribulations, the vicissitudes and tragedies in which they have played a part, the scenery amid which they were born and bred, and which has become a part of their nature, and, in fine, unfolds the simple but powerful dramas in which they are the unconscious actors. Mr. Craddock's stories have the charm of novelty and freshness. They are written with masculine grace, and they abound in situations which are invariably striking and picturesque, and often strongly dramatic. His delineations of individuals are noteworthy for the subtlety with which they discriminate fine and delicate shades of character, no less than for the boldness and originality with which they depict its coarser and severer lines. To all this he adds the wizard power of telling a story with straightforward earnestness and simplicity, and of investing it with absorbing pathos and tenderness.

MUCH that has been said in the preceding notice applies equally as well to four stories by Mr. Joel Chandler Harris, author of *Nights with Uncle Remus*, which he has grouped together under the title of *Mingo, and Other Sketches in Black and White*.[12] Less exclusively devoted than Mr. Craddock's tales to the portrayal of life in the mountains, Mr. Harris depicts some of the characteristic phases of the mountain life of northern Georgia, its romance and its reality, with the same bracing vigor and dramatic force that are visible in Mr. Crad-

[9] *The Globe Pronouncing Gazetteer of the World, Descriptive and Statistical, with Etymological Notes.* Being a Geographical Dictionary for Popular Use. With Thirty-two Maps. 12mo, pp. 500. New York: G. P. Putnam's Sons.
[10] *The Book of Psalms.* Translated by the Rev. T. K. Cheyne, M.A. "Parchment Library." 16mo, pp. 254. New York: D. Appleton and Co.

[11] *In the Tennessee Mountains.* By Charles Egbert Craddock. 16mo, pp. 331. Boston: Houghton, Mifflin, and Co.
[12] *Mingo, and Other Sketches in Black and White.* By Joel Chandler Harris. 16mo, pp. 273. Boston: James R. Osgood and Co.

dock's *In the Tennessee Mountains*, while his delineations of the plantation and village life that is rapidly dissolving before the influx of new social and industrial conditions at once preserve the memory of a vanishing phase of Georgia society, and delight the reader with his rare powers as a story-teller. It will not be easy to find in our home literature four more perfect or more thrilling stories than these of Mr. Harris's telling.

AFTER a comparatively long interval of silence Mr. Wilkie Collins has written another novel in his characteristic vein, but with less than his usual skill. Like the generality of his romances, the interest of his new novel, "*I Say No,*" or the *Love-Letter Answered*,[13] depends chiefly upon the development of a plot whose systematic intricacies pique the curiosity until the last moment, and upon the concealment of a mystery which baffles and defies solution until it shall have contributed to no end of cross purposes and caused a prodigious amount of incertitude and wretchedness. So far as this line of art is concerned Mr. Collins has no rival, and his reader is sure of being involved and absorbed in a plot whose pervading element is one of mystification and suspense most artfully and ingeniously sustained. In the higher requisites of romantic art the story before us is inferior to Mr. Collins's other novels. The characters are less definite, and their individuality is less strongly marked, its incidents and vicissitudes are more commonplace and conventional, and its situations are more purely sensational.

OF the other novels of the month, of which there has been a plenteous crop, several are of much more than ordinary merit. Among these are: *A Perilous Secret*,[14] the last, though far from the best, of Charles Reade's novels; *A Country Doctor*,[15] an exquisitely delicate and very subtle delineation, by Sarah Orne Jewett, of the evolution of character under the influence of simple and natural surroundings and of wise and wholesome guidance, coupled with some charming limnings of social phases, rural scenes, and village life and character; *Dissolving Views*,[16] a bright and kaleidoscopic romance of English society, with an engaging love story, by Mrs. Andrew Lang; *The Fate of Mansfield Humphreys*,[17] a delicious medley of love and

philology, by Richard Grant White; new editions respectively of Mr. Laurence Oliphant's *Piccadilly*[18] and Charles Reade's invigorating collection of *Good Stories*;[19] *Godfrey Helstone*,[20] a cheerful, changeful, and wholesome love story, by Georgiana M. Craik; and *The Miz Maze, or the Winkworth Puzzle*,[21] a brilliant tale, whose plot, resembling those of Wilkie Collins in its intricacy and mysterious involvements, is evolved through the medium solely of letters supposed to have been written by the imaginary actors, whose parts are personated by nine different writers, with the object in view of securing the difference in style and way of thinking that exists in real life. Each writer thus contributes not only her own individuality to the letters she writes, but gives her own special turns to the emotions and incidents of the story, while adhering to the general outlines of the plot. The novel which has resulted from this extensive copartnership is not less remarkable for its freshness and interest than for the ingenuity with which it has been executed by the numerous writers who were engaged upon it, and who, we may add, are the following well-known writers of fiction: Frances Hawley, Mary Bramston, Christabel R. Coleridge, A. E. Marcy Anderson Morshead, Charlotte M. Yonge, Frances M. Peard, Mary S. Lee, Eleanor S. Price, and Florence Wilford. The more deserving of the remaining novels are: *A Fair Country Maid*,[22] by E. Fairfax Byrrne; *My Ducats and My Daughter*,[23] by an anonymous author; *The Giant's Robe*,[24] by F. Anstey; *Miss Ludington's Sister*,[25] by Edward Bellamy; *Phœbe*,[26] by the author of *Rutledge*; *Stage-Struck*,[27] by Blanche Roosevelt; *Tinkling Cymbals*,[28] by Edgar Fawcett; and *The Crime of Henry Vane*,[29] by J. S. of Dale.

13 "*I Say No*;" or, *The Love-Letter Answered*. A Novel. By WILKIE COLLINS. 16mo, pp. 233. New York: Harper and Brothers.
The Same. "Franklin Square Library." 4to, pp. 62. New York: Harper and Brothers.
14 *A Perilous Secret*. By CHARLES READE. 16mo, pp. 160. New York: Harper and Brothers.
The Same. "Franklin Square Library." 4to, pp. 50. New York: Harper and Brothers.
15 *A Country Doctor*. By SARAH ORNE JEWETT. 16mo, pp 351. Boston: Houghton, Mifflin, and Co.
16 *Dissolving Views*. By Mrs. ANDREW LANG. 16mo, pp. 271. New York: Harper and Brothers.
17 *The Fate of Mansfield Humphreys*. With the Episode of Mr. Washington Adams in England. By RICHARD GRANT WHITE. 16mo, pp, 446. Boston: Houghton, Mifflin, and Co.
18 *Piccadilly*. A Fragment of Contemporary Biography. By LAURENCE OLIPHANT. 16mo, pp. 153. New York: Harper and Brothers.
19 *Good Stories*. By CHARLES READE. Illustrated. 16mo, pp. 319. New York: Harper and Brothers.
20 *Godfrey Helstone*. A Novel. By GEORGIANA M. CRAIK. "Franklin Square Library." 4to, pp. 57. New York: Harper and Brothers.
21 *The Miz Maze; or, The Winkworth Puzzle*. 16mo, pp. 212. New York: Harper and Brothers.
22 *A Fair Country Maid*. A Novel. By E. FAIRFAX BYRRNE. "Franklin Square Library." 4to, pp. 71. New York: Harper and Brothers.
23 *My Ducats and My Daughter*. A Novel, "Franklin Square Library." 4to, pp. 74. New York: Harper and Brothers.
24 *The Giant's Robe*. By F. ANSTEY. 16mo, pp. 427. New York: D. Appleton and Co.
25 *Miss Ludington's Sister*. A Romance of Immortality. By EDWARD BELLAMY. 16mo, pp. 260. Boston: James R. Osgood and Co.
26 *Phœbe*. A Novel. By the Author of "Rutledge." 16mo. pp. 332. Boston: Houghton, Mifflin, and Co.
27 *Stage-Struck; or, She Would be an Opera Singer*. By BLANCHE ROOSEVELT. 12mo, pp. 251. New York: Fords, Howard, and Hulbert.
28 *Tinkling Cymbals*. A Novel. By EDGAR FAWCETT. 12mo, pp. 332. Boston: James R. Osgood and Co.
29 *The Crime of Henry Vane*. By the Author of "Guerndale." 16mo, pp. 206. Boston: Charles Scribner's Sons.

Editor's Historical Record.

POLITICAL.

OUR Record is closed on the 17th of July. —The Democratic National Convention was held at Chicago, opening July 8. Colonel W. F. Vilas, of Wisconsin, was chosen permanent chairman. On the 11th, Hon. Grover Cleveland, of New York, was nominated for President, on the second ballot, and Hon. Thomas A. Hendricks, of Indiana, for Vice-President, without opposition. The ballots for President were as follows: *First*—Whole number of votes cast, 820; necessary to a choice, 547; for Grover Cleveland, of New York, 392; for Thomas F. Bayard, of Delaware, 168; for Allan G. Thurman, of Ohio, 88; for Samuel J. Randall, of Pennsylvania, 78; for Joseph E. McDonald, of Indiana, 56; for John G. Carlisle, of Kentucky, 27; for Roswell P. Flower, of New York, 4; for George Hoadly, of Ohio, 3; for Samuel J. Tilden, of New York, 1; for Thomas A. Hendricks, of Indiana, 1. *Second*—Whole number of votes cast, 820; necessary to a choice, 547; Cleveland, 684; Bayard, 81½; Thurman, 4; Randall, 4; McDonald, 1; Hendricks, 45½. The nomination was then made unanimous.

Congress adjourned July 7. The following bills were among those passed: The Utah Bill, Senate, June 18; Pacific Railroad Bill, House, June 19; Army Appropriation Bill, Senate, June 21; report of conference committee on Shipping Bill agreed to by House, June 21; Sundry Civil Bill, House, June 23; Mexican Pension Bill, Senate, June 24; Legislative, Executive, and Judicial Appropriation Bill, House, June 26; for a branch Soldiers' Home west of the Mississippi, Senate, July 1; Sundry Civil Bill, Senate, July 2; Fortifications Bill, House, July 2; conference report on Army Bill agreed to, House, July 2; Fortifications Bill, Senate, July 3; Anti-Chinese Bill, Senate, July 3; forfeiting Atlantic and Pacific Railroad unearned land grants, Senate, July 3; conference reports on Fortifications, Sundry Civil, and General Deficiency bills agreed to, House, July 6. Before adjournment the remaining appropriation bills were passed, and provision was made for the temporary support of the navy.

The President, July 2, vetoed the Fitz-John Porter Bill. It was passed over his veto by the House, July 2, but the Senate sustained the veto, July 3.

The President, July 4, nominated John A. Kasson to be Minister to Germany, Alphonso Taft to be Minister to Russia, John M. Francis to be Minister to Austria, Lewis Richmond to be Minister Resident to Portugal, Ward McAllister, Jun., to be United States Judge of Alaska; and John Jarrett to be Commissioner of Labor.

The Republican National Committee was organized, June 26, by the election of B. F. Jones as chairman.

The New York Democratic State Convention, June 18, instructed the delegates to the National Convention to vote as a unit, and renominated Judges Andrews (Republican) and Rapallo (Democrat) for the Court of Appeals, in accord with the similar non-partisan action of the Republican Convention.

The public debt was decreased $9,217,256 during the month of June.

The House of Lords, July 8, voted to postpone consideration of Mr. Gladstone's franchise bill until a redistribution of seats is included. This produced a political crisis, in which the question of the modification of the Upper House is involved. Mr. Gladstone announced that Parliament would be prorogued until October.

The Pan-Presbyterian Council was held at Belfast, Ireland, June 24 to July 3.

The Bartholdi statue was formally presented to the United States, Minister Morton receiving it, in Paris, July 4.

The cholera has made its appearance in France, many deaths being reported at Toulon and Marseilles.

An attack on French troops by Chinese troops at Lang-son, June 23, in violation of the treaty, provoked a demand from France for a heavy war indemnity.

The Conference on Egyptian Affairs met at London, June 28, and Earl Granville presented England's financial proposals. It then adjourned to permit examination of them by experts.

General Iglesias has resigned the Presidency of Peru, and has ordered a general election.

General Diaz has been declared President of Mexico.

DISASTERS.

June 19.—Several persons were fatally injured by the wrecking of a train on the Burlington and Missouri Railroad.

June 25.—Deaths from lightning were reported in New York, Pennsylvania, Ohio, and Wisconsin.

July 16.—Twenty-five persons were killed by the breaking of an engine axle on the Manchester and Sheffield Railway, England.

OBITUARY.

June 18.—At Philadelphia, Bishop Matthew Simpson, aged seventy-four years.

June 19.—At Berlin, John Gustavus Droysen, Professor of History in the University of Berlin, aged seventy-five years.

June 21.—At the Hague, the Prince of Orange, Crown Prince of the Netherlands, aged thirty-two years.

July 1.—At Chicago, Illinois, Allen Pinkerton, head of the detective agency, aged sixty-four years.

July 2.—General Francis Edward Todleben, the Russian engineer, aged sixty-six years.

Editor's Drawer.

THE Drawer is in want of information in regard to a characteristic New England custom that has a more or less remote bearing on the great question of the day, which is admitted to be the "conduct of life." Some persons may have the notion that the Drawer is only a fragmentary collection of anecdotes and smart sayings, the only purpose of which is to amuse the passing generation. In fact, it has an underlying philosophy and a deeper object than this. It gathers the anecdotes, the peculiar customs of localities, the odd freaks of human nature, the witticisms and the humors, and, above all, anything that illustrates the characteristic traits of the American people, traditions, manners, and character, in order to get a basis for a philosophy of life. And as the American people is a composite of every race and tribe that exists, the range of the Drawer necessarily takes in all creation. Ours is the inductive method, and in accordance with the prevailing fashion we have only to collect a sufficient number of facts in order to be able to set up and patent a theory which will enable us to understand human nature as perfectly as we now comprehend the development of a complete American university, with all its various activities and departments, out of certain inanimate and unintelligent ingredients or atoms, stirred together by a sort of indescribable cosmic spoon without a handle. If our collection of facts seems sometimes more humorous than facts ought to be on which to base a serious theory, that is because human nature can be best studied when it is, so to speak, off its guard, or stimulated into the brightest displays of its peculiarities. It is supposed by some philosophers that there is a fixed quantity of humor in the world, as there is a fixed quantity of wisdom (both so unequally distributed that the fools are always in a majority, especially in a popular election), and that this is the reason why all the witty sayings and funny anecdotes are successively borrowed by one generation from the preceding. But the fact is that no two people were ever created exactly alike, and almost every one is liable some time in his life to do or say something eccentric that has never been done or said before. Though it must be admitted that the doctrine of heredity comes in here, so that a joke made without intent to deceive turns out to have been made by an Aryan ancestor two or three thousand years before. Jokes are no doubt perpetuated, skipping entire generations, as physical traits are, and we recognize them by what we call "earmarks." We have in mind a child who has a slight slit in the lobe of each ear. Neither his father nor mother nor his grandparents had any such ear-mark, but it is remembered that his great-grandfather, who "fought into the Revolution," had exactly this birth-mark, and it is a tradition in the family that a remote ancestor of *his* had also this peculiarity. Now this boy should be watched; for if he ever makes a joke—that is, not a mere smart quibble of words, but achieves a characteristic piece of humor worthy to go into the Drawer—it will very likely be found that his great-grandfather perpetrated that very piece of humor, which probably also can be read in the ancient book of Greek jests. It is a solemn and interesting thought to us that children are born this very month who will grow up and try to get their jests and anecdotes into the future Drawers, and that the editor at the time will have to be on the watch for this heredity. For of all races the human race is the most deceiving.

But we have not been led away from our subject, as will appear from a statement of the information we desire in regard to a certain New England custom. We desire to know whether it is local or whether it prevailed elsewhere, whether it was invented in Massachusetts or was brought over from England or Holland, and whether it was practiced by any ancient peoples. The importance of this inquiry in the study of sociology will appear when we say that it relates to the most important concern in life, that is, courtship. In early New England days, as far back as the middle of the eighteenth century, when hospitality was a practice as well as a virtue, there was in most houses only one large assembly-room, and there the family and all the guests and chance callers gathered on winter nights about the blazing fire of logs. We know that youth was youth and love was love, and young men were timid and maidens were shy, and courtship went on in those days. How was courtship possible in this common room, where every word was heard and every look taken notice of? We read in the admirable volume on the recent centennial of Long Meadow, Massachusetts, by Professor Richard S. Storrs, of that town, that in the winter evenings, for the convenience of young lovers, since there was no "next room," courting-sticks were used; that is, long wooden tubes that could convey from lip to ear sweet and secret whispers. Was this an invention peculiar to Long Meadow?

It is a charming picture that this calls up of life in a Puritan household, this tubular love-making, the pretty girl (nearly every girl is pretty in the fire-light of long ago) seated in one stiff high-backed chair, and the staid but blushing lover in another, handling the courting-stick, itself an open confession of complacence, if not of true love. Would the young man dare to say, "I love you," through a tube, and would he feel encouraged by the laughing, tender eyes of the girl when she replied, through the same passage, "Do tell!"? Did they have two sticks, so that one end of one could be at the ear and the end of the other at the mouth all the while? How convenient, when the young man got more ardent than was seemly, as the flip went round, for the girl to put her thumb over the end of the tube, and stop the flow of soul! Did the young man bring his stick, and so announce his intention, or did the young lady always keep one or a pair on hand, and so reveal both willingness and expectation? It was so much more convenient than the telephone, with its "hello" and proclamation to all listeners at each end of the line. Lovers can make love with anything, even with a telephone; the successful courting of a deaf person (for there is one word that nearly everybody likes to hear), as we know, can go on through a speaking-trumpet; but these courting-sticks seem to us the *ne plus ultra* of tender communication—when a third party is present. They would be very useful now at large parties, where there is such a din and babble that one can only court a pretty girl at the risk of bronchitis or laryngitis. Sometimes in the jam you can not get near the girl; but with a long courting-stick you could wile her away from her too near admirer. This invention seems to us worthy of revival for many reasons, and we should be glad of any further information in regard to it. Civilization in its progress drops a good many things that ought to be retained.

In this same volume, in the speech of Professor Park, we find traced to its source a *mot* that has been attributed to John Randolph. Professor Park says: "A minister in this immediate neighborhood was once asked, in an insolent if not insulting way, 'Do you think you have got any religion?' He answered, 'None *to speak of*.' This apt reply was mentioned to John Randolph, who was pleased with it, and soon afterward said on the floor of our national House of Representatives, '*I* have no religion *to speak of*.' The felicitous remark has been ascribed to him as an original one."

DURING the time when New York and New Hampshire both claimed territorial jurisdiction over Vermont a newly married couple, named James and Rachel Leonard, came to the *verd mont* country to hew for themselves a fortune from the rocky wilderness.

Whether wafted by the dense cloud from the long pipes of their worthy Dutch parents, or by whatever combination of circumstances conveyed hither, they had come to stay; and when they heard that Colonel Ethan Allen was coming with a posse of soldiers to dispossess all who owned allegiance to the State of New York, they resolved not to be deprived of the little home which their mutual industry had reared.

When Allen arrived he found the young wife alone in the house. Asking her what jurisdic-

tion she recognized, she replied, "The State of New York."

He then told her that his errand was to dispossess all who claimed the protection of the State of New York, and that he must turn her out of her house.

"But I won't go," she answered.

Finding her determined in her resistance of authority, he said at last, "Well, you're not very heavy," and taking the plucky little woman in his arms, he carried her forcibly out of the house.

No sooner had he set her down, however, than she returned, the valiant Ethan calling after her, as she entered the door, "Remember that you go into that house under the jurisdiction of Vermont," and then riding away, his soldiers, no doubt, greatly amused to see the hero of Ticonderoga discomfited by a woman.

WHILE a certain Judge Greene was trying a civil case, Mr. X., the attorney for the defendant, had occasion to quote from Browne (a legal authority), but pronounced the final *e* in that name.

"Mr. X.," said the judge, "I believe that name is pronounced Brown, not Brown-e. Now my name is also spelled with a final *e*, but it is pronounced as one syllable, is it not?"

"Your honor," said Mr. X., "that depends entirely upon how you decide this case."

THE musical sense of the country choir is probably keener than their sense of the ludicrous and of the fitness of things. A correspondent heard the following extraordinary programme in a country Methodist church on the morning of Easter-Sunday. The organ prelude was from *Pinafore*—

> Farewell, my own—
> Light of my life, farewell.

The first hymn, in the midst of the radiant sunshine of that morning, was,

> Softly fades the twilight ray
> Of the blessed Sabbath day.

The anthem was the "Evening Hymn to the Virgin." The blissfully ignorant lads and lassies sang with as much unction to the peaceful congregation the

> Ave sanctissima—we lift our souls to thee;
> Ora pro nobis—'tis nightfall on the sea,

as they afterward put into the rousing hymn,

> I'm glad salvation's free,
> I'm glad salvation's free;
> Salvation's free for you and me—
> Bless God, salvation's free!

THIS anecdote of Virginia in the early days of reconstruction comes from a correspondent in Missouri, who heard it related by Chief Justice Miller, of Maryland:

Two elegant old-school Virginia gentlemen were seated one summer evening on the "hurricane" deck of a Rappahannock steamer. With their feet against the smoke-stack, chairs tilted back, and all the accessories to "old-school" comfort in the way of juleps and cigars, they were prepared to enjoy the sweet melancholy of the hour, and the pleasing panorama passing before their eyes, lighted by the last rays of the declining sun. Suddenly one of them speaks:

"Aw, majah, do you see that ar very fine mansion over thar?"

"Well, yes, colonel, I do. Belongs to Bob Kyarter, don't it?"

"Yes. You know Bob Kyarter? He was colonel of the Fifty-fifth; badly wounded at Chancellorsville."

"Yes, yes; I remember him now, majah."

"Well, you heard about that little legal affair of his'n lahst fall?"

"Seems to me I did. What was it?"

"Well, you know, Bob Kyarter is a fine old Virginia gentleman, good deal of land but vehy little cash, and there was a new postmahster appointed by Grahnt at the Landing here—Kyarter's Landing. And when Colonel Bob Kyarter, a gentleman of high social standin' and position in the community, of a good deal of land but vehy little cash, comes to this Yankee postmahster to' mail a lettah, why, the fellah says to Colonel Bob Kyarter that he was tired of mailin' lettahs for rebel brigadeahs, and onless he put a stamp on to the lettah it wouldn't go; that he spent his whole cussed salary paying for stahmps for rebel brigadeahs. He actually said that thing to Colonel Bob Kyarter, a gentleman of high social standin' and position in the community, of a good deal of land but vehy little cash—he did, sah, by gum, sah!"

"Well, what did Bob Kyarter do; he didn't suffah such cussed—"

"No, sah; he shot him, of course; and don't you know, majah, times is got so around heah that if it hadn't been for Colonel Bob Kyarter's high social standin' and position in the community, a Virginia gentleman of a good deal of land though vehy little cash, there would 'a been serious litigation over that little affair."

THE humor of this lies in its truth:

A gentleman, conductor on one of the main lines running between two of our prominent Western cities, was one Sunday persuaded to attend church by his cousin, who was then visiting at his house. The day was unusually warm, and he being very tired, having been in two railroad disasters through the week, he fell asleep. The minister, waxing warm with his subject, began to shout, and as he finished his sentence with a shout and stamp, the conductor rose at once, and shouted, "Put on the brakes, John, quick! we're off the track."

THE late Dr. De Koven, of Racine College, Wisconsin, was in the habit of giving his classes a weekly lecture upon religious subjects, questioning them beforehand in order to ascertain what they already knew. On one of these occasions the topic was the angels.

"Now," said the doctor, "before I begin, let some of you give me his notion of an angel."

A profound silence followed.

"Did none of you, for instance, ever hear of Lucifer?"

Thereupon a hand was lifted to reply.

"Well," said the doctor, "what have you to say of him?"

"Why," replied the student, "wasn't he the fellow that *started the German Reformation*, as they say?"

EVERY one who has read Mr. George Ticknor Curtis's *Life of Daniel Webster* will remember John Taylor, Mr. Webster's tenant and factotum at Franklin, New Hampshire, and Robert Wise, the old Revolutionary soldier who came home from the war with Captain Ebenezer Webster, Mr. Webster's father, and built for himself a little cottage on one corner of the Webster farm, where he lived and died. Skirting the Webster property, and passing by the spot where Robert Wise took up his humble abode, there had long been a ferryway, leading to a ferry across the Merrimac River. The ferry was established during the last century, and after Robert Wise had lived there for some time it came to be called Wise's Ferry. The ferryway was originally fenced on both sides, and it ran between the Webster farm and a farm belonging, at the time of which we are about to speak, to Deacon Farley. The fence on Webster's side of the ferryway had been allowed to fall into decay, but the fence on the Farley side had been well kept up. In the year 1848, after a bridge had been built across the river, the town voted to discontinue the ferryway and the ferry, and the land reverted, of course, to the original owner. Deacon Farley, assuming that the land belonged to himself, removed all traces of the fence on his own side, and included the whole of the land in his own territory up to the line where the Webster fence formerly stood.

Mr. Webster came up to Franklin soon after this had been done, and was greatly incensed by what he saw. He ordered John Taylor into his sitting-room, and said to him, sternly, "John Taylor, how came you to stand still and let Deacon Farley steal my land?" Mr. Webster was in one of his blackest moods. Poor Taylor was terribly frightened, for in all his life he had never seen his great friend in such a towering passion. Mr. Webster ordered him, in tones of thunder, to go and bring Deacon Farley.

The deacon came, and he too was saluted with a burst of wrath that made him tremble. He modestly replied that he believed the land was his; but Mr. Webster could not be pacified. Thereupon the deacon and John Taylor jumped into a wagon and drove in great alarm to see a young lawyer of the name of Pike (now Senator in Congress from New Hampshire), who lived two and a half miles up the river. They told Pike that he must go down and see Mr. Webster and endeavor to explain the matter.

Pike went, but as soon as he was in Mr. Webster's presence the latter roared out, "Young man, did you advise Deacon Farley to steal my land?"

"No, sir," said Pike; "I did not. But if the statements that were laid before me are true, the land belongs to the deacon."

"Well, sir," replied Webster, "if I can find a *lawyer* in this county, I shall bring an action."

"There is no need of that, Mr. Webster," said Pike. "I will get the proper documents and submit them to you, if you will hear me, and I believe you will be convinced that the land is not yours."

"You are a bold man, sir, if you propose to leave the case to me," said Mr. Webster. "But do as you please. I give you fair warning that I consider this land mine, and I will fight for every inch of my father's property."

Pike went away and procured a copy of the record which showed the laying out of the ferryway, and that all the land was taken from the property of Farley's grantor and none of it from the Webster property, a copy of the vote of the town discontinuing the ferry, and an affidavit of a former tenant of Webster's showing that the fence on the Webster side had been removed and the whole ferryway taken into the Webster field. The strip of land which the discontinuance of the ferryway took off from what Mr. Webster had always regarded as his own property extended the whole length of one of his best fields.

When Pike submitted the documents to Mr. Webster, the latter read them very carefully, and then said: "Mr. Pike, in half an hour the jury will be ready to render their verdict. Go and get Deacon Farley, that he may hear it."

In half an hour Pike returned with the deacon, who expected nothing but a repetition of what he had met before.

"Gentlemen," said Mr. Webster, "hearken to the verdict. The jury find that the land is Deacon Farley's, and is not the land of Daniel Webster. So says the foreman, so say all the jury. And now, Deacon Farley, I have an apology to make to you for having treated you very roughly. But I never dreamed that this land was not a part of my father's farm, and you know what my affection for this property is. I was very angry, but I hope you will excuse me."

ANOTHER new anecdote of Daniel Webster is recorded here merely to illustrate his unfailing dignity of manner and the magnificence of his liberality in common things. Journeying once from New York to Boston in the cars, he occupied a seat with a gentleman, who relates the story, to whom he said not a word until the train was approaching New Haven. Turning to him then, in his profoundest voice he asked, "Can you tell me, sir, of any place in New Ha-

ven where I can get a glass of first-rate brandy?—I am not feeling well."

His companion did happen to know a little house opposite the station, famous in those days to the initiated, where the unadulterated could be had, and it being without sign, he told his inquirer how to find it—to enter the door and go upstairs to the little front room, and ask for a glass of the best brandy. "And stay! tell the man to give it you out of the black bottle under the counter."

There was not much time to lose, but Webster found the place, and mounting to the little room, astonished the keeper by the magnificent depth of tone and air of authority with which he asked for a glass of brandy, and that, too, without delay. "And stop, sir," said the statesman, slowly raising his hand and pointing with his eloquent finger: "I want it from that black bottle under the counter."

The awed keeper obeyed. The great man poured out a nearly full tumbler, poured it down with expanding satisfaction, threw a bill on the counter, and turned to descend.

"Stop, sir," cried the man—"your change."

Webster turned with portentous solemnity, and in the tone that often thrilled the Senate, exclaimed: "No, sir. A man who gives a glass of brandy like that to a thirsty traveller should never give change for a dollar."

When the astonished bar-keeper related the incident, he learned who his imposing customer was.

A MINISTER of the Gospel who once journeyed on horseback through Virginia in the *ante bellum* days tells this story:

Overtaking an old negro on the road, and feeling in the mood for a chat with the old man, he slowed his horse to keep pace with him, when the following dialogue ensued:

"Do you live about here?"

"Yes, massa. I belongs to Colonel H——. He lib 'bout two miles from yer."

"It is a beautiful country. Are the people about here religious?"

"Yes, massa; dey is a powerful sight of 'ligions 'bout yer. Dere is Baptisses, Mefodesses, Presbyteriums, and some Quakers."

"Well, what religion did you choose?"

"Oh, laws, massa, I 'ain't no 'ligion at all—I's jest ole 'Piscopel."

JESSE DEEMS and Samuel Kemp, both about forty years old, had had many a quarrel and not a few combats. Finally Deems, who was the more pronounced and ardent character of the two, made a vow that he would never again speak to his adversary.

"Gentlemen," he would say, "he is nothing but a dog, and not worth a gentleman's speaking to. I would no more speak to him than I would to a dog."

Kemp, good-natured, heard of the remark, but smiled, and said nothing in response.

Not long afterward, Deems, having attended

a camp-meeting where there was a great revival of religion, became powerfully exercised
in his mind, and after some violent experience
was thought to have obtained religion. Deems
believed so himself, and having joined the
church, after the meeting was over rode along
home. Never had he been in so sweet a frame.
On the way, in the midst of pious and happy
meditations, he suddenly met his late adversary. He checked his horse, looked blandly
upon Kemp, and then said: "Kemp, we've had
many a quarrel and scuffle. I have said to
myself often, Kemp, that I honestly did believe
that you were the triflin'est, lowflungest hound
that I ever see, and that my intentions was
never to speak to you again. But, Kemp,
I've been to Big Spring Camp-meetin', where
they had a powerful rewiwal—powerful, Kemp
—and I've got religion, a thing I were afraid
I never would git, bein' hendered by jes sich
as you. And, Kemp, I now feels defferent. I
feels like I could speak to anything. I feels,
Kemp, like I could even speak to a dog. Good-
by, Kemp." Then Mr. Deems rode calmly on.

Go from home to get home information. A
St. Louis gentleman of Kentucky birth and education went recently to Montreal. Wanting
a cigar, he went to the stand in the hotel and
made known his desire. The dealer, a portly
side-whiskered person after the London pattern, asked him if he would "like to 'ave a
'Enry Clay," at the same time taking down a
box of that well-known brand. While making his selection, the Kentuckian said, "Henry
Clay—Clay—seems to me I've heard that
name. Pray, sir, who was Henry Clay?"
"'Enry Clay, sir?" replied the suave dealer;
"'e was a celebrated tobacco manufacturer
hover hin the States."
"Is he dead?"
"Hi think 'e his, sir; but 'is hestablishment
his kept hup by 'is sons."
The Kentucky St. Louisian smiled to himself, lit his cigar, and went out musing upon
the vanity of human greatness.

In Halifax County, Virginia, before the war,
lived an old negress named Lucretia, the property of the C—— estate. Her extreme old age
warranted the belief that she had seen the Father of her country, for he was a frequent visit-
or at the house of Mr. Isaac Coles, her first master. Aunt Crechy was very dignified, and so
proud of her birth and position, she regarded
every family not connected with her own (i. e.,
her master's) as beneath her notice.
One day somebody said, "Aunt Crechy, do
you remember General Washington when he
used to visit Mildendo?"
"I don' know, chile; he mighter come or he
mighter go. I know one thing, he warn't none
o' our folks."

There is a very pretty story about a couple
down in Prince William, on a plantation, illus-

trative of the old principle of women's preference, "I think him so because I think him so."
Charlotte, a bright-faced mulatto, with a
graceful figure and such nice lady-like ways
that she was a great favorite in the family, fell
in love with a great black coarse fellow, a
plantation hand, and, against the wishes of all
her friends, married him.
One day Billy came into the laundry to have
his hair cut; Charlotte in her fresh calico and
neat collar was sewing at the window. Even
Aunt Dilsey, the plantation barber, was struck
with the difference between the girl and her
husband, and fell to deriding Billy, and laughing at his hair.
"Don't you hurt Billy," cried Charlotte,
coming over to see the operation.
Billy showed all his white teeth in a delighted "ha! ha!"
"Ennybody think to see Charlotte, Billy
was prince."
"He prince to me," was the faithful and entirely feminine reply. F. O. H.

Dr. Terrell, a retired physician, rich and a
savant, besides other valuable property owned
a large plantation on the Ogeechee River,
Georgia. There had been a long, exhausting
drought, and reports had come that not only
the cotton was literally covering the ground
with "forms" it had shed, but the corn was
withered to such a degree that only a torch
was needed to start a conflagration that would
quickly consume every vestige of herbage of
all sorts on the hundreds of acres of some of
the most productive lowlands in the county.
Near by the Ogeechee plantation lived Jim
Bivins, who, though quite a small planter, was
a very large talker, and a most immense admirer of Dr. Terrell.
One day there came a great rain—plentiful,
benignant—such a rain as sometimes makes a
despondent small farmer, who has been trying
to prepare himself for the starvation that has
seemed imminent, rise with alacrity from his
slough and put on a new youth that acted as
if it expected to live in unlimited perennial
felicity.
Jim Bivins, early next morning, rode into
the town with the good news. For Jim, like
the condolers of the Persicus of Juvenal, bestowed his warmest sympathy upon the rich.
"Doctor," said Jim, who was in such haste
that he forgot to say good-morning, "you got
a superbongical good rain at your plantation
yistiday."
"What kind of a rain, Jim?" asked the doctor, in apparent great concern.
"A sup—a superbongical rain, sir."
"Am I to understand, Jim, that my plantation, and yours too as my nearest neighbor,
have both been washed away?"
"By no manner of means, doctor. Ef that
had of been so, you'd not of saw me here a-tellin'
of the doleful tale. Why, sir, it were the grandest kind of a rain. It were a light-'ood knot

floater of a rain; it were a rain that I could actilly hear your low-ground corn, as I rid by this mornin', a-crackin' as ef it were bent on makin' up for time los' in and durin' of the drowth."

"Ah, now I understand you, Jim; and I'm glad to get the news. At first you scared me with that word *sup*— What *was* that word, Jim?"

"I don't 'member it, doctor. Please, doctor, let me take that word back. I'll be obleeged to you if you will."

"Certainly, Jim; but the 'grand,' and the 'light-wood knot floater,' I hope *they* are all right?"

"That indeed they are, doctor. Hain't saw such a rain in I don't know when. You—you'll let me take that t'other word back, will you, doctor?"

"With pleasure, Jim, if you can honestly let me keep the others."

"Cert'nly, doctor; and I'm much obleeged to you."

"Not at all."

"Well, at leastways I thank you."

"You're entirely welcome, Jim."

An eccentric minister of the Methodist Episcopal Church in Ohio was once preaching in a very high pulpit. He was sailing along in his discourse, all eyes upon him, when suddenly he disappeared behind his barricade, causing the necks of the congregation to be stretched in pursuit of him. He soon came in sight again, and explained his absence by saying: "I just dropped my false teeth, and was looking for them. Thank God, when we get to heaven we will not need false teeth."

A GENUINE son of Erin called the other day at the shop of Mr. R——, who is a hearse-maker. "Cud I see Misther Murphy's hearse," said he—"the wan that's goin' to Clinton?" Mr. R—— replied that he could, and led the way through the wareroom. Pat looked around him; his eyes glistened.

"Is it wan o' these?" inquired he.

"Better-looking one than that," was the reply.

Pat began to grin, and his delight increased when he saw the completed vehicle with its immaculate varnish and silver fringes.

"Sure it's an iligint thing. Sure an' Murphy's the man fur stoyle," said he. He walked around it, hands in his pockets, head on one side, and finally burst out with, "Sure there'll be *suicides* in Clinton!"

MANY years ago the writer was judge of the Circuit Court in one of the mountain districts of Arkansas. In those regions Arcadian simplicity, sturdy honesty, and contempt for conventionalism are the prevailing characteristics.

In Carroll County John Doe was put to trial upon a criminal charge, one of the present Senators in Congress from Arkansas appearing as his counsel. The State's attorney was "to the manner born," imbibing with every breath of mountain air from boyhood up a love of freedom and independence, and a hearty contempt for shirt collars and the technicalities of the law.

In the progress of the trial it became necessary to prove a fact of which the records of an adjoining county was by statute made the best evidence.

Now these records had long since been destroyed by fire, and this fact was well known to judge, counsel, and public generally.

The State's attorney called a witness to prove his needed fact. Defendant's counsel objected to the evidence because it was secondary, and no foundation had been laid for its reception by proof of loss of the record, whereupon the following colloquy took place between the Court and prosecuting attorney:

JUDGE. "Mr. State's Attorney, before you can introduce this witness you must show the loss of the record."

STATE'S ATTORNEY. "I presumed your honor was aware of the fact that the records of Marion County were burned."

JUDGE. "As a private citizen I do know the fact, but as the Court I do not, and you must put the proof of the fact into your case."

STATE'S ATTORNEY. "Well, your honor, it strikes me as a little singular that your honor knows something off the bench, and don't know anything on it."

POOR TIRED MOTHER.

THEY were talking of the glory of the land beyond the skies,
Of the light and of the gladness to be found in paradise,
Of the flowers ever blooming, of the never-ceasing songs,
Of the wand'rings through the golden streets of happy white-robed throngs;
And said father, leaning cozily back in his easy-chair
(Father always was a master-hand for comfort everywhere):
"What a joyful thing 'twould be to know that when this life is o'er
One would straightway hear a welcome from the blessed shining shore!"
And Isabel, our eldest girl, glanced upward from the reed
She was painting on a water jug, and murmured, "Yes, indeed."
And Marian, the next in age, a moment dropped her book,
And "Yes, indeed!" repeated, with a most ecstatic look.
But mother, gray-haired mother, who had come to sweep the room,
With a patient smile on her thin face, leaned lightly on her broom—
Poor mother! no one ever thought how much she had to do—
And said, "I hope it is not wrong not to agree with you,
But seems to me that when *I* die, before I join the blest,
I'd like just for a little while to lie in my grave and rest."   MARGARET EYTINGE.

"JUDITH."—Illustrating William Black's "Judith Shakespeare."
From Drawing by E. A. Abbey.

HARPER'S
NEW MONTHLY MAGAZINE.

No. CCCCXIII.—OCTOBER, 1884.—Vol. LXIX.

THE HOME OF HANS CHRISTIAN ANDERSEN.

IT is a curious freak of fortune which has associated the little country of Denmark in most people's minds with two names representing the most contrasted personalities, Hamlet, the protagonist of human speculation, and Hans Christian Andersen, the first child-author. He was not the first to write for children, nor the first to introduce the child into literature; another distinction belongs to him: he was the first child who had contributed to literature. The work by which he is best known is nothing more nor less than an artistic creation of precisely the order which is common among children.

It is part of the common experience of men to endow inanimate things with more or less life through the operation of the imagination. Even mere symbols are made to have a superfluity of life. But the power of personifying that which seems to have no personality is strongest in childhood; it is very apt to die out or become indistinct in later years. Andersen never lost this power; he cultivated it; and that which with children is vivid but formless became with him even more vivid, but ordered and disposed as by the laws of art.

This, I think, may be taken as the peculiar contribution of Andersen to literature: he was the interpreter to the world of that creative power which is significant of childhood: the child spoke through him. He was himself, as his autobiography and the unvarying testimony of his friends show, a child all his life. The *naïveté* which is so large an element in his stories was an expression of his own artless nature; his was a condition almost of arrested development. He was an excessively vain man, but his vanity was the innocent egotism of a child who wants everybody to look at him when he is doing anything which pleases himself.

He bemoans with amusing simplicity the indifference which people showed to his philosophical writings; he avers with an air of injured innocence that he studied very hard, and was often reading difficult books at midnight, when people supposed he was amusing himself. He would have discontinued such trivial matters as writing his little tales, but they forced themselves from him.

It was hard for Andersen's contemporaries to withhold their ridicule of this strange figure, and it is still difficult for Danes to accept cordially the conspicuous position in their literature which he holds in the eyes of foreigners. He wrote novels, poems, books of travel, and dramas. He ranked as an artist and a man of creative power in these forms below others of his time and nation, yet it will be found that when Danish literature is named, Andersen is quite the only figure in it of familiar repute beyond the boundaries of his own country, and this not by virtue of these larger works, but through a few wonder-stories.

Andersen was by no means a man who preferred to associate with children. When it was proposed in his lifetime to erect in the Rosenborg Garden in Copenhagen a statue in his honor, various sculptors submitted designs. One of them was a pleasing one which would probably reflect the sentiment of most people regarding him; it represented the great story-teller with two children by his knee while he told them stories. Andersen objected positively to the conception, for he said he was not in the habit of taking children thus into his arms. The design which was chosen, and was presumably accepted by him, presents him in a curule chair, a cloak falling off his shoulders, while he bends forward, holding, with his finger between the leaves, a thin book, which

ROSENBORG CASTLE.

might contain one of his stories, and stretching forth the other hand with an eager gesture. This eagerness, too, is in his face and his parted lips; he is reciting one of his stories. The statue, which is of bronze, stands upon a pedestal bearing in front his name, with dates of his birth and death, and on the sides pretty reliefs, the one of the "Ugly Duckling" group, the other of a child borne upon a stork. A simple inscription states that the statue was erected in 1880 by the Danish people in memory of the wonder-story poet.

The statue was planned before Andersen's death in 1875, and his countrymen, who had been forced into a pride in his genius, and had adopted a good-natured tone of admiration toward him, somewhat as one might humor a spoiled child, entertained themselves with the thought that Andersen would every day take a walk in the Rosenborg Gardens and admire the bronze effigy of himself. I think they really regretted the loss of this reflected pleasure. Well, one might easily choose a less agreeable walk, even with somebody else's statue than his own at the end of it. The garden is the resort of nursery-maids and children, and there in the sunny afternoons of the long Northern summer days one may see children sporting in the long avenue overhung with grateful shade, at the end of which, in a little garden plat, stands Andersen's statue. Andersen had not a beautiful face, nor a graceful figure, but the sculptor, by giving the face the glow of animation and making the figure eager and unconscious, has achieved a signal triumph in a perfectly honest and truthful manner.

Boner's admirable translation—Boner is much the best translator Andersen has had—the beginning reads: "Every author has some peculiarity in his descriptions or in his style of writing. Those who do not like him magnify it, shrug their shoulders,

STATUE OF HANS CHRISTIAN ANDERSEN.

Intimate and extended mental association with the Danish story-teller rendered very trivial sights and incidents in Copenhagen and Odense interesting to me. Sentences out of his stories of no sort of intrinsic value remained in my head, and came up to entertain me as I walked through the streets. In the introduction, for instance, to *The Galoshes of Fortune*, in Charles

and exclaim, 'There he is again!' I, for my part, know very well how I can bring about this movement and this exclamation. It would happen immediately if I were to begin here, as I intended to do, with, 'Rome has its Corso, Naples its Toledo.' 'Ah, that Andersen! there he is again!' they would cry. Yet I must, to please my fancy, continue quite quietly,

VIEW ON HOLMENS KANAL.

length, simply because it was associated in my mind with the story of *The Old Bachelor's Night-Cap*, and I sought the Frederiks Hospital to see the dull, ordinary iron picket-fence in front of it, through which the unfortunate young man in *The Galoshes of Fortune* thrust his head. I even crossed over to Christianshavn, and set out on a walk to the east end of Amager, in order to reproduce for myself Andersen's first literary venture, when he published his *Journey on Foot from Holmens Kanal to the East Point of Amager*.

But, after all, it was the Copenhagen of Andersen's own fortune which interested me most. The story of his forlorn youth there, of the awkward, sensitive poet in his Ugly Duckling period, is one of the vivid sentences in modern literary history. Andersen wrote his experience for the Danish people, and he never had anything cosmopolitan about him, so that any one who reads sympathetically the early chapters of his autobiography must necessarily acquire a kind of intimacy with people who have very little historical significance. The names of Collin, Guldberg,

and add, 'but Copenhagen has its East Street.'"

As soon as I had chosen my quarters I sallied out, and struck at once into East Street, much pleased to find it as narrow, as winding, and as insignificant generally as Washington Street in Boston. What a charm and consolation it brings to us in our travels when the homely imagination which we have had proves to have been in excess of the fact! The people in East Street were innocent of any historic or literary consciousness. The shops were more ambitious to be French than to preserve Danish peculiarities, and it was only by repeopling the place with Andersen's characters and with himself that I could attain anything like an artistic satisfaction. It was thus that a perfectly commonplace street—Hyskenstraede (Smallhouses Street)—tempted me its whole

Dahlen, Colbjörnsen, come to have for him an individuality which is absolutely the gift of Andersen, while the better known names of Ingemann, Heiberg, Oersted, Ochlenschläger, Weyse, Hertz, and others are identified by the passing references in the book. The frequent recurrence of these names in Andersen's autobiography with familiar reference gives to the foreigner who is indebted to the book for his knowledge of Danish life a feeling as if he had known these people casually and under social conditions, not through literary history, so that Copenhagen, when he comes to visit the city, has been introduced to him by Andersen.

Of course such a knowledge is superficial enough, but it answers the agreeable purpose of making one feel at home in the city. Such a comfortable sensation is increased by what I may call the homeliness of Copenhagen. There is little that is striking in architectural feature. The Exchange with its twisted dragon spire is a picturesque red brick building of the Dutch Renaissance style, which is under careful restoration piece by piece. The Round Tower, attached to the Church of the Trinity, used once as an observatory for looking up, and now as an observatory for looking down and off, has only the character of a gigantic tube, up which one ascends by a paved roadway, rising in a gentle slope as it winds round a smaller tube. It would be possible to drive to the top, and emperors and queens and the like have amused themselves thus; but I followed the crowd, who clung to the inner wall going up, and trotted down by the larger outer circle. The walls, especially near the top, were scrawled with names and dates. I saw Rossini's name in very bold letters. The Church of Our Saviour has a curious spiral staircase winding outside of the spire, and there is a quaint old façade

from 1616 in the Amagertorv, but aside from these the public and private buildings would hold the eye accustomed to Flemish towns but a short time.

In the absence of any masterpieces of architecture, one returns to what I have characterized as the homeliness of the town. The churches are big, spacious, and hospitable houses. I remember especially the impression produced on me by Frederik's Church in Christianshavn, where the square auditorium had very few seats on the floor, but was surrounded in the oddest manner by three galleries, with curtains before them, so that, if the congregation chose, it could draw

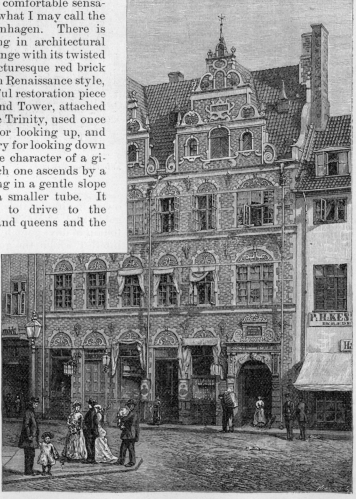

OLD HOUSE IN COPENHAGEN.

UNIVERSITY LIBRARY AND ROUND TOWER.

its curtains and go to sleep while the minister prosed in his pulpit. In another church—the one with a spiral staircase about its spire—there were four tiers of these private boxes in the transepts, and wood-carving of the most demoralized sort met the eye when gazing at the huge altarpiece and at the organ, which was held up by two huge wooden elephants that served as caryatides.

The palaces likewise, with no exterior splendor, but with gardens and honest-looking rooms, gave one the feeling that royalty made itself comfortable rather than spectacular. The museums were housed in palaces, the Thorwaldsen one only being in a building erected for the purpose; and inasmuch as the objects in the museums were largely the odds and ends of past royal living, one enjoyed the sense of being cheek by jowl with the titular great. Indeed, the principal museum, the famous Museum of Northern Antiquities, which occupies the Princes Palace,

owes its importance, after the indefatigable zeal of Mr. Thomsen, its great custodian in days gone by, to the unremitting interest which the government and people together have shown in its collections, so that an immense store of objects illustrating the whole range of Scandinavian life has been accumulated within its walls, and arranged with intelligent judgment. It seemed to me much the most popular museum which I ever visited. A living stream of visitors flowed through the rooms, and took a careful chronological course in its movement.

Thorwaldsen's Museum divides the honors with the Museum of Northern Antiquities, and the traveller, though he may have thought of the frequent reference which Andersen makes to the sculptor, does not need this introduction to a man who divides with Andersen the distinction of Danish fame in the minds of foreigners. The museum is devoted exclusively to originals or copies of Thorwaldsen's work, and to furniture or works of art which belonged to the sculptor, who made the Danish people his heirs. The first impression which one gets from walking through the galleries is of the astounding productiveness of the man, but the longer he looks the more he is likely to find the marvel comprehensible. Here is, indeed, a great array of statuary, but the same subject recurs repeatedly; the plaster reappears in the marble, and studies abound which indicate the variations upon a certain round of themes. It is a pity that the collection is not so arranged for the student that he may see in a group all the work produced by Thorwaldsen upon a single theme. Instead, the effort is apparently made to secure the widest variety of artistic grouping, so that the separate rooms shall each be agreeable little galleries of sculpture.

Aside from the portrait busts, the few illustrations of religious art for churches, and the occasional memorial sculpture, the great mass of works consists of illustrations of classic fable, and here again one discovers a further limitation in the constant recurrence by Thorwaldsen to the myth of Amor and Psyche, and the loveliest of his work was the marble group of Amor and Psyche reunited in heaven. There is a series of bass-reliefs entitled "Amor's Dominion over the World," and one is tempted to take it as expressing most completely the sculptor's conception of life. He was a man born with a love of sensuous beauty who came late to a knowledge of the Greek form, and seized upon it, and all the myths which it represented, as sufficient and satisfying. After that he desired chiefly to reproduce the Greek idea as it swayed his own life. There is thus little thought in his work, little attempt at losing himself in a great

idea, little imagination, but considerable fancy, and great fertility in the use of Greek examples. These he handled as the material which was familiar to him, and he never got far from the use of a few simple forms.

There was one curious invention as applied to Christian art, and that was in a whimsical illustration of the story of Adam and Eve. They are represented seated together, while Adam holds Abel on his knee. An altar fire burns near. Abel has an apple in his uplifted hand, and Cain, who is on the ground, spurns another apple with his foot, at the same time snatching at Abel's. The serpent looks upon this family group, which appears to have been Thorwaldsen's sculpturesque conception of an antithesis to the

CHURCH OF OUR SAVIOUR.

Holy Family. But in the treatment of the subject of Christian art one is apt to discover how completely Thorwaldsen was dominated by a Greek and, I may add, a pagan sense. He was often called upon for memorial stones, and his conception of Death was always one of fear. Such triumph as he delineated was always that of a sublimated human passion, as instanced in Psyche. In the direct subjects of the Christ and the Apostles the twelve are merely conventional figures, with scarcely any individuality springing from personal or typical traits, and the Christ was the *elegant* work of a man whose thought was controlled by Greek lines and inspired by a traditional Protestantism.

I have strayed a little from my subject, but Thorwaldsen and his work give a special significance to Danish life, which has a very lively interest in questions of art. The gallery, the ballet, the theatre, music, and literature are constantly making demands upon popular attention, and receiving the meed of discussion at any rate. Any one reading Andersen's life is struck by the village-like character of the society in which he moved, by the rough-and-tumble life which the followers of the arts endured, and the jostling

criticism which fell to every one's share. It was midsummer when I was in Copenhagen, and I had no opportunity to see some of the dramatic representations which give distinction to Denmark; but I went to Tivoli with every one else, and saw there a characteristic side of life.

Tivoli is not so unique a place as it once was, for the fashion which it set has been abundantly copied; but it remains as one of the most interesting of summer gardens, and this for the simple reason that Danish society is uncompromisingly democratic and homogeneous. There are absolutely no places of amusement in Copenhagen which have a class distinction. At Tivoli one sees the richest and most gentle by the side of the poorest and humblest. It is a social exchange where there is the most complete consideration for every one.

I went to Tivoli one evening when there was to be a series of entertainments especially for children. I can not say that there was very much novelty in the programme. There was a varied and skillful use of the customary sports; jugglers and strong men made the astonishing commonplace; brass bands and string bands played at judicious distance from each other; pantomime and comedy were housed under cover, while the audience stood outside; whirligigs went round, balloons went up, and there was one extraordinary amusement, which may have been reproduced elsewhere, but never chanced

MERCHANTS' EXCHANGE, COPENHAGEN.

to come in my way. It is called in Danish *Rutschban*, and may as well be dubbed in English rush-railway. A tower stands at either end of a railway, which is per-

stout, and holding two people with comfort. The wheels were in grooves, and the course extended over the descending and ascending slopes. Two people would

STATUE OF THORWALDSEN, BY HIMSELF.

haps a hundred and eighty feet in length, forty feet high at one extremity, and half as high at the other. I climbed the rude staircase of the higher tower, and found myself in a room crowded with people waiting their opportunity for a ride. At the entrance stood a phaeton-like car on four small iron wheels, the car being very

get into the car and be strapped in by a leathern boot; the car would be started down the inclined plane by an attendant, and away it would go down the first slope, and by its impetus rise to the next height, go over and down and up again, at each rise pitching a little lower, at each pitch rising to a lesser height, until the last

VESTIBULE OF THE THORWALDSEN MUSEUM.

slope, when it rushed up the hill, bumped against a buffer, and the two travellers got out. The car would then be seized, dragged aside, put upon a lift, hauled up to a height above, and sent back, with other passengers or empty, down a corresponding road parallel to the first, and terminating in a similar low tower by the side of the one I was in, where it would be hoisted again into place, and be ready to make the round of the rush-railway again.

I stood by the entrance where the car started down, watching the couples get into the vehicle and then go thundering down the slope. I saw sedate men who might have been bank presidents get in, and children, and ardent youths and maidens, two by two. They held each other in; they almost lost their hats; they bowed, and fell back upon the huge "thank-you-ma'ams"; they looked frightened, and they looked bold; they smiled, and they almost cried; but I heard no one scream. At length, when I had politely given way to those more eager, I was driven by shame and an inextinguishable curiosity to try this reckless "coast." I

paid the fare—about two and a half cents —and took my seat. I jammed my hat down over my brow, grasped the back of the car with one hand, and no doubt turned pale as the push was given and we began that awful descent. I felt that thrilling sensation of vibration in the pit of my stomach which one has in a swing when descending, and then we shot up the slope, saw a new abyss, and plunged into it. A delicious reprieve was followed by another fearful descent; four times we dashed in the face of fate, and then, with one triumphant rush, flew up the last incline. I got out of the car with my wits standing on end, and tumbled down the staircase in a bewildered, groggy way, anxious to get my legs upon the immovable earth again.

There was no mistaking the thorough enjoyment which everybody took in this amusing place, and the decorum and good feeling seemed to come by nature. The applause was enthusiastic and energetic, and one formed a most agreeable impression of the sociability of the people. No doubt something is due to the absence of a foreign element. All are Danes, and know each other as people do in a large village.

May I add that this democratic spirit was specially agreeable in the grave-yards? I went to the large cemetery where Andersen lies buried. Good taste was universally shown, and there was no display. Simple tablets and little family lots neatly ordered seemed to suggest no distinction of class or wealth. But it was odd to see how titles were always scrupulously placed on the stone, or if the man had no honorary title, then his occupation, so that one learned that Wine-merchant Pedersen lay buried here, Musical-instrument-maker Frederik Richter there, and in one place I read, "This stone is raised to the memory of the Veteran Chocolate-manu-facturer Reimer Timotheus Kehlet." I found Andersen's resting-place after considerable search. A neat Scotch granite stone stands in a small inclosure, where roses bloom in a box-bordered plat, and ivy vines and a prickly thorn give constant greenness. On the stone are Andersen's name, date of birth and death, and a stanza from one of his poems, which I venture to translate:

> The soul which in God's own image is made,
> Eternal is—can never fade;
> Eternity's seed in our life doth lie—
> The body may fall, the soul can not die.

A fading wreath lay at the foot of the stone, placed there ten days before, on the anniversary of his death. I was glad to think that he lay in so quiet a place.

It chanced to me to have entrance into

BELL'S HOLLOW.

the family life of Rolighed, upon the outskirts of the city, where Andersen spent many happy days, and where he died. I was in the midst there of familiar memories of Andersen, and got at his home life, as it may not be unfair to call it, if it was a borrowed home. Through the glimpses of sketches and photographs I saw him in the garden, lying upon the grass, talking with the painter Bloch, receiving a little child as she gravely brought him a stork and a doll, seated at his table, and among his books. Here he read his new stories as he wrote them, and listened, not always with patience, but always with instruction, to the criticisms offered, and so worked and reworked his little fancies. He had an odd genius for cutting out figures, and there was a drawing which he had made to preserve some view, curiously good and stiff, like the work of a very old master.

Andersen's life, when not spent in travel, was passed chiefly in Copenhagen. Thither he came to seek his fortune when a boy, and rarely did he go back to his birth-place in Odense; but the reader of his life will recall the early days there,

and the brief triumph when the city was illuminated and a celebration held on the seventieth anniversary of Andersen's birth. I spent a few hours in the old town before leaving Denmark, and traced the few signs not yet obliterated of the story-teller's childhood there. The house where he was born is pulled down, but the house associated with his childhood still stands, altered, as the neighborhood is. A tablet upon the side of the house commemorates the poet's connection with it, but I could not discover the corner in the roof where was the little garden which he describes so charmingly in *The Snow Queen*. The Bell's Hollow I saw in the deep shade of the Bishop's Garden, and the Monk's Mill still grinds its meal. Best of all, as I strolled along the river down to which the garden used to run from the house where Andersen lived, I saw a number of ducks paddling about, and to my supreme joy they all set upon one forlorn little duck and began to peck at it. I was content with this. It was worth the visit to Odense to see the veritable Ugly Duckling at the foot of Andersen's gooseberry-bush garden.

THE GREAT HALL OF WILLIAM RUFUS.

XIII.

WHEN James the First came down from Scotland, in 1603, to enter upon his new inheritance, he blew his horn for joy, just as if he had opened on the glades of a New Forest, and then proceeded to override everything, in the style of a man who had arrived upon his own particular preserves. James, as we all know, was a sporting character, fond of hawks and hounds, but especially of blowing his horn. This he did on every occasion, in the field or at court, alike among his dogs, his courtiers, and his subjects. In his reign all the dignity of majesty and dominion went to the dogs. No man who ever occupied a throne claimed more for the position and graced it less. He had inherited the whole arbitrary situation left by the Tudor dynasty, without the capacity to discern the signs of the times—the developing power of the Reformation, and its attendant growth, a democratic spirit. He breathed

in this miasm which enveloped the vacant throne, and it entered his blood like the plague which was raging round him when he was crowned at Westminster. But there was another thing which had taken an equal hold of his imagination, and fed an extraordinary delusion there. It seems surprising that historians have not made more of it in noticing the appearance of such a sudden and persistent phenomenon in one who had been so hampered and circumscribed in his former dominions.

What had been working in his brain needed only a crisis to turn his head. That crisis came when he found himself fairly seated, not only in "Edward's chair," but on the sacred Stone of Scone within it, which had been the seat of the Scottish kings for countless generations. The prediction that had been waiting for ages to be fulfilled had now come true in his own person:

"Where'er is found this sacred stone,
  The Scottish race shall reign."

If the genius of Shakespeare could have been so penetrated with this weird aspect of James's accession as to weave in his honor the fateful drama of *Macbeth*, certainly the "wisest fool in Christendom" may be pardoned for an assumption which *he* only lacked the genius to make good. Macbeth exclaims:

"And yet the eighth appears, who bears a glass,
Which shows me many more, and some I see
That twofold balls and treble sceptres carry."

It was the phantom of James himself which thus issued last in the procession from the witches' caldron, bearing the glass prefiguring the forms of his successors, and prophesying both the union of the two nations and the dominion of the three kingdoms. To James this "Stone of Destiny" was more his ancestral seat than to any previous king of England. It swung round through the line of his Scottish predecessors, past Kenneth MacAlpine in 840, past Fergus MacErc in 550, even to the dim Irish kings on the Hill of Tara, of a date, they say, before the Christian era. It had been wrested from his race three centuries before, and set up in this other realm, but only in the course of destiny and prophecy to bring him and his line at last to a higher throne and a double kingdom. In one way his throne was greater than his crown: his crown was the crown of England, but his throne was the throne both of England and of Scotland. It put one wise idea into his

JAMES I.
From painting by Paul Van Somer at Hampton Court.

head, which only his folly postponed— the union of both nations in a single kingdom; but it put also another into his head—an inconvenient interpretation of this union in his own person of Tudor despotism with his own accession, a theory of divine right, which was destined to be unceremoniously contradicted.

Singularly enough, now, we shall shortly see this occasion of his delusion, this very stone and chair of destiny, wheeled about, and made a conspicuous agency in completing the destruction of his house, taken for the first and only time out of the Abbey, and set high in the great Hall, in order to make the blow which had come at last to the royal race the more fatal to its assumption. This is one of the curiosities of history, and its oddity will fully appear at the critical moment when our story develops it.

The reign of James would seem to be more the tree upon which the arrow glanced than the object hit (though it was hit hard) when the great Hall got its impetus toward the heart of his dynasty. There are three or four branches in this tree which indicate how this divergent direction was both acquired and maintained. The scars remain there, though probably unnoticed at the time. One is the Gunpowder Plot, another the trial of Somerset, another the execution of Raleigh, and another the impeachment of Bacon. What was essential in each of these overlapped the future in a very significant way. We have room only to dwell upon this aspect of them rather than upon the scenic circumstances of each.

The Gunpowder Plot involved an attack on the nine-foot thick foundation walls of the ancient palace on the riverside, just below the chamber occupied by the House of Lords. The conspirators were all gentlemen, and they bloodied their delicate fingers at that point to no end. Their object was to put between thirty and forty barrels of gunpowder into the mine, and to blow the king and the Prince of Wales, the lords and the bishops, to atoms. They shortly found a cellar which answered their purpose better. Here they banked up their barrels under a suspicious quantity of coal and other fuel. When the train was laid, it led, however, to themselves, and when the explosion came, it was under their own feet. They were scattered to the four winds. When the fated members of the conspiracy were sought and found, a number were slain in the arrest, a few escaped, but the remainder were put to the torture and then tried. Guy Fawkes and seven others were arraigned before a special commission in Westminster Hall, and Coke, the Attorney-General, managed the proceedings against them. The result was, of course, an immediate and horrible execution in the rear of the Hall, and close to the scene of their labors. With very

natural injustice this infamous attempt was attributed to the Catholic party.

The consequence of all this was the immediate formation of an imaginary explosive compound, that went by another name than gunpowder—a threefold mixture of this popular rumor, some actual Catholic discontent, and some latent treason, the fright of which lasts, in form at least, to this day. Parliament always looks under the bed at the opening of every new session, the Prayer-book turns pale on the 5th of November, and Guy Fawkes is dishonored with a mock procession. But there was a period, and a good long one, when the memory of it revived in something more fiery than this now fossil ceremonial. In the nervous imagination of the people the explosive compound was always underneath the government. The mere spark of a suggestion was enough to set the whole train fizzing. This, for the most part, was after the Rebellion, at which time the throne was undermined and overturned by the Puritan party without exciting nearly so much scandal. The people were only afraid when the papists were at it. So when Titus Oates, seventy-four years after the Gunpowder Plot, told his enormous lie, they rushed, metaphorically speaking, to the cellars again to find the "popish plot," which had no existence, to seize and drag to judgment about as many supposed conspirators with supposed dark lanterns and supposed explosive materials concealed as Guy Fawkes had ever actually to do with, and again Westminster Hall had even more bloody work on its hands over this fiction of a malicious brain and this credulity of a suspicious people than it had over the veritable plot itself. It was a petard which, nevertheless, worked so undesignedly well that it nearly hoisted Charles the Second out of his throne because he had the best reason for not believing it, which did hoist all the papists out of Parliament so high that they never came down till George the Fourth's day, and the ring of the detonation was so loud that James the Second had afterward to put his hands to his ears and leave the kingdom to the Protestant triumph which has prevailed ever since. The extraordinary peculiarity of this gaseous version of the Gunpowder Plot was that it blew up the royal family after all, and with the nation's joyous consent. The mention of the topsy-turvy business here will render

THE GUY FAWKES CONSPIRATORS.

unnecessary any notice hereafter of the series of notable trials which ensued in the great Hall when first the supposed conspirators of the one side, and afterward the exposed liars of the other, were arraigned before its judges, as the Commons or the court alternately got into power.

XIV.

The next plot in King James the First's reign was a poisoning one. It did him more harm, in the long-run, than any amount of gunpowder could have done, because it blew out the windows of the court, and revealed to the world the foul condition in which he kept it.

James encouraged such an inundation of the Scotch into the metropolis that it produced a realization, on a small scale, of the union of the two countries. Westminster grew to such an extent that it joined itself to London. The people felt the intrusion like a visitation of the plague. It *was* a visitation of the Scotch fiddle. But they scratched the insides of their deprecating fingers, and bore the infliction loyally, until the favoritism, which invariably came to a head on the most worthless of the adventurers, centred upon one named Robert Carr. The king turned him into the Earl of Somerset, and took him so closely to his heart that finally the fellow wormed himself into his conscience, and then into the possession of some fatal secrets. The few facts which

afterward came to light reveal an amount of coarse vice in the interior of the royal breast which accounts for the open profligacy that spread itself through the palace. It swarms round this story of Carr. He fell in love with the Countess of Essex, and she with him. The obstacle to their union was that the Earl of Essex was still extant. The guilty pair desired a divorce. The complaisant king accordingly urged it. A servile Ecclesiastical Court then duly decreed it. The marriage took place amid great splendor. It was one of the great pageants of the reign. But Sir Thomas Overbury had opposed the whole proceeding, and the vengeance of the countess pursued him. While he was imprisoned in the Tower the incensed couple caused him to be poisoned. Years after, the murder came out, and now the offices of the great Hall were called in, but as much to the consternation and terror of James, so it proved, as to Somerset and his wife. Friendship was not at the bottom of it, for that had ended long ago, and only a hypocritical guise of it was left. But the royal solicitude hung about the rear and outskirts of the trial at every stage. It was helpless to save while the legal engine was at work. There was some dark secret which was in danger of coming out if the matter was pressed. The former favorite had the king in his power. The crown lawyers knew enough to know that they must manage the business with adroit and tender fingers. People were suspicious enough to whisper strange conjectures in connection with it—conjectures which touched their own heart very deeply, because incited by the sudden death of Henry, Prince of Wales, whose pure and dignified life had been a rebuke to that of his father, whose private court had drawn away from Whitehall the noblest spirits of the day, and who had given promise of repeating the splendid virtues of the Black Prince and of Henry the Fifth. His father had, most strangely, shown no grief at his loss.

The countess was first arraigned. She confessed the crime, and was condemned to the block. The next day, May 25, 1616, her equally guilty husband was to answer at the bar. But, on the night before, the lieutenant of the Tower was astonished and bewildered by the conduct of his prisoner. He was kept up all night. Somerset stormed in broad Scotch and broader hints. "The king durst not bring him to trial!" He would not appear in the Hall. He would stay in his bed, and they would have to take him there in it. The worried but discreet lieutenant thought it best to see the king privately, and went up to Whitehall in the dead hour of the night. He found his Majesty only too glad to talk with him, even in night-gown and slippers. The result of the hushed interview was that he undertook, under the promise of a rich reward, to manage the refractory ex-favorite. He returned to his room and beguiled him with encouraging words from the king. By this time it was three A.M. At eight o'clock Somerset was on his trial in the Hall. The coarse but incorruptible Coke showed symptoms of making his engine work without fear or favor. "God knows," he is reported to have muttered, "what became of that sweet babe Prince Henry, but I know somewhat." The danger now was that if the proceedings went harshly, the prisoner's rage would get the better of him, and he would "fly out upon the king." But the lieutenant had prepared a portable cell in which to ensconce him at the first sign of such an explosion. Two servants hovered near him with a cloak in their hands, and with instructions "to instantly hoodwink him with that cloak, take him violently from the bar, and carry him away." They were to be saved from the consequences, and bountifully rewarded. Bacon, the Attorney-General,

had also come prepared with a cloak of more subtle texture, with which to hoodwink the judges. "It shall be my care," he had said, "so to moderate the manner of charging him as it might make him not odious beyond the extent of mercy." His opportunity of distinguishing himself at the expense of his own character seemed to have run in this family. The criminal was the husband of the wife of Essex's son, the Essex whom he once took such particular care "to make odious beyond the extent of mercy." He did so manage it, Hallam says, "as to prevent him making any imprudent disclosure, or the judges from getting any insight into that which it was not meant to reveal." The cloudy Scotchman sustained the mist by silence, even though it parted enough about his own person to lay him open to the law. Was it not a pretty sight, worthy of the reign?—Justice blinking on the bench, the criminal nearly hooded at the bar, the sticky crime neatly rolled in flour, the pageant of the headsman's axe gone through as the prisoner retired, and then a royal pardon sent down from Whitehall to the Tower!

We lay no stress upon the darker intimations of the story, but here we have a part of that reign which left its loathsome trail on everything it touched, the church, the court, the bar, every pure interest of the realm, and destroyed the prestige of the crown in an age when the Puritan was rising among the people. "Somerset Ker!" exclaims Carlyle, in his contemptuous, significant way, "king's favorite, son of the Laird of Fermeherst, he and his extremely unedifying affairs—*except as they might transiently affect the nostril of some Cromwell of importance*—do not much belong to the history of England. Carrion ought at length to be buried."

XV.

In two years more—October, 1618—we come upon another scene in the great Hall, to the sight of another criminal at the bar of the king, before whom his Majesty is to undergo exposure of a different kind.

Sir Walter Raleigh stands there in his old age, but with the glory of his whole brilliant and heroic career at his back. Twelve years before, he had come under the vague suspicion of his unheroic sovereign. If we were to say that the author of the *Counter-blast* could not abide him because he smoked, we should be stating the grounds of his prejudice about as definitely as they were really in his mind.

Raleigh had been the captain of Queen Elizabeth's Guards. That was one ground.

Scotchman this was the very best ground, for upon that he could not only hate, but hold him. It was easy to arrest, and nearly as easy to procure his conviction and committal to the Tower on such a charge.

SIR WALTER RALEIGH AND HIS SON.

He had been the enemy of Essex, part of whose conspiracy against the queen had included a plan in James's favor. That was even better ground. He had been charged with conspiracy against his royal self. It could not be proved. But to the dense

It was done by overriding both facts and evidence with the sheer force of the royal will. Even lawyers personally inimical to Raleigh were shocked by this willful breaking of their web.

Raleigh remained in the Tower these

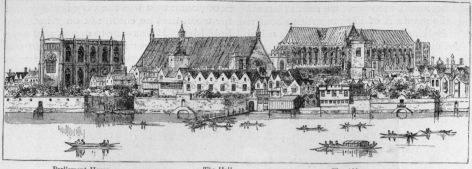

Parliament House.   The Hall.   The Abbey.

PLAN OF WESTMINSTER, 1647.—After a print by W. Hollar.

twelve years, doing as gallant work with his pen as he had already done with his sword; by the very heroism of his patience laying the foundations of a more deep and permanent regard among the people than even he had ever enjoyed. Out of his many retrospections during this long period there rose one which grew till it kindled in his mind a rational hope of liberty and returning glory. It was rational, chiefly because it was the only one with which he could kindle the mind of the king.

There was a gold mine in Guiana which had been discovered many years before. It was on English ground which had already been acquired for the crown. If there was anything in the world which the king wanted most at this time it was a gold mine. Rather would he that even his favorite criminal should find one in Guiana than that he himself should be put to any further quest for one in Parliament.

In fact, he was already out on his own hook in another direction for a gold mine that he thought *he* had discovered. Either one would make him gloriously independent of Parliament. His divine right would then have a yellow halo which would establish his pretensions before all men. Catholic Spain was his private El Dorado, and the Infanta, if affianced to Charles, would turn out to be a mine of untold wealth. But, on the other hand, the people were averse to Catholic and Spanish gold. Now he balanced the two projects, and, of course, preferred his own.

Sir Walter Raleigh had already sailed with his fleet, under full commission as admiral. Such a commission was itself a release from the impending axe of the Tower. The king now revealed his route and his plans to the Spanish ambassador in order to advance his own voyage into his Catholic Majesty's confidence and gratitude, his daughter and his ducats! Raleigh comes

EXTERIOR OF WESTMINSTER HALL AND SQUARE, 1647.—After a print by W. Hollar.

SIR FRANCIS BACON.—After Vandyck.

upon the unexpected obstruction of Spain thus treacherously laid for him. His opportunity is lost, and he returns to lose his life at the hands of both the English and the Spanish kings. Again he is committed to the Tower. Spies infest him there, but they get nothing out of him but the fragrance of his Indian pipe. It is the only real cloud he is under. The *Counterblast* king at last arraigns him again. He is required to show cause before the judges in the Hall why his former sentence should not now operate upon him. Raleigh, trembling with ague, but with nothing else, pleads the high commission which he had held. But Spanish revenge and Catholic venom have now entered the persecution. The people so understand it, but the court is the King's Bench, and it does the king's will. He is hurried into the room over the gate-house of the Abbey, his scaffold is made ready overnight in the rear of the Hall, and the next day, faint in body, but not in spirit, even under the depression of a coming chill, his ills are cured for this world by the "sharp medicine," as he called it, of the axe.

But the king had called down a sharper vengeance upon himself. The treacherous Spaniard played him false in his turn, and the way to the golden Infanta was obstructed by the now aroused alarm of his own nation. The Protestant interests of his own daughter on the Continent, it was resolved, should not suffer through this his Catholic friend. St. Stephen's rose in a body, with hats uplifted, to declare it so. When its committee waited upon him to state their respectful desire, he met this approach of their rightful sovereign share in his throne with a mocking wit which contained, unwittingly, a prophecy of the end: "Bring chairs for the ambassadors!" It was the very salt of that humor which was to be sown on the ruins of his house. It was the edge of that keen sarcasm which should descend on the neck of his son. It derisively recognized the very power which should finally place the descendants of that neglected Protestant daughter on a better-balanced throne.

XVI.

May 3, 1621. The fall of Bacon, Lord High Chancellor of England, on this memorable day, brought with it no concentrated or sensational scene in Westminster Hall, and yet the world agrees that it was a spectacle for both angels and men. As an event it was melancholy enough, but as a trial it was without the presence of the offender. When summoned to the bar, he sent his confession in his stead. When personally sought, he could only say: "It is my act, my hand, my heart. Oh, my lords, spare a broken reed!" When the sentence was given, he lay sick in his bed. It was the anguish of a great mind working death to a mean spirit.

He had reached the goal of what was, to such a one as he, an inadequate ambition. He had reached it through his genius as a lawyer, an orator, and a statesman. But he had reached it also through his crouching arts as a courtier. He lowered it, even in his own mind, by the means which he employed to get it. High as it intrinsically was as an office in the state, he was equal to a higher in the service of the world, and yet he could be tempted by its empty dignity and emolument in such a service as that of King James. He could lay aside the pageant of his thoughts for the pomp of this position. What has been called the most exquisitely constructed intellect ever given to man could yet be led aside by a judgment and perception so weak as to see meaning and glory in show and sham. The reflection of his strange infirmity is apparent in the very record of his imposing induction into his place. A letter of the time says: "To the Hall, besides his own retinue, did accompany him all the lords of his Majesty's Council and others, with all knights and gentlemen that could get horses and foot-cloths." "He was accompanied," says Chamberlain, "by most of the nobility, with other gallants to the number of more than two hundred horses, besides judges and the Inns of Court. . . . Both queen and prince sent all their following, and his other friends did their best to honor him." When he had arrived at his place, he made a speech to the multitude who had been attracted to the Hall. This might have done for the first day, and might well have been a spontaneous testimony of the public pleasure at the elevation of one already so illustrious; but he enjoyed, he desired it too much himself—how unlike Sir Thomas More in the self-same position under a greater and more showy king!—for he tried to keep up this splendid state, "exceeding all his predecessors in the bravery and multitude of his servants." The real grandeur of his office—what an incongruity in the author of the "Essays" that he did not see it! —was in its purity, not its pomp; and it was in trying to maintain its pomp instead of its purity that he fell.

If he did not rise to this conception, the people did; if he was dazzled by his own display, the people were not. It was one of the tremendous events of the time that their moral sense was equal to his overthrow. When the Commons impeached him at the bar of the Lords, it was the revolt of the people not so much at what he had done as at the bribery and corruption which filled the court of the king, the keeper of whose conscience he was. When his own conscience was set free

SIR THOMAS WENTWORTH AND SECRETARY.

by this enlightenment, he said, "I was the justest judge that was in England these fifty years; but it was the justest censure in Parliament that was there these two hundred years." That was the very point to which the public sentiment had risen, and it caught him where he ought not to have been. His meanness had made him the scapegoat of the king, when his greatness ought to have made him the sacrificing priest for the people. He crouched beneath the charge, not only from timidity and conscious guilt, but at the earnest desire of the frightened despot—frightened at an attitude of the Commons which revealed their consciousness of strength; frightened lest a worse inqui-

sition into wide-spread corruption should be provoked; frightened at what Bacon himself had prophesied, that if the attack upon him should be successful, the next movement would not stop short of the throne. If he had stood his trial, he himself, amid such an atmosphere, might have escaped, but it would have precipitated the revolution which was close at hand. Such was the significance of Bacon's forced exit from Westminster Hall.

XVII.

Charles was no banqueting king, but was, on the contrary, Rufus fined down to a quiet, pure, dignified gentleman—a most unaccountable son of his father. As a king, however, he was thoroughly derived from both of them, and in an accelerated ratio. He was a despot on principle, and the issue of principle, therefore, was made with him. It was an epoch when a question of principle was understood, and when the best men on both sides were prepared for any sacrifice to establish what they believed.

The struggle was precipitated the moment he came to the throne, because the issue had now matured in the mind of both parties. The king had resolved upon absolute despotism as the best for the peace of the kingdom; the Parliament had resolved to preserve all its own ancient rights as the best for the prosperity of the people. Four Parliaments, accordingly, went by the board in four years. They could not live if he took away their breath. The fourth had thus expired in 1629; but the last three died hard. There was a feeling in them and among the people that they had some vitality of their own.

After the first of these the king decided to enforce some subsidies it had not granted. The legal question came up in Westminster Hall. The crown judges decided for the king. There were five thousand people present, who shook the building with their shouts—"A Parliament! a Parliament! else no subsidies!" The king then tried a forced loan. Some imprisonments followed this. Now the question of "arbitrary detention" rose and went before the King's Bench, and again the Hall was thronged to hear the arguments of Selden and Noy for the liberty of the subject, and again the same uproar occurred. In the second of these Parliaments the chief scene was in St. Stephen's. The Commons had adjusted the scales of the great question by their "Petition of Right." In the one scale were the king's Prerogatives; in the other, the Parliament's Privileges. The equipoise was perfect, but it had not been reached without an agony of fury on both sides. It remained a law, and so hangs to this day in the senate-house. The king, however, left it dangling there by a prorogation. In the third of these Parliaments St. Stephen's was again the scene of a disturbance, both representative of the moment and designed to last. Pym brought up his famous "Remonstrance." Hollis and Valentine held down the Speaker in the chair until it was passed. These three men and several others were arrested. But they refused to plead in any lower court for what they had done in the High Court of Parliament.

Now the king took off his royal robes, and vowed he would have no more Parliaments; he would reign alone. St. Stephen's was struck dumb for eleven years; not a legislator haunted its precincts. The royal canopy at Whitehall was the only seat of power. Even Westminster Hall was made to abdicate its ancient throne, and sit at the feet of two courts which assumed its jurisdiction and overruled its decisions at will—the Civil Court of the Star Chamber, on the eastern side of the New Palace Yard, full in sight and within a stone's-throw of its venerable door, and the Ecclesiastical Court of High Commission, sitting in London, under the arches of St. Paul's. As there was to be no legislature, so there was to be no law, independent of the royal will.

His Majesty came to the front with two vigorous but not equally powerful hands. His right hand was Thomas Wentworth, afterward Earl of Strafford, a renegade from the party of liberty, and familiar with its spirit and plans. When the time came for him to decide between the two extremes, he had adopted the policy of despotism. The left hand of the king was William Laud, Archbishop of Canterbury. These two took intimate counsel together, and the maxim they agreed upon was "Thorough." His Majesty proved to be more muscular in these hands than in his brain.

The first necessity of such a throne was a standing army. The way to it was to raise funds for a standing navy, which funds, when procured, the king was to use as he pleased. Hence "ship-money" was demanded not only of the coast towns, as heretofore, but of all England. The judges in the Hall now degraded the bench and the laws by an extrajudicial opinion in its favor, and Wentworth was just preparing to raise his other horn of a "land army," when the whole question was taken by both horns in the same arena by a new champion, at whose appearing all the people rose. John Hampden, from among the Chiltern Hills, had come down to dispute the matter in the courts. He would not pay, and now what was to come of it? The Exchequer summoned all its judges to "the greatest cause that ever was tried in Westminster Hall." After a conflict of many months, on the

12th of June, 1637, eight of the twelve judges decided against Hampden. It made him "the most famous man in England."

We have now some curious doings to look at, which almost immediately took the Star Chamber, which haled them across the way to the pillories flanking the doorway of the Hall, to have their ears cut off. "The place was full of people," says an eye-witness, "who cried and

ARCHBISHOP LAUD.

place in front of the Hall, got up by the Archbishop of Canterbury, who fastened his grip with true ecclesiastic fervor on three offenders of the Church. The exhibition outside was hardly as dignified as that which had just taken place within. William Prynne, Henry Burton, and John Bastwick had all three been writing books of their own 'doxy, but not of Archbishop Laud's 'doxy. He haled them to howled terribly, especially when Burton was cropt. Dr. Bastwick was very merry; his wife got a stool, kissed him; his ears being cut off, she called for them, and put them in a clean handkerchief, and carried them away with her." Prynne had gone through the operation some years before in the same place, but his ears had been sewed on. As they were clipped off again, he uttered a solemn defiance to Laud, and challenged him to show whether this was according to the laws of England. Both men were taken to distant prisons, a hundred thousand people gathering together, in Burton's case, to see him pass, and showering his wife with money as she followed in a coach.

But Laud had only done this to get his hand in. He now put a trumpet to the king's lips, who blew a blast which awakened all Scotland. The faith of that nation must henceforth give way to the Church of England, which, like a car of Juggernaut, was coming with its mitred prelates and its embroidered robes and uniform service-books, and the terrible monster of the "Pope" looming up darkly behind all, and was to go crunching over their conventicles from one end of the land to the other! This, at any rate, was the way the trumpet sounded in the ears of Edinburgh. But now a worse mob gathered and howled; not in Palace Yard, but in and about St. Giles's Kirk. At the first sight of a mitre, at the first sound of the "collect for the day," "A pape! a pape!" went up in the loudest, broadest, most terrible burr that was ever heard in the Highlands. Laud kept up his hand, but the king trumpeted in vain. The sound thereof was drowned in the tumult he had raised. Now the mischief was done. The National Covenant suddenly lifted itself, as steep and as rough as Dumbarton rock. The pibroch sounded and the clans gathered. It was the first strong note for liberty. Canterbury should not "haul them all the way to Rome for their religion, or to Constantinople for their policy." The Scotch army invaded England with banners inscribed "For Christ's Crown and Covenant." Before it Charles's crown was to fall, and all *his* covenants were to be broken. When Scotland thus moved, as Hallam says, "it preserved the liberties and overthrew the monarchy of England." For the second time the action of an English king was to bring Scottish influence into the English constitution.

The son of James had not the "land army" he had desired at his disposal. He was obliged to call a Parliament to help him out of his difficulty. It met, but it did not suit him, and he dissolved it in three weeks. When he called another, in the fall of the same year, 1640, it took care to provide against such a sudden dissolution, and is known to this day as "the Long Parliament." The Hall presented a busy scene

when these legislators were assembling. With the courts all around them at work, the members stood in groups discussing the momentous issues soon to be precipitated upon them above-stairs in St. Stephen's. Pym met Hyde, the future Earl of Clarendon, there. His big, powerful eyes flashed as he said: "We must be now of another temper than we were the last Parliament. . . . We have now an opportunity to make the country happy by removing all grievances, and pulling up the causes of them by the roots." And root them up they did, one after the other. They rooted up the Star Chamber out of Palace Yard; they rooted up the High Commission in St. Paul's; they rooted up Finch, the Lord Keeper of the Great Seal, from his seat in the Hall; they rooted up Berkeley from the King's Bench, and laid hold also of five other judges with a like purpose, to the terror of all the rest. They had already rooted up Laud and flung him into the Tower, while Prynne, Burton, and Bastwick returned to the place of their mutilation with all London roaring a triumph into their cropped ears.

But the grandest historical scene was the first, when they had to pull with all their strength upon that deepest, mightiest root of all, the Earl of Strafford, and only then just barely got him out. When they did, they had undermined the throne. It is this scene which is the most widely known in picture and in story as connected with Westminster Hall.

The man who generated that business was Pym himself. He and Strafford had been intimate friends. When the latter deserted the cause, Pym had fiercely turned upon him: "You are going to be undone. But remember that though you leave us now, I will never leave you while your head is on your shoulders." He was now as good as his word. On the seventh morning of the session he caused the doors of St. Stephen's to be locked, lest the secret of his motion should take flight and forewarn his victim, and then, after a terrible arraigning speech, moved the impeachment of the Earl of Strafford. The motion met with unanimous consent, and the rest of the day was employed in preparing articles of impeachment. Then the doors were thrown open. Pym at the head of three hundred members proceeded along the corridor to the House of Lords, which was startled at the sudden visitation. Pym went up to the bar, and there in form impeach-

PRESENT EXTERIOR OF WESTMINSTER HALL.

ed the earl of high treason in the name of the Commons of England. The news flew to Strafford, who at once came to the House. He entered "with a proud, glooming countenance," and made for his seat. He was met with shouts "to void the place." In confusion he retired till he was called. They ordered him "to kneel, and on his knees to hear the sentence." In that attitude he was delivered to the keeper of the Black Rod.

We pass from his commitment on that 11th of November, 1640, to his trial on the following 22d of March.

Pym, the ablest man and the most eloquent speaker of the Commons, led in this dreadful pull of all hands when the bewildering noose of constructive treason—a rope twisted of many alleged misdemeanors—was thrown over the horns of the victim. At first they could not even stir the powerful man from the line of his defense. He put all his strength into his resistance, with an eloquence and agility of movement equal to any of theirs. Repeatedly did he sway them about as point after point was made, sometimes retreating, sometimes avoiding, even when forced to yield always boldly confronting, with but one object in view—to fling off or to break the one vital, fatal proof of high treason. The heroism of his defense, its dexterity, its ingenuity, its unflinching courage, his tact, his coolness, his ready resources, his bursts of manly feeling, finally broke the spell of prejudice in the multitude, and produced signs of revulsion in his favor. The ladies in the galleries restrained neither their tears nor exclamations. Even the bank of scarlet peers was moved, and the strength of the accusing Commons began to fail. It was evident that the charge of treason would not hold.

On the thirteenth day Pym tried another plan. He moved in the House of Commons that the proceedings should take the form of an act of attainder. It was retrospective, and therefore unjust, but he carried it through both Houses, though strongly opposed. This made both Houses his judges, and thus the bloody end for which they struggled was secured.

After long and agonized hesitation, Charles gave his consent to the retrospective ordinance, and Strafford went to the block. The consent was given under the tumult of the mob outside his palace, under the tears and terrors of Henrietta Maria within it, under what was worse, within himself a want of honor to the man he had compelled to face the danger with a solemn promise of his protection, and, worse still, a secret purpose to secure a foot-hold of peace from which to make another spring upon the liberties of the people.

There was now a momentary reaction. Two parties had begun to form, which almost equally divided the former unanimity against the king. The famous "Remonstrance" had passed, but only by eleven votes. Hampden and Cromwell were about taking passage to America. Conservative men, influential, wise, and pure, had received the king's pledge that he would only act after consultation with them. At this moment of peace and apparent security he suddenly burst upon the House of Lords with his personal impeachment of one of its peers, and upon the House of Commons with another of five of its members.

The king determined to arrest the five members himself. The exasperating point in the late doings of the Commons was a desire they had manifested to control the great army which was now to be raised to quell a rebellion in Ireland. The iron hand of Strafford having been withdrawn, that wild country had risen in revolt. So the oak of Shillelagh, the spirit of Turlogh O'Brien, was groaning in the rafters of Westminster Hall, when Charles, on the afternoon of January 4, 1642, entered it with a large body of armed men. They were more than his retinue—a throng of adventurers who had lately rallied around him—with halberds in their hands and swords by their sides. He had come in the very way which justified the suspicion that had so angered him, and revealed what a despot he would be if he held the power of the sword. While his guards grounded their halberds and rattled their swords in the Hall, he passed on into St. Stephen's. The Commons had got wind of his coming in this style. Some of the members drew their swords, but others, to avoid such a conflict, caused the five members to retire. The king now appeared at the door. Taking off his hat, he went up the aisle to the Speaker's chair. The Speaker rose to meet him. The king did not offer to sit down, but turned and stood on the step. Putting on his hat, he gazed sternly round the room. Pym, Hollis, Hampden, Hazlerig, and Strode were not to be seen. He continued this look for some time, amid the breathless hush which waited to see what he would do next. He then said that he had come for those five gentlemen; that treason had no privilege. He expected obedience to his demand of yesterday. He called for Pym and Hollis by name. No answer. He turned to the Speaker and asked "if they were here, or where they were." With a marvellous inspiration, the Speaker, as he fell on his knee, replied that "he was a servant to the House, and had neither eyes nor tongue to see or say anything but what they commanded him." Charles replied that "his own eyes were as good as his," and it was clear "his birds had flown." He declared his determination to find them, and taking off his hat, passed down between the graded benches to the door. Scarcely was he out before the astonished Commons found their voice, and the king could hear the fierce shouts which now filled the apartment, "Privilege!" "Privilege!" The House instantly adjourned.

The king, returning to the Hall, drew off his soldiers; but the mischief was done. He never entered its portals again until brought there by armed men to be arraigned at its bar for taking up arms against his Parliament and shedding the blood of his people. In less than a week he had fled from Whitehall, never, also, to enter its portals again, except to pass through the window of its banqueting-hall to confront the scaffold and the block.

NATURE'S SERIAL STORY.

XI.

NATURE was at last awakening from her long death-like repose with an energy that was startling. The thin skirmish line of vapor was followed by cloudy squadrons, and before sunset great masses of mist were pouring over Storm King, suggesting that the Atlantic had taken the drought in hand, and meant to see what it could do. The wind moaned and shrieked about the house as if trouble, and not relief, was coming. In spite of the young moon, the night grew intensely dark. Every moment they expected to hear the dash of rain, but it did not come.

Amy thought with a shudder of their desolate camping ground. Time must pass before pleasant associations could be connected with it. The intense darkness, the rush and roar of the coming storm, the agony, the death that might have occurred there, were now uppermost in her mind. She had found an opportunity to ask Webb questions similar to those of Miss Hargrove, and he had given Burt full credit for taking a fearful risk. A woman loves courage in the abstract, and when it is shown in behalf of herself or those whom she loves, he who has manifested it becomes heroic. But her homage troubled Burt, who was all at sea, uncertain of himself, of the future, of almost everything, but not quite uncertain as to Miss Hargrove. There was something in her look when they first met after their common peril that went straight to his deepest consciousness. He had before received, with not a little complacency, glances of preference, but none like that, in which a glimpse of feeling, deep and strong, had been revealed in a moment of

"THE EARLY TWILIGHT DEEPENED AROUND THEM."—[SEE PAGE 683.]

weakness. The thought of it moved him far more profoundly than the remembrance of his danger. Indeed, he scarcely thought of that, except as it was associated with a girl who now might have been dead or dying, and who, by a glance, had seemed to say, "What you saved is yours."

If this were true it was indeed a priceless, overwhelming gift, and he was terrified at himself as he found how his whole nature was responding. He also knew that it was not in his frank, impetuous spirit to disguise deep feeling. Should Miss Hargrove control his heart, he feared that all would eventually know it, as they had speedily discovered his other little affairs. And little indeed they now seemed to him, relating to girls as immature as himself. Some had since married, others were engaged, "and none ever lost their appetites," he concluded, with a grim smile.

But he could not thus dismiss the past so far as Amy was concerned, the orphan girl in his own home to whom he had promised fealty. What would be his feeling toward another man who had promised so much and had proved fickle? What would the inmates of his own home say? What would even his gentle mother, of whom he had made a confidante, think of him? Would not a look of pain, or, even worse, of scorn, come into Amy's eyes? He did love her dearly; he respected her still more as the embodiment of truth and delicacy. From Miss Hargrove's manner he knew that Amy had never gossiped about him, as he felt sure nine-tenths of his acquaintances would have done. He also believed that she was taking him at his word, like the rest of the family, and that she was looking forward to the future that he had once so ardently desired. Cost him what it might, he must be true to her.

She, little divining his tragic mood, which he sought to disguise with the whole force of his will, gave him an affectionate good-night kiss as she said, "Dear Burt, how happily the day has ended, after all!—and we know the reason why."

"Yes, Burt," added Webb, "no man ever did a braver thing."

His father's hearty praise, and even his mother's grateful and almost passionate embrace, only added to his deep unrest.

As he went to his room he groaned, "If they only knew!"

After very little and troubled sleep he awoke on the following morning depressed and exhausted. Mental distress was a new

"IDLEWILD."—[SEE PAGE 686.]

experience, and he showed its effects; but he made light of it as the result of over-excitement and fatigue. He felt that nature harmonized with his mood, for he had scarcely ever looked upon a gloomier sky. Yet, strange to say, no rain had fallen. It seemed as if the malign spell could not be broken. The wind that had been whirling the dust in clouds all night long grew fitful, and died utterly away, while the parched earth and withered herbage appeared to look at the mocking clouds in mute, despairing appeal. How could they be so near, so heavy, and yet no rain? The air was sultry and lifeless. Fall had come, but no autumn days as yet. Experienced Mr. Clifford looked often at the black, lowering sky, and predicted that a decided change was at hand.

"My fear is," he added, "that the drought may be followed by a deluge. I don't like the looks of the clouds in the southeast."

Even as he spoke a gleam of lightning shot athwart them, and was soon followed by a heavy rumble of thunder. It seemed that the electricity, or rather the concussion of the air, precipitated the dense vapor into water, for within a few moments down came the rain in torrents. As the first great drops struck the roads the dust flew up as if smitten by a blow, and then, with scarcely any interval, the gutters and every incline were full of tawny rills, that swelled and grew with hoarser and deeper murmurs, until they combined in one continuous roar with the downfall from clouds, that seemed scarcely able to lift themselves above the tree-tops. The lightning was not vivid, but often illumined the obscurity with a momentary dull red glow, and thunder muttered and growled in the distance almost without cessation.

The drought had been depressing. To Amy its gloomy, portentous ending was even more so. The arid noon-day heat and glare of preceding days had given place to a twilight so unnatural that it had almost the awe-inspiring effect of an eclipse. The hitherto brazen sky seemed to have become an overhanging reservoir from which poured a vertical cataract. The clouds drooped so heavily, and were so black, that they gave an impression of impending solid masses that might fall at any moment with crushing weight. Within an hour the beds of streams long dry were full and overflowing.

In spite of remonstrances, Webb put on a rubber suit and went to look after some little bridges on the place. He soon returned, and said: "If this keeps up until morning, there will be a dozen bridges lacking in our region. I've tried to anchor some of our little affairs by putting heavy stones on them, so that the water will pass over instead of sweeping them away. It makes one think that the flood was no myth."

To the general relief, the rain slackened in the late afternoon, and soon ceased. The threatening pall of clouds lifted a little, and in rocky channels on the mountains the dull gleam of rushing water could be seen. From every side its voices were heard, the scale running up from the gurgle in the pipes connected with the roof, to the roar of the nearest large stream. The drought was truly broken.

As the day advanced, Burt had grown very restless. Amy watched him curiously. The long day of imprisonment within-doors had given time for thought and a review of the past novel and exciting experiences. She had not seen the glances from Miss Hargrove which had suggested so much to Burt, but she had long since perceived that her friend greatly enjoyed his society. Had she loved him she would have seen far more. If this interest had been shown in Webb, she would have understood herself and Miss Hargrove also much better. Preoccupied as she was by her sense of loss and shortcoming produced by Webb's apparent absorption in pursuits which she did not share, the thought had repeatedly occurred to her that Miss Hargrove's interest in Burt might be more than passing and friendly. If this were true, she was sure the event of the preceding day must develop and deepen it greatly. And now Burt's manner, his fits of absent-mindedness, during which he stared at vacancy, awakened surmises also. "Where are his thoughts?" she queried, and she resolved to find out.

"Burt," she said, arousing him from one of the lapses into deep thought, which alternated with his restless pacings and rather forced gayety, "it has stopped raining. I think you ought to ride over and see how Gertrude is. I feel real anxious about her."

His face lighted up with eagerness. "Do you truly think I ought to go?" he asked.

A WOODLAND PATH.

"Certainly; and it would be a favor to me also," she added.

He looked at her searchingly for a moment, but there was nothing in her expression to excite his fears.

"Very well," he tried to say, quietly. "I'll go. A swift gallop would do me good, I believe."

"Of course it will, and so will a walk brighten me up."

"Let me go with you," he exclaimed, with an eagerness too pronounced.

"No, please. I'd rather hear how Gertrude is;" and she went to her room to prepare for her walk, smiling a little bit-

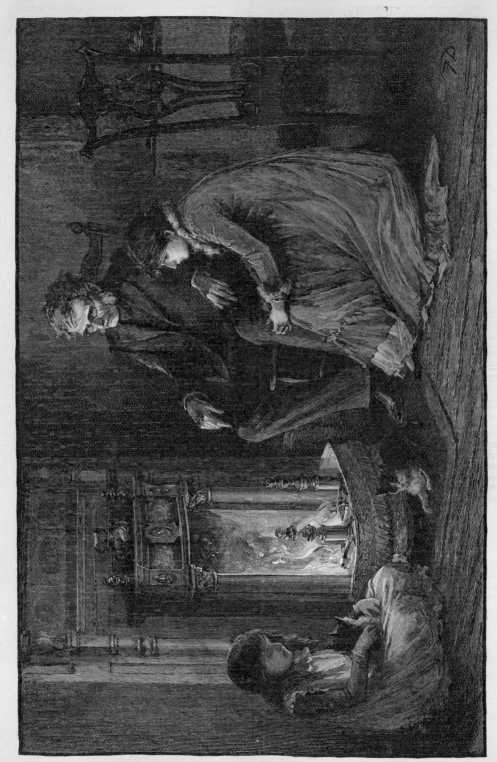

" AMY LOOKED AT THE PICTURE IN THE FLICKERING BLAZE."—[SEE PAGE 688.]

terly as she mused: "I now know where his thoughts were. I must be lacking indeed. Not only brother Webb, but also lover Burt, has grown weary of me. I can't entertain either of them through one rainy day." From her window she saw Burt riding away with a promptness that brought again the smile rarely seen on her fair features. In her light rubber suit she started on her ramble, her face almost as clouded as the sky. Another had been on the watch also, and Webb soon joined her, with the question, "May I not go too?"

"Oh, I fear it will take too much of your time," she said, in tones that were a little constrained.

He saw that she was depressed. He too had been interpreting Burt, and guessed his destination as he galloped away. His love for Amy was so deep that in a generous impulse of self-forgetfulness he was sorry for her, and sought to cheer her, and make what poor amends he could for Burt's absence, and all that it foreboded. "Since you don't say outright that I can't go," he said, "I think I'll venture;" and then, in a quiet, genial way, he began to talk about the storm and its effects. She would not have believed that even remarkable weather could be made so interesting a topic as it soon proved. Before long they stood upon the bank, and saw a dark flood rushing by where but yesterday had trickled a little rill. Now it would carry away horse and rider, should they attempt to ford it, and the fields beyond were covered with water.

"I don't like these violent changes," said Amy. "Tennyson's brook that 'goes on forever' is more to my taste than one like this, that almost stops, and then breaks out into a passionate, reckless torrent."

"It's the nature of this brook; you should not blame it," he answered. "But see, it's falling rapidly already."

"Oh, certainly; nothing lasts," and she turned away abruptly.

"You are mistaken, sister Amy," he replied, with strong, quiet emphasis.

The early twilight deepened around them, and gloomy night came on apace, but before Amy re-entered the house his unselfish efforts were rewarded. Burt's threatened disloyalty apparently had lost its depressing influence. Some subtle reassuring power had been at work, and the clouds passed from her face, if not from the sky.

That sombre day would ever be a memorable one to Miss Hargrove. Nature seemed weeping passionately over the summer that had gone with all its wealth of beauty and life. She knew that her girlhood had gone with it. She had cautioned her brother to say nothing of her escape on the previous day, for she was too unnerved to go over the scene again that night, and meet her father's questioning eyes. She wanted to be alone first and face the truth; and this she had done in no spirit of weak self-deception. The shadow of the unknown had fallen upon her, and in its cold gray light the glitter and tinsel of the world had faded, but unselfish human love had grown more luminous. The imminence of death had kindled rather than quenched it. It was seen to be something intrinsically precious, something that might survive even the deadliest poison.

Her father was disposed to regard Burt as one who looked upon life as a pleasure excursion, and who might never take it seriously. His laugh hereafter could never be so light and careless to her but that, like a minor key, would run the thought, "He risked his life for me; he might have died for me."

Her dark full eyes, the warm blood that her thoughts brought into her face even in the darkness and solitude of her chamber, did not belie her nature, which was intense, and capable of a strong and an abiding passion when once kindled.

Her father had watched her with the deepest solicitude on her return, and he felt rather than saw the change that had taken place in his idol. She had pleaded fatigue, and retired early. In the morning she was again conscious of his half-questioning scrutiny, and when he went to his study she followed, and told him what had occurred. He grew very pale, and drew a long, deep breath. Then, as if mastered by a strong impulse, he clasped her to his heart, and said, in trembling tones, "Oh, Trurie, if I had lost you!"

"I fear you would have lost me, papa, had it not been for Mr. Clifford."

He paced the room for a few moments in agitation, and at last stopped before her and said: "Perhaps in a sense I am to lose you after all. Has Mr. Clifford spoken?"

"No, papa; he has only risked his life to save mine."

"You are very grateful?"

"Yes."

"Do not think I underestimate his act, Trurie; but, believe me, if he should speak now or soon, you are in no condition to answer him."

She smiled incredulously.

"He did what any man would do for a woman in peril. He has no right to claim such an immense reward."

"Before I went to the mountains I said I was no longer a child; but I was, compared with what I am now. It seems to me that feeling, experience, more than years, measure our age. I am a woman to-day, one who has been brought so near the future world that I have been taught how to value what may be ours now. I have learned how to value you and your unselfish love as I never did before. Mr. Clifford will not speak very soon, if he ever does, and I have not yet decided upon my answer. Should it be favorable, rest assured more than gratitude will prompt me; and also be assured you would not lose me. Could I not be more to you were I happy than if I went through life with the feeling that I had missed my chance?"

"I fear your mother would never give her consent to so unworldly a choice," he said, with a troubled brow.

"I've yet to be convinced that it would be such a choice. It's scarcely unworldly to make the most and the best of the world one is in, and mamma must permit me to judge for myself, as she chose for herself. I shall never marry any one but a gentleman, and one who can give me a home. Have I not a right to prefer a home to an establishment, papa?"

"I should indeed be more than sorry if I ever saw you unhappy," he said, after another thoughtful pause. Then added, shaking his head, "I've seen those who gave their hearts even more disappointed with life than those who took counsel of prudence."

"I shall take counsel of prudence, and of you too, papa."

"I think it is as I feared—you have already given your heart."

She did not deny it. Before leaving him she pleaded: "Do not make much of my danger to mamma. She is nervous, and not overfond of the country at best. You know that a good many people survive in the country," she concluded, with a smile that was so winning and disarming that he shook his head at her as he replied:

"Well, Trurie, I foresee what a loving-ly obstinate little girl you are likely to prove. I think I may as well tell you first as last that you may count on me in all that is fairly rational. If with my years and experience I can be so considerate, I may hope that you will be also?"

Her answer was re-assuring, and she went to tell her mother. She had been forestalled. Fred was quite as confidential with his mother as she with her father, and the boy had been wild to horrify Mrs. Hargrove by an account of his sister's adventure. The injunction laid upon him was only for the previous evening, and Gertrude found her mother almost hysterical over the affair, and less inclined to commend Burt than to blame him as the one who had led her daughter into such "wild, harum-scarum experiences."

"It's always the way," she exclaimed, "when one goes out of one's own natural associations in life."

"I've not been out of my natural associations," Gertrude answered, hotly. "The Cliffords are as well-bred and respectable as we are;" and she went to her room.

It was a long, dismal day for her, but, as she had said to her father, she would not permit herself to drift. Her nature was too positive for idle, sentimental dreaming. Feeling that she was approaching one of the crises of her life, she faced it resolutely and intelligently. She went over the past weeks from the time she had first met Burt under the Gothic willow arch, and not only tried to analyze the power he had over her, but also the man himself. "I have claimed to papa that I am a woman, and I should act like one," she thought. A few things grew plain. Her interest in Burt had been a purely natural growth, the unsought result of association with one who had proved congenial. He was so handsome, so companionable, so vital with spirit and mirthfulness, that his simple presence was exhilarating, and he had won his influence like the sun in springtime. Had he the higher qualities of manhood, those that could sustain her in the inevitable periods when life would be no laughing matter? Could he meet the winter of life as well as the summer? She scarcely knew him well enough to be sure of this, but she was still sufficiently young and romantic to think, "If he should ever love me as I could him, I could bring out the qualities that papa fears are lacking." His courage seemed an earnest of all that she could desire.

Amy's feeling toward him, and the question whether he had ever regarded her in another light than that of a sister, troubled her the most. "If Amy loves him, and he has given her reason to do so, I shall not come between them, cost me what it may. I'll do without happiness rather than snatch it from a friend."

Therefore, although her heart gave a great bound as she saw Burt riding toward the house in the late afternoon, she went to her father and said: "Mr. Clifford is coming. I wish you would be present during his call."

The young fellow was received cordially, and Mr. Hargrove acknowledged his indebtedness so feelingly that Burt flushed like a girl, and was greatly embarrassed. He soon recovered himself, however, and chatted in his usual easy and spirited way. Before he left he asked, hesitatingly, "Would you like a souvenir of our little episode yesterday?" and took from his pocket the rattles of the snake he had killed.

"It was not a little episode," Gertrude replied, gravely. "I shall indeed value the gift, for it will remind me that I have a friend who did not count the cost in trying to help me."

Impetuous words rose to Burt's lips, but he checked them in time. Trembling for his resolutions, he soon took his departure, and rode homeward in deeper disquiet than he had ever known. He gave Amy her friend's messages, and he also, in spite of himself, afforded her a clearer glimpse of what was passing in his mind than she had received before.

The weather during the night and early on the following morning was puzzling. It might be that the storm was passing, and that the ragged clouds which still darkened the sky were the rear-guard or the stragglers that were following the sluggish advance of its main body; or it might be that there was a partial break in Nature's forces, and that heavier cloudy masses were still to come. Mr. Clifford inclined to the latter view. "Old Storm King is still shrouded," he said at the breakfast table, "and this heavy, sultry air does not indicate clearing weather."

Events soon confirmed his opinion. Nature seemed bent on repeating the programme of the preceding day, with the purpose of showing how much more she could do on the same line of action.

There was no steady wind from any quarter. Converging or conflicting currents in the upper air may have brought heavy clouds together in the highlands to the southwest, for although the rain began to fall heavily, it could not account for the unprecedented rise of the streams. In little over an hour there was a continuous roar of rushing water. Burt, restless and almost reckless, went out to watch the floods. He soon returned to say that every bridge on the place had gone, and that what had been dry and stony channels twenty-four hours before were now filled with resistless torrents.

Amy was pale and nervous. Johnnie was almost crying with terror, and she tremblingly asked her mother if Noah's flood could come again.

"No," said Maggie, confidently. "If there was to be another flood, grandpa would have been told to build an ark;" and this assurance had appeared so obviously true that the child's fears were quieted. Even Leonard's face was full of gloom and foreboding, when the children were not present, as he looked out on flooded fields, and from much experience estimated the possible injury to the farm and the town. Mr. and Mrs. Clifford were quiet and serene. They had attained a peace which was not easily disturbed, and the old gentleman remarked: "I have seen a worse storm even in this vicinity. You must remember it, Leonard."

"But this deluge isn't over," was the reply. "It seems a tremendous reaction from the drought, and where it will end it is hard to tell, unless this steady downpouring slackens soon."

Leonard's fears were not realized, however. The unusual and tropical manifestations of the storm at last ceased, and by night the rain fell softly and gently, as if Nature was penitent over her wild passion. The results of it, however, were left in all directions. Many roads were impassable; scores of bridges were gone. The passengers from the evening boats were landed on a wharf partially submerged, and some were taken in boats to a point whence they could reach their carriages.

In the elements' disquiet Burt had found an excuse for his own, and he had remained out much of the day. He had not called on Miss Hargrove again, but had ridden far enough to learn that the bridges in that direction were safe. All the family had remonstrated with him for his exposure, and Amy asked him, laughingly, if he had been "sitting on bridges to keep them from floating away."

"You are growing ironical," he answered, for he was not in an amiable mood, and he retired early.

In the morning Nature appeared to have forgotten both her passion and her penitence, and smiled serenely over the havoc she had made, as if it were of no consequence.

Amy said, "Let us take the strong rockaway, call for Miss Hargrove, and visit some of the streams"; and she noted that Burt's assent was too undemonstrative to be natural. Maggie decided to go also, and take the children; while Leonard proposed to devote the day to repairing the damage to the farm, his brothers promising to aid him in the afternoon.

When at last the party left their carriage at one of the entrances of Idlewild, the romantic glen made so famous by the poet Willis, a stranger might have thought that he had never seen a group more in accord with the open, genial sunshine. This would be true of Maggie and the children. They thought of what they saw, and uttered all their thoughts. The solution of one of life's deep problems had come to Maggie, but not to the others, and such is the nature of this problem that its solution can usually be reached only by long and hidden processes. Not one of the four young people was capable of an unfair deliberate policy; all, with the exception of Amy, were conscious whither Nature was leading them, and she had thoughts also of which she would not speak. There was no lack of truth in the party, and yet circumstances had brought about a larger degree of reticence than of frankness. To borrow an illustration from Nature, who, after all, was to blame for what was developing in each heart, a rapid growth of root was taking place, and the flower and fruit would inevitably manifest themselves in time. Miss Hargrove naturally had the best command over herself. She had taken her course, and would abide by it, no matter what she might suffer. Burt had mentally set his teeth, and resolved that he would be not only true to Amy, but also his old gay self. Webb, as usual, was quiet, observant, and not altogether hopeless. And so this merry party went down into the glen, and saw the torrent flashing where the sunlight struck it

through the overhanging foliage. Halfway down the ravine there was a rocky, wooded plateau from which they had a view of the flood for some distance as it came plunging toward them with a force and volume that appeared to threaten the solid foundations of the place on which they stood. With a roar of baffled fury it sheered off to the left, rushed down another deep descent, and disappeared from view. The scene formed a strange blending of peace and beauty with wild, fierce movement and uproar. From the foliage above and around them came a soft, slumberous sound, evoked by the balmy wind that fanned their cheeks. The ground and the surface of the torrent were flecked with waving, dancing light and shade as the sunlight filtered through innumerable leaves, on some of which a faint tinge of red and gold was beginning to appear. Beneath and through all thundered a dark, resistless tide, fit emblem of lawless passion, that, unchanged, unrestrained by gentle influences, pursues its downward course reckless of consequences. Although the volume of water passing beneath their feet was still immense, it was evident that it had been very much greater. "I stood here yesterday afternoon," said Burt, "and then the sight was truly grand."

"Why, it was raining hard in the afternoon!" exclaimed Miss Hargrove.

"Burt seemed even more perturbed than the weather yesterday," Amy remarked, laughing. "He was out nearly all the time. We were alarmed about him, fearing lest he should be washed away, dissolved, or something."

"Do I seem utterly quenched this morning?" he asked, in a light vein, but flushing deeply.

"Oh no, not in the least; and yet it's strange, after so much cold water had fallen on you."

"One is not quenched by such trifles," he replied, a little coldly.

They were about to turn away, when a figure sprang out upon a rock, far up the stream. They recognized Mr. Alvord, as he stood with folded arms and looked down on the flood that rushed by on either side of him. He had not seen them, and no greeting was possible above the sound of the waters. Webb thought, as he carried little Ned up the steep path, "Perhaps in the mad current he sees the counterpart of some period in his past."

The bridge across the mouth of Idlewild Brook was gone, and they next went to the landing. The main wharf was covered with large stones and gravel, the débris of the flood that had poured over it from the adjacent stream, whose natural outlet had been wholly inadequate. Then they drove to the wild and beautiful Mountainville road that follows the Moodna Creek for a long distance. They could not proceed very far, however, for they soon came to a place where a tiny brook had passed under a wooden bridge. Now there was a great yawning chasm. Not only the bridge but tons of earth were gone. The Moodna Creek, that had almost ceased to flow in the drought, had become a tawny river, and rushed by them with a sullen roar.

The fall season brought increased and varied labors on the farm and in the garden. As soon as the ground was dry after the tremendous storm, and its ravages had been repaired as far as possible, the ploughs were busy preparing for winter grain, turnips were thinned out, winter cabbages and cauliflowers cultivated, and the succulent and now rapidly growing celery earthed up. The fields of corn were watched, and as fast as the kernels within the husks—now becoming golden-hued— were glazed, the stalks were cut and tied in compact shocks. The earlier maize is cut the better, after it has sufficiently matured, for the leaves make more nutritious fodder if cured or dried while still full of sap. From some fields the shocks were wholly removed, that the land might be ploughed and seeded with grain and grass. Buckwheat, used merely as a green and scavenger crop, was ploughed under as it came into blossom, and that which was sown to mature was cut in the early morning, while the dew was still upon it, for in the heat of the day the grain shells easily, and is lost. After drying for a few days in compact little heaps it was ready for the threshing-machine. Then the black angular kernels—promises of many winter breakfasts—were spread to dry on the barn floor, for if thrown into heaps or bins at this early stage, they heat badly.

The Cliffords had long since learned that the large late peaches that mature after the Southern crop is out of the market are the most profitable, and scarcely a day elapsed but that Abram took to the landing a load of baskets full of downy beauties. An orange grove, with its deep green foliage and golden fruit, is beautiful indeed, but not less so an orchard laden with Crawford's Late, in their best development. Sharing the honors and attention given to the peaches were the Bartlett and other early pears. These latter fruits were treated in much the same way as the former. The trees were picked over every few days, and the largest and ripest specimens taken, their maturity being indicated by the readiness of the stem to part from the spray when the pear is lifted. The greener and imperfect fruit was left to develop, and the trees, relieved of much of their burden, were able to concentrate their forces on what was left. The earlier red grapes, like the Delaware, Brighton, Agawam, and others, not only furnished the table abundantly, but also a large surplus for market. Indeed, there was high and dainty feasting at the Cliffords' every day—fruit everywhere, hanging temptingly within reach, with its delicate bloom untouched, untarnished.

The storm and the seasonable rains that followed soon restored its fullness and beauty to nature's withered face. The drought had brought to vegetation partial rest and extension of root growth, and now with the abundance of moisture there was almost a spring-like revival. The grass sprung up afresh, meadows and fields grew green, and annual weeds from seeds that had matured in August appeared by the million.

"I am glad to see them," Webb remarked. "Before they can mature any seed the frost will put an end to their career of mischief, and there will be so many seeds less to grow next spring."

"There'll be plenty left," Leonard replied.

The Cliffords, by their provident system of culture, had prepared for droughts as mariners do for storms, and so they had not suffered so greatly as others; but busy as they were kept by the autumnal bounty of nature and the rewards of their own industry, they found time for recreation, and thoughts far removed from the material questions of profit and loss. The drama of life went on, and feeling, conviction, and love matured like the ripening fruits, although not so openly. As soon as his duties permitted, Burt took a rather abrupt departure for a hunting expedition in the northern woods, and a day or two later Amy received a note from Miss Hargrove saying that she had accepted an invitation to join a yachting party.

"Oh, Webb," she exclaimed, "I wish you were not so awfully busy all the time. Here I am thrown wholly on your tender mercies, and I am neither a crop nor a scientific subject."

He gave her little reason for complaint. The increasing coolness and exhilarating vitality of the air made not only labor agreeable, but out-of-door sports delightful, and he found time for an occasional gallop, drive, or ramble along roads and lanes lined with golden-rod and purple asters; and these recreations had no other drawback than the uncertainty and anxiety within his heart. The season left nothing to be desired, but nature, even in its perfection, is only an accompaniment of human life, which is often in sad discord with it.

Nature, however, is a harmony of many and varied strains, and the unhappy are always conscious of a deep minor key even on the brightest days. To Alf and Johnnie the fall brought unalloyed joy and promise; to those who were older, something akin to melancholy, which deepened with the autumn of their life; while to Mr. Alvord every breeze was a sigh, every rising wind a mournful requiem, and every trace of change a reminder that his spring and summer had passed forever, leaving only a harvest of bitter memories. Far different was the dreamy pensiveness with which Mr. and Mrs. Clifford looked back upon their vanished youth and maturity. At the same time they felt within themselves the beginnings of an immortal youth. Although it was late autumn with them, not memory, but hope, was in the ascendant.

During damp or chilly days, and on the evenings of late September, the fire burned cheerily on the hearth of their Franklin stove. The old gentleman had a curious fancy in regard to his fire-wood. He did not want the straight, shapely sticks from their mountain land, but gnarled and crooked billets cut from the fruit and other trees about the place that had required pruning and removal.

"I have associations with such fuel," he said, "and can usually recall the trees —many of which I planted—from which it came; and as I watch it burn and turn into coals, I see pictures of what happened many years ago."

One evening he threw on the fire a worm-eaten billet, the sound part of which was as red as mahogany; then drew Amy to him and said, "I once sat with your father under the apple-tree of which that piece of wood was a part, and I can see him now as he then looked."

She sat down beside him, and said, softly, "Please tell me how he looked."

In simple words the old man portrayed the autumn day, the fruit as golden as the sunshine, a strong, hopeful man, who had passed away in a far-distant land, but who was still a living presence to both. Amy looked at the picture in the flickering blaze until her eyes were blinded with tears. But such tears fall on the heart like rain and dew, producing richer and more beautiful life.

The pomp and glory of October were ushered in by days of such surpassing balminess and brightness that it was felt to be a sin to remain in-doors. The grapes had attained their deepest purple, and the apples in the orchard vied with the brilliant and varied hues of the fast-turning foliage. The nights were soft, warm, and resonant with the unchecked pipings of insects. From every tree and shrub the katydids contradicted each other with increasing emphasis, as if conscious that the time was drawing near when the last word must be spoken. The stars glimmered near through a delicate haze, and in the western sky the pale crescent of the moon was so inclined that the old Indian might have hung upon it his powder-horn.

On an evening like this the young people from the Cliffords' had gathered on Mr. Hargrove's piazza, and Amy and Gertrude were looking at the new moon with silver in their pockets, each making her silent wish. What were those wishes? Amy had to think before deciding what she wanted most, but not Miss Hargrove. Her face has grown thinner and paler during the last few weeks; there is unwonted brilliancy in her eyes to-night, but her expression is resolute. Her wish and her hope were at variance. Times of weakness, if such could be called, would come, but they should not appear in Burt's or Amy's presence.

The former had just returned, apparently gayer than ever. His face was bronzed from his out-of-door life in the Adirondacks. Its expression was also resolute, and his eyes turned oftenest toward Amy with a determined loyalty. As has been said, not long after the experiences following the storm, he had yielded to his impulse to go away and recover his poise. He felt that if he continued to see Miss Hargrove frequently he might reveal a weakness which would lead not only Amy to despise him, but also Miss Hargrove, should she become aware of the past. As he often took such outings, the family, with the exception of Webb and Amy, thought nothing of it. He had been at pains to take, in Amy's presence, a most genial and friendly leave of Miss Hargrove; but there was no trace of the lover in his manner. His smiles and cordial words had chilled her heart, and had strengthened the fear that in some way he was bound to Amy. Then had come an invitation to join a yachting party to Fortress Monroe, and she had eagerly accepted. With the half-reckless impulse of pride, she had resolved to throw away the dream that had promised so much, and yet had ended in such bitter and barren reality. She would forget it all in one brief whirl of gayety; and she had been the brilliant life of the party. But how often her laugh had ended in a stifled sigh! How often her heart told her, "This is not happiness, and never can be again"! Her brief experience of what is deep and genuine in life taught her that she had outgrown certain pleasures of the past, as a child outgrows its toys, and she had returned thoroughly convinced that her remedy was not in the dissipations of society.

The evening after her return, Burt, with Webb and Amy, had come to call, and as she looked upon him again she asked herself, in sadness, "Is there any remedy?" She was not one to give her heart in any half-way manner.

It seemed to her that he had been absent for years, and had grown indefinitely remote. Never before had she been so strongly impressed with the idea that he was in some way bound to Amy, and would abide by his choice. If this were true, she felt that the sooner she left the vicinity the better, and even while she chatted lightly and genially she was planning to induce her father to return to the city at an early date. Before parting, Amy spoke of her pleasure at her friend's return, and how much she had been missed, adding: "Now we shall make up for lost time. The roads are in fine condition for horseback exercise, nutting expeditions will soon be in

order, and we have a bee-hunt on the programme."

"I congratulate you on your prospects," said Miss Hargrove. "I wish I could share in all your fun, but fear I shall soon return to the city."

Burt felt a sudden chill at these words, and a shadow from them fell across his face. Webb saw their effect, and he at once entered on a rather new *rôle* for him. "Then we must make the most of the time before you go," he began. "I propose we take advantage of this weather and drive over to West Point, and lunch at Fort Putnam."

"Why, Webb, what a burst of genius!" Amy exclaimed. "Nothing could be more delightful. Let us go to-morrow, for we can't count on such weather long."

Miss Hargrove hesitated. The temptation was indeed strong, but she felt it would not be wise to yield, and began, hesitatingly, "I fear my engagements—" At this moment she caught a glimpse of Burt's face in a mirror, and saw the look of disappointment which he could not disguise. "If I return to the city soon," she resumed, "I ought to be at my preparations."

"Why, Gertrude," said Amy, "I almost feel as if you did not wish to go. Can't you spare one day? I thought you were to remain in the country till November. I have been planning so much that we could do together."

"Surely, Miss Hargrove," added Burt, with a slight tremor in his voice, "you can not nip Webb's genius in the very bud. Such an expedition as he proposes is an inspiration."

"But you can do without me," she replied, smiling on him bewilderingly.

It was a light arrow, but its aim was true. Never before had he so felt the power of her beauty, the almost irresistible spell of her fascination. While her lips were smiling there was an expression in her dark eyes that made her words, so simple and natural in themselves, a searching question, and he could not forbear saying, earnestly, "We should all enjoy the excursion far more if you went with us."

"Truly, Miss Hargrove," said Webb, "I shall be quenched if you decline, and feel that I have none of the talent 'for which I was beginning to gain a little credit."

"I can not resist such an appeal as that, Mr. Clifford," she said, laughingly.

"This is delightful!" cried Amy. "I anticipate a marvellous day to-morrow. Bring Fred also, and let us all vie with each other in encouraging Webb."

"Has that quiet Webb any scheme in his mind?" Miss Hargrove thought, after they had gone. "May to-morrow indeed be 'a marvellous day' for us all."

"*Can* I do without her?" was poor Burt's query. An affirmative answer was slow in coming, though he thought long and late.

LATITUDE AND LONGITUDE.

I WAS going from Boston to Philadelphia to see my aunt Rose. I was only a little shaver, so they sent me by steamer, under the captain's care—Captain Floy. Just the nicest man! A sailor every inch of him. Gray eyes, with the look in them that real sailors' eyes always have, and a brown beard, and such a kind, fresh look about his whole face. I wasn't going to talk about him, though—not yet—but about her.

She came down awhile before we sailed. I liked her at the first, for all she looked so tired and sorry. Her eyelids seemed too heavy to hold themselves up, and her cheeks were the whitest things you ever saw. They looked whiter yet against her black hair and lashes and dress. The captain and I were on the dock when she came down. He looked at her for a minute. Then he went up and touched his cap and said, "Are you going aboard, Miss—"

He stopped there, as if either he'd been going to say her name, or wanted to know what it was. She didn't take any notice, though; just said she was. Then he asked would I show her the way. So that was how I first came to speak to her.

There weren't many passengers that trip, for it was along in the fall, pretty late. Besides us there was only one old lady and her maid. She didn't have anything to say to us—the old lady didn't; but she talked to her maid a blue streak about how miserable it all was, and what a fool she was to come. I thought so too; but when I told the captain, he said he guessed she must enjoy being miserable, for she made the trip with him every spring and fall.

Of course I wanted to know her name (not the old lady's, you know), so I had to look in the book she had been reading for it. I was so surprised that, before ever I thought, I had blurted out, "Agnes May Wyvern! Are you Agnes Wyvern? Why, I've heard my mother talk about you ever so often."

She looked at me, sort of queer, and said, "What is your mother's name, Gus?"

I knew I'd made a big blunder, but it was too late to back out, so I said: "She's Mrs. Lawrence. No, she don't know you" (for she'd looked sort of surprised); "but she wanted to, the worst way. Say, Miss Wyvern, you're an awful swell, ain't you?"

The captain just laughed out. Then he made out he was very busy looking at a ship in the offing. She laughed too at first. Then she stopped and turned red.

"No, Gus," she said, "I'm not a 'swell,' as you call it."

"Then why did mamma want to know you?" I asked.

She hesitated a moment. Then she said, quite gravely, "It was very kind of your mother to wish to know me, Gus, but probably she is very glad now that she did not."

"Why," I said, "ain't you awful rich?"

"Not now," she said.

"But your uncle is?" I asked.

"My uncle—my uncle is dead," she said, and her face got white again, and the tears came into her eyes, till I was so sorry I didn't know what to do.

Then the captain began to talk to her, and I was glad enough to get out of the way.

We were up bright and early next day, me and Agnes. The sun came up behind clouds, but there was a sort of misty light over all the water, and the tops of the long ripples shone like the edge of a knife, and the white gulls flapped and screamed over our heads. Agnes had taken off her hat, and her head was all wrapped up in some sort of fleecy white thing. By-and-by the wind began to blow the pink into her cheeks, and the light into her eyes. It caught her hair too, and twisted it into little rings and curls around her forehead, and she looked just awful pretty. The captain came along, and he looked at her in such a pleasant sort of way, and then he leaned over the bulwarks beside her and began to talk. Agnes and I had both been to Florida, and we didn't think much of it. So had the captain, and he didn't think much of it too.

"The Windward Islands are better, Miss Wyvern," he said, and Agnes looked at him, sort of surprised.

"I was there once," she said, "in my uncle's yacht. We cruised about among them all winter."

"The *Agnes*," said the captain. "Yes, I remember her well."

"Remember?" said Agnes, looking puzzled. "But you—"

"Oh, you wouldn't recollect," said the captain. "I was only skipper of the *Agnes*."

"What! Captain Ben?" cried Agnes. "Why, how could I ever forget you? You were always so good to me, and I must have been a perfect plague. I was only fourteen, you know."

"Never a plague to me," said the captain, in a queer sort of half-voice, looking away to the horizon—"never a plague to me, and all the sailors worshipped you. It was a bright day to all when you came on board, with your eyes sparkling, and your black curls floating behind you, and your voice as bright and sweet and soft as the morning."

He stopped all of a sudden. Then Agnes said just, "You know?"

And the captain he said, "Yes, Miss Agnes, I know."

Then they both looked at me, and then they went on talking about those wonderful islands, Agnes and he.

Why do I call her Agnes? Because she told me to, of course. I called her Miss Wyvern till she gave a kind of shudder, and said, "Don't call me *that*, Gus. Call me Agnes, or, if you don't think that respectful, call me Miss May. I hate the name of Wyvern."

"Oh, I don't mind about respectful," I said. "I'd just as lief call you Agnes. But, I say, why don't you like Wyvern? It's no end of a jolly name, *I* think."

"People don't always like their own names," said Agnes. "Besides, May *is* my name."

"Yes, I know," I said, and I picked up the book where I had read it; but it wasn't there any longer. Fly-leaf and all were gone.

Along toward afternoon the captain brought up his quadrant, and began to teach Agnes how to hold it—in her left hand, you know, with the right on the screw.

"Now turn the screw gently," he said, "until you bring the sun down to the horizon, with just room to heave a sea-biscuit between. Then look where two lines exactly meet, and—"

It was all Greek to me, so I went off, while Agnes and the captain did sums. After the lesson was over, Agnes began telling the captain about some shipwreck. As I came up, I heard him say,

"So everything went down?"

There were tears in Agnes's eyes, but she only said: "Everything. No hope, and, worst of all, no pity."

"Was it a shipwreck, Agnes?" I said. "Who was wrecked? You?"

Agnes sort of jumped when I spoke, but she only said, "Yes," and I went on:

"Was the captain lost too? And only you saved? How funny! Who saved you?"

"I'm not sure that I was saved," said Agnes, with a sort of deep, dry sob.

I started. "Not saved?" I said. "Why, how could you be here, else? Tell a fellow about it. What was the captain's name?"

"Wyvern," said Agnes.

I was going to ask a lot more questions, but the captain caught me by the arm.

"See here, Gus," he said, when we were the other side of the deck. "Don't you know that sometimes when people have been through great danger they can't talk about it? Queer? Well, I don't know, but it is so. No, I'm not scolding you: only don't ask any more questions, and don't talk about this shipwreck to anybody—to *anybody*, mind."

I promised, and then I got to thinking. "Captain," I said, "you're not a bit like any of the captains I ever knew. Why is it?"

"I don't know, Gus," he said. "How am I different?"

That puzzled me. "You're *all* different?" I said. "You look different and you talk different—softer, somehow, and —and— Oh! I can't tell; but what makes you?"

The captain gave a sort of a smile. "Gus," he said, just as I thought he wasn't going to say any more, "suppose that once, for a little while, a bit of heaven had come into your life—"

"An angel, do you mean ?" I said; but he just smiled a deep, quiet sort of smile, and said:

"Call it an angel if you like. You didn't come into the angel's life, you know, only touched for a moment its outermost circle, but the angel came into yours, for all that. Even though it spread its wings and flew away, and you knew that most likely you would never, never, see it again, don't you think that the memory would stay by you, and that you would try to make yourself and your life worthier of it ?"

"Where did you see the angel, captain ?" I asked. "Was it in the Windward Islands ?"

For there seemed to be such queer things there that I thought maybe there was something the captain took for an angel. The captain didn't seem to understand, though, for he looked hard at me for a moment, and then he began to laugh.

"It doesn't do to talk in parables to you, youngster, I see," he said, and then he got up and went away.

Just then Agnes came up. "Come here, Gus," she said. "I want to give you a lesson. Some day, you know, you may be cast away at sea, and want to know where you are. How would you find out ?"

"Guess, I s'pose," I said; but Agnes put on a shocked face.

"Oh dear! that will never do," she said. "If you couldn't find your latitude and longitude, where would you be ?"

"Just where I should if I could," I said.

"Yes, but presently you'd find yourself just where you shouldn't," she said, laughing. "I want to teach you what the captain has taught me."

It was very good fun to peep through the little spy-hole, and turn the screw until the sun hung, a great red ball, just over the water, but when she began with the addings and that, I stopped her.

"Now, Agnes, it's no good," I said; "I never could do sums, and I'm not going to be a sailor, so where's the odds ?"

"But let me teach you—pray let me teach you," she begged, and I gave in.

"Teach away," I said; "but you won't make anything of it;" and she didn't.

When she'd gone on for half an hour about circles and degrees and chronometers and Greenwich time and that, I didn't

know quite as much as I did when she began, and I told her so. She just stopped short, and when I looked at her she was looking down at the quadrant, with the tears running down her cheeks.

"Why, Agnes," I said, "what's the matter? If you want to know the latitude and longitude so bad, I'll go ask the captain. He'll know."

"It isn't that," she said, laughing through all her tears. "The trouble is that I am to be a governess, and I wanted to see whether I knew how. I worked out the latitude and longitude this morning, but if I can't teach you how to do it, how can I teach my pupils anything ? That's what worries me."

Agnes Wyvern a governess! That stumped me.

"Who are you going to governess ?" I said. "Or don't you know yet ?"

"Of course I know. Do you think I am starting out to seek my fortune, like a princess in a fairy tale ? I'm going to 'governess' the children of a Mrs. Robert Caryl, in Philadelphia."

"Mrs. Robert Caryl! My eye! Cricky!" was all I could say.

"Why, do you know her ?" said Agnes. "What's the matter ?"

"Matter enough," says I. "Mrs. Robert Caryl's my aunt Rose, and her young ones are my cousins—worse luck. Of all the brats! You'll find out fast enough."

"Are they so bad ?" says Agnes, 'most crying. "Oh, Gus, what shall I do ?"

"Do ?" says I. "Why, don't go. Or, if you must go, just you give 'em a good thrashing first off. That 'll teach 'em what to look for if they're up to any of their shines. They ain't very big; I guess you can tackle 'em."

"Oh, do stop, Gus," said Agnes, laughing till she cried. "What a young barbarian you are !"

It had been getting rougher while we talked, and all of a sudden the ship gave such a lurch that the chairs we were sitting on went over like a shot, and landed us all in a heap in the middle of the hurricane deck.

"Hope you're not afraid of a little knocking about," said the captain, coming up to us. "It's coming on to blow. You two had better go below."

So he helped us down, while the ship began to wabble and dance and bump about at a great rate, and—well, that was the end of me for one while, you bet! Agnes staid with me 'most all day, and was in and out of my state-room a dozen times in the night, for I was just the sickest little shaver you ever did see. The old lady was sick too. Her state-room and mine both opened out of the same little passage, so that I could hear every word she said. Once in a while the captain came down; then the old lady used to pitch into him. Cricky! didn't she go it, though!

"What do you mean, captain, by taking us into weather like this? Couldn't help it? Of course you could help it. Don't tell *me*. Weather came to you, not you to the weather? Nonsense. Couldn't you have run out to sea, or run ashore, or something? Could have run ashore, certainly? Then why didn't you? Didn't know we'd care about it? Of course I care about it. Owners wouldn't? No, I suppose not. They never care how uncomfortable their passengers are made, so a little time is saved. But I'll tell you what it is, captain, the whole thing lies in a nutshell. You were so busy talking to that young woman on board that you couldn't see where you were going, and our lives are to be the sacrifice. Even to letting her navigate the ship! Oh! don't tell me. Didn't I see her myself with the quadrille, or whatever you call it, up to her eye? So unfeminine! Did you ever have such weather before in all the five years that I have sailed with you? Never! Very well, then. Did you ever let a young woman navigate the ship before? The inference is quite clear. Of course I shall consider it my duty to inform the owners of the line of the disgraceful circumstance if ever we reach the shore. As for the young woman, I leave her punishment to Providence, as I do not see my way to it at present."

"Abuse me, ma'am, as much as you please," said the captain, in a low, deep voice, something like the growl of a Newfoundland dog when he's in dead earnest. "It don't hurt me, and it may relieve you; but be kind enough to leave the young lady out."

I guess she was scared some, for she stopped a minute. Then she said: "Captain, I am starving—absolutely starving. Are you aware that they have let the kitchen fire go out, so that though I may be dying for a cup of tea, beef or otherwise, I can not have it?"

"I am aware, ma'am, that the fire is out," said the captain, sort of laughing.

"They haven't invented the sort of fire yet that will stay in when the waves are washing over the stove. But, ma'am, I thought you were seasick."

"Seasick?" said the lady, in a sort of squeal. "So I am, of course. Most unfeminine not to be seasick in such a storm as this. I always take to my bed when the wind blows, always, captain, and I have no opinion of people—of females, at least—who do otherwise. That young woman, now—but never mind that. Captain, don't you know that nature must be sustained? That I am sick is all the more reason why I should eat. A nice broiled partridge would be my choice, but I could make shift with a sweet-bread well larded, captain, or even a lamb fry."

"Oh dear!" I said, in a sort of groan. "I do wish she wouldn't talk about things to eat!"

I guess the captain heard me, for he began to laugh, and said, "All right, ma'am; I'll tell the steward."

Then he came into my state-room and just picked me up, bedclothes and all. "You'll never get well here, my little man," he said. "Just you come along with me—and Miss Agnes too, if she will."

Well, where do you think he took me? Why, into his own, his very own state-room, with its big bedstead and its lace curtains and its sofa and all—most as fine as the spare chamber at home.

"This is yours for the rest of the voyage," he said, as he dumped me down in the middle of the big bed. "It's no use to me, for I've got to spend my nights in the pilot-house till this gale blows itself out. There's a sofa for Miss Agnes, if she'll have it. You'll find it pleasanter taking care of the youngster up here."

Then he was off, before we could thank him.

"Say, Agnes," I said, "the captain thinks a lot of you, don't he?"

"Of you, you mean, Master Gus," she said. "It wasn't to me he gave this room."

"Oh, I'm not a bat," I said. "You knew him before, didn't you?"

"A long while ago," said Agnes. "He was skipper of my uncle's yacht on one cruise. Then my uncle took an interest in him and helped him up in the world, and I suppose he is—grateful."

That reminded me. "I say, Agnes," I said, "did you ever see anything like an angel in the Windward Islands?"

"What *do* you mean, Gus?" said Agnes, looking as if she thought I was off my head.

So then I told her what the captain had said about it. Agnes was still a minute, and then she began to laugh in an unsteady kind of way, and said:

"No; I think—I am sure there were no angels there. It was only the captain's fancy."

Then the ship began to wabble and dance and bump and roll worse than ever. There wasn't a thing a ship could do that that ship didn't do. And what with the howling and yelling of the wind, and the creaking of the ropes, and the groaning and straining of the timbers, you couldn't hear yourself think. It all didn't bother me much, though. All I knew was that there was a very sick little boy somewhere, and that Agnes May was taking care of him. I wasn't quite sure who the little boy was then, but, come to think of it now, I guess it must have been me. It was a long, long while before I began to wake up, or it seemed like that to me, and I found the ship was getting steadier. Then the captain came in.

"It's over at last," he said, "but I'm blessed if I know where we are. It's the first time I've ever had to take the latitude and longitude since I've been captain of this steamer, but I've got to do it now. Would you like to help me, Miss Agnes?"

So Agnes she said yes, if I didn't mind, and I didn't; so she went. When she came back the captain came with her as far as the door. I heard what he said to her:

"It is no new thing, and it will be the same forever. I never hoped, and under other circumstances I should never have dared to speak. Even now—"

"Oh, brave heart! true heart!" said Agnes, with a sort of sob; and when she came in her eyes were all soft and teary, and her lips quivering.

Lily and Angelo! I just wish you could have seen 'em. Lil was a skinny sort of a young one, with sharp snappy black eyes and straight black hair. In old times they'd have put her on a bed of hot coals and let her fly straight up the chimney, and serve her right! Angelo was fat and flabby, with big staring blue eyes and hair like tow. He was as stupid as a log, but Lily had brains enough for six—such as they were. Aunt Rose wasn't a bad sort of a fellow, if she hadn't been

so wrapped up in those brats. There wasn't any Uncle Rose. I wish there had been. He wouldn't have let her make such a fool of herself, I'll bet.

"Come here, darlings, and see their nice new governess that Mrs. Lovell sent them." (Just as if Agnes was a sugar elephant!) "She will make their lessons so easy that it will only be fun to learn them; won't she, my lammies? Miss May, I must warn you about these dear children. While I wish you to bring them on rapidly in their studies, I can not have them irritated or thwarted in any way. Above all, they must never be punished. If they require correction, I am the proper person to administer it, and I must request that such cases be always referred to me."

Angelo stood with his thumb in his mouth, staring at Agnes, and Lily she grinned from ear to ear, like an imp as she was. I was mad enough to whop 'em both, but that wouldn't have done any good, so I went off with Agnes.

"Oh, Gus! Gus!" says Agnes, putting both arms round me when we were outside the parlor door; "what shall I do? Oh, what shall I do?"

Something came up into my throat, but I choked it down, and said, "See here, Agnes, I guess I can do some good, if you'll teach me too, along with them."

"Oh, you dear boy!" says Agnes. "Let you spend your holidays shut up in a school-room? No, indeed."

"Now that's mean of you, Agnes," I said. "But we'll see."

So I went straight off to Aunt Rose and asked her, and next morning I was in the school-room.

First of all Agnes thought she'd find out what Lily knew.

"Lily," she said, "who signed the Magna Charta?"

"Floyd Ireson," says Lily, grave as a judge.

"Floyd Ireson? Lily, what do you mean?" says Agnes, not knowing whether to be angry or not.

"Well," says Lily, "doesn't it say,

'Floyd Ireson, for his hard heart,
    Tarred and feathered and carried in a *cart*'?

That was the Magna Charta, of course. Maybe it was 'the women of Marblehead' signed it, though. I don't know."

"What can you tell me about William the Conqueror?" asks Agnes.

"He wanted people to worship his hat," says Miss Lily; "but they just all opened their windows and prayed to the yeast instead. So then he said, 'England expects every man to do his duty,' and when they wouldn't, then he let fly at them, and his arrow hit the apple on his son's head, and then hit a tree, and flew back and struck him in the eye. So he died."

Agnes gave a kind of a sigh, and took up a geography.

"What is the capital of Connecticut?" she said.

"I don't know. Wooden nutmegs, I s'pose," says Lily.

"Lily!" cried Agnes, out of all patience. "There are two capitals. One is—"

"New Haven; I've been there," says Angelo, with his thumb in his mouth.

Agnes brightened right up.

"That's it," she said. "Now, Lily, what is on the bank of the Connecticut River?"

"I don't know," says Lily, slowly. "On the bank? Earth-worms, I s'pose. There most generally are. Or else crabs."

"Don't bother with her any more, Agnes," I said, too mad to hold in. "She's just trying to rile you. Then she'll yell, I know."

Didn't Lil give me a look, though! I didn't care. I just went on studying like a good fellow, while Agnes put Angelo through his paces. He didn't know enough to fool. The worst and the best he could do was to put his thumb in his mouth and goggle his eyes at Agnes.

It was as good as a play to hear Aunt Rose at dinner.

"Mamma's little lammies! Have they been good, Miss May? I needn't ask, though, for they are always good. You find them pretty equally balanced. Lily is the quickest, but Angelo excels in patience. Not that he is slow, either, only not quite so brilliant as Lily, but perhaps more profound. You find it so, don't you, Miss May?"

Poor Agnes, remembering Floyd Ireson and the earth-worms, could only blush and stammer out something, I don't know what, and I guess she didn't.

Well, I can't go over that time day by day, you know. I did what I could, but it wasn't much, Lily was so awful cute. Somehow it was never she that did things —spilled torpedoes about, and left pins in chairs, and such—but always Angelo, and there was no use scolding him. If Lil

had put him up to it, he never told, nor she either, you may bet your life on that. Sometimes Lil knew her lessons, and more times she didn't. When she didn't, she just went on with a lot of bosh, looking as wise as an owl and as innocent as a rabbit all the time. Angelo never knew his lessons, and never pretended to, but just looked stupid, and put his thumb in his mouth, and began to roar. Then Aunt Rose would come into the room like a whirlwind, with her eyes like blue blazes, and scold Agnes, and pity Lily (she was always yelling like mad too about that time), and carry Angelo off.

One day things had been going all contrary, contrarier than usual even, and Agnes was clean tuckered out. When Agnes opened her desk an ink-bottle upset. Of course it was nobody's fault that the bottle had been tilted up so that the least jar would send it over. Only Agnes was sure she hadn't left it so, and I saw Lily coming out of the school-room the night before, grinning fit to split. Lily had learned the wrong history lesson, and Angelo hadn't learned his at all. Then, of course, they both howled. For a wonder, Aunt Rose didn't come in, so after a while they shut up. Then Agnes set Angelo a multiplication sum on the blackboard, and then she began to hear Lily her French. Lil could translate well enough when she chose, but to-day she didn't choose. So she bungled and stammered and made hash of it generally. At last she came to the sentence, "*Blondine marcha dans un petit sentier*," and that she translated, "Blondine walked along in a little *smell*."

"Lily!" said Agnes, in a shocked kind of way. But Lil just looked up as innocent as you please.

"Well," she said, "haven't I just said *sentir*, and doesn't that mean to feel, or to smell? So what can *sentier* mean but a smell? It can't mean a *feel*, can it? And I'm sure *petit* means little. It always did before. I suppose it wasn't a very bad smell."

Agnes looked at her for a minute. Then she tried to speak, but she broke down, and laughed instead. The tears rolled down her cheeks, but she laughed on, for all she was sobbing at the same time. Then she just jumped up and ran out of the room. Lil she turned round and grinned at me—such a grin! It made me mad as hops.

"You just shut up, Lil Caryl," I said, "or I'll make you."

"Why, I didn't say a word," says Lil; and so she hadn't.

I went after Agnes, but I met her outside her own door. Her hair was all wet—soused, you know, like she had put it under a hydrant. She was quiet enough, only she looked sort of pale and quivery. Lil scuttled away from the blackboard as we came in, and picked up her book.

"Why, this is very strange, Angelo," said Agnes, when she had looked at his sum. "You have the answer right, but every figure of the working out is wrong. You must have copied the answer."

"Didn't," said Angelo, and that was all.

"It's a shame," says Lily, like as if she was talking to her book. "He did it, and he got the answer, and that's all about it."

Nobody took any notice, so she just fizzled herself out in mutters.

Just then Aunt Rose came in with her aunt, Mrs. Severance. She was awful rich, Mrs. Severance was, and Aunt Rose was as pleased as Punch to see her. I knew something as soon as ever I looked at Mrs. Severance, but I kept still. She was a fat old lady, with a crumpled-up face, all dressed off in satin and lace, with diamonds that winked and looked wicked like Lily's eyes.

"Here are my lammies," said Aunt Rose. "I have brought Mrs. Severance in to see them, Miss May. Aunt Ginevra, this is Miss May, the governess."

Mrs. Severance put up her gold eye-glasses and looked at Agnes, sort of puzzled, but she didn't say anything.

"And how are the lammies getting on?" said Aunt Rose, stooping down to kiss Angelo. "What a long, long sum for a little puzzle-pate. Isn't he a clever darling, Aunt Ginevra? And can he do it, Miss May?"

Agnes hesitated, but Lily she chipped in. "Oh yes, he can do it fast enough. He got the answer at once, but Miss May she said he must have copied it."

"Angelo copy his answers! Angelo, the soul of honor!" cried Aunt Rose. "Oh, Miss May, how could you?"

Lil jumped up. I saw it, for all she grabbed it so quickly and tucked it under her and sat down on it. I saw that arithmetic tumble out from under her apron, and then I remembered how she had scuttled away from the blackboard, and then I *knew*. There was no use trying to tell Aunt Rose, though. Bless you! no. She just wouldn't listen.

"This is Gus Lawrence, from Boston, Aunt Ginevra," she said, when she thought of me. "He must have been a fellow-passenger of yours upon the steamer."

Mrs. Severance put up her glasses and looked at me.

"I think I remember him," she said, slowly. "Miss May's face, too, struck me as familiar, but for the moment I could not place it. Now, however— You are the young woman who navigated the steamer, I think."

"Navigated the steamer? I?" said Agnes, struck all of a heap, and no wonder.

"Yes, my dear, certainly," said Mrs. Severance. "I saw you myself with the quadrille, or whatever you call it. I never can remember their sea terms—so unfeminine! It was you who ran us into that gale, into the very teeth of it. What possessed you to undertake such a thing?"

"I—I—" said Agnes; and then she went into a fit of laughing again; and then she said, "Oh! I beg your pardon." And then she laughed again; and then she began to cry, and just bolted out of the room.

Mrs. Severance and Aunt Rose looked at each other.

"Dear! dear!" said Aunt Rose, "I am afraid that I have been mistaken in Miss May; she seemed so gentle and modest."

"*Modest!*" said Mrs. Severance.

"Me and Angelo don't like her," piped up Lily, in her shrill little voice. "She laughed at me just like that when I made a mistake in my French this morning; and she scolds us awful when we don't say our lessons to suit her."

"Depend upon it, my dear, it's a mistake," Mrs. Severance said, nodding her head slowly. "Who sent her to you?"

"Mrs. Lovell, of Boston," said Aunt Rose. "It would never do to offend *her*, but—"

"A very unreliable person," said Mrs. Severance. "Philanthropic, you know; always taking up with doubtful people. Why, she is still hand and glove with the niece of that dreadful man with whose story all Boston is ringing. So unfeminine to encourage that sort of thing! I have no doubt that this Miss May is a mere adventurer."

Then I just blazed out. "I guess you don't know what you're talking about," I said. "If you knew she was Agnes Wyvern, you'd sing a different song." Well, they were astonished enough, but not just the way I'd meant.

"Agnes Wyvern!" squealed Mrs. Severance. "The very girl!"

"Agnes Wyvern!" squeaked Aunt Rose; "the niece of the forger, the embezzler, who would have been sent to State's-prison if he hadn't cut his own throat! Ugh!"

I was scared to death, I tell you. Before I had begun to get over my scare, Agnes came back. She began to apologize for the way she had left, but nobody listened. Aunt Rose had her young ones gathered up, one in each arm, and Mrs. Severance stood straight up, with her eye-glasses on her nose.

"Don't try to distract our attention from the main point, if you please," she said. "The question now is whether what Gus has just told us is correct. Is your name Wyvern?"

Agnes just gave me one quick look. It wasn't a cross look, but it 'most broke my heart, for all that.

"Oh, Agnes, I didn't mean—" I said; and then I just boo-hooed like a baby.

Agnes she gave a sort of little quivery smile, and said, "Never mind, Gus; it doesn't matter."

"Answer me, if you please," Mrs. Severance said; and Agnes turned to her.

"I was at one time known as Agnes Wyvern," she said, "but my real name is May. When my parents died, my uncle took me, and by his wish I bore his name. By Mrs. Lovell's advice I resumed my own, after—after—" Her lips quivered, and she stopped, and clasped her hands tight together.

"Of course, *Miss May*, you understand," said Mrs. Severance, after a pause.

"That I must go?" said Agnes. "Oh yes! I should have gone in any case, though, for I can not teach. I found that out on the steamer, you know, Gus," she said, turning to me with the weakest, poorest little smile, and the tears dripping fast over it.

Lily looked on, grinning her very wickedest. Angelo looked on too, till, all of a sudden, he began to roar. Now who'd 'a thought it? He'd got fond of Agnes, and didn't want her to go! The more Aunt Rose tried to hush him up, the louder he yelled, till she was 'most wild.

"Pray go, Miss May, and end this most distressing scene," she said at last. "This convinces me that your influence has been

very bad. The dear child never showed any temper before, never! Your money and your meals shall be sent to your room. It is too late for you to leave to-day, I suppose; but to-morrow—"

"To-morrow morning I will leave, madam," said Agnes.

"I'm going too, you know, Agnes," I said, when we were outside. "I can't stand it here after this."

"You dear boy!" said Agnes, squeezing my hand tight. "But what would your mother say, Gus?"

"The mammy?" I said. "Why, bless your heart! she'll be too glad to see me to say anything. Say, how are you going, Agnes? By steamer?"

Agnes just stopped short. "What day of the week is this, Gus?" she said.

"Friday," says I. "And, oh, jolly! why, the very steamer we came on goes back to-morrow. Are you going by her, Agnes? Say!"

"I suppose so," says Agnes, slowly; "yes, I must. I can not stay here, and the journey by land is so expensive; but—"

"Why, Captain Floy 'll be no end glad to see you. What's the row, Agnes?" I said; but she didn't answer.

We went off next morning, and the last thing we heard was Angelo's roars, and the last thing we saw was Lil's face grinning over the balusters. Agnes didn't talk much on the way down to the Pine Street wharf, but she kept turning red and white, and sometimes she smiled, and more times the tears came into her eyes.

When the captain saw us, it was as if a great light broke all over his face like sunrise. "Are you going back with me, Gus?" he said, but he only looked at Agnes.

"Yes," I said, "we're going back, me and Agnes. Aunt Rose was too many for us. And the brats. That Lil's a oner, I tell you what!"

"Lil?" said the captain, but he didn't seem to care about the answer, only looked at Agnes with all his eyes.

Agnes she was turning red and white as fast as winking, and after a minute Captain Floy said:

"Take her aboard, Gus. You can take your pick of state-rooms, for you are the only passengers this trip."

Then he pulled his cap a little further over his eyes, and went on overseeing the men.

That trip wasn't half as much fun as the other had been, for all it was as still as still all the way. Mrs. Severance herself couldn't have been sick, if she'd tried ever so hard. I wasn't, and I do it pretty easy. But Agnes was so queer. I didn't know what had come to her. First off she had to go and tell the captain she only came that way because she hadn't money enough to go by land. Of course he thought she didn't want to go with him, and he looked awful sorry, and didn't come near us again for ever so long.

"Agnes, what makes you so queer to the captain?" I said once.

Agnes turned all red, and she looked at me very sharp and quick. "Am I queer?" she said. "How?"

"Why, you're not a bit like you used to be," I said. "You don't even look at him if you can help it, and you are so still all the time. Say, Agnes, don't you like him any longer?"

Agnes was looking down into her lap, and she didn't look up.

"Like him? Yes, I like him," she said.

"As well as you used to?" I asked.

But Agnes she just said "Yes," and no more. So then I thought maybe he'd like to know it.

"I understand, Gus," he said, looking, oh! so kind and so sorry! "I know what she's afraid of, but she needn't be, bless her!"

I was glad enough we weren't going to be on the ship as long as we were before. We ought to get in Monday noon, the captain said; but something happened before that. Just as we got up on deck Monday morning there was an awful clatter, and a clatter that you don't know what it means scares you 'most to death on shipboard. The bell began to ring, not *ting-ting*, *ting-ting*, like it does when it strikes the half-hours, but hard and fast, like it was too scared to stop. Then the sailors came flying from every part of the ship. For one minute it just rained sailors—sprouted 'em too. The steward came up the cabin stairs in two jumps, and they all made straight for the pumps. They pumped like mad for a minute or two. Then the bell rang again, and they rushed to the boats.

"They can't put out the fire, and they're getting out the boats, Agnes," I said.

Scared? Of course I was scared. So would you be. Fire at sea's no joke, I don't guess. Just then I caught sight of the captain, and I grabbed Agnes and put for him, dragging her along.

"Captain, will you take care of us, me and Agnes?" I said; but the captain he just began to laugh.

"What a shame!" he said. "I thought you had been warned. It is only the drill we have to go through every fortnight, so that in case of accident there will be no confusion."

"And there is no fire?" said Agnes, very slowly, as if her lips were stiff with cold.

"None at all," said the captain.

Then Agnes she just sat down on the pump, and turned so white I thought she was going to faint. The captain caught her, for she sort of swayed over, and said, "Run for some water, Gus."

When he caught her, though, she held herself up a little, and turned a slow sort of pink, and quivered her eyelids, so I stopped.

"Don't be afraid, Miss Agnes," said the captain, in a sort of choked voice. "I will let you go as soon as you can stand."

"I am not afraid," said Agnes, softly, while the pink kept on coming back to her cheeks.

"I remember the distance between us, which once for a moment I forgot," he said. "Believe me, I will not grieve your sweet heart in that way again."

"*Won't* you?" said Agnes.

That was all, but she just lifted up her eyelids and looked at the captain, and the captain he started, and then looked down hard at her. Then she jumped up and covered her face with her hands and ran down the cabin stairs. The captain he looked like a man in a dream, just clean dazed. He rubbed his hand over his forehead once or twice, and then, all of a sudden, he broke into a smile that flowed all over his face, and the tears jumped into his eyes, and then he just turned on his heel and walked away.

Of course I asked Agnes what it all meant.

"The captain has been helping me to find my latitude and longitude," she said; "or else I've been helping him. I'm afraid, on the whole, that was the way of it. Dreadful, wasn't it, Gus?"

"Not if he couldn't find it without you," I said, wondering what she made such a fuss about that for.

She just laughed a happy sort of little laugh, and said, "Well, he didn't seem able."

ARTIST STROLLS IN HOLLAND.

Sebenth Paper.

ON our way to Zandvoort we had given a few of the morning hours to Zaandam, but I did not care to see again the long watery avenue of the place, with its hundreds of windmills "all a-blowing," nor did I wish to pay my duty visit to the shop of Peter the Great, so we took a good-natured-looking boatman at the ferry, and we floated lazily about on the broad, placid river, just above the locks, and peered into the queer, old-fashioned gardens, and into the comic summer-houses by the water's edge. It was not indiscreet, as there was no notion of any one's privacy being studied or considered in the matter of these leafy bowers and blooming banks of hollyhock and aster. The correct thing seemed to be to enjoy one's self as publicly as possible. The hedges seemed to be made low on purpose for the neighbors to step over and take part in any fun going, or at least to look over and see the others enjoy themselves. The trellis-work of the summer-houses was invitingly open to outside gazers, and there were little steps and landing-stages handy down at the water's edge, where boat-loads of friends might draw up and make themselves at home. It did not seem to be a place where the spirit of sport ever raged on the waters. I saw no sign of any one showing off in an outrigger or any other racing craft. The boats —such as I actually saw—were of the old-fashioned broad-bottomed, safety-assuring sort, highly painted and gilded, and scarlet-cushioned, but not sportive in the least.

Having now come pretty nearly to the end of the list of things to see in and about Amsterdam, I began to plan a jaunt, by way of Utrecht, to Arnheim, and then along through Brabant on to Maastricht. Of course other plans were thought of and weighed in the scale, but the balance was in favor of Brabant. Jacob was set to work to look up his trains, and find out anything of interest, and prepare generally. We found that we could spend a day or two at Utrecht with great profit, as there are so many fine things of artistic interest in and about the place generally.

I can't say much for the way Utrecht "leads up" to her attractions, from the Amsterdam side at least, for a more unin-

ARNHEIM.

teresting strip of country I never beheld. However, it is soon over—that's one comfort. I can't say of it as a friend said of his claret that his luncheon guests were rather shy of—"Do have some more; it isn't very good, but there's lots of it." Utrecht is gay and bright enough, but that impression may have been partly owing to the monotonous prelude to it, and partly to the fact that it was market-day.

There is a large and curious canal running through the town, with a kind of two-story quay alongside it. It seemed full of "go" and movement, and lots of color, and plenty of possibilities in the way of sketching. There was a lively fish market at a bustling corner of it, and there must have been a miraculous catch of prawns and shrimps the day before, somewhere near Utrecht. I never saw such an overflow of them. The very air was redolent and pink with them. They can't be very indigestible to Dutch folk, either, or many would have died that day, judging from the free and unstinted consumption of them by the general populace. They were carrying them away in paper sacks, and in their wide breeches pockets without any sack. It seemed to be only the very finicky, and those with spare time to kill, and those not hungry, who took the shells off before eating them. A good long fatiguing market-day will somehow make you feel as if you had been in the place a week when night comes on. Our inn was in the thick of the racket, and as the successful market people strayed in to moisten their parched shrimps, the din increased in speed and pitch. We had thought of staying overnight and going on to Arnheim early in the morning. As this row increased, Jacob was put in communion with his time-table. We could easily catch a nice train if we started then and there, and get to Arnheim for a quiet dinner, and, better still, a quiet night of it. We bade a hurried adieu to the gorged inn, whose flurried host seemed even glad to have our room, and we sped to our waiting train, and just in time. I should have enjoyed the daylight view of the country we were soon speeding through. It looked in the dim twilight to be of a more varied character than that we came past in the early morning.

Arnheim struck me as cool and fresh and calm after the racket of Utrecht. The hotel was of a different stamp, too. It was like a good Hague hotel, with a landlord welcoming you in good sound English, and all the servants were more or less up to a certain maltreatment of the language, so that one could make some sort of impression on them when out of Dutch for the moment. The hotel was not in the heart of the town, but just on the upland slope near to the Rhine. After our quiet little nicely served dinner we felt so refreshed and washed clean of "the toils of the day and the din of the

decided tone of the hosiers' startling goods, he can always keep his coin pretty intact about him in these places. If one has to be thought a fool in any given direction, he is safer from temptation if his foolery

MARKET-DAY AT ARNHEIM.

fair," that we took our soothing cigars and strolled out into the peaceful star-lit air.

The shops of Arnheim were still ablaze, and inviting the passer-by to indulge in all sorts of articles of luxury and superfluity. I never saw streets of shops filled with so many things I never hope to covet as I have remarked in some of the Dutch towns of minor import. If one is happily indifferent to the splendid but splurgy meerschaum, or qualmed by the show of fat confectionery, or undazed by the pretentious and hollow jewelry, or scared by the

be in things æsthetic. The tempting shops —nay, even the towns containing such— are few and far between, when once one has left the Hague and Amsterdam behind.

Arnheim is a very wealthy and exclusive town, with many costly and imposing residences therein (that is, the new part of it). There is little of Dutch character in any of the various orders of mixed architecture that one sees; the houses and villas are mostly modern, like the fortunes of the owners. The prevailing style is the French private hôtel of the provinces, but with certain classic variations. One is never led into charging them with inconsistency, as they never seemed to care to be consistent. They were built for convenience and for show, and if they have not

STREET URCHIN.

the first, they mostly have the latter attribute to a high degree. Having ceased to amuse or instruct ourselves in the gas-lighted streets of business, we had strolled into the quiet, tree-lined avenues beside the park and the long stretch of ornamental water that winds through that part of the town. Jacob tried to impress me with tales of the sudden rises to fortune he had heard of among these well-housed, opulent citizens, and I was glad to know of their prosperity, and to note the lavish way in which they adorned their palatial residences; but, when it was all said and done, it was not what I had come so far to see. For any special joy—except the quiet absence of any envy—it was giving me, I might as well have been walking down Park Lane. We left the scenes of select opulence, and wandered off to the other end of the town, down along the shadow-haunted streets about the great church. It was a massive looming old pile as we came upon it in the

moonlight, eloquent with musical clamor of pealing *carillon* every few minutes. The sacred precincts were rather damp and odorous, as well as impressive and grand, and after a certain time the damp and the "whiffs" seem to increase and grow out of all proportion to the original impressiveness; we left the narrow over-shadowed streets, and sought the great square near by. It was a fine open space, with borders of trees about it, and some good substantial old houses—nothing very ornate that I could make out in the dim half-light, but it was all open and fresh, and evidently well kept. The markets are held here, and to-morrow we will see a small one. So I agree to wait in patience. Jacob kept apologizing for the present desertion of the square. He was evidently disappointed with my tepid admiration of the "swell quarter" of the place, for he had given me to understand that such a spot was his dream in case he ever got rich (on petroleum shares, I fancy). We would just get a glimpse of the old gateway near the square on our way home. The moonlight did all it could to silver it with a romantic shimmer, but it didn't shimmer itself into anything very impressive, for all that. It had just been newly painted, as I soon discovered while fondly patting its rounded sides (after the manner of callow antiquaries). One might as well try to shake hands with it.

"Surely, Jacob, this is not a *very* old gateway, it looks so new and fresh."

"Oh, dot's de baint—you got zome on you klof—bot you *bet* she is old, dese gate! She is ever so many 'ondered year old if she's a day;" and he blew his nasal trumpet blast on his check bandana mainsail, and stood to his gate as if he were the defiant warder thereof.

"We will zee it better in de morning, and you will zay wot an old gate she is, and den you see dar oder gateway dere—de 'Deffil's 'Ouse,' and you see if you don't zay dot's ole enough too. Besides, *I* know de Deffil is an ole gate-'ouse anyway, because I've always been tole so."

There was no arguing with such convictions; and as it was getting rather late, and the old boy was getting tired and testy, we just strolled on home by way of the river, sitting down under the trees for a while to give him a rest, and enjoy the broad moon-lit river. The rising mists from it made the moored shipping look thin and weird; their twinkling lights wavered in snaky reflections on its slowly swirling tide.

> "On such a night stood Dido,
> With a willow in her hand."

I thought of a certain broad river miles and miles away, and in less than two minutes began to turn sadly homesick.

the like of for quaintness in fine weather, scurrying groups of figures with "clinging draperies" swishing with the wet. There are always friendly porchways to get under and out of it yourself; or sometimes, better still, one can find a convenient café "giving on" the biggest crowd on the square; there may be an

PORCH OF THE DEVIL'S HOUSE, ARNHEIM.

"Take me away, Jacob. This will serve for our first evening at Arnheim." There is nothing like a cozy, well-kept hotel to neutralize a tendency to homesickness. Ours was most comfortable and amusing. The landlord knew Jacob like a first cousin (as usual), and there was no lack of attention and kindness.

Next day was somewhat showery and blowy. We went out all the same, and enjoyed it. There are certain effects and incidents out in the rain that one never sees

unoccupied table by the window nearest the street, and by ordering a few cups of coffee and a cigar you have a splendid chance to sketch for hours unbothered. We often did this, as we got rest, refreshment, and shelter all at the same easy rate. And the waiter will not mind you if you tip him with a few mixed metals of the coinage. I once bought a new sketch-book (in fact we were always buying new sketch-books, Abbey and I, the Dutch paper is so enticing and cheap),

A WET SUNDAY AT ARNHEIM.

and I stood by the window of the shop to try it on a passer-by. The obliging bookseller offered me a chair, and I sat in that window bay all afternoon, and half filled that book, and bought a few more. Rainy days are the best for going into a crowded Dutch market-place. A railway station is a lovely place, too, to catch the fleeting types of costume and character; they sit and stand about at your mercy, waiting for their trains. One has only to get a corner seat and his back well jammed in a corner, so that he can't be overlooked, and, my word for it, there is good sport to be had.

The evil-reputed, grim "Devil's House" stands in the square just back of the cathedral. I was prepared with my most sympathetic shudder, after all the tales I had heard of it. We had come upon it unawares to me, and I found myself walking in and out under the archway trying to catch a bit of over the way, and be out of the rain. My bit finished, I began to look about me for the first time, and I then began to suspect that the huge, hideous caricatures of the "mortal enemy," each holding a mass of overhanging doorway on his wicked horned head, and grinning a grin of acute suffering, rather than menace to affright the average child of man, was the "arch-fiend" himself. I

began to suspect, also, some dreadful flash of humor in the by-gone builder of the house in thus making him support his character of *arch* fiend. Anyway, joke or no, there they were, the poor devils, and had been for centuries, grinning under their load of ponderous arch for their sins. The good people of the town were in no way disposed to treat the effigies with scorn or contumely; in fact, they had given them every kindly care that images could expect. Each long-enduring demon had just had the fresh ointment of healing putty jammed into his gaping wounds and cracks, and his parched and scaling hide treated to a salve of fawn-colored paint; and both the devils and the archway, and even the whole house front, shone again from the effects of that restoring agency. I stood under the porch and sketched it and various other things, and managed to imprint a large blotch of fresh fawn-color on my shoulder, and that was about all the awful impression the house of the demons made on me. It has a long and grisly history. I went into it no further than the various guide-books could take me. It seemed veiled in more mystery than I had time or desire to fathom just then. I shall always think pleasantly of the awful house, on account of its kindly sheltering archway, so useful to me on that day of drizzle and damp. I could there gather in the picturesque passer-by when the figures happened to be worth while, which was not often. There is not much in the way of distinctive dress to be noted, especially among the natives. Down along the quays, among the sailor folk, a few stray mariners from far-off Zeeland or Duiveland may enliven the scene, but most of the others fail entirely. Even the street urchin is far too conventional to invite a second glance. The market-place had a few rustics of an amusing pattern from the surrounding country, but at the best nothing to begin with the most ordinary in a Zeeland market town.

The next day was not only rainy again, but it was Sunday; and though that day is rather a restless than a restful one in the Low Countries, bringing out gay groups of holiday-clad people, sporting their best old family plate, in their filmy lace caps, and jewelled heirlooms about their ample throats and swinging in their rosy ears. Here, somehow, most of the people seemed to think such gauds "bad form," and only made a parade of sober blacks or sad grays, and jackets of the fash-

ion before the last. There was scarcely a bright green, or even the most modest scarlet, or retiring light blue umbrella, to give a bit of point to the color of the slowly moving groups smoking their way to church or back from it.

Down by the river, however, there were the inevitable groups of Sunday anglers. Rain, nor hail, nor fear of scandal, awed them in the least. They seemed a sociable set among themselves; there was no seeking out a retired spot, and each selfishly trying to lure away his neighbor's gudgeon. They got closely together in pleasantly arranged groups, and chatted and laughed and tangled each other's lines, and lied enormously, no doubt, about the fish they caught "the other day," and seemed to rather enjoy the rain than not.

Now and again the sun would struggle through the shifting skeins of drizzle, and turn to golden haze the vapor from the slow dun-colored stream, and light up with a wan blush the sere and yellow trees across the river, on the flat green meadows beyond. The scene was a good background for the eager groups of fishers with their waving rods at every angle against the sky and water. Jacob sadly

NYMEGEN.

wanted me to drive out into the country to some wood or "bosch," but I too keenly remembered a certain drive through a certain Prince's Wood, on a damp autumn day, to wish to try such joys again. He then suggested the old town of Nymegen. On that very day they would celebrate with all their remaining vigor the closing carnival of a week's kermesse.

Alas! I had a too sorrowful remembrance of just such a powwow at Purmerend, the year before, to spring to this proposal at once. A year, however, is a long time to harbor animosity. I had often laughed during it over some of the wild scenes of that long rackety night. Months afterward, while "deep in the velvet sinking" of a luxurious couch near to a gilded ball-room, I watched the twinkling flash of dainty satin shoes, mingled with the larger and more sustaining effort of manly patent-leather, "chasing the weary hours with flying feet," to the strains of the Coldstream Band. Suddenly there came the wild refrain of that pandemonium of a fair at Dutch Purmerend—"Le Beau Nicholas." I could but smile a smile of kindly greeting to it. I could hear the lusty Dutch voices shouting, howling, *hurling* out the words in broken French: "*Nicko*-lar! NEEK-o-laar! Ah-ah-*ah!*" that rent the maddened air all that wild night. How lovely it seemed now as it spun about the swishing coat tails and lace frillings in that swift "galop." And to think of how these wildly prancing North Dutch revellers had tried to splinter the floors with their great clogs to every salient note of it!

It was not far to Nymegen; we could be there in time for luncheon, and then see the town and such of the kermessing as we liked, and then, if need be, escape the terrors of the inevitable midnight racket by taking the train to Bois-le-Duc. I felt that I was not doing quite all my duty to Arnheim, for I had heard that the surrounding country is simply delightful. I consoled my conscience with a short mem.: "Do this place another time earlier in the season." And then we gathered our belongings, and trained off to festive Nymegen. It was not very far, but it seemed hundreds of miles away in differences of character and people.

There was not the same form and primness, the same devotion to starch and brilliantine, or even to clothes-brush and hair-brush, in Nymegen. Perhaps it was hardly fair to remark these things without crediting the good folk of Nymegen with a whole week's "jubilation." The town itself looked messy and "traipsed," with clinging greasy mud of a sandy yellow. This sad condition of things also needs an apology, and, I might say, a sigh of regret for. They were laying shovel and pick and blasting powder to the ancient walls and ramparts of the town. Bastions and towers and gateways and moats were disappearing in dust and mud. They were toppling over their ancient and honorable defenses into the weedy ditch, and filling in the stray holes with any extra rubbish to give it consistency and flavor, and then smoothing it all nicely down and planting wispy trees and setting out some chilly iron seats, and flattering their stupid but honest souls with the idea that the new boulevard they were making would break the hearts of the modernizing burghers of Arnheim or Bois-le-Duc.

It was a splendid day for fleeting effects of light and shade, for wind-blown movement and unstudied action. How the vivid umbrellas were fluttered about, and the beribboned caps and gay kerchiefs flapped in the breeze! and how jolly and good-natured they all were!—not a little tangled and battered and high-tinted after their week's hilarity, some few of them, but still even these seemed to have a good stock of endurance left. Whenever the pulse of revelry was likely to beat a little slowly there was always ready a fresh influx of new blood to be let into the veins of fun. The train we came by was brimming over with a merry crowd from the country round, eager to let out its rich flow of pent-up animal spirits wherever the revels might seem to lag. The refreshment booths were full; there was not much noise; every one seemed quietly laying in a supply of "motive power" for the midnight fandango, or to repair the lost tissue wasted in the whirling fray of the previous night. The choice spirits of Arnheim and the roistering lads and lasses of Bois-le-Duc had evidently come in force to dance for the palm of endurance with what was left of the revellers of Nymegen. There was a fine touch of the old fire of mediæval rivalry of town and town in it all; but it was rather sad and sinful on the whole. I felt as if I had gone knowingly out of my way from

A DAUGHTER OF THE SOIL.

peaceful, quiet, prim Arnheim on purpose to be shocked. The only concession I could well make to any outraged sense of propriety was to get out of the thick of the revellers as soon as I had satisfied a modest amount of shocked curiosity. We went to an excellent and quiet place for lunch—the Hôtel Boggia, in the market square, the landlord speaking excellent English.

After that we strolled around the outer fringe of the fair, and into some of the old churches and some of the civic buildings in the by-squares. The old town-hall is very picturesque, and is mostly uninjured in its best portions of ancient work. The old houses in the streets are very numerous and good; in fact, some of them strikingly so. The town slopes upward from the river Waal to what is quite a notable hill in these parts. We mounted this up a straggling tree-shaded street to a fair "outsight" looking over miles of level river-laced country. There is an old watch-tower on this hill of rather good lines, and generally picturesque. We sat on a convenient bench by the tower, and looked down upon the tree-shaded river and town. Nymegen was seemingly rich in parks and gardens, and the whole panorama was warmed and gilded with the bronzed tones of the October foliage. The distant hum of the fair seemed like the buzz of some great hive of bees, and it was far more restful. There was a certain sense-enchantment being lent to the murmur of the far-off throng by the wide intervening stretch of russet-leaved tree-tops. There was a promise of something to note down by the river-side, where a couple of large ferry-boats were plying to and fro from the other shore with more revellers for the kermesse. We wended our way to the river to see about it. Naturally the boats were not things to enjoy, but the passengers were, many of them, a rare treat. I regretted to note that a few had already been "treated," and not wisely, but too well. They were all happy, however, and good-tempered even to a fault, if one may find a slight error in their ways.

The Dutch are so genial and industrious and "decent" generally, that one can afford to come upon a kermesse, especially if he goes out of his way to it now and then, and look at the jovial side of their picturesque carouse, much as Teniers and Brouwer did.

The ferry amused us until it was time to ramble over to the station, along the sad line where the ancient donjons and ramparts were grovelling in the *fosse* before the coming steam tram and the asphalted promenade. The train had just arrived from some near-by town, gorged with jubilant kermessers, and as they streamed out of the station and went prancing townward, I was tempted to chant with the old cynic in the comic opera:

(*Aloud:*)
"Happy villagers, dance away!"
(*Aside, with glee:*)
"Too much exercise brings on cramp,
Fits, convulsions, sudden death!"

It was a quiet ride to Bois-le-Duc, or "s'Bosch," as you might say if a native. We arrived at the Golden Lion just in time for its "*dobble dote,*" as Jacob fondly hoped we would. That worthy had not been enjoying the day at all. I fancy that by dint of showing the ker-

messe to the wandering tourist too often he was getting aweary of it himself.

Although a quiet place is usually grateful after the turmoil of a fair, I must say that Bois-le-Duc is too much of a change. The silent church-yard would not seem very cold and lonesome after an hour or two of the chill, stagnant, lifeless air that hung over and about us on that sad, grewsome evening.

The squeak of the fiddles and the general racket still sung in my ears; perhaps I should have been glad of the buzzing echo, as it kept my thoughts from being loaded down by the all-prevailing gloom of the ancient inn. It was old enough, but it had been robbed of all the charm that comes of antiquity. It was a senile, weak old inn, with foolish stairways and doddering dim passages, clean enough and tolerably well kept, and the people sufficiently willing and attentive; enough of everything except the charm that should go with its "period." When the sad, serious *table d'hôte* had run its courses, the depressed guests produced their damp green cigars and favored us with a generous stifle of acrid smoke. They meant it all kindly and socially enough, but we did not care to join in the general reek. The chill outside air was as near the point of complete saturation as the rain-gauge would go without a deluge; however, we ventured out into it for a change of atmosphere. There was a brilliant café open, and in there we turned to take our coffee, and to see such life as might be stirring. The waiter, as a delicate compliment to me, brought a London paper weeks old. I read it all with an approach to wild joy. We then sought our chilly inn. Jacob had had the happy forethought to order a fire in the great rambling bedroom, and as we opened the door it was worth anything as a cheering surprise. We sat down before it for an hour or two, and Jacob actually warmed to himself again, and told me a few "bonny chokes" as a pleasant wind-up to the dreary evening.

The next day was a kind of market-day for butter and eggs and other good things from the fat farms about. The sun was dispersing the clinging mists, and things generally were emerging from the chill dullness. The streets were alive with movement and color, and pleasant with busy chatter. Jacob was beaming as brightly as the rosy morn itself. He had discovered that our host was uncle to a cousin's brother-in-law, or some such involved kin and kind, and we were to have *such* a breakfast to ourselves in a little private room "as will mek your eye wot-

fine positive reds and blues. They are, perhaps, inordinately vain of their great spreading lace caps (and often is the lace of good old "point"), and their long pendent ear-rings flashing in the sun; their

OLD GATEWAY, NYMEGEN.

ter." We would just take a turn around the market square. Would I go and see the pigs or the butter? I thought the latter might best suit the dainty whims of our early morning appetite for savor and suggestiveness of color. Besides, it was farther away, and would give us more of a trot. It turned out to be the freshest, crispest, dewiest-looking array of the fat o' the land that we could well see anywhere. There were rows of brilliantly clear pink-and-white-complexioned dames and damsels with great flat baskets of golden butter, the deftly patted and stamped rolls just peeping out of the neatly folded snowy napkins, and all cooled on beds of fresh green leaves. More flat baskets of new-laid eggs, so new that the shells looked the *mat*-color of a white rose.

The market women were mostly inside the market proper, but many were outdoors under great tent-like umbrellas of

fat pink hands, folded patiently over the handles of the baskets, are ringed heavily with wide hoops of barbaric gold. Wide necklets of coral or deep garnets are clasped about the throat with archaic clasps, often set with precious stones. Many of them had brushed the morning dew from the fields tramping here with the produce of their snug farms. They were all bright-eyed and merry and strong, and all too much engaged, I found, with the serious pursuit of selling butter or eggs to mind being sketched in the least.

What a different-looking Bois-le-Duc from last evening, and what another sight after yesterday's revel! It was like a breath of pure crisp air after a stifling room. After the promised "little breakfast," which was really a picture of sparkling freshness after the stodgy *table d'hôte* of the night before, we went back to the butter market again. Somehow the first freshness seemed to have gone off everything. The dew had dried from the hems of the manifold and ample skirts of the dairy-maids, and their crisp produce seemed wilting under the blare and heat of the throng. I hastened away before the first crisp impression on my memory wilted also.

There was an odd corner of the market-place for "antiques" in the shape of odds and ends of all sorts of dejected rubbish. All of it had been carefully sorted over by the keen eye of the small experts, and there was nothing left, even for the most simple and confiding beginner in bric-à-brac. There was much clanging and booming of the many church bells every few minutes, which reminded us that the splendid old cathedral was far better worth our seeing than the turmoil of the butter market. I remembered that we were in the very thick of the cream of Catholic Holland, in the capital of Brabant itself, which has always been the stronghold of the faith in the Netherlands. All through Protestant Holland the great churches and the cathedrals are generally the most bare and uninviting temples that one can imagine, but here they seem living, fervent things. There is no mistaking the spirit of devotion and earnest faith one sees here on every side, whether one believes in it or not. There is always some grand old music to hear, and generally something picturesque and impressive in the way of ceremonial to see. It was pleasant wandering in and out as one listed; the great baize-covered door was always swinging to and fro, and crowds meandered in and out as if the church was part of the highway. The church itself is one of the most important in size and architectural claims of any of those of the Netherlands. It is not so very old, as churches go, being built in the early fifteenth century, but it looks so crumbled and mumbled by nibbling Time that one would not be surprised (except judging from its style) to hear that it was many hundreds older. The stone of which it is built is so soft and sandy that it seems powdering away at every blast of wind. There are some very good bits of wood and stone carving inside, but there, too, the stone is gradually being dusted away by the very action of the air upon it.

The people who were thronging the place took my interest almost entirely away from the building itself. They went about their devotions as if they gave their whole being up to what they were doing. From out the dimly lighted fane, filled with musky incense and the thrill of young singing voices and deep organ tones, into the sunny air again.

We wandered out toward a park-like place and sat under the tall trees. We were on part of the old battlements commanding a sweep of the surrounding country for many miles. It was a low, swampy waste, too, most of it—so low and watery that for many of the rainy months of the year it will be like a vast shallow lake, entirely surrounding the town. It was then fairly dried up, and I hear they have done much to drain it in late years. It was all very picturesque and agreeable in arrangement of pool, canal, and river—a joy to the soul above fears of malaria. There are some good old gateways and parts of the old defenses still standing, and I really fancy that as yet they are unthreatened with improvement. The town-hall is a good worthy edifice, with no direct claims on our gratitude for anything in the way of delightful architecture.

We turned off from the mart down to a long tree-lined quay. There was a good show of movement and traffic up and down. Bois-le-Duc is not a "dead city," evidently. We sat down on a shaded seat for a while to watch the unloading of a brick barge. This work was being done by a gang of about twenty lusty women. They had to run up and down a rather steep incline from the low-laden boat to the top of the high embankment with a creel of bricks that would have winded many a stevedore. They did not seem to mind it; they even wasted their useful breath in superfluous laughter and chatter; their rosy faces were smirched with the inharmonious raw reds of brick dust; but they were happy. I was allowed to sketch them in peace, for a wonder. They were too busy to wish to look on, or even to shy a section of brick in our direction. It was a scene of picturesque and often statuesque poses of strong, striking, but mostly unlovely movements.

If a Watteau nymph could come to life and step from her sylvan groves in her glow of satin and snow of filmy lace to this scene, how her peach-and-cream flesh would shudder, her arched eyebrows and her violet eyes hide behind her azure fan, when she heard that these were but low-

CUTTING HERBAGE.

A WAY-SIDE CROSS.

lier sisters of her own race! And yet, if a worthy picture could be painted of this scene as I saw it, how well it would hang beside a good Watteau! They would only be characters in the same old fable, "La Cigale et la Fourmi."

There was much in Bois-le-Duc to tempt me to stay longer, but there was still stronger attraction toward distant Maastricht to tempt me onward. We therefore took the early train next day, and the slow—though, for the matter of that, the express itself in Holland leaves nothing to desire in the way of quiet deliberation. The ordinary slow train had for me two advantages: it would stop at nearly every station, and I could look about me; besides, it was cheaper, and consequently better filled with the people of the country. We nearly always went second or third class for this very reason, and were always in certain respects the better for it —at least I found my note-book the fuller for it. In our second-class compartment on that day there was a delightful old couple. She in full Holland bravery, with the inevitable modern bonnet stuck on the top of her national head-gear, of course; but the head-gear by itself was lovely, great filigree gold pendants hanging from the golden bosses at either temple, and a broad blade of chased gold set with scrolls of brilliants went across the forehead, and over it all a flowing cap of old Flemish lace. Jacob engaged them in sweet converse, as usual, and in no time they were interchanging snuff and on the best of terms. I was incidentally referred to by him, and my calling explained, and embroidered with romance and mystery, no doubt. We all got on delightfully together, and it ended in our being both invited to come and stay with them in North Holland for a few days, and they would show us the biggest dairy-farm in the country. Jacob elicited that they had been on a visit to a married daughter at Bois-le-Duc, and it was the first time the old lady had ever been so far from home. She furthermore declared that it would be about her last trip, as she did not care for strange countries or ways.

I was missing something of the country through my interest in our fellow-travellers. Occasionally, however, I would look out, but there would be little of marked variation from the usual Dutch landscape to note. The cottages were not so flourishing, or the land itself quite so fat and fertile, as the best, but it was all very pleasant and tidy. The fields were filled with workers, mostly women, of course, digging, delving, harrowing, weed - burning, manure-spreading, cutting cabbages, and sacking the potatoes. We waited for a good two hours at a way station. I forgot to note its name. I struck out into the country roads, and made a few notes of the lusty field hands who lend themselves so easily and well to the sketcher's needs. The landscape itself was here rather more Belgian, or even French, in character than Dutch; the low white cottages with the thatched roofs, the tall wispy trees with the tuft of sparse foliage atop, the shapes and colors of the distant church towers and spires, the blue blouses of the men, the close caps of the women and children, were good enough, but not quite like Holland. The many way - side shrines and *calvaires* told of a different race and faith in the strong ascendant. The closely shaven parish priest was no infrequent figure along the road, listening to the plaints of the poor, giving spiritual comfort, patting the fluffy heads of the children, and going on his various village duties. We always had a cheery return of our " Good-day" from them, and any information or pleasant chat in French that we might desire. I was making a sketch of a little maid, down on her knees cutting herbs for the rabbits at home, when the good curé strayed upon the scene, and took an interest in the proceeding, even so far as to bid the maid to keep a little quiet, and he would have favored us with her family history if I had had time. He pointed out his church spire from among a knot of roofs straggling up a sandy eminence in the middle distance. I made a mem., "to go back some day to investigate that village," it looked so filled with possibilities in sketching matter. We had many changes of scene on that day. It was not all smiling landscape and rich teeming fields. We passed by miles of bog and swamp, stunted forests of dwarf birch and scraggy pine, and acres of rich peat land, with groups of the diggers laboring in the black trenches, and looking as if they were digging so many soppy graves. They were not without a certain impressiveness,

such scenes, especially in the waning light of the afternoon, just as the crows were wending their way toward the scraggy wood. The streeling lines of flapping wings and their rasping bronchial note accorded well with the lines and the color note of the picture. We arrived at Wyk, the over-the-river suburb of Maastricht, just as the sun was going down. It gave us the kindly chance of seeing the finely varied outlines of the ancient city under the enhanced value of an evening effect. As we turned to go over the massive old stone bridge we got all the "relative values" of the gray old town with its fringe of belfries, towers, and pinnacles, its rambling roofs, and scrolly weathercocks cutting sharp against the twilight sky. The old town itself,

CATHEDRAL AT DORDRECHT.

dim and blurred with hazy smoke, was reflected in the tawny stream that runs past it. I had not much time to admire it. A hotel omnibus conductor, chilled with waiting at the station, is usually impelled with a strong desire to show the unexpected guests to his hotel landlady as soon as possible. It did not take us long to see our rooms, order a late dinner, and rush out again to see the last of the rosy light before it faded to ashen gray among the roofs and spires of the old capital of Lemburg. We first sought the great square to see the cathedral, said to have been commenced in the days of the Roman occupation. The ponderous masses of crumbling stone forming the bulk of the structure were built in the fashion of that time, but it looks more like a great work of defense, a citadel rather than a church. The late additions to it, during the fifteenth and sixteenth centuries, are those that give it its ecclesiastical character. On the wide open square, lined with spreading shade trees, are held the fairs and kermesse revels. It was at one time the cathedral cemetery, but many years ago they quietly flagged the dead over with their own grave-stones, and made the place what it is. Here the old mediæval pageants and processions occurred, and here during the days of conflicting creeds and faiths did "Christians burn each other, quite persuaded that the apostles would have done as *they* did."

The old town is far more German and Flemish in its architectural features than Dutch. The people are far behind the Hollanders in cleanliness and other good qualities. The outside views of the town, the old walls and the gardens straying down to the river, the quaint shipping, and all that, are quite worth going to see. The old churches, and the one old gate, called "De Helpoort," are very picturesque; but, for all that it has to show of strictly *Dutch* character, the sketcher in that direction had better keep to Haarlem, Middelburg, and Dordrecht. For all the combined good qualities of a fine old Netherlandish town, such as churches, houses, shipping, people, and country round about, I should say that Dordrecht would take the medal. I fain would have gone there again on my way home, for at last I heard of my long straying companion of last year as being there among a set of hard sketchers stopping at the "White Nag." But my own time was up, and I made the interesting bit of country between Maastricht and Flushing a sacrifice to my need to be at home. I parted with the faithful Jacob at Roosendaal. It was all I could do to prevent him from straying with me down to Flushing—"to mek shoor you kitz de right boat."

PRESIDENT JOHNSON TEACHING HIS FIRST CLASS.

KING'S COLLEGE.

THERE was a time when "God Save the King" was the national anthem for America as well as England. Then came the change to "Hail Columbia." The change was reflected directly in that home of learning which is now taking its proper place in New York as the metropolitan university. Until 1784, "C-o-l-u-m-b-i-a," as the college men now shout it, was called King's College, a name which it shared with an older sister in old England, whose lovely chapel is one of the fairest sights on the banks of the quiet Cam. A younger sister of the same name stands on the shore of a busier stream, the Strand, London, and is, in its modest way, also a metropolitan university.

The earliest mention of King's College, New York, is to be found in the records of Trinity Church, in the year 1703, when the rector and wardens were directed to wait upon Lord Cornbury, then Governor of the Province of New York, to know what part of "the King's Farme," then vested in Trinity Church, had been intended for the proposed college.

The answer does not appear, and nothing seems to have been done till 1746, when an act was passed "for raising the sum of £2250 by a public lottery for this colony, for the encouragement of learning, and toward the founding of a college within the same." By 1751, £3443 18s. had been collected for the expenses of a college;

SAMUEL JOHNSON.

forms led him finally to the Prayer-book, which caused his conversion to Episcopacy. His enforced voyage to England for the purpose of being ordained brought him into contact with the most cultivated of the English clergy, and their letters, still extant, show the very high esteem and regard they entertained for him.

Returning after an absence of ten months, he settled down to his parish work. His two sons were born in 1727 and 1731. Wishing them to be thoroughly educated, he concluded to educate them himself, and for their advantage, as well as his own, he took also as pupils the sons of several gentlemen of New York and Albany. At the age of thirteen each of his sons was admitted to Yale College.

Though earnestly besought by the founders of King's College, Dr. Johnson was very loath, much as he loved colleges and college life, to leave the literary ease and calm repose of his rural parish for the turmoil of a great city and the vicinity of the small-pox. The dread of this disease was itself a disease with the worthy gentleman, and seems almost ludicrous to us of to-day, who forget what a dreadful scourge this was in the early days of New York. His correspondence is so full of small-pox that his very letters seem to need vaccination. The small-pox seems to have known his weakness, and to have followed him up mercilessly.

He was, however, much consulted by the trustees, giving them excellent advice, and thus becoming more and more interested in the undertaking, so that at last, when all concerned declared that unless he would accept the presidency they would entirely abandon the enterprise, he yielded.

Meanwhile the projectors of the college had been fiercely assailed by those who were hostile to the Episcopal Church, on the ground that they were about to sacrifice the public good to that of a sect.

The charter of King's College made the best possible reply to this charge of sectarianism by placing among the first governors ministers of the Reformed Dutch, the Lutheran, the French Protestant, and the Presbyterian churches, as well as, at the suggestion of the Rev. Mr. Ritzema, senior minister of the Reformed Dutch Church, establishing a professor in divinity according to the doctrines of that

and finally, October 31, 1754, the charter was granted by James De Lancey, the Lieutenant-Governor.

The Rev. Dr. Samuel Johnson was appointed first president. This remarkable man seems to have been considered an expert in starting colleges; he had been first tutor of Yale College, when it was established at New Haven; he was first president of King's College; and he declined being first president of the Philadelphia College, though warmly pressed thereto by Benjamin Franklin. Born in 1696 in Guilford, Connecticut, at fourteen he entered Yale College, which was then at Saybrook. On graduating (1714) he took charge of a high school at Guilford, and began to preach, though only eighteen. Two years after, he was elected by the trustees as tutor of Yale College, then removed to New Haven, and took entire charge of that institution, having under him fifteen students. Four years after, he resigned, was ordained, and settled at West Haven, where he was near the college and its library. Though prejudiced by education against the Church of England, he felt a growing dislike for extempore prayers, and his search for fixed

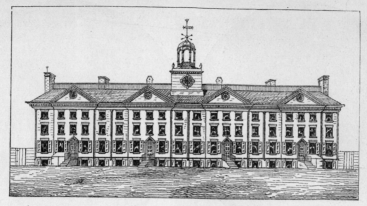

KING'S COLLEGE.——From an Old Print.

Church. The charter also provided that the governors should make no laws "to exclude any Person of any religious Denomination whatever from equal Liberty and Advantages, or from any of the Degrees, Liberties, Privileges, Benefits, or Immunities of the said College, on Account of his particular Tenets in Matters of Religion."

President Johnson, also, in his first advertisement in the New York *Gazette*, of June 3, 1754, said:

"And as to the daily worship in the College, Morning and Evening, it is proposed that it should ordinarily consist of such a collection of Lessons, Prayers, and Praises of the Liturgy of the Church as are for the most Part taken out of the Holy Scriptures, and such as are agreed on by the Trustees to be in the best Manner expressive of our common Christianity; and as to any peculiar Tenets, every one is left to judge freely for himself, and to be required only to attend constantly at such Places of Worship, on the Lord's Day, as their Parents or Guardians shall think fit to order or permit."

In this same advertisement the charge for tuition is named as twenty-five shillings per quarter. As provincial currency was worth about one-third less than sterling, this would be about $4 25, making the entire annual charge about $17. The salary of the president was £250. Trinity Church made him an assistant minister, with light duties and a salary of £150, making in all £400, equal to about $1300. His assistant, Mr. Chauncey Whittlesey, was given a salary of £200.

On the 17th of July, 1754, the worthy president might have been seen in the vestry-room in the school-house attached to Trinity Church, teaching the eight students who then constituted King's College. Their names were Samuel Verplanck, Rudolph Ritzema, Philip Van Cortlandt, Robert Bayard, Samuel Provoost, Thomas Marston, Henry Cruger, and Joshua Bloomer. When a second class was admitted, his younger son was employed as an assistant.

In 1755, Trinity Church granted to the college a piece of ground "in the West Ward," bounded by Church, Barclay, and Murray streets, and running down to the North River, on condition that the president should always be a member of the Episcopal Church, and that the college prayers should be drawn from the Prayer-book. The consideration was the sum of ten shillings, and an annual rental of a pepper-corn. It is suspected that the

COPPER CROWN ON CUPOLA.

trustees have not paid their rent as promptly as they should have done, and if Trinity Church should claim the arrearages at compound interest, the consequences might be appalling.

In this same year the charter was finally delivered to the governors, who were sworn in by Mr. Daniel Horsmanden, one

SILVER MEDAL OF KING'S COLLEGE.

of the judges of the Supreme Court. Besides the sixteen *ex officio* governors, the following twenty-four gentlemen had been appointed: Joseph Murray, Henry Beekman, John Watts, James De Lancey, Oliver De Lancey, David Clarkson, Joseph Robinson, Joseph Reade, Leonard Lispenard (whose names still live in the names of our streets), Benjamin Nicoll (a step-son of President Johnson), Archibald Kennedy, Josiah Martin, Paul Richard, John Cruger, Henry Cruger, William Walton, Philip Verplanck, Frederic Philipse, James Livingston, William Livingston, John Livingston, Nathaniel Marston, Joseph Haynes, and Abraham Lodge. They held their first meeting May 17, 1755, and June 3 adopted the college seal now so familiar.

The governors decided to build, for college purposes, a "lime house," 180 feet by 30. Two plans were presented. With reckless liberality they selected that which had a cupola. This cupola was long surmounted by a copper crown, still to be seen in the library of Columbia College. Sir Stratford Canning, who, under the name of Lord Stratford de Redcliffe, was for so many years all-powerful at Constantinople, and who was himself a scholar of King's College, Cambridge, was shown this old crown of our King's College by Professor McVickar in 1820. Turning gravely to the professor, he said, "You should preserve that crown carefully, sir, for you republicans will by-and-by need a crown." It was determined to locate the

college building "in the skirts of the city," on the land granted by Trinity Church, and the first stone, with a suitable inscription,* was laid on the 23d of August, 1756, by the Governor, Sir Charles Hardy, the bluff old sea-captain, who next year was made Rear-Admiral of the Blue. When he came first to the province the enemies of the college tried hard to win him over, but he decided in its favor, and emphasized his decision by presenting to it £500.

In November, 1755, President Johnson's younger son went to England to be ordained, and Mr. Leonard Cutting, a graduate of Eton and of Oxford, took his place as tutor. In September following, President Johnson received the terrible news of his son's death by small-pox in London, and the appearance of that disease in New York city drove him to Westchester. He left the thirty pupils in the three classes in charge of Mr. Cutting, to whom Mr. Daniel Treadwell, a graduate of Harvard College, was added as an assistant, with the title of Professor of Mathematics and Natural Philosophy.

The president's enemy did not desert him even in his rural retreat, for in March, 1758, he wrote, with grim humor, to his son:

"The young fellows here purposely take the small-pox so much, that I believe we can not be any longer safer here than at town."

---

* When the old college was torn down, in 1857, this corner-stone was preserved, and it is now carefully imbedded in the wall of the college chapel.

But in running away from small-pox he had invited more insidious danger, for his wife, to whom he was tenderly attached, died on the 1st of June, 1758, of consumption, following upon malarial fever contracted in Westchester.

As it had already "been decided to hold the first Commencement of the college on the 21st of June, and President Johnson was desirous of having his students make a good appearance, he turned resolutely from his domestic grief, and set himself seriously at work to prepare for this occasion. The graduating class numbered eight, and the two tutors, Cutting and Treadwell, with eleven other gentlemen, were admitted to the degree of Master of Arts."*

The second Commencement of the college, in 1759, was necessarily private, only one student being admitted to the degree of Bachelor of Arts. How lonesome Epenetus Townsend must have been!

In the records of the college are some quaint remarks about certain of his companions who began their college life with him, but afterward left him in the lurch. Of one it is said that "in his third year he went to Philadelphia College"; of another, that " about the middle of his second year he went into the army"; of another, that he, "after three years, went to merchandise"; of another, that "after about two years he went privateering";† and of

---

* Beardsley's excellent life of Dr. Johnson.

† Privateering was at this time fashionable on both sides of the Atlantic. The Manual of the Common Council for 1870 gives a list of those engaged in privateering from the port of New York, which includes the names of almost all the best families in the city.

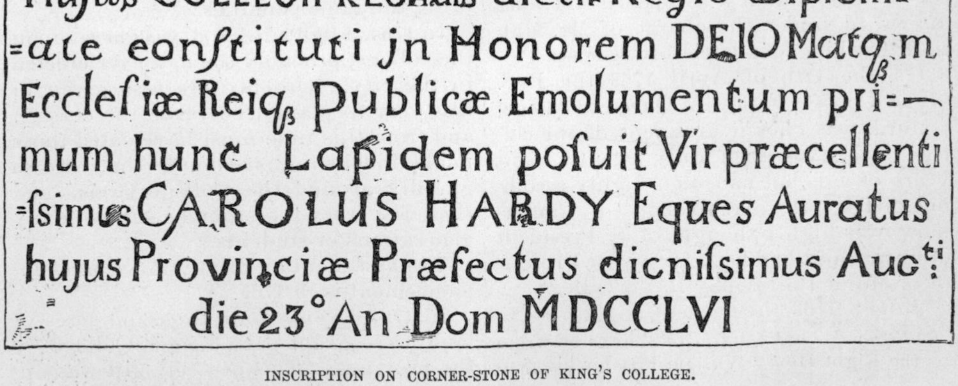

---

another, that "after three years he went to nothing."

Meanwhile the college building "was going on vigorously," and soon afterward the Board of Foreign Missions granted the college £500.

In the fall of 1759 President Johnson again ran away from the small-pox, this time to Stratford. Returning to the city in May, he found that his long absence and the loss of his "best tutor" had been a serious detriment to the institution. Several of the students withdrew, and the future was gloomy. All his energy was needed to recover from these losses, and get back the confidence of those who had grown lukewarm.

The college building, three stories high, "in a delightful situation" near the river, was so far completed that he moved into it, and "set up housekeeping and tuition there," being the first to live in King's College, as he had been the first to live in Yale College, "a little more than forty years before." The officers and students also began this year (1760) to mess in the college.

In May, 1762, Dr. James Jay was made solicitor for the college in England. This arrangement brought nearly £6000, including a special donation of £600 from his Majesty George III. About this time also Mr. Joseph Murray bequeathed his estate of £9000 to the college. This helped to furnish the library already started, Rev. Dr. Bristowe, of England, having previously bequeathed his own library of 1500 volumes.

At the fifth Commencement Dr. Johnson was carried to the chapel in a close

INSCRIPTION ON CORNER-STONE OF KING'S COLLEGE.

MYLES COOPER.

erous Donation to the College, for the Regard he expresses for the Institution and the Interest of America in General, and hope that he will continue the same on future occasions."

In this year also new statutes were carefully made, which ordered "an habitation to be assigned to each student in the college," and a penalty of five shillings for a student's first night of absence, eight for the second, "twelve for the third (or adequate exercises)," and finally expulsion. Within fourteen days of his entrance "a proper Academical Habit" must be procured, "in which he shall always appear (unless he have leave from the president or tutors), under the penalty of two shillings for the first offence, and so in proportion (or adequate exercises)." Each student must "attend morning and evening prayers in the college, and also public worship on the Lord's Day. . . . under penalty of four pence for each omission, or proportionate exercise." Three-quarters of an hour were allowed for breakfast, an hour and a half for dinner, and from evening prayers to bed-time for recreation.

The money from fines is to be spent in books to reward the diligent. Tardiness at "studying-time" shall bring a fine of "two Pence for the first half-hour," four for the second, etc. The outer gates are to be locked at 10 P.M. in summer and 9 in winter. Coming in after this shall bring a fine of sixpence for the first hour, one shilling for the second, etc. Getting through the college fence or over it shall bring the same penalties.

In 1764, a lightning-rod was placed upon the college, probably the first ever erected in the city. Orders were also given in this year to plant trees near the college, and from this time must have dated those noble lindens and sycamores that rose so grandly around the College Green, and sheltered from the summer sun so many generations of students.

The first mention of any music at Commencement is in 1765.

In 1767, twenty-four thousand acres of land were granted to King's College by the province. This princely gift was un-

carriage, through fear of the small-pox. The next year the dreaded disease seized upon his second wife (the mother of his son's wife), and her loss hastened the execution of his previous decision to resign his post as president. After reluctantly accepting his resignation, the governors voted him a yearly pension of £50—a sum very much more in accordance with their income than their wishes. At the same meeting at which Dr. Johnson's resignation was announced, a plan was adopted for the establishment of a grammar school in connection with the college, and it was opened not long afterward under the charge of Mr. Matthew Cushing, of Charlestown, Mass.

On the 12th of April, 1763, the Rev. Myles Cooper, Fellow of Queen's College, Oxford, was chosen president of the college. He was then only twenty-eight years of age, but had been highly recommended by the Archbishop of Canterbury, was highly thought of by President Johnson, and had been for a year Professor of Moral Philosophy in the college.

June 2, 1763, the trustees

"Resolved, That a letter of thanks be wrote to the Right Honble William Pitt for his gen-

fortunately located in the eastern part of the State, and was ultimately included in lands ceded to the people of Vermont, without any compensation at the time being made to the college. The system of leasing the property in the city for twenty-one years, as allowed by charter, seems to have been begun the previous year.

In 1769 the first medical college was founded under the auspices of King's College, and partly in consequence of the enthusiasm aroused by an address of Dr. Bard at the college Commencement. From his eloquent discourse also sprang our present New York Hospital.

"A Book of Misdemeanors, *alias* Black Book," which is now preserved in the library of the college, purports to have been commenced in January, 1771, and ends April 24, 1775. From this it is evident that the pranks of our progenitors were wonderfully like our own. The following extracts will suffice:

"*Feb.*, 1771.—S—— reprimanded publicly for having come through a hole in the College Fence at twelve o'clock at night."

"*July* 9, 1772.—V——, D——, and N——, who had gone over the College Fence the preceding Tuesday, between the hours of 3 and 4 P.M., to bathe, were reprimanded, confined to College until Saturday, and each directed to translate into Latin four pages of Dr. Chandler's Charity Sermon."

"*Dec.* 23, 1774.—W——, for not performing his exercise the last Vacation, as ordered by ye preceding visitation, to finish that, and also to translate half of the eighth Æneid of Virgil into English by ye first day of next term."*

In 1774, it was ordered that no more wood should be used as fuel, coal taking its place.

The most distinguished student of King's College, Alexander Hamilton, matriculated in 1774. At that time all men's minds were deeply moved by the great question of the Revolution. President Cooper sided with the mother country, talking and writing with all his power against the freedom of the colonies. The tide of indignation rising higher and higher against such doctrines, it was finally determined to hold a public meeting in the

---

* It is interesting to know that Marinus Willett, the W—— above referred to, was afterward presented with an elegant sword by Congress for a gallant sortie from a beleaguered fort, and after the war was made Mayor of our city.

open fields just above Dey Street, on the 6th of July, 1774, for the purpose of protesting against the acts of the authorities.

Young Hamilton was urged to address the meeting, and as he closed a brilliant and impassioned address, the cry of surprise, "It is a collegian," with which his youthful appearance was received, gave way to loud expressions of wonder and applause.

Young Hamilton presently crossed swords, or pens, with his college president, who could not believe at first that so young a man could be so strong a pamphleteer. In one of the periods of the excitement a liberty mob approached the college with the purpose of laying vio-

MARINUS WILLETT.

lent hands on the Tory president. As they drew near his residence, Hamilton and Robert Troup, a fellow-student, ascended the steps, and fearful lest in this moment of irritation they might commit some excess, Hamilton, in order to give the president time to escape, harangued the mob with great eloquence and animation "on the excessive impropriety of their conduct, and the disgrace they were bringing on the cause of liberty, of which they professed to be the champions."

In the mean time another student, who had preceded the throng, had warned the president of his danger, just in time to

HAMILTON ADDRESSING THE MOB.

save him. "He escaped only half dressed over the college fence, reached the shore of the Hudson, and wandered along the river-bank till near morning, when he found shelter in the house of his friend Mr. Stuyvesant, where he remained for that day, and during the night following took refuge on board the *Kingfish-* *er*, an English ship of war, in which soon afterward he sailed for England."

Six days after his escape, the Rev. Benjamin Moore, an alumnus of the college, was appointed Praeses *pro tempore*. Owing to the state of affairs there was no public Commencement, but the degree of Bachelor of Arts was conferred on seven students, that of Master of Arts on two alumni of the college, and eight students were admitted.

On the 6th of April, 1776, a message was sent to the treasurer of the college, signed by Robert Benson, and purporting to be from a number of men who styled themselves "The Committee of Safety," desiring the governors to prepare the college within six days for the reception of troops. The students were consequently dispersed, the library and apparatus were deposited in the City Hall, or elsewhere, and the college edifice was thenceforth devoted to military purposes until the arrival of the British. By them it was used as a military prison.

They crossed to New York on Sunday, September 15, 1776. On Saturday, September 21, a great fire broke out about 2 A.M., and raged from the Battery to St. Paul's Church and the college, having been "arrested by the College Green and a change of wind," but not before it had destroyed "four hundred and ninety-three houses—nearly one-third of the city."

The college was doubtless used for military purposes until the British evacuated the city, in November, 1783. The history of King's College ends of course with the evacuation, and no establishment of learning could win a higher eulogy than that bestowed by the Hon. Benjamin F. Butler, who stood for so many years in the front rank of the New York bar: "The influence of that institution on the literary character of the State was truly wonderful; for though the whole number of students educated in the college prior to 1775 was but one hundred, many of them attained to the highest distinction in their respective professions and in public life."

A HOME OF TOMMY ATKINS.

IT is a bright sunny morning, one of those rare English summer days, peaceful and calm, the blue sky broken with fleecy, drifting clouds casting their shadows on the purple heather-covered hills and tawny sandy valleys, and by the ever-changing masses of light and shade lending even to the monotonous rows of brown huts and yellow brick barracks of Aldershot camp something of color and of the picturesque. There is little stirring in the straight side streets running at right angles with our road, and lined with their rows of huts, intersecting each other with the regularity of the squares on a checker-board, as it is the hour of drill, and the troops are out on the parades or off at musketry drill, and we can hear now and then the far-off reports of their rifles or the distant blare of a bugle, while behind the white tents, gleaming brightly in the sunlight away over under Peak Hill, where some troops are lying under canvas, the cloud of dust rising from the "Dust Hole" betokens the presence there of the artillerymen at their morning exercises. We pass a guard-house where the sentry, rifle in hand, paces up and down his beat, and the soldiers of the guard sit on benches on the shady side of the hut, lazily dozing or sucking at their short pipes. Now and then we meet a soldier engaged on some fatigue duty; a working party in their canvas overalls, picks and shovels on their shoulders, crosses the road; a smart hussar orderly, his busby strapped under his chin, and trappings clanking on his horse's flanks, trots by; the hum of children's voices from the school-house near the married soldiers' quarters of some regiment strikes our ears; and in the trim little gardens about the officers' houses a man is working about the flower beds. Passing the green lawns and well-trimmed hedges of the officers' club grounds, we roll over the bridge crossing the canal, catching a glimpse, as we do so, of some boating man leisurely sculling over the smooth glassy surface, or an occasional angler, his red jacket reflected in the still water. Down in a pretty green valley, relieving picturesquely against dark masses of trees, lies an infantry camp, and on its edge some of the men are busy about the earthen ovens preparing the noonday meal.

As we turn a corner I catch sight of a body of troops coming toward us, their band playing an almost forgotten tune, an air that I had often heard in my own country, and it carries my memory back to the time when the sound of martial music was almost as familiar to American ears as the ringing of the church bells. By their dark green uniforms, so dark as to be almost black, I know them

A MEASURE OF DISCIPLINE.

to be riflemen. They form one of the battalions of the "King's Royal Rifles," the "Royal Americans," raised originally in America, and which served there in the French and Indian war, still proudly bearing on its record the names of some of the bloody battles of that conflict, the result of which assured to the British crown the possession of the Canadas. We stop as they pass, marching with a quick, cadenced step, middle-sized sturdy fellows, their Glengarries cocked rakishly on one side of their heads, their shining black leathers and the silver ornaments on the officers' trappings gleaming brightly in the sunlight. There is a smart, tidy look about the men in spite of their hard morning's drill in the "Long Valley," and the consequent powdering of yellow dust they have received. I watch them as they wheel off the road, moving over the level surface of the "Queen's Parade," now being crossed in various directions by returning battalions, winding in scarlet-hued and glittering columns over the green turf, while the air is filled with the scream of the fifes and the stirring rattle of the drums. As it nears the lines of huts the battalion halts, and a group of men, who have been awaiting its approach, advances and takes position facing it, while at a command from their chief the officers sheathe their sabres, and leaving the ranks, form an irregular semicircle about him. A measure of discipline is to be enforced, and the men are to witness the punishment and disgrace of one of their number. The man, a sergeant, a rather good-looking young fellow, with crisp, curling blonde hair and sunburned face, seems keenly to feel his position, as, under guard of a soldier with drawn bayonet, he stands with bowed head and cap in hand facing his comrades, while the adjutant in monotonous, formal tones reads aloud the record of his offense, his trial, and his sentence. Hardly has the sound of the last words of the officer died away, when the sergeant-major, with a few rapid cuts of his knife, severs the chevrons from the sleeves of the culprit's tunic, and as the badges of his former rank drop to the ground, the latter, bringing his hand to his forehead in salute to his officers, rapidly marches down the front of the line, and returns to his quarters. It was a painful scene, and seems to have made an impression on the men as they are dismissed and move silently off the ground.

My friends, stationed at the camp, receive me with the frank, generous hospitality of the English officer, and their kind and friendly treatment soon makes me feel thoroughly at home among them, free to come and go as I please, and to

pipe-clay and brush, can make them, proud of their position and of their profession, and often exercising fully as much authority over the men under them as the best of their officers.

A canteen where the soldier can purchase at moderate rates many of the little luxuries of life, libraries, reading, smoking, and recreation rooms, are attached to the large barracks at Aldershot. Here theatrical performances, often of considerable merit, are frequently given by the men, and the soldiers can always rely upon

ON THE CAMP GROUND.

make my acquaintance with Tommy Atkins at my leisure. All branches of the service are represented here—engineers, artillery, "horse, foot, and dragoons," and all the varied types of character in the army are to be met with, from the little drummer-boy born in the service to the hardened non-commissioned officer of a dozen campaigns. Magnificent types of the soldier these latter, as they pass through the streets with ringing strides, straight as arrows, neat as soap and water,

the generous support of their officers in their amusements. The theatre or music hall at the Royal Artillery Barracks is generally well attended almost any evening, and a good "song and dance" man enjoys no mean degree of popularity among his comrades.

But it is in the innate love that all Englishmen bear for athletic sports that "Tommy" comes out in his full glory, and his officers do not disdain to meet him on equal grounds at cricket, foot-ball, and

A BATHING POST.

other out-door games. Different branches of the service frequently meet in friendly rivalry, and many a match is played on the grounds of the officers' club between teams of various regiments or corps, selected from among the officers and men, irrespective of their military rank. It is not an unusual sight to see a game among the officers "umpired" by some veteran non-commissioned officer, skilled in all the intricacies of the national game of cricket.

The most interesting of the purely martial sports—if I can use the word in reference to what forms part of the drill of the cavalry and mounted artillery—are the exciting contests of sabre *versus* sabre, or sabre *versus* lance, and the like, when some rival "rough - riders" are pitted against one another. One can easily imagine how the tournaments of old appeared, to see these active fellows, mounted on their fine horses, which seem to sympathize with and enter into the spirit of their riders, as, clad in stout leather tunics, their heads protected with strong wire masks, they charge down on one another, cutting, thrusting, and parrying, retreating

and pursuing. Hard knocks are given and received with apparent good-humor, though I doubt not that long habits of discipline restrain many an honest fellow's temper when his blood is up. It is rough but manly work, and one does not wonder, on seeing what training they go through, that the British horsemen are renowned for their courage and dexterity. Another sport in which the nerve and coolness that go so far toward making a good cavalier are displayed to great advantage is tent-pegging, introduced, I believe, into the British army by the native cavalrymen of the Indian service. The player, armed with a light bamboo lance, puts his horse at full gallop over the course, and strikes with his lance head a tent peg protruding a few inches out of the ground, into which one end has been firmly driven. See how firmly yet lightly the soldier sits his horse, body bent forward, lance couched, thundering forward at the top of his horse's speed. Lower down on his charger's neck, a tighter clasp of the legs, nearer and nearer—the exact moment must be rightly chosen—a slight turn of the wrist of the practiced bridle hand—

now! crash!—and he swings back upright into the saddle, waving the light lance triumphantly above his head, with the splintered piece of wood transfixed on its iron point.

of admiring friends; their cries and laughter, a burst of applause at some more than usually dexterous play, mingle with the music of the band standing under the overhanging branches of the trees near

TENT-PEGGING.

A favorite resort of the officers of the garrison and their families is the park-like inclosure of the "Club Grounds," with its pleasant groups of shade trees, its green velvety lawns and winding paths, and the scene here on any sunny summer afternoon is an animated one. A large space is devoted to the game of lawn tennis, and the swift, graceful movements of the players, among whom are many ladies, are watched with interest by little knots

the cricket grounds, or in the pagoda-like band stand. Every one, with the exception of an occasional soldier, servant, or bandsman, is in plain clothes—for the English officer, unlike those of the Continental armies, wears his uniform only while actually on duty or at mess—and nearly every one is accompanied by his faithful four-footed companion, his dog.

A quiet row late in the afternoon, with one or two agreeable companions, on the smooth waters of the canal, now in disuse, is a pleasure not soon to be forgotten. Gliding between its pretty banks, with their overhanging fringe of bushes and beds of water-weeds, one would scarcely realize that one is really in the midst of a vast camp, with all its busy bustle of military life, were it not for the occasional redcoat, asleep in the shade of some group of trees, or idly angling in the still, calm waters. We pass a group disporting in the water, and the scarlet coats hanging on the trees, over the other heaps of clothing scattered about, show plainly enough that it is composed of soldiers.

There are miles of pretty walks about Aldershot, through lovely country lanes or past sleeping ponds of water, up to the purple, fir-topped Fox Hills, or along the Hog's Back on the road to Guildford, past little way-side inns, old vine-covered cottages with latticed windows and blooming flower gardens, quiet country churches in the centre of a little colony of grassy graves, marked with moss-covered stones, green hedges with wide-spreading yew-trees and scarlet-berried holly.

And now the quiet of the summer season, with its round of drills, parades, inspections, and all the daily recurring episodes of the life of the camp, is broken by darkening thunder-clouds of war, sweeping up in gloomy, threatening masses and flashes of lurid lightning from the eastward of the political horizon.

Marching orders from the Horse-Guards have arrived. Aldershot is in a state of excitement and bustle, preparing and mustering the forces for departure for the seat of war, and Tommy, ever ready for a fight, or a change in the monotony of his daily existence, is filled with enthusiasm and eager for the fray.

It is between three and four o'clock in the morning, and the gray light is just stealing through the mist of the gently falling rain, as I stand in the Farnsborough station listening to the distant cheering and the plaintive strains of "Auld Lang Syne," which betoken the approach of some departing regiment. A long line of railway carriages and horse trucks, their wet tops glistening, and the black smoke from the locomotive curling over them, stands in readiness alongside the platform. Some porters are engaged taking off the tarpaulins that have covered a little pile of luggage, and are stowing it

away in one of the vans, and the stationmaster and his assistants are hurrying about, busy in their preparations for the reception of their freight. Up the station road two horsemen, trotting rapidly along, loom up through the mist; further behind them we can see a dark mass moving slowly toward us, and the sound of the music grows louder and more distinct as the troops come forward and halt on the brow of the hill above the station. They are cavalry, and as the leading squadron breaks from the column and marches in through the gates we see that they are hussars. The men are clad in their campaign dresses—dark blue serge blouses, white sun helmets and "puggarees," well-filled haversacks and canteens, untanned leather boots, carbines, and sabres. Their saddles are packed in heavy marching order, and there is a decidedly business-like look about both men and horses. They dismount and form their horses into line, unbuckle their sabres, and together with the carbines place them on the ground in their rear, and immediately commence the business of embarking. One by one the horses are led forward, and driven, pushed, and forced into the trucks. Gradually the inclosure about the station is filling up. A general officer with his aide and a couple of orderlies has arrived, a brake filled with officers who have come to bid their friends farewell drives up, and here and there a poor soldier's wife with tear-stained face, perhaps two or three tow-headed children clinging to her skirts, sobs on the shoulder of some stalwart fellow. The scene becomes livelier as the awakening day sheds fuller light on the busy crowd, and troop after troop enters the station as the horses of the preceding ones are put on board the train; bundles of hay and forage for the baiting of the horses during the journey to the coast are handed into the cars from the heavy wagons of the Army Service Corps, luggage is stowed away under the seats in the carriages, or corded firmly under the tarpaulins on the tops. Near the first-class carriage at the head of the train the officers are smoking a parting cigar with their friends, sergeants and corporals and busy orderlies are moving about, and the men, picking up their weapons, are falling in again preparatory to embarking in their turn. The colonel is receiving a few parting directions from the general, a fine, aristocratic, middle-aged gentleman with

THE GIRL I LEFT BEHIND ME.

soldierly bearing and gray military mustache and whiskers, the gold-braided peak of his cap drawn down over his eyes, and his overcoat covering his plain, tasteful, undress uniform. The last horse has been shut in; the last straggling soldier has taken his place in the carriages, the windows of which are crowded with heads; the last good-byes are said; sobbing women and children watch husband and father with streaming eyes; the younger and more thoughtless of the soldiers are cracking their parting jokes. The colonel touches his helmet, and with a shake of the general's hand turns to the train. "Get on board, gentlemen!" to the officers. "All ready." The station-master raises his hand, the whistle of the locomotive shrieks, the band on the platform strikes up "Auld Lang Syne" again. Slowly the great driving-wheels of the engine begin to move. Good-by, Mary, Tom, Katie. God bless you! Good luck! And amid loud cheers the long train glides down the long line of glistening rails and disappears around a curve.

CHARLES STEWART.

MY LIFE AS A SLAVE.

THE following autobiographical narrative has been taken down almost verbatim from the lips of its hero, an old negro man, who has dictated or told the whole of it with absolutely no help but his own memory. He does not read at all, or, of course, write either, though he once knew his alphabet, and there are none of his contemporaries alive in this part of the country, all the older members of his last owner's family, with whom he still remains, being dead, and none of those among them, to whom old Charles has been a life-long servant and friend, I might almost say necessity, knowing anything about the names and dates of races and race-horses, which are given exactly as he remembers them. Nothing throughout has been altered in any way except to make the details as consecutive and the dialect as intelligible as possible, and perhaps it may be as well to add here the facts necessary to complete his story. He does not exaggerate in any way his life in Virginia; he was the favorite and trusted servant of Colonel Johnson during his whole career with him, was in charge of first one training stable, then another, and for several years was employed with the entire care of valuable race-horses and stud-horses, which he took from place to place and course to course in Kentucky, among others, as he mentions, Monsieur Tonson and Medley. At such a distance from his master, and unable even to read his letters of instruction himself, he yet discharged his duties excellently, keeping long accounts in his head, and handling the large sums of money which were constantly passing through his hands with scrupulous accuracy and care. All these facts about him are gathered from letters, family tradition, and the direct report of his masters to the writer's mother, all of which confirm his own perfectly literal and impartial statements. When purchased by Judge Porter, of Louisiana, he was at once placed in charge of a racing establishment where there were never less than twelve horses in training, and which kept forty or forty-five men and boys constantly employed. It was a position of much care and responsibility, for there was a race-course on the plantation which was a favorite centre for turfmen, and Charles was called upon to train horses for this or that gentleman so frequently that he was compelled to establish a system, and undertake so much and no more.

After Judge Porter's death, in 1843, Charles remained in his new home in the service of his late owner's brother, who left him where he found him, as head trainer; and in that position, travelling every spring and autumn to one course or another as the horses went to fulfill their engagements, he continued until his master's death, and the consequent breaking up of the racing establishment, reduced him to the less glorious level of family coachman, and general "boss" of everything in the way of horseflesh on the place. During the war he never left his mistress, who was alone on the plantation during the whole period, for a single day, and since its close he has been the constant, never-failing factotum, adherent, and, as he calls it, "'pendence" of the whole family.

About ten days ago the writer said to him: "Uncle Charles, I want you to come in this evening and tell me all you can remember that ever happened to you, from the very beginning, and let me see if I can not write it down so that people can read it. You have told me so many things about when you were young, I want to put it all down together in black and white." The old man was deeply interested at once, and when he fully understood the object in view, his pride and delight exceeded all bounds. He went off to his own house, which is quite near, and for the rest of the day refused to speak or be spoken to, on the plea that he was "studyin'." In the evening, at what he calls early candle-light, he appeared, arrayed in his Sunday clothes, and it being a warm night in June, the feeling of self-respect must have been genuine indeed which compelled him to put on a plush waistcoat reaching nearly to his knees, heavy white velveteen trousers ending in a pair of shooting gaiters, the whole surmounted by a long black frock-coat, a spotted silk cravat of vast size, and a small jockey's cap. It was a brilliant, clear evening, and his own cabin not two hundred yards off, yet he carried a blue cotton umbrella of the very largest size. In this costume he has presented himself every evening since for the *séances* whose results are given in this sketch, although during the day he works about the place in an airy suit of guinea blue much better adapted to the weather. In spite of his eighty-four or five years, Charles is an extremely active, hard-working man, always busy at carpentering, gardening, shoe-making, or "horse-doctoring," in which branch of medicine he is a great authority. His third wife, whom he married after he came to Louisiana, is still living, and has three grown children, who are of little assistance or profit to their father. But he has a nice little homestead of five or six acres, with a cabin on it, which he has almost entirely built himself within the past two years, and he has already planted the place, of which he only two years ago became owner, with fruit trees and vines and shrubs of every description.

De fust thing dat I remembers of is de little town of Pocahontas, 'crost de river from Petersburg, en Virginia, an' ef you sarched dat whole town troo from eend to eend you couldn't ha' lit down on no big-

ger little yaller rascal dan me when I fust
begin to take good notice of myself.　Dat
I was!　A rascal, hide an' hyar, sho's you
born.　My father—dat is, I hear folks say
dat was my daddy, an' he 'lowed so his-
self; but mammy she lived with Aunt
Mary Stevens, an' 'cept fur her being his
full sister she neber let on no more'n dat
—he lived en a good, large house, an' he
was a sea-farrin man, a mighty light
mulatter; he looked like one o' dese yere
Mexikin somebodies.　His wife an' chillen staid right dar all de time, an' I 'vid-
ed my time 'twixt dar an' Aunt Mary Stevens's, whar mammy staid when she
warn't out home at ole Marster Enoch
Vaughan's, what she belonged to, an' I
took a spell o' stayin' out dar sometimes.
Mammy's name was Sally; father his
name was Charles Stewart; he was free,
an' so was all his folks.　I lived amongst
'em all, jes' as limber an' mischievious
as any little 'coon dat eber stole corn.
Colonel Enoch Vaughan's place was two
miles from town, on de heights near Major Butts's, ole Gin'ral Harrison's father-
in-law.　I neber knowed which I liked de
best: to hear de white gen'lemen out dar
tellin' 'bout de rebelspishonary wars, an'
all de ely*ments* dat tuk place when dey
was fightin' agin the British mens, or to
set en de chimbley-corner en my daddy's
house an' hear him a-tellin' an' narratin'
all about dem whalin' vyages he went on,
whar de fishes has got calves, an' gives
milk same as cows, and cuts up *dat fat!*
dar ain't no hog ever wallered in de mud
dat could give a drap for a bucket, *even
countin'*, wid one o' dem almighty fat
critters.　He was mighty good to me, an'
I kin ricolleck now how it was share an'
share alike wid his yother chillen, an' how
his sister, Aunt Mary Stevens, was allers
givin' me cake an' clo's an' candy.

You see, de ole Colonel Vaughan died
when I was a baby-child, an' de 'state was
sort of all sproshered [mixed] up, so dey
jes' left me at my daddy's, an' he tried time
an' agin to buy me; but dey wouldn't sell
me, nor hear about it.　Well, arter I
was goin' on 'bout ten or 'leven year old,
my young mistis, Miss Lizzie Pace, what
used to be Miss Lizzie Vaughan, dat I done
fell arr to when her pa done died, she got
broke en conserkerwenz of her husband
losin' money—something I neber could
unnerstan', kase I allers heerd he neber
had none, nohow—an 'so my daddy he was
gone, an' dey jes' up an' sole me en my

tracks ter Colonel William R. Johnson.
De Napoleon of de Turf was de name he
went by from Dandy to Queen o' Sheba.
Lord! he was a great man, sho enuff.　Ef
he didn't hab more stables an' more
horses!　De place where he lived was a
mighty fine farm an' house named Oakland, jes' eighteen mile fum Petersburg an'
twenty-two fum Richmond; but I neber
staid dar—no, sir.　De Colonel he jes' dashed his eyes ober me—I was monst'ous lean
an' peart fur twelve year ole—an' says to
some of de quality dat was a-settin' 'long-
side: "Here's a light weight for my New
Market stables, an' Arthur Taylor's handling.　Do you know a horse when you
see one, boy?"　"Yas, sir," I says; "I
knows a horse fum a mule jes' as far as I
kin see 'em bofe walk."　Dey all larfs at
dat, an' de nex' thing dey gives me some
new clo's all fixed up, an' I was sarnt
down to de great big training stables my
new marster owned at New Market, an' I
was set to wuk—de fust wuk I eber done
sence I was foaled—to rub down Reality,
own sister to Vanity, what was owned by
Colonel Allen.　De head manager of de
stable den was a Englishman named Arthur Taylor, an' dough he only had eight
horses en trainin' at dat time, dar was a
big force of boys an' men at wuk on 'em,
two boys to each horse, an' another white
man second in charge, named Peter.
Jehu! how we did wuk on dem horses!
Dey was John Stanley, sired by Sir Harry,
imported by Harry Haxall, Esq., an' dar
was a Sir Archy gray filly dat I can remember well kase she warn't no 'count till
she was four year ole, when she jumped
ober creation.　We had another dar belonging to Collyer Minn, named Moses,
half-brother to John Stanley by Sir Harry.

How I did love dem horses!　It 'peared
like dey loved me too, an' when dey turned deir rainbow necks, all slick an' shinin',
aroun' sarchin' fur me to come an' give
'em deir gallops, whew-e-e! how we did
spin along dat old New Market course,
right arter sunrise in de cool summer
mornings!　In dem times New Market
was 'bout de head place in de Nu-ninted
States fur horse-racin', an' all de gen'lemen fum far an' near used to come.　Nobody dat was anybody staid away, an' it
was a fine sight when de spring an' autumn races come, I tell you.　My marster
was de picter of a fine ole gen'leman; he
was a fa'r-lookin' man, with thick white
hyar, an' eyes dat jes' snapped fire at you;

he was what you call a plain gen'leman, an' didn't b'lieve his coat an' pants was de makin' of him; he treated his servants like dey was de prime cut, an' dey all loved him. He was a yearthly gen'leman, an' ef dere is any good place anywhere, it 'pears to me like he ought to be in it. An' as fur horses, ef he jes' only walked by a horse to look at it, he could tell you jes' how far dat horse could run. Why, dere was a mar' named Clary Fisher, an' a nag called Bonnets of Blue, dat I raised myself, which was Reality's daughter. When dey was runnin', de ole man walked by Clary Fisher an' looked at her fore-legs, an' he seed a sign in one of her fore-legs dat she would lay down in runnin' a mile an' three-quarters; he tole Mr. Crowell to go back an' bet every dollar he had, an' Mr. Crowell went back an' bet his three plantations, an' won de wuth of 'em, jes' as Colonel Johnson tole him. Den dere was General Wynne an' Billy Wynne, Billy Badger and Sam Badger, John C. Stevens, Mr. Van Rance, an' plenty more what used to fotch deir stables down to New Market ebery spring an' autumn, jes' as reg'lar as clock-wuk, de second Tuesdays in May an' October. Dem was de grandest times dat eber lived. King of Heaven! it was a sight to see my ole marster, an' yothers like him, a-struttin' up an' down wid deir shirts all frilled an' ruffled down de front. Why, den you could build a ball-room as long as fum here to de stable, an' fill it wid folks, an' ebery one of 'em de real stuff. But nowadays what's it like? Name o' Heaven! blue trash, red trash, green trash, speckled trash, dar's plenty of ebery qualinfication, but nary one dat washes in lye soap an' dries on de grass widout fadin'. Why, dar was Otway Hare, Parker Hare, John C. Goode, Mr. Corbin, Mr. Taylor, Colonel Peter Mason (we used to walk our horses ebery evenin' pas' his house), John Drummond an' Allen Drummond, the two brothers dat raised Sir Charles, all belonged to the New Market Jockey Club. Lord! how proud dis nigger was when dey called me "Johnson's Charles," an' I used to come a-clippin' down de track en a two-mile heat! De fust real race eber I rid was in a sweepstake, a mile an' a repeat, on John Stanley, trained by Arthur Taylor, when I was 'bout thirteen year ole, an' weighed in at seventy pounds. I was one o' dese yer fever-an'-ague little fellers what ain't got no flesh to take off

nohow; an' ef I warn't de proudest nigger! One of de horses was Mr. Green's nag fum Norfolk. My king! it skeers me a'most to talk 'bout it all, it looks so fur back; it looks wicked to ricolleck all dese yere dead an' buried things. It seems kin' o' like shakin' up de speerits too hard.

It warn't long arter dis here fust race when I was sarnt down to Norf Kyallina to ride fur Mr. Peter Davis, an' dat was de fust journey eber I tuk. I went all alone, an' when I got up on de stage at Petersburg in my new suit o' store clo's, wid ten dollars in my pocket an' more to come, I was "high come up," I tell you. De stage was a high flyer, an' I was sorry enough when she stopped at Warrenton, whar I got out, right at Mars' William Faulkner's, Colonel Johnson's sister's son. A heap o' fine folks lived 'bout dar besides him in dem times—ole Major Dancy, Bob Ransom, Judge Jones, an' Heyward Johnson, an' John Johnson, besides ole Marmaduke Johnson, de daddy of 'em all, what was married three times, an' imported Diomed, the sire of Sir Archy, an' one of de finest horses—dough dey tell me he was twenty-one year old when dey fotched him fum England—dat eber knocked de wind in de face. De race I rid was on a nag called Aggy-up, agin a chestnut colt named Scott, by Timoleon. Dar was three o' dem Aggy nags. Dey was Aggy-up, Aggy-down, an' Oh-Aggy, an' dey was all three sarnt up to New Market to be trained even-tully. I staid down dar near Warrenton fur nigh on to six months, an' den I got a notion to go home, an' I done went. Den I staid pretty quiet at home, clost to marster, trainin' en de stables under Arthur Taylor, an' goin' back an' forth 'twixt de stables an' Oakland, or Petersburg, or maybe Richmond, wharsomeber me an' de Colonel mought be livin' en residence at de time. Ebery spring an' autumn I rid stakes for him, an' 'bout dese years we trained Bonnets o' Blue, Black Star, Jeannette Lafayette, Flyin' Childers, Betsey Richards, John Richards, an' Sir Henry. John Warlin an' me was de two best light weights. I kep' down to eighty pound. De day of de great race on Long Island 'twixt Eclipse an' Henry, me an' marster an' all on us was there en course. My king! what a crowd an' noise an' screechin' an' hallooin' dar was dat day! When de third heat come roun', Arthur Taylor rid Sir Henry, what John Warlin had rid de two fust, an' ole Purdy he jumped on

Eclipse, kase he 'lowed dat Sam Laird couldn't git de jump out of him dat he could. Dat same time I rid de stake fur John C. Stevens on his Young Sir Archy, an' los' it by jes' eighteen inches; but I made my three hundred dollars an' de fines' suit o' clo's you eber see. I tell you, I walked roun' like a ole gobbler wid a red flannel tail tied on to his hind-leg when we got back home agin. By de time I was twenty year ole, 'bout de time Van Buren was President, marster he calls to me one day, an' he says: "Charley, my boy, I has layed out fur you to hab a stable of your own separate 'pinting. You is ole enough, an' done seed de rights of things long enough, to be my depritty yourself, so I is goin' to send you ober to my stable one mile fum New Market, an' I specs you to take everything into your own keer, an' send home some o' dem lazy scoundrels dat is hidin' out dar, too thick to shake a stick at, an' jes' waiting fur me to go an' scrattle [scatter] 'em home."

So sho' enough I went to de stable outside o' New Market, an' dar I was de "boss" ober nine little niggers an' four big ones, 'sides two white trash dey called "helpers." Wa'al, I had a nice stable full of nags. Dar was Medley, an' Slender, an' Tariff, an' Arab, an' more too, but I disricollecks de oders now. Dat was de fust of my turnin' out, an' I tell you I felt so fine dat my own mudder wouldn't ha' knowed me fur her son. I had plenty o' money, an' nobody to say nothin' to me. I jes' had to train an' exercise my horses, an' send 'em up when dey was wanted. Wa'al, arter a couple of year pass away, I begin to think 'bout gittin' married. I says to myself dat I was lonesome en dat big harnsome cabin, dat I was well off fur eberything 'ceptin' a good nigger to cook an' wash fur me, an' as I neber had no notion o' wastin' victuals on a woman I didn't love, or pomperin' up one wid love an' victuals *bofe* what didn't belong to me, hide an' hyar, I jes' made up my mind to ax Colonel Burford to let me look ober a lot of mighty likely young gals he had on a place not very far fum whar I lived. It was a little slip of a farm, clost to Rock Spring meetin'-house, an' he had put a whole lot of South Kyallina nigger wenches dar till he could git 'em settled on his yother places. I had done looked all roun' Chesterfield County all ready to pick up de fust dat 'peared like she would suit; but de minute I drove

up to de quarters on Colonel Burford's place I see de gal fur me. She was standin' on de step of de corn-crib sharpenin' a hoe, an' I seed dat she was as strong as a mule an' as sharp as pepper seeds, befo' I lit down out of de buggy. I axed her her name, an' she 'lowed dat dey called her Betsey Dandridge; so I axed fur de honor of pursentment to her daddy, ole nigger Dandridge dey called him, an' by sundown de mahter was fixed dat I was to git Colonel Burford's say-so right off, an' we would hab de weddin' when de corn was bent, for Scripter says, "As de corn is bent, so is de wife inclined," an' also, "Feed me wid food convenient fur me," an' 'bout dat time de summer apples would be ripe, an' de peaches.

So I started off to Petersburg, but while I was huntin' all round fur Colonel Burford, lo an' git up! what does I hear but Sim Jackson a-tellin' somebody dat he heerd dat Colonel Burford was goin' to sell de whole kit an' bilin' of 'em, track o' land an' all, to Major Isham Puckett, Esq. So I jes' rid ober de nex' day to whar ole nigger Dandridge an' his folks was a-waitin' fur me to come an' be 'fianced—what dey allers does up in Virginny befo' de marriage—an' de ole gen'leman he steps out, wid his ole black head a-shinin' like a Kentucky walnut, an' says to me, "Why, Colonel Stewart," says he (kase I had done tuk my marster's title), "we expected to see you here dis mornin' sooner dan dis; you is not so peryactical en yo' courtin' as we had expected." So wid dat I jes' steps up an' makes him a low bow, an' says I, "Mr. Dandridge, sir, you will allow me de privily of obsarvin' dat I intends to be 'fianced to yo' darter, Miss Betsey, when I gits ready, an' not befo'; an' let me tell you, sir, dar is a heap o' difference 'twixt axin' a lady fur to be your spouse, an' buyin' a gal dat you don't know de price of." Kase, you see, dat was what was troublin' me. I knowed Colonel Burford like a book, an' could calkilate on his sayin', "Wa'al, Stewart, you can hab Betsey a year or so fust to see ef she will suit you, an' den we kin talk 'bout de price," but Major Puckett an' me was on diff'unt sort o' tums. He was an old-school Whig, I was one of de new-school ones, an' we had to git acquainted better befo' I could tell what kind o' bargain he would make. But, hi! I needn't ha' bothered none 'bout dat. Jes' as soon as I steps up to him en Richmond, whar I found him en front o' de Court-house, an' interjuces myself as being "Colonel Johnson's Charles," he was jes' as affable as a settin' hen. I seed two or three gen'lemen I knowed well a-standin' by, but I didn't ax nobody to speak fur me; I up an' speaks for myself, an' jes' as soon as I had sensed him wid what I was sayin', he laughs an' says, "Why, Charley, you can have her jes' as she stands fur three hundred and fifty dollars." I tell you I was pleased. Befo' a mule could kick, I jumped round to Mr. Jefferson Balls's office (he was Major Puckett's brother-in-law, an', besides dat, he was de money agent for Colonel Johnson, an' dat's how come he was my agent too). I drawed out three hundred an' fifty dollars, fur I had made a heap dat las' year, more'n I could spend in clo's an' tobacco, more spesherly, too, by reason dat de Colonel always give 'em bofe to me; so as soon as I had drawed de money out I jes' hands it back agin to Mr. Balls for Major Puckett, an' says, "Dis yere sum is for de ackisition of Miss Betsey Dandridge, an' all de chillen we can raise: is dat so, Mr. Balls, sir?" An' he arnsers "yes," an' give me de papers, to hab an' to hole her as long as she behave herself.

So jes' as soon as I could I put back to de Rock Spring farm, an' sho enough we was married at de 'pinted time, an' I tuk her home. I had de best kind of a house ajinin' my trainin' stable, an' you neber seed de like of all de grand things as was give to us. I hauled home three cart-loads o' weddin' presents. Sech furniture an' fixin's was as fine as dey *could* be. Lord! when I look back to dem days an' think 'bout all de money, an' dogs, an' chickens, an' ducks, an' geese, an' pigs I had, an' whole chists full of fine clo's, an' more chaney dan we could eat out of en a year, an' de Colonel ready to hand me out a hundred dollars ebery time I ax fur it, an' think no more 'bout 'em dan 'bout spittin' out a chaw of tobacco! I neber did treat none o' my wives arter dat wid de same respex, kase I was right dar whar all de folks knowed me, an' I had a heap more truck dan I eber could colleck arter I lef' Virginny. I don' know perzackly what year dat was, but it was somewhars 'bout eight year 'fo' I married my second wife down en Kentucky, an' I know de year *dat* happened was de same year Queen Victoriore tuk up wid Prince Albert an' married him, an' made sech a talkin' an' palaveerin' as

neber was heered befo'. Wa'al, dar I was married, an' I mought jes' as well espress my disappintment fust as last. Treatment makes all de respex dat can happen responseful in de world, but a woman ought to tell some of de trufe once a day, ef it's only to limber up her tongue. It was a good while fust befo' I foun' out what make all Betsey's promises an' arnsers all de time fallin' flat and flatter, like bad dough or mean pie-crust, but when I seed how 'twas, I jes' sets to wuk to see ef I could cure her. I tried 'suasion an' finery, birch rods split fine, an' a light hickory stick 'bout as thick as my littlest finger, an' I tried makin' her kin an' my kin dat had religion pray fur her at de big camp-meetin'. But it warn't no use. She had three likely arrs, 'bout a year betwixt 'em, an' I neber had but dat one fault to find wid her; she cooked as good biskits, hoe-cake, bacon fry, hominy mush, an' coffee as any gal I seed; den, moreober, she could iron an' wash my shirts, an' keep things a-goin' right smart; but she couldn't seem to tell de trufe to save her life, an' it got to be so dat I jes' made my mind up to 'vorce her as quick as eber I could. In course an' sartinly I couldn't be out o' pocket for no sech a hussy as she was; an' den de question was wedder it was wuf while to keep de arrs an' raise 'em; but I says, "No, she must ha' come of a bad breed, an' a colt is mos' apt to take arter de dam, anyhow; I better git shet of de whole gang of 'em, an' try a new cross." Dar was a horse-dealer t'other side o' Petersburg by de name of Jones, what had de finest nag I had seen in a year fur sale at jes' de bery price I paid fur Betsey. De horse was named Brown Jim, an' he was wuf de money, I tell you; so I jes' says to Major Puckett dat he could have Betsey back at de same price I paid fur her, an' lowin' fur de war an' tar of de four year I had done kep' her, I would throw de boys into de bargain. Wa'al, I neber was sorry fur dat 'vorcement, nohow, an' dat autumn de Colonel sarnt me out to Kentucky, whar I had Monsieur Tonson and Medley, 'sides Black Elk, Glencoe, Leviathan, an' yothers.

Our head-quarters was in Paris, Kentucky, an' I staid dar a long time, an' was jes' as happy as a king. In de spring an' fall of de year I would take de horses 'bout fum place to place, en 'cordance wid marster's orders, an' I was jes' as free an' independent as any gen'leman en de land.

I had my helpers an' jockeys, grooms an' stablemen, under me, nobody was ober me, an' de squire or de jedge was always somewhar 'bout to read marster's letters to me. I neber had no book-larnin' myself, kase I neber was willin', fur I knowed my brain was too smart for to stand it. When anybody has got as much sense en de head as I had, dey must take great keer not to be foolin' round tryin' to stuff more en, or de fust thing dey'll bust it open. I lef' all dat fur folks dat wanted fillin' up an' patchin' on to. Yes, I was mighty happy at Paris an' at Bowling Green, whar I staid jes' about de same, 'vidin' my time 'cordin' to de horses. Dar was a heap o' rich gen'lemen all through dat country. Dar was Squire Oglen, whar Monsieur Tonson stood some time, an' was showed in the State Fair, wid me standin' alongside, an' we tuk de prizes of three fifty-dollar tankards. Ole Henry Clay was always aroun', an' mighty peart an' perlite de ole man was, too, an' knowed a horse when he seed him, I tell you. His son, Henry Clay junior, dey called him, he thought dat much of me he offered Colonel Johnson $3500 fur me himself, but de Colonel he tole him money couldn't buy me; an' he made jes' de bery same arnser to Wade Hampton, what offered him de bery same price. I had a heap of people after me, I tell you, an' some on 'em used to beg me jes' to say so as I wanted to go wid 'em an' leave my ole marster; but I would neber 'gree to dat ar scheme wid any of 'em; I was too well off fur dat, an' I heerd folks say as how "betwixt a two-edged sword you falls to de groun'," an' all sech sayin's as has sense en 'em. Whilst I was a-livin' at Paris I foun' anoder good reason fur stayin' jes' how I was an' whar I was. I 'come acquainted wid de likeliest-lookin' an' fa'rest-behavin' light-colored mulatter gal I eber seed in my life. Lord! I tell you dar ain't no sech niggers now as she was! An' dat genteel an' handy, an' sech snappin' black eyes an' coal-black hyar, like an Injun's, an' a pretty slim shape, wid sich a smooth light yaller skin, 'mos' de color of a ripe pumpkin seed. You may sarch dis world ober, but as sho as de Lord is de secret Jedge you won't eber find any 'oman as pretty an' as good as my little Kentucky sweetheart. Her name was Mary Jane Mallory, an' her owner, Mr. Robertson, tole me to marry her an' welcome, an' he would neber say nothin' to part us. She had a

brother dat hired himself out as a locksmith, an' all her folks was nice, pursentable pussons nobody could be shamed by. So I married her, an' tuk her to a little house I had fixed up near de stables, an' she clear-starched an' sewed an' 'broidered an' wukked wid de hand-loom, an' made more pretty things dan I could count. She paid her marster, en course, reg'lar, so much a month fur her hire, but, lor', she neber touched her airnin's fur dat. I had plenty of money to hire as many wives as I wanted, but dis one was de onliest one I eber did want, an' so it was easy enough.

I kin see dat little house now, wid de big white bed, all clean an' sweet an' hung wid ruffled curtains, in one corner, de cupboard full of flowered chaney an' shinin' metal an' glass opposite, an' de bright wood fire, piled up wid hickory an' ash logs, blazin' on de h'arth, an' Mary Jane settin' in front by de candle wid her fine white sewin' an' her pink caliker dress an' slick black hyar, lookin' so kind o' quiet till I speaks to her, an' den you kin see de fire-light a-glimpsin' on her white teeth. Arter a while she had a arr, sech a fine boy it was a picter to see him, an' as smart an' cunnin' as a little 'coon, an' jes' as like his daddy, what was me, you know, as a ole rabbit is like a young one. Dis was little Johnny; we named him arter her folks, her daddy an' her brother; an' I kept on a-reckonin' an' thinkin' that arter a while when marster sarnt for me to take Monsieur Tonson an' Medley back home to Virginny I would fetch Mary Jane and Johnny along wid me, an' show 'em to my folks in Petersburg, kase my mammy she was livin' dar, an' so was my brothers an' sisters an' a heap of kin, an' I wanted 'em all to see my wife an' boy. But it was 'bout six months arter Johnny was born, an' I was jest beginnin' to think 'bout buyin' Mary Jane in good arnest, so as to be all ready fur de time to start, when I begin to notice dat she hab got a mighty bad-soundin' cough, an' den her mammy says, "Why don't you eat, darter? you don't eat enough." An' den yother folks say, "What make Mary Jane look so poorly an' git so lean ?" I was badly skeered, an' I sarnt for de doctor, an' he says she mus' eat a heap an' drink port-wine, an' 'muse herself; so I takes her to see a ole friend at de springs, an' I buys good victuals, an' de gen'lemen, sich as Squire Oglen an' all of 'em, sends her port-wine, an' de doctor gives her quinine an' bark an' everything, but none of it was any use; her time was come, her hour for her to go had done been struck in heaven, an' de time was short. It warn't two year arter our weddin' when I laid her in her coffin, wid her big eyes shet foreber, an' I neber grieved so ober anybody in all de world. She was jes' as fond o' me as I was of her, an' it did 'pear hard luck to lose her jes' as I was makin' up my mind to buy her out an' out, only en course it was a fortunate thing I hadn't bought her, as long as she had to die, kase den I would ha' lost her an' de money too. Arter she was in de ground it jes' 'peared to me like eberything was different; I tuk a dislikement to Paris, an' I didn't feel like goin' home to Virginny. It got so arter a while dat I got de squire to write home to marster an' tell him I wanted to go to some strange place, an' marster he writ back dat "ef I could find *a owner to suit me, dat would pay his price fur me,* I could go, dough he had neber expected to part wid me *by sale.*" It jes' happened 'bout dat time dat Jedge Porter fum 'way down en Louisiana was in de Nu-ninted States, an' trabelling aroun' fur pleasure. He was one of de Washington Sennyters, an' was a great jedge (dey *said* he was a great jedge of de South, an' could make laws like a book, an' I *knows* he was a great jedge of a horse), so when he come to Bowling Green him an' me got acquainted, an' he says to me dat he was lookin' arter a head trainer fur his stables in de South, an' would I like to go wid him ef he would buy me. So I tuk a week or two to consider de mahter, an' him an' me had a heap o' talk, an' de more I thinks to myself 'bout stayin' in Kentucky widout Mary Jane, de more I says to myself dat I can't on no 'count do it.

De eend of de mahter was I tuk sech a likin' to de Jedge dat we fixed it up disaway: I was to go an' stay six months to see how I liked it, an' den, ef I didn't like it, he promised to send me back home, an' ef I did like it, he would pay Colonel Johnson $3500 fur me. Dat's what I sole for when I was young, an' I bet dar ain't many folks wuf dat 'mount o' money Norf or South. Arter dis bargain was made, I went out to Mr. Robertson's, whar my little Johnny was wid his grandmammy; an' Miss Mary Robertson she had jes' tuk sech a likin' to de little feller dat she had him roun' de house harf de time; an' now

when I went up to de house wid Mother-in-law Mallory, what was totin' him in her arms, he reached out his two little fisses to her as quick as he seed her a-settin' on de piazzy. I tole her an' Mr. Robertson all 'bout my new prospex, an' when I was done, de ole gen'leman stretched ober an' picked Johnny up, an' stood him on de little stool by him, and says, "Well, Stewart, I see what you want is dis little man, an' you shall hab him for $150, an' not one penny more." I tell you I *was* pleased, sho enough, an' I paid de money, an' got de receipt, an' we toted Johnny in to Bowling Green dat bery day. You see, de reason why I neber bought him befo' was dat I had to leave him wid his grandmammy. An' some folks is so cur'ous dat I wa'n't sho dey would let a free nigger, or rader a nigger dat belonged to his own daddy, stay on de place; so Mary Jane's sister she offered to keep him fur me till I could send fur him, kase en course I couldn't trabel wid a baby like dat; but I 'lowed to send fur him jes' as soon as I could git settled. An' de eend of de mahter was I lef' him; an' I ain't neber seed dat chile sence. Wa'al, my new marster an' me we started off for Louisiana, an' I 'clar' to Moses I thought we warn't neber goin' to git dar. We was goin' an' goin', en steamboats an' stages, stages an' steamboats, fur weeks an' days, till we come to New Orleans. It warn't as big as New York, but dar was a sight of oranges an' banarnas, an' more oder kinds of fruit dan I could call de names of. But de wust of de place was ef you axed anybody a question dey arnsered you in French, an' you might screech till you was deef befo' dey would let on dat dey knowed what you was talkin' 'bout. I stood dat kind o' nonsense fust-rate fum white folks: ef dey couldn't talk no Christian langwidge, I jes' felt sorry fur 'em: but when it come to a great big fool nigger a-doin' me dat way, I jes' hits him a lick in his ole black jaws dat shet 'em up for dat day. So marster an' me we soon left New Orleans, an' come on ober here to de 'Takapas country, whar he got sech a big fine plantation, so much of it, so many trees, an' de fields is so broad, an' de lakes is so big, I felt kind o' skeered an' lonesome de fust week. But it didn't take me long to git ober dat feelin' when I seed de race-course, de stables, an' de horses what was waitin' fur me on de Teche.

It was de prettiest picter of a place,

an' as fine a lot of horses as eber I seed togedder, twelve of 'em always en trainin', wid more brood marrs, outsiders, an' colts dan you could dream 'bout en one night. I had a mighty good large house at de top of de stable yard, an' my bell rung en de oberseer's house, de head helper's, an' de stable; besides, I had a boy to sleep en ebery stall. I was jes' put right at de head of eberything; nobody could say nothin' to me at all. Ef I said I wanted *dis*, I got it, or must hab *dat*, I got it too. He was jes' as open-handed an' gin-'rous, but he wouldn't stand no foolin' neither, I tell you. Things had to be jes' so, but dar warn't no naggin' nor scoldin'; it was jes' stiddy management.

Arter my marster, Jedge Porter, died, I belonged to his brother, Mr. James Porter, what done arred [heired] de place an' de niggers, an' ef dar eber was a good man walked en shoe-leather, he was one. Dey tells me dat

"'Twixt de saddle an' de ground
De sinner hab salvation found;"

an' en course we all knows 'bout dat dar horse-thief what our Saviour done pardon arter he was hung up; but I neber had no 'pinion of dis yere way of jumpin' into heaven ober de fence, 'stid of goin' right 'long by de road an' through de toll-gate, whar St. Peter takes de pennies; but dar was none o' dat wild kind of religion 'bout Mars' Jeames. He was good all through, both outsides an' down de middle, an' him an' me, an', arter he died, his folks an' me, we jes' went on peaceful an' happy till de war come an' rooted ebery blessed thing up by de roots.

A PROVIDENCE THWARTED.

IT was after ten o'clock, and there was work to do at home that ought to be finished before dinner, as old Mr. Willets knew, "but his grist wa'n't ready, and he couldn't start before it was, and it was kinder pleasant, too, settin' there—fellers passin' putty often, and men gittin' their loads weighed on the scales, or their oxen, and it was warm out there on the south side of the mill," as he explained to his wife when she came to the door, on his return home, to see why he staid so long.

Harlan's grist-mill did more business than any for twenty miles around, and there were always men hanging about the door meditatively chewing kernels of wheat, or sitting on the bench that ran along the side of the mill. It was quite a social luxury for the farmers of the region to visit it.

It was a delightful September morning —a golden haze hung over plain and hill. The air was like wine, and so clear that the cock-crowing from both neighboring and distant farm-yards rang sharply on the ear, and the blue jays' cries and the chirr of the chipmunks were to be heard in every direction. The dropping of the yellow leaves of the chestnuts and elms that overhung the mill-pond kept up a soft pattering murmur that made it pleasant for the farmer to listen with his eyes shut, and his hat canted over them to keep out the hot sunshine.

Hearing the rattle of wheels, Mr. Willets straightened himself up, and looking down the road, saw a man driving a poor old black horse, harnessed to a shackling buggy.

Mr. Willets gazed intently after him as he passed, and rose to his feet to see the last of him. As the buggy disappeared he settled down again, and looking around him as if in search of some one to whom he could free his mind, ejaculated, in a dazed manner, "I swow!" and remained lost in thought until roused by the appearance of a farmer with corn to grind, of whom he excitedly inquired, "Say, did you meet a man just now comin' from the Holler?"

"Don' know but I may hev. Afoot or drivin'?" asked the farmer, as he prepared to get his bags of corn from out the end of his wagon.

"Drivin' a black hoss—a reg'lar crow-bate?"

"B'lieve I did"—slowly getting one of the bags on his shoulder and carrying it into the mill. Stopping in the doorway on his way back for another, he took off his hat, and taking out a red handkerchief, he wiped his head, which was thinly thatched with sandy locks, and said, "Come to think of it, I guess it was William Lane, wasn't it?"

"Why, yes," rejoined Mr. Willets. "I know it was; but what's he doin' here?"

"Why, he hez come and bought back

the old place; that is, it would be goin' too fur to say he's actually bought it, for he's paid very little down, as I understand it; and most folks as poor as he appears to be, should say, they'd stand a poor chance of ever payin' for't; but you know the family; and if there's any one that can fat sheep on the inside of a quarry, probably he can do it, and presume he will;" and he shouldered another bag of corn and started toward the door.

Mr. Willets followed him into the mill, and twitching his sleeve, said, "Are you goin' to wait for your grist?"

"Depends on how soon it will be ready. I might wait a spell, but I don't mean to spend the day."

"Well," drawled Silas, "it'll be ready so'st you can git home by dinner-time."

"Well, I've got too much on my shoulders to wait here, and I shall take the mare down to the blacksmith's and have her for'ard shoes set."

"I don't care if I go down with ye," said Mr. Willets, eagerly.

"Get in, then."

"Well, about William," said Mr. Willets, "how d'ye know he was so poor, and how come he so? I knew they'd hed losses, but I'd no idee how 'twas with 'em. Hain't heard anythin' about 'em for the last five year."

"Well, William he told me. I was one of his securities in buying back the old place, and he told me. I've allus known William, and liked him—liked him when he was a boy, and when he come to be a man I hadn't altered my idees. It ain't my way. I s'pose you can remember back to when they left this town, fifteen year ago. William was fifteen years old then. You've heard how the old man went and kep' a hotel to Cleveland, sold liquor, and made money accordingly. It was a trial to the rest of the family, but they'd allus hed to put up with his ways, and they did then. Well, he bought, or partly bought, a steamer, and traded between there and Detroit. Did an amazin' business, and picked up money like chips. But I never see a family go down as they hev," continued the farmer, drawing up at the blacksmith's shop.

Mr. Gibbs went in, leaving Mr. Willets to follow at his leisure.

"Anything for you, Mr. Gibbs?" sung out the smith.

"You don't seem to be drivin' with work this mornin'?" said Mr. Gibbs.

"Yes, I want Sukey's for'ard shoes set; I see she's loosened both of 'em;" and he went out again, followed by the smith, and soon had the mare unharnessed, and under the smith's hands.

"S'pose you heard that William Lane hed got back onto the old place?" said the smith.

"Yes," briefly responded Mr. Gibbs.

"Is he as poor as they say?" said one of the men.

"I don' know what they say," Mr. Gibbs replied, "but he's poor enough."

"Well, I presume you know as much as any one. They say his father died an awful death," suggestively remarked another.

"Is that so?" eagerly inquired Mr. Willets.

"Well, yes, they say so. Ben Nevins said he read the account in a Cleveland paper at the time. Paper said they was consid'able of a temperance movement, and he went out and was talkin', and the men was tellin' him how the leaders of the movement was raidin' on the bars, and how, likely, he'd be visited — purpose to rile him up, you know—and he was awful mad, and sez he, 'I shall sell liquor as long as I please, and the Almighty sha'n't stop me.' And just as he got that out he flushed up awfully, and fell over onto his face in a fit, and they took him home and laid him onto a table in his own bar-room, and he died there that night—never come to a minit."

"And I presume to say," remarked one of the men, after a silence, "that his wife mourned for him as much as if he'd been one of the best men that ever lived."

"We've all of us read the sayin', 'Riches take to themselves wings and fly away.' How true it is!" remarked Deacon Harris, with a sigh, from the doorway, where he had been listening unobserved for a few minutes. Deacon Jabez Harris was a man of fifty-five, hale and well preserved, with an ingratiating, though perhaps what some might term a sanctimonious, manner, a shrewd face, on which always hovered a slight smile, belied by the hard glint of his eye—a man never known to lose his temper, or do a generous deed. Looking about him, he continued, "Now the way that man's accumulated riches melted away, as it were, in a moment, is a series of remarkable providences that should be a lesson and a warning to all of us."

"That's so," assented the smith.

"Well," observed the deacon, "I asked William how it was. He came to me for help, with my friend Mr. Gibbs here"—Mr. Gibbs bowed—"and I said to him that I could not feel free to aid him unless I was convinced that this loss of property was not due to laxness on his part. William told me, that, beginning with his sister's death, there seemed to be a fatality following them."

"I presume some of you have heard of the eldest son falling into ways of sin ?"

As he waited for a response from some one, Mr. Gibbs said, "Yes."

"Just so, and the awful death of the father. It seems that Mr. Lane died in October, and the lake steamers are not insured after the 1st of November, but the captain who was running their boat was a self-willed man, and loaded up at Detroit for a return trip, and started from port. A fearful gale coming up, the boat was destroyed, with all on board, it being a total loss. And now to see how the providences of God follow up the doings of sinful men, although in this case it seems mysterious, and falling on the innocent instead of the guilty."

"Providence hez allus been blind, kinder," softly remarked Mr. Willets.

"The following December," resumed the deacon, "the hotel took fire, and was consumed, and as the heft of Mr. Lane's means was placed in the boat and the house, they were left comparatively penniless."

"What they livin' on now ?" asked the smith—"the widder and the rest of the children ?"

"There was a small portion left, on which the relict and her younger children will get on. I understand from William that he has established them in a modest home in Cleveland. There seems to be an impressive lesson in these dealings for all of us," said the deacon.

"I don' know," said one of the men. "I was just thinkin' it didn't apply to any in this circle. There ain't any of us that's hampered with worldly goods, unless it's you, deacon. You know how that is better than I do," he added, slyly.

"Well, now, I guess you'll find them shoes all right. If they ain't, I won't charge you," said the smith.

"Time they was," said Mr. Gibbs, as he paid for them. "It's past twelve now," consulting a large silver watch.

"There can't nobody tell where this mornin' has gone to, but I don' know but what it's been pleasant, too," said one, as they all rose to go to their respective homes. "It's allus kinder interestin' to hear of your neighbors' misfortun's, though I don' know anybody," he added, looking through the door after the deacon, who could be seen just entering his house, across the green, "that sets 'em out in such a hard way, without no lightenin' to 'em, as the deacon doos."

"That's so," assented the smith.

William Lane had always wished to return to the farm, and was now free to do so.

The old unpainted house standing on its rocky knoll, with the great elm drooping over it, the bouncing-bets and sweet-williams on either side of the front door, the old well-sweep, the trout brook, the starved meadow that lay on the south side, and the uncared-for orchard that stretched along the half-deserted by-road—all were dear to him.

He had partly forgotten that his father had been hard with him there, and rather remembered the freedom of the farm, the long walks through the forest, the trout fishing and woodchuck hunts with old Towser, and fancied that, once there again, he should be happy.

He was very poor; a small sum, barely enough to buy the necessary stock, was all he had; but Mr. Gibbs, an old friend of his mother's, lent him most of the money he needed, and Deacon Harris furnished the remainder. By the time the early September frosts came on William found himself the virtual owner of the place, and set to work with might and main. Long before the sun rose he was at work, and had need to be, for with one man's help he did all, both in-doors and out. William's neighbors, like himself, were hard-working men, but his diligence was felt to be out of the ordinary, and was the subject of much comment.

Mr. Gibbs proved the best of advisers, and aided him in many ways, and by the time two years had gone by he found himself getting on, much to his own satisfaction. After serious consideration he sought him a wife, and offered his heart and the chances of life on a hill farm to Lizzie Spencer, a high-spirited and sensible young girl in a neighboring town.

All went smoothly with Lizzie, but when William applied to her father and mother for their consent, it was withheld. When he questioned them the mother said she had nothing against it, but "father didn't favor it." The father openly offered his objections.

"The reason I don't wish you for a son-in-law, William, is because I want to have nothing to do with your family. I know your folks through and through. Your father was a man that never hesitated to do a mean thing when he saw a dollar in it. He never knew what it was to spare a man he had at his mercy. He was a hard man and a bad man, and what's 'bred in the bone'—you know the saying."

"It's unfair to judge me by my father, Mr. Spencer.'

"Well, I don't know; I don't trust you. You seem fair enough, but your name is Lane, and I never heard of a Lane that I could trust."

"Then you forbid your daughter marrying me simply because I bear the name of Lane."

"That's reason enough for me. Lizzie will do as she likes; every one must marry to suit themselves; but I never 'll give my consent, nor, what is more to the purpose, the portion I would have settled on her if she'd married to suit me."

"I don't wish the money, Mr. Spencer," William replied, with a moderation in tone and manner that rather abashed the other. "I shall be able to get on as I have done, I trust, with no one's help. If Lizzie will marry me I shall have all I wish."

When the alternative was placed before Lizzie of parting with her lover or her fortune, she announced, with a spirit of determination that matched her father's, that she could easier do without money, hampered with conditions, than William. So she married him, and they were very happy.

William's lot, he found, was easier as well as happier. Lizzie had "faculty," and proved a notable housekeeper. The food, though as frugal as ever, was not so monotonous in its routine, the milking and butter-making fell to her share, and she did not disdain to don her sun-bonnet and "rake after" the cart in hay-making.

Affairs prospered with them, so that they laid a little—a very little, but still something—by, toward paying for the place, and the only drawback to their happiness was the fact that Lizzie's father still held out against them, and never visited the farm.

As years went by they were blessed with two children. The little girl, who promised to be as pretty as her mother, was William's darling, and the boy, who had the blue eyes and wavy curls of his father, Lizzie fondly hoped might grow up to be as good a man as William.

As time passed on William still worked as untiringly as ever, but showed signs of losing his vigorous strength, and Lizzie insensibly fell into the habit of thinking of him as almost an old man, and when, one wet September, he succumbed to an attack of rheumatism, it left him bent and haggard, and discouraged also. The fields missed the master's care, and much that he had planned to do was left undone. The neighbors were kind, and now and again lent a helping hand, but it was the busy season of the year, and they had their own crops to harvest.

Early in December William was sent for in a great hurry to go to Mr. Gibbs. Lizzie heated a stone to keep his feet warm, and wrapped him up, and having tucked him well into the sleigh, hoped the ride would do him good, though she owned to herself with a sigh, as she watched the sleigh disappear, that William looked very old and feeble.

Arrived at Mr. Gibbs's house, he found his old friend very ill, battling for his life with a severe attack of congestion of the lungs. As William entered the bedroom where the sick man lay, his old friend lifted his fevered eyes to his, and signed to William to come near, and as he took his hand began at once to address him as if he felt his time was short.

"William, I've been pitying you all along this fall, but I'm the worst off to-day."

William began to express his sorrow at his sad condition, but the farmer cut him short.

"I see you feel for me, but I've no time to talk. But your affairs—that note of yourn I hed. I don' know but I've done you an injury, spite of my feeling toward you." He rested a little; then went on. "I never pressed you for't."

"I know that," said William.

"No," gasped the farmer, painfully, "'n' I hope he won't."

"Who?" inquired William, as Mr. Gibbs waited to gather a little strength.

"The deacon. I hadn't no choice,

William. I thought of wife. She hain't no head for business—'n' the deacon happened to call early this morning, 'n' he offered to take the note—'n' I didn't know what to do—'n' I let him have it—the note 'n' the mortgage. He's a hard man," he said, anxiously, as he noted William's look of apprehension; "but he's allus been fair with me—'n' he said he'd do the right thing by you—promised he would—'n' I knew I was dying, 'n' I thought of wife."

William, seeing how troubled he was, urged him not to think of it, and reminded him of his great kindnesses toward himself.

"I hev—I've set store by ye, William—'n' I hope I hain't hurt ye now. The deacon give me his word," he gasped again, as William rose to leave him, after bidding him farewell.

In January the interest fell due, and William went to the deacon's to pay it. Deacon Harris was very amiable, and inquired in his most affable manner after wife and children, and William was about taking his leave with a lightened heart, —for he had dreaded lest the principal might be called for—when, as if an afterthought had struck him, the deacon said, as William opened the door to go out, "By-the-way, William, I hope it wouldn't put you out too much if I was to ask you to pay off part of what you owe me—say the note of six hundred that I took of Mr. Gibbs to oblige him; the other, for three hundred, that I've held all along, can lie longer. But I put myself out to take it up for our friend; only did it to lighten a dying man's last moments; and now I feel the need of the money. I should like it —say the 18th of next month;" and he smiled benevolently upon William.

William turned pale as he answered that he was afraid he couldn't possibly raise it. "You know," he said, "what bad luck I have had this year. I can't raise it," he said, desperately; "I hain't the money, and can't get it."

"I think you'll have to find it, William. It's a matter of necessity with me."

The next morning William went out among his friends, with a faint hope that he might find help, but it was a fruitless errand.

Most of the farmers of that region had all they could do to live; many owed money they were hopeless of repaying; the taxes bore heavily on the most fortu-

nate, and although they would have been glad to have assisted him, were powerless to do so, and could only give doubtful shakes of the head over his chances.

When William had applied to every one likely to have money, and failed, his wife suggested as a last resort that they should sell their sheep. They had a fine flock. William had begun by buying a few at a time, as he could, and now, with the natural increase of numbers, he counted them by scores. He had taken great care of them, and Lizzie had brought up many a poor deserted lamb to be a credit to the flock. Their sheep were gaining them quite a reputation; but now it was decided they must go, and William went to the county town the next market-day.

He succeeded better than he had hoped to do, and came home quite cheered, to be met by the hired man, who carried him to the sheep-fold to "see what in natur' ailed the critters. He thought it must be the distemper."

William's heart sank within him as he glanced over the poor creatures, and separated those that had sickened already— quite a number—from the others.

It was in vain that the men worked over them, and Lizzie let the house-work go, and left the children to get on as they could, while she tried one remedy after another. In the course of a fortnight there were but a poor half-dozen left, and William and his wife looked at each other in despair.

The 18th of February came, and bright and early came the deacon. Without appearing to be aware of their losses (although he knew of them as well as any one), he asked William if he was ready to pay the note. On William's answering "No," he frowned, and inquired, civilly, what the reason might be.

"I told you, Mr. Harris, that I couldn't raise the money. I have tried every way," said William. "I should have been able to get it if my sheep had not died. I hope you will not be hard upon me, but extend the time until I can find some other way," he added, feeling himself at the mercy of a man who he knew *meant* to be hard.

"Extend the time! That's what a defaulting debtor always wants," sneered the deacon, with his smile quite gone, and his small eyes drawn together. "You knew the money was due to-day, didn't you? And I warned you I must have it, and I intend to, too."

Here Lizzie, who had been listening in the next room, came in, to see if her entreaties might not soften him. She had always been called "a real putty girl," and she had not lost her pink cheeks yet; she had brushed her glossy hair until it shone like a chestnut, and put on a red bow at her throat, and William thought, as she came in, that she looked charming enough to touch the heart of any man.

The deacon, who was very gallant toward women, answered her "Good-morning" very graciously, and inquired after her health and that of the children. But when she came to the subject of his call, he hardened at once. As she said, "I hope you will not be hard upon us, Mr. Harris; we will pay you in time, if you will only have patience with us now; we have been so unfortunate this year," her voice trembled so that she stopped to steady it.

"That's bad for you; very sad indeed," said the deacon, coldly; "but still it scarcely concerns me. The question is," he added, sharply, "can you pay the money?"

"No," said Lizzie, "we can't. William has tried every way."

"Just so," observed the deacon, settling himself back more comfortably in the arm-chair by the fire. "I supposed you couldn't. All that I can see, then, for me to do is just to foreclose."

"You can't mean it!" exclaimed William. "You wouldn't do that, and rob me of my home."

"I shall do it," rejoined the deacon, looking from the husband to the wife and back again, with evident satisfaction, "if the money isn't forth-coming in a week. It's more consideration than I owe you, but Scripter says, 'Thou shalt not distress thy brother without cause,' and I have always been strictly just in all my dealings, and you can have the advantage of a week."

"Only a week to raise six hundred dollars in, when I haven't been able to do it in a month!" said William, in despair.

"Oh, Mr. Harris, be merciful to us!" cried Lizzie, all in tears. "I've heard," she went on, as well as her crying would let her, "that when you were young you had a hard time to get on, and know what it is to be pinched. What would have become of you if any one had treated you as you do us?"

"Well, Mrs. Lane, just this very thing did happen to me, and it's made me what I am. I hope the discipline will prove as valuable to your husband," he added, with a bland smile.

"If you have been in such a place yourself, then surely you will have compassion on us now," urged William.

"*Why* should I?" asked the deacon, as if amused at the absurdity of the idea. "Now I'll tell you something, William, that may help you to see things in a different light. When I was twenty-five years old I had bought me a farm in Exeter; I'd had my time since I was twenty-one, and had laid by a little something. I didn't trifle away my time in useless pursuits, as young men now do. I never knew what it was to take a leisure hour; all my energies were bent on paying for my farm.

"Well, I had to borrow money, and Providence led me in the way of your father. Your father always had money to lend, on good security, and he let me have all I wanted. That was kind, eh, William? I worked as few men have done. I was very strong, and I put my heart into it. I was engaged to the prettiest girl in the place, and I wanted to have the neatest farm and the prettiest house in the county, to please her.

"You remind me of her some," he said, turning toward Lizzie, who sat by the fire plaiting and unplaiting the hem of her apron: "I've often thought of it when I see you in meeting.

"Well," he resumed, with a sigh, after a pause, "I put all the money I could raise into improvements; I was foolish, but when I'd feel worried about it, as I did once in a while, and speak about the money to your father, he would always say, 'Go on, go on; I like to see you ambitious about your place. I don't care how many years the money lies; I've no call to use it;' and so I was caught in my own trap, and went on. I have never encouraged *you* in any foolishness, have I, William?

"Well, it went on until about three months before I was to have married, and Eunice was working her wedding gown."

"Eunice!" broke in Lizzie. "I thought your wife's name was Chloe."

"Yes: I didn't marry Eunice. Mrs. Harris is an excellent woman," he said, dryly. "I didn't marry *her* for a pretty face. However, my wife is not concerned in this.

"I said it was three months before I was to have been married, when your father came to me with a plausible story, was sorry to trouble, but he wanted the money, the *whole* of it. He wasn't so easy as I am with you, William.

"There's no need to go into particulars. He wouldn't hear to anything, but took the place, and I lost everything—yes, everything," he said, bitterly, "for Eunice wouldn't marry a beggar.

"Well, I had the world to begin again, with all my life, up to that time, lost to me, and I knew whom I had to thank for it, and I took an oath then to be revenged upon your father.

"I never had a chance with him. He was too sharp for me, and prospered in everything he did; but when you came to me, William, to borrow money, I saw what you were—not like your father in smartness, though I know you've his meanness in you. It can't be buried so deep but what it's there."

"Then you have deliberately ruined me for a mean revenge on a dead man!" broke out William.

"The *injury* is a living one, William. I am sorry your father couldn't see that I've paid myself off," said the deacon, with a world of gratified malice speaking through his eyes.

The deacon paused, and noting the looks of horror that both William and his wife cast upon him, smoothed out his face into its wonted lines, and said, dryly: "What have you to complain of ? When a man incurs a money liability he knows he must meet it. Doesn't the money legally belong to me ?"

"You can take it by law, but if the Christian mercy I've heard you expatiate upon in prayer-meetings has a living principle with you, you would extend it now toward us."

"Young man," said the deacon, reprovingly, "religious matters are one thing, and money matters are another, and I never mix them."

He rose, and as he buttoned up his coat, added: "You've had your notice, and you'll see that I shall keep my word. Good-day to you."

There wanted but one day of the sale, when Lizzie's father, having some business in the town in which she lived, betook himself in good season to the place. A fifteen-mile drive was of little consequence to his smart-stepping horse; but, when nearing the village, Billy cast a shoe, and he turned toward the blacksmith's to have it set.

Driving up from the side road, and stopping to unharness his horse, he overheard the conversation going on just within the door of the smithy.

"Do you know whether it's likely there'll be smart biddin' on the prop'ty to-morrow ?" he heard Mr. Willets's voice asking.

"Don' know," responded some unknown person. "'Tain't likely anybody 'll have spunk enough to bid agin the deacon. Everybody understands that he intends to git the place into his own hands, I guess."

"If there *was* any one that hed money to spare," one added, suggestively, "I s'pose they wouldn't lose to git it, and let them poor creeturs try an' buy it back; but money is awful scarce. I know 'tis with me, anyway."

Mr. Spencer stopped unharnessing, and listened more attentively, wondering whom the men were talking of. As he had very slight intercourse with any of the towns-people, and did not take the county paper (his interest lying in other directions), he had not heard of William's recent straits. He started as he heard another voice say, "I never'd thought that the last of the Lanes, as you might say, would come to this, and the only decent one I ever heard of, too. William is a first-rate man."

"That's so," assented the smith, heartily; "he's real clever, too; and so's his wife. She's just as smart as a steel-trap, and kind."

"I don' know any one I'd go to, if I was in trouble, quicker than I would to her, or him either," said another. "They'd help you in a minute, if 'twas so they could."

"I should think *her* folks would step in now and give 'em a hist. What's the reason they don't ?" queried Mr. Willets.

"They say they didn't favor the weddin' anyway, and hain't never been near 'em. Her mother's been dead some time, I believe, and there ain't any family, 'cept her father, and he's as hard as that hammer that Jones is strikin' with. That's what I've heard," the speaker added, cautiously.

Mr. Spencer winced as he heard these speeches, and he took a step toward the shop to interrupt them, but stopped as the next speaker lifted his voice. What he had heard was a revelation to him.

"I don't s'pose," said Mr. Willets, "that there'd anything hurt the deacon so, as to have somebody pay off William's note, and let him keep his place. He's awful hard, the deacon is, but he allus keeps within the law; so he can take it well enough, and no one can say, 'Why do ye so?'—'ceptin' Providence."

Mr. Spencer smiled grimly to himself, and taking the bridle of his horse, led him up to the door, and summoning the smith by a nod, asked Mr. Jones if he would see to his horse, and loan him another in the mean time to drive to the county town, some five miles distant — casting sharp looks around the circle of men gathered in the smithy while he spoke.

The smith answered in the affirmative to both questions, and Mr. Spencer was soon seen to drive off at a speedy trot.

As Mr. Jones returned he was accosted by Mr. Willets, who demanded, excitedly, "Say, who was that man?"

"Hem! well, that was William's father-in-law, as it happens," said the smith, with a grin, at the dashed looks of those around him.

"You don't! well, if that ain't the crowner!" ejaculated one, as all united in blocking up the doorway, in their anxiety to see the last of him. When he had disappeared, Mr. Willets expressed the mind of all in the observation, "Well! it hain't hurt him none. Perhaps it will stir him up to do for 'em. He could if he favored it."

Meantime Mr. Spencer hurried to town, and to the bank, where he had a comfortable bit of money laid up, drew out the necessary amount (having privately questioned the smith as they fastened the latter's horse to the sleigh), and hastened back with it. Avoiding the smithy, he went up the hill to William and Lizzie's home. As he neared the house he spied a team standing before the sitting-room door, and conjecturing it to be the deacon's, hurried in through the back kitchen.

He opened the kitchen door softly, and looked in. There stood Lizzie washing out a few things at the sink, and sprinkling the garments with her tears. She looked up, and saw her father. "Oh, father!" she cried, and giving a hasty wipe to her hands with her apron, ran and threw her arms around her father's neck, and burst into tears on his shoulder.

Mr. Spencer was distressed. Lizzie had been a girl that never cried. "She must have broken down considerable," he thought to himself. He smoothed her hair down once or twice, and said, "There, there!" as he had done when she was a baby. Then, as she continued to sob, "Lizzie, don't ye know you're jammin' in the crown of my hat?"

Lizzie immediately withdrew herself, took the hat from his hand, said, with compunction, "I am so sorry!" and began to smooth it.

After a moment's pause, during which Mr. Spencer noted her changed appearance, he said, abruptly, "Who's in there?" indicating the sitting-room by a gesture.

"William and the deacon. He's going to sell the farm to-morrow," she said, with another burst of tears, this time bestowed upon her apron.

Without another word he went across the floor to the door leading into the sitting-room, softly lifted the latch, listened for a while, and entered, closing the door after him.

Standing by the stove, with one foot resting on the hearth, was the deacon, while William sat dejectedly at a table, with his head upon his hands.

Going past William with a curt nod, Mr. Spencer addressed himself to the subject in hand:

"Mr. Harris, if I'm not mistaken?" The deacon bowed. "I've never met you before, I believe. My name is Spencer."

"How do you do, sir?" said the deacon, at a loss what to expect.

"There's to be a foreclosure sale here to-morrow, as I understand, to satisfy your claim."

"Exactly," said the deacon, in his silkiest tones, "unless Mr. Lane here can pay me to-day. He has just told me he could not."

"Just so. If he could, you'd be glad to release him?" said Mr. Spencer, dryly.

The deacon had no choice but to answer "Yes."

"Very well. How much is the sum?"

The deacon gave it. Mr. Spencer sat down, extracted a fat pocket-book from an inner pocket of his coat, and slowly counted over a pile of bills by the aid of an occasionally moistened thumb. Securing the bills between his knees, he drew out a small purse, and told out silver. Putting up purse and pocket-book, he handed bills and silver to William, saying, briefly, "Might as well settle with him right off."

William looked up, scarcely knowing what was meant, and Mr. Spencer forcing the money into his hand, he mechanically looked it over, and all at once realized that he was delivered. He was about to spring up to express, if he was capable, his thankfulness, but Mr. Spencer, checking him, said, quietly, "Don't keep the deacon waiting any longer. His time is probably precious."

William rose, and handing the money to the deacon, received the note and mortgage, reluctantly parted with.

"Now you're satisfied, I presume, Mr. Harris, though you don't look so either," said Mr. Spencer, enjoying the other's looks of discomfiture and rage. "As I've been the instrument of Providence in delivering my son," turning to indicate William, "I propose to continue in that capacity, and give you an honest man's opinion of your dealings. I've never been an eavesdropper but twice: both times to-day. Once I heard reflections on myself and appreciation of my son here that took the scales off my eyes, and let me see where I was and where William stood.

"I'm a set man," he continued, "but when I'm convinced, I know what to do, and I made up my mind if I could make matters right between me and my son-in-law and my daughter, I'd do it, if it was the eleventh hour.

"I've been hard on William. I had as much reason to despise his father as any man could, and I've been mean enough to let that feeling stand between us and make us all miserable. But—enough said before you. I'll say what I hev to say when you are gone.

"The second time I listened was to hear you," pointing a big forefinger at the deacon, his voice rising with wrath and contempt, "making yourself out to be the meanest creature that is on God's footstool this minit."

"I have not overstepped the law; no one can say that," exclaimed the deacon, in self-defense.

"Not human law—no, you hain't; but Divine law says, 'Thou shalt not grind the face of the poor.' You're great on Scripter. You've read that text, and can find it, and there's plenty more just like it."

"I gave William every chance to redeem his place. I extended the time to him," said the deacon.

"You can say that, but you know it isn't so. You gave him no chance. Why, I *heard* you," he broke out, fiercely, as the deacon was about to speak, "I tell you; I listened at the door. I heard William here pleadin' with you, and you tell him you'd ruin him.

"For six hundred dollars you meant to rob him of a home he has all but killed himself to win." He stopped to view the look of baffled malice and rage that made the deacon's face anything but a pleasant sight to see. As he was about to speak, Mr. Spencer stopped him with the remark:

"I haven't a doubt but you are capable of speaking of this as a providential dispensation, and being enough of a hypocrite to ask the Lord in your evening prayers to bless this 'visitation.'"

"He owed the money. It was a righteous debt," said the deacon.

"You didn't take a righteous way to collect it, and you didn't want the money. You claimed it because you saw your opportunity to ruin him. You have been planning it all this time, and would have worked it out but for my stepping in at the last moment, as it were—and I really believe it was Providence that led my steps this morning—but spoiled yours, deacon," he added, with a smile.

"Don't you offer a word in your defense! You quit this house, and don't you ever find your way here again.— William," he added, "I'll take the privilege of showing the deacon the door."

He waited in grim silence while the deacon put up the money and took up his hat; then accompanied him to the door, and going out after him, said, in a low grunt, that no one else might hear him:

"What *I* ask and expect of you, Deacon Harris, is, that you'll take the trouble to just mention to the blacksmith's that there won't be no sale here to-morrow. They'll understand it," he added, with a chuckle.

"Now, William," he said, as he went in again, "the deacon's gone." He shook William's hand heartily, and they stood regarding each other for a little in silence, while William's face worked, and Mr. Spencer's eyes shone with a suspicious brightness.

There were no words spoken, nor were any needed. Each understood the other, and forgiveness and reconciliation were offered and accepted in a look.

THE GATEWAY OF THE SIERRA MADRE.

ar-cane, and garden vegetables. The residue of water, after many a devious wandering, and re-enforced by several similar streams that, rising in the very heart of the city, meander through its streets and gardens, is turned into its original channel, only to perform like services for the rich sugar *haciendas* of the valleys below.

It is this alternation of town and county, the union of city life with all the charms and associations of rural surroundings, that forms one of the chief attractions of Monterey.

More than three decades and a half have elapsed since this name first became famous, as associated with the early battles of the Mexican war, the theatre of the gallant exploits of Worth and Taylor, and now, by a curious coincidence, it is again prominently brought before the public, the first-fruits, as it were, of the new invasion of Mexico—a movement almost phenomenal in its character, and which threatens the speedy yet peaceful commercial conquest of the country.

The 16th of September last, the anniversary of Mexican independence, was celebrated at Monterey by the formal opening of railway communication with the United States: for the first time in their history the two republics, through their representative cities, were united by bands of steel.

The central and more settled portions of Mexico have for some time enjoyed a limited railroad system, constructed by English and native capital, but the vast regions to the north, comprising more than two-thirds of the country, had, up to the past year of American construction, known no better means of communication than the clumsy ox cart and pack train of by-gone days. In all the earlier international concessions it was especially stipulated by the government that construction should begin from the capital northward, and in no event from the frontier into the interior. The suspicion and distrust of American aggrandizement, inherent in the heart of every Mexican, feared to open up the sparsely settled States of the north to foreign enterprise while they were yet isolated from the centres of power and population in their own country. It is a significant fact, evidence of the new and better feeling, that the anniversary of independence, which to the

NE hundred and fifty miles south of the Rio Grande frontier, at the gateway of the rugged range of the Sierra Madre, lies the beautiful city of Monterey. Here the detached spurs of the "Mother Mountains" converge together to form the great plateau of the table-lands, leaving but a narrow pass through which all the roads from the coast and Rio Grande, uniting in one at Monterey, wind through the gorge to Saltillo and the group of central cities in the interior. From this pass, fed by countless mountain springs, emerges the Arroyo San Juan, a beautiful stream of rapid water, clear as crystal, and cool from the mountains even in the hottest days of midsummer. Although skirting the city in a semicircle and close along the foot-hills of the Sierra, its channel is dry except in time of freshet, every drop of water being diverted from above into the *acequias*, or irrigating ditches, that permeate for miles the fertile plains of the valley. Here are thousands of acres of the richest lands, much of it level as a well-kept lawn, and fruitful in maize, sug-

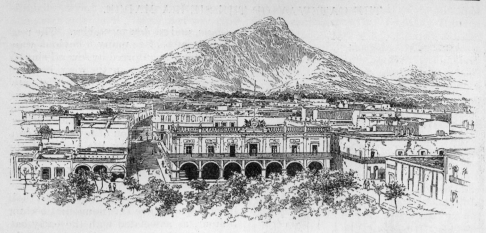

VIEW OF MONTEREY.

ultra-patriotic Mexican means more than liberty or even national prosperity, should be signalized by the union of the two principal cities of the north* with the railway system of the United States.

American signs, among which "saloon" figures with suggestive prominence, are displayed at various points, notably on the principal plaza, and English is to be heard on the streets in common with the vernacular tongue; a street railway has been inaugurated, with the innovation of forming a freight transfer as well for the narrow-gauge cars of the Mexican National, a telephone exchange opened, and wires stretched for lighting the city with the electric light. But these things are all alien to the soil, and, like fresh shoots grafted on to an old trunk, must have time to assimilate with the long-established order of things.

Ever since the opening of the road a constant stream of visitors—tourists, invalids, and prospectors—has poured down from the north, crowding the hotels to suffocation, and taking absolute possession of the plazas and other places of public resort. At first the old citizens—those who were born and raised here, with their fathers and grandfathers before them— were disposed to look upon this invasion with stolid indifference, while the curiosity of the visitors, who stared at everything they saw, from the ridiculous little *burros*

loaded with wood from the mountains until only their long ears are visible, to the mud-walled, grass-thatched *jacals* of the suburbs, was put down by the average Mexican as the natural amazement of the *gringo** (greenhorn) at beholding these evidences of a civilization so far superior to anything he could ever have seen before: even when the editorial excursions began to discharge their hordes of hungry scribes upon them, they still looked on with good-natured stoicism; but when at last a recent convention of some six hundred hard-shell Baptists adjourned in a body to Monterey, then the patience of the long-suffering Mexicans gave way entirely, and loud and deep were the anathemas hurled by the faithful against the invading host of profaning heretics.

In the good old days, when Texas and Nuevo Leon were sister States of the "Eastern Internal Provinces," both loyal to his Majesty of Spain, San Antonio and Monterey were kindred cities, linked together by a community of interests, and the "old San Antonio road," that for three hundred miles wound among the rugged mountains and barren plains of a desert country, was swept by bands of savage Indians, and exposed to all the vicissitudes of a wild frontier. Then the seat of government was at Monterey, and San Luis Potosi, still further to the south, and from that direction came everything of power and civilization the country yet

---

* Chihuahua, capital of the State of like name, was reached at the same time by the Mexican Central Railroad, a continuation of the Atchison, Topeka, and Santa Fe.

* A term of ridicule and obloquy applied to Americans throughout all Mexico.

had known. How wonderfully has the current changed! The populous, ever-restless regions of the North have again asserted their supremacy, and over the same old road, now bound with bands of steel, rolls a returning flood that threatens soon to sweep away every vestige of the past.

Monterey, the capital of Nuevo Leon, and metropolis of northern Mexico, is picturesquely situated in a sort of amphi-theatre among the mountains, their huge, rugged forms towering over it in every direction save the north, where the valley widens out into the great plains lying blue and purple in the distance. Along the southern vista, beyond the green val-ley of the arroyo, and the gentle foot-hills crowned with white-towered chapels and suburban villas, extends the main range of the Sierra, here flanked on either side by the bold, detached peaks of La Mitra and Silla (the Mitre and Saddle), both most appropriately named, as is made ev-ident at a glance. The Sierra proper lifts itself in three distinct chains, one serrated line above another, until they fairly seem to lean against the sky, with the summer clouds drifting lazily below. Especially is this true of an early morning, when the rising mists of the val-ley unite with them in produc-ing the fairy-like landscapes above the clouds that form one of the chief charms of Alpine scenery. In gazing down any of the nar-row streets, and indeed in every view of Monterey, this rugged background is ever before the eyes, distance being al-most annihilated by the rarefied atmos-phere of the mountains.

To the new-comer, especially if escap-ing from the rigors of a Northern winter, the first night in Monterey offers a scene of enchantment. The narrow streets, with their dead-walls of massive masonry, flat-roofed, parapeted houses, with balconies and windows barred with iron gratings; the slouching groups of loungers at the street corners, wrapped to their eyes in gaudy *serape*, and shaded by sombreros of

immense dimensions—all have a delight-fully foreign look. Even the execrable pavements over which he is tortured in a decrepit old hack propelled by two deplor-able specimens of horseflesh, compared with which Don Quixote's Rozinante was a noble steed, are pronounced unique, as they undoubtedly are. But when the hotel is reached, and the traveller ushered into the cool, shaded corridors of the "Iturbide" or "Monterey," with its Moorish arched col-onnades and court-yard filled with tropic shrubbery—well, then his impressions of Monterey are, perhaps, a little more rose-colored than they may be a day or two later, when the novelty has a little worn away. We might almost say, "an *hour* or two later," for one of these hostelries is located in the convent of the Capu-chinos, and, however romantic the situa-tion, the bare stone cells, cement-floored and windowless, afford but sorry guest chambers. Buried in their depths, a lamp is necessary even at mid-day; however, as the artist observed, they are just the thing for a convention of photographers, where each would have his own "dark room" without extra trouble or expense.

Brought by the new railroad within a

PRIMITIVE SUGAR MILL.

few hours' travel of the United States, Monterey is yet essentially as strange and foreign to American eyes as if the broad Atlantic rolled between, and it were in the heart of Andalusian Spain. Not only are the scenery, architecture, language, very picturesque, but the varied dress and cus-toms of the people, as exemplified in the daily panorama of street life, are even more so, and are a constant source of in-terest to the new-comer. The bells of the numerous churches still keep up their continual jangle throughout the day; but the shovel-hatted *padres* and other en-signed members of the priesthood who formerly constituted the most picturesque figure of Mexican street life, have disappeared before the laws of reform, together with the convents and monasteries that gave them shelter. While the Church has thus gone to decay, the State is flourishing at its expense, for soldiers are to be met with everywhere, and uniforms are as common as in the strongest garrisoned towns on the Continent. Hardly to be distinguished from the regular troops are the city police: clothed in a sort of undress uniform, and a little brief authority, armed with a rusty old Toledo in lieu of the regulation locust club, they are a veritable terror to evil-doers, and, in truth, a most formidable body of men. To them it is due that Monterey is to-day the most quiet and orderly of cities; indeed, more so than most towns of its size in the United States. Then there are the *cargadores*, or porters, who, numbered and licensed like drays, of which they are the only substitute, may be seen bending under the most tremendous burdens. Provided with only a straw pad to protect the head, they will move piano-fortes and other heavy articles of furniture from one end of the town to the other, and this with apparent ease, and for the most trifling compensation. Another interesting character is the *sereno*, or night-watchman, who is always going about with a lantern, though, unlike his famous predecessor, looking for a *dishonest* man. In storm or calm, throughout the long watches of the night, his shrill voice may be heard calling off the hours, with the monotonous concluding formula of "*y todo es bueno*" (and all is well)—a custom brought down through force of tradition from the old Moorish times in Spain, when every city was an armed fortress, and its inhabitants lived in constant dread of being surprised by the turbaned moslem.

The market-place is a scene of bustle and animation that is as amusing as it is novel to Northern eyes. Here may be found a little of everything that enters into the every-day economy of Mexican life—economy indeed, where, as here, each necessary is doled out by the *tlaco* and *cuartillo*'s worth, (the eighth and quarter of a shilling). Patient donkeys, laden with every imaginable commodity, even to milk cans slung in panniers, stand disconsolately about, their long ears lapped down in utter despondency, while scores of hucksters cry their various wares in a

Babel of tongues that at times threatens to drown the sonorous voices of their long-eared rivals. Oranges from Linares, apples and peaches from Saltillo, eggs, each wrapped in corn husk, with vegetables of all sorts from nearer at home, even pottery and singing-birds, are all brought burro-back, packed in little crates of the carrizo cane. Of the pottery, many specimens would attract attention from the devotees of the late ceramic craze: while mostly of simple Indian workmanship, some few patterns, especially those brought from Guadalajara, in the interior, are of beautiful design both in moulding and ornamentation, and would rank as real works of art anywhere.

We have alluded to the picturesque aspect of Monterey street life, but to see it at its best one should select the harvest season, when the sugar is being marketed, and country provincialism turns out in all the gaudy display of Spanish dress and accoutrements. The streets are blocked with great lumbering carts drawn by long trains of bullocks, yoked, or rather fastened, with rawhide thongs about the horns, and all day long the ungreased axles may be heard groaning under their heavy loads of sugar, *frejoles*, and corn, baled in the coarse sacking of the ixtle plant.

Monterey, with its 40,000 inhabitants, has stores sufficient for treble that number; indeed, by virtue of its situation and the large amount of capital invested in business, it has long been the chief emporium of trade for an immense extent of country, including, besides its own, considerable portions of the neighboring States of Coahuila, Zacatecas, and Tamaulipas. Here is the purchasing and distributing point for all the native products which supply most of the wants of the lower classes, and are numerous and characteristic enough to warrant more than a passing notice. The sugar of Nuevo Leon, some 4,500,000 pounds, even with the present almost entirely domestic market, with half as much more from Tamaulipas, all put up on the plantations in little cakes of a pound each (*piloncillos*), wrapped in its own leaves; maize for *tortillas*, a national dish, and substitute for bread among the common people; *frejoles*, a large red bean, peculiar to the country, and one of its staple productions, by the hundreds of cart-loads; *chile* peppers, another national dish *par excellence; mes-*

BISHOP'S PALACE, MONTEREY.

cal, distilled from the maguey; cotton, wool, wheat, and barley from more temperate Coahuila; also the fine wines and brandies for which the district of Paris is celebrated—all these, with many other articles too numerous to mention, seek a purchaser at Monterey, in exchange for the bulky eagle dollars that here are literally handled by the "barr'l," two of the huge specie sacks being sufficient to fill one.

We must not omit to mention the maguey, yuca, and other fibrous plants which grow wild and in great profusion all over the country. They are manufactured with the most primitive appliances into cordage and various kinds of coarse sacking—an industry yet in its in-

fancy, but which promises great things for the future. This same industry further south, particularly in Yucatan, has developed into an extensive business, building railroads, subsidizing steamships, and bringing general wealth and prosperity to the land.

Even far-away Chihuahua sends her quota of live stock, hides, and skins across the desert; though silver she has in abundance, she is lacking in the productions of

PLAZA DE ZARAGOZA.

her more fruitful sister States. Here we would mention a curious instance of the commercial changes brought about even now by the advent of the railroads. Many cars of sugar and other products are being shipped from Monterey to Chihuahua, in bond, through the United States. No better proof could be given of the delays and vexations incident to ox-cart transportation.

But the foreign trade is the great reliance of Monterey, in which many of her merchants have grown to wealth and independence. A few months ago this was principally carried on through the port of Matamoras, by means of wagon trains and treasure *conductas*, but the completion of the railroad from Laredo has entirely changed the course of trade. Now everything is shipped over the Corpus Christi bonded route. Matamoras hopes to regain her lost supremacy through her railroad, now under construction, to Monterey; but that is for the future to decide.

Dry hides and skins, wool, ixtle, live stock, lead, and specie—this last far in excess of all others—are among the principal articles of export; while dry-goods and notions of every description, hardware, agricultural implements, and machinery, French wines and fancy groceries, petroleum, musical instruments, stationery, drugs and medicines—in fact, a

little of almost everything known to commerce is imported, often smuggled, into the country, and distributed over the interior at exorbitant prices. Cotton goods, particularly prints and calicoes, which form more than one-half of the entire imports, amounting to millions in the aggregate, are almost entirely of English manufacture, brought in bond through our territory; not but that the American goods are just as cheap, and of confessedly better quality, but the English dealers have long held a monopoly of the trade, understand the people, their peculiar ways of credit and doing business, and the goods required. This is the great secret of their success, and that of the French, German, and other foreign merchants who control the trade of Mexico: they understand the peculiar wants of their customers, and humor them accordingly. This is just what our own manufacturers will have to do before they can hope to make much headway against their rivals, nor are they at all backward in seizing the present opportunity. Those pioneers of commerce, the drummers, are making their appearance in Monterey, and manufacturers' goods are sold there cheaper than to the jobbers in our own country. Some few American manufactures—sewing-machines, arms and ammunition, for instance —have long been in great demand, and sold at extravagant prices. Improved agricultural implements are beginning to be used by the larger proprietors, but have to encounter the strong prejudice of the peasantry, who render them as ineffectual as possible, even to breaking or refusing to work with them. The ploughs most in use, such as are to be daily seen in the Monterey valley, are simply a crooked stick, sometimes shod with iron, and fastened to a long pole—an instrument whose ineffectual scratching would provoke the

shall be made good at any cost. Failures are almost unknown, and are not recognized commercially or in law.

Many articles that formerly were among the principal imports are now largely produced in the country, the result of the government's liberal policy toward manufacturers. Monterey has three cotton factories in successful operation, all provided with the most improved machinery, print-works where the poorly paid operatives receive less day wages than the price

A MEXICAN TAN-YARD.

mingled amazement and derision of any energetic Yankee rooster. They will be readily recognized as the exact counterparts of the ploughs pictured forth in illustrations of old Biblical times. Threshing is still carried on through the agency of half-wild horses driven about the grain in a paved inclosure, and the sugar mills are mainly of the most primitive pattern, with wooden rollers slowly manipulated through the labors of a pair of stout bullocks.

The Mexican merchants are of a very high order of integrity. Whatever else they may be or do, Castilian pride requires that their obligations and plighted word

of a single yard of the cloth they manufacture, several flouring mills, an ice factory, a score or more of tanneries, with manufactories of boots and shoes, saddles, hats, candles, matches, mining chemicals, and many others of less importance. A large and expensive sugar refinery stands idle, principally because of the prejudice of the people in favor of old methods. The passing of the proposed reciprocal treaty may give it renewed activity. A long street in the eastern suburbs is given up to the tan-yards, where the almost naked workmen wade about the vats spearing refractory hides as a Western river "driver" does his logs. The *encina*, or live-oak, affords material for tannin, the bark first pulverized under a ponderous stone wheel dragged around by a disconsolate mule that was only too glad to rest from his enforced labors for the artist to better take his picture.

Monterey is regularly laid out after the old Spanish style, with spacious plazas, narrow streets paved with a sort of conglomerate of cobble-stones and cement, and a once beautiful *alameda*, now sadly gone to decay. Of the former, some half a dozen are scattered throughout the city, several ornamented with trees and shrubbery, with shaded walks and flowing fountains, a grateful resort for the tired wayfarer during the heat of the day—all lending an air of ease and refinement to the often somewhat incongruous surroundings. The principal square, or Plaza de Zaragoza, as it is called, in honor of the hero of Pueblo, is in reality an extensive oblong in the heart of the city, with the Capitol, or "palace" of the government, cutting it in the centre. Here, as in every Mexican town, is the grand centre of Church and State, the emporium of the business and social life of the community. The venerable cathedral, with its huge pile of chiselled stone and elaborate stucco-work, would attract attention anywhere, even when, as here, it suffers from the contrast with nature's mighty monument, the Saddle Mountain, in the background. Without any regular order of architecture, but rather that mixture of the Moresque and Italian Renaissance so much in vogue throughout all Spanish America, the general effect is pleasing, and even imposing. Especially is this true of the interior, where in the subdued light scores of penitents may be seen at all hours of the day kneeling prone upon the floor, while the stained windows, the rich carving and painting of the altar, the whispered responses and chanting of the choir echoing along the vaulted roof, all tend to promote those feelings of awe and devotion which lie deep down in every human heart. The chancel—indeed, almost the entire body of the cathedral—is paved with a sort of giant mosaic of time-stained cedar, each panel ceiling the tomb of some one of the faithful, who thus in death rests under the very shadow of the sanctuary.

Up in the towers among the fourteen bells that almost deafen one with their clatter, after toiling over the shaky, worm-eaten stairs that threaten to tumble with every renewed gust of wind, a magnificent prospect of the city, with its fertile plain and towering mountain ramparts, rewards the adventurous climber for his toil. Hard by is the once flourishing monastery of the Franciscans, now degraded to the base office of a city prison, with its one lordly palmetto that the "Padre José" loved and cared for so tenderly in days of yore. In front, beyond the clustering house-tops, towers, and orchard-gardens, the Bishop's Palace rears itself in bold relief, commanding both the city and the dark defile leading away to Saltillo, in the background. This forms a salient point in most views of Monterey, and is the shrine to which every American first makes his pilgrimage. As he climbs the steep rocky ascent, the mind involuntarily goes back to that other day, thirty-six years ago, when all the hill was wreathed in sulphurous smoke, and his country's flag borne in triumph to crown the fortress on its summit. Even on a peace footing the tramp is tiresome enough; what was it, then, when in the face of determined resistance from superior numbers intrenched behind stone walls, the works were stormed and taken at the point of the bayonet! Now the old fortress is strangely quiet; at its feet lies the smiling valley, the city over which it dominates; but here, as in another world not yet awakened, no sign of life or animation disturbs the memories of the past. A few antiquated cannon, old veterans of the Bishop's Palace, lie in picturesque confusion about the summit. Spiked and broken, their formidableness has long since departed, the long grass half hides their rusting forms, and the birds build their nests undisturbed in the long-silent mouths. Between the palace and the city proper may be seen "the house in the tree," a sort of Swiss chalet built high up in the branches of an immense pecan-tree. This is one of the sights of the city, and from its sixty-six feet of altitude a fine view may be had of its surroundings. The new order of "improvements" has utilized it for a beer garden.

Before the advent of the railroad, not one-tenth of even the more intelligent classes of the population had ever seen a locomotive; and the most exaggerated ideas, derived from vague rumors of the phenomenal growth of Western towns under the magic impetus of Yankee enterprise, were popularly current as to the

A COURT-YARD IN MONTEREY.

wonderful era of building and prosperity about to be inaugurated. The whole western suburbs, and far out on to the level, irrigated plain, were to spring up, mushroom-like, into a city by itself—a veritable American quarter of staked-out streets, wooden shanties, and corner lots of fabulous value. So the long, romantic lanes that from time immemorial had been at once the pride and glory of Monterey were laid waste, their grateful shade of lordly pecan and sycamore, many of them of half a century's growth, even the very hedges, ruthlessly cut down by their "enterprising" owners. Now the white, glaring roads, half smothered in dust and deprived of their wonted shade, the murmuring canals fast drying up under the fervid beams of the sun, the once-fruitful fields lying so bare and brown—all give mournful testimony to the aggressive march of modern "progress." The railroad has come and gone, but the few very ordinary buildings pertaining to it, with the inevitable "American House," recognizable anywhere, are all that go to mark the site of the new city that is yet to be. Fallen cypresses still cumber the ground as they fell—fit emblems of the destruction they exemplify—the only occupants of the lots, whose far-seeing purchasers now mourn over their permanent investments. It may be questioned if this one act of vandalism has not fully compensated for every benefit, present and future, the railroad has brought or will bring to Monterey. To fully appreciate it, it must be remembered that this is essentially a barren country, deficient alike in wood and water, the very name Nuevo Leon given in remembrance of that part of treeless Spain whose barrenness is most deplorable. In truth, Monterey has heretofore had a superfluity of room, the population falling away with the decay of the country after the expulsion of the Spaniard and succeeding period of wars and revolutions. Houses already built were rather suffered to go to decay than new ones begun, and retrogression was the general order of the day up to the present infusion of new blood and energy.

A whitish stone found near by is used almost exclusively for building, so soft when first taken from the quarry as to work readily with ordinary carpenter's tools, but afterward hardening through exposure to the air.

The houses of the better class are all built in the form of a hollow square, inclosing the *patio*, or court-yard, the latter generally surrounded with an arched colonnade planted with flowers and tropical plants. Here, too, is found the well, with its wall of masonry and leathern bucket. The water is always cool and clear as crystal, as well it may be, for the wells are cut through the living rock to an immense depth, the work of the old Spanish times. Some few buildings are of considerable pretension, indeed, embellished in a style of almost Oriental magnificence. Noticeable among them is the house of Don Patricio Milmo, with its double arched gallery and court-yard adorned with fountain, seats, and shrubbery—a veritable

little plaza of itself. Here, as also in the large fountain on the Zaragoza Plaza, may be seen specimens of the beautiful variegated marble of Nuevo Leon. Monterey has but comparatively few of the *jacals*, or hovels, so common about the outskirts of most Mexican towns.

Resting under the arched colonnade of the "palace" on the plaza may be seen the Monterey Fire Department—an institution of amusing interest to most American visitors, who, however, hardly view it with those feelings of awe and admiration ascribed to them by the native lookers-on. A wheezy little hand-engine that was out of date a century ago, with a few feet of rotten hose, comprises the entire force. Yet even this is very seldom called into service, and is comparatively much more adequate to answer all demands than are the best paid fire departments of our largest cities. A serious conflagration is out of the question in Monterey, everything being fire-proof, from the cement floor to the roof of cement, stone, and tiles. In the event of fire, as at every other time of public interest or calamity, the soldiers are ordered out, who soon smother the flames with dirt in regular sapper-and-miner style.

Monterey, from a military stand-point, is the key of northern Mexico, and has always played an important part in the various wars and revolutions that have afflicted the country. The surrounding heights are crowned with the ruins of old fortifications, now dismounted and fast crumbling away, while scarcely a street or square in the city but bears marks of the conflict, the stone doors in many instances showing the holes where the locks have been blown open with musketry. Here are the head-quarters of the Military Division of the North, under the command of General Treviño, ex-Minister of War, and one of the famous men of his country under the new and liberal Diaz administration. Born and bred in Nuevo Leon, he is emphatically a man of the people, the idol of the army he has so often led to victory during the troublous times succeeding Maximilian's usurpation. But it is in the romantic incidents of the general's "international" marriage that Americans will take the most interest, out of which, indeed, a very pretty romance might be drawn. At the close of 1877, when Mexican border affairs were in a most critical and unsatisfactory condition,

President Hayes's celebrated order authorizing the invasion of Mexico by our troops, when "in hot pursuit" of raiders, was promulgated. The opposing frontiers were under the respective commands of General Treviño and the late lamented General Ord. To the good judgment and moderation of these two officers was largely due

nineteen, and the usual result soon followed. Negotiations for the betrothal were carried on with all the form of a foreign potentate suing for a princess of the blood, and soon the old cathedral of San Fernando saw a wedding such as it had never seen before. General Treviño is generally conceded to be the coming man,

GLIMPSE OF SANTA CATARINA.

the fact that the existing irritation did not ripen into open hostilities, and out of their necessarily close social and business relations there sprang a warm friendship, founded on mutual respect and esteem. At the house of General Ord in San Antonio his guest met the oldest daughter, a beautiful and interesting girl of sweet

and next successor of Diaz to the Presidency; so there is every probability that in the near future an American lady will be called upon to do the honors of the Presidential mansion at the city of Mexico.

To see Monterey at its best one should view it from the house-tops on one of the glorious moonlight nights so common in these latitudes. The sentinel mountains stand out in bold relief against the azure sky, their summits half veiled in fleecy clouds, as if keeping guard over the sleeping city at their feet. Apparently within pistol-shot, they are in reality many miles away, yet every rocky gorge and sheer descent, even the giant pines that crown their rugged sides, are shadowed forth in bold relief—such is the marvellous purity of this atmosphere. Below, the white-walled city, with its flat roofs, towers, and domes, lies spread out as if upon a map, every arch, column, crenellated parapet, and jaloused window magnified in the flood of misty light.

At least one-third of the city is in ruins, and this not confined to any particular quarter, but distributed throughout the whole, some of the most extensive lying in picturesque confusion within a stone's-throw of the main centre of business on the plaza. Everywhere are broken columns, fragments of long lines of graceful arches, the crumbling ruins of once pretentious buildings, now dismantled and covered with a luxuriant growth of tangled vegetation. But the ill wind which blows nobody good has had no hand in this, for the wretched hovels are the refuge of thousands of the poorer class, this doubtless accounting for the scarcity of *jacals* on the outskirts, before referred to.

In truth, here as everywhere else in Mexico the day of the expulsion of the Spaniards was the beginning of a decadence in every material interest of the country—a decadence only arrested through the present invasion of foreign brains and capital. We remember to have seen recently at Santa Catarina, on the road to Saltillo, droves of cattle driven through the carved portals of one of the finest fronts on the plaza. The former mansion of a Spanish grandee had become a corral for wild cattle.

The business prospects of Monterey are very promising. It is already a railroad centre, and well able to hold and extend the trade already tributary to its capital and position. Nor can the great stream of travel and immigration—invalids, tourists, and prospectors—even now pouring into Monterey, and sure to be increased tenfold another season, prove anything but beneficial to the city, and money into the pockets of its citizens. Long before November's frosts begin to prompt the invalids and pleasure-seekers from the North to find a milder clime, the road will be completed to Saltillo and beyond, and here, at an elevation of 4500 feet, sheltered among the mountains, and far removed from the chill "northers" that sweep over Florida and the coast, will be found a climate of perpetual spring, the most perfect on this continent, if not in the world.

NATIVE POTTERY.

A REMINISCENCE OF MR. DARWIN.

EARLY in 1871, while passing a few months in London, it being my good fortune to know Sir Charles Lyell, I, through his introduction, made the personal acquaintance of Mr. Darwin. At that time the state of Mr. Darwin's health was regarded by his family and friends as very delicate; and absorbed as he was in scientific and literary pursuits, he spent most of his time in the retirement of his country home in Kent, and very rarely saw strangers. Under these circumstances I had no reason to expect the pleasure of a personal interview with him. It so happened, however, that, some ten or twelve years before, I had made a long cruise in the South Pacific Ocean, and had visited many of the coral islands of that region. Talking of these islands with Sir Charles Lyell, and expressing something of the deep interest with which I at that time had read Mr. Darwin's *Voyage of the Beagle*, and especially his studies of coral islands, he was kind enough to say, doubtless in response to a wish of mine, implied if not expressed, that if a favorable occasion offered he would gladly procure for me an opportunity of talking with Darwin himself on the subject. Accordingly, not long after, I received a message from Sir Charles saying that Mr. Darwin, accompanied by some of his family, was spending a few days in town at his brother's house in Queen Anne Street, where he would be pleased to see me at luncheon on the following Sunday. This pleasant invitation was accompanied with a thoughtful warning in a note from Lady Lyell to the effect that although I might find Mr. Darwin looking well and strong, I should remember his really delicate health, and not stay too long.

On my arrival at the door, at the appointed hour, the servant evidently recognized the name of an expected visitor, and took me upstairs at once to a small library room, where I found Darwin alone. He came forward very cordially, putting out his hand in a way to make a stranger feel welcome, and entered directly into conversation in a manner lively enough to relieve any apprehension of his suffering as a great invalid. At that time he was about sixty-two, and he already wore the full gray beard visible in the portraits taken in his later years. We had a little

to say about his health, and he spoke of the opinion of some of his friends that its present rather feeble state might be attributed to long-continued seasickness on his voyages years ago; and then said, "So you've been a voyager too?" and asked me in what part of the Pacific Ocean I had been, and what islands I had seen. I thereupon related to him some of my experiences and observations, which led to a pleasant talk on his part about the coral islands. He spoke with great vivacity and interest of his voyage in the *Beagle*, and especially of his work on coral reefs and atolls, of the wonderful impression that those islands make upon the mind of an observer, and of the charm and poetry they possess in their singular beauty and their peculiar origin and structure.

We were presently joined by two of Mr. Darwin's sons (George, now Professor of Astronomy and Experimental Philosophy at Cambridge, England, and Francis, for several years his father's secretary and co-laborer in botanical researches), and soon after went down to luncheon, where we met Miss Darwin, his daughter, Mrs. Darwin's absence being excused on account of illness. In the course of conversation I expressed to Mr. Darwin the regret I had ever since felt that when I went out to the South-sea Islands I was so poorly qualified to observe many of the most interesting features of the places visited, as I had studied very little of natural history, and knew nothing of birds, fishes, corals, shells, or anything of that sort. "Well," said he, "you need not think yourself unique in that respect. I never knew a man who had a rare opportunity for observation who did not regret his imperfect qualifications. It was my own experience. If I could only go now, with my head sixty years old and my body twenty-five, I could do something." Then he said that his visit to the Pacific, or rather his voyage in the *Beagle*, was the beginning of his scientific career; that he had not before given much serious attention to science, or studied with a definite purpose; that when the *Beagle* was fitting out he was a young man, fond of sport, shooting and fishing, and with a strong liking for natural history; and it seemed to him a pleasant thing to go as volunteer on the party with his friend Captain Fitzroy. Even after he came back, he said, it was only after many talks with Lyell, who always heard with interest whatever he had to say, and who urged him to work up and publish his results, that he determined to devote himself to scientific studies.

After a while he spoke of some of his American friends, saying that Mr. Charles Eliot Norton and family had been his neighbors in the country for a time, and that he had enjoyed their society very much. He also mentioned visits which he had received from the younger Agassiz and from Dr. Gray, saying of the latter, "Gray often takes me to task for making hasty generalizations; but the last time he was here talking that way I said to him: 'Now, Gray, I have one more generalization to make, which is not hasty, and that is, the Americans are the most delightful people I know.'"

The conversation having turned upon his last book, *The Descent of Man*, which had made its first appearance only shortly before, he spoke of the reviews which he had so far seen, saying that most of them were, of course, somewhat superficial, and doubtless others might come later of a different tone, but he had been much impressed by the general assent with which his views had been received. "Twenty years ago," said he, "such ideas would have been thought subversive of everything good, and their author might have been hooted at, but now not only the press, but, from what my friends who go into society say, everybody, is talking about it without being shocked."

"That is true," I said, "but, according to Mr. *Punch*, while the men seem to accept it without dissent, the women are inclined to protest."

"Ah, has *Punch* taken me up?" said Mr. Darwin, inquiring further as to the point of the joke, which, when I had told him, seemed to amuse him very much. "I shall get it to-morrow," he said: "I keep all those things. Have you seen me in the *Hornet*?" As I had not seen the number referred to, he asked one of his sons to fetch the paper from upstairs. It contained a grotesque caricature representing a great gorilla having Darwin's head and face, standing by the trunk of a tree with a club in his hand. Darwin showed it off very pleasantly, saying, slowly and with characteristic criticism, "The head is cleverly done, but the gorilla is bad: too much chest; it couldn't be like that."

The humorists have done much to make Mr. Darwin's features familiar to the public, in pictures not so likely to inspire respect for the author of *The Descent of Man* as they are to imply his very close relation to some slightly esteemed branches of the ancestry he claims; but probably no one has enjoyed their fun more than he.

Luncheon was already over, and, mindful of Lady Lyell's caution, I took an early leave.

To this short narrative I may add the following concerning a subsequent occasion upon which I had the pleasure of seeing Mr. Darwin with his family at their home in Kent. Being again in London in 1878, I was very glad to receive one day about the middle of May a message from Mrs. Darwin inviting me to go down into the country to dine and pass the night at their house in company with one other guest, Colonel T. W. Higginson, of Boston. Leaving town about four or five o'clock in the afternoon, a railway ride of an hour or a little less through one of the most beautiful parts of England brought us to Orpington, from which station we had to make a drive of three or four miles to Darwin's house, near the old and picturesque village of Down. Meeting Mr. George Darwin on the train, we got into a dogcart which was awaiting us at Orpington station, and drove pleasantly for half an hour through a charming succession of pretty lanes and country roads on our way to Down. The day was showery, and before reaching our destination we got something of a wetting; but the intervals of bright sunshine between the showers lit up a most beautiful landscape, and gave a wonderfully brilliant effect to the foliage, glistening with the freshly fallen rain. The trees, the hedges, the shrubbery, and the grass all seemed on that May day, with alternating sun and shower, to be in a state of absolute perfection. Just before arriving we got a pretty view of Down, and passed within sight of the country-seat of Darwin's friend and fellow-worker in scientific pursuits, Sir John Lubbock.

The dwelling of the Darwin family, as I recall it, is a spacious and substantial old-fashioned house, square in form and plain in style, but pleasing in its comfortable and home-like appearance. The approach seems now to my memory to have been by a long lane, as though the house stood remote from any much-travelled highway, and without near neighbors, surrounded by trees and shrubbery, and commanding a far-reaching view of green fields and gently undulating country. A portion of the house, the front, has, I believe, been built long enough to be spoken of as old even in England, to which in the rear some modern additions have been made. Entering a broad hall at the front, we passed, on the right, the door of the room the interior of which has since been made known in pictures as "Mr. Darwin's Study"; and a little further on were welcomed immediately by Mr. and Mrs. Darwin to a spacious and cheerful parlor or family room, whose broad windows and outer door opened upon a wide and partly sheltered piazza at the rear of the house, evidently a favorite sitting-place, judging from the comfortable look of easy-chairs assembled there, beyond which was a pleasing vista of fresh green lawn, bright flower beds, and blossoming shrubbery, gravel-paths, and a glass greenhouse, or perhaps botanical laboratory, and, further yet, a garden wall, with a gate leading to pleasant walks in fields beyond. All this one could see standing before the hearth, from which, although past the middle of May, a slowly smouldering fire gave out a pleasant warmth, by no means unwelcome to one whose clothing had been dampened by the brisk shower encountered on the way from the station.

The interior of the room wore a delightfully comfortable and every-day look, with books and pictures in profusion, and a large table in the middle covered with papers, periodicals, and literary miscellany. At a smaller round table, bearing a shaded lamp not yet lit and a work-basket, Mrs. Darwin—a lady of agreeable presence, perhaps eight or ten years younger than her husband (whose cousin she is), and of slightly larger stature than the average English woman of her age—resumed the place from which she had evidently risen to welcome her guests, occupying her hands with some light embroidery or other feminine handiwork, while joining in the general conversation with an occasional remark.

Mr. Darwin sat by the fireside, where he seemed to have been reading. Dressed in an easy-fitting, short, round coat, he looked as though he might have spent the day at work in the garden or laboratory. Though seven years had passed since I had seen him in London, he appeared as

well as then and hardly older. We had some pleasant personal chat for a little while, when Colonel Higginson, whose arrival had been delayed, came in, and, soon after, we went to our rooms to dress for dinner, Mr. Darwin himself going on before to show his guests the way, and to see that their needs had been duly provided for.

Re-assembled a half-hour later, we were soon seated at the dinner table, six in all, George and Francis being the only younger members of the family then at home. The dining-room was a handsome, spacious apartment, with windows opening upon the lawn in the rear of the house; its walls hung with pictures, among which I seem to recall some dim, dark portraits of the Darwin ancestry, though nothing, if I remember rightly, more remote than the distinguished grandfather, Dr. Erasmus. Our dinner, though noteworthy for its wholesome simplicity in these days of excessive luxury, was served with care and elegance by two men-servants in livery, the elder butler, a man of advanced years, being evidently of long service in the family. The dinner-table talk was for the greater part light, cheerful, personal; to some extent political, suggested by current events in England and the United States; and touching somewhat upon social reforms, as might indeed be readily imagined in the presence of my distinguished *vis-à-vis*, Colonel Higginson. To this, however, the way was, perhaps, more directly led by the coincidence of a temperance lecture being given that evening in the public hall at Down, in which good work the family evidently felt some interest; and partly, too, by the experience of Colonel Higginson at the railway station, where he had narrowly escaped being called upon to appear in the rôle of a reformer. The lecturer, it seems, had come down from London by an early evening train, and upon Mr. Francis Darwin had devolved the duty of meeting him at the station, taking him to the hall, and seeing him fairly started upon his praiseworthy mission before returning to join us at dinner. As I now recall the affair, Colonel Higginson, having been delayed in town, had arrived at Orpington station by the same train with the lecturer, and while seeking some means of reaching his further destination, fell in with Mr. Francis Darwin, who, not then knowing him per-

CHARLES DARWIN.

From photograph by Maull and Fox, 187 Piccadilly, London.

sonally, and anxiously looking for the lecturer, supposed the colonel was his man, and was about whisking him off to leave him at the public hall when he discovered his mistake. Doubtless the colonel would have graced the platform as well as the dinner table, at which the incident, as he related it, afforded us some amusement.

When Mrs. Darwin rose to leave the gentlemen with their cigars, she reminded her husband that he too must go and take his customary nap. He accordingly withdrew, but about half an hour later rejoined us in the drawing-room, where he remained until half past ten or eleven. During this time he made inquiry for American friends, mostly of Cambridge, but also Marsh, of New Haven. He spoke, too, with particular interest of Mark Twain, from whose writings he had evidently derived much entertainment.

We broke up for the night with the understanding that Colonel Higginson, who had a morning engagement in town, should be called for an earlier breakfast than the rest, and go by a train leaving soon after eight o'clock, while my departure was deferred till noon. Happening to waken early, I dressed and went downstairs soon after seven, but to my surprise Mr. Darwin was there, fresh as a lark, ready to breakfast with the colonel, and speed the parting guest. When he had gone, the later members of the family gathered at their leisure about the breakfast table, while Mr. Darwin disappeared for an hour's work in his study.

During this interval I accepted the invitation of Francis Darwin to go with him for a walk about the grounds, in the course of which we followed some of his father's favorite rambles along shaded paths in a neighboring field, coming back finally to the greenhouse, where some interesting experiments on the revolving movement of plants were at that time in progress. The work of the forenoon was the careful observation of a number of tender shoots that were growing in pots, each under a separate bell-glass, and all ranged on a table exposed to the morning sun. To the growing tip of each plant there had been attached by wax or some other adhesive substance one end of a straight piece of very finely drawn glass thread, in such a manner that its other end projected about two inches, horizontally or nearly so, from the point of attachment, where any revolving movement of the stem must be imparted to the glass thread, and cause it to turn like a radial arm from a central point. The ends of the glass thread were made conspicuous by little "blobs" of color, thus giving two easily distinguished points in one straight line. By marking then upon the outer surface of the bell-glass a third point in line with the two "blobs," the subsequent departure of the outer "blob" from that line, caused by the turning of the stem of the plant, very soon became distinctly visible.

At the moment of departure the family gathered at the door, each with a parting word and good wish, and I came away filled with pleasant memories of a charming home and gracious hospitality.

EVENING.

I FEEL the cool breath of the coming night,
    Sweet with the scent of meadows and new hay,
And subtly as a failing of the sight
    The dusk invisibly dissolves the day.
Still in the west an arc of primrose light
    Crowns like an aureole the mountain's brow,
Flecked with thin sprays of palest red and gold,
    And through its lambent heart is piercing now
The point of one large star, keen, still, and cold.

The east lies in the arms of night; the eye
    No longer marks the lines of hedge and lane,
The russet stacks and squares of husbandry,
    The shaven stubble and the furrowed plain;
But over all a clear obscurity—
    A pearly gloom lit from the lucid skies—
Hangs like a tenuous veil, through which is seen
    A world transformed to unfamiliar guise
Of darkling loveliness, cool, dim, serene.

CHAPTER XXVIII.

RENEWALS.

AS yet she was all unconscious; and indeed the dullness following her father's departure was for her considerably lightened by this visit to her grandmother's cottage, where she found a hundred duties and occupations awaiting her. She was an expert needle-woman, and there were many arrears in that direction to be made up: she managed the cooking, and introduced one or two cunning dishes, to the wonder of the little Cicely; she even tried her hand at carpentering, where a shelf, or the frame of a casement, had got loose; and as a reward she was occasionally invited to assist her grandmother in the garden. The old dame herself grew wonderfully amiable and cheerful in the constant association with this bright young life; and she had a great store of ballads with which to beguile the tedium of sewing—though, in truth, these were for the most part of a monotonous and mournful character, generally reciting the woes of some poor maiden in Oxfordshire or Lincolnshire who had been deceived by a false lover, and yet was willing to forgive him even as she lay on her death-bed. As for Judith, she took to this quiet life quite naturally and happily; and if she chanced to have time for a stroll along the wooded lanes or through the meadows, she was now right glad that there was no longer any fear of her being confronted by Master Leofric Hope—or Jack Orridge, as he had called himself. Of course she thought of him often, and of his courteous manners, and his eloquent and yet modest eyes, and she hoped all was going well with him, and that she might perchance hear of him through her father. Nor could she forget (for she was but human) that the young man, when disguised as a wizard, had said that he had heard her named as the fairest maid in Warwickshire; and subsequently, in his natural character, that he had heard Ben Jonson speak well of her looks, and she hoped that if ever he recalled these brief interviews, he would consider that she had maintained a sufficiency of maidenly dignity, and had not betrayed the ignorance or awkwardness of a farm-bred wench. Nay, there were certain words of his that she put some store by—as coming from a stranger. For the rest, she was in no case likely to undervalue her appearance: her father had praised her hair, and that was enough.

One morning she had gone down to the little front gate, for some mischievous boys had lifted it off its hinges, and she wanted to get it back again on the rusty iron spikes. But it had got jammed somehow, and would not move; and in her pulling, some splinter of the wood ran into her hand, causing not a little pain. Just at this moment—whether he had come round that way on the chance of catching a glimpse of her it is hard to say—Tom Quiney came by; but on the other side of the road, and clearly with no intention of calling at the cottage.

"Good-morrow, Judith," said he, in a kind of uncertain way, and would have gone on.

Well, she was vexed and impatient with her fruitless efforts, and her hand smarted not a little; so she looked at him and said, half angrily,

"I wish you would come and lift this gate."

It was but a trifling task for the tall and straight-limbed young fellow who now strode across the highway. He jerked it up in a second, and then set it down again on the iron spikes, where it swung in its wonted way.

"But your hand is bleeding, Judith!" he exclaimed.

"'Tis nothing," she said. "It was a splinter. I have pulled it out."

But he snatched her hand peremptorily, before she could draw it away, and held it firmly and examined it.

"Why, there's a bit still there; I can see it."

"I can get it out for myself," said she.

"No, you can not," he answered. "'Tis far easier for some one else. Stay here a second, and I will fetch out a needle."

He went into the cottage, and presently re-appeared, not only with a needle, but also with a tin vessel holding water, and a bit of linen and a piece of thread. Then he took Judith's soft hand as gently as he could in his muscular fingers, and began to probe for the small fragment of wood just visible there. He seemed a long time about it: perhaps he was afraid of giving her pain.

"Do I hurt you, Judith?" he said.

"No," she answered, with some color of embarrassment in her face. "Be quick."

"But I must be cautious," said he. "I would it were my own hand; I would make short work of it."

"Let me try myself," said she, attempting to get away her hand from his grasp.

But he would not allow that; and in due time he managed to get the splinter out. Then he dipped his fingers in the water and bathed the small wound in that way; and then he must needs wrap the piece of linen round her hand—very carefully, so that there should be no crease—and thereafter fasten the bandage with the bit of thread. He did not look like one who could perform a surgical operation with exceeding delicacy; but he was as gentle as he could be, and she thanked him—in an unwilling kind of way.

Then all at once her face brightened.

"Why," said she, "I hear that you gave my father a riding-whip on his going."

"Did you not see it, Judith?" he said, with some disappointment. "I meant you to have seen it. The handle was of ivory, and of a rare carving."

"I was not at the door when they went away—I met my father as they passed along the road," said she. "But I shall see it, doubtless, when he comes home again. And what said he? Was he pleased? He thanked you right heartily, did he not?"

"Yes, truly; but 'twas a trifling matter."

"My father thinks more of the intention than of the value of such a gift," said she—"as I would."

It was an innocent and careless speech, but it seemed to suddenly inspire him with a kind of wild wish.

"Ah," said he, regarding her, "if you, Judith, now, would but take some little gift from me—no matter what—that would be a day I should remember all my life."

"Will you not come into the house?" said she, quickly. "My grandam will be right glad to see you."

She would have led the way; but he hesitated.

"Nay, I will not trouble your grandmother, Judith," said he. "I doubt not but that she hath had enough of visitors since you came to stay with her."

"Since I came?" she said, good-naturedly—for she refused to accept the innuendo. "Why, let me consider, now. The day before yesterday my mother walked over to see how we did; and before that—I think the day before that—Mistress Wyse came in to tell us that they had taken a witch at Abbots Morton; and then yesterday Farmer Bowstead called to ask if his strayed horse had been seen anywhere about these lanes. There, now, three visitors since I have come to the cottage: 'tis not a multitude."

"There hath been none other?" said he, looking at her with some surprise.

"Not another foot hath crossed the threshold to my knowledge," said she, simply, and as if it were a matter of small concern.

But this intelligence seemed to produce a very sudden and marked alteration in his manner. Not only would he accompany her into the house, but he immediately became most solicitous about her hand.

"I pray you be careful, Judith," said he, almost as if he would again take hold of her wrist.

"'Tis but a scratch," she said.

"Nay, now, if there be but a touch of rust, it might work mischief," said he, anxiously. "I pray you be careful; and I would bathe it frequently, and keep on the bandage until you are sure that all is well. Nay, I tell you this, Judith: there are more than you think of that would liefer lose a finger than that you should have the smallest hurt."

And in-doors, moreover, he was most amiable and gentle and anxious to please, and bore some rather sharp sayings of the old dame with great good-nature; and whatever Judith said, or suggested, or approved of, that was right, once and for all. She wished to hear more of the riding-whip also. Where was the handle carved? Had her father expressed any desire for such ornamentation?

"Truly 'twas but a small return for his kindness to us the other day," said the young man, who was half bewildered with delight at finding Judith's eyes once more regarding him in the old frank and friendly fashion, and was desperately anxious that they should continue so to regard him (with no chilling shadow of the parson intervening). "For Cornelius Greene being minded to make one or two more catches," he continued—and still addressing those eyes that were at once so gentle and so clear and so kind—"he would have me go to your father and beg him to give us words for these, out of any books he might know of. Not that we thought of asking him to write the words himself—far from that—but to choose them for us: and right willingly he did so. In truth, I have them with me," he added, searching for and producing a paper with some written lines on it. "Shall I read them to you, Judith?"

He did not notice the slight touch of indifference with which she assented; for when once she had heard that these compositions (whatever they might be) were not her father's writing, she was not anxious to become acquainted with them. But his concern, on the other hand, was to keep her interested and amused and friendly; and Cornelius Greene and his doings were at least something to talk about.

"The first one we think of calling 'Fortune's Wheel,'" said he; "and thus it goes:

' Trust not too much, if prosperous times do smile,
  Nor yet despair of rising, if thou fall:
The Fatal Lady mingleth one with th' other,
  And lets not fortune stay, but round turns all.'

And the other one—I know not how to call it yet—but Cornelius takes it to be the better of the two for his purpose; thus it is:

' Merrily sang the Ely monks
  When rowed thereby Canute the King.
" Row near, my Knights, row near the land,
  That we may hear the 'good monks sing.'"

See you now how well it will go, Judith —Merrily sang—merrily sang—the Ely monks — the Ely monks — when rowed thereby—CANUTE THE KING!" said he, in a manner suggesting the air. "'Twill go excellent well for four voices, and Cornelius is already begun. In truth, 'twill be something new at our merry-meetings—"

"Ay, and what have you to say of your business, good Master Quiney?" the old dame interrupted, sharply. "Be you so busy with your tavern catches and your merry-makings that you have no thought of that?"

"Indeed, I have enough regard for that, good Mistress Hathaway," said he, in perfect good-humor; "and it goes forward safely enough. But methinks you remind me that I have tarried here as long as I ought; so now I will get me back to the town."

He half expected that Judith would go to the door with him; and when she had gone so far, he said,

"Will you not come a brief way across the meadows, Judith?—'tis not well you should always be shut up in the cottage—you that are so fond of out-of-doors."

He had no cause for believing that she was too much within-doors; but she did not stay to raise the question; she good-naturedly went down the little garden path with him, and across the road, and so into the fields. She had been busy at work all the morning; twenty minutes' idleness would do no harm.

Then, when they were quite by themselves, he said, seriously:

"I pray you take heed, Judith, that you let not the blood flow too much to your hand, lest it inflame the wound, however slight you may deem it. See, now, if you would but hold it so, 'twould rest on mine, and be a relief to you."

He did not ask her to take his arm, but merely that she should rest her hand on his; and this seemed easy to do, and natural (so long as he was not tired). But also it seemed very much like the time when they used to go through those very meadows as boy and girl together, the tips of their fingers intertwined: and so she spoke in a gentle and friendly kind of fashion to him.

"And how is it with your business, in good sooth?" she asked. "I hope there be no more of these junketings, and dancings, and brawls."

"Dear Judith," said he, "I know not who carries such tales of me to you. If you knew but the truth, I am never in a brawl of mine own making or seeking; but one must hold one's own, and the more that is done, the less are any likely to interfere. Nay," he continued, with a modest laugh, "I think I am safe for quiet now with any in Warwickshire; 'tis only a strange lad now and again that may come among us and seek cause of quarrel; and surely 'tis better to have it over and done with, and either he or we to know our place? I seek no fighting for the love of it; my life on that; but you would not have any stranger come into Stratford a-swaggering, and biting his thumb at us, and calling us rogues of fiddlers?"

"Mercy on us, then," she cried, "are you champion for the town—or perchance for all of Warwickshire? A goodly life to look forward to! And what give they their watch-dog? Truly they must reward him that keeps such guard, and will do battle for them all?"

"Nay, I am none such, Judith," said he: "I but take my chance like the others."

He shifted her hand on his that it might rest the more securely, and his touch was gentle.

"And your merchandise — pray you who is so kind as to look after that when you are engaged in those pastimes?" she asked.

"I have no fault to find with my merchandise, Judith," said he. "That I look after myself. I would I had more inducement to attend to it, and to provide for the future. But it goes well; indeed it does."

"And Daniel Hutt?"

"He has left the country now."

"And his vagabond crew: have they all made their fortunes?"

"Why, Judith, they can not have reached America yet," said he.

"I am glad that you have not gone," she remarked, simply.

"Well," he said, "why should I strive to push my fortunes there more than here? To what end? There be none that I could serve either way."

And then it seemed to him that this was an ungracious speech, and he was anxious to stand well with her, seeing that she was disposed to be friendly.

"Judith," he said, suddenly, "surely you will not remain over at Shottery to-morrow, with all the merriment of the fair going on in the town? Nay, but you must come over—I could fetch you, at any hour that you named, if it so pleased you. There is a famous juggler come into the town, as I hear, that can do the most rare and wonderful tricks, and hath a dog as cunning as himself; and you will hear the new ballads, to judge which you would have; and the peddlers would show you their stores. Now, in good sooth, Judith, may not I come for you?—why, all the others have some one to go about with them; and she will choose this or that posy or ribbon, and wear it for the jest of the day; but I have no one to walk through the crowd with me, and see the people, and hear the bargainings and the music. I pray you, Judith, let me come for you. It can not be well for you, always to live in such dullness as is over there at Shottery."

"If I were to go to the fair with you," said she, and not unkindly, "methinks the people would stare, would they not? We have not been such intimate friends of late."

"You asked me not to go to America, Judith," said he.

"Well, yes," she admitted. "Truly I did so. Why should you go away with those desperate and broken men? Surely 'tis better you should stay among your own people."

"I staid because you bade me, Judith," said he.

She flushed somewhat at this; but he was so eager not to embarrass or offend her that he instantly changed the subject.

"May I, then, Judith? If you would come but for an hour!" he pleaded; for he clearly wanted to show to everybody that Judith was under his escort at the fair; and which of all the maidens (he asked himself) would compare beside her? "Why, there is not one of them but hath his companion, to buy for her some brooch, or pretty coif, or the like—"

"Are they all so anxious to lighten their purses?" said she, laughing. "Nay, but truly I may not leave my grandmother, lest the good dame should think that I was wearying of my stay with her. Pray you get some other to go to the fair with you—you have many friends, as I know, in the town—"

"Oh, do you think 'tis the fair I care about?" said he, quickly. "Nay, now, Judith, I would as lief not go to the fair at all—or but for a few minutes—if you will let me bring you over some trinket in the afternoon. Nay, a hundred times would I rather not go, if you would grant me such a favor. 'Tis the first I have asked of you for many a day."

"Why," she said, with a smile, "you must all of you be prospering in Stratford, since you are all so eager to cast abroad your money. The peddlers will do a rare trade to-morrow, as I reckon."

This was almost a tacit permission, and he was no such fool as to press her for more. Already his mind ran riot—he saw himself ransacking all the packs and stalls in the town.

"And now," she said, as she had come within sight of the houses—"I will return now, or the good dame will wonder."

"But I will walk back with you, Judith," said he, promptly.

She regarded him, with those pretty eyes of hers clearly laughing.

"Methought you came away from the cottage," said she, "because of the claims of your business; and now you would walk all the way back again?"

"Your hand, Judith," said he, shame-facedly—"you must not let it hang down by your side."

"Nay, for such a dangerous wound," said she, with her eyes gravely regarding him, "I will take precautions; but can not I hold it up myself—so—if need were?"

He was so well satisfied with what he had gained that he would yield to her now as she wished. And yet he took her hand once more—gently and timidly—and as if unwilling to give up his charge of it.

"I hope it will not pain you, Judith," he said.

"I trust it may not lead me to death's door," she answered, seriously; and if her eyes were laughing, it was with no un-kindness.

And then they said good-by to each other, and she walked away back to Shottery, well content to have made friends with him again, and to have found him for the time being quit of his dark suspicions and jealousies of her; while as for him, he went on to the town in a sort of foreknowledge that all Stratford Fair would not have anything worthy to be offered to Judith, and wondering whether he could not elsewhere, and at once, and by any desperate effort, procure something fine and rare and beautiful enough to be placed in that poor wounded hand.

CHAPTER XXIX.

"THE ROSE IS FROM MY GARDEN GONE."

Now when Parson Blaise set forth upon the mission that had been intrusted to him, there was not a trace of anger or in-dignation in his mind. He was not even moved by jealous wrath against the person with whom Judith had been holding these clandestine communications; nor had he any sense of having been himself injured by her conduct. For one thing, he knew enough of Judith's pride and self-reliance to be fairly well satisfied that she was not likely to have compromised herself in any serious way; and for an-other, his own choice of her, from among the Stratford maidens, as the one he wish-ed to secure for helpmate, was the result not so much of any overmastering pas-sion as of a cool and discriminating judg-ment. Nay, this very complication that had arisen—might he not use it to his own advantage? Might it not prove an argu-ment more powerful than any he had hitherto tried? And so it was that he set out, not as one armed to punish, but with the most placable intentions; and the bet-ter to give the subject full consideration, he did not go straight across the meadows to the cottage, but went through the town, and away out the Alcester road, before turning round and making for Shottery.

Nor did it occur to him that he was ap-proaching this matter with any mean or selfish ends in view. Far from that. The man was quite honest. In winning Ju-dith over to be his wife, by any means whatever, was he not adding one more to the number of the Lord's people? Was he not saving her from her own undisci-plined and wayward impulses, and from all the mischief that might arise from these? What was for his good was for her good, and the good of the Church also. She had a winning way; she was friends with many who rather kept aloof from the more austere of their neighbors; she would be a useful go-between. Her cheer-fulness, her good temper, nay, her comely presence and bright ways—all these would be profitably employed. Nor did he for-get the probability of a handsome mar-riage portion, and the added domestic comfort and serenity that that would bring himself. Even the marriage por-tion (which he had no doubt would be a substantial one) might be regarded as coming into the Church in a way; and so all would work together for good.

When he reached the cottage he found the old dame in the garden, busy with her flowers and vegetables, and was told that Judith had just gone within-doors. In-deed, she had but that minute come back from her stroll across the fields with Qui-ney, and had gone in to fetch a jug so that she might have some fresh water from the well in the garden. He met her on the threshold.

"I would say a few words with you, Judith, and in private," said he.

She seemed surprised, but was in no ill-humor; so she said, "As you will, good sir," and led the way into the main apart-ment, where she remained standing.

"I pray you be seated," said he.

She was still more surprised; but she obeyed him, taking her seat under the window, so that her face was in shadow, while the light from the small panes fell full on him, sitting opposite her.

"Judith," said he, "I am come upon a serious errand, and yet would not alarm you unnecessarily. Nay, I think that when all is done, good may spring out of the present troubles—"

"What is it?" she said, quickly. "Is any one ill?—my mother—"

"No, Judith," he said. "'Tis no trial of that kind you are called to face. The Lord hath been merciful to you and yours these several years; while others have borne the heavy hand of affliction, and lost their dearest at untimeous seasons, you have been spared for many years now all but such trials as come in the natural course: would I could see you as thankful as you ought to be to the Giver of all good. And yet I know not but that grief over such afflictions is easier to bear than grief over the consequences of our own wrong-doing: memory preserves this last the longer; sorrow is not so enduring, nor cuts so deep, as remorse. And then to think that others have been made to suffer through our evil-doing— that is an added sting: when those who have expected naught but filial obedience and duty, and the confidence that should exist between children and their parents—"

But this phrase about filial obedience had struck her with a sudden fear.

"I pray you what is it, sir? What have I done?" she said, almost in a cry.

Then he saw that he had gone too fast and too far.

"Nay, Judith," he said, "be not over-alarmed. 'Tis perchance but carelessness and a disposition to trust yourself in all circumstances to your own guidance that have to be laid to your charge. I hope it may be so; I hope matters may be no worse; 'tis for yourself to say. I come from your mother and sister, Judith," he continued, in measured tones. "I may tell you at once that they have learned of your having been in secret communication with a stranger who has been in these parts, and they would know the truth. I will not seek to judge you beforehand, nor point out to you what perils and mischances must ever befall you so long as you are bent on going your own way,

without government or counsel; that you must now perceive for yourself, and I trust the lesson will not be brought home to you too grievously."

"Is that all?" Judith had said, quickly, to herself, and with much relief.

"Good sir," she said to him, coolly, "I hope my good mother and Susan are in no bewilderment of terror. 'Tis true, indeed, that there was one in this neighborhood whom I met and spoke with on several occasions. If there was secrecy, 'twas because the poor young gentleman was in hiding; he dared not even present the letter that he brought commending him to my father. Nay, good Master Blaise, I pray you comfort my mother and sister, and assure them there was no harm thought of by the poor young man."

"I know not that, Judith," said he, with his clear, observant eyes trying to read her face in the dusk. "But your mother and sister would fain know what manner of man he was, and what you know of him, and how he came to be here."

Then the fancy flashed across her mind that this intervention of his was but the prompting of his own jealousy, and that he was acting as the spokesman of her mother and sister chiefly to get information for himself.

"Why, sir," said she, lightly, "I think you might as well ask these questions of my grandmother, that knoweth about as I do concerning the young man, and was as sorry as I for his ill fortunes."

"I pray you take not this matter so heedlessly, Judith," he said, with some coldness. "'Tis of greater moment than you think. No idle curiosity has brought me hither to-day; nay, it is with the authority of your family that I put these questions to you; and I am charged to ask you to answer them with all of such knowledge as you may have."

"Well, well," said she, good-naturedly, "his name—"

She was about to say that his name was Leofric Hope; but she checked herself, and some color rose to her face—though he could not see that.

"His name, good sir, as I believe, is John Orridge," she continued, but with no embarrassment; indeed, she did not think that she had anything very serious either to conceal or to confess; "and I fear me the young man is grievously in debt, or otherwise forced to keep away from those that would imprison him; and being come to Warwickshire, he brought a letter to my father, but was afraid to present it. He hath been to the cottage here certain times, for my grandmother, as well as I, was pleased to hear of the doings in London; and right civil he was, and well-mannered; and 'twas news to us to hear about the theatres and my father's way of living there. But why should my mother and Susan seek to know aught of him?—surely Prudence hath not betrayed the trust I put in her?—for indeed the young man was anxious that his being in the neighborhood should not be known to any in Stratford. However, as he is now gone away, and that some weeks ago, 'tis of little moment, as I reckon; and if ever he cometh back here, I doubt not but that he will present himself at New Place, that they may judge of him as they please. That he can speak for himself, and to advantage and goodly showing, I know right well."

"And that is all you can say of this man, Judith," said he, with some severity in his tone—"of this man that you have been thus familiar with?"

"Marry is it!" she said, lightly. "But I have had guesses, no doubt; for first I thought him a gentleman of the court, he being apparently acquainted with all the doings there; and then methought he was nearer to the theatres, from his knowledge of the players. But you would not have had me ask the young man as to his occupation and standing, good sir? 'Twould have been unseemly in a stranger, would it not? Could I dare venture on questions, he being all unknown to any of us?"

And now a suspicion flashed upon him that she was merely befooling him, so he came at once and sharply to the point.

"Judith," said he, endeavoring to pierce with his keen eyes the dusk that enshrouded her, "you have not told me all. How came he to have a play of your father's in his possession?"

"Now," said she, with a quick anger, "that is ill done of Prudence. No one but Prudence knew; and for so harmless a secret—and that all over and gone, moreover, and the young man himself away I know not where—nay, by my life, I had not thought that Prudence would serve me so. And to what end? Why, good sir, I myself lent the young man the sheets of my father's writing—they were the sheets that were thrown aside—and I got

each and all of them safely back, and replaced them. Prudence knew what led me to lend him my father's play; and where was the harm of it? I thought not that she would go and make trouble out of so small a thing."

By this time the good parson had come to see pretty clearly how matters stood—what with Prudence's explanations and Judith's present confessions. And he made no doubt that this stranger—whether from idleness, or for amusement, or with some more sinister purpose, he had no means of knowing—had copied the play when he had taken the sheets home with him to the farm; while as to the appearance in London of the copy so taken, it was sufficiently obvious that Judith was in complete ignorance, and could afford no information whatever. So that now the first part of his mission was accomplished. He asked her a few more questions, and easily discovered that she knew nothing whatever about the young man's position in life, or whether he had gone straight from the farm to London, or whether he was in London now. As to his being in possession, or having been in possession, of a copy of her father's play, it was abundantly evident that she had never dreamed of any such thing.

And now he came to the more personal part of his mission; that was for him much more serious.

"Judith," said he, "'tis not like you should know what sad and grievous consequences may spring from errors apparently small. How should you? You will take no heed or caution. The advice of those who would be nearest and dearest to you is of no account with you. You will go your own way, as if one of your years and experience could know the pitfalls that lie in a young maiden's path. The whole of life is but a jest to you—a tale without meaning—something to pass the hour withal. And think you that such blindness and willfulness bring no penalty? Nay, sooner or later the hour strikes; you look back and see what you have done, and the offers of safe guidance that you have neglected or thrust aside."

"I pray you, sir, what is it now?" she said, indifferently (and with a distinct wish that he would go away and release her, and let her get out into the light again). "Methought I had filled up the measure of my iniquities."

"Thus it is—thus it will be always,"

said he, with a kind of hopelessness, "so long as you harden your heart, and have no thought but for the vanities of the moment." And then he addressed her more pointedly. "But even now methinks I can tell you what will startle you out of your moral sloth, which is an offense in the eyes of the Lord, as it is a cause for pity and almost despair to all who know you. It was a light matter, you think, that you should hold this secret commerce with a stranger, careless of the respect due to your father's house, careless of the opinion and the anxious wishes of your friends, careless even of your good name—"

"My good name?" said she, quickly and sharply. "I pray you, sir, have heed what you say."

"Have heed to what I have to tell you, Judith," said he, sternly. "Ay, and take warning by it. Think you that I have pleasure in being a bearer of evil tidings?"

"But what now, sir? What now? Heaven's mercy on us, let us get to the end of the dreadful deeds I have done!" she exclaimed, with some anger and impatience.

"I would spare you, but may not," said he, calmly. "And now, what if I were to tell you that this young man whom you encouraged into secret conversation —whose manners seemed to have had so much charm for you—was a rascal thief and villain? How would your pride bear it if I told you that he had cozened you with some foolish semblance of a wizard?"

"Good sir, I know it," she retorted. "He himself told me as much."

"Perchance. Perchance 'twas part of his courteous manners to tell you as much!" was the scornful rejoinder. "But he did not tell you all—he did not tell you that he had copied out every one of those sheets of your father's writing; that he was about to carry that stolen copy to London, like the knave and thief that he was; that he was to offer it for money to the booksellers? He did not tell you that soon your father and his associates in the theatre would be astounded by learning that a copy of the new play had been obtained in some dark fashion, and sold; that it was out of their power to recover it; that their interests would be seriously affected by this vile conspiracy; or that they would by-and-by discover that this purloined play, which was like to cause them so much grievous loss and vexation of mind,

had been obtained here, in this very neighborhood, and by the aid of no other than your father's daughter."

"Who—told—you—this?" she asked, in a strange, stunned way: her eyes were terror-stricken, her hands all trembling.

"A good authority," said he. "Your father. A letter is but now come from London."

She uttered a low, shuddering cry; it was a moan almost.

"See you now," said he (for he knew that all her bravery was struck down, and she entirely at his mercy), "what must ever come of your willfulness and your scorn of those who would aid and guide you? Loving counsel and protection are offered you—the natural shield of a woman; but you must needs go your own way alone. And to what ends? Think you that this is all? Not so. For the woman who makes to herself her own rule of conduct must be prepared for calumnious tongues. And bethink you what your father must have thought of you—the only daughter of his household now— when he learned the story of this young man coming into Warwickshire, and befooling you with his wizard's tricks, and meeting you secretly, and cozening you of the sheets of your father's play. These deeds that are done in the dark soon reach the daylight; and can you wonder, when your father found your name abroad in London—the heroine of a common jest, a by-word—that his vexation and anger should overmaster him? What marvel that he should forthwith send to Stratford demanding to know what further could be learned of the matter, perchance fondly trusting — who knows ?— to find that rumor had lied? But there is no such hope for him—nor for you. What must your mother say in reply? What excuse can she offer? Or how make reparation to those associates of your father who suffer with him? And how get back your good name, that is being bandied about the town as the heroine of a foolish jest? Your father may regain possession of his property—I know not whether that be possible or no—but can he withdraw the name of his daughter from the ribald wit of the taverns? And I know which he valueth the more highly, if his own daughter know it not."

He had struck hard; he knew not how hard.

"My father wrote thus?" she said; and

her head was bent, and her hands covering her face.

"I read the letter no more than an hour ago," said he. "Your mother and sister would have me come over to see whether such a story could be true; but Prudence had already admitted as much—"

"And my father is angered," she said, in that low strange voice.

"Can you wonder at it?" he said.

Again there came an almost inarticulate moan, like that of an animal stricken to death.

As for him, he had now the opportunity of pouring forth the discourse to her that he had in a measure prepared as he came along the highway. He knew right well that she would be sorely wounded by this terrible disclosure; that the proud spirit would be in the dust; that she would be in a very bewilderment of grief. And he thought that now she might consent to gentle leading, and would trust herself to the only one (himself, to wit) capable of guiding her through her sorrows; and he had many texts and illustrations apposite. She heard not one word. She was as motionless as one dead; and the vision that rose before her burning brain was the face of her father as she had seen it—for a moment—in the garden on the morning of his departure. That terrible swift look of anger toward old Matthew she had never forgotten—the sudden lowering of the brows, the flash in the eyes, the strange contraction of the mouth; and that was what she saw now—that was how he was regarding her; and that, she knew, would be the look that would meet her always and always as she lay and thought of him in the long wakeful nights. She could not go to him. London was far away. She could not go to him, and throw herself at his feet, and beg and pray with outstretched and trembling hands for but one word of pity. The good parson had struck hard.

And yet in a kind of way he was trying to administer consolation—at all events, counsel. He was enlarging on the efficacy of prayer. And he said that if the Canaanitish woman of old had power to intercede for her daughter, and win succor for her, surely that would not be denied to such a one as Judith's mother, if she sought for her daughter strength and fortitude in trouble where alone these could be found.

"The Canaanitish woman," said he,

"had but the one saving grace—but that an all-powerful one—of faith; and even when the disciples would have her sent away, she followed, worshipping, and saying, 'Lord, help me.' And the Lord himself answered and said, 'It is not good to take the children's bread, and to cast it to whelps.' But she said, 'Truth, Lord; yet indeed the whelps eat of the crumbs which fall from their master's table.' Then our Lord answered and said, 'O woman, great is thy faith: be it to thee as thou desirest.' And her daughter was made whole at that hour."

Judith started up—she had not heard a single word.

"I pray you pardon me, good sir," she said—for she was in a half-frantic state of misery and despair—"my—my grandmother will speak with you. I—I pray you pardon me—"

She got up into her own little chamber—she scarce knew how. She sat down on the bed. There were no tears in her eyes; but there was a terrible weight on her chest that seemed to stifle her, and she was breathless, and could not think aright, and her trembling hands were clinched. Sometimes she wildly thought she wanted Prudence to come to her, and then a kind of shudder possessed her, and a wish to go away—she cared not where—and be seen no more. That crushing weight increased, choking her; she could not rest; she rose and went quickly down the stair, and through the garden into the road.

"Judith, wench!" called her grandmother, who was talking to the parson.

She took no heed. She went blindly on; and all these familiar things seemed so different now. How could the children laugh so? She got into the Bidford road; she did not turn her eyes toward any whom she met, to see whether she knew them or no: there was enough within her own brain for her to think of. She made her way to the summit of Bardon Hill; and there she looked over the wide landscape; but it was toward London that she looked—and with a strange and trembling fear. And then she seemed anxious to hide away from being seen, and went down by hedge-rows and field paths; and at last she was by the river. She regarded it, flowing so stealthily by, in the sad and monotonous silence. Here was an easy means of slipping away from all this dread thing that seemed to surround her and overwhelm her—to glide away as noislessly and peacefully as the river it-self, to any unknown shore, she cared not what. And then she sat down—still look-ing vaguely and absently at the water—and began to think of all that had hap-pened to her on the banks of this stream; and she looked at these visionary pictures and at herself in them as if they were apart and separated from her, and she never to be like that again. Was it pos-sible that she ever could have been so care-less and so happy, with no weight at all resting on her heart, but singing out of mere thoughtlessness, and teaching Willie Hart the figures of dances, herself laugh-ing the while? It seemed a long time ago now; and that he was cut off from her too, and all of them, and that there was to be no expiation for evermore for this that she had done.

How long she sat there she knew not. Everything was a blank to her but this crushing consciousness that what had hap-pened could never be recalled; that her father and she were forever separated now —and his face regarding her with the ter-rible look she had seen in the garden; that all the happy past was cut away from her, and she an outcast, and a by-word, and a disgrace to all that knew her. And then she thought, in the very weariness of her misery, that if she could only walk away anywhere—anywhere alone, so that no one should meet her or question her—un-til she was broken and exhausted with fatigue, she would then go back to her own small room, and lie down on the bed, and try if sleep would procure some brief spell of forgetfulness, some relief from her aching head and far heavier heart. But when she rose she found that she was trembling from weakness; and a kind of shiver as of cold went through her, though the autumn day was warm enough. She walked slowly, and almost dragged her-self, all the way home. Her hand shook so that she could scarce undo the latch of the gate. She heard her grandmother in the inner apartment; but she managed to creep noiselessly upstairs into her own little chamber; and there she sank down on the bed, and lay in a kind of stupor, pressing her hands on her throbbing brow.

It was some two hours afterward that her grandmother, who did not know that Judith had returned, was walking along the little passage, and was startled by hear-ing a low moaning above—a kind of dull cry of pain, so slight that she had to listen again ere she could be sure that it was not mere fancy. Instantly she went up the few wooden steps and opened the door. Judith was lying on the bed, with all her things on, just as she had seen her go forth. And then—perhaps the noise of the open-ing of the door had wakened her—she started up, and looked at her grandmother in a wild and dazed kind of way, as if she had just shaken off some terrible dream.

"Oh, grandmother," she said, springing to her and clinging to her like a child, "it is not true—it is not true—it can not be true!"

But then she fell to crying—crying as if her heart would break. The whole weight of her misery came back upon her; and the hopelessness of it; and her despair.

"Why, good lass," said her grandmo-ther, smoothing the sun-brown hair that was buried in her bosom, and trying to calm the violence of the girl's sobbing, "thou must not take on so. Thy father may be angered, 'tis true; but there will come brighter days for thee. Nay, take not on so, good lass."

"Oh, grandmother, you can not under-stand," she said, and her whole frame was shaken with her sobs. "You can not understand. Grandmother, grandmother, there was—there was but the one rose—in my garden—and that is gone now."

CHAPTER XXX.

IN TIME OF NEED.

LATE that night, in the apartment be-low, Tom Quiney was seated by the big fire-place, staring moodily into the chips and logs that had been lit there, the even-ings having grown somewhat chill now. There was a little parcel lying unopened and unheeded on the table. He had not had patience to wait for the fair of the morrow; he had ridden all the way to Warwick to purchase something worthy of Judith's acceptance; and he had come over to the cottage in high hopes of her being still in that kindly mood that re-minded him of other days. Then came the good dame's story of what had befall-en, and how that the parson had been over, bringing with him these terrible ti-dings; and how that since then Judith would not hear of any one being sent for, and would take no food, but was now lying there, alone in the dark, moaning to herself at times. And the good dame— as this tall young fellow sat there listening to her, with his fists clinched, and the look on his face ever growing darker— went on to express her fear that the parson had been over-hard with her grandchild; that probably he could not understand how her father had been the very idol of her life-long worship; that the one thing she was ever thinking of was how to win his approval, to be rewarded by even a nod of encouragement.

"Nay, I liked not the manner of his speaking, when he wur come to me in the garden," the old dame continued. "I liked it not. He be sharp of tongue, the young pahrson; and there wur too much to my mind of discipline, and chastening of proud spirits, and the like o' that. To my mind he have not years enough to be placed in such authority."

"The Church is behind him," said this young fellow, almost to himself, and his eyes were burning darkly as he spoke. "I may not put hand on him. The Church is behind him. Marry, 'tis a goodly shelter for men that be of the woman kind."

Then he looked up quickly, and his words were savage.

"What think you, good grandmother, were one to seize him by neck and heel and break his back on the rail of Clopton's bridge? Were it not well done?—by my life, I think it were well done!"

"Nay, nay, now," said she, quickly, for she was somewhat alarmed, seeing his face set hard with passion and his eyes afire. "I would have no brawling. There be plenty of harm done already. Perchance the good pahrson hath not spoken so harshly after all. In good sooth, now, none but her own people can understand how the wench hath ever looked up to her father for a word or a nod commending her, as I say, and when she be told now that she hath wrought mischief, and caused herself to be talked about, and her father vexed, and all the rest of the tale, why, 'tis like to drive her out of her mind. And now this be all her cry—that she may see no one of her people any more; she would bide with me here. 'Grandmother, grandmother,' she saith, 'I will bide with you, if you will suffer me. I will show myself in Stratford no more; they shall have no shame through me.' Nay, but the wench be half out of her senses, as I think; and

saith wild things—that she would go and sell herself to be a slave in the Indies, could she restore the money to her father or bring him back this that he hath lost. 'Tis a terrible plight for the poor wench; and always she saith, 'Grandmother, grandmother, let me bide with you; I will never go back to New Place; grandmother, I can work as well as any, and you will let me bide with you.' Poor lass—poor lass!"

"But how came the parson to interfere?" Quiney said, hotly. "I'll be sworn Judith's father did not write to him. How came he to be preaching his discipline and chastisement? How came he to be intrusted with the task of abusing her and crushing the too proud spirit? By Heavens, now, there may be occasion ere long to tame some one's proud spirit, but not the spirit of a defenseless young maid— marry, that is work fit only for parsons. Man to man is the better way, and it will come ere long."

"Nay, softly, softly, good Master Quiney," said the old dame, in her gentlest tones. "Would you mar all the good opinion that Judith hath of you? Why, to-day, now, just ere the pahrson came, I wur in the garden, putting things straight a bit, and as she came through she says to me, quite pleasant like, 'I have just been across the fields, grandmother, with Master Quiney'—or Tom Quiney, as she said, being friendly and pleasant like— 'and I hear less now of his quarrelling and fighting among the young men; and his business goeth on well; and to-morrow, grandmother, he is going to buy me something at the fair.'"

"Said she all that?" he asked, quickly, and with a flush of color rushing to his face.

"Marry, did she; and looked pleased; for 'tis a right friendly wench and good-natured withal," the old dame said, glad to see that these words had for the moment scattered his wrath to the winds; and she went on for some little time talking to him in her garrulous easy fashion about Judith's frank and honest qualities, and her good-hearted ways, and the pretty daintinesses of her coaxing when she was so inclined. It was a story he was not loath to listen to, and yet it seemed so strange: they were talking of her almost as of one passed away—as if the girl lying there in that darkened room, instead of torturing her brain with incessant and lightning-like visions of all the harm she had caused in London, were now far removed from all such troubles, and hushed in the calm of death.

He went to the table and opened the box, and took out the little present he had brought for Judith. It was a pair of lace cuffs, with a slender silver circle at the wrist; the lace going back from that in a succession of widening leaves. It was not only a pretty present; it was also (in proportion to his means) a costly one, as the old dame's sharp eyes instantly saw.

"I think she would have been pleased with them," he said, absently.

And then he said,

"Good grandmother, it were of no use to lay them near her in the morning—on a chair or at the window—that perchance she might look at them?"

"Nay, nay," the grandmother said, shaking her head: "'tis no child's trouble that hath befallen the poor wench, that she can be comforted with pretty trifles."

"I meant not that," said he, flushing somewhat. "'Tis that I would have her know that—that there were friends thinking of her all the same; those that would rather have her gladdened and tended and made much of rather than—than—chidden with any chastisement."

This word chastisement seemed to recall his anger.

"I say that Judith hath done no wrong at all," he said, as if he were confronting some one not there; "and that I will maintain; and let no man in my hearing say aught else. Why, now, the story as you tell it, good grandmother—'tis as plain as daylight—a child can see it: all that she did was done to magnify her father and his writing; and if the villain sold the play, or let it slip out of his hands, was that her doing? Doubtless it is a sore mischance; but I see not that Judith is to be blamed for it; and right well I know that if her father were to hear how she is smitten down with grief, he would be the first to say: 'Good lass, there is no such harm done. A greater harm would be your falling sick; get you up and out; seek your friends again; and be happy as you were before.' That is what he would say, I will take my oath of it; and if the parson and his chastisements were to come across him, by my life I would not seek to be in the parson's shoes!"

"I must make another trial with the poor wench," said the good grandmother,

rising, "that hath eaten nothing all the day. In truth, her only cry is to be left alone now, and that hereafter I am to let her bide with me. It be a poor shelter, I think, for one used to live in a noble house; but there 'tis, so long as she wisheth it."

"Nay, but this can not be suffered to go on, good Mistress Hathaway," said he, as he rose and got his cap. "For if Judith take no food, and will see no one, and be alone with her trouble, of a surety she will fall ill. Now to-morrow morning I will bring Prudence over. If any can comfort her, Prudence can; and that she will be right willing, I know. They have been as sisters."

"That be well thought of, Master Quiney," said the grandmother, as she went to the door with him. "Take care o' the ditch the other side of the way; it be main dark o' nights now."

"Good-night to you, good grandmother," said he, as he disappeared in the darkness.

But it was neither back home nor yet to Stratford town that Tom Quiney thought of going all that long night. He felt a kind of constraint upon him (and yet a constraint that kept his heart warm with a secret satisfaction) that he should play the part of watch-dog, as it were—as if Judith were sorely ill, or in danger, or in need of protection somehow; and he kept wandering about in the dark, never at any great radius from the cottage. His self-imposed task was the easier now that as the black clouds overhead slowly moved before the soft westerly wind, gaps were opened, and here and there clusters of stars were visible, shedding a faint light down on the sombre roads and fields and hedges. Many strange fancies occurred to him during that long and silent night as to what he could do, or would like to do, for Judith's sake. Breaking the parson's neck was the first and most natural, and the most easily accomplished; but fleeing the country, which he knew must follow, did not seem so desirable a thing. He wanted to do something—he knew not what. He wished he had been less of a companion with the young men, and less careful to show, with them, that Stratford town, and the county of Warwick, could hold their own against all comers. If he had been more considerate and gentle with Judith, perhaps she would not have sought the society of the parson? He knew he had not the art of winning her

over, like the parson. He could not speak
so plausibly. Nor had he the authority
of the Church behind him. It was natural for women to think much of that, and
to be glad of the shelter of authority.
Parsons themselves (he considered) were
a kind of half-women, being in women's
secrets, and entitled to speak to them in
ghostly confidence. But if Judith, now—
wanted some one to do something for her,
no matter what, in his rough-and-ready
way—well, he wondered what that could
be that he would refuse. And so the dark
hours went by.

With the gray of the dawn he began to
cast his eyes abroad, as if to see if any one
were stirring, or approaching the cluster
of cottages nestled down there among the
trees. The daylight widened and spread
up in the trembling east; the fields and
the woods became clear; here and there
a small tuft of blue smoke began to arise
from a cottage chimney. And now he
was on Bardon Hill, and could look abroad
over the wide landscape lying between
Shottery and Stratford town; and if any
one—any one bringing lowering brows
and further cruel speech to a poor maid
already stricken down and defenseless—
had been in sight, what then? Watchfully and slowly he went down from the
hill, and back to the meadows lying between the hamlet and Stratford, there to
interpose, as it were, and question all comers. And well it was, for the sake of peace
and charity, that the good parson did not
chance to be early abroad on this still
morning; and well it was for the young
man himself. There was no wise-eyed
Athene to descend from the clouds and
bid this wrathful Achilles calm his heart.
He was only an English country youth—
though sufficiently Greek-like in form;
and he was hungry, and gray-faced with
his vigil of the night, and not in a placable mood. Nay, when a young man is
possessed with the consciousness that he
is the defender of some one behind him
—some one who is weak, and feminine,
and suffering—he is apt to prove a dangerous antagonist; and it was well for
all concerned that he had no occasion to
pick a quarrel on this morning in these
quiet meadows. In truth, he might have
been more at rest had he known that the
good parson was in no hurry to follow up
his monitions of the previous day; he
wished these to sink into her mind and
take root there, so that thereafter might

spring up such wholesome fruits as re-
pentance, and humility, and the desire of
godly aid and counsel.

By-and-by he slipped away home,
plunged his head into cold water to banish the dreams of the night; and then,
having swallowed a cup of milk to stay
his hunger, he went along to Chapel Street,
to see if he could have speech of Prudence.
He found that not only were all of the
household up and doing, but that Prudence
herself was ready to go out, being bent on
one of her charitable errands. And it
needed but a word to alter the direction
of her kindness: of course she would at
once go to see Judith.

"Truly I had fears of it," said she, as
they went through the fields, the pale,
calm face having grown more and more
anxious as she listened to all that he had
to tell her. "Her father was as the light
of the world to her. With the others of
us she hath ever been headstrong in a
measure and careless—and yet so lovable
withal and merry that I for one could
never withstand her: nay, I confess I tried
not to withstand her, for never knew I of
any willfulness of hers springing from anything but good-nature and her kind and
generous ways. But that she was ever
ready to brave our opinions I know, and
perchance make light of our anxieties, we
not having her courage; and in all things
she seemed to be a guide unto herself, and
to walk sure, and have no fear. In all
things but one. Indeed, 'tis true what her
grandmother told you, and who should
know better than I, who was always with
her? The slightest wish of her father's
—that was law to her. A word of commending from him, and she was happy
for days. And think what this must be
now—she that was so proud of his approval—that scarce thought of aught else.
Nay, for myself, I can see that they have
told him all a wrong story in London,
that know I well; and 'tis no wonder that
he is vexed and angry; but Judith—poor
Judith—"

She could say no more just then; she
turned aside her face somewhat.

"Do you know what she said to her
grandmother, Prudence, when she fell
a-crying?—that there had been but the one
rose in her garden, and that was gone
now."

"'Tis what Susan used to sing," said
Prudence, with rather trembling lips.
"'The rose is from my garden gone,'

'twas called. Ay, and hath she that on her mind now? Truly I wish that her mother and Susan had let me break this news to her; none know as well as I what ·it must be to her."

And here Tom Quiney quickly asked .her whether it was not clear to her that the parson had gone beyond his mission altogether, and that in a way that would have to be dealt with afterward, when all these things were amended. Prudence, with some faint color in her pale face, defended Master Blaise to the best of her power, and said she knew he could not have been unduly harsh; nay, had she not herself, just as he was setting forth, besought him to be kind and considerate with Judith? Hereupon Quiney rather brusquely asked what the good man could mean by phrases about discipline and chastenings and chastisements; to which Prudence answered gently that these were but separate words, and that she was sure Master Blaise had fulfilled what he undertook in a merciful spirit, which was his nature. After that there was a kind of silence between these two; perhaps Quiney considered that no good end could be served at present by stating his own ideas on that subject. The proper time would come in due course.

At length they reached the cottage. But here, to their amazement, and to the infinite distress of Prudence, when Judith's grandmother came down the wooden steps again, she shook her head, saying that the wench would see no one.

"I thought as 'twould be so," she said. "But me, good grandmother!—me!" Prudence cried, with tears in her eyes. "Surely she will not refuse to see me!"

"No one, she saith," was the answer. "Poor wench, her head do ache so bad! And when one would cheer her or comfort her a morsel, 'tis another fit of crying —that will wear her to skin and bone, if she do not pluck up better heart. She hath eaten naught this morning neither; 'tis for no willfulness, poor lass, for she tried an hour ago; and now 'tis best, as I think, to leave her alone."

"By your leave, good grandmother," said Prudence, with some firmness, "that will I not. If Judith be in such trouble, 'tis not likely that I should go away and leave her. It hath never been the custom between us two."

"As you will, Prudence," the grandmother said. "Young hearts have their confidences among themselves. Perchance you may be able to rouse her."

Prudence went up the stairs silently, and opened the door. Judith was lying on the bed, her face turned away from the light, her hands clasped over her forehead.

"Judith!"

There was no answer.

"Judith," said her friend, going near, "I am come to see you."

There was a kind of sob—that was all.

"Judith, is your head so bad? Can I do nothing for you?"

She put over her hand—the soft and cool and gentle touch of which had comforted many a sick-bed—and she was startled to find that both Judith's hands and forehead were burning hot.

"No, sweetheart," was the answer, in a low and broken voice, "you can do nothing for me now."

"Nay, nay, Judith, take heart," Prudence said, and she gently removed the hot fingers from the burning forehead, and put her own cooler hand there, as if to dull the throbbing of the pain. "Sweetheart, be not so cast down. 'Twill be all put right in good time."

"Never—never," the girl said, without tears, but with an abject hopelessness of tone. "It can never be undone now. He said my name was become a mockery among my father's friends. For myself, I would not heed that—nay, they might say of me what they pleased; but that my father should hear of it—a mockery and scorn—and they think I cared so little for my father that I was ready to give away his papers to any one pretending to be a sweetheart and befooling me and my father to know it all, and to hear such things said—no, that can never be undone now. I used to count the weeks and the days and the very hours when I knew he was coming back; that was the joy of my life to me; and now if I were to know that he were coming near to Stratford I should fly, and hide somewhere—anywhere—in the river as lief as not. Nay, I make no complaint. 'Tis my own doing, and it can not be undone now."

"Judith! Judith! you break my heart!" her friend cried. "Surely to all troubles there must come an end."

"Yes, yes," was the answer, in a low voice, and almost as if she were speaking to herself. "That is right. There will come an end. I would it were here now."

All Prudence's talking seemed to be of no avail. She reasoned and besought, oftentimes with tears in her eyes; but Judith remained quite listless and hopeless; she seemed to be in a stunned and dazed condition after the long sleeplessness of the night, and Prudence was afraid that further entreaties would only aggravate her headache.

"I will go and get you something to eat now," said she. "Your grandmother says you have had nothing since yesterday."

"Do not trouble; 'tis needless, sweetheart," Judith said. And then she added, with a brief shiver, "But if you could fetch a thick cloak, dear Prudence, and throw it over me—surely the day is cold somewhat."

A few minutes after (so swift and eager was everybody in the house), Judith was warmly wrapped up; and by the side of the bed, on a chair, was some food the good grandmother had been keeping ready, and also a flask of wine that Quiney had brought with him.

"Look you, Judith," said Prudence, "here is some wine that Thomas Quiney hath brought for you—'tis of a rare quality, he saith—and you must take a little—nay, you must and shall, sweetheart; and then perchance you may be able to eat."

She sipped a little of the wine—it was but to show her gratitude and send him her thanks. She could not touch the food. She seemed mostly anxious for rest and quiet; and so Prudence noiselessly left her, and stole down the stair again.

Prudence was terribly perplexed, and in a kind of despair almost.

"I know not what to do," she said. "I would bring over her mother and Susan, but that she begs and prays me not to do that—nay, she can not see them, she says. And there is no reasoning with her. 'It can not be undone now'—that is her constant cry. What to do I can not tell. For surely, if she remain so, and take no comfort, she will fall ill."

"Ay, and if that be so, who is to blame?" said Quiney, who was walking up and down in considerable agitation. "I say that letter should never have been put into the parson's hands. Was it meant to be conveyed to Judith? I warrant me it was not! Did her father say that he wished her chidden? did he ask any of you to bid the parson go to her with his upbraidings? would he himself have been so quick and eager to chasten her proud spirit? I tell you no. He is none of the parson kind. Vexed he might have been; but he would have taken no vengeance. What?—on his own child? By heavens, I'll be sworn, now, that if he were here, at this minute, he would take the girl by the hand, and laugh at her for being so afraid of his anger—ay, I warrant me he would —and would bid her be of good cheer, and brighten her face, that was ever the brightest in Warwickshire, as I have heard him say. That would he—my life on it!"

"Ah," said Prudence, wistfully, "if you could only persuade Judith of that!"

"Persuade her?" said he. "Why, I would stake my life that is what her father would do!"

"You could not persuade her," said Prudence, with a hopeless air. "No; she thinks it is all over now between her father and her. She is disgraced and put away from him. She hath done him such injury, she says, as even his enemies have never done. When he comes back again, she says, to Stratford, she will be here; and she knows that he will never come near this house; and that will be better for her, she says, for she could never again meet him face to face."

Well, all that day Judith lay there in that solitary room, desiring only to be left alone, taking no food, the racking pains in her head returning from time to time; and now and again she shivered slightly as if from cold. Tom Quiney kept coming and going to hear news of her, or to consult with Prudence as to how to rouse her from this hopelessness of grief; and as the day slowly passed he grew more and more disturbed and anxious and restless. Could nothing be done? could nothing be done? was his constant cry.

He remained late that evening, and Prudence staid all night at the cottage. In the morning he was over again early, and more distressed than ever to hear that the girl was wearing herself out with this agony of remorse—crying stealthily when that she thought no one was near, and hiding herself away from the light, and refusing to be comforted.

But during the long and silent watches he had been taking counsel with himself.

"Prudence," said he, regarding her with a curious look, "do you think, now, if some assurance were come from her father himself—some actual message from him—a kindly message—some token that he was far indeed from casting her away from him—think you Judith would be glad to have that ?"

"'Twould be like giving her life back to her," said the girl, simply. "In truth, I dread what may come of this: 'tis not in human nature to withstand such misery of mind. My poor Judith, that was ever so careless and merry !"

He hesitated for a second or two, and then he said, looking at her, and speaking in a cautious kind of way:

"Because, when next I have need to write to London, I might beg of some one —my brother Dick, perchance, that is now in Bucklersbury, and would have small trouble in doing such a service—I say I might beg of him to go and see Judith's father, and tell him the true story, and show him that she was not so much to blame. Nay, for my part, I see not that she was to blame at all, but for overkindness and confidence, and the wish to exalt her father. The mischief that hath been wrought is the doing of the scoundrel and villain, on whose head I trust it may fall ere long; 'twas none of hers. And if her father were to have all that now put fairly and straight before him, think you he would not be right sorry to hear that she had taken his anger so much to heart, and was lying almost as one dead at the very

thought of it ? I tell you, now, if all this be put before him, and if he send her no comfortable message—ay, and that forthwith and gladly—I have far misread him. And as for her, Prudence, 'twould be welcome, say you ?"

"'Twould be of the value of all the world to her," Prudence said, in her direct and earnest way.

Well, he almost immediately thereafter left (seeing that he could be of no further help to these women-folk), and walked quickly back to Stratford, and to his house, which was also his place of business. He seemed to hurry through his affairs with speed; then he went upstairs and looked out some clothing; he took down a pair of pistols and put some fresh powder in the pans; and made a few other preparations. Next he went round to the stable, and the stout little Galloway nag whinnied when she saw him at the door.

"Well, Maggie, lass," said he, going into the stall, and patting her neck and stroking down her knees, "what sayst thou ? Wouldst like a jaunt that would carry thee many a mile away from Stratford town ? Nay, but if you knew the errand, I warrant me you would be as eager as I ! What, then—a bargain, lass ? By my life, you shall have many a long day's rest in clover when this sharp work is done !"

MUNICIPAL FINANCE.

IT will be remembered of Lord Beaconsfield that he never lost an opportunity to attack philosophical politics, and to declare against the introduction into what he called the practical business of life of the highest kind—namely, politics—of "philosophical ideas instead of political principles." While this attitude is in some respects an admirable one, and while the unpractical side of philosophical and professional politics is apparent to all men of real experience, it is nevertheless true that so-called statesmen and practical politicians themselves prefer vague and attractive theories to the serious discussion of the great but difficult and intricate questions of government. This is the reason why, notwithstanding the fact that it is in national, State, and municipal budgets that thoughtful men find the best index to our political condition, the poli-

ticians and great body of voters pass carelessly over budgetary problems. As set forth in figures they are exactly, although coldly and unattractively, presented, and demand more of careful and intelligent study than the politicians and the people can or are willing to give them, so long as passion, prejudice, tradition, and selfishness suggest so much easier and more natural ways of dealing with political questions. We see our budgets carelessly or even extravagantly made up, we see waste or theft of public moneys, we see the real needs of the community neglected, and the treasury pillaged for the maintenance of office-holders, and no one ever denies even for a moment the necessity of reforming the evils. Nevertheless no one moves, or if perhaps something for reform is really undertaken, half measures only are applied. The community is conservative, and dislikes to interfere radically with the things which are established, even with the established machinery of admitted fraud or wastefulness. Investigations are undertaken, and quashed when they begin to show too much. The press clamors for and inquires into suspicious transactions, but the politicians defeat the public accountants, and the people stand neutral as between the parties. We read calmly one day of a defalcation in office, feel a temporary shame or chagrin at the thought of what can be done under our very eyes by way of well-planned theft, hope that some one—not ourselves—will bring the wrong-doer to justice, and to-morrow forget all about it, and have not enough public spirit to attend a meeting to denounce the crime. We all admit the necessity of placing some check upon municipal expenditure, of devising some fraud-proof system in our municipal bureaus. Day by day we feel an increasing mistrust of our public officials, and still we suffer the wrong, and refuse to take any definite steps to introduce order into our municipal system, or to insist on administrative economy. Why such is the case has been recently pointed out by a French author, who has the same things to complain of in his own country. It is because, as he says, "besides the financial work which has to be accomplished—the elements of which leave no room for uncertainty and doubt, the calculations lending themselves neither to complaisancy nor to delays—there is, as in the past, political work to be pursued, passions to be played upon, cupidity to be provided for, because universal suffrage, save in exceptional circumstances, *does not permit itself to be persuaded by figures, but obeys prejudices,* and the existence of Deputies depends upon this suffrage."

In this country prejudice and tradition maintain in existence two great political parties, neither of which is willing to take a definite stand upon either side of any great administrative or financial question, and this notwithstanding the fact that nowhere in the nation are we confronted by a single question which is political as contradistinguished from economical, for our political emancipation was won long ago, and leaves little to be desired, while our economical emancipation has yet to be achieved. Worst of all, these party divisions reach down even to the wards of

cities, and prevent or nullify the effects of any co-operation among citizens as such, acting together for the reduction of a local tax rate. The public book-keeping attracts but few, and those few go to the polls on election day and vote against each other because some twenty years ago there were national issues which transcended all book-keeping. The people are like the members of a great stock company who own a few shares each, and knowing that any loss must be distributed *pro rata,* are willing to remain ignorant of the company's accounts, and trust to luck and their subordinates. Our municipalities are such joint-stock companies, and are the only ones which our business men treat in this way. It is one of the peculiarities of our form of government in cities that those who should be and ultimately are most interested in them fail in the inclination to study their finances, although they have to meet the demands of the budgets, and although the budgets are the summary of the conditions and possibilities of municipal life. In physics we are taught the laws of statics before we take up those of dynamics, but in politics this is completely reversed, and we talk continually of what may be and of what should be, without knowing or caring to know what actually is. The people simultaneously demand small tax rates and a larger expenditure for public works, or an enlargement of the functions of the government. To again quote Lord Beaconsfield, who saw this very clearly: "If you establish a democracy, you must in due season reap the fruits of a democracy. You will in due season have great impatience of the public burdens, combined in due season with great increase of the public expenditure."

This is certainly true, but, from one motive or another, the people, if deeds and not words be taken as symptoms, are more patient of the increase of public expenditure than they are impatient of the public burden, even when they know that with the public moneys the politicians are doing those things which they ought not to do, and leaving undone those things which they ought to do. So true is this that in some parts of the country, in New Jersey and Maine, the people have permitted the municipalities to be extravagant to the point of bankruptcy. If one were to say that the remedy for such a disease of the public mind is the study of statistics, he might be roundly laughed at, and yet he would be by no means wide of the mark. If our voters would devote but a little time to the matter, and disregarding altogether the splendid principles or the appeals to their passions and prejudices which are the basis of the claims of political parties to their consideration, and having familiarized themselves somewhat with the machinery of government rather than with the government of the machine, study the budgets themselves, and then judge and act as they do when looking over their own balance-sheets, the much-cried-for reforms would not be so slow in coming. Such a study of the figures robs political questions of their personal, traditional, and contingent character, shows the real tendency of affairs, and gives the stamp of truth or of falsehood to the promises of politicians, whom we follow too largely for what they say rather than for what they do. Furthermore, it goes without saying that if the great problems which are fraught with danger for our country are really economical and administrative, this is the only way to study them, for the figures are not apt at lying, which is more than can be said for the politicians, who distort their true meaning when they notice them at all. The ordinary occupation of the politician when he is not in office is trying to get there, by educating his constituents into the belief that if they will only prefer him to his opponents he will work some sort of financial miracle, unless he can appeal to them more directly by a promise of division of the spoils. No one declares so frequently as he that figures are no partisans, and then proceeds directly to make them tell the most outrageous of lies in his particular interest.

The story of our political methods for the last twenty-five years is soonest told by the immense increase in our municipal indebtedness. This phenomenon of debt growth is, however, a universal one, and is apparent not only in the case of municipalities, but of states and nations as well, and goes a long way toward showing that the so-called rudder of government is, after all, just what Carlyle described it, namely, "the spigot of taxation," wherewith, in place of steering, the politicians may "tap, and the more cunningly the nearer the lees." While, according to Mulhall, the earnings of nations rose during the ten years 1870–1880 in twice the

ratio of the increase of population, the ratio of increase of taxation was more than twice, and the ratio of increase of public indebtedness more than four times, that of the ratio of increase of public wealth. The result of Mulhall's inquiries shows that the percentage of increase during those years was as follows:

Population .... 9.76 per cent.
Earnings of nations......19.84   "
Public wealth...........10.57   "
Taxes ....22.34   "
Public debt ....43.39   "

If these figures be correct, it is at once apparent that throughout the civilized world taxes and public indebtedness have increased out of all proportion to the increase in population, the earnings of nations, and the mass of wealth. The most noteworthy feature of the situation, however, is this, that the ratio of increase of taxation and public indebtedness is thus large notwithstanding the fact that in a majority of the leading states of the world there has been but a proportionately small increase, and in some an actual decrease, of the national debt. It is to the increase in local expenditure that the very enormous increase of 43.39 per cent. in public debt is due, this item including all public debts whatsoever. The figures will have to stand upon the authority of Mulhall, but, whether absolutely accurate or not, that they point out with approximate correctness the tendency of the times can be shown by even a slight study of the facts.

This increase of municipal expenditure and debt is a fact to which public financiers in all countries have long been calling attention. M. Leroy Beaulieu, one of the greatest living authorities, has not scrupled to say that "there is scarcely a country in the civilized world where the provinces, and particularly the cities, have not been given over to a lamentable wastefulness of the public funds." After asserting that the experience of France is not unique in this respect, and that England, Italy, the United States, and even Belgium are in like case, he goes on to recite the experience of his own country. The details will not interest us, but it is certainly a startling fact that the local taxes in France have increased almost 550 per cent. since the beginning of the century, and increased about 50 per cent. between the years 1864 and 1877. In Great Britain, while the national debt fell from 798 millions sterling in 1870 to 774 millions in 1880, or 24 millions in ten years, the municipal and other local debts rose from 84 to 140 millions sterling during the same period.

According to Mr. Robert P. Porter, in his volume on the statistics of public indebtedness, etc., the last census shows that "the minor civil divisions of the United States number in round figures about 2400 counties; 311 cities and towns with a population of 7500 and upward; about 8000 incorporated cities, villages, and other small places with a population below 7500; about 12,000 townships having a financial existence; and 105,000 school districts possessing a debt-creating power." A study of the indebtedness of these localities shows that while since 1870 the indebtedness of the national government as well as that of the State governments has been gradually reduced, the debts of the localities have been steadily growing in volume. During the ten years from 1870 to 1880 the national debt fell from $2,480,672,428 to $2,120,415,371, being a decrease of $360,257,057, or 14.5 per cent. During the same period the aggregate gross debt of all the States and Territories was reduced from $351,296,784 to $260,179,-723, or 25.9 per cent., as will more fully appear in the following table, which also shows the amount in the sinking fund for the payment of the State debts, and the net State indebtedness in 1880:

1880.

	Population.	Total Municipal Debt as above.	Per Capita.
United States	50,155,783	$698,270,199	$13.922
New England	4,010,529	125,937,193	31.152
Middle States	11,756,053	350,377,635	29.804
Southern States ..	15,257,393	71,064,858	4.657
Western States...	18,524,989	150,644,180	8.131
Territories	606,819	246,333	2.463

INCREASE FROM 1870 TO 1880.

	Increase.	Per Cent. of Increase.	Increase per Capita.
United States......	$370,025,679	112.7	5.41
New England......	54,414,451	76.07	10.646
Middle States......	234,861,803	203.31	18.071
Southern States*...	.....	....	....
Western States	84,368,212	127.298	3.221
Territories.........	222,013	912.88	1.942

* Decrease of $3,840,800; of 5.127 per cent.; of 2.001 per capita.

It thus appears that the local debt has grown from $328,244,520 to $698,270,199, the increase of $370,025,679 showing that it has somewhat more than doubled itself in the decade. The actual difference, however, is somewhat greater, inasmuch as the figures for 1870 are the gross, while those for 1880 are the net indebtedness.

The diverging tendencies of the national and State debts on the one hand, and of those of the minor political divisions on the other, will be disclosed with peculiar emphasis if we stop to consider the proportion of each class of indebtedness to the total public debt of the United States in each of the two years 1870 and 1880. In

STATE INDEBTEDNESS.

	Total Debt, 1870.	Total Debt, 1880.	Decrease.	Per Cent. of Decrease.	Sinking Fund, 1880.	Net Debt, 1880.
United States...	$351,296,784	$260,179,723	$91,117,061	25.9	$25,743,462	$234,436,261
New England...	50,348,550	49,950,926	397,624	0.8	14,743,444	35,207,482
Middle States...	79,834,481	44,604,511	35,229,970	44.1	7,029,401	37,575,110
Southern States.	174,486,407	125,728,155	48,758,252	27.9	1,924,920	123,803,235
Western States .	46,013,358	39,707,953	6,305,405	13.7	2,036,697	37,671,256
Territories	*613,988	188,178	425,810	69.3	9,000	179,178

* Exclusive of Colorado.

While this marked reduction has been going on in State and national indebtedness, the debt of the municipalities shows more than a proportionate increase, as shown in the following tables:

MUNICIPAL DEBT, INCLUDING TOWNSHIP AND SCHOOL DISTRICT.

1870.

	Population.	Total Municipal Debt as above.	Per Capita.
United States	38,558,371	$328,244,520	$8.5129
New England	3,487,924	71,522,742	20.506
Middle States	9,848,415	115,515,832	11.733
Southern States ..	11,250,411	74,905,658	6.658
Western States...	13,700,455	66,275,968	4.91
Territories	271,166	24,320	0.521

1870 the total public debt was $3,349,349,186, made up as follows:

National...............	$2,480,672,428
State.................	352,866,698
County	187,565,540
City and town	328,244,520
	$3,349,349,186

Of this total gross indebtedness the national debt was accordingly about 74 per cent., the State debt 10.5 per cent., the county debt 5.8 per cent., and the municipal debt 9.7 per cent. Deducting the national debt from this total of over 3349 millions, we have for the total gross indebtedness of the United States in 1870, other than that incurred by the general government, $868,676,758, of which 40.62 per cent. was State debt, 21.59 per cent. county debt, and 37.79 per cent. city and town debt.

In 1880, the total indebtedness of the United States, *for all purposes*, was $2,998,756,441, distributed as follows: national, $1,942,172,295; State, $234,436,261; county, $123,877,686; city and town, $698,270,199.

This shows a *decrease* of $350,592,745 over 1870, allowance to be made for the fact that the aggregate of indebtedness here given is net. It will be seen, therefore, that the net debt of the general government was only 66.7 per cent. of the total net indebtedness in 1880, as against about 74 per cent. in 1870; the State indebtedness 7.8 per cent. in 1880, as against 10.5 per cent. in 1870; the county indebtedness 4.4 per cent. in 1880, as against 5.8 per cent. in 1870; and the municipal indebtedness 23.2 per cent. of the total indebtedness of the county in 1880, as against 9.7 per cent. in 1870.

The total net indebtedness of the United States in 1880, *after deducting the national debt*, was $1,056,584,146—an *increase* of $187,907,388, or 22 per cent. Of this sum the State debt was 22.2 per cent., as against 40.6 per cent. in 1870, showing a decrease of 18.4 per cent.; the county debt 11.7 per cent., as against 21.5 per cent. in 1870, showing a decrease of 9.9 per cent.; and the municipal debt 66 per cent., as against 37.7 per cent., showing an increase of 28.3 per cent. over 1870.

We then have the following result: that while national, State, and county indebtedness was steadily decreasing from 1870 to 1880, the municipal debt was more than doubled, and is now 23.2 per cent. of the total indebtedness of the country, as against 9.7 per cent. in 1870; and 66 per cent. of the aggregate of State, county, and municipal indebtedness, as against 37.7 per cent. in 1870. It is more than three times as large as the State debt, and more than five and a half times as large as the combined county, township, and school district indebtedness of the entire country.

I have reproduced a diagram from the report, already referred to, in the last census, showing the relative total national, State, and municipal indebtedness of the United States for 1880, and have drawn another upon the same scale for 1870, for purposes of comparison, which will show the facts more graphically than the simple figures can do:

PUBLIC INDEBTEDNESS OF THE UNITED STATES IN 1880.

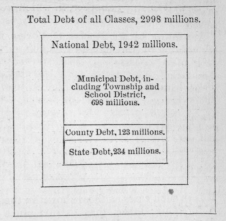

Total Debt of all Classes, 2998 millions.

National Debt, 1942 millions.

Municipal Debt, including Township and School District, 698 millions.

County Debt, 123 millions.

State Debt, 234 millions.

PUBLIC INDEBTEDNESS OF THE UNITED STATES IN 1870.

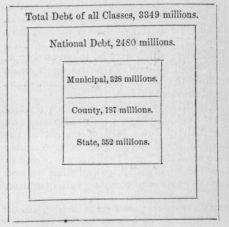

Total Debt of all Classes, 3349 millions.

National Debt, 2480 millions.

Municipal, 328 millions.

County, 187 millions.

State, 352 millions.

While as a matter of course the heaviest aggregate municipal indebtedness is to be found in the great cities, the most burdensome debt is found in the smaller ones. Taking the figures from the census of 1880, I find the following to be the ten most heavily burdened cities in the Union:

Cities.	Population.	Debt per Capita.
Bath, Maine	7,874	$216 69
Elizabeth, New Jersey	28,229	195 28
Brookline, Massachusetts	8,057	164 99
Bangor, Maine	16,856	157 87
Memphis, Tennessee	33,592	135 58
Rockland, Maine	7,599	129 88
Portland, Maine	33,810	127 84
District of Columbia	177,624	127 66
Jersey City, New Jersey	120,722	127 45
Middletown, Connecticut	11,732	119 97

This table will show the extent to which official extravagance has gone in localities. In addition, however, to this table showing the debt per capita of population, it will be well to study another, in which we can see the absolute debt of our ten largest cities:

Cities.	Population, 1870.	Population, 1880.	Debt, 1880.	Debt per Capita, 1880.
New York	942,292	1,206,299	$109,425,414	$90 71
Philadelphia	674,022	847,170	54,223,844	64 01
Brooklyn	396,099	566,663	38,040,000	67 13
Chicago	298,977	503,185	12,794,271	25 43
Boston	250,526	362,839	28,244,018	77 84
St. Louis	310,864	350,518	22,847,761	65 18
Baltimore	267,354	332,313	854,466	2 57
Cincinnati	216,289	255,139	21,992,500	86 20
San Francisco	149,473	233,959	3,059,285	13 08
New Orleans	191,418	216,090	17,736,509	82 08

It is in such cases as those shown in the two foregoing tables that extravagance and misgovernment have resulted in burdening our cities with debts larger in proportion to their population than can be found in any other country in the world. But in the matter of details we may go a step further, and study the debt of New York city, which may be taken as a type, in respect both of its alarming increase during the last twenty years, and of its absolute magnitude.

The history of the permanent debt of New York city begins with the passage on the 12th of June, 1812, of an act of the Legislature authorizing the city, to enable it to meet the "great expenses incurred in the erection of buildings and wharves, and for the purpose of carrying into operation the plan for laying out the said city into streets, avenues, and public squares, to raise upon its bonds the sum of $900,000 as a *permanent arrangement of the finances of the city*." The population of the city was still less than 100,000, and the thrifty legislators of those days could scarcely even in their dreams have looked forward to the time when, within little more than half a century, the population should have increased more than twelvefold, and the debt more than one hundred and twelvefold. This loan of 1812 was followed in 1820 by one of $400,000, and in 1825 by another of $700,000, the larger part of the earlier debt having been meanwhile extinguished. In 1830 the debt was still below a million dollars, as it continued to be till 1835. By 1840, however, the Croton water having been meanwhile introduced, the debt had risen to over 10 millions, which was about 4.25 per cent. of the assessed value of property within the city for that year, as against only 0.62 the ratio of debt to valuation in 1830.

STATEMENT SHOWING THE DEBT OF THE CITY AND COUNTY OF NEW YORK OTHER THAN REVENUE BONDS, WITH THE VALUATION OF TAXABLE PROPERTY OF THE SAME, FROM 1860 TO 1881, INCLUSIVE.

Year.	Gross Debt.	Net Debt.	Increase.	Decrease.	Ratio.	Valuation of Taxable Property.	Ratio of Net Debt to Valuation.	Bonds of Annexed Territory added to Debt.
1860	$22,264,044 00	$18,194,349 45	....	....	..	$576,631,706 97	3.1553	....
1861	25,268,944 00	20,141,543 00	$1,947,193 55	....	10.7000	581,579,971 00	3.4633	....
1862	28,068,042 00	21,357,541 00	1,215,998 00	....	6.0372	517,655,045 00	4.1258	....
1863	34,170,342 00	26,438,841 00	5,081,300 00	....	23.7916	594,196,693 00	4.4327	....
1864	41,880,924 50	33,441,723 50	7,002,882 50	....	26.4871	634,615,890 00	5.2696	....
1865	43,366,624 50	33,848,523 50	406,800 00	....	1.2167	608,827,855 00	5.5596	....
1866	44,196,776 50	33,569,189 50	....	$279,334 00	0.8253	736,989,908 00	4.5549	....
1867	46,577,474 45	32,978,231 50	....	590,958 00	1.7604	830,594,713 00	3.9704	....
1868	48,982,730 80	32,869,258 50	....	108,973 00	0.3304	907,815,529 00	3.6207	....
1869	63,627,452 22	45,548,039 92	12,678,781 42	....	38.5733	965,326,614 00	4.7184	....
1870	79,523,246 51	61,840,783 50	16,292,743 58	....	35.7704	1,047,388,449 00	5.9043	....
1871	102,182,608 51	82,513,845 50	20,673,062 00	....	33.4295	1,076,253,805 00	7.6667	....
1872	110,701,032 27	88,592,967 25	6,079,121 75	....	7.3674	1,104,098,087 00	8.0240	....
1873	121,419,592 02	96,646,045 22	8,053,077 97	....	9.0900	1,129,291,023 00	8.5581	....
1874	140,351,057 24	113,735,279 24	17,089,234 02	....	17.6824	1,154,029,176 00	9.8555	....
1875	141,580,203 54	113,953,852 15	218,572 91	....	0.1912	1,100,943,699 00	10.3506	$1,258,500 00
1876	143,123,213 28	114,944,110 51	990,258 36	....	0.8690	1,111,054,343 00	10.3455	1,201,100 00
1877	143,835,133 15	112,755,125 61	....	2,188,984 90	1.9043	1,101,092,093 00	10.2403	1,120,500 00
1878	140,645,815 82	109,371,674 50	....	3,383,451 11	3.0008	1,098,387,775 00	9.9575	1,065,500 00
1879	137,406,433 66	104,795,883 59	....	4,575,790 91	4.1837	1,094,069,335 00	9.5785	1,035,500 00
1880	134,488,519 87	101,591,455 42	....	3,204,428 17	3.0749	1,143,765,727 09	8.8081	999,000 00
1881	134,400,507 07	98,768,705 00	....	2,822,750 42	2.7603	1,185,948,098 96	8.3283	915,500 00

In 1850 the debt had risen to 12 millions and upward, and in 1860 to a little less than 19 millions, the ratio of debt to valuation in the two years being respectively 4.26 per cent. and 3.21 per cent. It rose steadily until 1877, when it was about 10.25 per cent. of the assessed valuation of all property, real and personal, within the city. It then began to decline, and is now about 8 per cent. of the assessed valuation. The table at the foot of the preceding page, carefully compiled from official documents, will show its history since 1860.

This table suggests some comparisons which will show how great the indebtedness of New York city really is. For the purpose of making these comparisons we will confine ourselves to the year 1880. In that year the net debt of the city will be seen to have been $101,591,455, or more than one-nineteenth of the entire national debt, which was then $1,942,172,295. The last census shows the net indebtedness of all municipalities in the United States to have been as follows: of cities, towns, etc., of over 7500 population, $593,344,418; of cities, towns, etc., of less than 7500 population, $55,817,126, making a total of $649,161,544, of which total we see at a glance that the debt of New York city alone was nearly one-sixth. The census shows that the indebtedness of cities of over 7500 population, aggregating $593,344,418, was divided as follows in 1880:

All of the Southern States $64,912,431
All of the Western States........... 111,484,430
All of the New England States 99,181,223
All of the Middle States 317,699,334
All of the Territories 67,000

Looking at these figures, it will be readily seen that in 1880 the indebtedness of New York city was larger than that of all of the cities of over 7500 population in all of the Southern States, than that of all those of New England, nearly as large as that of all the Western cities together, and about one-third of that of all of the cities of the Middle States. It was larger by nearly eight millions of dollars than the debt of all of the cities of Alabama, Arkansas, California, Colorado, Delaware, Florida, Georgia, Indiana, Iowa, Kansas, Kentucky, Maryland, Michigan, Minnesota, Mississippi, Missouri, Nebraska, Nevada, New Hampshire, North Carolina, Oregon, Rhode Island, South Carolina, Tennessee, Texas, Utah, Vermont, Virginia, West Virginia, and Wisconsin, which aggregate but $93,693,000.

In 1880 the gross State indebtedness of all the States in the Union was $260,179,723, which was about twice as much as the gross debt of New York city, and not three times as much as its net debt. In 1880 and 1881 the tax budgets of all the States together, for State purposes, aggregated only $61,921,144, while that of New York city alone was $30,259,202. The tax rate for State purposes in 1881 varied from 10 cents on $100 in Tennessee to 25 cents in New York, and 70 cents in Florida, while the municipal rate in New York city was $2 62. In 1882 the city debt of New York city was more than ten times as large as the State debt, which was but $9,109,054, all of which was canal debt but about $122,694, and on account of which there was $2,422,981 in the sinking fund. In 1882 the State raised by taxation only $6,820,022 29, as against about 28 millions raised by the city for the same time. The total ordinary expenses of the national government for the year 1881, including over 50 millions for pensions, 82 millions for interest on the public debt, 55 millions for the army and navy, 41 millions for public buildings, light-houses, collecting the revenue, etc., and 17 millions for civil expenses, was $260,712,887, or a little more than eight times the expenditure of New York city for the same year. Of the $30,259,205 raised by taxation in New York city for 1881, $13,176,102 were required for the payment of State taxes and the interest and redemption of the city debt, leaving $17,183,103 for administration. For the same year the amount expended by the national government for Congress, the Executive, the judiciary, the government of the Territories, the sub-treasuries, public land offices, inspection of steam vessels, and the Mint and assay offices, was but $17,941,177, and of which amount $6,878,442 was charged against the Executive alone. Our city debt is now larger than that of the nation was at any time from 1791 to 1815. In 1816 the national debt was only 127 millions, and had fallen by 1819 to 95 millions, from which time it gradually declined until it was extinguished in 1836. It was not until the outbreak of the war in 1861 that it rose to anywhere near the proportions of the present city debt of New York, and in that year it was only $90,580,873.

To those who have never stopped to seriously consider the financial situation of the city of New York the foregoing figures will show to what a pass it has actually come. Looked at by the light of these comparisons, we realize how truly enormous the indebtedness and annual taxation of the city are. How it came to be what it is, is matter of history, the story of official frauds, of decrease of public spirit, and of increased neglect on the part of the citizens, far more than of the increased needs for municipal expenditure. It may be interesting, however, to see just where the increase has taken place, and we are enabled to do this through a "comparative statement of expenses of the corporation in 1860 and 1880," which is given in the report of the Comptroller of August 1, 1881, and which is as follows:

the taxable valuation of property about 100 per cent. greater, ... the annual expenses, as shown in the above table, have increased about 145 per cent."

It is unnecessary to go more fully into detail. The figures speak plainly enough, and demand such attention as they have never yet received. The financial problem in our States and in the nation is a comparatively simple one; not so in the municipalities, much less so in the city of New York. The people of the metropolis are the most expensively governed in the world, and yet year after year they pay their millions and do nothing to cure the evil. They elect their city officials at the same time as State and national ones, and they vote for them all

	Expenses in 1860.	Expenses in 1880.
State Taxes	$1,311,399 44	$3,571,322 91
For expenses of city and county government, viz.:		
Interest on the city debt, including amount paid from Sinking Fund	1,360,718 04	9,056,588 46
Redemption of city debt*	71,657 36	221,610 57
The Common Council (and Board of Supervisors, 1860)	181,273 03	122,712 86
The Mayoralty	28,198 59	39,701 61
Department of Finance	131,629 50	262,127 99
Law Department	45,574 40	160,186 51
Department of Public Works	3,420,456 58	3,308,546 11
(This department was created in 1870. The expenses of 1860 are those of the Street Department, the Croton Aqueduct Department, and for building and repairs of docks.)		
Department of Docks	....	589,889 48
Department of Public Parks	908,661 17	694,400 67
Department of Buildings (including amount under Fire Department)	....	55,392 78
Department of Public Charities and Correction	746,199 00	1,318,793 03
Health Department	163,130 06	256,425 33
Police Department	1,398,132 64	3,277,069 20
Cleaning streets	325,371 37	809,703 01
Fire Department	152,730 11	1,373,723 08
Board of Education	1,278,781 00	3,422,307 71
College of the City of New York	....	138,905 31
Department of Taxes and Assessments	58,515 80	107,784 33
The Judiciary	323,185 56	1,291,771 31
Advertising, printing, stationery, and blank books	153,473 31	166,352 67
Asylums, reformatories, and charitable institutions	110,257 89	1,344,916 35
Election expenses	148,913 84	177,469 31
Judgments and claims	89,548 70	533,299 48
New York and Brooklyn Bridge	....	421,900 00
Street openings	786,811 59	82,626 50
Miscellaneous purposes	508,371 30	707,136 48
Totals	$13,702,990 28	$33,512,663 05

* Amount raised by tax, exclusive of the amount paid from "the Sinking Fund for the Redemption of the City Debt," and also exclusive of amount of bonds refunded.

The Comptroller, after giving this table, states that since 1860 there have been radical changes in the organization of several city departments; that the Fire Department and Dock Department did not then exist; and that the present Public Works Department embraces what was then the Street and Croton Aqueduct departments. He makes a long explanation of the differences between the two years—an explanation too long for repetition here, and which, although it is comparatively thorough, leaves the fact remaining that while "the population of the city in 1880 was about 50 per cent. more than in 1860, and

alike from the same principle, namely, political partisanship, the dividing lines of which spring out of national tradition instead of national or local needs. They consent year after year to surrender their rights to party machines, and to be governed from their State Capitol rather than at home. They devote themselves to money-getting, and lose all sense of civic pride, while the hungry professionals in politics are making their municipal budgets and confiscating their property. Occasionally they strive to mend matters by revolution, and then fall back into their old ways. Once in a great while they ask the Legislature plaintively for spring elections, and the constitutional right to local self-government, then tire out and relapse into their careless ways. But the politician never tires. It remains to be seen whether a remedy can be effected before the evil of misgovernment and official wrong-doing assumes such proportions that one after another our municipalities, and particularly the city of New York, are driven by the succession of frauds, extravagances, and thefts into a political revolution, which shall at last compel the States to give constitutional home rule to the cities, and the Legislatures to frame charters upon business- and statesman-like principles. The relief can never come through professorial or professional politicians, but through the well-directed and untiring business-like action of business men. Carlyle truly divined our case. As the matter stands to-day, the rudder of government is but the spigot of taxation.

"In 1790," say the officers of the last census, "one-thirtieth of the population of the United States lived in cities of 8000 inhabitants and over; in 1800, one twenty-fifth; in 1810, and also in 1820, one-twentieth; in 1830, one-sixteenth; in 1840, one-twelfth; in 1850, one-eighth; in 1860, one-sixth; and in 1870, a little over one-fifth." The ratio is now nearly one-quarter. This unparalleled growth of cities, and the startlingly disproportionate increase in the cost of governing them, sufficiently show where the really troublesome questions of government are to arise in the future, and that any sacrifice of municipal interests to national or State politics will strengthen the hands of professional politicians, and increase the burden of the people where that burden is already heaviest.

A GATHERER OF SIMPLES.

A DAMP air was blowing up, and the frogs were beginning to peep. The sun was setting in a low red sky. On both sides of the road were rich green meadows intersected by little canal-like brooks. Beyond the meadows on the west was a distant stretch of pine woods, that showed dark against the clear sky. Aurelia Flower was going along the road toward her home, with a great sheaf of leaves and flowers in her arms. There were the rosy spikes of hardhack; the great white corymbs of thoroughwort, and the long blue racemes of lobelia. Then there were great bunches of the odorous tansy and pennyroyal in with the rest.

Aurelia was a tall, strongly built woman; she was not much over thirty, but she looked older. Her complexion had a hard red tinge from exposure to sun and wind, and showed seams as unreservedly as granite. Her face was thin, and her cheek-bones high. She had a profusion of auburn hair, showing in a loose slipping coil beneath her limp black straw hat. Her dress, as a matter of fashion, was execrable; in point of harmony with her immediate surroundings, very well, though she had not thought of it in that way. There was a green under-skirt, and a brown over-skirt and basque of an obsolete cut. She had worn it for a good many years just so, and never thought of altering it. It did not seem to occur to her that though her name was Flower, she was not really a flower in regard to apparel, and had not its right of unchangeableness in the spring. When the trees hung out their catkins, she flaunted her poor old greens and browns under them, rejoicing, and never dreamed but what they looked all right. As far as dress went, Aurelia was a happy woman. She went along the road to-night at a good pace, her armful of leaves and blossoms nodding; her spare muscular limbs bore her along easily. She had been over a good many miles since noon, but she never thought of being tired.

Presently she came in sight of her home, a square unpainted building, black with age. It stood back a little from the road on a gentle slope. There were three great maple-trees in front of the house; their branches rustled against the roof. On the left was a small garden; some tall poles thickly twined with hops were prominent in it.

Aurelia went round to the side door of the house with her armful of green things. The door opened directly into the great kitchen. One on entering would have started back as one would on seeing unexpected company in a room. The walls were as green as a lady's bower with bunches and festoons of all sorts of New

England herbs. There they hung, their brave blossoms turning gray and black, giving out strange half-pleasant, half-disgusting odors. Aurelia took them in like her native air. "It's good to get home," murmured she to herself, for there was no one else: she lived alone.

She took off her hat and disposed of her burden; then she got herself some supper. She did not build a fire in the cooking stove, for she never drank tea in warm weather. Instead, she had a tumbler of root-beer which she had made herself. She set it out on one end of her kitchen table with a slice of coarse bread and a saucer of cold beans. She sat down to it and ate with a good appetite. She looked better with her hat off. Her forehead was an important part of her face; it was white and womanly, and her reddish hair lay round it in pretty curves; then her brown eyes, under very strongly arched brows, showed to better advantage. Taken by herself, and not compared with other women, Aurelia was not so bad-looking; but she never was taken by herself in that way, and nobody had ever given her any credit for comeliness. It would have been like looking at a jack-in-the-pulpit and losing all the impression that had ever been made on one by roses and hyacinths, and seeing absolutely nothing else but that one flower's fine green and brown lines: it is doubtful if it could be done.

She had finished her supper, and was sorting her fresh herbs, when the door opened and a woman walked in. She had no bonnet on her head: she was a neighbor, and this was an unceremonious little country place.

"Good-evenin', 'Relia," said she. There was an important look on her plain face, as if there was more to follow.

"Good-evenin', Mis' Atwood. Take a chair."

"Been herbin' again?"

"Yes; I went out a little while this afternoon."

"Where'd you go?—up on Green Mountain?"

"No; I went over to White's Woods. There were some kinds there I wanted."

"You don't say so! That's a matter of six miles, ain't it? Ain't you tired?"

"Lor', no," said Aurelia. "I reckon I'm pretty strong, or mebbe the smell of the herbs keeps me up;" and she laughed. So did the other. "Sure enough—well,

mebbe it does. I never thought of that. But it seems like a pretty long tramp to me, though my bein' so fleshy may make a difference. I could have walked it easier once."

"I shouldn't wonder if it did make a difference. I 'ain't got much flesh to carry round to tire me out."

"You're always pretty well, too, ain't you, 'Relia?"

"Lor', yes; I never knew what 'twas to be sick. How's your folks, Mis' Atwood? Is Viny any better than she was?"

"I don't know as she is, much. She feels pretty poorly most of the time. I guess I'll hev you fix some more of that root-beer for her. I thought that seemed to 'liven her up a little."

"I've got a jug of it all made, down cellar, and you can take it when you go home, if you want to."

"So I will, if you've got it. I was in hopes you might hev it."

The important look had not vanished from Mrs. Atwood's face, but she was not the woman to tell important news in a hurry, and have the gusto of it so soon over. She was one of the natures who always dispose of bread before pie. Now she came to it, however.

"I heard some news to-night, 'Relia," said she.

Aurelia picked out another spray of hardhack. "What was it?"

"Thomas Rankin's dead."

Aurelia clutched the hardhack mechanically. "You don't mean it, Mis' Atwood! When did he die? I hadn't heard he was sick."

"He wasn't, long. Had a kind of a fit this noon, and died right off. The doctor—they sent for Dr. Smith from Alden—called it sun-stroke. You know 'twas awful hot, and he'd been out in the field to work all the mornin'. I think 'twas heart trouble; it's in the Rankin family; his father died of it. Doctors don't know everything."

"Well, it's a dreadful thing," said Aurelia. "I can't realize it. There he's left four little children, and it ain't more'n a year since Mis' Rankin died. It *ain't* a year, is it?"

"It ain't a year into a month and sixteen days," said Mrs. Atwood, solemnly. "Viny and I was countin' of it up just before I come in here."

"Well, I guess 'tisn't, come to think of it. I couldn't have told exactly. The oldest of those children ain't more than eight, is she?"

"Ethelind is eight, coming next month: Viny and I was reckinin' it up. Then Edith is six, and Isadore is five, and Myrtie ain't but two, poor little thing."

"What do you s'pose will be done with 'em?"

"I don't know. Viny an' me was talking of it over, and got it settled that her sister, Mis' Loomis, over to Alden, would hev to hev 'em. It'll be considerable for her, too, for she's got two of her own, and I don't s'pose Sam Loomis has got much. But I don't see what else can be done. Of course strangers ain't goin' to take children when there is folks."

"Wouldn't his mother take 'em?"

"What, old-lady Sears? Lor', no. You know she was dreadful put out 'bout Thomas marryin' where he did, and declared he shouldn't hev a cent of her money. It was all her second husband's, anyway. John Rankin wasn't worth anything. She won't do anything for 'em. She's livin' in great style down near the city, they say. Got a nice house, and keeps help. She might hev 'em jest as well as not, but she won't. She's a hard woman to get along with, anyhow. She nagged both her husbands to death, an' Thomas never had no peace at home. Guess that was one reason why he was in such a hurry to get married. Mis' Rankin was a good-tempered soul, if she wasn't quite so drivin' as some."

"I do feel dreadfully to think of those children," said Aurelia.

"'Tis hard; but we must try an' believe it will be ruled for the best. I s'pose I must go, for I left Viny all alone."

"Well, if you must, I'll get that rootbeer for you, Mis' Atwood. I shall keep thinking 'bout those children all night."

A week or two after that, Mrs. Atwood had some more news; but she didn't go to Aurelia with it, for Aurelia was the very sub-essence of it herself. She unfolded it gingerly to her daughter Lavinia—a pale, peaked young woman, who looked as if it would take more than Aurelia's root-beer to make her robust. Aurelia had taken the youngest Rankin child for her own, and Mrs. Atwood had just heard of it. "It's true," said she; "I see her with it myself. Old-lady Sears never so much as sent a letter, let alone not coming to the funeral, and Mis' Loomis was glad enough to get rid of it."

Viny drank in the story as if it had been so much nourishing jelly. Her too narrow life was killing her as much as anything else.

Meanwhile Aurelia had the child, and was actively happy, for the first time in her life, to her own naïve astonishment, for she had never known that she was not so before. She had naturally strong affections, of an outward rather than an inward tendency. She was capable of much enjoyment from pure living, but she had never had anything to be so very fond of. She could only remember her father as a gloomy, hard-working man, who never noticed her much. He had a melancholy temperament, which resulted in a tragical end when Aurelia was a mere child. When she thought of him, the same horror which she had when they brought him home from the river crept over her now. They had never known certainly just how Martin Flower had come to die; but folks never spoke of him to Aurelia and her mother, and the two never talked of him together. They knew that everybody said Martin Flower had drowned himself; they felt shame and a Puritan shrinking from the sin.

Aurelia's mother had been a hard, silent woman before; she grew more hard and silent afterward. She worked hard, and taught Aurelia to. Their work was peculiar; they hardly knew themselves how they had happened to drift into it; it had seemed to creep in with other work, till finally it usurped it altogether. At first, after her husband's death, Mrs. Flower had tried millinery: she had learned the trade in her youth. But she made no headway then in sewing rose-buds and dainty bows on to bonnets; it did not suit with tragedy. The bonnets seemed infected with her own mood; the bows lay flat with stern resolve, and the rose-buds stood up fiercely; she did not please her customers, even among those uncritical country folk, and they dropped off. She had always made excellent root-beer, and had had quite a reputation in the neighborhood for it. How it happened she could not tell, but she found herself selling it; then she made hop yeast, and sold that. Then she was a woman of a fertile brain, and another project suggested itself to her.

She and Aurelia ransacked the woods thereabouts for medicinal herbs, and disposed of them to druggists in a neighboring town. They had a garden of some sorts too—the different mints, thyme, lavender, coriander, rosemary, and others. It was an unusual business for two women to engage in, but it increased, and they prospered, according to their small ideas. But Mrs. Flower grew more and more bitter with success. What regrets and longing that her husband could have lived and shared it, and been spared his final agony, she had in her heart, nobody but the poor woman herself knew; she never spoke of them. She died when Aurelia was twenty, and a woman far beyond her years. She mourned for her mother, but although she never knew it, her warmest love had not been called out. It had been hardly possible. Mrs. Flower had not been a lovable mother; she had rarely spoken to Aurelia but with cold censure for the last few years. People whispered that it was a happy release for the poor girl when her mother died; they had begun to think she was growing like her husband, and perhaps was not "just right."

Aurelia went on with the business with calm equanimity, and made even profits every year. They were small, but more than enough for her to live on, and she paid the last dollar of the mortgage which had so fretted her father, and owned the old house clear. She led a peaceful, innocent life, with her green herbs for companions; she associated little with the people around, except in a business way. They came to see her, but she rarely entered their houses. Every room in her house was festooned with herbs; she knew every kind that grew in the New England woods, and hunted them out in their season and brought them home; she was a simple, sweet soul, with none of the morbid melancholy of her parents about her. She loved her work, and the greenwood things were to her as friends, and the healing qualities of sarsaparilla and thoroughwort, and the sweetness of thyme and lavender, seemed to have entered into her nature, till she almost could talk with them in that way. She had never thought of being unhappy; but now she wondered at herself over this child. It was a darling of a child; as dainty and winsome a girl baby as ever was. Her poor young mother had had a fondness for romantic names, which she had bestowed, as the only heritage within her power, on all her children. This one was Myrtilla—Myrtie for short. The little thing clung to Aurelia from the first, and Aurelia found that she had another way of loving besides the way in which she loved lavender and thoroughwort. The comfort she took with the child through the next winter was unspeakable. The herbs were banished from the south room, which was turned into a nursery, and a warm carpet was put on the floor, that the baby might not take cold. She learned to cook for the baby—her own diet had been chiefly vegetarian. She became a charming nursing mother. People wondered. "It does beat all how handy 'Relia is with that baby," Mrs. Atwood told Viny.

Aurelia took even more comfort with the little thing when spring came, and she could take her out with her; then she bought a little straw carriage, and the two went after herbs together. Home they would come in the tender spring twilight, the baby asleep in her carriage, with a great sheaf of flowers beside her, and Aurelia with another over her shoulder.

She felt all through that summer as if she was too happy to last. Once she said so to one of the neighbors. "I feel as if it wa'n't right for me to be so perfectly happy," said she. "I feel some days as if I was walkin' an' walkin' an' walkin' through a garden of sweet-smellin' herbs, an' nothin' else; an' as for Myrtie, she's a bundle of myrtle an' camphor out of King Solomon's garden. I'm so afraid it can't last."

Happiness had seemed to awake in Aurelia a taint of her father's foreboding melancholy. But she apparently had no reason for it until early fall. Then, returning with Myrtie one night from a trip to the woods, she found an old lady seated on her door-step, grimly waiting for her. She was an old woman and tremulous, but still undaunted and unshaken as to her spirit. Her tall, shrunken form was loaded with silk and jet. She stood up as Aurelia approached wondering, and her dim old eyes peered at her aggressively through fine gold spectacles, which lent an additional glare to them.

"I suppose you are Miss Flower?" began the old lady, with no prefatory parley.

"Yes," said Aurelia, trembling.

"Well, my name's Mrs. Matthew Sears, an' I've come for my grandchild there."

Aurelia turned very white. She let her herbs slide to the ground. "I—hardly understand—I guess," faltered she. "Can't you let me keep her?"

"Well, I guess I won't have one of my grandchildren brought up by an old yarb woman—not if I know it."

The old lady sniffed. Aurelia stood looking at her. She felt as if she had fallen down from heaven, and the hard reality of the earth had jarred the voice out of her. Then the old lady made a step toward the carriage, and caught up Myrtie in her trembling arms. The child screamed with fright. She had been asleep. She turned her little frightened face toward Aurelia, and held out her arms, and cried, "Mamma! mamma! mamma!" in a perfect frenzy of terror. The old lady tried to hush her in vain. Aurelia found her voice then. "You'd better let me take her and give her her supper," she said, "and when she is asleep again I will bring her over to you."

"Well," said the old lady, doubtfully. She was glad to get the frantic little thing out of her arms, though.

Aurelia held her close and hushed her, and she subsided into occasional convulsive sobs, and furtive frightened glances at her grandmother.

"I s'pose you are stopping at the hotel?" said Aurelia.

"Yes, I am," said the old lady, stoutly. "You kin bring her over as soon as she's asleep." Then she marched off with uncertain majesty.

Some women would have argued the case longer, but Aurelia felt that there was simply no use in it. The old lady was the child's grandmother: if she wanted her, she saw no way but to give her up. She never thought of pleading, she was so convinced of the old lady's determination.

She carried Myrtie into the house, gave her her supper, washed her, and dressed her in her little best dress. Then she took her up in her lap and tried to explain to her childish mind the change that was to be made in her life. She told her she was going to live with her grandmother, and she must be a good little girl, and love her, and do just as she told her to. Myrtie sobbed with unreasoning grief, and clung to Aurelia; but she wholly failed to take the full meaning of it all in.

She was still fretful and bewildered by her rude wakening from her nap. Presently she fell asleep again, and Aurelia laid her down while she got together her little wardrobe. There was a hop pillow in a little linen case, which Myrtie had always slept on; she packed that up with the other things.

Then she rolled the little sleeping girl up in a blanket, laid her in her carriage, and went over to the hotel. It was not much of a hotel—merely an ordinary two-story house, where two or three spare rooms were ample accommodation for the few straggling guests who came to this little rural place. It was only a few steps from Aurelia's house. The old lady had the chamber of honor, a large square room on the first floor, opening directly on to the piazza. In spite of all Aurelia's care, Myrtie woke up and began to cry when she was carried in. She had to go off and leave her screaming piteously after her. Out on the piazza, she uttered the first complaint, almost, of her life, to the hostess, Mrs. Simonds, who had followed her there.

"Don't feel bad, 'Relia," said the woman, who was almost crying herself. "I know it's awful hard, when you was taking so much comfort. We all feel for you."

Aurelia looked straight ahead. She had the bundle of little clothes and the hop pillow in her arms: the old lady had said, in a way that would have been funny if it had not been for the poor heart that listened, that she didn't want any yarb pillows, nor any clothes scented with yarbs nuther.

"I don't mean to be wicked," said Aurelia, "but I can't help thinking that Providence ought to provide for women. I wish Myrtie was *mine*."

The other woman wiped her eyes at the hungry way in which she said "mine."

"Well, I can't do anything; but I'm sorry for you, if that's all. You'd make enough sight better mother for Myrtie than that cross old woman. I don't b'lieve she more'n half wants her, only she's *sot*. She doesn't care anything about having the other children; she's going to leave them with Mis' Loomis; but she says her grandchildren ain't going to be living with strangers, an' she ought to hev been consulted. After all you've done for the child, to treat you as she has to-night, she's the most ungrateful— I know one thing: I'd charge her for Myrtie's board—a good price, too."

"Oh, I don't want anything of that sort," said poor Aurelia, dejectedly, listening to her darling's sobs. "You go in an' try to hush her, Mis' Simonds. Oh!"

"So I will! her grandmother can't do

anything with her, poor little thing! I've got some peppermints. I do believe she's spankin' her—the—"

Aurelia did not run in with Mrs. Simonds; she listened outside till the pitiful cries hushed a little; then she went desolately home.

She sat down in the kitchen, with the little clothes in her lap. She did not think of going to bed; she did not cry or moan to herself; she just sat there still. It was not very late when she came home—between eight and nine. In about half an hour, perhaps, she heard a sound outside that made her heart leap—a little voice crying pitifully, and saying, between the sobs, "Mamma! mamma!"

Aurelia made one spring to the door. There was the tiny creature in her little night-gown, shaking all over with cold and sobs.

Aurelia caught her up, and all her calm was over. "Oh, you darling! you darling! you darling!" she cried, covering her little cold body all over with kisses. "You sha'n't leave me—you sha'n't! you sha'n't! Little sweetheart—all I've got in the world. I guess they sha'n't take you away when you don't want to go. Did you cry, and mamma go off and leave you? Did they whip you? They never shall again—never! never! There, there, blessed, don't cry; mamma'll get you all warm, and you shall go to sleep on your own little pillow. Oh, you darling! darling! darling!"

Aurelia busied herself about the child, rubbing the little numb limbs, and getting some milk heated. She never asked how she came to get away; she never thought of anything except that she had her. She stopped every other minute to kiss her and croon to her; she laughed and cried. Now she gave way to her feelings; she was almost beside herself. She had the child all warm and fed and comforted by the kitchen fire, when she heard steps outside, and she knew at once what was coming, and a fierce resolve sprang up in her heart: they should not have that child again to-night. She cast a hurried glance around; there was hardly a second's time. In the corner of the kitchen was a great heap of herbs which she had taken down from the walls where they had been drying; the next day she had intended to pack them and send them off. She caught up Myrtie and covered her with them. "Lie still, darling!" she

whispered. "Don't make a bit of noise, or your grandmother will get you again." Myrtie crouched under them, trembling.

Then the door opened; Mr. Simonds stood there with a lantern. "That little girl's run away," he began—"slipped out while the old lady was out of the room a minute. Beats all how such a little thing knew enough. She's here, ain't she?"

"No," said Aurelia, "she ain't."

"You don't mean it?"

"Yes."

"'Ain't you seen her, though?"

"No."

Mr. Simonds, who was fat and placid, began to look grave. "Then, all there is about it, we've got to have a hunt," said he. "'Twon't do to have that little tot out in her night-gown long. We hadn't a thought but that she was here. Must have lost her way."

Aurelia watched him stride down the yard. Then she ran after him. "Mr. Simonds!" He turned. "I told you a lie. Myrtie's in the corner of the kitchen under a heap of herbs."

"Why, what on earth—"

"I wanted to keep her so to-night." Aurelia burst right out in loud sobs.

"There, 'Relia! It's a confounded shame. You shall keep her. I'll make it all right with the old lady somehow. I reckon, as long as the child's safe, she'll be glad to get rid of her to-night. She wouldn't have slept much. Go right into the house, 'Relia, and don't worry."

Aurelia obeyed. She hung over the little creature all night, asleep in her little crib. She watched her every breath. She never thought of sleeping herself—her last night with Myrtie. The seconds were so many grains of gold-dust. Her heart failed her when day broke. She washed and dressed Myrtie at the usual time, and gave her her breakfast. Then she sat down with her and waited. The child's sorrow was soon forgotten, and she played about as usual. Aurelia watched her despairingly. She began to wonder at length why they did not come for her. It grew later and later. She would not carry her back herself, she was resolved on that.

It was ten o'clock before any one came; then it was Mrs. Simonds. She had a strange look on her face.

"'Relia," she said, standing in the door and looking at her and Myrtie, "you 'ain't heard what's happened to our house this mornin', hev you?"

"No," said Aurelia, awed.

"Old Mis' Sears is dead. Had her third shock: she's had two in the last three years. She was took soon after Mr. Simonds got home. We got a doctor right off, but she died 'bout an hour ago."

"Oh," said Aurelia, "I've been a wicked woman."

"No, you 'ain't, Aurelia; don't you go to feeling so. There's no call for the living to be unjust to themselves because folks are dead. You did the best you could. An' now you're glad you can keep the child; you can't help it. I thought of it myself the first thing."

"Oh, I was such a wicked woman to think of it myself," said Aurelia. "If I could only have done something for the poor old soul! Why didn't you call me?"

"I told Mr. Simonds I wouldn't; you'd had enough."

There was one thing which Aurelia found to do, though—a simple and touching thing, though it probably meant more to her than to most of those who knew of it.

On the day of the funeral the poor old woman's grave was found lined with fragrant herbs from Aurelia's garden—thyme and lavender and rosemary. She had cried when she picked them, because she could not help being glad, and they were all she could give for atonement.

Editor's Easy Chair.

THE general and almost affectionate sympathy with which the news of the recovery of a part of the Greely arctic expedition was received shows how profound is the interest which attends the persistent efforts of heroic men to extend the area of scientific knowledge and to dissipate the mystery that surrounds the pole. The news of Lieutenant Greely's safe return was telegraphed from Newfoundland, and reached New York about noon. The bulletin-boards were instantly surrounded with eager crowds. The tidings flew through the city. They were known in every office and discussed in every circle. Simultaneously the people of the whole country knew that part at least of the long-lost party had returned safely. England knew it at the same time, and the Queen and the President exchanged telegrams of congratulation upon the happy event. Lieutenant Greely was justly the hero of the hour, and for a moment the angry passions of the Presidential campaign were mitigated by the unanimous pleasure that the brave officer and his men had escaped the doom which has befallen so many of their heroic predecessors.

The details of their story are like those of every similar expedition. They include every form of exposure and suffering, and, like the earlier narratives, such as those of Parry and Back, which captivated the imagination of youth half a century ago, and cast a glamour of fascinating romance over the arctic voyage, they are unconscious tributes to the heroism and the noblest qualities of human nature. The object of the Greely expedition was not the gratification of curiosity, nor the desire to discover the Northwest Passage. It was undertaken in concert with expeditions from other countries to determine certain scientific points, and was open to the charge of foolhardiness in no other way than all undertakings in the interest of scientific research which involve peril are open to the same charge.

The long series of arctic voyages has now fully demonstrated that there is no practicable Northwest Passage. It was to discover this way that many of them were undertaken, and they have shown that while a sea doubtless surrounds the pole, and that in that sense such a passage exists, yet that it is not practically navigable because of the ice. Nordenskjöld has made the circuit from Europe through the polar sea, along the north of Asia and past Behring Strait, into the Pacific. But, that voyage successfully accomplished, there is no reason for undertaking it again for that purpose. Until Fourier's millennial age of harmony shall melt the ice that guards the pole, mere curiosity may be considered to be satisfied, and further exploration is not probable except for the love of wild adventure and for the interests of science.

But we may be sure that the alluring spell of the pole has not spent its force. The same charm that in the face of danger and death has drawn so many brave men to do what others have dared will appeal to other Kanes, Halls, and Hayeses as to those who are gone. The old remonstrance will be unheeded. The warnings of previous failure will but kindle greater zeal. Imagination, hope, ambition, will repeat again and again the old heroic arctic story. Governments may refuse to authorize the voyage. But governments will hardly refuse to try to rescue the voyagers.

Long ago the Easy Chair was keeping the watch with an American sailor upon the Mediterranean off the coast of Spain. The huge mountains of Granada glimmered through the moonlight, and as the quiet talk went on, the sailor owned the resistless fascination of the sea. He was an inland boy, but at midnight when he awoke and heard the wind sighing or roaring through the trees, he seemed to hear the dash of the ocean imperiously calling him to come away. "I could not stay upon the farm," he said; "and here I am, and here I shall always be." That is the call which the predestined arctic explorer hears, and although the peril be great, it is not greater than in other marine service. In his late work upon arctic exploration, Professor Nourse says, what we had previously heard, that the loss of life in arctic exploration has been remarkably small. All the deaths upon all the Franklin relief expeditions up to 1873 did not equal two per cent. of all the officers and men employed, "nor have the casualties in the recent German, English, Swedish, and American expeditions equalled those ordinarily occurring among the ships on naval duty in other regions of the globe." He quotes Professor Maury as saying that the losses by wreckage around the British Isles during a single year exceed the aggregate of all losses within the history of arctic explorations.

In three hundred years there have been some two hundred arctic voyages, for various purposes and with various fates. The Greely expedition was but one of thirteen expeditions. Five hundred men passed two winters within the polar circle, and nineteen of them only were lost. And Lieutenant Ray says that the result of the observations of all these expeditions will be the doubling of the world's knowledge of the magnetic forces. That is to say, as the Rev. Brooke Herford states in his admirable sermon upon this subject, "Not one of all the thousand and ten thousand craft sailing to and fro among the many lands of earth but will be a little surer of its compass, a little closer in its reckoning, a little safer, than it ever was before." Is this worth nothing? Is not the risk, the loss, even amply recompensed? But also, as Mr. Herford points out, the moral qualities, the patience, the courage, the self-denial, the faith, the endurance, developed by these Northern researches are incomparable. "There is simply no other chapter in the history of human doings to be compared with it. Beside it the adventures of commerce and conquest look greedy and base, the stories of chivalry are mere tinsel, the long heroism of the Crusades seems a fevered frenzy." Cui bono? is not an argument to discourage the restless soul which the prospect of peril inspires, nor will the pathetic story of the patient and generous endurance, amid apparently remediless suffering, which the record of the Greely expedition discloses dismay or deter other Greelys from daring the same dangers. The arctic story is one of the saddest, but it is also one of the noblest, in the annals of human heroism.

WHEN photography began to make the faces and figures and dress of the most famous of living people familiar, and at last emperors and kings and princes were shown precisely as they were, plain men and women, with no glamour of robe or coronet or visible state, it was a question whether the divinity that doth hedge a king, and which, according to Bagehot, is still believed in by the mass of subjects, would not disappear. The Queen of England, he says, is known, of course, to the rural Englishman to be a woman, but she is nevertheless a figure of the imagination. She is not as other women, and he sees her sitting in perpetual state, robed in ermine and gold, crowned, and bearing a sceptre. This figure his imagination exalts into a being more than woman, and it is to her, England incarnate, or the tutelary genius of his country, that his heart is loyal, and brings him to his feet when "God save the Queen" is played or sung.

This glamour of royalty, however, has departed from the minds of those who have read Hervey's memoirs or Madame D'Arblay's, or Thackeray's Georges, or, indeed, any book of memoirs that deals with courts and courtiers. There is a dreadful "disillusioning" in such works, and human nature never appears more sordid and mean and contemptible than in such pictures of what are called the higher classes of human beings. That personal loyalty should survive such revelations, and that a Borgia should be gravely accepted as the divine vicegerent, shows how possible it is to regard a man, wholly regardless of his own qualities, as the symbol of something to which he is entirely foreign. The clear perception of official as distinguished from personal character enables a man to behave toward another man whom he despises as if he were a superior being. It is easy to imagine what Robert Walpole's real opinion was of the little German prince whom he disturbed in his after-dinner nap, and before whom he fell upon one knee as he announced to him that he was King of England.

The royal personages, however, appeared in the portraits and pictures in due and impressive pomp. The crown, the robe, the uniform, the ribbon, were all set forth with the cunning of art, and sought to confirm the impression of the imagination. But the photograph is relentlessly accurate, and the loyal soul in the remote English country-side must have been a little tried when the picture of an elderly lady in a widow's cap, such as he had seen a hundred times in the country, was presented to him as the portrait of the Queen. It was a most levelling stroke, for nothing could suggest to him the essential equality, which is the distinctive democratic doctrine, more clearly than such a picture. The memoirs of courts, although fatally undeceiving, were yet full of ceremony and a certain social splendor which could easily catch the loyal imagination. So far as the royal personages were involved, they were descriptions. But when the startling photograph began to speak, when the lady in the widow's cap published her diary or her letters, and the loyal soul in the country seclusion not only saw precisely how she looked, but in her printed diary saw also what she was, there was, of course, little left for the imagination, and royalty must then be judged, not by its ceremonial significance, but by its essential human quality.

It is this consideration which gives a singular interest to the Queen's diary and letters, and to the letters of her daughter, the Princess Alice, Grand Duchess of Hesse-Homburg, which have been recently published. They are such intimate glimpses of royalty and of royal life as were practically unknown until the publication of the Queen's diary a few years since, and the earlier autobiography of the Margravine of Anspach. From one point of view the diary of the Queen is certainly the chronicling of very small beer, but from another it is exceedingly interesting. The evident delight of a great public personage, a permanent official ceremony, a form even more than a human being, in the privacy of common life, is very touching. At Balmoral the Queen can almost forget that she is a Queen and become a woman. The little commonplace details of daily life in the country, the walks, the drives, the strolls in the garden, the shopping in the village, the "nice" breakfast, the "good cold dinner," the gossip and the twaddle, are all pleasant because they are all expressions of unaffected enjoyment of the simplicities of a country life. There is no pastoral drama like that of Marie Antoinette at the Petit Trianon; there is no operatic and spectacular unreality of rural life, a pastoral affectation, a mere resource of satiety; but the book is the record of a truly English matronly pleasure in the common sights and incidents of the country, and as hearty a relish of them as the poets feign in Daphne and Chloris.

Therefore, while nothing would seem more certainly to destroy the fond illusion which wraps royalty in the imagination of the village and the farm-house than its appearance under the ordinary and familiar human conditions, the book of the Queen's diary will probably strengthen her hold upon the hearts of her subjects, who will now see in her not only the august sovereign, but the plain and sympathetic matron of simple and domestic tastes, of the very qualities, indeed, that commended so warmly her grandfather, "Farmer George," to the love of England.

There is also a reflected light thrown upon the character of the Queen by the letters of the Princess Alice. They are full of a devoted and ardent affection and respect which only genuine domestic worth and tender maternal thoughtfulness could inspire. They reveal the incidents and proofs of these qualities, and with their reverence for the Princess's father, Prince Albert, they contain glimpses of a simple and affectionate domestic interior which is very beautiful. The character of the Princess herself which the letters disclose is such as to justify the feeling with which she was regarded. The Crown Princess of Prussia was regarded as the "clever one" of the family, we believe, but if her loveliness and

force of character are more striking than those of this young Princess, who died some years since, still a very young woman and mother, the Crown Princess of Prussia is a singularly charming woman.

The husband of the Princess Alice, whom she loved fondly, was the Grand Duke who lately figured as the hero of a morganatic marriage. He was the governing prince of a small duchy, and there are glimpses in the letters of a straitened royalty which recall Thackeray's amusing sketches of the court of Pumpernickel. There is the same gratitude to the Queen, the Princess's mother, for furnishing the dining-room, and the same doubt whether a journey can be undertaken because of the expense, which might be found in the correspondence of any young and thrifty and affectionate mother who was not a royal princess and a reigning duchess.

But the charm and value of the letters lie in their revelation of the fact that the simple human sense of duty, the active sympathy for others, the conviction that rank and power and wealth are not meant for self-indulgence, but divine trusts for a common benefit, were as active and vital in this young princess as in any private woman who consecrates her life to the service of her kind. She goes quietly and unrecognized into dirt and squalor to visit and succor the suffering. She gives her friendly favor to a suspected heretic like Dr. Strauss. She thanks her mother for portraits of her granduncle George the Fourth and others of the royal family, but wishes for a portrait of her father rather than of "all these good people whom I do not like."

The royal mother's diary and the royal daughter's letters offer a singular contrast with Hervey's memoirs of the Queen's grandfather's grandfather. And the general character of the court and of the ministers during Victoria's long reign might certainly reconcile the most resolute British republican to a longer trial of the monarchy whose spirit has undergone so great a change in so short a time. The license of George the Second's court, the venality of that of George the Third, the vulgarity of George the Fourth's, have disappeared in that of the matron of Balmoral.

———

Mr. John Morley, for many years editor of the *Fortnightly Review*, one of the most accomplished students of history and literature in England, and a very advanced radical in religion and politics, passed two or three years ago from the editorship of the *Pall Mall Gazette* to Parliament. This English scholar recently addressed a meeting of coal miners in Durham, a body of men probably as illiterate as any in the kingdom, and more so than any American political orator addresses, and he asked them whether they, whose forefathers would not endure the tyranny and misgovernment of kings, should submit to the oppression and stupidity of peers. The House of Lords, he said, which was merely a hereditary Tory club with the power of unlimited veto in a free government, was nothing more than a very bad practical joke. It was not the Lords, he declared, who had covered the fair country of the north of England with marvels of ingenuity and skill. Not at all. They had been from the first the rallying-point of all that was stupid, selfish, and obstructive in the currents of this country.

This shows the spirit and the vigor and plainness of speech with which the House of Lords is now assailed in England. The tone of Mr. Morley's address to a body of miners would seem to be revolutionary, but probably neither he nor John Bright nor any other Liberal orator anticipates a revolution. There is no line in English literature more exactly truthful than that of Tennyson that England is the country in which

> "Freedom broadens slowly down
> From precedent to precedent."

The national stock is so little modified by immigration that the national temperament remains virtually unchanged, and the national movement may be generally predicted. The Lords will yield. They will not push resistance to extremity, and when they have made their protest, and have arrayed themselves in line of battle, they will politely withdraw, and leave the field to the Commons. They made their last threatening stand against the Reform Bill of 1832, and for some time there was a prospect of serious trouble. But the Whig ministry controlled the King, and the King by the power of creating peers controls the House of Lords. The King intimated his wishes, and the Lords acquiesced.

They are not likely to make another contest for a veto upon the action of the House of Commons, for the reason that there is so much intelligence and good sense among them. A British peer has certain class prejudices and peculiarities, but he knows perfectly well that the real governing power in England is the House of Commons, which is the direct and elected representative of the whole body of English voters. When he perceives plainly the will of that body, he knows that to resist it to the end would be to invite the demolition of his order. Nobody knows better than he that Disraeli's pictures of a possible English society in which hereditary lords are the actual leaders of the people are dreams of romance, and that it is a society no more possible in England than in the United States.

Moreover, My Lord's position, when stripped of the veto, has its "extreme compensations." Even the power of the veto will not be abolished. It will merely become obsolete, like that of the crown. It will still remain as a decoration of his position, as the King of England still bore the title of King of France long after he had ceased to assert any claim to the French crown. But the actual power of the noble class arising from tradition and long habit, from enormous possessions, high

education and trained ability, and from the natural conservatism of English feeling, will be immense. The peerage has become an essential part of the fabric of British society, and it can be no more effectually abolished by law than taste and feelings and traditions. Its hold is beyond the law.

Mr. Frederic Harrison has shown that practically the government of England is that of the people, as in the United States, and that effectively England is a republic and not a monarchy. Mr. John Morley says felicitously that the House of Lords is a Tory club with a hereditary veto. The descriptions are good, but they are not exhaustive. In Mr. Harrison's English republic, loyalty to the sovereign is one of the strongest national feelings, and Mr. Morley's Tory club possesses very much more than a hereditary veto. The Lords will yield. They will not attempt to exercise their veto. But they will certainly exercise their other powers, and it is doubtful if John Bright himself would wish to turn them out of their chamber, as he would not wish to overthrow the throne.

Mr. Matthew Arnold says that he has been obliged to decline the honor of several interviews with the reporters of several journals who wished to know what he had to say of America. What he has to say of America he has promised to give to the *Nineteenth Century*, but at present he has nothing to say. Yet in declining the interview he still said some pleasant things, which will not be surprising to those who know his essential kindliness of nature and his entire simplicity. It was doubtless a mistake for a noted man who is not a public speaker to present himself to a foreign audience as an orator. Mrs. Browning's line that

> "Poets never read their own verses to their worth"

is as true of many essayists and men of letters; and it is not often that a purely literary man has the singular charm in the public reading of his essays which distinguished Mr. Emerson. The seraphic serenity of his aspect in earlier years, the rich musical modulation of his voice, the air of immediate inspiration, the natural refinement and elegance of his manner despite its want of conventional grace, and a certain rustic and homely simplicity, made his reading of his discourses in his earlier years very memorable. The impression, indeed, was always that of the scholar and the student rather than of the orator, but compared with its charm much popular oratory of the time seemed utterly meagre and insincere.

But Mr. Arnold is especially an author who should be read, and the disparity between his easy mastery in his natural position as an essayist and the inadequacy of his public address explains much of the kind of disappointment which, with all the admiration and even affection with which he was regarded, he produced upon this side of the water. The image of a cultivated scholar, who, with incomparable felicity of expression and an unsurpassed lightness of exact touch, poises and points and shades and exquisitely colors his thought, so that the whole effect is that of smiling supremacy and unchallenged command, was quite lost in the public speaker, although the substance of the discourse, as in the opening of the paper upon Emerson, and in the motive and treatment of that upon Numbers, was very characteristic. Mr. Arnold, indeed, is purely a man of letters, versed in the great works of literature, a sagacious observer of the currents of cultivated thought in his own time, a critic of large and generous sympathies, with complete intellectual independence in moral discussion, judging literary and mental achievement by well-defined canons. He is master of the art of arts in literary and moral criticism, the art of "putting things," which is simply the gift of saying what he has to say in a manner which commands attention.

This is a gift of the highest value. For important and original observations of truth in any department of knowledge or thought do not become known because of their intrinsic worth, but because of the consummate skill and attractiveness with which they are told. This is a branch of the clothes philosophy with which Herr Teufelsdröckh does not adequately deal. Literary style is the garment of thought. But not only is it true that only well-dressed thoughts arrest attention, but so deep and instinctive is the regard for fine clothes that a beautiful literary garment with nothing in it often commands universal admiration. There are popular books which in this sense are only wardrobes of exquisitely laced and embroidered garments. The gift of speech, as it is called, by which is not meant the orator's gift only, but the power of literary expression, is one of the choicest gifts which the fairy godmother can bring to the cradle. Its power is seen very conspicuously in the books of Mr. Henry George. Except for the lucid and eloquent style, the literary felicity, which is as innate as a fine voice or an ear for music, and which endeavor and cultivation may develop and diversify, but never create,

the latest important contribution to politico-economical suggestion would have been hardly known.

The Easy Chair has often heard a brilliancy and fluency of private talk which would have been invaluable to a public speaker, but the talker could not command the power of public expression, and the possible statue slept forever in the quarry. So it was hard to recognize in the lecturer whom we heard the author whom we knew as Matthew Arnold. Should he write a book of American reminiscences we may be sure of the old charm of treatment, the grace, the felicity, the sparkle, which are familiar in all his work. In speaking to a reporter of Chicago, he recently said: "I would not go to see the pig-sticking at the stock-yards. Certainly not! Why should I wish to see pig-sticking?" He prefers Philadelphia to any American city, but everywhere he found kindness and affectionateness. The Americans, however, he thinks, are a commercial people, with the intellectual limitations of such. This struck him, as the insular limitations and the thinly veneered Berserker in the English race struck Taine.

But the American ladies Mr. Arnold most warmly praises. "While many of the gentlemen have the tone of feeling and the speech of English gentlemen, the ladies are much more engaging than English ladies, are better informed, and more capable in conversation." Poor man! he must settle that remark with his own country-women. It will not disturb those who are accustomed to such homage. We hope that Mr. Arnold will give us the article. America lies like a great good-natured giant on the Western continent, smiling in his shaggy strength at the crowd of pilgrims who come in every mood of prejudice, or admiration, or simple wonder, amused by their angry and vehement comments, but recognizing readily the word that really hits or rebukes, and weighing with unchanged aspect everything that is said. Nobody knows so well as he the value of De Tocqueville, and the worthlessness of other books that have been written about him. It is because Matthew Arnold's view would be worthy of attention that intelligent Americans would be glad to know it.

Editor's Literary Record.

MR. F. W. ROBINSON'S *A Fair Maid*[1] is one of those rare novels that defy criticism by disarming the critic. So full and rapid is the rush of its narrative, so racy and spirited the flow of its dialogue, so manifold and various the alternations and transitions of its incidents, and so marked and attractive the personality of its characters, that the censor is in no mood to criticise, but insensibly surrenders himself to the developments of the plot, and is carried away by the absorbing movement of the story. Its scene is laid in the same rich English county of Kent with which we have been made so delightfully familiar in several of Mr. Blackmore's most engrossing tales, but it is presented to us under widely different aspects. Instead of the lush fields of waving

[1] *A Fair Maid.* A Novel. By F. W. ROBINSON. "Franklin Square Library." 4to, pp. 72. New York: Harper and Brothers.

grain, the thrifty orchards bending under golden fruit, the luxuriant meadows dotted with hay-cocks and lazy kine, the bright landscapes flecked with swiftly chasing sun and shade, the ample and well-stored barns, the cool and inviting dairies, the troops of hard-working but joyous farm lads and lasses, and the roomy and substantial homesteads, whose wide-open doors are eloquent of hospitality and overflowing creature comforts, on which Mr. Blackmore lavishes the wealth of his descriptive powers, Mr. Robinson introduces us to the dark and seamy side of Kentish-land, to unlovely hop fields, to swarms of lawless, screaming, fighting male and female hop-pickers, to troops of drunken and abandoned women, worse even than the brutes of men who keep them company, tramping hither and yon on the lookout for another job, and forming black blots upon the green country round about, to weird and stifling oast-houses, half-ruined lime-kilns, empty and dismantled barns, and gloomy and forbidding homesteads. Not exclusively, however, does Mr. Robinson confine himself to this sombre side of Kentish rural life. It is but the effective foreground of a picture in which all the moods and phases of Kentish life and scenery are vividly limned, its brightness and sunshine as well as its cloud and gloom. Unlike Mr. Wilkie Collins and novelists of his school, who jealously nurse a secret or a mystery lest the reader should surprise and penetrate it before the supreme moment arrives when it is predestined that the curtain shall be raised, Mr. Robinson generously takes the reader into his confidence at the outset, and shares with him the secret upon which the action of his story hinges while its actors are still perplexed and entangled by it, and are ignorantly or intelligently engaged in unravelling it. In this way we are enabled to form our own estimate, long in advance, of the probability or improbability of their escape from their entanglements, and to follow their movements with a new and livelier interest. We shall not presume to give an outline of this fine story, since its nature is such that an exposure of its plot would be to ungenerously forestall it with the reader, and rob him of much of his enjoyment. We shall only lift the curtain so far as to say that among the actors in the story the reader will encounter several remarkably impressive or attractive characters, remarkable for their massive originality and individuality, and for their brightness, sweetness, grace, and supreme self-forgetfulness and self-devotion.

So widely dissimilar are the methods and the requirements of science and art, that it might be naturally supposed that the life-long studies and investigations which have been prosecuted by Dr. William A. Hammond in the difficult scientific specialties of his profession would be an unfriendly preparatory training for the production of a work in the department

of romance. Nevertheless, he has produced a novel which has many substantial and some very striking merits, although it may be safely predicted of it that it will not gain for him that distinction in the world of romantic art that his professional labors have won for him in that of science. Clever, vigorous, and at times brilliant and dramatic as Lal[2] must be conceded to be, it is yet unmistakably the work of a neophyte in art, and as unmistakably bears the stamp of amateurship. Its descriptions are spirited and vivid, but hard and unfinished; its conceptions and delineations of character almost invariably lack those subtle elements that constitute individuality; and its narrative is varied and eventful, but unequal, and too often and even tediously interrupted by scientific or philosophical reflections and digressions which provokingly retard the action of the story, and are evidently introduced as merely mechanical contrivances intended to throw light on the motives and acts, or to give a clew to the idiosyncrasies and character, of some of the leading personages.

The scene of the story is laid in the mountain-peaks and table-lands and amid the gulches and cañons of one of our far Western Territories, whither its hero, John Tyscovus, a Polish nobleman, had been drawn by a dream. Of the early years of this man, and of the influences that entered into the growth and development of his character, nothing is revealed, but when he is introduced to the reader he is in the plenitude of his vigorous prime, and is represented as an accomplished man of the world, gifted with a lofty and courageous nature, endowed with great physical strength and rare powers of endurance, and withal a scholar, a thinker, a philosopher, a mystic, and a dreamer. For many years he had brooded over his conception of a great literary work which was to revolutionize thought and be productive of untold benefits to mankind. He had meditated over this work in the quiet of his native home, while enduring the hardships of exile in Siberia, and while travelling or residing in various European states. But owing to his absorption in the work of collecting materials, and in his observations, thoughts, and speculations, he had made no headway with it. In reality the work was yet to be begun, so far as the reduction of the thoughts and reflections that he had accumulated to writing was concerned; and instead of realizing that he was overburdening himself with materials and heaping up difficulties which made the task of writing more formidable, he suddenly sprung to the conclusion that it was the fault of his environments, that he had exhausted all that the Old World could give him, that the peculiar character of its civilization stifled originality of thought, that his whole nature must be changed if he would

---

[2] Lal. A Novel. By WILLIAM A. HAMMOND. 12mo, pp. 466. New York: D. Appleton and Co.

succeed with his work, and that he must seek the originality he coveted and the change he needed in some new land, where the physical surroundings were more inspiring, where he could cut himself loose from the influences that paralyzed his constructive and inventive energies, and where, in the vastness and solitude of nature, he could give himself up to the abstract and introspective thought which he conceived to be essential to the production of his *magnum opus*. While our philosophic scholar was in this mood, not realizing or caring to realize that he had already cogitated too much, and that in reality he dreaded to begin the work of writing up his "abstract and introspective thought," and would gladly put it off, as the "most noble Felix" put off St. Paul, to a more "convenient season," the spirit of Zimmermann, the celebrated mystical philosopher and writer on solitude, who had been dead for nearly a hundred years, appeared to him in a sleeping or waking vision, and revealed to him that it would be impossible for him to accomplish his great work in the air of the corrupt and effete civilization of the Old World; that if he would prosecute it successfully he must turn his back on Europe and go to that new continent beyond the sea in whose mountain heights the air is so highly rarefied that the lungs are forced to extreme expansion in order to get enough oxygen to serve the purposes of life, where the ozonized atmosphere would destroy the impurities that the atmosphere of Europe had incorporated into his system, and where, consequently, thought would be more profound, and above all purer and freer. The shade of the defunct philosopher wound up these and similar scientific pedantries by pointing out on a globe the precise spot in America where all the features were in consonance with the spiritual needs of Tyscovus, and by charging him to go thither, accompanying his command with explicit directions for finding the highly favored spot, even to its exact longitude and latitude, and such other minute landmarks as would have satisfied the most methodical of surveyors. Tyscovus lost no time in his quest, and the real action of the story begins with his appearance upon the spot described by the spirit of Zimmermann, and his identification of it down to the most minute detail. Here a great change indeed awaited him. In lieu of the "effete civilization" of Europe, he is brought at once in contact with that rude and lawless, but exceedingly vigorous, civilization of America which is represented by its cow-boys, cattle thieves, and murderers, with their corollaries of regulators, vigilance committees, and the summary methods of Judge Lynch. He finds the spot that had been described in his dream occupied by the cabin of a red-handed homicide, with whom he speedily struck a bargain for its ownership. Indeed, he had just come in the nick of time to do this promptly, and even advantageously, for the ruffian had most opportunely received a warning that "the committee," meaning the regulators, would visit him that evening and hang him to the nearest tree, in retaliation, not for a recent murder that he had perpetrated in cold blood—that being a comparatively venial escapade according to their code—but for the unpardonable offense of cattle-stealing. Mr. Bosler—for that was the classical name of the scoundrel—had barely time to close the sale of his premises, pocket the proceeds, and disappear with his family and household belongings in one of the neighboring gulches or cañons, when the regulators appeared upon the scene, and in their prompt and dead-earnest way had almost made an innocent victim of Tyscovus before they discovered that he was not the man they were after. His narrow escape from death by hanging at their hands brought its compensations, however, for his courageous bearing in the emergency, and the great muscular power he displayed, to the discomfiture of some of their number, converted his would-be executioners into his fervent admirers, and in connection with a flogging that he administered in a hand-to-hand fight to one of the most powerful desperadoes of the vicinity, who had visited him on burglarious thoughts intent, made him at a single bound, as it were, not only a popular hero, but the most popular man in the region. But, besides these, another element now entered into the experience of Tyscovus, which was destined to effect a more pronounced change in him and a greater expansion of his ideas than was effected by the oxygen and ozone predicted by Zimmermann. He had another vision, in which he saw no unsubstantial shade, but a woman of superb physical beauty and strength. It was Lal, the rude, crassly ignorant, and thoroughly uncultured daughter of Bosler, pure amidst the hardest, coarsest, and most vulgar surroundings, endowed with an instinctive delicacy and refinement, a native intelligence, and an intuitive perception of the right, the true, and the womanly that no evil associations could efface, combined with a fearlessness that no danger could daunt, a courage and resolution that no brutality could subdue, and a reserve of love and tenderness that nothing could exhaust. This figure came between him and his studies: nay, it was his study; and although another figure interposed—again that of a woman, loving, beautiful, cultivated, accomplished, and learned above her sex—to distract his attention temporarily, his study of this perfect product of the highest civilization served only to heighten his admiration for Lal, the wild and untutored child of nature, until at last it ripened into overmastering and enduring love. The unfolding of the character and conscience, the taste and intelligence, of this frontier wild flower, the brutal ordeals to which she is subjected, and from which she extricates herself unharmed by her own pluck and energy, the blossoming of her love for the hero of the tale, and the discovery that she was not the child of the ruffian Bosler, but had been stolen by him in infancy from parents of great refinement and intelligence, are woven into a romance of genuine but unequal power, and in which, besides this growth of a soul and birth of love, are also depicted some dramatic scenes of far Western life, illustrative of its lawlessness and sense of honor, its fierceness and gentleness, its strange commingling of vices and virtues, its hospitality, generosity, and quick recognition of physical or intellectual excellence. This synopsis makes some of the grotesque absurdities and pedantries of the tale more apparent than they will be to the reader, whose attention will be interested and absorbed by its rapidly shifting scenes, its stirring and novel incidents, and its striking contrasts of life and character.

VERY delicate and fragrant are the flowers of fancy which Queen Elizabeth of Roumania (better known by her literary *sobriquet* of " Carmen Sylva") has wreathed together in the "cycle of tales" to which she has given the general title *Pilgrim Sorrow*.[3] Although they are not formally so announced, these charming little tales are in part autobiographical, and under the guise of some figurative or imaginary characters reproduce many pleasing, or tender, or pathetic passages in the life of this exemplary queen and true gentlewoman, or, couched beneath some translucent allegory, give utterance to her hopes, fears, and aspirations, and to her experiences of the joys and sorrows, the trials and temptations, the victories and the defeats, of life. Each of the tales is a separate but related allegory, in which the intangible external influences and internal emotions that affect the heart and mould the character are personified and invested with human attributes, while still retaining their own special traits and qualities. In this way Life and Death, Strife and Peace, Love and Happiness, Work and Patience, Doubt and Truth, Innocence, Courage, Ambition, Pain, and Sorrow are symbolized, their relations to and associations with mankind are defined and illustrated, and helpful lessons are inculcated for the conduct of life under all the joyous or painful vicissitudes to which it may be subjected. Although the title of the group of stories is *Pilgrim Sorrow*, and although sorrow in some one of its forms is a constant factor in them, it must not be concluded that they are sombre or morbid. On the contrary, they are so laden with wise and beautiful thoughts and examples from which the consolations and alleviations of hope may be drawn, and sorrow itself is shown to be so pitiful and gentle and wholesome, that they minister rather to cheerful but quiet pensiveness than to feelings of

sadness and dejection. A graceful biographical sketch by the translator is prefixed to the tales.

ALTHOUGH it can not in any strict sense be considered the fruit of original research, since its materials have been long and well known to geographical and historical scholars, Mr. Arthur J. Weise's account of *The Discoveries of America to the Year* 1525[4] is a work of real value and great interest, and has involved the study and collation of many old, rare, and not easily accessible books, maps, and manuscripts, a careful review and comparison of the various reports that have been made by early writers of the voyages of those whom they believed to have been the first discoverers of those portions of the coast of America lying between Baffin Bay and Tierra del Fuego, and a diligent perusal of the large accumulations of recent papers and publications on the subject. The chief merit of Mr. Weise's book, and its distinguishing feature, is the compression in a single convenient volume, in a continuous narrative arranged in chronological sequence, of all the authenticated records of voyages in North American waters and of discoveries on the mainland prior to 1525, and the elimination from contemporaneous and recent accounts of whatever is now conceded to be erroneous or apocryphal. To the general reader, who has neither the time nor the opportunity to consult, much less to study and compare, the multitude of scattered books and manuscripts in which the narratives of the early voyagers and discoverers, or of their historiographers, are preserved in minute and oftentimes tedious detail, Mr. Weise's epitome will prove an acceptable substitute, sufficiently full for all practical purposes, and more trustworthy and intelligible than most of the early relations, especially since many of them were written in foreign languages. Not inappropriately, we think, Mr. Weise prefaces the special task he has set himself to perform with two introductory chapters embodying the traditions and legends that were in vogue among the ancients preserving the memory of a vast continent lying to the westward of Europe, the theories that have been current respecting the origin of the aboriginal American races, an outline account of the alleged discovery of America by the Northmen—a discovery, by-the-way, which in his opinion rests more upon conjecture than upon evidence—and brief summaries of the wonderstories of Marco Polo and Sir John Mandeville, and of the attempts that were made by the Portuguese and others prior to the advent of Columbus to discover a direct water route to India. Having thus disposed of fable and tradition, and also of the partial discoveries before 1492, Mr. Weise enters upon a series of historical sketches and summaries describing the va-

[3] *Pilgrim Sorrow.* A Cycle of Tales. By (Carmen Sylva) Queen ELIZABETH of Roumania. Translated by HELEN ZIMMERN. 16mo, pp. 262. New York: Henry Holt and Co.

[4] *The Discoveries of America to the Year* 1525. By ARTHUR JAMES WEISE, M.A. 8vo, pp. 380. New York: G. P. Putnam's Sons.

rious expeditions that were fitted out under Spanish, Portuguese, English, Dutch, and French auspices, under the leadership of Columbus, Cabot, Amerigo Vespucci, Verrazzano, and other discoverers, and giving full accounts of their discoveries on the mainland of the North American continent and in the adjacent waters. Mr. Weise has made large use of the reports of the original discoverers,which he presents to the reader in the form of careful translations when needed, and which give us their fresh and genuine impressions both as to the people and countries visited and their own several claims to priority of discovery. His work is a model of carefulness and candor, especially when dealing with rival or controverted claims. Its chiefest interest, however, centres upon his account of the discoveries by Verrazzano in 1524, crediting that enterprising navigator with the first discovery and description of all that portion of the American coast which extends from the Carolinas to Maine, and which he named New France, and establishing the fact that he discovered and sailed up the Hudson, or, as he styled it, the Grand or Great River (una Grandissima Riviera), as far as the Palisades nearly a century before it was visited by Hendrik Hudson in the *Half-Moon.* In this connection Mr. Weise broaches a new theory of the origin of the name Manhattan, afterward applied by the Dutch to the site of New York. His claim is that instead of this name having been first given to the island by the Dutch, it was in reality a corruption of the title given to the inhabitants by Verrazzano nearly a hundred years before, and imperfectly handed down by the natives.

The elegance and consequent expensiveness of Mr. Weise's volume will be a bar to the popular use for which it is otherwise admirably adapted. It will, however, be prized by scholars, and especially by those who are interested in geographical and historical investigations, for the fullness and fidelity of its summaries, the copiousness of its citations and annotations, the excellence of its translations, and its valuable maps.

THE researches and discoveries of science during the last half a century, and the materialistic and rationalistic theories and hypotheses built upon them that have obtained large credence, have rendered necessary a thorough revision of the theological methods and a careful restatement of the theological doctrines and opinions that were once generally accepted and considered satisfactory. Indeed, so wide is the difference between the theology of to-day and that of fifty or a hundred years ago, that it amounts almost to a revolution— a revolution as great as that which, in another sphere of human activity, has been wrought in the weapons and missiles of war. So that the theologian who should now confine himself to the use of the proofs, arguments, and reasonings that were relied upon as effective by the theologian of a century or half a century ago would be as far behind the age, and as completely at the mercy of his adversaries, as the soldier who should trust to the old-time firelock or the ineffective smooth-bore cannon of the same era, in opposition to the unerring long-range rifles and artillery of the present day. Such a revision and restatement have been made with great candor and learning, in an important department of the theological field, by Professor George T. Ladd, of Yale College, in a comprehensive work, whose title— *The Doctrine of Sacred Scripture : a Critical, Historical, and Dogmatic Inquiry into the Origin and Nature of the Old and New Testaments*[5]—very accurately defines its scope and bearing. The work is an inquiry into the origin and nature of the Sacred Scriptures in the accepted canon, as considered in the totality of their phenomena and in their complete history ; and in the course of this inquiry it discusses in the largest sense of the words, What are the claims of the Bible? and What is the Bible? The inquiry is opened with a thorough and comprehensive induction, which includes an investigation, first, into the claims of the Bible, and second, into its different classes of phenomena. In examining the question, What does the Bible claim to be? the infallibility of the claims made by the Bible for itself is not advanced or assumed by Dr. Ladd, but the claims themselves are critically scrutinized as constituting one class of those facts which must be taken into account by a complete induction. After an exegetical exposition of these claims they are tested, corrected, and amplified by an examination of the various orders of phenomena which have entered into the concrete reality of the Bible; a classification is made of the different contents of the Biblical writings; and the discussion of these contents is followed by dissertations, in successive chapters, upon their language, style, and authorship, and upon the canon and text of the Bible, the aim being kept constantly in mind to lay in a thorough and comprehensive induction of the foundations of a doctrine of Sacred Scripture. The discussion involves an investigation of the nature of the Old Testament Scripture as determined by the *teaching* of Christ, of the nature of the New Testament Scripture as determined by the *promises* of Christ, of the claims of the Old Testament as put forth in its own writings, of the claims made for the Old Testament by the writers of the New Testament, and of the claims made for the New Testament by its own writers; also an examination of all the principal classes of phenomena which belong to the whole Bible as a concrete and historic product, and a searching inquiry into the doctrine of Sacred

5 *The Doctrine of Sacred Scripture : a Critical, Historical, and Dogmatic Inquiry into the Origin and Nature of the Old and New Testaments.* By GEORGE T. LADD, D.D. In Two Volumes, 8vo, pp. 761 and 765. New York: Charles Scribner's Sons.

Scripture as related to or dependent upon the scientific, miraculous, historical, predictive, and ethico-religious contents of the Bible, and as exhibited by its style, principles of composition, and authorship. This exhaustive investigation and examination constitute the first volume, or the entire inductive half, of the work. The second volume, pursuing the inquiry as if it were proposed before the tribunal of our ethical and religious consciousness, institutes a careful historical investigation of the questions: first, What has the Church Catholic believed to be true concerning the Bible? and second, What doctrine of Sacred Scripture accords with all the most closely allied Christian doctrines, and with the common experiences of men in the direction and growth of the religious life? As the result of the inquiry the conclusion is satisfactorily established that the essential claims of the Bible for itself are not negatived, but rather are confirmed, by all the discoveries of modern historical and critical researches, so that a certain view of the Biblical writings may be inductively established, which view is further expanded and confirmed by the ancient permanent opinion of the Church Catholic.

ONE of the most interesting incidents of our home literature at this juncture is the great attention that is given by earnest and able thinkers and writers to the preparation, and by enterprising publishers to the publication, of *small* and inexpensive books on *large* subjects. Many of the books in the class to which we refer are scarcely larger than a primer, but their subject-matter is of large and permanent interest, and excellent in quality. Embracing a wide range of topics, which are treated with equal brevity and thoroughness, these publications have reached large proportions, and promise to constitute a valuable educational agency, directed to the popular diffusion of knowledge in many branches from which the great body of the people have been hitherto debarred. The character of these cheap and unpretending books may be divined from a glance at the contents of half a score of them which we shall take promiscuously from their number, and which are fairly representative of the quality of this interesting class of publications.

Lying nearest to our hand are three brief and instructive essays[6] in the department of mental and moral philosophy, by Dr. McCosh, in which he exposes with characteristic cogency and candor the fallacy of the wide-spread impression that the advance of thought, and

especially of natural science, has overthrown the old and fundamental truths of philosophy and religion, and demonstrates that while some of these truths must necessarily be put in a new and more correct form, and the defense of them must proceed in a wiser way, their radical principle remains as deeply and firmly established as ever. In the course of this series of essays Dr. McCosh examines the doubts and difficulties that have proceeded from philosophy or metaphysics, from natural science, from ethics, and from cosmogonical theories, with their consequences of agnosticism and skepticism, and he subjects each of them to a brief but searching criticism and analysis. In the first of the series, on *Certitude, Providence, and Prayer*, he gives a more sober account than is usually given of first or *a priori* truths, vindicates the belief in a special Providence who hears and answers prayer, and institutes an inquiry as to what is the character of our world, showing that it is neither optimist nor pessimist, but is going on toward perfection. In the other two essays he defends and further exemplifies his position with regard to *a priori* truths by a historical and critical survey and review of the philosophy of Locke, Berkeley, and Hume, all of whom, as he shows, have exposed prevailing errors, and have caught glimpses of important truths, but have promulgated serious error; and he accompanies his recapitulation of the truths they held, and his demonstration of the errors into which they fell, with succinct sketches of their lives and literary achievements, and with condensed outlines of their general theories. The essays are valuable aids to faith, and are admirably adapted for training the mind in those habits of close and accurate reasoning which are all-essential in the study or intelligent perusal of metaphysical subjects.

ANOTHER field of philosophic thought is traversed in four lucid and well-written essays by T. Nelson Dale, grouped together under the title of *The Outskirts of Physical Science*.[7] They are addressed respectively to Christians and naturalists, marking out the harmony between Christian faith and physical science; to classical and scientific teachers, discussing the value and importance of scientific studies, and assigning them their place and use in education; to Biblical and geological students, suggesting and enforcing the principles of interpretation which should be resorted to for a true comprehension of the nature and object of the first chapter of Genesis; and to creationists and evolutionists, setting forth and analyzing the vital questions that are at issue in the conflict between religious and physical science, and establishing the conclusion that physical science does afford some ground for a belief in the existence of God, and that both religious

[6] "Philosophic Series." *Certitude, Providence, and Prayer*. By JAMES McCOSH, D.D., etc. 8vo, pp. 46. New York: Charles Scribner's Sons.
The Same. *Locke's Theory of Knowledge*. With a Notice of Berkeley. By JAMES McCOSH, D.D., etc. 8vo, pp. 77. New York: Charles Scribner's Sons.
The Same. *Agnosticism of Hume and Huxley*. With a Notice of the Scottish School. By JAMES McCOSH, D.D., etc. 8vo, pp. 77. New York: Charles Scribner's Sons.

[7] *The Outskirts of Physical Science*. By T. NELSON DALE. 16mo, pp. 187. Boston: Lee and Shepard.

and physical science point unerringly to unity of method and to unity of source in one master mind.

ONE of the best intellectual exercises that can be presented to the attention of those who have an ambition to excel as close thinkers and reasoners, and at the same time one of the most graphic presentments that is extant of the life, habits, manners, and usages of the philosophers and philosophic youth of Greece in the times of Socrates and Plato, is supplied in a modest little volume by an anonymous editor, entitled, *A Day in Athens with Socrates.*[8] It comprises scholarly translations of Plato's celebrated dialogues, the *Protagoras*, directed against the specious but fallacious reasoning and the defective philosophy of the Sophists, and exposing their charlatanry, their paradoxes, and their practical abuse of rhetoric and of metaphysical discussion by subjecting them to a rigid cross-examination ; and the *Republic*, in which Plato makes Socrates the medium for a presentation of his idea of a perfect commonwealth, and unfolds the mystery of perfect justice in language which is at once the most poetical and the most philosophical of prose compositions. The editor has prefixed to these dialogues a chastely written preface introducing the reader to the actors in each of them, and explaining the motives that underlie them, and in an appendix he supplies a large body of valuable notes explanatory of the local, historical, and classical allusions in the text.

THE history of the influential event which forms the dividing line between modern and ancient thought and institutions has been ably epitomized by Bishop Hurst, of the Methodist Episcopal Church, in a modest little pocket volume entitled, *A Short History of the Reformation.*[9] Within the briefest compass Dr. Hurst has condensed all the salient incidents and principles of that marvellous revolution, without sacrificing grace of style or clearness and continuity of narrative. The volume is a comprehensive historical outline, in which the causes that led to and the principles that lay at the root of the Reformation are traced and defined, the events that paved the way for and attended it are passed carefully under review, the religious, intellectual, and political movements of the times that prepared Europe for the adoption of the ideas that culminated in civil and religious liberty are vigorously outlined, and brief and animated biographical portraits are given of the pioneers who cleared the way for the Reformation, and of the great reformer and his friends and coadjutors who precipitated and established it.

THE theory of storms is discussed with marked ability by Mr. William M. Davis, of Harvard College, in a scientific monograph, adapted to the popular understanding, on *Whirlwinds, Cyclones, and Tornadoes.*[10] In this admirable little treatise the equilibrium of the atmosphere is explained and illustrated, the action of whirlwinds, tropical cyclones, and water vapor in cyclones is described, an exposition of barometric gradients is given, the effect of the earth's rotation and of rain on the course of storms is considered and expounded, the forces in cyclones are estimated, rules are furnished for avoiding storms at sea, and a series of studies is prosecuted of the storm floods, storms, and tornadoes that occur in the United States, the whole concluding with a statement in outline of the theory of tornadoes first proposed by Mr. Ferrel a few years ago, and now generally conceded by meteorologists to be the most ingenious and satisfactory of any of the theories that have been broached.

OTHERS of these unpretending volumes are upon subjects which have a direct and practical bearing upon the needs and exigencies of every-day life in the household, the family, the library, and the neighborhood. In this class is a sterling little emergency hand-book prepared by Dr. Robert B. Dixon, of the Boston Dispensary, whose title, *What is to be Done? A Hand-Book for the Nursery, with Useful Hints for Children and Adults,*[11] furnishes a key to its contents. Its hints and directions for the prompt treatment of accidents and sudden attacks of disease are not only eminently safe and judicious, but are such as may be easily extemporized in the absence of a physician by any person of ordinary coolness and intelligence, and its suggestions with reference to ventilation and the use of sanitary agencies for the prevention or alleviation of disease and to insure against its spread are thoroughly wise and practical.—Equally safe and judicious is a treatise by Dr. J. K. Shirk on *Female Hygiene and Female Diseases,*[12] written in plain and untechnical language suited to the understanding and intended for the general guidance of parents.— Besides the above are the following, each of which, we are able to say after a careful perusal, is excellent of its kind : *Notes on the Opium Habit,*[13] describing its causes, symptoms, remedies, and general treatment, by Asa P. Meylert, M.D. ; *A Hand-Book of Tree-Planting,*[14] in which Mr. Nathaniel H. Egleston, chief of the Forestry Division in the Department of Agriculture,

---

[8] *A Day in Athens with Socrates.* Translations from the Protagoras and the Republic of Plato. 16mo, pp. 145. New York : Charles Scribner's Sons.
[9] *Short History of the Reformation.* By JOHN F. HURST, D.D. 18mo, pp. 125. New York : Harper and Brothers.
[10] *Whirlwinds, Cyclones, and Tornadoes.* By WILLIAM MORRIS DAVIS. 18mo, pp. 90. Boston : Lee and Shepard.
[11] *What is to be Done?* A Hand-Book for the Nursery, etc. By ROBERT B. DIXON, M.D. 18mo, pp. 67. Boston : Lee and Shepard.
[12] *Female Hygiene and Female Diseases.* By J. K. SHIRK, M.D. 16mo, pp. 102. Lancaster : Lancaster Publishing Co.
[13] *Notes on the Opium Habit.* By ASA P. MEYLERT, M.D. 16mo, pp. 37. New York : G. P. Putnam's Sons.
[14] *Hand-Book of Tree-Planting.* By N. H. EGLESTON. 16mo, pp. 126. New York : D. Appleton and Co.

considers and answers with great fullness and particularity the practical questions why, where, what, and how to plant forest and other trees; *A Modern Proteus*,[15] or list of books published under more than one title, a convenient reference-book for the library, by James L. Whitney; *A Dictionary of Electricity*,[16] being a hand-book of reference for electricians, which includes all recent electrical and technical terms, with explanations of their meaning and application, and descriptions of new inventions in electricity, magnetism, etc.; and the *Hand-Book of the St. Nicholas Agassiz Association*,[17] a sensible and handy manual prepared by the principal of Lenox Academy, designed to awaken a taste for the observation of natural objects, and to promote the formation of affiliated associations for the systematic study of natural history, to which end it embodies a large amount of practical information for the collection, preservation, classification, and exchange of plants, insects, birds, reptiles, minerals, and other specimens.

SCARCELY ten years have elapsed since it was supposed that the application of electricity to practical uses was exclusively confined to telegraphy and electroplating. Outside of these two uses it was considered merely as a costly curiosity, and it seemed destined to remain so. But since then the rapidity of its application to other uses, and especially to artificial lighting, has resulted in the invention of a multiplicity of methods and instruments for its cheap and practical utilization, which have followed each other in quick succession, or have been simultaneously revealed to the researches of indefatigable inventors and students of physical science, until the accumulation of discoveries of processes, methods, and machines has become so enormous that few, even among the inventors and scientists who have been most active in the work, have been able to keep track of all that has been attempted or accomplished. The activity with which the investigation of the electric light has been prosecuted, the great number of those who have been engaged in it, and the immense mass of experiments that have been made and of results that have been obtained, have also operated to invest the relation of the history of electric lighting with great and increasing difficulties; so that unless a systematic effort were soon made to complete the record of it up to the present time by some one possessing the requisite scientific and mechanical knowledge, it would shortly become impossible to trace its progress step by step from its early beginnings with anything like accuracy, to

form a correct judgment of its present status, or to give due credit to those who have contributed to it with greater or less effectiveness. Fortunately the subject has attracted the attention of two gentlemen who are competent to deal with it scientifically, yet in a manner sufficiently popular to enable the intelligent general reader to understand the essential features of electric lighting, and to appreciate the difficulties that had to be encountered and the problems to be solved before it could become practical and industrial. Messrs. E. Alglave and J. Boulard, two accomplished French physicists, whose unremitting attention has been given to this specialty from an early day, have prepared an able and comprehensive treatise on *The Electric Light*,[18] which, in connection with the changes and additional chapters that have been introduced by their American editor, Professor Lungren, is a highly satisfactory, if not an absolutely exhaustive, presentation of the subject. After an interesting historical sketch of artificial lighting in ancient and modern times by oils, candles, and gas, the subject of electric lighting is treated in the order of its historical development under the heads of the voltaic arc, the incandescent light, the production of electrical currents, the distribution of electricity, and the application of the electric light. Under these divisions the principles involved are announced and explained, the difficulties that were encountered are stated, and the history is given of the particular discoveries, inventions, improvements, and applications that were made by the various mechanicians and scientists who have contributed more or less largely to the utilization of the electric light, and to whom the world is indebted for its present state of perfection. Apart from its scientific and industrial interest, the work is a striking illustration of the interesting fact that the development of electric lighting has not resulted in any of its forms, from the fortunate guesses or clever conjectures of enterprising charlatans and empirics, but that its principles and applications have been patiently and laboriously worked out by strictly scientific methods, and that every step that has been gained has been at the cost of severe reasoning, and of close and unremitting scientific research and investigation.

THOSE who were interested in the brief sketch of Rochester[19] in the Editor's Easy Chair for August, will find a complete and entertaining history of that city in a volume recently published, prepared by Jenny Marsh Parker, profusely illustrated.

[15] *A Modern Proteus.* Books Published under more than One Title. By JAMES L. WHITNEY. 18mo, pp. 106. New York: F. Leypoldt.
[16] *A Dictionary of Electricity.* By HENRY GREER. 16mo, pp. 192. New York: College of Electrical Engineering.
[17] *Hand-Book of the St. Nicholas Agassiz Association.* By H. H. BALLARD. 16mo, pp. 109. Lenox, Massachusetts: The Author.

[18] *The Electric Light: its History, Production, and Applications.* By EM. ALGLAVE and J. BOULARD. Translated from the French by T. O'CONNOR SLOANE, E.M. Edited, with Notes and Additions, by C. M. LUNGREN, C.E. Illustrated. 8vo, pp. 458. New York: D. Appleton and Co.
[19] *Rochester: a Story Historical.* By JENNY MARSH PARKER. Illustrated. 8vo, pp. 412. Rochester, New York: Scranton, Wetmore, and Co.

Editor's Historical Record.

POLITICAL.

OUR Record is closed on the 15th of August. —The following nominations were made by State Conventions: Kansas Republicans, July 17, Colonel John A. Martin, for Governor; Indiana Prohibitionists, July 24, R. S. Dwiggins, Governor; West Virginia Democrats, July 24, E. W. Wilson, Governor; West Virginia Republicans and Greenbackers, July 30, Edwin Maxwell, Governor; Georgia Democrats, August 13, H. O. McDaniel, Governor (renominated); Missouri Democrats, August 13, General J. S. Marmaduke, Governor.

The Alabama State election, August 4, resulted in the return of Governor E. A. O'Neal, Democrat, for another term.

The National Prohibition Convention met in Pittsburgh July 23, and nominated for President ex-Governor St. John, of Kansas, and for Vice-President William Daniel, of Maryland.

The news of the rescue of Lieutenant A. W. Greely, the arctic explorer, and a number of his party by the relief expedition under command of Captain Schley reached the Secretary of the Navy July 17. The leading points of the official story are as follows: At 9 P.M. on June 22, five miles off Cape Sabine, in Smith's Sound, the *Thetis* and *Bear* rescued the following alive: Lieutenant A. W. Greely, Sergeant Brainerd, Sergeant Fredericks, Sergeant Long, Hospital Steward Beiderback, Private Connell, and Sergeant Ellison. They are the only survivors of the Lady Franklin Bay expedition. Sergeant Ellison had lost both hands and feet by frost-bite, and died July 6, at Godhavn, three days after amputation, which had become imperative. Seventeen of the twenty-five persons composing this expedition perished by starvation at the point where found. One was drowned while sealing to procure food. Twelve bodies of the dead were brought on board the ships. Five were swept out to sea, and could not be recovered. Greely abandoned Fort Conger on August 9, 1883, and reached Baird Inlet on August 29 following, with the entire party well. He abandoned all his boats, and was adrift for thirty days on an ice-floe in Smith's Sound. His permanent camp was established on October 21, 1883, at the point where he was found. The expedition reached a higher point than any other had ever done—83° 24′ north, 44° 5′ west. The credit belongs to Lieutenant Lockwood and Sergeant Brainerd.

The corner-stone of the pedestal for Bartholdi's statue of Liberty was laid on Bedloe's Island, New York Harbor, on the afternoon of August 6. William Allen Butler delivered the oration.

An earthquake occurred on Sunday, August 10, in thirteen of the United States. The shock was felt from Richmond, Virginia, to Portland, Maine, and from the Atlantic coast to Ohio. Its greatest strength seems to have been along the New Jersey and Long Island coast. No serious damage was done.

A motion to consider the Franchise Bill in the English House of Lords, July 17, was defeated by a vote of 182 to 132.—The House of Commons, August 2, passed the Irish Constabulary Bill, and on August 6 voted a credit of £300,000 for an expedition to relieve General Gordon.

Henry M. Stanley, the African explorer, reached England July 28, having completed the work of establishing satisfactory trading stations along the Congo River from its mouth to Stanley Pool, 1400 miles by river.

The French Chamber of Deputies, July 31, adopted the Revision of the Constitution Bill, as it passed the Senate, by a vote of 294 to 191.

The official record shows that 2200 of the inhabitants in the south of France have died of cholera during the present outbreak.

Both Houses of the Parliament of Holland met in joint congress August 1, and passed, by a vote of 97 to 3, a bill naming Queen Emma regent during the minority of the Princess Wilhelmina.

DISASTERS.

July 21.—Spanish steamer *Gijon* and British steamer *Laxham* sunk off coast of Corunna. One hundred and thirty lives lost.

July 30.—Steamer *Amsterdam*, of Netherlands and American Navigation Company's Line, wrecked on Sable Island in a fog. Three passengers lost.

OBITUARY.

July 22.—At Swissdale, Pennsylvania, Jane Grey Swisshelm, aged sixty-eight years.

July 23.—In Syracuse, New York, ex-Attorney-General Daniel Pratt, aged seventy-eight years.—In Princeton, New Jersey, Rear-Admiral George F. Emmons, aged seventy-five years.

July 24.—In Boonton, New Jersey, ex-Congressman John Hill, aged sixty-three years.

July 25.—At Concord, New Hampshire, ex-Governor Walter Harriman, aged sixty-seven years.

July 30.—In New York, Royal Phelps, merchant, aged seventy-five years.—In London, England, George Brittingham Sowerby, artist and naturalist, aged seventy-two years.

July 31.—At Morristown, New Jersey, Thomas Dickson, President Delaware and Hudson Canal Company, aged sixty years.

August 1.—In Vienna, Austria, Henri Laube, poet, aged seventy-eight years.

August 4.—In Elizabeth, New Jersey, Levi B. Chatfield, ex-Attorney-General of New York, aged seventy-six years.

August 13.—At Brighton, England, Arthur Richard Wellesley, second Duke of Wellington, aged seventy-seven years.

Editor's Drawer.

THE Drawer is not given to statistics, and is never an alarmist, but a study of the United States census of 1880 gives some cause for anxiety. It revealed a population, a good deal mixed, and only partially good, of 50,000,000. The results of the census are not yet all tabulated and published, but already the figurers say that since the census there has been an increase to 55,000,000; and if —— is elected President, as there is every reason at this writing to believe that he will be, the population by December will be no one knows what, nor in what condition. The people are increasing, in short, faster than we can number them or convert them to right principles. The mathematicians, who take into account no moral or economic cause, and calculate that we shall double about once in a generation, expect that the United States will have 100,000,000 of people shortly after the year 1900, and that by the year 2000 there will be 400,000,000 of us, and that at least a fourth of these will be black. On the face of it there is nothing improbable in these figures. Our territory (not reckoning in now Mexico, Cuba, and Canada) has a greater proportion of arable, productive land than that occupied by any other people in the world, and we could more easily support 400,000,000, indeed 600,000,000 (it is so easy to make figures), than China can sustain her 300,000,000 or 350,000,000. How our successors will like being packed in like Chinese, with no chance to swarm anywhere, all the world being in like manner overcrowded by that time, is another matter. But it will be a very interesting country for a traveller to look at. One of the most peculiar sights will be the sea-coast during the summer season. The inland population will, of course, feel the same necessity as now for going down to the ocean once a year. The border of the Atlantic (to say nothing of the Pacific) will be one continuous camp-meeting from Mount Desert to St. Augustine. There will be a great roaring multitude camped along it, extending some distance inland. All the islands and sand spits will be occupied, and monster floating hotels, like islands, with gardens and probably polo grounds, will be anchored out along the shore. Of course every available spot will be occupied with private palaces and gigantic hotels and summer theatres, and a hundred devices for amusement and health, and all the bays will present something of the appearance of luxury and splendor of the Roman Baiæ and Pozzuoli. Still, with all these appliances, there will not be room enough for all those who will want a salt bath in August. Science will come to their aid. Vast reservoirs will be formed in the interior, into which ocean water will be pumped any distance, and great funnels will be constructed through which to drive the sea air inland to play over these artificial salt lakes, and create a sea-side illusion. Along the Jersey coast screens will be placed at the mouth of these funnels to catch the mosquitoes, which will thus be collected in heaps, and used for fertilizing the land.

There is nothing alarming in all this. The government will by that time be "reformed" (indeed, it is a wonder that it is not already, both the great parties being so eager for that, and nothing else), and everybody will be content in the consciousness that he is a part of a nation so big, powerful, and perfectly organized that it only need to shake itself a little to carry terror and admiration round the globe. Our private anxiety is of another sort. The census shows that in some sections illiteracy gains faster than the increase in population, and it is found that generally intelligence does not grow in proportion to our increase in numbers. And a still more important point for us is that anecdotes do not bear any ratio to the growth of population. Anecdotes are the result of peculiar and original character. The elements that blossom into a good story, a queer situation, or into wit, do not increase in the proportion that numbers do, or by that crowding together and multiplicity of population which some consider civilization. We believe it is the experience of the Drawer that more characteristic stories come from the South than from the more thickly settled North. The people go on increasing like rabbits, but the power to produce good anecdotes does not keep pace with that increase. The latter capacity seems limited, if not fixed, in human development. There are fewer good stories produced in any given time than good people. The supply is never equal to the demand, and it is suspected that only a certain amount of anecdote and wisdom was given to the world in the beginning, to last for all time. This would account for the fact that there are so few new and so many old stories and jokes and facetiæ turning up year after year. Now few people have any idea of the difficulty the Drawer has in furnishing fresh anecdotes for 55,000,000 of people. What will it be when it is obliged to find new anecdotes for 400,000,000 of people? If the anecdote faculty (not factory) would only keep pace with the growth of the population, we should have no forebodings.

———

IN the village of —— there is a Presbyterian church, several of whose members are Scotch-Irish. Their views and their practices on the subject of temperance are not in strict accord with the notions of their pastor. Some years ago he preached them a sermon in which he "came down pretty heavy," as the younger brethren described it, upon the habits of that portion of his flock which came from the province of Ulster. One in particular, McA——, a good old man, with but one failing, who occupied a pew at the side of the pulpit, was so clearly hinted at that all eyes were upon him. Even the minister expected that Mac's "Irish blood would be up." The offending brother was slightly deaf, but the preacher was so much in earnest that even the deaf could hear. But McA—— knew how to turn his infirmity to account. The benediction was scarcely ended when he had the pastor by the hand.

"Brother W——," he exclaimed, "an' it is dauncing ye are gieing it to the young folk about?"

Brother W—— waited some time before he ventured another temperance sermon.

A SOURCE OF EDITORIAL MIRTH.

In a certain New York family one of the servants, a recent importation from Ireland, if not strictly an object of beauty, is one of great joy, and her original sayings are duly reported at the dinner table each day, much to the delectation of the family.

The master of the house is an editor, whose duties do not require his presence at the office until afternoon, though they keep him there until late at night. Soon after her arrival, Maggie asked her mistress, "Plaze, mum, phat do be the master's occipation?"

"He is an editor," was the reply.

"Oho! an iditor is it? I thought maybe he was a Bobby."

Referring to a much-valued pin of oxidized silver worn by her mistress, Maggie said: "'Tis a pity, mum, that yer brooch is so dirty. I think, wid a bit av sapoliho, I could clane it, if I was let thry."

She was much attracted by the stylish appearance of a young gentleman who came to call one evening, and afterward described him as having been "dressed up to the door-knob."

She has never seen a mosquito, but has heard such terrible stories of their ferocity that she looks forward to their advent with grave apprehensions. One Sunday she was overheard to say to the cook that while in church she had prayed to be preserved from sin and "muskittys."

Although she is always neatly and tidily dressed, her wardrobe is limited, and she is obliged to be very careful of her clothes. Upon one occasion she had just answered the door-bell, and still wore the neat white apron which she always dons for this service. Her mistress called her to come and sweep the parlor, and she answered,

"Yes, mum, if ye'll wait till I take off me only bit of dacency."

She is now having such a laughable and at the same time desperate flirtation with the ice man that the editorial family are apprehensive that she may soon be removed to another sphere of usefulness, and be lost to them forever. C. K. M.

CORN-SHUCKING SONG.

Shuck erlong, niggers, shuck dis co'n!
　Dar's menny er bar'l in dis ya pile;
Dar's menny er rashin, sho's yo bo'n,
　Ter feed all de han's wid arter 'wile.
　　Luk at Susing, dat fat gal!
　　Whar she git dat ballymeral?
　　Mus' er got hit fum ole Miss Sal.
　　Shuck erlong, shuck dis co'n.

Chorus.

　Shuck a ruck a shuck! shuck a ruck a shuck!
　　Pars dat tickler down dis way.
　Shuck a ruck a shuck! shuck a ruck a shuck!
　　Ain' gwine home ez long ez I stay.

Hyar dat bo' pig, how he squeal!
Wishin' fo' de slops ter-morrer mo'n;
Ef he hatter got in dat dere fiel',
　Niggers, we'd neber bin shuckin' dis co'n.
　　Luk at Moses, how he grin!
　　Ain' nuffin ob him but he wool an' chin;
　　Mouf ez big ez dat co'n bin.
　　Shuck erlong, shuck dis co'n.

Chorus.

　Shuck a ruck a shuck! shuck a ruck a shuck!
　　Pars dat tickler down dis way.
　Shuck a ruck a shuck! shuck a ruck a shuck!
　　Ain' gwine home ez long ez I stay.
　　　　　　S. C. CROMWELL.

The things that used to amuse the people of the seventeenth century were much the same —some of them the very same—that are put forward to amuse us. A specimen or two from John Ashton's curious collection of *Humor, Wit, and Satire of the Seventeenth Century* (Chatto and Windus, London) will make this quite apparent:

Meg and her husband Tom, not long agoe,
Were at it close, exchanging blow for blow.
Both being eager, both of a stout heart,
Endured many a bang ere they would part.
Peter lookt on, and would not stint the strife;
He's curst (quoth he) that parteth man and wife.

John came to Thomas his house to speak with him; but Thomas came to the door, and bade his Maid say he was not at home, which John overheard. Two or three days after, Thomas came to speak with John, and John looks out a window and told him he was not at home.

"Why do you say so? Do I not see you at home?"

"Heyday!" says John. "I believed your Maid you were not at home, and you will not believe me my own self!"

A Man, being very much diseased and weak, was bemoaning himself to his only Son, whom he loved very well. "For, Jack," says he, "if I stand, my Legs ake; if I kneel, my Knees ake; if I go, my Feet ake; if I lie, then my Back akes; if I lean, my Elbows ake."

"Why, truly, Father," says he (like a good, dutiful Child), "I advise you, Father, to hang yourself an hour or two, and if that does not do, then come to me again."

King James, riding a-hunting in Essex, comes to a Gate which he must go through, and seeing a Country Clown at it, he says to him, "Prithee, good Fellow, open the Gate." But he, knowing who it was, answered, "No; an't please your Grace, I am not worthy to be in that office; but I'll run and fetch Mr. Johnson, who is a Justice of the Peace, and lives a mile off, and he shall open it for your Grace." So he ran away as fast as he could, and left the King to open it himself.

Deacon Archibald—known also as the Squire—began his political life as a worshipper of General Jackson. For a few months preceding every important election he talked and thought and dreamed of nothing else than politics. The result of the "hard-cider" campaign almost killed him. His neighbors, even his Whig ones, rejoiced that it did not, as they affirmed that the deacon would be better prepared for the change if it would come during an "off year" in politics. It seemed as if their pious concern for the Squire was to be respected. On the 3d of March, 1845, they were gathered in to see their friend take his departure. Close by the bedside sat his former political opponent, D——, expressing contrition for the ill-advised epithets which he had applied to neighbor A. during the heat of a recent political discussion. The deacon had lain motionless for some time, when, suddenly opening his eyes, he exclaimed, "To-morrow will be a glorious day."

"Yes, brother," replied D——, in lugubrious tones—it was the first time he had ever applied this fraternal epithet to the Squire— "yes, brother, to-morrow will be a glorious day for you: you will then be in heaven."

"I perceive, gentlemen, that you do not understand me. To-morrow James K. Polk will be President."

It need scarcely be added that the deacon didn't die at that time. Indeed, he lived to rejoice over the inauguration of the last Democratic President, and to have his spirit so chastened by the successive defeats of his party that an "off year" was not needed for his peaceful departure.

In the very entertaining *Life of Alaric A. Watts*, the poet and annalist, by his son, Mr. Alfred A. Watts, there is a (to us) new anecdote of Lady Holland. Henry Howard, the painter, contemporary of Constable, was the only person who ever ventured to tackle that gracious and overbearing hostess.

One day at dinner at Woburn Abbey, where they happened to be both on a visit, Lady Holland, in one of her periodical spasms of temper, saw fit to make an especial butt or victim of Mr. Howard, whom she treated with imperious and ill-mannered discourtesy. He chanced to

offer a remark on some work of art in Rome, when she turned upon him and, in a tone of indescribable effrontery, said, "And pray, Mr. Howard, when and how came you in Rome?" as who should say, "How is it that persons in your condition of life have the presumption to go to Rome?"

He replied: "I was an Academy student in Rome, Lady Holland; I was there in 1795," adding, after a moment's pause, "at the same time as your ladyship."

There was a dead silence for a moment; everybody knew what must be in everybody's mind, that when Lady Webster ran away from her husband with Lord Holland, under circumstances more than usually fluttering to the dove-cotes of society, it was in the month of February of that year, and to that place that the lovers directed their flight from Florence. Lady Holland was perfectly civil to Mr. Howard during the remainder of the visit, and, to do her justice, he believed bore him no malice.

Another anecdote is told of her which shows how very grand great ladies were in that day of so much theoretical equality. When she was dissatisfied, or fancied she was, with her trades-people, it was her pleasure to have them summoned to her presence, and to discourse with the creatures, mediately, through her page, as it were, thus:

"I am much displeased with Mr. Dill" (her ladyship's chief baker); "his biscuits are as dry as shavings, and his rolls are uneatable. If he doesn't make a change, I shall."

Page, addressing Mr. Dill, then and there in present attendance, and hearing every word: "Mr. Dill, my lady is much displeased with you. She says your biscuits are as dry as shavings, and your rolls uneatable. My lady says, Mr. Dill, if you don't make a change, she will."

Dill, the delinquent, tenders to the page propitiation, which is similarly translated to her ladyship, supposed to be in entire ignorance of Dill's presence, then and there standing in front of her, and the conversation so proceeds until by the same vicarious process he receives his deliverance.

Some stories are also told of Constable. In the country one day he had set himself down before a picturesque cottage to make a sketch of it, when the good woman of the house, who had seen him at a little distance, came out and said, "It's no use; we don't want anything, my good man," mistaking him for a peddler. Nothing disconcerted, Constable went on with his preparations, telling her that he was a painter, not a peddler, and that if she would go away and stand afar off at her cottage door, he would put her into his picture. "Ah, sir," she said, "now would you really! If you had only seen me before I had the small-pox!"

One day, coming out of the Academy, Constable met Sam, the porter, who had just been moving into its place one of Constable's landscapes, painted in his characteristic manner, with those spotty lights in it which he was so fond of introducing into his pictures.

"Well, Mr. Constable, sir, that is a picture of yours, sir! Wonderful, sir!"

"Glad you approve of it, Sam," said Constable, feeling in his pocket for a shilling wherewith to encourage Sam's taste.

"Wonderful, sir! I never see snow painted so natural in all *my* life!"

One of the contributors to the *United Service Gazette* when Mr. Watts was editor, a man instant in prayer and exhortation, and full of benevolent work, who wrote a series of instructive papers, was a distinguished "gunner" *en retraite*, and author of a tract for the conversion to Christian courses of flymen at Brighton, under the Baxterian title of "Cobwebs to catch Horseflies."

A royal anecdote was communicated to the mother of Mr. Alfred A. Watts by Mr. Westall, an artist of that day. Mr. Westall had the honor of teaching drawing to her present Majesty. One day, after the lesson, the young princess said to him, "Mr. Westall, what do you do on Sunday?"

The courtly but conscientious painter replied, "Your Royal Highness, I'm afraid I do very often what I am sure you never do, and would not approve—I paint on Sunday!"

"Oh, do you?" said Mr. Westall's pupil. "I'm so glad; because sometimes, do you know, when I can get a little time to myself on Sunday, I paint too!"

EVERY one about Alexandria, Virginia, before the late war, knew Captain Charley P——, and many knew him to their sorrow, for he was an inveterate joker (says a correspondent). Poor fellow! I saw the notice of his death in Memphis in the papers of last week, and that made me think of what I am going to write. During the war he was clerk for Captain W——, who was depot quartermaster, in charge of the coffins, in the city of Richmond, for the Confederate government. The office was in the rear of a store-house, and the front of the house was filled with coffins. One warm Sunday morning in summer Captain P—— thought that he would take a wash and put on a change of clothing. The office being closed on that day, he did so, and the day being very warm, he thought he would take a nap, and proceeded to look for a good place. He decided at last that a nice clean coffin would be the best then at hand; so he got into one, and went to sleep. He was awakened after a while by a knocking at the front door. He called out, "Come in." The door was opened, and a head thrust in, and he heard a voice saying, "Nobody in." The captain had his coat off, and his hair and whiskers were snow-white. Placing a hand on each side of the coffin, he raised himself to a sitting position, exclaiming, as he did so, "Ha!" The door was slammed to hurriedly, and he ran to it as fast as he could, and, on looking out, saw a countryman dashing up the street as fast as he could, but not standing upon the order of his going. He was rushing over everything in his path, and people thought he was mad. He had evidently seen a ghost.

THE following letter, which was passed around the House during the late session of Congress was, we are sorry to say, not acted on. Congress, was so much taken up with politics that it could pay little attention to the real wants of the people, and it adjourned without doing anything to lessen the spavin of the land. This is the more singular since it evinced a disposition to establish "bureaus" for everything else:

——, February, 1884.

Hon. ——, *House of Representatives:*

DEAR SIR,—I have some desire to lurn through you some remidy for spavin in Hosses you being at the head of the government and aught to use all endevers to help the poore farming class of this Distress land. I have a fine mar that have spavin. She has had it for foure years I have tride everthinge for it I could here of I have examin a good many Ferrers some say it incuible some gives remidys but all in vain affter consiringe the matter I have determin to adress you on the subject to see if thar be any remidy in reach of the poore farmer in the United States. Put this to the House to see if thay is any remidy or not any information will be thankfully received on the subject.

I have the honer to be yours obediant survant,

ONE Sunday, at an Ohio camp-meeting, when the excursion trains had brought in immense crowds, a good proportion of them being bent on having a jolly good time without regard to the day or the place, a disturbance arose, and the policemen of the grounds were attracted by the shout of "A fight! a fight!" They got to the spot too late to see for themselves who had been fighting; but one man was marched off and locked up in the log jail, notwithstanding his protests that he had been only a looker-on, and that by chance. In a short time the managers discovered that the man was, indeed, innocent, and they went immediately in person to the jail to release their prisoner. But the man, seeing by their profuse apologies how the land lay, refused to be released, telling them that he was simply following the example set by Paul and Silas when they were in the same situation. To that the managers had nothing to say, but walked off. When they had gone, the prisoner walked out, and at the next term of the Common Pleas Court he brought suit against the trustees of the camp ground for false imprisonment. He retained as counsel Judge C——, and to assist him a young lawyer who had then just been admitted to the bar. While the trial was in progress, and just before the time came for Judge C—— to make his speech to the jury, he bethought himself of the remark about Paul and Silas that his client had made to the officers when arrested. It would give effect to his argument, he thought, if he were to read to the jury the passage of Scripture concerning the release of the apostles. While busy with other preparations, he sent his colleague to the clerk's office, where, he told him, he would find a Bible, to look up for him the passage he wanted. The time for him to open his speech arrived, but his colleague had not appeared, and Judge C—— excused himself for a minute, hurried out, and stormed into the clerk's office. There he found the young man lying on the floor, with his head on his hand, and an enormous Bible spread open before him, while he was running his finger down the columns.

"Haven't you found that place yet?" demanded the judge.

His colleague turned another page without looking up, and said, "No; I can not find anything about Paul or Silas either, and I am *half-way through Exodus.*"

"TWO SIDES TO EVERY PICTURE."

"My dear," remarked a gentleman, gloomily, to his wife, "I consider myself the most unfortunate man that ever existed. I have spent my whole life so far in running after nothing."

"On the contrary," replied his wife, briskly, "I consider your life a splendid success, for you have certainly succeeded in getting nothing, and have no need to run after it any longer."

That gentleman was silenced, but not convinced.

THE DUKE OF WELLINGTON'S EXPERIMENT.

In a ground-floor room in one of the large public buildings of London a man sat writing at a table covered with papers. He was a short, strongly built figure, with a prominent nose, and a face hard and massive as a granite statue, wearing the set look peculiar to men who have surmounted great difficulties and confronted great perils. Few, indeed, had had more practice in both than this man, for he was no other than the Duke of Wellington, and his crowning victory at Waterloo was still but a few years old.

There was the tinkle of a bell outside, and then a murmur of voices in the anteroom; but the Duke never raised his head from his writing, even when his secretary entered and said:

"If it please your Grace, that man with the bullet-proof breastplate has called again, and wishes very much to see your Grace for a moment."

The Duke's face darkened, as well it might, for the man in question was the most pertinacious bore whom he had ever encountered. The bullet-proof cuirass was his own invention, and he never lost a chance of declaring that the safety of the whole British army depended upon its instant adoption of this "unparalleled discovery," which he carried about with him, and exhibited at all times and in all places.

Had this been all, he would soon have been disposed of; but, unluckily, he had contrived to interest in his invention one or two of the Duke's personal friends, and to get from them letters of recommendation which even Wellington could not easily disregard. Something must clearly be done, however; for although the fellow had hitherto been kept at bay, he was evidently determined to give the Duke no peace till the matter had been fully gone into.

For a moment Wellington looked so grim that the secretary began to hope for the order which he would gladly have obeyed, viz., to kick the inventor into the street forthwith. But the next instant the iron face cleared again, and over it played the very ghost of a smile, like a gleam of winter sunshine upon a precipice.

"Show him in," said he, briefly.

The observant secretary noted both the tone and the smile that accompanied it; and he inwardly decided that it would have been better for that inventor if he had *not* insisted on seeing the Duke.

In came the great discoverer—a tall, slouching, shabby, slightly red-nosed man, with a would-be jaunty air, which gave way a little, however, before the "Iron Duke's" penetrating glance.

"I am glad to think that your Grace appreciates the merits of my invention," said he, in a patronizing tone. "They are, indeed, too important to be undervalued by any great commander. Your Grace can not fail to remember the havoc made by your gallant troops at Waterloo among the French cuirassiers, whose breast-plates were *not* bullet-proof; whereas, if—"

"Have you got the thing with you?" interrupted Wellington.

The inventor unwrapped a very showy-looking cuirass of polished steel, and was just beginning a long lecture upon its merits, when the Duke cut him short by asking,

"Are you quite sure it *is* bullet-proof?"

"Quite sure, your Grace."

"Put it on, then, and go and stand in that corner."

The other wonderingly obeyed.

"Mr. Temple," shouted Wellington to his secretary, "tell the sentry outside to load with ball-cartridge, and come in here to test this cuirass. Quick, now!"

But quick though the secretary was, the inventor was quicker still. The moment he realized that he had been set up there on purpose to be fired at, and to be shot dead on the spot if his cuirass turned out to be *not* bullet-proof after all, he leaped headlong through the open window with a yell worthy of a Blackfoot Indian, and darting like a rocket across the court-yard, vanished through the outer gateway; nor did the Duke of Wellington, from that day forth, ever see or hear of him again.

DAVID KER.

CHARLES I. AND HENRIETTA MARIA.

Engraved by W. R. Gleason from the original painting by Vandyck.

COLUMBIA COLLEGE.

WHEN "God save the King" had given place to "Hail Columbia," and the clouds of war were cleared away, the thoughtful people of the new nation saw that they must build on deep and wide foundations of education. The several colleges existing at the opening of the Revolution — Harvard (founded 1638), William and Mary (1693), Yale (1701), Princeton (1746), the University of Pennsylvania (1748), King's (1754), Brown (1764), Dartmouth (1769), Rutgers (1770) —had suffered more or less from the war, and King's not least among them. Her men had done good service in the patriot cause. "There were early found Jay and Livingston, Morris and Benson, Van Cortlandt and Rutgers, and Troup and Hamilton." The college building had been seized for a barracks, and afterward used as a hospital, and worthy Mr. Lispenard meanwhile loaned a house for the use of Mr. Moore, President *ad interim*, until Tory President Cooper should return. The class of '76 was graduated with six men, and two students were matriculated in 1777, but except for an occasional meeting of the governors, the college seems to have slept a sleep very like death during the turmoil of the war.

In 1784 came a vigorous awakening. In response to an earnest recommendation of Governor Clinton, the Assembly passed an act granting new privileges to King's College, and providing for the establishment of a university.

The scheme which it embodied was a grand one. The "Colledge of the Province of New York," as revived, was to be called Columbia College, and was to be "the Mother of an University" whose influence should be felt throughout the State. In fact, it was at first proposed to name the institution the State College. Accordingly, eight State and city offi-cials, and twenty-four persons, two from each county, were incorporated "by the Name and Stile of the Regents of the University of the State of New York," and were made the governing body of the revived college, as well as supervisors of the schools and colleges which they were expected to found in different parts of the State. The clergy of each religious denomination in the State were authorized to designate a regent from their own body, and the president and a second representative of each school connected with this university system were also to be regents. The regents might hold "Estates to the annual Amount of forty thousand Bushels of Wheat"— to which strait of financial nomenclature the new nation was driven by the confusion of the colonial currency—but might not levy a fine above "the Value of one Bushel of Wheat," nor expel or "resticate" a student without fair hearing. The regents lost no time. Three days after the passage of the act they met at the house of Mr. John Simmons, in the city of New York, and the next day elected Governor Clinton, Chancellor, Hon. Pierre Van Cortlandt, Vice-Chancellor, Brockholst Livingston, Esq., Treasurer, and Robert Harpur, Esq., Secretary to the university. Mr. Livingston, who served the college faithfully for forty years, was, curiously enough, a son of the William Livingston who had so bitterly opposed King's College thirty years before, and Mr. Harpur had been a professor therein seventeen years back. Thus began, a hundred years ago, the first of those repeated attempts to make Columbia a metropolitan university, whose history we shall trace to their successful realization in our own day.

France was then the sister country to our new nation, and the regents promptly expressed their patriotic sentiments at this first meeting by appointing the Rev. J. P. Tetard as Professor of French. The classics were obliged to wait a few days, when Mr. William Cochran was appointed master of the proposed grammar school and college teacher of Latin and Greek. On the 17th of May the first student presented himself in the person of the Governor's nephew, De Witt Clinton—a name afterward illustrious in the Empire State—and being duly examined in the august presence of the Chancellor, the Vice-Chancellor, the Secretary, the Mayor of New York, and Professor Tetard, he was admitted, at the age of fifteen, to the Junior class. His memory is held in great reverence by his *alma mater*, and the chair in which he died, presented by his son, stands, with the chair of Benjamin Franklin, among her especial treasures.

The regents not only examined, through a committee of their body, all candidates for admission, but they drove ahead in the most approved modern fashion. The income of the college was reported at but £1000, yet by December our fearless regents had organized "the four faculties of Arts, Divinity, Medicine, and Law, making the first to comprise seven professorships; the second to consist of such as might be established by the different religious societies within the State, pursuant to the act instituting the university; the third to be composed of seven professors; and the last of three; besides which there were to be nine extra professors, a president, a secretary, and a librarian." The staff of the college during the period of the regency, which lasted until separate trustees were provided by the act of 1787, really consisted of Acting President Moore, Professors Tetard, Cochran (Greek and Latin), Kunze (Oriental Languages), Gross (German and Geography), Bard (Natural Philosophy and Astronomy), Moyes (Natural History and Chemistry), and Tutor Kemp (Mathematics), besides Professors Bard, Kissam, McKnight, Crosby, and Romaine in the School of Medicine. No president was appointed, for lack of funds—though Colonel Clarkson had been sent to France and the Netherlands to procure donations — and the professors took turns in filling the executive chair.

"The Plan of Education," as drawn by the regents, shows what was the real literary standing of our colleges at the close of the war of Independence. Candidates were required to be able only to construe Cæsar, Cicero against Catiline, four books of Virgil, and the Gospels in Greek, "to turn English into grammatical Latin," and "to understand the four first [*sic*] Rules of Arithmetic, with the Rule of Three." The curriculum was essentially classical: for the Freshmen, twice a day, Livy and more of Cicero, Xenophon, Lucian, and Demosthenes, with written Latin exercises daily, and written translations into English once a week; for the Sophomores, once a day, Tacitus, Sallust, Virgil again, more Demosthenes, Homer, Euripides, and Sophocles, and they were "to continue to make Latin every day"; for the Juniors, these or other authors, at the choice of the professor, with Latin compositions; for the Seniors, Longinus, Quintilian, etc., "in their chambers."

In mathematics the student learned vulgar and decimal fractions, extracting the roots, and algebra in his Freshman year, and soared in the Sophomore to Euclid, trigonometry, and conic sections; the Freshman's tasks were completed with English grammar, and "the art of reading and speaking English with propriety and elegance"; the Sophomore's with geography. The Juniors were to be taught logic and natural philosophy; the Seniors, ethics, universal grammar, and criticism.

But a hundred years ago the plan of making Columbia "the Mother of an University," which is now being realized, was premature; and the scheme proved too grand. The original act and others succeeding were codified in 1787, as is witnessed by a copy of the charter and statutes printed "at the Bible, in Pearl Street, M,DCC,XCVI," now among the treasures of the college library. The Regents of the University, as they are still curiously called, became what they now are, a useful supervisory body, to visit, inspect, and report upon the colleges, academies, and schools established within the State; and a separate body of trustees was established "in perpetual succession" for the government of the college. This act, passed April 13, 1787, is said to have been drawn by Alexander Hamilton.

In May, 1787, the trustees found a worthy first president for Columbia in the person of the son of the worthy first president of King's, and elected to that office William Samuel Johnson, LL.D., one of the most distinguished citizens of the young nation. He was then sixty years old. He had en-

WILLIAM SAMUEL JOHNSON.

tered Yale at thirteen, and was the "scholar of the house" who won the Berkeley bounty in the graduating class of 1744. His father said of his two boys: "It was a great damage that they entered so young, and that when they were there they had so little to do, their classmates being so far behind them." After graduating at Yale, the future president attended law lectures at Harvard, and was in 1747 made a Master of Arts by that university, having to pay, as he wrote to his father with great sorrow, £10 for a proper wig and £8 for his degree. In 1766, having already been a member of the Connecticut Assembly, he was honored by his State with the appointment of special commissioner to England to secure the claim to a large tract of land. During his five years' residence abroad he made many friends amongst noted men, and sought out his namesake, the great Dr. Johnson, "as odd a mortal," he wrote to his father, "as you ever saw. You would not, at first sight, suspect he had ever read or thought in his life, or was much above the degree of an idiot. But, *nulla fronti fides*, when he opens himself after a little acquaintance, you are abundantly repaid for these first unfavorable appearances." A family tradition says that when he introduced himself as an American, the gruff old doctor retorted: "The Americans! What do they know, and what do they read?" "They read, sir, *The Rambler*," was the polite

Johnson set sail from Gravesend August 3, 1771, and reached Stratford October 1. His State thanked him "for his constant endeavors to promote the general cause of American liberty," made him a judge, and sent him to the Colonial Congress which met in New York, September 5, 1774, but his appointment as arbitrator on the Van Rensselaer estate at Albany caused him to resign this honor in favor of Silas Deane. In the war of Independence he did good work at home, sending a substitute to the front, and in the constructive period that followed he was one of our ablest statesmen. He represented Connecticut in Congress from 1784 to 1787, and in the Constitutional Convention of the latter year, and he was named first on the committee, with Hamilton, Morris, Madison, and King as his associates, appointed "to revise the style of and arrange the articles agreed to by the House." He was elected President of Columbia College, May 21,

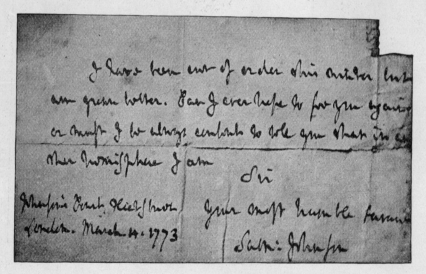

PART OF LETTER OF DR. SAMUEL JOHNSON TO PRESIDENT JOHNSON.

and apt reply, which so won the doctor that before his namesake left London he presented him with "an elegantly bound copy of his large folio dictionary, and an engraving of himself from a painting by Sir Joshua Reynolds, which he considered his best likeness." The two became lifelong correspondents, and some of the letters are still preserved at the Stratford homestead.

At last, successful in his mission, Mr.

1787, and held that office conjointly with that of Senator from Connecticut until after the removal of Congress to Philadelphia in 1793. The bill for reorganizing the judiciary was drawn by him and his colleague, Oliver Ellsworth.

Columbia has good reason to be proud of its patriot first president, and he proved himself as vigorous for the college as for the country. But in 1799, returning through a snow-storm from the meeting

JOHN RANDOLPH.

held in Trinity vestry to lament the death of General Washington, he fell ill; and July 16, 1800, he resigned his post and retired to Stratford. But he lived to marry a second wife that same year, and to pass his ninety-second birthday in 1819.

At the time of Dr. Johnson's accession there were thirty-nine students in the college, nearly half of whom were in the Freshman class. Five of them lodged and boarded in the college, and five more had rooms and studied there. Among those who entered in 1788 were John Randolph of Roanoke, then a pretty and attractive lad, and his brother Theodoric; but the latter left in the Sophomore and the former in the Junior year. The income of the college was about £1330. The faculties of Arts and of Medicine consisted of three professors each; there were no faculties of Law and Divinity, and the only extra professor was a German who served without salary. In 1792, however, the Medical Society of the State urged the trustees to establish the Medical School on a broader basis, and accordingly seven medical professors were appointed, with Dr. Samuel Bard as their dean. A grant was obtained from the Legislature of £7900, and £750 annually for five years, new professors were appointed, an addition was made to the library, and the foundations laid for two new buildings at right angles to the old. But again the authorities seemed to have gone ahead too fast, and when the five years had passed and the grant was not renewed, they were obliged to consolidate the professorships, and, instead of completing the buildings, to sell the materials they had on hand.

BENJAMIN MOORE.

chased of the corporation of the city of New York twenty acres of ground, situated on the middle road, between Bloomingdale and Kingsbridge, and distant from the city about three miles and a half." By the autumn of 1806 he was able to publish a catalogue of about two thousand species, and in 1810 he succeeded in obtaining from the Legislature an agreement of purchase by the State. Various experts appraised the land at about $2500 per acre, and for the ground and improvements, aside from plants worth above $12,500, for which no charge was made, the doctor received $74,268 75. This tract, then called Elgin, is the property between Forty-seventh and Fifty-first streets and between Fifth and Sixth avenues, no longer "near the fourth mile-stone," but in the very centre of the city. In 1814, to replace certain property ceded to Vermont at the settlement of the boundary, the State gave this land to the college, with the proviso that the buildings should be removed thither within twelve years; but five years later it rescinded this condition, besides granting to the college $10,000 in cash, and the ground-rents of a portion of this property are now one of the chief sources of revenue of the college.

In 1810 the college made a great stride forward. A committee of the trustees, headed by Rufus King, had reported during the previous year in favor of bettering the literary standing of the college. The requisites of admission were accordingly raised with the opening of the college year 1810–11, and a more advanced course of studies was adopted. The Legislature had granted in the spring of 1810 a new charter, one of its provisions permitting the trustees to lease property for sixty-three instead of for twenty-one years, and the trustees, who at this time reported 135 students, expressed their intention "to lay a broader and stronger basis for sound and thorough education than (as they believe) has hitherto been known in these States."

The committee presented a strong and able report, which was for some years printed with the college statistics, and is still of value. It laid down as "the primary principle of all sound education, *the evolution of faculty and the formation*

On Dr. Johnson's retirement the senior professor filled his place at the Commencement. Rev. Dr. Wharton, of Philadelphia, was elected to fill the vacancy in May of 1801, but resigned early in December, and it was not till the last day of the year that, in accordance with an understanding that professional duties should be detached from the presidency, Right Rev. Benjamin Moore, Bishop of New York, an alumnus who had been President Cooper's whilom successor six-and-twenty years before, was again made president. The professors were intrusted with the daily charge of affairs, and the college prospered, receiving a fresh grant of lands from the regents in 1802, and completing the hall and recitation-rooms on the north end of the new foundation.

The Medical College enjoyed at this time the vigorous services of Dr. David Hosack as Professor of Botany and Materia Medica. The good doctor, though he got together an excellent library of books, wisely insisted that his students ought to be taught from the living plants, and after several almost successful attempts to induce the State Legislature to provide for a botanical garden, he himself in 1801 "pur-

of habit"—a definition curiously in line with the scientific nomenclature as well as the best scientific thought of to-day. It disclaimed any intention "to try that most fruitless and mischievous experiment, the added rhetoric and algebra to the Sophomore; gave the Juniors spherical trigonometry and conic sections from the Freshman studies, ethics from those of the Seniors, and history and chronology;

JOHN McVICKAR.

experiment of educating either the naturally stupid or the incurably idle." The changes in the course of study from the "plan of education" of 1784 added two books of Xenophon and two of Homer, and decimal and vulgar fractions, to the entrance requirements, advanced the classical course so as to leave the Senior studies to the discretion of the provost, transferred Euclid and part of geography from the Sophomore to the Freshman year, and and in the Senior year provided for fluxions, natural philosophy, and astronomy; criticism and universal grammar; history and chronology; intellectual philosophy, logic, and the "law of nature and nations."

To make way for a more concentrated and vigorous administration, Bishop Moore resigned in 1811. Dr. Mason, an energetic leader in the college affairs, was the general choice for the headship of the college;

but the president must by the charter be an Episcopalian, and the doctor was "the champion of the Presbyterians." The office of provost was therefore created for him, and the honorary position was given to Rev. Dr. William Harris—"worthy, paternal Dr. Harris"—"a man," said Professor McVickar at his death, "of a tender heart, great firmness, and deep piety." In 1816, Dr. Mason having resigned the provostship, that office was abolished, and President Harris reigned *de facto* as well as *de jure*, till his death in 1829. During Dr. Mason's administration the medical school had been given up (1813) in favor of a new institution established by the regents under the title of the College of Physicians and Surgeons, which returned to the fold in 1860.

In 1817 the trustees began the long-contemplated improvements in the college building. Two wings, each fifty feet square, were added to the main building, providing residence for four professors, and room for a chapel and library was found in the old building. "How grand," wrote Dr. Haight, in later reminiscences of his Freshman days of this time— "how grand everything about the college seemed!—the stately sycamores on the green, venerable from age, overshadowing the edifice, the old building, the great staircase, the chapel with its strange hanging gallery, the dais at the east end, and the white-haired president in his robes, and the professors on his either hand."

Among the professors of Columbia in these years were many men of strength and note. Dr. Robert Adrain—"Old Bobbie," the students called him—was one of these, serving the college from 1813 to 1825 as Professor of Mathematics. He was "an Irish gentleman, of large size, broad, beaming face, and silvery voice"—a genial soul, and a great lover of chess. Once having heard of an old salt who had "checkmated" pretty well around the world, he put on his old clothes, invaded the sailor's boarding-house *incog.*, and, on beating the old fellow, was amply rewarded with the spontaneous praise, "You must be the devil or Dr. Adrain!" Chancellor Kent, who had been a professor from 1793 to 1798, was re-appointed in 1823 to the chair of Law, and delivered the famous lectures that became the chief commentary on the Constitution.

The college was very proud of the fact that Professors McVickar, Moore, Anthon,

Renwick, and Anderson, who for some years constituted the entire faculty, were all alumni. Professor Anderson, who succeeded Dr. Adrain, and served till 1843, is spoken of as a man whose character approached as near to perfection as is permitted to poor humanity. He was strong, able, modest, so versatile in his knowledge of languages that his students were afraid to wager what language he did not know. One day he was noticed listening to a strange conversation on the street; it proved to be Bohemian, which he had quietly added to his stock of tongues. His mathematical ability was still more noteworthy. Mr. A. S. Hewitt tells that he once went with the professor to make some observations at the Observatory at West Point, when it was found that they had left behind some necessary and elaborate formulas. It was ten o'clock at night, and their only chance for the observations was early the next day. "Never mind," said the professor; "go to bed, and I'll see what I can do." By morning he had reconstructed all the formulas from the material furnished by his marvellous memory, and the observations were successfully made. His classical attainments commanded the exacting respect of Dr. Anthon, and he had found time also to train himself in out-of-door work, so that he had several times walked fifty miles in a day.

Dr. Charles Anthon was another of the giants of those days. His father, born in Germany, came to the New World as a British officer during the French war, and was Surgeon-General at Detroit. His mother was the daughter of a French officer. The father was a practicing physician in New York during and after the Revolution, and in 1796 he was made a trustee of Columbia College. The son, born in 1797, entered Columbia at fourteen, and so far surpassed his classmates that he took the gold medal twice, and was accordingly "excluded from competition," as are the pictures of the great artists in the Paris Salon. On graduation he studied law in the office of his elder brother, but though admitted to the bar, it was his appointment in 1820, at the age of twenty-three, to the adjunct professorship of Greek and Latin that determined his life-work. Thenceforward for forty-seven years, till he died in harness in 1867, he devoted an iron frame, an obstinate and unflagging industry, an extraordinary knowledge,

CHARLES ANTHON.

and a patient habit of accumulation, to the instruction of his students and the editing of books. His Horace is believed to be the "first attempt at a critical edition of an ancient author in this country," and his series of text-books, dictionaries, and manuals of antiquities, amounting to forty volumes, covered almost the whole field of the educational classics. The students of to-day scarcely know how much they are indebted to him for making easy and delightful paths which previous writers had blocked with difficulties on the principle that "struggling makes strong." His works, republished in England, made him almost as well known there as here. The *Athenæum* said: "Dr. Anthon has done more for sound classical school literature than any half-dozen Englishmen." Wedded only to his work, he knew no respite and no other cares. His working day was from four in the morning till ten at night. With his students he showed a curious mixture of harshness and friendliness, so that some—probably the lazy ones—recall him as a monstrous tyrant, and others as the embodiment of kindness. One of his chief services to the college was the training of his coadjutor and successor, Professor Henry Drisler, who began his college service in 1843, and is now the honored senior of the faculty.

Professor McVickar graduated at the head of his class in 1804, at the age of seventeen, and at thirty was made full professor. As Professor of Political Economy, which subject was introduced, at his desire, as a Senior study, about 1817, he is said to have given the first course of lectures on this subject delivered in any American college, and in 1825 he published what is said to have been the first work on political economy from an American pen. His *Hints on Banking*, published in 1827, unfolded the principle of free banking under a general statute which is at the foundation of our national-bank system. "Quiet perseverance" was his secret of success. He preached as well as taught, and he had some very clear ideas about churches. "Decorate construction, never construct decoration," said he, strikingly ; and he was a great advocate of free seats: "No proprietorship in the house of God." He also served the college forty-seven years, until he was made an *emeritus* professor in 1864, four years before his death. The roll of Columbia is, in fact, so full of honor-men that it is impossible to continue the roster.

On Dr. Harris's death, in 1829, Hon. William A. Duer, LL.D., "a respectable layman who deservedly stands high in the confidence of the community," became the fifth president of Columbia, and at once the venerable college was called upon to show its prowess. The proposal in 1830 to establish the University of the City of New York roused the trustees—who demurred to two institutions within the city while Columbia lacked $2000 per year of its expenditure—to lay fresh claim to a university *status* by the establishment, in addition to the "full course" for matriculated students, of a "scientific and literary course," open to such persons as might be pleased to attend. For the full course the requisites for admission had in the intervening years been raised by adding algebra. The mathematical subjects were strengthened in the Freshman year. The Sophomores now studied analytical

geometry, descriptive geometry and linear drawing, mensuration, surveying, and navigation ; they had a well - balanced course in physics, including "the *relations* of heat, electricity, magnetism, and light"; their English compositions were to be criticised by the professor in the presence of the class, and they were each to make a weekly analysis of their work in history. The Juniors had reached practical astronomy with the use of instruments, chemistry applied to the arts, and mineralogy and geology, and enjoyed lectures on English and modern literature, "with references to authorities." And the Senior class had undertaken the calculus, mechanics, architecture, and engineering, the history of philosophy, the evidences, and political economy, besides attending lectures from Professor Kent on the constitutional jurisprudence of the United States and on international law. All this marked an advance corresponding to that of knowledge and of the country. The "scientific and literary course" was planned to cover three years, and, as gradually developed, aimed to be "a complete system of instruction for young men designed for civil or military engineers, architects, superintendents of manufactories of all kinds, or for mercantile or nautical pursuits." The applicant was required to have a knowledge of French, and some mathematical and geographical information; he then entered upon a course of studies selected from the regular curriculum, with the French language in place of the classics, and the addition of chemical manipulation, assaying, book-keeping, perspective drawing, and the use of water-colors, and technical drawing "according to the intended profession of the student."

The new scheme introduced many other changes ; nearly a score of public lectureships were provided for, whose incumbents should fix and receive the fees for their lectures; various societies, the religious denominations, and all schools sending at least four students, and any person paying $1000, were to have free scholarships; and any religious denomination or person paying $20,000 endowment might found a professorship and nominate the professor. In the classes students were to be seated, as before, according to their grade of merit, but now a gold medal, awarded to the best student of each class, was to give him individual precedence in the first grade. Two gold medals put the student on an honor list "beyond competition," as a sort of student *emeritus*. Here was, in fact, the germ of a real university, as well as of the scientific school rian as well as professor for some years, became his successor in 1842. He was "a refined scholar," and highly cultivated gentleman of the old school, living a

HENRY DRISLER.

afterward started as the School of Mines; but the scheme came to an untimely end in 1843, when some of the studies were adopted into the regular course, and German added.

On the resignation of President Duer, "the high-toned gentleman," Professor N. F. Moore, LL.D., who had been libra-

bachelor's life in the world of books, "of a pleasant petulance and an engaging earnestness," a model of good-breeding. He is described by Dr. Haight as "tall, spare, lithe, with a firm, intellectual face, bearing the marks of years of hard study and close application." He resigned in 1849, and was succeeded by Hon. Charles

King, LL.D., a representative of one of the historic families of New York, and another gentleman and scholar of the good old days, who served the college for fifteen years, till the inauguration of President Barnard in 1864. In 1857 there was established a "post-graduate course," in which Professor Arnold Guyot lectured on physical geography, and Professor George P. Marsh on the English language; but this continued only a year. Nevertheless, the foundations of a university were again laid, and this time more permanently, by the establishment of the School of Law in 1858, with Professor Theodore W. Dwight as warden, by the re-adoption of the Medical College in 1860, and by the modest beginning of the School of Mines in 1863–5, under the vigorous inspiration and efforts of Professor Thomas Egleston, Jun.

For nearly a hundred years the college had found its home in that fine "limehouse" with the cupola which the trustees had proudly completed in 1760. There had been extensions and additions, and the college was proud of its site, its grounds, and that umbrageous and delightful College Place into which old Chapel Street had been transformed; but now commerce was crowding it. The Botanic Gardens were the destined site, and when in 1851 a resolution was passed to "lay out building lots, with space for a church and college," the plot west of Fifth Avenue between Forty-ninth and Fiftieth streets was left at its original level for the college buildings, for which Upjohn was preparing a design. Pending their erection, that portion of the Trinity gift on which the college actually stood was sold, and a temporary investment of the proceeds was made in the old Deaf-and-dumb Asylum and its grounds, between Madison and Fourth avenues and Forty-ninth and Fiftieth streets. The college moved into this temporary home in 1857, and appears to have made this site its permanent one. The east dormitory became the chapel and library, the west one homes for the professors. In 1862 a President's House was completed on the grounds. The war put a stop to the new plans, and now the college is anchored. The old Asylum, with its columned portico, still exists, and is known to irreverent undergrads as the *maison de punk*, but it will soon give way to the new buildings which are to replace it. This site is estimated to be worth over $400,000.

Columbia, under the administrations of Presidents Moore and King, preserved her easy equanimity even into the stirring times of the war, though she was sending many a brave boy to the field, as she had done a century before. But with the inauguration of President F. A. P. Barnard, in 1864, a new era began. He was then a veteran educator, having been graduated at Yale in 1828, and he had been Chancellor of the University of Mississippi until the war drove all Northern sympathizers out of the South, and sent him to Washington. Years before he had been connected with the Deaf-and-dumb Asylum, little thinking that he would be called back to the old halls with this great future opening before them. His inaugural address showed a far look ahead. He was deeply impressed with the university idea, and with the educational needs of the metropolis, and his faith has been justified by works. At his coming, there were but one hundred and fifty students in the college proper, the School of Mines was in an inchoate state, the schools of Law and of Medicine were connected with the School of Arts by the merest thread of association. To-day, a thousand students, under-graduate, graduate, and professional, throng the college grounds, and, with the exception of the Medical College (which has five hundred students in its building on Twenty-third Street, and whose connection with the university consists chiefly in the signing of its diplomas by the President), all the schools are part of a compact and centrally governed university, to which a splendid future is assured.

The trustees had foreseen the need of more room, and each member of the faculty had been requested to furnish an estimate of what the future would demand in his special department. A building was erected for the School of Mines in 1865, but only as a temporary expedient; and in 1871 the trustees appointed a Committee on Site, who examined various locations, and presented three plots to the board for their choice. But in 1873 the pressure for room became insistent, and against the judgment of the president, who entered a written protest on the minutes, the die was cast by the erection of a solid and permanent building for the School of Mines on the old grounds. Columbia has found her permanent home, and her architect has had to meet the difficult problem of housing a great and grow-

FREDERICK A. P. BARNARD.

ing university within the contracted limits of a city block.

The difficulty has been very well met by planning a double quadrangle, both "quads" being open on the south side. Throughout, the architect, Mr. C. C. Haight, has had the good sense to plan from within outward, instead of cramping interior accommodations to provide for architectural effects, and the result of "decorating construction and not constructing decoration" has been as happy as it is honestly reached. The general style of the new buildings is the English collegiate—of whose early examples at the English universities Mr. Haight has been a careful student—worked out in red brick and Potsdam sandstone. Hamilton Hall, which occupies the western or Madison Avenue frontage, is the home of the School of Arts, or college proper, and contains the president's, faculty, and trustees' rooms. In planning it, each professor was given opportunity to state his needs, and the windows, and consequently the entire façade, were worked accordingly. A graceful and slender bastion tower at the upper corner and a hanging bay give variety of effect to this front, and make it, although there are no doorways to provide striking features, an architectural adornment of Madison Avenue. The Fourth Avenue frontage is occupied by the new building of the School of Mines, with fine halls for the geological, chemical, and other collections, and for the drawing-room; and the present site of the President's House will give place for the organic laboratory provided for in the munificent Phœnix bequest, and for large lecture-rooms for the scientific professors. The Fiftieth Street side is now occupied by the older School of Mines building, and by the original asylum edifice, with the chapel and old library adjoining. The site of the asylum will afford room for the graduate schools of Political Science, etc., and the chapel will be replaced either by a new chapel and a college hall, to hold a thousand hearers, or by additional stack-rooms for the library. The Law School below, and the library above, with the observatory in the top of the adjoining tower, occupy the very striking building dividing one quadrangle from the other, which is one of the chief architectural features of this notable group of buildings. It has been completed during the past year at a cost of about $200,000. The interior of this building is finished in brick, and it is altogether a most honest and noble piece of work. The present library building is separated from the old college by a space of only a few inches, which the boys have christened the Pass of Thermopylæ. Under the east quadrangle is the engine-room, connected with the library and the School of Mines by under-ground passages, and the high chimney forms a noteworthy architectural feature of the new School of Mines building.

The most important interior feature of the new building is the noble library hall, a room of grand proportions, with a triple-arch roof supported by iron truss-work, so that the floor space—113 by 75 feet—is unbroken by divisions. A gallery makes the circuit of it, and the walls, within reaching distance of the floor and of the gallery, are lined with that best of decorations, books. The Phœnix collection, of above 7000 valuable and rare books, occupies the entire south gallery. The general arrangement is by subjects, and every frequenter of the library has unquestioned access to the 25,000 volumes here shelved as a reference library. The floor is dotted with tables, to which the reader may freely take as many books as he requires, and as the dusk comes on, a tap of the bell from the librarian's room to the engineer puts at his disposal a movable electric light, which he may turn on or off at will. All the tables have individual lights, and the shades for these burners and for those about the room were so arranged, in consultation with Dr. C. R. Agnew, who is one of the trustees, that all the light falls on the books or tables, and no ray glares into the reader's eye. The assistant librarians have their desks on the main floor, and are ready to put their knowledge of their special subjects at the service of the reader. It is pleasant to note that the conveniences of this library are to be extended not only to the 1600 members of the university and its alumni, but to such other scholars as may rightly seek its privileges; so that what the Astor and Lenox libraries have not given to New-Yorkers, Columbia will

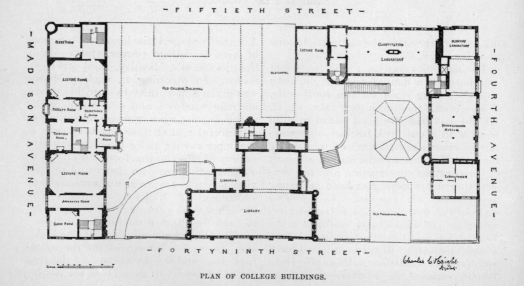

PLAN OF COLLEGE BUILDINGS.

give—a working library open every day in the year except Sundays and Good-Friday, and from eight, morning, till ten, night.

modern library co-operation, of which the new librarian, Mr. Melvil Dewey, has been a leading apostle.   The modern librarian

A BIT OF OLD AND NEW.

Such facilities as these are made possible only by the adoption of the improved library methods and fittings resulting from the

aims, above all, to have his books used, to give them the greatest accessibility at the least possible inconvenience to the reader, albeit to the dire disturbance of the old-fashioned book-keeper, who fears his precious books will be hurt by using. In respect of facility of use, the Columbia College library promises to be the most notable in the country. The libraries of the several schools are now brought together under one administration, and the law librarian, the science librarian, and other specialists are staff officers of the university librarian. They, in turn, have the help of a staff of bright Wellesley girls, of the class of 1883, who are trained as cataloguers and library assistants. The staff hours are so arranged that no one need work more than seven hours. Catalogueing goes on without closing any part of the library; it will require three years to complete the work.

The system of registry, which makes free use possible, is centred in a desk at the very entrance, in the transept of the great hall. This desk is in easy communication, by means of sliding-boxes, with the stack-rooms, in which the body of the collection not needed for reference is packed with such economy of space that a low room, 61 by 22 feet, houses 40,000 volumes. These are, indeed, catacombs of books, with lettered avenues and numbered streets but twenty-six inches wide, so that a book can be had instantly when called for from the card directory below. Each book has pasted inside its cover a pocket, into which slips a book-card; each reader is represented also by a card arranged according to his initials in a case at the registry desk. The book's number is entered on the reader's card; the reader signs his initials on the book's card, which, while the book is out, is kept in a second case at the registry desk, arranged by subjects. Thus any book "out" can be instantly traced, and the receipt for it produced. When a reader wishes to return a book, he has only to hand it in at the registry desk; and if he is in a super-American hurry, he need not wait even the instant required to make sure that the attendant, by stamping the date of return on the book card, has cancelled his receipt. There is no field in which modern organization has achieved a greater triumph than in this single example of library administration.

The library itself has been of slow growth, that of King's College, which should have been its nucleus, having apparently been dispersed during the Revolution, by the seizure of the college build-ings for military purposes. In 1806 six hundred volumes from it came to light in a room in St. Paul's Chapel. Several donations and purchases had increased the collection in 1862 to 16,000 volumes, valued at $34,000. In 1882 the munificent bequest of Stephen Whitney Phœnix brought to the college his superb collection. The united libraries in 1883 numbered 50,000 volumes, and the accessions this year add about 12,000 more. In the upper stack-room is housed the fine Torrey herbarium, covering 60,000 specimens, and valued at over $25,000. Above the wing of the library building is the tower and paper dome of the astronomical observatory, with the Rutherfurd telescope and transit instrument.

After many false starts, Columbia College has at last physically and intellectually begun to build thoroughly the foundation of a true metropolitan university. Her system now includes "a School of Arts, a School of Mines, a School of Law, a School of Political Science, and a School of Medicine, employing a president and one hundred and twenty professors, instructors, and assistants"—almost as many as her students in old days—and numbering over fifteen hundred students. To this the trustees have voted to add a School of Library Economy, for the training of librarians, of which the librarian will be the chief professor.

The progress made in the School of Arts since "the plan of education" first cited is interestingly shown by an examination of the present course. The classical course is bettered in the selection of authors, but the chief change has naturally been in rounding out education with the new studies. For entrance, the would-be Freshman must construe more of Cæsar, Cicero, and Virgil than a hundred years ago, and something of Xenophon and Homer in place of the Greek Gospels; he must be versed in English, Latin, and Greek grammar, prosody and composition, writing an English paper off-hand in the examination-room; he must know the elements of ancient and modern geography, of ancient history, of arithmetic, algebra, and geometry. In the Freshman class, the classic authors are Horace and Cicero, Homer and Herodotus; in the Sophomore, Horace (Satires) and Livy, Euripides and Xenophon (*Memorabilia*). In both, the student must elect one modern language, having choice of German, French, Italian, and

THE LIBRARY.

Spanish. The Freshman completes algebra and geometry, with conic sections; the Sophomore reaches trigonometry, mensuration, and surveying, and has a course in general chemistry. The Freshman studies English grammar and analysis, and the history of English literature, with special attention to the prose of Addison and Thackeray; the Sophomore, historical grammar and the poetry of Shakespeare. Rhetoric is a study of both years, and the Sophomore adds German and French history. The elective system was introduced in 1869, and now Junior and Senior studies are chiefly elective, with the exception of, for the Junior year, English, with Anglo-Saxon grammar and the special study of Bacon, Milton, and Spenser, English history, and political economy; for the Senior class, Anglo-Saxon literature and Chaucer, and the constitutional history of the United States. The Junior elective studies include Juvenal and Cicero, a drama of Sophocles, and a dialogue of Plato; analytical geometry and mechanics; heat and electricity; botany, logic, psychology, and a modern language. The Senior elective studies include Terence and Cicero's epistles, archaic Latin and the Latin inscriptions, Æschylus and Demosthenes (On the Crown), comparative philology, differential and integral calculus, astronomy (practical as well as theoretical), and the higher physics, chemistry, botany, geology and lithology, psychology and the history of philosophy, the constitutional history of England and Europe, and political economy. The choice of elective studies is coupled only with the provisions that there must be altogether not less than fifteen hours of college work per week, and that students shall not change their elective studies without permission from the faculty.

STAIRWAY LEADING TO LIBRARY.

After six years of development a competent authority declared that "among all the most famous schools in the world there is not one so well supplied with apparatus, and not one where all the departments are carried on with the same equal care."

The interesting and admirable feature of summer work includes classes in practical mining, started in 1877, in which the men go with pick and drill into the mines alongside the working miners; in mechanical engineering, in which they visit the great foundries and machine-shops of New York city, making working drawings, handling tools, and listening to work-shop lectures from their instructors, in which the workmen, during their noonings, show equal interest; and in geodesy, in which valuable field work is done on the New York State Survey. The membership of the school now includes nearly three hundred students, and it has a capable faculty, of which Professor C. F. Chandler is dean.

The School of Mines is a partial title for what is really a very broad school of science, with six specific courses in mining engineering, civil engineering, metallurgy, geology and paleontology, analytical and applied chemistry, and architecture. For the first of the four years all students pursue a common course, which is a general training in the elements of science and in French, German, and drawing. Thereafter each must select his specialty, and hold to it. The school arose from small beginnings, for Mr. Thomas Egleston, its projector, in his first proposals of 1863, promised that the college should not be asked to support it. A room was provided in the basement of the old college building as a laboratory, to accommodate but twelve students. Twenty-five, however, applied for admission, and during the session of 1864-5 the number reached forty-eight.

The School of Medicine—the College of Physicians and Surgeons on Twenty-third Street, having over five hundred students, with Dr. Alonzo Clark as president—has but a nominal connection with the university; but the School of Law, under the management of its distinguished warden, Professor Theodore W. Dwight, with its home on Lafayette Place, is now housed with the other schools, and is entirely under the government of the college authorities. Its success has been so great that two sets of lectures are required from Professor Dwight, one in the morning and one in the afternoon. Two moot-courts are held each week, for which printed slips containing the case to be discussed are given out to the students in advance, and in which questions of law are argued by six or eight students, and a decision is given by the professor acting as judge;

and these are supplemented by debating clubs, in which students discuss more fully the same cases. The course occupies two years, and above four hundred students are in attendance.

The School of Political Science, the youngest child of the group, which was an outgrowth of the School of Law, has become, under the headship of Professor John W. Burgess, a distinguished member of the university family. It was established in 1880, "to prepare young men for the duties of public life." It requires for admission the qualifications necessary for the Junior class in college, and it awards the degree of Ph.D., after a prescribed three years' course in physical and political geography, the history of philosophy, the history of the literature of the political sciences, the constitutional history of Europe, England, and the United States, Roman jurisprudence, the comparative constitutional law of European states, the United States, and the several States of the Union, the history of diplomacy, administrative law, political economy, statistical and social science. Provision is made for special students in any of these departments. The school has already attracted an attendance of forty students, and it shows growth.

Columbia decided in 1883 to extend its examinations so as to grant certificates of proficiency to such women as prepared themselves elsewhere to pass them. The university idea was further advanced by the establishment in 1871 of two fellowships, in literature and science, which secured to members of the graduating class $500 per year for three years, to enable them to continue their studies at the college or elsewhere, under the direction of the president.

The future should see Columbia, under wise management, one of the great universities of the world. Her "physical basis of life" is a magnificent endowment of real estate valued at over $5,000,000. The progress of the last ten years points to the possibility of a university in this great commercial city which, like the great city universities of the Renaissance, shall attract thousands of students by the facilities for study which only a great centre of civilized activity can supply. With the resources of great libraries, of music, and of art, at her disposal, with the other great educational institutions of the city acknowledging her university character as giving a centre and head to a general educational system, with a true spirit of scholarship which permits no jealousy but always inspires union to a common end, Columbia University ought to be in the next century a source of intellectual and moral strength whose influence shall be felt, through New York, by the whole of America.

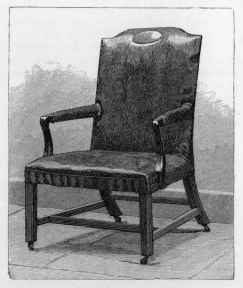

FRANKLIN'S CHAIR.

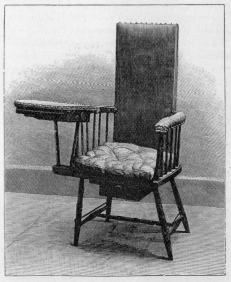

DE WITT CLINTON'S CHAIR.

KEW GREEN.

A DAY WITH SIR JOSEPH HOOKER AT KEW.

THE past and the present meet at Kew in quaint red brick houses and modern stucco villas, in village green and suburban railway station, in Georgian reminiscences and Victorian progress; and as the old and the new combine to adapt imperial Kew to current nineteenth-century ideas, it may also be said that the temperatures, if not the climates, of the world are concentrated here, each with its specimen of tree and plant, of fruit and flower.

George the Third and his Queen were more intimately associated with Kew than were any other royal personages, though Caroline, the persecuted wife of the second George, began the gardens. It was in the autumn of 1786, after an attack had been made upon the King, that the good people of the hamlet solaced him with a rural demonstration that is recorded by Madame D'Arblay as follows: "An exceedingly pretty scene was exhibited to-day to their Majesties. We came, as usual on every alternate Tuesday, to Kew. The Queen's lodge is at the end of a long meadow surrounded with houses, which is called Kew Green, and this was quite filled with all the inhabitants of the place—the lame, old, blind, sick, and infants—who all assembled, dressed in their Sunday garb, to line the sides of the road through which their Majesties passed, attended by a band of musicians arranged in the front, who began "God save the King" the moment they came upon the Green, and finished it with loud huzzas. This affected the Queen to tears; and speaking of it afterward, she said, 'I shall always love little Kew for this.'" In those days of a simple unintellectual royalty the Green was not railed in; nor, it would seem, was the hamlet walled out of the royal lodge and gardens. But London had a comparatively small population then, and, so far as transit is concerned, was quite a distance from Kew, which did not need the defenses now necessary against holiday "roughs" and midnight marauders. Few coaches, I suspect, travelled thither in the last century. Thames barges and wherries carried but few pleasure-seekers so far. The Green must invariably have had the same aspect of sober somnolence as that which you may now once in a way observe there on autumn days. You may picture the royal squire and his wife acknowledging the loyal greeting of the motley little crowd of a hundred years ago; or, entering the gardens in imagination, with a certain clownish boy having three halfpence in his pocket and Swift's *Tale of a Tub* in his hand, recall William Cobbett's pleasant interview with the English King.

When you are tired of ruminating in this wise you may step aside to the banks of the Thames and recall the regal processions of boat and barge which, through several reigns, passed to and fro between London and Hampton Court. Or, what is still better, come with me and be introduced to the modern master of Kew Gardens, and the world's best authority on botany, theoretical and practical.

outlook upon one of those rich, velvet-like lawns that have a continual and never-ending charm for Americans. A desk covered with letters and reports, a pot of strange flowers, several colored facsimiles of rare plants. Over the mantel-shelf there is a medallion bust of Sir John Franklin, the arctic explorer, a vase of

SIR JOSEPH HOOKER.

We do not enter by the public gates. This "old Kensington" style of house, with odd nooks and corners of brick half hidden by ivy and other creepers, has an entrance from the Green, and its front gives upon the Gardens inside. We are received by a house-maid in the light print dress which obtains in country houses. Piloted along a passage adorned with old engravings, we enter Sir Joseph Hooker's study. It is a simple room, with an

white chrysanthemums, a study of the characteristic head of Professor Darwin. On the walls there are portraits of Sir Joseph's father (the first curator of Kew), John Lindley, and other men of note. There is a book-case full of miscellaneous literature, and here and there, on bracket and table, several Wedgwood plaques and bits of old Nankin "blue." It is the room of a man of taste, of a busy man whose avocations lie among beautiful things.

SIR JOSEPH HOOKER'S STUDY.

With an open forehead, a prominent nose, a firm mouth, Sir Joseph looks his life and career, which has been one of study, research, and exploration. Sixty-three years of age, he walks with the elastic step of a young man, and talks like most busy men, as if the future had nothing in store for him but a repetition of his past days of work, except, however, that they are full of new plans and developments.

The medallion of Franklin and other arctic memorials upon which our eyes fall emphasize the fact that Sir Joseph, then Dr. Hooker, in 1839 went out on board Sir James Ross's ship, the *Erebus*, to the Antarctic Ocean. The young medico's object was botanical research, and on his return he published his *Flora Antarctica*, which at once became a text-book. Ten years later the author made an excursion into the Himalayas for the purpose of investigating tropical vegetation. He was captured and imprisoned by a border rajah, who affected to see something more serious than botanizing in the adventurous

scientist's work. He returned to England from his perilous and varied travels in 1852, and published his famous *Himalayan Journals*, followed by some other well-known works on Indian plants and flowers. But it is no part of our plan to write his biography. He and his works are known in all countries. His name is familiar among botanists and gardeners in America, as it also is in India, Australia, New Zealand, and wherever the English language is spoken, and in many other countries where it is not.

Kew Gardens cover several hundred acres. They are diversified with wood and water. They contain specimens of forest trees and examples of plants and flowers from every part of the world, civilized and uncivilized. They include in a ring-fence the old palace built in the reign of James the First, and occupied by George the Third and Queen Charlotte. They have miles of glass houses, many interesting museums, a remarkable Chinese pagoda tower, and a palm house filled with the rarest of tropical growths. There is a special botanical garden where Sir Joseph, the curator, conducts his experiments in propagation and cultivation.

ing swept up into little brown hillocks upon the green grass.

"Letters represent a good deal of my work," he answers; "they come to Kew

IN THE ARBORETUM.

The pleasure-grounds are laid out with great care. Affording delight to the eye, they are also more or less made to contribute to the scientific uses of the institution.

"You must have a heavy correspondence," I remark, as we step out into the Gardens, where the falling leaves are be-

from all parts of Europe, Asia, Africa, and America, in reference to trees and plants. In the Herbarium you will find our people naming plants from the most unfrequented places. Many are sent to us in duplicate, and in return for additions to our collection we give them the names of plants which they have been unable to identify."

IN THE PALM HOUSE.

"You have had some rather remarkable successes in the introduction of useful and commercial plants in British colonies and dependencies?"

"Yes; we have been fortunate in the propagation of Colombian barks in India, more particularly in regard to the soft Colombian and hard Carthagena barks of commerce. We have grown some forty or fifty plants from cuttings which Mr. Cross brought from New Granada. We have introduced with great success the cinchona in Jamaica, the bark having come thence to England to be sold at a good price. We sent some cork oaks to the Punjab, which are doing well. We have established the rubber-yielding plants of South America in Ceylon and India, and Dr. Thwaites, of Ceylon, has distributed the seed in Feejee, Jamaica, Java, Sydney, Trinidad, Zanzibar, and Queensland."

"With regard to the cinchona, it is used as a substitute for quinine?"

"And proves an excellent

one," answered Sir Joseph. "It is not as pleasant as quinine, but taken in moderate doses the nauseating effects which used to be charged against it disappear. The cinchona plantations introduced from Kew in British Sikkim, Bengal, have paid four and a half per cent. on the capital outlay. I am informed that recently in India a method of making the sulphate itself has been discovered."

"Do medical men consider cinchona as good a febrifuge, for all practical purposes, as quinine?"

"Quite; and the price is a question of great importance, the pure sulphate being fifteen shillings an ounce, the other, three shillings."

"What kinds of seeds are most asked for by your correspondents at the present time?"

"The eucalyptus. We have good reports of the results of our propagation and distribution of this Australian genus from Assouan, Bengal, Bombay, Jamaica, Saharunpoor, Singapore, Zanzibar, and other places. We have also made great advances in the introduction of various fodder grasses. Another matter that will interest you is our progress in regard to the culture of Liberian coffee, which several of the Eastern colonies are now growing from our plants. The great demand for Liberian coffee is in New York. Lord Kimberley first mentioned the subject to me, and lately we have had some very gratifying reports of its profitable growth."

"What do you regard as your special work just now at Kew, that upon which you may be said to concentrate your efforts?"

"The raising of plants and seeds for the colonies and for other countries. Communication is now so rapid that the effect of our experiments is soon known. By-the-way, one of our latest records of success is the cultivation of mahogany in the Old World. We raised it from seed here at Kew, and have given it a home among the forest trees of India, Burmah, Singapore, and other places. Sometimes we have little difficulties placed in our way, but not often. We do not wait for the colonial or Indian governments to ask us for plants; we send them whatever is good for them."

This work of finding out what is desirable for a colony and providing it is the labor upon which Sir Joseph is chiefly engaged at Kew. In answering our questions he hardly once spoke in the first person singular, but invariably made a point of including his lieutenants and other subordinates in the administration of this great national institution.

While we talked we walked past beds of varied colors, chrysanthemum and other autumn flowers, over a vast carpet of closely mown grass, under the boughs of magnificent trees. Once in a way a positive red or yellow would suggest the fall foliage of America, but only to be made conspicuous by the sombre surroundings of the English tints. That portion of the Gardens called the Arboretum is a paradise of noble trees. It was originally a mere game preserve covered with rough timber and undergrowth. Five-and-twenty years of careful attention has converted it into a lovely park of lawns and walks and wood, in which every tree is named, and many of them are the outcome of the curator's planting. The Thames runs along this locality, and the gardens go down to the river in lawn and terrace, in tree and flower. What is here called "the old oak collection" contains a hundred trees upward of thirty years old, chiefly Asiatic and American. Recently a fine grove of American oaks at the bottom of Sion Avenue has been brought prominently in view by the removal of a collection of shrubs.

Among the buildings (and they are numerous), the most interesting to the general sight-seer, and probably not the least to the scientist, is the Palm House. It is situated almost in the centre of the grounds, with a broad terrace that looks upon a pond, picturesque with fringing weeds and willows. On summer days crowds of children and well-dressed people haunt this favorite spot, rambling at will through the great galleries of the crystal house of palms. The sheet-glass with which the house is glazed is tinted with green to modify the direct heat of the sun. The building is 362 feet long, 100 feet wide, and 66 feet high, with wings 50 feet wide and 30 feet high. The iron ribs of the structure are secured in heavy blocks of granite placed in solid concrete. The house is heated by six boilers, connected with a system of 20,000 feet of hot-water piping. It has an under-ground railway for the conveyance of coal and the removal of ashes. Sir Joseph conducted us around the galleries in the central por-

IN THE ORCHID HOUSE.

er and fruit. One of these marvels of vegetation is the *Arenga saccharifera* of the Indian Archipelago, of which it is said, "when the natives want wine they cut a branch of this tree, and attach a great pot to the stem at the place where the branch is cut, and in a day and night they find the pot filled: the wine is an excellent drink, and is got both white and red." Perhaps the best known and not the least beautiful of the palms in this house is the *Mauritia flexuosa*, which is found throughout the basins of the Amazon and Orinoco. "The earliest American voyagers and missionaries noticed its abundance in the delta of the Orinoco, and how in the season of inundations the natives dwelt on stages supported by the growing trunks, whose fruit afforded their chief food; so that to them it was truly *arbol de la vida*, or tree of life." There were very graceful specimens of the vegetable-ivory palm (*Phytelephas macrocarpa*), the banyan (*Ficus indica*), a superb *Crinum asiaticum*, and many other beautiful productions of tropical lands, including the mango, the coffee shrub, the tamarind, the orange, the cocoa-nut, the fig-tree, the coral plant, the bread-tree, the betel, and the wax palm. Sir Joseph spoke of these and other specimens as a man who loves them. He was more particularly concerned as to the ultimate fate of the finest specimen of the *Pandanaceæ* in Europe, which is gradually becoming too big for its new home. It has been lopped and cut in various directions, but it puts out new arms which already press against the roof.

"The truth is," said Sir Joseph, "since 1877 we have used here a new system of heating, under the influence of which many plants now flourish which formerly led only a languishing life. The tub in which this luxurious tree is growing stands on the iron grating over the hot-water pipes, and the tree fairly revels, as you see, in the genial warmth."

I have seen many stove-houses, including those of Chatsworth and Brussels, but none where the plants give such evident proof of thorough acclimatization as at Kew; and I have frequently noticed that English travellers who go out to hot countries invariably turn for their best illustrations of the vegetable

tion of the building, where we looked down upon a little world of palms and other tropical products that presented the most wonderful combination of leafy plumes and strange suggestions of flow-

and floral features of the tropics to Kew Gardens.

Next to the great Palm House, visitors to Kew seem most interested in the neighboring home of the great water-maize of Central America, named by English discoverers, in compliment to the Queen, *Victoria regia*. It was first successfully cultivated at Kew, and is still seen here in greater perfection than elsewhere, though Chatsworth has a beautiful rival in one of the hot-houses of the Duke of Devonshire's gardens. It is in the summer when the marvellous water-plant is in full bloom at Kew, its gigantic flowers and leaves covering the water space of 18,000 square feet there allotted to it. In the autumn it is little less wonderful to look upon, its great oval leaves lying upon the still water like enormous trays or tables, with delicately turned and carved edges. Flourishing in the same house with the Victoria are numerous examples of tropical as well as temperate plants, a curious palm being the *Nipa fructicans*, of which Sir Joseph Hooker writes in his *Himalayan Journals*, that "every now and then the paddles of the steamer [at the mouth of the Ganges] tossed up the large fruits of this low, stemless palm that grows in the tidal waters of the Indian Ocean, and bears a large head of nuts. It is a plant of no interest to the common observer, but of much to the geologist, from the nuts of a similar plant abounding in the tertiary formations at the mouth of the Thames,

and having floated about there, in as great profusion as here, till buried deep in the silt and sand that now form the island of Sheppey." The *Carludovica palmata* is worth noting. Of the leaves of this singular and picturesque grass the familiar Panama hat is made, touching which Sir Joseph mentioned some recent investigations into some reports of the British consul at Ning-Po, China, describing the trade in "Ning-Po hats," woven by hand from a species of *carex* (sedge), and which had grown into an important industry, 15,000,000 of them having been exported in 1878. Sir Joseph tells us that these hats were very abundant in London a year ago, and on examination he finds that the plant used in their manufacture is identical with that from which China matting is made, the only difference being that in making the hats the culms are used whole, while for matting they are split in two.

Sir Joseph never seemed more pleased than when discoursing upon the benefits that accrue from the propagation and cultivation of the economic plants, though he was equally at home among the more curious and eccentric specimens of nature's handiwork, some of which are to be found in the tropical stove-house near the Victoria tank previously mentioned, though they are more numerous in

THE BIG WATER-LILY.

THE ROYAL COTTAGE.

the eastern wing of the Orchid House. Here will be found the *sesquipedale*, of Madagascar, the spur of the flower of which is nearly as long as the name implies. Close by is the *Peristeria elata*, of Central America, where the people call it "El Espiritu Santo," because the column of the flower and its appendages are shaped somewhat like a dove. The pitcher-plants near the door leading into the central area occupied by the Victoria tank are among the lions of this department. These singular and beautiful plants are natives of southeastern Asia and the Indian Archipelago. It was while among the Bornean examples of these orchids that Mr. Burbridge went into ecstasies in *The Gardens of the Sun*, and one of which, the *Nepenthes bicalcarata*, the "two-spurred pitcher-plant," he has for the first time introduced into Europe alive. It may now be seen among the Veitch collection at Chelsea. Some species bear pitchers twelve inches long and six in diameter, large enough to hold two quarts of water. Wallace, in his *Malay Archipelago*, speaks of finding in the pitcher-plants on Mount Ophir, Malacca, half a pint in each, from which he and his companions, after ejecting many drowned insects, quenched their thirst. The inner surface of the jug-like formation is glandular, and during active vegetation secretes a fluid in which insects meet with "watery graves." There are other vegetable productions which are equally inimical to flies, the small plants called the American "side-saddle flower" (*Sarracenia*) and the *Darlingtonia*, for example. One has here at Kew an opportunity of verifying in a small way the observations of Dr. Torrey, who in their wild growth found the cavity of the leaves often partly full of water, apparently derived from rain or dews. It always contained dead insects, and sometimes so many that he has known their putrescence to render the swamps where the plants grow quite offensive. The insect comes to grief in this way: in creeping over the hairy surface of the lamina its feet become entangled in the hairs which extend beyond the orifice of the cavity, and it finds it difficult to return. Passing over the smooth upper surface of the tube, it is again detained by the hairs below, where it is either drowned or starved to death. "It has never been determined," says the botanist, "what purpose in the economy of the plant is thus accomplished." The Venus fly-trap (*Dionæa muscipula*) is a popular attraction in this house. A little crowd of curious gazers may often be seen here, as in the fly-catching lizards' house at the "Zoo," waiting for the immolation of an unfortunate fly. The plant so erroneously named after Venus is indigenous only in the eastern part of North Carolina.

The Temperate House, Miss North's new museum, the enlarged Botanical Museum, the Herbarium, and the other buildings of the place are full of interesting things.

Sir Joseph spoke with great satisfaction of his visit to America. "I accompanied the surveying party of the Topographical and Geological Surveys of the United States, on the invitation of the chief," he said, "in Colorado and Utah. During my travels I noted the most distinctive features of the vegetation of the middle regions of the continent from the Atlantic to the Pacific, including the eastern forests extending to the Mississippi, the prairies, the temperate, sub-alpine, and alpine zones of the Rocky Mountains and the Sierra Nevada, and the 'sequoia' and other coniferous forests of California." During these journeys he says he saw nearly every form of natural phenomena, and he spoke of the great park projected by the state as covering a region which would include examples of the leading physical phenomena of the earth, in addition to many of its most striking examples of vegetation. "Among the results of my journey," he added, "were a large collection of seeds and museum specimens, and a herbarium of about a thousand species, together with notes on the distribution of the North American trees in particular, as also several new correspondents in parts of the country whence I have since obtained some novelties."

There is a portion of the Gardens unchanged from the days when that rural crowd cheered the third George and his wife in the autumn years ago. Queen Victoria, when she dedicated Kew to the public, reserved this little plot—about half a dozen acres. It is railed in and kept apart from the rest of the grounds. The royal cottage where the King and Queen used to play at being poor people still remains. It is closed, and has not been opened for years. The park round about it is almost in a wild state. One day in the spring I walked over it, and it was a little world of bluebells; the wild hyacinth literally covered every yard of ground. The great trees grew up, as it were, out of them, hiding the sky, and keeping down the perfume which every breeze seemed to stir into a delicious activity.

All the red and gold of the sunset has gone out of the sky as we gradually leave Kew behind us and the cozy-looking houses on the Green. Lights begin to appear in the windows, and lamps to dot the roadway, where we linger to take a last glimpse of the sylvan scene, and to realize something of the soft, tender influences of the English twilight.

IN THE CACTUS HOUSE.

FRINGING the Channel coast, and against the background of laughing hills and cool orchard slopes, is a succession of fishing villages inhabited by a hardy sea-faring race. Although Normandy extends her arms and embraces the towns of Rouen, Caen, and Bayeux, the Norman, the lineal descendant of the Norseman, hugs the indented coast. Behind him lie the green luxuriance and nestling rose-embowered thatches. His gaze is seaward, piercing the salt spray, the veiling mist, the fury of the storm, or braving with undaunted eye the majesty of the sun upon the waters. He wears the tints of the rocks and the water—*le couleur du travail*—with the same instinct that a stone's-throw back clads the ploughman in the hues of the upturned furrow. But with the ploughman and his he never intermarries, and thus he has kept his race customs and traditions pure for centuries.

In summer the coasts of Normandy flower with the life from gay casinos and coquettish villas. Parisian toilets flutter down the narrow streets, and the shrill voices of the boulevard, and those not less shrill of the Faubourg St. Germain, penetrate the low, gloomy interiors, and surmount the sound of the incoming tide dashing against the cliff. But to the breath of high fashion and the sense of luxurious idleness the fisher-folk are alike insensible. But one sound is in their ears, to but one voice they hearken.

The gay idlers about them don the costume of the mussel-gatherer and the shrimper, and wade in the salt pools left by the tide, or bury their feet with delight in the black slime. The yachtsman hastens to exchange the luxuries of his craft for the rough fare of the fishing smack. They affect the Norman tongue, and the curt phrases intended to cut the blast and override the sound of the waves run trippingly from their tongues. But the fascinations of the airy, easy life about them make no mark on the fisher-folk, except, perhaps, to whet the keen edge of their love of gain.

Their harmony with their environment gives them pictorial interest, and attracts to the shores of Normandy that artistic life which has brought fashion and luxury in its train. Whether the fishing-boats come in with the tide, or the mussel-gatherers go out as it flows back, the composition is at hand, the moving groups dissolving from picture into picture.

The life of the fisher people, their unwritten laws, constitute a republic in a republic, the one in fact, the other in name. Each fishing craft is a corporation. Its owner is its captain. One man brings the rigging, another the nets, a third the tackle, a young boy the service of his strong arms and legs. Each, for his capital, whether in stock or labor, assumes his part of the risks, and receives a corresponding share in the haul. While the men are masters at sea, the women rule on land. Their labors are equally responsible and more varied. They comprehend the more intricate questions of finance, the condition of the market, and the state of competition. These are delicate matters, but their broad shoulders and lusty sinews fit them also for sterner work.

The Seine divides Normandy in twain. On the left side the magnificent sweep of beach dips gently into the water beneath the cliffs. At Honfleur and Trouville the fishing-boats ride at anchor in the finely constructed basins, for each is also a commercial port. But in the intervening villages the fishing life is much more characteristic, since it can only adjust itself to natural conditions. At Villersville the beach lies like a sandy plain, broken by low brown rocks extending far into the bay. The fishing-boats go out and come in with the tide. The boats lying at their ease among the rocks, like sentient things at rest, are righted as the waters flow around them. When they are thus afloat the men are carried out to them on the sturdy backs of their broad-hipped wives. When the tide calls them home, the wives are gathered on the beach, babes in arms, and children playing on the sand. Long since, the lookout has spied them with her glass. Every sail and spar is known. As they skim over the water, the rowers quicken their speed, and a deft hand furls the sails. They glide into the anchorage, and the fishermen's labor is over. Then the women, the stout-limbed mussel-gatherers, wade out to the boat. They carry the baskets to land, and returning, bring the men pickback triumphantly to shore. The lithe young girls seize the baskets and hurry up the cliffs, their quick commercial instincts alive to the need of fore-

RETURN OF THE MUSSEL-GATHERERS.

MENDING NETS AT LOW TIDE.

stalling competition. The fisherman goes slowly homeward, his wife and children about him, and the baby in his arms.

Here are the most important mussel grounds of the coast, and on these the women reign supreme. As the tide runs quickly out, the procession of mussel-gatherers, their baskets on their back, begins its descent. In a short time the great plain lies revealed, with here and there shining shallow pools, and is swarming with gray stooping figures. From the cliff above they seem part of the landscape, so perfectly they assimilate with it. The path to the mussel grounds is treacherous. The brown rocks are covered with sea-weed, and suddenly lose themselves in black slime, shining like polished marble, but offering unknown depths to the false step. But the mussel-gatherer walks with sure step, and keeps close to the receding tide.

The mussel of the Channel coast is one of its most dainty products. The tide leaves it clinging in clusters among the sea-weed to the hidden rocks. Twice a day it seems to have blossomed and borne fruit like a miraculous plant in this great garden of the sea. The mussel-gatherer with her sharp knife detaches them, and throws them into her basket. To the dull eye, slime, weed, shells, all is vague, but she works with that sort of instinct that is bred in our own manufactories.

The mussel ground, like the washing pool, is the village newspaper and Dorcas society. The younger women and the older gossips gather together, and the noise of their chatter rises above the sound of the waves; the doings of the village are discussed, and the presence of the stranger offers opportunity to the village wit to exercise

A SHRIMPER.

her powers of humor under her breath, and to the unqualified delight of her neighbors. Down the cliff and out among the rocks come the carts, drawn by stout Norman horses. The women throw the cords around their necks, and dexterously swinging the heaping baskets on to their backs, carry them to the carts. Returning empty, they begin their work again, until the tide comes creeping in, and drives them shoreward, working as they go.

The shrimper is always a lonely figure, following the tide through pools knee-deep, waving her net like a great-winged bird. The labor is light, but each sweep of her vigorous arm and the dip of her net in the water is the throw of a die. That element of uncertainty which accompanies so closely the fisherman's calling drives her on until stout legs and arms are weary. The deep cone-shaped net comes up brimming, and as the water drops in shining showers, her eager eyes peer into its depths. The shrimp is her silver and gold. The shining *crevette* is the stake for which she plays, and now the capricious waves line her net with its silver gleam, and now fill it with worthless refuse.

The fishing life on the other side of the Seine has more striking characteristics. The conformation of the coast is altogether different. The very cliffs confront the Channel waves, a sturdy wall defending the green fields and hoary farms of Caux. Here and there the inland streams have bitten their way through the cliffs. The beach is strewn with the débris, which the waves have licked into great round pebbles. Étretat, Fécamp, Yport, St.-Valery-en-Caux, are but morsels bitten out of the cliffs, where the semicircular sweep of beach, guarded at each end by the lofty rock, makes landing, not harbor, for the fishing-boats. The peculiarity of the coast makes the fisherman wary. In the sudden storms which sweep up and down the Channel the inhospitable cliffs afford him no refuge. Unless he can make his port, he must keep to the open sea, or run the peril of the rocks. Thus the fishing life on this coast is full of sharp contrasts, and in the midst of calm, danger and anxiety on sea and land always lie near the surface.

The beach at Étretat is very picturesque. The encroachments of fashion have seized half of this, and bestrewed it with sum-mer hotels, a casino, and all those gay surroundings which supply the diversions of the idle summer days. The dividing line is sharp which separates those who work from those who play. From the Hôtel Hauteville to the lofty cliff the beach at Étretat is a constant scene of picturesque industry: the launching of boats; the sharp grate of the keel upon the pebbles as, impelled by the swift rowers, it leaps on the shore; the groups mending nets; the mossy old hulks on the banks, the receptacles for nets and tackle, giving forth odors of tarred rope; the women harnessed to the capstan dragging the boats up the steep pebbly terraces to await the incoming tide; the washer-women holding a high carnival of cleanliness at the fountain; the babies crowing in the idle boats while the mothers work; and the children running like young cherubs from shore to sea.

From without, the gloomy dark interior of the fishing hut is significant of the drudgery and apparent joylessness of the fisherman's life. But this view is superficial. The Norman wife has also her housewifely ambitions. Poverty, as we understand it, has here no meaning. Her home is the abode of decency and cleanliness. Of such, Mère Gradot is a type. In front of the dingy gray hut, with its little windows hap-hazard breaking through the stone, her fish-market stands, newly built of brick, with pots of geranium brightening the air. The narrow, crazy stairs pierce the gloom of the interior. Below, half buried in the ground, is the kitchen, with its wide-mouthed fire-place and *petit four*, on which the *pot au feu* fills the air with its savory smell. The brick floor shines with frequent scouring. Old Rouen faience, such as the bric-à-brac dealers on the Rue Alphonse Karr tempt the summer loiterers with, makes bands of color ranged endwise on the buffet shelves, and two silver tankards are conspicuously displayed. The buffet of shining yellow wood is brilliantly polished, and with the great armoire, curiously wrought as to hinges and fastenings, is here as elsewhere the joy of every Norman fish-wife's heart. Above the fire-place hang a few kitchen utensils of copper, as resplendent as decorative plaques. The light from the window, half above-ground, falls through blue curtains, and thus softly subdued the room is full of deep rich color, yel-

A TYPE.

low, red, blue, in harmonies that artistic resources with definite purpose can not always compel.

"But perhaps ma'm'selle will prefer her own room," said Mère Gradot, half disdaining her own pride in the stranger's astonished admiration.

"Denise will show ma'm'selle, and Jehan will go to the diligence and bring her things, and all will be arranged." The crazy stairs wind aloft. Denise, smiling, thoughtful-faced, opens the door gently.

"Does ma'm'selle think she can be comfortable here? Perhaps the Hôtel Hauteville is too crowded for the contentment of the guests."

The little room is decked like a shrine. There is a sense of sacrilege in profaning its purity with a traveller's dusty belongings. Everything is virginal white. Snowy draperies flutter at the window in the warm sea-laden air. The toilet-table is dressed in white, with knotted fringes swaying. The bed with its tent-like hangings rises like a mound of snow in one corner. There are curious shell-like ornaments, and childish balls of gilt and colored glass on the mantel, and pictures of the Virgin and the Bleeding Heart upon the walls. Denise unlocks the great armoire, piled full of fragrant linen, and brings out an armful of towels that shed an odor of lavender throughout the room.

The *patron* is a small man with bronzed and wrinkled face, and a pair of kindly blue eyes under shaggy beetling brows. His presence in the house diffuses a sort of mild joy. Henri sits by his knee and strokes his rugged hand, and Denise makes excuse to linger that he may lay his hand on her hair. Even the loud tones of the great blonde cousin Margot soften in his presence.

In Calvados and the western shore the fish-wives are in the employ of the dealers, and take a large share of the rough work. Here the beaching of the boats spares them much of the drudgery, and they themselves approach the dignity of *commerçantes*.

Each morning Mère Gradot's counter is spread with shining mackerel, the rosy mullet, and much-prized sole, amid heaps of *éperlans* and bouquets; and twice a week Denise goes to Havre for *langoustes*, a species of lobster rarely found here. Grim, rough-favored Mère Gradot, with a sort of artistic instinct almost universal

along the coast, gives her fish-market a festal air which nearly atones for its fishy odors. But she holds her own with shrewd tenacity among the airy Parisian toilets and white-capped cooks which make here daily rendezvous. In the afternoon Denise and Margot take the fish that are left and carry them in baskets from door to door, and to the remoter quarters of the peasantry. From morning to evening there is no respite to their labor, for the house is kept immaculately clean, and Denise finds time to broil and serve in unknown and toothsome fashion the mackerel and mullet, and toss with deft hand the savory omelet. All these duties are performed with serious gravity. No angry word is heard in Mère Gradot's home, but never also a merry laugh.

"Do you always work so hard, Denise? Do you never amuse yourself?"

"In summer, ma'm'selle, one must work, but in winter we amuse ourselves."

"And when do you marry, Denise?"

Denise blushed. "After the herring fishing is over, then we may marry, ma'm'-selle."

"That is in October. In three months, then, Denise?" since her consciousness had made the question personal.

"Yes, ma'm'selle. And would you really like to know? I will have a white gown, and a wreath of flowers on my head. After we have been to the mayoralty we will go to the church and be married. Then we will drive as far down as Ernestine's, and perhaps through the forest to Yport. In the evening we will dance. At the Casino? Oh no. The Place du Maire will be so clean, and the stones be sprinkled with fine sand, and we will dance in the open air. Oh, it will be gay after the herring fishing. Louis and Madeleine, Jehan and Liszen, Pierre and Véronique, I know not how many, are waiting for the herring fishing."

"And Margot—is Margot not waiting?"

"Ah, Margot. Margot must grow wearier, for Georges Duroc has gone with the men from Fécamp after cod, away in the North among the summer ice."

"And do all the girls marry, Denise?"

"Why, yes, ma'm'selle. Even Suzanne, the *donne*, married. It would be a weary life for the women without the going and the home-coming."

"But the danger and the anxiety?"

"Ah, ma'm'selle, that keeps René closer in my heart."

AN INTERIOR.

The home-coming of *La Sainte du Cœur d'Or* is due. Toinette, the "look-out," has been on the beach all day with her long glass, while Toto is in glorious liberty within the safe confines of an idle boat. When Toinette throws down her glass with a joyful cry, Henri, hovering near, brings the news, and we hasten to

ON THE LOOKOUT.

the beach. Toinette and Toto are on the brink, and as the boat flies like a bird on to the shore, Louis leaps out and catches Toto in his arms. Toinette clings to his arm, and with the *patron* holding Henri by the hand, his mild blue eyes shining, we go up the bank, where Mère Gradot waits, harnessed to the capstan.

"C'est bien, mon ami?"

"Bien, Marthe."

The capstan has four arms. The *patron* and Louis place themselves behind two, and Pierre and Grandjean lend their strong arms to the other two. In front of the *patron* is Mère Gradot with a leather strap around her neck, and Toinette slips another across her shoulders, attached to the arm that Louis commands. The capstan creaks as they begin their slow rounds, and the cable grows taut. At the water's edge Jehan and Pierre have greased guttered boards, which they slip under the keel; these give place to billets of wood, changed as frequently as the slow movements of the capstan may require. At length *La Sainte du Cœur d'Or* reaches her moorings high up on the rocky terrace, and the men hasten to take charge of the haul.

The fish are piled in baskets, but the last haul lies in the nets. These are tossed out on the pebbles, full of live writhing things struggling to free themselves from the inextricable meshes. Several are dead, bruised to death in their efforts to escape. The arrival of a boat attracts a crowd, and the gay population from the Casino flutter thitherward. The fish are thrown out one by one, and the bidding begins. The competition is open, and the prudent householder from the villa takes his chances with the fish-wife here rather than on her own ground. They struggle hand to hand over the sole. The sole is, during the season, the chief prize of the fisherman, and the swarms of cat and more pugnacious fish have made the sole wary. There are but four or five in the net, and the *patron* has reckoned that they shall bring him more than they would fetch at Havre, or even at Les Halles. The demands of Paris have largely increased the trade at Havre, Fécamp, and

ment, but the *patron* speaks low, and the fish-wives are curt and otherwise silent. The children pick out the refuse with nimble fingers, and the visiting dogs sport with the crabs in a sort of fearful fascination. When the nets are cleared, the baskets are taken to the house, and the fish packed among straw in the tall crates and sent by the diligence to Havre.

The Fountain, at low tide, is one of the picturesque sights of Étretat. In fact, except at low tide, the Fountain does not exist. It is here the subterranean river finds its way into the Channel. As soon as the tide releases the spot, the women have gathered, and with their spades and strong arms scoop out large round basins in the pebbles, and into these the fresh, clear water of the river bubbles up. Into

SUNDAY MORNING.

Dieppe, and drained the length of the coast. Of late years there has been ill success on the Channel coast among the fishermen, and the summer appetite at Étretat is great. The bidding is more animated since it brings in a different ele-

these basins the women put their clothes, and, if need be, the smooth round pebbles serve as wash-boards. But each woman has with her a long bottle filled with a whitish fluid, with which she deluges the obstinate stain. It is the insidious liquid washing soda that has made its way into a community which is singularly free from other forms of vice.

As the tide recedes, the women follow it with their spades, and build barriers against the lap of the waves into their pebbled tubs. There is no choice of places except as the personal preferences and social qualities of the workers indicate. The flow of water is so abundant that the basins are clustered closely together, leaving only space enough for the kneeling women. When the sun shines, the gray and white figures, the piles of white and shining clothes on the pebbles, the sparkling sea, make a scene of dazzling light and beauty, which the cool shadowy sides of the tall cliff throw into greater relief.

For a week the sky has been filled with summer brightness, but now the shifting clouds betoken rain. In the evening René comes up to bid Denise good-by, as his boat is to leave that night at three for a longer cruise after fish that are wary of the coast. The morning is lowering, and a breeze beats up the Channel. To the eye every phase of the Channel is beautiful, but the fishermen linger on the beach in the thickening weather, and the boats that are to start in the afternoon do not put out. The gale increases, and the waves dash through the great ogive windows which the waters have licked through the cliff and bespatter its side with foam. The idlers of the Casino, wrapped in water-proofs, hang over the sides of the promenade, and, sheltered behind the glass windows of the conversation-room, watch the waves tearing down and building up the pebbled terraces of the beach. It is only another spectacle more grand and imposing than the rest which nature has kindly produced to ward off some possible *ennui* of the long summer days.

On the heights above, by the side of the high-road, yet commanding the view up and down the Channel, is one of those calvaries so associated with the landscape of Catholic countries, and which to the foreigner is one of its novel and consequently interesting features.

It is the Man of sorrows, acquainted with grief, with hands outstretched upon the cross. The details of the carving are rude and commonplace, and from the top of a diligence, or seen through the dust of flying wheels, the lachrymose visage, begrimed with dust, only awakens the thoughtless jest. With other eyes there is something touching in the ungainly figure patiently waiting, through mud and weather, laughter and mockery, for the possible day of sorrow and tears. It has come. The rain falls furiously, and, driven by the strong west wind, the drops have stinging force. Wrapped in water-proofs, with Denise's cousin, Margot, her fair hair flying from under the fichu she has wound about her head, we struggle up the road. Upon the steps which lead up to the calvary the women whose men are out in the boats have thrown themselves with tears and prayers. Standing on the topmost step is Denise, her arms flung about the cross, and her tearless eyes raised in an agony of supplication. Her wrappings, unloosed by the fierce wind, have fallen in sculpturesque folds about her slender figure. Denise herself might be some statue, so immovable she stands. The artistic relation of the figures, the composition, as it were, is striking, and the service which the natural expression of the emotions renders to art obtrudes like a sacrilegious thought.

"Denise! Denise!" Margot calls, but can scarcely make her voice heard through the storm.

"It is useless. Let us go back for the *patron*. Denise will get her death. The wind has torn her fichu from her neck, and her throat is bare."

Margot smiled. "No; let her be. It will give her rest. There is nothing else now."

Nothing was heard from the boats all day.

"Life or death, I must get some mussels for Madame De Hautepin. The tide is low at four in the morning, and I will take L'Épine the donkey, and go by L'Aiguille d'Étretat down near Ernestine's, where one can find mussels if they can be found."

In the night the wind lulls, and only the sound of the waves is heard beating against the pebbles. In the struggling light Mère Gradot starts with L'Épine for her lonely walk beneath the cliff.

To the rest of us the night is heavy with sleep. Denise, overcome by exhaustion, has not wakened. Some time during the morning Mère Gradot comes into the little white room. Her stern, hard face is softer. She sits down, after those little polite salutations are made which no French woman, gentle or lowly, omits.

A FUNERAL.

"René has come," she says, simply.

"Oh, Mère Gradot!"

"With me."

"Have you told Denise?"

"One would not wake her for this. See. I took L'Épine and went for the mussels. It was dark; we could scarcely see. The path beneath the cliff is narrow, and the waves broke over it, so L'Épine and I had to keep close to the cliff. When we reached Ernestine's the tide had fallen a little, but it was hard finding mussels; the water had been too rough. I had to wait, and after a while I saw a heap of stuff wedged in between the rocks which the water had left. The sea sometimes brings strange things. I went to the place. It was dark, but I saw it was a man drowned. I pulled off the sea-weed. The face was downward. I turned the body, but it was bruised—so bruised I could not see it; but in the shirt was a little pin. Denise had given such a pin to René. I lifted the body up—it was hard work—and laid it on the poor beast's back. L'Épine and I brought poor René home."

"Oh, Mère Gradot! Alone in the darkness by that wild sea!"

"Yes. Was it not fortunate? It will be better for Denise."

The details of the catastrophe came later. The fishing-boat had been run over by a packet from Southampton to Havre, driven out of her course by the gale.

A funeral among the fisher people is as much a matter of consolatory pride as among other folk. By the wise provisions of the Church the funeral train which bore René from his home to the church is composed of participants, not spectators. Even the little ones bear their candles, and identify themselves with the solemn ceremonies.

Denise goes through all the scenes with that sort of stoicism which is peculiar to the Norman blood.

"She is cut deep, that girl," says Mère Gradot. "We must spare her, and send her to her aunt Leyrand, at Boulogne. Ma'm'selle will perhaps see her there."

The fishing quarter of Boulogne is over the hill, by the Rue de Constantine—a winding road, carrying in its name, as one finds elsewhere in Boulogne, reminiscences of the old Roman occupation. It is a compact, well-built little brick village, on the slope of the hill. The place is deserted.

Following the street until it overlooks the sandy beach beneath, a strange sight is presented. All the women of the village are on their knees making wide circles in the sand with their vigorous arms and sturdy fingers. When they have loosened enough sand, they gather it into their baskets, and swing them on to their backs and toil up the hill. Their movements are those of instinct in animals, but their social instincts are those of women. It is their afternoon rendezvous, and this gathering of sand daily to sand their floors their lighter and more elegant recreation.

Denise is not here, but at the herring factory near the Quai des Paquebots.

At six o'clock the streets are filled with the fisher girls going home from their work among the herrings—a picturesque procession which always allures the stranger, flitting never so hurriedly from train to steamer. Among them is Denise.

"Oh, Denise, how pretty you look!"

She wears the costume of the Boulogne fisher girl, the most piquant of the coast. Her brown dress is cut low, and laced over the white shirt beneath. About her waist a blue apron is tied, and her blue fichu, crossed low on her breast, is knotted behind with careless grace. On her head is a white cap, with a snowy frill standing erect like a halo around her head, and framing her sad face, which brightens a little at my involuntary praise.

"You like it here, Denise?"

"For myself, well enough; but my father misses me, and my mother with the accounts, and Margot finds the basket heavy without Denise."

"We all missed you, Denise; but the patron has had great luck with his sole, and Mère Gradot sends fish to the château every day, and Henri helps Margot with the basket."

"I go back in two months. The girl is better with the mother. I miss the dear kind hand of the father on my hair, and Margot and little Henri. I go back, yes, in two months. Then we will all miss ma'm'selle," she added, with her thoughtful politeness.

"And ma'm'selle. Do you think she can ever forget the patron, Mère Gradot, Denise, Margot, or the little Henri, or cease to remember the peaceful hours in the little white room of the fishing hut at Étretat?"

Ah, no, Denise!

CHRYSANTHEMUMS.

IF the chrysanthemum does not actually share the honors of popularity with the rose, it certainly has characteristics and distinctions the rose does not possess. The remarkable variations of the different types are so conspicuous as to almost make us believe, in many instances, they have no relation, so entirely different in structure is each of the family groups. It matters not whether we admire most the tiny flowers of the pompons which individually are not more than three-quarters of an inch in diameter, yet so numerous as to cover the entire plant with a solid sheet of bloom, or the largest Japanese varieties with their grotesquely shaped ragged flowers of six or more inches, or the Chinese varieties with their symmetrical globular forms which are often four or five inches in diameter, there is a fascination so irresistible as to make their cultivation, when once begun, almost a mania. Again, the range of colors is very great, especially in neutral tints, which are

introduction being evidently from Japan, under the name of *Matricaria japonica maxima*, having large flowers of yellow, white, blush, purple, and crimson. Breynius, a great botanist, thus describes them as having been brought to Holland in 1689. We should infer that these were single-flowered kinds. The pompon type, with single flowers, was figured by Rheede in 1699. Linnæus, in 1753, refers to *sineuse*, with large white flowers, and to *indicum*, with small yellow flowers, double and single. They are again noticed by Thunberg, in 1784, as *matricaria*. In all probability their introduction was not considered of much interest. Like many other plants introduced in those times, their economical or commercial value was the object, rather than decoration, as the great order of Compositæ to which they belong had furnished many valuable additions to medicine. In the beginning of the present century, when the flower began to receive some attention as a decorative plant, disputes arose as to whether it was a *matricaria*, *anthemis*, or *artemisia*, to end which it was decided to make a new species, and to call it *Chrysanthemum*, from *chrysos*, gold or golden, and *anthos*, a flower. The commerce with China having grown to considerable proportions about 1800, many plants and seeds found their way to different countries through merchants. Though we have no record of their introduction into America, undoubtedly they were known here as early as 1820, for from facts brought to notice of late we find many varieties are to be found in old gardens on Long Island that have been there for over fifty years. These differ but little from the varieties described at that time in some old periodicals, and were probably raised from

made up of whites, yellows, all shades of bronze, chromes, and ambers, rich browns, deep purples, rose, and pink shades.

The introduction and history of the flower is one of unusual interest. We find it has been known to the gardens of Europe for two centuries, the first

TUBULIFLORA.

seed direct from China. In France the raising of numerous seedlings and selecting of the largest double-flowered, with petals curving inward, was carried on with great vigor after 1820, and these are the immediate ancestors of the Chinese in-curved type as grown to-day. The pompons would seem to have been lost, or at least were not grown by florists previous to 1845, when Robert Fortune re-introduced them as Chusan daisies. To him also we are indebted for the introduction of the immediate progenitors of the present Japanese kinds directly from Japan in 1859. The Japanese varieties are now at the head of the family in popularity. So variable are they in shape and coloring as to defy description, and, while each flower is beautiful by itself, they present very attractive groups; many kinds with one or two rows of petals and large yellow disks, resembling giant flowers of the ox-eye daisies—some as regular and flat in form as though stamped from some geometrical design, others with the outer rays quite flat, and the inner ones curved and twisted in fantastic shapes.

The chrysanthemum in China and Japan is the national emblematic flower, receiving the most reverential care and attention, surpassing by far in devotion that accorded to the fleur-de-lis, lilies, roses, and thistles, the emblems of other countries. Each recurring year, in November, in all large cities in Japan, and on nearly every street, thousands of plants are sold, trained generally to one stem, with a solitary large flower of immense size, often ten to twelve inches across. A very ordinary flower of some six inches is sold for five cents, the very largest specimens being sold for twenty-five cents, pot included.

POMPONS AND MARGUERITES.

The chrysanthemum is thoroughly cosmopolitan, thriving alike in smoky cities or suburban villages, and no plant is so much at home in large towns. One of the great attractions of London in November is the display at the Temple and Inner Temple Gardens, several thousand plants being grown and arranged in beds and borders, their only protection being a simple muslin awning drawn over them each evening. Thousands of people visit the display daily. These annual exhibitions have been given regularly since 1850, and in 1859 there were grown at the Temple Gardens over five hundred varieties, apparently a very great number; but these sink into insignificance by the side of over two thousand varieties that are to be found in the catalogues of to-day. In this multiplicity of varieties there are many apparently identical, or lacking distinctiveness, to the casual observer, whereas those

intimately acquainted with them have no difficulty in
determining individual kinds. Of course so many
kinds are in most cases produced from seed, and as
each *seedling* is undoubtedly, in the chrysanthemum,
as in all other plants, physiologically a distinct individual, where many are engaged in raising and distributing any particular family of
plants the varieties become numerous
and conflicting. It is not by seed
alone that new varieties of chrysanthemums are obtained, as many are
produced by bud variation, known in

the vernacular
of gardeners as
sports. This change
takes place frequently
after a variety has been
cultivated a few years. Branches bearing entirely different-col-
ored flowers, and sometimes of
quite a distinct form, occur on
the same plant, and if the branch
is allowed to mature, and the
young shoots from the base of
this branch are propagated, the
variation becomes a fixed form.
Indeed, some of the most popular and handsome kinds that are
found to-day were obtained in
this way, and no plant or class
of plants *sports* as much. There
does not seem to be any rule as to this
sporting, though the majority of sports
have been from white to yellow and from
white to pink, and *vice versa*.

The cultivation of the chrysanthemum
as compared with the cultivation of the
rose is of the most simple description, re-

JAPANESE VARIETIES.

quiring only a rich soil, a sunny or a partially sunny position, and occasional waterings in extreme droughts. Young plants set in the ground during April and May will with some little attention make specimens of two feet in diameter. The tops of the leading or strongest growths should be removed by pinching, after the shoots have grown four or five inches long, and this should be continued until the end of July, after which the entire plant should be allowed to grow. The flower buds begin to form about the end of August or beginning of September. If it is desirable to have them flower in the house or conservatory—a plan which is highly recommended—they should be dug up carefully about the first of October, and placed in pots according to the size of each plant. For the very largest plants pots ten or twelve inches in diameter are required. The plants should be well drenched with water at once, and set in some shady place for a few days, after which they can be exposed to the full sun. They must be protected before the appearance of frost, but should not be subjected to artificial heat, a temperature of forty-five to fifty degrees Fahrenheit being quite high enough. Where they are intended to flower out-of-doors it is best either to plant them at first in some sheltered position, or to dig carefully and remove to such a place after the middle of October. With this simple care they are among the most satisfactory of all flowers. With such popularity of course the chrysanthe-

mum is an exhibition flower, and for this purpose many very large specimens are grown in comparatively small pots in various shapes. Some, grown as bushes, are to be seen from four to six feet in diameter; others, grown as small trees, on stems four or five feet high, are surmounted with heads two or more feet in diameter, literally covered with flowers. Others, again, are trained in severe pyramidal and convex forms. The flowers are also grown individually for exhibition, and attain a very large size, the plant being allowed to carry but few buds, which are removed from time to time during September, until the largest plants have only a half-dozen flowers to support. These are obtained by strict attention to watering and stimulating with manure water three or four times each day during the growing season.

As to hardiness, many of the varieties will endure the severest winter weather in climates as cold as New York State, providing they are slightly protected by loose leaves and a few branches of evergreens to keep the leaves in position. The covering of snow is a sufficient protection in winter. The older kinds, as a rule, are somewhat hardier than those of modern date, but in cases where they are winter-killed they are easily replaced at very slight cost. Where plants are already in pots, a sure and simple way of keeping them is to place them in any cool light cellar, a cool pit, or out-house, where the extreme weather is somewhat tempered.

XVIII.

THE flight of Charles from Whitehall did not more really empty the royal seat, in the view of the Parliament, than had already his armed intrusion upon the sanctity of the House of Commons.

Accordingly, now, the Parliament began to take off the robes of his prerogatives, one by one, and as there was no Henry of Bolingbroke just then about the precincts of Westminster Hall, they proceeded to hang them upon a dummy king, an office and authority without either body, soul, or spirit. So they legislated and decreed for a while "in the king's name."

But those of them who could not bring their imagination to such a metaphysical point left the speculative region of Westminster, and sought the denuded son of James, whom they found making martial efforts to get back into his own again. He secured a "land army" at last, but by that time it was unhappily opposed by another. There were two "powers of the sword" in the field, and a great duel was preparing between "the crown" and "the cause."

The civil war, for a while, was very much like the American in the outset, "bushwhacking on a large scale." Neither side, thanks to the pacific James, had had any military experience, and there was consequently a good deal of gallant blundering on the part of the one, and of indefinite struggling on the part of the other. The style of it had already been anticipated in the great Hall at Westminster during the days before the crisis was precipitated, when the nicknames "Roundhead" and "Cavalier" were roared out under its roof, as Colonel Lunsford and his curled adventurers rode in to drive out the close-cropped London apprentices on one day, to find themselves beset and surrounded on the next with cries of "Slash us now!"

In the same way the royalist army had the advantage until Cromwell came to the front, and, with him, organized victory. Then the Cavaliers were cut down, and the kingdom was cleared.

Long before this, however, the Commons had put aside their dummy, and the way was getting open to an actual empty throne, and to a king with no claim to the name. Even the Church of England had gone by the board. Laud was beheaded. There was nowhere a mitre to be seen. Westminster Abbey was a Presbyterian meeting-house. At last Charles, who had stood out for episcopacy as the main bulwark of his throne, gave himself up to the Presbyterian Scots. The Scots gave him up to the Presbyterian Parliament. Then the army of Independents took him away from the Parliament, and now Cromwell had him in hand.

Charles was brought from Hurst Castle, which he had feared was to be his Berkeley or his Pontefract, and brought conveniently near to Westminster. The Commons were above any scandal of an assassination. They were resolved upon a more open and impressive way of putting an end to him than on the former occasions of Edward of Carnarvon and Richard of Bordeaux. Westminster Hall should be the preliminary scene of it again, but they would go about it in all the formal majesty of the law.

On January 20, 1649, this "high (or high-handed) Court of Justice" was opened in the great Hall. One hundred and thirty-five persons had been fixed upon by the Independent Commons to compose it. Only sixty-nine or seventy could be got to sit. Some were officers in the army, some members of the Commons; the remainder were citizens of London. It was, to a man, a court of the people.

The spectacle was as bare of scenic grandeur as of everything else. In the absence of everything else, they were not at all indisposed to make as great a show as they could. There was the usual blaze of scarlet and crimson over the graded seats of the judges, which ran up against the southern wall. Bradshaw, the "Lord President," sat in a crimson velvet chair on a platform in front of and below them, enveloped in a scarlet robe, and wearing a great broad-brimmed hat. A desk with a crimson velvet cushion was before him. In the middle of the space in front was a large square table, covered with a rich Turkey carpet, on which lay the golden mace and the sword of state across one another. The steel halberds of a numerous guard were seen gleaming on either side and down the length of the Hall. Inside the bar—a partition running across some distance below, and inclosing the court—at the very centre, was the crim-

TRIAL OF CHARLES I.—After John Barnett.

son chair for the king, with its back to the bar, and directly facing the Lord President, over the intermediate table where the "regalia" lay, and the two clerks sat. This was all that could come down to them in the tradition of the now extinct realm. The splendors of royalty could not descend to this: the king was in the shadow of death. There were none of the rich robes of the nobility: the nobles were exiled or dead. There were no ermined judges: the judges had refused to sit. The brilliant insignia of the kingdom, which once had been wont to flash from every side in this Hall of kings, lay in total eclipse. Not an armorial bearing, except those wrought in the roof, was to be seen, save the new "arms of the Commonwealth," the red cross of England and the gold harp of Ireland, emblazoned on a huge escutcheon which hung under the great southern window, and shone over the topmost tier of those who composed the regicide court. We have forgotten two ornaments: there, high up against the wall, directly under the new arms, sat Oliver Cromwell and Henry Martin.

On either side, looking down upon the hatted heads of the court, was a double gallery. The rest of the Hall was also prepared for the vast concourse that was sure to be there.

When the court had been seated and all was ready, the gates were thrown open, and the multitude thronged in, filling the galleries, the scaffoldings, and the immense open area of the floor. Then Bradshaw ordered the sergeant-at-arms "to bring in the prisoner." The king entered, and proceeded up the side next the Thames, under the guard of thirty-two officers, bearing halberds. He was attended also by his servants. The sergeant-at-arms with his men received him and conducted him within the bar. There were none so poor to do him reverence. Not a sign of respect was shown. Amid the awful hush he stood for a moment facing the court with a stern, steadfast gaze. Then he looked up at the galleries in front and on either side of him. He had suffered his hair and beard to grow, and they had become gray. His once handsome, pensive face looked pale and worn under the shadow of his hat. The banners of Marston Moor, of Naseby, and of Preston hung over his head. He sat down, then immediately rose again, as if he had forgotten something, turning com-

pletely round and gazing down the long vista of the Hall, crowded with ten thousand of his subjects, among whom on every side gleamed the bright axes of the halberdiers. The moment he resumed his seat the blazing escutcheon of the Commonwealth caught his eye, with Cromwell's eyes beneath it fastened intently on him. It was eight years since Strafford here fought his accusers, at last to die by his hand. It was twenty-four years since his coronation banquet in this room, when the steel gauntlet of his champion had rung upon this floor. And here was he now, king, by hereditary right, of England and of Scotland, the heir of Egbert, and Kenneth, and William the Conqueror, with the blood of all these in his veins. Was there no one to befriend or defend him?

There was a disturbance in his favor at the very outset. When the crier called over the court, amid the blank hush of many absences, there came the name of Sir Thomas Fairfax, the General of the Parliament. A voice answered for him from the gallery above, "He has too much wit to be here!"

Bradshaw now addressed the king: "Charles Stuart, King of England, the Commons of England, being deeply sensible of the calamities that have been brought upon this nation, which are fixed upon you as the principal author of them, have resolved to make inquisition for blood."

When the charge was read, "in the name of the people of England," the same voice spoke from the gallery: "It is a lie —not a tenth part of them." Axtell, the officer of the guard, ordered his men to fire into the box. But the muskets were soon lowered. It was Lady Fairfax!

Charles himself, when he heard himself accused of being "a tyrant and traitor, a murderer and a public enemy," laughed in the face of the court. Once during the reading he stretched out his gold-headed cane and touched Coke, the Solicitor-General, lightly on the shoulder, saying, "Hold!" The head of the cane dropped off. No one moved to pick it up. He stooped and picked it up himself, showing no embarrassment at the moment, though he afterward told Bishop Juxon that the omen deeply affected him. The president ordered the clerk to go on, saying to Charles that "if he had anything to say afterward, the court would hear him."

When called upon to answer the charges,

OLIVER CROMWELL.

From bust in National Portrait Gallery, modelled from life by Edward Pierce, Jun.

he declined to recognize the jurisdiction of the court, or its competency, giving his reasons, and declaring his readiness, before a properly constituted tribunal, to answer in his defense. His bearing was dignified, his manner ready.

On two other days the court sat with a like result. On the last of these more general signs of sympathy with him broke out. Cries of "God save the king!" were heard, which others tried to drown by shouts of "Justice!" "Justice!" "Execution!" "Execution!" "Poor souls," said the king, "for a little money they would do as much against their commanders!"

On the 27th there was another public sitting of the court. They had agreed upon the sentence, Bradshaw now announced. The king desired, before it was given, to meet the two Houses in the Painted Chamber. After consultation this was refused. The sentence was read from a long roll of vellum. It was "that his head should be severed from his body," each of the commissioners testifying his assent by standing up.

The king exclaimed, "Will you hear me a word, sir?"

"Sir," replied Bradshaw, "you are not to be heard after the sentence."

"No, sir?" exclaimed the king.

"No, sir, by your favor," replied Bradshaw. "Guards, withdraw your prisoner."

Charles then exclaimed again, with deep emotion: "I may speak after the sentence! By your favor, sir, I may speak after the sentence! Even, by your favor—"

"Hold!" said Bradshaw, sternly, signing to the guards.

The king broke out again in passionate

entreaty. "The sentence, sir! I say, sir, I do—"

"Hold!" said Bradshaw again.

The king was taken out exclaiming, "*I* am not suffered to speak! Expect what justice other people will have!"

As he went out a soldier asked his blessing. An officer struck him down to the floor. "Methinks, sir," said the king, "the punishment exceeds the offense." Then passed he out from the door of the Banqueting Hall of William Rufus, to die in front of the Banqueting Hall of his own palace.

XIX.

The dynasty had received a shock, but the despotism was by no means overthrown. The spirit was still the spirit of Charles, but the face was the face of Cromwell. The spirit had reason to be rampant, for in this man was now centred the authority of king, Lords, and Commons. He was girded with the power of the sword, and he wielded a mighty bow. Nothing was wanting to him but the crown.

On December 16, 1653, four years after the execution of the king, four days after the dissolution of the Parliament, a double line of soldiers was to be seen winding through the streets from the palace of Whitehall to the doors of Westminster Hall. The cavalcade which passed at high noon through this military avenue had somewhat of the pomp, though none of the splendor, which had formerly attended the processions of kings and queens that way. First came the Lords Commissioners of the Great Seal in official robes, then the scarlet judges of Westminster Hall, then the Council of State, then the Lord Mayor and Aldermen in scarlet vestments and state carriages. Then followed a body-guard. After them a large number of gentlemen walking bare-headed. Now it was time for the state carriage of Oliver Cromwell. He sat in it, dressed in a black velvet suit, long boots, and a hat with a broad gold band. The carriage was surrounded by the principal officers of the army, each carrying his sword in his hand.

On arriving at the Hall, Cromwell alighted and entered, passing through the array which had preceded him there. The length of the Hall was a long walk, but he moved on with a dignity of bearing which was very becoming, though quite new, and finally reached the Court of Chancery, where a chair of state awaited him. "Usually he was very ordinarily apparelled," says Warwick; "but the dignity of his position had grown upon him, and having had a better tailor, and more converse among good company, he was of a great and majestic deportment and comely presence."

Now he removed his hat, and stood before the chair. As soon as the chiefs of the assembly were seated, Major-General Lambert, "in the name of the army, of the three nations, and of the exigencies of the time, prayed the Lord General to accept the office of Protector of the Commonwealth of England, Scotland, and Ireland." After a moment's pause Cromwell "expressed his readiness to undertake the charge." The oath of the new office was read, and he signed it. Then Lambert, falling on his knee, presented the civil sword in the scabbard. Cromwell laid aside his own war sword, and received it as a token that "he intended to govern no longer by military law alone." He was now desired to take his seat in the Chair of State. Thereupon he put on his hat and sat down, all present remaining, as before, uncovered. The inauguration now being over, the procession formed again, and escorted him on his return, the people looking on curiously, but making little demonstration. Soon the booming of guns was heard. It announced that the Lord Protector had taken up his residence in the palace of Whitehall.

Four years more passed—no longer than the official term of an American President. There had come a wondrous change. Both the military and the civil swords had been well used. England was at peace, and in such prosperity as she had never known. Justice had risen to its height in Westminster Hall. The three kingdoms were one. England was supreme on the ocean, the most formidable power on the globe. It was time to make him "a prince" who, as Macaulay says, "had made England the dread of all the world; who had been the chief founder of her maritime greatness and of her colonial empire; who had conquered Scotland and Ireland; who had humbled Holland and Spain; the terror of whose name had been a guard round every English traveller in remote countries, and round every Protestant congregation in the heart of Catholic empires."

Parliament would have made him king, but the army would have withheld the

CHARLES II
From painting by John Greenhill in the National Portrait Gallery.

crown. He accepted all that was attainable and safe. On the 26th of June, 1657, he was enthroned in Westminster Hall, receiving every mark of royalty except the crown.

In fifteen months from that day, with "a pomp," says Guizot, far "exceeding all that had ever been displayed at the funeral of kings," the body of Oliver Cromwell, a "prince" who had wielded more absolute power than any sovereign of England, passed the door of the Hall stretched upon a velvet bed of state in a magnificent funeral car, his effigy, also above him, clad in a royal robe, with crown and sceptre and globe—to be laid among the kings in Westminster Abbey.

But in three years from that same inaugural day his body was torn from its splendid tomb, and hung from the gallows at Tyburn, and his head, pierced with an ashen pike, was placed on the south gable of Westminster Hall, over the very spot, as it happened, where he had sat at the trial of Charles the First. There it swayed in the winds of twenty years, till one stormy night it fell to the pavement, to be picked up by a sentinel, to pass thereafter from hand to hand, to be curiously examined and identified, at last to find what repose it might in a private cabinet as all that was left of Oliver Cromwell—all but what he had bequeathed to the glory of England.

XX.

On the morning of the 8th of May, 1660, to all appearances the Commonwealth had passed away like a dream, and the restored

THE HANGMAN IN THE HALL.
From drawing by H. M. Paget.

monarchy acted as if it had been suddenly roused from walking in its sleep. New Palace Yard is thronged with people who have reason to be rubbing their eyes. The gates of the great Hall are thrown open. What is this? The van of an old-time royal pageant fills the arch. Heralds and pursuivants, in gorgeous tabards emblazoned all over with lions and such things, are coming forth with great flourishes of clarions and trumpets. Out also from the self-same door come pouring the very House of Lords, the very House of Commons, which had met in the days of Charles the First. Nowhere is the sour face, the black coat, the steeple crown, of an Independent to be seen. They all look as bright as the sunbeams which are playing about them, and stand bare-headed, while with another flourish the heralds proclaim his Majesty Charles the Second.

The Hall had been furbished anew. The banners of Marston Moor, of Naseby, and of Preston had been swept like cobwebs out of the roof. Rich hangings on the walls, a new dais on the western side, a new canopy of state over it, new galleries one upon another, and some pieces of a new regalia lying on the new table under the new canopy, and a new crimson chair behind the table, waiting for the old dynasty to come in and take possession. It was on the 23d of April, 1661, when this formally took place. It was only a tall dark man, with a pleasant face and gracious ways, seated in the chair, and receiving the throng of richly dressed nobles and richly coped ecclesiastics, bringing in the rest of the regalia with obeisances and genuflections, and then a marshalling of the whole into a procession for the Abbey.

One ceremony yet remained to be gone through with. It was in keeping with the general vivacity of the restored monarchy. They had already hanged, drawn, and quartered all the regicides they could lay their hands on that were alive, and had dug up and gibbeted all who were dead. About a month after the coronation the Lords and Commons, in Parliament assembled, opened formal communication with the common hangman. That active and conspicuous functionary was notified to be in attendance at a certain hour on a certain day in Westminster Hall. The courts were in session. The grave judges raised their heads from their work, the lawyers stopped their pleading and turned round. What was the public executioner of the lowest grade standing about and staring here for? They always sent him his commissions at Tyburn. But now appeared another officer in the centre of the Hall. The smoke curled away toward the roof, the smell made its way to the nostrils of justice. The lawyers choked with emotion, and loyally held their noses. Was it not im-

JAMES II.
After painting by Sir Godfrey Kneller.

of state with a bundle of parchments. He had come in the name of the High Court of Parliament. These lower courts had nothing to do but endure. Was there to be a hanging of sheep in this shape? Not so. There was to be a burning—and a burning bad smell. These were the parchments of the late "Commonwealth." This was the "Act for the Trial of Charles the First"; this, the "Act for the Abolishing of the House of Lords"; this, "for the Establishing the Commonwealth"; this, "for the Renunciation of the Stuarts"; and, last of all, this, "for the Security of the Protector's Person." Each of these was received in turn by Mr. Ketch, and solemnly laid upon a fire he had just lit

pressive? This was the odor of the Commonwealth! The Commonwealth was now extinct! "God save the king!"

XXI.

The next smell of momentous consequence was of *incense*. It was a long time after, say about twenty-five years. James the Second busied himself with burning clouds of it in Whitehall, and the "noise" of it, after a while, floated into Westminster Hall. The Pope was *in*censed, but the people were *in*censed. King James found out that it was exceedingly dangerous to play with fire.

To a nation with whom the Protestant religion was quite as much the law as it was the gospel, it was more than offensive that the representative of the restored monarchy should spend his time in swinging the censer and counting his beads in the royal chapel. It said nothing, however, until he showed a disposition to introduce the fragrant ceremonial into every church in the kingdom. His attempt to bring this about was a covert and highly ingenious one. But the unfortunate feature of his plan, for him, was that it brought out the whole disease of despotism with which his family were afflicted, and of which his father died.

He raised the question of prerogative in the King's Bench, and then appointed the judges who were to decide it. It decreed, as he desired, that it lay in his prerogative to abrogate any express law of the realm. The Chief Justice declared that the crown was absolute, that the government of England was vested in the king. Pretty well for Westminster Hall, after all it had witnessed of the bloody consequences of that doctrine! So much for reaction.

Now, as might have been foreseen, rose up the spectre of Henry the Eighth, but with the brains and views of James the Second. The Supreme Head of the Church at once made a most generous announcement. There should be universal toleration. This, of course, gave a foothold to the very Church which was against the law. And it enabled the Supreme Head of the Church to make of the Established Church just what he most desired. And, moreover, he was entirely free to withdraw from the general arrangement whenever he chose. Still the nation looked on and did nothing.

The Supreme Head then took another step. He ordered his "Declaration of Indulgence" to be read in all the churches. Now he would make the clergy a party to it. This was the empty censer he proposed first to swing before each altar. But the bishops and clergy, smelling the incense before, rose up, and would none of it. Despotism at last, in touching the Faith, had touched the quick—and the dead too, as it turned out. The whole nation was roused from its lethargy when the seven bishops came to the front and were thrown into the Tower. For the first time Churchman and Nonconformist stood shoulder to shoulder. For the last time the people were as one against the king. The battle of Liberty with Despot-

ism was fought out finally on the floor of Westminster Hall. It was a bloodless question of law. It produced, nevertheless, one of the most exciting scenes ever beheld under its ancient roof. Now the arrow struck the heart of the despotism, and the dynasty died.

We may omit a full account of the public excitement: Tower Hill black with tens of thousands of people, the space round the Tower gates blocked up with the carriages of the nobility, the Thames covered with boats, the very guards of the prison cheering the bishops and drinking their health. The bonfires, too, the guns, the bells, the shouts, the blessings, at the mere rumor afterward of their acquittal in the Hall, because "enlarged on their own recognizance," the multitude thronging New Palace Yard, kneeling about them as they came out, kissing their hands and their robes.

June 29, 1688, was the day set for the trial. The king would not yield. "Indulgence ruined my father," said he. The Hall was thronged to its utmost capacity. Outside, it stood up amid an ocean of heads, a dense mass not only filling both the old and the new Yards, but every street which led to it, as far as the eye could reach.

The next morning, when the jury brought in the verdict, "Not guilty," "Halifax sprang up and waved his hat." There was a huzza, a shout of joy so tremendous that it sounded, says Mackintosh, "like a crack of the ancient massy roof of Westminster Hall." "It is a rebellion in noise," exclaimed one. The members of the jury were embraced, with tears of joy, as deliverers. The multitude outside caught up the news, and it spread with electric rapidity. It ran down the streets in a continuous roar. It ran down the Thames in answering huzzas. All London was informed in a moment. Couriers dashed away along the country roads to carry it over the realm. The king was reviewing his standing army on Hounslow Heath. It broke forth in resounding cheers almost in his face.

That night, while the sky over London was red with bonfires and burning effigies of the Pope, there sped across the Channel to the Hague that message to the Prince of Orange which resulted in the flight of James, "the Revolution of 1688," the accession, through the elective power, of William and Mary to the throne.

WESTMINSTER HALL.—LORD MAYOR'S DAY.—After painting, "Departure of the Lord Mayor (1844)," by David Roberts.

GEORGE III.—After Ramsay.

XXII.

We have a breathing-place just here to look about us. How did the old Hall look in those days of the Stuarts? We have been too much engaged with it as a theatre and stage of a historic drama to have the opportunity to note some minor points which will fill in and add new interest to the pictures we have drawn.

It now bore the weight of nearly six hundred years. It had suffered neglect and misuse. Very different was it in appearance and environment in 1688 from the day when it stood up like a Norman temple in the meadows of an ancient palace and monastery, a magnificent addition to the one, a profane rival to the other. Very different was it from the day when it had newly put on its Gothic vesture, three cen-

turies later, and was still conspicuous in all the landscape round as the fit companion of the new Abbey, as part of its now enormous pile, and girt by the gardens and tilt-yards of a sumptuous king. Now the city of Westminster had grown up all about it. Royalty no longer dwelt near by. It was sought only in its pageants and its affairs. It had become the home of the Law. Its quadrangle was built up with the offices of state. Now only its noble front could be seen, for it was flanked with buildings on either side, and only its lofty sloping roof and long ridge-pole, like a high back amid the imbedding mass, told of the volume of space it inclosed.

But the interior presented the strangest sight of all, especially during term-time. All along its walls, on either side, were ranged the stalls of seamstresses, milliners, instrument-makers, law-stationers, second-hand booksellers, and even publishers, the courts being in session all the time, and, in fact, drawing the crowd with which these petty merchants plied their trade. Laud mentions in his diary how the Hall once came near being burned down, February, 1630, through some of the little shops taking fire.

The extraordinary, if not scandalous, incongruity of the spectacle under this elegant roof, where the stately law courts of the realm, with red-gowned and heavily bewigged justices, and "gentlemen of the long robe," met to transact business of the gravest nature, amid the din, confusion and distraction incident to the less worthy uses of "Rufus's roaring Hall," as Pope calls it, did not escape certain sharp eyes in that day, and has more than once been embalmed in the literature of the period.

But our space diminishes. We would like to revive several other historic events which assumed a picturesque interest in the Hall, notably the trial of Sacheverell, in Queen Anne's day, and of the rebel lords, Kilmarnock, Balmerino, Cromartie, and Lovat, after the battle of Culloden, in the reign of George the Second; but we shall hardly have room for the two or three which are necessary to the symmetrical completion of the sketch we have undertaken.

XXIII.

Twenty-seven years after the coronation of George the Third, but only five after the close of the conflict in the Western wing of the empire, Westminster Hall was to take upon itself a most memorable protest against tyranny in the Eastern wing also. In February, 1788, Warren Hastings was impeached, for misgovernment in India, by the House of Commons at the bar of the House of Lords. The splendor of the spectacle, as depicted by the great master of historical narrative, familiar as it is to the reader, may now acquire new inter-

SHOPS IN WESTMINSTER HALL.

est when brought into the current of the larger consciousness with which we have tried to invest the Hall.

"Every step in the proceedings carried the mind either backward, through many troubled centuries, to the days when the foundations of the constitution were laid, or far away, over boundless seas and deserts, to dusky nations, living under strange stars, worshipping strange gods, and writing strange characters from right to left. The High Court of Parliament was to sit, according to forms handed down from the days of the Plantagenets, on an Englishman accused of exercising tyranny over the lord of the city of Benares and the ladies of the princely house of Oude.

"The place was worthy of such a trial. It was the great Hall of William Rufus; the Hall which had resounded with acclamations at the inauguration of thirty kings; the Hall which had witnessed the just sentence of Bacon, and the just absolution of Somers; the Hall where the eloquence of Strafford had for a moment awed and melted a victorious party inflamed with a just resentment; the Hall where Charles had confronted the High Court of Justice with the placid courage which has half redeemed his fame.

"Neither military nor civil pomp was wanting. The avenues were lined with grenadiers. The streets were kept clear by cavalry. The peers, robed in gold and ermine, were marshalled by the heralds under Garter King-at-arms. The judges, in their vestments of state, attended to give advice on points of law. Near a hundred and twenty lords, three-fourths of the Upper House, as the Upper House then was, walked in solemn order from their usual place of assembling to the tribunal. The junior baron present led the way, George Eliott, Lord Heathfield, recently ennobled for his memorable defense of Gibraltar against the fleets and armies of France and Spain. The long procession was closed by the Duke of Norfolk, Earl Marshal of the realm, by the great dignitaries, and by the brothers and the sons of the king. Last of all came the Prince of Wales, conspicuous by his fine person and noble bearing. . . .

"The sergeants made proclamation. Hastings advanced to the bar, and bent his knee. The culprit was, indeed, not unworthy of that great presence. He had ruled an extensive and populous country, had made laws and treaties, had sent forth armies, had set up and pulled down princes, and in his high place he had so borne himself that all had feared him, that most had loved him, and that hatred itself could deny him no title to glory except virtue. He looked like a great man, and not like a bad man; a person small and emaciated, yet deriving dignity from a carriage which, while it indicated deference to the court, indicated also habitual self-possession and self-respect; a high and intellectual forehead; a brow pensive, but not gloomy; a mouth of inflexible decision; a face pale and worn, but serene—such was the aspect with which the great proconsul presented himself to his judges.

"His counsel accompanied him, ... the bold and strong-minded Law, afterward Chief Justice of the King's Bench; the more humane and eloquent Dallas, afterward Chief Justice of the Common Pleas; and Plomer, who, nearly twenty years later, successfully conducted in the same high court the defense of Lord Melville, and subsequently became Vice-Chancellor and Master of the Rolls.

"But neither the culprit nor his advocates attracted so much notice as his accusers. In the midst of the blaze of red drapery, a space had been fitted up with green benches and tables for the Commons. The managers, with Burke at their head, appeared in full dress. . . . The box in which the managers stood contained an array of speakers such as perhaps had not appeared together since the great age of Athenian eloquence. There were Fox and Sheridan; . . . . there was Burke; . . . . there, with eyes reverently fixed on Burke, appeared the finest gentleman of his age, ... the ingenious, the chivalrous, the high-souled Windham. . . .

"On the third day Burke rose. Four sittings were occupied by his opening speech. . . . The energy and pathos of the great orator extorted expressions of unwonted admiration from the stern and hostile Chancellor, and for a moment seemed to pierce the resolute heart of the defendant. The ladies in the galleries, unaccustomed to such displays of eloquence, excited by the solemnity of the occasion, and perhaps not unwilling to display their taste and sensibility, were in a state of uncontrollable emotion. Handkerchiefs were pulled out, smelling-bottles were handed round, hysterical cries and sobs were heard, and Mrs. Sheridan was carried out in a fit. At length the orator concluded. Raising his voice till the old arches of Irish oak resounded, 'Therefore,' said he, 'hath it with all confidence been ordered by the Commons of Great Britain that I impeach Warren Hastings of high crimes and misdemeanors. I impeach him in the name of the ture, in the name of both sexes, in the name of every age, in the name of every rank, I impeach the common enemy and oppressor of all. "

XXIV.

The trial of Warren Hastings, if not the last—and it was nearly the last—was the most splendid and imposing arraign-

WARREN HASTINGS.—After Sir Thomas Lawrence.

Commons House of Parliament, whose trust he has betrayed. I impeach him in the name of the English nation, whose ancient honors he has sullied. I impeach him in the name of the people of India, whose rights he has trodden under foot, and whose country he has turned into a desert. Lastly, in the name of human na- ment of a criminal which ever took place in Westminster Hall. Our story of the Hall might fitly end as it began, with a banquet, and a banquet, too, on such a scale as no previous king had either the means or the ambition to attain. It was a worthy successor of Rufus, who spent one-and-fifty thousand pounds of the people's money in order to give himself the fleeting glory of such a pageant. Contrast it, as you may imagine it, for we shall not attempt to describe it, with the coronation feast of Henry the First. Then Henry sat beside Edith-Maud, his Saxon bride; now George the Fourth sat alone, his queen driven thrice that day from the Abbey doors.

So Westminster Hall, as a banqueting hall, came in with a king, and went out with a king. William the Second built it, Richard the Second remodelled it, and George the Fourth restored it. When George the Fourth, after the biggest banquet of them all, proceeded to fit it up anew, its glory both as a banqueting hall and as a judgment hall departed at once and together. Its long galleries were taken down, the curtained inclosures of its courts were removed, all the familiar features which had grown up in it and distinguished it for ages disappeared. The face of the ancient walls was chiselled away, and the mason-work of Rufus and of Richard was veiled from sight by a thin ashlering of stone, the windows were new glazed, the cornice, the corbels, the statues, the niches, the sculptures within and without, were all furbished anew. A pavement of uniform square stones replaced its aged floor. Forty loads of oaken timber, taken from some broken-up men-of-war at Portsmouth, were worked into the northern part of its mighty roof, where it had always been incomplete. Seven doors were cut through its western wall, as entrances into the rooms in an adjoining building, erected from the designs of Sir John Soane, 1820–1825, where now the courts were destined to sit until the great Palace of Justice should rise on the hill midway between the Abbey and St. Paul's. On the 4th of December, 1882, these new "Royal Courts of Justice," as they are officially called, were formally opened by the Queen, and the Strand, instead of Westminster Palace Yard, became the seat of English justice. The materials of the building erected by Soane were soon after sold at auction, so that by its removal the old Hall might assume its former architectural dignity.

The great Hall of William Rufus is to-day the noble vestibule of the Houses of Parliament, and as the members of the government traverse its long extent between a double row of marble statesmen, the busts and statues of those who likewise once walked this way in flesh and blood, they pass over a bridge whose archways are the centuries which have spanned the history of their country. The Palace confers dignity upon the Hall, and the Hall confers antiquity upon the Palace.

To Americans and to Englishmen alike it is common ground. Within these walls and beneath this roof the foundation stones of the Constitution of the United States as well as the foundation stones of the British Empire were laid. It is as much the vestibule of the Capitol at Washington as of the Parliament Houses of Westminster, and the customs, the traditions, the very language, of the ancient courts which for ages held their sessions here are familiar and effectual to-day in every tribunal which is known to the daughter nation across the sea.

Westminster Hall is old England. Kings may have founded it, but the people now reign in it. It is the area where the great events of the kingdom not only concentrated their force, but developed into picturesque scenes. Unlike the Abbey, it has no tombs ; unlike the Tower, it has no dungeons; its memories, like spirits, are not visible in its interior to-day; and yet if they could all revive in the breadth of their association, if they could all speak from the depth of their occasion, neither Tower nor Abbey could exceed its power both to move and to impress the mind which stands within its gates.

THE POET'S FAME.

As some slow spark leaps to a ruddy beam
That burns and brightens in a constant fire,
Whose brilliant lights mount ever high and
  higher,
Until against the farthest sky they seem
To be reflected in a roseate gleam,
So soars the song sung with a grand desire,
So burn the words the poet's thoughts inspire,
  And, lo! the world is lighted by his theme.
    Sweet in his eager ear the plaudit rings;
He sees his fame a shining beacon-star,
  The halo of whose glory lights the earth.
    And yet he is not happiest who sings.
Ye know not, for ye see not from afar,
  The heap of ashes on his lonely hearth.

TO A HAGGIS.

Fair fa' your honest, sonsie face,
Great chieftain o' the puddin' race:
Aboon them a' ye tak your place.
          Painch, tripe, or thairm;
Weel are ye wordy of a grace
          As lang's my arm.

The groaning trencher there ye fill,
Your hurdies like a distant hill;
Your pin wad help to mend a mill
          In time o' need,
While through your pores the dews distill
          Like amber bead.

His knife see rustic labor dight,
And cut you up wi' ready slight,
Trenching your gushing entrails bright
          Like ony ditch;
And then, oh what a glorious sight,
          Warm-reekin', rich!

Then horn for horn they stretch and strive,
Deil tak the hindmost, on they drive,
Till a' their weel-swall'd kytes belyve
          Are bent like drums;
Then auld guidman, maist like to rive,
          "Bethankit!" hums.

Is there that owre his French *ragout,*
Or *olio* that wad staw a sow,
Or *fricassee* wad mak her spew
          Wi' perfect scunner,
Looks down wi' sneering, scornfu' view
          On sic a dinner!

Poor devil! see him owre his trash,
As feckless as a withered rash,
His spindle-shank a guid whip-lash,
          His nieve a nit;
Through bloody flood or field to dash,
          Oh how unfit!

But mark the rustic, haggis-fed;
The trembling earth resounds his tread;
Clap in his walie nieve a blade,
          He'll mak it whissle;
And legs, and arms, and heads will sned,
          Like taps o' thrissle.

Ye Powers wha mak mankind your care,
And dish them out their bill o' fare,
Auld Scotland wants nae skinking ware
          That jaups in luggies;
But, if ye wish her gratefu' prayer,
          Gie her a Haggis!

THE HAGGIS.

From a drawing by E. A. Abbey.—[See preceding page.]

THE ACADIAN TRAGEDY.

AT the head of the Bay of Fundy, on the isthmus that joins Nova Scotia, or the Acadian peninsula, to the mainland, stands a hill which once bore the name of Beauséjour. On this hill, overlooking on one side the great marsh of Missaguash, and on the other the still greater marsh of Tantemar, there stood, in the year 1755, a strong fortified work, the heavy earthen ramparts of which still remain. Over it floated the white flag of the Bourbons. Some two miles distant, across the marsh of Missaguash, was a rising ground, crowned with the palisades and embankments of another fort, above which waved the red cross of St. George. Fort Beauséjour and Fort Lawrence were the advance-guards of two rival nations, just then on the point of deadly conflict for ascendency on this continent, each hotly denying the claims of the other, and each with the sword half drawn to enforce its own. Diplomacy had failed. There was no resource but in the last argument of kings.

The two crowns were nominally at peace, but the British authorities of Nova Scotia had proof that the French were preparing to attack Fort Lawrence, rouse the Acadian population to revolt, and seize upon the whole or a part of the province, which had been forty years under the British flag. Shirley, Governor of Massachusetts, and Lawrence, Governor of Nova Scotia, with the approval of the cabinet of London, had resolved to anticipate the blow by seizing upon Fort Beauséjour. It was a part of the scheme of operation, audacious as it was comprehensive, by which the British and colonial authorities resolved this year to anticipate a declaration of war, and force back the French along the whole line of their alleged encroachments. Braddock was to attack Fort Duquesne on the Ohio, Johnson was to attack Crown Point on Lake Champlain, Shirley was to attack Fort Niagara, and Monckton was to attack Fort Beauséjour.

Monckton, a British officer, had a small force of regular troops, but his chief reliance was on two thousand New England men, whom Shirley was to send from Boston, under Colonel John Winslow. Winslow was sprung from the early Governors of Plymouth colony; but though well born, he was indifferently educated, which did not prevent him from being both popular and influential. He had strong military inclinations, had led a company of his own raising at the luckless attack on Carthagena, and on various other occasions had left his Marshfield farm to serve his country. The men enlisted readily at his call. They gathered at Boston early in April. The muster-rolls still preserve their names, vocations, birth-places, and abode. Obadiah, Nehemiah, Jedediah, Jonathan, Ebenezer, Joshua, and the like Old Testament designations abound upon the list. They are set down as farmers, fishermen, shop-keepers, laborers, and handicraftsmen of various trades, including wigmakers. While the vessels that were to carry them lay at Long Wharf, the order went forth on a Saturday afternoon: "The men will behave very orderly on the Sabbath day, and either stay on board their transports or else go to church, and not stroll up and down the streets."

They sailed at last, anchored at the head of the bay, landed at Fort Lawrence, marched over the marsh to the hill of Beauséjour, dug trenches, mounted a few small mortars, and began to bombard the fort. The defense was of the feeblest. The fleur-de-lis was lowered, the British cross was raised in its stead, and the place was christened anew, under the name of Fort Cumberland. In it, along with the regular garrison, were found three hundred Acadians, self-styled neutrals, fighting against the power of whom most of them were legally the subjects.

Now was begun a dismal tragedy, famous in prose and verse, yet ill understood, both in its causes and its events. The removal of the Acadians was the result of influences that had been at work for forty years, and which had now mounted to a crisis. Abbé Reynal, who knew nothing of this people except from hearsay, has drawn an ideal picture of them, which later writers have copied and embellished, till Acadia has become Arcadia. The plain realities of their condition and fate are touching enough to need no such exaggeration. They were a simple and very ignorant peasantry, industrious and frugal, till evil days came to discourage them; living aloof from the world, with little of that spirit of adventure which marked their Canadian kindred; having few wants, and those of the rudest; fishing a little, and hunting in the winter, but chiefly employed in cultivating the meadows along the river Annapolis, or rich marshes reclaimed by dikes from the tides of the Bay of Fundy. The British government left them entirely free of taxation. They made clothing of flax or wool of their own raising, hats of similar materials, and shoes or moccasins of moose or seal skin. They bred cattle, sheep, hogs, and horses in abundance, and the valley of the Annapolis, then as now, was known for the profusion and excellence of its apples. For drink they made cider or brewed spruce-beer. French officials describe their dwellings as wretched wooden boxes, without ornaments or conveniences, and scarcely supplied with the most necessary furniture. Two or more families often occupied the same house, and their way of life, though simple and virtuous, was by no means remarkable for cleanliness. Such as it was, contentment reigned among them, undisturbed by what modern America calls progress. Marriages were early, and population grew apace. This humble society had its disturbing elements, for, like the Canadians, they were a litigious race, and neighbors often quarrelled about their boundaries. Nor were they without a bountiful share of jealousy, gossip, and backbiting to relieve the monotony of their lives; and every village had its turbulent spirits, sometimes by fits, though rarely long, contumacious even to the curé, the guide, counsellor, and ruler of his flock. Enfeebled by hereditary mental subjection, and too long kept in leading-strings to walk alone, they needed him, not for the next world only, but for this; and their submission, compounded of love and fear, was commonly without bounds. He was their true government; to him they gave a frank and full allegiance, and dared not disobey him if they would. Of knowledge he gave them nothing, but he taught them to be true to their wives, and constant at confession and mass, to stand fast for the Church and King Louis, and to resist heresy and King George; for, in one degree or another, the Acadian priest was always the agent of a double-headed foreign power, the Bishop of Quebec allied with the Governor of Canada.

Nova Scotia, under the name of Acadia, had been ceded by France to the British crown in 1713. By the terms of the cession, its inhabitants were to retain the free exercise of the Roman Catholic religion.

It was now more than forty years since they had become British subjects, and the greater part of the population had been born under the British flag. It is the testimony of the French themselves that the British rule had been an exceedingly mild one; that the colonial authorities, recognizing the value of a frugal and industrious population, had labored to reconcile them to a change of allegiance which, on the whole, was to their advantage; that no burdens were imposed on them; and that they had not been oppressed or molested in matters spiritual or temporal. The British on the peninsula were, in fact, too few to rule by force. Until the settlement at Halifax in 1749 they consisted only of a feeble garrison at Annapolis, with three or four others, yet feebler, scattered here and there over the country; and the Acadian population was left substantially to the government of its own priests. This population had its chief centres in the valley of the river Annapolis, and at Grand Pré, Cobequid, Pisiquid, and other settlements around the Basin of Mines, which forms one of the two heads of the Bay of Fundy.

After the cession of the country the British authorities required the Acadians to take an oath of fidelity and obedience to their new sovereign. This, after a delay of many years, they did at last, with an understanding, as they alleged, that they should not be forced to bear arms against their former countrymen, the French. When war began again in 1745, many of them broke their oath, and sometimes openly, sometimes in the disguise of Indians, joined the French in attacks on British garrisons, while others acted as spies, or aided the enemy with information and provisions. When, in 1748, the war ended, the French officials prophesied some signal act of vengeance on the part of the British against the offending Acadians. On the contrary, they showed great forbearance, and only insisted that all the adult male population should take an oath of allegiance, without any reserve or restriction whatever.

This they would have done if they had been let alone; but they were not let alone. Another war was plainly at hand, and France meditated the reconquest of Acadia. To this end the Acadians must be kept French at heart, and ready, at a signal given, to rise against the English. France had acknowledged them as British subjects, but this did not prevent the agents of Louis XV. from seeking by incessant intrigue to stir them into bitter hostility against the British government. Before me are two large volumes of papers, about a thousand pages in all, copied from the archives of the Colonial Department at Paris. They relate to these French efforts to rouse the Acadians to revolt; and they consist of the journals, dispatches, reports, and letters of officers military, civil, and ecclesiastical, from the Governor of Canada to a captain of bush-rangers, and from the Bishop of Quebec to the curé of Cobequid. They show, by the evidence of the actors themselves, the scope and methods of the machination, to which the King himself appears, in his languid way, as an accessory. The priests of Acadia were the chief agents employed. They taught their parishioners that fidelity to King Louis was inseparable from fidelity to God, and that to swear allegiance to the British crown would be eternal perdition. Foremost among these apostles of revolt was Le Loutre, missionary to the Micmac Indians, and Vicar-General for Acadia under the Bishop of Quebec. His fanatical hatred of the English and the natural violence of his character impelled him to extremes which alarmed his employers, and drew upon him frequent exhortations to caution. He threatened the Acadians with excommunication if they obeyed the King of England. In connection with French officers across the line, he encouraged them to put on the disguise of Indians and join his Micmacs in pillaging and killing English settlers on the outskirts of Halifax when the two nations were at peace. He drew on one occasion from a French official 1800 livres to pay his Indians for English scalps. With a reckless disregard of the welfare of the unhappy people under his charge, he spared no means to embroil them with the government under which, but for him and his fellow-conspirators, they would have lived in peace and contentment. An entire heartlessness marked the dealings of the French authorities with the Acadians. They were treated as mere tools of policy, to be used, broken, and flung away.

The loss of Acadia had been gall and wormwood to France. That she would soon seek to recover it was certain; and with the temper which her agents had infused into the population there could be no doubt that at the appearance of a French squadron in the Bay of Fundy the whole country would rise in arms. With Fort Beauséjour on the border of the colony, the danger was redoubled; and hence the chief motive that had led Shirley and Lawrence to advise the seizure of that stronghold.

When Monckton and the Massachusetts men laid siege to it, Governor Lawrence thought the moment favorable for exacting from the Acadians the unqualified oath of allegiance which up to that time they had absolutely refused. The presence of a superior and victorious force would help, he thought, to bring them to reason. Lawrence had not the good-nature and conciliating temper which had marked his predecessors Cornwallis and Hopson. His energetic will was not apt to relent under the softer sentiments, and the behavior of the Acadians was fast exhausting his patience. More than a year before, the Lords of Trade had instructed him that they had no right to their lands if they persisted in refusing the oath. Lawrence replied, enlarging on their obstinacy, treachery, and "ingratitude for the favor, indulgence, and protection they have at all times so undeservedly received from his Majesty's government," declaring at the same time that "while they remain without taking the oath, and have incendiary French priests among them, there are no hopes of their amendment," and that "it would be much better, if they refuse the oath, that they were away." "We were in hopes," again wrote the Lords of Trade, "that the lenity which had been shown to those people by indulging them in the free exercise of their religion and the quiet possession of their lands would by degrees have gained their friendship and assistance, and weaned their affections from the French; but we are sorry to find that this lenity has had so little effect, and that they still hold the same conduct." This conduct was that of an enemy in disguise, encamped in the heart of the province, leagued with its enemies without, and so numerous as to require as security against them a body of troops stronger than the authorities had at command; for the Massachusetts men were enlisted only for the campaign, and would go home at the end of it. The presence of this disaffected population was for the French commanders a continual inducement to invasion, and Lawrence could not cope at once with attack from without and insurrection from within. Such are the reasons which explain and palliate measures too harsh to be wholly justified.

Still, the Acadians would have remained safe and unmolested had they but consented to take the oath; and to the last Lawrence and his Council labored, in manifest good faith, to persuade them to do so. Early in June, about the time when the siege of Fort Beauséjour was begun, the principal inhabitants of Grand Pré and other settlements about the Basin of Mines brought a memorial, signed with their crosses, to Captain Murray, the military commandant in their district, and desired him to send it to Governor Lawrence, to whom it was addressed. Murray reported that when they brought it to him they behaved with the greatest insolence, though just before they had been unusually submissive. He thought that this change of demeanor was caused by a report which had lately got among them of a French fleet in the Bay of Fundy; for it had been observed that any rumor of an approaching French force always had a similar effect. The deputies who brought the memorial were sent with it to Halifax, where they laid it before the Governor and Council. It declared that the signers had kept the qualified oath they had taken, "in spite of the solicitations and dreadful threats of another power," and that they would continue to prove "an unshaken fidelity to his Majesty, provided that his Majesty shall allow us the same liberty that he has [hitherto] granted us." Their memorial then demanded, in terms highly offensive to the Council, that the guns, pistols, and other weapons which they had lately been required to give up should be returned to them. They were told in reply that they had been protected for many years in the enjoyment of their lands, though they had not complied with the terms on which the lands were granted; "that they had always been treated by the government with the greatest lenity and tenderness, had enjoyed more privileges than other English subjects, and had been indulged in the free exercise of their religion;" all which they acknowledged to be true. The Governor then told them that their conduct had been undutiful and ungrateful; "that they had discovered a constant disposition to assist his Majesty's enemies and to distress his

subjects; that they had not only furnished the enemy with provisions and ammunition, but had refused to supply the [English] inhabitants or government, and when they did supply them, have exacted three times the price for which they were sold at other markets." The hope was then expressed that they would no longer obstruct the settlement of the province by aiding the Indians to molest and kill English settlers; and they were rebuked for saying in their memorial that they would be faithful to the King only on certain conditions. The Governor added that they had some secret reason for demanding their weapons, and flattered themselves that French troops were at hand to support their insolence. In conclusion, they were told that now was a good opportunity to prove their sincerity by taking the oath of allegiance, in the usual form, before the Council. They replied that they had not made up their minds on that point, and could do nothing till they had consulted their constituents. Being reminded that the oath was personal to themselves, and that six years had already been given them to think about it, they asked leave to retire and confer together. This was granted, and at the end of an hour they came back with the same answer as before, whereupon they were allowed till ten o'clock on the next morning for a final decision.

At the appointed time the Council again met, and the deputies were brought in. They persisted stubbornly in the same refusal. "They were then informed," says the record, "that the Council could no longer look on them as subjects to his Britannic Majesty, but as subjects to the King of France, and as such they must hereafter be treated; and they were ordered to withdraw." A discussion followed in the Council. It was determined that the Acadians should be ordered to send new deputies to Halifax, who should answer for them, once for all, whether they would accept the oath or not; that such as refused it should not thereafter be permitted to take it; and "that effectual measures ought to be taken to remove all such recusants out of the province."

The deputies, being then called in and told this decision, became alarmed, and offered to swear allegiance in the terms required. The answer was that it was too late; that as they had refused the oath under persuasion, they could not be trusted when they took it under compulsion. It remained to see whether the people at large would profit by their example.

"I am determined," wrote Lawrence to the Lords of Trade, "to bring the inhabitants to a compliance, or rid the province of such perfidious subjects." First in answer to the summons of the Council, the deputies from Annapolis appeared, declaring that they had always been faithful to the British crown, but flatly refusing the oath. They were told that, far from having been faithful subjects, they had always secretly aided the Indians, and that many of them had been in arms against the English; that the French were threatening the province; and that its affairs had reached a crisis when its inhabitants must either pledge themselves without equivocation to be true to the British crown, or else must leave the country. They all declared that they would lose their lands rather than take the oath. The Council urged them to consider the matter seriously, warning them that if they now persisted in refusal, no farther choice would be allowed them, and they were given till ten o'clock on the following Monday to make their final answer.

When that day came, another body of deputies had arrived from Grand Pré and other settlements of the Basin of Mines; and being called before the Council, both they and the former deputation absolutely refused to take the oath of allegiance. These two bodies represented nine-tenths of the Acadian population within the peninsula. "Nothing," pursues the record of the Council, "now remained to be considered but what measures should be taken to send the inhabitants away, and where they should be sent to." If they were sent to Canada, Cape Breton, or neighboring islands, they would strengthen the enemy, and still threaten the province. It was therefore resolved to distribute them among the various English colonies, and to hire vessels for the purpose with all dispatch.

The oath the refusal of which had brought such consequences was a simple pledge of fidelity and allegiance to King George II. and his successors. Many of them had already taken an oath of fidelity, though with the omission of the word "allegiance," and, as they insisted, with a saving clause exempting them from bearing arms. The effect of this was that they did not regard themselves as British subjects, and claimed, falsely as regards most of them, the character of neutrals. It was to put an end to this anomalous state of things that the oath without reserve had been demanded of them. Their rejection of it, reiterated in full view of the consequences, is to be ascribed partly to a fixed belief that the English would not execute their threats, partly to ties of race and kin, but mainly to superstition. They feared to take part with heretics against the King of France, whose cause, as already stated, they had been taught to regard as one with the cause of God. They were constrained by the dread of perdition. "If the Acadians are miserable, remember that the priests are the cause of it," writes the French officer Boishébert to the missionary Manach.

The Council having come to a decision, Lawrence acquainted Monckton with the result, and ordered him to seize all the adult males in the neighborhood of Beauséjour, and this he promptly did. It remains to observe how the rest of the sentence was carried into effect.

Instructions were sent to Winslow to secure the inhabitants on or near the Basin of Mines and place them on board transports, which, he was told, would soon arrive from Boston. His orders were stringent: "If you find that fair means will not do with them, you must proceed by the most rigorous measures possible, not only in compelling them to embark, but in depriving those who shall escape of all means of shelter or support, by burning their houses and by destroying everything that may afford them the means of subsistence in the country." Similar orders were given to Major Handfield, the regular officer in command at Annapolis.

On the 14th of August Winslow set out from his camp at Fort Beauséjour, or Cumberland, on his memorable errand. He had with him but two hundred and ninety-seven men. His mood of mind was not serene. He was chafed because the regulars had charged his men with stealing sheep, and he was doubly vexed by an untoward incident that happened on the morning of his departure.

Thus ruffled in spirit, he embarked with his men, and sailed down Chignecto Channel to the Bay of Fundy. Here, while they waited the turn of the tide to enter the Basin of Mines, the shores of Cumberland lay before them, dim in the hot and hazy air, and the promontory of Cape Split, like some misshapen monster of primeval chaos, stretched its portentous length along the glimmering sea, with head of yawning rock and ridgy back, bristled with forests. Borne on the rushing flood, they soon drifted through the inlet, glided under the rival promontory of Cape Blomedon, passed the red sandstone cliffs of Lyon's Cove, and descried the mouths of the rivers Canard and Des Habitants, where fertile marshes, diked against the tide, sustained a numerous and thriving population. Before them spread the boundless meadows of Grand Pré, waving with harvests or alive with grazing cattle. The green slopes behind were dotted with the simple dwellings of the Acadian farmers, and the spire of the village church rose against a background of woody hills. It was a peaceful, rural scene, soon to become one of the most wretched spots on earth. Winslow did not land for the present, but held his course to the estuary of the river Pisiquid, since called the Avon. Here, where the town of Windsor now stands, there was a stockade called Fort Edward, where a garrison of regulars under Captain Alexander Murray kept watch over the surrounding settlements. The New England men pitched their tents on shore, while the sloops that had brought them slept on the soft bed of tawny mud left by the fallen tide.

Winslow found a warm reception, for Murray and his officers had been reduced too long to their own society not to welcome the coming of strangers. The two commanders conferred together. Both had been ordered by Lawrence to "clear the whole country of such bad subjects," and the methods of doing so had been outlined for their guidance. Having come to some understanding with his brother officer concerning the duties imposed on both, and begun an acquaintance which soon grew cordial on both sides, Winslow embarked again, and retraced his course to Grand Pré, the station which the Governor had assigned him. "Am pleased," he wrote to Lawrence, "with the place proposed by your Excellency for our reception [the village church]. I have sent for the elders to remove all sacred things to prevent their being defiled by heretics." The church was used as a store-house and place of arms; the men pitched their tents between it and the grave-yard, while Winslow took up his quarters in the house of the priest. They agreed that Winslow should summon all the male inhabitants about Grand Pré to meet him at the church and hear the King's orders, and that Murray should do the same for those around Fort Edward. Winslow then called in his three captains, Adams, Hobbs, and Osgood, made them swear secrecy, and laid before them his instructions and plans, which latter they approved. Murray then returned to his post, and on the next day sent Winslow a note containing the following: "I think the sooner we strike the stroke the better; therefore will be glad to see you here as soon as conveniently you can. I shall have the orders for assembling ready wrote for your approbation, only the day blank, and am hopeful everything will succeed according to our wishes. The gentlemen join me in our best compliments to you and the doctor."

On the next day, Sunday, Winslow and the doctor, whose name was Whitworth, made the tour of the neighborhood, with an escort of fifty men, and found a great quantity of wheat still on the fields. On Tuesday, Winslow "set out in a whale-boat with Dr. Whitworth and Adjutant Kennedy to consult with Captain Murray in this critical conjuncture." They agreed that three in the afternoon of Friday should be the time of assembling; then, between them, they drew up a summons to the inhabitants, and got one Beauchamp, a merchant, to "put it into French." It ran as follows:

"By John Winslow, Esq., Lieutenant-Colonel and Commander of his Majesty's troops at Grand Pré, Mines, River Canard, and places adjacent,

"To the inhabitants of the districts above named, as well ancients as young men and lads:

"Whereas his Excellency the Governor has instructed us of his last resolution respecting the matters proposed lately to the inhabitants, and has ordered us to communicate the same to the inhabitants in general in person, his Excellency being desirous that each of them should be fully satisfied of his Majesty's intentions, which he has also ordered us to communicate to you, such as they have been given him;

"We therefore order and strictly enjoin by these presents to all the inhabitants as well of the above-named districts as of all the other districts, both old men and young men, as well as all the lads of ten years of age, to attend at the church in Grand Pré on Friday, the 5th instant, at three of the clock in the afternoon, that we may impart what we are ordered to communicate to them. Declaring that no excuse will be admitted on any pretense whatsoever, on pain of forfeiting goods and chattels in default.

"Given at Grand Pré the 2d of September, in the twenty-ninth year of his Majesty's reign, A.D. 1755."

A similar summons was drawn up in the name of Murray for the inhabitants of the district of Fort Edward.

Captain Adams made a reconnaissance of the rivers Canard and Des Habitants, and reported "a fine country, and full of inhabitants, a beautiful church, and abundance of the goods of the world." Another reconnaissance by Captains Hobbs and Osgood among the settlements behind Grand Pré brought reports equally favorable. On the 4th another letter came from Murray: "All the people quiet, and very busy at their harvest; if this day keeps fair, all will be in here in their barns. I hope to-morrow will crown all our wishes." The Acadians, like the bees, were to gather a harvest for others to enjoy. The summons was sent out that afternoon. Powder and ball were served to the men, and all were ordered to keep within the lines.

On the next day the inhabitants appeared at the hour appointed, to the number of four hundred and eighteen men. Winslow ordered a table to be set in the middle of the church, and placed on it his instructions and the address he had prepared. Here he took his stand, in his laced uniform, with one or two subalterns from the regulars at Fort Edward, and such of the Massachusetts officers as were not on guard duty—strong, sinewy figures, bearing, no doubt, more or less distinctly, the peculiar stamp with which toil, trade, and Puritanism had imprinted the features of New England. Their commander was not of the prevailing type. He was fifty-three years of age, with double chin, smooth forehead, arched eyebrows, close powdered wig, and round rubicund face, from which the weight of an odious duty had probably banished the smirk of self-satisfaction that dwelt there at other times. Nevertheless, he had manly and estimable qualities. The congregation of peasants, clad in rough homespun, turned their sunburned faces upon him, anxious and intent, and Winslow "delivered them by interpreters the King's orders in the following words,"

which, retouched in orthography and syntax, ran thus:

"Gentlemen, I have received from his Excellency Governor Lawrence the King's instructions, which I have in my hand. By his orders you are called together to hear his Majesty's final resolution concerning the French inhabitants of this his province of Nova Scotia, who for almost half a century have had more indulgence granted them than any of his subjects in any part of his dominions. What use you have made of it you yourselves best know.

"The duty I am now upon, though necessary, is very disagreeable to my natural make and temper, as I know it must be grievous to you, who are of the same species. But it is not my business to animadvert on the orders I have received, but to obey them; and therefore, without hesitation, I shall deliver to you his Majesty's instructions and commands, which are that your lands and tenements and cattle and live stock of all kinds are forfeited to the crown, with all your other effects, except money and household goods, and that you yourselves are to be removed from this his province.

"The peremptory orders of his Majesty are that all the French inhabitants of these districts be removed, and through his Majesty's goodness I am directed to allow you the liberty of carrying with you your money and as many of your household goods as you can take without overloading the vessels you go in. I shall do everything in my power that all these goods be secured to you, and that you be not molested in carrying them away, and also that whole families shall go in the same vessel, so that this removal, which I am sensible must give you a great deal of trouble, may be made as easy as his Majesty's service will admit, and hope that in whatever part of the world your lot may fall you may be faithful subjects and a peaceable and happy people.

"I must also inform you that it is his Majesty's pleasure that you remain in security under the inspection and direction of the troops that I have the honor to command."

He then declared them prisoners of the King. "They were greatly struck," he says, "at this determination, though I believe they did not imagine that they were actually to be removed." After delivering the address he returned to his quarters at the priest's house, whither he was followed by some of the elder prisoners, who begged leave to tell their families what had happened, "since they were fearful that the surprise of their detention would quite overcome them." Winslow consulted with his officers, and it was arranged that the Acadians should choose twenty of their number each day to revisit their homes, the rest being held answerable for their return.

A letter, dated some days before, now came from Major Handfield at Annapolis, saying that he had tried to secure the men of that neighborhood, but that many of them had escaped to the woods. Murray's report from Fort Edward came soon after, and was more favorable: "I have succeeded finely, and have got a hundred and eighty-three into my possession." To which Winslow replies, "I have the favor of yours of this day, and rejoice at your success, and also for the smiles that have attended the party here." But he adds, mournfully, "Things are now very heavy on my heart and hands." The prisoners were lodged in the church, and notice was sent to their families to bring them food. "Thus," says the diary of the commander, "ended the memorable 5th of September —a day of great fatigue and trouble."

There was one quarter where fortune did not always smile. Major Jedediah Preble, of Winslow's battalion, wrote to him that Major Frye had just returned from Chipody, whither he had gone with a party of men to destroy the settlements, and bring off the women and children. After burning two hundred and fifty-three buildings he had embarked, leaving fifty men on shore at a place called Petticodiac to give a finishing stroke to the work by burning the "mass-house," or church. While thus engaged they were set upon by three hundred Indians and Acadians, led by the partisan officer Boishébert. More than half their number were killed, wounded, or taken. The rest ensconced themselves behind the neighboring dikes, and Frye, hastily landing with the rest of his men, engaged the assailants for three hours, but was forced at last to re-embark. Captain Speakman, who took part in the affair, also sent Winslow an account of it, and added, "The people here are much concerned for fear your party should meet with the same fate (being in the heart of a numerous devilish crew), which I pray God avert."

Winslow had, indeed, some cause for anxiety. He had captured more Acadians since the 5th, and had now in charge nearly five hundred able-bodied men, with scarcely three hundred to guard them. As they were allowed daily exercise in the open air, they might, by a sudden rush, get possession of arms, and make serious trouble. On the Wednesday after the scene in the church, some unusual movements were observed among them, and Winslow and his officers became convinced that they could not safely be kept in one body. Five vessels, lately arrived from Boston, were lying within the mouth of the neighboring river. It was resolved to place fifty of the prisoners on board each of these, and keep them anchored in the Basin. The soldiers were all ordered under arms, and posted on an open space beside the church and behind the priest's house. The prisoners were then drawn up before them, ranked six deep, the young unmarried men, as the most dangerous, being told off and placed on the left, to the number of a hundred and forty-one. Captain Adams, with eighty men, was then ordered to guard them to the vessels. Though the object of the movement had been explained to them, they were possessed with the idea that they were to be torn from their families and sent away at once; and they all in great excitement refused to go. Winslow told them that there must be no parley or delay; and as they still refused, a squad of soldiers advanced toward them with fixed bayonets, while he himself, laying hold of the foremost young man, commanded him to move forward. "He obeyed, and the rest followed, though slowly, and went off praying, singing, and crying, being met by the women and children all the way (which is a mile and a half) with great lamentation, upon their knees, praying." When the escort returned, about a hundred of the married men were ordered to follow the first party, and, "the ice being broken," they readily complied. The vessels were anchored at a little distance from shore, and six soldiers were placed on board each of them as a guard. The prisoners were offered the King's rations, but preferred to be supplied by their families, who, it was arranged, should go in boats to visit them every day; "and thus," says Winslow, "ended this troublesome job." He was not given to effusions of feeling, but he wrote to Major Handfield: "This affair is more grievous to me than any service I was ever employed in."*

Murray sent him a note of congratulation. "I am extremely pleased that things are so clever at Grand Pré, and that the poor devils are so resigned. Here they are more patient than I could have expected for people in their circumstances, and what surprises me still more is the indifference of the women, who really are, or seem, quite unconcerned. I long much to see the poor wretches embarked, and our affair a little settled, and then I will do myself the pleasure of meeting you and drinking their good voyage."

This agreeable consummation was still distant. There was a long and painful delay. The provisions for the vessels which were to carry the prisoners did not come, nor did the vessels themselves, excepting the five already at Grand Pré. In vain Winslow wrote urgent letters to George Saul, the commissary, to bring the supplies at once. Murray at Fort Edward, though with less feeling than his brother officer, was quite as impatient of the burden of suffering humanity on his hands. "I am amazed what can keep the transports and Saul. Surely our friend at Chignecto is willing to give us as much of our neighbors' company as he well can." Saul came at last with a ship-load of provisions, but the lagging transports did not appear. Winslow grew heart-sick at the daily sight of miseries which he himself had occasioned, and wrote to a friend at Halifax: "I know they deserve all and more than they feel, yet it hurts me to hear their weeping and wailing and gnashing of teeth. I am in hopes our affairs will soon put on another face, and we get transports, and I rid of the worst piece of service that ever I was in."

After weeks of delay seven transports came from Annapolis, and Winslow sent three of them to Murray, who joyfully responded: "Thank God, the transports are come at last. So soon as I have shipped off my rascals I will come down and settle matters with you, and enjoy ourselves a little."

* Haliburton, the source from which writers on the removal of the Acadians have drawn most of their information, but who knew Winslow's journal only by imperfect extracts, erroneously states that the men put on board the vessels were sent away immediately. They remained at Grand Pré several weeks, and were then sent off at intervals with their families.

Winslow prepared for the embarkation. The Acadian prisoners and their families were divided into groups answering to their several villages, in order that those of the same village might, as far as possible, go in the same vessel. It was also provided that the members of each family should remain together, and notice was given them to hold themselves in readiness. "But even now," he writes, "I could not persuade the people I was in earnest." Their doubts were soon ended. The first embarkation took place on the 8th of October, under which date the diary contains this entry: "Began to embark the inhabitants, who went off very solentarily [sic] and unwillingly, the women in great distress, carrying off their children in their arms; others carrying their decrepit parents in their carts, with all their goods; moving in great confusion, and appeared a scene of woe and distress."

Though a large number embarked on this occasion, still more remained; and as the transports slowly arrived, the dismal scene was repeated at intervals, with more order than at first, as the Acadians had learned to accept their fate as a certainty. So far as Winslow was concerned, their treatment seems to have been as humane as was possible under the circumstances; but they complained of the men, who disliked and annoyed them. One soldier received thirty lashes for stealing fowls from them; and an order was issued forbidding soldiers or sailors, on pain of summary punishment, to leave their quarters without permission, "that an end may be put to distressing this distressed people." Two of the prisoners, however, while trying to escape, were shot by a reconnoitring party.

At the beginning of November, Winslow reported that he had sent off fifteen hundred and ten prisoners in nine vessels, and that more than six hundred still remained in his district. The last of these were not embarked till late in December. Murray finished his part of the work at the end of October, having sent from the district of Fort Edward eleven hundred persons in four frightfully crowded transports. At the close of that month sixteen hundred and sixty-four had been sent from the district of Annapolis, where many others escaped to the woods. A detachment which was ordered to seize the inhabitants of the district of Cobequid failed entirely, finding the settlements abandoned. In the country about Fort Cumberland, Monckton, who directed the operation in person, had very indifferent success, catching in all but little more than a thousand. Le Guerne, missionary priest in this neighborhood, gives a characteristic and affecting incident of the embarkation. "Many unhappy women, carried away by excessive attachment to their husbands, whom they had been allowed to see too often, and closing their ears to the voice of religion and their missionary, threw themselves blindly and despairingly into the English vessels; and now was seen the saddest of spectacles, for some of these women, solely from a religious motive, refused to take with them their grown-up sons and daughters." They would expose their own souls to perdition among heretics, but not those of their children.

When all, or nearly all, had been sent off from the various points of departure, such of the houses and barns as remained standing were burned, in obedience to the orders of Lawrence, that those who had escaped might be forced to come in and surrender themselves. The whole number removed from the province, men, women, and children, was a little above six thousand. Many remained behind; and while some of these withdrew to Canada, Isle St. Jean, and other retreats, the rest lurked in the woods or returned to their old haunts, whence they waged for several years a guerrilla warfare against the English. Yet their strength was broken, and they were no longer a danger to the province.

Of their exiled countrymen, one party overpowered the crew of the vessel that carried them, ran her ashore at the mouth of the St. John, and escaped. The rest were distributed among the colonies, from Massachusetts to Georgia, the master of each transport having been provided with a letter from Lawrence addressed to the Governor of the province to which he was bound, and desiring him to receive the unwelcome strangers. The provincials were vexed at the burden imposed upon them, and though the Acadians were not in general ill-treated, their lot was a hard one. Still more so was that of those among them who escaped to Canada. The chronicle of the Ursulines of Quebec, speaking of these last, says that their misery was indescribable, and attributes it to the poverty of the colony. But there were other causes. The exiles found less pity from kindred and fellow-Catholics than from the heretics of the English colonies. Some of them, who had made their way to Canada from Boston, whither they had been transported, sent word to a gentleman of that place, who had befriended them, that they wished to return. Bougainville, the celebrated navigator, then aide-de-camp to Montcalm, says concerning them: "They are dying by wholesale. Their past and present misery, joined to the rapacity of the Canadians, who seek only to squeeze out of them all the money they can, and then refuse them the help so dearly bought, are the cause of this mortality."

Many of the exiles eventually reached Louisiana, where their descendants now form a numerous and distinct population. Some, after incredible hardships, made their way back to Acadia, where, after the peace, they remained unmolested, and, with those who had escaped seizure, became the progenitors of the present Acadians now settled in various parts of the British maritime provinces, notably at Madawaska, on the upper St. John, and at Clare, in Nova Scotia. Others were sent from Virginia to England, and others again, after the complete conquest of the country, found refuge in France.

In one particular the authors of the deportation were disappointed in its results. They had hoped to substitute a loyal population for a disaffected one, but they failed for some time to find settlers for the vacated lands. The Massachusetts soldiers, to whom they were offered, would not stay in the province, and it was not till five years later that families of British stock began to occupy the waste fields of the Acadians. This goes far to show that a longing to become their heirs had not, as has been alleged, any considerable part in the motives for their removal.

New England humanitarianism, melting into sentimentality at a tale of woe, has been unjust to its own. Whatever judgment may be passed on the cruel measure of wholesale expatriation, it was not put in execution till every resource of patience and persuasion had been tried and failed. The agents of the French court, civil, military, and ecclesiastical, had made some act of force a necessity. The government of Louis XV. began with making the Acadians its tools, and ended with making them its victims.

THREE QUIET LADIES OF THE NAME OF LUCE.

THREE quiet ladies of the name of Luce —Miss Maria, Miss Margaret, and Miss Martha Luce. Perhaps you would not have called them precisely old; yet there seemed to be no time within the Highfields memory when they had not looked exactly as they did now. But then people grow up with such indecent haste, and people who have grown up remain so long without changing their masks, that they become a sort of landmark. If the young people of the place, nevertheless, who regarded the Misses Luce as immemorial monoliths had been told of the superior contempt with which the Misses Luce regarded them for their insolence in growing up, and their brazen forwardness in marrying, and wheeling their children about the streets, they would no more have believed it than if told that the old witch-stone in the edge of the forest, on which many an uncanny measure had been trodden, had risen from its mossy bed to testify.

Ah, it was an old witch-stone! Seated upon this stone, under the flickering green shade and sun—how many years ago!—had the father of the Misses Luce first kissed their mother. That is, allowing that it was not merely tradition, and that old Squire Luce, rest his soul! had ever so far forgotten himself as to condescend to such lightness. Here, with a sweet superstition regarding it, had Miss Maria led the reluctant steps of a swain who once went home from singing-school with her, remembering, perhaps, that history repeats itself—as it might have done, indeed, had not the swain, mistaking the cry of a child in the farm beyond the wood for that of the panther which had been reported in the neighborhood, fled incontinently, leaving her to her fate. She had despised men ever since. Here, too, had Miss Margaret come with some of her companions on an All-hallow-eve night to try a spell, leaving them on the skirt of the wood, just within reach; and, sitting on the stone, she had seen a stranger walking in the broad moonbeam and turning upon her so dark and splendid a face as he passed that she could not be sure whether it was her future lover or the Evil One, and had herself fled as incontinently as her sister's swain had done, and never dared lift her eyes again to the face of man. Here, too, had Miss Martha hap-

pened, ignorant of the ventures of her sisters, to see the youth who had sat on the edge of a parlor chair alone with her all one evening, till her father had called out that it was time decent folks were at home —(to make Bethiah Brigham believe he was again visiting her, which he never did, her elder sister, Maria, had, how many a night! set a candle in the window of the empty parlor) — here had she happened, only to see the unfaithful wretch sit with his arm about Bethiah, and her head upon his shoulder, the day before their banns were called in meeting. It was not much of a love experience, you may say; yet it was quite enough for the fancy of poor Miss Maria and Miss Margaret, and they always appealed to Miss Martha whenever any amatory question arose, as the one having sufficient knowledge and experience of the subject to discourse. It was in this view that they pounced upon Marion, their niece, when, in one of her vacations, she was found upon this witch-stone reading a letter, which she hastily tucked into her dress, and haled her before Miss Martha and left them alone together, receiving Miss Martha's subsequent dictum, that Marion might keep the letter, as law, if not gospel.

Marion was the child of the brother who, having run away from Highfields to live, had one day come back there to die, and had brought with him his little child, who had seemed to her three aunts something just out of heaven's gates. It was a subject of pride to them that their brother had married at all; it was the only wedding in the family. To be sure, they had had nothing to do with it, and had never seen his wife; but in some mysterious way it took off the reproach of their spinsterhood; it made them one with the race, not individuals aside from it; and if one of Squire Luce's children had married, the rest were as good as married, especially with this child to bring up. They brought her up according to their own notions, which notions seemed born of a belief that there were lions in the way, ready at every opportunity to devour young girls. It was only by the intervention of the family physician that Marion was allowed at last to go to boarding-school, where she afterward remained as a teacher of elocution, coming home only in her vacations, or when, for some reason known only to the currents of the blood, her heart yearned for some of her own kin.

And after Marion went away, their life relapsed into its former preternatural stillness. There was absolutely nothing to disturb it, nobody to come in, nothing to expect, nothing to do. The week was broken by Sunday, of course, and in a measure by Wednesday evening prayer-meeting, and there was the Missionary Sewing Society every other week — all agreeable dissipations, but not absorbing ones. The town was so thrifty that their charities were not exhausting; and they had few gossips, and were too innocent to know how to talk scandal well if they had had more. In the vacuity they clung with a fatuous expectation to the mail, and the possibilities it might bring to them from the great world beyond, in a way that gave a flavor of romance to their lives. Every morning one of them stalked gauntly down to the post-office in the corner of the variety store, where nothing was ever handed out to them, with the exception of Marion's weekly letter and the *Puritan Messenger*. But that never daunted them; they immediately possessed themselves of a fund of fresh hope for the morrow, and rising, found every morning bright with expectation of something, they knew not what, arriving by the mail.

Their pocket-handkerchiefs, too, formed an important element in their lives. Bridget, all unaware of it, dwelt under an unlifting cloud of suspicion regarding those handkerchiefs. Not that, even among themselves, they ever accused her of the pure fact of theft, but the circumstance that their best handkerchiefs did not come out of the wash till week after next pointed rather fixedly to such a probability as that Bridget thought she owned the handkerchiefs, and kindly allowed them to use the articles once in every week or two. It was of no use to mark them severely with an L, for all their last names, of course, began with L, and so, sooth to say, did Bridget's. It was a queer way to spell O'Connell, but Bridget said it was the right way, and Bridget had lived with them so many years that they never thought of disputing her. Nor was it of any use to mark them with an M, for all their first names began with an M, and not only that, but with M-a-r. Their sole refuge was to write out their names in full, with their best glasses on, and

in their finest script and most indelible ink; the affair being one of much ceremony, with warm flat-irons, and drying in the sun, and always attended by the final breaking down and retiring of Miss Martha to her own room, indelible ink being a subject of tearful memory with her, she having been engaged with it on the day that news arrived of Bethiah Brigham's marriage. And when she descended again to the lower regions, how the cushions were shaken up in the best chair for her, and fresh coals were put in the foot-stove, and a delicious hot sangaree was stirred and tasted and improved and stirred again, Miss Maria grimly thinking that no man alive was worth it all, yet joining Margaret, who, in her starved life, hailed this bit of emotion as the prisoner did the flower growing up between the flags of his cell, and, unconsciously it may be, perfectly happy in having the thing to pity. For the rest, they sometimes took their handkerchiefs on Bridget's afternoon out and washed them themselves; but as this hastier method tended to yellow them, they did not often attempt it, and contented themselves with hanging over the clothes-horse on Tuesdays, and quietly removing them as fast as they accumulated, never quite satisfied that they had them all. On the whole, the handkerchiefs were a real godsend.

Another godsend was their superstition. For the good souls, who pinched themselves to send missionaries to the heathen, had a score or so of small superstitions that did not vary greatly from the worship of stocks and stones. The moon was a prolific source of them. What would the poor women have thought if anybody had told them that their solicitude as to seeing the new moon over their left shoulders, and with silver in their pockets, and not through glass, and never failing to wish, was a relic of the heathen worship of the silver-horned goddess Astarte?—especially that part of it all which obliged them to bow nine times, wishing with each bow, on the first glimpse of her, in expectation each of a gift within the month as recompense for the act of complaisance. The old farmer, jogging along in his pung one November evening, who saw them just setting out over the snow, single file, for missionary meeting, with Rosy, the little table girl carrying their lantern—the old farmer who saw them all stop deliberately at the first sight of the golden blossom of the new moon dropping down the violet depths of the west, and bow nine times with solemn angularity, little Rosy doing just as they did, may not have thought they were heathen, but he might have thought that they were inmates of a lunatic asylum out for a walk.

Then, besides, if a dog bayed at night, they looked for a death as much as if it had been a banshee; the breaking of a looking-glass, and the shattering of the image within it, also foretold death to them; nothing would induce them to cut their nails on Sunday, lest they should do something they were ashamed of before the week was over; if they put on a garment wrong side out, they would wear it so all day, for fear of turning their luck if they turned the garment; they threw the salt over their shoulders, this way and that, for nothing if not in propitiation of evil powers, when they spilled it at table; in a sort of Oriental divination they always turned their tea-cups, too, after the tea-drinking which they loved to prolong in soft sweet summer evenings, with honeysuckle smells coming in the door, and the sound of distant bells from the next village below making gentle music; I do not know as to their feelings regarding thirteen at table, since that was something they never had a chance to try. All this gave them a great deal to talk about, the more as they added to it the telling of their dreams at breakfast, although the visions of the night became more ghostly and unreal than before when recited on a bright winter's morning, with the crisp creak of logs hauled over the snow by steaming oxen outside for an accompaniment. Miss Martha even had a dream-book, but it was felt among them that that was going a little too far; it was pardoned to her on account of her sentimental experience; but it was kept in her own room, and only now and then consulted by the sisters in a secret manner, when a Welsh rare-bit or a bit of cold apple-pie had wrought dreams of unusual portent; but such harmless shibboleths as "Dream of the dead and you'll hear of the living," or "Fruit out of season is trouble out of reason," or "Dream of a death and go to a wedding," were justified to them by history and habit, although Miss Maria looked at them askance, and occupied herself oftener in finding their exceptions than in proving their rule.

The sisters had, however, some other unfailing topics of conversation. Miss Maria, years ago, when rumor of bacteria first reached the vulgar ear, had mounted the germ theory, mention of which by some strange accident she had chanced to pick up, but only mention, so that she was at liberty to develop the theory after any manner that struck her fancy. She tied up her mouth when sweeping was in progress; she burned coffee and vinegar and sugar till the house had an odor of its own; she declined to kiss people except on rare occasions; she would not breathe the night air without a respirator, regardless of Miss Margaret's irritating insinuation that there was no other air to breathe at night; she took snuff to create a volcanic escape for any deleterious inhalation; and one could not have a toothache or a rheumatism without a rehearsal of all the possibilities of germs, till it seemed to all of them, as Bridget expressed it, as much as your life was worth to live. Miss Maria had fine ideals of that millennium when all poisonous germs were to have been exterminated, and such absolute health was to reign in their place that mankind were to be practically immortal; but at that point of development she was rebuked by Miss Margaret, who shivered at profanity, the idea tending to assert that men themselves were gods. But then Miss Maria always fell back on her strong point of the mosquitoes —mosquitoes that she held to be only conveyers of malaria, in spite of her niece Marion's declaration that there were mosquitoes in swarms both at Highfields and at the North Pole, and not an atom of malaria at either. She fell like a fury upon the doomed marauder that dared to invade her nettings, maintaining it was not the sting of the thing she minded, but the germs of leprosy and all diseases with which that sting inoculated her; and it was idle for Miss Martha to look up with her round astonished eyes and declare that she hadn't got the leprosy: it only gave Miss Maria a chance to talk all day about the theory.

And that would not suit Miss Margaret at all; for Miss Margaret did the murders for the family. Not that the stainless woman committed, herself, overt acts of felony, nor that there were so many of them, all told—only those which happened to filter through the careful columns of the *Messenger*, or which were so redolent of all the disagreeable odors belonging to the murder-committing class by the time they reached her in poor Bridget's newspaper, worn and soiled by the touch of all its co-subscribers. There was a singular outreaching to the world in the way in which this simple and white-hearted person made herself familiar with crime, and although she had never hurt a fly in her life, pursued the murderers with a morbid fascination till they ascended rejoicing into heaven. The matter did not interest her sisters, but they listened with a vague feeling that Margaret was a woman of the world, acquainted with human nature; and it ended in their turning over the tramps to her for treatment when any paused at their door, if, indeed, the sight of Bridget's face—where the most prominent feature presented an open view of the Thames Tunnel—had not already frightened them away.

As for Miss Martha, her contribution to the family conversation was the state of the tides and the quarters of the moon, concerning which she perpetually consulted her almanac. It did not signify in the least that they dwelt a hundred miles inland; the fact that down on the coast the great sea rose and fell, and that the mysterious power pushed slowly up the rivers twice a day, was the most alluring fact in the universe to her imagination. She lay awake sometimes in the dark, thinking that now the midnight tide was sounding its thunders along the shore; and she was always saying that now the moon was in such a quarter, or that if it rose so many minutes past five this morning, it must set within so many minutes past five this afternoon, and announcing that it was a dry moon, or a wet moon, or that with this moon there must be a course of very high tides. Certainly the almanac occupied a good part of her attention; if it also occupied the same shelf with her dream-book and her Bible, it was only because there was no other shelf in her room. Miss Martha had also some window flowers and some chickens. Miss Maria objected vigorously to the chickens, as she also did to the cat, on account of germs; but they all had a trick of indulging Miss Martha. As to the flowers, Miss Maria vibrated between the opposing theories that they consumed carbon and eliminated oxygen, and that they made malaria. You knew which idea she was advocating by the silent presence of a bottle of the solution of sulphate of quinine upon the

mantel. It was a source of great conversational flow with Miss Martha when one of the plants pouted out a new bud; a blossom made her radiant as long as it lasted; and when by any stretch of good fortune she found two eggs in one of her hens' nests she felt rich enough to have one of her old gowns made over for Rosy.

And that was about all there was in their lives. One could not call them very full. To Marion, before she went away to school, and coming back on her vacations, in the rebound of her protesting nature, they seemed bitterly empty. "It is mere vegetation," she cried to herself, never thinking of the time when merely to grow like a flower in the sun would seem blest to her.

Miss Maria, the eldest of the three, was not a church member, although her sisters were. She went with them to evening and missionary meeting because there was nothing else to go to, and because she liked to fight, if only in her silent thoughts. Wisely, she did not spend much time in reviling religious methods, perhaps because she rather envied her sisters' peace of mind, and did not wish to disturb it; yet she gave voice now and then without regard to persons. It may have been because she felt herself rather on scientific ground that she cherished her germ theory in place of a religious creed. Somehow she got a great deal of discomfort out of her germ theory, while her sisters got a great deal of comfort out of their peace of mind. Her unbelief, so far as it was unbelief, was of a mild type, it is true; but it was enough to give a great deal of trouble to Miss Margaret and Miss Martha, who could not bear to see her take out her knitting on Sundays, but who knew that if they said a word about it she would go to her own room with it and stay there, as she did on Thanksgiving-days, when she always had tea and toast upstairs, refusing to eat the sacrificial turkey or to take any part in the Thanksgiving, for she saw not what and knew not to whom, as she phrased it.

"I am sure," Miss Martha would mildly say on the eve of every Thanksgiving, "we have a great deal to be thankful for. We have each other—"

"No thanks to anybody for that," Miss Maria would answer, glumly, with an eye to the germs. "The arrangement of things—you may call it Providence, or Fate, or Nature, or what you will—has put so many traps and snares and pitfalls of accident and disease in the way that we shouldn't have each other if it could be hindered."

"And we have Marion," Miss Martha resumed, more timidly, on one occasion.

"Much we have Marion!" cried out Miss Maria then, with a great voice. "Marion in love with a play-actor, going to marry a play-actor, going to be a play-actor herself, going to perdition!"

Then Miss Martha shed a few tears over the prospect for Marion, and over her sister's inconsistency. And yet the tears had the savor of the dew in the rose, for Marion's marrying at all was something so altogether interesting as not to be altogether regrettable. "At any rate, she will come back to us sometimes," she murmured.

"Never!" said Miss Maria. "Dismiss that flattering unction. We are three dull old women, unspeakably tiresome, and she is in the swim of the world, turning night into day with the ungodly glee of her new sort. And never will she be received by me," added Miss Maria, more vehemently yet, "though she were dear as my heart's blood, while that man is beside her—that man who has tolled her away from respectability with his arts."

"Well," urged Miss Martha, who would make the best of things, "I don't look at it that way. There are very good play-actors. There was Shakespeare—"

"Shakespeare lived three hundred years ago," interpolated Miss Margaret. "And it isn't likely there's another, you know."

"Shakespeare was Shakespeare," said Miss Maria, emphatically; "and so was Mrs. Siddons, maybe," although she alone knew what she meant. "But as for these French hussies— Oh, don't talk to me!" cried Miss Maria. "I've no patience!" which was a patent fact.

"At all events," said Miss Martha, returning to the original thesis, "we have a comfortable home to be thankful for."

"I am thankful for it!" exclaimed Miss Maria—"thankful to my own father and mother in the flesh, who earned it, and left me my share of it. And if you prefer to take the credit of it away from your own hard-working parents—"

Here Miss Martha, who might have known that if Miss Maria was seldom positively aggressive, yet she never failed to follow up the foe who offered battle, discreetly and gently withdrew from the

room. And Miss Maria tossed her head, and said, "The idea!" and went out the other way to see that Bridget did not forget to-morrow the particular jelly that Martha always found so toothsome.

So life went on with the three quiet ladies of the name of Luce, and six more winters neither added snow to their hair nor lines to their faces, nor took them away. They had but one anxiety or sorrow in their lives, and that was concerning Marion, from whom of late they had not heard at all. Miss Margaret and Miss Martha had many a long talk together, in which many tears fell over her; but Miss Maria locked her pain in her stern old breast, and only once in a while gave herself a season of relaxation with it, when she took out a little blurred daguerreotype, which she had to hold all sorts of ways to see at all. It was a sweet little child's face, with large pathetic eyes that seemed to see already some prophecy of fate—of the fate that had come to Marion at last with a husband whose affections and whose principles were as light as thistle-down. Miss Maria knew all about it. And if she agonized over her darling if, in her sorrow sometimes she fell upon her knees and implored help of some unknown power, wrestling mightily for her release from pain worse than all bodily pain, there was no one there to see or hear of it.

Miss Maria, I say, knew all about Marion's troubles, at least as much as she could interpret of them. She had pretended once that she was going to spend a night, or possibly two, with Rosy's mother, who lived further up among the hills, with whom she wished to consult as to that young person's future, the carpenter having lately come home from meeting with her. She had left Rosy's mother in half an hour, and betaken herself to the great city, where it had not been difficult for her to trace Marion's husband and learn of his career. Ignorant as she was of the ways of the world, she heard enough to make her heart stand still, before it broke out in its indignant moan. In the distance, too, she saw the pale proud face of her suffering darling; but she gave no sign. When Marion wanted them, she must come back of her own will, and not because any urged her. And when Miss Maria returned to Highfields, I know not by what subtle sense her sisters knew the errand she had been about, for she told them no syllable. Nor, perhaps, if she had, could they, could either of them, have comprehended much of what filled the bald outline of the plain fact which she had learned—the fact that Marion was wretched, with a dissolute husband.

But of the first delight of the dawning of art on her horizon, with her lofty ideals smitten to fresh glory in its ray; of its slow deadening and darkening in her want of power to forget her own sorrows in those of her mimic part; of her self-abnegation and abandonment then in her husband's career, giving him all the strength of her being; of the slow and withering amazement when she found that art was with him but a craft, fidelity but a delusion, good fame but a lie—of all that they could comprehend nothing. Still less could they, with their ignorance and inexperience, comprehend the torture she endured in seeing the one she loved grow each day more degraded; the torture to a haughty spirit of suffering public disgrace from city to city—public to her, although her husband's fame and popularity had so waned together that few knew and fewer cared whether he was beside himself with wine or not; the torture to a proud, pure nature of seeing other women than his wife his associates; the torture of feeling the slow shrivelling of love till it became only a black disgust. Nor could they have understood why still she clung to him—perhaps with that divine pity which in some women takes the place of love. Noble friends, whom she met pursuing their common art highly, helped her to bear her lot; but its alternations of fever and despair, with his sinning and repenting, his indifference and his passion, gave her an unutterable longing for rest. Yet while he lived she remembered that she had vowed to live with him. And that was all. Their wanderings, their poverty, their pain, made it impossible to write home and say nothing of it all; she chose silence. But as she thought of morning rising over the soft low hills, of gentle days going by on their quiet wings, of radiant evenings and still dark in a land that seemed assoiled of stain, there, in the midst of her noisome life, the thought was as delicious as a dream of death with its eternal rest and peace.

It was the day before Thanksgiving, and the early dark was shutting down over the land, bathed in misty rose under the bloom of the young setting moon, as Miss Martha began her yearly sentence: "It would seem so much more like Thanksgiving, sister, if you enjoyed it with us, that—"

"I don't know why it should seem like Thanksgiving, Martha."

"Oh, Maria! If we haven't all we want, we have so much! And if we are grateful to the Lord for what we have, He may add the rest—"

"Is He that sort of a power?" cried Miss Maria, her sunken eyes flashing scorn. "Is He to be bought? We have nothing," she said. "There is neither health nor hope in the house, nor, so far as I can see, in the world—"

And just then the door softly opened and closed, and Marion, clad in black, came in and stood among them. "I have come home to stay," she murmured, brokenly, "if you will let me. To rest—to rest—to rest." And Miss Maria fell upon her knees and wept aloud.

The next morning Miss Martha put her head inside the kitchen door, as she came down the back stairs, saying, "Bridget, you had better have Miss Maria's tea and toast ready for Rosy to take to her room," when a voice from the dining-room beyond accosted her, and Miss Maria, busy over the table, with its broiled chicken and raised biscuit and waffles, was calling out, "The idea of being late at breakfast on a Thanksgiving-day, the only real Thanksgiving-day I ever knew in my life!" And without glancing up again, Miss Maria was bending her head and saying a blessing over the cups, and then looking across the table at Marion as if a miracle were going on before her eyes. "The angel of the Lord has come down and troubled the waters," she said. "I am going to meeting with you, sisters. If my prayers have been heard, then there is Something to hear them, and I am going to find out all there is to know. And meanwhile I give thanks." And her sisters gave thanks with her, while Marion, so lately "tortured with winter's storms and tossed with a tumultuous sea," now lying on the lounge that had been drawn up to the table, conscious that life was going on here in the same way, still, still, so still, with nothing to change its gentle ripple but the fact that there had been three quiet ladies in the house and now there were four, secure in the tranquillity of the household, felt in her heart only a perpetual thanksgiving.

SYDNEY SMITH.

"GOOD-BY, Mr. Smith. I have enjoyed your hospitality extremely. You constantly remind me of Sam Brown, whom in our country we consider quite our most remarkable buffoon."

This speech, according to a perfectly apocryphal legend, was made by an American guest to Sydney Smith. The story, though absolutely without foundation, does illustrate a very common and erroneous view of the great Canon of St. Paul's and immortal Rector of Foston. In England, at least, the public are apt to forget Sydney Smith's great services to rational freedom, and to think of him only as "quite our most remarkable buffoon." We remember him as the wit who told the child who stroked the tortoise that she "might as well stroke the dome of St. Paul's by way of pleasing the Dean." He lives as the author of the innocent query, "On whose?" when he was told by his doctor to "take a walk on an empty stomach." He is the stout humorist who in a hot summer desired "to take off his flesh and sit in his bones." He it was who, when attempts, ultimately successful, were made to warm the cathedral

of St. Paul's, observed, "You might as well try to warm the county of Middlesex." These and a thousand other anecdotes of the same kind keep Sydney Smith's jocund memory green, but always in the character of "our most remarkable buffoon." The Scotch less pleasantly remember the Canon for the saying that it requires a surgical operation to get a joke into a Caledonian head. One can rarely take up a Scotch newspaper without finding an angry protest against that remark, which is only true of a minority of my countrymen, but of them true as Gospel. Sydney Smith was no better liked for the geographical remark that Scotland was only "the knuckle-bone of England." Did Bruce and Wallace bleed for a knuckle-bone?

It is not impossible that some American readers, like our patriotic Scots, knew Sydney Smith best by the tart things he said about their country sixty years since. "Literature the Americans have none—native literature we mean: it is all imported." "Some pieces of pleasantry by Mr. Irving"—Washington Irving—he admits, do exist, and he notes the appearance of an epic poem "by Mr. Timothy Dwight." "In the four quarters of the globe, who reads an American book, or goes to an American play?" Sydney Smith asked in the *Edinburgh Review* (1818–1820). The development of sixty years has taken all the sting out of these antique gibes, but perhaps they are remembered when another saying of the Canon's is forgotten. In 1820 an Englishman was a liberal indeed who could write thus of America : "We look with unqualified pleasure to such a land of freedom, and such a magnificent spectacle of human happiness."

This last observation (which surely may be set off against sneers at Mr. Dwight) is in the true spirit of that large, noble, clear-sighted intellect and good heart of which Mr. Stewart J. Reid has told the history anew. At a time when Sydney Smith's fame is dwindling into that of a japer of japes, Mr. Reid's biography is of high value and interest. He has sought earnestly for fresh information, and unused documents have been intrusted to him by the descendants of many of the friends of Sydney Smith. Lord Lansdowne, Lord Morley, Sir Michael Hicks-Beach (in a parish of whose family manor Sydney Smith was a curate), Mr. George Howard, and many other people have permitted the biographer to ransack their family archives. He has also visited, in the spirit of a devout pilgrim, the remote and quiet rustic shrines, the parishes where Sydney Smith passed so much of his life among the country poor. He describes the little-changed scenes, the churches and parsonages, and collects the last echoes of local traditions. Throughout his biography Mr. Reid has always made it his business to remind us of Sydney Smith's sterling virtues, his courage, energy, hatred of oppression, scorn of foolish public opinion, kindness, and genial wisdom. The result is a very agreeable record, a picture like that praised by Horace, in which "the whole life of the old man is displayed" without artifice, and with manifest veracity.

When Scott wrote *Waverley* he was greatly impressed by the changes which two generations had seen. In the "sixty years" that had passed between Forty-five and the composition of the romance, the northern part of the island had changed from a warlike and pastoral stage, almost like that of the Zulus, to a modern

pacific existence. "'Tis sixty years since" the prime of Sydney Smith's career, and the alterations, though less striking, have been almost as great as in the two generations that went before. Young and even middle-aged men can scarcely believe that the England of Sydney Smith's youth was so different from the England of to-day. When Sydney Smith was the life of the *Edinburgh Review*, Catholics were still under disabilities inherited from the time of Elizabeth. Members of Parliament were returned for decayed villages by five or six venal voters, while places like Birmingham had no representatives at all. Everything everywhere was ordered for the greater glory of "the squire and his relations, who keep us in our proper stations," as the rural hymn says. In the squire's interest, foreign grain was under a prohibitive tax. In the squire's interest, it was forbidden to sell game, and the richest merchant or banker, if landless, could only see a partridge at dinner by helping to break the game laws.

> "He loves the dappled deer
> As he their father were ;
> For maiming hart or hind,
> Full many a man goes blind,"

said the old English rhyme about William the Conqueror. The same lines (substituting rabbits and hares for stags and hinds) applied to the British squire of Sydney Smith's time. To protect his game he was permitted by law, if not to blind the lieges, at least to make his park about as safe to walk in as the outskirts of Plevna during the siege. In the Museum of Scotch Antiquaries, when I was a boy, there used to be an object which was very attractive to youths. It was a large block of heavy wood, in which was accommodated a stout gun-barrel, with an old-fashioned flint-lock. This mechanism was attached to wires and chains, and the whole was called a "spring-gun." These spring-guns the squire was permitted to conceal in his covers, with the wires cunningly spread, so that the trespasser—artist, poacher, or whoever he was—might trip in the meshes, pull the trigger, and so get himself shot. The law, as one studies it in Sydney Smith's essays, appears only to have required that due notice should be given. "Beware of spring-guns," the warning used to run; and man-traps, with or without sharp-toothed edges, were also employed to capture the wayfarer. The printed warnings (though attended to by Mr. Jingle's learned dog Ponto, in *Pickwick*) could be of little service to a peasantry destitute of elementary education.

While these were the amenities of the country, the towns were not free from barbarism. Sydney Smith draws a horrible picture of a great London party—every one merry, the table bountifully set forth with flowers, glass, and silver, the dinner exquisite, and a small "climbing boy" being roasted to death up the chimney! When chimneys caught fire (as they seem often to have done on festive occasions), the practice was to send "a little lad who clomb and crope" up the flue to extinguish the flames. This was but one of the dangers incident to the lives of young chimney-sweeps. Of smaller social changes, those produced by steam, electricity, gas, education (a weaver need no longer be "a beast," as Sydney Smith says he too commonly was), it is not necessary to speak. Not one of the changes, from the emancipation of the Catholics to the abolition of spring-guns and man-traps, from humanity to climbing boys to the drainage of that then horribly malodorous city, Edinburgh, was unaided by the humor and eloquence of Sydney Smith. As Cervantes "laughed Spain's chivalry away," so the Rector of Foston laughed spring-guns, Catholic disabilities, Methodist miracles, the worst features of the game laws, dirt, ignorance, snobbishness, if not quite "away," still into dark corners and a subterranean life of shame. In doing all this, Sydney Smith deliberately placed himself for the time beyond the reach of clerical preferment. He was an ambitious man, a man fond of power, and yet he threw in his lot with the side which, though certain to win in the long-run, was by no means certain to win during his lifetime. His chosen mode of attack, ridicule, "shooting abuses with sparrow-shot," he probably could not help choosing. His splendid endowments of wit and intellectual high spirits left him no other course. But he knew as well as any one that his wit was all but fatal to his professional chances. His daughter, Lady Holland, used to say that among her earliest recollections was the following incident. An acquaintance met her and said, "Tell your father that the King has been reading his books, and says, 'Mr. Smith is a clever fellow, but he will never be a bishop.'" He never was a bishop;

he laughed at the Bench as French wits laugh at the Academy, but he would have been just as glad to wear lawn sleeves as a Frenchman to don the gold-embroidered coat of the Immortals.

Before attempting any general criticism of the genius and character of Sydney Smith, we may offer, by the aid of Lady Holland's *Memoirs* and the new biography which lies before us, a brief sketch of the life of this English humorist. Only the author of *The English Humorists*, only Thackeray, could have done justice to the subject in one of his immortal sketches. The following essay may at least send readers interested in the topic to Mr. Reid's volume.

Essex is not, in the opinion of its local rivals, a county opulent in genius. "Essex calves," the neighbors call these East Saxons, and Essex appears to be looked on as the Bœotia of England. Sydney Smith did his best to remove the reproach from the foggy county by being born there, at Woodford, on June 3, 1771. His father, Robert, was a capricious, eccentric

GATEWAY OF WINCHESTER SCHOOL.

humorist, who left his beautiful wife, Sydney Smith's mother, at the church door and went off to America. He returned in the course of time, and became the sire of Sydney, and Bobus, and other less famous children.

The young Smiths were encouraged by their father to be argumentative and disputatious—"a most intolerable and overbearing set of boys," according to Sydney.

REV. SYDNEY SMITH'S HOUSE, 56 GREEN STREET, GROSVENOR SQUARE, LONDON.

The father judiciously sent them to different public schools. Sydney and Courtenay went to Winchester. In the foundation of William of Wykeham, Sydney found, like a modern school-boy elsewhere, "that the dinners were execrable," but he does not seem to have also thought "that the company made up for them." Winchester was then a terribly rough place, full of cruel mediæval traditions. Sydney Smith, though successful in form, appears to have been tolerably miserable there. It is characteristic of human nature that he was inclined, in his manhood, to hold lightly his son's complaints of unhappiness at school. The parable of Mr. Anstey's *Vicè Versa* is illustrated afresh in every generation. Mr. Reid remarks that, even in old age, Sydney Smith was wont "to kindle into indignant eloquence when he was led to recount his schoolboy experiences of hunger, hardship, and abuse.

While Sydney was wretched at Winchester, Bobus was probably quite jolly at Eton. There Bobus made friends among the children of earls, whom Sydney came to know later, and hence his introduction to Holland House, and the origin of his share of "the caresses of the great." Sydney Smith became, in later days, the *Voiture* of the *Précieuses* of Holland House, but this social success of wit and engaging manners was only the affair of his play hours. His brother Bobus was a wit like himself. Bobus was a barrister. "Your profession certainly does not make angels of men," said Sir Henry Holland, the physician. "No, but *yours* does," replied Bobus, with an innocent air, adding another to the many jests against doctors. As for Courtenay Smith, he was a little spendthrift at school. By pinching and starving, Sydney paid his debts, and long afterward inherited from him a considerable fortune. From Winchester Sydney Smith went to New College, Oxford, where he has left no tradition: few men do in the brief course of the flying terms. He got a fellowship, worth, at that time, only £100 a year, and never drew another penny from his father. It was before quitting Oxford, we presume, in 1794, that Sydney Smith went to live at Mont Villiers, in France. For the sake of safety, this orthodox young Whig joined the local Jacobin club, where he was known as *le Citoyen Smees*. Probably no other Jacobin ever became a Canon of St. Paul's, or wrote stately in the *Edinburgh Review*.

Perhaps Sydney Smith would never have chosen the Church as a profession had the choice been his. He was put in one of the priests' offices that he might earn a morsel of bread, for his father could not afford to educate him, like Bobus, for the bar. Being a priest, Sydney Smith did his duty manfully by Church and people: perhaps in no career could his example and his work have been so profitable to his country and his kind. His first curacy (1794) was that of Nether Avon, "six miles from a lemon," if, indeed, that ingredient of punch and element of a happy life could be bought even in the drowsy old town of Amesbury. How sleepy an English clerical "Sleepy Hollow" could be in 1796 may be partly understood from the following contemporary fact. In a county much less slumbrous than Wiltshire is a parsonage not far from a famous university. The parson's family (not poor people) took in no newspaper during the great war of 1870. On Sundays the parson used to have a look at the county weekly paper at the squire's. This little fact may do more than a ream of writing to show American readers how lazily indifferent to the world's affairs an English rural district may still contrive to be. Almost wholly destitute of society, except when the Hicks-Beaches were at home, Sydney Smith struggled with the idle "wretchedness of most unclean living," as the Prayer-book calls it, that prevailed in his parish. He opened Sunday-schools, where the ragged boys came in the most airy garments, "ready for a whipping," like fowls ready trussed for cooking.

Such were—unhappily such too often are—the dwellers in our English Arcadia. In the "profound, immeasurable, awful dullness of this place" Sydney Smith lay buried, but by no means idle, till he became travelling tutor, "bear-leader," as they said then, to the young heir of all the Hicks-Beaches. In 1798 Sydney took his pupil to Edinburgh, where they found "odious smells, barbarous sounds, bad suppers, excellent hearts, and most enlightened and cultivated understandings."

These were the days of Dugald Stewart, of Sir Walter's glorious youth, of Adam Ferguson and Henry Erskine, Jeffrey and Campbell. Sydney Smith and his pupil lived on the windy crest of the New Town, in George Street. Sydney says that he once rescued a man who was black in the face, having been blown by the wind flat against the door of his lodgings. I myself have seen a lady lifted up about three feet off the ground by the wind in Edinburgh, while pallid bailies clung trembling round the solid pedestals of the monuments in George Street, and fathers of families who had to cross Dean Bridge crawled on their hands and knees. Sydney Smith's legend of the victim flattened against his door is hardly an exaggeration. As one should read *Humphrey Clinker* to understand the malodorous Edinburgh just before Sydney Smith's time, so, for Edinburgh a little later, Hogg's *Life of Shelley* should be studied. Sydney was particularly struck (like Heine in Göttingen) by the prodigious

feet, like "family Bibles," of the servant-girls in respectable families.

In Edinburgh Sydney Smith laid the foundation of his fame as an eloquent, amusing, and courageous preacher. In 1802 he became one of the original staff of the *Edinburgh Review*, and *his* articles, at least, retain all the sparkle and effervescence which have died out of the essays of his comrades.

When young Hicks-Beach's education was finished, Sydney took other pupils. In Edinburgh was the first home of his married life—a life of few adventures, mere "changes from the blue room to the brown," from one rectory or vicarage to another. In 1803 Sydney Smith left Edinburgh for London, where he almost at once became a popular preacher and lecturer. No one ever filled like Sydney Smith the somnolent benches of the Royal Institution in Albemarle Street with a delighted and wide-awake company. He now became and remained the guest and friend of Holland House. Like Carlyle, Sydney Smith could not always afford a cab, and he was compelled to trudge through the rainy streets, and change his muddy boots on his arrival. Thackeray has drawn for us, in "Mrs. Perkins's Ball," a picture of the proud porter sneering at this harmless action on the part of Mr. Frederick Minchin. Carlyle has confessed and groaned over his own loss of temper when Mrs. Carlyle's draggled shoe-laces needed to be tied up. But Sydney Smith, with his invincible spirits, made even the solemn disapproval of pampered lackeys relax in shouts of laughter.

These years of danger from abroad, years when a day's mastery of the Channel would have made Napoleon master of England, were evil times for Liberals. Somehow Tories do seem to make the best rulers in seasons of war, and Tories of the most strenuous and benighted sort checked all domestic reforms during Sydney Smith's residence in London, and kept France on the far side of the blessed narrow seas. The country had enough to do to defend her shores, without troubling about Catholic emancipation. However, the Grenville ministry and Sydney Smith's friends had a brief lease of power in 1806. For their ingenuous supporter, Sydney Smith, they secured a living, that of Foston, in the deepest depths of Yorkshire. The living was worth £500 a year, and was a certainty which a poor man could

FOSTON RECTORY.

not refuse, however much he might regret leaving London for the Cimmerian darkness of the country, and for dinner parties where the servant threw away the soup, "supposing it was dirty water." From the Yorkshire retreat, where he was parson, doctor, magistrate, and architect of his own new vicarage, Sydney Smith published the "Letters of Peter Plymley." These anonymous epistles advocated the claims of the Catholics to complete liberty, and especially took the side of the Irish. Sydney Smith could not foresee that the concession of all the reforms he demanded would still leave the Ireland of to-day in a condition more distressing than open rebellion. He was sanguine about the future of Ireland, and while his hopes have not been fulfilled, a criminal anomaly has been removed from English life, and perhaps no writer contributed so much to this result as did Sydney Smith. The government in vain tried to discover the author of the "Plymley Letters"—epistles unmatched in destructive wit except by the infinitely finer banter of Pascal.

The use of his pen, and the society of Lord Grey and the family at Howick, kept the intellectual high spirits of Sydney Smith alive during his long premature burial at Heslington, where he lived while building his new parsonage, and at Foston. He found Foston a parish where there had been no resident parson for more than a century and a half, and where the parsonage-house was valued at £50. He built a parsonage-house and farm-steading at the cost of £4000, brought one hundred acres under cultivation, and spent upon the living more than it was worth. All this while he was fighting the mediæval survivals of our law and society in the *Edinburgh Review.* "If a man injured Westminster Bridge, he was hanged; if he appeared disguised on a public road, he was hanged; if he cut down young trees, *if he shot at rabbits*, if he stole anything at all from a wheat field, ... for any of these offenses he was hanged"—so savage was the law of England in the early part of what the clergyman described as "this so-called nineteenth century." In his warfare against abuses up to this date Sydney Smith had been a writer only. In 1825 he appeared for the first time as a speaker on a public platform, to support the claims of the Catholics. But his brother clergy were too strong for him. "A poor clergyman whispered to me," he writes, "that he was quite of my way of thinking, but had nine children. I begged he would remain a Protestant." In 1828 Sydney Smith left Foston for preferment at Bristol, where he preached to a Protestant mayor and corporation an unpardonable and unpardoned sermon about the duty of Christian charity toward persons differing from us in creed. For twenty years the corporation never returned to the cathedral where they had listened to such subversive doctrines. Perhaps the ferocity of Bristol orthodoxy made Sydney Smith all the better pleased to migrate to the beautiful west Somerset parish of Combe Florey, "the vale of flowers," where he had leisure to throw himself into the final struggle for Parliamentary reform. The triumph of his party enabled them to offer him a canonry of St. Paul's, and this prize, which some men win long before they are forty, was the high-water mark of Sydney Smith's professional promotion. He made up his mind "to grow old merrily," and his letters, like Charles Lamb's, are now touched with the melancholy of humorous old age. "I sleep with Cough and Cramp," wrote Lamb; "we lie three in a bed." Sydney Smith, too, could tell how he and Mrs. Smith fared at the hands of physicians. "We take something every hour," he says, convivially, "and pass the mixture." But at sixty-three he was still "burly but active-looking, with dark complexion and iron-gray hair." "I suspect," he said, "that the fifth act of life should be in great cities; it is there, in the long death of old age, that a man most forgets himself and his infirmities, receives the greatest consolation from the attentions of friends, and the greatest diversions from external circumstances."

On Saturday evening, February 22, 1845, came the Saturday evening of the life of Sydney Smith, and he entered on the Sabbath of his rest. When he was dying, some one came to see him and said, "I fear, Mr. Smith, you are very ill." "Yes," replied Sydney Smith; "not enough of me left to make a curate."

When one tries to estimate the genius of Sydney Smith, what strikes one most is his humor unaccompanied by melancholy. Most great humorists have been melancholy men, like Molière.

Sydney Smith, on the other hand, was not a jester only in his books and in society. His wonderful high spirits were almost constantly with him in the home which they filled with happiness and laughter. The essence of his wit is this volatile and airy spirit, soaring without trammel high above the laboring world, and discovering, from its familiar heights, mirthful resemblances in things where other men only saw incongruities. Boldness, freedom, vivacity, these are the characteristics of his humor. He had an extraordinary audacity in venturing almost on the verge of nonsense. He was daring in humorous exaggeration. This buoyant courage and gayety of fancy sometimes give his good things the character of American humor.

He began his *History of Ethics* with Socrates, and avowed that "Aristotle was not such a fool as many people think who have never read him." The early philosophers, he declared, "were gallant gentlemen, for whose company, I confess, I have never had any great relish." Again:

INTERIOR OF FOSTON CHURCH.

"If Orpheus or Linus sang, in bad verse, such advice as a grandmother would now give a child of six years old, he was thought to be inspired by the gods, and statues or altars were erected to his memory." This good-humored irreverence to the mighty shades of Orpheus and Linus reminds one, in its frank Philistinism, of Mark Twain and the *Innocents Abroad.* I am accustomed to take Orpheus very seriously, and do not quite enjoy this cavalier treatment of Linus. But the gayety of Sydney Smith becomes more boisterous than ever when he tries to account for the superiority of man over the beasts. To these he allows the rudiments of our faculties. But *we,* he remarked, live longer, collect more experience, and are gregarious, so that we communicate our valuable discoveries to each other. How different is the conduct, he says, of the unprogressive lion! "A lion lives under a hole in a rock, and if any other lion happens to pass by, they fight. Now whoever gets a habit of lying under a hole in a rock, and fighting with every gentleman who passes near him, can not possibly make any progress." Again, lions are uncommunicative, very; hence their stationary culture. "If lions would only come together and growl out the observations they have made about killing sheep and shepherds, and the most likely places for catching a calf grazing, they could not fail to improve." This is quite in "Mark's way," as Lord Tennyson says. Again, when the Catholics were oppressed in Ireland, Sydney Smith said to the clergy and the government: "Why do you choose these fierce people to bully? Why don't you torment William Wilberforce and the Clapham saints? Why torture a bulldog when you can get a frog or a rabbit?" Again he writes, on pulpit oratory: "Why are we natural everywhere but in the pulpit? *Why call in the aid of paralysis to piety?* Is sin to be taken from man, as Eve was from Adam, by casting him into a deep sleep?" Yet, with all his audacious humor, his friends could only once remember that Sydney Smith made a jest bordering on irreverence toward things Scriptural, and he instantly withdrew it, and seemed ashamed of his words.

He was a great lover of light; he rejoiced, like Scott, in the discovery of gas, a flaring mode of lighting which we do not much admire nowadays. This love of light, of shadowless views and clear-cut distinctions, was part of his intellectual nature. "We are all for orthodoxy and common-sense," he exclaimed, in the *Edinburgh Review,* and he was convinced that common-sense and orthodoxy were at one in their decisions. His mind was of the eighteenth century. He had no more mercy on Methodists and missionaries (guilty, both of them, of "enthusiasm") than on "Puseyites," those ambiguous creatures. the bats of the modern twilight of the gods.

In parting with Sydney Smith, one can not but hold him *felix opportunitate vitæ*—happy in the span allotted to him of life. Liberalism was triumphant in his later days. What would he think of the "enthusiasms" of modern Liberalism? How would his orthodoxy regard Darwinism, now that Evolution has passed beyond the reach of facile ridicule? Many things in which Sydney Smith rejoiced seem now to have the drawbacks inseparable from his beloved gas. He might have been less assured in all his ideas had he lived in our time; but how we miss his wisdom, his wit, his mirth!—we who live in an age of stolidity and frivolity, when instruction, as Sydney Smith said of Hallam's books, is "clear of every particle of amusement."

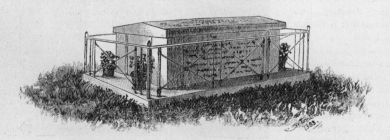

TOMB OF THE REV. SYDNEY SMITH, KENSAL GREEN CEMETERY, LONDON.

THE HUDSON, FROM FORT PUTNAM.

NATURE'S SERIAL STORY.

XII.

MR. HARGROVE had welcomed the invitation that took his daughter among some of her former companions, hoping that a return to brilliant fashionable life would prove to her that she could not give it up. It was his wish that she should marry a wealthy man of the city. His wife did not dream of any other future for her handsome child, and she looked forward with no little complacency to the ordering of a new and elegant establishment.

At the dinner table Gertrude had given a vivacious account of her yachting experience, and all had appeared to promise well; but when she went to the library to kiss her father good-night he looked at her inquiringly, and asked, "You enjoyed every moment, I suppose ?"

She shook her head sadly, and after a moment said : "I fear I've grown rather tired of that kind of thing. We made much effort to enjoy ourselves. Is there not a happiness which comes without so much effort ?"

"I'm sorry," he said, simply.

"Perhaps you need not be. Suppose I find more pleasure in staying with you than in rushing around ?"

"That would not last. That is contrary to nature."

"I think it would be less contrary to *my* nature than forced gayety among people I care nothing about."

He smiled at her fondly, but admitted to himself that absence had confirmed the impressions of the summer, instead of dissipating them, and that if Burt became her suitor he would be accepted.

When she looked out on the morning of the excursion to Fort Putnam it was so radiant with light and beauty that hope sprung up within her heart. Disappointment that might last through life could not come on a day like this. Silvery mists were rising from the river down among the Highlands. The lawn and many of the fields were as green as they had been in June, and on every side were trees like immense bouquets, so rich and varied were the colors of their leaves. There was a dewy freshness in the air, a genial warmth in the sunshine, a spring-like blue in the sky; and in these was no suggestion that the November of her life was near. "And yet it may be," she thought. "I must face my fate soon, and I must be true to Amy."

Mrs. Hargrove regarded with discontent the prospect of another long mountain expedition; but Fred, her idol, was wild for it, and in a day or two he must return to his school in the city, from which, at his earnest plea, he had been absent too long already; so she smiled her farewell at last upon the fateful excursion.

He, with his sister, was soon at the Cliffords', and found the rockaway—the strong old carry-all with which Gertrude already had tender associations — in readiness. Maggie had agreed to chaperon the party, little Ned having been easily bribed to remain with his father.

Miss Hargrove had looked wistfully at the Clifford mansion as she drew near to it. Never had it appeared to her more home-like, with its embowering trees and laden orchards. And when Mr. Clifford met her at the door, and took her in to see the invalid, who greeted her almost as affectionately as she would have welcomed Amy after absence, Miss Hargrove knew in the depths of her heart how easily she could be at home there.

Never did a pleasure party start under brighter auspices. Even Mrs. Clifford came out, on her husband's arm, to wave them a farewell.

The young men had their alpenstocks,

for it was their intention to walk up the steep places. Webb was about to take Alf and Johnnie on the front seat with him, when Amy exclaimed: "I'm going to drive, Mr. Webb. Johnnie can sit between us, and keep me company when you are walking. You needn't think that because you are the brilliant author of this expedition you are going to have everything your own way."

Indeed, not a little guile lurked behind her laughing eyes, which ever kept Webb in perplexity—though he looked into them so often—whether they were blue or gray. Miss Hargrove demurely took her seat with Maggie, and Burt had the two boys with him. Fred had brought his gun, and was vigilant for game, now that the "law was up."

They soon reached the foot of the mountain, and there was a general unloading, for at first every one wished to walk. Maggie good-naturedly climbed around to the front seat and took the reins, remarking that she would "soon have plenty of company again."

Burt had not recognized Amy's tactics, nor did he at first second them, even unconsciously.

One of the objects of the expedition was to obtain an abundant supply of autumn leaves and ferns for pressing. "I intend to make the old house look like a bower this winter," Amy remarked.

"That would be impossible with our city home," Miss Hargrove said, "and mamma would not hear of such an attempt. But I can do as I please in my own room, and shall gather my country *souvenirs* to-day."

The idea of decorating her apartment with feathery ferns and bright-hued leaves took a strong hold upon her fancy, for she hoped that Burt would aid her in making the collection. Nor was she disappointed, for Amy said:

"Burt, I have gathered and pressed nearly all the ferns I need already. You know the shady nooks where the most delicate ones grow, and you can help Gertrude make as good a collection as mine. You help too, won't you, Webb?" added the innocent little schemer, who saw that Burt was looking at her rather keenly.

So they wound up the mountain, making long stops here and there to gather sylvan trophies and to note the fine views. Amy's manner was so cordial and natural that Burt's suspicions had been allayed, and the young fellow, who could do nothing by halves, was soon deeply absorbed in making a superb collection for Miss Hargrove, and she felt that, whatever happened, she was being enriched by everything he obtained for her. Amy had brought a great many newspapers folded

ceedingly dull after such brilliant experiences as that of your yachting excursion."

"Do you find to-day exceedingly dull?"

"But I am used to the quiet country, and a day like this is the exception."

"I do not imagine you have ever lived a tame life."

THE HUDSON AT WEST POINT.

together so that leaves could be placed between the pages, and Webb soon noted that his offerings were kept separate from those of Burt. The latter tried to be impartial in his labors in behalf of the two girls, bringing Amy bright-hued leaves instead of ferns, but did not wholly succeed, and sometimes he found himself alone with Miss Hargrove as they pursued their search a short distance on some diverging and shaded path. On one of these occasions he said,

"I like to think how beautiful you will make your room this winter."

"I like to think of it too," she replied. "I shall feel that I have a part of my pleasant summer always present."

"Has it been a pleasant summer?"

"Yes; the pleasantest I ever enjoyed."

"I should think you would find it ex-

"Isn't that about the same as calling me wild?"

"There's no harm in beginning a little in that way. Time sobers one fast enough."

"You are so favored that I can scarcely imagine life bringing sobering experiences to you very soon."

"Indeed? Have you forgotten what occurred on these very mountains at no great distance? I assure you I never forget it;" and her eyes were eloquent as she turned them upon him.

"One does not forget the most fortunate event of one's life. Since you were

to meet that danger, I would not have missed being near for the world. I had even a narrower escape, as you know, on this mountain. The spot where Webb found me is scarcely more than a mile from here."

She looked at him very wistfully, and her face grew pale, but she only said, "I don't think either of us can forget these Highlands."

"I shall never forget that little path," he said, in a low tone, and he looked back at it lingeringly as they came out into the road and approached the rest of the party.

They made a long pause to enjoy the view looking out upon Constitution Island, West Point, the southern mountains, and the winding river, dotted here and there with sails, and with steamers, seemingly held motionless by their widely separated train of canal boats.

"What mountain is this that we are now to descend?" Miss Hargrove asked.

"Cro'nest," Burt replied. "It's the first high mountain that abuts on the river above West Point, you will remember."

They were soon winding down the S's by which the road overcame the steep declivity.

The road from the foot of the mountain descends gradually through wild, beautiful scenery to West Point. Cro'nest rose abruptly on the left, and there was a wooded valley on the right, with mountains beyond. The trees overhung the road with a canopy of gold, emerald, and crimson foliage, and the sunlight came to them as through stained-glass windows. Taking a side street at the back of the military post, they soon reached a point over which frowned the ruins of the fort, and here they left their horses. After a brief climb to the northward they entered on an old road, grass-grown and leaf-carpeted, and soon passed through the gaping sally-port, on either side of which cone-like cedars stood as sentinels. Within the fort nature had been busy for a century softening and obliterating the work of man. Cedar-trees—some of which were dying from age—grew everywhere, even on the crumbling ramparts.

All but Amy had visited the spot before, and Burt explored the place with her while the rest prepared for lunch. She had asked Gertrude to accompany them, but the latter had sought refuge with Maggie, and at her side she proposed to remain. She scarcely dared trust herself with Burt, and as the day advanced he certainly permitted his eyes to express an interest that promised ill for his inexorable purpose of constancy.

It had become clear to Miss Hargrove that he was restrained by something that had occurred between him and Amy, and both her pride and her sense of truth to her friend decided her to withdraw as far as possible from his society, and to return to the city.

She and Burt vied with each other in gayety at lunch. When it was over they all grouped themselves in the shade of a clump of cedars, and looked away upon the wide prospect, Webb pointing out objects of past and present interest. Alf and Fred speedily grew restless, and started off with the gun; Johnnie's head sunk into her mother's lap; Miss Hargrove and Burt grew quiet and preoccupied, their eyes looking off into vacancy. Webb was saying: "By one who had imagination, how much more could be seen from this point than meets the eye! There on the plain below us would rise the magnificent rustic colonnade, two hundred and twenty feet long and eighty wide, beneath which Washington gave the great banquet in honor of the birth of the Dauphin of France, and on the evening of the same day these hills blazed with musketry and rolled back the thunder of cannon with which the festivities of the evening were begun. Think of the 'Father of his country' being there in flesh and blood, just as we are here! In the language of an old military journal, 'he carried down a dance of twenty couple on the green grass, with a graceful and dignified air, having Mrs. Knox for his partner.' In almost a direct line across the river you can see the Beverly Robinson house, from which Arnold carried on his correspondence with André. You can look into the window of the room to which, after hearing of the capture of André, he hastened from the breakfast table. To this upper room he immediately summoned his wife—who had been the beautiful Margaret Shippen, you remember—and told her of his awful peril, then rushed away, leaving the poor terror-stricken woman unconscious on the floor. Would you not like to look through the glass at the house where the tragedy occurred, Miss Hargrove?"

At the sound of her name the young girl started visibly, and Webb saw that

IN THE APPLE ORCHARD.

there were tears in her eyes; but she complied without a word, and he so directed the glass that it covered the historic mansion.

"How full of sensibility she is!" thought innocent Webb, taking her quickly suppressed emotion as a tribute to his moving reminiscences.

"Oh, Webb, have done with your lugubrious ancient history!" cried Burt, springing up.

"It's time we were getting ready for a homeward move," said Maggie. "I'll go and pack the things."

"And I'll help you," added Miss Hargrove, hastily following her.

"Let me look at the house too," said Amy, taking the glass. Then she added, after a moment: "Poor Margaret Arnold! It was indeed a tragedy, as you said, Webb —a sadder one than these old preparations for war can suggest. In all his career of war and treachery, Arnold never inflicted a more cruel wound."

"How much feeling Miss Hargrove showed!" Webb remarked, musingly.

"Yes," said Amy, quietly; "she was under strong emotion evidently." Her thought was, "I don't believe she heard a word that Webb said." Then, seeing that Burt was helping Maggie and Miss Hargrove, she added, "Please point out to me some other interesting places."

Webb, well pleased, talked on to a listener who did not give him her whole attention. She could not forget her friend's paleness and manner, her alternations from extreme gayety to a look of such deep sadness as to awaken not a little sympathetic curiosity. Amy loved her friend truly, and it did not seem strange to her that Miss Hargrove was deeply interested in Burt, since they had been much thrown together, and since she probably owed her life to him.

By the time they were ready to start homeward, the southern side of Cro'nest was in deep blue shadow. They bowled along rapidly till they came to the steep ascent, and then the boys and the young men sprang out. "Would you like to walk, Gertrude?" Amy asked, for she was bent on throwing her friend and Burt together during the witching twilight that was coming on apace.

"I fear I am too tired, unless the load is heavy," she replied.

"Oh no, indeed," said Webb. "It does not take long to reach the top of the mountain on this side, and then it's chiefly downhill the rest of the way."

Amy, who had been sitting with Webb and Johnnie as before, said to Miss Hargrove, "Won't you step across the seats and keep me company?"

She complied, but not willingly. She was so utterly unhappy that she wished to be left to herself as far as possible. In her realization of a loss that seemed immeasurable, she was a little resentful toward Amy, feeling that she had been more frank than her friend in her confidences. If Amy had claims on Burt, why had she not spoken of them? why had she permitted her, for whom she professed such strong friendship, to drift almost wholly unwarned upon so sad a fate? and why was she now clearly trying to bring together Burt and the one to whom even he felt that he had no right to speak in more than a friendly manner? While she was making such immense self-sacrifice to be true, she felt that Amy was maintaining an unfair reticence, if not actually beguiling them into a display of weakness for which they would be condemned, or at least Burt would be, and love identifies itself with its object. These thoughts, having once been admitted, grew upon her mind rapidly, for it is hard to suffer through another and maintain a gentle charity. Therefore she was silent when she took her seat by Amy, and when the latter turned and gave a look that was like a caress, she did not return it.

"You are tired, Gertrude," Amy began, gently. "Indeed, you look ill. You must stay with me to-night, and I'll watch over you like Sairy Gamp."

So far from responding to Amy's playful and friendly words, Miss Hargrove said, hastily: "Oh no; I had better go on home. I don't feel very well; and I must begin preparations to-morrow for my return to the city."

Amy would not be repulsed, but putting her arm around her friend, she looked into her eyes and asked: "Why are you so eager to return to New York? Are you tiring of your country friends? You certainly told me that you expected to stay till November."

"Fred must go back to school to-morrow," said Gertrude, in a constrained voice, "and I do not think it is well to leave him alone in the city house."

"You are withdrawing your confidence from me," said Amy, sadly.

"Have you ever truly given me yours?" was the low, impetuous response. "No. If you had, I should not be the unhappy girl I am to-night. Well, since you wish to know the whole truth, you shall. You said you could trust me implicitly, and I promised to deserve your trust. If you had said to me that Burt was bound to you when I told you that I was heart-whole and fancy-free, I should have been on my guard. Is it natural that I should be indifferent to the man who risked his life to save mine? Why have you left me so long in his society without a word of warning? But I shall keep my word. I shall not try to snatch happiness from another."

Johnnie's tuneful little voice was piping a song, and the rumble of the wheels over the stony road prevented Maggie, on the last seat, from hearing anything.

The clasp of Amy's arm tightened. "Now you shall stay with me to-night," she said. "I can not explain here and now. See, Burt has turned, and is coming toward us. I pledge you my word he can never be to me more than a brother. I do not love him except as a brother, and never have, and you can snatch no happiness from me except by treating me with distrust, and going away."

They soon reached the summit, and paused to give the horses a rest. The young moon hung in the west, and its silver crescent symbolized to Miss Hargrove the hope that was growing in her heart.

Burt in the mean time was occupied with some disagreeable reflections. Perhaps both the girls had at last understood him, and had been comparing notes to his infinite disadvantage. His fickleness and the dilemma he was in may have become a jest between them. What could he do? Resentment, except against himself, was impossible. If Amy understood him, in what other way could she meet any approach to sentiment on his part than by a laughing scorn? If Miss Hargrove had divined the past, or had received a hint concerning it, why should she not shun his society? He was half desperate, and yet felt that any show of embarrassment or anger would only make him appear more ridiculous.

When they arrived at home, they found Mr. Hargrove's carriage in waiting; and Amy, after a brief conference with her friend in her room, came down prepared to accompany Miss Hargrove home after supper. Burt was still distraught, and in spite of all his efforts at ease and gayety, his embarrassment and trouble were evident. He had observed Miss Hargrove's pallor and her effort to keep up at Fort Putnam, and could not banish the hope that she sympathized with him; but now the young girl was demurely radiant. Her color had come again, and the lustre of her beautiful eyes was dazzling. Yet they avoided his, and she had far more to say to Webb and the others than to him. Webb, too, was perplexed, for during the day Amy had been as bewildering to him as to Burt. But he was in no perplexity as to his course, which was simply to wait. He, with Burt, saw the girls to the carriage, and the latter said good-night rather coldly and stiffly. Alf and Fred parted regretfully, with the promise of a correspondence which would be as remarkable for its orthography as for its natural history.

Mr. Hargrove greeted Amy cordially, but his questioning eyes rested oftenest on his daughter. Her expression and manner caused him to pace his study long and late that night. Mrs. Hargrove was very polite and a little stately. She felt that she existed on a plane above Amy.

The young girls soon pleaded fatigue, and retired. Once in the seclusion of their room, they forgot about their innocent fib, and there was not a trace of weariness in their manner. While Burt was staring at his dismal, tangled future, seeing no solution of his difficulties, a fateful conference relating to him was taking place. Amy did not look like a scorner, as with a sister's love and a woman's tact she pleaded his cause and palliated his course to one incapable of harsh judgment. But she felt that she must be honest with her friend, and that the whole truth would be best and safest in the end. Her conclusion was: "No man who loved *you*, and whom you encouraged, would ever change. I know now that I never had a particle of such feeling as you have for Burt, and can see that I naturally chilled and quenched his regard for me."

Miss Hargrove's dark eyes flashed ominously as she thought of Burt, or of any man, proving faithless after she had given encouragement.

"But it wasn't possible for me to give him any real encouragement," Amy persisted. "I've never felt as you do, and am not sure that I want to for a long time."

"How about Webb?" Miss Hargrove almost said, but she suppressed the words, feeling that since he had not revealed his secret, she had no right to do so. Indeed, as she recalled how sedulously he had guarded it, she was sure he would not thank her for suggesting it to Amy before she was ready for the knowledge. Impetuous as Miss Hargrove was at times, she had too fine a nature to be careless of the rights and feelings of others.

Her decision, after this portentous conference, was: "Mr. Burt must seek me, and seek very zealously. I know you well enough, Amy, to be sure that you will give him no hints. It's bad enough to love a man before I've been asked to do so. What an utterly perverse and unmanageable thing one's heart is!"

Burt entertained half a dozen wild and half-tragic projects before he slept that night, but finally, in utter self-disgust, settled down on the prosaic and not irrational one of helping through with the fall work on the farm, and then of seeking some business or profession to which he could give his whole mind. "As to ladies' society," he concluded, savagely, "I'll shun it hereafter till I'm grown up."

Burt always attained a certain kind of peace and the power to sleep after he had reached an irrevocable decision.

During the night the wind veered to the east, and a cold, dismal rain-storm set in. Dull and dreary indeed the day proved to Burt. He could not go out and put his resolution into force. He fumed about the house, restless yet reticent. He would rather have fought dragons than keep company with his own thoughts in inaction. All supposed he missed Amy, except Webb, who hoped he missed some one else.

"Why don't you go over and bring Amy home, Burt?" his mother asked at the dinner table. "The house seems empty without her, and everybody is moping. Even father has fretted over his newspaper, and wished Amy was here."

"Why can't they print an edition of the paper for old men and dark days?" said the old gentleman, discontentedly.

"Well," remarked Leonard, leaning

"INDEED, BURT, I CARE FOR YOU."

back in his chair, and looking humorously at Maggie, "I'm sorry for you young fellows, but I'm finding the day serene."

"Of course you are," snapped Burt. "With an arm-chair to doze in and dinner to look forward to, what more do you wish ? As for Webb, he can always get astride of some scientific hobby, no matter how bad the weather is."

"As for Burt, he can bring Amy home, and then every one will be satisfied," added his mother, smiling.

Thus a new phase of his dilemma presented itself to poor Burt. He must either face those two girls, after their night's conclave, with all its possible revelations, or else awaken at once very embarrassing surmises. Why shouldn't he go for Amy ? all would ask. "Well, why shouldn't I ?" he thought. "I may as well face it out." And in a mood of mingled recklessness and fear he drove through the storm. When his name was announced the girls smiled significantly, but went down looking as unconscious as if they had not spoken of him in six months, and Burt could not have been more suave, non-committal, and impartially polite if these ladies had been as remote from his thoughts as one of Webb's theories. At the same time he intimated that he would be ready to return when Amy was.

At parting the friends gave each other a little look of dismay, and he caught it from the same tell-tale mirror that persisted in taking a part in this drama.

"Aha!" thought the young fellow, "so they *have* been exchanging confidences, and my manner is disconcerting—not what was expected. If I have become a jest between them, it shall be a short-lived one. Miss Hargrove, with all her city experience, shall find that I'm not so young and verdant but that I can take a hand in this game also. As for Amy, I now know that she never cared for me, and I don't believe she ever would." And so he went away with laughing repartee, and did not see the look of deep disappointment with which he was followed.

Burt treated Amy in an easy, fraternal manner. He engaged actively in the task of gathering and preparing for market the large crop of apples, and he openly broached the subject of going into a business of some kind away from home, where, he declared, with a special meaning for Amy, he was not needed, adding: "It's time I was earning my salt, and settling down to

something for life. Webb and Len can take care of all the land, and I don't believe I was cut out for a farmer."

He not only troubled Amy exceedingly, but he perplexed all the family, for it seemed that he was decidedly taking a new departure. One evening, a day or two after he had broached the project of going elsewhere, his father, to Amy's dismay, suggested that he should go to the far West and look after a large tract of land which the old gentleman had bought some years before. It was said that a railroad was to be built through it, and if so, the value of the property would be greatly enhanced, and steps should be taken to get part of it into the market. Burt entered into the scheme with eagerness, and was for going as soon as possible. Looking to note the effect of his words upon Amy, he saw that her expression was not only reproachful, but almost severe. Leonard heartily approved of the plan. Webb was silent and in deep despondency, feeling that if Burt went now, nothing would be settled. He saw Amy's aversion to the project also, and misinterpreted it.

The more, however, Burt thought of his long western journey, the more serious it appeared to him. At first he had welcomed it as promising a diversion of excitement and change, now it began to appear like exile. He dreaded to think of the memories he must take with him; still more he deprecated the thoughts he would leave behind him. His plight made him so desperate that he suddenly put on his riding suit, and in a few moments was galloping furiously away on his black horse. With a renewal of hope, Webb watched his proceedings; and with many surmises, Amy, from a distant hill-side, saw him passing at a break-neck pace.

For the first two or three miles Burt rode as if he was trying to leave care behind him, scarcely heeding what direction he took. When at last he reined in his reeking horse he found himself near the entrance of the lane over which the willows met in a Gothic arch. He yielded to the impulse to visit the spot which had seen the beginning of so fateful an acquaintance, and had not gone far when a slight turn in the road revealed a group whose presence almost made his heart stand still for a moment. Miss Hargrove had stopped her horse on the very spot where he had aided her in her awkward predicament.

Her back was toward him, and her great dog was at her side, looking up into her face as if in mute sympathy with his fair mistress.

Hope sprung up in Burt's heart. She could not be there with bowed head if she despised him. Her presence seemed in harmony with that glance by which when weak and unnerved after escaping from deadly peril she had revealed possibly more than gratitude to the one who had rescued her. His love rose like an irresistible tide, and he resolved that before he left his home Amy and Miss Hargrove should know the whole truth, whatever might be the result. Meanwhile he was rapidly approaching the young girl, and the dog's short bark of recognition was her first intimation of Burt's presence. Her impulse was to fly, but in a second she saw the absurdity of this course, and yet she was greatly embarrassed, and would rather have been discovered by him at almost any other point of the globe. She was going to the city on the morrow, and as she had drawn rein on this spot, and realized the bitterness of her disappointment, tears would come. She wiped them hastily away, but dreaded lest their traces should be seen.

Turning her horse, she met Burt with a smile that her moist eyes belied, and said, "I'm glad you do not find me in such an awkward dilemma as when we first met here. I've been giving my horse a rest. Do you not want a gallop?" and away like the wind she started homeward.

Burt easily kept at her side, but conversation was impossible. At last he said: "My horse is very tired, Miss Hargrove. At this pace you will soon be home, and I shall feel that you are seeking to escape from me. Have I fallen so very low in your estimation?"

"Why," she exclaimed, in well-feigned surprise, as she checked her horse, "what have you done that you should fall in my estimation?"

"I shall tell you before very long," he said, with an expression that seemed almost tragic.

"Mr. Clifford, you surprise me. Your horse is all of a foam, too. Surely this brief gallop can not have so tired your superb beast. What has happened? Amy is not ill, or any one?"

"Oh no," he replied, with a grim laugh. "Every one is well and complacent. I had been riding rapidly before I met you.

My horse has been idle for some days, and I had to run his spirit out of him. Amy wishes to have a chestnutting party to-morrow. Won't you join us?"

"I'm sorry, Mr. Clifford, but I return to the city to-morrow afternoon, and was coming over in the morning to say good-by to Amy and your father and mother."

"I am very sorry too," he said, in tones that gave emphasis to his words.

She turned upon him a swift, questioning glance, but her eyes instantly fell before his intent gaze.

"Oh, well," she said, lightly, "we've had a very pleasant summer, and all things must come to an end, you know." Then she went on speaking in a matter-of-fact way of the need of looking after Fred, who was alone in town, and of getting the city house in order, and of her plans for the winter, adding: "As there is a great deal of fruit on the place, papa does not feel that he can leave just yet. You know he goes back and forth often, and so his business does not suffer. But I can just as well go down now, and nearly all my friends have returned to town."

"All your friends, Miss Hargrove?"

"Amy has promised to visit me soon," she said, hastily.

"It would seem that I am not down on your list of friends," he began, gloomily.

"Why, Mr. Clifford, I'm sure papa and I would be glad to have you call whenever you are in town."

"I fear I shall have to disappoint Mr. Hargrove," he said, a little satirically. "I'm going West the last of this month, and may be absent much of the winter. I expect to look about in that section for some opening in business."

"Indeed!" she replied, in tones which were meant to convey but little interest, yet which had a slight tremor in spite of her efforts. "It will be a very great change for you."

"Perhaps you think that constitutes its chief charm."

"Mr. Clifford," she said, "what chance have I had to think about it at all? You have never mentioned the matter." (Amy had, however, and she had not only thought about, but dreamed of it, as if she had been informed that on a certain date the world would end.) "Is it not a rather sudden plan?" she asked, a little hesitatingly.

"Yes, it is. My father has a large tract of land in the West, and it's time it was looked after. Isn't it natural that I should think of doing something in life? I fear I've given you the impression that I have few thoughts beyond having a good time."

"To have a good time in life," she said, smiling at him, "is a very serious matter—one worthy of any one's attention. It would seem that few accomplish it."

"And I greatly fear that I shall share in the ill success of the majority."

"You are much mistaken. A man has no end of resources. You will soon be enjoying the excitement of travel and enterprise in the West."

"And you the excitement of society and conquest in the city. Conquests, however, must be almost wearisome to you, Miss Hargrove, you make them so easily."

"You overrate my power. I certainly should soon weary of conquests were I making them. Women are different from men in this respect. Where in history do we read of a man who was satiated with conquests? Well, here we are at home. Won't you come in? Papa will be glad to see you."

"Are you going to the city to-morrow?"

"Yes."

"May I call on you this evening?"

"Certainly. Bring Amy with you, won't you?"

"Will you forgive me if I come alone?"

"I'll try to."

He did not reply, but lifted his hat gravely, mounted his horse, and galloped away as if he were an aide bearing a message that might save a battle.

Miss Hargrove hastened to her room, and took off her hat with hands that trembled. Burt's pale, resolute face told her that the crisis in her life had come. And yet she did not fully understand him. If he meant to speak, why had he not spoken? why had he not asked permission to speak to her father?

Mr. Hargrove, from his library window, saw Burt's formal parting, and concluded that his fears or hopes—he scarcely knew which were uppermost, so deep was his love for his daughter, and so painful would it be to see her unhappy—were not to be fulfilled. By a very great effort Gertrude appeared not very *distraite* at dinner, nor did she mention Burt, except in a casual manner, in reply to a question from her mother, but her father thought he detected a strong and suppressed excitement.

She excused herself early from the table, and said she must finish packing for her departure.

Burt's black horse was again white with foam before he approached his home. In the distance he saw Amy returning, the children running on before, Alf whooping like a small Indian to some playmate who was answering farther away. The gorgeous sunset lighted up the still more brilliant foliage, and made the scene a fairyland. But Burt had no more eye for nature then than a man would have who had staked his all on the next throw of the dice. Amy was alone, and now was his chance to intercept her before she reached the house. Imagine her surprise as she saw him make his horse leap the intervening fences, and come galloping toward her.

"Burt," she cried, as he, in a moment or two, reined up near her, "you will break your neck!"

"It wouldn't matter much," he said, grimly. "I fear a worse fate than that."

"What do you mean?" she asked, in alarm. "What has happened?"

He threw the bridle over a stake in the fence, and the horse was glad to rest with drooping head. Then he came and stood beside her, his face flushed, and his mouth twitching with his strong feeling and excitement. For a moment he could not speak.

"Burt," she said, "what *is* the matter? What do you fear?"

"I fear your scorn, Amy," he began, impetuously; "I fear I shall lose your respect forever. But I can't go on any longer detesting myself, and feeling that you and Miss Hargrove both despise me. I may seem to you both a fickle fool, a man of straw, but you shall both know the truth. I sha'n't go away a coward. I can at least be honest, and then you may think what you please of my weakness and vacillation. You can not think worse things than I think myself, but you must not imagine that I am a cold-blooded, deliberate trifler, for that has never been true. I know you don't care for me, and never did."

"Indeed, Burt, you are mistaken. I do care for you immensely," said Amy, eagerly clasping his arm with both her hands.

"Amy, Amy," said Burt, in a low, desperate tone, "think how few short months have passed since I told you I loved you, and protested I would wait till I was gray!

You have seen me giving my thoughts to another, and in your mind you expect to see me carried away by half a dozen more. You are mistaken, but it will take a long time to prove it."

"No, Burt, I understand you better than you think. Gertrude has inspired in you a very different feeling from the one you had for me. I think you are loving now with a man's love, and that you won't get over it very soon, if you ever do. You have seen, you must have felt, that my love for you was only that of a sister, and of course you soon began to feel toward me in the same way. I don't believe I would have married you had you waited an age. Don't you fret. I'm not going to break my heart about you."

"I should think not, nor will any one else. Oh, Amy, I so despised myself that I have been half desperate."

"Despised yourself because you love a girl like Gertrude Hargrove! I never knew a man to do a more natural and sensible thing, whether she gave any encouragement or not. If I were a man I would make love to her, rest assured, and she would have to refuse me more than once to be rid of me."

Burt took a long breath of immense relief. "You are heavenly kind," he said. "Are you sure you won't despise me? I could not bear that. It seems to me that I have done such an awfully mean thing in making love to you in my own home, and then in changing."

Her laugh rang out merrily. "Fate has been too strong for you, and I think—I mean I hope—it has been kind."

"But you will be my loving sister as long as you live, Amy? You will believe that I have a little manhood if given a chance to show it?"

"I believe it now, Burt, and I can make you a hundredfold better sister than wife. The idea! It seems but the other day I was playing with dolls. Here, now, cheer up. You have judged yourself too harshly." And she looked at him so smilingly and affectionately that he took her in his arms and kissed her again and again, exclaiming: "You can count on one brother to the last drop of his blood. Oh, Amy, whatever happens now, I won't lose courage. Miss Hargrove will have to say no a dozen times before she is through with me."

At this moment Webb, from the top of a tall ladder in the orchard, happened to glance that way, and saw the embrace. He instantly descended, threw down his basket of apples, and with it all hope. Burt had won Amy at last. The coolness between them had been but a misunderstanding, which apparently had been banished most decidedly. He mechanically took down his ladder and placed it on the ground, then went to his room to prepare for supper.

He appeared at the supper table the personification of quiet geniality, but Amy thought she had never seen him look so hollow-eyed. The long strain was beginning to tell on him decidedly, and to-night he felt as if he had received a mortal blow. But with indomitable courage he hid his wound, and seemed absorbed in a conversation with Leonard and his father about the different varieties of apples and their relative value. Amy saw that his mother was looking at him anxiously, and she did not wonder. He was growing thin even to gauntness.

Burt also was an arrant dissembler, and on rising from the table remarked casually that he was going over to bid Miss Hargrove good-by, as she would return to town on the morrow.

"She'll surely come and see us before she goes," Mrs. Clifford remarked. "It seems to me she hasn't been very social of late."

"Certainly," said Amy; "she'll be over in the morning. She told me she was coming to say good-by to us all, and she has asked me to visit her. Come, Webb, you look all tired out to-night. Let me read to you. I'll stumble through the driest scientific treatise you have if I can see you resting on the sofa."

"That's ever so kind of you, Amy, and I appreciate it more than you imagine, but I'm going out this evening."

"Oh, of course, sisters are of no account. What girl are _you_ going to see?"

"No girl whatever. I am too old and dull to entertain the pretty creatures."

"Don't be fishing. You know one you could entertain, if she isn't a pretty creature; but then she's only a sister who doesn't know much."

"I'm sorry—I must go," he said, a little abruptly, for her lovely, half-laughing, half-reproachful face, turned to his, contained such mocking promise of happiness that he could not look upon it.

What was his urgent business? His rapid steps as he walked mile after mile indicated that the matter was pressing indeed, but although it was late before he returned, he had spoken to no one. The house was dark and silent except that a light was burning in Burt's room. And it is his momentous fortunes that the reader must now follow.

Miss Hargrove, with a fluttering heart, heard the rapid feet of his horse as he rode up the avenue. Truly he was coming at a lover's pace. The door-bell rang, she heard him admitted, and expected the maid's tap at her door to follow. Why did it not come? Were the tumultuous throbs of her heart so loud that she could not hear it? What had become of him? She waited and listened in vain. She opened her door slightly; there was no sound. She went to her window. There below, like a shadow, stood a saddled horse. Where was the knight? Had the stupid girl shown him into the drawing-room and left him there? Surely the well-trained servant had never been guilty of such a blunder before. Could it have been some one else who had come to see her father on business? She stole down the stairway in a tremor of apprehension, and strolled into the parlor in the most nonchalant manner imaginable. It was lighted, but empty, and her expression suddenly became one of troubled perplexity. She returned to the hall, and started as if she had seen an apparition. There on the rack hung Burt's hat as natural as life. Voices reached her ear from her father's study. She took a few swift steps toward it, then fled to her room, and stood panting before her mirror, which reflected a young lady in a costume charmingly ill adapted for "packing."

How swiftly the minutes passed! how eternally long they were! Would she be sent for? *When* would she be sent for? "It was honorable in him to speak to papa first, and papa would not, could not, answer him without consulting me. I can not be treated as a child any longer," she muttered, with flashing eyes. "Papa loves me," she murmured, in swift alternation of gentle feeling. "He would not make my happiness secondary to a paltry sum of money."

Meanwhile Burt was pleading his cause. Mr. Hargrove had greeted him with no little surprise. The parting of the young people had not promised any such interview.

"Have you spoken to my daughter on this subject?" Mr. Hargrove asked, gravely, after the young fellow had rather incoherently made known his errand.

"No, sir," replied Burt; "I have not secured your permission. At the same time," he added, with an ominous flash in his blue eyes, "sincerity compels me to say that I could not take a final refusal from any lips except those of your daughter, and not readily from hers. I would not give up the effort to win her until convinced that any amount of patient effort was useless. I should not persecute her, but I would ask her to reconsider an adverse answer as often as she would permit, and I will try with all my soul to render myself more worthy of her."

"In other words," began Mr. Hargrove, severely, "if I should decline this honor, I should count for nothing."

"No, sir, I do not mean that, and I hope I haven't said it even by implication. Your consent that I should have a fair field in which to do my best would receive from me boundless gratitude. What I mean to say is that I could not give her up; I should not think it right to do so. This question is vital to me, and I know of no reason," he added, a little haughtily, "why I should be refused a privilege which is considered the right of every gentleman."

"I have not in the slightest degree raised the question of your being a gentleman, Mr. Clifford. Your course in coming to me before revealing your regard to my daughter proves that you are one. But you should realize that you are asking a great deal of me. My child's happiness is my first and only consideration. You know the condition of life to which my daughter has been accustomed. It is right and natural that I should also know something of your prospects, your ability to meet the obligations into which you wish to enter."

Poor Burt flushed painfully and hesitated. After a moment he answered with a dignity and an evident sincerity which won golden opinions from Mr. Hargrove: "I shall not try to mislead you in the least on this point. For my own sake I wish that your daughter were far poorer than I am. I can say little more than that I could give her a home now and every comfort of life. I could not now give her the luxury to which she has been accustomed. But I am willing to wait and eager to work. In youth and health and a fair degree of education I have some capital, in addition to the start in life which my father has promised to his sons. What could not Miss Hargrove inspire a man to do ?"

The man of experience smiled in spite of himself at Burt's frank enthusiasm and *naïveté*. The whole affair was so different from anything that he had ever looked forward to. Instead of a few formalities between himself and a wealthy suitor whom his wife, and therefore all the world, would approve of, here he was listening to a farmer's son, with the consciousness that he must yield, and not wholly unwilling to do so. Moreover, this preposterous young man, so far from showing any awe of him, had almost defied him from the start, and had plainly stated that the father's wealth was the one and only objection to the daughter. Having seen the drift of events, Mr. Hargrove had long since informed himself thoroughly about the Clifford family, and had been made to feel that the one fact of his wealth, which Burt regretted, was almost his only claim to superiority. Burt was as transparent as a mountain brook, and quite as impetuous. The gray-haired man sighed, and felt that he would give all his wealth in exchange for such youth. He knew his daughter's heart, and felt that further parley was vain, although he foresaw no easy task in reconciling his wife to the match. He was far from being heart-broken himself, however, for there was such a touch of nature in Burt, and in the full strong love awaiting to reward the youth, that his own heart was stirred, and in the depths of his soul he knew that this was better than giving his child to a jaded millionaire. "I have money enough for both," he thought. "It's a pity if we can't afford an old-fashioned love-match."

Burt was respectfully impatient under Mr. Hargrove's deep thought and silence.

At last the father arose and gave him his hand, saying, "You have been honest with me, and that with an old merchant counts for a great deal. I also perceive you love my daughter for herself. If she should ever inform me that you are essential to her happiness I shall not withhold my consent."

Burt seized his hand with a grasp that made it ache, as he said, "Every power I have, sir, shall be exerted that you may never regret this kindness."

"If you make good that promise, Mr. Clifford, I shall become your friend, should your wooing prove successful. If you will come to the parlor, I will tell Miss Hargrove that you are here."

He went up the stairs slowly, feeling that he was crossing the threshold of a great change. How many thoughts passed through his mind as he took those few steps! He saw his child a little black-eyed baby in his arms; she was running before him trundling her hoop; she came to him with contracted brow and half-tearful eyes bringing a knotty sum in fractions, and insisting petulantly that they were very "vulgar" indeed; she hung on his arm, a shy girl of fifteen, blushingly conscious of the admiring eyes that followed her; she stood before him again in her fresh, radiant beauty as a *débutante*, and he had dreamed of the proudest alliance that the city could offer; she looked into his eyes, a pale earnest woman, and said, "Papa, he saved my life at the risk of his own." True, true. Mr. Clifford had not spoken of that, and he had not thought of it in the interview so crowded with considerations, and his heart relented toward the youth as it had not done before. Well, well, since it was inevitable, he was glad to be the one who should first bring the tidings of this bold wooer's purpose. "Trurie will never forget this moment," he muttered, as he knocked at her door, "nor my part in her little drama." Oh love! how it craves even the crumbs that fall from the table of its idol!

"Trurie," he began, as he entered, "you had better dress. Bless me! I thought you were packing."

"I—I was."

"You were expecting some one ?"

"Mr. Clifford said he would call—to bid me good-by, I suppose."

"Was that all you supposed, Trurie ?"

"Indeed, papa, I told him I was going to town to-morrow, and he asked if he might call."

"Did he speak of his object ?"

"No, papa. I'm sure it's quite natural he should call, and I have been packing."

"Well, I can assure you that he has a very definite object. He has asked me if he might pay his addresses to you, and in the same breath assured me that he would in any event."

"Oh, papa," she said, hiding her face on his shoulder, "he was not so unmannerly as that."

"Indeed he went much further, declaring that he would take no refusal from you either; or rather that he would take it so often as to wear out your patience, and secure you by proving that resistance was useless. He had one decided fault to find with you also. He much regrets that you have wealth."

"Oh, papa, tell me what he did say." And he felt her heart fluttering against his side like that of a frightened bird.

"Why, Trurie, men have offered you love before."

"But I never loved before, nor knew what it meant," she whispered. "Please don't keep me in suspense. This is all so strange, so sacred to me."

"Well, Trurie, I hope your match may be one of those that are made in heaven. Your mother will think it anything but worldly-wise, but I will reconcile her to it, and I'm glad to be the one with whom you will associate this day. Long after I am gone it may remind you how dear your happiness was to me, and that I was willing to give up my way for yours. Mr. Clifford has been straightforward and manly, if not conventional, and I've told him that if he could win you, and would keep his promise to do his best for you and by you, I would be his friend, and that, you know, means much. Of course it all depends upon whether you accept him. You are not committed in the least."

"Am I not, papa? Here is an organ" (with her hand upon her heart) "that knows better. But I shall not throw myself at him. Must I go down now?"

"Oh no; I can excuse you," he said, with smiling lips, but moist eyes.

"Dear papa, I will indeed associate you with this hour, and every pleasant thing of life. You will find that you have won me anew instead of having lost me;" and looking back at him with her old filial love shining in her eyes, she went slowly away to meet the future under the sweet constraint of nature's highest law.

If Burt had been impatient in the library, he grew almost desperate in the parlor. Horrible doubts and fears crossed his mind. Might not Miss Hargrove's pride rise in arms against him? Might she not even now be telling her father of his fickleness, and declaring that she would not listen to a "twice-told tale"? Every moment of delay seemed ominous, and many moments passed. The house grew sepulchral in its silence, and the wind without sighed and moaned as if nature foreboded

and pitied him in view of the overwhelming misfortune impending. At last he sprung up and paced the room in his deep perturbation. As he turned toward the entrance he saw a picture framed in the doorway that appeared like a radiant vision. Miss Hargrove stood there looking at him so intently that for a second or two he stood spell-bound. She was dressed in some soft white clinging material, and, with her brilliant eyes, appeared in the uncertain light too beautiful and wraith-like to be a human girl. She saw her advantage, and took the initiative instantly. "Mr. Clifford," she exclaimed, "do I seem an apparition?"

"Yes, you do," he replied, coming impetuously toward her. She held out her hand, proposing that their interview should at least begin at arm's-length. Nevertheless the soft fire in his eyes and the flush on his handsome face made her tremble with a delicious apprehension.

"Ah, Mr. Clifford," she cried, "you ought to know that you are not crushing a ghost's hand."

"Pardon me. What I meant was that I thought I had seen you before, but you are a new revelation every time I see you."

"I can't interpret visions."

"Please don't say that, for I must ask you to interpret one to-night. What does Shakespeare say about those who have power? I hope you will use yours mercifully. Oh, Miss Hargrove, you are so beautiful that I believe I should lose my reason if you sent me away without hope."

"Mr. Clifford, you are talking wildly," was her faint response.

"I fear I am. I am almost desperate from fear, for I have a terribly hard duty to perform."

"Indeed!" she said, withdrawing her hand, which he relinquished most reluctantly, dreading that he might never receive it again.

"Do not assume that attitude, Miss Hargrove, or I shall lose courage utterly."

"Truly, Mr. Clifford," she said, a little satirically, seating herself on a sofa, "I never imagined you deficient in courage. Is it a terrible duty to entertain me for a half-hour, and say good-by?"

"Yes. Nothing could be worse than that, if that were all;" and he looked at her so appealingly and in such perplexed distress that she laughed outright.

"I am very much in earnest, Miss Hargrove."

"You are very enigmatical, Mr. Clifford. Must I be present while you perform this terrible duty?"

"I think you know what I must confess already, and have a world of scorn in store for me. Do not judge me harshly. Whatever the end may be, and my sense of ill desert is heavy indeed, I shall begin on the basis of absolute truth. You shall know the worst. I've asked your father for the privilege of winning your love;" and then he hesitated, not knowing how to go on.

"Is that the worst?" she asked, demurely.

"No; I fear it will be the best, for he kindly gave his consent, and I know it would be hard for him to do as much for any man, much more so for one not wholly to his mind. Miss Hargrove, I must appear awkwardness and incoherency personified. I hardly know how to go on. I shall appear to you fickle and unmanly. How can I excuse myself to you, when I have no excuse except the downright truth that I love you better than my life, better than my own soul, better than all the world and everything in it? I never knew what love was until you became unconscious in my arms on the mountain. Forgive me for referring to it. I'm only trying to explain myself; and yet I had thought that I knew, and had spoken words of love to your friend, Amy Winfield, who is worthy of the love of the best and noblest man that ever breathed. She did not welcome my words—they only wounded her—and she has never cared for me except as a true and gentle sister cares. But I promised to wait till she did care. I can't keep that promise. You fascinated me from the first hour of our meeting. I feel now that I cherished an unworthy purpose toward you. I thought that by attentions to you I could make Amy care; I thought that you were but a brilliant society girl; but every hour I spent with you increased my admiration, my respect: I saw that you were better and stronger than I was. On the first day we went into camp on the mountain I saw whither my heart was leading me, and from that hour until to-day I have tried to conquer my love, feeling that I had no right to give it, that you would despise it if I did. You can't have any confidence in me now. All my hope is that you will give me a chance to prove that I am not a fickle wretch. I will ac-

cept of any probation, I will submit to any terms. I can't take an absolute refusal now, for I feel you are seeing me at my worst, and I know that you could do with me anything you pleased."

Her head bowed lower and lower as he poured out these words like a torrent. "Does Amy—have you told her that you can not keep your promise to her?" she faltered, in a low tone.

"Yes; I told her so a few hours ago—since I met you this afternoon. I was going away to the West, like a coward, to escape from my dilemma, for I felt you would never listen to me after you knew I had broken my word to Amy. I feared that I had already become a by-word of all that was weak and fickle between you. But after I saw you I could not go till I spoke. I determined to reveal the whole truth, and if you ever gave me a chance to retrieve myself, gratitude would be no name for my deep feeling."

"Did—did Amy release you?"

"Yes: she was kindness itself. She told me in good plain English that she wanted neither me nor my promise, that she didn't think that she ever could have loved me, no matter how long I might have waited. But I could not look into your clear eyes and say, I love you, and know that you might learn from her or any one that I had said this before. If you won't trust me, having had the whole truth, then I must bear my hard fate as best I can."

"How long would you be willing to wait for me?" she asked, in tones so low that he could scarcely catch the words.

He bounded to her side, and took her unresisting hand. "Oh, Gertrude," he pleaded, "prove me; give me a chance; let me show that I am not without manhood and constancy. Believe me, I know the priceless gift I'm asking, but what else can I do? I have tried for weeks to conquer the feeling you have inspired—tried with all the help that pride and sense of duty and honor could give, but it has been utterly useless. I now am free; I have the right to speak. I have concealed nothing from you. I'm wholly at your mercy."

At last she raised her downcast eyes and averted face to his, and for a moment he was dazed at its expression. In tones sweet, low, and deep with her strong emotion, she said: "Burt, how glad I am that you men are blind! I found out that I loved you before we went to our mountain camp." She sprung up and gave him her other hand as she continued: "Can love impose such hard conditions as you suggest—months of doubtful waiting for one who risked his life for me without a second's hesitation? That is not my nature, Burt. If I have power over you, I shall show it in another way."

She would never forget his look as he listened to these words, nor his humility as he bowed his head upon her shoulder, and murmured, "I am not worthy of this." It touched the deepest and tenderest chord in her heart. His feeling was not the exultation of success, but a gratitude too deep for words, and a half-conscious appeal that she would use her woman's power to evoke a better manhood. It was not mere acknowledgment of her beauty, or the impulse of his passion; it was homage to the best and noblest part of her nature, the expression of his absolute trust. Never had she received such a tribute, and she valued it more than if Burt had laid untold wealth at her feet.

A great joy is often as sobering as a great sorrow, and they talked long and earnestly together. Gertrude would not become engaged until she had told her mother, and shown her the respect that was her due. "You must not be resentful," the young girl said, "if mamma's consent is not easily won. She has set her heart on an establishment in town; I've set my heart on you; so there we differ, and you must give me time to reconcile her to a different programme."

The clock on the mantel chimed eleven, and Burt started up, aghast at the flight of time. Gertrude stole to her father's library, and found that he was pacing the floor. "I should not have left him alone so long to-night," she thought, with compunction. "Papa," she said, "Mr. Clifford is going. Will you not come and speak to him?"

He looked into his daughter's flushed, happy face, and needed no further explanation, and with her hands on his arm he went to the drawing-room. Burt said but few and very simple words, and the keen judge of men liked him better than if he had been more exuberant. There was evidence of downright earnestness now that seemed a revelation of a new trait.

"You spoke of going to the West soon," Mr. Hargrove remarked, as they lingered in parting. "Have you any objection to telling me of your purpose?"

Burt explained. Mr. Hargrove's face soon expressed unusual interest. "I must talk with you further about this," he said. "I have land in the same locality, and also an interest in the railroad to which you refer. Perhaps I can make your journey of mutual service."

"Oh, papa," cried his daughter, "you are my good genius!" for she well understood what that mutual service meant.

After Burt had gone, Mr. Hargrove said: "Well, well, this Western land business puts a new aspect on the affair, and mamma may have little ground for complaint. I think the Cliffords will realize a very respectable fortune out of that land."

"Papa," said the young girl, "Burt gave me something better than wealth to-night—better even than love in the usual sense of the word. He gave me his faith. He acted as if he saw in me the power to help him to be a true man, and what higher compliment can a woman receive? He did not express it so much by word as by an unconscious manner that was so sincere and unpremeditated that it thrilled my very soul. Oh, papa, you have helped me to be so very happy!"

THE ART COMPETITIONS.

THE failure of both the art competitions instituted by Harper and Brothers has doubtless been a surprise to all interested parties, and to none more than to the firm itself. It was apparent from the character of the undertaking that it was the purpose of the firm to bring out, if possible, any native talent which circumstance and situation prevented from developing, to recognize this talent and to encourage it in a substantial manner. As one of the judges in these competitions, I feel called upon, not to endeavor to explain nor to apologize for the unanimous decision of the judges that there was no work worthy of a prize, but to draw a lesson from the competitions which may be of service both to those who entered it in the hope of reward and to the public at large.

The first competition was confined, it will be remembered, to the illustration of Alfred Domett's "Christmas Hymn" which was published in 1837. The only conditions of the competition were that those who contributed to it should be Americans, not over twenty-five years of age, and that the drawings should be suitable for publication in Harper and Brothers' periodicals. Over three hundred drawings were sent in response to ten times that number of circulars which were distributed, announcing the subject and terms of the competition. A large number of these drawings were made in pencil upon small sheets of note-paper or bits of drawing paper, and were sent through the post without any protection except a piece of paper or an envelope wrapped about them. This may appear to be a trifling detail, but it was a sure indication of inexperience on the part of these aspirants, and proved that they either undervalued their productions with an inexcusable modesty, or else trusted largely to luck in their expectation of securing the three thousand dollar prize or one of the three lesser ones. In consequence of this and of other careless packing, a great many drawings arrived crushed and disfigured. However, there were no accidents of this kind serious enough to prevent a fair judgment of the work, and the result was doubtless the same as if they had all been forwarded in packing cases. The first thing that attracted our attention from an artistic stand-point was the great similarity of the drawings both in the conception of the subject and in the execution of it. By far the larger proportion of them were finished in the most precise and painful way without the remotest idea of the requirements of illustration. The hackneyed compositions of the Babe in the Manger and of the Shepherds and the Star in the East were elaborated with the most minute and careful stipple, showing that the aspirant was only in that stage of progress when the perfection of finish is the most hopeful accomplishment, the greatest triumph. In many cases the competitors had simply taken the figures from well-known engravings, had surrounded them with original accessories, and had placed them in a landscape or in an interior of their own design. This was too evident copying to be done with an idea of deception, and we were forced to believe that they were submitted with a simple-minded faith in the value of the execution. They were usually accompanied by an unsigned note to the judges calling their attention to the

fact that these were the first attempts of the competitors, and that, without any instruction or assistance, and in the midst of the cares of business or of household occupation, they had developed their skill to a degree which they hoped would be found sufficiently promising to warrant encouragement. We could not fail to find genuine sincerity and earnestness in a great deal of the work of this kind. Its very faithfulness made the results all the more painful and discouraging, for we, even if we had known the names of the competitors, could not have undertaken the immense task of giving personal encouragement or advice to all whose work showed one simple condition of progress, and oftentimes the only one to be discovered in first productions—earnestness of purpose. From the remote ranches of Colorado to the boudoirs of Fifth Avenue first attempts and the productions of untrained amateurs came to testify with indisputable force that the present popularity of art, to which we are accustomed to refer with pride as a sure sign that we are soon to have a national school of painters, is only the superficial result of an enthusiasm largely based on fashion, and that we must look much further and deeper for the real gauge of the possibilities of our nation in the direction of the fine arts. The contributions of which I speak were not the work of ignorant and uncultivated people, and they had none of the rude strength of the beginners who stand afar off and gaze at the temples of art with awe, but they were, rather, the attempts of people who had mistaken interest and delight in art for an indication of talent, or who, from familiarity with it in some form or other, had been seized with a desire to undertake to produce it. The careful imitation of a mezzotint engraving or of a lithograph was apparently their chief ambition, and with this preoccupation they of course forgot, if they ever considered at all, that the highest triumph of art is the result, not the method.

Apart from the class of contributions to which I have just referred, there was another and a perfectly distinct division to be made in the list of drawings sent in. This was the work of those who, having entered the competition with all seriousness, labored to express their conceptions of the subject without regard to manner or material. It was among these that we found the most interesting performances.

Taking them as a class, they apparently were the work of those to whom art is chiefly valuable as a means of illustrating ideas of religion. The devout and primitive manner in which these competitors endeavored to illustrate the subject of the Christmas Hymn can be described in no better way than by comparing it with the style of the early German school. The Northern quality of the art—if art it may properly be called—was shown by the rigidity and formality of the poses, the quaint and forcible expression of the faces, the absence of all attempt at beauty, and the introduction of a prominent *genre* element, no less than by an uncompromising literary tendency in the composition. It was surprising to find such a close relation existing between compositions produced more than four centuries apart. A description of a single example will give some idea of the character of this class of the competitive drawings, although it is more complex than the most of them, and I can not hope to give, without the aid of illustration, an accurate notion of the earnest and devout spirit which guided the hand of the one who conceived and executed the composition. It was a large sheet of paper covered with what appeared at first sight to be an irregular combination of small drawings. Close examination disclosed the fact that these pictures were borne on the branches of a great tree, as if they were the cross sections of large fruit or the sides of broad leaves. At the bottom of the paper the trunk of the tree entered the ground, and there it was dissected to show a great acorn embraced by the roots. The acorn was in turn cut across so as to show the infant Jesus asleep in the manger inside it. This discovered, the key to the composition was plain enough. The tree was the tree of life, the acorn the vital germ, and the ramifications of the branches represented the variety of the phases of human life. The birth of the Saviour having had such an influence on human life, the tree bore as its fruit illustrations of the observances of Christmas-time as representing the civilizing influences of the Christian religion. Here on one side was a winter landscape with Santa Claus and his reindeer; opposite was a view of a great city, and the side of one of the houses was removed to show a party of happy children around the Christmas tree, and so on for a score of small pictures. The literary element of

the illustration was, as may be surmised, by far the best part of it, for the execution was only distinguished by a painful elaboration of details. Accompanying this drawing were several sheets of manuscript explaining the scheme of the composition, and calling attention to the comprehensive manner in which the subject was illustrated.

The Throne of Grace, with adoring angels and pleading sinners, the Adoration of the Lamb, the Crucifixion, and other common religious subjects were probably believed to have a close relation to the subject of the Christmas Hymn, for there were a number of drawings of this character. An ideal portrait of Christ, accompanied by a portrait of the artist, heads of Cupids and angels, bits of landscape and still-life studies, and indeed scores of other drawings as remotely related as these to the subject given for illustration, were entered for competition. There was a certain desperate humor about one of the unfinished contributions which could scarcely pass unnoticed. This drawing was very much worn and rubbed, and had evidently been worked at over and over again, until all the original surface had been destroyed. The composition was a moon-lit landscape with figures, and the latter had been cut from another drawing and pasted on over the much-rubbed and formless figures of the original. On the back of the paper was written the following legend: "From one who, alas! having drawn his outline with all circumspection and care, finds, when all too late, the dancing moonlight and the flitting shadows a delusion and a snare to his unpracticed brush." It was impossible, notwithstanding the comic aspect of the matter, not to feel some sympathy for the student, who, having been so oppressed by the importance of the work, had labored with nervous zeal until he had used up all his time and had ruined his paper, and then, after all, had been obliged to make a shift to present some kind of a drawing to ease his conscience from the reproach of total failure. As a contrast to this ragged and worn contribution was a beautiful Russia leather portfolio, with a monogram and an Arabic seal in gold on the outside, and accompanied by a dainty closed envelope bearing the same devices on the back. Inside the portfolio was a small drawing.

The result of the first competition seemed to indicate that the subject was too difficult to illustrate because the poem was so broad in its scope, and also that the limit of age was too low to admit those who had already had some experience in illustration. In accordance, therefore, with the intimation given in the announcement of the first competition, and in harmony with the suggestion of the judges, Messrs. Harper and Brothers reopened the competition, increasing the age of the competitors to twenty-seven, limiting the subject for illustration only to some one appropriate to Christmas, and extending the time nine months, that is, to March 1, 1884.

If the first competition was remarkable for a certain uniformity of expression in the classes into which the works naturally divided themselves, the second was equally noticeable for a great variety of conception of subject and of manner of execution. The great class of religious compositions almost entirely disappeared from the lists, and the *genre* class came prominently to the front. Notwithstanding the increase in the limit of age, the freedom in choice of subject apparently tempted a larger proportion of first beginners than the poem did, and amateur work predominated even more than before. The spectacle of hundreds of drawings—for the number sent in for each competition was about the same—mostly of the young ladies' boarding-school variety, with only here and there a variation in the substitution of oil-color or pen-and-ink for the crayon or the pencil, was too discouraging to be reviewed now with profit to any one. I need only say that there were attempts in the whole range of figure and landscape art. From the most wonderful mountain scenery and wild marine views to studies of flowers and marvellous architectural combinations, sometimes with, but often without, any reference to a Christmas idea, the whole domain of landscape art was boldly entered on. Not even the fantastic flights of Doré's fancy nor the weirdness of Blake's imagination excelled the vagaries which found illustration in the composition of angels and shepherds, heavenly hosts, and unearthly effects of light, which were submitted to our judgment. The *genre* class, although it did not present many hopeful examples, still was so much less pretentious than the imaginative drawings just alluded to, that it was a relief to meet with such common subjects as the

well-filled stockings, or Santa Claus in the fire-place, although they were illustrated with more patience than with skill and originality. Many of this class were downright exact plans of interiors of the most commonplace aspect, with the wall-paper patterns and the carpet figures all carefully drawn out, and the whiskers of the cat sitting by the grate perhaps the most offensively prominent detail, except the darned patches on the heels of the stockings which were carefully pinned to the fire-place jambs. One large and ambitious work still haunts me. It was quite alone by itself in originality of conception, although the subject found other illustrators. The drawing represented a statue of a half-dressed child standing in a niche holding an empty stocking in one hand. Everything was white, and an effect of light had been chosen which cast the smallest amount of shadow. On one cheek of the marble face stood an ink-black tear, shining in prominent relief. There was no mistaking the sentiment. The title, "The Empty Stocking," carved in the base, was scarcely necessary. But it was a first attempt. Only a scant half-score out of the hundreds examined caused any hesitation on the part of the judges. Among these several were remarkably well done; but all, unfortunately, failed to satisfy the conditions of the competition in combining sufficiency of illustration with satisfactory execution, and we could not, therefore, award a prize.

The result of the two competitions was as great a disappointment to the judges as to any one. I may frankly say that, at the start, we were certain that the opportunity for recognition would bring into notice at least a few struggling students whose acquirements would warrant their encouragement. We shared the common opinion that the establishment of art schools, the popularization of art in the magazines and in the illustrated papers, and the recent great increase of public interest in the production of art must have developed a large class of talented students who only needed recognition to start them on the road of rapid progress. The result proved that we were totally mistaken in our estimation of the general standard of art culture, and that we had not sufficiently considered the difference which exists between our own country and the older civilizations in respect to the quality and quantity of inherited artistic disposition.

At the period of the Centennial Exhibition it was a common prophecy that there would follow a great wave of art popularization similar to the one which swept over England after the great exhibition of thirty years ago. The prophecy has been more than fulfilled, and various branches of the fine arts have been not only popularized, but even vulgarized, by the contagion which has seized all classes of minds, and encouraged the production of an incalculable amount of artistic rubbish. The rage for painting on drain-pipe and for embroidering kitchen crash has filled the remotest farm-houses with specimens of this species of decoration. The useless spinning-wheel has been given a place of honor in the parlor, and the three-legged kettle, resplendent with a coat of red paint, hangs, filled with flowers, on a rustic tripod in the front yard. Few houses are now without some specimens of original work in chalk or in color, the gift of an aspiring friend or the triumph of one of the family. The number of art teachers has grown to be myriad; schools of art of more or less importance have sprung up in every large town, and the passion for the practice of the fine arts in its various branches has seized multitudes without regard to sex, age, or previous turn of mind. This condition of things has its encouraging and its disheartening side. It is disheartening because the results are so far from being commensurate with the time, money, and labor employed, and because it is not productive of sufficiently serious work to indicate a hopeful state of progress. But to find encouragement in this vulgarization of the methods of producing works of art we must remember that this state of preoccupation with the material and the methods is possibly as necessary to the development of a genuine feeling for art as are other and more dignified phases of education. How many artists are there who do not vividly remember the great interest and joy which their first color-box and palette excited in them, or what delight and what possibilities there were for them in the first sketching materials or canvases? How many will ever forget the pleasure of the first flushes of enthusiasm, when materials and methods were the great objects of investigation and study? And yet how little did this common zeal and fervor indicate the result which further growth and higher purposes brought about?

The contagion of dabbling in art—for it is difficult to give it another or more descriptive name—is more powerful than most fashions of the kind, because it adds the attraction of some definite and tangible production to the charm of an agreeable household occupation. The American mind naturally inclines to the practical and the productive. It is ordinarily best satisfied with something which can be pointed to as a material result accomplished. This is just what comes out of the household art craze, and in satisfying this natural desire for fruitful and absorbing occupation the fashion for art work has changed the current of thought, elevated the purposes, and brightened the lives of those who have gone with the wave, and it has in a great measure fertilized the waste which the rigid Puritanism of our forefathers made of every-day life.

It is undoubtedly too soon to begin to look for better results of the popularization of art than the great increase in the number of students and teachers. The youth of America have been brought up, we may say, outside the influence of art. There are here none of the monuments of past centuries to excite the youthful imagination or to fill the mind with an appreciation of art; there are but meagre means, indeed, of developing that love of art which grows unconsciously like other human tastes and inclinations. In the present generation of artists there are few who have had the benefit of association with works of art, either good or bad, from early childhood. Many of them passed their childhood and youth in country towns, where such a thing as an original picture, or even a good reproduction, was perhaps never seen; some are from the West, where they never felt an influence more civilizing than that of the colored print or the lithograph; those, indeed, who have been reared in cities remember only that in their early years art was a remote and a mysterious thing, possessed by few, understood by a limited number of favored beings, and the profession of artist was too closely associated with the name of Bohemian to be more than a fairly respectable, much less than an honorable, calling. The faculty of acquiring a trade or a profession which is characteristic of Americans is exemplified in the readiness with which our students abroad often take leading rank in the competitions with native students who have had the advantage of longer and more thorough training. It is worth while, however, to remember that with the speedy acquirement of mechanical dexterity the superiority of the American generally ends, for he has not that unconscious knowledge of the requirements and limitations of art which is commonly the birthright of the foreign student of perhaps less education and culture in other directions. Not that our young painters abroad do not show genuine artistic feeling and real power, but it is generally the case that they are enabled to supplement their technical training by a more extended study of the different Old World galleries than is possible for their foreign companions, and in this way they partially supply the deficiency of their inherited culture or youthful impressions.

There is one great advantage in foreign art study which it is difficult to define without making use of a phrase which has become almost meaningless—art atmosphere. But it is a fact that our students abroad find themselves surrounded by those whose life is in art, who think, talk, and dream about it, who, in fact, have never known another life. The indescribable influence of this absorption in art is invaluable in creating a singleness of purpose which is not a common attribute of the American mind. This is one thing we lack here to produce a school of painters which shall make a mark in the history of art. In the present popularization of art we may discover the remote beginning of a general acquaintance with and regard for art for its own sake, which will bring about sooner or later just such a condition of feeling as is conducive to the growth of the artist, so far, indeed, as this may be created without the background of an old and indigenous art, which is a constant and most useful aid to progress.

The art competitions not only proved that there was very little hidden talent anxiously seeking recognition, but also decided without question that the art student here is several years older than the foreign student of equal attainments—a fact generally overlooked in the establishment of schools, and in the institution of prizes for art wherever age enters as a condition of competition. This is accounted for readily enough. The rudimentary training is not commonly undertaken at the same time with the ordinary schooling, as it should be, but begins later, and usually as a separate and distinct course of study. Then, too, we have neither the Continental system of free art schools, nor the establishment of town and state subsidies for art students, which is of such importance abroad. It is a common impression here that the study of art is like the study of any trade or profession, that its necessary duration can be gauged as accurately as in the acquirement of any trade, and that there should be quite as speedy substantial returns. Frequently without any assistance from parents or friends, never with any public subsidy or scholarship, the art student is forced to consider, first, where he can get that instruction which will bring him forward most rapidly; next, how he can turn his acquired skill into a means of paying his expenses. Consequently his attention is often fixed more on the practical question of profitable production than on the real progress in art. Such a situation is, of course, not only fatal to the best advancement of the student in the technique of the profession, but also makes it impossible for him to acquire that knowledge and culture outside the immediate range of his studies which is necessary to his real success as an artist. A little incident which came within my own observation will illustrate this statement in regard to self-supporting students.

I was talking with a prominent art-dealer near the front door of his establishment, when a young man entered with a newspaper parcel in his hand, and inquired for the proprietor. After he had learned that the gentleman before him was the one he sought, he introduced himself as a student of such and such a school of art, saying that he had been through the antique class, and was now drawing from life. He explained that he was obliged to try to get work to do in his spare hours to support himself and pay for his instruction, and that he had brought something which he would like to show, to see if it was salable. He then unrolled the newspaper, and disclosed a piece of sheet brass which had been screwed down upon a piece of soft plank, and then hammered with a tool so as to bring a human figure into low relief. This was, of course, only the ordinary method of domestic brass-working just now the rage. If the design had been at all attractive or meritorious some use might have been found for the article, notwithstanding its character, but the student had, with painstaking zeal, simply copied one of his own class studies.

The failure of the art competitions will show to the disappointed contributors the folly of expecting compensation for work which has no better claim to recognition than that of personal sympathy, and will also, in a measure, teach the value of making a rigid comparison of their own work with examples of art which are of recognized value—a method of securing gratuitous instruction of the best kind, and one which is always serviceable. To those interested in art schools the result of the competitions ought to prove the value of a wider range of instruction, so that the consideration of subject may, in a measure, advance with the technical skill, in order that the student may not find himself at the end with a good stock of tools and a knowledge of their use, but with no definite desire or purpose before him. The special training of the illustrator is undoubtedly of the greatest assistance in the production of pictures. This faculty of illustrating an idea is the one the least developed in the art schools, as the work of the students shows. It is a perfectly reasonable and straightforward way of learning to paint to continually attempt to make use of any degree of technical skill whatsoever in illustrating some subject. The facility and power of execution will be better gained when there is a definite reason for acquiring them than by stupidly plodding on to develop manual dexterity in imitation. But if the student is preoccupied with the execution alone, he never gains the facility, if he does not entirely lose the faculty, of expression.

The funds set aside by Harper and Brothers for prizes in the art competition have been increased by them to the sum of five thousand dollars, and placed in the hands of trustees as a permanent art scholarship fund, the interest of which is to be devoted to the support of deserving art students in whatever way the trustees may decide. For the present it has been thought best to join the interest with that of a like sum left by the late Julius Hallgarten for a similar purpose, and to send a student abroad for a term of years. It is to be hoped that this is but the small beginning of a system of art scholarships and subsidies, which will result in securing for our art students the opportunity for the pursuit of their studies which the nature of the case demands, and will encourage the acquirement of that larger culture and more generous education which seems at present next to impossible. With a penalty placed by government on the importation of works of art, we can not have the advantages of an acquaintance with the modern which is best worth study, and even if this penalty were removed, it will always be necessary for artists to familiarize themselves with the great productions of past centuries. But it is quite as important to the growth of an artist that he should acquire the rudiments of his profession under the best possible conditions as it is that he should have later advantages of study and training. If the failure of the art competitions result in any improvement in the training of art students, or impress upon them the value of applying their skill to the expression of ideas or the illustration of subjects, it must really be considered an unqualified success.

JUDITH SHAKESPEARE:
HER LOVE AFFAIRS AND OTHER ADVENTURES.

CHAPTER XXXI.
A LOST ARCADIA.

IT was on this same morning that Judith made a desperate effort to rouse herself from the prostration into which she had fallen. All through that long darkness and despair she had been wearily and vainly asking herself whether she could do nothing to retrieve the evil she had wrought. Her good name might go—she cared little for that now; but was there no means of making up to her father the actual money he had lost? It was not forgiveness she thought of, but restitution. Forgiveness was not to be dreamed of; she saw before her always that angered face she had beheld in the garden; and her wish was to hide away from that, and be seen of it no more. Then there was another thing: if she were to be permitted to remain at the cottage, ought she not to show herself willing to take a share of the humblest domestic duties? Might not the good dame begin to regard her as but a useless encumbrance? If it were so that no work her ten fingers could accomplish would ever restore to her father what he had lost through her folly, at least it might win her grandmother's forbearance and patience. And so it was on the first occasion of her head ceasing to ache quite so badly she struggled to her feet (though she was so languid and listless and weak that she could scarcely stand), and put round her the heavy cloak that had been lying on the bed, and smoothed her hair somewhat, and went to the door. There she stood for a minute or two listening; for she would not go down if there were any strangers about.

The house seemed perfectly still. There was not a sound anywhere. Then, quite suddenly, she heard little Cicely begin to sing to herself—but in snatches, as if she were occupied with other matters—some well-known rhymes to an equally familiar tune—

> *"By the moon we sport and play;*
> *With the night begins our day;*
> *As we drink, the dew doth fall—*
> *Trip it, dainty urchins all!*
> *Lightly as the little bee,*
> *Two by two, and three by three,*
> *And about go we, go we"*

—and she made no doubt that the little girl was alone in the kitchen. Accordingly she went down. Cicely, who was seated near the window, and busily engaged in plucking a fowl, uttered a slight cry when she entered, and started up.

"Dear Mistress Judith," she said, "can I do aught for you? Will you sit down? Dear, dear, how ill you do look!"

"I am not at all ill, little Cicely," said Judith, as cheerfully as she could, and she sat down. "Give me the fowl—I will do that for you; and you can go and help my grandmother in whatever she is at."

"Nay, not so," said the little maid, definitely refusing. "Why should you?"

"But I wish it," Judith said. "Do not vex me now. Go and seek my grandmother, like a good little lass."

The little maid was thus driven to go; but it was with another purpose. In about a couple of minutes she had returned, and preceding her was Judith's grandmother.

"What, art come down, wench?" the old dame said, patting her kindly on the shoulder. "That be so far well—ay, ay, I like that, now; that be better for thee than lying all alone. But what would you with the little maid's work, that you would take it out of her hands?"

"Why, if I am idle and do nothing, grandmother, you will be for turning me out of the house," the girl answered, looking up with a strange kind of smile.

"Turn thee out of the house?" said her grandmother, who had just caught a better glimpse of the wan and tired face. "Ay, that will I—and now. Come thy ways, wench; 'tis time for thee to be in the fresh air. Cicely, let be the fowl now. Put some more wood on the fire, and hang on the pot—there's a clever lass. And thou, grandchild, come thy ways with me into the garden; and I warrant me, when thou comest back, a cupful of barley broth will do thee no harm."

Judith obeyed, though she would fain have sat still. And then, when she reached the front door, what a bewilderment of light and color met her eyes! She stood as one dazed for a second or two. The odors of the flowers and the shrubs were so strange, moreover—pungent, and strange, and full of memories. It seemed so long a time since she had seen this wonderful glowing world, and breathed this keen air, that she paused on the stone flag to collect her senses, as it were. And then a kind of faintness came over her, and perhaps she might have sunk to the ground but that she laid hold of her grandmother's arm.

"Ay, ay, come thy ways and sit thee down, dearie," the old dame said, imagining that the girl was but begging for a little assistance in her walking. "I be main glad to see thee out again. I liked not that lying there alone—nay, I wur feared of it, and I bade Prudence send your mother and Susan to see you—"

"No, no, good grandmother—no, no," Judith pleaded, with all the effort that remained to her.

"But, yea, yea," her grandmother said, sharply. "Foolish wench, that would hide away from them that can best aid thee! Ay, and knowest thou how the new disease, as they call it, shows itself at the beginning?—why, with a pinching of the face, and sharp pains in the head. Wouldst thou have me let thee lie there, and perchance go from bad to worse, and not send for them—ay, and for Susan's husband, if need were? Nay, but let not that fright thee, good wench," she said, in a gentler way. "'Tis none so bad as I thought, else you would not be venturing down the stairs—nay, nay, there be no harm done as yet, I warrant me; 'tis a breath of fresh air to sharpen thee into a hungry fit that will be the best doctor for thee. Here, sit thee down and rest, now; and when the barley broth be warm enough, Cicely shall bring thee out a dish of it. Nay, I see no harm done. Keep up thy heart, lass; thou wert ever a brave one: ay, what was there ever that could daunt thee?—and not the boldest of the youths but was afraid of thy laugh and thy merry tongue! Heaven save us, that thou should take on so! And if you would sell yourself to work in slavery in the Indies, think you they would buy a poor weak trembling creature? Nay, nay; we will have to fetch back the roses to your cheeks ere you make for that bargain, I warrant me!"

They were now seated in the little arbor. On entering, Judith had cast her eyes round it in a strange and half-frightened fashion; and now, as she sat there, she was scarcely listening to the good-natured garrulity of the old dame, which was wholly meant to cheer her spirits.

"Grandmother," said she, in a low voice, "think you 'twas really he that took away with him my father's play?"

"I know not how else it could have been come by," said the grandmother; "but I pray you, child, heed not that for the present. What be done and gone can not be helped—let it pass. There, there, now, what a lack of memory have I, that should have shown thee the pretty lace cuffs that Thomas Quiney left for thee—fit for a queen, they be, to be sure—ay, and the fine lace of them, and the silver too. He hath a free hand, he hath; 'tis a fair thing for any that will be in life-partnership with him; 'twill not away—marry 'twill not; 'twill bide in his nature—that will never out of the flesh that's bred in the bone, as they say; and I like to see a young man that be none of the miser kind, but ready forth with his money where 'tis to please them he hath a fancy for. A brave lad he is, too, and one that will hold his own; and when I told him you were pleased that his business went forward well, why, saith he, as quick as quick, 'Said she that?'—and if my old eyes fail me not, I know of one

that setteth greater share by your good word than you imagine, wench."

She but half heard; she was recalling all that had happened in this very summer-house.

"And think you, grandmother," said she, slowly, and with absent eyes, "that when he was sitting here with us, and telling us all about the court doings, and about my father's friends in London, and when he was so grateful to us, or saying that he was so, for our receiving of him here—think you that all the time he was planning to steal my father's play and to take it and sell it in London? Grandmother, can you think it possible? Could any one be such a hypocrite? I know that he deceived me at the first; but 'twas only a jest, and he confessed it all, and professed his shame that he had so done. But, grandmother, think of him—think of how he used to speak, and ever so modest and gentle: is't possible that all the time he was playing the thief, and looking forward to the getting away to London to sell what he had stolen?"

"For love's sake, sweetheart, heed that man no more!—'tis all done and gone; there can come no good of vexing thyself about it," her grandmother said. "Be he villain or not, 'twill be well for all of us that we never hear his name more. In good sooth I am as much to blame as thou thyself, child, for the encouraging him to come about, and listening to his gossip—beshrew me, that I should have meddled in such matters, and not bade him go about his business! But 'tis all past and gone now, as I say—there be no profit in vexing thyself—"

"Past and gone, grandmother!" she exclaimed, and yet in a listless way. "Yes—but what remains? Good grandmother, perchance you did not hear all that the parson said. 'Tis past and gone, truly, and more than you think."

The tone in which she uttered these words somewhat startled the good dame, who looked at her anxiously. And then she said:

"Why, now I warrant me the barley broth will be hot enough by this time. I will go fetch thee a cupful, wench. 'Twill put warmth in thy veins, it will—ay, and cheer thy heart too."

"Trouble not, good grandmother," she said. "I would as lief go back to my room now. The light hurts my eyes strangely."

"Back to your room?—that shall you not!" was the prompt answer, but not meant unkindly. "You shall wait here, wench, till I bring thee that will put some color in thy white face—ay, and some of Thomas Quiney's wine withal; and if the light hurt thee, sit further back, then: of a truth 'tis no wonder, after thou hast hid thyself like a dormouse for so long."

And so she went away to the house. But she was scarcely gone when Judith—in this extreme silence that the rustling of a leaf would have disturbed—heard certain voices; and listening more intently, she made sure that the new-comers must be Susan and her mother, whom Prudence had asked to walk over. Instantly she got up, though she had to steady herself for a moment by resting her hand on the table; and then, as quickly as she could, and as noiselessly, she stole along the path to the cottage, and entered, and made her way up to her own room. She fancied she had not been heard. She would rather be alone. If they had come to accuse her, what had she to answer? Why, nothing: they might say of her what they pleased now; it was all deserved: only the one denunciation of her that she had listened to—the one she had heard from the parson—seemed like the ringing of her death-knell. Surely there was no need to repeat that? They could not wish to repeat it, did they but know all it meant to her.

Then the door was quietly opened, and her sister appeared, bearing in one hand a small tray.

"I have brought you some food, Judith, and a little wine, and you must try and take them, sweetheart," said she. "'Twas right good news to us that you had come down, and gone into the garden for a space. In truth, making yourself ill will not mend matters; and Prudence was in great alarm."

She put the tray on a chair, for there was no table in the room; but Judith, finding that her sister had not come to accuse her, but was in this gentle mood, said, quickly and eagerly:

"Oh, Susan, you can tell me all that I would so fain know! You must have heard, for my father speaks to you of all his affairs; and at your own wedding you must have heard, when all these things were arranged. Tell me, Susan—I shall have a marriage portion, shall I not?—and how much, think you? Perchance not

so large as yours, for you are the elder, and Doctor Hall was ever a favorite with my father. But I shall have a marriage portion, Susan, shall I not?—nay, it may already be set aside for me?"

And then the elder sister did glance somewhat reproachfully at her.

"I wonder you should be thinking of such things, Judith," said she.

"Ah, but 'tis not as you imagine," the girl said, with the same pathetic eagerness. "'Tis in this wise, now: would my father take it in a measure to repay him for the ill that I have done? Would it make up the loss, Susan, or a part of it? Would he take it, think you? Ah, but if he would do that!"

"Why, that were an easy way out of the trouble, assuredly!" her sister exclaimed. "To take the marriage portion that is set aside for thee—and if I mistake not, 'tis all provided; ay, and the Rowington copyhold, which will fall to thee, if 'tis not thine already—truly, 'twere a wise thing to take these to make good this loss, and then, when you marry, to have to give you your marriage portion all the same!"

"Nay, nay, not so, Susan," her sister cried, quickly. "What said you? The Rowington copyhold also? and perchance mine already? Susan, would it make good the loss? Would all taken together make good the loss? For, as Heaven is my witness, I will never marry—nor think of marrying—but rejoice all the days of my life, if my father would but take these to satisfy him of the injury I have done him. Nay, but is't possible, Susan? Will he do that for me?—as a kindness to me? I have no right to ask for such; but—but if only he knew!—if only he knew!"

The tears were running down her face; her hands were clasped in abject entreaty.

"Sweetheart, you know not what you ask," her sister said, but gently. "When you marry, your marriage portion will have to be in accordance with our position in the town; my father would not have it otherwise. Were you to surrender that now, would he let one of his daughters go forth from his house as a beggar, think you? Or what would her husband say, to be so treated? You might be willing to give up these, but my father could not, and your husband would not."

"Susan, Susan, I wish for no marriage," she cried; "I will stay with my grandmother here; she is content that I should bide with her; and if my father will take these, 'twill be the joy of my life; I shall wish for no more, and New Place shall come to no harm by me; 'tis here that I am to bide. Think you he would take them, Susan?—think you he would take them?" she pleaded; and in her excitement she got up and tried to walk about a little, but with her hands still clasped. "If one were to send to London, now—a message—or I would walk every foot of the way did I but think he would do this for me—oh, no! no! no! I durst not—I durst never see him more; he has cast me off, and—and I deserve no less!"

Her sister went to her and took her by the hand.

"Judith, you have been in sore trouble, and scarce know what you say," she said, in that clear, calm way of hers. "But this is now what you must do. Sit down and take some of this food. As I hear, you have scarce tasted anything these two days. You have always been so wild and wayward: now must you listen to reason and suffer guidance."

She made her sit down. The girl took a little of the broth, some of the spiced bread, and a little of the wine; but it was clear that she was forcing herself to it. Her thoughts were elsewhere. And scarcely had she finished this make-believe of a repast when she turned to her sister and said, with a pathetic pleading in her voice:

"And is it not possible, Susan? Surely I can do something! It is so dreadful to think of my father imagining that I have done him this injury, and gone on the same way, careless of what has happened. That terrifies me at night!—oh, if you but knew what it is in the darkness, in the long hours, and none to call to, and none to give you help; and to think that these are the thoughts he has of me—that it was all for a sweetheart I did it, that I gave away his writing to please a sweetheart, and that I care not for what has happened, but would do the like again to-morrow! It is so dreadful in the night!"

"I would comfort you if I could, Judith," said her sister, "but I fear me you must trust to wiser counsel than mine. In truth I know not whether all this can be undone, or how my father regards it at the moment; for at the time of the writing they were all uncertain. But surely now you would do well to be ruled by some one better able to guide you than any of us women-folk: Master Blaise hath been most kind and serviceable in this, as in all other matters, and hath written to your father in answer to his letter, so that we have had trust and assurance in his direction. And you also—why should you not seek his aid and counsel?"

At the mere mention of the parson's name, Judith shivered instinctively, she scarce knew why.

"Judith," her sister continued, regarding her watchfully, "to-morrow, as I understand, Master Blaise is coming over here to see you."

"May not I be spared that? He hath already brought his message," the girl said, in a low voice.

"Nay, he comes but in kindness—or more than kindness, if I guess aright. Bethink you, Judith," she said, "'tis not only the loss of the money—or great or small I know not—that hath distressed my father. There was more than that. Nay, do not think I am come to reproach you; but will it not be ever thus so long as you will be ruled by none, but must always go your own way? There was more than merely concerned money affairs in my father's letter, as doubtless Master Blaise hath told you; and then, think of it, Judith, how 'twill be when the bruit of the story comes down to Stratford."

"I care not," was the perfectly calm answer. "That is for me to bear. Can Master Blaise tell me how I may restore to my father this that he hath lost? Then his visit might be more welcome, Susan."

"Why will you harden your heart so?" the elder sister said, with some touch of entreaty in her tone. "Nay, think of it, Judith! Here is an answer to all. If you but listen to him, and favor him, you will have one always with you as a sure guide and counsellor; and who then may dare say a word against you?"

"Then he comes to save my good name?" the girl said, with a curious change of manner. "Nay, I will give him no such tarnished prize."

And here it occurred to the elder sister, who was sufficiently shrewd and observant, that her intercession did not seem to be producing good results; and she considered it better that the parson should speak for himself. Indeed, she hoped she had done no mischief; for this that she now vaguely suggested had for long been the dream and desire of both her mother and herself; and at this moment, if ever, there was a chance of Judith's being obedient and compliant. Not only did she forthwith change the subject, but also she managed to conquer the intense longing that possessed her to learn something further about the young man who (as she imagined) had for a time captured Judith's fancies. She gave her sister what news there was in the town. She besought her to take care of herself, and to go out as much as possible, for that she was looking far from well. And finally, when the girl confessed that she was fain to lie down for a space (having slept so little during these two nights), she put some things over her, and quietly left, hoping that she might soon get to sleep.

Judith did not rest long, however. The question whether the sacrifice of her marriage portion might not do something toward retrieving the disaster she had caused was still harassing her mind; and then, again, there was the prospect of the parson coming on the morrow. By-and-by, when she was certain that her mother and sister were gone, she went downstairs, and began to help in doing this or the other little thing about the house. Her grandmother was out-of-doors, and so did not know to interfere, though the small maid-servant remonstrated as best she might. Luckily, however, nature was a more imperative monitress; and again and again the girl had to sit down from sheer physical weakness.

But there came over a visitor in the afternoon who restored to her something of her old spirit. It was little Willie Hart, who, having timidly tapped at the open door without, came along the passage, and entered the dusky chamber where she was.

"Ah, sweetheart," said she (but with a kind of sudden sob in her throat), "have you come to see me?"

"I heard that you were not well, cousin," said he, and he regarded her with troubled and anxious eyes as she stooped to kiss him.

"Nay, I am well enough," said she, with as much cheerfulness as she could muster. "Fret not yourself about that. And what a studious scholar you are, Cousin Willie, to be sure, that must needs bring your book with you! Were I not so ignorant myself, I should hear you your tasks; but you would but laugh at me—"

"'Tis no task-book, Judith," said he, diffidently. "'Twas Prudence who lent it to me."

And then he hesitated, through shyness. "Why, you know, Judith," he said, "you have spoken to me many a time about Sir Philip Sidney; and I was asking this one and the other at times; and Prudence said she would show me a book he had written, that belongs to her brother. And then to-day, when I went to her, she bade me bring the book to you, and to read to you, for that you were not well, and might be pleased to hear it, she not being able to come over till the morrow."

"In truth, now, that was well thought of and friendly," said she; and she put her hand in a kindly fashion on his shoulder. "And you have come all the way over to read to me—see you how good a thing it is to be wise and instructed! Well, then, we will go and sit by the door, that you may have more of light; and if my grandmother catch us at such idleness, you shall have to defend me—you shall have to defend me, sweetheart—for you are the man of us two, and I must be shielded."

So they went to the door, and sat down on the step, the various-colored garden and the trees and the wide heavens all shining before them.

"And what is the tale, Cousin Willie?" said she, quite pleasantly (for indeed she was glad to see the boy, and to chat with one who had no reproaches for her, who knew nothing against her, but was ever her true lover and slave). "Nay, if it be by Sir Philip Sidney, 'twill be of gallant and noble knights assuredly."

"I know not, Cousin Judith," said he; "I but looked at the beginning as I came through the fields. And this is how it goes."

He opened the book, and began to read:

"It was in the time that the Earth begins to put on her new apparel against the approach of her lover, and that the sun, running a most even course, becomes an indifferent arbiter between the night and the day, when the hopeless shepherd Strephon was come to the sands which lie against the island of Cithera, where, viewing the place with a heavy kind of delight, and sometimes casting his eyes to the isleward, he called his friendly rival the pastor Claius unto him; and, setting first down in his darkened countenance a doleful copy of what he would speak, 'O my Claius,' said he—"

Thus he went on; and as he read, her face grew more and more wistful. It was a far-off land that she heard of; and beautiful it was; it seemed to her that she had been dwelling in some such land, careless and all unknowing.

"The third day after," she vaguely heard him say, "in the time that the morning did strew roses and violets in the heavenly floor against the coming of the sun, the nightingales, striving one with the other which could in most dainty variety recount their wrong-caused sorrow, made them put off their sleep; and, rising from under a tree, which that night had been their pavilion, they went on their journey, which by-and-by welcomed Musidorus' eyes with delightful prospects. There were hills which garnished their proud heights with stately trees; humble valleys whose base estate seemed comforted with the refreshing of silver rivers; meadows enamelled with all sorts of eye-pleasing flowers; thickets which, being lined with most pleasant shade, were witnessed so to by the cheerful disposition of many well-tuned birds; each pasture stored with sheep, feeding with sober security, while the pretty lambs, with bleating oratory, craved the dams' comfort: here a shepherd's boy piping, as though he should never be old; there a young shepherdess knitting, and withal singing: and it seemed that her voice comforted her hands to work, and her hands kept time to her voice-music."

Surely she had herself been living in some such land of pleasant delights, without a thought that ever it would end for her, but that each following day would be as full of mirth and laughter as its predecessor. She scarcely listened to the little lad now. She was looking back over the years. So rare and bright and full of light and color were they—and always a kind of music in them, and laughter at the sad eyes of lovers. She had never known how happy she had been. It was all distant now—the idle flower-gathering in the early spring-time; the afternoon walking in the meadows, she and Prudence together (with the young lads regarding them askance); the open casements on the moon-lit nights, to hear the madrigal-singing of the youths going home; or the fair and joyous mornings that she was allowed to ride away, in the direction of Oxford, to meet her father and his companions coming in to Stratford town. And now, when next he should come, to all of them, and all of them welcoming him—even neighbors and half-strangers—and he laughing to them all, and getting off his horse, and calling for a cup of wine as he strode into the house, where should she be? Not with all of these, not laughing and listening to the merry stories of the journey, but away by herself, hiding herself, as it were, and thinking, alone.

"Dear Judith, but why are you crying?" said the little lad, as he chanced to look up; and his face was of an instant and troubled anxiety.

"Why, 'tis a fair land—oh, indeed, a fair land!" said she, with an effort at regarding the book, and pretending to be wholly interested in it. "Nay, I would hear more of Musidorus, sweetheart, and of that pretty country. I pray you continue the reading—continue the reading, sweetheart Willie. Nay, I never heard of a fairer country, I assure thee, in all the wide world!"

CHAPTER XXXII.

A RESOLVE.

THEN that night, as she lay awake in the dark, her incessant imaginings shaped themselves toward one end. This passion of grief she knew to be unavailing and fruitless. Something she would try to do, if but to give evidence of her contrition; for how could she bear that her father should think of her as one having done him this harm and still going on light-hearted and unconcerned? The parson was coming over on the morrow. And if she were to put away her maidenly pride (and other vague dreams that she had sometimes dreamed), and take it that her consent would re-establish her in the eyes of those who were now regarding her askance, and make her peace with her own household? And if the surrender of her marriage portion and her interest in the Rowington copyhold (whatever it might be) were in a measure to mitigate her father's loss? It was the only thing she could think of. And if at times she looked forward with a kind of shudder (for in the night-time all prospects wear a darker hue) to her existence as the parson's wife, again there came to her the reflection that it was not for her to repine. Some sacrifice was due from her. And could she not be as resolute as the daughter of the Gileadite? Oftentimes she had heard the words read out in the still afternoon:

"Now when Iphtah came to Mizpeh unto his house, behold his daughter came out to meet him with timbrels and dances: which was his only child; he had none other son nor daughter. And when he saw her he rent his clothes, and said, Alas, my daughter! thou has brought me low, and art of them that trouble me." The Jewish maiden had done no ill, and yet was brave to suffer: why should she repine at any sacrifice demanded of her to atone for her own wrong-doing? What else was there? She hoped that Susan and her mother would be pleased now, and that her father and his friends in London would not have any serious loss to regret. There was but the one way, she said to herself again and again. She was almost anxious for the parson to come over, to see if he would approve.

With the daylight her determination became still more clear; and also she saw more plainly the difficulties before her. For it could not be deemed a very seemly and maidenly thing that she, on being asked to become a bride (and she had no doubt that was his errand), should begin to speak of her marriage portion. But would he understand? Would he help her over her embarrassment? Nay, she could not but reflect, here was an opportunity for his showing himself generous and large-minded. He had always professed, or at least intimated, that his wish to have her for wife was based mostly on his care for herself and his regard for the general good of the pious community to which he belonged. She was to be a helpmeet for one laboring in the Lord's vineyard; she was to be of service in the church; she was to secure for herself a constant and loving direction and guidance. And now, if he wished to prove all this—if he wished to show himself so noble and disinterested as to win for himself her life-long gratitude—what if he were to take over all her marriage portion, as that might be arranged, and forthwith and chivalrously hand it back again, so that her grievous fault should so far be condoned? If the girl had been in her usual condition of health and spirits, it is probable that she would have regarded this question with a trifle of skepticism (for she was about as shrewd in such matters as Susan herself)—nay, it is just probable that she might have experienced a malicious joy in putting him to the proof. But she was in despair; her nerves were gone, through continual wake-fulness and mental torture; this was the only direction in which she saw light before her, and she regarded it, not with her ordinary faculty of judgment, but with a kind of pathetic hope.

Master Blaise arrived in the course of the morning. His reception was not auspicious; for the old dame met him at the gate, and made more than a show of barring the way.

"Indeed, good sir," said she, firmly, "the wench be far from well now, and I would have her left alone."

He answered that his errand was of some importance, and that he must crave a few minutes' interview. Both her mother and sister, he said, were aware he was coming over to see her, and had made no objection.

"No, no, perchance not," the grandmother said, though without budging an inch, "but she be under my care now, and I will have no harm befall her—"

"Harm, good Mistress Hathaway?" said he.

"Well, she be none so strong as she were, and—and perchance there hath been overmuch lecturing of the poor lass. Nay, I doubt not 'twas meant in kindness, but there hath been overmuch of it, as I reckon; and what I say is, if the wench have done amiss, let those that have the right to complain come to her. Nay, 'twas kindness, good sir; 'twas well meant, I doubt not; and 'tis your calling belike to give counsel and reproof; I say naught against that; but I am of a mind to have my grandchild left alone at present."

"If you refuse me, good Mistress Hathaway," said he, quite courteously and calmly, "there is no more to be said. But I imagine that her mother and sister will be surprised. And as for the maiden herself—go you by her wishes?"

"Nay, not I," was the bold answer. "I know better than all of them together. For to speak plain with you, good master parson, your preaching must have been oversharp when last you were within here, and was like to have brought the wench to death's door thereafter—marry, she be none so far recovered as to risk any further of such treatment. Perchance you meant no harm; but she is proud and high-spirited, and, by your leave, good sir, we will see her a little stronger and better set up ere she have any more of the discipline of the church bestowed on her."

It was well that Judith appeared at this juncture; for the tone of the old dame's voice was growing more and more tart.

"Grandmother," said she, "I would speak with Master Blaise."

"Get thee within-doors at once, I tell thee, wench!" was the peremptory rejoinder.

"No, good grandmother, so please you," Judith said, "I must speak with him. There is much of importance that I have to say to him. Good sir, will you step into the garden?"

The old dame withdrew, sulky and grumbling, and evidently inclined to remain within ear-shot, lest she should deem it necessary to interfere. Judith preceded Master Blaise to the door of the cottage, and asked the little maid to bring out a couple of chairs. As she sat down, he could not but observe how wan and worn her face was, and how listless she was in manner; but he made no comment on that: he only remarked that her grandmother seemed in no friendly mood this morning, and that only the fact that his mission was known to Susan and her mother had caused him to persist.

It was clear that this untoward reception had disconcerted him somewhat; and it was some little time before he could recover that air of mild authority with which he was accustomed to convey his counsels. At first he confined himself to telling Judith what he had done on behalf of her mother and Susan—in obedience to their wishes; but by-and-by he came to herself, and her own situation; and he hoped that this experience through which she had passed, though it might have caused her bitter distress for the time, would eventually make for good. If the past could not be recalled, at least the future might be made safe. Indeed, one or two phrases he used sounded as if they had done some previous service; perhaps he had consulted with Mistress Hall ere making this appeal; but in any case Judith was not listening so particularly as to think of that—she seemed to know beforehand what he had to say.

To tell the truth, he was himself a little surprised at her tacit acquiescence. He had always had to argue with Judith; and many a time he had found that her subtle feminine wit was capable of extricating herself from what he considered a defenseless position. But now she sat almost silent. She seemed to agree to everything.

There was not a trace left of the old audacious self-reliance, nor yet of those saucy rejoinders which were only veiled by her professed respect for his cloth. She was at his mercy.

And so, growing bolder, he put in his own personal claim. He said little that he had not said, or hinted, on previous occasions; but now all the circumstances were changed; this heavy misfortune that had befallen her was but another and all too cogent reason why she should accept his offer of shelter and aid and counsel, seeing into what pitfalls her own unguided steps were like to lead her.

"I speak the words of truth and soberness," said he, as he sat and calmly regarded her downcast face, "and make no appeal to the foolish fancies of a young and giddy-headed girl, for that you are no longer, Judith. The years are going by. There must come a time in life when the enjoyment of the passing moment is not all in all; when one must look to the future, and make provision for sickness and old age. Death strikes here and there; friends fall away; what a sad thing it were to find one's self alone, the dark clouds of life thickening over, and none by to help and cheer! Then your mother and sister, Judith—"

"Yes, I know," she said, almost in despair—"I know 'twould please them."

And then she reflected that this was scarcely the manner in which she should receive his offer, that was put before her so plainly and with so much calm sincerity.

"I pray you, good sir," said she, in a kind of languid way, "forgive me if I answer you not as frankly as might be. I have been ill; my head aches now; perchance I have not followed all you said. But I understand it—I understand it; and in all you say there is naught but good intention."

"Then it is yes, Judith?" he exclaimed, and for the first time there was a little brightness of ardor—almost of triumph —in this clearly conceived and argued wooing.

"It would please my mother and sister," she repeated, slowly. "They are afraid of some story coming from London about—about what is passed. This would be an answer, would it not?"

"Why, yes," he said, confidently, for he saw that she was yielding (and his own susceptibilities were not likely to be wounded in that direction). "Think you we should heed any tavern scurrility? I trow not! There would be the answer plain and clear—if you were my wife, Judith."

"They would be pleased," again she said, and her eyes were absent. And then she added: "I pray you pardon me, good sir, if I speak of that which you may deem out of place; but—but if you knew —how I have been striving to think of some means of repairing the wrong I have done my father, you would not wonder that I should be anxious, and perchance indiscreet. You know of the loss I have caused him and his companions. How could I ever make that good with the work of my own hands? That is not possible; and yet when I think of how he hath toiled for all of us, late and early, as it were—why, good sir, I have myself been bold enough to chide him, or to wish that I were a man, to ride forth in the morning in his stead and look after the land: and then that his own daughter should be the means of taking from him what he hath earned so hardly—that I should never forget; 'twould be on my mind year after year, even if he were himself to try to forget it."

She paused for a second; the mere effort of speaking seemed to fatigue her.

"There is but the one means, as I can think, of showing him my humble sorrow for what hath been done—of making him some restitution. I know not what my marriage portion may be—but 'twill be something—and Susan saith there is a part of the manor of Rowington, also, that would fall to me. Now, see you, good Master Blaise, if I were to give these over to my father in part quittance of this injury, or if belike—my—my—husband would do that—out of generosity and nobleness—would not my father be less aggrieved?"

She had spoken rather quickly and breathlessly (to get over her embarrassment), and now she regarded him with a strange anxiety, for so much depended on his answer! Would he understand her motives? Would he pardon her bluntness? Would he join her in this scheme of restitution?

He hesitated only for a moment.

"Dear Judith," he said, with perfect equanimity, "such matters are solely within the province of men, and not at the disposition of women, who know less of the affairs of the world. Whatever arrangements your father may have made in respect of your marriage portion—truly I have made no inquiry in that direction— he will have made with due regard to his own circumstances, and with regard to the family, and to your future. Would he be willing to upset these in order to please a girlish fancy? Why, in all positions in life, pecuniary losses must happen, and a man takes an account of these; and is he likely to recover himself at the expense of his own daughter?"

"Nay, but if she be willing! If she would give all that she hath, good sir!" she cried, quickly.

"'Twould be but taking it from one pocket to put it in the other," said he, in his patient and forbearing way. "I say not, if a man were like to become bankrupt, that his family might not forego their expectations in order to save him; but your father is one in good position. Think you that the loss is so great to him? In truth, it can not be."

The eagerness fell away from her face. She saw too clearly that he could not understand her at all. She did not reckon her father's loss in proportion to his wealth —in truth she could not form the faintest notion of what that loss might be: all her thought was of her winning back (in some remote day, if that were still possible to her) to her father's forgiveness, and the regarding of his face as no longer in dread wrath against her.

"Why," said he, seeing that she sat silent and distraught (for all the hope had gone out of her), "in every profession and station in life a man must have here or there a loss, as I say; but would he rob his family to make that good? Surely not. Of what avail might that be? 'Tis for them that he is working; 'tis not for himself; why should he take from them to build up a property which must in due course revert and become theirs? I pray you put such fancies out of your head, Judith. Women are not accustomed to deal with such matters; 'tis better to have them settled in the ordinary fashion. Were I you I would leave it in your father's hands."

"And have him think of me as he is thinking now!" she said, in a kind of wild way. "Ah, good sir, you know not!— you know not! Every day that passes is but the deeper misery; for—for he will be hardened in the belief—'twill be fixed in his mind forever—that his own daughter did him this wrong, and went on lightly, not heeding, perchance to seek another sweetheart. This he is thinking now; and I—what can I do?—being so far away, and none to help!"

"In truth, dear Judith," said he, "you make too much of your share in what happened. 'Tis not to you your father should look for reparation of his loss, but to the scoundrel who carried the play to London. What punishment would it be for him, or what gain to your father, that your father should upset the arrangements he has made for the establishment and surety of his own family? Nay, I pray you put aside such a strange fancy, dear heart, and let such things take their natural course."

"In no wise! in no wise!" she exclaimed, almost in despair. "In truth, I can not. 'Twould kill me were nothing to be done to appease my father's anger; and I thought that if he were to learn that you had sought me in marriage, and—and agreed that such restitution as I can make should be made forthwith—or afterward, as might be decided—but only that he should know now that I give up everything he had intended for me—then I should have greater peace of mind."

"Indeed, Judith," said he, somewhat coldly, "I could be no party to any such foolish freak—nay, not even in intention, whatever your father might say to it. The very neighbors would think I was bereft of my senses. And 'twould be an ill beginning of our life together—in which there must ever be authority and guidance as well as dutiful obedience—if I were to yield to what every one must perceive to be an idle and fantastic wish. I pray you consult your own sober judgment: at present you are ailing and perturbed; rest you awhile until these matters have calmed somewhat, and you will see them in their true light."

"No, no," she said, hurriedly and absently—"no, no, good sir; you know not what you ask. Rest? Nay, one way or the other, this must be done, and forthwith. I know not what he may have intended for me, but be it large or small, 'tis all that I have to give him—I can do no more than that; and then, then there may be some thoughts of rest."

She spoke as if she were scarcely aware of the good parson's presence; and in truth, though he was not one to allow any wounded self-love to mar his interests, he could not conceal from himself that she was considering the proposal he had put before her mainly, if not wholly, with a view to the possible settlement of these troubles and the appeasing of her friends. Whether, in other circumstances, he might not have calmly overlooked this slight need not now be regarded; in the present circumstances—that is to say, after her announced determination to forego every penny of her marriage portion—he did take notice of it, and with some sharpness of tone, as if he were truly offended.

"Indeed, you pay me no compliment, Judith," said he. "I come to offer you the shelter of an honest man's home, an honorable station as his wife, a life-long guidance and protection; and what is your answer?—that perchance you may make use of such an offer to please your friends, and to pay back to your father what you foolishly think you owe him. If these be the only purposes you have in view—and you seem to think of none other—'twould be a sorry forecast for the future, as I take it. At the very beginning an act of madness! Nay, I could be no party to any such thing. If you refuse to be guided by me in great matters, how could I expect you to be guided in small?"

These words, uttered in his clear and precise and definite manner, she but vaguely understood (for her head troubled her sorely, and she was tired and anxious to be at rest) to be a withdrawal of his proposal; but that was enough; and perhaps she even experienced some slight sense of relief. As for his rebuking of her, she heeded not that.

"As you will, sir—as you will," she said, listlessly; and she rose from her chair.

And he rose too. Perhaps he was truly offended; perhaps he only appeared to be; but at all events he bade her farewell in a cold and formal manner, and as if it were he who had brought this interview to an end, and that for good.

"What said he, wench, what said he?" her grandmother asked (who had been pretending all the time to be gathering peas, and now came forward). "Nay, I caught but little—a word here or there—and yet methinks 'tis a brave way of wooing they have nowadays, that would question a maid about her marriage portion. Heaven's mercy! did ever any hear the like? 'Twas not so when I was young— nay, a maid would have bade him go hang that brought her such a tale. Oh, the good parson!—his thoughts be not all bent on heaven, I warrant me! Ay, and what said he? And what saidst thou, wench? Truly you be in no fit state to answer him; were you well enough, and in your usual spirits, the good man would have his answer—ay, as sharp as need be. But I will say no more; Master Quiney hath a vengeful spirit, and perchance he hath set me too much against the good man; but as for thyself, lass, there be little cause for talking further of thy offenses, if 'tis thy marriage portion the parson be after, now!"

"Good grandmother, give me your arm," Judith said, in a strange way. "My head is so strange and giddy. I know not what I have said to him—I scarce can recollect it: if I have offended, bid him forgive me; but—but I would have him remain away."

"As I am a living woman," said the old dame (forgetting her resolve to speak smooth words), "he shall not come within the door, nor yet within that gate, while you bide with me and would have him kept without! What, then? More talk of chastenings? Marry, now, Thomas Quiney shall hear of this—that shall he —by my life he shall!"

"No, no, no, good grandmother; pray you blame no one," the girl said; and she was trembling somewhat. "'Tis I that have done all the harm to every one. But I know not what I said. I—I would fain lie down, grandmother, if you will give me your arm so far; 'tis so strangely cold—I understand it not—and I forget what was't he said to me, but I trust I offended him not—"

"Nay, but what is it, then, my dearie?" the old woman said, taking both the girl's hands in hers. "What is it that you should fret about? Nay, fret not, fret not, good wench; the parson be well away, and there let him bide. And would you lie down?—well, come, then; but sure you shake as if 'twere winter. Come, lass— nay, fret not; we will keep the parson away, I warrant, if 'tis that that vexes thee!"

"No, grandmother, 'tis not so," the girl said, in a low voice. "'Twas down by the river, as I think; 'twas chilly there —I have felt it ever since from time to time—but 'twill pass away when I am lain down and become warm again."

"Heaven grant it be no worse!" the old dame said to herself, as she shrewdly re-garded the girl; but of course her outward talk, as she took her within-doors, was ostensibly cheerful. "Come thy ways, then, sweeting, and we shall soon make thee warm enough. Ay, ay, and Prudence be coming over this afternoon, as I hear; and no doubt Thomas Quiney too; and thou must get thyself dressed prettily, and have supper with us all, though 'tis no treat to offer to a man of his own wine. Nay, I warrant me he will think naught of that, so thou be there, with a pleasant look for him; he will want nor wine nor aught else if he have but that, and a friendly word from thee, as I reckon; ay, and thou shalt put on the lace cuffs, now, to do him fair service for his gift to thee—that shalt thou, and why not?—I swear to thee, my brave lass, they be fit for a queen!"

And she would comfort her and help her (just as if this granddaughter of hers, that always was so bright and gay and radiant, so self-willed and self-reliant, with nothing but laughter for the sad eyes of the stricken youths, was now but a weak and frightened child, that had to be guarded and coaxed and caressed), and would talk as if all her thinking was of that visit in the afternoon; but the only answer was:

"Will you send for Prudence, grandmother? Oh, grandmother, my head aches so! I scarce know what I said."

Swiftly and secretly the old dame sent across to the town; and not to Prudence only, but also (for she was grown anxious) to Mistress Hall, to say that if her husband were like to return soon to Stratford, he might come over and see Judith, who was far from well. As for Prudence, a word was sufficient to bring her; she was there straightway.

She found Judith very much as she had left her, but somewhat more restless and feverish perhaps, and then again hopelessly weak and languid, and always with those racking pains in the head. She said it was nothing—it would soon pass away; it was but a chill she had caught in sitting on the river-bank: would not Prudence now go back to her duties and her affairs in the house?

"Judith," said her friend, leaning over her and speaking low, "I have that to tell thee will comfort thee, methinks."

"Nay, I can not listen to it now," was the answer—and it was a moan almost. "Dear mouse, do not trouble about me;

but my head is so bad that I—that I care not now. And the parson is gone away thinking that I have wronged him also. 'Tis ever the same now— Oh, sweetheart, my head! my head!"

"But listen, Judith," the other pleaded. "Nay, but you must know what your friends are ready to do for you—this surely will make thee well, sweetheart. Think of it, now: do you know that Quiney is gone to see your father?"

"To my father?" she repeated, and she tried to raise her head somewhat, so that her eyes might read her friend's face.

"I am almost sure of it, dear heart," Prudence said, taking her hot hand in hers. "Nay, he would have naught said of it. None of his family know whither he is gone; and I but guess. But this is the manner of it, dear Judith—that he and I were talking, and sorely vexed he was that your father should be told a wrong story concerning you—ay, and sorry to see you so shaken, Judith, and distressed; and said he, 'What if I were to get a message to her from her father—that he was in no such mood of anger, and had not heard the story aright, and that he was well disposed to her, and grieved to hear she had taken it so much to heart —would not that comfort her?' he said. And I answered that assuredly it would, and even more, perchance, than he thought of; and I gathered from him that he would write to some one in London to go and see your father and pray him to send you assurance of that kind. But now— nay, I am certain of it, dear Judith—I am certain that he himself is gone all the way to London to bring thee back that comfort; and will not that cheer thee, now, sweetheart?"

"He is doing all that for me?" the girl said, in a low voice, and absently.

"Ah, but you must be well and cheerful, good mouse, to give him greeting when he comes back," said Prudence, striving to raise her spirits somewhat. "Have I not read to thee many a time how great kings were wont to reward the messengers that brought them good news? —a gold chain round their neck, or lands, perchance. And will you have no word of welcome for him? Will you not meet him with a glad face? Why, think of it, now—a journey to London, and the perils and troubles by the way, and all done to please thee! Nay, he would say naught of it to any one, lest they might wonder

at his doing so much for thee, belike; but when he comes back 'twere a sorry thing that you should not give him a good and gracious welcome."

Judith lay silent and thinking for a while; and then she said, but as if the mere effort to speak were too much for her:

"Whatever happens, dear Prudence— nay, in truth, I think I am very ill—tell him this, that he did me wrong: he thought I had gone to meet the parson that Sunday morning in the church-yard. 'Twas not so—tell him it was not so; 'twas but a chance, dear heart; I could not help it."

"Judith, Judith," her friend said, "these be things for thine own telling. Nay, you shall say all that to himself; and you must speak him fair—ay, and give him good welcome and thanks that hath done so much for thee."

Judith put her head down on the pillow again, languidly; but presently Prudence heard her laugh to herself in a strange way.

"Last night," she said, "'twas so wonderful, dear Prue. I thought I was going about in a strange country, looking for my little brother Hamnet, and I knew not whether he would have any remembrance of me. Should I have to tell him my name, I kept asking myself. And 'Judith, Judith,' I said to him when I found him; but he scarce knew; I thought he had forgotten me; 'tis so long ago now. 'Judith, Judith,' I said; and he looked up, and he was so strangely like little Willie Hart that I wondered whether it was Hamnet or no."

But Prudence was alarmed by these wanderings, and did her best to hush them. And then, when at length the girl lay silent and still, Prudence stole down-stairs again and bade the grandmother go to Judith's room, for that she must at once hurry over to Stratford to speak with Susan Hall.

CHAPTER XXXIII.
ARRIVALS.

SOME few mornings after that, two travellers were standing in the spacious archway of the inn at Shipston, chatting to each other, and occasionally glancing toward the stable-yard, as if they were expecting their horses to be brought round.

"The wench will thank thee for this service done her," the elder of the two said; and he regarded the younger man in a shrewd and not unkindly way.

"Nay, I am none well pleased with the issue of it all," the young man said, moodily.

"What, then?" his companion said. "Can nothing be done and finished but with the breaking of heads? Must that ever crown the work? Mercy on us!— how many would you have slaughtered? Now 'tis the parson that must be thrown into the Avon; again it is Gentleman Jack you would have us seek out for you; and then it is his friend—whose very name we know not—that you would pursue through the dens and stews of London town. A hopeful task, truly, for a Stratford youth! What know you of London, man? And to pursue one whose very name you know not—and all for the further breaking of heads, that never did any good anywhere in the world."

"You are right, sir," the younger man said, with some bitterness. "I can brag and bluster as well as any. But I see not that much comes of it. 'Tis easy to break the heads of scoundrels—in talk. Their bones are none the worse."

"And better so," the other said, gravely. "I would have no blood shed. What, man, are you still fretting that I would not leave you behind in London?"

"Nay, sir, altogether I like not the issue of it," he said, but respectfully enough. "I shall be told, I doubt not, that I might have minded my own business. They will blame me for bringing you all this way, and hindering your affairs."

"Heaven bless us!" said the other, laughing, "may not a man come to see his own daughter without asking leave of the neighbors?"

"'Tis as like as not that she herself will be the first to chide me," the younger man answered. "A message to her was all I asked of you, sir. I dreamt not of hindering your affairs so."

"Nay, nay," said Judith's father, good-naturedly. "I can make the occasion serve me well. Trouble not about that, friend Quiney. If we can cheer up the wench and put her mind at rest—that will be a sufficient end of the journey; and we will have no broken heads withal, so please you. And if she herself should have put aside these idle fears, and become her usual self again, why, then,

there is no harm done either. I mind me that some of them wondered that I should ride down to see my little Hamnet when he lay sick; for 'twas no serious illness that time, as it turned out; but what does that make for now? Now, I tell you, I am right glad I went to see the little lad; it cheered him to be made so much of; and such small services or kindnesses are pleasant things for ourselves to think of when those that are dearest to us are no longer with us. So cease your fretting, friend Quiney. For the hindering of my affairs I take it that I am answerable to myself, and not to the good gossips of Stratford town. And if 'tis merely to say a kind word to the lass—if that is all that need be done—well, there are many things that are of different value to different people; and the wench and I understand each other shrewdly well."

The horses were now brought round; but, ere they mounted, Judith's father said, again regarding the youth in that observant way,

"Nay, I see how it is with you, good lad; you are anxious as to how Judith may take this service you have done her —is't not so?"

"Perchance she may be angry that I called you away, sir," he said,

"Have no fear. 'Twas none of thy doing. 'Twas but a whim of mine own— nay, there be other and many reasons for my coming, that need not to be explained to her. What, must I make apology to my own daughter? She is not the guardian of Stratford town? I am no rogue; she is no constable. May not I enter? Nay, nay, have no fear, friend Quiney; when that she comes to understand the heavy errand you undertook for her, she will give you her thanks, or I know nothing of her. Her thanks?—marry, yes!"

He looked at the young man again.

"But let there be no broken heads, good friend, I charge you," said he, as he put his foot in the stirrup. "If the parson have been overzealous, we will set all matters straight, without hurt or harm to any son of Adam."

And now as they rode on together the younger man's face seemed more confident and satisfied; and he was silent for the most part. Of course he would himself be the bearer of the news; it was but natural that he should claim as much. And as Judith's father intended to go first to New Place, Quiney intimated to him that he would rather not ride through the town; in fact, he wanted to get straightway (and unobserved, if possible) to Shottery, to see how matters were there.

When he arrived at the little hamlet, Willie Hart was in the garden, and instantly came down to the gate to meet him. He asked no questions of the boy; but begged of him to hold the bridle of his horse for a few minutes; then he went into the house.

Just within the threshold he met Judith's sister.

"Ah," said he, quickly, and even joyously, "I have brought good news. Where is Judith? May I see her? I want to tell her that her father is come, and will be here to see her presently."

And then something in the scared face that was regarding him struck him with a sudden terror.

"What is it?" he said, with his own face become about as pale as hers.

"Judith is very ill," was the answer.

"Yes, yes," he said, eagerly, "and that she was when I left. But now that her father is come, 'twill be all different—'twill be all set right now. And you will tell her, then, if I may not? Nay, but may not I see her for a moment—but for a moment—to say how her father is come all the way to see her—ay, and hath a store of trinkets for her—and is come to comfort her into assurance that all will go well? Why, will not such a message cheer her?"

"Good Master Quiney," Susan said, with tears welling into her eyes, "if you were to see her, she would not know you; she knows no one; she knows not that she is ill; but speaks of herself as some other—"

"But her father!" he exclaimed, in dismay, "will she not know him? Will she not understand? Nay, surely 'tis not yet too late!"

But here Doctor Hall appeared; and when he was told that Judith's father was come to the town and would shortly be at the cottage, he merely said that perchance his presence might soothe her somewhat, or even lead her delirious wanderings into a gentler channel, but that she would almost certainly be unable to recognize him. Nor was the fever yet at its height, he said, and they could do but little for her. They could but wait and hope. As for Quiney, he did not ask to be admitted to the room. He seemed stunned. He sat down in the kitchen—heeding no one—and vaguely wondering whether any lengthening of the stages of the journey would have brought them in better time. Nay, had he not wasted precious hours in London in vainly seeking to find himself face to face with Jack Orridge?

Prudence chanced to come down-stairs. As she entered the kitchen he forgot to give her any greeting; he only said, quickly:

"Think you she will not understand that her father is come to see her? Surely she must understand so much, Prudence! You will tell her, will you not?—and if she sees him standing before her?"

"I know not—I am afraid," said Prudence, anxiously. "Perchance it may frighten her the more; for ever she says that she sees him; and always with an angry face toward her; and she is for hiding herself away from him, and even talking of the river. Good lack! 'tis pitiful that she should be so struck down, and almost at death's door, and all we can do of so little avail!"

"Prudence," said he, starting to his feet, "there is her father just come; I hear him; now take him to her, and you will see—you will see. I may not go; a strange face might frighten her; but I know she will recognize him, and understand; and he will tell her to have no longer any fear of him—"

Prudence hurried away to meet Judith's father, who was in the doorway, getting such information as was possible from the doctor. And then they all of them (all but Quiney) stole gently upstairs; and they stood at the door in absolute silence, while Judith's father went forward to the bed—so quietly that the girl did not seem to notice his approach.

The grandmother was there, sitting by the bedside, and speaking to her in a low voice.

"Hush thee now, sweeting, hush thee now," she was saying, and she patted her hand. "Nay, I know 'twas ill done; 'tis quite right what thou sayst; they treated her not well—and the poor wench anxious to please them all. But have no fear for her; nay, trouble not thy head with thoughts of her: she be safe at home again, I trust. Hush thee now, sweeting; 'twill go well with her, I doubt not. I swear to thee her father be no longer angry with the wench; 'twill go well with her, and well. Have no fear."

The girl looked at her steadily, and yet with a strange light in her eyes, as if she saw distant things before her, or was seeking to recall them.

"There was Susan, too," she said, in a low voice, "that sang so sweet—oh, in the church it was so sweet to hear her!—but when it was '*The rose is from my garden gone*,' she would not sing that—though that was ever in her sister's mind after she went away down to the river-side; I can not think why they would not sing it to her—perchance the parson thought 'twas wicked : I know not now. And when she herself would try it with the lute, nothing would come right, all went wrong with her—all went wrong; and her father came angry and terrible to seek her—and 'twas the parson that would drag her forth—the bushes were not thick enough. Good grandam, why should the bushes in the garden be so thin that the terrible eyes peered through them, and she tried to hide, and could not?"

"Nay, I tell thee, sweetheart," said the grandmother, whispering to her, "that the poor wench you speak of went home, and all were well content with her, and her father was right pleased—indeed, indeed, 'twas so."

"Poor Judith! poor Judith!" the girl murmured to herself, and then she laughed slightly. "She was ever the stupid one; naught would go right with her; ay, and evil-tempered she was, too, for Quiney would ride all the way to London for her, and she thanked him with never a word or a look—never a word or a look—and he going all the way to please her. Poor wench, all went wrong with her somehow; but they might have let her go, she was so anxious to hide; and then to drag her forth from under the bushes. Grandam, it was cruelly done of them, wasn't it?"

"Ay, ay, but hush thee now, dearie," her grandmother said, as she put a cool cloth on the burning forehead. "'Tis quite well now with the poor wench you speak of."

Her father drew nearer, and took her hand quietly.

"Judith," said he, " poor lass, I am come to see you."

For an instant there was a startled look of fear in her eyes; but that passed, and she regarded him at first with a kind of smiling wonder, and thereafter with a contented satisfaction, as though his presence was familiar. Nay, she turned her attention altogether toward him now, and addressed him—not in any heart-broken way, but cheerfully, and as if he had been listening to her all along. It was clear that she did not in the least know who he was.

"There, now, lass," said he, "knowest thou that Quiney and I have ridden all the way from London to see thee?—and thou must lie still and rest, and get well again, ere we can carry thee out into the garden."

She was looking at him with those strangely brilliant eyes.

"But not into the garden," she said, in a vacant kind of way. "That is all gone away now—gone away. 'Twas long ago—when poor Judith used to go into the garden—and right fair and beautiful it was—ay, and her father would praise her hair, and the color of it—until he grew angry, and drove her away far from him—and then—and then—she wandered down to the river—and always Susan's song was in her mind—or the other one, that was near as sad as that, about the western wind—was it not? How went it, now?

'*Western wind, when will you blow?*'

Nay, I can not recall it—'tis gone out of my head, grandam, and there is only fire there—and fire—and fire—

'*Western wind, when will you blow?*'

it went; and then about the rain next—what was it?

'*So weary falls the rain!*'

Ay, ay, that was it, now—I remember Susan singing it:

'*Western wind, when will you blow?*
So weary falls the rain!
O if my love were in my arms,
Or I in my bed again!'"

And here she turned away from them and fell a-crying, and hid from them, as it were, covering her face with both her hands.

"Grandmother, grandmother," they could hear her say through her sobbing, "there was but the one rose in my garden, and that is gone now—they have robbed me of that—and what cared I for aught else? And Quiney is gone too, without a word or a look; and ere he be come back—well, I shall be away by then —he will have no need to quarrel with me and think ill of me that I chanced to meet the parson. 'Tis all over now, grandmother, and done with, and you will let me bide with you for just a little while longer—a little while, grandmother; 'tis no great matter for so little a while, though I can not help you as I would; but Cicely is a good lass, and 'twill be for a little while, for last night again I found Hamnet—ay, ay, he hath all things in readiness now—all in readiness." And then she uttered a slight cry, or moan rather. "Grandmother, grandmother, why do you not keep the parson away from me?—you said that you would."

"Hush, hush, child," the grandmother said, bending over her and speaking softly and closely. "You are overconcerned about the poor lass that was treated so ill. Take heart now; I tell thee all is going well with her; her father hath taken her home again; and she is as happy as the day is long. Nay, I swear to thee, good wench, if thou lie still and restful, I will take thee to see her some of these days. Hush thee now, dearie; 'tis going right well with the lass now."

The doctor touched the arm of Judith's father; and they both withdrew.

"She knew you not," said he. "And the fewer people around her the better—they set her fancies wandering."

They went down-stairs to where Quiney was awaiting them; and the sombre look on their faces told its own tale.

"She is in danger!" he said, quickly.

The doctor was busy with his own thoughts, but he glanced at the young man, and saw the burning anxiety of his eyes.

"The fever must run its course," said he, "and Judith hath had a brave constitution these many years that I fear not will make a good fight. 'Twas a sore pity that she was so distressed and stricken down in spirits, as I hear, ere the fever seized her."

Quiney turned to the window.

"Too late—too late!" said he. "And yet I spared not the nag."

"You have done all that man could do," her father said, going to him. "Nay, had I myself guessed that she was in such peril—but 'tis past recall now."

And then he took the young man by the hand, and grasped it firmly.

"Good lad," said he, "this that you did for us was a right noble act of kindness, and I trust in Heaven's mercy that Judith herself may live to thank you. As

for me, my thanks to you are all too poor and worthless; I must be content to remain your debtor—and your friend."

CHAPTER XXXIV.

AN AWAKENING.

IT was going ill with her. Late one night, Quiney, who had kept hovering about the house, never able to sit patiently and watch the anxious coming and going within-doors, and never able to tear himself away but for a few hundred yards, wandered out into the clear star-lit darkness. His heart was full. They had told him the crisis was near at hand. And almost it seemed to him that it was already over. Judith was going away from them. And those stars overhead—he knew but little of their names; he understood but little of the vast immensities and deeps that lay between them; they were to him but as grains of light in a darkened floor; and far above that floor rose the wonderful shining city that he had heard of in the Book of Revelation. And already—so wild and unstrung were his fancies—he could see the foursquare walls of jasper, and the gates of pearl, and the wide white steps leading up to these; and who was that who went all alone—giving no backward thought to any she was leaving behind—up those shining steps, with a strange light on her forehead and on her trembling hands? He saw her slowly kneel at the gate; her head meekly bowed, her hands clasped. And when they opened it, and when she rose and made to enter, he could have cried aloud to her for one backward look, one backward thought, toward Stratford town and the friends of her childhood and her youth. Alas! there was no such thing. There was wonder on her face, as she turned to this side and to that, and she went hesitatingly; and when they took her hands to lead her forward, she regarded them, this side and that, pleased, and wondering, and silent; but there was never a thought of Stratford town. Could that be Judith that was going away from them so—she that all of them had known so dearly? And to leave her own friends without one word of farewell! Those others there—she went with them smiling and wondering, and looking in silence from one to the other; but she knew them not. Her friends were here—here—with breaking hearts because she had gone away and forgotten them, and vanished within those far-shining gates.

And then some sudden and sullen thought of the future would overtake him. The injunctions laid on him by Judith's father could not be expected to last forever. And if this were to be so; if the love and desire of his youth were to be stolen away from him; if her bright young life, that was so beautiful a thing to all who knew her, was to be extinguished, and leave instead but a blankness and an aching memory through the long years —then there might arrive a time for a settlement. The parson was still coming about the house, for the women-folk were comforted by his presence; but Judith's father regarded him darkly, and had scarce ever a word for him. As for Quiney, he moved away or left the house when the good man came near: it was safer so. But in the future—when one was freer to act—for those injunctions could not be expected to last forever—and what greater joy could then be secured than the one fierce stroke of justice and revenge? He did not reason out the matter much; it was a kind of flame in his heart whenever he thought of it.

And in truth that catastrophe was nearly occurring now. He had been wandering vaguely along the highways, appealing to the calmness of the night, as it were, and the serenity of the star-lit heavens, for some quieting of his terrible fears; and then in his restlessness he walked back toward the cottage, anxious for further news, and yet scarcely daring to enter and ask. He saw the dull red light in the window, but could hear no sound. And would not his very footfall on the path disturb her? They all of them went about the house like ghosts. And were it not better that he should remain here, so that the stillness dwelling around the place should not be broken even by his breathing? So quiet the night was, and so soundless, he could have imagined that the wings of the angel of mercy were brooding over the little cottage, hushing it, as it were, and bringing rest and sleep to the sore-bewildered brain. He would not go near. These were the precious hours. And if peace had at last stolen into the sick-chamber, and closed the troubled eyelids, were it not better to remain away, lest even a whisper should break the charm?

Suddenly he saw the door of the cottage open, and in the dull light a dark figure appeared. He heard footsteps on the garden path. At first his heart felt like stone, and he could not move, for he thought it was some one coming to seek him with evil news; but presently, in the clear starlight, he knew who this was that was now approaching him. He lost his senses. All the black night went red.

"So, good parson," said he (but he clinched his fists together, so that he should not give way), "art thou satisfied with thy handiwork?"

There was more of menace in the tone than in the taunt. At all events, with some such phrase as, "Out of the way, tavern-brawler!" the parson raised his stick as if to defend himself. And then the next instant he was gripped firm, as in a vise; the stick was twisted from his grasp and whirled away far into the dark; and forthwith—for it all happened in a moment—five fingers had him by the back of the neck.

There was one second of indecision— what it meant to this young athlete, who had his eyes afire and his mind afire with thoughts of the ill that had been done to the one he loved the dearest, can well be imagined. But he flung his enemy from him, forward, into the night.

"Take thy dog's life, and welcome— coward and woman-striker!"

He waited; there was no answer. And then—all shaking from the terrible pressure he had put on himself, and still hungering and athirst to go back and settle the matter then and there—he turned and walked along the road, avoiding the cottage. and still with his heart aflame, and wondering whether he had done well to let the hour of vengeance go.

But that did not last long. What cared he for this man, that any thought of him should occupy him at such a moment? All his anxieties were elsewhere—in that hushed small chamber, where the lamp of life was flickering low, and all awaiting, with fear and trembling, what the dawn might bring. And if she were to slip away so— escaping from them, as it were—without a word of recognition? It seemed so hard that the solitary figure going up those far, wide steps should have no thought for them she had left behind. As he saw her there, content was on her face, and a mild radiance, and wonder; and her new companions were pleasant to her. She

"'AND HER THANKS TO WHOM?' SAID PRUDENCE, SMILING."—[See Page 949.]

would go away with them; she was content to be with them; she would disappear amongst them, and leave no sign. And Sunday morning after Sunday morning he would look in vain for her coming through the church-yard, under the trees; and there would be a vacant place in the pew; no matter who might be there, one face would be wanting; and in the afternoon the wide meadows would be empty. Look where he might, from the foot-bridge over the river, from Bardon Hill, from the Weir Brake, there would be no more chance of his descrying Judith walking with Prudence—the two figures that he could make out at any distance almost. And what a radiance there used to be on her face!—not that mild wonder that he saw as she passed away with her companions within the shining gates, but a happy, audacious radiance, so that he could see she was laughing long ere he came near her. That was Judith; that was the Judith he had known, laughing, radiant, in summer meadows, as it seemed to him, careless of the young men, though her eyes would regard them, and always with her chief secrets and mystifications for her friend Prudence. That was Judith; not this poor worn sufferer, wandering through darkened ways, the frail lamp of her life going down and down, so that they dared not speak in the room. And that message that she had left for him with Prudence—was it a kind of farewell? They were about the last words she had spoken ere her speech lost all coherence and meaning—a farewell before she entered into that dark and unknown realm. And there was a touch of reproach in them, too: "Tell him he did me wrong to think I had gone to meet the parson in the church-yard; 'twas but a chance." The Judith of those former days was far too proud to make any such explanation; but this poor stricken creature seemed anxious to appease every one and make friends. And was he to have no chance of begging her forgiveness for doing her that wrong, and of telling how little she need regard it, and how that she might dismiss the parson from her mind altogether, as he had done? The ride to London: she knew nothing of that; she knew nothing of her father having come all the way to see her. Why, as they came riding along, by Uxbridge, and Wycombe, and Woodstock, and Enstone, many a time he looked forward to telling Judith of what he had done; and he hoped that she would go round to the stable, and have a word for the Galloway nag, and pat the good beast's neck. But all that was over now, and only this terrible darkness and the silence of the roads and the trees; and always the dull, steady, ominous light in the small window. And still more terrible that vision overhead—the far and mystic city, and Judith entering with those new and strange companions, regarding this one and that, and ever with a smile on her face and a mild wonder in her eyes, they leading her away by the hand, and she timid, and looking from one to the other, but pleased to go with them into the strange country. And as for her old friends, no backward look or backward thought for them: for them only the sad and empty town, the voiceless meadows, the vacant space in the pew, to which many an eye would be turned as week by week came round. And there would be a grave somewhere, that Prudence would not leave untended.

But with the first gray light of the dawn there came a sudden trembling joy, that was so easily and eagerly translated into a wild audacious hope. Judith had fallen into a sound sleep—a sleep hushed and profound, and no longer tortured with moanings and dull low cries as if for pity. A slumber profound and beneficent, with calmer breathing and a calmer pulse. If only on the awakening she might show that the crisis was over, and she started on the road—however long and tedious that might be—toward the winning back of life and health!

It was Prudence who brought him the news. She looked like a ghost in the wan light, as she opened the door and came forth. She knew he would not be far away; indeed, his eyes were more accustomed to this strange light than hers, and ere she had time to look about and search for him he was there. And when she told him this news, he could not speak for a little while; for his mind rushed forward blindly and wildly to a happy consummation; he would have no misgivings; this welcome sleep was a sure sign Judith was won back to them; not yet was she to go away all alone up those wide, sad steps.

"And you, Prudence," said he, or rather he whispered it eagerly, that no sound should disturb the profound quiet of the house, "now you must go and lie down

—you are worn out. Why, you are all trembling."

"The morning air is a little cold," said she; but it was not that that caused her trembling.

"You must go and lie down and get some sleep too," said he (but glancing up at the window, as if all his thoughts were there). "What a patient watcher you have been! And now, when there is this chance, do, dear Prudence, go within and lie down for a while—"

"Oh, how could I?—how could I?" she said; and unknown to herself she was wringing her hands—not from grief, but from mere excitement and nervousness. "But for this sleep, now, the doctor was fearing the worst. I know it, though he would not say it. And she is so weak! Even if this sleep calm her brain, or if she come out of it in her right mind, one never knows: she is so worn away, she might waken only to slip away from us."

But he would not hear of that. No, no; this happy slumber was but the beginning of her recovery. Now that she was on the turn, Judith's brave constitution would fight through the rest. He knew it; he was sure of it; had there ever been a healthier or happier wench, or one with such gallant spirits and cheerfulness?

"You have not seen her these last two days," Prudence said, sadly.

"Nay, I fear not now; I know she will fight through," said he, confidently (even with an excess of confidence, so as to cheer this patient and gentle nurse). "And what a spite it is I can do nothing? Did you ask the doctor, Prudence? Is there nothing that I can fetch him from Warwick?—ay, or from London, for that matter? 'Tis well for you that can do so much for your friend; what can I do but wait about the lanes? I would take a message anywhere, for any of you, if you would but tell me; 'tis all that I can do. But when she is getting better, that will be different—that will be all different then; I shall be able to get her many things to please her and amuse her, and —and—think of this, Prudence," said he, his fancies running away with him in his eagerness "Do you not think, now, that when she is well enough to be carried into the garden—do you not think that Pleydell and I could devise some kind of couch—to be put on wheels, see you, and slung on leather bands, so that it would go easily? Why, I swear it could be made,

and might be in readiness for her. What think you, Prudence? No one could object if we prepared it—ay, and we should get it to go as smooth as velvet, so that she could be taken along the lanes or through the meadows."

"I would there were need of it," Prudence said, wistfully. "You go too fast. Nay, but if she come well out of this deep sleep, who knows? Pray Heaven there be need for all that you can do for her."

The chirping of a small bird close by startled them—it was the first sound of the coming day.

And then she said, regarding him:

"Would you like to see Judith for a moment? 'Twould not disturb her."

He stepped back, with a sudden look of dismay on his face.

"What mean you, Prudence?" he said, quickly. "You do not think—that—there is fear?—that I should look at her now?"

"Nay, not so; I trust not," she said, simply. "But if you wished, you might slip up the stair—'twould do no harm."

He stooped and took off his shoes and threw them aside; then she led the way into the house, and they went stealthily up the short wooden stair. The door was open an inch or two; Prudence opened it still further, but did not go into the room. Nor did he; he remained at the threshold; for Judith's mother, who was sitting by the bedside, and who had noticed the slight opening of the door, had raised her hand quietly, as if in warning. And was this Judith, then, that the cold morning light, entering by the small casement, showed him—worn and wasted, the natural radiance of her face all fled, and in place of that a dull hectic tone that in no wise concealed the ravages the fever had made? But she slept sound. The bent arm, that she had raised to her head ere she fell asleep, lay absolutely still. No, it was not the Judith he had known—so gay and radiant and laughing in the summer meadows; but the wasted form still held a precious life; and he had no mistrust—he would not doubt; there was there still what would win back for him the Judith that he had known—ay, if they had to wait all through the winter for the first silver-white days of spring.

They stole down-stairs again, and went to the front door. All the world was awaking now; the light was clear around them; the small birds were twittering in the bushes.

"And will you not go and get some sleep now, Prudence?" said he. "Surely you have earned it; and now there is the chance."

"I could not," she said, simply. "There will be time for sleep by-and-by. But now, if you would do us a service, will you go over to the town and tell Susan that Judith is sleeping peacefully, and that she need not hurry back, for there be plenty of us to watch and wait? And Julius would like to hear the good news—that I know. Then you yourself—do you not need rest?—why—"

"Heed not for me, dear Prudence," said he, quickly, as if it were not worth while wasting time on that topic. "But is there naught else I can do for you? Naught that I can bring for you—against her getting well again?"

"Nay, 'tis all too soon for that," was Prudence's answer. "I would the occasion were here, and sure."

Well, he went away over to the town, and told his tale to those that were astir, leaving a message for those who were not; and then he passed on to his own house, and threw himself on his bed. But he could not rest. It was too far away, while all his thoughts were concentrated on the small cottage over there. So he wandered back thither; and again had assurance that Judith was doing well; and then he went quietly up to the summer-house, and sat down there; and scarcely had he folded his arms on the little table and bent forward his head than he was in a deep sleep—nature claiming her due at last.

The hours passed; he knew nothing of them. He was awakened by Judith's father; and he looked round him strangely, for he saw by the light that it was now afternoon.

"Good lad," said he, "I make no scruple of rousing you. There is better news. She is awake, and quite calm and peaceable, and in her right mind—though sadly weak and listless, poor wench."

"Have you seen her—have you spoken with her?" he said, eagerly.

"Nay, not yet," Judith's father said. "I am doubtful. She is so faint and weak. I would not disturb her."

"I pray you, sir, go and speak with her," Quiney entreated. "Nay, I know what will give her more peace of mind than anything. And if she begin to recall what happened ere she fell ill— I pray you, sir, of your kindness go and speak with her."

Judith's father went away to the house slowly, and with his head bent in meditation. He spoke to the doctor for a few minutes. But when, after some deliberation, he went upstairs, and into the room, it was his own advice, his own plan, he was acting on.

He went forward to the bedside, and took the chair that the old grandmother had instantly vacated, and sat down just as if nothing had occurred.

"Well, lass, how goes it with thee?" he said, with an air of easy unconcern. "Bravely well, I hear. Thou must haste thee now, for soon we shall be busy with the brewing."

She regarded him in a strange way—perhaps wondering whether this was another vision. And then she said, faintly:

"Why are you come back to Stratford, father?"

"Oh, I have many affairs on hand," said he; "and yet I like not the garden to be so empty. I can not spare thee over here much longer. 'Tis better when thou art in the garden, and little Bess with thee—nay, I swear to thee thou disturbest me not—and so must thou get quickly well and home again."

He took her hand—the thin, worn, white hand—and patted it.

"Why," said he, "I hear they told thee some foolish story about me. Believe them not, lass. Thou and I are old friends, despite thy saucy ways, and thy laughing at the young lads about, and thy lecturing of little Bess Hall—oh, thou hast thy faults, a many of them too; but heed no idle stories, good lass, that come between me and thee. Nay, I will have a sharp word for thee an thou do not as the doctor bids; and thou must rest thee still and quiet, and trouble not thy head, for we want thee back to us at New Place. Why, I tell thee I can not have the garden left so empty: wouldst have me with none to talk with but goodman Matthew? So now farewell for the moment, good wench; get what sleep thou canst, and take what the doctor bids thee; why, knowst thou not of the ribbons and gloves I have brought thee all the way from London?—I warrant me they will please thee."

He patted her hand again, and rose and left—as if it were all a matter of course. For a minute or two after, the girl looked dazed and bewildered, as if she were trying to recall many things; but always she kept looking at the hand that he had held, and there was a pleased light in her sad and tired eyes. She lay still and silent, for so she had been enjoined.

But by-and-by she said, in a way that was like the ghost of Judith's voice of old:

"Grandmother, I can scarce hold up my hand—will you help me? What is this that is on my head?"

"Why, 'tis a pretty lace cap that Susan brought thee," the grandmother said, "and we would have thee smart and neat ere thy father came in."

But she had got her hand to her head now, and then the truth became known to her. She began to cry bitterly.

"Oh, grandmother, grandmother," she said, or sobbed, "they have cut off my hair, and my father will never look with favor on me again. 'Twas all he ever praised."

"Dearie, dearie, thy hair will grow again as fair as ever—ay, and who ever had prettier?" the old grandmother said. "Why, surely; and the roses will come to thy cheeks too, that were ever the brightest of any in the town. Thy father?—heardst thou not what he said a moment ago—that he could not bear to be without thee? Nay, nay, fret not, good lass; there be plenty that will right gladly wait for the growing of thy hair again—ay, ay, there be plenty and to spare that will hold thee in high favor, and think well of thee, and thy father most of all of them—have no fear."

And so the grandmother got her soothed and hushed, and at last she lay still and silent. But she had been thinking.

"Grandmother," said she, regarding her thin wasted hand, "is my face like that?"

"Hush thee, child; thou must not speak more now, or the doctor will be scolding me."

"But tell me, grandmother," she pleaded.

"Why, then," she answered, evasively, "it be none so plump as it were; but all that will mend—ay, ay, good lass, 'twill mend surely."

Again she lay silent for a while; but her mind was busy with its own fears.

"Grandmother," she said, "will you promise me this—to keep Quiney away? You will not let him come into the room, good grandmother, should he ever come over to the cottage?"

"Ay, and be this thy thanks, then, to him that rode all the way to London town to bring thy father to thee?" said the old dame, with some affectation of reproach. "Were I at thy age, I would have a fairer message for him."

"A message, grandmother?" the girl said, turning her languid eyes to her with some faint eagerness. "Ay, that I would send him willingly. He went to London for me, that I know; Prudence said so. But perchance he would not care to have it, would he, think you?"

The old dame listened, to make sure that the doctor was not within hearing—for this talking was forbidden; but she was anxious to have the girl's mind pleased and at rest; and so she took Judith's hand and whispered to her:

"A message? Ay, I warrant me the lad would think more of it than of aught else in the world. Why, sweetheart, he hath been never away from the house all this time—watching to be of service to any one—night and day it hath been so; and that he be not done to death passes my understanding. Ay, and the riding to London, and the bringing of thy father, and all—is't not worth a word of thanks? Nay, the youth hath won to my favor, I declare to thee; if none else will speak for him, I will; a right good honest youth, I warrant. But there now, sweeting, hush thee; I may not speak more to thee, else the doctor will be for driving me forth."

There was silence for some time; then Judith said, wistfully,

"What flowers are in the garden now, grandmother?"

The old dame went to the window—slowly—it was an excuse for not having too much talking going on.

"The garden be far past its best now," said she; "but there be marigolds, and Michaelmas daisies—"

"Could you get me a bit of rosemary, grandmother?" the girl asked.

"Rosemary!" she cried in affright—for the mention of the plant seemed to strike a funeral note. "Foolish wench, thou knowst I can never get the rosemary bushes through the spring frosts. Rosemary, truly! What wantest thou with rosemary?"

"Or a pansy, then?"

"A pansy, doubtless—ay, ay, that be better, now—we may find thee a pansy somewhere, and plenty of other things, so thou lie still and get well."

"Nay, I want but the one, grandmother," she said, slowly. "You know I can not write a message to him; and yet I would send him some token of thanks for all that he hath done. And would not that do, grandmother?—could you but find me a pansy, if there be one left anywhere, and a small leaf or two; and if 'twere put in a folded paper, and you could give it him from me, and no one knowing? I would rest the happier, grandmother, for I would not have him think me ungrateful—no, no, he must not think me that. And then, good grandmother, you will tell him that I wish him not to see me; only—only, the little flower will show him that I am not ungrateful; for I would not have him think me that."

"Rest you still now, then, sweeting," the old dame said. "I warrant me we will have the message conveyed to him; but rest you still, rest you still, and ere long you will not be ashamed to show him the roses coming again into your cheeks."

CHAPTER XXXV.

TOWARD THE LIGHT.

THIS fresh and clear morning, with a south wind blowing, and a blue sky overhead, made even the back yard of Quiney's premises look cheerful, though the surroundings were mostly empty barrels and boxes. And he was singing, too, as he went on with his task; sometimes,

"*Play on, minstrèl, play on, minstrèl,*
My lady is mine only girl,"

and sometimes,

"*I bought thee petticoats of the best,*
The cloth so fine as fine might be;
I gave thee jewels for thy chest,
And all this cost I spent on thee,"

or again, he would practice his part in the new catch:

"*Merrily sang—the Ely monks—*
*When rowed thereby—*CANUTE THE KING!"

And yet this that he was so busy about seemed to have nothing to do with his own proper trade. He had chalked up on the wall a space about the size of an ordinary cottage window; at each of the upper corners he had hammered in a nail; and now he was endeavoring to suspend from these supports, so that it should hang parallel with the bottom line, an oblong basket roughly made of wire, and pretty obviously of his own construction. His dinner—of bread and cheese and ale—stood untouched and unheeded on a bench hard by. Sometimes he whistled, sometimes he sang; for the morning air was fresh and pleasant, and the sunlight all about was enlivening.

Presently Judith's father made his appearance, and the twisting and shaping of the wire hooks instantly ceased.

"She is still going on well?" the lad said, with a rapid and anxious glance.

"But slowly—slowly," her father answered. "Nay, we must not demand too much. If she but hold her own now, time is on our side, and the doctor is more than ever hopeful that the fever hath left no serious harm behind it. When that she is a little stronger, they talk of having her carried down-stairs—the room is larger, and the window hath a pleasant outlook."

"I heard of that," said Quiney, glancing at the oblong basket of wire.

"I have brought you other news this morning," Judith's father said, taking out a letter and handing it to Quiney. "But I pray you say nothing of it to the wench; her mind is at rest now; we will let the past go."

"Nay, I can do no harm in that way," said the younger man, in something of a hurt tone, "for they will not let me see her."

"No, truly? Why, that is strange, now," her father said, affecting to be surprised, but having a shrewd guess that this was some fancy of the girl's own. "But they would have her kept quiet, I know."

Quiney was now reading the letter. It was from one of Judith's father's companions in London, and the beginning of it was devoted to the imparting of certain information that had apparently been asked from him touching negotiations for the purchase of a house in Blackfriars. Quiney rightly judged that this part had naught to do with him, and scanned it briefly, and as he went on he came to that which had a closer interest for him.

The writer's style was ornate and cumbrous and confused, but his story in plainer terms was this: The matter of the purloined play was now all satisfactorily ascertained and settled, except as regarded Jack Orridge himself, whom a dire mischance had befallen. It appeared that having married a lady possessed of considerable wealth, his first step was to ransom—at what cost the writer knew not—the play that had been sold to the booksellers, not by himself, but by one Francis Lloyd. It was said that this Lloyd had received but a trifle for it, and had, in truth, parted with it in the course of a drunken frolic; but that Gentleman Jack, as they called him, had to disburse a goodly sum ere he could get the manuscript back into his own hands. That forthwith he had come to the theatre, and delivered up the play, with such expressions of penitence and shame that they could not forbear to give him full quittance for his fault. But that this was not all; for, having heard that Francis Lloyd had in many quarters been making a jest of the matter, and telling of Orridge's adventures in Warwickshire, and naming names, the young man had determined to visit him with personal chastisement, but had been defeated in this by Lloyd being thrust into prison for debt. That thereafter Lloyd, being liberated from jail, was sitting in a tavern with certain companions, and there "Gentleman Jack" found him, and dealt him a blow on the face with the back of his hand, with a mind to force the duello upon him. But that here again Orridge had ill fortune, for Lloyd, being in his cups, would fight then and there, and flung himself on him, without a sword or anything, as they thought; but that presently, in a struggle, Orridge uttered a cry, "I am stabbed!" and fell headlong, and they found him with a dagger wound in his side, bleeding so that they thought he would have died ere help came. And that, in truth, he had been nigh within death's door, and was not yet out of the leech's hands; while, as for Lloyd, he had succeeded in making good his escape, and was now in Flanders, as some reported. This was the gist of the story, as far as Quiney was interested; thereafter came chiefly details about the theatre; and the writer concluded with wishing his correspondent all health and happiness, and bidding him remember "his true loving friend, Henry Condell."

Quiney handed back the letter.

"I wish the dagger had struck the worser villain of the two," said he.

"'Tis no concern of ours," Judith's father said. "And I would have the wench hear never a word more of the matter. Nay, I have already answered her that

'twas all well and settled in London, and no harm done; and the sooner 'tis quite forgotten the better. The young man hath made what amends he could; I trust he may soon be well of his wound again. And married, is he?—perchance his hurt may teach him to be more of a stay-at-home."

Judith's father put the letter in his pocket, and was for leaving, when Quiney suggested that if he were going to the cottage, he would accompany him, as some business called him to Bidford. And so they set out together—the younger man having first of all made a bundle of the wire basket, and the nails and hooks and what not, so that he could the more easily carry them.

It was a clear and mild October day; the wide country very silent; the woods turning to yellow and russet now, and here and there golden leaves fluttering down from the elms. So quiet and peaceful it all was in the gracious sunlight; the steady ploughing going on; groups of people gleaning in the bean fields; but not a sound of any kind reaching them, save the cawing of some distant rooks. And when they drew near to Shottery, Quiney had an eye for the cottage gardens, to see what flowers or shrubs were still available; for of course the long wire basket, when it was hung outside Judith's window, must be filled—ay, and filled freshly at frequent intervals. If the gardens or the fields or the hedge-rows would furnish sufficient store, there would be no lack of willing hands for the gathering.

They went first to the front door (the room that Judith was to be moved into looked to the back); and here, ere they had crossed the threshold, they beheld a strange thing. The old grandmother was standing at the foot of the wooden stair, with a small looking-glass in her hand. She had not heard them approach; so it was with some amazement they saw her deliberately let fall the glass on to the stone passage, where naturally it was smashed into a hundred fragments. And forthwith she began to scold and rate the little Cicely; and that in so loud a voice that her anger must have been heard in the sick-room above.

"Ah, thou mischief, thou imp, thou idle brat, that must needs go break the only looking-glass in the house! A handy wench, truly, that can hold nothing with thy silly fingers, but must break cup, and platter, and pane; and now the looking-glass—'twere well done to box thine ears, thou mischief!"

And with that she patted the little girl on the shoulder, and shrewdly winked, and smiled, and nodded her head; and then she went up the stair, and again loudly bewailing her misfortune.

"What a spite be this, now!" they could hear her say, at the door of Judith's room. "The only looking-glass in the house—and just as thou wouldst have it sent for! That mischievous idle little wench—heard you the crash, sweetheart? Well, well, no matter; I must still have the tiring of thee—against any one coming to see thee; ay, and I would have thee brave and smart, when thou art able to sit up a bit; ay, and thy hair will soon be growing again, sweeting. And then the trinkets that thy father brought, and the lace cuffs that Quiney gave thee—these and all thou must wear. Was ever such a spite, now?—our only looking-glass to be broken so; but thou shalt not want it, sweetheart—nay, nay, thou must rest in my hands. I will have thee smart enough; when any would come to see thee—"

That was all they heard—for now she shut the door; but both of them guessed readily enough why the good dame had thrown down and smashed the solitary mirror of the house.

Then they went within, and heard from Prudence that Judith was going on well, but very slowly; and that her mind was in perfect calm and content, only that at times she seemed anxious that her father should return to London, lest his affairs should be hindered.

"And truly I must go ere long," said he; "but not yet. Not until she is more fairly on the highway."

They were now in the room that was to be given up to Judith, because of its larger size.

"Prudence," said Quiney, "if the bed were placed so — by the window — she might be propped up so that when she chose she could look abroad. Were not that a simple thing, and cheerful for her? And I have arranged a small matter so that every morning she may find some fresh blossoms awaiting her, and yet not disturbing her with any one wishing to enter the room. Methinks one might better fix it now, ere she be brought down, so that the knocking may not harm her."

"I would she were in a fit state to be brought down," Prudence said, rather sadly. "For never saw I any one so weak and helpless."

All the same, he went away to see whether the oblong basket of wire and the fastenings would fit; and although (being a tall youth) he could easily reach the foot of the window with his hands, he had to take a chair with him in order to gain the proper height for the nails. Prudence from within saw what he was after; and when it was all fixed up, she opened one of the casements to speak to him, and her face was well pleased.

"Truly, now, that was kindly thought of," said she. "And shall I tell her of this that you have contrived for her?"

"Why, 'tis in this way, Prudence," said he, rather shamefacedly: "she need not know whether 'tis this one or that that puts a few blossoms in the basket; 'twill do for any one—any one that is passing along the road or through the meadows, and picks up a pretty thing here or there. 'Twill soon be hard to get such things, save some red berries or the like; but when any can stop in passing and add their mite, 'twill be all the easier, for who that knows her but hath good-will toward her?"

"And her thanks to whom?" said Prudence, smiling.

"Why, to all of them," said he, evasively. "Nay, I would not have her even know that I nailed up the little basket—perchance she might think I was too officious."

"And can you undo it?" she asked. "Can you take it down?"

"Surely," he answered; and he lifted the basket off the hooks to show her.

"For," said she, "if you would bring it round, might we not put a few flowers in it, and have them carried up to Judith, to show her what you have designed for her? In truth it would please her."

He was not proof against this temptation. He carried the basket round; and they fell to gathering such blossoms as the garden afforded—marigolds, monthly roses, Michaelmas daisies, and the like—with some scarlet hips from the neighboring hedges, and some broad green leaves to serve as a cushion for all of these. But he did not stay to hear how his present was received. He was on his way to Bidford, and on foot, for he had kept his promise with the Galloway nag.

So he bade Prudence farewell, and said he would call in again on his way back in the evening.

The wan, sad face lit up with something like pleasure when Judith saw this little present brought before her; it was not the first by many of similar small attentions that he had paid her—tokens of a continual thoughtfulness and affection—though he was not even permitted to see her, much less to speak with her. How his business managed to thrive during this period they could hardly guess; only that he seemed to find time for everything. Apparently he was content with the most hap-hazard meals, and seemed able to get along with scarcely any sleep at all; and always he was the most hopeful one in the house, and would not admit that Judith's recovery seemed strangely slow, but regarded everything as happening for the best, and tending toward a certain and happy issue. One result of his being continually in or about the cottage was this—that Master Walter Blaise had not looked near them since the night on which the fever reached its crisis. The women-folk surmised that, now there was a fair hope of Judith's recovery, he perchance imagined his ministrations to be no longer necessary, and was considerately keeping out of the way, seeing that he could be of no use. At all events, they did not discuss the subject much; for more than one of them had perceived that, whenever the parson's name was mentioned, Judith's father became reticent and reserved—which was about his only way of showing displeasure—so that they got into the habit of omitting all mention of Master Blaise, for the better preserving and maintaining the serenity of the domestic atmosphere.

And yet Master Blaise came to be talked of—and to Judith herself—this very morning. When Prudence went into the room, carrying Quiney's flowers, the old grandmother said she would go down and see how dinner was getting forward (she having more mouths to feed than usual), and Prudence was left in her place, with strict injunctions to see that Judith took the small portions of food that had been ordered her at the proper time. Prudence sat down by the bedside. These two had not had much confidential chatting of late, for Judith had been forbidden to talk much, and was indeed far too weak and languid for that, while generally there was some third person about in attendance. But now they were alone, and Prudence had a long tale to tell of Quiney's constant watchfulness and care, and all of the little things he had thought of and arranged for her, up to the construction of the wire flower-basket.

"But what he hath done, Judith, to anger Parson Blaise I can not make out," she continued; "ay, and to anger him sorely; for yesternight, when I went over to see how my brother did, I met Master Blaise, and he stayed me and talked with me for a space. Nay, he spoke too harshly of Quiney, so that I had to defend him, and say what I had seen of him—truly, I was coming near to speaking with warmth—and then he went away from that. And think you what he came to next, Judith?"

The pale quiet face of the speaker was overspread with a blush, and she looked timidly at her friend.

"What, then, sweetheart?"

"Perchance I should not tell you," she said, with some hesitation, and then she said, more frankly: "nay, why should there be any concealment between us, Judith? And he laid no charge of secrecy on me—in truth, I said that I would think of it, and might even have to ask for counsel and guidance. He would have me be his wife, Judith."

Judith betrayed no atom of surprise; nay, she almost instantly smiled her approval—it was a kind of friendly congratulation, as it were—and she would have reached out her hand only that she was so weak.

"I am glad of that, dear mouse," said she, as pleasantly as she could. "There would you be in your proper place—is't not so? And what said you?—what said you, sweetheart? Ah, they all would welcome you, be sure; and a parson's wife—a parson's wife, Prudence—would not that be your proper place? would you not be happy so?"

"I know not," the girl said, and she spoke wistfully, and as if she were regarding distant things. "He had nearly persuaded me, good heart, for indeed there is such power and clearness in all he says; and it was almost put before me as a duty, and something incumbent on me, for the pleasing of all of them, and the being useful and serviceable to so many; and then—and then—"

There was another timid glance, and she took Judith's hand, and her eyes were downcast as she made the confession:

"Nay, I will tell thee the truth, sweetheart. Had he spoken to me earlier, I—I might not have said him nay—so good a man and earnest withal, and not fearing to give offense if he can do true service to the Master of us all: Judith, if it be unmaidenly, blame me not, but at one time I had thoughts of him; and sometimes, ashamed, I would not go to your house when that he was there in the afternoon, though Julius wondered, seeing that there was worship and profitable expounding. But now—now 'tis different."

"Why, dear mouse, why?" Judith said, with some astonishment. "You must not flout the good man. 'Tis an honorable offer."

Prudence was looking back on that past time.

"If he had spoken then," said she, absently, "my heart would have rejoiced; and well I knew 'twould have been no harm to you, dear Judith, for who could doubt how you were inclined—ay, through all your quarrels and misunderstandings? And if 'twas you the good parson wished for in those days—"

"Prudence," her friend said, reproachfully, "you do ill to go back over a bygone story. If you had thoughts of him then, when as yet he had not spoken, why not now, when he would have you be his wife? 'Tis an honorable offer, as I say; and you—were you not meant for a parson's wife, sweetheart?"

Then Prudence regarded her with her honest eyes.

"I should be afraid, Judith. Perchance I have listened overmuch to your grandmother's talking, and to Quiney's; they are both of them angered against him. They say he wrought you ill, and was cruel when he should have been gentle with you, and was overproud of his office. Nay, I marked that your father had scarce ever a word for him when he was coming over to the cottage, but would get away somehow and leave him. And—and methinks I should be afraid, Judith; 'tis no longer as it used to be in former days; and then—without perfect confidence—how should one dare to venture on such a step? No, no, Judith—I should be afraid."

"In truth I can not advise thee, then,

dear heart," her friend said, looking at her curiously. "For more than any I know should you marry one that would be gentle with you, and kind. And think you that the parson would overlord it?"

"I know not—I know not," she said, in the same absent way. "But with doubt, with hesitation, without perfect confidence, how could one take such a step?"

And then she bethought her.

"Why, now, all this talking over my poor affairs!" she said, more cheerfully. "A goodly nurse I am proving myself! 'Tis thy affairs are of greater moment; and thou must push forward, sweetheart, and get well more rapidly, else they will say we are careless and foolish that can not bring thee into firmer health."

"But I am well content," said Judith, with a perfectly placid smile.

"Content? But you must not be content!" Prudence exclaimed. "Would you remain within-doors until your hair be grown? Vanity is it, then? Ah, for shame—you that always professed to be so proud, and careless of what they thought! Content, truly! Look at so thin a hand—are you content to remain so?"

"I am none so ill," Judith said, pleasantly. "The days pass well enough; and every one is kind."

"But I say you must not be content," Prudence again remonstrated. "Did ever any one see such a poor, weak, white hand as that? Look at the thin, thin veins!"

"Ah, but you know not, sweetheart," Judith said, and she herself looked at those thin blue veins in the white hand. "They seem to me to be running full of music and happiness ever since I came out of the fever, and found my father talking to me in the old way."

CHAPTER XXXVI.

"WESTERN WIND, WHEN WILL YOU BLOW?"

THERE was much laughing among the good folk of Stratford town—or rather among those of them allowed to visit Quiney's back yard—over the nondescript vehicle that he and his friend Pleydell were constructing there. But that was chiefly at the first, when the neighbors would call it a coffin on wheels, or a grown-up cradle; afterward, when it grew into shape, and began to exhibit traces of decoration (the little canopy at the head, for example, was covered over with blue taffeta, that made a shelter from the sun), they moderated their ridicule, and at last declared it a most ingenious and useful contrivance, and one that went as easily on its leather bands as any king's coach that ever was built. And they said they hoped it would do good service; for they knew it was meant for Judith; and she had won the favor and good-will of many in that town—in so far as an unmarried young woman was deemed worthy of consideration.

But that was an anxious morning when Quiney set forth with this strange vehicle for the cottage. Little Willie Hart was there, and Quiney had flung him inside, saying he would give him a ride as far as Shottery; but thereafter he did not speak a word to the boy. For this was the morning on which he was to see Judith for the first time since the fever had left her; and not only that, but he had been appointed to carry her down-stairs to the larger room below. This was by the direct instructions of the doctor. Judith's father was now in London again; the doctor was not a very powerful man; the staircase was overnarrow to let two of the women try it between them: who, therefore, was there but this young athlete to gather up that precious charge and bear her gently forth? But when he thought of that first meeting with Judith he trembled, and dismay and apprehension filled his heart lest he should show himself in the smallest way shocked by her appearance. Careless as she might have been of other things, she had always put a value on that; she knew that she had good looks, and she liked to look pretty and dainty, and to wear becoming and pretty things. And again and again he schooled himself and argued with himself. He must be prepared to find her changed—nay, had he not already had one glimpse of her, as she lay asleep, in the cold light of the dawn? He must be prepared to find the happy and radiant face no longer that, but all faded and white and worn; the clear-shining eyes no longer laughing, but sunken and sad; and the beautiful sun-brown hair—that was her chiefest pride of all— no longer clustering round her neck. Not that he himself cared: Judith was for him always and ever Judith, whatever she

might be like; but his terror was lest he should betray, in the smallest fashion, some pained surprise. He knew how sensitive she was; and as an invalid she would be even more so; and what a fine thing it would be if her eyes were suddenly to fill with tears on witnessing his disappointment? And so he argued and argued, and strove to think of Judith as a ghost—as anything rather than her former self; and when he reached the cottage he asked whether Judith was ready to be brought down in so matter-of-fact a way that he seemed perfectly unconcerned.

Well, she was not ready, for her grandmother had the tiring of her; and the old dame was determined that, if she had her way, her grandchild should look none too like an invalid. If the sun-brown curls were gone, at least the cap that she wore should have pretty blue ribbons where it met under the chin. And she would have her wear the lace cuffs, too, that Quiney had brought her from Warwick: did not she owe it to him to do service for the gift? And when all that was done, she made Judith take a little wine and water —to strengthen her for the being carried down-stairs—and then she sent word that Quiney might come up.

He made his appearance forthwith—a little pale, perhaps, and hesitating and apprehensive as he crossed the threshold. And then he came quickly forward, and there was a sudden wonder of joy and gladness in his eyes.

"Judith!" he exclaimed, quite involuntarily, and forgetting everything, "why, how well you are looking! indeed, indeed you are! Sweetheart, you are not changed at all!"

For this was Judith: not any of the spectral phantoms he had been conjuring up, but Judith herself, regarding him with friendly (if yet timid) eyes; and her face, as he looked at her in this glad way, was no longer pale, but had grown rose-red as the face of a bride. Her anxiety and nervousness had been far greater than she dared to tell any of them; but now his surprise and delight were surely real; and then— for she was very weak, and she had been anxious and full of fear, and this joy of seeing him, of seeing a strange face that belonged to the former happy time, was too much for her. Her lips were tremulous; tears rose to her eyes, and she would have turned away to hide her crying, but that all at once he recalled his scattered senses, and inwardly cursed himself for a fool, and forthwith addressed her in the most cheerful and simple way:

"Why, now, what stories they have been telling me, Judith! I should scarce know you had been ill. You are thinner—oh yes, you are a little thinner; and if you went to the woods to gather nuts, I reckon you would not bring home a heavy bag; but that will all mend in time. In honest truth, dear Judith, I am glad to see you looking none so ill; now I marvel not at your father going away to see after his affairs—so sure he must have been."

"I am glad that he went, I was fretting so," she said (and it was so strange to hear Judith's voice—that always stirred his heart as if with the vibration of Susan's singing); and then she added, timidly regarding him—"And you—I have caused you much trouble also."

He laughed; in truth he was so bewildered with the delight of seeing this real living Judith before him that he scarce knew what he said.

"Trouble!—yes, trouble indeed, that I could do nothing for you, and all the others waiting with you and cheering you. But now, dear Judith, I have something for you—oh, you shall see it presently; and you may laugh, but I warrant me you will find it easy and comfortable when that you are allowed to go forth into the garden. 'Tis a kind of couch, as it were, but on wheels—nay, you may call it your chariot, Judith, if you would be in state; and if you may not go further than the garden at first, why, then you may lie in it, and have some one read to you; and there is a small curtain if you would shut them all out and go to sleep; ay, and when the time comes for you to go along the lanes, then you may sit up somewhat, for there are pillows for your head, and for your back. As for the drawing of it, why, little Willie Hart can pull me when I am in it, and surely he can do the same for you, that are scarce so heavy as I, as I take it. Oh, I warrant you, you will soon get used to it; and 'twill be so much pleasanter for you than being always within-doors; and the fresher air—the fresher air will soon bring back your color, Judith."

For now that the first flush of embarrassment was gone, he could not but see (though still he talked in that cheerful strain) how pale and worn was her face; and her hands, that lay listlessly on the coverlet, with the pretty lace cuffs going back from the wrists, were spectral hands, so thin and white were they.

"Master Quiney," said the old dame, coming to the door, "it be all ready now below, if you can carry the wench down. And take time—take time; there be no hurry."

"You must come and help me, good grandmother," said he, "to get her well into my arms."

In truth he was trembling with very nervousness as he set about this task. Should some mischance occur?—some stumble?—and then he found himself all too strong and uncouth and clumsy, with her so frail and delicate and weak. But her grandmother lifted the girl's hand to his shoulder—or rather to his neck—and bade her hold on so, as well as she might; and then he got his arms better round her; and with slow and careful steps made his way down to the room below. There the bed was near the window, and when he had gently placed her on it, and propped up her head and shoulders, so that she was almost sitting, the first thing that she saw before her was the slung box of flowers and leaves outside the little casement. She turned to him, and smiled, and looked her thanks with grateful eyes: he sought for no more than that.

Of course they were all greatly pleased at this new state of affairs: it seemed a step on the forward way, a hopeful thing. Moreover, there was a brighter animation in the girl's look—whether that was owing to the excitement of the change or the pleasure at seeing the face of an old friend. And as the others seemed busy among themselves, suggesting small arrangements and the like, Quiney judged it was time for him to go: his services were no longer needed.

He went forward to her.

"Judith," said he, "I will bid you good-day now. If you but knew how glad I am to have seen you—ay, and to find you going on so well! I will take away a lighter heart with me."

She looked up at him, hesitating and timid; and then she gathered courage.

"But why must you go?" said she—with some touch of color in the pale face.

He glanced at the others.

"Perchance they may not wish me to stay; they may fear your being tired with talking."

"But if I wish you to stay—for a little while?" she said, gently. "If your business call you not?"

"My business!" he said. "My business must shift for itself on such a day as this. Think you 'tis nothing for me to speak with you again, Judith, after so long a time?"

"And my chariot," she said, brightly: "may not I see my chariot?"

"Why, truly!" he cried. "Willie Hart is in charge of it without. We will bring it along the passage, and you will see it at the door: and you must not laugh, dear Judith—'tis a rude-made thing, I know, but serviceable; you shall have comfort from it, I warrant you."

They wheeled it along the passage, but could not get it within the apartment; however, through the open door she could see very easily the meaning and construction of it. And when she observed with what care and pretty taste it had been adorned for her, even to the putting ribbons at the front corners of the little canopy (but this was not the work of men's fingers; it was Prudence who had contributed these), she was not in the least inclined to laugh at the efforts of these good friends to be of use to her and to gratify her. She beckoned him to come to her.

"'Tis but a patchwork thing to look at," said he, rather shamefacedly, "but I hope you will find it right comfortable when you use it. I hope soon to hear of you trying it, Judith."

"Give me your hand," said she.

She took his hand and kissed it.

"I can not speak my thanks to you," she said, in a low voice, "for not only this, but for all that you have done for me."

There were tears in her eyes; and he was so bewildered, and his heart so wildly aflame, that he could only touch her shoulder and say:

"Be still now, Judith. Be still and quiet; and perchance they may let me remain with you a little space further."

Well, it was a long and a weary waiting. She seemed too content with her feeble state; there were so many who were kind to her; and her father sending her messages from London; and Quiney coming every morning to put some little things—branches of evergreens, or the like, when flowers were no longer to be had—in the little basket outside the window. He could reach to that easily; and when she happened to hear his footsteps coming near, even when she could not see him, she would tap with her white fingers on the window-panes—that was her thanks to him, and morning greeting.

It was a bitter winter; and ever they were looking forward to the milder weather, to see when they might risk taking her out-of-doors, swathed up in her chariot, as she called it; but the weeks and weeks went by, hard and obdurate, and at last they found themselves in the new year. But she could get about the house a little now, in a quiet way; and so it was that, one morning, she and Quiney were together standing at the front window, looking abroad over the wide white landscape. Snow lay everywhere, thick and silent; the bushes were heavy with it; and far beyond those ghostly meadows—though they could not see it—they knew that the Avon was fixed and hard in its winter sleep, under the hanging banks of the Weir Brake.

"'Western wind, when will you blow?'" she said, and yet not sadly, for there was a placid look in her eyes: she was rather complaining, with a touch of the petulance of the Judith of old.

The arm of her lover was resting lightly on her shoulder—she was strong enough to bear that now, and did not resent the burden. And she had got her soft sunny-brown curls again, though still they were rather short; and her face had got back something of its beautiful curves; and her eyes, if they were not so cruelly audacious as of old, were yet clear-shining and gentle, and with abundance of kind messages for all the world, but with tenderer looks for only one.

"'Western wind,'" she repeated, with that not oversad complaint of injury, "'when will you blow—when will you blow?'"

"All in good time, sweetheart, all in good time," said he; and his hand lay kindly on her shoulder, as if she were one to whom some measure of gentle tending and cheering words were somehow due. "And guess you now what they mean to do for you when the milder weather comes?—I mean the lads at the school. Why, then, 'tis a secret league and compact—I doubt not that your cousin Willie may have been at the suggesting of it, but 'twas some of the bigger lads who came to me. And 'tis all arranged now, and all for the sake of you, dear heart. For when the milder weather comes, and the year begins to wake again, why, they are all of them to keep a sharp and an eager eye here and there—in the lanes or in the woods—for the early peeping up of the primroses. And then 'tis to be a grand whole holiday that I am to get for them, as it appears; and all the school is to go forth to search the hedge-rows and the woods and the banks—all the country-side is to be searched and searched—and for what, think you?—why, to bring you a spacious basketful of the very first primroses of the spring! See you, now, what it is to be the general favorite!—nay, I swear to you, dear Judith, you are the sweetheart of all of them; and what a shame it is that I must take you away from them all!"

THE END.

GRANDMOTHER'S STORY.

WHEN I was a boy, a house possessing some pretensions to elegance stood on Main Street, in Plymouth, Massachusetts, which had been occupied many years by successive generations of the Lothrop family. When it was taken down, I was attracted, on my way to school one day, by a pile of old papers which the carpenters had thrown out of one of its attic windows, and which had lodged on the heap of bricks and plaster lying in the street below. As the boy is father to the man, in obedience to a love of everything old, which has since grown into a passion, I gathered up these already scattering relics, and depositing them in my school satchel, packed them away afterward in an old secretary, where for many years they remained unexamined and almost unnoticed. In the course of time, during the leisure hours of an irksome convalescence, they came for the first time again under my observation, and then proved to be antiquarian treasures. Most of them were original papers of the period of King Philip's war, among which were letters of Josiah Winslow, commander of the united forces of Plymouth, Massachusetts, and Connecticut, and of Major William Bradford, the son of the Governor of the Old Colony. One, however, not so ancient as the rest, a perfect manuscript, in the handwriting of a lady, especially attracted my attention. It was entitled "Grandmother's Story," and purported to be a true narration of some of the incidents in the life of the writer. No name was attached to the manuscript, but its author was disclosed in the course of the narrative. I found on inquiry that her name was Priscilla Thomas, and that the incidents of the story were a familiar tradition among her descendants. Its incorrectness of style, which is to be attributed rather to her advanced age than to an imperfect education, I have taken the liberty to amend, and trust that readers will feel an interest equal to my own in the perusal of the following story:

I was born in Marshfield, in the State of Massachusetts, on the 5th of April, 1705, and was the daughter of Jeremiah and Priscilla Thomas of that town. My father was the grandson of William Thomas, one of the merchants of London who by their aid and influence enabled the Pilgrims to found a successful colony in New England. He was a large landed proprietor, and his estate adjoined that of Isaac Winslow, the grandson of Edward Winslow of the *Mayflower*. John Winslow, a son of Isaac, was my school and play mate, and after he had become distinguished as commander of the Massachusetts forces in the expedition against the Acadians, I often saw him and admired his military and gentlemanly bearing.

My childhood and youth were passed without any special event to disturb their monotony, my parents giving me the benefit of the short seasons of the single public school of the town, and the rarer privilege of attending such private schools as were occasionally taught during the winter months by either students or graduates of the college at Cambridge. Though Marshfield was on the road from Plymouth to Boston, there was little communication with either, and the mails were carried to each place on horseback only twice in each week. Much of my time was spent in the ordinary occupations of spinning and weaving, as all the outer clothing worn by members of the family was—as was the custom of the day in all country towns—made from cloth spun and woven at home. There were two fulling-mills in the village, and the only work on the cloth used by the household which we did not ourselves perform was that done in these establishments, which found abundant support from contributions of domestic industry.

As may be supposed, to those leading a quiet country life the arrival of strangers was a great event. Whether old or young, and of whichever sex, they were looked upon as in these later times the barbarous inhabitants of some distant island look upon casual visitors from more civilized shores. But if at any time by chance a strange young man should visit our town, I am not ashamed to confess that the female heart was thrown into a state of excitement and perturbation. And now and then such was the case in the form, as I have said before, of some student or graduate of Harvard, who came on a prospecting tour in search of a school. Though some of my school-mates surrendered to these sieges laid to their hearts by these young men, I was fortunate or unfortunate enough to escape an attack from these foes to the peace of our firesides until I was nineteen years of age.

But my turn was soon to come. At that time a young man named Noah Hobart, a graduate of Cambridge, in the summer of 1724 came to Duxbury to teach a winter school, and brought letters of introduction to my father. Duxbury was but three miles distant, and soon after his arrival he came to present his letters, and was urged to take his cup of tea with us and spend the evening. He belonged to one of the old families of Massachusetts Colony, his great-grandfather having been Edward Hobart, one of the early settlers of Hingham in 1635. On the occasion of his first visit I was much impressed with his manly beauty and entertaining conversation, and, maiden-like, thought that I discovered in his somewhat distant and dignified manner of addressing me that he had received as favorable an impression of myself. Though perfectly free and unrestrained in his bearing toward others, his treatment of me from the first, as he afterward acknowledged, was as if I were a shrine too holy for him to approach with levity on his tongue. I long ago discovered that love is sober and serious in its manifestations, and that the merry voice directed to merely friendly ears gives way to a tenderness akin to sadness in the presence of the one beloved. With me it was love at first sight—the only true love in the world, as I believe, a love which has no chilly morn nor dusky eve, but is from first to last meridian day. When he left us on that first evening, I thought, in bidding him good-night, I felt a pressure of his hand, which the will by which his tongue had been controlled had no power to repress. I know not why it is, but women read the hearts of men more clearly than men read theirs. It may be that men are more pronounced in the signals of their affection, or that they are less perfectly educated in the language which lovers use. It was not until after repeated visits that he discovered the interest I felt in him, and even then he was reserved in his attentions, oppressed as he was by the conviction that his worldly prospects were not sufficiently established to warrant the declaration of his love. But at length the strength of his affection overcame his fears, and with no thought beyond the happiness of the hour I promised to become his wife. The fear, however, that a long time must elapse before we could be married continued to harass him, and mingled with this fear was the still greater one that he might be depriving me of more favorable opportunities of marriage.

Such was the state of things between us when one day, during the summer of 1727, my mother called me into her chamber, telling me that she had an important communication to make which concerned my future welfare and happiness. With a feeling of half hope and half fear I followed her, and both hope and fear were soon overwhelmed in the astonishment I felt at her announcement. She told me that John Watson, a gentleman of Plymouth, had, through my father, solicited my hand in marriage. Mr. Watson was a merchant in his native town, living with abundant means and in comparative luxury, and though long a friend of our family, was so much older than myself that I had looked upon him rather as the associate and companion of my father than of those of my own age. He had married, in 1715, Sarah Rogers, of Ipswich—a descendant of John Rogers, the martyr—who had died, leaving him a widower with two children, John and George, both of whom are now living. My father had told him, in reply to his solicitation, that

I was already engaged to Mr. Hobart, and with the instincts of an honorable man he had urged the withdrawal of his offer. My father, however, deeply impressed with the advantages of the proposed alliance, insisted on communicating his wishes, with the distinct understanding, however, that all parties should be informed of the circumstances attending their expression. It was the earnest wish, my mother told me, both of herself and my father, that I should terminate the engagement with Mr. Hobart, which promised to be of indefinite duration, and accept Mr. Watson. Mr. Hobart, she said, was poor, and if he should ever be able to make me his wife, he could hardly be expected to maintain a family in the comfort and luxury to which I had been accustomed. But the prudential reasons stated by my mother had no influence on my mind. It was enough for me that I was living in a world of happiness and love, and the future was beyond the horizon of my daily thoughts and feelings. This happiness surrounded me as the atmosphere surrounds the earth, and I felt that wherever destiny might lead, it would always follow me through the orbit of my life.

But in those days, in matrimonial affairs, the wishes of parents were a law for the children—a law which, so far as I was concerned, was sanctified by the filial affection which the untiring devotion of my father and mother had planted in my breast. The conflict between love and duty which now raged within me no one knew but him who had become the joy of my life and the centre of my being. To him I told all, and poured out my heart until it became only an aching void. He met the occasion as only a noble and self-sacrificing nature could. His love for me was so sincere that he was ready to make any sacrifice to insure my happiness, even that of the surrender of all claim to my hand. Though he felt that the loss of his beloved was the loss of happiness and even of hope, he was able to bear it, as for my sake he would lay down life itself. I can not recall, without a shudder, the ensuing hours of tender companionship, the tears we shed, and the separation which we were at last called on to endure. It is enough to say that he gave me with his kisses a final blessing, and left me never to be seen again for many years.

After rallying somewhat from my affliction I met Mr. Watson, and formally accepted his hand. I told him frankly that my heart was exhausted of its love, but that such as it was, it was his, and that the respect which I entertained for his character would make me at least a dutiful wife, even if its failure to ripen into a warmer feeling could never make me a loving one. I soon married and removed to Plymouth, where I occupied the house in Leyden Street fronting Hanover, the main street of the town. Mr. Watson was the owner of Clark's Island in Plymouth Harbor, and there he had built a house, which was our home during the summer months.

At that time Plymouth had a population of about twelve hundred, chiefly supported by foreign trade and the fisheries. The whale-fishery was carried on to some extent, mainly in small sloops and schooners, along the neighboring shores, not more than a day's sail from home. The stream of water running through the town, now vexed by the wheels of industry, flowed unobstructed to the sea, except by a single corn mill, and a fulling-mill which fulled the cloth manufactured in the houses of the inhabitants. In comparison with the quiet fields and woods surrounding my old home, Plymouth seemed full of bustle and excitement. Amidst its novel scenes and my family cares my old love became chilled upon its surface, though, as it afterward proved, flowing deep and strong beneath, as the brook runs on below the crust of ice by which it is concealed.

In 1730 my first child, William, was born, and in 1732 my second, named Elkanah after his grandfather, son of George Watson, who came to Plymouth from England in 1635. In the autumn previous to the birth of my second child my husband died, leaving me with a family of four sons—John, fifteen years of age, George, thirteen, William, one year old, and Elkanah, an infant. The first two were children by Mr. Watson's first wife. The season of sorrow through which I passed after the death of my husband, whom during the three years of our married life I had grown to love, was fully occupied by family cares. From the burden of these, however, I was somewhat relieved by the thoughtful attentions of my step-sons, for whom I had formed an attachment only less than that which I felt for my own children.

My youngest child was, as I have said,

an infant, and my good health and vigorous constitution, which afforded me a more exuberant supply of maternal food than my nursing child required, were the means of evolving the next important incident in my eventful life. It happened that soon after the death of my husband, Colonel Isaac Lothrop, of Plymouth, lost his wife, who died in giving birth to a child, which thus became motherless. Our families had long been intimate, and after the idea had once suggested itself, I did not long hesitate to offer to nurse the Lothrop infant with my own. Colonel Lothrop was two years younger than myself, I being at that time twenty-seven and he twenty-five. Mr. Watson having been twenty-seven years older, I hardly looked upon Colonel Lothrop as a contemporary, and never thought of him as a possible husband. In the lives of all of us, however, there seem to be special providences, and in our small community two families in the same social circle had been stricken by the hand of death, one left without a husband, and the other without a wife. The circumstance, too, that I was acting vicariously in the capacity of mother to his child doubtless had some influence on the mind of Colonel Lothrop. His frequent visits to see his child, who with its attendant had been installed in my house, brought us in confidential relations, and hastened an event which I soon saw was inevitable. The death of the child, which was an only one, and our communion of sympathies, added still further in its consummation. Two years later, in 1734, I became his wife, and moved into his house opposite the head of Queen Street, in Plymouth, which had been built by his father, Major Isaac Lothrop, in 1709. The father was a descendant in the fourth generation from Rev. John Lothrop, pastor of the Southwark Church, in London, now flourishing as the parent Congregational Church of England, who came to New England in 1634, and settled in Scituate.

Thus far in life I had reason to take pride in my matrimonial connections, and in the social position I had occupied. I was blessed with an abundance of this world's goods, and surrounded with every comfort and luxury conducive to happiness. My husband was a man respected by his neighbors and friends, and occupied the position of Justice of the Court of Common Pleas. The life I led under his roof was like the lives of most mothers and wives, and beyond the birth of five children, and the performance of duties incident to a large family, nothing occurred until the death of my husband in 1750 to break its monotony. The loss of my husband added another blow to my naturally buoyant spirits, thus for a third time stricken with sorrow, as I had been accustomed to look back on the rupture of my engagement with Mr. Hobart as my first widowhood.

I had now reached the age of forty-five, and my only remaining duty in life seemed to be the education of my children and the promotion of their welfare. The aged mother of my husband was an inmate of my household, and on his death-bed I had made to him the promise that I would be her protector in what remained to her of life. In the performance of this promise my responsibilities were increased, but I taught myself to look upon every act of tenderness toward her as the best tribute I could pay to the memory of her son.

As the freshness of my grief wore away, and the image of my husband, with whom I had passed many happy years, receded into the past, the memory of him whom I had first loved would often rise in my mind. Since the time we parted, twenty-three years before, I had never seen him nor heard directly from him. I knew that he had studied for the ministry, had married, and been settled in Fairfield, in the State of Connecticut. Now I began to wonder what his journey through life had been; whether his path had been strewn with flowers or had proved the rugged road over which so many are obliged to pick their weary way. Had he been happy? had he ever thought of me? had he ever in his dreams seen visions of her whom he had once loved, as I had so often seen visions of him? These were questions which I found myself oftener and oftener, as time passed by, endeavoring to answer in a way to satisfy my hopes and allay my fears. But whenever these thoughts occurred to my mind I sought to silence them, and finally settled down in seeming forgetfulness of the past. But Providence was still directing my steps, and these passing reveries proved to be premonitions of the future.

About a year after the death of my husband I was summoned one day into my parlor to meet a gentleman who wished to see me. I know not why, but the vision of my dreams at once swept by. I went below, and the vision, now a reality, stood before me. With a smiling face and cheerful greeting, he whom I had first and only devoutly loved met me as if it were only yesterday we had parted, and I had expected his arrival. The first words he spoke melted the ice which had so long incased my love, and I found the stream still flowing as strong and pure and sweet as ever. During all these years it had sped its way unseen and unknown, but was now once more revealed to the light of day. As he pressed me to his heart I felt the current of sympathy and love passing between us, as sometimes the electric spark passes in a completed circuit from hand to hand. Words were not necessary to convey our meaning. Without a motion of our lips he had asked, Do you love me still? and I had answered, Yes. He then told me of his life. He had married, as I had heard, had two children, a daughter Ellen and a son John, and had lost his wife near the time of my husband's death. He was still at Fairfield, had acquired a competency, and was living in comfort and ease. He had heard of the death of Colonel Lothrop, and as soon as the rule of propriety would permit, had come to reclaim his long-lost bride. I told him of my promise to remain with my mother-in-law, now feeble with age, and that my promise was too sacred to be violated even in response to the yearnings of love. The noble spirit which he possessed in his youth had not died out, and again upon the altar of duty he laid his sacrifice, and bade me keep my promise to the end. I remember that it was on a Wednesday he called, having driven from Hingham in the morning, whither he was obliged to return to preach for his friend Rev. Mr. Shute the Thursday lecture on the following day.

Again we parted, and from this unexpected and fleeting sunlight I went back into the shadow of my daily cares. That night my mother died. Peaceful and calm she passed from life through sleep into the valley of death, and we found her in the morning without a trace of suffering on her brow. The rest of my story is soon told. Mr. Hobart preached his Thursday lecture, and on his way home from church with his friend met a horseman riding into the village, who drew up by the road-side and engaged in conversation with Mr. Shute. He said that he had ridden from Plymouth, and when asked the news, spoke of the death of Mrs. Lothrop, which had occurred the night before. As the reader may imagine, the course of Mr. Hobart was no longer homeward, as he had intended. He returned to Plymouth on the same day, and as soon after the funeral as seemed fit and proper, I became his wife, thus consummating my vows of twenty-six years before.

And now began the happiest season of my life, covering a period of twenty-two years, until 1773, when my husband died, and for the third time I was left a widow. My son Nathaniel Lothrop had in the mean time married the daughter of Mr. Hobart, and was now living in the old mansion at Plymouth. After the death of my husband I returned to Plymouth to live with him, and for seventeen years have been a member of his household. I am now eighty-five years of age, with all my children living and happy, and am waiting in serene expectation of that final change which shall end a life whose early and later years seem a happy reality, with all between a dream.

Editor's Easy Chair.

AS a mild censor of minor morals and manners, the Easy Chair is asked whether it will not aid the movement against the twirling of canes and umbrellas in the streets and in the faces of innocent pedestrians. This "movement" was not known to the Easy Chair, but it sympathizes with it fully, and hopes that the interest of all well-conducted persons will be attracted to it. There is no one who, hastening along the street, has found his eyes suddenly threatened by the gyrations of a cane or umbrella leisurely brandished by a forerunner upon the pavement but will warmly agree that the performance is a nuisance and a peril which ought summarily to be stopped by a "movement" or otherwise. So the hapless citizen who, in close quarters with another citizen before him, is unexpectedly confronted by the point of an umbrella or of a cane which the citizen in front of him suddenly whips up under his arm, that he may the more conveniently blow his nose, will gladly seek relief from any "movement," even one that should propel the offender from the sidewalk. There are other street malefactors who grasp their umbrellas resolutely by the handle, and thrust, poke, and stab with them toward the rear as if they were musing upon Queen Elizabeth at Tilbury hurling foul scorn at Parma and at Spain, or as if the whole world behind them were full of foes or wild beasts to be defied, prodded, and pierced with unceasing energy.

Some movement, but of another kind, is imperatively necessary to correct this evil. The citizen coming up behind, who is assailed in this unprovoked manner by his fellow-pedestrian in front, if he chance to be armed with an umbrella or cane, may, of course, at once return the attack, and prick, pierce, stab, thrust, and poke in self-defense. He may regard all other pedestrians who are liable to sin in this way as *hostes humani generis*, and proceed to general reprisals by twirling his cane or umbrella, and annoying and imperiling everybody else. But this would be an extreme measure. It would too much resemble a general dissolution of society and the flight of Astræa. The days of the French Fronde would have come again, and the only safety would be in never venturing into the street. Indeed, the only effectual "movement" under such circumstances would be a sumptuary code which would absolutely prohibit the carrying of canes and umbrellas, and that would inevitably produce a counter-movement of revolution.

Indeed, what form of action the movement against the twirling of canes and umbrellas has taken, the Easy Chair has not been informed. It is not represented as aggressive, and probably it contemplates only a moral appeal. That is the better way, for this offense is not a class in itself. It belongs to the great class of offenses against good manners in public—the behavior which is becoming to public places and upon public occasions.

Among such offenses are to be reckoned noisy walking and loud talking in hotel corridors at night, slamming doors, and flinging shoes out of them to be blacked, loud whispering and laughing at concerts and theatres during the performance, occupying more seats than the one for which you pay in railroad cars, and other similar conduct for which the great family of Hog is distinguished, and which is very familiar. Endangering eyes and bodies by brandishing canes and umbrellas belongs to this class, and you may safely assume that a man who punches at his neighbors in the street with the weapon that he carries in his hand will laugh boisterously as he passes chamber doors at midnight, and chatter in a box at the opera, and engross more than his rightful seat in a car.

There has always been a "movement" against such malefactors. Their offenses are not crimes to be dealt with by severely repressive laws, by fines, imprisonments, exile,

stripes, and the halter. They are the petty annoyances which laws are too solemn to touch, and to repress which the duello or mortal combat of two is too savage. There is, indeed, the wild justice of immediate revenge, which is very sweet, and which many aggrieved persons find to be full of solace, as when a man advancing briskly upon a slow-going pedestrian before him, who bears a cane sticking horizontally out from under his arm, strikes it down with a sure and vigorous blow, or who seizes a similarly offending umbrella, and twisting it out from its perch, hands it to the amazed owner with an energy and a severity of politeness which intimate distinctly, "If you don't carry your umbrella properly, I'll—"

It was this kind of remedy which was sought by a traveller on the steamboat who, seeing his opposite neighbor at the tea table constantly licking his spoon, and then dipping it in the common sugar bowl, offered him again and again a separate spoon for that purpose. But the offender persisting, either from willfulness or stupidity, the traveller arose, and leaning over the table, thrust his forefinger in his mouth, and then taking it out, put it into his neighbor's cup and stirred the tea violently, and as he resumed his seat exclaimed, defiantly, "There! how do you like it?" The beneficiary of that demonstration probably remembered to use the sugar spoon upon the next occasion, even if in the mean time he had privately dispatched his mentor. But it is not every victim of twirling canes and umbrellas who has the courage to resort to such summary redress; and indeed it is undoubtedly open to the objection of the retort in kind that we have already mentioned. The streets would become practically battle-fields; and again we reach the conclusion that either the carrying of umbrellas and canes must be prohibited, or the twirlers of them and the active opponents of twirling must be exterminated, which would be much the same thing.

The anti-umbrella-and-cane-twirling movement, therefore, it may be safely assumed, is a moral movement. It appeals to the love of justice, to the forbearance, to the good manners, of all persons who carry these weapons to remember our common humanity, to reflect that, great and superior as they are, there are others who have some rights, and that among them are the rights to the use of their eyes and, so far as others are concerned, to the undisturbed comfort of their bodies. It begs the bearers of belligerent canes and umbrellas to consider that when they wish to twirl them, or thrust, prod, poke, and stab with them, it may be presumptuous for others to venture to put their eyes and bodies in the way, but that it is sometimes necessary for such persons to make use of the public highway, and that therefore it would be more humane to twirl, brandish, shove, push, pass, lunge, drive, prick, prod, urge, goad, spur, transfix, and spear with their canes and umbrellas in some private room of their houses, or in some public hall which might be erected by the community and dedicated to that purpose.

THE Easy Chair was lately reading some charming sketches of loitering among the Italian lakes. Their very names are musical in that melodious tongue—Maggiore, Lugano, Como, Orta—and every one is a key to rich treasures of memory. That is the double delight of travel, that you have not only the present pleasure, but the consciousness of the future pleasure which you will enjoy in recollection. Indeed, the old traveller, as he sits upon his piazza in summer or before the bright fire in winter, musing upon the days that are no more, upon old scenes and old comrades and a passed happiness, is much like the meditative mother of the herd who lies comfortably in the clover field calmly chewing the cud, and renewing all the sweetness of the fresh grazing.

Every famous name of travel is a mystic word, an *open sesame,* to the old traveller. He reads of Lago Maggiore, and at once the apple orchard upon which he is looking as he lifts his eyes from his book, the distant rounded hill dotted with trees, the "mowing," the old wooden meeting-house with the airy Palladian tower transformed into a town-hall, the maple-shaded village street, the barns, the roof of the academy—all these disappear, and he is rowing across the placid Italian water, and climbing the terraces, and gazing with romantic eagerness upon the villas and the rich picturesqueness of the Italian scene. And is that the statue of the good San Carlo Borromeo? and is it into its head, with infinite pains, discomfort, and danger, that Uncle Samuel climbed in his heroic youth because he thought that Uncle Eleazer said that when he was making the grand tour he had climbed there, but learned upon returning to his native land that he was mistaken, and that he had had his pains and discomforts and dangers all for naught?

But as the old traveller turns the toothsome cud he is half aware that even at the moment it was not the scene itself so much as the general consciousness that this was Italy which was the supreme pleasure. Italy to the young imagination was the land of faery, the gardens of Armida, the enchanted isles. Memory holds few more rapturous moments than that of the Alpine descent to the south; of the first glimpses of almonds, oleanders, figs; of the softened outlines, the vineyards, the "diviner air." Was it in the eye or in the mind, in the fancy, in the faith? Who shall say? But wherever it was, there was the blissful vision of Italy, and every glowing anticipation was fulfilled.

"O Love, what hours are thine and mine,
In lands of palm and southern pine,
  In lands of palm, of orange blossom,
Of olive, aloe, and maize and vine!
    *   *   *   *   *   *

"How faintly flushed, how phantom fair,
Was Monte Rosa hanging there!
A thousand shadowy pencilled valleys,
And snowy dells in a golden air."

This last stanza is the vision of the Val Anzasca, the long, narrow, luxuriant vale up which you rapidly climb through all the semi-tropical richness of that region toward Monte Rosa, which fills the skyward perspective, and which, with the *open sesame* in his hand or in his eye, the old traveller sees as distinctly as he sees Monadnoc from the neighboring upland pasture on a bright September day. Or—as he reads, as he reads—the wayward voyager, swinging at ease in his hammock, crosses from Lago Maggiore to Lago Lugano, and skirting the wooded shores, hears far up over the chestnuts and the silvery gray slopes of olive groves the convent bell chiming vespers; and at the little landings he sees the brilliant costumes of the peasants, unchanged in form for how long? What life is this? Those priests above, these peasants below, what do they know of the storms which are shaking off crowns in France, and bringing Germany to its feet, and whirling Metternich out of Austria, and presently bringing Radetzky to Milan, not far away? For this lake voyage is not of to-day. There is no time in such retrospective travel, and yesterday and to-day are the same.

Is it a moonlight evening in summer when we arrive at Bellagio, upon Lake Como, crossing in a row-boat from the shore at Sommariva? Does Bellagio seem to be the most Italian spot in Italy? Is it the little promontory that divides the two long lower reaches of the lake, at the end of one of which is the village of Como, and Lecco at the end of the other? And are all the shores soft with characteristic verdure and cultivation, and toward the north does the beautiful lake stretch away, overhung with the lofty Alps, rising even to glistening glimpses of peaks of snow and ice? And from that northern end of the lake shall the traveller some day turn to climb the pass of the Stelvio, the highest of the passes, winding under the awful summit of the Orteler Spitz? And as we sit under the arbor in the terraced garden at Bellagio, and look out upon the enchanted moonlight night, and hear the sounds of laughter, and the measured beat of oars, and the throb of guitars, and snatches of singing near and far, is it all a world of beauty and delight into which no serpent ever entered, and in which great Pan still lives?

As he chews, as he chews (reference is here made to the cud of reflection), the old traveller, turning the cud and still holding the book and swinging in the hammock, once more starts in the late evening from the village of Como, and with his comrades walks all night toward Milan, which the Austrian army has just occupied. The night is bright with stars, but the road most solitary. There is a general panic, and every man is afraid of every other, and when toward morning the pedestrians knock at a *locanda* not far from Milan, knowing that it would be impossible to enter the city until day, it is with the utmost difficulty that, after long and doubtful parley through the door, they are admitted to an interior so dismal and forbidding that every old story of entrapped travellers is at once verified; and being shown to their forlorn and suspicious quarters, they begin immediately to bar and barricade, determined to do battle to the last, and to sell their lives dearly, as becomes true-born sons of Columbia.

—There is no end to these recollections of the old traveller. His memory is like the famous Green Vaults of Dresden, piled with all kinds of treasures from all parts of the world, and every little allusion, every name of mark, is a golden key which opens it. Or it is an endless gallery of unfading pictures in which he is perpetually walking and looking and rejoicing, and blessing that kind Providence which, having once shown us a lovely island, or an Alpine peak, or a beautiful building—*Isola Bella*, for instance, or Mont Blanc, or the Milan Cathedral—or having once permitted us to hear the *Ranz-des-vaches*, or the vesper bell, or Jenny Lind, suffers us to see them and hear them forever.

Charles Lamb proposed that the reading of books should be preceded with a grace of music. Before Boccaccio it should be some toccata of Galluppi's, before Milton some solemn organ voluntary. So, as the old traveller beholds the great steamers sailing for Europe crowded with passengers bent upon their various purposes and delights in foreign travel, he thinks of all the various strains which, according to the many moods of those wanderers, might fitly prelude the voyage. But he who is not of them is yet even happier than they, because as watching them he sets forth again to see in memory all that they shall see "with eyes," his embarkation is saluted with the pensive and tender music that sings from the heart of a fellow-voyager. Together they travelled. Together they travel still. The Atlantic and the Mediterranean, Leghorn and Florence, the Campagna and Rome, are all blended with that happy travel, that abiding friendship, and as the anniversary of their departure returns, the poet sings to his friend:

"Still shines our August day, as calm, as bright,
    As when, long years ago, we sailed away
Down the blue Narrows and the widening bay
Into the wrinkling ocean's flashing light.
And the whole universe of sound and sight
    Repeats the radiance of that festal day.
    But for the inward eye no power can slay
The fleeting splendor of our youth's delight.
Still shines our August day, but not for me
    The olden chantment, when lay care and sorrow
Untried, the hopeful heart was ever free
    To greet the morn as herald of the morrow.
Yet shine, fair day, and let my soul from thee
    Hope, faith, and strength for life's dim future
        borrow."

WHEN one singer asks five thousand dollars for a single appearance in Italian opera, the nature of Italian opera as a fabulous luxury is clearly demonstrated. But when this demand is made in the plain decline of public interest in Italian opera, the continuance of that luxury becomes exceedingly doubtful. The provision for this opera in New York last winter was more profuse than in any other city of the world. There were two houses, and almost all of the famous singers were assembled in the city. It was, however, undeniable that there was a general feeling that all of them were a little beyond the *prima gioventu*, the golden prime, which even the queens of song and the first *tenori* know. The times, also, were sober, and there was less money for luxurious amusement. Besides this, there was the most lavish rivalry between the houses, and at the new Metropolitan house riches seemed to be squandered, although a great audience was seldom seen there, and it was alleged that it was a very difficult house in which to sing or to hear.

The drop fell at the close of the season amid rumors of disastrous loss, and as the autumn advances it is not even known who is to sing during the coming season, or whether, indeed, there is to be a season. It is understood that the *diva assoluta* will still not sing for less than the amazing honorarium for every appearance, and that the *donna nobile*—for who should dare to say *seconda?*—declares that if the *diva* be worth a guinea, she herself is certainly worth a pound. Then it was said, and we hope incorrectly, that the *primo tenore* proposed to organize a peripatetic opera company, and strike for fortune as a wandering star. Meanwhile the hapless managers are supposed to be sucking their burned fingers and gazing doubtfully at the fire.

But the fascination of opera management is not less than that of arctic exploration. Shrewd sportsmen would probably wager that the burned fingers will try the fire again. As actors themselves can not stay away from the theatre on off nights, but go to sit in the boxes when they are not upon the stage, or as the old habitués of Baden and of Homburg hang around the tables when their purses are empty, so the old managers seem to be irresistibly drawn to the desperate undertaking, and while there is a dollar left it is a dollar ventured. No task, indeed, could seem more thankless. The care of infinite and vexatious and petty detail, the adjustment of perpetual internecine war in the greenroom, the caprice of fashion, the chance of the weather, the whims of the press—all these are to be managed; and when all is done, what is the reward? Not fame, nor riches, nor public gratitude, for of all these what does the opera manager gather? The reward is the excitement of the game, the gratification of an appetite. Here as elsewhere the worker is subdued to his work. He may begin with the hope of making money. He ends with the pleasure of managing.

In the midst of all the speculation about the opera season Dr. Damrosch departed for Europe, and Mrs. Grundy immediately declared that Italian opera had succumbed, and that Wagner and the Wagnerians were to rule where Bellini, Verdi, and Rossini had reigned. But so great a change will not occur suddenly. The Italian opera is essentially an amusement, a relaxation, a pleasant entertainment. It charms the ear and pleases the mind with marked melody and a simple situation. It is like a fashionable novel which makes no demand upon the mind or conscience and wiles away an hour. It is the melodious accompaniment of gay conversation, like the murmur of the organ during a service. Society has adjusted the Italian opera to itself. It is a decoration, an ornamented part of the factitious life of fashion and the drawing-room.

But the modern German opera, the Wagnerian opera, is a serious business. It may be totally neglected, but it can hardly be subordinated to the ease and enjoyment of a volatile society murmuring and ogling in the boxes. There is an earnest, religious motive and feeling in the new opera, and its conception is radically different from that of the series of florid arias and concerted *scenas* which make up the rival opera. It would be singularly strange and *caviare* to the gay throng that flutters about the house; for whatever good may be said of the new opera, it is in no sense whatever "easy," and therefore no sudden transfer of taste could be made from one to the other.

But these speculations are superfluous. The character of the coming season will be announced by the time that these words are printed, and whatever it may prove to be, whether the old Italian divinities are still to be worshipped or the new German deities are to be enthroned, there is one thing not to be forgotten: that is that good manners will remain, and that good manners are founded in good feeling for our neighbors. Consequently if that party from Oshkosh or some remoter frontier strays again into the new opera-house, as it strayed last year, and hums and babbles and buzzes in the box, as it did last year, disturbing with its uncouth behavior the intelligent and well-bred people who come to hear, it is earnestly to be hoped that the same kind fate will provide another gentleman to arise in the parquet and audibly to request the barbarians from the outer world who prattle and giggle in the boxes "to stop their noise," and to try to imitate the behavior of well-bred people whom they can see all around them.

———

A RECENT writer protests against the fashion, "too common among city ladies, of aping male attire and demeanor," and he cites certain familiar instances of famous women who have dressed or behaved like men. The two offenses, however, are essentially different. Dress and behavior are not subject to the same general rules, except that both should be modest and becoming. We can all join heartily in protesting against the imitation by women of much of the behavior of men, whether the word be used in a more serious or in a lighter sense. The free and easy manner of many young men toward young women as it displays itself in lounging, swaggering, smoking, and, in general, the Sultan style of behavior, would be hardly beautiful in the other sex.

The other evening, after watching Florio for some time, an elder friend asked him, "How would you like Horatio to treat your sister as you treat his?" Florio looked at the elder friend as a pasha might look at a critic who remarked upon the pasha's treatment of his harem. Now Florio's is a kind of behavior which it would not be agreeable to see "aped" by the gentler sex, and the party of the recent writer who deplored it would be very large. But why not take the next step, which is the really important one, and protest against any behavior in a young man which any young woman might not properly " ape"? Of course behavior does not include certain pursuits and sports, such as shooting, or cricket, or curling, which require muscular strength. By behavior let us mean conduct and manner, and then why should a young man not conform to the standard which is equally becoming in a young woman?

Courtesy, thoughtfulness, kind consideration, respectful bearing in action and posture and tone, all the little details that comprise manner or good-breeding, these are all as becoming to a man as to a woman. Strutting and swelling, and strident talking and laughing, and "slangwhanging," and every form of selfish and boisterous and rude behavior, are not to be "aped" by women, not because they are common among men, but because they are in themselves disagreeable and intolerable. The excellent author whose protest we are considering would agree that profanity is an offense which is singularly shocking and repulsive in a woman, and, in fact, almost unknown except among the most abandoned women. But would he hold that it is to be shunned by women because it is a peculiarly manly vice? Certainly not, but because, whether in men or women, it is disgusting.

And as for dress, why should so vigilant a commentator bring all his broadsides to bear upon a sparrow? How many women of his acquaintance are inclined to "ape" the dress of men? Some pretty little suggestion of a man's waistcoat there may be, some trim and coy little bobs behind that recall the lappets or "tails" of the manly coat. But these are not invasions or raids, still less are they spoliations upon the domain of masculine attire. There were, indeed, heroic Mrs. Amelia Bloomer and the daring Mrs. Dr. Mary Walker, but among fifty millions of persons, half of them women, they enjoyed an unshared distinction. Their sisters were not decoyed from skirts, nor inveigled into stove-pipe hats. No, no; something may be left to the natural sense of taste and grace and propriety. Indeed, the most cogent argument for that equal liberty which is known as "woman's rights" is that the "sphere" of woman needs no more to be guarded and defined by laws made by men than their dress. It is not necessary to forbid women to wear pantaloons, and it is for the same general reason unnecessary to limit their freedom of choice in more important affairs.

And while our author is troubled about the possibility that women may wear the dress of men, why not turn his diamond-pointed pen toward the Eastern lands where all men wear more or less flowing skirts like women? He will be sorry to find that the manly pantaloon is still practically unknown in much of the earliest and longest civilized parts of the globe.

IF the old French chronicler should watch the pleasure parties that go forth from New York and other cities in "slow-trailing barges," or upon excursion trains, or otherwise, he would surely shake his head with sympathy, and sigh that his fellow-men of the English blood and speech still take their pleasure sadly. Why are we so awkward at it? Why do we have a secret feeling that people who deliberately set out to enjoy themselves are either foolish children or simple squanderers of time? Is there some inherent Puritan drop in the national blood? Is enjoyment in itself a wrong? Ought we to add to the Litany a supplication to be delivered from all pleasure and delightful recreation, from joy, gladness, and glee?

If you ever go to Dresden, you will naturally saunter upon the Brühl Terrace over the Elbe, and it is quite probable that you will enter the spacious café to take a light refection. You will watch the loitering groups, and listen to the excellent music, and your musing mind will follow your eyes toward Pillnitz, and the Saxon Switzerland there below, and push on toward Prague and the Oriental *Hradschin*, the stately palace, and the lovely dark-eyed Jewess—*eheu! eheu!* is it of you who are to do all this that the Easy Chair is speaking, or of himself who did it, who loitered and sat and listened and mused and beheld, how many thousand years ago!

But sitting in that café you will perhaps observe the worthy citizen of Dresden who

has come out with his wife and children to take his evening pleasure. He sits gravely reading his paper and sipping his beer. The good frau is knitting and drinking coffee. The children sit peaceably by and watch the crowd, and beat time to the music. Their enjoyment is so sincere and tranquil that you—restless and morbidly introspective American vagabond—you take your pleasure in watching them. The sight rests you like a far-stretching and gentle rural landscape, like those broad-sided, wooded, massive ranges of hills beyond the Westfield—hills of Worthington and Cummington and distant Peru, which you see from that smooth lawn, that hospitable home in Chesterfield.

Why can not we take our pleasure like that Dresden family? or will not the generalization hold, and is it not "we," but only a few of us, who do not know how to enjoy? Is the secret, after all, not in temperament, but in fire-water? And if we could have a real prohibition, would not fire companies and charitable societies and other associations go forth upon their annual picnics and pleasure excursions as quietly and cheerfully as the Dresden family? However this may be, nothing is plainer than that a great city breeds a dangerous class whose members can not be safely allowed at their own will to join public pleasure parties, and who must be restrained in some way. It may not be possible to forbid pleasure-seekers and "roughs" to carry a private bottle of ardent spirits, but it is possible to prohibit a public bar upon barge excursions, and to provide a capable police guard.

It may be that we mistake the shaking head and the sighing of old Froissart as he watches the barges carrying the picnic parties across the bay and up the rivers of New Amsterdam, and that he is saying, with melancholy truth, they take their pleasure savagely. But no truer word has been spoken of us for many a year than that of Herbert Spencer, that we need the habit of relaxation and recreation; and as the abused dumb animals have found their friend and protector who in this neighborhood at least has taught everybody to be more considerate and to stay the tormenting hand, so some happy morning the overworked and anxious people who "scorn delight and live laborious days" will awaken to find that some beneficent Bergh is resolved that they shall enjoy themselves, and that he is dedicating himself to teach them how to do it.

Editor's Literary Record.

AS it has been customarily treated, general or universal history has been very commonly, and not altogether unjustly, considered one of the driest and least engaging departments of literature, despite the learning and industry that have been exhibited in its compilation. And herein, that for the most part

it has been little more than a barren *compilation* of the husks of history, of facts, dates, and events, arranged methodically and even perspicaciously according to certain epochs, eras, or subjects, is to be found the reason alike for the low esteem in which it has been held by historical scholars, the distaste with which it has been regarded by general readers, and the aversion that has been felt for it by youths at school or college into whose unwilling hands it has been placed, in one or other of its forms, as a text-book. It has lacked both the spice of novelty and freshness that accompanies original historical research and investigation, and the penetrating philosophical insight which vitalizes the facts of history by its sifting analysis and its effective marshalling and grouping of distant but related principles and occurrences.

Hitherto universal history, as has been well and concisely stated by Lord Woodhouselee, has been projected on three general lines or plans. Of these, one epitomized all the remarkable events that have occurred since the creation, and being little more than a mere catalogue of facts, was characterized by method, without any reflection; another regarded general history in no other light than as furnishing documents and proofs illustrative of a particular subject, as, for instance, the science of politics, the law of nations, or the influence of a language, a family, or a race, and was consequently freighted with a great deal of theory and reflection, without any method; and the third, pursuing a middle course, rejected both these methods, and paying more attention to the connection of subject than to that of time, has sought to exhibit to view the predominant nations or empires, to which all the rest bear, as it were, an under part, and whose history, being the most important, is therefore entitled to be more fully delineated, while the rest, as subordinate, are brought into view only when they have an obvious connection with their principal, and their antecedent and current histories figure only as episodes, so introduced as not to violate the unity of the narrative. This latter method, which was that of Lord Woodhouselee himself, was a material improvement upon the previous ones, and an approach to the more perfect method we shall soon consider, but its great defect was that it merged the general and universal in the particular, and was a universal history in the sense only that it gave synchronous epitomes of the history of individual nations, while it left the general connection and movement of things very greatly obscured.

In the hands of the veteran historian Leopold von Ranke, general history is now clothed with a new spirit and meaning. This greatest of living historians has devoted the closing years of his long and illustrious life to the preparation of a universal history, in which, recognizing the general connection of things to which we have adverted, and treating the broad facts of history rather than its details, he undertakes to trace the sequence of those events, whether great or small, which link all nations together, and materially control their destinies; and to investigate the universal life of mankind, including in this last the first beginnings of culture and civilization, the growth of the germs of art and literature, and of social and political institutions, the historical development of nations as they appear on the stage of action, and are combined into progressive communities, and their rivalry for the soil or for political or military supremacy, by means of which empires are evolved, and the peculiar characteristics of each nation are modified, and at the same time resist and react upon universal tendencies. Herr Von Ranke loses himself neither in the mists of generalization nor in the bewildering intricacies of petty details. He holds that universal history would degenerate into mere theory and speculation if it were to desert the firm ground of national history, but that just as little can it afford to cling to this ground alone; that the history of each separate nation throws light on the history of humanity at large, but that there is a general historical life which moves progressively from one nation or group of nations to another; and finally, that while our attention must always be fixed upon the universal, it must not overlook the individual and particular. His point of view throughout is tersely stated by himself as follows: That in the course of ages the human race has won for itself a sort of heirloom in the material and social advance which it has made, but still more in its intellectual and religious development; that one portion of this heritage, the most precious jewel of the whole, consists of those immortal works of genius in poetry and literature, science and art, which, while modified by the local conditions under which they were produced, yet represent what is common to all mankind; that with this possession are inseparably combined the memories of events, of ancient institutions, and of great men who have passed away; and that one generation hands on this tradition to another that it may from time to time be revived and recalled to the minds of men for their encouragement and instruction. Keeping these thoughts constantly in his mind, the venerable philosopher and historian throws aside all that is fabulous or held merely on trust and speculation, and scanning the period that has intervened and the peoples and nations that have played their part on the world's stage since history first took exact and authentic note of them, he gives a luminous outline of the career of each, and extracts from all whatever is known of those principles and motives of action and of those movements and developments in every department of industrial and national life which have become the common heritage and possession. It is amazing with what skill and clearness he traces the thread of religious, social, and political development, and gathers up the seminal principles of art, literature, and morals from amidst the mutations and wrecks of nations and dynasties; and even still more amazing are the transparent simplicity and reasonableness of his arguments, deductions, and conclusions. Of course we speak only of the installment of his work which is now before us. The entire work, when completed, will be a universal history of the world from the earliest historic period until our own day. Of this great undertaking he has completed four volumes, covering the earlier periods, and the volume[1] now published relates exclusively to the oldest historical group of nations—the Egyptians, the Hebrews, the Assyrian and other Asiatic nations—and the Greeks. Every page is instinct with broad and philosophic generalization, and the statement of unexpected but most convincing facts and conclusions. Its style is perfect; the reader is delighted by the charm of its steadily flowing narrative, while he is instructed by its revelations of the origins and development of things which have exerted, and continue to exert, a powerful influence upon mankind, and have thus a universal interest and application. Those who are curious may here find the record of the first development of small independent communities into nations, of the first maritime expedition and the first systematic war by land, of the first endowment of the individual in society with those rights and immunities which are the foundation of all civil order, of the first tragic personage in history, of the first establishment of the principles of hereditary monarchy and democracy, of the first conquering power which we encounter in the history of the world, of the first time that the power of money made itself felt in the internal affairs of an important community, of the first employment of mercenary troops, and a multiplicity of other "first things" in history, whose analogues, parallels, and counterparts are traced by the great historian down through the centuries to our own day. The volume before us brings the history down to the struggle of Hellas and Carthage for the supremacy, and the rise of the new power, Rome, that was destined to vanquish both; and we are apprised in a prefatory note by the capable English editor and translator, Mr. G. W. Prothero, that it must depend on the reception of this installment by the public whether the translation of the remaining five or six volumes will be continued. Unless we greatly mistake the impression that this admirable installment will make upon the public, the translation and publication of the entire work will not be long deferred.

MR. WILLIAM O. STODDARD, who was one of President Lincoln's secretaries during the war of the rebellion, has prepared a *Life of Lincoln*[2]

which has strong claims upon the interest and attention of every American. A popular and strictly personal biography, it is so simply and tersely written as to be adapted to readers of every age and degree of intelligence; and it recites in brief, vigorous, and nervous sentences the story of a life which comprises many of the elements of true greatness, and is eminently worthy of contemplation as a practical example of the potent possibilities that reside in our republican institutions. It may not be reserved for many men to be confronted by circumstances like those which moulded, trained, and tested Mr. Lincoln. Not many youths are, like him, eager to learn, prompt to observe, persistent, industrious, not afraid of work; nor are there many adults who have the patient steadfastness of purpose, the single-mindedness, sincerity, honesty, sagacity, and simple patriotism that formed the grain and fibre of his sinewy character. But though circumstances may not be invented or improvised, life and character may be imitated and emulated; and all things being considered, there has been no man of recent times whose life and character, in all their conditions and possibilities, were more truly and representatively American than the life and character of Mr. Lincoln, or more susceptible of very general and successful imitation. There are few intelligent American lads who will enter upon life with a scantier equipment of education and this world's goods than did young Lincoln. What he accomplished and became is possible to all; and if any considerable portion of the youth of America can be persuaded to make themselves familiar with his life as boy and man, and with the steps of his growth and development into manhood, as delineated in Mr. Stoddard's suggestive biography, it will be the better for them and for the republic. Aside from its value in this direction, Mr. Stoddard's volume is a graphic and entertaining biography, as rich in incident as any romance, and sparkling with wise wit and racy anecdote. It comprises a large mass of valuable and judiciously epitomized information concerning the momentous political and social events that preceded the war, and the still more momentous military and political occurrences that attended and immediately followed it. However materially one may differ from some of Mr. Stoddard's judgments of men and measures, and from his criticisms of military leaders and policies, the occasions for such difference are so rare, and his views are so candidly and temperately stated, that only a morbidly captious spirit of partisanship can seriously object to them.

THERE is a marked difference in the grain and quality of the poems in Mr. Edgar Fawcett's *Song and Story*;[3] and singularly enough those among them which are the most note-

---

[1] *Universal History.* The Oldest Historical Group of Nations and the Greeks. By LEOPOLD VON RANKE. Edited by G. W. PROTHERO, Fellow and Tutor of King's College, Cambridge. 8vo, pp. 494. New York: Harper and Brothers.

[2] *Abraham Lincoln.* The True Story of a Great Life. Showing the Inner Growth, Special Training, and Peculiar Fitness of the Man for his Work. By WILLIAM O. STODDARD. With Illustrations. 8vo, pp. 508. New York: Fords, Howard, and Hulbert.

[3] *Song and Story.* Later Poems. By EDGAR FAWCETT. 12mo, pp. 181. Boston: James R. Osgood and Co.

worthy for their originality, imaginativeness, and other poetic qualities are the least perfect in their finish and execution. The most finished compositions in the volume, as relates to their exterior form and structure, are his songs and sonnets; but there is nothing in either of these that betrays the possession of any very exalted poetic gifts. The songs are very far from being prosaic or commonplace, but still lack the airiness, the glow of passion and emotion, the depth of tenderness and pathos, the gayety, the abandon, the sense of exhilaration, and the suggestions of music and movement that have characterized the best English songs from the time of Shakespeare and Ben Jonson to the present day; and the sonnets, though admirable in their form and replete with intellectuality as to their matter, in like manner lack the brilliancy, point, and compactness, the power of cumulative thought, and the many-hued fancies and imaginings that are found in the best examples of that gem-like verse. In strong contrast with his songs and sonnets are his longer poems. These are as fervid and imaginative as the others are coldly intellectual, and their rich and sustained narrative and finely poetic descriptions fully justify the appellative of "Story," under which the author classifies them, and which he uses to distinguish them from their companions. Especially affluent of these qualities is the vigorous narrative poem "Alan Eliot." Belonging to the same class are the poems entitled "The Singing of Luigi," "A Mood of Cleopatra," "The Girl at the Crossing," and "A Vengeance." These are narrative poems of great force and beauty, less elaborate and less dramatic than "Alan Eliot," but all marked by the same ripe and versatile imagination that distinguishes it. With one exception, however —being that of the delicious Italian love tale, "The Singing of Luigi"—the perfection of all these poems is marred by a grandiloquence of style which recalls the bombastic mouthings against which Shakespeare directed the battery of his raillery in the persons of Malvolio, Sir John Falstaff, and honest Nick Bottom, and also reminds us of a poetic style that was much affected at a much later day by some of our own poets, among others by Carlos Wilcox, Henry Ware, Jun., and even by Bryant in a few of his earlier poems. There are several other poems of considerable merit in Mr. Fawcett's volume which do not strictly belong either to "song" or "story." Of these the best examples are "The Republic" and "The Rivers," the first-named being a sonorous pæan emphasizing the true glories of our country, and the other a series of soliloquies supposed to have been uttered by certain historic rivers, reciting their claims to greatness on the score of the important events that had happened on or beside them, and their alliance with human interests and sympathies. Their versification is nearly faultless, and they are enriched with many lofty thoughts and much splendid imagery; but in the main they are the product of the brain rather than of the fancy or the imagination.

RARELY does it fall to the lot of the critic to meet with verse as redolent as that of Mr. Maurice Thompson of the fragrant breath of flower and leaf and field, or as suggestive of the noise of waters, the song of birds, and the manifold sounds, movements, and colors of nature. His *Songs of Fair Weather* may[4] be classed among the most perfect of our briefer homespun pastorals and idyls, whether regard be had to the liquid melody of their style, the delicate thoughts and fine fancies with which they are laden, or the *naïveté* and expressiveness of the language in which they are clothed. Not in vain does the poet, in a felicitous prelude to his poems, invoke the "spirit that moves the sap in spring" to inform his words and make his lines "as sweet as flowers" and "as strong as vines," to endue him with "the freshening power of rain on grass or dew on flower," and to inspire him with the power to voice his thoughts in "fertilizing song, nut-flavored, racy," and "as keen as wine." To analyze these delightful poetic morsels would be as ungracious and as ruinous as to dissect the lily or to subject the rose to the crucible. For such a task we have no taste, and prefer to leave them with their exquisite bloom and beauty unimpaired for the enjoyment of such of our readers as may choose to possess themselves of the writings of one whom a brother poet has not inaptly styled "a new Theocritus."

EARLIEST among the harbingers of the approaching holidays are new and very attractive editions of Scott's *Marmion*[5] and *The Lay of the Last Minstrel*,[6] of an English anthology[7] from Chaucer to the present day, of the *Poems*[8] of Dante Gabriel Rossetti, and of *Selections from the Poetical Works of Algernon C. Swinburne.*[9] Upon *Marmion* and *The Lay of the Last Minstrel* criticism has long since exhausted itself, and the poems in the other volumes we have named have been so generally appraised that a particular criticism of them may be dispensed with at this time. Superbly printed on fine calendered paper, and gayly and even resplendently bound, they have been specially designed by the publishers for holiday gifts, and are highly attractive specimens of such souvenirs. The volume containing Swinburne's

---

[4] *Songs of Fair Weather.* By MAURICE THOMPSON. 12mo, pp. 99. Boston: James R. Osgood and Co.
[5] *Marmion.* By Sir WALTER SCOTT, Bart. 12mo, pp. 312. New York: Thomas Y. Crowell and Co.
[6] *The Lay of the Last Minstrel.* By the Same. 12mo, pp. 222. New York: Thomas Y. Crowell and Co.
[7] *Red-letter Poems by English Men and Women.* 12mo, pp. 648. New York: Thomas Y. Crowell and Co.
[8] *Poems.* By DANTE G. ROSSETTI. 12mo, pp. 294. New York: Thomas Y. Crowell and Co.
[9] *Selections from the Poetical Works of A. C. Swinburne.* Edited by R. H. STODDARD. Sq. 8vo, pp. 634. New York: Thomas Y. Crowell and Co.

poems has a new feature of special interest from the fact that it has been edited by Mr. R. H. Stoddard, whose taste and judgment are manifest in the choice of the selections reprinted, and who has further enhanced its value by a scholarly and finely discriminating critical essay upon the genius of Swinburne and the characteristic features of his poetry.

THE almost countless number of strong novels that flow in a steady stream from the pens of a goodly number of clever and entertaining authors pretty clearly demonstrates that the art of writing that kind of fiction which is enlivened with dramatic scenes and incidents, and which delineates striking phases of character and manifestations of passion, is not an uncommon gift. A much rarer gift—indeed, a most rare one—is the faculty of writing a *quiet* novel, whose interest does not depend upon these highly spiced and stimulating excitements. To write such a novel without lapsing into insipidity or tameness is one of the most difficult tests to which a writer of romance can be subjected, and to write one that will be successful with the public is a genuine triumph of art. On more than one occasion Miss Mulock has shown that along with the creative and dramatic power which signalizes her efforts in the higher walk of romantic fiction she also possesses the faculty of touching the heart and quickening the sensibilities through the medium of these more modest and unpretending performances, but never more successfully than in the latest and most delightful of her many delightful minor tales, *Miss Tommy*.[10] This tale is an exceedingly simple one; its unaffected narrative is undisturbed by any exciting passages, and quietly unfolds a story within a story—of two young lives whose prosperous love is interrupted by some transient adversities, and of two other and older lives which had drifted asunder when life was young, and had come together again when it was old, but was still rich in the capacity for tranquil happiness. Miss Tommy is one of those truly heroic characters, not uncommon among true-hearted women, who cherish the secret of unrequited love in their "heart of hearts," not brooding over it repiningly until they become hard and soured, but so keeping its memory green that it softens and beautifies their whole nature, and renders them unobtrusively but effectively sympathetic with human suffering, but more especially helpfully alive to the hopes and fears that beset the paths of young lovers, and actively ministrant to their mutual trust and constancy. The character of Miss Tommy is a charming conception, and is delineated with

exquisite fineness, firmness, and delicacy, and the drama in which she plays her quiet part is keyed in a tone of gentle cheerfulness blended with mild pathos.

MISS VIRGINIA W. JOHNSON'S latest novel, *The Fainalls of Tipton*,[11] will be less popular than her previous romances in the proportion that it is less richly imaginative than they have been, not so lavishly supplied with picturesque descriptions and piquant situations, and more sober and restrained in its style. Still, it is a skillful and ingenious performance of a more difficult task than she has hitherto undertaken, and evinces a wider and nearer experience of human nature than was required for the production of either of her former romances, and a clearer perception of the motives and springs of action that enter into and differentiate character. The tale deals with the average run of men and women—people who live the uneventful life of an out-of-the-way country village, who are stirred by those petty passions and emotions and ruffled by those trivial incidents and vicissitudes which are often underestimated because they are common, but which, nevertheless, are of the kind that contributes to the pangs and joys and constitutes the prose and the romance of life the world over. With the earnestness of a conscientious artist, and with the graceful skill of a practiced one, Miss Johnson has constructed out of these simple and unpromising materials a finished realistic story, dealing, it is true, with ordinary and even commonplace people and every-day incidents and emotions, but in which she manages to keep the expectation of the reader on tiptoe, and to compel his interest by the ingenious, the humorous, and the unexpected transitions of its narrative, and its graphic delineations of characters such as we are wont to meet in real life.

MR. THOMAS W. KNOX is an indefatigable and successful caterer of instructive and entertaining information for our intelligent and inquisitive youth. Having carried them in his sterling "Boy Travellers" series through Asia and Africa, he now invites them to accompany two youths in their adventures in the arctic regions. The volume in which these adventures are recorded, and which the author has entitled *The Voyage of the "Vivian" to the North Pole and Beyond*,[12] is constructed upon the same plan as his *Boy Travellers in the East*, and like it consists of an array of facts embroidered upon a ground-work of fiction. The ship and the crew, as well as the adventurous youths who are the heroes of the narrative, are fictitious, but with the exception of several chapters

[10] *Miss Tommy: A Mediæval Romance;* and *In a House-Boat: A Journal.* By the author of John Halifax, Gentleman. Illustrated. Paper, 16mo, pp. 253. New York: Harper and Brothers.
The Same. Library Edition. 16mo, pp. 253. New York: Harper and Brothers.

[11] *The Fainalls of Tipton.* By VIRGINIA W. JOHNSON. 16mo, pp. 482. New York: Charles Scribner's Sons.
[12] *Adventures of Two Youths in the Open Polar Sea. The Voyage of the "Vivian" to the North Pole and Beyond.* By THOMAS W. KNOX. Illustrated. 8vo, pp. 297. New York: Harper and Brothers.

which give an imaginary account of a voyage from Herald Island to the north pole, and thence to Grant Land, and which record the discovery of an open polar sea, the scenes of the voyages, and the incidents and adventures described, are based upon fact, and are a faithful transcript of the experiences of various travellers and explorers from the time of Frobisher to the present. So, likewise, the scientific discoveries that are recorded have a solid basis in reality, having been digested from the works of eminent explorers and voyagers, and incorporated in the account of the voyage of the *Vivian* in order to give verisimilitude to the narrative, and at the same time bring into succinct form all that is known of arctic discovery. In this way the youthful reader is put substantially in possession, and in a most agreeable manner, of the contents of many rare and costly books of travel and exploration, and of all the results that have been achieved in polar regions by the arctic explorers of the last and the present centuries. The geographical, ethnological, and scientific statements that are made, always excepting those which are woven into the text of the apocryphal chapters referred to above, have been carefully verified by Mr. Knox, and may be accepted as scrupulously accurate. There is no volume to which young readers can be referred which gives so full, clear, and condensed a view of arctic exploration and discovery as that which may be derived from Mr. Knox's graphic and entertaining narrative of *The Voyage of the " Vivian."*

MR. HORACE E. SCUDDER has prepared a *History of the United States*[13] for the use of schools and academies, which embodies every requirement that is essential in a historical text-book for the young. Chastely and concisely written, its brief and epigrammatic paragraphs contain the pith of our history, stated so simply and clearly as to be easily fixed in the memory, and presented so attractively as to engage the attention and excite the patriotic interest of the youthful reader. Mr. Scudder has the rare faculty of being able to condense a narrative of events within the smallest compass without destroying its flavor or impairing the continuity of its outline. It would be impossible in fewer words than have been employed by Mr. Scudder to delineate the great events that have contributed to our national life, to depict the illustrious patriots, soldiers, and statesmen who have adorned and exemplified it, or to announce the great principles which have made an impression upon or have been illustrated by it. Each chapter is preceded by a table of the definition and pronunciation of the novel or more difficult words that occur in it, and the text is accompanied and explained by a number of excellent maps which give a clear idea of the geographical relations and the physical conditions of our country at different periods, and of the countries that were most closely associated with its history. In an appendix is a body of questions adjusted to the contents of each of the chapters, together with the full texts of the Declaration of Independence and of the Constitution. The volume brings the history of the United States down from the discovery of America to the present year. It is written in a tone of quiet earnestness appropriate to the gravity and significance of the subjects involved, and is admirably calculated to arouse the patriotism of the reader while it adds to his store of precise and accurate knowledge concerning his native land.

MR. ANDREW CARNEGIE'S *Round the World*[14] differs from the conventional books of travel in its abstinence from labored attempts at fine writing and ambitious description on the one hand, and on the other from a too prosaic and commonplace array of statistics and useful information. And yet not anything that is worth seeing escapes him, and in a few crisp touches he reproduces what he sees, and places it before the reader with all the glow and freshness of reality. Before taking up his sparkling and exhilarating book we fancied that we knew all that could be known about those much-bewritten countries, Japan and China, India and Egypt, but at every step of his rapid peregrinations he flashes before us, in words fit though few, some new fact or thing vividly descriptive of phases of character, and specialties of manners, customs, business, institutions, and scenery, which heretofore we have but imperfectly apprehended. His gayety and good-humor are contagious. We share his unclouded animal spirits, his abounding and resounding hilarity, and his tireless dash and activity. He is thoroughly practical, too, when it pleases him, but never tiresomely so; so that when his shrewd glance rests, as it often does, upon some suggestive business topic, we find ourselves pausing beside him and putting on a look as intent and penetrating as his own. Mr. Carnegie has given us a bright, breezy, and thoughtful volume, redolent with life and movement, with sound sense and hearty comradeship. Of course there are flaws and specks in it, but these are few and far between, and generally not worthy of mention—generally, but not always, as, for instance, where, in a letter ostensibly written from the Great American Desert of Utah, in October, 1878, he interjects a rather spiteful fling, the only really ill-natured *skit* in his book, at Tennyson for masquerading as a British peer. And this was nearly six years before the event!

---

[13] *A History of the United States of America.* Preceded by a Narrative of the Discovery and Settlement of North America, and of the Events which led to the Independence of the Thirteen English Colonies. By HORACE E. SCUDDER. With Maps and Illustrations. 12mo, pp. 510. Philadelphia: J. H. Butler.

[14] *Round the World.* By ANDREW CARNEGIE. 8vo, pp. 360. New York: Charles Scribner's Sons.

Editor's Historical Record.

POLITICAL.

OUR Record is closed on the 18th of September.—The following nominations were made by State Conventions: Connecticut Republican, Governor, Henry B. Harrison; Lieutenant-Governor, Lorren D. Cooke; Secretary of State, Charles A. Russell; Treasurer, Valentine B. Chamberlain; Comptroller, Luzerne J. Munson; Michigan Greenback, Governor Begole renominated; Iowa Republican, Secretary of State, F. D. Jackson; Treasurer, V. P. Twombly; Kansas Democratic, Governor Glick renominated; Michigan Prohibition, Governor, David Preston; Missouri Prohibition, Governor, Rev. John A. Brooks; Texas Democratic, Governor John Ireland renominated; Nebraska Republican, Governor James W. Dawes renominated; Wisconsin Greenback, Governor, Colonel William L. Utley; Vermont Independent Republican, Governor, C. M. Stone; Michigan Prohibition, Governor, David Preston; Connecticut Democratic, Governor Waller renominated; New Hampshire Republican, Governor, Moody Currier; Massachusetts Republican, Governor George D. Robinson renominated; Massachusetts Democratic, Governor, W. C. Endicott; Wisconsin Republican, Governor, Jeremiah M. Rusk; Wisconsin Prohibition, Governor, S. D. Hastings; New Hampshire Prohibition, Governor, L. D. Mason; Missouri Republican, Governor, Nicholas Ford; Wisconsin Democratic, Governor, W. D. Fratt; Colorado Republican, Governor, B. H. Eaton; New Hampshire Democratic, Governor, Hon. J. M. Hill; Massachusetts Prohibition, Governor, President J. H. Seelye; Connecticut People's, Governor, Major J. L. Curtiss.

The Arkansas State election, September 1, resulted in a victory by the Democrats, with a large majority.

The Vermont election, September 2, was carried by the Republicans, with a majority of 21,413.

The Maine election, September 8, gave the Republican candidate for Governor a plurality of about 20,000.

The public debt of the United States was reduced during the month of August $8,542,852.

The British Budget shows a decrease in revenue receipts for the year of £1,439,172, and a decrease in expenditure of £2,917,688.

The French Chamber of Deputies, August 15, voted the Tonquin credit of 38,000,000 francs.

The French flag was hoisted over the citadel at Hué, the capital of Anam, August 17. The same day, the new King of Anam was crowned with great pomp.

Foo-Chow was bombarded by the French fleet August 23. The arsenal was destroyed after a four hours' fire. Nine Chinese gunboats and twelve junks were sunk, and two escaped. On the 25th a second bombardment took place, and on the day following a number of forts on the river Min were reduced.

DISASTERS.

August 19.—Seventeen workmen suffocated in an under-ground canal at Braye, France.

August 20.—United States ship *Tallapoosa* sunk in a collision off Martha's Vineyard. Two lives lost.

August 21.—Eight lives lost by gas in Greenback Colliery, near Shamokin, Pennsylvania.

August 29.—Steamer *City of Merida* burned at Havana. No lives lost.—Transfer steamer *Belmont* sunk in a storm near Evansville, Indiana. Sixteen lives lost.

September 7.—Destructive fire in Cleveland, Ohio.

September 10.—Nine persons killed in an accident on the Mexican Central Railroad.—Distillery explosion, Pekin, Illinois. Several killed.

September 10–11.—A rapid rise in the Eau Claire and Chippewa rivers, destroying over $4,000,000 worth of property.

September 15.—Report by mail to San Francisco that the province of Kiang-See had been inundated, and seventy thousand lives lost.

OBITUARY.

August 15.—In Newburgh, New York, Rev. John Brown, aged ninety-three years.

August 16.—In Washington, D.C., John Pool, ex-United States Senator, aged fifty-eight years.

August 18.—Near Philadelphia, Colonel J. J. Woodward, Surgeon U.S.A., aged fifty-one years.—In Cairo, Sultan Pasha, President of the Egyptian Legislative Council.—In Washington, D.C., Mary Clemmer Hudson.

August 24.—In England, Henry George Bohn, publisher, aged eighty-eight years.

August 25.—In Berlin, Lord Ampthill, Ambassador to Prussia, in his fifty-sixth year.—In Philadelphia, J. L. Claghorn, aged sixty-seven years.

August 28.—In Marion, Massachusetts, Rear-Admiral A. A. Harwood, U.S.N., aged eighty-two years.

August 29.—At Fort Hamilton, New York, R. Cornell White, aged fifty-nine years.

September 1.—In Nyack, New York, Smith Sheldon, publisher, aged seventy-two years.

September 2.—In Providence, Rhode Island, United States Senator Henry B. Anthony, aged sixty-nine years.

September 3.—In Sparta, Georgia, Bishop George F. Pierce, aged seventy-three years.

September 4.—In Geneva, New York, Hon. Charles J. Folger, Secretary of the Treasury, aged sixty-six years.

September 13.—In Tarrytown, New York, Robert Hoe, of the firm of R. Hoe and Co., of this city, in his seventieth year.

Editor's Drawer.

ONE of the most pleasing signs of the cordial relations existing between the North and the South—which were recently testing each other's muscle and endurance — is the frank and even forward admission by the former that Mount Mitchell, the highest peak in the Black Mountains of North Carolina, is higher by several hundred feet than Mount Washington, in New Hampshire, and the modest manner in which the South admits this glory, as if reluctant to wound Northern sensibilities. It may be a regret on both sides that the highest point of land east of the Rocky Mountains does not bear the name of Washington. The peak in New Hampshire was allotted to him in good faith that it was the highest, and his shade must be content with the good intention. Even the Father of his Country can not be permitted to sprawl all over the continent to the exclusion of all other aspirants for high honor ; and we must be satisfied with giving him (in the Washington Monument) the tallest pile of stone built by anybody since the Tower of Babel, and let Professor Mitchell sleep in peace on his mountain in the lonesomest if not the highest-placed grave in the republic. On the summit of that wooded peak, 6711 feet above the Atlantic, and almost that height above Mount Vernon, Mitchell lies amid the clouds and thunder-storms and aerial battles of the Black Mountains. This individual eminence is a stroke of fortune. Washington did what he could for his personal elevation : he cut his initials as high up on the buttress of the Natural Bridge as he could climb in his stocking feet, and in other ways he deserved well of his country ; but a professor of chemistry, by a lucky chance of first measuring this peak and announcing his discovery, and by the equally lucky chance (for his immortality) of losing his life in attempting to establish the assertion that this was the peak he had first measured, and not a neighboring one, as Senator Clingman insisted, has secured an eminence which all the character and correctness of life possessed by George Washington could not give him.

North Carolina, of course, has a justifiable pride in this mountain — although she has probably twenty peaks about as high as Mount Washington — and before the war this may have been an arrogant pride ; but now this is one of the old North State's contributions to the glory of the republic. Before the war the Northern States might have been ready to fight for the superiority of the New Hampshire hill, or at least to have insisted that an admission of its inferiority should be considered as one of the compromises of the Constitution ; but now they take as much national pride in the bigness of Mitchell as if it were situated on Boston Common. It is one of the amiable traits of human nature that people should take a sort of credit to themselves for such excrescences on the surface of the earth in the places they inhabit. The inflation of Western people about their eminences is as harmless as it is pleasing, and we dwellers in lower regions feel that their importance in the world is increased by the noble height of their mountains ; and we know that what some Englishmen call boastfulness in them is merely the reflection of the generous scale on which nature is laid out west of the Mississippi River. We all share, in a way, in the distinction which the Rockies and Sierras give our country. If the time comes when we shall desire the annexation of Mexico, the possession of Popocatepetl will be a weight in the scale of our desire.

We can not leave this fruitful theme without a suggestion that may serve to moderate any lingering feeling of sectional rivalry or envy in ignoble minds in regard to the respective heights of these two respectable mountains. The White Mountains are of granite, and even in their frost-trying climate likely to outlast the republic in their integrity. But the Black Mountains are built of a softer material, and would be subject to a more rapid degradation if they were stripped of their protecting vegetation and subject to the wash of the frequent rains. Even the best mountains are slowly wearing away, and the pride that the American must feel in Mitchell as he stands upon its green summit must be moderated by regret that it was not made of granite. The geologists alone can tell how soon it will sink to the altitude of a common hill, but even the geologists can not sensibly lessen our feeling of security that Mitchell will long continue a source of national pride. If Professor Mitchell were now living and were a candidate for the Presidency, his mountain would not escape detraction, and probably venal surveyors would be found to depreciate its height in the interest of party. We have reason, at any rate, to congratulate ourselves, as we begin to feel more keenly the political hurricane of November, that there are some things safe from the devastation of a Presidential campaign.

In 18— the artist Ary Scheffer read the story of Little Nell, and was so much pleased with that graceful and touching creation that he expressed a desire to paint a portrait of the author. Arrangements were made with Mr. Dickens to give him a sitting on his next visit to Paris. On the appointed day the author presented himself at the artist's house, and was refused entrance on the ground that the day had been set apart for Mr. Dickens. On receiving assurances that this was the veritable Mr. Dickens, the attendant admitted the visitor to his master's studio. No sooner had the painter of " Dante and Beatrice in Paradise" caught sight of the chin whiskers and watch chain, and the figure so different from the ideal creator of Little Nell, than he covered his eyes with his hands and exclaimed, in a broken voice, "You are not Charles Dickens!"

Mr. Dickens replied, in his dreary voice, "Assuredly it is Charles Dickens."

In a broken voice the artist moaned, with covered eyes, "Oh, mon Dieu!—oh, mon Dieu! Withdraw yourself, in the name of Heaven, and come not again till I have forgotten the Charles Dickens of my dreams."

Mr. Dickens withdrew himself, and it is to be presumed permanently, for the Charles Dickens of the poet's dreams was never painted—standing on a cloud in a night-gown, holding Little Nell's hand, and pointing heavenward.

ONE bright morning many years ago an elderly country couple rang the bell at the house of William C. Bryant, and asked if they could see Mr. Bryant. On being told it was impossible, they seemed much cast down, and the old lady said tearfully that they had come fifty miles on purpose to see him. Their disappointment was so evident, and the fact that these simple children of nature had made so long a pilgrimage to see the "poet of the woods" was so touching, they were told they might see his study. Here they were much interested, and their reverential, subdued manner confirmed the good impression they had already made. Finally they begged to be allowed "to look at Mr. Bryant just once."

"But Mr. Bryant is dressing. It is impossible."

"Dressing!" exclaimed the old couple in a breath. "Why, we came to see the corpse!"

Dan Bryant, "the minstrel," was dead, and the worthy people recognized but one form of minstrelsy—the burnt cork variety.

ONE of the recent Governors of Michigan was the late John J. Bagley, who, before assuming the Executive chair, had made a fortune as a tobacconist. Near the close of one of the legislative sessions, the law-makers, accompanied by his Excellency, indulged in an excursion to some of the Lake Superior islands, and during the speech-making and other festivities which usually attend on such occasions the Governor told the following story, drawn from his own experience.

One day while engaged in the Executive Chamber there was rather a peculiar knock at the door, indicating that at least the caller was not of the usual sort. On the door being opened by an attendant, the caller was discovered to be one of the seediest, dirtiest, most loaferish-looking tramps that ever slept under a hay-stack. His clothes were not only shabby and dirty, but stained with tobacco juice, while a liberal stream of that fluid meandered from each corner of his mouth.

As the door opened, the tramp eyed the attendant rather curiously, and after a little delay said, "Is this the place whar Guv'ner Bagglely stops?"

"Yes, sir," said the attendant; "this is his office."

"Is he tu hum?" added the visitor.

"Yes, sir. Would you like to see him?" said the rather amused attendant, opening wide the Executive portal.

Just then the Governor, who was seated at a desk, caught sight of his odd caller, and thinking there might be some amusement in store, called out to him, "Come in, neighbor; come right in."

"Air you Guv'ner Bagglely?" said the tramp, awkwardly ambling toward the desk of the ruler of Michigan, with hat on, and hands in his pockets.

"Yes, sir; that's what they call me."

"That's so, is it? I swan I'm glad ter see you."

"Thank you," said the Governor. "Now what can I do for you, my friend?"

The tramp took a pretty thorough survey of the State Executive, upward, downward, and sideways, chewing vigorously all the while, and then, as if pretty well satisfied, said, as he began to edge away: "Oh, nothin', I reckon. B'lieve I never seed you afore; often thought I'd like to, 'cause *I've chawed lots uv yer tobakker.*"

As this is the month of Thanksgiving, and there is nothing better to be thankful for than a maiden's "Yes," said at the right time, we find appropriate to the season these verses on

THE WISH-BONE.

Slender and shining, prophetic bone,
　We pulled it the future to divine;
Her bare pink palm, the bit in my own,
　Told that wish and wish-bone both were mine.

"What did you ask for?" whispered my Rose,
　Looking up shyly with eyes so true.
"I wished," I answered, drawing her close,
　"The woman I win might look like you:

"Her eyes as brown as a forest brook,
　Her cheek as pink as a sea-shell's tint,
A tender mouth, and a saucy look,
　And pale brown hair with a golden glint;

"In short, that my future wife might be
　You, dear little Rose, and only you."
Hiding her face in my breast, said she,
　"Isn't it funny?—I wished that too."

RUTH HALL.

WHILE Mary Anderson was playing Ingomar to an appreciative audience in Detroit not long ago, they were amused by some unconscious but audible comments passed upon the hero by one of the country's yeomen.

When Ingomar bids farewell to Parthenia, within sight of the walls of her native city, and disappears toward his mountain home, our countryman gave a sigh of relief as he said, "There, he's gone!" But when, in response to Parthenia's pathetic "Ingomar! oh, Ingomar!" he sees that barbarian come sneaking back, a look of mingled disgust and astonishment spread over his face, and he ejaculates, "The derned fool has come back again!"

The pathos of that scene was wasted upon most of that audience.

If Mr. Bergh wants peace of mind, he should move to Cape May, where the city ordinance with regard to the disposition of unmuzzled dogs is drawn with a most tender consideration for their feelings. It directs that if dogs are left unsecured for five hours, "it shall be the duty of the marshal or any of the policemen to have them transferred from their present state of existence in as humane a manner as possible."

Perhaps the most ingenious form of appeal for rich people to come to the aid of education is "A Prayer for Royer's Academy," printed on a slip of paper, and sent about as a circular. It opens with an invocation to the Almighty and the All-Wise, and thanks Him that He has put it into the hearts of men "to build this academy," and that "amid all the discouragements the work has gone forward," until the edifice, "now a temple of beauty, lifts its proud turrets above the oaks of the forest." But this pæan abruptly changes into a confession, as follows:

"But, O Lord, nothing is hid from thine eye. Thou canst look down through its comely Mansard roof, and through its thick walls of brick and mortar. Thou knowest its hideous incompleteness within. There is no floor upon which to walk through its lovely corridors or its magnificent halls, no winding stairs by which to ascend its heights, no plaster to hide its grinning walls, no seats, no bell, no furnace, no musical instrument, no library."

And with this confession the prayer takes the form of intercession: "O Lord, send us friends. Thou hast made many of our people rich. Now, O Lord, make them liberal. Teach them to speak to us through the A. H. M. S., O Lord!"

A well-known New York artist and his wife made their appearance at an evening party last winter. As they entered the drawing-room the hostess hastened to greet them with effusion, and exclaimed: "I'm so glad to see you! We've been ransacking the very highways and by-ways to get people to come here to-night."

The same artist has a little place in the country that is his pride and delight, and upon which he spends all his spare time in manual labor. One day he met some of his neighbors, among whom was a lady who at every meeting insisted upon talking art. She at once accosted him with, "Oh, Mr. ——, so glad to see you! Upon what work are you engaged now?"

"One of the greatest of my life, madam," replied the artist, impressively.

"Indeed! Do tell us all about it. I do so

love to know of such things before they are given to the general public! What is the nature of the work?"

"Its nature, madam, is heroic, and the treatment demanded is of the boldest. I am now engaged in washing the surface, which is so large that even this simple task will occupy me several days."

"Why, Mr. ——, you surprise me. How large is the canvas?"

"It is not canvas, madam; it is wood; and in the four sides of the barn that I am white-washing are about 3600 square feet."

At the Centennial Lunch of the Athena Literary Society of Chicago in 1876 one of the toasts given was, "The matrons of the Revolution." In the response to the toast Mrs. Haven read a letter written (November 9, 1778) by her grandmother to the husband of the latter, Captain Daniel Emerson, who was serving in the army in Rhode Island. The letter is a simple one, reciting the difficulties of her situation:

"I do not know what I shall do. I have paid out almost all of my money for salt and other necessaries, things being very dear, and growing dearer very fast. I have but little wood, and few candles."

A lady hearing this remarked, "What common people they must have been to be so poor!"

Little Lyman Beecher Stowe, grandson of Mrs. Harriet Beecher Stowe, recently received a miniature tea set, which pleases him more than any of his toys. A night or two after it came into his possession, as his mother was about to leave him for the night, she said, "God bless my darling," whereupon the scion of the Beechers replied, "Don't fordet to say, Dod bless my dishes too, mamma."

A lady displayed with pardonable pride a very ancient piece of house linen to her servant, saying, as she held it up for inspection, "Look, Katie, at this table-cloth; it has been in our family for over two hundred years."

Katie eyed the article in question over carefully, and then, stepping close up to her mistress, remarked, in a most confidential tone: "Shure never mind, Mrs. Arthurs dear. If you just kape quiet about it, and don't let on to anybody, who would know but what it was bought bran'-new out of the shop?"

A Liverpool (England) reader who appreciates American facetiæ writes:

I am impelled to offer you for insertion a brace of the sayings of a coachman who once honored me by affecting, for a consideration, to take an interest in some horses of mine.

I had purchased a small property, and enlarged the house upon it, without interfering much with the garden and grounds, which had been very well planned. An iron trellis in the form of an arch spanned the carriage drive, and the branches of a weeping-elm tree had been trained over it, making, with the shrubbery, an effectual screen between the hall door and the gates which opened from the public road.

Driving up to the door for the first time after the house had been made ready for occupation, I stepped out of the carriage, and said something to the effect that I hoped the horses would like their new quarters. James touched his hat, and remarked that they ought to. "But," said he, "I don't like that arch over the drive."

"Why, what is the matter with that?"

"You can never drive a hearse under there without taking the plumes out," was his cheering reply.

The laundry was connected with the coachman's cottage, and obviously it would have been a convenience to have the coachman's wife do the laundry-work. I said something like this to James one day, adding that if I could hear of a coachman whose wife was a good laundress, he (James) would have to look for another situation, to which he replied: "Oh, I don't think you will find one. It's the gardeners as takes up with the laundry-maids; coachmen takes cooks."

———

IN the Editor's Drawer of *Harper's Monthly* for September, 1851, appeared an item stating that a distinguished clergyman of the Church of England, "of unique mind, and in his manners not a copyist of others, had been imprisoned in a lunatic asylum, not three hundred miles from New York, on the alleged ground that he was crazy. The truth, however, was soon discovered, and he was liberated, but the result arose from a mere accident."

Having been refused permission to attend church on a Sunday, and having been threatened with closer confinement if the request was repeated, he asked for writing materials, and wrote some lines, which found their way outside the asylum walls. They produced the impression everywhere that there was some "method" in the writer's "madness," and instantly the requisite steps were taken to procure his release. The lines began:

> Go on, go on; your prison den
> No terrors has for me:
> God is my shield. Why fear I, then,
> A moment's tyranny?

The above narrates how he came out, but few have ever known how he went in. When carried to the asylum he met the distinguished physician in charge of the institution, and said to him, in his own peculiar manner, and in decided, almost courtly, tones: "Doctor, I have a word to say to you. I am not going to make any trouble. I know I am unjustly deprived of my liberty; but that may not be your fault, and I shall conform to all your rules. But I wish to ask you a question. I know your patients are classified according to the nature of their maladies. Now, sir, I want to know to what class do I belong: what type of insanity do you call mine?"

The doctor replied, cautiously, "I should call yours insanity induced by excessive mental activity."

The reverend gentleman fixed upon the doctor his piercing glance, and said, in tones of great solemnity, "Be profoundly thankful to Almighty God, doctor, that you are in no danger of ever becoming insane from such a cause."

———

THE following occurred in one of the village schools of Rhode Island. Several of the pupils were the children of French Canadians. One little girl had the following sentence in her reading lesson: "Here is the heir; come, let us kill him." She read it as follows: "Here is the *hair-comb;* let us kill him." A class in geography stood up to recite. The question, "Name some of the animals of Asia," was answered as follows: "They be the lion, the tiger, the rhy-nasty-ros, and the hippo-crite." Whereupon the teacher remarked, "We need not go to Asia for the last; we can find them nearer home."

"Yes," said a little fellow; "there be two of um up to the college."

———

A CLERGYMAN of the Episcopal Church sends us the following:

I was located in my first parish, in the suburbs of Boston. One Monday evening, twenty-five years ago, a young man called upon me, whom I knew but slightly. He was a mechanic, and was earning good wages. The call was very long, and he seemed greatly embarrassed, and really seemed to have nothing to say. I did not suspect that he came for any special purpose. At length he asked,

"Have you any engagement for next Thursday?"

"None that will prevent me from making others," I replied.

"I am to be married to Miss H——, and we thought we would like Thursday."

"All right," I answered.

"Could you marry us early in the day? We are going away, and would like to be married early," he went on.

"Any hour will suit me," I replied, "provided I know it beforehand."

"Would nine o'clock in the morning be too early?" he continued.

"It will be perfectly convenient for me," I said.

"You see," he added, "we are going away, and we should like to be married early."

He placed such emphasis on the "going away" that I thought it only courteous to ask,

"Where do you intend to go?"

"Well," said he, "we haven't quite made up our minds, but I *think* we shall go to Mount Auburn."

And so they did, and spent their wedding day in that cheerful cemetery.